THE BLAIR READER

THE BLAIR READER

Second Edition

EDITED BY

Laurie G. Kirszner
Philadelphia College of Pharmacy and Science

Stephen R. Mandell
Drexel University

A Blair Press Book

Prentice Hall, Upper Saddle River, NJ 07458

Library of Congress Cataloging-in-Publication Data

The Blair reader /edited by Laurie G. Kirszner, Stephen R. Mandell.—
 –2nd ed.
    p. cm.
    "A Blair Press book."
    Includes index.
    ISBN 0–13–400110–9
    1. College readers. 2. English language—Rhetoric. I. Kirszner, Laurie G.
    II. Mandell, Stephen R.
    PE1417.B54, 1996
    808'.0427—dc20   96-16883
                                                        CIP

Editorial/production supervision: Electronic Publishing Services Inc.
Cover design: Tom Nery
Cover image: Van Gogh/Les Livres Jaunes
Buyer: Robert Anderson

A BLAIR PRESS BOOK

© 1996 and 1992 by Prentice-Hall, Inc.
Simon & Schuster/A Viacom Company
Upper Saddle River, New Jersey 07458

Printed in the United States of America

10 9 8 7 6 5 4 3 2 1

ISBN 0-13-400110-9

Acknowledgments appear on pages 817–822,
which constitute an extension of the copyright page.

Prentice-Hall International (UK) Limited, *London*
Prentice-Hall of Australia Pty. Limited, *Sydney*
Prentice-Hall Canada, Inc., *Toronto*
Prentice-Hall Hispanoamericana, S.A., *Mexico*
Prentice-Hall of India Private Limited, *New Delhi*
Prentice-Hall of Japan, Inc., *Tokyo*
Simon & Schuster Asia Pte. Ltd., *Singapore*
Editora Prentice-Hall do Brasil, Ltda., *Rio de Janeiro*

PREFACE

After more than twenty years of teaching composition, we have come to believe that students will be most enriched and engaged by the reading and writing they do if they view them as a way of participating in a public discussion about subjects that matter. Being involved in this manner enables students to discover their own ideas and to see how these ideas fit into a larger social context, where ideas gain meaning and value. We created *The Blair Reader* to encourage students to make their own contribution to the public discussion and to help them realize that ideas take shape only in response to other ideas.

Another reason we decided to create *The Blair Reader* was that we could not find a reader that truly addressed our needs as teachers. We—like you—expect (and believe we are entitled to) compelling reading selections that engage both instructors and students in a spirited dialogue. We also expect selections that reflect (and are enriched, not limited, by) the cultural diversity that characterizes our schools and our society. We expect writers to speak in distinctive voices, to treat issues that concern us deeply, and to use language that challenges and provokes us. In addition, we expect questions that accompany readings to ask readers, "What does this mean *to you?*" not simply "What does this mean?" In short, we expect a book that stimulates discussion and that encourages students to discover new ideas and to see familiar ideas from new perspectives. These expectations led us to develop *The Blair Reader* and to enhance its usefulness in this new edition.

The Reading Selections and Their Arrangement

At the heart of every reader, of course, are its selections. Keeping this in mind, we began work on *The Blair Reader* determined that it would include readings that composition instructors really enjoyed teaching. To accomplish this goal, we surveyed hundreds of instructors and asked them what essays they thought were the most readable and teachable. To their selections we added our own favorite classic and contemporary essays, fiction, and poetry. After we assembled our table of contents, teachers from all over the country tested the readings and apparatus. The result of this effort was a reader that contained the most readable and teachable essays, stories, and poems we could find.

To create the second edition, we followed a similar process, relying on our own experience as users of the first edition in the classroom as well as on the thoughtful comments of the many other teachers who generously shared their reactions to the first edition with us. The result is a more concise text, one that includes 99 essays, 8 short stories, and 8 poems. In this edition we have added a new chapter on the impact of the media on our lives and expanded the chapter on environmental issues. The readings are now arranged in ten more tightly focused units: Family and Memory, Issues in Education, The Politics of Language, The Media's Message, Women and Men, The American Dream, The Way We Live Now, Medical Practice and Responsibility, Earth in the Balance, and Making Choices. These thematic groupings, representing subjects of interest to composition instructors and to their students, are diverse enough to allow many options yet focused enough for meaningful discussion and writing.

New to this edition are two features designed to increase the flexibility of the book by presenting alternatives to its main thematic arrangement. **Perspectives on . . .** groups two (and, in one case, three) readings that present complementary perspectives on an issue, thus helping students learn to make connections and improve their critical thinking skills. These paired readings, with a single set of "Responding to Reading" questions, appear in every chapter. A **Rhetorical Table of Contents**, located in the front of the book on pages xvii–xxiii, groups the text's readings in categories that reflect their arrangement of material—narrative, description, comparison and contrast, and so on. The Perspectives on. . . and Rhetorical Table of Contents, along with the popular **Topical Clusters** (pp. 823–830), now revised and expanded, offer teachers and students a variety of options for pairing and grouping individual readings and a number of perspectives from which to view the text's issues and themes.

As we worked to tighten the focus of each chapter, we also took pains to add readings that represented varied viewpoints and issues. Among the selections new to this edition are Seamus Heaney's "Digging," Lynda Barry's "The Sanctuary of School," William A. Henry III's "In Defense of Elitism," Dinesh D'Souza's "The Visigoths in Tweed," Jonathan Kozol's "Savage Inequalities," Stephen L. Carter's "Racial Preferences? So What?" Terry McMillan's "The Movie That Changed My Life," Deborah Tannen's "Marked Women," Judith Ortiz Cofer's "The Looking-Glass Shame," Mary Tsukamoto and Elizabeth Pinkerton's "May 29, 1942," Lars Eighner's "On Dumpster Diving," Abraham Verghese's "My Own Country," Al Gore's "The Wasteland," and Deborah Lipstadt's "Denying the Holocaust." To enable students to see differences in a single author's style, voice, and perspective on different issues, we include two reading selections by each of six authors: Martin Luther King, Jr., Amy Tan, Deborah Tannen, Jonathan Kozol, Chief Seattle, and George Orwell.

These and other new readings were selected with care to introduce students to the ongoing ethical debates surrounding issues like political correctness, inequalities in education, the problems of the disabled and the homeless, stereotyping in the media, the death penalty, euthanasia and assisted suicide, the gay and lesbian experience, affirmative action, the rain forests, AIDS, and animal rights. The result of our revision is a table of contents that combines time-tested favorites with provocative new pieces, thereby illustrating to students that ideas can continue to be "relevant" long after a selection was written.

Finally, the selections in *The Blair Reader*, second edition, continue to represent a wide variety of rhetorical patterns and types of discourse as well as a variety of themes, issues, and positions. In addition to essays, *The Blair Reader* contains speeches, meditations, newspaper and magazine articles, short stories, and poems. The level of diction ranges from the relaxed formality of E. B. White's "Once More to the Lake" to the biting satire of Marge Piercy's "Barbie Doll." Every effort has been made, too, to include a diverse selection of voices, because we believe that the only way students can discover their own voices is by becoming acquainted with the voices of others.

Resources for Students

We designed the apparatus in *The Blair Reader* to involve students and to encourage them to respond critically to what they read. Their reactions can then become the basis for more focused thinking and writing. In order to facilitate this process, we included the following special features:

- **Introduction: Becoming a Critical Reader** explains and illustrates the process of reading and reacting critically to texts and formulating varied and original responses.

- **Student Voices**, a collection of brief, informal student responses to the unit's theme, opens each chapter.

- A brief chapter introduction, **Preparing to Read and Write**, places each chapter's broad theme in a narrower social or political context, helping students connect with the chapter's specific ideas and issues. A series of questions at the end of these chapter introductions helps students to focus their intellectual and emotional reactions to individual selections in the context of the chapter's larger issues.

- **Headnotes** that accompany each selection provide useful biographical information and often offer insight into the writer's motivation or purpose.

- **Responding to Reading** questions that follow each selection engage students on a personal level so that they have an incentive to write about the ideas they encounter. At the same time, these questions encourage students to respond critically to the material they have read. By asking students to do more than read essays simply for facts or information, the "Responding to Reading" questions help them realize that reading is an interactive and intellectually stimulating process and that they have something valuable to contribute.

- **Writing Suggestions** at the end of each chapter ask students to respond in writing to the various ideas they have encountered. These questions encourage students to explore relationships among readings and to connect readings to their own lives.

- The **Appendix: Student Writing** contains five student essays written in response to the text's themes and readings. These essays offer realistic models inspired by different topics and assignments and illustrate a variety of formats and styles.

Resources for Instructors

Because we wanted *The Blair Reader* to be a rich and comprehensive resource for instructors, we developed an **Instructor's Resource Manual** to accompany the text. This manual, designed to serve as a useful and accessible classroom companion, incorporates teaching techniques drawn from our more than twenty years in the classroom as well as reactions of our own students to the essays, stories, and poems, and additional creative approaches to the material developed by Libby Miles of Purdue University.

The **Instructor's Resource Manual** includes the following features:

- **Setting up the Unit** begins each chapter by focusing on a rhetorical or pedagogical strategy that instructors can use in their discussion of the chapter.

- **Confronting the Issues** offers a range of activities—most of them collaborative—designed to explore some of the issues suggested by the chapter's readings.

- **For Openers**, the first prompt for each selection, is designed to initiate class discussion after students have read the selection.

- **Teaching Strategies** for each selection provide suggestions for eliciting students' response to the reading, stimulating their discussions, and providing further information on the writer or the writing selection.

- **Collaborative Activities** present group activities through which students can develop insight and understanding by exchanging ideas with others.

- **Writer's Options** offer possibilities for exploring (in a journal entry or a longer piece of writing) personal responses, stylistic techniques, or thematic issues suggested by the selection.

- **Multimedia Resources** point to "texts" outside the scope of the anthology—movies, songs, cartoons, and the like—that address either the selection itself or the issues it raises.

- **Suggested Answers for "Responding to Reading"** questions provide possible responses to the questions that follow the selection.

- **Additional "Responding to Reading"** questions are supplementary questions for those instructors who want more editorial apparatus than the book includes.

- **Teaching Perspectives** prompts facilitate using the two or three readings in the chapter that have been grouped together because they provide complementary perspectives on an issue.

We encourage you to use the Instructor's Resource Manual to complement your own proven strategies. We also encourage you to let us know your reactions to the Manual and your suggestions for making it better. We are especially interested in hearing about classroom strategies that you use successfully and reading selections that have consistently appealed to your students. In future editions of the Instructor's Resource Manual, we would like to include these suggestions along with the names of the individuals who submitted them. Just write us in care of Blair Press (One Lake Street, Upper Saddle River, NJ 07458).

Acknowledgments

The Blair Reader is the result of a fruitful collaboration between the two of us, between us and our students, between us and Blair Press, and between us and you—our colleagues who told us what you wanted in a reader. (We consider ourselves especially fortunate to have had students who shared their thoughts with us so honestly for the "Student Voices" feature—and colleagues who shared their students' papers with us for the Appendix.) Because we worked so closely with so many generous people, we have a long list of thank yous.

First, we wish to express our gratitude to Nancy Perry for doing her usual thorough, professional job—and for somehow always managing to see both the forest and the trees. Also at Blair Press, we want to thank Rosanna Rodriguez for her cheerful efficiency and amazing poise. We also appreciate the organizational skills of Mary Rottino at Prentice Hall and Colleen Quinn at Electronic Publishing Services, Inc., and we thank them for their patience and professionalism as they guided the book through production.

As always, Mark Gallaher's editorial instincts were exactly right; as always, his contributions are much appreciated. (And, as always, he deserves his own paragraph.)

In preparing *The Blair Reader*, second edition, we benefited at every stage from the assistance and suggestions of colleagues from across the country: Janice Albert, Las Positas Community College; Faith Barrett, University of Iowa; Hilda P. Barrow, Pitt Community College; Linda Bensel-Meyers, The University of Tennessee, Knoxville; Jon G. Bentley, Albuquerque Technical-Vocational Institute; Carol M. Bradley, Las Positas Community College; Nancy J. Brown, Lourdes College; Lorelle Browning, Pacific University; Michael Cochran, Santa Fe Community College; Collett B. Dilworth, East Carolina University; Susan F. Fitzgerald, University of Memphis; Beverly Galvan, Clark College; Cherry Grisham, Santa Rose Junior College; Michael Hennessy, Southwest Texas State University; Linda Holman, Kingsborough Community College, CUNY; JoAnne James, Pitt Community College; Emily Jahn, Berkshire Community College; Martha Kallstrom, Georgia Southern University; Jane Keller, Pitt Community College; Lynne B. Koch, Marist College; Michael Lackey, Harper College; Joseph A. Leone, Bergen Community College; Nick Mauriello, Bergen Community College; Kelly McQuain, Temple University; Esther L. Panitz, William Paterson College of New Jersey; Jon F. Patton, University of Toledo; Joan E. Perisse, State University of New York, New Paltz; Vicki G. Russell, University of California, Irvine; Victoria Vetro, Temple University; Ethel Weisberg, Bergen Community College; James B. Willis, Las Positas Community College; and Linda Woodson, The University of Texas at San Antonio.

On the home front, we once again round up the usual suspects to thank—Mark, Adam, and Rebecca Kirszner and Demi, David, and Sarah Mandell. And, of course, we thank each other: It really has been a "beautiful friendship."

Laurie G. Kirszner
Stephen R. Mandell

CONTENTS

RHETORICAL CONTENTS

DESCRIPTION

PROCESS

EXAMPLE

CAUSE AND EFFECT

COMPARISON AND CONTRAST

CLASSIFICATION AND DIVISION

DEFINITION

ARGUMENT AND PERSUASION

THE BLAIR READER

INTRODUCTION:
BECOMING A
CRITICAL READER

In his autobiographical essay "The Library Card" (p. 406), Richard Wright describes his early exposure to the world of books. He says, "The plots and stories in the novels did not interest me so much as the point of view revealed. I gave myself over to each novel without reserve, without trying to criticize it; it was enough for me to see and feel something different. Reading was like a drug. . . ."

It is a rare person today for whom reading holds this magic or inspires this awe. Most of us take the ability to read and the access to books for granted. As a student, you've probably learned to be pragmatic about your reading. In fact, for many students "reading" has come to mean reading assigned pages in a textbook. Whether the book's subject is modern American history, principles of corporate management, or quantum mechanics, students tend to read just for information, assuming that a book's ideas will be accessible and free of ambiguity and that the book will be clearly written and logically organized. If these expectations are met, they expect to have no trouble understanding the ideas they are reading.

In addition to reading textbooks, however, students also read essays and journal articles, fiction and poetry. These present special challenges to you as a student because you read them not just for information but also to discover your own ideas about what the writer is saying—what the work means to you, how you react to it, why you react as you do, and how your reactions differ from the responses of other readers. And, because the writers express opinions and convey impressions as well as facts, your role as a reader must be more active than it is when you read a textbook. Here, reading becomes not only a search for information, but also a search for meaning.

Reading and Meaning

Like many readers, you may assume that meaning is hidden somewhere between the lines and that if you only ask the right questions or unearth the appropriate clues, you will be able to discover exactly what the writer is getting at. But reading is not a game of hide-and-seek in which you must find ideas that have been hidden by the writer. As current reading theory demonstrates, readers play a key role in creating meaning. In fact, meaning is not contained within a text; rather, it is created by the interaction between a reader and a text.

One way to explain this interactive process is to draw an analogy between a **text**—a work being read—and a **word.** A word is not the one natural equivalent of the thing it signifies. The word *dog,* for example, does not evoke the image of a furry, four-legged animal in all parts of the world. To speakers of Spanish, the word *perro* elicits the same mental picture *dog* does in English-speaking countries. Not only does the word *dog* have meaning only in a specific cultural context, but even within that context it evokes different images in different people. Some people may picture a collie, others a poodle, and still others a particular pet named Rex or a snarling attack dog.

Like a word, a text can have different meanings in different cultures—or even in different historical time periods. Each reader brings to the text associations that come from the cultural community in which he or she lives. These associations are determined by experience and education as well as by ethnic group, class, religion, gender, and many other factors. Each of these factors contributes to the way a person views the world. Each reader also brings to the text a host of expectations, desires, and prejudices that influence how he or she reacts to and interprets it. Therefore, it is entirely possible for two readers to have very different, yet equally valid, interpretations of the same text. (This does *not* mean, of course, that a text can mean whatever any individual reader wishes it to mean. Any valid interpretation must be supported by what actually appears in the text.)

To get an idea of the range of individual interpretations that can be suggested by a single text, consider some of the possible responses different readers might have to E. B. White's classic essay "Once More to the Lake" (p. 41).

In "Once More to the Lake" White tells a story about his visit with his son to a lake in Maine in the 1940s. White compares this visit with one he made with his own father in 1904. Throughout the essay White describes the changes that have occurred since he was there as a boy—changes that frustrate his desire to "revisit old haunts." Memories from the past flood his consciousness and lead him to remember things he did when he was a boy. At one point, after he and his son have been feeding worms to fish, he remembers doing the same thing with his father and has trouble separating the past from the present. As a result, White realizes that he will soon be just a memory in his son's mind—as his father is just a memory in his.

White had specific goals in mind in this essay. His title, "Once More to the Lake," indicates that he intended to compare his childhood and adult visits to the lake. The organization of ideas in the essay, the use of flashbacks, and the choice of particular transitional phrases reinforce this structure. In addition, descriptive detail—such as the image of the tarred road that replaced the dirt road—reminds readers, as well as the narrator, that the years have made the lake site different from what it once was. The essay ends not on an idyllic note but with the image of the son standing on the dock in cold, dripping bathing trunks and the father suddenly feeling the "chill of death."

Despite White's specific intentions, each person reading "Once More to the Lake" will respond to it somewhat differently. Male readers might identify with the boy. If they have ever spent a vacation at a lake, they might have experienced the "peace and goodness and jollity" of the whole summer scene. Female readers might also want to share these experiences, but they might feel excluded because only males are described in the essay. Urban readers who have never been on a camping trip might not feel the same nostalgia for the woods that White feels. To them camping in the woods away from the comforts of home might seem to be an unthinkably uncomfortable ordeal. Older readers might identify with White, sympathizing with his efforts to recapture the past and seeing his son as naively innocent of the hardships of life.

Thus, although each person who reads White's essay will read the same words, each will be likely to *interpret* it differently and to see different things as important. This is because much is left open to interpretation. All essays leave *blanks* or *gaps*—missing words, phrases, or images—that readers have to fill in. In "Once More to the Lake," for example, readers must imagine what happened in the years that separated the narrator's last visit to the lake and the trip he takes with his son.

These gaps in the text create *ambiguities*—words, phrases, descriptions, or ideas that need to be interpreted by the reader. For instance, when you read the words "One summer, along about 1904, my father rented a camp on a lake," how do you picture the camp? White's description of the setting contains a great deal of detail, but no matter how many sensory impressions he conveys, he cannot begin to provide a complete verbal representation of the lakeside camp. He must rely on the reader's ability to visualize the setting and supply details from his or her own experience.

Readers also bring their own *emotional associations* to a text. For example, how readers react to White's statement above depends, in part, on their feelings about their own fathers. If White's words bring to mind a parent who is loving, strong, protective, and considerate, they will respond favorably; if the essay calls up memories of a parent who is distant, bad-tempered, excitable, or even abusive, they may respond negatively.

Because each reader views the text from a slightly different angle, each may also see a different *focus* as central to "Once More to the Lake." Some might see nature as the primary element in the essay and believe that White's purpose is to condemn the gradual encroachment of human beings on the environment. Others might see the passage of time as the central focus. Still others might see the initiation theme as being the most important element of the essay: Each boy is brought to the wilderness by his father, and each eventually passes from childhood innocence to adulthood.

Finally, each reader may *evaluate* the essay differently. Some readers might think "Once More to the Lake" is impossibly boring because it has little action and deals with a subject in which they have no interest. Others might believe the essay is a brilliant meditation that makes an impact through its vivid description and imaginative figurative language. Still others might see the essay as a mixed bag—admitting, for example, that although White is an excellent stylist, he is also self-centered and self-indulgent. After all, they might argue, the experiences he describes are available only to those in relatively privileged segments of society and are irrelevant to those who must struggle every day with unemployment, discrimination, or poverty. Beyond the denotative meaning of words on a page, then, a text will elicit a variety of responses and judgments from its readers.

Reading Critically

Reading critically means interacting with a text, keeping an open mind that permits you to question its assumptions and to formulate and reformulate judgments about its ideas. Think of reading as a dialogue between you and the text: Sometimes the author will assert himself or herself, and at other times you will dominate the conversation. Remember, though, that a critical voice is a thoughtful and responsible one, not one that shouts down the opposition. Deborah Tannen makes this distinction clear in her essay "The Triumph of the Yell" (p. 274):

> In many university classrooms, "critical thinking" means reading someone's life work, then ripping it to shreds. Though critique is surely one form of critical thinking, so are integrating ideas from disparate fields and examining the context out of which they grew. Opposition does not lead to truth when we ask only "What's wrong with this argument?" and never "What can we use from this in building a new theory, a new understanding?"

In other words, being a critical reader does not necessarily mean quarreling and contradicting; more often, it means asking questions, exploring reactions, and remaining open to new ideas.

Asking the following questions as you read will help you to become aware of the relationships between the writer's perspective and your own.

What audience does the writer address? Does the work offer clues to the writer's intended audience? For example, the strong title of Susan Estrich's essay on women's colleges, "Separate Is Better" (p. 132), not only states her position but also suggests that the author is questioning her readers' preconceived notions about the value of coed versus single-sex education. The way her arguments challenge these notions indicates that she sees her readers as knowledgeable but probably not inclined to agree with her position.

What is the writer's purpose? What is the writer trying to accomplish in his or her essay? For example, is he or she attempting to explain, persuade, justify, evaluate, describe, debunk, entertain, preach, browbeat, threaten, or frighten? What strategies does the writer use to achieve this purpose? Does the writer, like Amitai Etzioni in "HIV Sufferers Have a Responsibility" (p. 585) or Rachel Carson in "The Obligation to Endure" (p. 656), try to move readers to action? To achieve his or her objective, does the writer use logic, emotion, or a combination of the two? Also consider whether the writer appeals to the prejudices or fears of readers, engages in name calling, or in any other way attempts to influence readers unfairly.

What kind of voice does the writer use? Is the writer close to his or her subject? Does the writer seem to talk directly to readers? Does the writer's subjectivity get in the way, or does it help to involve readers? Does the writer's voice seem distant, even formal? Writers have many options, and each can have a different effect on readers. For example, an emotional tone, like the one Martin Luther King, Jr., uses in "I Have a Dream" (p. 397), can inspire; an intimate tone, like the one Ursula K. LeGuin uses in "The Ones Who Walk Away from Omelas" (p. 797), can involve readers and create empathy. A straightforward, forthright voice, like those of Vine Deloria in "We Talk, You Listen" (p. 295) and Lars Eighner in "On Dumpster Diving" (p. 521), can make the writer's ideas seem reasonable and credible. An ironic tone can amuse readers or alienate them; a distant, reserved tone can inspire awe or discomfort.

What emotional response is the writer trying to evoke? In "We May Be Brothers" (p. 400) and in "Letter to President Pierce, 1855" (p. 647), Chief Seattle maintains a calm, unemotional tone even though he is describing the defeat of his people and the destruction of their land. By maintaining a dignified tone and avoiding bitterness and resentment, he succeeds in evoking sympathy and respect in his readers rather than forcing them to take a defensive stance. Other writers may attempt to evoke other emotional responses: amusement, nostalgia, curiosity, wonder over the grandeur or mystery of the world that surrounds us, even anger or fear.

What position does the writer take on the issue? Barbara Grizzuti Harrison's title "Getting Away with Murder" (p. 492) clearly reveals her position on murder defendents who claim to be society's victims; Martin Luther King, Jr. conveys his position in equally unambiguous terms when, in "Letter from Birmingham Jail" (p. 741), he asserts that people have a responsibility to disobey laws they consider unjust. Keep in mind, though, that a writer's position may not always be as obvious as it is in these two examples. As you read, look carefully for statements that suggest the writer's position on a particular subject or issue—and be sure you understand how you feel about that position, particularly if it is an unusual or controversial one. Do you agree or disagree? Can you explain your reasoning? Remember, however, that a writer's support for a particular position, even if it is at odds with your own, does not automatically render the work suspect or its ideas invalid. A writer's ideas may have been shaped by his or her geographical, cultural, religious, historical, or ethnic context, and ideas that you might consider shocking or absurd may be readily accepted by many other readers. Rather than limiting you, the realization that writers may take unexpected, puzzling, or even repellent positions should encourage you to read carefully and thoughtfully, trying to understand the larger historical and cultural context in which they write.

How does the writer support his or her position? Just as important as determining what the writer's position is and how you respond to it is determining whether the writer supports that position convincingly. What kind of support does the writer use? Does the writer use a series of individual examples, as Alleen Pace Nilsen does in "Sexism in English: A 1990s Update" (p. 220), or an extended example, as Mary Gordon does in "Mary Cassatt" (p. 341)? Does the writer use statistics, as Arthur Levine does in "The Making of a Generation" (p. 481), or does he or she rely primarily on personal experiences, as Brent Staples does in "Just Walk on By" (p. 499)? Does the writer quote experts, as Deborah Tannen does in "Marked Women" (p. 362), or present anecdotal information, as Jenny Lyn Bader does in "Larger Than Life" (p. 471)? Why does the writer choose a particular kind of support? Does he or she supply enough information to support his or her points? Are the examples given relevant to the issues being discussed? Is the writer's reasoning valid, or do the arguments seem forced or unrealistic? Are any references in the work unfamiliar to you? If so, do they arouse your curiosity, or do they discourage you from reading further?

What beliefs, assumptions, or preconceived ideas do you have that color your responses to a work? Does the writer challenge any ideas that you accept as "natural" or "obvious"? For example, does Garrett Hardin's controversial stand in "Lifeboat Ethics: The Case against Helping the Poor" (p. 756) shock you or violate your sense of fair play? Does the fact that you do not like horror movies prevent you from appreciating the perspective of Stephen King's essay "Why We Crave Horror Movies" (p. 286)?

What experiences have you had that enable you to understand or interpret the writer's ideas? Does your background give you any special insights? Are the writer's experiences similar to or different from your own? Is the writer like or unlike you in terms of age, ethnic background, gender, and social class? How do the similarities and differences between you and the writer affect your reaction to the work? For example, you may be able to understand Richard Rodriguez's "Aria" (p. 169) better than other students because you too speak one language at home and another in public. You may have a unique perspective on the problems Raymond Carver examines in "My Father's Life" (p. 69) because you too have an alcoholic parent. Or, your volunteer work delivering meals to homebound AIDS patients may have helped shape your position on the issue of the media's characterization of people with AIDS as either "innocent" or "guilty," as described by Michael Bronski in "Magic and AIDS: Presumed Innocent" (p. 315). Any experiences you have can help you to understand a writer's ideas and shape your response to them.

Recording Your Reactions

It is always a good idea to read a work at least twice: the first time to get a general sense of the writer's ideas and the second to think critically about them. As you read critically, you interact with the text and respond in ways that will help you to develop an interpretation of it. This process of coming to understand the text will in turn prepare you to discuss the work with others and, perhaps, to write about it.

As you read and reread, be sure to record your responses; if you do not, you will forget many of your best ideas. Two activities can help you keep a record of the ideas that come to you as you read: **highlighting**— using a system of symbols and underlining to identify key ideas—and **annotating**—writing down your responses and interpretations.

When you react to what you read, do not be afraid to go against the grain of a text and question or challenge the writer's ideas. As you read and make annotations, you might find that you are bothered by or disagree with some of the writer's ideas. Jot your responses down in the margin; when you have time, you can think more about what you have written. These informal responses may be the beginning of a thought process that will lead you to an original insight—and, perhaps, to an interesting piece of writing.

Highlighting and annotating helped a student to understand the passage below, which is excerpted from Jane Goodall's essay "A Plea for the Chimps" (p. 588). As she prepared to write about Goodall's essay, the student identified the writer's key points, asked pertinent questions, made a connection with another essay (Meir Shalev's "If Bosnians Were Whales") (p. 710), and eventually reached her own conclusions. As she read, she underlined some of the passage's important words and ideas, using arrows to indicate relationships between them. She also circled the word *physiology*, to remind her to look up its meaning later on, and she wrote down questions and comments as they occurred to her.

> The chimpanzee is more like us, genetically, than any other animal. It is because of similarities in physiology, in biochemistry, in the immune system, that medical science makes use of living bodies of chimpanzees in its search for cures and vaccines for a variety of human diseases.
>
> *(What us?)*
>
> There are also behavioral, psychological and emotional similarities between chimpanzees and humans, resemblances so striking that they raise a serious ethical question: are we justified in using an animal so close to us—an animal, moreover, that is highly endangered in its African forest home—as a human substitute in medical experimentation?
>
> *Is there an alternative? Other animals? Computer models?*
>
> In the long run, we can hope that scientists will find ways of exploring human physiology and disease, and of testing cures and vaccines, that do not depend on the use of living animals of any sort. A number of steps in this direction have already been taken, prompted in large part by growing public awareness of the suffering that is being inflicted on millions of animals. More and more people are beginning to realize that nonhuman animals—even rats and guinea pigs—are not just unfeeling machines but are capable of enjoying their lives, and of feeling fear, pain and despair.
>
> *Compare human suffering? (Shaky essay) (Like humans)*
>
> But until alternatives have been found, medical science will continue to use animals in the battle against human disease and suffering. And some of those animals will continue to be chimpanzees.
>
> *Is this justified? Does Goodall think it is?*

Reading to Write

Much of the reading you will do as a student will prepare you for writing. Writing helps you focus your ideas about various issues; in addition, the process of writing can lead you in unexpected directions, thereby enabling you to discover new insights. In fact, the most rewarding way to examine a particular text is not just to read and think about it but also to write about it. With this in mind, we have included in *The Blair Reader* a number of special features that can help you as you read and prepare to write about its selections.

The readings in *The Blair Reader* are arranged in ten thematic chapters, each offering a variety of different vantage points from which to view the theme. Although most of the selections are essays, one or more works of short fiction or poetry in each chapter enable you to become acquainted with a wider range of intellectual perspectives and styles.

Each chapter in the book opens with a collection of "Student Voices," brief comments by college students about the theme the chapter explores. Next, a brief introduction, "Preparing to Read and Write," provides a context for the theme and lists some questions designed to guide your thinking as you read the works in the chapter. These questions encourage you to see the reading selections from many different angles and thus enable you to sharpen your critical skills and begin to apply those skills effectively. As you become accustomed to reading in an academic environment, the process of reading critically will become natural to you.

Following each reading selection are three questions designed to help you think about and respond—in discussion and perhaps in writing—to what you have read. These "Responding to Reading" questions focus on the reader's side of the interaction, encouraging you to make personal connections with the writer's ideas or to reexamine your own values and beliefs. In "Dirty Needle," (p. 779) for example, Nicholas Jenkins argues against capital punishment. A question that follows this essay asks you to consider your own thoughts about capital punishment in light of Jenkins's comments.

You should consider keeping a record of your responses to the "Responding to Reading" questions—as well as any other ideas that occur to you as you read and highlight each selection—in a **writing journal.** Your journal will not only help you maintain a record of your reactions but will also serve as a sourcebook of ideas that you can use later in your writing.

Concluding each chapter are ten writing suggestions that expand upon the ideas developed by the "Preparing to Read and Write" and "Responding to Reading" questions. Writing suggestions are designed to further the interaction between reader and text: They invite you to relate the chapter's theme to your own experiences and encourage you to make connections among different works in the chapter, or between selections in different chapters.

At the end of the text, an appendix collects five student essays written in response to *The Blair Reader's* first edition. These essays illustrate a variety of stylistic and structural options for writing projects.

As you read the selections in this book and write about the ideas they suggest, remember that you are learning ways of thinking about yourself and about the world. By considering and reconsidering the ideas of others, by rejecting easy answers and set conclusions, by considering a problem from many different angles, and by appreciating the many factors that can influence your responses, you develop critical thinking skills you will use throughout your life. In addition, you participate in an ongoing conversation that has been taking place for centuries within the community of scholars and writers who care deeply about the issues that shape our world.

FAMILY AND
MEMORY

Student Voices

"My parents did not have very much money when I was born. I am their first child, so they were just beginning their life together when I became a part of it. They worked hard to make ends meet until they were finally able to find better jobs and make our lives more comfortable. Eventually, my sister and brother were born, and my parents were able to buy a bigger house. They have taught me that hard work does pay off.

"There were times, when I was younger, when I was ashamed of my parents. The fact that our traditions and foods were different embarrassed me at times, and I did not want to show my friends what my true life was like. Now I realize I should be proud of my parents. They have worked hard to raise their children, and now they are sending me to college. When I have grown up, I will work hard, as my parents did, so that I can be proud of myself and my family."

—*Cynthia Denise Padilla*

"I have only met eight or nine of my relatives. My parents have told me that many of our other relatives are dead or overseas and that I am the last of the male Jamersons left to carry on our name in this country. However, I have never met most of my relatives, and so I have little respect for or concern with my family's name or heritage or history. It is for this reason that I feel no desire to have children just to carry on the family name."

—*Matthew Hunter Jamerson*

"The most negative thing that ever happened to me was when my father moved out of the house. My mother took my three sisters and me out to a movie, and when we returned, my father was gone. My sisters and my mom sat there and cried for a long time, but I did nothing. I wasn't upset at him for leaving, but I was angry because of the financial situation that he left my mother in. I was young and didn't know much about money, but I knew that a single parent couldn't take care of four kids on a part-time job. What made the whole situation worse was that my father tried to avoid paying child support. This event took place when I was 7 or 8, and I haven't seen or talked to my father since."

—*Charles Guittar*

───────────── **Preparing to Read and Write** ─────────────

In autobiographical essays, stories, and poems, writers often reconsider the past, trying to understand it, to recapture it, or to recreate it. In each selection in this chapter a narrator—sometimes the writer, sometimes the writer's **persona**, or fictional creation—concentrates on seeing across the barriers imposed by time. In some cases memories appear in sharp focus; in others, they are blurred, confused, or even partially invented. Many writers focus on parents or other family members, struggling to close generational gaps, to replay events, to see through the eyes of others—and thus to understand their families and themselves more fully.

As you read and prepare to write about the selections in this chapter, you may consider the following questions.

- Does the selection focus on a single person, on a relationship between two people, or on family dynamics?

- Do you think the narrator's perspective is *subjective*—informed by his or her emotional responses or personal opinions—or *objective*—based mainly on observation and fact rather than on personal impressions? What makes you think so?

- Does the selection recount events from the perspective of an adult looking back at his or her childhood? Does the narrator seem to have more insight now than when the events occurred? What has the narrator learned—and how?

- What strengths and weaknesses do adult children see in their parents?

- Are family members presented in a favorable, unfavorable, neutral, or ambivalent light?

- Does one family member seem to have a great influence over others in the family? If so, is this influence positive or negative?

- Does the narrator feel close to or distant from family members? Does the narrator identify with a particular family member?

- Are two individuals—or two generations—compared? How are they alike? How are they different?

- What social, political, economic, or cultural forces influence the way the family functions?

- To what degree is the selection about a specific historical time, a place, or a culture rather than about an individual?

- Is the selection's purpose observation, exploration, self-discovery, explanation, rationalization, or something else?

- Do you identify with the narrator or with another person depicted in the selection? What makes you identify with that person?

ON GOING HOME

Joan Didion

Joan Didion (1934–), a native of California, is an essayist, novelist, and
screenwriter. She is best known for her nonfiction, which is reflective
and personal and, at the same time, journalistic and spare in style. Her
nonfiction books include three essay collections, *Slouching Toward Bethlehem* (1968), *The White Album* (1979), and *After Henry* (1992), and two
works of reportage, *Salvador* (1983) and *Miami* (1987). She has said of
her writing, "There is always a point in the writing of a piece where I
sit in a room literally papered with false starts and cannot put one
word after another." In the following essay, characteristically full of
personal anecdotes and introspection, Didion explores what she means
by *home*.

I am home for my daughter's first birthday. By "home" I do not
mean the house in Los Angeles where my husband and I and the baby
live, but the place where my family is, in the Central Valley of California. It is a vital although troublesome distinction. My husband likes my
family but is uneasy in their house, because once there I fall into their
ways, which are difficult, oblique, deliberately inarticulate, not my husband's ways. We live in dusty houses ("D-U-S-T," he once wrote with
his finger on surfaces all over the house, but no one noticed it) filled with
mementos quite without value to him (what could the Canton dessert
plates mean to him? how could he have known about the assay scales,[1]
why should he care if he did know?), and we appear to talk exclusively about people we know who have been committed to mental hospitals,
about people we know who have been booked on drunk-driving
charges, and about property, particularly about property, land, price per
acre and C-2 zoning and assessments and freeway access. My brother
does not understand my husband's inability to perceive the advantage
in the rather common real-estate transaction known as "sale-leaseback,"
and my husband in turn does not understand why so many of the people he hears about in my father's house have recently been committed
to mental hospitals or booked on drunk-driving charges. Nor does he
understand that when we talk about sale-leasebacks and right-of-way
condemnations we are talking in code about the things we like best, the
yellow fields and the cottonwoods and the rivers rising and falling and
the mountain roads closing when the heavy snow comes in. We miss
each other's points, have another drink and regard the fire. My brother

1

---

[1] Scales used to weigh ore. [Eds.]

refers to my husband, in his presence, as "Joan's husband." Marriage is the classic betrayal.

Or perhaps it is not anymore. Sometimes I think that those of us who are now in our thirties were born into the last generation to carry the burden of "home," to find in family life the source of all tension and drama. I had by all objective accounts a "normal" and a "happy" family situation, and yet I was almost thirty years old before I could talk to my family on the telephone without crying after I had hung up. We did not fight. Nothing was wrong. And yet some nameless anxiety colored the emotional charges between me and the place that I came from. The question of whether or not you could go home again was a very real part of the sentimental and largely literary baggage with which we left home in the fifties; I suspect that it is irrelevant to the children born of the fragmentation after World War II. A few weeks ago in a San Francisco bar I saw a pretty young girl on crystal take off her clothes and dance for the cash prize in an "amateur-topless" contest. There was no particular sense of moment about this, none of the effect of romantic degradation, of "dark journey," for which my generation strived so assiduously. What sense could that girl possibly make of, say, *Long Day's Journey into Night?*[2] Who is beside the point?   2

That I am trapped in this particular irrelevancy is never more apparent to me than when I am home. Paralyzed by the neurotic lassitude engendered by meeting one's past at every turn, around every corner, inside every cupboard, I go aimlessly from room to room. I decide to meet it head-on and clean out a drawer, and I spread the contents on the bed. A bathing suit I wore the summer I was seventeen. A letter of rejection from *The Nation*, an aerial photograph of the site for a shopping center my father did not build in 1954. Three teacups hand-painted with cabbage roses and signed "E.M.," my grandmother's initials. There is no final solution for letters of rejection from *The Nation* and teacups hand-painted in 1900. Nor is there any answer to snapshots of one's grandfather as a young man on skis, surveying around Donner Pass in the year 1910. I smooth out the snapshot and look into his face, and do and do not see my own. I close the drawer, and have another cup of coffee with my mother. We get along very well, veterans of a guerrilla war we never understood.   3

Days pass. I see no one. I come to dread my husband's evening call, not only because he is full of news of what by now seems to me our remote life in Los Angeles, people he has seen, letters which require at-   4

---

[2] Semi-autobiographical play by American dramatist Eugene O'Neill (1888–1953) written in 1941 and published after his death. The play is about a troubled family. The mother is a drug addict and one son is an alcoholic. [Eds.]

tention, but because he asks what I have been doing, suggests uneasily that I get out, drive to San Francisco or Berkeley. Instead I drive across the river to a family graveyard. It has been vandalized since my last visit and the monuments are broken, over-turned in the dry grass. Because I once saw a rattlesnake in the grass I stay in the car and listen to a country-and-Western station. Later I drive with my father to a ranch he has in the foothills. The man who runs his cattle on it asks us to the roundup, a week from Sunday, and although I know that I will be in Los Angeles I say, in the oblique way my family talks, that I will come. Once home I mention the broken monuments in the graveyard. My mother shrugs.

I go to visit my great-aunts. A few of them think now that I am my ⁵ cousin, or their daughter who died young. We recall an anecdote about a relative last seen in 1948, and they ask if I still like living in New York City. I have lived in Los Angeles for three years, but I say that I do. The baby is offered a horehound drop, and I am slipped a dollar bill "to buy a treat." Questions trail off, answers are abandoned, the baby plays with the dust motes in a shaft of afternoon sun.

It is time for the baby's birthday party: a white cake, strawberry- ⁶ marshmallow ice cream, a bottle of champagne saved from another party. In the evening, after she has gone to sleep, I kneel beside the crib and touch her face, where it is pressed against the slats, with mine. She is an open and trusting child, unprepared for and unaccustomed to the ambushes of family life, and perhaps it is just as well that I can offer her little of that life. I would like to give her more. I would like to promise her that she will grow up with a sense of her cousins and of rivers and of her great-grandmother's teacups, would like to pledge her a picnic on a river with fried chicken and her hair uncombed, would like to give her *home* for her birthday, but we live differently now and I can promise her nothing like that. I give her a xylophone and a sundress from Madeira, and promise to tell her a funny story.

Responding to Reading

1. Didion characterizes family life as full of "ambushes" (6). What does she mean? Have such "ambushes" occurred in your own life?
2. How does her daughter's first birthday affect Didion's attitude toward older family members?
3. Didion believes that her generation may be the last "to carry the burden of 'home,' to find in family life the source of all tension and drama" (2). What implications does her idea have for children born in this decade? Does your own experience support or contradict her generalization?

INDELIBLE MARKS: GROWING UP
～ IN A CHINESE LAUNDRY

Joyce Howe

Joyce Howe (1958–), a journalist and book critic who frequently writes on issues relating to Asian Americans, grew up in New York, where her father was a laundryman. In 1983 she published the following essay in the *Village Voice* about her memories of the laundry. She no longer lives in New York, but she visits regularly and continues to pass by the building in which she grew up and where her late father worked.

It is a Sunday afternoon, and I am in a friend's East Village apartment, watching him sort laundry. He and his roommate throw a month's worth of dirty wash into large white drawstring bags and stretched-out pillowcases for the short trek down Second Avenue to a laundry where for four dollars the owner will wash 15 pounds. [1]

The sheets, underwear, socks, towels, polos, and T's are bundled up into their bags, but the long-sleeved cotton shirts—the young professional uniforms—are set aside. The next day, these will be brought around the corner to the Chinese laundry, to the featureless man behind the counter, Mr. Lee or Mr. Chan, whose English is bad, who irons out the creases, and promises they will be ready next Wednesday. [2]

"Oh, you're going to the Chinks!" laughs a visitor from the Upper West Side, whom I have just met. My face reddens. "In Riverdale, that's how we said we were going to the Chinese laundry," he says. I laugh. As the daughter of a former Chinese laundryman, I figure I have learned how. [3]

My older sisters and I grew up in the back of laundries. In 1964, when I was six years old, we moved from my father's first laundry on Amsterdam Avenue to his last, in Jackson Heights. All of us lived in the rear rooms of the business just as the nearly 8000 mostly lone laundrymen in New York did at the turn of the century. A single long curtain divided the workplace from home. [4]

I grew up with the sight of my stocky father wringing the milky, handmixed starch solution, that turned even the limpest collar stiff, from a clean shirt into a pail. Or my father was bent low over the "hong-chong," an ironing bed, built waist-high along the laundry wall from planks and boards and covered with a felt pad and muslin hammered in with tacks. (The "hong-chong" was traditionally used for storage too; a sheet of cloth hung down from it, hiding boxes of tickets, starch, and [5] other tools.) In his right hand, the old heavy wood-handled electric iron glided across the front of a customer's button-down shirt or smoothed the corner of a cotton handkerchief.

My father preferred the dull smooth-bottomed irons with their own   6
metal plates to the modern chrome steam irons, and he wet the wrinkled cloth with spray from two triggered hoses hanging overhead. As children, my sisters and I had terrific water-gun fights with those hoses.

My father, now 66, ran a laundry for almost 30 years. Born in Al-   7
bany in 1916, he learned the business from his father, a former farmer from Canton who, with his wife, had sailed to America that same year. His father (my Goong, or paternal grandfather) had come to Albany with the same hopes of a prosperous life that all immigrants bring. Still, I know very little about him, and very little about my father's youth. What I, the youngest of four daughters, know comes only from an old gilt-framed photograph sitting on my parents' dresser and from those occasions, perhaps fewer than 10, when I have asked questions and my father has answered.

The black-and-white photograph is a formal portrait of my grand-   8
parents and their three children—my father and his two younger sisters—taken sometime in the late 1920s. Goong sits tall; his thin body is hidden in a dark, American suit, a bow tie tight at his throat. There is a gentle look about his mouth, the barest smile on a long face which I like to think was kind. My father does not look like him at all. In the photo, he stands as an adolescent, in short pants and suit jacket, to the right of my seated grandmother; her bound feet are not noticeable. It is she whom my father resembles—the same broad forehead and nose, the full lips and heavy brows, the face set tight, betraying nothing.

What *do* I know? I know that my father, who raised his children as   9
agnostics, was once an altar boy in an Albany Catholic church, and that after finishing the eighth grade he left school to work full time in his ailing father's store. I know that neighborhood children ran in and out of that store, calling Goong and my father names, like "Chink" or "Chinaman." Even now, when I bring up discrimination, he remembers the name-calling. He is insistent that such things no longer happen, certain that things are now better. He has told me that when he was 18, Goong sent him off to China with a family friend, a laundryman from nearby Mechanicsville, for Chinese education. While there, according to his father's wishes, he met and married the friend's youngest daughter, my mother. Goong died during the year or so my father was away. A short time later, my grandmother died.

My father sailed back to the U.S. alone. He sold his father's laundry.   10
After service in the army, he apprenticed with an uncle in Manhattan. This bachelor uncle, who'd arrived in New York years before, was debilitated by an old opium habit begun long ago to relieve the tedium of his work day.

My mother, because of strict immigration laws forbidding the entry [11] of Chinese females into the country, was still in Canton. The pretty young wife, whom he hardly knew, wrote letters to my father, describing how she and my oldest sister, who was born after he left, fled their rural village to escape the invading Japanese—how for days, they stayed with whoever would take them in. In each letter she asked for money, and my father always sent it. His literacy in Chinese was limited, so his uncle read my mother's letters aloud, translating my father's prompt responses into delicate Chinese script.

After his uncle's death (my father blames it on the opium), the laun- [12] dry at 966 Amsterdam Avenue, on whose plate-glass window was painted the name "Jim Lee Laundry" in red for luck, was left to him. In 1949 my mother and oldest sister, then 12 years old, arrived in New York. My sister later married a young Chinese immigrant and for $4500, they soon bought their own laundry, 20 blocks south of my father's. They are still there, and the laundry is one of the few remaining in the area.

In Queens, on the block where we moved, my father was known as [13] the man who ran the Chinese laundry, like Ernie who ran the deli, Benny the upholsterer, and the butcher a few doors down. To all of his customers he was Joe. And they—middle-aged housewives, young bachelors and students, mainly white—were known to him by a first name or by the unique indelible "mark" on their collars and hems. (This "mark," consisting of one or more characters, was written on each item for the duration of a customer's patronage; if he switched laundries, the new establishment usually did not bother changing it.) With all of them, as tickets, laundry bills, and change passed from hand to hand over the wide counter, my father exchanged comments: "Too much of this rain, huh?", "Yeah, the Mets looked lousy last night," or "How's the wife and the kids?"

Saturday was his busiest day. It was not only the day more cus- [14] tomers came in and out, but it was also one of the three days on which the long and tedious job of laundry-sorting was done. The entire floor of the store became a dumping ground for soiled clothes. My father divided the laundry into piles: 10 to 15 sheets and pillow-cases were bundled up into one sheet and the ticket stubs of the customers whose laundry made up the bundle were then stapled together and put aside for later identification. "Wet items," such as towels, underwear, and socks were separated into two categories—light and dark; shirts were separated into four categories—colored, white, starch, and no starch. Each pile of "wet items" and shirts was then placed in a laundry bag with its respective tag.

The bags and bundles were picked up Sunday morning by the truck [15] drivers, who had names like Rocky and Louie, from the wholesale laundry or "wet wash" contracted by my father. ("Hand laundry" has been a misnomer since the late 1930s and '40s, when a whole new industry of Chinese-operated wholesale laundries and pressing concerns sprang up and contracted to do the actual washing and pressing for laundrymen.) Every Sunday, we were awakened from our sleep by the sound of the drivers' keys turning in the front door's locks.

When the "wet wash" drivers returned Monday with the previous [16] day's load, the sheets and pillowcases, or "flat pieces," were wrapped in a heavy brown paper which my mother later would use for tablecloths. The shirts returned in the same bags they went out in. My father pulled out the bag of shirts to be starched and hand-ironed, leaving the rest for the shirt-press truck to pick up that night. On Tuesday night, they returned—clean, pressed, folded—in large square cardboard boxes, each shirt ringed in its own pale blue paper band.

For a short time, we had our own automatic dryer to take care of the [17] damp "wet items" when they returned. After it broke down, irreparably, the dryer retired, and was left to hold stacks of comic books and board games. My sisters and I took turns making pilgrimages to the local laundromat, our metal shopping cart bent from the weight of the load. We wheeled those three blocks three times a week. On my turn, I always hoped that no one I knew would see me as I struggled with two hands to keep laundry and cart intact when maneuvering the high curbs. Even then, the irony of going from the laundry to the laundromat was not lost.

Of course, there were days when the system was off, when the [18] shirt press might return its load late, or when my father didn't feel well enough to wrap every package. On those days, we were all expected to help. We made sure that the promise my father had made to customers on Saturday that their shirts would be ready by Wednesday was kept. Behind the tan curtain drawn across our plate-glass window every evening at seven and the door's pulled venetian blind, we settled into a tableau. My family formed a late-night assembly line, each member taking his place amid the shelves, boxes, white cones of string, rolls of wrapping paper, and the familiar fragrance of newly laundered cloth.

There were those customers who took an interest in my father's life [19] and in his children, who gave my sisters and me candy, and asked how we were doing in school. Without offering any of his own, my father heard their problems, while making sure it was only a little starch they wanted or that their shirts should be hung rather than folded.

I was always glad when these customers came in. In my child's eyes, [20] their interest somehow legitimized us. My sisters and I, who often wished our father ran a candy store instead, were not just seen as three faceless Chinese daughters with braids, dutifully making change, delivering laundry or cleaning up. We became individuals, known by our first names, with other concerns.

Hearing my father converse with the customers reassured me that ²¹ not everyone saw his life revolving entirely around his livelihood. His identity was not solely that of the role of Chinese laundryman. He had interests in the outside world. He read the *Daily News* and the *Post*. He bet on the harness races with Benny the upholsterer, who drove him to the track. During the baseball season, he sat in the back, on the orange vinyl couch discarded from a friend's take-out restaurant, and watched the day games on TV, getting up at the sound of the front door's chimes as someone came in.

I needed the reassurance of others. It seemed as if it would be easi- ²² er, on those endless forms handed out in school, to fill in "candy store owner" in the space for "father's occupation." Instead of "Chinese laun- dryman," my sisters taught me to write "Chinese laundry proprietor," as if the latter were somehow more respectable. No one else we knew at school lived behind a store.

Shouldn't our American-born father—who drank beer with his rice ²³ at dinner, who took us to James Bond movies and amusement parks, to LaGuardia airport to watch the planes take off—be something more than another laundryman? He wasn't an immigrant like his father, an- other Chinaman who came to find gold but found the washing indus- try instead.

My father retired when he was 60. I was a sophomore away at col- ²⁴ lege; my family had bought a three-family brick house three years be- fore. His average weekly income of $400 (considered "good business" for a hand laundry) had gradually plummeted to a low of $175 as the racial and economic face of our Jackson Heights neighborhood changed from middle-class whites to lower-income Hispanics. When his rent ($200 when he moved in 14 years earlier) threatened to double, my fa- ther let the laundry go.

There would have been no one to pass it on to. No only son to try ²⁵ and make a go of it. His younger children—who had spent hours after school and during weekends learning to sort laundry, count change quickly, and securely tie string—were all too grown, all too educated.

According to the New York Chinatown History Project, which has ²⁶ put together a traveling exhibit on the history of Chinese laundry workers in the United States, only an estimated 1000 hand laundries re- main in the New York metropolitan area. The city's Department of Con- sumer Affairs, which licenses all "establishments which take in laun- dry" (except for dry cleaners) every two years, reports that as of September 13, there were only 305 licensed hand laundries in New York.

When my father retired, he referred his remaining customers to an- ²⁷ other laundry, owned by friends, two blocks away. His laundry and for- mer home have since become in turn, a dry cleaner, a dress shop, a bode- ga, and another dress shop named "Fuego." On the few times I've driven by, I've looked carefully for its latest occupant, catching a quick glimpse of an iron gate instead.

I have a favorite photo of my father. It is in color. Taken two or three [28] years ago in the garden that he and my mother tend behind the family house, my shirt-sleeved father is kneeling among the leafy green cabbage, tomato plants, and other vegetables growing in straight rows. His fine white hair is combed back from the broad forehead, black-rimmed spectacles frame his eyes. Looking straight at the camera, he is smiling.

I showed it once to my friend, laughing proudly, "Doesn't he look [29] like a Russian dissident intellectual here?" But of course, he is not. The man in the photograph is my father. He used to run a Chinese laundry.

Responding to Reading

1. Howe writes, "In Queens, on the block where we moved, my father was known as the man who ran the Chinese laundry . . ." (13). How do his customers view him? How does his occupation shape their perception of him?
2. Does Howe admire her father? Is she disappointed in him? Or does she simply accept him for what he is?
3. Howe provides a good deal of background information about her father's family. What purpose does this information serve in the essay? What would you like to know about your parents' and grandparents' lives?

ONE LAST TIME

Gary Soto

Gary Soto (1952–) was raised in the San Joaquin valley of California, where he worked for a time as a migrant laborer. He studied geography in college but then turned to poetry, often using his childhood locale in poems about poverty and desolation among Mexican-Americans. His lean, simple prose shows his characters' struggles to rise above their difficult situations. In 1985 Soto won the American Book Award for his autobiographical prose work *Living Up the Street: Narrative Recollections*. In an unpublished interview about this book, Soto says, "I would rather show and not tell about certain levels of poverty, of childhood; I made a conscious effort not to tell anything but just present the stories and let the reader come up with assumptions." His most recent books have been novels and poetry collections for children and young adults. The following essay about picking grapes for a raisin company is from *Living Up the Street*.

Yesterday I saw the movie *Gandhi*[1] and recognized a few of the peo- [1]
ple—not in the theater but in the film. I saw my relatives, dusty and thin
as sparrows, returning from the fields with hoes balanced on their shoulders. The workers were squinting, eyes small and veined, and were
using their hands to say what there was to say to those in the audience
with popcorn and Cokes. I didn't have anything, though. I sat thinking
of my family and their years in the fields, beginning with Grandmother who came to the United States after the Mexican revolution to settle
in Fresno where she met her husband and bore children, many of them.
She worked in the fields around Fresno, picking grapes, oranges, plums,
peaches, and cotton, dragging a large white sack like a sled. She worked
in the packing houses, Bonner and Sun-Maid Raisin, where she stood at
a conveyor belt passing her hand over streams of raisins to pluck out
leaves and pebbles. For over twenty years she worked at a machine that
boxed raisins until she retired at sixty-five.

Grandfather worked in the fields, as did his children. Mother also [2]
found herself out there when she separated from Father for three weeks.
I remember her coming home, dusty and so tired that she had to rest on
the porch before she trudged inside to wash and start dinner. I didn't
understand the complaints about her ankles or the small of her back,
even though I had been in the grape fields watching her work. With my
brother and sister I ran in and out of the rows; we enjoyed ourselves and
pretended not to hear Mother scolding us to sit down and behave ourselves. A few years later, however, I caught on when I went to pick
grapes rather than play in the rows.

Mother and I got up before dawn and ate quick bowls of cereal. She [3]
drove in silence while I rambled on how everything was now solved,
how I was going to make enough money to end our misery and even
buy her a beautiful copper tea pot, the one I had shown her in Long's
Drugs. When we arrived I was frisky and ready to go, self-consciously
aware of my grape knife dangling at my wrist. I almost ran to the row
the foreman had pointed out, but I returned to help Mother with the
grape pans and jug of water. She told me to settle down and reminded
me not to lose my knife. I walked at her side and listened to her explain
how to cut grapes; bent down, hands on knees, I watched her demonstrate by cutting a few bunches into my pan. She stood over me as I tried
it myself, tugging at a bunch of grapes that pulled loose like beads from
a necklace. "Cut the stem all the way," she told me as last advice before
she walked away, her shoes sinking in the loose dirt, to begin work on
her own row.

I cut another bunch, then another, fighting the snap and whip of [4]
vines. After ten minutes of groping for grapes, my first pan brimmed

---

[1] 1982 film biography of the nonviolent revolutionary Mohandas Gandhi (known as Mahatma),
which was set in part among the peasants of India. [Eds.]

with bunches. I poured them on the paper tray, which was bordered by a wooden frame that kept the grapes from rolling off, and they spilled like jewels from a pirate's chest. The tray was only half filled, so I hurried to jump under the vines and begin groping, cutting, and tugging at the grapes again. I emptied the pan, raked the grapes with my hands to make them look like they filled the tray, and jumped back under the vine on my knees. I tried to cut faster because Mother, in the next row, was slowly moving ahead. I peeked into her row and saw five trays gleaming in the early morning. I cut, pulled hard, and stopped to gather the grapes that missed the pan; already bored, I spat on a few to wash them before tossing them like popcorn into my mouth.

So it went. Two pans equaled one tray—or six cents. By lunchtime   5
I had a trail of thirty-seven trays behind me while mother had sixty or more. We met about halfway from our last trays, and I sat down with a grunt, knees wet from kneeling on dropped grapes. I washed my hands with the water from the jug, drying them on the inside of my shirt sleeve before I opened the paper bag for the first sandwich, which I gave to Mother. I dipped my hand in again to unwrap a sandwich without looking at it. I took a first bite and chewed it slowly for the tang of mustard. Eating in silence I looked straight ahead at the vines, and only when we were finished with cookies did we talk.

"Are you tired?" she asked.   6

"No, but I got a sliver from the frame," I told her. I showed her the   7
web of skin between my thumb and index finger. She wrinkled her forehead but said it was nothing.

"How many trays did you do?"   8

I looked straight ahead, not answering at first. I recounted in my   9
mind the whole morning of bend, cut, pour again and again, before answering a feeble "thirty-seven." No elaboration, no detail. Without looking at me she told me how she had done field work in Texas and Michigan as a child. But I had a difficult time listening to her stories. I played with my grape knife, stabbing it into the ground, but stopped when Mother reminded me that I had better not lose it. I left the knife sticking up like a small, leafless plant. She then talked about school, the junior high I would be going to that fall, and then about Rick and Debra, how sorry they would be that they hadn't come out to pick grapes because they'd have no new clothes for the school year. She stopped talking when she peeked at her watch, a bandless one she kept in her pocket. She got up with an *"Ay, Dios,"* and told me that we'd work until three, leaving me cutting figures in the sand with my knife and dreading the return to work.

Finally I rose and walked slowly back to where I had left off, again   10
kneeling under the vine and fixing the pan under bunches of grapes. By that time, 11:30, the sun was over my shoulder and made me squint and think of the pool at the Y.M.C.A. where I was a summer member. I saw

myself diving face first into the water and loving it. I saw myself gleaming like something new, at the edge of the pool. I had to daydream and keep my mind busy because boredom was a terror almost as awful as the work itself. My mind went dumb with stupid things, and I had to keep it moving with dreams of baseball and would-be girlfriends. I even sang, however softly, to keep my mind moving, my hands moving.

I worked less hurriedly and with less vision. I no longer saw that [11] copper pot sitting squat on our stove or Mother waiting for it to whistle. The wardrobe that I imagined, crisp and bright in the closet numbered only one pair of jeans and two shirts because, in half a day, six cents times thirty-seven trays was two dollars and twenty-two cents. It became clear to me. If I worked eight hours, I might make four dollars. I'd take this, even gladly, and walk downtown to look into store windows on the mall and long for the bright madras shirts from Walter Smith or Coffee's, but settling for two imitation ones from Penney's.

That first day I laid down seventy-three trays while Mother had a [12] hundred and twenty behind her. On the back of an old envelope, she wrote out our numbers and hours. We washed at the pump behind the farm house and walked slowly to our car for the drive back to town in the afternoon heat. That evening after dinner I sat in a lawn chair listening to music from a transistor radio while Rick and David King played catch. I joined them in a game of pickle, but there was little joy in trying to avoid their tags because I couldn't get the fields out of my mind: I saw myself dropping on my knees under a vine to tug at a branch that wouldn't come off. In bed, when I closed my eyes, I saw the fields, yellow with kicked up dust, and a crooked trail of trays rotting behind me.

The next day I woke tired and started picking tired. The grapes [13] rained into the pan, slowly filling like a belly, until I had my first tray and started my second. So it went all day, and the next, and all through the following week, so that by the end of thirteen days the foreman counted out, in tens mostly, my pay of fifty-three dollars. Mother earned one hundred and forty-eight dollars. She wrote this on her envelope, with a message I didn't bother to ask her about.

The next day I walked with my friend Scott to the downtown mall [14] where we drooled over the clothes behind fancy windows, bought popcorn, and sat at a tier of outdoor fountains to talk about girls. Finally we went into Penney's for more popcorn, which we ate walking around, before we returned home without buying anything. It wasn't until a few days before school that I let my fifty-three dollars slip quietly from my hands, buying a pair of pants, two shirts, and a maroon T-shirt, the kind that was in style. At home I tried them on while Rick looked on enviously; later, the day before school started, I tried them on again wondering not so much if they were worth it as who would see me first in those clothes.

Along with my brother and sister I picked grapes until I was fifteen, [15] before giving up and saying that I'd rather wear old clothes than stoop like a Mexican. Mother thought I was being stuck-up, even stupid, because there would be no clothes for me in the fall. I told her I didn't care, but when Rick and Debra rose at five in the morning, I lay awake in bed feeling that perhaps I had made a mistake but unwilling to change my mind. That fall Mother bought me two pairs of socks, a packet of colored T-shirts, and underwear. The T-shirts would help, I thought, but who would see that I had new underwear and socks? I wore a new T-shirt on the first day of school, then an old shirt on Tuesday, than another T-shirt on Wednesday, and on Thursday an old Nehru shirt that was embarrassingly out of style. On Friday I changed into the corduroy pants my brother had handed down to me and slipped into my last new T-shirt. I worked like a magician, blinding my classmates, who were all clothes conscious and small-time social climbers, by arranging my wardrobe to make it seem larger than it really was. But by spring I had to do something—my blue jeans were almost silver and my shoes had lost their form, puddling like black ice around my feet. That spring of my sixteenth year, Rick and I decided to take a labor bus to chop cotton. In his old Volkswagen, which was more noise than power, we drove on a Saturday morning to West Fresno—or Chinatown as some call it—parked, walked slowly toward a bus, and stood gawking at the winos, toothy blacks, Okies, *Tejanos*[2] with gold teeth, whores, Mexican families, and labor contractors shouting "Cotton" or "Beets," the work of spring.

We boarded the "Cotton" bus without looking at the contractor who [16] stood almost blocking the entrance because he didn't want winos. We boarded scared and then were more scared because two blacks in the rear were drunk and arguing loudly about what was better, a two-barrel or four-barrel Ford carburetor. We sat far from them, looking straight ahead, and only glanced briefly at the others who boarded, almost all of them broken and poorly dressed in loudly mismatched clothes. Finally when the contractor banged his palm against the side of the bus, the young man at the wheel, smiling and talking in Spanish, started the engine, idled it for a moment while he adjusted the mirrors, and started off in slow chugs. Except for the windshield there was no glass in the windows, so as soon as we were on the rural roads outside Fresno, the dust and sand began to be sucked into the bus, whipping about like irate wasps as the gravel ticked about us. We closed our eyes, clotted up our mouths that wanted to open with embarrassed laughter because we couldn't believe we were on that bus with those people and the dust attacking us for no reason.

---

[2] Texans. [Eds.]

When we arrived at a field we followed the others to a pickup where [17] we each took a hoe and marched to stand before a row. Rick and I, self-conscious and unsure, looked around at the others who leaned on their hoes or squatted in front of the rows, almost all talking in Spanish, joking, lighting cigarettes—all waiting for the foreman's whistle to begin work. Mother had explained how to chop cotton by showing us with a broom in the backyard.

"Like this," she said, her broom swishing down weeds. "Leave one [18] plant and cut four—and cut them! Don't leave them standing or the foreman will get mad."

The foreman whistled and we started up the row stealing glances at [19] other workers to see if we were doing it right. But after awhile we worked like we knew what we were doing, neither of us hurrying or falling behind. But slowly the clot of men, women, and kids began to spread and loosen. Even Rick pulled away. I didn't hurry, though. I cut smoothly and cleanly as I walked at a slow pace, in a sort of funeral march. My eyes measured each space of cotton plants before I cut. If I missed the plants, I swished again. I worked intently, seldom looking up, so when I did I was amazed to see the sun, like a broken orange coin, in the east. It looked blurry, unbelievable, like something not of this world. I looked around in amazement, scanning the eastern horizon that was a taut line jutted with an occasional mountain. The horizon was beautiful, like a snapshot of the moon, in the early light of morning, in the quiet of no cars and few people.

The foreman trudged in boots in my direction, stepping awkward- [20] ly over the plants, to inspect the work. No one around me looked up. We all worked steadily while we waited for him to leave. When he did leave, with a feeble complaint addressed to no one in particular, we looked up smiling under straw hats and bandanas.

By 11:00, our lunch time, my ankles were hurting from walking on [21] clods the size of hardballs. My arms ached and my face was dusted by a wind that was perpetual, always busy whipping about. But the work was not bad, I thought. It was better, so much better, than picking grapes, especially with the hourly wage of a dollar twenty-five instead of piece work. Rick and I walked sorely toward the bus where we washed and drank water. Instead of eating in the bus or in the shade of the bus, we kept to ourselves by walking down to the irrigation canal that ran the length of the field, to open our lunch of sandwiches and crackers. We laughed at the crackers, which seemed like a cruel joke from our Mother, because we were working under the sun and the last thing we wanted was a salty dessert. We ate them anyway and drank more water before we returned to the field, both of us limping in exaggeration. Working side by side, we talked and laughed at our predicament because our Mother had warned us year after year that if we didn't get on track in school we'd have to work in the fields and then we would see. We mimicked Mother's whining voice and smirked at her smoky view of the future in which we'd be trapped by marriage and screaming kids. We'd eat beans and then we'd see.

Rick pulled slowly away to the rhythm of his hoe falling faster and smoother. It was better that way, to work alone. I could hum made-up songs or songs from the radio and think to myself about school and friends. At the time I was doing badly in my classes, mainly because of a difficult stepfather, but also because I didn't care anymore. All through junior high and into my first year of high school there were those who said I would never do anything, be anyone. They said I'd work like a donkey and marry the first Mexican girl that came along. I was reminded so often, verbally and in the way I was treated at home, that I began to believe that chopping cotton might be a lifetime job for me. If not chopping cotton, then I might get lucky and find myself in a car wash or restaurant or junkyard. But it was clear; I'd work, and work hard.   22

I cleared my mind by humming and looking about. The sun was directly above with a few soft blades of clouds against a sky that seemed bluer and more beautiful than our sky in the city. Occasionally the breeze flurried and picked up dust so that I had to cover my eyes and screw up my face. The workers were hunched, brown as the clods under our feet, and spread across the field that ran without end—fields that were owned by corporations, not families.   23

I hoed trying to keep my mind busy with scenes from school and pretend girlfriends until finally my brain turned off and my thinking went fuzzy with boredom. I looked about, no longer mesmerized by the beauty of the landscape, no longer wondering if the winos in the fields could hold out for eight hours, no longer dreaming of the clothes I'd buy with my pay. My eyes followed my chopping as the plants, thin as their shadows, fell with each strike. I worked slowly with ankles and arms hurting, neck stiff, and eyes stinging from the dust and the sun that glanced off the field like a mirror.   24

By quitting time, 3:00, there was such an excruciating pain in my ankles that I walked as if I were wearing snowshoes. Rick laughed at me and I laughed too, embarrassed that most of the men were walking normally and I was among the first timers who had to get used to this work. "And what about you, wino," I came back at Rick. His eyes were meshed red and his long hippie hair was flecked with dust and gnats and bits of leaves. We placed our hoes in the back of a pickup and stood in line for our pay, which was twelve fifty. I was amazed at the pay, which was the most I had ever earned in one day, and thought that I'd come back the next day, Sunday. This was too good.   25

Instead of joining the others in the labor bus, we jumped in the back 26
of a pickup when the driver said we'd get to town sooner and were welcome to join him. We scrambled into the truck bed to be joined by a heavy-set and laughing *Tejano* whose head was shaped like an egg, particularly so because the bandana he wore ended in a point on the top of his head. He laughed almost demonically as the pickup roared up the dirt path, a gray cape of dust rising behind us. On the highway, with the wind in our faces, we squinted at the fields as if we were looking for someone. The *Tejano* had quit laughing but was smiling broadly, occasionally chortling tunes he never finished. I was scared of him, though Rick, two years older and five inches taller, wasn't. If the *Tejano* looked at him, Rick stared back for a second or two before he looked away to the fields.

I felt like a soldier coming home from war when we rattled into Chi- 27
natown. People leaning against car hoods stared, their necks following us, owl-like; prostitutes chewed gum more ferociously and showed us their teeth; Chinese grocers stopped brooming their storefronts to raise their cadaverous faces at us. We stopped in front of the Chi Chi Club where Mexican music blared from the juke box and cue balls cracked like dull ice. The *Tejano*, who was dirty as we were, stepped awkwardly over the side rail, dusted himself off with his bandana, and sauntered into the club.

Rick and I jumped from the back, thanked the driver who said *de* 28
nada and popped his clutch, so that the pickup jerked and coughed blue smoke. We returned smiling to our car, happy with the money we had made and pleased that we had, in a small way, proved ourselves to be tough; that we worked as well as other men and earned the same pay.

29
We returned the next day and the next week until the season was over and there was nothing to do. I told myself that I wouldn't pick grapes that summer, saying all through June and July that it was for Mexicans, not me. When August came around and I still had not found a summer job, I ate my words, sharpened my knife, and joined Mother, Rick, and Debra for one last time.

Responding to Reading

1. How does work bring Soto closer to an understanding of his family? Has your own work experience helped you to understand your family better?
2. In paragraph 1 Soto says he recognizes his relatives in the characters he sees in the film *Gandhi*. What does he mean? Do you recognize any of your own relatives in the essay "One Last Time"?
3. Why would Soto at age fifteen "rather wear old clothes than stoop like a Mexican" (15)? Does the adult Soto understand the reasons for this sentiment? What does this comment reveal about the society in which Soto lived?

Oak Ridge, Tennessee

Bob Summer

Before becoming a writer, Bob Summer (1937–) had a long career in publishing, working for several university presses and serving as one of the founders of the Publishers Association of the South. Author of *Getting Strong, Looking Strong: A Guide to Successful Bodybuilding,* he also writes about travel, art, authors, and the book industry. He is currently the southeast correspondent for *Publishers Weekly,* the major trade magazine for publishers, booksellers, and libraries. The following essay was written for the collection *Hometowns: Gay Men Write About Where They Belong,* edited by John Preston. Here, Summer recalls how his emerging homosexuality set him apart from the East Tennessee community where he grew up, a town founded by the U.S. government in 1942 at the beginning of World War II as part of the Manhattan Project to develop and manufacture the nuclear material that powered the first atomic bomb.

"Oh, Uncle Bob, this looks like 'Happy Days,'" my niece gleefully [1] exclaimed when she discovered the 1955 *Oak Log* on the closet shelf where my mother kept the high school yearbooks of my older brother, Jimmy, my younger sister, Barbara, and myself. Each of us had gone through the school system in Oak Ridge, the small East Tennessee city to which our family moved in 1945, and the three of us were graduates of Oak Ridge High School. So Mama had in her little archive an unbroken record of life at ORHS from the late forties to 1960, years covering a relatively large chunk of the history of the town that was built over several months straddling 1942 and 1943 on the 59,000-acre reservation in the Cumberland foothills that General Leslie R. Groves selected to play a strategic role in the Manhattan Project. Bordered on the southeast and southwest by the meandering Clinch River, Oak Ridge processed the uranium that would be used in the atomic bombs that incinerated Hiroshima and Nagasaki in the world's first clouds of nuclear destruction.

My own years at Oak Ridge High School were 1952 to 1955, the [2] ninth grade still being held at Jefferson Junior High. And in our yearbook pictures I guess we do look something like Richie, Potsie, Ralph, and Joanie, the boys with their flattop haircuts, saddle oxfords, and rolled-up jeans, the girls in their swirling appliquéd skirts, sweaters, furry collars, and bobby sox. And yes, we even had a few Fonzies, with their looked-down-upon ducktails. So my niece, a child of the first full TV generation, was right in her "Happy Days" analogy. Nevertheless I do not recall those years, nor any I spent growing up in Oak Ridge, as happy days. From the time I entered third grade, after we had moved into a small boxlike flattop house unlike any I had ever seen, I always felt I belonged somewhere else.

Later—sometime in high school, I think—when I came across 3 Gertrude Stein's famous "When you get there, there isn't any there there" quote, I felt the same could be said about Oak Ridge. Certainly the town, which never really overcame the military-base look its army builders gave it, was a far cry from Milwaukee, the older city where Marion and Howard Cunningham, Richie and Joan's mom and dad on the popular TV sitcom, kept their cheerfully fiftyish middle-American home.

The new "secret" town, surrounded by a chain and barbed-wire 4 fence, where until 1949 you had to show a badge or other documentation to be admitted (often after a car check) was also far different from the mid-South Carolina rural community where my parents came from or even Columbia, that state's capitol, where I was born. When my parents, during all the years they lived in Oak Ridge, referred to "home," what they meant was their native community, called the Dutch Fork ever since Germans had settled there between the V of the Broad and Saluda rivers in the eighteenth century.

It wasn't until well into the fifties, when the U.S. government began 5 selling the houses (economically designed by the architectural firm of Skidmore, Owings, and Merrill) in Oak Ridge to the people who lived in them, that Oak Ridgers began to think of the place as home, however. At Christmas, I recall from the few we spent there, the town was virtually deserted; most families had gone "home" for the holidays. Lucky ones from nearby Appalachian towns and farms went "home" more often. And every summer when my father got his vacation from K-25, the huge (42.6 acres under one roof!) gaseous-diffusion plant where he worked for Union Carbide as an electrician, we could drive over the dizzying, curvy, pre-Interstate route crossing the Tennessee-North Carolina mountains down to the flatter Dutch Fork and home.

The couple of weeks we spent there were what I lived for with long- 6 ing the rest of the year. The warmth of my grandmother Ma Ellen's hug and laugh, the large family (uncles and aunts and cousins would be there, too) gathered around the big kitchen table at breakfast, the noon dinner, and supper, with Pa Joe, my grandfather, reigning at its head and everyone by turns regaling one another with stories—that, to me, symbolized home. At Grandmother's, my father's home place in another part of the Dutch Fork, meals were more taciturn, but the food would be deliciously plentiful and unlike any served in Oak Ridge, except at Mama's table or, in a lesser way, at that of my more "modern" aunt, Fannie Belle. My mother's younger sister, Aunt Fannie Belle and Uncle Otis and Pat, their daughter, had moved to Oak Ridge just before we did when Uncle Otis, like my father, joined the hordes of workers drawn by the many jobs the Clinton Engineer Works (named after the nearby seat of Anderson County) provided in a part of the nation that only recently had been claimed from the Depression by the Tennessee Valley Authority[1] and the war effort.

Indeed, my father had been a TVA man. And before he went to work at Oak Ridge for Union Carbide, we lived in Fontana, the town built for the workers' families when TVA was constructing Fontana Dam in western North Carolina. I began school there, although my memories of first grade are hazy. Neither do I recall much about my second grade in Knoxville, the city some twenty miles east of Oak Ridge where we lived temporarily while waiting for our name to come to the top of the list for housing assignments in the new town. But I *do* vividly recall helping my brother with his *Knoxville News Sentinel* paper route the afternoon the headline heralded the death of President Roosevelt, whose name I was raised to revere; he had made TVA possible, "saved the South" (my parents said), and nurtured the Manhattan Project. Then several months later, on August 6, the *News Sentinel* boldly announced the dropping of the atomic bomb on Hiroshima. Suddenly we and the rest of the world knew what Oak Ridge was all about.

Third grade is more firm in my memory, because by then, our name having come up on the housing list, we had moved to that prefabricated flattop in Oak Ridge. It was on a lane just off Louisiana Avenue, then the westernmost of the major north-south throughways running up the ridge from the Turnpike, which ran east to west and was the town's main highway. Miss Pippin, my teacher, told us wonderful "lessons" whether we were learning reading, writing, or arithmetic. And although she had a class filled with widely diverse speech peculiarities and economic backgrounds to work with, she somehow molded us into the oneness of rudimentary English grammar.

Except for one of her charges, whose name, I recall, was Bobby Joe. He was a sometimes playmate of mine—I was called Bobby, too—who lived in a neighboring flattop. I really didn't care to spend much time with him because of his harsh East Tennessee twang, which was so foreign to the South Carolina sounds I loved. And I didn't care at all for his fondness for daredevil roughness. Mama said he was "a real boy" while, I must admit, I wasn't yet very far from the time when my greatest pleasure was dressing up paper dolls with Marlene, my favorite cousin, upstairs in Ma Ellen and Pa Joe's big white frame house where we delightedly whiled away the long afternoons, out of sight and lost in make-believe. My brother Jimmy, whom Mama called her "little man," scorned such "sissy" things, much preferring action involving a football, baseball, rifle, or rod and reel. Those were his ideas of what a boy should

7

8

9

---

[1] A government agency created in the 1930s to develop the Tennessee River basin through a system of dams and other installations. [Eds.]

be attracted to. Bobby Joe's involved a bike that would run over things, including animals and, sometimes, people.

But after my year with Miss Pippin, we moved eastward to the sec- [10] tion of the town centered by Pine Valley, one of the several elementary schools around which various parts of town were clustered. Each section had a small convenience shopping area, also, although to buy groceries at the A&P or Tulip Town or take in movies Oak Ridgers had to go to Townsite or Grove Center. We moved into an "A" house, the smallest of the Skidmore, Owings, and Merrill cemesto designs; others increased in size the farther down the alphabet they went. But there were only a few "F" houses, the largest individual family units ("E"s being apartment houses), and they were situated atop the ridge and were reserved for local Atomic Energy Commission administrators, managers of the K-25, Y-12, and X-10 plants, and top scientists at the Oak Ridge National Laboratory.

Still, we saw our "A" house on Vermont Avenue as a great leap up- [11] ward. We had a real roof (pitched, not flat), a brick fireplace, a porch, a yard large enough for Daddy to have a vegetable garden and enclosed tool shed, and a coal furnace, instead of the space heater that so spottily heated our drafty flattop. And soon we got our first telephone. Sure, we were on a party line—but so were most Oak Ridgers. Just to have it hanging on a wall in our narrow kitchen was, to us, proof of our elevated status.

It did not really matter that my brother and I had to share a small [12] bedroom, or that Mama and Daddy had to find room for my sister's bed in their only slightly larger one, or that we all used one bathroom, that we still had boardwalks to the street, or that we didn't have a tree in our yard. Most Oak Ridgers didn't either; ironically, the trees identified in the town's name had largely been uprooted and bulldozed away when the town was being built. But there were other civic amenities nearby for us to enjoy. In supposedly classless Oak Ridge, everyone—except the relatively few blacks who were relegated to Gamble Valley on the other side of the Turnpike and out of sight after their jobs as janitors and maids were done for the day—could use the large, centrally located municipal swimming pool, the town's few tennis courts, and the recreation centers at Grove Center and Ridge Hall, where the public library was located.

We even joined a church, Grace Lutheran, although its Sunday ser- [13] vices were not held in a real church—not like the Chapel on the Hill, one of Oak Ridge's two actual church buildings in those early years—but in Ridge Hall, just as First Methodist's larger congregation gathered in the Ridge Theatre before the movies began later Sunday afternoon. The Summers and the Lowmans, my mother's family, were traditionally Lutheran, so I assume my parents thought that since they were putting down roots they should support the mission church their denomination was establishing in a state that was predominantly Baptist and Methodist. Never mind that the few Lutheran faithful gathered into the small Oak Ridge flock were in large part Midwesterners, one of whom my mother, at a woman's circle meeting, overheard talking derisively about Southerners.

Once when Mama's brother Paul, then a Nabisco executive head- [14] quartered in New York City, and his wife drove through Oak Ridge with their two children on their way south, Daddy was chagrined too when Aunt Vivian proclaimed that the town was full of "floaters." Daddy was loyal to the place, even if it was not "home," and Mama was peeved too but let it pass. The Lowmans had never liked Uncle Paul's wife, and this was just another example of her flightiness, I suppose my mother reasoned. I let it pass, too, since I was much more interested in hearing my cousin Peggy tell all about the Broadway musicals she had seen, Radio City Music Hall, and movie stars she had glimpsed. Already a big fan of such radio shows as Tallulah Bankhead's "Big Show" and "The Lux Radio Theatre" ("Lux presents Hollywood," the announcer intoned each week), I was bedazzled by the glamour of show business.

"Let's Pretend," a nationally broadcast show that came over a [15] Knoxville station—WATO, Oak Ridge's own new station, had mostly local programs—on Saturday morning was another favorite, and weekly I would be glued to it after we had gone to see the Oak Ridge High Wildcats play a football rival the night before. Daddy was a big booster, as were most plant workers; there were pregame parades through town to whip up spirit. But at Blankenship Field, where the games were played, I was more interested in seeing what the girls and women in the crowd were wearing, the half-time show, and looking at the players pictured in the printed program with their exaggeratedly masculine scowls, padded shoulders, and form-fitting pants. I even drew some of them when I got home, though I kept my sketches hidden and never showed them to anyone.

Ever since I had realized my attraction to the visual, I had kept a [16] scrapbook in which I pasted appealing pictures clipped from magazines. And when we learned how to use the library at Pine Valley and were allowed to check out books, I would first look to see if those I pulled off the shelves were illustrated. I quickly became an N. C. Wyeth snob, and if he was not the illustrator I assumed the book was not worth my time. But Mama, seeing my enthusiasm for books, had an unillustrated edition of *Heidi* for me on Christmas morning one year, along with the usual gifts of clothes and shoes plus my customary stocking filled with oranges, tangerines, and pecans (South Carolina style). Neither she nor my father cared much for books, and the only ones we had in our house were a Webster's dictionary, a United States atlas, and a King James Bible, which I liked to peak into to gaze at an illustration of a heavily muscled Samson wrestling with the lions.

I also adored Mrs. Cunningham, my fourth-grade teacher. A North [17]
Carolinian, she was actually from Ava Gardner's[2] hometown. But
what proved more enduring in my memory was the mesmerizing way
in which she indulged my fascination for historical tales. To her, history was synonymous with murals, and that year we painted several,
including one of the Parthenon[3] reconstructed in Nashville (the
"Athens of the South") late in the nineteenth century. Of course, few
of Mrs. Cunningham's students had actually seen it, but she brought
in lots of brochures and other illuminating information. And we must
have done a pretty good job of following the pictures we painted from,
since the mural was prominently hung in Pine Valley's main hallway,
where it remained for several years—perhaps until the school was
later closed because of a shift in Oak Ridge's population after it declined from a wartime high of over 80,000 and stabilized at around
29,000.

Becoming a budding muralist under the guidance of Mrs. Cun- [18]
ningham and Pine Valley's art teacher, I preferred to dawdle over our
painting of the month while my classmates hurried out for recess to the
large playing field behind the school. I guess I figured that once again
when teams were divided up for the day's sport I would not be chosen
until last; paints and brushes, probably, were subterfuges to hide my
physical awkwardness. But whatever the reason, they held greater attraction for me than a football, basketball, or baseball, even though my
brother was beginning to win fame as one of Oak Ridge's best all-
around athletes. Back in South Carolina I would close my ears to the *ohs*
and *ahs* about him, anxiously awaiting the "old-time" stories told at Ma
Ellen and Pa Joe's table, or on their sprawling front porch.

The only stories Oak Ridgers told each other concerned the mud, [19]
coal soot, and other inconveniences of living there. Although the fenced-
in area included several older cemeteries and other vestiges of the rural
people who earlier lived among the hills and valleys upon which the
reservation was superimposed, that preceding culture was seldom mentioned. Not until I was in high school did I become aware of John Hendrix, the psychic Ridger from an earlier era who predicted that something like Oak Ridge would replace the area's traditional ways of life.

One of the vestiges of an older culture was a brick school that was [20]
left standing to become a part of the added-on structure built to house
Jefferson Junior High, which I became increasingly apprehensive about
entering as time grew closer for me to leave Pine Valley at the end of
sixth grade. My brother had cut a swathe there and I was terrified of

---

[2] Glamorous film star of the 1940s and 1950s. [Eds.]

[3] Ancient Greek temple still surviving in Athens, a replica of which is located in Nashville, Tennessee. [Eds.]

having to follow his shadowing reputation. The only things I excelled in were checking out library books, mural painting, and going to movies, usually alone. Daddy had bought a piano for me and my sister (and perhaps as another badge of our improving economic situation), but deep down I knew he would much prefer that I play football. And I was reluctant to bring home a new friend I somehow lucked out in making after Mama commented that he "was nothing but a sissy." So I tried hard to memorize sports scores, batting averages, and so forth when I poured over the *News Sentinel* sports pages each afternoon after I had finished my paper route. I wanted—passionately—to impress my male classmates with my sports knowledge.

I doubt I ever really did, but at least I found a couple of boys I could [21] sit comfortably beside on the school bus and go to football games with, no longer having to tag along with my parents. And I was even invited to join a group of paired boys and girls to go to Saturday afternoon serials at the Center Theatre on Jackson Square. I thought of it as my first date, and somehow mustered the courage to put my arm around my "girlfriend" when I noticed, there in the flickering dark, the other boys doing that with theirs.

The member of the group I eventually became closest to, however, [22] was a shy boy who *was* good at sports but didn't make a big deal out of it, preferring instead quieter, more individual pursuits. Oh, we never grew to be best friends, but we did become well-acquainted enough to trade sly jokes in the hallway between classes; his low-key and easy sense of humor appealed to me. And as he began making his passage through puberty, Jack—a fictitious name—began filling out his body so muscularly that when he went to the Oak Ridge Swimming Pool during the summer, pubescent girls would clamor to find ways to get close to him. But although he played team sports at Jefferson and on through high school, there was something about his self-mocking way that kept him from being one of the boys who hung out at the Wildcat Den, ORHS's recreation center where football victories were celebrated on Friday nights, or who cruised (in cars borrowed from their parents) around the Blue Circle diner on the Turnpike, where everyone who was thought to matter went after the movies on Saturday night.

Occasionally I swung by the Blue Circle also to see the football play- [23] ers, cheerleaders, majorettes, and other ORHS stars shining there. Although Jefferson was a social fizzle for me, I nonetheless held tightly to my fantasy that my status would markedly improve at Oak Ridge High, which by the time I entered had moved into a sprawling brick-and-glass building that was the town's pride. After all, I convinced myself, everyone there would respect who I was: Jimmy Summer's brother. President of the student council, football team captain, the "most outstanding" male senior in the yearbook's superlatives, and a prize catch for a string of Oak Ridge's prettiest girls, he was *the* big man on campus.

Alas, little of that brilliance touched me. Oh, I did get elected to [24] student council, but not as an officer. And I was chosen by my homeroom class to meet Eleanor Roosevelt when the peripatetic former First Lady stopped in Oak Ridge—then a Democratic outpost in staunchly Republican East Tennessee—and visited ORHS in February 1955. I was a prom attendant the year the decorating committee (on which I served) transformed the school cafeteria with blue lights and crepe paper finely shredded to resemble—supposedly—Spanish moss, and, completing the "southern nights" theme, built an ersatz pillored veranda at the large room's end, where the prom king and queen, together with also-rans (including me), were presented. And in the 1955 *Oak Log*, the one that later delighted my niece, I'm pictured among the class superlatives as the "most courteous" boy. That was also the year I became a lifeguard at the Oak Ridge Swimming Pool, another of my little glories.

By then we had moved to a larger house, a "C" at the corner of [25] Pennsylvania Avenue and West Pawley Road. Later, when the federal government offered the town's houses to the families that lived in them, Daddy and Mama bought it, the first and only house they ever owned. Oak Ridge had steadily become what was locally thought to be more normal since the opening of the gates in 1949, a big celebration that, for some curious reason, was attended by Adolfe Menjou, Adele Jergens, Marie "the Body" McDonald, and cowboy Rod Cameron, all lesser movie stars of varying brilliance.

And by 1954 television finally was being beamed through the East [26] Tennessee hills vividly enough that Daddy bought us our first set, though he grumbled that TV was a fad that wouldn't last. Now we too could watch "I Love Lucy," "Howdy Doody," and Dick Clark's "American Bandstand," the latter to learn the new R&R dance steps. Too, we all stayed home to watch the "Ed Sullivan Show" that Sunday night Elvis the Pelvis shook up the nation. Mama and Daddy were shocked, and I thought that was the end for our TV set.

In the mid-fifties, also, Oak Ridge got its first large shopping center, [27] ironically named Downtown. That meant Oak Ridgers no longer had to drive to Knoxville to shop for clothes, shoes, home furnishings, and other items unavailable in satisfactory selections in "the Atomic City," the town's sobriquet increasingly appearing on tourist brochures. Now we had our own Sears, J. C. Penney, Miller's (a Knoxville-based department store), and Gateway, which sold books and the largest variety of magazines I had yet seen. It was there I discovered bodybuilding magazines, one of which I secretly bought from my paper route income and showed to Jack the next day. ORHS did not have any weights among its gym facilities when we were there—the pumping iron era was a couple decades in the future—but he knew what bodybuilders were. "They lift barbells out in California," he explained, "to develop big arms and chests larger than a woman's tits."

I heard about other things, too, from my ORHS classmates that [28] would later crop up in my life. One day when Mr. X assigned his class to read one of Oscar Wilde's[4] better-known plays, a girl in the back of the classroom giggled. In the hall after class I asked her what was so funny. "Don't you know?" she said; "He"—and she dropped her voice to a whisper—"was a homosexual." I had never heard that word spoken before, although I knew that was what "queer" referred to when I heard it bantered around the locker room during my dreaded gym classes, or saw it scrawled on a men's room wall. I had even heard it applied to Mr. X, who was labeled a "queer" in that locker-room talk, although we knew he was married and a father, as well as one of the Wildcats' most vocal cheerleaders; he was always in the bleachers or stands at every football or basketball game and track meet.

I was in Mr. X's homeroom class when the *Brown* vs. *Board of Edu-* [29] *cation of Topeka* decision came down from the Supreme Court, destroying the separate-but-equal doctrine that had prevailed in the South for generations. Mr. X asked us how we would feel about going to school with Negroes, and when it came my turn to answer I smugly drew on my sophomoric "Madly for Adlai" liberalism that had blossomed when the Democrats first ran Stevenson for president. It, I said, would give "us" the opportunity to be good examples to "them." The memory of that, I confess, never ceases to shame me.

I graduated from ORHS, however, before integration; that came [30] during my sister's time. And although comparatively few blacks initially enrolled in Oak Ridge's schools—generally acclaimed as among Tennessee's best—several were in my sister Barbara's graduating class. It upset my parents to see their pretty young daughter walking down the auditorium's aisles with them to receive their diplomas.

I had gone to college at the University of Tennessee in Knoxville, not [31] because I chose it but because my father told me he wouldn't help pay for me to go anywhere else and the in-state tuition was too good a deal to pass up. (Besides, he was a Vol football fan, and once named a couple of beagles we owned after sensational halfback Hank Lauricella; the male was called Hank and the bitch Laura.) But each summer I returned to Oak Ridge to resume my lifeguard duties, although the pool we had once been so proud of was less a public draw, now that there was a country club to the west of town and some subdivisions of new houses with swimming pools.

I had lost track of Jack, since he had gone to another college and [32] spent his summers elsewhere. And I had little social life, aside from the

---

[4] Irish playwright (1854–1900), acclaimed for his witty and sophisticated works, who was imprisoned at the height of his career because of his homosexuality. [Eds.]

movies and an occasional play at the Oak Ridge Community Playhouse, which together with the town's public library, the Oak Ridge Civic Musical Association (founded by music-loving, classically-bent scientists during Oak Ridge's beginning years), and the Art Center, provided a "cultural" outlet for Oak Ridgers inclined that way.

I continued to be a constant patron of the public library those summers, going through Hemingway and Fitzgerald one year, and Thomas Wolfe the next. But I read other authors also, including Gore Vidal. It was during my Wolfe summer that I picked up a paperback copy of Vidal's *The City and the Pillar* at Gateway. Mama, Daddy, and Barbara had gone "home" to South Carolina, and I was alone in Oak Ridge. Before going to the pool for the evening lifeguard shift, I stretched out on the chaise longue on our porch and read the paperback from cover to cover, excitedly turning the pages. Nevertheless, the ending was shattering, and I headed up Pennsylvania Avenue to sort out the book's impact on me. As I neared the top of the hill in the late afternoon sunlight, it hit me: That book is about what I am, I admitted to myself for the first time—a homosexual. In that second of self-realization, I was pierced with an intensity greater than any I have ever known. 33

I did not have the boldness, however, to act on my awareness until some years later, guiltily resolving each New Year's to grow out of it. And I never saw Jack again, although I randomly followed him through items I saw in *The Oak Ridger* newspaper when I returned to visit my parents from places I subsequently lived. But one night, at a park on Melton Hill Lake, just outside of town, a furtive police raid on an alleged homosexual ring gathered there nabbed some prominent Oak Ridge men, including, to my stunned surprise, Jack, who had made his home in Oak Ridge and was married and, I think, a father. The resulting scandal was big news in *The Oak Ridger*, and the identified men were forced out of their jobs and out of the area to rebuild their lives elsewhere. Finally, Oak Ridge as home had eluded them too. 34

Responding to Reading

1. Throughout his autobiographical essay, Summer develops two themes—his sense of being different from other boys his age and his family's need for roots. How are these two themes related? Are they ever reconciled?
2. In paragraphs 12 and 29–30 Summer briefly (and somewhat offhandedly) comments on the status of blacks in Oak Ridge. What purpose do these comments serve? Do they add something important to the essay, or could they be deleted?
3. Not until paragraph 33 does Summer reveal that he is a gay man. Do you think his sexual orientation is central or incidental to the ideas his essay expresses about home and family? Explain your conclusion.

Once More to the Lake

E. B. White

One of the America's best-loved essayists, E. B. White (1899–1986) enjoyed an almost idyllic childhood in Mt. Vernon, New York, graduated from college in 1921, and embarked on a career writing for newspapers. Soon he was writing essays for *The New Yorker* and *Harper's Magazine.* White wrote the children's classic *Charlotte's Web* (1952); in 1959 he expanded Will Strunk's grammar book, which White had used as his student, into the now classic *The Elements of Style;* and he published essays in the collections *One Man's Meat* (1944) and *Essays of E. B. White* (1977). In his nostalgic "Once More to the Lake," White revisits the lake in Maine where he vacationed as a boy with his family and explores the themes of time and change.

One summer, along about 1904, my father rented a camp on a lake 1
in Maine and took us all there for the month of August. We all got ringworm from some kittens and had to rub Pond's Extract on our arms and legs night and morning, and my father rolled over in a canoe with all his clothes on; but outside of that the vacation was a success and from then on none of us ever thought there was any place in the world like that lake in Maine. We returned summer after summer—always on August 1st for one month. I have since become a salt-water man, but sometimes in summer there are days when the restlessness of the tides and the fearful cold of the sea water and the incessant wind which blows across the afternoon and into the evening make me wish for the placidity of a lake in the woods. A few weeks ago this feeling got so strong I bought myself a couple of bass hooks and a spinner and returned to the lake where we used to go, for a week's fishing and to revisit old haunts.

I took along my son, who had never had any fresh water up his nose 2
and who had seen lily pads only from train windows. On the journey over to the lake I began to wonder what it would be like. I wondered how time would have marred this unique, this holy spot—the coves and streams, the hills that the sun set behind, the camps and the paths behind the camps. I was sure the tarred road would have found it out and I wondered in what other ways it would be desolated. It is strange how much you can remember about places like that once you allow your mind to return into the grooves which lead back. You remember one thing, and that suddenly reminds you of another thing. I guess I remembered clearest of all the early mornings, when the lake was cool and motionless, remembered how the bedroom smelled of the lumber it was made of and of the wet woods whose scent entered through the screen.

The partitions in the camp were thin and did not extend clear to the top of the rooms, and as I was always the first up I would dress softly so as not to wake the others, and sneak out into the sweet outdoors and start out in the canoe, keeping close along the shore in the long shadows of the pines. I remembered being very careful never to rub my paddle against the gunwale for fear of disturbing the stillness of the cathedral.

The lake had never been what you would call a wild lake. There 3 were cottages sprinkled around the shores, and it was in farming country although the shores of the lake were quite heavily wooded. Some of the cottages were owned by nearby farmers, and you would live at the shore and eat your meals at the farmhouse. That's what our family did. But although it wasn't wild, it was a fairly large and undisturbed lake and there were places in it which, to a child at least, seemed infinitely remote and primeval.

I was right about the tar: it led to within half a mile of the shore. But 4 when I got back there, with my boy, and we settled into a camp near a farmhouse and into the kind of summertime I had known, I could tell that it was going to be pretty much the same as it had been before—I knew it, lying in bed the first morning, smelling the bedroom, and hearing the boy sneak quietly out and go off along the shore in a boat. I began to sustain the illusion that he was I, and therefore, by simple transposition, that I was my father. This sensation persisted, kept cropping up all the time we were there. It was not an entirely new feeling, but in this setting it grew much stronger. I seemed to be living a dual existence. I would be in the middle of some simple act, I would be picking up a bait box or laying down a table fork, or I would be saying something, and suddenly it would be not I but my father who was saying the words or making the gesture. It gave me a creepy sensation.

We went fishing the first morning. I felt the same damp moss cov- 5 ering the worms in the bait can, and saw the dragonfly alight on the tip of my rod as it hovered a few inches from the surface of the water. It was the arrival of this fly that convinced me beyond any doubt that everything was as it always had been, that the years were a mirage and there had been no years. The small waves were the same, chucking the rowboat under the chin as we fished at anchor, and the boat was the same boat, the same color green and the ribs broken in the same places, and under the floor-boards the same freshwater leavings and débris—the dead helgramite,[1] the wisps of moss, the rusty discarded fishhook, the dried blood from yesterday's catch. We stared silently at the tips of our rods, at the dragonflies that came and went. I lowered the tip of mine into the water, tentatively, pensively dislodging the fly, which darted two feet away, poised, darted two feet back, and came to rest again a lit-

---

[1] The nymph of the May-fly, used as bait. [Eds.]

tle farther up the rod. There had been no years between the ducking of this dragonfly and the other one—the one that was part of memory. I looked at the boy, who was silently watching his fly, and it was my hands that held his rod, my eyes watching. I felt dizzy and didn't know which rod I was at the end of.

We caught two bass, hauling them in briskly as though they were   6
mackerel, pulling them over the side of the boat in a businesslike manner without any landing net, and stunning them with a blow on the back of the head. When we got back for a swim before lunch, the lake was exactly where we had left it, the same number of inches from the dock, and there was only the merest suggestion of a breeze. This seemed an utterly enchanted sea, this lake you could leave to its own devices for a few hours and come back to, and find that it had not stirred, this constant and trustworthy body of water. In the shallows, the dark, water-soaked sticks and twigs, smooth and old, were undulating in clusters on the bottom against the clean ribbed sand, and the track of the mussel was plain. A school of minnows swam by, each minnow with its small individual shadow, doubling the attendance, so clear and sharp in the sunlight. Some of the other campers were in swimming, along the shore, one of them with a cake of soap, and the water felt thin and clear and unsubstantial. Over the years there had been this person with the cake of soap, this cultist, and here he was. There had been no years.

Up to the farmhouse to dinner through the teeming, dusty field, the   7
road under our sneakers was only a two-track road. The middle track was missing, the one with the marks of the hooves and the splotches of dried, flaky manure. There had always been three tracks to choose from in choosing which track to walk in; now the choice was narrowed down to two. For a moment I missed terribly the middle alternative. But the way led past the tennis court, and something about the way it lay there in the sun reassured me; the tape had loosened along the backline, the alleys were green with plantains and other weeds, and the net (installed in June and removed in September) sagged in the dry noon, and the whole place steamed with midday heat and hunger and emptiness. There was a choice of pie for dessert, and one was blueberry and one was apple, and the waitresses were the same country girls, there having been no passage of time, only the illusion of it as in a dropped curtain— the waitresses were still fifteen; their hair had been washed, that was the only difference—they had been to the movies and seen the pretty girls with the clean hair.

Summertime, oh summertime, pattern of life indelible, the fade-   8
proof lake, the woods unshatterable, the pasture with the sweetfern and the juniper forever and ever, summer without end; this was the background, and the life along the shore was the design, the cottagers with their innocent and tranquil design, their tiny docks with the flagpole and the American flag floating against the white clouds in the blue sky, the

little paths over the roots of the trees leading from camp to camp and the paths leading back to the outhouses and the can of lime for sprinkling, and at the souvenir counters at the store the miniature birch-bark canoes and the post cards that showed things looking a little better than they looked. This was the American family at play, escaping the city heat, wondering whether the newcomers in the camp at the head of the cove were "common" or "nice," wondering whether it was true that the people who drove up for Sunday dinner at the farmhouse were turned away because there wasn't enough chicken.

It seemed to me, as I kept remembering all this, that those times and those summers had been infinitely precious and worth saving. There [9] had been jollity and peace and goodness. The arriving (at the beginning of August) had been so big a business in itself, at the railway station the farm wagon drawn up, the first smell of the pine-laden air, the first glimpse of the smiling farmer, and the great importance of the trunks and your father's enormous authority in such matters, and the feel of the wagon under you for the long ten-mile haul, and at the top of the last long hill catching the first view of the lake after eleven months of not seeing this cherished body of water. The shouts and cries of the other campers when they saw you, and the trunks to be unpacked, to give up their rich burden. (Arriving was less exciting nowadays, when you sneaked up in your car and parked it under a tree near the camp and took out the bags and in five minutes it was all over, no fuss, no loud wonderful fuss about trunks.)

Peace and goodness and jollity. The only thing that was wrong now, [10] really, was the sound of the place, an unfamiliar nervous sound of the outboard motors. This was the note that jarred, the one thing that would sometimes break the illusion and set the years moving. In those other summertimes all motors were inboard; and when they were at a little distance, the noise they made was a sedative, an ingredient of summer sleep. They were one-cylinder and two-cylinder engines, and some were make-and-break and some were jump-spark,[2] but they all made a sleepy sound across the lake. The one-lungers throbbed and fluttered, and the twin-cylinder ones purred and purred, and that was a quiet sound too. But now the campers all had outboards. In the daytime, in the hot mornings, these motors made a petulant, irritable sound; at night, in the still evening when the afterglow lit the water, they whined about one's ears like mosquitoes. My boy loved our rented outboard, and his great desire was to achieve singlehanded mastery over it, and authority, and he soon learned the trick of choking it a little (but not too much), and the adjustment of the needle valve. Watching him I would remember the things you could do with the old one-cylinder engine with the heavy fly-

---

[2] Methods of ignition timing. [Eds.]

wheel, how you could have it eating out of your hand if you got really close to it spiritually. Motor boats in those days didn't have clutches, and you would make a landing by shutting off the motor at the proper time and coasting in with a dead rudder. But there was a way of reversing them, if you learned the trick, by cutting the switch and putting it on again exactly on the final dying revolution of the flywheel, so that it would kick back against compression and begin reversing. Approaching a dock in a strong following breeze, it was difficult to slow up sufficiently by the ordinary coasting method, and if a boy felt he had complete mastery over his motor, he was tempted to keep it running beyond its time and then reverse it a few feet from the dock. It took a cool nerve, because if you threw the switch a twentieth of a second too soon you would catch the flywheel when it still had speed enough to go up past center, and the boat would leap ahead, charging bull-fashion at the dock.

We had a good week at the camp. The bass were biting well and the [11] sun shone endlessly, day after day. We would be tired at night and lie down in the accumulated heat of the little bedrooms after the long hot day and the breeze would stir almost imperceptibly outside and the smell of the swamp drift in through the rusty screens. Sleep would come easily and in the morning the red squirrel would be on the roof, tapping out his gay routine. I kept remembering everything, lying in bed in the mornings—the small steamboat that had a long rounded stern like the lip of a Ubangi, and how quietly she ran on the moonlight sails, when the older boys played their mandolins and the girls sang and we ate doughnuts dipped in sugar, and how sweet the music was on the water in the shining night, and what it had felt like to think about girls then. After breakfast we would go up to the store and the things were in the same place—the minnows in a bottle, the plugs and spinners disarranged and pawed over by the youngsters from the boys' camp, the fig newtons and the Beeman's gum. Outside, the road was tarred and cars stood in front of the store. Inside, all was just as it had always been, except there was more Coca-Cola and not so much Moxie and root beer and birch beer and sarsaparilla. We would walk out with a bottle of pop apiece and sometimes the pop would backfire up our noses and hurt. We explored the streams, quietly, where the turtles slid off the sunny logs and dug their way into the soft bottom; and we lay on the town wharf and fed worms to the tame bass. Everywhere we went I had trouble making out which was I, the one walking at my side, the one walking in my pants.

One afternoon while we were there at that lake a thunderstorm came [12] up. It was like the revival of an old melodrama that I had seen long ago with childish awe. The second-act climax of the drama of the electrical disturbance over a lake in America had not changed in any important respect. This was the big scene, still the big scene. The whole thing was so familiar, the first feeling of oppression and heat and a general air around camp of not wanting to go very far away. In midafternoon (it was all the same) a curious darkening of the sky, and a lull in everything that had made life tick; and then the way the boats suddenly swung the other way at their moorings with the coming of a breeze out of the new quarter, and the premonitory rumble. Then the kettle drum, then the snare, then the bass drum and cymbals, then crackling light against the dark, and the gods grinning and licking their chops in the hills. Afterward the calm, the rain steadily rustling in the calm lake, the return of light and hope and spirits, and the campers running out in joy and relief to go swimming in the rain, their bright cries perpetuating the deathless joke about how they were getting simply drenched, and the children scream-ing with delight at the new sensation of bathing in the rain, and the joke about getting drenched linking the generations in a strong indestructible chain. And the comedian who waded in carrying an umbrella.

When the others went swimming my son said he was going in too. He [13] pulled his dripping trunks from the line where they had hung all through the shower, and wrung them out. Languidly, and with no thought of going in, I watched him, his hard little body, skinny and bare, saw him wince slightly as he pulled up around his vitals the small, soggy, icy garment. As he buckled the swollen belt suddenly my groin felt the chill of death.

Responding to Reading

1. How is White's "holy spot" different when he visits it with his son? Is the essay primarily about his visits as a child or about his return? Is there a place that has the same kind of special significance for you or for your family?
2. Does this essay focus primarily on a time, a place, or a relationship? Explain.
3. Why does White feel "the chill of death" (13) as he watches his son? Do you think you have to be a parent to share White's sentiments?

No Name Woman

Maxine Hong Kingston

Maxine Hong Kingston (1940–), a native of California, is a nonfiction writer who has taught English in high school and at the University of Hawaii. She also contributes to *Ms., The New Yorker, American Heritage,* and other publications. Her most recent work is the novel *Tripmaster Monkey: His Fake Book* (1989). In her autobiography, *The Woman Warrior: Memoirs of a Girlhood Among Ghosts* (1976), and in *China Men* (1980)

Kingston explores her Chinese ancestry. She said of *The Woman Warrior* in a 1983 interview, "One of the themes in *Warrior* was: what is it that's a story and what is it that's life? . . . Sometimes the boundaries are very clear, and sometimes they interlace and we live out stories." In the following selection from *The Woman Warrior*, Kingston tells the story of her aunt in China, who disgraced her family and suffered neglect and despair.

"You must not tell anyone," my mother said, "what I am about to 1
tell you. In China your father had a sister who killed herself. She jumped into the family well. We say that your father has all brothers because it is as if she had never been born.

"In 1924 just a few days after our village celebrated seventeen hurry- 2
up weddings—to make sure that every young man who went 'out on the road' would responsibly come home—your father and his brothers and your grandfather and his brothers and your aunt's new husband sailed for America, the Gold Mountain. It was your grandfather's last trip. Those lucky enough to get contracts waved good-bye from the decks. They fed and guarded the stowaways and helped them off in Cuba, New York, Bali, Hawaii. 'We'll meet in California next year,' they said. All of them sent money home.

"I remember looking at your aunt one day when she and I were 3
dressing; I had not noticed before that she had such a protruding melon of a stomach. But I did not think, 'She's pregnant,' until she began to look like other pregnant women, her shirt pulling and the white tops of her black pants showing. She could not have been pregnant, you see, because her husband had been gone for years. No one said anything. We did not discuss it. In early summer she was ready to have the child, long after the time when it could have been possible.

"The village had also been counting. On the night the baby was to 4
be born the villagers raided our house. Some were crying. Like a great saw, teeth strung with lights, files of people walked zigzag across our land, tearing the rice. Their lanterns doubled in the disturbed black water, which drained away through the broken bunds. As the villagers closed in, we could see that some of them, probably men and women we knew well, wore white masks. The people with long hair hung it over their faces. Women with short hair made it stand up on end. Some had tied white bands around their foreheads, arms, and legs.

"At first they threw mud and rocks at the house. Then they threw 5
eggs and began slaughtering our stock. We could hear the animals scream their deaths—the roosters, the pigs, a last great roar from the ox. Familiar wild heads flared in our night windows; the villagers encircled us. Some of the faces stopped to peer at us, their eyes rushing like searchlights. The hands flattened against the panes, framed heads, and left red prints.

"The villagers broke in the front and the back doors at the same [6] time, even though we had not locked the doors against them. Their knives dripped with the blood of our animals. They smeared blood on the doors and walls. One woman swung a chicken, whose throat she had slit, splattering blood in red arcs about her. We stood together in the middle of our house, in the family hall with the pictures and tables of the ancestors around us, and looked straight ahead.

"At the time the house had only two wings. When the men came [7] back, we would build two more to enclose our courtyard and a third one to begin a second courtyard. The villagers pushed through both wings, even your grandparents' rooms, to find your aunt's, which was also mine until the men returned. From this room a new wing for one of the younger families would grow. They ripped up her clothes and shoes and broke her combs, grinding them underfoot. They tore her work from the loom. They scattered the cooking fire and rolled the new weaving in it. We could hear them in the kitchen breaking our bowls and banging the pots. They overturned the great waist-high earthenware jugs; duck eggs, pickled fruits, vegetables burst out and mixed in acrid torrents. The old woman from the next field swept a broom through the air and loosed the spirits-of-the-broom over our heads. 'Pig.' 'Ghost.' 'Pig,' they sobbed and scolded while they ruined our house.

"When they left, they took sugar and oranges to bless themselves. [8] They cut pieces from the dead animals. Some of them took bowls that were not broken and clothes that were not torn. Afterward we swept up the rice and sewed it back up into sacks. But the smells from the spilled preserves lasted. Your aunt gave birth in the pigsty that night. The next morning when I went for the water, I found her and the baby plugging up the family well.

"Don't let your father know that I told you. He denies her. Now that [9] you have started to menstruate, what happened to her could happen to you. Don't humiliate us. You wouldn't like to be forgotten as if you had never been born. The villagers are watchful."

Whenever she had to warn us about life, my mother told stories that [10] ran like this one, a story to grow up on. She tested our strength to establish realities. Those in the emigrant generations who could not reassert brute survival died young and far from home. Those of us in the first American generations have had to figure out how the invisible world the emigrants built around our childhoods fit in solid America.

The emigrants confused the gods by diverting their curses, mis- [11] leading them with crooked streets and false names. They must try to confuse their offspring as well, who, I suppose, threaten them in similar ways—always trying to get things straight, always trying to name the unspeakable. The Chinese I know hide their names; sojourners take new names when their lives change and guard their real names with silence.

Chinese-Americans, when you try to understand what things in you [12] are Chinese, how do you separate what is peculiar to childhood, to poverty, insanities, one family, your mother who marked your growing with stories, from what is Chinese? What is Chinese tradition and what is the movies?

If I want to learn what clothes my aunt wore, whether flashy or or- [13] dinary, I would have to begin, "Remember Father's drowned-in-the-well sister?" I cannot ask that. My mother has told me once and for all the useful parts. She will add nothing unless powered by Necessity, a riverbank that guides her life. She plants vegetable gardens rather than lawns; she carries the odd-shaped tomatoes home from the fields and eats food left for the gods.

Whenever we did frivolous things, we used up energy; we flew high [14] kites. We children came up off the ground over the melting cones our parents brought home from work and the American movie on New Year's Day—*Oh, You Beautiful Doll* with Betty Grable one year, and *She Wore a Yellow Ribbon* with John Wayne another year. After the one carnival ride each, we paid in guilt; our tired father counted his change on the dark walk home.

Adultery is extravagance. Could people who hatch their own chicks [15] and eat the embryos and the heads for delicacies and boil the feet in vinegar for party food, leaving only the gravel, eating even the gizzard lining—could such people engender a prodigal aunt? To be a woman, to have a daughter in starvation time was a waste enough. My aunt could not have been the lone romantic who gave up everything for sex. Women in the old China did not choose. Some man had commanded her to lie with him and be his secret evil. I wonder whether he masked himself when he joined the raid on her family.

Perhaps she encountered him in the fields or on the mountain where [16] the daughters-in-law collected fuel. Or perhaps he first noticed her in the marketplace. He was not a stranger because the village housed no strangers. She had to have dealings with him other than sex. Perhaps he worked an adjoining field, or he sold her the cloth for the dress she sewed and wore. His demand must have surprised, then terrified her. She obeyed him; she always did as she was told.

When the family found a young man in the next village to be her [17] husband, she stood tractably beside the best rooster, his proxy, and promised before they met that she would be his forever. She was lucky that he was her age and she would be the first wife, an advantage secure now. The night she first saw him, he had sex with her. Then he left for America. She had almost forgotten what he looked like. When she tried to envision him, she only saw the black and white face in the group photograph the men had had taken before leaving.

The other man was not, after all, much different from her husband. [18] They both gave orders: she followed. "If you tell your family, I'll beat you. I'll kill you. Be here again next week." No one talked sex, ever. And she might have separated the rapes from the rest of living if only she did not have to buy her oil from him or gather wood in the same forest. I want her fear to have lasted just as long as rape lasted so that the fear could have been contained. No drawn-out fear. But women at sex hazarded birth and hence lifetimes. The fear did not stop but permeated everywhere. She told the man, "I think I'm pregnant." He organized the raid against her.

On nights when my mother and father talked about their life back [19] home, sometimes they mentioned an "outcast table" whose business they still seemed to be settling, their voices tight. In a commensal[1] tradition, where food is precious, the powerful older people made wrongdoers eat alone. Instead of letting them start separate new lives like the Japanese, who could become samurais and geishas, the Chinese family, faces averted but eyes glowering sideways, hung on to the offenders and fed them leftovers. My aunt must have lived in the same house as my parents and eaten at an outcast table. My mother spoke about the raid as if she had seen it, when she and my aunt, a daughter-in-law to a different household, should not have been living together at all. Daughters-in-law lived with their husbands' parents, not their own; a synonym for marriage in Chinese is "taking a daughter-in-law." Her husband's parents could have sold her, mortgaged her, stoned her. But they had sent her back to her own mother and father, a mysterious act hinting at disgraces not told me. Perhaps they had thrown her out to deflect the avengers.

She was the only daughter; her four brothers went with her father, [20] husband, and uncles "out on the road" and for some years became western men. When the goods were divided among the family, three of the brothers took land, and the youngest, my father, chose an education. After my grandparents gave their daughter away to her husband's family, they had dispensed all the adventure and all the property. They expected her alone to keep the traditional ways, which her brothers, now among the barbarians, could fumble without detection. The heavy, deep-rooted women were to maintain the past against the flood, safe for returning. But the rare urge west had fixed upon our family, and so my aunt crossed boundaries not delineated in space.

The work of preservation demands that the feelings playing about in [21] one's guts not be turned into action. Just watch their passing like cherry blossoms. But perhaps my aunt, my forerunner, caught in a slow life, let dreams grow and fade and after some months or years went toward what persisted. Fear at the enormities of the forbidden kept her desires delicate,

---

[1] Eating at the same table; sharing meals as table companions. [Eds.]

wire and bone. She looked at a man because she liked the way the hair was tucked behind his ears, or she liked the question-mark line of a long torso curving at the shoulder and straight at the hip. For warm eyes or a soft voice or a slow walk—that's all—a few hairs, a line, a brightness, a sound, a pace, she gave up family. She offered us up for a charm that vanished with tiredness, a pigtail that didn't toss when the wind died. Why, the wrong lighting could erase the dearest thing about him.

It could very well have been, however, that my aunt did not take [22] subtle enjoyment of her friend, but, a wild woman, kept rollicking company. Imagining her free with sex doesn't fit, though. I don't know any women like that, or men either. Unless I see her life branching into mine, she gives me no ancestral help.

To sustain her being in love, she often worked at herself in the mir- [23] ror, guessing at the colors and shapes that would interest him, changing them frequently in order to hit on the right combination. She wanted him to look back.

On a farm near the sea, a woman who tended her appearance [24] reaped a reputation for eccentricity. All the married women blunt-cut their hair in flaps about their ears or pulled it back in tight buns. No nonsense. Neither style blew easily into heart-catching tangles. And at their weddings they displayed themselves in their long hair for the last time. "It brushed the backs of my knees," my mother tells me. "It was braided, and even so, it brushed the backs of my knees."

At the mirror my aunt combed individuality into her bob. A bun [25] could have been contrived to escape into black streamers blowing in the wind or in quiet wisps about her face, but only the older women in our picture album wear buns. She brushed her hair back from her forehead, tucking the flaps behind her ears. She looped a piece of thread, knotted into a circle between her index fingers and thumbs, and ran the double strand across her forehead. When she closed her fingers as if she were making a pair of shadow geese bite, the string twisted together catching the little hairs. Then she pulled the thread away from her skin, ripping the hairs out neatly, her eyes watering from the needles of pain. Opening her fingers, she cleaned the thread, then rolled it along her hairline and the tops of her eyebrows. My mother did the same to me and my sisters and herself. I used to believe that the expression "caught by the short hairs" meant a captive held with a depilatory string. It especially hurt at the temples, but my mother said we were lucky we didn't have to have our feet bound when we were seven. Sisters used to sit on their beds and cry together, she said, as their mothers or their slave removed the bandages for a few minutes each night and let the blood gush back into their veins. I hope that the man my aunt loved appreciated a smooth brow, that he wasn't just a tits-and-ass man.

Once my aunt found a freckle on her chin, at a spot that the almanac [26] said predestined her for unhappiness. She dug it out with a hot needle and washed the wound with peroxide.

More attention to her looks than these pullings of hairs and pickings [27] at spots would have caused gossip among the villagers. They owned work clothes and good clothes, and they wore good clothes for feasting the new seasons. But since a woman combing her hair hexes beginnings, my aunt rarely found an occasion to look her best. Women looked like great sea snails—the corded wood, babies, and laundry they carried were the whorls on their backs. The Chinese did not admire a bent back; goddesses and warriors stood straight. Still there must have been a marvelous freeing of beauty when a worker laid down her burden and stretched and arched.

Such commonplace loveliness, however, was not enough for my [28] aunt. She dreamed of a lover for the fifteen days of New Year's, the time for families to exchange visits, money, and food. She plied her secret comb. And sure enough she cursed the year, the family, the village, and herself.

Even as her hair lured her imminent lover, many other men looked [29] at her. Uncles, cousins, nephews, brothers would have looked, too, had they been home between journeys. Perhaps they had already been restraining their curiosity, and they left, fearful that their glances, like a field of nesting birds, might be startled and caught. Poverty hurt, and that was their first reason for leaving. But another, final reason for leaving the crowded house was the never-said.

She may have been unusually beloved, the precious only daughter, [30] spoiled and mirror gazing because of the affection the family lavished on her. When her husband left, they welcomed the chance to take her back from the in-laws; she could live like the little daughter for just a while longer. There are stories that my grandfather was different from other people, "crazy ever since the little Jap bayoneted him in the head." He used to put his naked penis on the dinner table, laughing. And one day he brought home a baby girl, wrapped up inside his brown western-style greatcoat. He had traded one of his sons, probably my father, the youngest, for her. My grandmother made him trade back. When he finally got a daughter of his own, he doted on her. They must have all loved her, except perhaps my father, the only brother who never went back to China, having once been traded for a girl.

Brothers and sisters, newly men and women, had to efface their sex- [31] ual color and present plain miens.[2] Disturbing hair and eyes, a smile like no other, threatened the ideal of five generations living under one roof. To focus blurs, people shouted face to face and yelled from room to room. The immigrants I know have loud voices, unmodulated to American

---

[2] Appearances. [Eds.]

tones even after years away from the village where they called their friendships out across the fields. I have not been able to stop my mother's screams in public libraries or over telephones. Walking erect (knees straight, toes pointed forward, not pigeon-toed, which is Chinese-feminine) and speaking in an inaudible voice, I have tried to turn myself American-feminine. Chinese communication was loud, public. Only sick people had to whisper. But at the dinner table, where the family members came nearest one another, no one could talk, not the outcasts nor any eaters. Every word that falls from the mouth is a coin lost. Silently they gave and accepted food with both hands. A preoccupied child who took his bowl with one hand got a sideways glare. A complete moment of total attention is due everyone alike. Children and lovers have no singularity here, but my aunt used a secret voice, a separate attentiveness.

She kept the man's name to herself throughout her labor and dying; 32 she did not accuse him that he be punished with her. To save her inseminator's name she gave silent birth.

He may have been somebody in her own household, but intercourse 33 with a man outside the family would have been no less abhorrent. All the village were kinsmen, and the titles shouted in loud country voices never let kinship be forgotten. Any man within visiting distance would have been neutralized as a lover—"brother," "younger brother," "older brother"—one hundred and fifteen relationship titles. Parents researched birth charts probably not so much to assure good fortune as to circumvent incest in a population that has but one hundred surnames. Everybody has eight million relatives. How useless then sexual mannerisms, how dangerous.

As if it came from an atavism[3] deeper than fear, I used to add 34 "brother" silently to boys' names. It hexed the boys, who would or would not ask me to dance, and made them less scary and as familiar and deserving of benevolence as girls.

But, of course, I hexed myself also—no dates. I should have stood 35 up, both arms waving, and shouted out across libraries, "Hey, you! Love me back." I had no idea, though, how to make attraction selective, how to control its direction and magnitude. If I made myself American-pretty so that the five or six Chinese boys in the class fell in love with me, everyone else—the Caucasian, Negro, and Japanese boys—would too. Sisterliness, dignified and honorable, made much more sense.

Attraction eludes control so stubbornly that whole societies de- 36 signed to organize relationships among people cannot keep order, not even when they bind people to one another from childhood and raise them together. Among the very poor and the wealthy, brothers married their adopted sisters, like doves. Our family allowed some romance, paying adult brides' prices and providing dowries so that their sons and

---

[3] The reappearance of a characteristic after a long absence. [Eds.]

daughters could marry strangers. Marriage promises to turn strangers into friendly relatives—a nation of siblings.

In the village structure, spirits shimmered among the live creatures, [37] balanced and held in equilibrium by time and land. But one human being flaring up into violence could open up a black hole, a maelstrom that pulled in the sky. The frightened villagers, who depended on one another to maintain the real, went to my aunt to show her a personal, physical representation of the break she had made in the "roundness." Misallying couples snapped off the future, which was to be embodied in true offspring. The villagers punished her for acting as if she could have a private life, secret and apart from them.

If my aunt had betrayed the family at a time of large grain yields [38] and peace, when many boys were born, and wings were being built on many houses, perhaps she might have escaped such severe punishment. But the men—hungry, greedy, tired of planting in dry soil, cuckolded— had had to leave the village in order to send food-money home. There were ghost plagues, bandit plagues, wars with the Japanese, floods. My Chinese brother and sister had died of an unknown sickness. Adultery, perhaps only a mistake during good times, became a crime when the village needed food.

The round moon cakes and round doorways, the round tables of [39] graduated size that fit one roundness inside another, round windows and rice bowls—these talismans had lost their power to warn this family of the law: a family must be whole, faithfully keeping the descent line by having sons to feed the old and the dead, who in turn look after the family. The villagers came to show my aunt and her lover-in-hiding a broken house. The villagers were speeding up the circling of events because she was too shortsighted to see that her infidelity had already harmed the village, that waves of consequences would return unpredictably, sometimes in disguise, as now, to hurt her. This roundness had to be made coin-sized so that she would see its circumference: punish her at the birth of her baby. Awaken her to the inexorable. People who refused fatalism because they could invent small resources insisted on culpability. Deny accidents and wrest fault from the stars.

After the villagers left, their lanterns now scattering in various di- [40] rections toward home, the family broke their silence and cursed her. "Aiaa, we're going to die. Death is coming. Death is coming. Look what you've done. You've killed us. Ghost! Dead ghost! Ghost! You've never been born." She ran out into the fields, far enough from the house so that she could no longer hear their voices, and pressed herself against the earth, her own land no more. When she felt the birth coming, she thought that she had been hurt. Her body seized together. "They've hurt me too much," she thought. "This is gall, and it will kill me." With forehead and knees against the earth, her body convulsed and then relaxed. She turned on her back, lay on the ground. The black well of sky and stars went out and out and out forever; her body and her complexity seemed to disappear. She was one of the stars, a bright dot in blackness, without home, without a companion, in eternal cold and silence. And agoraphobia[4] rose in her, speeding higher and higher, bigger and bigger; she would not be able to contain it; there would be no end to fear.

Flayed, unprotected against space, she felt pain return, focusing her 41
body. This pain chilled her—a cold, steady kind of surface pain. Inside, spasmodically, the other pain, the pain of the child, heated her. For hours she lay on the ground, alternately body and space. Sometimes a vision of normal comfort obliterated reality: she saw the family in the evening gambling at the dinner table, the young people massaging their elders' backs. She saw them congratulating one another, high joy on the mornings the rice shoots came up. When these pictures burst, the stars drew yet further apart. Black space opened.

She got to her feet to fight better and remembered that old-fash- 42
ioned women gave birth in their pigsties to fool the jealous, pain-deal-ing gods, who do not snatch piglets. Before the next spasms could stop her, she ran to the pigsty, each step a rushing out into emptiness. She climbed over the fence and knelt in the dirt. It was good to have a fence enclosing her, a tribal person alone.

Laboring, this woman who had carried her child as a foreign 43
growth that sickened her every day, expelled it at last. She reached down to touch the hot, wet, moving mass, surely smaller than anything human, and could feel that it was human after all—fingers, toes, nails, nose. She pulled it up on to her belly, and it lay curled there, butt in the air, feet precisely tucked one under the other. She opened her loose shirt and buttoned the child inside. After resting, it squirmed and thrashed and she pushed it up to her breast. It turned its head this way and that until it found her nipple. There, it made little snuffling noises. She clenched her teeth at its preciousness, lovely as a young calf, a piglet, a little dog.

She may have gone to the pigsty as a last act of responsibility: she 44
would protect this child as she had protected its father. It would look after her soul, leaving supplies on her grave. But how would this tiny child without family find her grave when there would be no marker for her anywhere, neither in the earth nor the family hall? No one would give her a family hall name. She had taken the child with her into the wastes. At its birth the two of them had felt the same raw pain of sepa-ration, a wound that only the family pressing tight could close. A child with no descent line would not soften her life but only trail after her, ghost-like, begging her to give it purpose. At dawn the villagers on their way to the fields would stand around the fence and look.

---

[4] Pathological fear of of being helpless or embarrassed in a public situation, characterized by avoid-ance of public places. [Eds.]

Full of milk, the little ghost slept. When it awoke, she hardened her   45
breasts against the milk that crying loosens. Toward morning she picked
up the baby and walked to the well.

Carrying the baby to the well shows loving. Otherwise abandon it.   46
Turn its face into the mud. Mothers who love their children take them
along. It was probably a girl; there is some hope of forgiveness for boys.

"Don't tell anyone you had an aunt. Your father does not want to   47
hear her name. She has never been born." I have believed that sex was
unspeakable and words so strong and fathers so frail that "aunt" would
do my father mysterious harm. I have thought that my family, having
settled among immigrants who had also been their neighbors in the ancestral land, needed to clean their name, and a wrong word would incite the kinspeople even here. But there is more to this silence: they want
me to participate in her punishment. And I have.

In the twenty years since I heard this story I have not asked for de-   48
tails nor said my aunt's name; I do not know it. People who can comfort
the dead can also chase after them to hurt them further—a reverse an-
cestor worship. The real punishment was not the raid swiftly inflicted by
the villagers, but the family's deliberately forgetting her. Her betrayal so
maddened them, they saw to it that she would suffer forever, even after
death. Always hungry, always needing, she would have to beg food
from other ghosts, snatch and steal it from those whose living descendants give them gifts. She would have to fight the ghosts massed at
crossroads for the buns a few thoughtful citizens leave to decoy her
away from village and home so that the ancestral spirits could feast un-
harassed. At peace, they could act like gods, not ghosts, their descent
lines providing them with paper suits and dresses, spirit money, paper
houses, paper automobiles, chicken, meat, and rice into eternity—
essences delivered up in smoke and flames, steam and incense rising
from each rice bowl. In an attempt to make the Chinese care for people
outside the family, Chairman Mao[5] encourages us now to give our
paper replicas to the spirits of outstanding soldiers and workers, no matter whose ancestors they may be. My aunt remains forever hungry.
Goods are not distributed evenly among the dead.

My aunt haunts me—her ghost drawn to me because now, after fifty   49
years of neglect, I alone devote pages of paper to her, though not
origamied into houses and clothes. I do not think she always means me
well. I am telling on her, and she was a spite suicide, drowning herself
in the drinking water. The Chinese are always very frightened of the
drowned one, whose weeping ghost, wet hair hanging and skin bloated, waits silently by the water to pull down a substitute.

---

[5] Mao Zedong (1893–1976), founder and leader from 1949 until his death of the communist People's
Republic of China.

Responding to Reading

1. How accurate do you imagine Kingston's "facts" are? Do you think strict accuracy is important in this essay? Why or why not?
2. Kingston never met her aunt. In what sense is this essay nevertheless about her relationship with her aunt (and with other family members, both known and unknown)?
3. Is there a family member other than your parents who has had a profound effect on your life? In what way is this relationship like and unlike the one Kingston has with her aunt?

The Way to Rainy Mountain

N. Scott Momaday

N. Scott Momaday (1934–) is a poet, novelist, and nonfiction writer who won the Pulitzer Prize for his novel *House Made of Dawn* (1968). Critic Baine Kerr in *Southwest Review* describes this book as an attempt to "transliterate Indian culture, myth, and sensibility into an alien art form without loss." Momaday grew up on a reservation in New Mexico and now teaches at the University of Arizona. His work chronicles Native American experience and portrays Indian culture as strongly identified with the land. Recent works include a novel, *The Ancient One* (1989), and a collection of stories and poems spanning his thirty-year writing career, *In the Presence of the Sun* (1992). In the following selection from his collection of autobiographical essays *The Way to Rainy Mountain* (1969), Momaday describes Kiowa culture through the stories and legends his grandmother told him.

A single knoll rises out of the plain in Oklahoma, north and west of   1
the Wichita Range. For my people, the Kiowas, it is an old landmark, and they gave it the name Rainy Mountain. The hardest weather in the world is there. Winter brings blizzards, hot tornadic winds arise in the spring, and in summer the prairie is an anvil's edge. The grass turns brittle and brown, and it cracks beneath your feet. There are green belts along the rivers and creeks, linear groves of hickory and pecan, willow and witch hazel. At a distance in July or August the steaming foliage seems almost to writhe in fire. Great green and yellow grasshoppers are everywhere in the tall grass, popping up like corn to sting the flesh, and tortoises crawl about on the red earth, going nowhere in the plenty of time. Loneliness is an aspect of the land. All things in the plain are isolate; there is no confusion of objects in the eye, but *one* hill or *one* tree or

one man. To look upon that landscape in the early morning, with the sun at your back, is to lose the sense of proportion. Your imagination comes to life, and this, you think, is where Creation was begun.

I returned to Rainy Mountain in July. My grandmother had died in the spring, and I wanted to be at her grave. She had lived to be very old and at last infirm. Her only living daughter was with her when she died, and I was told that in death her face was that of a child.   2

I like to think of her as a child. When she was born, the Kiowas were living the last great moment of their history. For more than a hundred years they had controlled the open range from the Smoky Hill River to the Red, from the headwaters of the Canadian to the fork of the Arkansas and Cimarron. In alliance with the Comanches, they had ruled the whole of the southern Plains. War was their sacred business, and they were among the finest horsemen the world has ever known. But warfare for the Kiowas was preeminently a matter of disposition rather than of survival, and they never understood the grim, unrelenting advance of the U.S. Cavalry. When at last, divided and ill-provisioned, they were driven onto the Staked Plains in the cold rains of autumn, they fell into panic. In Palo Duro Canyon they abandoned their crucial stores to pillage and had nothing then but their lives. In order to save themselves, they surrendered to the soldiers at Fort Sill and were imprisoned in the old stone corral that now stands as a military museum. My grandmother was spared the humiliation of those high gray walls by eight or ten years, but she must have known from birth the affliction of defeat, the dark brooding of old warriors.   3

Her name was Aho, and she belonged to the last culture to evolve in North America. Her forebears came down from the high country in western Montana nearly three centuries ago. They were a mountain people, a mysterious tribe of hunters whose language has never been positively classified in any major group. In the late seventeenth century they began a long migration to the south and east. It was a journey toward the dawn, and it led to a golden age. Along the way the Kiowas were befriended by the Crows, who gave them the culture and religion of the Plains. They acquired horses, and their ancient nomadic spirit was suddenly free of the ground. They acquired Taime, the sacred Sun Dance doll, from that moment the object and symbol of their worship, and so shared in the divinity of the sun. Not least, they acquired the sense of destiny, therefore courage and pride. When they entered upon the southern Plains they had been transformed. No longer were they slaves to the simple necessity of survival; they were a lordly and dangerous society of fighters and thieves, hunters and priests of the sun. According to their origin myth, they entered the world through a hollow log. From one point of view, their migration was the fruit of an old prophecy, for indeed they emerged from a sunless world.   4

Although my grandmother lived out her long life in the shadow of [5]
Rainy Mountain, the immense landscape of the continental interior lay
like memory in her blood. She could tell of the Crows, whom she had
never seen, and of the Black Hills, where she had never been. I wanted
to see in reality what she had seen more perfectly in the mind's eye, and
traveled fifteen hundred miles to begin my pilgrimage.

Yellowstone, it seemed to me, was the top of the world, a region of [6]
deep lakes and dark timber, canyons and waterfalls. But, beautiful as it
is, one might have the sense of confinement there. The skyline in all directions is close at hand, the high wall of the woods and deep cleavages
of shade. There is a perfect freedom in the mountains, but it belongs to
the eagle and the elk, the badger and the bear. The Kiowas reckoned
their stature by the distance they could see, and they were bent and
blind in the wilderness.

Descending eastward, the highland meadows are a stairway to the [7]
plain. In July the inland slope of the Rockies is luxuriant with flax and
buckwheat, stonecrop and larkspur. The earth unfolds and the limit of
the land recedes. Clusters of trees, and animals grazing far in the distance, cause the vision to reach away and wonder to build upon the
mind. The sun follows a longer course in the day, and the sky is immense
beyond all comparison. The great billowing clouds that sail upon it are
shadows that move upon the grain like water, dividing light. Farther
down, in the land of the Crows and Blackfeet, the plain is yellow. Sweet
clover takes hold of the hills and bends upon itself to cover and seal the
soil. There the Kiowas paused on their way; they had come to the place
where they must change their lives. The sun is at home on the plains. Precisely there does it have the certain character of a god. When the Kiowas
came to the land of the Crows, they could see the dark lees of the hills at
dawn across the Bighorn River, the profusion of light on the grain
shelves, the oldest deity ranging after the solstices. Not yet would they
veer southward to the caldron of the land that lay below; they must wean
their blood from the northern winter and hold the mountains a while
longer in their view. They bore Tai-me in procession to the east.

A dark mist lay over the Black Hills, and the land was like iron. At [8]
the top of a ridge I caught sight of Devil's Tower upthrust against the
gray sky as if in the birth of time the core of the earth had broken
through its crust and the motion of the world was begun. There are
things in nature that engender an awful quiet in the heart of man;
Devil's Tower is one of them. Two centuries ago, because they could not
do otherwise, the Kiowas made a legend at the base of the rock. My
grandmother said:

> Eight children were there at play, seven sisters and their brother. Sud-
> denly the boy was struck dumb; he trembled and began to run upon
> his hands and feet. His fingers became claws, and his body was cov-
> ered with fur. Directly there was a bear where the boy had been. The

sisters were terrified; they ran, and the bear after them. They came to the stump of a great tree, and the tree spoke to them. It bade them climb upon it, and as they did so it began to rise into the air. The bear came to kill them, but they were just beyond its reach. It reared against the tree and scored the bark all around with its claws. The seven sisters were borne into the sky, and they became the stars of the Big Dipper.

From that moment, and so long as the legend lives, the Kiowas have kinsmen in the night sky. Whatever they were in the mountains, they could be no more. However tenuous their well-being, however much they had suffered and would suffer again, they had found a way out of the wilderness.

My grandmother had a reverence for the sun, a holy regard that now is all but gone out of mankind. There was a wariness in her, and an ancient awe. She was a Christian in her later years, but she had come a long way about, and she never forgot her birthright. As a child she had been to the Sun Dances; she had taken part in those annual rites, and by them she had learned the restoration of her people in the presence of Tai-me. She was about seven when the last Kiowa Sun Dance was held in 1887 on the Washita River above Rainy Mountain Creek. The buffalo were gone. In order to consummate the ancient sacrifice—to impale the head of a buffalo bull upon the medicine tree—a delegation of old men journeyed into Texas, there to beg and barter for an animal from the Goodnight herd. She was ten when the Kiowas came together for the last time as a living Sun Dance culture. They could find no buffalo; they had to hang an old hide from the sacred tree. Before the dance could begin, a company of soldiers rode out from Fort Sill under orders to disperse the tribe. Forbidden without cause the essential act of their faith, having seen the wild herds slaughtered and left to rot upon the ground, the Kiowas backed away forever from the medicine tree. That was July 20, 1890, at the great bend of the Washita. My grandmother was there. Without bitterness, and for as long as she lived, she bore a vision of deicide.[1]

Now that I can have her only in memory, I see my grandmother in the several postures that were peculiar to her: standing at the wood stove on a winter morning and turning meat in a great iron skillet; sitting at the south window, bent above her beadwork, and afterwards, when her vision failed, looking down for a long time into the fold of her hands; going out upon a cane, very slowly as she did when the weight of age came upon her; praying. I remember her most often at prayer. She made long, rambling prayers out of suffering and hope, having seen many things. I was never sure that I had the right to hear, so exclusive were they of all mere custom and company. The last time I saw her she prayed standing by the side of her bed at night, naked to the waist, the light of a kerosene

9

10

---

[1] The killing of a god. [Eds.]

lamp moving upon her dark skin. Her long, black hair, always drawn and braided in the day, lay upon her shoulders and against her breasts like a shawl. I do not speak Kiowa, and I never understood her prayers, but there was something inherently sad in the sound, some merest hesitation upon the syllables of sorrow. She began in a high and descending pitch, exhausting her breath to silence; then again and again—and always the same intensity of effort, of something that is, and is not, like urgency in the human voice. Transported so in the dancing light among the shadows of her room, she seemed beyond the reach of time. But that was illusion; I think I knew then that I should not see her again.

Houses are like sentinels in the plain, old keepers of the weather watch. There, in a very little while, wood takes on the appearance of great age. All colors wear soon away in the wind and rain, and then the wood is burned gray and the grain appears and the nails turn red with rust. The windowpanes are black and opaque; you imagine there is nothing within, and indeed there are many ghosts, bones given up to the land. They stand here and there against the sky, and you approach them for a longer time than you expect. They belong in the distance; it is their domain. [11]

Once there was a lot of sound in my grandmother's house, a lot of coming and going, feasting and talk. The summers there were full of excitement and reunion. The Kiowas are a summer people; they abide the cold and keep to themselves, but when the season turns and the land becomes warm and vital they cannot hold still; an old love of going returns upon them. The aged visitors who came to my grandmother's house when I was a child were made of lean and leather, and they bore themselves upright. The wore great black hats and bright ample shirts that shook in the wind. They rubbed fat upon their hair and wound their braids with strips of colored cloth. Some of them painted their faces and carried the scars of old and cherished enmities. They were an old council of warloads, come to remind and be reminded of who they were. Their wives and daughters served them well. The women might indulge themselves; gossip was at once the mark and compensation of their servitude. They made loud and elaborate talk among themselves, full of jest and gesture, fright and false alarm. They went abroad in fringed and flowered shawls, bright beadwork and German silver. They were at home in the kitchen, and they prepared meals that were banquets. [12]

There were frequent prayer meetings, and great nocturnal feasts. When I was a child I played with my cousins outside, where the lamplight fell upon the ground and the singing of the old people rose up around us and carried away into the darkness. There were a lot of good things to eat, a lot of laughter and surprise. And afterwards, when the quiet returned, I lay down with my grandmother and could hear the frogs away by the river and feel the motion of the air. [13]

Now there is funeral silence in the rooms, the endless wake of some final word. The walls have closed in upon my grandmother's house. [14]

When I returned to it in mourning, I saw for the first time in my life how small it was. It was late at night, and there was a white moon, nearly full. I sat for a long time on the stone steps by the kitchen door. From there I could see out across the land; I could see the long row of trees by the creek, the low light upon the rolling plains, and the stars of the Big Dipper. Once I looked at the moon and caught sight of a strange thing. A cricket had perched upon the handrail, only a few inches away from me. My line of vision was such that the creature filled the moon like a fossil. It had gone there, I thought, to live and die, for there, of all places, was its small definition made whole and eternal. A warm wind rose up and purled[2] like the longing within me.

The next morning I awoke at dawn and went out on the dirt road to 15 Rainy Mountain. It was already hot, and the grasshoppers began to fill the air. Still, it was early in the morning, and the birds sang out of the shadows. The long yellow grass on the mountain shone in the bright light, and a scissortail hied above the land. There, where it ought to be, at the end of a long and legendary way, was my grandmother's grave. Here and there on the dark stones were ancestral names. Looking back once, I saw the mountain and came away.

Responding to Reading

1. Does Momaday portray his grandmother as an individual or as a symbol meant to stand for some larger idea? Explain.
2. Does the background Momaday provides make his grandmother's life easier or harder for you to understand? What other information would be helpful?
3. This essay focuses on Momaday's grandmother, not on his own relationship with her. In what sense is the essay about the author as well as about his grandmother?

BEAUTY: WHEN THE OTHER
~ DANCER IS THE SELF

Alice Walker

Alice Walker (1944–) was born in Eatonton, Georgia, where her parents were sharecroppers. A writer of stories since childhood, she is today known as a poet, fiction writer, essayist, biographer, and editor.

---

[2] Flowed; rippled. [Eds.]

Walker often writes about the experiences of poor black women and the effects of racism and sexism. An advocate of African-American women writers, she helped revive the literary reputation of writer and folklorist Zora Neale Hurston by editing a collection of her writing, *I Love Myself When I Am Laughing* (1979). Walker is also the author of five novels, including the Pulitzer-Prize-winning *The Color Purple* (1982), and several collections of poetry, stories, and essays. In the following essay from her collection *In Search of Our Mothers' Gardens* (1983), she traces the changes she experienced in her self-image after a childhood accident left her blind and disfigured in one eye.

It is a bright summer day in 1947. My father, a fat, funny man with beautiful eyes and a subversive wit, is trying to decide which of his eight children he will take with him to the county fair. My mother, of course, will not go. She is knocked out from getting most of us ready: I hold my neck stiff against the pressure of her knuckles as she hastily completes the braiding and then beribboning of my hair. [1]

My father is the driver for the rich old white lady up the road. Her name is Miss Mey. She owns all the land for miles around, as well as the house in which we live. All I remember about her is that she once offered to pay my mother thirty-five cents for cleaning her house, raking up piles of her magnolia leaves, and washing her family's clothes, and that my mother—she of no money, eight children, and a chronic earache—refused it. But I do not think of this in 1947. I am two and a half years old. I want to go everywhere my daddy goes. I am excited at the prospect of riding in a car. Someone has told me fairs are fun. That there is room in the car for only three of us doesn't faze me at all. Whirling happily in my starchy frock, showing off my biscuit-polished patent-leather shoes and lavender socks, tossing my head in a way that makes my ribbons bounce, I stand, hands on hips, before my father. "Take me, Daddy," I say with assurance; "I'm the prettiest!" [2]

Later, it does not surprise me to find myself in Miss Mey's shiny black car, sharing the back seat with the other lucky ones. Does not surprise me that I thoroughly enjoy the fair. At home that night I tell the unlucky ones all I can remember about the merry-go-round, the man who eats live chickens, and the teddy bears, until they say: that's enough, baby Alice. Shut up now, and go to sleep. [3]

It is Easter Sunday, 1950. I am dressed in a green, flocked, scalloped-hem dress (handmade by my adoring sister, Ruth) that has its own smooth satin petticoat and tiny hot-pink roses tucked into each scallop. My shoes, new T-strap patent leather, again highly biscuit-polished. I am six years old and have learned one of the longest Easter speeches to be heard that day, totally unlike the speech I said when I was two: "Easter lilies/pure and white/blossom in/the morning light." When I rise to give my speech I do so on a great wave of love and pride and expecta- [4]

tion. People in the church stop rustling their new crinolines. They seem to hold their breath. I can tell they admire my dress, but it is my spirit, bordering on sassiness (womanishness), they secretly applaud.

"That girl's a little *mess*," they whisper to each other, pleased.   5

Naturally I say my speech without stammer or pause, unlike those   6 who stutter, stammer, or, worst of all, forget. This is before the word "beautiful" exists in people's vocabulary, but "Oh, isn't she the *cutest* thing!" frequently floats my way. "And got so much sense!" they gratefully add . . . for which thoughtful addition I thank them to this day.

It was great fun being cute. But then, one day, it ended.   7

I am eight years old and a tomboy. I have a cowboy hat, cowboy   8 boots, checkered shirt and pants, all red. My playmates are my brothers, two and four years older than I. Their colors are black and green, the only difference in the way we are dressed. On Saturday nights we all go to the picture show, even my mother; Westerns are her favorite kind of movie. Back home, "on the ranch," we pretend we are Tom Mix, Hopalong Cassidy, Lash LaRue (we've even named one of our dogs Lash LaRue); we chase each other for hours rustling cattle, being outlaws, delivering damsels from distress. Then my parents decide to buy my brothers guns. These are not "real" guns. They shoot "BBs," copper pellets my brothers say will kill birds. Because I am a girl, I do not get a gun. Instantly I am relegated to the position of Indian. Now there appears a great distance between us. They shoot and shoot at everything with their new guns. I try to keep up with my bow and arrows.

One day while I am standing on top of our makeshift "garage"—   9 pieces of tin nailed across some poles—holding my bow and arrow and looking out toward the fields, I feel an incredible blow in my right eye. I look down just in time to see my brother lower his gun.

Both brothers rush to my side. My eye stings, and I cover it with my   10 hand. "If you tell," they say, "we will get a whipping. You don't want that to happen, do you?" I do not. "Here is a piece of wire," says the older brother, picking it up from the roof; "say you stepped on one end of it and the other flew up and hit you." The pain is beginning to start. "Yes," I say, "Yes, I will say that is what happened." If I do not say this is what happened, I know my brothers will find ways to make me wish I had. But now I will say anything that gets me to my mother.

Confronted by our parents we stick to the lie agreed upon. They   11 place me on a bench on the porch and I close my left eye while they examine the right. There is a tree growing from underneath the porch that climbs past the railing to the roof. It is the last thing my right eye sees. I watch as its trunk, its branches, and then its leaves are blotted out by the rising blood.

I am in shock. First there is intense fever, which my father tries to   12 break using lily leaves bound around my head. Then there are chills: my mother tries to get me to eat soup. Eventually, I do not know how, my parents learn what has happened. A week after the "accident" they take me to see a doctor. "Why did you wait so long to come?" he asks, looking into my eye and shaking his head. "Eyes are sympathetic," he says. "If one is blind, the other will likely become blind too."

This comment of the doctor's terrifies me. But it is really how I look   13
that bothers me most. Where the BB pellet struck there is a glob of whitish scar tissue, a hideous cataract, on my eye. Now when I stare at people—a favorite pastime, up to now—they will stare back. Not at the "cute" little girl, but at her scar. For six years I do not stare at anyone, because I do not raise my head.

Years later, in the throes of a mid-life crisis, I ask my mother and sis-   14
ter whether I changed after the "accident." "No," they say, puzzled. "What do you mean?"

What do I mean?   15

I am eight, and, for the first time, doing poorly in school, where I   16
have been something of a whiz since I was four. We have just moved to the place where the "accident" occurred. We do not know any of the people around us because this is a different county. The only time I see the friends I knew is when we go back to our old church. The new school is the former state penitentiary. It is a large stone building, cold and drafty, crammed to overflowing with boisterous, ill-disciplined children. On the third floor there is a huge circular imprint of some partition that has been torn out.

"What used to be here?" I ask a sullen girl next to me on our way   17
past it to lunch.

"The electric chair," says she.   18

At night I have nightmares about the electric chair, and about all the   19
people reputedly "fried" in it. I am afraid of the school, where all the students seem to be budding criminals.

"What's the matter with your eye?" they ask, critically.   20

When I don't answer (I cannot decide whether it was an "accident"   21
or not), they shove me, insist on a fight.

My brother, the one who created the story about the wire, comes to   22
my rescue. But then brags so much about "protecting" me, I become sick.

After months of torture at the school, my parents decide to send me   23
back to our old community, to my old school. I live with my grandparents and the teacher they board. But there is no room for Phoebe, my cat. By the time my grandparents decide there *is* room, and I ask for my cat, she cannot be found. Miss Yarborough, the boarding teacher, takes me under her wing, and begins to teach me to play the piano. But soon she marries an African—a "prince," she says—and is whisked away to his continent.

At my old school there is at least one teacher who loves me. She is [24] the teacher who "knew me before I was born" and bought my first baby clothes. It is she who makes life bearable. It is her presence that finally helps me turn on the one child at the school who continually calls me "one-eyed bitch." One day I simply grab him by his coat and beat him until I am satisfied. It is my teacher who tells me my mother is ill.

My mother is lying in bed in the middle of the day, something I have [25] never seen. She is in too much pain to speak. She has an abscess in her ear. I stand looking down on her, knowing that if she dies, I cannot live. She is being treated with warm oils and hot bricks held against her cheek. Finally a doctor comes. But I must go back to my grandparents' house. The weeks pass but I am hardly aware of it. All I know is that my mother might die, my father is not so jolly, my brothers still have their guns, and I am the one sent away from home.

"You did not change," they say. [26]

Did I imagine the anguish of never looking up? [27]

I am twelve. When relatives come to visit I hide in my room. My [28] cousin Brenda, just my age, whose father works in the post office and whose mother is a nurse, comes to find me. "Hello," she says. And then she asks, looking at my recent school picture, which I did not want taken, and on which the "glob," as I think of it, is clearly visible, "You still can't see out of that eye?"

"No," I say, and flop back on the bed over my book. [29]

That night, as I do almost every night, I abuse my eye. I rant and [30] rave at it, in front of the mirror. I plead with it to clear up before morning. I tell it I hate and despise it. I do not pray for sight. I pray for beauty.

"You did not change," they say. [31]

I am fourteen and baby-sitting for my brother Bill, who lives in [32] Boston. He is my favorite brother and there is a strong bond between us. Understanding my feelings of shame and ugliness he and his wife take me to a local hospital, where the "glob" is removed by a doctor named O. Henry. There is still a small bluish crater where the scar tissue was, but the ugly white stuff is gone. Almost immediately I become a different person from the girl who does not raise her head. Or so I think. Now that I've raised my head I win the boyfriend of my dreams. Now that I've raised my head I have plenty of friends. Now that I've raised my head classwork comes from my lips as faultlessly as Easter speeches did, and I leave high school as valedictorian, most popular student, and *queen*, hardly believing my luck. Ironically, the girl who was voted most beautiful in our class (and was) was later shot twice through the chest by a male companion, using a "real" gun, while she was pregnant. But that's another story in itself. Or is it?

"You did not change," they say. [33]

It is now thirty years since the "accident." A beautiful journalist ³⁴ comes to visit and to interview me. She is going to write a cover story for her magazine that focuses on my latest book. "Decide how you want to look on the cover," she says. "Glamorous, or whatever."

Never mind "glamorous," it is the "whatever" that I hear. Sudden- ³⁵ ly all I can think of is whether I will get enough sleep the night before the photography session: if I don't, my eye will be tired and wander, as blind eyes will.

At night in bed with my lover I think up reasons why I should not ³⁶ appear on the cover of a magazine. "My meanest critics will say I've sold out," I say. "My family will now realize I write scandalous books."

"But what's the real reason you don't want to do this?" he asks.   ³⁷

"Because in all probability," I say in a rush, "my eye won't be ³⁸ straight."

"It will be straight enough," he says. Then, "Besides, I thought you'd ³⁹ made your peace with that."

And I suddenly remember that I have.   ⁴⁰

I remember: ⁴¹

I am talking to my brother Jimmy, asking if he remembers anything ⁴² unusual about the day I was shot. He does not know I consider that day the last time my father, with his sweet home remedy of cool lily leaves, chose me, and that I suffered and raged inside because of this. "Well," he says, "all I remember is standing by the side of the highway with Daddy, trying to flag down a car. A white man stopped, but when Daddy said he needed somebody to take his little girl to the doctor, he drove off."

I remember: ⁴³

I am in the desert for the first time. I fall totally in love with it. I am ⁴⁴ so overwhelmed by its beauty, I confront for the first time, consciously, the meaning of the doctor's words years ago: "Eyes are sympathetic. If one is blind, the other will likely become blind too." I realize I have dashed about the world madly, looking at this, looking at that, storing up images against the fading of the light. *But I might have missed seeing the desert!* The shock of that possibility—and gratitude for over twenty-five years of sight—sends me literally to my knees. Poem after poem comes—which is perhaps how poets pray.

On Sight
I am so thankful I have seen
The Desert
And the creatures in the desert
And the desert Itself.

The desert has its own moon   5
Which I have seen
With my own eye.
There is no flag on it.

Trees of the desert have arms
All of which are always up   10
That is because the moon is up
The sun is up
Also the sky
The stars
Clouds   15
None with flags.

If there were flags, I doubt
the trees would point.
Would you?

But mostly, I remember this: 45

I am twenty-seven, and my baby daughter is almost three. Since her   46
birth I have worried about her discovery that her mother's eyes are different from other people's. Will she be embarrassed? I think. What will
she say? Every day she watches a television program called "Big Blue
Marble." It begins with a picture of the earth as it appears from the
moon. It is bluish, a little battered-looking, but full of light, with whitish
clouds swirling around it. Every time I see it I weep with love, as if it is
a picture of Grandma's house. One day when I am putting Rebecca
down for her nap, she suddenly focuses on my eye. Something inside me
cringes, gets ready to try to protect myself. All children are cruel about
physical differences, I know from experience, and that they don't always
mean to be is another matter. I assume Rebecca will be the same.

But no-o-o-o. She studies my face intently as we stand, her inside   47
and me outside her crib. She even holds my face maternally between her
dimpled little hands. Then, looking every bit as serious and lawyerlike
as her father, she says, as if it may just possibly have slipped my attention: "Mommy, there's a *world* in your eye." (As in, "Don't be alarmed,
or do anything crazy.") And then, gently, but with great interest:
"Mommy, where did you get that world in your eye?"

For the most part, the pain left then. (So what, if my brothers grew   48
up to buy even more powerful pellet guns for their sons and to carry real
guns themselves. So what, if a young "Morehouse man"[1] once nearly
fell off the steps of Trevor Arnett Library because he thought my eyes
were blue.) Crying and laughing I ran to the bathroom, while Rebecca
mumbled and sang herself off to sleep. Yes indeed, I realized, looking
into the mirror. There was a world in my eye. And I saw that it was possible to love it: that in fact, for all it had taught me of shame and anger
and inner vision, I *did* love it. Even to see it drifting out of orbit in boredom, or rolling up out of fatigue, not to mention floating back at atten-

---
[1] A student at Morehouse College, a historically black college in Atlanta, Georgia. [Eds.]

tion in excitement (bearing witness, a friend has called it), deeply suitable to my personality, and even characteristic of me.

That night I dream I am dancing to Stevie Wonder's song "Always" [49] (the name of the song is really "As," but I hear it as "Always"). As I dance, whirling and joyous, happier than I've ever been in my life, another bright-faced dancer joins me. We dance and kiss each other and hold each other through the night. The other dancer has obviously come through all right, as I have done. She is beautiful, whole and free. And she is also me.

Responding to Reading

1. How does Walker's physical appearance affect the way she was treated by her parents? Do you think your physical appearance affected your parents' attitude toward you in any way? Explain.
2. At several points in the essay Walker repeats the words her relatives used to reassure her: "You did not change." Why does she repeat this phrase? Were her relatives correct?
3. What circumstances or individuals does Walker blame for the childhood problems she describes? Who do you think is responsible for her misery? Would you be as forgiving as Walker seems to be?

My Father's Life

~

Raymond Carver

Raymond Carver (1939–1988) was a fiction and poetry writer who grew up in a working-class family in the Pacific Northwest. Influenced by his father's storytelling, he began writing stories himself as a boy. Collections of Carver's stories include *Will You Please Be Quiet, Please?* (1976), *What We Talk About When We Talk About Love* (1981), *Cathedral* (1984), and *Short Cuts* (1993). Usually about desperate people struggling for daily survival, Carver's stories often have enigmatic endings. In "My Father's Life," which originally appeared in *Esquire* in 1984, Carver tells how his father first struggled financially during the Great Depression and later suffered from psychological depression.

My dad's name was Clevie Raymond Carver. His family called him [1] Raymond and friends called him C. R. I was named Raymond Clevie Carver Jr. I hated the "Junior" part. When I was little my dad called me Frog, which was okay. But later, like everybody else in the family, he began calling me Junior. He went on calling me this until I was thirteen or fourteen and announced that I wouldn't answer to that name any longer. So he began calling me Doc. From then until his death, on June 17, 1967, he called me Doc, or else Son.

When he died, my mother telephoned my wife with the news. I was   2
away from my family at the time, between lives, trying to enroll in the School of Library Science at the University of Iowa. When my wife answered the phone, my mother blurted out. "Raymond's dead!" For a moment, my wife thought my mother was telling her that I was dead. Then my mother made it clear *which* Raymond she was talking about and my wife said, "Thank God. I thought you meant *my* Raymond."

My dad walked, hitched rides, and rode in empty boxcars when he   3
went from Arkansas to Washington State in 1934, looking for work. I don't know whether he was pursuing a dream when he went out to Washington. I doubt it. I don't think he dreamed much. I believe he was simply looking for steady work at decent pay. Steady work was meaningful work. He picked apples for a time and then landed a construction laborer's job on the Grand Coulee Dam.[1] After he'd put aside a little money, he bought a car and drove back to Arkansas to help his folks, my grandparents, pack up for the move west. He said later that they were about to starve down there, and this wasn't meant as a figure of speech. It was during that short while in Arkansas, in a town called Leola, that my mother met my dad on the sidewalk as he came out of a tavern.

"He was drunk," she said. "I don't know why I let him talk to me.   4
His eyes were glittery. I wish I'd had a crystal ball." They'd met once, a year or so before, at a dance. He'd had girlfriends before her, my mother told me. "Your dad always had a girlfriend, even after we married. He was my first and last. I never had another man. But I didn't miss anything."

They were married by a justice of the peace on the day they left for   5
Washington, this big, tall country girl and a farmhand-turned-construction worker. My mother spent her wedding night with my dad and his folks, all of them camped beside the road in Arkansas.

In Omak, Washington, my dad and mother lived in a little place not   6
much bigger than a cabin. My grandparents lived next door. My dad was still working on the dam, and later, with the huge turbines producing electricity and the water backed up for a hundred miles into Canada, he stood in the crowd and heard Franklin D. Roosevelt when he spoke at the construction site. "He never mentioned those guys who died building that dam," my dad said. Some of his friends had died there, men from Arkansas, Oklahoma, and Missouri.

---

[1] On the Columbia River, northwest of Spokane, Washington. [Eds.]

He then took a job in a sawmill in Clatskanie, Oregon, a little town   7
alongside the Columbia River. I was born there, and my mother has a
picture of my dad standing in front of the gate to the mill, proudly holding me up to face the camera. My bonnet is on crooked and about to
come untied. His hat is pushed back on his forehead, and he's wearing
a big grin. Was he going in to work or just finishing his shift? It doesn't
matter. In either case, he had a job and a family. These were his salad
days.

In 1941 we moved to Yakima, Washington, where my dad went to   8
work as a saw filer, a skilled trade he'd learned in Clatskanie. When war
broke out, he was given a deferment because his work was considered
necessary to the war effort. Finished lumber was in demand by the
armed services, and he kept his saws so sharp they could shave the hair
off your arm.

After my dad had moved us to Yakima, he moved his folks into the   9
same neighborhood. By the mid-1940s the rest of my dad's family—his
brother, his sister, and her husband, as well as uncles, cousins, nephews,
and most of their extended family and friends—had come out from
Arkansas. All because my dad came out first. The men went to work at
Boise Cascade, where my dad worked, and the women packed apples
in the canneries. And in just a little while, it seemed—according to my
mother—everybody was better off than my dad. "Your dad couldn't
keep money," my mother said. "Money burned a hole in his pocket. He
was always doing for others."

The first house I clearly remember living in, at 1515 South Fifteenth   10
Street, in Yakima, had an outdoor toilet. On Halloween night, or just any
night, for the hell of it, neighbor kids, kids in their early teens, would
carry our toilet away and leave it next to the road. My dad would have
to get somebody to help him bring it home. Or these kids would take the
toilet and stand it in somebody else's backyard. Once they actually set
it on fire. But ours wasn't the only house that had an outdoor toilet.
When I was old enough to know what I was doing, I threw rocks at the
other toilets when I'd see someone go inside. This was called bombing
the toilets. After a while, though, everyone went to indoor plumbing
until, suddenly, our toilet was the last outdoor one in the neighborhood.
I remember the shame I felt when my third-grade teacher, Mr. Wise,
drove me home from school one day. I asked him to stop at the house
just before ours, claiming I lived there.

I can recall what happened one night when my dad came home late   11
to find that my mother had locked all the doors on him from the inside.
He was drunk, and we could feel the house shudder as he rattled the
door. When he'd managed to force open a window, she hit him between
the eyes with a colander and knocked him out. We could see him down
there on the grass. For years afterward, I used to pick up this colander—

it was as heavy as a rolling pin—and imagine what it would feel like to be hit in the head with something like that.

It was during this period that I remember my dad taking me into the [12] bedroom, sitting me down on the bed, and telling me that I might have to go live with my Aunt La Von for a while. I couldn't understand what I'd done that meant I'd have to go away from home to live. But this, too—whatever prompted it—must have blown over, more or less, anyway, because we stayed together, and I didn't have to go live with her or anyone else.

I remember my mother pouring his whiskey down the sink. Some- [13] times she'd pour it all out and sometimes, if she was afraid of getting caught, she'd only pour half of it out and then add water to the rest. I tasted some of his whiskey once myself. It was terrible stuff, and I don't see how anybody could drink it.

After a long time without one, we finally got a car, in 1949 or 1950, [14] a 1938 Ford. But it threw a rod the first week we had it, and my dad had to have the motor rebuilt.

"We drove the oldest car in town," my mother said. "We could have [15] had a Cadillac for all he spent on car repairs." One time she found someone else's tube of lipstick on the floorboard, along with a lacy handkerchief. "See this?" she said to me. "Some floozy left this in the car."

Once I saw her take a pan of warm water into the bedroom where [16] my dad was sleeping. She took his hand from under the covers and held it in the water. I stood in the doorway and watched. I wanted to know what was going on. This would make him talk in his sleep, she told me. There were things she needed to know, things she was sure he was keeping from her.

Every year or so, when I was little, we would take the North Coast [17] Limited across the Cascade Range from Yakima to Seattle and stay in the Vance Hotel and eat, I remember, at a place called the Dinner Bell Cafe. Once we went to Ivar's Acres of Clams and drank glasses of warm clam broth.

In 1956, the year I was to graduate from high school, my dad quit his [18] job at the mill in Yakima and took a job in Chester, a little sawmill town in northern California. The reasons given at the time for his taking the job had to do with a higher hourly wage and the vague promise that he might, in a few years' time, succeed to the job of head filer in this new mill. But I think, in the main, that my dad had grown restless and simply wanted to try his luck elsewhere. Things had gotten a little too predictable for him in Yakima. Also, the year before, there had been the deaths, within six months of each other, of both his parents.

But just a few days after graduation, when my mother and I were [19] packed to move to Chester, my dad penciled a letter to say he'd been sick for a while. He didn't want us to worry, he said, but he'd cut himself on a saw. Maybe he'd got a tiny sliver of steel in his blood. Anyway, something had happened and he'd had to miss work, he said. In the same mail was an unsigned postcard from somebody down there telling my mother that my dad was about to die and that he was drinking "raw whiskey."

When we arrived in Chester, my dad was living in a trailer that be- [20] longed to the company. I didn't recognize him immediately. I guess for a moment I didn't want to recognize him. He was skinny and pale and looked bewildered. His pants wouldn't stay up. He didn't look like my dad. My mother began to cry. My dad put his arm around her and patted her shoulder vaguely, like he didn't know what this was all about, either. The three of us took up life together in the trailer, and we looked after him as best we could. But my dad was sick, and he couldn't get any better. I worked with him in the mill that summer and part of the fall. We'd get up in the mornings and eat eggs and toast while we listened to the radio, and then go out the door with our lunch pails. We'd pass through the gate together at eight in the morning, and I wouldn't see him again until quitting time. In November I went back to Yakima to be closer to my girlfriend, the girl I'd made up my mind I was going to marry.

He worked at the mill in Chester until the following February, when [21] he collapsed on the job and was taken to the hospital. My mother asked if I would come down there and help. I caught a bus from Yakima to Chester, intending to drive them back to Yakima. But now, in addition to being physically sick, my dad was in the midst of a nervous break-down, though none of us knew to call it that at the time. During the en-tire trip back to Yakima, he didn't speak, not even when asked a direct question. ("How do you feel, Raymond?" "You okay, Dad?") He'd com-municate if he communicated at all, by moving his head or by turning his palms up as if to say he didn't know or care. The only time he said anything on the trip, and for nearly a month afterward, was when I was speeding down a gravel road in Oregon and the car muffler came loose. "You were going too fast," he said.

Back in Yakima a doctor saw to it that my dad went to a psychiatrist. [22] My mother and dad had to go on relief,[2] as it was called, and the coun-ty paid for the psychiatrist. The psychiatrist asked my dad. "Who is the President?" He'd had a question put to him that he could answer. "Ike," my dad said. Nevertheless, they put him on the fifth floor of Valley Memorial Hospital and began giving him electroshock treatments. I was married by then and about to start my own family. My dad was still locked up when my wife went into this same hospital, just one floor down, to have our first baby. After she had delivered, I went upstairs to give my dad the news. They let me in through a steel door and showed

---

[2] What would today be called "public assistance" or "welfare." [Eds.]

me where I could find him. He was sitting on a couch with a blanket over his lap. *Hey,* I thought. *What in hell is happening to my dad?* I sat down next to him and told him he was a grandfather. He waited a minute and then he said, "I feel like a grandfather." That's all he said. He didn't smile or move. He was in a big room with a lot of other people. Then I hugged him, and he began to cry.

Somehow he got out of there. But now came the years when he [23] couldn't work and just sat around the house trying to figure what next and what he'd done wrong in his life that he'd wound up like this. My mother went from job to crummy job. Much later she referred to that time he was in the hospital, and those years just afterward, as "when Raymond was sick." The word *sick* was never the same for me again.

In 1964, through the help of a friend, he was lucky enough to be [24] hired on at a mill in Klamath, California. He moved down there by himself to see if he could hack it. He lived not far from the mill, in a one-room cabin not much different from the place he and my mother had started out living in when they went west. He scrawled letters to my mother, and if I called she'd read them aloud to me over the phone. In the letters, he said it was touch and go. Every day that he went to work, he felt like it was the most important day of his life. But every day, he told her, made the next day that much easier. He said for her to tell me he said hello. If he couldn't sleep at night, he said, he thought about me and the good times we used to have. Finally, after a couple of months, he regained some of his confidence. He could do the work and didn't think he had to worry that he'd let anybody down ever again. When he was sure, he sent for my mother.

He'd been off from work for six years and had lost everything in [25] that time—home, car, furniture, and appliances, including the big freezer that had been my mother's pride and joy. He'd lost his good name too—Raymond Carver was someone who couldn't pay his bills—and his self-respect was gone. He'd even lost his virility. My mother told my wife, "All during that time Raymond was sick we slept together in the same bed, but we didn't have relations. He wanted to a few times, but nothing happened. I didn't miss it, but I think he wanted to, you know."

During those years I was trying to raise my own family and earn a [26] living. But, one thing and another, we found ourselves having to move a lot. I couldn't keep track of what was going down in my dad's life. But I did have a chance one Christmas to tell him I wanted to be a writer. I might as well have told him I wanted to become a plastic surgeon. "What are you going to write about?" he wanted to know. Then, as if to help me out, he said, "Write about stuff you know about. Write about some of those fishing trips we took." I said I would, but I knew I wouldn't. "Send me what you write," he said. I said I'd do that, but then I didn't. I wasn't writing anything about fishing, and I didn't think he'd particularly care about, or even necessarily understand, what I was writing in those days. Besides, he wasn't a reader. Not the sort, anyway, I imagined I was writing for.

Then he died. I was a long way off, in Iowa City, with things still to [27] say to him. I didn't have the chance to tell him goodbye, or that I thought he was doing great at his new job. That I was proud of him for making a comeback.

My mother said he came in from work that night and ate a big sup- [28] per. Then he sat at the table by himself and finished what was left of a bottle of whiskey, a bottle she found hidden in the bottom of the garbage under some coffee grounds a day or so later. Then he got up and went to bed, where my mother joined him a little later. But in the night she had to get up and make a bed for herself on the couch. "He was snoring so loud I couldn't sleep," she said. The next morning when she looked in on him, he was on his back with his mouth open, his cheeks caved in. *Graylooking,* she said. She knew he was dead—she didn't need a doctor to tell her that. But she called one anyway, and then she called my wife.

Among the pictures my mother kept of my dad and herself during [29] those early days in Washington was a photograph of him standing in front of a car, holding a beer and a stringer of fish. In the photograph he is wearing his hat back on his forehead and has this awkward grin on his face. I asked her for it and she gave it to me, along with some others. I put it up on my wall, and each time we moved, I took the picture along and put it up on another wall. I looked at it carefully from time to time, trying to figure out some things about my dad, and maybe myself in the process. But I couldn't. My dad just kept moving further and further away from me and back into time. Finally, in the course of another move, I lost the photograph. It was then that I tried to recall it, and at the same time make an attempt to say something about my dad, and how I thought that in some important ways we might be alike. I wrote the poem when I was living in an apartment house in an urban area south of San Francisco, at a time when I found myself, like my dad, having trouble with alcohol. The poem was a way of trying to connect up with him.

Photograph of My Father in His Twenty-Second Year

October. Here in this dank, unfamiliar kitchen
I study my father's embarrassed young man's face.
Sheepish grin, he holds in one hand a string
of spiny yellow perch, in the other
a bottle of Carlsberg beer.   5

In jeans and flannel shirt, he leans
against the front fender of a 1934 Ford.
He would like to pose brave and hearty for his posterity,
wear his old hat cocked over his ear.
All his life my father wanted to be bold.   10

But the eyes give him away, and the hands
that limply offer the string of dead perch
and the bottle of beer. Father, I love you,
yet how can I say thank you, I who can't hold my liquor either
and don't even know the places to fish.   15

The poem is true in its particulars, except that my dad died in June 30
and not October, as the first word of the poem says. I wanted a word
with more than one syllable to it to make it linger a little. But more than
that, I wanted a month appropriate to what I felt at the time I wrote the
poem—a month of short days and failing light, smoke in the air, things
perishing. June was summer nights and days, graduations, my wedding
anniversary, the birthday of one of my children. June wasn't a month
your father died in.

After the service at the funeral home, after we had moved outside, 31
a woman I didn't know came over to me and said, "He's happier where
he is now." I stared at this woman until she moved away. I still remember the little knob of a hat she was wearing. Then one of my dad's
cousins—I didn't know the man's name—reached out and took my
hand, "We all miss him," he said, and I knew he wasn't saying it just to
be polite.

I began to weep for the first time since receiving the news. I hadn't 32
been able to before. I hadn't had the time, for one thing. Now, suddenly, I couldn't stop. I held my wife and wept while she said and did what
she could do to comfort me there in the middle of that summer afternoon.

I listened to people say consoling things to my mother, and I was 33
glad that my dad's family had turned up, had come to where he was. I
thought I'd remember everything that was said and done that day and
maybe find a way to tell it sometime. But I didn't. I forgot it all, or nearly. What I do remember is that I heard our name used a lot that afternoon, my dad's name and mine. But I knew they were talking about my
dad. *Raymond,* these people kept saying in their beautiful voices out of
my childhood. *Raymond.*

Responding to Reading

1. Why does Carver include details about his father's work history? His drinking? His mental illness? The photograph? Do you think these details are necessary?
2. What information is provided by the poem in paragraph 29 that is not provided by the essay itself?
3. What aspects of your father's life do you find hard to understand? Why?
   What does Carver finally come to realize about his father, and about himself?

THREE PERSPECTIVES ON FAMILY AND MEMORY

Here, three poets reflect on family ties and the persistence of memory. Oklahoma-born Linda Hogan (1947–) is a teacher and writer of poetry and fiction who is active in the Native American movement. Her collections include *Calling Myself Home* (1979) and *The Big Woman* (1987). In "Heritage," from *Calling Myself Home,* she connects her physical appearance and understanding of the world to those of the two generations that precede her. Detroit-born African American Robert Hayden (1913–1980), who taught at Fisk University and the University of Michigan and whose *Complete Poems* were collected in 1985, once said that "writing poetry is one way of coming to grips with both inner and external realities"; in "Those Winter Sundays," from *Angle of Ascent* (1975), he recalls his distant father with sadness and love. Irish poet and critic Seamus Heaney (1939–), whose father and grandfather both worked the earth as farmers and turf cutters, writes about his heritage from these two men in "Digging," from his first collection of poetry, *Death of a Naturalist* (1966); other collections include *Field Work* (1979) and *Seeing Things* (1991).

HERITAGE

Linda Hogan

From my mother, the antique mirror
where I watch my face take on her lines.
She left me the smell of baking bread
to warm fine hairs in my nostrils,
she left the large white breasts that weigh down   5
my body.

From my father I take his brown eyes,
the plague of locusts that leveled our crops,
they flew in formation like buzzards.

From my uncle the whittled wood   10
that rattles like bones
and is white
and smells like all our old houses

that are no longer there. He was the man
who sang old chants to me, the words   15
my father was told not to remember.

From my grandfather who never spoke
I learned to fear silence.
I learned to kill a snake
when you're begging for rain.   20

And grandmother, blue-eyed woman
whose skin was brown,
she used snuff.
When her coffee can full of black saliva
spilled on me   25
it was like the brown cloud of grasshoppers
that leveled her fields.
It was the brown stain
that covered my white shirt,
my whiteness a shame.   30
That sweet black liquid like the food
she chewed up and spit into my father's mouth
when he was an infant.
It was the brown earth of Oklahoma
stained with oil.   35
She said tobacco would purge your body of poisons.
It has more medicine than stones and knives
against your enemies.

That tobacco is the dark night that covers me.
She said it is wise to eat the flesh of deer   40
so you will be swift and travel over many miles.
She told me how our tribe has always followed a stick
that pointed west
that pointed east.

From my family I have learned the secrets   45
of never having a home.

THOSE WINTER SUNDAYS

Robert Hayden

Sundays too my father got up early
and put his clothes on in the blueblack cold,
then with cracked hands that ached
from labor in the weekday weather made
banked fires blaze. No one ever thanked him.   5

I'd wake and hear the cold splintering, breaking,
When the rooms were warm, he'd call,
and slowly I would rise and dress,
fearing the chronic angers of that house,

Speaking indifferently to him,   10
who had driven out the cold
and polished my good shoes as well.
What did I know, what did I know
of love's austere and lonely offices?

DIGGING

Seamus Heaney

Between my finger and my thumb
The squat pen rests; snug as a gun.

Under my window, a clean rasping sound
When the spade sinks into gravelly ground:
My father, digging. I look down   5

Till his straining rump among the flowerbeds
Bends low, comes up twenty years away
Stooping in rhythm through potato drills
Where he was digging.

The coarse boot nestled on the lug, the shaft   10
Against the inside knee was levered firmly.
He rooted out tall tops, buried the bright edge deep
To scatter new potatoes that we picked
Loving their cool hardness in our hands.
By God, the old man could handle a spade.   15
Just like his old man.

My grandfather cut more turf in a day
Than any other man on Toner's bog.
Once I carried him milk in a bottle
Corked sloppily with paper. He straightened up   20
To drink it, then fell to right away

Nicking and slicing neatly, heaving sods
Over his shoulder, going down and down
For the good turf. Digging.

The cold smell of potato mould, the squelch and slap   25
Of soggy peat, the curt cuts of an edge

Through living roots awaken in my head.
But I've no spade to follow men like them.

Between my finger and my thumb
The squat pen rests.   30
I'll dig with it.

Responding to Reading

1. What feelings does the speaker in Hogan's poem have about her family's past? Do you have conflicting feelings toward your own heritage?
2. Other than having "driven out the cold," what has the father in Hayden's poem done for his son? To what might the "chronic angers" (line 9) refer?
3. How would you characterize the speaker's attitude toward his father and grandfather in Heaney's poem? In what sense does he see himself as like them?
4. What important lessons has each speaker learned? Are these lessons primarily practical or theoretical? Explain.
5. What traits, abilities, values, habits, or fears have you inherited from your parents? What do you think you will pass on to your children?
6. What do you know now about your parents' responsibilities and sacrifices that you did not know when you were a child?

--------------------- **WRITING** ---------------------

Family and Memory

1. When Joan Didion looks at a snapshot of her grandfather as a young man, she says, "I . . . do and do not see my own [face]" (3). What does she mean? Write an essay in which you discuss in what respects this sentiment is true for one or two other writers represented in this chapter—for instance, for Raymond Carver or Gary Soto. If you prefer, you may discuss instead how you are like or unlike a member of your family.

2. What role does setting play in essays about family? For example, how is the concept of *home* defined? How important is the geographical location? The landscape? Discuss the development of setting in two or three of the selections in this chapter; or, consider the role of setting in shaping your own memories about your family.

3. What is your earliest memory of your family? It is a pleasant memory or an unpleasant one? Who are the central characters in the scene you picture? Why do you think the scene is so clear today? Write an essay in which you describe the scene exactly as you remember it. If you like, you may use present tense (as Alice Walker does in her essay) to make the scene more immediate and more real.

4. Several of the writers represented in this chapter—for example, Kingston, Momaday, and Carver—present fairly detailed biographical sketches of their subjects. Using these essays as guides, write a detailed biographical sketch of a member of your family. If you can, prepare for this assignment by interviewing several family members.

5. Have you ever returned as an adult to a place that was important to you when you were a child? Write two brief descriptions, one from the point of view of your adult self and one from the point of view of your childhood self. In each description, consider both the physical appearance of the place and its significance to you. Then, expand your descriptions into an essay by writing an introduction and a conclusion that compare the two views.

6. In many of the selections in this chapter, central figures are portrayed as outsiders, even outcasts. Sometimes these people have chosen to isolate themselves, sometimes they have been set apart by their behavior, and sometimes they have been ostracized by the society or by their own family. Analyze the factors that might have caused various individuals portrayed in this chapter to be isolated.

7. How do your parents' notions of success and failure affect you? Do you think your parents tend to expect too much of you? Explore these ideas in an essay, referring to one selection in this chapter and one in Chapter 6, "The American Dream."

8. Some writers—for example, Alice Walker and Raymond Carver—seem to have good reason to feel anger toward their parents. Are there negative events or situations in your own life for which you blame your parents? Identify several such events, and write a letter to your parents explaining why you believe your anger is justified.

9. Both Joyce Howe and Gary Soto come to understand their parents better by seeing them in the role of workers. Discuss these two writers' changing attitudes toward their parents' work. If you like, you can also refer in your essay to ideas expressed by Scott Russell Sanders in "The Men We Carry in Our Minds" in Chapter 5. Or, you can write an essay in which you discuss how your experience as a worker has helped you to understand or appreciate your own parents.

10. Read the poem "Photograph of My Father in His Twenty-Second Year" in paragraph 29 of Raymond Carver's essay. Write an essay in which you compare and contrast this poem with "Those Winter Sundays" (p. 78).

2

ISSUES IN EDUCATION

Student Voices

"Because so much emphasis is placed on grade point averages, students may actually forget that school is a place to learn and to have fun. It should not just be an institution that prepares people to get good jobs and high salaries. Schools should open students up to the possibilities around them."

—Celeste Armenti

"I believe I have gotten more out of school than what was taught in class. I have learned discipline and how to manage my time. I have also learned how to test myself on what I've learned. In some classes I've taken, I've gotten nothing more than a letter grade. In others, I've gotten much more, even though my grade might not have reflected it."

—Brett Kendall

"Coming from a small town, I never knew what living in a city was all about. Many of my friends at home will never experience living with people from many different parts of the country. They go to high school, graduate, get a job, and spend all their lives in one place. Also, many of my hometown friends are not accustomed to living together with people from many different racial and ethnic backgrounds. I consider this an important part of my education at college."

—Kim Thompson

"Last year when I decided to go back to school, I encountered many obstacles. Basically, I had been away from college for over five years, and during that time I had not used my mind much. But as I grew older, I began to realize what I was missing. I knew that it was about time for me to prove to myself that I could do college-level work. At first the adjustment was difficult. I went from working a fifty-hour week to working only on weekends. Eventually, however, I began to enjoy the new challenge of college material. I could feel my mind expanding and my confidence growing."

—*Robert Joiner*

——————————— **Preparing to Read and Write** ———————————

It may seem odd to us today, when education is touted as a remedy for all the problems of modern society, that one hundred years ago Mark Twain could imply that becoming educated means paying a price: forfeiting youthful innocence and happiness. Yet that is precisely what he suggests in his essay "Reading the River," where he examines two different ways of viewing the world: one innocent and naive, the other experienced and educated; one accepting, the other questioning.

It is this view of education—as a process that radically changes a person from an unthinking child to a cognizant adult—that is largely missing from today's educational systems. In fact, more emphasis seems to be placed on increasing self-esteem and avoiding controversy than on challenging students to discover new ways of thinking and new contexts for viewing the world. As a result, ideas are sanitized, classic books are censored or rewritten, and scientific theories are "balanced" with religious doctrine. The result is an educational environment that has all the excitement of elevator music. Many people—educators included—seem to have forgotten that ideas must be unsettling if they are to make us think. What is education, after all, but a process that encourages us to think critically about the world and develop a healthy skepticim—to question, evaluate, and synthesize ideas and events?

As you read and prepare to write about the selections in this chapter, you may consider the following questions.

- How does the writer define education? Is this definition consistent with yours?

- What does the writer think the main goals of education should be? Do you agree?

- Does the writer believe informal education is more important than formal education?

- On what aspect or aspects of education does the writer focus? Should the writer have discussed any additional aspects?

- What obstacles to education does the writer identify? How does he or she explain their existence and suggest they may be overcome?

- Who does the writer believe bears primary responsibility for a student's education? The student? The school? The community? The government?

- Does the writer use personal experience to support his or her ideas? Or does he or she use facts and statistics or expert opinion as support? Do you find the writer's ideas convincing?

- What changes in the educational system does the writer recommend? Do you agree with the writer's recommendations?

TWO PERSPECTIVES
ON EDUCATION

The following two essays describe a striking contrast between public schools in the early 1960s and public schools today. The first is by Lynda Barry, the cartoonist and chronicler of adolescent angst who is best known for her syndicated strip *Ernie Pook's Comeek* and her auto-biographical comic-strip novel *The Good Times Are Killing Me* (1988), later turned into a successful musical play. In "The Sanctuary of School," she remembers her Seattle grade school in a racially mixed neighborhood as a nurturing safe haven from her difficult family life. The second essay is by Antonio Strano, a junior high art teacher who has taught in San Francisco public schools for more than twenty-five years. Rather than a haven, the school where he teaches today is a pow-derkeg where students and faculty live in constant fear of guns and vi-olence, a fear that Strano laments can "kill the spirit of learning."

THE SANCTUARY OF SCHOOL

Lynda Barry

I was 7 years old the first time I snuck out of the house in the dark. [1] It was winter and my parents had been fighting all night. They were short on money and long on relatives who kept "temporarily" moving into our house because they had nowhere else to go.

My brother and I were used to giving up our bedroom. We slept on [2] the couch, something we actually liked because it put us that much clos-er to the light of our lives, our television.

At night when everyone was asleep, we lay on our pillows watch- [3] ing it with the sound off. We watched Steve Allen's mouth moving. We watched Johnny Carson's mouth moving. We watched movies filled with gangsters shooting machine guns into packed rooms, dying sol-diers hurling a last grenade and beautiful women crying at windows. Then the sign-off finally came and we tried to sleep.

The morning I snuck out, I woke up filled with a panic about need- [4] ing to get to school. The sun wasn't quite up yet but my anxiety was so fierce that I just got dressed, walked quietly across the kitchen and let myself out the back door.

It was quiet outside. Stars were still out. Nothing moved and no one ⁵
was in the street. It was as if someone had turned the sound off on the
world.

I walked the alley, breaking thin ice over the puddles with my ⁶
shoes. I didn't know why I was walking to school in the dark. I didn't
think about it. All I knew was a feeling of panic, like the panic that
strikes kids when they realize they are lost.

That feeling eased the moment I turned the corner and saw the dark ⁷
outline of my school at the top of the hill. My school was made up of
about 15 nondescript portable classrooms set down on a fenced concrete
lot in a rundown Seattle neighborhood, but it had the most beautiful
view of the Cascade Mountains. You could see them from anywhere on
the playfield and you could see them from the windows of my classroom—Room 2.

I walked over to the monkey bars and hooked my arms around the ⁸
cold metal. I stood for a long time just looking across Rainier Valley. The
sky was beginning to whiten and I could hear a few birds.

In a perfect world my absence at home would not have gone unno- ⁹
ticed. I would have had two parents in a panic to locate me, instead of
two parents in a panic to locate an answer to the hard question of survival during a deep financial and emotional crisis.

But in an overcrowded and unhappy home, it's incredibly easy for ¹⁰
any child to slip away. The high levels of frustration, depression and
anger in my house made my brother and me invisible. We were children
with the sound turned off. And for us, as for the steadily increasing
number of neglected children in this country, the only place where we
could count on being noticed was at school.

"Hey there, young lady. Did you forget to go home last night?" It ¹¹
was Mr. Gunderson, our janitor, whom we all loved. He was nice and
he was funny and he was old with white hair, thick glasses and an unbelievable number of keys. I could hear them jingling as he walked
across the playfield. I felt incredibly happy to see him.

He let me push his wheeled garbage can between the different ¹²
portables as he unlocked each room. He let me turn on the lights and
raise the window shades and I saw my school slowly come to life. I saw
Mrs. Holman, our school secretary, walk into the office without her orange lipstick on yet. She waved.

I saw the fifth-grade teacher Mr. Cunningham, walking under the ¹³
breezeway eating a hard roll. He waved.

And I saw my teacher, Mrs. Claire LeSane, walking toward us in a ¹⁴
red coat and calling my name in a very happy and surprised way, and
suddenly my throat got tight and my eyes stung and I ran toward her
crying. It was something that surprised us both.

It's only thinking about it now, 28 years later, that I realize I was cry- ¹⁵
ing from relief. I was with my teacher, and in a while I was going to sit

at my desk, with my crayons and pencils and books and classmates all around me, and for the next six hours I was going to enjoy a thoroughly secure, warm and stable world. It was a world I absolutely relied on. Without it, I don't know where I would have gone that morning.

Mrs. LeSane asked me what was wrong and when I said "Nothing," [16] she seemingly left it at that. But she asked me if I would carry her purse for her, an honor above all honors, and she asked if I wanted to come into Room 2 early and paint.

She believed in the natural healing power of painting and drawing [17] for troubled children. In the back of her room there was always a drawing table and an easel with plenty of supplies, and sometimes during the day she would come up to you for what seemed like no good reason and quietly ask if you wanted to go to the back table and "make some pictures for Mrs. LeSane." We all had a chance at it—to sit apart from the class for a while to paint, draw and silently work out impossible problems on 11 x 17 sheets of newsprint.

Drawing came to mean everything to me. At the back table in Room [18] 2, I learned to build myself a life preserver that I could carry into my home.

We all know that a good education system saves lives, but the people [19] of this country are still told that cutting the budget for public schools is necessary, that poor salaries for teachers are all we can manage and that art, music and all creative activities must be the first to go when times are lean.

Before- and after-school programs are cut and we are told that pub- [20] lic schools are not made for baby-sitting children. If parents are neglectful temporarily or permanently, for whatever reason, it's certainly sad, but their unlucky children must fend for themselves. Or slip through the cracks. Or wander in a dark night alone.

We are told in a thousand ways that not only are public schools not [21] important, but that the children who attend them, the children who need them most, are not important either. We leave them to learn from the blind eye of a television, or to the mercy of "a thousand points of light"[1] that can be as far away as stars.

I was lucky. I had Mrs. LeSane. I had Mr. Gunderson. I had an abun- [22] dance of art supplies. And I had a particular brand of neglect in my home that allowed me to slip away and get to them. But what about the rest of the kids who weren't as lucky? What happened to them?

By the time the bell rang that morning I had finished my drawing [23] and Mrs. LeSane pinned it up on the special bulletin board she reserved for drawings from the back table. It was the same picture I always drew—a sun in the corner of a blue sky over a nice house with flowers all around it.

---

[1] Catchphrase for former President George Bush's plan to substitute volunteerism for government programs. [Eds.]

Mrs. LeSane asked us to please stand, face the flag, place our right [24] hands over our hearts and say the Pledge of Allegiance. Children across the country do it faithfully. I wonder now when the country will face its children and say a pledge right back.

Incident in Room 3

Antonio Strano

"Be on the lookout for a .357 magnum" were strange words to read [1] in a memo from the principal's office. As news got around, it cast an eerie cloud over Westlake Junior High School in Oakland, where I teach.

This wasn't the first memo about guns on campus. For weeks this [2] winter the school was plagued by guns: students would report seeing them passed around in classes, or out in the hall. Thankfully, none had been fired.

Silent guns, however, also have a way of killing: they can kill the [3] spirit of learning. The fear that prevails on our streets has taken root in our school. Too many of my students now pack weapons along with their lunch and homework. When kids are caught with guns, cops arrest them. But usually nothing comes of it, and they are back in school in no time. The juvenile justice system is overwhelmed by more important problems.

We're trying to address the problem on our own. In January, we had [4] a "gun assembly." We've had other "crisis" assemblies: one was about AIDS prevention, another was a panel discussion by a group called Parents of Murdered Children. In a twist, a student of mine acquired a gun on campus during the assembly on guns. In a botched holdup the next day, he shot at the fleeing victim and at the cop who came after him. He was sentenced to a year in a juvenile detention center.

During another assembly on violence, one of my best art students [5] was savagely beaten in a back corridor by a group of boys. He was carted off on a gurney by paramedics.

Then came Washington's Birthday. After the four-day weekend, the [6] students seemed relaxed. But at the start of the second period, two friends, Darryl and Michelle, 15 years old, entered my class embroiled in a shoving match. I separated them, but was suddenly disoriented by a blow to my head. They kept trying to hit each other, but I was in the way. A punch broke my glasses.

It was over in 30 seconds. Michelle bolted from the room promising [7] swift retribution. Shortly after, the vice principal came in and told Darryl to fill out a statement about the incident. Darryl sat down and the vice principal left.

Ten minutes later, two grown men suddenly appeared at my class- 8
room door. One had a hand in his pocket as if gripping a gun. A gun ornament dangled from his partner's neck.

I blocked the door but the thug with his hand in his pocket pushed 9
me backward. I put my hands in the air, retreating.

"Where's the boy?" he asked matter-of-factly. 10

"He's not here," I answered, my voice breaking. 11

"The office said he was here filling out a statement," he said. 12

I now became very frightened. I suddenly recalled my dinner the 13
night before with my daughter, Carina, who would be entering college
in the fall. I had suggested she might want to consider becoming an art
teacher like me. One bullet from this man's gun and my kid would never
consider teaching.

In the dead silence of room 3 my fear turned to anger. If I was going 14
to be shot, I thought, I refused to die meekly. I lowered my hands. "He's
not here," I said, looking at Darryl, who sat frozen like a sphinx. I had
to move quickly before the thugs noticed him. "You'll have to go now,"
I said, escorting them to the door, surprised they went so docilely. I
locked it and called the principal to tell him to call the cops.

Later, I angrily demanded to know who had told the men that Dar- 15
ryl was in my classroom. The principal, looking shaken, described a terrible scene in his office with Michelle's mother and the two men, one of
whom was Michelle's brother; she had called home for help. Her brother
kept shoving the principal in the face, while her mother cursed him out.

I asked why the men weren't arrested, and the principal explained 16
police department triage[1] in Oakland: when no one is hurt and no blood
is spilled, they just let it go. I understood. It was nothing urgent.

Responding to Reading

1. Is Barry's elementary school like the one you remember? What information
   has she left out of her description? How can you explain these omissions?
2. In "Incident in Room 3" Strano's reaction to being confronted by two men
   changes from fear to anger. Why does he become angry? Would you have
   handled the situation the same way he did?
3. Both essays end on a somewhat cynical note. How effective are these conclusions? What does each writer gain or lose with this concluding strategy?
4. The two writers view school from different perspectives. Are their views really as different as they seem? In what ways are the authors' views similar?
5. Both writers use a personal experience to make a point about school. How
   else could they have conveyed their views?
6. Did you see school as a dangerous place, a refuge, or something else? Explain.

---

[1] The act of sorting injured people into groups according to the severity of their injuries. [Eds.]

GRADUATION

Maya Angelou

Maya Angelou (1928–) was born in St. Louis, where her mother lived, but was raised in Arkansas by her grandmother, who ran a general store. She began a theatrical career when she toured with *Porgy and Bess* in 1954–55, but now Angelou is a poet, writer, lecturer, civil rights leader, and teacher. She read her poem "On the Pulse of Morning" at the 1993 inauguration of Bill Clinton. A critic in *Southern Humanities Review* has said that "her genius as a writer is in her ability to recapture the texture of the way of life in the texture of its idioms, its idiosyncracies, and especially its process of image-making." Angelou's many books include *Oh Pray My Wings Are Gonna Fit Me Well* (poetry, 1975) and *I Know Why the Caged Bird Sings* (autobiography, 1969). In "Graduation," Angelou remembers the anger and pride of graduation day at her segregated high school in Stamps, Arkansas.

The children in Stamps trembled visibly with anticipation. Some [1] adults were excited too, but to be certain the whole young population had come down with graduation epidemic. Large classes were graduating from both the grammar school and the high school. Even those who were years removed from their own day of glorious release were anxious to help with preparations as a kind of dry run. The junior students who were moving into the vacating classes' chairs were tradition-bound to show their talents for leadership and management. They strutted through the school and around the campus exerting pressure on the lower grades. Their authority was so new that occasionally if they pressed a little too hard it had to be overlooked. After all, next term was coming, and it never hurt a sixth grader to have a play sister in the eighth grade, or a tenth-year student to be able to call a twelfth grader Bubba. So all was endured in a spirit of shared understanding. But the graduating classes themselves were the nobility. Like travelers with exotic destinations on their minds, the graduates were remarkably forgetful. They came to school without their books, or tablets or even pencils. Volunteers fell over themselves to secure replacements for the missing equipment. When accepted, the willing workers might or might not be thanked, and it was of no importance to the pregraduation rites. Even teachers were respectful of the now quiet and aging seniors, and tended to speak to them, if not as equals, as beings only slightly lower than themselves. After tests were returned and grades given, the student body, which acted like an extended family, knew who did well, who excelled, and what piteous ones had failed.

Unlike the white high school, Lafayette County Training School dis- 2
tinguished itself by having neither lawn, nor hedges, nor tennis court,
nor climbing ivy. Its two buildings (main classrooms, the grade school
and home economics) were set on a dirt hill with no fence to limit either
its boundaries or those of bordering farms. There was a large expanse to
the left of the school which was used alternately as a baseball diamond
or basketball court. Rusty hoops on swaying poles represented the permanent recreational equipment, although bats and balls could be borrowed from the P.E. teacher if the borrower was qualified and if the diamond wasn't occupied.

Over this rocky area relieved by a few shady tall persimmon trees 3
the graduating class walked. The girls often held hands and no longer
bothered to speak to the lower students. There was a sadness about
them, as if this old world was not their home and they were bound for
higher ground. The boys, on the other hand, had become more friendly, more outgoing. A decided change from the closed attitude they projected while studying for finals. Now they seemed not ready to give up
the old school, the familiar paths and classrooms. Only a small percentage would be continuing on to college—one of the South's A & M (agricultural and mechanical) schools, which trained Negro youths to be carpenters, farmers, handymen, masons, maids, cooks and baby nurses.
Their future rode heavily on their shoulders, and blinded them to the
collective joy that had pervaded the lives of the boys and girls in the
grammar school graduating class.

Parents who could afford it had ordered new shoes and ready-made 4
clothes for themselves from Sears and Roebuck or Montgomery Ward.
They also engaged the best seamstresses to make the floating graduating dresses and to cut down secondhand pants which would be pressed
to a military slickness for the important event.

Oh, it was important, all right. Whitefolks would attend the cere- 5
mony, and two or three would speak of God and home, and the Southern way of life, and Mrs. Parsons, the principal's wife, would play the
graduation march while the lower-grade graduates paraded down the
aisles and took their seats below the platform. The high school seniors
would wait in empty classrooms to make their dramatic entrance.

In the Store I was the person of the moment. The birthday girl. 6
The center. Bailey[1] had graduated the year before, although to do so
he had had to forfeit all pleasures to make up for his time lost in Baton
Rouge.

My class was wearing butter-yellow piqué dresses, and Momma 7
launched out on mine. She smocked the yoke into tiny crisscrossing

---

[1] Angelou's brother. The Store was run by Angelou's grandmother, whom she called Momma, and
Momma's son, Uncle Willie.

puckers, then shirred the rest of the bodice. Her dark fingers ducked in and out of the lemony cloth as she embroidered raised daisies around the hem. Before she considered herself finished she had added a crocheted cuff on the puff sleeves, and a pointy crocheted collar.

I was going to be lovely. A walking model of all the various styles 8 of fine hand sewing and it didn't worry me that I was only twelve years old and merely graduating from the eighth grade. Besides, many teachers in Arkansas Negro schools had only that diploma and were licensed to impart wisdom.

The days had become longer and more noticeable. The faded beige 9 of former times had been replaced with strong and sure colors. I began to see my classmates' clothes, their skin tones, and the dust that waved off pussy willows. Clouds that lazed across the sky were objects of great concern to me. Their shiftier shapes might have held a message that in my new happiness and with a little bit of time I'd soon decipher. During that period I looked at the arch of heaven so religiously my neck kept a steady ache. I had taken to smiling more often, and my jaws hurt from the unaccustomed activity. Between the two physical sore spots, I suppose I could have been uncomfortable, but that was not the case. As a member of the winning team (the graduating class of 1940) I had outdistanced unpleasant sensations by miles. I was headed for the freedom of open fields.

Youth and social approval allied themselves with me and we tram- 10 meled memories of slights and insults. The wind of our swift passage remodeled my features. Lost tears were pounded to mud and then to dust. Years of withdrawal were brushed aside and left behind, as hanging ropes of parasitic moss.

My work alone had awarded me a top place and I was going to be 11 one of the first called in the graduating ceremonies. On the classroom blackboard, as well as on the bulletin board in the auditorium, there were blue stars and white stars and red stars. No absences, no tardinesses, and my academic work was among the best of the year. I could say the preamble to the Constitution even faster than Bailey. We timed ourselves often: "WethepeopleoftheUnitedStatesinordertoformamoreperfectunion . . ." I had memorized the Presidents of the United States from Washington to Roosevelt in chronological as well as alphabetical order.

My hair pleased me too. Gradually the black mass had lengthened 12 and thickened, so that it kept at last to its braided pattern, and I didn't have to yank my scalp off when I tried to comb it.

Louise and I had rehearsed the exercises until we tired out our- 13 selves. Henry Reed was class valedictorian. He was a small, very black boy with hooded eyes, a long, broad nose and an oddly shaped head. I had admired him for years because each term he and I vied for the best grades in our class. Most often he bested me, but instead of being disappointed I was pleased that we shared top places between us. Like many Southern Black children, he lived with his grandmother, who was as strict as Momma and as kind as she knew how to be. He was courteous, respectful and soft-spoken to elders, but on the playground he chose to play the roughest games. I admired him. Anyone, I reckoned, sufficiently afraid or sufficiently dull could be polite. But to be able to operate at a top level with both adults and children was admirable.

His valedictory speech was entitled "To Be or Not to Be." The rigid [14] tenth-grade teacher had helped him write it. He'd been working on the dramatic stresses for months.

The weeks until graduation were filled with heady activities. A [15] group of small children were to be presented in a play about buttercups and daisies and bunny rabbits. They could be heard throughout the building practicing their hops and their little songs that sounded like silver bells. The older girls (nongraduates, of course) were assigned the task of making refreshments for the night's festivities. A tangy scent of ginger, cinnamon, nutmeg and chocolate wafted around the home economics building as the budding cooks made samples for themselves and their teachers.

In every corner of the workshop, axes and saws split fresh timber as [16] the woodshop boys made sets and stage scenery. Only the graduates were left out of the general bustle. We were free to sit in the library at the back of the building or look in quite detachedly, naturally, on the measures being taken for our event.

Even the minister preached on graduation the Sunday before. His [17] subject was, "Let your light so shine that men will see your good works and praise your Father, Who is in Heaven." Although the sermon was purported to be addressed to us, he used the occasion to speak to backsliders, gamblers and general ne'er-do-wells. But since he had called our names at the beginning of the service we were mollified.

Among Negroes the tradition was to give presents to children going [18] only from one grade to another. How much more important this was when the person was graduating at the top of the class. Uncle Willie and Momma had sent away for a Mickey Mouse watch like Bailey's. Louise gave me four embroidered handkerchiefs. (I gave her crocheted doilies.) Mrs. Sneed, the minister's wife, made me an undershirt to wear for graduation, and nearly every customer gave me a nickel or maybe even a dime with the instruction "Keep on moving to higher ground," or some such encouragement.

Amazingly the great day finally dawned and I was out of bed before [19] I knew it. I threw open the back door to see it more clearly, but Momma said, "Sister, come away from that door and put your robe on."

I hoped the memory of that morning would never leave me. Sun- [20] light was itself young, and the day had none of the insistence maturity would bring it in a few hours. In my robe and barefoot in the backyard, under cover of going to see about my new beans, I gave myself up to the gentle warmth and thanked God that no matter what evil I had done in my life He had allowed me to live to see this day. Somewhere in my fatalism I had expected to die, accidentally, and never have the chance to walk up the stairs in the auditorium and gracefully receive my hard-earned diploma. Out of God's merciful bosom I had won reprieve.

Bailey came out in his robe and gave me a box wrapped in Christ- [21] mas paper. He said he had saved his money for months to pay for it. It felt like a box of chocolates, but I knew Bailey wouldn't save money to buy candy when we had all we could want under our noses.

He was as proud of the gift as I. It was a soft-leather-bound copy of [22] a collection of poems by Edgar Allan Poe, or, as Bailey and I called him, "Eap." I turned to "Annabel Lee" and we walked up and down the garden rows, the cool dirt between our toes, reciting the beautifully sad lines.

Momma made a Sunday breakfast although it was only Friday. [23] After we finished the blessing, I opened my eyes to find the watch on my plate. It was a dream of a day. Everything went smoothly and to my credit. I didn't have to be reminded or scolded for anything. Near evening I was too jittery to attend to chores, so Bailey volunteered to do all before his bath.

Days before, we had made a sign for the Store, and as we turned out [24] the lights Momma hung the cardboard over the doorknob. It read clearly: CLOSED. GRADUATION.

My dress fitted perfectly and everyone said that I looked like a sun- [25] beam in it. On the hill, going toward the school, Bailey walked behind with Uncle Willie, who muttered, "Go on, Ju." He wanted him to walk ahead with us because it embarrassed him to have to walk so slowly. Bailey said he'd let the ladies walk together, and the men would bring up the rear. We all laughed, nicely.

Little children dashed by out of the dark like fireflies. Their crepe- [26] paper dresses and butterfly wings were not made for running and we heard more than one rip, dryly, and the regretful "uh uh" that followed.

The school blazed without gaiety. The windows seemed cold and [27] unfriendly from the lower hill. A sense of ill-fated timing crept over me, and if Momma hadn't reached for my hand I would have drifted back to Bailey and Uncle Willie, and possibly beyond. She made a few slow jokes about my feet getting cold, and tugged me along to the now-strange building.

Around the front steps, assurance came back. There were my fellow [28] "greats," the graduating class. Hair brushed back, legs oiled, new dresses and pressed pleats, fresh pocket handkerchiefs and little handbags, all homesewn. Oh, we were up to snuff, all right. I joined my comrades and didn't even see my family go in to find seats in the crowded auditorium.

The school band struck up a march and all classes filed in as had ²⁹
been rehearsed. We stood in front of our seats, as assigned, and on a signal from the choir director, we sat. No sooner had this been accomplished than the band started to play the national anthem. We rose again
and sang the song, after which we recited the pledge of allegiance. We
remained standing for a brief minute before the choir director and the
principal signaled to us, rather desperately I thought, to take our seats.
The command was so unusual that our carefully rehearsed and smooth-
running machine was thrown off. For a full minute we fumbled for our
chairs and bumped into each other awkwardly. Habits change or solid-
ify under pressure, so in our state of nervous tension we had been ready
to follow our usual assembly pattern: the American national anthem,
then the pledge of allegiance, then the song every Black person I knew
called the Negro National Anthem. All done in the same key, with the
same passion and most often standing on the same foot.

Finding my seat at last, I was overcome with a presentiment of ³⁰
worse things to come. Something unrehearsed, unplanned, was going to
happen, and we were going to be made to look bad. I distinctly remember being explicit in the choice of pronoun. It was "we," the graduating class, the unit, that concerned me then.

The principal welcomed "parents and friends" and asked the Bap- ³¹
tist minister to lead us in prayer. His invocation was brief and punchy,
and for a second I thought we were getting on the high road to right action. When the principal came back to the dais, however, his voice had
changed. Sounds always affected me profoundly and the principal's
voice was one of my favorites. During assembly it melted and lowed
weakly into the audience. It had not been in my plan to listen to him, but
my curiosity was piqued and I straightened up to give him my attention.

He was talking about Booker T. Washington, our "late great leader," ³²
who said we can be as close as the fingers on the hand, etc. . . . . Then he
said a few vague things about friendship and the friendship of kindly
people to those less fortunate than themselves. With that his voice nearly faded, thin, away. Like a river diminishing to a stream and then to a
trickle. But he cleared his throat and said, "Our speaker tonight, who is
also our friend, came from Texarkana to deliver the commencement address, but due to the irregularity of the train schedule, he's going to, as
they say, 'speak and run.'" He said that we understood and wanted the
man to know that we were most grateful for the time he was able to give
us and then something about how we were willing always to adjust to
another's program, and without more ado—"I give you Mr. Edward
Donleavy."

Not one but two white men came through the door off-stage. The ³³
shorter one walked to the speaker's platform, and the tall one moved to
the center seat and sat down. But that was our principal's seat, and already occupied. The dislodged gentleman bounced around for a long

breath or two before the Baptist minister gave him his chair, then with more dignity than the situation deserved, the minister walked off the stage.

Donleavy looked at the audience once (on reflection, I'm sure that [34] he wanted only to reassure himself that we were really there), adjusted his glasses and began to read from a sheaf of papers.

He was glad "to be here and to see the work going on just as it was [35] in the other schools."

At the first "Amen" from the audience I willed the offender to im- [36] mediate death by choking on the word. But Amens and Yes, sir's began to fall around the room like rain through a ragged umbrella.

He told us of the wonderful changes we children in Stamps had in [37] store. The Central School (naturally, the white school was Central) had already been granted improvements that would be in use in the fall. A well-known artist was coming from Little Rock to teach art to them. They were going to have the newest microscopes and chemistry equip-ment for their laboratory. Mr. Donleavy didn't leave us long in the dark over who made these improvements available to Central High. Nor were we to be ignored in the general betterment scheme he had in mind.

He said that he had pointed out to people at a very high level that [38] one of the first-line football tacklers at Arkansas Agricultural and Me-chanical College had graduated from good old Lafayette County Train-ing School. Here fewer Amen's were heard. Those few that did break through lay dully in the air with the heaviness of habit.

He went on to praise us. He went on to say how he had bragged that [39] "one of the best basketball players at Fisk[2] sank his first ball right here at Lafayette County Training School."

The white kids were going to have a chance to become Galileos and [40] Madame Curies and Edisons and Gauguins,[3] and our boys (the girls weren't even in on it) would try to be Jesse Owenses and Joe Louises.[4]

Owens and the Brown Bomber were great heroes in our world, but what school official in the white-goddom of Little Rock had the right to decide that those two men must be our only heroes? Who decided that for Henry Reed to become a scientist he had to work like George Wash-ington Carver, as a bootblack, to buy a lousy microscope? Bailey was ob-viously always going to be too small to be an athlete, so which concrete angel glued to what country seat had decided that if my brother want-ed to become a lawyer he had to first pay penance for his skin by pick-ing cotton and hoeing corn and studying correspondence books at night for twenty years?

---

[2] Highly regarded, predominately black university in Nashville. [Eds.]

[3] Inventors, scientists, and artists. [Eds.]

[4] The black track star and Olympic gold medalist; and the longtime world heavyweight boxing champion, known as the "Brown Bomber." [Eds.]

The man's dead words fell like bricks around the auditorium and [42] too many settled in my belly. Constrained by hard-learned manners I couldn't look behind me, but to my left and right the proud graduating class of 1940 had dropped their heads. Every girl in my row had found something new to do with her handkerchief. Some folded the tiny squares into love knots, some into triangles, but most were wadding them, then pressing them flat on their yellow laps.

On the dais, the ancient tragedy was being replayed. Professor Par- [43] sons sat, a sculptor's reject, rigid. His large, heavy body seemed devoid of will or willingness, and his eyes said he was no longer with us. The other teachers examined the flag (which was draped stage right) or their notes, or the windows which opened on our now-famous playing diamond.

Graduation, the hush-hush magic time of frills and gifts and con- [44] gratulations and diplomas, was finished for me before my name was called. The accomplishment was nothing. The meticulous maps, drawn in three colors of ink, learning and spelling decasyllabic words, memorizing the whole of *The Rape of Lucrece*[5]—it was for nothing. Donleavy had exposed us.

We were maids and farmers, handymen and washerwomen, and [45] anything higher that we aspired to was farcical and presumptuous.

Then I wished that Gabriel Prosser and Nat Turner[6] had killed all [46] whitefolks in their beds and that Abraham Lincoln had been assassinated before the signing of the Emancipation Proclamation, and that Harriet Tubman[7] had been killed by that blow on her head and Christopher Columbus had drowned in the *Santa Maria*.

It was awful to be a Negro and have no control over my life. It was [47] brutal to be young and already trained to sit quietly and listen to charges brought against my color with no chance of defense. We should all be dead. I thought I should like to see us all dead, one on top of the other. A pyramid of flesh with the whitefolks on the bottom, as the broad base, then the Indians with their silly tomahawks and teepees and wigwams and treaties, the Negroes with their mops and recipes and cotton sacks and spirituals sticking out of their mouths. The Dutch children should all stumble in their wooden shoes and break their necks. The French should choke to death on the Louisiana Purchase (1803) while silkworms ate all the Chinese with their stupid pigtails. As a species, we were an abomination. All of us.

Donleavy was running for election, and assured our parents that if [48] he won we could count on having the only colored paved playing field

---

[5] *The Rape of Lucrece* is a long narrative poem by Shakespeare. [Eds.]

[6] Prosser and Turner both led slave rebellions. [Eds.]

[7] Harriet Tubman (1820–1913) was an African-American abolitionist who became one of the most successful guides on the Underground Railroad. [Eds.]

in that part of Arkansas. Also—he never looked up to acknowledge the grunts of acceptance—also, we were bound to get some new equipment for the home economics building and the workshop.

He finished, and since there was no need to give any more than the [49] most perfunctory thank-you's, he nodded to the men on the stage, and the tall white man who was never introduced joined him at the door. They left with the attitude that now they were off to something really important. (The graduation ceremonies at Lafayette County Training School had been a mere preliminary.)

The ugliness they left was palpable. An uninvited guest who would- [50] n't leave. The choir was summoned and sang a modern arrangement of "Onward, Christian Soldiers," with new words pertaining to graduates seeking their place in the world. But it didn't work. Elouise, the daughter of the Baptist minister, recited "Invictus,"[8] and I could have cried at the impertinence of "I am the master of my fate, I am the captain of my soul."

My name had lost its ring of familiarity and I had to be nudged to [51] go and receive my diploma. All my preparations had fled. I neither marched up to the stage like a conquering Amazon, not did I look in the audience for Bailey's nod of approval. Marguerite Johnson,[9] I heard the name again, my honors were read, there were noises in the audience of appreciation, and I took my place on the stage as rehearsed.

I thought about colors I hated: ecru, puce, lavender, beige and [52] black.

There was shuffling and rustling around me, then Henry Reed was [53] giving his valedictory address, "To Be or Not to Be." Hadn't he heard the whitefolks? We couldn't *be*, so the question was a waste of time. Henry's voice came out clear and strong. I feared to look at him. Hadn't he got the message? There was no "nobler in the mind" for Negroes because the world didn't think we had minds, and they let us know it. "Outrageous fortune"? Now, that was a joke. When the ceremony was over I had to tell Henry Reed some things. That is, if I still cared. Not "rub," Henry, "erase." "Ah, there's the erase." Us.

Henry had been a good student in elocution. His voice rose on tides [54] of promise and fell on waves of warnings. The English teacher had helped him to create a sermon winging through Hamlet's soliloquy. To be a man, a doer, a builder, a leader, or to be a tool, an unfunny joke, a crusher of funky toadstools. I marveled that Henry could go through with the speech as if we had a choice.

---

[8] An inspirational poem written in 1875 by William Ernest Henley (1849–1903). Its defiant and stoic sentiments made it extremely popular with nineteenth-century readers. [Eds.]

[9] Angelou's given name. [Eds.]

I had been listening and silently rebutting each sentence with my [55] eyes closed; then there was a hush, which in an audience warns that something unplanned is happening. I looked up and saw Henry Reed, the conservative, the proper, the A student, turn his back to the audience and turn to us (the proud graduating class of 1940) and sing, nearly speaking,

"Lift ev'ry voice and sing
Till earth and heaven ring
Ring with the harmonies of Liberty . . ."

It was the poem written by James Weldon Johnson. It was the music composed by J. Rosamond Johnson. It was the Negro national anthem. Out of habit we were singing it.

Our mothers and fathers stood in the dark hall and joined the hymn [56] of encouragement. A kindergarten teacher led the small children onto the stage and the buttercups and daisies and bunny rabbits marked time and tried to follow:

"Stony the road we trod
Bitter the chastening rod
Felt in the days when hope, unborn, had died.
Yet with a steady beat
Have not our weary feet
Come to the place for which our fathers sighed?"

Each child I knew had learned that song with his ABC's and along [57] with "Jesus Loves Me This I Know." But I personally had never heard it before. Never heard the words, despite the thousands of times I had sung them. Never thought they had anything to do with me.

On the other hand, the words of Patrick Henry had made such an [58] impression on me that I had been able to stretch myself tall and trembling and say, "I know not what course others may take, but as for me, give me liberty or give me death."

And now I heard, really for the first time: [59]

"We have come over a way that with tears
has been watered,
We have come, treading our path through
the blood of the slaughtered."

While echoes of the song shivered in the air, Henry Reed bowed his [60] head, said "Thank you," and returned to his place in the line. The tears that slipped down many faces were not wiped away in shame.

We were on top again. As always, again. We survived. The depths [61] had been icy and dark, but now a bright sun spoke to our souls. I was no longer simply a member of the proud graduating class of 1940; I was a proud member of the wonderful, beautiful Negro race.

Oh, Black known and unknown poets, how often have your auc-   62
tioned pains sustained us? Who will compute the lonely nights made less
lonely by your songs, or the empty pots made less tragic by your tales?

If we were a people much given to revealing secrets, we might raise   63
monuments and sacrifice to the memories of our poets, but slavery
cured us of that weakness. It may be enough, however, to have it said
that we survive in exact relationship to the dedication of our poets (include preachers, musicians and blues singers).

Responding to Reading

1. Angelou's graduation took place in 1940. Do you think educators still have
   limited expectations for members of minority groups? What expectations
   did the teachers in your high school have for you and your fellow students?
2. In what way does Mr. Donleavy's speech educate the graduates? How does
   Angelou's thinking change as she listens to him?
3. What has their formal education taught the graduates? What more subtle
   lessons have they learned as citizens of Stamps, Arkansas? What lessons did
   you learn in the classroom? What lessons have you learned outside the classroom?

SAVAGE INEQUALITIES

∼

Jonathan Kozol

Born in Boston into a "privileged and isolated" environment, Jonathan
Kozol (1936-) received his B.A. in literature from Harvard and drifted
into the civil rights movement in 1964. In 1967 he published *Death at an
Early Age: The Destruction of the Hearts and Minds of Negro School Children
in the Boston Public Schools*. Based on his experiences as a fourth grade
teacher in an inner city school from which he was fired for "curriculum
deviation," this controversial book led to a number of specific reforms.
Since then, Kozol has divided his time between academia and social activism, noting "It is a simple matter of humanity to use our limited resources in the places where they're the most needed." His books include *Illiterate America* (1985), an excerpt from which appears on page
203; *Rachel and Her Children* (1988), a study of homeless families; and
Savage Inequalities (1991), an eye-opening examination of the unequal
resources available to suburban and inner city public schools. In this
chapter from *Savage Inequalities*, Kozol looks at two grade schools only
a few miles apart in the Bronx, New York, where differences based on
race and class could not be more apparent.

"In a country where there is no distinction of class," Lord Acton [1]
wrote of the United States 130 years ago, "a child is not born to the station of its parents, but with an indefinite claim to all the prizes that can
be won by thought and labor. It is in conformity with the theory of
equality . . . to give as near as possible to every youth an equal state in
life." Americans, he said, "are unwilling that any should be deprived in
childhood of the means of competition."

It is hard to read these words today without a sense of irony and [2]
sadness. Denial of "the means of competition" is perhaps the single
most consistent outcome of the education offered to poor children in
the schools of our large cities; and nowhere is this pattern of denial
more explicit or more absolute than in the public schools of New York
City.

Average expenditures per pupil in the city of New York in 1987 were [3]
some $5,500. In the highest spending suburbs of New York (Great Neck
or Manhasset, for example, on Long Island) funding levels rose above
$11,000, with the highest districts in the state at $15,000. "Why . . .," asks
the city's Board of Education, "should our students receive less" than do
"similar students" who live elsewhere? "The inequity is clear."

But the inequality to which these words refer goes even further than [4]
the school board may be eager to reveal. "It is perhaps the supreme
irony," says the nonprofit Community Service Society of New York, that
"the same Board of Education which perceives so clearly the inequities"
of funding between separate towns and cities "is perpetuating similar
inequities" right in New York. And, in comment on the Board of Education's final statement—"the inequity is clear"—the CSS observes,
"New York City's poorest . . . districts could adopt that eloquent statement with few changes."

New York City's public schools are subdivided into 32 school dis- [5]
tricts. District 10 encompasses a large part of the Bronx but is, effectively, two separate districts. One of these districts, Riverdale, is in the
northwest section of the Bronx. Home to many of the city's most sophisticated and well-educated families, its elementary schools have relatively few low-income students. The other section, to the south and
east, is poor and heavily nonwhite.

The contrast between public schools in each of these two neighbor- [6]
hoods is obvious to any visitor. At Public School 24 in Riverdale, the
principal speaks enthusiastically of his teaching staff. At Public School
79, serving poorer children to the south, the principal says that he is
forced to take the "tenth-best" teachers. "I thank God they're still breathing," he remarks of those from whom he must select his teachers.

Some years ago, District 10 received an allocation for computers. [7]
The local board decided to give each elementary school an equal number of computers, even though the schools in Riverdale had smaller
classes and far fewer students. When it was pointed out that schools in

Riverdale, as a result, had twice the number of computers in proportion to their student populations as the schools in the poor neighborhoods, the chairman of the local board replied, "What is fair is what is determined . . . to be fair."

The superintendent of District 10, Fred Goldberg, tells the *New York* [8] *Times* that "every effort" is made "to distribute resources equitably." He speculates that some gap might exist because some of the poorer schools need to use funds earmarked for computers to buy basic supplies like pens and paper. Asked about the differences in teachers noted by the principals, he says there are no differences, then adds that next year he'll begin a program to improve the quality of teachers in the poorer schools. Questioned about differences in physical appearances between the richer and the poorer schools, he says, "I think it's demographics."[1]

Sometimes a school principal, whatever his background or his pol- [9] itics, looks into the faces of the children in his school and offers a disarming statement that cuts through official ambiguity. "These are the kids most in need," says Edward Flanery, the principal of one of the low-income schools, "and they get the worst teachers." For children of diverse needs in his overcrowded rooms, he says, "you need an outstanding teacher. And what do you get? You get the worst."

In order to find Public School 261 in District 10, a visitor is told to [10] look for a mortician's office. The funeral home, which faces Jerome Avenue in the North Bronx, is easy to identify by its green awning. The school is next door, in a former roller-skating rink. No sign identifies the building as a school. A metal awning frame without an awning supports a flagpole, but there is no flag.

In the street in front of the school there is an elevated public transit [11] line. Heavy traffic fills the street. The existence of the school is virtually concealed within this crowded city block.

In a vestibule between the outer and inner glass doors of the [12] school there is a sign with these words: "All children are capable of learning."

Beyond the inner doors a guard is seated. The lobby is long and nar- [13] row. The ceiling is low. There are no windows. All the teachers that I see at first are middle-aged white women. The principal, who is also a white woman, tells me that the school's "capacity" is 900 but that there are 1,300 children here. The size of classes for fifth and sixth grade children in New York, she says, is "capped" at 32, but she says that class size in the school goes "up to 34." (I later see classes, however, as large as 37.) Classes for younger children, she goes on, are "capped at 25," but a school can go above this limit if it puts an extra adult in the room. Lack

---

[1] Marketing term for the statistical characteristics—such as income and education—of particular population groups. [Eds.]

of space, she says, prevents the school from operating a pre-kindergarten program.

I ask the principal where her children go to school. They are en-   14
rolled in private school, she says.

"Lunchtime is a challenge for us," she explains. "Limited space   15
obliges us to do it in three shifts, 450 children at a time."

Textbooks are scarce and children have to share their social stud-   16
ies books. The principal says there is one full-time pupil counselor
and another who is here two days a week: a ratio of 930 children to
one counselor. The carpets are patched and sometimes taped together to conceal an open space. "I could use some new rugs," she
observes.

To make up for the building's lack of windows and the crowded   17
feeling that results, the staff puts plants and fish tanks in the corridors. Some of the plants are flourishing. Two boys, released from
class, are in a corridor beside a tank, their noses pressed against the
glass. A school of pinkish fish inside the tank are darting back and
forth. Farther down the corridor a small Hispanic girl is watering the
plants.

Two first grade classes share a single room without a window, di-   18
vided only by a blackboard. Four kindergartens and a sixth grade class
of Spanish-speaking children have been packed into a single room in
which, again, there is no window. A second grade bilingual class of 37
children has its own room but again there is no window.

By eleven o'clock, the lunchroom is already packed with appetite   19
and life. The kids line up to get their meals, then eat them in ten minutes.
After that, with no place they can go to play, they sit and wait until it's
time to line up and go back to class.

On the second floor I visit four classes taking place within another   20
undivided space. The room has a low ceiling. File cabinets and movable
blackboards give a small degree of isolation to each class. Again, there
are no windows.

The library is a tiny, windowless and claustrophobic room. I count   21
approximately 700 books. Seeing no reference books, I ask a teacher if
encyclopedias and other reference books are kept in classrooms.

"We don't have encyclopedias in classrooms," she replies. "That is   22
for the suburbs."

The school, I am told, has 26 computers for its 1,300 children. There   23
is one small gym and children get one period, and sometimes two, each
week. Recess, however, is not possible because there is no playground.
"Head Start,"[2] the principal says, "scarcely exists in District 10. We have
no space."

---

[2] Government program for disadvantaged preschoolers that has lost significant amounts of funding
in recent years. [Eds.]

The school, I am told, is 90 percent black and Hispanic; the other 10 [24] percent are Asian, white or Middle Eastern.

In a sixth grade social studies class the walls are bare of words or [25] decorations. There seems to be no ventilation system, or, if one exists, it isn't working.

The class discusses the Nile River and the Fertile Crescent. [26]

The teacher, in a droning voice: "How is it useful that these civi- [27] lizations developed close to rivers?"

A child, in a good loud voice: "What kind of question is that?" [28]

In my notes I find these words: "An uncomfortable feeling—being [29] in a building with no windows. There are metal ducts across the room. Do they give air? I feel asphyxiated. . . ."

On the top floor of the school, a sixth grade of 30 children shares a [30] room with 29 bilingual second graders. Because of the high class size there is an assistant with each teacher. This means that 59 children and four grown-ups—63 in all—must share a room that, in a suburban school, would hold no more than 20 children and one teacher. There are, at least, some outside windows in this room—it is the only room with windows in the school—and the room has a high ceiling. It is a relief to see some daylight.

I return to see the kindergarten classes on the ground floor and feel [31] stifled once again by lack of air and the low ceiling. Nearly 120 children and adults are doing what they can to make the best of things: 80 children in four kindergarten classes, 30 children in the sixth grade class, and about eight grown-ups who are aides and teachers. The kindergarten children sitting on the worn rug, which is patched with tape, look up at me and turn their heads to follow me as I walk past them.

As I leave the school, a sixth grade teacher stops to talk. I ask her, "Is [32] there air conditioning in warmer weather?"

Teachers, while inside the building, are reluctant to give answers to [33] this kind of question. Outside, on the sidewalk, she is less constrained: "I had an awful room last year. In the winter it was 56 degrees. In the summer it was up to 90. It was sweltering."

I ask her, "Do the children ever comment on the building?" [34]

"They don't say," she answers, "but they know." [35]

I ask her if they see it as a racial message. [36]

"All these children see TV," she says. "They know what suburban [37] schools are like. Then they look around them at their school. This was a roller-rink, you know. . . . They don't comment on it but you see it in their eyes. They understand."

On the following morning I visit P.S. 79, another elementary school [38] in the same district. "We work under difficult circumstances," says the principal, James Carter, who is black. "The school was built to hold one thousand students. We have 1,550. We are badly overcrowded. We need smaller classes but, to do this, we would need more space. I can't add five teachers. I would have no place to put them."

Some experts, I observe, believe that class size isn't a real issue. He [39] dismisses this abruptly. "It doesn't take a genius to discover that you learn more in a smaller class. I have to bus some 60 kindergarten children elsewhere, since I have no space for them. When they return next year, where do I put them?

"I can't set up a computer lab. I have no room. I had to put a class [40] into the library. I have no librarian. There are two gymnasiums upstairs but they cannot be used for sports. We hold more classes there. It's unfair to measure us against the suburbs. They have 17 to 20 children in a class. Average class size in this school is 30.

"The school is 29 percent black, 70 percent Hispanic. Few of these [41] kids get Head Start. There is no space in the district. Of 200 kindergarten children, 50 maybe get some kind of preschool."

I ask him how much difference preschool makes. [42]

"Those who get it do appreciably better. I can't overestimate its im- [43] pact but, as I have said, we have no space."

The school tracks children by ability, he says. "There are five to [44] seven levels in each grade. The highest level is equivalent to 'gifted' but it's not a full-scale gifted program. We don't have the funds. We have no science room. The science teachers carry their equipment with them."

We sit and talk within the nurse's room. The window is broken. [45] There are two holes in the ceiling. About a quarter of the ceiling has been patched and covered with a plastic garbage bag.

"Ideal class size for these kids would be 15 to 20. Will these children [46] ever get what white kids in the suburbs take for granted? I don't think so. If you ask me why, I'd have to speak of race and social class. I don't think the powers that be in New York City understand, or want to understand, that if they do not give these children a sufficient education to lead healthy and productive lives, we will be their victims later on. We'll pay the price someday—in violence, in economic costs. I despair of making this appeal in any terms but these. You cannot issue an appeal to conscience in New York today. The fair-play argument won't be accepted. So you speak of violence and hope that it will scare the city into action."

While we talk, three children who look six or seven years old come [47] to the door and ask to see the nurse, who isn't in the school today. One of the children, a Puerto Rican girl, looks haggard. "I have a pain in my tooth," she says. The principal says, "The nurse is out. Why don't you call your mother?" The child says, "My mother doesn't have a phone." The principal sighs. "Then go back to your class." When she leaves, the principal is angry. "It's amazing to me that these children ever make it with the obstacles they face. Many *do* care and they *do* try, but there's a feeling of despair. The parents of these children want the same things for their children that the parents in the suburbs want. Drugs are not the cause of this. They are the symptom. Nonetheless, they're used by people in the suburbs and rich people in Manhattan as another reason to keep children of poor people at a distance."

I ask him, "Will white children and black children ever go to school together in New York?" [48]

"I don't see it," he replies. "I just don't think it's going to happen. It's a dream. I simply do not see white folks in Riverdale agreeing to cross-bus with kids like these. A few, maybe. Very few. I don't think I'll live to see it happen." [49]

I ask him whether race is the decisive factor. Many experts, I observe, believe that wealth is more important in determining these inequalities. [50]

"This," he says—and sweeps his hand around him at the room, the garbage bag, the ceiling—"would not happen to white children." [51]

In a kindergarten class the children sit cross-legged on a carpet in a space between two walls of books. Their 26 faces are turned up to watch their teacher, an elderly black woman. A little boy who sits beside me is involved in trying to tie bows in his shoelaces. The children sing a song: "Lift Every Voice." On the wall are these handwritten words: "Beautiful, also, are the souls of my people." [52]

In a very small room on the fourth floor, 52 people in two classes do their best to teach and learn. Both are first grade classes. One, I am informed, is "low ability." The other is bilingual. [53]

"The room is barely large enough for one class," says the principal. [54]

The room is 25 by 50 feet. There are 26 first graders and two adults on the left, 22 others and two adults on the right. On the wall there is the picture of a small white child, circled by a Valentine, and a Gainsborough painting of a child in a formal dress. [55]

"We are handicapped by scarcity," one of the teachers says. "One fifth of these children may be at grade level by the year's end." [56]

A boy who may be seven years old climbs on my lap without an invitation and removes my glasses. He studies my face and runs his fingers through my hair. "You have nice hair," he says. I ask him where he lives and he replies, "Times Square Hotel," which is a homeless shelter in Manhattan. [57]

I ask him how he gets here. [58]

"With my father. On the train," he says. [59]

"How long does it take?" [60]

"It takes an hour and a half." [61]

I ask him when he leaves his home. [62]

"My mother wakes me up at five o'clock." [63]

"When do you leave?" [64]

"Six-thirty." [65]

I ask him how he gets back to Times Square. [66]

"My father comes to get me after school."   67

From my notes: "He rides the train three hours every day in order   68
to attend this segregated school. It would be a shorter ride to Riverdale.
There are rapid shuttle-vans that make that trip in only 20 minutes.
Why not let him go to school right in Manhattan, for that matter?"

At three o'clock the nurse arrives to do her recordkeeping. She tells   69
me she is here three days a week. "The public hospital we use for an
emergency is called North Central. It's not a hospital that I will use if I
am given any choice. Clinics in the private hospitals are far more likely
to be staffed by an experienced physician."

She hesitates a bit as I take out my pen, but then goes on: "I'll give   70
you an example. A little girl I saw last week in school was trembling and
shaking and could not control the motions of her arms. I was concerned
and called her home. Her mother came right up to school and took her
to North Central. The intern concluded that the child was upset by 'family matters'—nothing more—that there was nothing wrong with her.
The mother was offended by the diagnosis. She did not appreciate his
words or his assumptions. The truth is, there was nothing wrong at
home. She brought the child back to school. I thought that she was ill. I
told her mother, 'Go to Montefiore.' It's a private hospital, and well respected. She took my advice, thank God. It turned out that the child had
a neurological disorder. She is now in treatment.

"This is the kind of thing our children face. Am I saying that the city   71
underserves this population? You can draw your own conclusions."

Out on the street, it takes a full half hour to flag down a cab. Taxi dri-   72
vers in New York are sometimes disconcertingly direct in what they say.
When they are contemptuous of poor black people, their contempt is un-
adorned. When they're sympathetic and compassionate, their observations often go right to the heart of things. "Oh . . . they neglect these children," says the driver. "They leave them in the streets and slums to live
and die." We stop at a light. Outside the window of the taxi, aimless men
are standing in a semicircle while another man is working on his car.
Old four-story buildings with their windows boarded, cracked or missing are on every side.

I ask the driver where he's from. He says Afghanistan. Turning in   73
his seat, he gestures at the street and shrugs. "If you don't, as an American, begin to give these kids the kind of education that you give the kids
of Donald Trump, you're asking for disaster."

                                                                              74
Two months later, on a day in May, I visit an elementary school in
Riverdale. The dogwoods and magnolias on the lawn in front of P.S. 24
are in full blossom on the day I visit. There is a well-tended park across
the street, another larger park three blocks away. To the left of the
school is a playground for small children, with an innovative jungle
gym, a slide and several climbing toys. Behind the school there are two

playing fields for older kids. The grass around the school is neatly trimmed.

The neighborhood around the school, by no means the richest part [75] of Riverdale, is nonetheless expensive and quite beautiful. Residences in the area—some of which are large, free-standing houses, others condominiums in solid red-brick buildings—sell for prices in the region of $400,000; but some of the larger Tudor houses on the winding and tree-shaded streets close to the school can cost up to $1 million. The excellence of P.S. 24, according to the principal, adds to the value of these homes. Advertisements in the *New York Times* will frequently inform prospective buyers that a house is "in the neighborhood of P.S. 24."

The school serves 825 children in the kindergarten through sixth [76] grade. This is approximately half the student population crowded into P.S. 79, where 1,550 children fill a space intended for 1,000, and a great deal smaller than the 1,300 children packed into the former skating rink; but the principal of P.S. 24, a capable and energetic man named David Rothstein, still regards it as excessive for an elementary school.

The school is integrated in the strict sense that the middle- and [77] upper-middle-class white children here do occupy a building that contains some Asian and Hispanic and black children; but there is little integration in the classrooms since the vast majority of the Hispanic and black children are assigned to "special" classes on the basis of evaluations that have classified them "EMR"—"educable mentally retarded"— or else, in the worst of cases, "TMR"—"trainable mentally retarded."

I ask the principal if any of his students qualify for free-lunch pro- [78] grams. "About 130 do," he says. "Perhaps another 35 receive their lunches at reduced price. Most of these kids are in the special classes. They do not come from this neighborhood."

The very few nonwhite children that one sees in mainstream class- [79] es tend to be Japanese or else of other Asian origins. Riverdale, I learn, has been the residence of choice for many years to members of the diplomatic corps.

The school therefore contains effectively two separate schools: one [80] of about 130 children, most of whom are poor, Hispanic, black, assigned to one of the 12 special classes; the other of some 700 mainstream students, almost all of whom are white or Asian.

There is a third track also—this one for the students who are labeled [81] "talented" or "gifted." This is termed a "pull-out" program since the children who are so identified remain in mainstream classrooms but are taken out for certain periods each week to be provided with intensive and, in my opinion, excellent instruction in some areas of reasoning and logic often known as "higher-order skills" in the contemporary jargon of the public schools. Children identified as "gifted" are admitted to this program in first grade and, in most cases, will remain there for six years. Even here, however, there are two tracks of the gifted. The regular gifted classes are provided with only one semester of this specialized instruction yearly. Those very few children, on the other hand, who are identified as showing the most promise are assigned, beginning in the third grade, to a program that receives a full-year regimen.

In one such class, containing ten intensely verbal and impressive [82] fourth grade children, nine are white and one is Asian. The "special" class I enter first, by way of contrast, has twelve children of whom only one is white and none is Asian. These racial breakdowns prove to be predictive of the schoolwide pattern.

In a classroom for the gifted on the first floor of the school, I ask a [83] child what the class is doing. "Logic and syllogisms," she replies. The room is fitted with a planetarium. The principal says that all the elementary schools in District 10 were given the same planetariums ten years ago but that certain schools, because of overcrowding, have been forced to give them up. At P.S. 261, according to my notes, there was a domelike space that had been built to hold a planetarium, but the planetarium had been removed to free up space for the small library collection. P.S. 24, in contrast, has a spacious library that holds almost 8,000 books. The windows are decorated with attractive, brightly colored curtains and look out on flowering trees. The principal says that it's inadequate, but it appears spectacular to me after the cubicle that holds a meager 700 books within the former skating rink.

The district can't afford librarians, the principal says, but P.S. 24, un- [84] like the poorer schools of District 10, can draw on educated parent volunteers who staff the room in shifts three days a week. A parent organization also raises independent funds to buy materials, including books, and will soon be running a fund-raiser to enhance the library's collection.

In a large and sunny first grade classroom that I enter next, I see 23 [85] children, all of whom are white or Asian. In another first grade, there are 22 white children and two others who are Japanese. There is a computer in each class. Every classroom also has a modern fitted sink.

In a second grade class of 22 children, there are two black children [86] and three Asian children. Again, there is a sink and a computer. A sixth grade social studies class has only one black child. The children have an in-class research area that holds some up-to-date resources. A set of encyclopedias (World Book, 1985) is in a rack beside a window. The children are doing a Spanish language lesson when I enter. Foreign languages begin in sixth grade at the school, but Spanish is offered also to the kindergarten children. As in every room at P.S. 24, the window shades are clean and new, the floor is neatly tiled in gray and green, and there is not a single light bulb missing.

Walking next into a special class, I see twelve children. One is white. [87] Eleven are black. There are no Asian children. The room is half the size of mainstream classrooms. "Because of overcrowding," says the principal, "we have had to split these rooms in half." There is no computer and no sink.

I enter another special class. Of seven children, five are black, one is [88] Hispanic, one is white. A little black boy with a large head sits in the far corner and is gazing at the ceiling.

"Placement of these kids," the principal explains, "can usually be [89] traced to neurological damage."

In my notes: "How could so many of these children be brain-dam- [90] aged?"

Next door to the special class is a woodworking shop. "This shop is [91] only for the special classes," says the principal. The children learn to punch in time cards at the door, he says, in order to prepare them for employment.

The fourth grade gifted class, in which I spend the last part of the [92] day, is humming with excitement. "I start with these children in the first grade," says the teacher. "We pull them out of mainstream classes on the basis of their test results and other factors such as the opinion of their teachers. Out of this group, beginning in third grade, I pull out the ones who show the most potential, and they enter classes such as this one."

The curriculum they follow, she explains, "emphasizes critical [93] thinking, reasoning and logic." The planetarium, for instance, is employed not simply for the study of the universe as it exists. "Children also are designing their own galaxies," the teacher says.

A little girl sitting around a table with her classmates speaks with [94] perfect poise: "My name is Susan. We are in the fourth grade gifted program."

I ask them what they're doing and a child says, "My name is Lau- [95] rie and we're doing problem-solving."

A rather tall, good-natured boy who is half-standing at the table tells [96] me that his name is David. "One thing that we do," he says, "is logical thinking. Some problems, we find, have more than one good answer. We need to learn not simply to be logical in our own thinking but to show respect for someone else's logic even when an answer may be technically incorrect."

When I ask him to explain this, he goes on, "A person who gives an [97] answer that is not 'correct' may nonetheless have done some interesting thinking that we should examine. 'Wrong' answers may be more useful to examine than correct ones."

I ask the children if reasoning and logic are innate or if they're things [98] that you can learn.

"You know some things to start with when you enter school," Susan [99] says. "But we also learn some things that other children don't."

I ask her to explain this.   [100]

"We know certain things that other kids don't know because we're [101] *taught* them."

She has braces on her teeth. Her long brown hair falls almost to her [102] waist. Her loose white T-shirt has the word TRI-LOGIC on the front. She tells me that Tri-Logic is her father's firm.

Laurie elaborates on the same point: "Some things you know. Some [103] kinds of logic are inside of you to start with. There are other things that someone needs to teach you."

David expands on what the other two have said: "Everyone can [104] think and speak in logical ways unless they have a mental problem. What this program does is bring us to a higher form of logic."

The class is writing a new "Bill of Rights." The children already [105] know the U.S. Bill of Rights and they explain its first four items to me with precision. What they are examining today, they tell me, is the very *concept* of a "right." Then they will create their own compendium of rights according to their own analysis and definition. Along one wall of the classroom, opposite the planetarium, are seven Apple II computers on which children have developed rather subtle color animations that express the themes—of greed and domination, for example—that they also have described in writing.

"This is an upwardly mobile group," the teacher later says. "They [106] have exposure to whatever New York City has available. Their parents may take them to the theater, to museums. . . ."

In my notes: "Six girls, four boys. Nine white, one Chinese. I am [107] glad they have this class. But what about the others? Aren't there ten black children in the school who could enjoy this also?"

The teacher gives me a newspaper written, edited and computer- [108] printed by her sixth grade gifted class. The children, she tells me, are provided with a link to kids in Europe for transmission of news stories.

A science story by one student asks if scientists have ever falsified [109] their research. "Gergor Mendel," the sixth grader writes, "the Austrian monk who founded the science of genetics, published papers on his work with peas that some experts say were statistically too good to be true. Isaac Newton, who formulated the law of gravitation, relied on un-seemly mathematical sleight of hand in his calculations. . . . Galileo Galilei, founder of modern scientific method, wrote about experiments that were so difficult to duplicate that colleagues doubted he had done them."

Another item in the paper, also by a sixth grade student, is less es- [110] oteric: "The Don Cossacks dance company, from Russia, is visiting the United States. The last time it toured America was 1976. . . . The Don Cossacks will be in New York City for two weeks at the Neil Simon The-ater. Don't miss it!"

The tone is breezy—and so confident! That phrase—"Don't miss [111] it!"—speaks a volume about life in Riverdale.

"What makes a good school?" asks the principal when we are talk- [112] ing later on. "The building and teachers are part of it, of course. But it isn't just the building and the teacher. Our kids come from good families and the neighborhood is good. In a three-block area we have a public library, a park, a junior high. . . . Our typical sixth grader reads at eighth-grade level." In a quieter voice he says, "I see how hard my colleagues work in schools like P.S. 79. You have children in those neighborhoods who live in virtual hell. They enter school five years behind. What do they get?" Then, as he spreads his hands out on his desk, he says: "I have to ask myself why there should be an elementary school in District 10 with fifteen hundred children. Why should there be an elementary school within a skating rink? Why should the Board of Ed allow this? This is not the way that things should be."

Responding to Reading

1. Do you agree that today's educational system denies children "the means of competition" (2)? Do you think your education has given you the ability to compete?
2. Kozol's essay focuses on the schools in New York. Do you think the inequalities he describes also exist in the schools in your community?
3. At the end of his essay Kozol describes a program for "talented" or "gifted" children. What are the advantages and disadvantages of such programs? Do you think children should be grouped according to their ability?

COLLEGE PRESSURES

William Zinsser

William Zinsser (1922–) is a critic, writer, editor, and teacher who advocates clear and simple prose. He was a columnist for *Look, Life,* and the *New York Times;* he taught at Yale University from 1970 to 1979; and he served as general editor of the Book-of-the-Month Club. His current work includes articles on travel and the environment in the United States. Zinsser has written nine books, including *Pop Goes America* (1963), *The Lunacy Boom* (1970), and *Writing with a Word Processor* (1983). One of his most popular books, which explains good writing to beginners, is *On Writing Well* (4th edition, 1994). Zinsser first published the following article in *Blair and Ketchum's Country Journal* (1979). In it, he defines four kinds of pressure that college students face and argues that most college students are rigidly goal-oriented young people too fearful "to imagine allowing the hand of God or chance to nudge them down some unforeseen trail."

Dear Carlos: I desperately need a dean's excuse for my chem midterm which will begin in about 1 hour. All I can say is that I totally blew it this week. I've fallen incredibly, inconceivably behind.

Carlos: Help! I'm anxious to hear from you. I'll be in my room and won't leave it until I hear from you. Tomorrow is the last day for . . .

Carlos: I left town because I started bugging out again. I stayed up all night to finish a take-home make-up exam & am typing it to hand in on the 10th. It was due on the 5th. P.S. I'm going to the dentist. Pain is pretty bad.

Carlos: Probably by Friday I'll be able to get back to my studies. Right now I'm going to take a long walk. This whole thing has taken a lot out of me.

Carlos: I'm really up the proverbial creek. The problem is I really *bombed* the history final. Since I need that course for my major I . . .

Carlos: Here follows a tale of woe. I went home this weekend, had to help my Mom, & caught a fever so didn't have much time to study. My professor . . .

Carlos: Aargh! Trouble. Nothing original but everything's piling up at once. To be brief, my job interview . . .

Hey Carlos, good news! I've got mononucleosis.

Who are these wretched supplicants, scribbling notes so laden with [1] anxiety, seeking such miracles of postponement and balm? They are men and women who belong to Branford College, one of the twelve residential colleges at Yale University, and the messages are just a few of the hundreds that they left for their dean, Carlos Hortas—often slipped under his door at 4 A.M.—last year.

But students like the ones who wrote those notes can also be found [2] on campuses from coast to coast—especially in New England and at many other private colleges across the country that have high academic standards and highly motivated students. Nobody could doubt that the notes are real. In their urgency and their gallows humor they are authentic voices of a generation that is panicky to succeed.

My own connection with the message writers is that I am master of [3] Branford College. I live in its Gothic quadrangle and know the students well. (We have 485 of them.) I am privy to their hopes and fears—and also to their stereo music and their piercing cries in the dead of night ("Does anybody *ca-a-are?*"). If they went to Carlos to ask how to get through tomorrow, they come to me to ask how to get through the rest of their lives.

Mainly I try to remind them that the road ahead is a long one and ⁴
that it will have more unexpected turns than they think. There will be
plenty of time to change jobs, change careers, change whole attitudes
and approaches. They don't want to hear such liberating news. They
want a map—right now—that they can follow unswervingly to career
security, financial security, Social Security and, presumably, a prepaid
grave.

What I wish for all students is some release from the clammy grip ⁵
of the future. I wish them a chance to savor each segment of their education as an experience in itself and not as a grim preparation for the
next step. I wish them the right to experiment, to trip and fall, to learn
that defeat is as instructive as victory and is not the end of the world.

My wish, of course, is naïve. One of the few rights that America does ⁶
not proclaim is the right to fail. Achievement is the national god, venerated in our media—the million-dollar athlete, the wealthy executive—
and glorified in our praise of possessions. In the presence of such a potent state religion, the young are growing up old.

I see four kinds of pressure working on college students today: eco- ⁷
nomic pressure, parental pressure, peer pressure, and self-induced pressure. It is easy to look around for villains—to blame the colleges for
charging too much money, the professors for assigning too much work,
the parents for pushing their children too far, the students for driving
themselves too hard. But there are no villains; only victims.

"In the late 1960s," one dean told me, "the typical question that I got ⁸
from students was 'Why is there so much suffering in the world?' or
'How can I make a contribution?' Today it's 'Do you think it would look
better for getting into law school if I did a double major in history and
political science, or just majored in one of them?'" Many other deans
confirmed this pattern. One said: "They're trying to find an edge—the
intangible something that will look better on paper if two students are
about equal."

Note the emphasis on looking better. The transcript has become a ⁹
sacred document, the passport to security. How one appears on paper
is more important than how one appears in person. *A* is for Admirable
and *B* is for Borderline, even though, in Yale's official system of grading,
A means "excellent" and *B* means "very good." Today, looking very
good is no longer good enough, especially for students who hope to go
on to law school or medical school. They know that entrance into the
better schools will be an entrance into the better law firms and better
medical practices where they will make a lot of money. They also know
that the odds are harsh. Yale Law School, for instance, matriculates 170
students from an applicant pool of 3,700; Harvard enrolls 550 from a
pool of 7,000.

It's all very well for those of us who write letters of recommendation ¹⁰
for our students to stress the qualities of humanity that will make them

good lawyers or doctors. And it's nice to think that admission officers are really reading our letters and looking for the extra dimension of commitment or concern. Still, it would be hard for a student not to visualize these officers shuffling so many transcripts studded with As that they regard a B as positively shameful.

The pressure is almost as heavy on students who just want to grad- [11] uate and get a job. Long gone are the days of the "gentleman's C," when students journeyed through college with a certain relaxation, sampling a wide variety of courses—music, art, philosophy, classics, anthropology, poetry, religion—that would send them out as liberally educated men and women. If I were an employer I would rather employ graduates who have this range and curiosity than those who narrowly pursued safe subjects and high grades. I know countless students whose inquiring minds exhilarate me. I like to hear the play of their ideas. I don't know if they are getting As or Cs, and I don't care. I also like them as people. The country needs them, and they will find satisfying jobs. I tell them to relax. They can't.

Nor can I blame them. They live in a brutal economy. Tuition, room, [12] and board at most private colleges now comes to at least $7,000, not counting books and fees. This might seem to suggest that the colleges are getting rich. But they are equally battered by inflation. Tuition covers only 60 percent of what it costs to educate a student, and ordinarily the remainder comes from what colleges receive in endowments, grants, and gifts. Now the remainder keeps being swallowed by the cruel costs—higher every year—of just opening the doors. Heating oil is up. Insurance is up. Postage is up. Health-premium costs are up. Everything is up. Deficits are up. We are witnessing in America the creation of a brotherhood of paupers—colleges, parents, and students, joined by the common bond of debt.

Today it is not unusual for a student, even if he works part time at [13] college and full time during the summer, to accrue $5,000 in loans after four years—loans that he must start to repay within one year after graduation. Exhorted at commencement to go forth into the world, he is already behind as he goes forth. How could he not feel under pressure throughout college to prepare for this day of reckoning? I have used "he," incidentally, only for brevity. Women at Yale are under no less pressure to justify their expensive education to themselves, their parents, and society. In fact, they are probably under more pressure. For although they leave college superbly equipped to bring fresh leadership to traditionally male jobs, society hasn't yet caught up with this fact.

Along with economic pressure goes parental pressure. Inevitably, [14] the two are deeply intertwined.

I see many students taking pre-medical courses with joyless tenaci- [15] ty. They go off to their labs as if they were going to the dentist. It saddens me because I know them in other corners of their life as cheerful people.

"Do you want to go to medical school?" I ask them.   16

"I guess so," they say, without conviction, or "Not really."   17

"Then why are you going?"   18

"Well, my parents want me to be a doctor. They're paying all this   19
money and . . ."

Poor students, poor parents. They are caught in one of the oldest   20
webs of love and duty and guilt. The parents mean well; they are trying
to steer their sons and daughters toward a secure future. But the sons
and daughters want to major in history or classics or philosophy—subjects with no "practical" value. Where's the payoff on the humanities?
It's not easy to persuade such loving parents that the humanities do indeed pay off. The intellectual faculties developed by studying subjects
like history and classics—an ability to synthesize and relate, to weigh
cause and effect, to see events in perspective—are just the faculties that
make creative leaders in business or almost any general field. Still, many
fathers would rather put their money on courses that point toward a
specific profession—courses that are pre-law, pre-medical, pre-business,
or, as I sometimes heard it put, "pre-rich."

But the pressure on students is severe. They are truly torn. One part   21
of them feels obligated to fulfill their parents' expectations; after all, their
parents are older and presumably wiser. Another part tells them that the
expectations that are right for their parents are not right for them.

I know a student who wants to be an artist. She is very obviously an   22
artist and will be a good one—she has already had several modest local
exhibits. Meanwhile she is growing as a well-rounded person and taking humanistic subjects that will enrich the inner resources out of which
her art will grow. But her father is strongly opposed. He thinks that an
artist is a "dumb" thing to be. The student vacillates and tries to please
everybody. She keeps up with her art somewhat furtively and takes
some of the "dumb" courses her father wants her to take—at least they
are dumb courses for her. She is a free spirit on a campus of tense students—no small achievement in itself—and she deserves to follow her
muse.

Peer pressure and self-induced pressure are also intertwined, and   23
they begin almost at the beginning of freshman year.

"I had a freshman student I'll call Linda," one dean told me, "who   24
came in and said she was under terrible pressure because her roommate,
Barbara, was much brighter and studied all the time. I couldn't tell her
that Barbara had come in two hours earlier to say the same thing about
Linda."

The story is almost funny—except that it's not. It's symptomatic of   25
all the pressures put together. When every student thinks every other
student is working harder and doing better, the only solution is to study
harder still. I see students going off to the library every night after dinner and coming back when it closes at midnight. I wish they would

sometimes forget about their peers and go to a movie. I hear the clacking of typewriters in the hours before dawn. I see the tension in their eyes when exams are approaching and papers are due: *"Will I get everything done?"*

Probably they won't. They will get sick. They will get "blocked." 26 They will sleep. They will oversleep. They will bug out. *Hey Carlos, help!*

Part of the problem is that they do more than they are expected to 27 do. A professor will assign five-page papers. Several students will start writing ten-page papers to impress him. Then more students will write ten-page papers, and a few will raise the ante to fifteen. Pity the poor student who is still just doing the assignment.

Once you have 20 or 30 percent of the student population deliber- 28 ately overexerting," one dean points out, "it's bad for everybody. When a teacher gets more and more effort from his class, the student who is doing normal work can be perceived as not doing well. The tactic works, psychologically."

Why can't the professor just cut back and not accept longer pa- 29 pers? He can, and he probably will. But by then the term will be half over and the damage done. Grade fever is highly contagious and not easily reversed. Besides, the professor's main concern is with his course. He knows his students only in relation to the course and doesn't know that they are also overexerting in their other courses. Nor is it really his business. He didn't sign up for dealing with the student as a whole person and with all the emotional baggage the student brought along from home. That's what deans, masters, chaplains, and psychiatrists are for.

To some extent this is nothing new: a certain number of professors 30 have always been self-contained islands of scholarship and shyness, more comfortable with books than with people. But the new pauperism has widened the gap still further, for professors who actually like to spend time with students don't have as much time to spend. They also are overexerting. If they are young, they are busy trying to publish in order not to perish, hanging by their finger nails onto a shrinking profession. If they are old and tenured, they are buried under the duties of administering departments—as departmental chairmen or members of committees—that have been thinned out by the budgetary axe.

Ultimately it will be the students' own business to break the circles 31 in which they are trapped. They are too young to be prisoners of their parents' dreams and their classmates' fears. They must be jolted into believing in themselves as unique men and women who have the power to shape their own future.

"Violence is being done to the undergraduate experience," says Car- 32 los Hortas. "College should be open-ended: at the end it should open many, many roads. Instead, students are choosing their goal in advance, and their choices narrow as they go along. It's almost as if they think that the country has been codified in the type of jobs that exist—that they've got to fit into certain slots. Therefore, fit into the best-paying slot.

"They ought to take chances. Not taking chances will lead to a life 33 of colorless mediocrity. They'll be comfortable. But something in the spirit will be missing."

I have painted too drab a portrait of today's students, making them 34 seem a solemn lot. That is only half of their story; if they were so dreary I wouldn't so thoroughly enjoy their company. The other half is that they are easy to like. They are quick to laugh and to offer friendship. They are not introverts. They are unusually kind and are more considerate of one another than any student generation I have known.

Nor are they so obsessed with their studies that they avoid sports 35 and extracurricular activities. On the contrary, they juggle their crowded hours to play on a variety of teams, perform with musical and dramatic groups, and write for campus publications. But this in turn is one more cause of anxiety. There are too many choices. Academically, they have 1,300 courses to select from; outside class they have to decide how much spare time they can spare and how to spend it.

This means that they engage in fewer extracurricular pursuits than 36 their predecessors did. If they want to row on the crew and play in the symphony they will eliminate one; in the '60s they would have done both. They also tend to choose activities that are self-limiting. Drama, for instance, is flourishing in all twelve of Yale's residential colleges as it never has before. Students hurl themselves into these productions—as actors, directors, carpenters, and technicians—with a dedication to create the best possible play, knowing that the day will come when the run will end and they can get back to their studies.

They also can't afford to be the willing slave of organizations like the 37 *Yale Daily News.* Last spring at the one-hundredth anniversary banquet of that paper—whose past chairmen include such once and future kings as Potter Stewart,[1] Kingman Brewster,[2] and William F. Buckley, Jr.[3]— much was made of the fact that the editorial staff used to be small and totally committed and that "Newsies" routinely worked fifty hours a week. In effect they belonged to a club; Newsies is how they defined themselves at Yale. Today's student will write one or two articles a week, when he can, and he defines himself as a student. I've never heard the word Newsie except at the banquet.

If I have described the modern undergraduate primarily as a driven 38 creature who is largely ignoring the blithe spirit inside who keeps trying to come out and play, it's because that's where the crunch is, not only at Yale but throughout American education. It's why I think we

---

[1] Potter Stewart is an Associate Justice of the United States Supreme Court. [Eds.]

[2] Kingman Brewster is a former president of Yale. [Eds.]

[3] William F. Buckley, Jr., is a columnist and founder of the conservative journal *The National Review.* [Eds.]

should all be worried about the values that are nurturing a generation so fearful of risk and so goal-obsessed at such an early age.

I tell students that there is no one "right" way to get ahead—that [39] each of them is a different person, starting from a different point and bound for a different destination. I tell them that change is a tonic and that all the slots are not codified nor the frontiers closed. One of my ways of telling them is to invite men and women who have achieved success outside the academic world to come and talk informally with my students during the year. They are heads of companies or ad agencies, editors of magazines, politicians, public officials, television magnates, labor leaders, business executives, Broadway producers, artists, writers, economists, photographers, scientists, historians—a mixed bag of achievers.

I ask them to say a few words about how they got started. The stu- [40] dents assume that they started in their present profession and knew all along that it was what they wanted to do. Luckily for me, most of them got into their field by a circuitous route, to their surprise, after many detours. The students are startled. They can hardly conceive of a career that was not pre-planned. They can hardly imagine allowing the hand of God or chance to nudge them down some unforeseen trail.

Responding to Reading

1. Zinsser wrote this essay in 1979. Do you think it accurately portrays today's college students? Do you feel the same pressures Zinsser describes?
2. Zinsser uses students who attend Yale University as his examples. How representative are these examples? Do you think students from other types of colleges face the same pressures? What pressures, for example, might a student in a community college or a large urban university face that the students in Zinsser's sample might not encounter?
3. What purpose does Zinsser think college should serve? What purpose do *you* think college should serve?

IN DEFENSE OF ELITISM

William A. Henry III

William A. Henry III (1950–1994), a reporter and critic who served for many years as the culture and theater critic for *Time* magazine, also wrote stories for *Time* about American society. He was the recipient of two Pulitzer Prizes in journalism, one in 1980 for criticism and a shared prize in 1975 for reporting on desegregation in the Boston public schools. Author of *The Great One: The Life and Legend of Jackie Gleason* (1992), he also produced a PBS documentary, "Bob Fosse: Steam Heat," which received an Emmy in 1990. In his posthumously published *In Defense of Elitism* (1994), Henry argues that the United States is in decline at least in part because of Americans' increasing lack of respect for true intellectual and cultural accomplishment and, more important, because of a growing unwillingness "to assert unyieldingly that one idea, contribution, or attainment is better than another." In the following chapter from that book, Henry focuses specifically on higher education, arguing that the egalitarian attempt to make a college education available to large numbers of Americans is a costly mistake and has resulted in a serious decline in overall educational standards.

While all the major social changes in post-war America reflect egalitarianism of some sort, no social evolution has been more willfully egalitarian than opening the academy. Half a century ago, a high school diploma was a significant credential, and college was a privilege for the few. Now high school graduation is virtually automatic for adolescents outside the ghettos and barrios, and college has become a normal way station in the average person's growing up. No longer a mark of distinction or proof of achievement, a college education is these days a mere rite of passage, a capstone to adolescent party time.   1

Some 63% of all American high school graduates now go on to some form of further education, according to the Department of Commerce's *Statistical Abstract of the United States,* and the bulk of those continuing students attain at least an associate's degree. Nearly 30% of high school graduates ultimately receive a four-year baccalaureate degree. A quarter or so of the population may seem, to egalitarian eyes, a small and hence elitist slice. But by world standards this is inclusiveness at its most extreme—and its most peculiarly American.   2

For all the socialism of British or French public policy and for all the paternalism of the Japanese, those nations restrict university training to a much smaller percentage of their young, typically 10% to 15%. Moreover, they and other First World nations tend to carry the elitism over into judgments about precisely which institution one attends. They rank their universities, colleges and technical schools along a prestige hierarchy much more rigidly gradated—and judged by standards much more widely accepted—than we Americans ever impose on our jumble of public and private institutions.   3

In the sharpest divergence from American values, these other countries tend to separate the college-bound from the quotidian masses[1] in early adolescence, with scant hope for a second chance. For them, higher education is logically confined to those who displayed the most aptitude for lower education.   4

---

[1] "Ordinary people." [Eds.]

The opening of the academy's doors has imposed great economic ⁵
costs on the American people while delivering dubious benefits to many
of the individuals supposedly being helped. The total bill for higher education is about $150 billion per year, with almost two-thirds of that
spent by public institutions run with taxpayer funds. Private colleges and
universities also spend the public's money. They get grants for research
and the like, and they serve as a conduit for subsidized student loans—
many of which are never fully repaid. President Clinton refers to this sort
of spending as an investment in human capital. If that is so, it seems reasonable to ask whether the investment pays a worthwhile rate of return.
At its present size, the American style of mass higher education probably ought to be judged a mistake—and one based on a giant lie.

Why do people go to college? Mostly to make money. This reality is ⁶
acknowledged in the mass media, which are forever running stories and
charts showing how much a college degree contributes to lifetime income (with the more sophisticated publications very occasionally noting
the counterweight costs of tuition paid and income forgone during the
years of full-time study.)

But the equation between college and wealth is not so simple. Col- ⁷
lege graduates unquestionably do better on average economically than
those who don't go at all. At the extremes, those with five or more years
of college earn about triple the income of those with eight or fewer years
of total schooling. Taking more typical examples, one finds that those
who stop their educations after earning a four-year degree earn about 1
1/2 times as much as those who stop at the end of high school. These
outcomes, however, reflect other things besides the impact of the degree
itself. College graduates are winners in part because colleges attract people who are already winners—people with enough brains and drive that
they would do well in almost any generation and under almost any circumstances, with or without formal credentialing.

The harder and more meaningful question is whether the medioc- ⁸
rities who have also flooded into colleges in the past couple of generations do better than they otherwise would have. And if they do, is it because college actually made them better employees or because it simply
gave them the requisite credential to get interviewed and hired? The
U.S. Labor Department's Bureau of Labor Statistics reports that about
20% of all college graduates toil in fields not requiring a degree, and this
total is projected to exceed 30% by the year 2005. For the individual, college may well be a credential without being a qualification, required
without being requisite.

For American society, the big lie underlying higher education is ⁹
akin to Garrison Keillor's description of the children in Lake Wobegon:²

---

² Fictional community that is the setting of Keillor's popular public radio program. [Eds.]

they are all above average. In the unexamined American Dream rhetoric promoting mass higher education in the nation of my youth, the implicit vision was that one day everyone, or at least practically everyone, would be a manager or a professional. We would use the most élitist of all means, scholarship, toward the most egalitarian of ends. We would all become chiefs; hardly anyone would be left a mere Indian. On the surface, this New Jerusalem appears to have arrived. Where half a century ago the bulk of jobs were blue collar, now a majority are white or pink collar. They are performed in an office instead of on a factory floor. If they still tend to involve repetition and drudgery, at least they do not require heavy lifting.

But the wages for them are going down virtually as often as up. And 10 as a great many disappointed office workers have discovered, being better educated and better dressed at the workplace does not transform one's place in the pecking order. There are still plenty more Indians than chiefs. Lately, indeed, the chiefs are becoming even fewer. The major focus of the "downsizing" of recent years has been eliminating layers of middle management—much of it drawn from the ranks of those lured to college a generation or two ago by the idea that a degree would transform them from the mediocre to magisterial.

Yet our colleges blithely go on "educating" many more prospective 11 managers and professionals than we are likely to need. In my own field, there are typically more students majoring in journalism at any given moment than there are journalists employed at all the daily newspapers in the U.S. A few years ago, there were more students enrolled in law school than there were partners in all law firms. As trends shift, there have been periodic oversupplies of M.B.A.-wielding financial analysts, of grade school and high school teachers, of computer programmers, even of engineers. Inevitably many students of limited talent spend huge amounts of time and money pursuing some brass-ring occupation, only to see their dreams denied. As a society we consider it cruel not to give them every chance at success. It may be more cruel to let them go on fooling themselves.

Just when it should be clear that we are already probably doing too 12 much to entice people into college, Bill Clinton is suggesting we do even more. In February 1994, for example, the President asserted that America needs a greater fusion between academic and vocational training in high school—not because too many mediocre people misplaced on the college track are failing to acquire marketable vocational skills, but because too many people on the vocational track are being denied courses that will secure them admission to college. Surely what Americans need is not a fusion of the two tracks but a sharper division between them, coupled with a forceful program for diverting intellectual also-rans out of the academic track and into the vocational one. That is where most of them are heading in life anyway. Why should they wait until they are older and must enroll in high-priced proprietary vocational programs of often dubious efficacy—frequently throwing away not only their own funds but federal loans in the process—because they emerged from high school heading nowhere and knowing nothing that is useful in the marketplace?

If the massive numbers of college students reflected a national boom [13] in love of learning and a prevalent yen for self-improvement, America's investment in the classroom might make sense. There are introspective qualities that can enrich any society in ways beyond the material. But one need look no further than the curricular wars to understand that most students are not looking to broaden their spiritual or intellectual horizons. Consider three basic trends, all of them implicit rejections of intellectual adventure. First, students are demanding courses that reflect and affirm their own identities in the most literal way. Rather than read a Greek dramatist of 2,000 years ago and thrill to the discovery that some ideas and emotions are universal, many insist on reading writers of their own gender or ethnicity or sexual preference, ideally writers of the present or the recent past.

The second trend, implicit in the first, is that the curriculum has [14] shifted from being what professors desire to teach to being what students desire to learn. Nowadays colleges have to hustle for students by truckling trendily. If the students want media-studies programs so they can all fantasize about becoming TV news anchors, then media studies will abound. There are in any given year some 300,000 students enrolled in undergraduate communications courses.

Of even greater significance than the solipsism of students and the [15] pusillanimity of teachers is the third trend, the sheer decline in the amount and quality of work expected in class. In an egalitarian environment the influx of mediocrities relentlessly lowers the general standards at colleges to levels the weak ones can meet. When my mother went to Trinity College in Washington in the early 1940s, at a time when it was regarded more as a finishing school for nice Catholic girls than a temple of discipline, an English major there was expected to be versed in Latin, Anglo-Saxon and medieval French. A course in Shakespeare meant reading the plays, all 37 of them. In today's indulgent climate, a professor friend at a fancy college told me as I was writing this chapter, taking a half semester of Shakespeare compels students to read exactly four plays. "Anything more than one a week," he explained, "is considered too heavy a load."

This probably should not be thought surprising in an era when most [16] colleges, even prestigious ones, run some sort of remedial program for freshmen to learn the reading and writing skills they ought to have developed in junior high school—not to mention an era when many students vociferously object to being marked down for spelling or grammar. Indeed, all the media attention paid to curriculum battles at Stanford, Dartmouth and the like[3] obscures the even bleaker reality of American higher education. As Russell Jacoby points out in his book *Dogmatic Wisdom*, most students are enrolled at vastly less demanding institutions, where any substantial reading list would be an improvement.

My modest proposal is this: Let us reduce, over perhaps a five-year   17
span, the number of high school graduates who go on to college from nearly 60% to a still generous 33%. This will mean closing a lot of institutions. Most of them, in my view, should be community colleges, current or former state teachers' colleges and the like. These schools serve the academically marginal and would be better replaced by vocational training in high school and on-the-job training at work. Two standards should apply in judging which schools to shut down. First, what is the general academic level attained by the student body? That might be assessed in a rough-and-ready way by requiring any institution wishing to survive to give a standardized test—say, the Graduate Record Examination—to all its seniors. Those schools whose students perform below the state norm would face cutbacks or closing. Second, what community is being served? A school that serves a high percentage of disadvantaged students (this ought to be measured by family finances rather than just race or ethnicity) can make a better case for receiving tax dollars than one that subsidizes the children of the prosperous, who have private alternatives. Even ardent egalitarians should recognize the injustice of taxing people who wash dishes or mop floors for a living to pay for the below-cost public higher education of the children of lawyers so that they can go on to become lawyers too.

Some readers may find it paradoxical that a book arguing for greater   18
literacy and intellectual discipline should lead to a call for less rather than more education. Even if college students do not learn all they should, the readers' counterargument would go, surely they learn something, and that is better than learning nothing. Maybe it is. But at what price? One hundred fifty billion dollars is awfully high for deferring the day when the idle or ungifted take individual responsibility and face up to their fate. Ultimately it is the yearning to believe that anyone can be brought up to college level that has brought colleges down to everyone's level.

Responding to Reading

1. What does Henry mean by the term *elitism?* Do you think his use of this term suggests his snobbery or his insight?
2. Do you agree with Henry when he says, "the curriculum has shifted from

---

[3] Universities that sparked "political correctness" controversies by proposing greater cultural diversity in course reading lists. See the essays by Dinesh D'Souza (p.136) and Huntly Collins (p. 308) [Eds.].

being what professors desire to teach to being what students desire to learn" (14)? Do any of the courses at your school reflect the trend Henry describes?

3. A review of Henry's book in the *New York Times* states that his main point is that in the United States equality of opportunity has come to mean equality of outcome. What do you think this statement means? Do you agree?

RACIAL PREFERENCES?
~ SO WHAT?

Stephen L. Carter

Yale law professor Stephen L. Carter (1954–) attended Stanford University and the Yale Law School. One of the growing number of black commentators labeled politically conservative, Carter is the author of *The Culture of Disbelief: How American Law and Politics Trivialize Religious Devotion* (1993) and *The Confirmation Mess: Cleaning Up the Federal Appointments Process* (1994). He has said that he and other blacks today should "commit ourselves to battle for excellence, to show ourselves able to meet any standard, . . . to form ourselves into a vanguard of black professionals who are simply too good to ignore." In the following opening chapter from his provocative critique of affirmative action, *Reflections of an Affirmative Action Baby* (1991), Carter argues that proponents of affirmative action err when they try to pretend affirmative action policies do not benefit minority students at the expense of white students whose credentials are better.

I got into law school because I am black. As many black professionals think they must, I have long suppressed this truth, insisting instead that I got where I am the same way everybody else did. Today I am a professor at the Yale Law School. I like to think that I am a good one, but I am hardly the most objective judge. What I am fairly sure of, and can now say without trepidation, is that were my skin not the color that it is, I would not have had the chance to try.

For many, perhaps most, black professionals of my generation, the matter of who got where and how is left in a studied and, I think, purposeful ambiguity. Some of us, as they say, would have made it into an elite college or professional school anyway. (But, in my generation, many fewer than we like to pretend, even though one might question the much-publicized claim by Derek Bok, the president of Harvard University, that in the absence of preferences, only 1 percent of Harvard's entering class would be black.) Most of us, perhaps nearly all of us, have learned to bury the matter far back in our minds. We are who we are and where we are, we have records of accomplishment or failure, and there is no rational reason that anybody—employer, client, whoever—should care any longer whether racial preference played any role in our admission to a top professional school.

When people in positions to help or hurt our careers *do* seem to care, [3] we tend to react with fury. Those of us who have graduated professional school over the past fifteen to twenty years, and are not white, travel career paths that are frequently bumpy with suspicions that we did not earn the right to be where we are. We bristle when others raise what might be called the qualification question—"Did you get into school or get hired because of a special program?"—and that prickly sensitivity is the best evidence, if any is needed, of one of the principal costs of racial preferences. Scratch a black professional with the qualification question, and you're likely to get a caustic response, such as this one from a senior executive at a major airline: "Some whites think I've made it because I'm black. Some blacks think I've made it only because I'm an Uncle Tom. The fact is, I've made it because I'm good."

Given the way that so many Americans seem to treat receipt of the [4] benefits of affirmative action as a badge of shame, answers of this sort are both predictable and sensible. In the professional world, moreover, they are very often true: relatively few corporations are in a position to hand out charity. The peculiar aspect of the routine denial, however, is that so many of those who will bristle at the suggestion that they themselves have gained from racial preferences will try simultaneously to insist that racial preferences be preserved and to force the world to pretend that no one benefits from them. That awkward balancing of fact and fiction explains the frequent but generally groundless cry that it is racist to suggest that some individual's professional accomplishments would be fewer but for affirmative action; and therein hangs a tale.

For students at the leading law schools, autumn brings the recruit- [5] ing season, the idyllic weeks when law firms from around the country compete to lavish upon them lunches and dinners and other attentions, all with the professed goal of obtaining the students' services—perhaps for the summer, perhaps for a longer term. The autumn of 1989 was different, however, because the nation's largest firm, Baker & McKenzie, was banned from interviewing students at the University of Chicago Law School, and on probation—that is, enjoined to be on its best behavior—at some others.

The immediate source of Baker & McKenzie's problems was a [6] racially charged interview that a partner in the firm had conducted the previous fall with a black third-year student at the school. The interviewer evidently suggested that other lawyers might call her "nigger" or "black bitch" and wanted to know how she felt about that. Perhaps out of surprise that she played golf, he observed that "there aren't too many golf courses in the ghetto." He also suggested that the school was admitting "foreigners" and excluding "qualified" Americans.

The law school reacted swiftly, and the firm was banned from in- [7] terviewing on campus. Other schools contemplated taking action against the firm, and some of them did. Because I am black myself, and teach in a law school, I suppose the easiest thing for me to have done would have been to clamor in solidarity for punishment. Yet I found myself strangely reluctant to applaud the school's action. Instead, I was disturbed rather than excited by this vision of law schools circling the wagons, as it were, to defend their beleaguered minority students against racially insensitive remarks. It is emphatically not my intention to defend the interviewer, most of whose reported questions and comments were inexplicable and inexcusable. I am troubled, however, by my suspicion that there would still have been outrage—not as much, but some—had the interviewer asked only what I called at the beginning of the chapter the qualification question.

I suspect this because in my own student days, something over a [8] decade ago, an interviewer from a prominent law firm addressed this very question to a Yale student who was not white, and the student voices—including my own—howled in protest. "Racism!" we insisted. "Ban them!" But with the passing years, I have come to wonder whether our anger might have been misplaced.

To be sure, the Yale interviewer's question was boorish. And be- [9] cause the interviewer had a grade record and résumé right in front of him, it was probably irrelevant as well. (It is useful here to dispose of one common but rather silly anti-affirmative action bromide: the old question, "Do you really want to be treated by a doctor who got into medical school because of skin color?" The answer is, or ought to be, that the patient doesn't particularly care how the doctor got *into* school; what matters is how the doctor got *out*. The right question, the sensible question, is not "What medical school performance did your grades and test scores predict?" but "What was your medical school performance?") But irrelevance and boorishness cannot explain our rage at the qualification question, because lots of interviewers ask questions that meet the tests of boorishness and irrelevance.

The controversy is not limited to outsiders who come onto campus [10] to recruit. In the spring of 1991, for example, students at Georgetown Law School demanded punishment for a classmate who argued in the school newspaper that affirmative action is unfair because students of color are often admitted to law school on the basis of grades and test scores that would cause white applicants to be rejected. Several universities have considered proposals that would deem it "racial harassment" for a (white?) student to question the qualifications of nonwhite classmates. But we can't change either the truths or the myths about racial preferences by punishing those who speak them.

This clamor for protection from the qualification question is pow- [11] erful evidence of the terrible psychological pressure that racial preferences often put on their beneficiaries. Indeed, it sometimes seems as though the programs are not supposed to have any beneficiaries—or, at least, that no one is permitted to suggest that they have any.

And that's ridiculous. If one supports racial preferences in profes- [12] sional school admissions, for example, one must be prepared to treat them like any other preference in admission and believe that they make a difference, that some students would not be admitted if the preferences did not exist. This is not a racist observation. It is not normative in any sense. It is simply a fact. A good deal of emotional underbrush might be cleared away were the fact simply conceded, and made the beginning, not the end, of any discussion of preferences. For once it is conceded that the programs have beneficiaries, it follows that some of us who are professionals and are not white must be among them. Supporters of preferences must stop pretending otherwise. Rather, some large segment of us must be willing to meet the qualification question head-on, to say, "Yes, I got into law school because of racial preferences. So what?"—and, having said it, must be ready with a list of what we have made of the opportunities the preferences provided.

Now, this is a costly concession, because it carries with it all the bag- [13] gage of the bitter rhetorical battle over the relationship between preferences and merit. But bristling at the question suggests a deep-seated fear that the dichotomy might be real. Indeed, if admitting that racial preferences make a difference leaves a funny aftertaste in the mouths of proponents, they might be more comfortable fighting against preferences rather than for them.

So let us bring some honesty as well as rigor to the debate, and begin [14] at the beginning. I have already made clear my starting point: I got into a top law school because I am black. Not only am I unashamed of this fact, but I can prove its truth.

As a senior at Stanford back in the mid-1970s, I applied to about half [15] a dozen law schools. Yale, where I would ultimately enroll, came through fairly early with an acceptance. So did all but one of the others. The last school, Harvard, dawdled and dawdled. Finally, toward the end of the admission season, I received a letter of rejection. Then, within days, two different Harvard officials and a professor contacted me by telephone to apologize. They were quite frank in their explanation for the "error." I was told by one official that the school had initially rejected me because "we assumed from your record that you were white." (The words have always stuck in my mind, a tantalizing reminder of what is expected of me.) Suddenly coy, he went on to say that the school had obtained "additional information that should have been counted in your favor"—that is, Harvard had discovered the color of my skin. And if I had already made a deposit to confirm my decision to go elsewhere, well, that, I was told, would "not be allowed" to stand in my way should I enroll at Harvard.

Naturally, I was insulted by this miracle. Stephen Carter, the white [16] male, was not good enough for the Harvard Law School; Stephen Carter, the black male, not only was good enough but rated agonized telephone calls urging him to attend. And Stephen Carter, color unknown, must have been white: How else could he have achieved what he did in college? Except that my college achievements were obviously not sufficiently spectacular to merit acceptance had I been white. In other words, my academic record was too good for a black Stanford University undergraduate, but not good enough for a white Harvard law student. Because I turned out to be black, however, Harvard was quite happy to scrape me from what it apparently considered somewhere nearer the bottom of the barrel.

My objective is not to single out Harvard for special criticism; on the [17] contrary, although my ego insists otherwise, I make no claim that a white student with my academic record would have been admitted to any of the leading law schools. The insult I felt came from the pain of being reminded so forcefully that in the judgment of those with the power to dispose, I was good enough for a top law school only because I happened to be black.

Naturally, I should not have been insulted at all; that is what racial [18] preferences are for—racial preference. But I was insulted and went off to Yale instead, even though I had then and have now absolutely no reason to imagine that Yale's judgment was based on different criteria than Harvard's. Hardly anyone granted admission at Yale is denied admission at Harvard, which admits a far larger class; but several hundreds of students who are admitted at Harvard are denied admission at Yale. Because Yale is far more selective, the chances are good that I was admitted at Yale for essentially the same reason I was admitted at Harvard—the color of my skin made up for what were evidently considered other deficiencies in my academic record. I may embrace this truth as a matter of simple justice or rail against it as one of life's great evils, but being a member of the affirmative action generation means that the one thing I cannot do is deny it. I will say it again: I got into law school because I am black. So what?

Responding to Reading

1. Carter opens his essay with the statement, "I got into law school because I am black" (1). What is your reaction to this statement? Do you think he should have used another opening strategy?
2. Do you agree with Carter's observation "that the patient doesn't particularly care how the doctor got *into* school; what matters is how the doctor got *out*" (9)?

3. Were you, like Carter, ever offered preferential treatment because of what or who you were? Do you believe this treatment was fair? Explain.

SEPARATE IS BETTER

Susan Estrich

Born in suburban Boston in 1953, Susan Estrich attended Wellesley College and Harvard Law School. After clerking for Supreme Court Justice John Paul Stevens, she returned to Harvard, becoming one of the youngest tenured professors on the Law School faculty. While there, she wrote *Real Rape* (1987), an examination of the social and legal issues surrounding the subject of sexual assault, which had its roots in her own earlier experience as a rape victim. She later served as the campaign manager for Michael Dukakis's 1988 presidential bid, the first woman in the country to hold such a position. Now a professor of law and political science at the University of Southern California, Estrich writes often about issues related to gender and politics. In the following essay, she presents what she sees as the benefits for female students of attending an all-women's college.

Twenty years ago, when I attended Wellesley College, an all-women's college, coeducation fever was gripping America. Yale and Princeton had just "gone"; Dartmouth "went" next. My freshman year, we were polled on whether we thought Wellesley should join the stampede. What did I know? I said yes. But now I know I was wrong, and I'm glad my vote didn't change anything. [1]

This year, 60 percent of the National Merit Scholarship finalists are boys, because boys outscored girls on the Preliminary Scholastic Assessment Test (P.S.A.T.), which determines eligibility for the scholarships. The test doesn't ask about sports; it does ask about math and science, though, and that's where the differences between boys and girls are most pronounced. The American Civil Liberties Union and the National Center for Fair and Open Testing filed a Federal civil rights suit in February charging that the test discriminates against women. The plaintiffs want more girls to get National Merit Scholarships. So do I. But I want to see the girls earn them, in schools that give them a fair chance. [2]

I didn't win a Merit Scholarship either, although if the Fair Test people had their way, I might have. My grades were near perfect. But I didn't take the tough math and science courses. I had different priorities. [3]

I started junior high as the only girl on the math team. By high school, I'd long since quit. Instead, I learned to twirl a baton, toss it in the air and catch it while doing a split in the mud or the ice. The problem wasn't the P.S.A.T., but me, and my school.

Things have changed since then, but not as much as one would   4 hope. The American Association of University Women did a major study in 1992 about how schools shortchange girls and concluded that even though girls get better grades (except in math), they get less from school. Teachers pay less attention to girls and give them less encouragement. Two American University researchers, Myra and David Sadker, reached a similar conclusion after 20 years of study. Girls are the invisible students; boys get the bulk of the teachers' time. Boys call out eight times as often as girls do. When the boys call out, they get answers; when the girls do, they're often admonished for speaking out. And that's true whether the teacher is a man or a woman. Even the new history textbooks devote only about 2 percent of their pages to women. What is happening, says Elisabeth Griffith, a historian and headmistress of the Madeira School in McLean, Va., is that "boys learn competence, girls lose it."

If schools shortchange girls, why is it surprising when the tests show   5 that they're doing less well? It isn't just the P.S.A.T.'s, where 18,000 boys generally reach the top categories and only 8,000 girls do. While the gap has narrowed, boys also outscore girls on 11 of the 14 College Board Achievement tests, and on the A.C.T. exams and on the S.A.T.'s. It is possible to jimmy selection standards to make sure girls win more scholarships, but equal results don't count for much if those results are forced. Instead of declaring equality, society should be advancing it. The challenge isn't to get more scholarships for baton twirlers but to get more baton twirlers to take up advanced mathematics.

One place that happens is in girls' schools and women's colleges.   6 Sometimes separate isn't equal; it's better. Changing the way teachers teach in coed schools, changing the textbooks to make sure they talk about women as well as men, educating parents about raising daughters—all of these things make sense, since most girls will be educated in coed classrooms. But we've been talking about them for a decade, and the problems of gender bias stubbornly persist. In the meantime, for many girls, single-sex education is working.

In girls' schools, 80 percent of the girls take four years of science and   7 math, compared with the national average of two years in a coed environment. Elizabeth Tidball, a George Washington University researcher, found that graduates of women's colleges did better than female graduates of coed colleges in terms of test scores, graduate school admissions, number of earned doctorates, salaries and personal satisfaction. One-third of the female board members of Fortune 1,000 companies are graduates of women's colleges, even though those colleges contribute less than 4 percent of total graduates. Forty-three percent of the math doctorates and 50 percent of engineering doctorates earned by female liberal-arts college students go to graduates of Barnard, Bryn Mawr, Mount Holyoke, Smith or Wellesley—all women's colleges. Graduates of women's colleges outnumber all other female entries in Who's Who.

I stopped twirling my baton when I got to Wellesley. I'd like to say [8] that I knew I needed a women's college after all those years in the mud at football games, but it doesn't always work that way. I went to Wellesley because they gave me a generous scholarship, and because Radcliffe rejected me (the test scores, maybe). I was actually miserable a good deal of the time I was there, particularly during the long winters when the janitor was the only man around. But what I learned was worth it. I spent the better part of four years in a world in which women could do anything, because no one told us we couldn't. I even took some math courses. By senior year, somehow, I'd become an accomplished test-taker. When I got to Harvard Law School, where men vastly outnumbered women and sexism was the rule, a professor told me on the first day that women didn't do very well. I laughed and decided to prove he was wrong. That's a Wellesley education.

I'm not proposing that coed public schools be replaced with a net- [9] work of single-sex academies. But if the problem is that women don't do well in math or science, then single-sex classes, and single-sex schools, may be part of the answer.

The evidence, though scant, is promising. In Ventura, Calif., the [10] public high school has begun offering an all-girls Algebra II course. The girls, one teacher says, think so little of their ability that the teacher spends her time not only teaching math but also building self-confidence, repeatedly telling the girls that they're smart and that they can do it. The Illinois Math and Science Academy in Aurora is experimenting with a girls-only calculus-based physics class for the first semester, with the girls joining the coed class at midyear. In the girls-only class, the students report that they are jumping up to ask and answer questions instead of sitting back, hoping that the teacher doesn't call on them. One student said she was worried about the transition to a coed classroom: "We need to make sure we don't lose our newfound physics freedom." "Physics freedom" for girls—what a wonderful concept.

The biggest obstacles to such classes, or even to all-girls public [11] schools, are erected by lawyers bent on enforcing legal equality. In the 1954 case of Brown v. Board of Education, the Supreme Court declared that "separate but equal" was inherently unequal. That was certainly true in Topeka, Kan., whose school system was challenged. It was true of the black-only law school established to keep blacks out of the University of Texas law school. It is not necessarily true of the Ventura High School math class for girls or the Aurora Academy calculus-based physics class, whose futures are in jeopardy because of the knee-jerk application of Brown.

Classes like those in Ventura County or Aurora, Ill., survive constitutional challenge by formally opening their doors to men, with a wink and a nod to keep them from coming in. Otherwise, the schools could be stripped of Federal support, and even enjoined under the Constitution by Federal court order, because they are "discriminating." Private schools may open their doors only to boys or girls under an exemption from Federal laws mandating "equality." But public schools enjoy no such freedom. The reality is that if you need a Wellesley education in America, you have to pay for it. That's the price of committing to formal equality instead of committing to real opportunity.   12

Boys may pay the price as well. Some educators in the African-American community believe that all-boys classes may be part of the solution to the dismal failure and dropout rates of African-American boys in school. But the courts prevented the Detroit school district from establishing three public all-boys schools, effectively stopping similar projects planned in other cities. Nonetheless, all-boys classes are being held quietly in as many as two dozen schools around the country, mostly in inner cities.   13

Such programs may or may not succeed in the long run. Research and careful study are plainly needed. But research and careful study are difficult when classes are held in near secrecy for fear of discovery by lawyers and Government officials intent on shutting them down in the name of equality.   14

If girls don't want to go to all-girls schools, or if parents don't want to send them, that's their choice. If the experiments with girls-only math classes or boys-only classes should fail, then educators can be trusted to abandon them. But short of that, let the educators and the parents and the students decide, and leave the lawyers and judges out of it.   15

Responding to Reading

1. Estrich argues in favor of all-women's colleges. Does she effectively apply her arguments to single-sex high schools? Could the same arguments be applied to historically black colleges? To all-men's colleges?
2. At various points in her essay, Estrich uses statistics to support her argument. How effective is this support? Would examples from her personal experience have been equally effective? More effective?
3. Do you agree with Estrich's position on single-sex education? Can you see any problems with her recommendations?

THE VISIGOTHS IN TWEED

Dinesh D'Souza

Born in Bombay, India, Dinesh D'Souza (1961–) came to the U.S. in 1978. He attended Dartmouth College, where from 1982 through 1983 he edited the controversial *Dartmouth Review*, an independent student newspaper funded in part by William F. Buckley's highly conservative opinion magazine, *The National Review*. After graduation, D'Souza authored a biography of television evangelist Jerry Falwell and *My Dear Alex: Letters from a KGB Agent* (1987, with Gregory Fossedale), a satire on Soviet manipulation of U.S. politicians and the American press. A former policy advisor to Presidents Reagan and Bush, he is a research fellow at the American Enterprise Institute. In 1991 he published the widely read *Illiberal Education: The Politics of Race and Sex on Campus*, a scathing attack on what D'Souza calls higher education's "attempted brainwashing [of students] that deprecates Western learning and exalts a neo-Marxist ideology promoted in the name of multiculturalism." The following essay, which originally appeared in the business magazine *Forbes*, is adapted from that book and presents D'Souza's central thesis. (For another report on the multiculturalism controversy, see Huntly Collins's essay "PC and the Press" on page 308.)

"I am a male WASP who attended and succeeded at Choate   1
(preparatory) School, Yale College, Yale Law School, and Princeton Graduate School. Slowly but surely, however, my life-long habit of looking, listening, feeling, and thinking as honestly as possible has led me to see that white, male-dominated, western European culture is the most destructive phenomenon in the known history of the planet.

"[This Western culture] is deeply hateful of life and committed to   2
death; therefore, it is moving rapidly toward the destruction of itself and most other life forms on earth. And truly it deserves to die. . . . We have to face our own individual and collective responsibility for what is happening—our greed, brutality, indifference, militarism, racism, sexism, blindness. . . . Meanwhile, everything we have put into motion continues to endanger us more every day."

This bizarre outpouring, so reminiscent of the "confessions" from   3
victims of Stalin's show trials,[1] appeared in a letter to *Mother Jones* magazine and was written by a graduate of some of our finest schools. But the truth is that the speaker's anguish came not from any balanced as-

---

[1] During his brutal assumption of totalitarian control over the Soviet Union in the 1930s, Joseph Stalin purged many of his enemies in mock trials where they were forced to confess their "crimes" before they were executed. [Eds.]

sessment but as a consequence of exposure to the propaganda of the new barbarians who have captured the humanities, law, and social science departments of so many of our universities. It should come as no surprise that many sensitive young Americans reject the system that has nurtured them. At Duke University, according to the *Wall Street Journal,* professor Frank Lentricchia in his English course shows the movie *The Godfather* to teach his students that organized crime is "a metaphor for American business as usual."

Yes, a student can still get an excellent education—among the best 4 in the world—in computer technology and the hard sciences at American universities. But liberal arts students, including those attending Ivy League schools, are very likely to be exposed to an attempted brainwashing that deprecates Western learning and exalts a neo-Marxist ideology promoted in the name of multiculturalism. Even students who choose hard sciences must often take required courses in the humanities, where they are almost certain to be inundated with an anti-Western, anticapitalist view of the world.

Each year American society invests $160 billion in higher education, 5 more per student than any nation in the world except Denmark. A full 45 percent of this money comes from the federal, state, and local governments. No one can say we are starving higher education. But what are we getting for our money, at least so far as the liberal arts are concerned?

A fair question? It might seem so, but in university circles it is con- 6 sidered impolite because it presumes that higher education must be accountable to the society that supports it. Many academics think of universities as intellectual enclaves, insulated from the vulgar capitalism of the larger culture.

Yet, since the academics constantly ask for more money, it seems 7 hardly unreasonable to ask what they are doing with it. Honest answers are rarely forthcoming. The general public sometimes gets a whiff of what is going on—as when Stanford alters its core curriculum in the classics of Western civilization—but it knows very little of the systematic and comprehensive change sweeping higher education.

An academic and cultural revolution has overtaken most of our 8 3,535 colleges and universities. It's a revolution to which most Americans have paid little attention. It is a revolution imposed upon the students by a university elite, not one voted upon or even discussed by the society at large. It amounts, according to University of Wisconsin-Madison Chancellor Donna Shalala, to "a basic transformation of American higher education in the name of multiculturalism and diversity."

The central thrust of this "basic transformation" involves replacing 9 traditional core curricula—consisting of the great works of Western culture—with curricula flavored by minority, female, and Third World authors.

Here's a sample of the viewpoint represented by the new curriculum. Becky Thompson, a sociology and women's studies professor, in a teaching manual distributed by the American Sociological Association, writes: "I begin my course with the basic feminist principle that in a racist, classist, and sexist society we have all swallowed oppressive ways of being, whether intentionally or not. Specifically, this means that it is not open to debate whether a white student is racist or a male student is sexist. He/she simply is." 10

Professors at several colleges who have resisted these regnant dogmas about race and gender have found themselves the object of denunciation and even university sanctions. Donald Kagan, dean of Yale College, says: "I was a student during the days of Joseph McCarthy,[2] and there is less freedom now than there was then." 11

As in the McCarthy period, a particular group of activists has cowed the authorities and bent them to its will. After activists forcibly occupied his office, President Lattie Coor of the University of Vermont explained how he came to sign a sixteen-point agreement establishing, among other things, minority faculty hiring quotas. "When it became clear that the minority students with whom I had been discussing these issues wished to pursue negotiations *in the context of occupied offices . . .* I agreed to enter negotiations." As frequently happens in such cases, Coor's "negotiations" ended in a rapid capitulation by the university authorities. 12

At Harvard, historian Stephan Thernstrom was harangued by student activists and accused of insensitivity and bigotry. What was his crime? His course included a reading from the journals of slave owners, and his textbook gave a reasonable definition of affirmative action as "preferential treatment" for minorities. At the University of Michigan, renowned demographer Reynolds Farley was assailed in the college press for criticizing the excesses of Marcus Garvey and Malcolm X; yet the administration did not publicly come to his defense. 13

University leaders argue that the revolution suggested by these examples is necessary because young Americans must be taught to live in and govern a multiracial and multicultural society. Immigration from Asia and Latin America, combined with relatively high minority birth rates, is changing the complexion of America. Consequently, in the words of University of Michigan President James Duderstadt, universities must "create a model of how a more diverse and pluralistic community can work for our society." 14

---

[2] The notorious U.S. senator of the late 1940s and early 1950s who instigated a search for suspected Communists and others with "un-American" leanings in government, academia, and the entertainment industry, ruining many careers. McCarthy was eventually censured by the U.S. Senate. [Eds.]

No controversy, of course, about benign goals such as pluralism or [15] diversity, but there is plenty of controversy about how these goals are being pursued. Although there is no longer a Western core curriculum at Mount Holyoke or Dartmouth, students at those schools must take a course in non-Western or Third World culture. Berkeley and the University of Wisconsin now insist that every undergraduate enroll in ethnic studies, making this virtually the only compulsory course at those schools.

If American students were truly exposed to the richest elements of [16] other cultures, this could be a broadening and useful experience. A study of Chinese philosophers such as Confucius or Mencius would enrich students' understanding of how different peoples order their lives, thus giving a greater sense of purpose to their own. Most likely, a taste of Indian poetry such as Rabindranath Tagore's *Gitanjali* would increase the interest of materially minded young people in the domain of the spirit. An introduction to Middle Eastern history would prepare the leaders of tomorrow to deal with the mounting challenge of Islamic culture. It would profit students to study the rise of capitalism in the Far East.

But the claims of the academic multiculturalists are largely phony. [17] They pay little attention to the Asian or Latin American classics. Rather, the non-Western or multicultural curriculum reflects a different agenda. At Stanford, for example, Homer, Plato, Dante, Machiavelli, and Locke[3] are increasingly scarce. But often their replacements are not non-Western classics. Instead the students are offered exotic topics such as popular religion and healing in Peru, Rastafarian poetry, and Andean music.

What do students learn about the world from the books they are required to read under the new multicultural rubric? At Stanford one of [18] the non-Western works assigned is *I, Rigoberta Menchú,* subtitled "An Indian Woman in Guatemala."

The book is hardly a non-Western classic. Published in 1983, *I, Rigob-* [19] *erta Menchú* is the story of a young woman who is said to be a representative voice of the indigenous peasantry. Representative of Guatemalan Indian culture? In fact, Rigoberta met the Venezuelan feminist to whom she narrates this story at a socialist conference in Paris, where, presumably, very few of the Third World's poor travel. Moreover, Rigoberta's political consciousness includes the adoption of such politically correct causes as feminism, homosexual rights, socialism, and Marxism. By the middle of the book she is discoursing on "bourgeois youths" and "Molotov cocktails," not the usual terminology of Indian peasants. One chapter is titled "Rigoberta Renounces Marriage and Motherhood," a norm that her tribe could not have adopted and survived.

---

[3] European writers and philosophers from ancient times through the 17th century. [Eds.]

If Rigoberta does not represent the convictions and aspirations of [20] Guatemalan peasants, what is the source of her importance and appeal? The answer is that Rigoberta seems to provide independent Third World corroboration for Western left-wing passions and prejudices. She is a mouthpiece for a sophisticated neo-Marxist critique of Western society, all the more powerful because it seems to issue not from some embittered American academic but from a Third World native. For professors nourished on the political activism of the late 1960s and early 1970s, texts such as *I, Rigoberta Menchú* offer a welcome opportunity to attack capitalism and Western society in general in the name of teaching students about the developing world.

We learn in the introduction of *I, Rigoberta Menchú* that Rigoberta is [21] a quadruple victim. As a person of color, she has suffered racism. As a woman, she has endured sexism. She lives in South America, which is— of course—a victim of North American colonialism. She is also an Indian, victimized by Latino culture within Latin America.[4]

One of the most widely used textbooks in so-called multicultural [22] courses is *Multi-Cultural Literacy*, published by Graywolf Press in St. Paul, Minnesota. The book ignores the *The Tale of Genji*, the Upanishads and Vedas, the Koran and Islamic commentaries. It also ignores such brilliant contemporary authors as Jorge Luis Borges, V.S. Naipaul, Octavio Paz, Naguib Mahfonz, and Wole Soyinka. Instead it offers thirteen essays of protest, including Michele Wallace's autobiographical "Invisibility Blues" and Paula Gunn Allen's "Who Is Your Mother? The Red Roots of White Feminism."

One student I spoke with at Duke University said he would not [23] study *Paradise Lost* because John Milton was a Eurocentric white male sexist. At the University of Michigan, a young black woman who had converted to Islam refused to believe that the prophet Muhammad owned slaves and practiced polygamy. She said she had taken courses on cultural diversity and the courses hadn't taught her that.

One of the highlights of this debate on the American campus was a [24] passionate statement delivered a few years ago by Stanford undergraduate William King, president of the Black Student Union, who argued the benefits of the new multicultural curriculum before the faculty senate of the university. Under the old system, he said, "I was never taught . . . the fact that Socrates, Herodotus, Pythagoras, and Solon studied in Egypt and acknowledged that much of their knowledge of astronomy, geometry, medicine, and building came from the African civilization in and around Egypt. [I was never taught] that the Hippocratic oath acknowledges the Greeks' 'father of medicine,' Imhotep, a black Egyptian pharaoh whom they called Aesculapius. . . . I was never informed when it was found that the 'very dark and wooly haired' Moors

---

[4] Menchú was awarded the Nobel Peace Prize in 1992, shortly after this article was published.

in Spain preserved, expanded, and reintroduced the classical knowledge that the Greeks had collected, which led to the 'renaissance.' . . . I read the Bible without knowing Saint Augustine looked black like me, that the Ten Commandments were almost direct copies from the 147 Negative Confessions of Egyptian initiates. . . . I didn't learn Toussaint L'Ouverture's defeat of Napoleon in Haiti directly influenced the French Revolution, or that the Iroquois Indians in America had a representative democracy which served as a model for the American system."

This statement drew wild applause and was widely quoted. The [25] only trouble is that much of it is untrue. There is no evidence that Socrates, Pythagoras, Herodotus, and Solon studied in Egypt, although Herodotus may have traveled there. Saint Augustine was born in North Africa, but his skin color is unknown, and in any case he could not have been mentioned in the Bible; he was born over 350 years after Christ. Viewing King's speech at my request, Bernard Lewis, an expert on Islamic and Middle Eastern culture at Princeton, described it as "a few scraps of truth amidst a great deal of nonsense."

Why does multicultural education, in practice, gravitate toward [26] such myths and half-truths? To find out why, it is necessary to explore the complex web of connections that the academic revolution generates among admissions policies, life on campus, and the curriculum.

American universities typically begin with the premise that in a de- [27] mocratic and increasingly diverse society the composition of their classes should reflect the ethnic distribution of the general population. Many schools officially seek "proportional representation," in which the percentage of applicants admitted from various racial groups roughly approximates the ratio of those groups in society at large.

Thus universities routinely admit black, Hispanic, and American In- [28] dian candidates over better-qualified white and Asian American applicants. As a result of zealously pursued affirmative action programs, many selective colleges admit minority students who find it extremely difficult to meet demanding academic standards and to compete with the rest of the class. This fact is reflected in the dropout rates of blacks and Hispanics, which are more than 50 percent higher than those of whites and Asians. At Berkeley a study of students admitted on a preferential basis between 1978 and 1982 concluded that nearly 70 percent failed to graduate within five years.

For affirmative action students who stay on campus, a common [29] strategy of dealing with the pressures of university life is to enroll in a distinctive minority organization. Among such organizations at Cornell University are Lesbian, Gay & Bisexual Coalition; La Asociacion Latina; National Society of Black Engineers; Society of Minority Hoteliers; Black Students United; and Simba Washanga.

Although the university brochures at Cornell and elsewhere con- [30] tinue to praise integration and close interaction among students from different backgrounds, the policies practiced at these schools actually encourage segregation. Stanford, for example, has "ethnic theme houses" such as the African house called Ujaama. And President Donald Kennedy has said that one of his educational objectives is to "support and strengthen ethnic theme houses." Such houses make it easier for some minority students to feel comfortable but help to create a kind of academic apartheid.

The University of Pennsylvania has funded a black yearbook, even [31] though only 6 percent of the student body is black and all other groups appeared in the general yearbook. Vassar, Dartmouth, and the University of Illinois have allowed separate graduation activities and ceremonies for minority students. California State University at Sacramento has just established an official "college within a college" for blacks.

Overt racism is relatively rare at most campuses, yet minorities are [32] told that bigotry operates in subtle forms such as baleful looks, uncorrected stereotypes, and "institutional racism"—defined as the underrepresentation of blacks and Hispanics among university trustees, administrators, and faculty.

Other groups such as feminists and homosexuals typically get into [33] the game, claiming their own varieties of victim status. As Harvard political scientist Harvey Mansfield bluntly puts it, "White students must admit their guilt so that minority students do not have to admit their incapacity."

Even though universities regularly accede to the political demands [34] of victim groups, their appeasement gestures do not help black and Hispanic students get a genuine liberal arts education. They do the opposite, giving the apologists of the new academic orthodoxy a convenient excuse when students admitted on a preferential basis fail to meet academic standards. At this point student activists and administrators often blame the curriculum. They argue that it reflects a "white male perspective" that systematically depreciates the views and achievements of other cultures, minorities, women, and homosexuals.

With this argument, many minority students can now explain why [35] they had such a hard time with Milton in the English department, Publius in political science, and Heisenberg in physics. Those men reflected white male aesthetics, philosophy, and science. Obviously, nonwhite students would fare much better if the university created more black or Latino or Third World courses, the argument goes. This epiphany leads to a spate of demands: Abolish the Western classics, establish new departments such as Afro-American Studies and Women's Studies, hire minority faculty to offer distinctive black and Hispanic "perspectives."

Multicultural or non-Western education on campus frequently [36] glamorizes Third World cultures and omits inconvenient facts about them. In fact, several non-Western cultures are caste-based or tribal, and often disregard norms of racial equality. In many of them feminism is virtually nonexistent, as indicated by such practices as dowries, widow-burning, and genital mutilation; and homosexuality is sometimes regarded as a crime or mental disorder requiring punishment. These nasty aspects of the non-Western cultures are rarely mentioned in the new courses. Indeed, Bernard Lewis of Princeton argues that while slavery and the subjugation of women have been practiced by all known civilizations, the West at least has an active and effective movement for the abolition of such evils.

Who is behind this academic revolution, this contrived multicul-   37 turalism? The new curriculum directly serves the purposes of a newly ascendant generation of young professors, weaned in the protest culture of the late 1960s and early 1970s. In a frank comment, Jay Parini, who teaches English at Middlebury College, writes, "After the Vietnam War, a lot of us didn't just crawl back into our library cubicles. We stepped into academic positions. . . . Now we have tenure, and the work of reshaping the university has begun in earnest."

The goal that Parini and others like him pursue is the transformation   38 of the college classroom from a place of learning to a laboratory of indoctrination for social change. Not long ago most colleges required that students learn the basics of the physical sciences and mathematics, the rudiments of economics and finance, and the fundamental principles of American history and government. Studies by the National Endowment for the Humanities show that this coherence has disappeared from the curriculum. As a result, most universities are now graduating students who are scientifically and culturally impoverished, if not illiterate.

At the University of Pennsylvania, Houston Baker, one of the most   39 prominent black academics in the country, denounces reading and writing as oppressive technologies and celebrates such examples of oral culture as the rap group N.W.A. (Niggers With Attitude). One of the group's songs is about the desirability of killing policemen. Alison Jaggar, who teaches women's studies at the University of Colorado, denounces the traditional nuclear family as a "cornerstone of women's oppression" and anticipates scientific advances enabling men to carry fetuses in their bodies so that child-bearing responsibilities can be shared between the sexes. Duke professor Eve Sedgwick's scholarship is devoted to unmasking what she terms the heterosexual bias in Western culture, a project that she pursues through papers such as "Jane Austen and the Masturbating Girl" and "How To Bring Your Kids Up Gay."

Confronted by racial tension and Balkanization on campus, univer-   40 sity leaders usually announce that, because of a resurgence of bigotry, "more needs to be done." They press for redoubled preferential recruitment of minority students and faculty, funding for a new Third World or Afro-American center, mandatory sensitivity education for whites, and so on. The more the university leaders give in to the demands of minority activists, the more they encourage the very racism they are supposed to be fighting. Surveys indicate that most young people today hold fairly liberal attitudes toward race, evident in their strong support for the civil rights agenda and for interracial dating. However, these liberal attitudes are sorely tried by the demands of the new orthodoxy: many undergraduates are beginning to rebel against what they perceive as a culture of preferential treatment and double standards actively fostered by university policies.

Can there be a successful rolling back of this revolution, or at least [41] of its excesses? One piece of good news is that blatant forms of racial preference are having an increasingly tough time in the courts, and this has implications for university admissions policies. The Department of Education is more vigilant than it used to be in investigating charges of discrimination against whites and Asian Americans. With help from Washington director Morton Halperin, the American Civil Liberties Union has taken a strong stand against campus censorship. Popular magazines such as *Newsweek* and *New York* have poked fun at "politically correct" speech. At Tufts University, undergraduates embarrassed the administration into backing down on censorship by putting up taped boundaries designating areas of the university to be "free speech zones," "limited speech zones," and "Twilight Zones."

Even some scholars on the political left are now speaking out [42] against such dogmatism and excess. Eugene Genovese, a Marxist historian and one of the nation's most respected scholars of slavery, argues that "too often we find that education has given way to indoctrination. Good scholars are intimidated into silence, and the only diversity that obtains is a diversity of radical positions." More and more professors from across the political spectrum are resisting the politicization and lowering of standards. At Duke, for example, sixty professors, led by political scientist James David Barber, a liberal Democrat, have repudiated the extremism of the victims' revolution. To that end they have joined the National Association of Scholars, a Princeton, New Jersey-based group devoted to fairness, excellence, and rational debate in universities.

But these scholars need help. Resistance on campus to the academ- [43] ic revolution is outgunned and sorely needs outside reinforcements. Parents, alumni, corporations, foundations, and state legislators are generally not aware that they can be very effective in promoting reform. The best way to encourage reform is to communicate in no uncertain terms to university leadership and, if necessary, to use financial incentives to assure your voice is heard. University leaders do their best to keep outsiders from meddling or even finding out what exactly is going on behind the tall gates, but there is little doubt that they would pay keen attention to the views of the donors on whom they depend. By threatening to suspend donations if universities continue harmful policies, friends of liberal learning can do a lot. In the case of state-funded schools, citizens and parents can pressure elected representatives to ask questions and demand more accountability from the taxpayer-support-ed academics.

The illiberal revolution can be reversed only if the people who foot 44 the bills stop being passive observers. Don't just write a check to your alma mater; that's an abrogation of responsibility. Keep abreast of what is going on and don't be afraid to raise your voice and even to close your wallet in protest. Our Western, free-market culture need not provide the rope to hang itself.

Responding to Reading

1. Do you agree with D'Souza when he says, "An academic and cultural rev-olution has overtaken most of our 3,535 colleges and universities" (8)? Is there any evidence of such a revolution at your college or university?
2. With which points in this essay do you agree? With which do you disagree? On the whole, do you find D'Souza's arguments convincing or unconvinc-ing?
3. A review of D'Souza's book in *Time* said that students on most campuses are untouched by the academic debates that take place around multiculturalism and political correctness. Does your experience support this statement?

READING THE RIVER

Mark Twain

Samuel Clemens (1835–1910) grew up in Hannibal, Missouri. He is known by his pen name, Mark Twain, a phrase, meaning "two fathoms deep," that indicates the navigating depth of a river. Twain became a riverboat pilot in 1859, but he practiced this trade only until 1861, when the Civil War ended commercial river transportation. His writing is known for its wit, satire, and irony. He wrote humorous sketches of his travels to Europe and the Holy Land (*Innocents Abroad*, 1869) and of his prospecting days in the Nevada Territory and California (*Roughing It*, 1872). After settling in Hartford, Connecticut, in 1871, Twain used the rich material of his midwestern childhood to write his best-known works, *The Adventures of Tom Sawyer* (1876) and *The Adventures of Huck-leberry Finn* (1884). Later, Twain lived abroad for many years and trav-eled extensively as a lecturer. "Reading the River" is an excerpt from his autobiographical narrative *Life on the Mississippi* (1883).

Now when I had mastered the language of this water and had [1] come to know every trifling feature that bordered the great river as familiarly as I knew the letters of the alphabet, I had made a valuable acquisition. But I had lost something, too. I had lost something which could never be restored to me while I lived. All the grace, the beauty, the poetry, had gone out of the majestic river! I still kept in mind a certain wonderful sunset which I witnessed when steamboating was new to me. A broad expanse of the river was turned to blood; in the middle distance the red hue brightened into gold, through which a solitary log came floating, black and conspicuous; in one place a long, slanting mark lay sparkling upon the water; in another the surface was broken by boiling, tumbling rings, that were as many-tinted as an opal; where the ruddy flush was faintest, was a smooth spot that was covered with graceful circles and radiating lines, ever so delicately traced; the shore on our left was densely wooded and the somber shadow that fell from this forest was broken in one place by a long, ruffled trail that shone like silver; and high above the forest wall a clean-stemmed dead tree waved a single leafy bough that glowed like a flame in the unobstructed splendor that was flowing from the sun. There were graceful curves, reflected images, woody heights, soft distances, and over the whole scene, far and near, the dissolving lights drifted steadily, enriching it every passing moment with new marvels of coloring.

I stood like one bewitched. I drank it in, in a speechless rapture. The [2] world was new to me and I had never seen anything like this at home. But as I have said, a day came when I began to cease from noting the glories and the charms which the moon and the sun and the twilight wrought upon the river's face; another day came when I ceased altogether to note them. Then, if that sunset scene had been repeated, I should have looked upon it without rapture, and should have commented upon it inwardly after this fashion: "This sun means that we are going to have wind to-morrow; that floating log means that the river is rising, small thanks to it; that slanting mark on the water refers to a bluff reef which is going to kill somebody's steamboat one of these nights, if it keeps on stretching out like that; those tumbling 'boils' show a dissolving bar and a changing channel there; the lines and circles in the slick water over yonder are a warning that that troublesome place is shoaling up dangerously; that silver streak in the shadow of the forest is the 'break' from a new snag and he has located himself in the very best place he could have found to fish for steamboats; that tall dead tree, with a single living branch, is not going to last long, and then how is a body ever going to get through this blind place at night without the friendly old landmark?"

No, the romance and beauty were all gone from the river. All the [3] value any feature of it had for me now was the amount of usefulness it could furnish toward compassing the safe piloting of a steamboat. Since those days, I have pitied doctors from my heart. What does the lovely flush in a beauty's cheek mean to a doctor but a "break" that ripples above some deadly disease?[1] Are not all her visible charms sown thick with what are to him the signs and symbols of hidden decay? Does he ever see her beauty at all, or doesn't he simply view her professionally and comment upon her unwholesome condition all to himself? And doesn't he sometimes wonder whether he has gained most or lost most by learning his trade?

Responding to Reading

1. Which of the two ways of looking at nature does Twain seem to believe is more valuable? Why? Do you agree?
2. Would you define Twain's view of education as optimistic or pessimistic? What leads you to this conclusion?
3. As you have become more educated, have you found yourself seeing the "usefulness" of information and experiences instead of their "romance and beauty"? Explain.

WHEN I HEARD THE LEARN'D
~ ASTRONOMER

Walt Whitman

Walt Whitman (1819–1892) was a bold, eccentric character who wrote radical poetry about sexuality, technology, and nature to unsettle "all the settled laws." He first published his best-known work, *Leaves of Grass,* in 1855 with no author's name on the title page. Whitman was also a journalist who reported on the Civil War and an essayist who commented on American society and democracy. He wrote about and for working-class Americans, but his work appealed mostly to intellectuals. In the poem "When I Heard the Learn'd Astronomer," Whitman unites two of his favorite and seemingly incompatible themes: science and nature.

> When I heard the learn'd astronomer,
> When the proofs, the figures, were ranged in columns before me,

---

[1] Red cheeks are one of the signs of tuberculosis. [Eds.]

When I was shown the charts and diagrams, to add, divide, and measure them,
When I sitting heard the astronomer where he lectured with much applause in the lecture-room,
How soon unaccountable I became tired and sick,   5
Till rising and gliding out I wander'd off by myself,
In the mystical moist night-air, and from time to time,
Look'd up in perfect silence at the stars.

Responding to Reading

1. This poem could be divided into two 4-line segments. What kinds of ideas are expressed in each segment? How are the two kinds of ideas related?
2. What attitudes toward education are expressed in the poem? Do you agree with the speaker's sentiments?
3. What courses have you taken that have changed the way you look at the world? Were these changes positive or negative? Explain.

GRYPHON

Charles Baxter

Charles Baxter (1947–), born in Minneapolis, is a fiction writer and professor of English who now teaches at the University of Michigan. Baxter has published two novels, *First Light* (1987) and *Shadow Play* (1993), and three short story collections, *Harmony of the World* (1984), *Through the Safety Net* (1985), and *Relative Stranger* (1990). He has said that his writing career was inspired by a bohemian aunt. "Gryphon," a story from *Through the Safety Net*, looks through the eyes of a fourth grader to tell a tale of a substitute teacher with an eccentric and often unbalanced imagination.

On Wednesday afternoon, between the geography lesson on ancient   1
Egypt's hand-operated irrigation system and an art project that involved drawing a model city next to a mountain, our fourth-grade teacher, Mr. Hibler, developed a cough. This cough began with a series of muffled throat clearings and progressed to propulsive noises contained within Mr. Hibler's closed mouth. "Listen to him," Carol Peterson whispered to me. "He's gonna blow up." Mr. Hibler's laughter—dazed and infrequent—sounded a bit like his cough, but as we worked on our model cities we would look up, thinking he was enjoying a joke, and see Mr.

Hibler's face turning red, his cheeks puffed out. This was not laughter. Twice he bent over, and his loose tie, like a plumb line, hung down straight from his neck as he exploded himself into a Kleenex. He would excuse himself, then go on coughing. "I'll bet you a dime," Carol Peterson whispered, "we get a substitute tomorrow."

Carol sat at the desk in front of mine and was a bad person—when she thought no one was looking she would blow her nose on notebook paper, then crumble it up and throw it into the wastebasket—but at times of crisis she spoke the truth. I knew I'd lose the dime.

"No deal," I said.

When Mr. Hibler stood us up in formation at the door just prior to the final bell, he was almost incapable of speech. "I'm sorry, boys and girls," he said. "I seem to be coming down with something."

"I hope you feel better tomorrow, Mr. Hibler," Bobby Kryzanowicz, the faultless brown-noser said, and I heard Carol Peterson's evil giggle. Then Mr. Hibler opened the door and we walked out to the buses, a clique of us starting noisily to hawk and cough as soon as we thought we were a few feet beyond Mr. Hibler's earshot.

Five Oaks being a rural community, and in Michigan, the supply of substitute teachers was limited to the town's unemployed community college graduates, a pool of about four mothers. These ladies fluttered, provided easeful class days, and nervously covered material we had mastered weeks earlier. Therefore it was a surprise when a woman we had never seen came into the class the next day, carrying a purple purse, a checkerboard lunchbox, and a few books. She put the books on one side of Mr. Hibler's desk and the lunchbox on the other, next to the Voice of Music phonograph. Three of us in the back of the room were playing with Heever, the chameleon that lived in the terrarium and on one of the plastic drapes, when she walked in.

She clapped her hands at us. "Little boys," she said, "why are you bent over together like that?" She didn't wait for us to answer. "Are you tormenting an animal? Put it back. Please sit down at your desks. I want no cabals this time of the day." We just stared at her. "Boys," she repeated, "I asked you to sit down."

I put the chameleon in his terrarium and felt my way to my desk, never taking my eyes off the woman. With white and green chalk, she had started to draw a tree on the left side of the blackboard. She didn't look usual. Furthermore, her tree was outsized, disproportionate, for some reason.

"This room needs a tree," she said, with one line drawing the suggestion of a leaf. "A large, leafy, shady, deciduous . . . oak."

Her fine, light hair had been done up in what I would learn years later was called a chignon, and she wore gold-rimmed glasses whose lenses seemed to have the faintest blue tint. Harold Knardahl, who sat across from me, whispered "Mars," and I nodded slowly, savoring the imminent weirdness of the day. The substitute drew another branch with an extravagant arm gesture, then turned around and said, "Good morning. I don't believe I said good morning to all you yet."

Facing us, she was no special age—an adult is an adult—but her face [11] had two prominent lines, descending vertically from the sides of her mouth to her chin. I knew where I had seen those lines before: *Pinocchio.* They were marionette lines. "You may stare at me," she said to us, as a few more kids from the last bus came into the room, their eyes fixed on her, "for a few more seconds, until the bell rings. Then I will permit no more staring. Looking I will permit. Staring, no. It is impolite to stare, and a sign of bad breeding. You cannot make a social effort while staring."

Harold Knardahl did not glance at me, or nudge, but I heard him [12] whisper "Mars" again, trying to get more mileage out of his single joke with the kids who had just come in.

When everyone was seated, the substitute teacher finished her tree, [13] put down her chalk fastidiously on the phonograph, brushed her hands, and faced us. "Good morning," she said. "I am Miss Ferenczi, your teacher for the day. I am fairly new to your community, and I don't believe any of you know me. I will therefore start by telling you a story about myself."

While we settled back, she launched into her tale. She said her [14] grandfather had been a Hungarian prince; her mother had been born in some place called Flanders, had been a pianist, and had played concerts for people Miss Ferenczi referred to as "crowned heads." She gave us a knowing look. "Grieg," she said, "the Norwegian master, wrote a concerto for piano that was," she paused, "my mother's triumph at her debut concert in London." Her eyes searched the ceiling. Our eyes followed. Nothing up there but ceiling tile. "For reasons that I shall not go into, my family's fortunes took us to Detroit, then north to dreadful Saginaw, and now here I am in Five Oaks, as your substitute teacher, for today, Thursday, October the eleventh. I believe it will be a good day: All the forecasts coincide. We shall start with your reading lesson. Take out your reading book. I believe it is called *Broad Horizons,* or something along those lines."

Jeannie Vermeesch raised her hand. Miss Ferenczi nodded at her. [15] "Mr. Hibler always starts the day with the Pledge of Allegiance," Jeannie whined.

"Oh, does he? In that case," Miss Ferenczi said, "you must know it [16] *very* well by now, and we certainly need not spend our time on it. No, no allegiance pledging on the premises today, by my reckoning. Not with so much sunlight coming into the room. A pledge does not suit my mood." She glanced at her watch. "Time *is* flying. Take out *Broad Horizons.*"

She disappointed us by giving us an ordinary lesson, complete with ¹⁷
vocabulary word drills, comprehension questions, and recitation. She
didn't seem to care for the material, however. She sighed every few minutes and rubbed her glasses with a frilly perfumed handkerchief that she
withdrew, magician style, from her left sleeve.

After reading we moved on to arithmetic. It was my favorite time of ¹⁸
the morning, when the lazy autumn sunlight dazzled its way through
ribbons of clouds past the windows on the east side of the classroom,
and crept across the linoleum floor. On the playground the first group
of children, the kindergartners, were running on the quack grass just beyond the monkey bars. We were doing multiplication tables. Miss Ferenczi had made John Wazny stand up at his desk in the front row. He
was supposed to go through the tables of six. From where I was sitting,
I could smell the Vitalis soaked into John's plastered hair. He was doing
fine until he came to six times eleven and six times twelve. "Six times
eleven," he said, "is sixty-eight. Six times twelve is . . ." He put his fingers to his head, quickly and secretly sniffed his fingertips, and said,
"seventy-two." Then he sat down.

"Fine," Miss Ferenczi said. "Well now. That was very good." ¹⁹

"Miss Ferenczi!" One of the Eddy twins was waving her hand des- ²⁰
perately in the air. "Miss Ferenczi! Miss Ferenczi!"

"Yes?" ²¹

"John said that six times eleven is sixty-eight and you said he was ²²
right!"

"*Did* I?" She gazed at the class with a jolly look breaking across her ²³
marionette's face. "Did I say that? Well, what *is* six times eleven?"

"It's sixty-six!" ²⁴

She nodded. "Yes. So it is. But, and I know some people will not en- ²⁵
tirely agree with me, at some times it is sixty-eight."

"When? When is it sixty-eight?" ²⁶

We were all waiting. ²⁷

"In higher mathematics, which you children do not yet understand, ²⁸
six times eleven can be considered to be sixty-eight." She laughed
through her nose. "In higher mathematics numbers are . . . more fluid.
The only thing a number does is contain a certain amount of something.
Think of water. A cup is not the only way to measure a certain amount
of water, is it?" We were staring, shaking our heads. "You could use
saucepans or thimbles. In either case, the water *would be the same*. Perhaps," she started again, "it would be better for you to think that six
times eleven is sixty-eight only when I am in the room."

"Why is it sixty-eight," Mark Poole asked, "when you're in the ²⁹
room?"

"Because it's more interesting that way," she said, smiling very ³⁰
rapidly behind her blue-tinted glasses. "Besides, I'm your substitute

teacher, am I not?" We all nodded. "Well, then, think of six times eleven equals sixty-eight as a substitute fact."

"A substitute fact?"   31

"Yes." Then she looked at us carefully. "Do you think," she asked,   32 "that anyone is going to be hurt by a substitute fact?"

We looked back at her.   33

"Will the plants on the windowsill be hurt?" We glanced at them.   34 There were sensitive plants thriving in a green plastic tray, and several wilted ferns in small clay pots. "Your dogs and cats, or your moms and dads?" She waited. "So," she concluded, "what's the problem?"

"But it's wrong," Janice Weber said, "isn't it?"   35

"What's your name, young lady?"   36

"Janice Weber."   37

"And you think it's wrong, Janice?"   38

"I was just asking."   39

"Well, all right. You were just asking. I think we've spent enough   40 time on this matter by now, don't you, class? You are free to think what you like. When your teacher, Mr. Hibler, returns, six times eleven will be sixty-six again, you can rest assured. And it will be that for the rest of your lives in Five Oaks. Too bad, eh?" She raised her eyebrows and glinted herself at us. "But for now, it wasn't. So much for that. Let us go to your assigned problems for today, as painstakingly outlined, I see, in Mr. Hibler's lesson plan. Take out a sheet of paper and write your names in the upper left-hand corner."

For the next half hour we did the rest of our arithmetic problems.   41 We handed them in and went on to spelling, my worst subject. Spelling always came before lunch. We were taking spelling dictation and look-ing at the clock. "Thorough," Miss Ferenczi said. "Boundary." She walked in the aisles between the desks, holding the spelling book open and looking down at our papers. "Balcony." I clutched my pencil. Some-how, the way she said those words, they seemed foreign, Hungarian, mis-voweled and mis-consonanted. I stared down at what I had spelled. *Balconie.* I turned my pencil upside down and erased my mistake. *Bal-coney.* That looked better, but still incorrect. I cursed the world of spelling and tried erasing it again and saw the paper beginning to wear away. *Balkony.* Suddenly I felt a hand on my shoulder.

"I don't like that word either," Miss Ferenczi whispered, bent over,   42 her mouth near my ear. "It's ugly. My feeling is, if you don't like a word, you don't have to use it." She straightened up, leaving behind a slight odor of Clorets.

At lunchtime we went out to get our trays of sloppy joes, peaches in   43 heavy syrup, coconut cookies, and milk, and brought them back to the classroom, where Miss Ferenczi was sitting at the desk, eating a brown sticky thing she had unwrapped from tightly rubber-banded wax paper. "Miss Ferenczi," I said, raising my hand. "You don't have to eat with us."

You can eat with the other teachers. There's a teachers' lounge," I ended up, "next to the principal's office."

"No, thank you," she said. "I prefer it here." [44]

"We've got a room monitor," I said. "Mrs. Eddy." I pointed to [45] where Mrs. Eddy, Joyce and Judy's mother, sat silently at the back of the room, doing her knitting.

"That's fine," Miss Ferenczi said. "But I shall continue to eat here, [46] with you children. I prefer it," she repeated.

"How come?" Wayne Razmer asked without raising his hand. [47]

"I talked with the other teachers before class this morning," Miss [48] Ferenczi said, biting into her brown food. "There was a great rattling of the words for the fewness of ideas. I didn't care for their brand of hilarity. I don't like ditto machine jokes."

"Oh," Wayne said. [49]

"What's that you're eating?" Maxine Sylvester asked, twitching her [50] nose. "Is it food?"

"It most certainly *is* food. It's a stuffed fig. I had to drive almost [51] down to Detroit to get it. I also bought some smoked sturgeon. And this," she said, lifting some green leaves out of her lunchbox, "is raw spinach, cleaned this morning before I came out here to the Garfield-Murry school."

"Why're you eating raw spinach?" Maxine asked. [52]

"It's good for you," Miss Ferenczi said. "More stimulating than soda [53] pop or smelling salts." I bit into my sloppy joe and stared blankly out the window. An almost invisible moon was faintly silvered in the daytime autumn sky. "As far as food is concerned," Miss Ferenczi was saying, "you have to shuffle the pack. Mix it up. Too many people eat . . . well, never mind."

"Miss Ferenczi," Carol Peterson said, "what are we going to do this [54] afternoon?"

[55]

"Well," she said, looking down at Mr. Hibler's lesson plan, "I see that your teacher, Mr. Hibler, has you scheduled for a unit on the Egyptians." Carol groaned. "Yessss," Miss Ferenczi continued, "that is what we will do: the Egyptians. A remarkable people. Almost as remarkable as the Americans. But not quite." She lowered her head, did her quick smile, and went back to eating her spinach.

After noon recess we came back into the classroom and saw that [56] Miss Ferenczi had drawn a pyramid on the blackboard, close to her oak tree. Some of us who had been playing baseball were messing around in the back of the room, dropping the bats and the gloves into the playground box, and I think that Ray Schontzeler had just slugged me when I heard Miss Ferenczi's high-pitched voice quavering with emotion. "Boys," she said, "come to order right this minute and take your seats. I do not wish to waste a minute of class time. Take out your geography books." We trudged to our desks and, still sweating, pulled out *Distant Lands and Their People.* "Turn to page forty-two." She waited for thirty seconds, then looked over at Kelly Munger. "Young man," she said, "why are you still fossicking in your desk?"

Kelly looked as if his foot had been stepped on. "Why am I what?" [57]

"Why are you . . . burrowing in your desk like that?" [58]

"I'm lookin' for the book, Miss Ferenczi." [59]

Bobby Kryzanowicz, the faultless brown-noser who sat in the first [60] row by choice, softly said, "His name is Kelly Munger. He can't ever find his stuff. He always does that."

"I don't care what his name is, especially after lunch," Miss Ferenczi [61] said. *"Where is your book?"*

"I just found it." Kelly was peering into his desk and with both [62] hands pulled at the book, shoveling along in front of it several pencils and crayons, which fell into his lap and then to the floor.

"I hate a mess," Miss Ferenczi said. "I hate a mess in a desk or a [63] mind. It's . . . unsanitary. You wouldn't want your house at home to look like your desk at school, now, would you?" She didn't wait for an answer. "I should think not. A house at home should be as neat as human hands can make it. What were we talking about? Egypt. Page forty-two. I note from Mr. Hibler's lesson plan that you have been discussing the modes of Egyptian irrigation. Interesting, in my view, but not so interesting as what we are about to cover. The pyramids and Egyptian slave labor. A plus on one side, a minus on the other." We had our books open to page forty-two, where there was a picture of a pyramid, but Miss Ferenczi wasn't looking at the book. Instead, she was staring at some object just outside the window.

"Pyramids," Miss Ferenczi said, still looking past the window. "I [64] want you to think about the pyramids. And what was inside. The bodies of the pharaohs, of course, and their attendant treasures. Scrolls. Perhaps," Miss Ferenczi said, with something gleeful but unsmiling in her face, "these scrolls were novels for the pharaohs, helping them to pass the time in their long voyage through the centuries. But then, I am joking." I was looking at the lines on Miss Ferenczi's face. "Pyramids," Miss Ferenczi went on, "were the repositories of special cosmic powers. The nature of a pyramid is to guide cosmic energy forces into a concentrated point. The Egyptians knew that; we have generally forgotten it. Did you know," she asked, walking to the side of the room so that she was standing by the coat closet, "that George Washington had Egyptian blood, from his grandmother? Certain features of the Constitution of the United States are notable for their Egyptian ideas."

Without glancing down at the book, she began to talk about the [65] movement of souls in Egyptian religion. She said that when people die, their souls return to Earth in the form of carpenter ants or walnut trees, depending on how they behaved—"well or ill"—in life. She said that the Egyptians believed that people act the way they do because of magnetism produced by tidal forces in the solar system, forces produced by the sun and by its "planetary ally," Jupiter. Jupiter, she said, was a planet, as we had been told, but had "certain properties of stars." She was speaking very fast. She said that the Egyptians were great explorers and conquerors. She said that the greatest of all the conquerors, Genghis Khan, had had forty horses and forty young women killed on the site of his grave. We listened. No one tried to stop her. "I myself have been in Egypt," she said, "and have witnessed much dust and many brutalities." She said that an old man in Egypt who worked for a circus had personally shown her an animal in a cage, a monster, half bird and half lion. She said that this monster was called a gryphon and that she had heard about them but never seen them until she traveled to the outskirts of Cairo. She said that Egyptian astronomers had discovered the planet Saturn, but had not seen its rings. She said that the Egyptians were the first to discover that dogs, when they are ill, will not drink from rivers, but wait for rain, and hold their jaws open to catch it.

"She lies." [66]

We were on the school bus home. I was sitting next to Carl Whiteside, who had bad breath and a huge collection of marbles. We were arguing. Carl thought she was lying. I said she wasn't, probably. [67]

"I didn't believe that stuff about the bird," Carl said, "and what she told us about the pyramids? I didn't believe that either. She didn't know what she was talking about." [68]

"Oh yeah?" I had liked her. She was strange. I thought I could nail him. "If she was lying," I said, "what'd she say that was a lie?" [69]

"Six times eleven isn't sixty-eight. It isn't ever. It's sixty-six, I know for a fact." [70]

"She said so. She admitted it. What else did she lie about?" [71]

"I don't know," he said. "Stuff." [72]

"What stuff?" [73]

"Well." He swung his legs back and forth. "You ever see an animal that was half lion and half bird?" He crossed his arms. "It sounded real fakey to me." [74]

"It could happen," I said. I had to improvise, to outrage him. "I read in this newspaper my mom bought in the IGA about this scientist, this mad scientist in the Swiss Alps, and he's been putting genes and chromosomes and stuff together in test tubes, and he combined a human being and a hamster." I waited, for effect. "It's called a humster." [75]

"You never." Carl was staring at me, his mouth open, his terrible bad breath making its way toward me. "What newspaper was it?" [76]

"The *National Enquirer*," I said, "that they sell next to the cash registers." When I saw his look of recognition, I knew I had bested him. "And this mad scientist," I said, "his name was, um, Dr. Frankenbush." [77]

I realized belatedly that this name was a mistake and waited for Carl to notice its resemblance to the name of the other famous mad master to permutations, but he only sat there.

"A man and a hamster?" He was staring at me, squinting, his mouth [78] opening in distaste. "Jeez. What'd it look like?"

When the bus reached my stop, I took off down our dirt road and [79] ran up through the back yard, kicking the tire swing for good luck. I dropped my books on the back steps so I could hug and kiss our dog, Mr. Selby. Then I hurried inside. I could smell Brussels sprouts cooking, my unfavorite vegetable. My mother was washing other vegetables in the kitchen sink, and my baby brother was hollering in his yellow playpen on the kitchen floor.

"Hi, Mom," I said, hopping around the playpen to kiss her, "Guess [80] what?"

"I have no idea." [81]

"We had this substitute today, Miss Ferenczi, and I'd never seen her [82] before, and she had all these stories and ideas and stuff."

"Well. That's good." My mother looked out the window behind the [83] sink, her eyes on the pine woods west of our house. Her face and hairstyle always reminded other people of Betty Crocker, whose picture was framed inside a gigantic spoon on the side of the Bisquick box; to me, though, my mother's face just looked white. "Listen, Tommy," she said, "go upstairs and pick your clothes off the bathroom floor, then go outside to the shed and put the shovel and ax away that your father left outside this morning."

"She said that six times eleven was sometimes sixty-eight!" I said. [84] "And she said she once saw a monster that was half lion and half bird." I waited. "In Egypt, she said."

"Did you hear me?" my mother asked, raising her arm to wipe her [85] forehead with the back of her hand. "You have chores to do."

"I know," I said. "I was just telling you about the substitute." [86]

"It's very interesting," my mother said, quickly glancing down at [87] me, "and we can talk about it later when your father gets home. But right now you have some work to do."

"Okay, Mom." I took a cookie out of the jar on the counter and was [88] about to go outside when I had a thought. I ran into the living room, pulled out a dictionary next to the TV stand, and opened it to the G's. *Gryphon:* "variant of griffin." *Griffin:* "a fabulous beast with the head and wings of an eagle and the body of a lion." Fabulous was right. I shouted with triumph and ran outside to put my father's tools back in their place.

Miss Ferenczi was back the next day, slightly altered. She had pulled [89] her hair down and twisted it into pigtails, with red rubber bands holding them tight one inch from the ends. She was wearing a green blouse and pink scarf, making her difficult to look at for a full class day. This time there was no pretense of doing a reading lesson or moving on to arithmetic. As soon as the bell rang, she simply began to talk.

She talked for forty minutes straight. There seemed to be less con-[90] nection between her ideas, but the ideas themselves were, as the dictionary would say, fabulous. She said she had heard of a huge jewel, in what she called the Antipodes, that was so brilliant that when the light shone into it at a certain angle it would blind whoever was looking at its center. She said that the biggest diamond in the world was cursed and had killed everyone who owned it, and that by a trick of fate it was called the Hope diamond. Diamonds are magic, she said, and this is why women wear them on their fingers, as a sign of the magic of womanhood. Men have strength, Miss Ferenczi said, but no true magic. That is why men fall in love with women but women do not fall in love with men; they just love being loved. George Washington had died because of a mistake he made about a diamond. Washington was not the first *true* President, but she did not say who was. In some places in the world, she said, men and women still live in the trees and eat monkeys for breakfast. Their doctors are magicians. At the bottom of the sea are creatures thin as pancakes which have never been studied by scientists because when you take them up to the air, the fish explode.

There was not a sound in the classroom, except for Miss Ferenczi's [91] voice, and Donna DeShano's coughing. No one even went to the bathroom.

Beethoven, she said, had not been deaf; it was a trick to make him-[92] self famous, and it worked. As she talked, Miss Ferenczi's pigtails swung back and forth. There are trees in the world, she said, that eat meat: their leaves are sticky and close up on bugs like hands. She lifted her hands and brought them together, palm to palm. Venus, which most people think is the next closest planet to the sun, is not always closer, and, besides, it is the planet of greatest mystery because of its thick cloud cover. "I know what lies underneath those clouds," Miss Ferenczi said, and waited. After the silence, she said, "Angels. Angels live under those clouds." She said that angels were not invisible to everyone and were in fact smarter than most people. They did not dress in robes as was often claimed but instead wore formal evening clothes, as if they were about to attend a concert. Often angels *do* attend concerts and sit in the aisles where, she said, most people pay no attention to them. She said the most terrible angel had the shape of the Sphinx. "There is no running away from that one," she said. She said that unquenchable fires burn just under the surface of the earth in Ohio, and that the baby Mozart fainted dead away in his cradle when he first heard the sound of a trumpet. She said that someone named Narzim al Harrardim was the greatest writer who ever lived. She said that planets control behavior, and anyone conceived during a solar eclipse would be born with webbed feet.

"I know you children like to hear these things," she said, "these se- [93] crets, and that is why I am telling you all this." We nodded. It was better than doing comprehension questions for the readings in *Broad Horizons*.

"I will tell you one more story," she said, "and then we will have to [94] do arithmetic." She leaned over, and her voice grew soft. "There is no death," she said. "You must never be afraid. Never. That which is, can- not die. It will change into different earthly and unearthly elements, but I know this as sure as I stand here in front of you, and I swear it: you must not be afraid. I have seen this truth with these eyes. I know it be- cause in a dream God kissed me. Here." And she pointed with her right index finger to the side of her head, below the mouth, where the verti- cal lines were carved into her skin.

Absent-mindedly we all did our arithmetic problems. At recess the [95] class was out on the playground, but no one was playing. We were all standing in small groups, talking about Miss Ferenczi. We didn't know if she was crazy, or what. I looked out beyond the playground, at the rusted cars piled in a small heap behind a clump of sumac, and I want- ed to see shapes there, approaching me.

On the way home, Carl sat next to me again. He didn't say much, [96] and I didn't either. At last he turned to me. "You know what she said about the leaves that close up on bugs?"

"Huh?" [97]

"The leaves," Carl insisted. "The meat-eating plants. I know it's true. [98] I saw it on television. The leaves have this icky glue that the plants have got smeared all over them and the insects can't get off 'cause they're stuck. I saw it." He seemed demoralized. "She's tellin' the truth."

"Yeah." [99]

"You think she's seen all those angels?" [100]

I shrugged. [101]

"I don't think she has," Carl informed me. "I think she made that [102] part up."

"There's a tree," I suddenly said. I was looking out the window at [103] the farms along County Road H. I knew every barn, every broken wind- mill, every fence, every anhydrous ammonia tank, by heart. "There's a tree that's . . . that I've seen . . ."

"Don't you try to do it," Carl said. "You'll just sound like a jerk." [104]

I kissed my mother. She was standing in front of the stove. "How [105] was your day?" she asked.

"Fine." [106]

"Did you have Miss Ferenczi again?" [107]

"Yeah." [108]

"Well?" [109]

"She was fine. Mom," I asked, "can I go to my room?" [110]

"No," she said, "not until you've gone out to the vegetable garden [111] and picked me a few tomatoes." She glanced at the sky. "I think it's going to rain. Skedaddle and do it now. Then you come back inside and watch your brother for a few minutes while I go upstairs. I need to clean up before dinner." She looked down at me. "You're looking a little pale, Tommy." She touched the back of her hand to my forehead and I felt her diamond ring against my skin. "Do you feel all right?"

"I'm fine," I said, and went out to pick the tomatoes. [112]

Coughing mutedly, Mr. Hibler was back the next day, slipping [113] lozenges into his mouth when his back was turned at forty-five minute intervals and asking us how much of the prepared lesson plan Miss Ferenczi had followed. Edith Atwater took the responsibility for the class of explaining to Mr. Hibler that the substitute hadn't always done exactly what he would have done, but we had worked hard even though she talked a lot. About what? he asked. All kinds of things, Edith said. I sort of forgot. To our relief, Mr. Hibler seemed not at all interested in what Miss Ferenczi had said to fill the day. He probably thought it was woman's talk; unserious and not suited for school. It was enough that he had a pile of arithmetic problems from us to correct.

For the next month, the sumac turned a distracting red in the field, [114] and the sun traveled toward the southern sky, so that its rays reached Mr. Hibler's Halloween display on the bulletin board in the back of the room, fading the scarecrow with a pumpkin head from orange to tan. Every three days I measured how much farther the sun had moved toward the southern horizon by making small marks with my black Crayola on the north wall, ant-sized marks only I knew were there, inching west.

And then in early December, four days after the first permanent [115] snowfall, she appeared again in our classroom. The minute she came in the door, I felt my heart begin to pound. Once again, she was different: this time, her hair hung straight down and seemed hardly to have been combed. She hadn't brought her lunchbox with her, but she was carrying what seemed to be a small box. She greeted all of us and talked about the weather. Donna DeShano had to remind her to take her overcoat off.

When the bell to start the day finally rang, Miss Ferenczi looked out [116] at all of us and said, "Children, I have enjoyed your company in the past, and today I am going to reward you." She held up the small box. "Do you know what this is?" She waited. "Of course you don't. It is a tarot pack."

Edith Atwater raised her hand. "What's a tarot pack, Miss Fer- [117] enczi?"

"It is used to tell fortunes," she said. "And that is what I shall do this [118] morning. I shall tell your fortunes, as I have been taught to do."

"What's fortune?" Bobby Kryzanowicz asked. [119]

"The future, young man. I shall tell you what your future will be. I [120] can't do your whole future, of course. I shall have to limit myself to the five-card system, the wands, cups, swords, pentacles, and the higher arcanes. Now who wants to be first?"

There was a long silence. Then Carol Peterson raised her hand.   [121]

"All right," Miss Ferenczi said. She divided the pack into five small- [122] er packs and walked back to Carol's desk, in front of mine. "Pick one card from each of these packs," she said. I saw that Carol had a four of cups, a six of swords, but I couldn't see the other cards. Miss Ferenczi studied the cards on Carol's desk for a minute. "Not bad," she said. "I do not see much higher education. Probably an early marriage. Many children. There's something bleak and dreary here, but I can't tell what. Perhaps just the tasks of a housewife life. I think you'll do very well, for the most part." She smiled at Carol, a smile with a certain lack of interest. "Who wants to be next?"

Carl Whiteside raised his hand slowly.   [123]

"Yes," Miss Ferenczi said, "let's do a boy." She walked over to [124] where Carl sat. After he picked his five cards, she gazed at them for a long time. "Travel," she said. "Much distant travel. You might go into the Army. Not too much romantic interest here. A late marriage, if at all. Squabbles. But the Sun is in your major arcana, here, yes, that's a very good card." She giggled. "Maybe a good life."

Next I raised my hand, and she told me my future. She did the same [125] with Bobby Kryzanowicz. Kelly Munger, Edith Atwater, and Kim Foor. Then she came to Wayne Razmer. He picked his five cards, and I could see that the Death card was one of them.

"What's your name?" Miss Ferenczi asked.   [126]

"Wayne."   [127]

"Well, Wayne," she said, you will undergo a *great* metamorphosis, [128] the greatest, before you become an adult. Your earthly element will leap away, into thin air, you sweet boy. This card, this nine of swords here, tells of suffering and desolation. And this ten of wands, well, that's certainly a heavy load."

"What about this one?" Wayne pointed to the Death card.   [129]

"That one? That one means you will die soon, my dear." She gath- [130] ered up the cards. We were all looking at Wayne. "But do not fear," she said. "It's not really death, so much as change." She put the cards on Mr. Hibler's desk. "And now, let's do some arithmetic."

At lunchtime Wayne went to Mr. Faegre, the principal, and told [131] him what Miss Ferenczi had done. During the noon recess, we saw Miss Ferenczi drive out of the parking lot in her green Rambler. I stood under the slide, listening to the other kids coasting down and landing in the little depressive bowl at the bottom. I was kicking stones and tugging at my hair right up to the moment when I saw Wayne come out to the playground. He smiled, the dead fool, and with the fingers of his right hand he was showing everyone how he had told on Miss Ferenczi.

I made my way toward Wayne, pushing myself past two girls from another class. He was watching me with his little pinhead eyes. [132]

"You told," I shouted at him. "She was just kidding." [133]

"She shouldn't have," he shouted back. "We were supposed to be doing arithmetic." [134]

"She just scared you," I said. "You're a chicken. You're a chicken, Wayne. You are. Scared of a little card," I singsonged. [135]

Wayne fell at me, his two fists hammering down on my nose. I gave him a good one in the stomach and then I tried for his head. Aiming my fist, I saw that he was crying. I slugged him. [136]

"She was right," I yelled. "She was always right! She told the truth!" Other kids were whooping. "You were just scared, that's all!" [137]

And then large hands pulled at us, and it was my turn to speak to Mr. Faegre. [138]

In the afternoon Miss Ferenczi was gone, and my nose was stuffed with cotton clotted with blood, and my lip had swelled, and our class had been combined with Mrs. Mantei's sixth-grade class for a crowded afternoon science unit on insect life in ditches and swamps. I knew where Mrs. Mantei lived: she had a new house trailer just down the road from us, at the Clearwater Park. She was no mystery. Somehow she and Mr. Bodine, the other fourth-grade teacher, had managed to fit forty-five desks into the room. Kelly Munger asked if Miss Ferenczi had been arrested, and Mrs. Mantei said no, of course not. All that afternoon, until the buses came to pick us up, we learned about field crickets and two-striped grasshoppers, water bugs, cicadas, mosquitoes, flies, and moths. We learned about insects' hard outer shell, the exoskeleton, and the usual parts of the mouth, including the labrum, mandible, maxilla, and glossa. We learned about compound eyes and the four-stage metamorphosis from egg to larva to pupa to adult. We learned something, but not much, about mating. Mrs. Mantei drew, very skillfully, the internal anatomy of the grasshopper on the blackboard. We learned about the dance of the honeybee, directing other bees in the hive to pollen. We found out about which insects were pests to man, and which were not. On lined white pieces of paper we made lists of insects we might actually see, then a list of insects too small to be clearly visible, such as fleas; Mrs. Mantei said that our assignment would be to memorize these lists for the next day, when Mr. Hibler would certainly return and test us on our knowledge. [139]

Responding to Reading

1. What connotations does the phrase *substitute teacher* have to you? In what ways is Miss Ferenczi like and unlike your idea of a substitute teacher?
2. As the story goes on, Miss Ferenczi's remarks become increasingly unorthodox. Is she eccentric or unstable, or do you think that her comments are not random but calculated to provoke a particular response?
3. Have you ever had a teacher who undercut and challenged your ideas? How did you react to this challenge? Do you think teachers like Miss Ferenczi are necessary or dangerous to education?

--- **Writing** ---

Issues in Education

1. Both Lynda Barry and Maya Angelou describe personal experiences related to their education. Write an essay in which you describe a positive or negative experience you had with your education. Be specific, and make sure you include plenty of specific details.

2. Stephen L. Carter suggests that people should care less about how a person got into a school and more about what he or she learned there. Write an essay in which you evaluate this idea. Would your response be the same regardless of a person's profession? For example, would it matter if the person was a teacher? A lawyer? A political candidate?

3. One question that is never resolved in Charles Baxter's "Gryphon" is whether Miss Ferenczi is a good or bad teacher. Imagine you are the principal of the school in which Miss Ferenczi taught. Write an evaluation of her performance. As an alternative, you might write an evaluation from the point of view of a student.

4. Both Maya Angelou in "Graduation" and Jonathan Kozol in "Savage Inequalities" look at ways race affects the educational experience. In what ways do your high school and college experiences support or contradict their views?

5. Write a letter to your college newspaper in which you discuss the steps that should be taken to make an education at your college or university a more positive and meaningful experience.

6. Write an essay in which you describe a teacher who had a significant effect (positive or negative) on you. In what ways was this teacher like and unlike the teachers mentioned in the selections by Lynda Barry, Jonathan Kozol, and Charles Baxter?

7. Both Mark Twain in "Reading the River" and Walt Whitman in "When I Heard the Learn'd Astronomer" seem to value innocence. Miss Ferenczi in "Gryphon," however, goes to great lengths to challenge her students' innocent views. Write an essay in which you compare either Twain's or Whitman's ideas about education with Miss Ferenczi's. Be sure you use specific examples from each work to support your ideas.

8. In his essay "In Defense of Elitism," William A. Henry III argues that too many unqualified students go to college. To remedy this solution, he proposes limiting the number of high school students who are allowed to attend college. Referring to "Savage Inequalities" by

Jonathan Kozol and Stephen L. Carter's "Racial Preferences? So What?" argue for or against Henry's proposal.

9. Write an essay in which you consider which elements of formal and informal education are most valuable. Base your essay on your own experiences as well as on the readings in this chapter.

10. In his essay "The Visigoths in Tweed," Dinesh D'Souza argues that at many U.S. colleges and universities anti-Western viewpoints are being forced on students. According to Huntly Collins in "PC and Press" (p.308), however, the popular press has exaggerated the influence of political correctness on American campuses. After reading both essays, write an essay in which you support either D'Souza's or Collins's position. (If you wish, you may take a position that falls between the two.) Whatever the case, be specific and support your points with references to both essays and to your own experience as a college student.

3

THE POLITICS OF LANGUAGE

Student Voices

"I think a person learns language at home and at school. If a person is well educated and comes from a family that speaks well, then that person will speak well too. If the person comes from a bad school or from a family in which the language is not spoken well, then that person will have trouble. My parents come from Vietnam and do not speak English well. . . . All through school I have had difficulty speaking and writing correct English."

—*Din Ngoc Dang*

"I basically speak in slang. I enjoy being different, and language is one way to separate myself from others. I regularly use words like *chill, sweet, right on,* and *excellent.* People know who's talking when they hear these words. The language I use not only catches their attention, but it also makes it easier for me to express myself. To me, language is just one of many ways to set myself apart."

—*Todd Snellenburg*

"Words can be sexist or racist. I personally am offended when I hear a male refer to women as *chicks* or *babes.* We are not just *chicks* or *babes.* We are *women* or *females.* Racist remarks also offend me. I once heard a young child, a fourth grader, shout a racist term out of a school bus window at an old man working in his garden.

"There is no way to stop sexist or racist remarks. To do so, we would have to limit free speech, and this would be a violation of our constitutional rights. I suppose this means that we must all put up with offensive terms so we can preserve our right to express ourselves freely."

—*Megan Seely*

"When I first heard the question, "Should any limits be placed on free speech?" I thought the sky was falling down. How could anyone question the great American dream of freedom of speech? Later, however, I saw neofascists on television preaching racism, hate, and the superiority of a 'higher race'. Is this what freedom of speech means? I don't think that remarks such as these should be allowed on television. Maybe there should be some limitations on what people can say. Maybe American society has entered a stage where limiting hate speech could help protect human rights."

—*Gennadiy Levit*

─────────────── **Preparing to Read and Write** ───────────────

During the years he spent in prison, political activist Malcolm X became increasingly frustrated by his inability to express himself in writing, so he began the tedious and often frustrating task of copying words from the dictionary—page by page. The eventual result was that for the first time he could pick up a book and read it with understanding. "Anyone who has read a great deal," he says, "can imagine the new world that opened." In addition, by becoming a serious reader, Malcolm X was able to develop the ideas about politics and economics that he would present so forcefully after he was released from prison.

In our society, language is constantly manipulated for political ends. This fact should come as no surprise if we consider the potential power of words. Often the power of a word comes not from its dictionary definitions or *denotations* but from its *connotations*, the associations that surround it. Often these connotations are subtle, giving language the power to confuse and even to harm. For example, whether a doctor who performs an abortion is "terminating a pregnancy" or "murdering a preborn child" is not just a matter of intellectual interest but a political issue, one that has provoked not only debate, but also violence. This potential for danger makes careful word choice all the more important.

As you read and prepare to write about the selections in this chapter, you may consider the following questions.

- Does the selection deal primarily with written or spoken language?
- Does the writer place more emphasis on the denotations or the connotations of words?
- Does the writer make any distinctions between language as it is applied to males and to females? Do you consider such distinctions valid?
- Does the writer discuss language in the context of a particular culture? Does he or she see language as a unifying or a divisive factor?
- In what ways would the writer like to change or reshape language? What do you see as the possible advantages or disadvantages of these changes?
- Does the writer believe that people are shaped by language or that language is shaped by people?
- Does the writer see language as having a particular social or political function? In what sense?

- Does the writer make assumptions about the status of individuals on the basis of their use of language? Do these assumptions seem justified?
- Does the writer make a convincing case for the importance of language?
- In what ways are your ideas about the power of words similar to or different from the writer's?

TWO PERSPECTIVES ON THE POLITICS OF LANGUAGE

In the following two essays, Richard Rodriguez and Barbara Mellix both consider the differences between "public" and "private" languages. Rodriguez, who grew up in San Francisco the son of Mexican-American immigrants and holds a graduate degree from Stanford University in Renaissance literature, has written extensively about Hispanic-American culture. An opponent of bilingual education, he uses his own experiences as a child to argue in "Aria" that immigrant children must become proficient in the "public" language of English if they are to achieve full individuality in U.S. society; this 1981 essay later appeared in his collection *Hunger of Memory: The Education of Richard Rodriguez* (1982). In "From Outside, In" South Carolina-born Mellix, an academic who holds a master's degree in creative writing, describes the conflicts raised in her childhood between the black English she spoke within her family and the standard English she was expected to master to communicate with the "others"; her essay originally appeared in *The Georgia Review* in 1987.

ARIA[1]

Richard Rodriguez

Supporters of bilingual education today imply that students like me [1] miss a great deal by not being taught in their family's language. What they seem not to recognize is that, as a socially disadvantaged child, I considered Spanish to be a private language. What I needed to learn in school was that I had the right—and the obligation—to speak the public language of *los gringos*.[2] The odd truth is that my first-grade classmates could have become bilingual, in the conventional sense of that word, more easily than I. Had they been taught (as upper-middle-class children are often taught early) a second language like Spanish or French, they could have regarded it simply as that: another public language. In my case such bilingualism could not have been so quickly achieved. What I did not believe was that I could speak a single public language.

---

[1] Solo vocal piece with instrumental accompaniment or melody. [Eds.]

[2] Foreigners, especially Americans. [Eds.]

Without question, it would have pleased me to hear my teachers address me in Spanish when I entered the classroom. I would have felt much less afraid. I would have trusted them and responded with ease. But I would have delayed—for how long postponed?—having to learn the language of public society, I would have evaded—and for how long could I have afforded to delay?—learning the great lesson of school, that I had a public identity. 2

Fortunately, my teachers were unsentimental about their responsibility. What they understood was that I needed to speak a public language. So their voices would search me out, asking me questions. Each time I'd hear them, I'd look up in surprise to see a nun's face frowning at me. I'd mumble, not really meaning to answer. The nun would persist, "Richard, stand up. Don't look at the floor. Speak up. Speak to the entire class, not just to me!" But I couldn't believe that the English language was mine to use. (In part, I did not want to believe it.) I continued to mumble. I resisted the teacher's demands. (Did I somehow suspect that once I learned public language my pleasing family life would be changed?) Silent, waiting for the bell to sound, I remained dazed, diffident, afraid. 3

Because I wrongly imagined that English was intrinsically a public language and Spanish an intrinsically private one, I easily noted the difference between classroom language and the language of home. At school, words were directed to a general audience of listeners. ("Boys and girls.") Words were meaningfully ordered. And the point was not self-expression alone but to make oneself understood by many others. The teacher quizzed: "Boys and girls, why do we use that word in this sentence? Could we think of a better word to use there? Would the sentence change its meaning if the words were differently arranged? And wasn't there a better way of saying much the same thing?" (I couldn't say. I wouldn't try to say.) 4

Three months. Five. Half a year passed. Unsmiling, ever watchful, my teachers noted my silence. They began to connect my behavior with the difficult progress my older sister and brother were making. Until one Saturday morning three nuns arrived at the house to talk to our parents. Stiffly, they sat on the blue living room sofa. From the doorway of another room, spying the visitors, I noted the incongruity—the clash of two worlds, the faces and voices of school intruding upon the familiar setting of home. I overheard one voice gently wondering, "Do your children speak only Spanish at home, Mrs. Rodriguez?" While another voice added, "That Richard especially seems so timid and shy." 5

That Rich-heard! 6

With great tact the visitors continued, "Is it possible for you and your husband to encourage your children to practice their English when they are home?" Of course, my parents complied. What would they not do for their children's well-being? And how could they have questioned 7 the Church's authority which those women represented? In an instant, they agreed to give up the language (the sounds) that had revealed and accentuated our family's closeness. The moment after the visitors left, the change was observed, "*Ahora*, speak to us *en inglés*,[3] my father and mother united to tell us.

At first, it seemed a kind of game. After dinner each night, the fam- 8
ily gathered to practice "our" English. (It was still then *inglés*, a language foreign to us, so we felt drawn as strangers to it.) Laughing, we would try to define words we could not pronounce. We played with strange English sounds, often overanglicizing our pronunciations. And we filled the smiling gaps of our sentences with familiar Spanish sounds. But that was cheating, somebody shouted. Everyone laughed. In school, mean-while, like my brother and sister, I was required to attend a daily tutor-ing session. I needed a full year of special attention. I also needed my teachers to keep my attention from straying in class by calling out, *Rich-heard*—their English voices slowly prying loose my ties to my other name, its three notes, *Ri-car-do*. Most of all I needed to hear my mother and father speak to me in a moment of seriousness in broken—sudden-ly heartbreaking—English. The scene was inevitable: One Saturday morning I entered the kitchen where my parents were talking in Span-ish. I did not realize that they were talking in Spanish however until, at the moment they saw me, I heard their voices change to speak English. Those *gringo* sounds they uttered startled me. Pushed me away. In that moment of trivial misunderstanding and profound insight, I felt my throat twisted by unsounded grief. I turned quickly and left the room. But I had no place to escape to with Spanish. (The spell was broken.) My brother and sisters were speaking English in another part of the house.

Again and again in the days following, increasingly angry, I was 9
obliged to hear my mother and father: "Speak to us *en inglés*" (*Speak.*) Only then did I determine to learn classroom English. Weeks after, it happened: One day in school I raised my hand to volunteer an answer. I spoke out in a loud voice. And I did not think it remarkable when the entire class understood. That day, I moved very far from the disadvan-taged child I had been only days earlier. The belief, that calming assur-ance that I belonged in public, had at last taken hold.

Shortly after, I stopped hearing the high and loud sounds of *los grin-* 10
gos. A more and more confident speaker of English, I didn't trouble to listen to *how* strangers sounded, speaking to me. And there simply were too many English-speaking people in my day for me to hear American accents anymore. Conversations quickened. Listening to persons who sounded eccentrically pitched voices, I usually noted their sounds for an initial few seconds before I concentrated on *what* they were saying. Con-versations became content-full. Transparent. Hearing someone's *tone* of

---

[3] "Now, speak to us in English." [Eds.]

voice—angry or questioning or sarcastic or happy or sad—I didn't distinguish it from the words it expressed. Sound and word were thus tightly wedded. At the end of a day, I was often bemused, always relieved, to realize how "silent," though crowded with words, my day in public had been. (This public silence measured and quickened the change in my life.)

At last, seven years old, I came to believe what had been technically true since my birth: I was an American citizen.   11

But the special feeling of closeness at home was diminished by then.   12
Gone was the desperate, urgent, intense feeling of being at home, rare was the experience of feeling myself individualized by family intimates. We remained a loving family, but one greatly changed. No longer so close; no longer bound tight by the pleasing and troubling knowledge of our public separateness. Neither my older brother nor sister rushed home after school anymore. Nor did I. When I arrived home there would often be neighborhood kids in the house. Or the house would be empty of sounds.

Following the dramatic Americanization of their children, even my   13
parents grew more publicly confident. Especially my mother. She learned the names of all the people on our block. And she decided we needed to have a telephone installed in the house. My father continued to use the word *gringo*. But it was no longer charged with the old bitterness or distrust. (Stripped of any emotional content, the word simply became a name for those Americans not of Hispanic descent.) Hearing him, sometimes, I wasn't sure if he was pronouncing the Spanish word *gringo* or saying gringo in English.

Matching the silence I started hearing in public was a new quiet at   14
home. The family's quiet was partly due to the fact that, as we children learned more and more English, we shared fewer and fewer words with our parents. Sentences needed to be spoken slowly when a child addressed his mother or father. (Often the parent wouldn't understand.) The child would need to repeat himself. (Still the parent misunderstood.) The young voice, frustrated, would end up saying, "Never mind"—the subject was closed. Dinners would be noisy with the clinking of knives and forks against dishes. My mother would smile softly between her remarks; my father at the other end of the table would chew and chew at his food, while he stared over the heads of his children.

My *mother!* My *father!* After English became my primary language,   15
I no longer knew what words to use in addressing my parents. The old Spanish words (those tender accents of sound) I had used earlier—*mamá* and *papá*—I couldn't use anymore. They would have been too painful reminders of how much had changed in my life. On the other hand, the words I heard neighborhood kids call their parents seemed equally unsatisfactory. *Mother* and *Father; Ma, Papa, Pa, Dad, Pop* (how I hated the all American sound of that last word especially)—all these terms I felt

were unsuitable, not really terms of address for my parents. As a result, I never used them at home. Whenever I'd speak to my parents, I would try to get their attention with eye contact alone. In public conversations, I'd refer to "my parents" or "my mother and father."

My mother and father, for their part, responded differently, as their [16] children spoke to them less. She grew restless, seemed troubled and anxious at the scarcity of words exchanged in the house. It was she who would question me about my day when I came home from school. She smiled at small talk. She pried at the edges of my sentences to get me to say something more. (What?) She'd join conversations she overheard, but her intrusions often stopped her children's talking. By contrast, my father seemed reconciled to the new quiet. Though his English improved somewhat, he retired into silence. At dinner he spoke very little. One night his children and even his wife helplessly giggled at his garbled English pronunciation of the Catholic Grace before Meals. Thereafter he made his wife recite the prayer at the start of each meal, even on formal occasions, when there were guests in the house. Hers became the public voice of the family. On official business, it was she, not my father, one would usually hear on the phone or in stores, talking to strangers. His children grew so accustomed to his silence that, years later, they would speak routinely of his shyness. (My mother would often try to explain: Both his parents died when he was eight. He was raised by an uncle who treated him like little more than a menial servant. He was never encouraged to speak. He grew up alone. A man of few words.) But my father was not shy, I realized, when I'd watch him speaking Spanish with relatives. Using Spanish, he was quickly effusive. Especially when talking with other men, his voice would spark, flicker, flare alive with sounds. In Spanish, he expressed ideas and feelings he rarely revealed in English. With firm Spanish sounds, he conveyed confidence and authority English would never allow him.

The silence at home, however, was finally more than a literal silence. [17] Fewer words passed between parent and child, but more profound was the silence that resulted from my inattention to sounds. At about the time I no longer bothered to listen with care to the sounds of English in public, I grew careless about listening to the sounds family members made when they spoke. Most of the time I heard someone speaking at home and didn't distinguish his sounds from the words people uttered in public. I didn't even pay much attention to my parents' accented and ungrammatical speech. At least not at home. Only when I was with them in public would I grow alert to their accents. Though, even then, their sounds caused me less and less concern. For I was increasingly confident of my own public identity.

I would have been happier about my public success had I not some- [18] times recalled what it had been like earlier, when my family had conveyed its intimacy through a set of conveniently private sounds. Sometimes in public, hearing a stranger, I'd hark back to my past. A Mexican farmworker approached me downtown to ask directions to somewhere, "*¿Hijito . . .?*"[4] he said. And his voice summoned deep longing. Another time, standing beside my mother in the visiting room of a Carmelite convent, before the dense screen which rendered the nuns shadowy figures, I heard several Spanish-speaking nuns—their busy, singsong overlapping voices—assure us that yes, yes, we were remembered, all our family was remembered in their prayers. (Their voices echoed faraway family sounds.) Another day, a dark-faced old woman—her hand light on my shoulder—steadied herself against me as she boarded a bus. She murmured something I couldn't quite comprehend. Her Spanish voice came near, like the face of a never-before-seen relative in the instant before I was kissed. Her voice, like so many of the Spanish voices I'd hear in public, recalled the golden age of my youth. Hearing Spanish then, I continued to be a careful, if sad, listener to sounds. Hearing a Spanish-speaking family walking behind me, I turned to look. I smiled for an instant, before my glance found the Hispanic-looking faces of strangers in the crowd going by.

Today I hear bilingual educators say that children lose a degree of [19] "individuality" by becoming assimilated into public society. (Bilingual schooling was popularized in the seventies, that decade when middle-class ethnics began to resist the process of assimilation—the American melting pot). But the bilingualists simplistically scorn the value and necessity of assimilation. They do not seem to realize that there are *two* ways a person is individualized. So they do not realize that while one suffers a diminished sense of *private* individuality by becoming assimilated into public society, such assimilation makes possible the achievement of *public* individuality.

The bilingualists insist that a student should be reminded of his [20] difference from others in mass society, his heritage. But they equate mere separateness with individuality. The fact is that only in private—with intimates—is separateness from the crowd a prerequisite for individuality. (An intimate draws me apart, tells me that I am unique, unlike all others.) In public, by contrast, full individuality is achieved, paradoxically, by those who are able to consider themselves members of the crowd. Thus it happened for me: Only when I was able to think of myself as an American, no longer an alien in *gringo* society, could I seek the rights and opportunities necessary for full public individuality. The social and political advantages I enjoy as a man result from the day that I came to believe that my name, indeed, is *Rich-heard Road-ree-guess*. It is true that my public society today is often impersonal. (My public society is usually mass society). Yet despite the anonymity of

---

[4] "Little boy. . . .?" [Eds.]

the crowd and despite the fact that the individuality I achieve in public is often tenuous—because it depends on my being one in a crowd—I celebrate the day I acquired my new name. Those middle-class ethnics who scorn assimilation seem to me filled with decadent self-pity, obsessed by the burden of public life. Dangerously, they romanticize public separateness and they trivialize the dilemma of the socially disadvantaged.

My awkward childhood does not prove the necessity of bilingual [21] education. My story discloses instead an essential myth of childhood—inevitable pain. If I rehearse here the changes in my private life after my Americanization, it is finally to emphasize the public gain. The loss implies the gain: The house I returned to each afternoon was quiet. Intimate sounds no longer rushed to the door to greet me. There were other noises inside. The telephone rang. Neighborhood kids ran past the door of the bedroom where I was reading my school-books—covered with shopping-bag paper. Once I learned public language, it would never again be easy for me to hear intimate family voices. More and more of my day was spent hearing words. But that may only be a way of saying that the day I raised my hand in class and spoke loudly to an entire roomful of faces, my childhood started to end.

FROM OUTSIDE, IN

Barbara Mellix

Two years ago, when I started writing this paper, trying to bring [1] order out of chaos, my ten-year-old daughter was suffering from an acute attack of boredom. She drifted in and out of the room complaining that she had nothing to do, no one to "be with" because none of her friends were at home. Patiently I explained that I was working on something special and needed peace and quiet, and I suggested that she paint, read, or work with her computer. None of these interested her. Finally, she pulled up a chair to my desk and watched me, now and then heaving long, loud sighs. After two or three minutes (nine or ten sighs), I lost my patience. "Looka here, Allie," I said, "you too old for this kinda carryin' on. I done told you this is important. You wronger than dirt to be in here haggin' me like this and you know it. Now git on outta here and leave me off before I put my foot all the way down."

I was at home, alone with my family, and my daughter understood [2] that this way of speaking was appropriate in that context. She knew, as a matter of fact, that it was almost inevitable; when I get angry at home, I speak some of my finest, most cherished black English. Had I been speaking to my daughter in this manner in certain other environments, she would have been shocked and probably worried that I had taken leave of my sense of propriety.

Like my children, I grew up speaking what I considered two distinctly different languages—black English and standard English (or as I thought of them then, the ordinary everyday speech of "country" coloreds and "proper" English)—and in the process of acquiring these languages, I developed an understanding of when, where, and how to use them. But unlike my children, I grew up in a world that was primarily black. My friends, neighbors, minister, teachers—almost everybody I associated with every day—were black. And we spoke to one another in our own special language: *That sho is a pretty dress you got on. If she don' soon leave me off I'm gon tell her head a mess. I was so mad I could'a pissed a blue nail. He all the time trying to low-rate somebody. Ain't that just about the nastiest thing you ever set ears on?*

Then there were the "others," the "proper" blacks, transplanted relatives and one-time friends who came home from the city for weddings, funerals, and vacations. And the whites. To these we spoke standard English. "Ain't?" my mother would yell at me when I used the term in the presence of "others." "You *know* better than that." And I would hang my head in shame and say the "proper" word.

I remember one summer sitting in my grandmother's house in Greeleyville, South Carolina, when it was full of the chatter of city relatives who were home on vacation. My parents sat quietly, only now and then volunteering a comment or answering a question. My mother's face took on a strained expression when she spoke. I could see that she was being careful to say just the right words in just the right way. Her voice sounded thick, muffled. And when she finished speaking, she would lapse into silence, her proper smile on her face. My father was more articulate, more aggressive. He spoke quickly, his words sharp and clear. But he held his proud head higher, a signal that he, too, was uncomfortable. My sisters and brothers and I stared at our aunts, uncles, and cousins, speaking only when prompted. Even then, we hesitated, formed our sentences in our minds, then spoke softly, shyly.

My parents looked small and anxious during those occasions, and I waited impatiently for our leave-taking when we would mock our relatives the moment we were out of their hearing. "Reeely," we would say to one another, flexing our wrists and rolling our eyes, "how dooo you stan' this heat? Chile, it just too hy*ooo*-mid for words." Our relatives had made us feel "country," and this was our way of regaining pride in ourselves while getting a little revenge in the bargain. The words bubbled in our throats and rolled across our tongues, a balming.

As a child I felt this same doubleness in uptown Greeleyville where the whites lived. "Ain't that a pretty dress you're wearing!" Toby, the town policeman, said to me one day when I was fifteen. "Thank you very much," I replied, my voice barely audible in my own ears. The words felt wrong in my mouth, rigid, foreign. It was not that I had never spoken that phrase before—it was common in black English, too—but I was extremely conscious that this was an occasion for proper English. I had taken out my English and put it on as I did my church clothes, and I felt as if I were wearing my Sunday best in the middle of the week. It did not matter that Toby had not spoken grammatically correct English. He was white and could speak as he wished. I had something to prove. Toby did not.

Speaking standard English to whites was our way of demonstrating   8
that we knew their language and could use it. Speaking it to standard-English-speaking blacks was our way of showing them that we, as well as they, could "put on airs." But when we spoke standard English, we acknowledged (to ourselves and to others—but primarily to ourselves) that our customary way of speaking was inferior. We felt foolish, embarrassed, somehow diminished because we were ashamed to be our real selves. We were reserved, shy in the presence of those who owned and/or spoke *the* language.

My parents never set aside time to drill us in standard English. Their   9
forms of instruction were less formal. When my father was feeling particularly expansive, he would regale us with tales of his exploits in the outside world. In almost flawless English, complete with dialogue and flavored with gestures and embellishment, he told us about his attempt to get a haircut at a white barbershop; his refusal to acknowledge one of the town merchants until the man addressed him as "Mister"; the time he refused to step off the sidewalk uptown to let some whites pass; his airplane trip to New York City (to visit a sick relative) during which the stewardesses and porters—recognizing that he was a "gentleman"—addressed him as "Sir." I did not realize then—nor, I think, did my father— that he was teaching us, among other things, standard English and the relationship between language and power.

My mother's approach was different. Often, when one of us said,   10
"I'm gon wash off my feet," she would say, "And what will you walk on if you wash them off?" Everyone would laugh at the victim of my mother's "proper" mood. But it was different when one of us children was in a proper mood. "You think you are so superior," I said to my oldest sister one day when we were arguing and she was winning. "Superior!" my sister mocked. "You mean I am acting 'biggidy'?" My sisters and brothers sniggered, then joined in teasing me. Finally, my mother said, "Leave your sister alone. There's nothing wrong with using proper English." There was a half-smile on her face. I had gotten "up-pity," had "put on airs" for no good reason. I was at home, alone with the family, and I hadn't been prompted by one of my mother's proper moods. But there was also a proud light in my mother's eyes; her children were learning English very well.

Not until years later, as a college student, did I begin to understand [11] our ambivalence toward English, our scorn of it, our need to master it, to own and be owned by it—an ambivalence that extended to the public-school classroom. In our school, where there were no whites, my teachers taught standard English but used black English to do it. When my grammar-school teachers wanted us to write, for example, they usually said something like, "I want y'all to write five sentences that make a statement. Anybody git done before the rest can color." It was probably almost those exact words that led me to write these sentences in 1953 when I was in the second grade:

The white clouds are pretty.

There are only 15 people in our room.

We will go to gym.

We have a new poster.

We may go out doors.

Second grade came after "Little First" and "Big First," so by then I [12] knew the implied rules that accompanied all writing assignments. Writing was an occasion for proper English. I was not to write in the way we spoke to one another: The white clouds pretty; There ain't but 15 people in our room; We going to gym. We got a new poster; We can go out in the yard. Rather I was to use the language of "other": clouds *are, there are, we will, we have, we may.*

My sentences were short, rigid, perfunctory, like the letters my [13] mother wrote to relatives:

Dear Papa,
How are you? How is Mattie? Fine I hope. We are fine. We will come
to see you Sunday. Cousin Ned will give us a ride.

Love,
Daughter

The language was not ours. It was something from outside us, something we used for special occasions.

But my coloring on the other side of that second-grade paper is dif- [14] ferent. I drew three hearts and a sun. The sun has a smiling face that radiates and envelops everything it touches. And although the sun and its world are enclosed in a circle, the colors I used—red, blue, green, purple, orange, yellow, black—indicate that I was less restricted with drawing and coloring than I was with writing standard English. My valentines were not just red. My sun was not just a yellow ball in the sky.

By the time I reached the twelfth grade, speaking and writing stan- [15] dard English had taken on new importance. Each year, about half of the newly graduated seniors of our school moved to large cities—particularly in the North—to live with relatives and find work. Our English teacher constantly corrected our grammar: "Not 'ain't,' but 'isn't.'" We seldom wrote papers, and even those few were usually plot summaries of short stories. When our teacher returned the papers, she usually lectured on the importance of using standard English: "I *am;* you *are;* he, she, or it *is,*" she would say, writing on the chalkboard as she spoke. "How you gon git a job talking about 'I is,' or 'I isn't' or 'I ain't?'"

In Pittsburgh, where I moved after graduation, I watched my aunt 16 and uncle—who had always spoken standard English when in Greeleyville—switch from black English to standard English to a mixture of the two, according to where they were or who they were with. At home and with certain close relatives, friends, and neighbors, they spoke black English. With those less close, they spoke a mixture. In public and with strangers, they generally spoke standard English.

In time, I learned to speak standard English with ease and to switch 17 smoothly from black to standard or a mixture, and back again. But no matter where I was, no matter what the situation or occasion, I continued to write as I had in school:

> Dear Mommie,
> How are you? How is everybody else? Fine I hope. I am fine. So are Aunt and Uncle. Tell everyone I said hello. I will write again soon.
>
> > Love,
> > Barbara

Responding to Reading

1. Rodriguez has been criticized by those who favor teaching Spanish-speaking children in both Spanish and English. Do you agree with Rodriguez's contention that Spanish-speaking children should be taught only in English? Explain your position.
2. In what sense is Mellix's essay as much about class and race as it is about language?
3. Both Rodriguez and Mellix feel ambivalent about speaking standard English. With what do they associate standard English? With what do they associate Spanish and black English, respectively? Are these associations reasonable?
4. What preconceptions do Rodriguez and Mellix have about people who speak standard English? Do you agree with these assumptions?
5. What do you think Rodriguez and Mellix lose by adopting standard English as their primary language? What do you think they gain?
6. Do you, like Mellix and Rodriguez, speak one way at home and with close friends and another way at school and in "public" generally? Does your private language cause you to feel ambivalent about speaking standard English?

LEARNING TO READ AND WRITE

Frederick Douglass

Frederick Douglass (1818–1895)—editor, author, lecturer, U.S. minister
to Haiti—was born a slave in agricultural Maryland and later served a
family in Baltimore. In the city, he had opportunities for personal improvement—and the luck to escape to the North in 1838. He settled in
New Bedford, Massachusetts, where he became active in the abolitionist movement. In 1845 Douglass wrote his most famous work, *Narrative of the Life of Frederick Douglass.* Like other such narratives, exten-
sions of the storytelling oratory and drama of former slaves in the
abolitionist movement, it was distributed to a large and diverse audience. In the following excerpt from his *Narrative,* Douglass writes of
outwitting his owners to become literate and find "the pathway from
slavery to freedom."

I lived in Master Hugh's family about seven years. During this time,   1
I succeeded in learning to read and write. In accomplishing this, I was
compelled to resort to various stratagems. I had no regular teacher. My
mistress, who had kindly commenced to instruct me, had, in compliance
with the advice and direction of her husband, not only ceased to instruct, but had set her face against my being instructed by any one else.
It is due, however, to my mistress to say of her, that she did not adopt
this course of treatment immediately. She at first lacked the depravity indispensable to shutting me up in mental darkness. It was at least necessary for her to have some training in the exercise of irresponsible power,
to make her equal to the task of treating me as though I were a brute.

My mistress was, as I have said, a kind and tender-hearted woman;   2
and in the simplicity of her soul she commenced, when I first went to
live with her, to treat me as she supposed one human being ought to
treat another. In entering upon the duties of a slaveholder, she did not
seem to perceive that I sustained to her the relation of a mere chattel,[1]
and that for her to treat me as a human being was not only wrong, but
dangerously so. Slavery proved as injurious to her as it did to me. When
I went there, she was a pious, warm, and tender-hearted woman. There
was no sorrow or suffering for which she had not a tear. She had bread
for the hungry, clothes for the naked, and comfort for every mourner
that came within her reach. Slavery soon proved its ability to divest her
of these heavenly qualities. Under its influence, the tender heart became
stone, and the lamblike disposition gave way to one of tigerlike fierceness. The first step in her downward course was in her ceasing to in-

---

[1] Property. [Eds.]

struct me. She now commenced to practise her husband's precepts. She finally became even more violent in her opposition than her husband himself. She was not satisfied with simply doing as well as he had commanded; she seemed anxious to do better. Nothing seemed to make her more angry than to see me with a newspaper. She seemed to think that here lay the danger. I have had her rush at me with a face made all up of fury, and snatch from me a newspaper, in a manner that fully revealed her apprehension. She was an apt woman; and a little experience soon demonstrated, to her satisfaction, that education and slavery were incompatible with each other.

From this time I was most narrowly watched. If I was in a separate 3 room any considerable length of time, I was sure to be suspected of having a book, and was at once called to give an account of myself. All this, however, was too late. The first step had been taken. Mistress, in teaching me the alphabet, had given me the *inch,* and no precaution could prevent me from taking the *ell.*

The plan which I adopted, and the one by which I was most suc- 4 cessful, was that of making friends of all the little white boys whom I met in the street. As many of these as I could, I converted into teachers. With their kindly aid, obtained at different times and in different places, I finally succeeded in learning to read. When I was sent on errands, I always took my book with me, and by going one part of my errand quickly, I found time to get a lesson before my return. I used also to carry bread with me, enough of which was always in the house, and to which I was always welcome; for I was much better off in this regard than many of the poor white children in our neighborhood. This bread I used to bestow upon the hungry little urchins, who, in return, would give me that more valuable bread of knowledge. I am strongly tempted to give the names of two or three of those little boys, as a testimonial of the gratitude and affection I bear them; but prudence forbids;—not that it would injure me, but it might embarrass them; for it is almost an unpardonable offence to teach slaves to read in this Christian country. It is enough to say of the dear little fellows, that they lived on Philpot Street, very near Durgin and Bailey's ship-yard. I used to talk this matter of slavery over with them. I would sometimes say to them, I wished I could be as free as they would be when they got to be men. "You will be free as soon as you are twenty-one, *but I am a slave for life!* Have not I as good a right to be free as you have?" These words used to trouble them; they would express for me the liveliest sympathy, and console me with the hope that something would occur by which I might be free.

I was now about twelve years old, and the thought of being *a slave* 5 *for life* began to bear heavily upon my heart. Just about this time, I got hold of a book entitled "The Columbian Orator."[2] Every opportunity I

---

[2] A popular textbook that taught the principles of effective public speaking. [Eds.]

got, I used to read this book. Among much of other interesting matter, I found in it a dialogue between a master and his slave. The slave was represented as having run away from his master three times. The dialogue represented the conversation which took place between them, when the slave was retaken the third time. In this dialogue, the whole argument in behalf of slavery was brought forward by the master, all of which was disposed of by the slave. The slave was made to say some very smart as well as impressive things in reply to his master—things which had the desired though unexpected effect; for the conversation resulted in the voluntary emancipation of the slave on the part of the master.

In the same book, I met with one of Sheridan's might speeches on and in behalf of Catholic emancipation.[3] These were choice documents to me. I read them over and over again with unabated interest. They gave tongue to interesting thoughts of my own soul, which had frequently flashed through my mind, and died away for want of utterance. The moral which I gained from the dialogue was the power of truth over the conscience of even a slaveholder. What I got from Sheridan was a bold denunciation of slavery, and a powerful vindication of human rights. The reading of these documents enabled me to utter my thoughts, and to meet the arguments brought forward to sustain slavery; but while they relieved me of one difficulty, they brought on another even more painful than the one of which I was relieved. The more I read, the more I was led to abhor and detest my enslavers. I could regard them in no other light than a band of successful robbers, who had left their homes, and gone to Africa, and stolen us from our homes, and in a strange land reduced us to slavery. I loathed them as being the meanest as well as the most wicked of men. As I read and contemplated the subject, behold! that very discontentment which Master Hugh had predicted would follow my learning to read had already come, to torment and sting my soul to unutterable anguish. As I writhed under it, I would at times feel that learning to read had been a curse rather than a blessing. It had given me a view of my wretched condition, without the remedy. It opened my eyes to the horrible pit, but to no ladder upon which to get out. In moments of agony, I envied my fellow-slaves for their stupidity. I have often wished myself a beast. I preferred the condition of the meanest reptile to my own. Any thing, no matter what, to get rid of thinking! It was this everlasting thinking of my condition that tormented me. There was no getting rid of it. It was pressed upon me by every object within sight or hearing, animate or inanimate. The silver

6

---

[3] Richard Brinsley Sheridan (1751–1816), British playwright and statesman who made speeches supporting the right of English Catholics to vote. Full emancipation was not granted to Catholics until 1829. [Eds.]

trump of freedom had roused my soul to eternal wakefulness. Freedom now appeared, to disappear no more forever. It was heard in every sound, and seen in every thing. It was ever present to torment me with a sense of my wretched condition. I saw nothing without seeing it, I heard nothing without hearing it, and felt nothing without feeling it. It looked from every star, it smiled in every calm, breathed in every wind, and moved in every storm.

I often found myself regretting my own existence, and wishing my- ⁷ self dead; and but for the hope of being free, I have no doubt but that I should have killed myself, or done something for which I should have been killed. While in this state of mind, I was eager to hear any one speak of slavery. I was a ready listener. Every little while, I could hear something about the abolitionists. It was some time before I found what the word meant. It was always used in such connections as to make it an interesting word to me. If a slave ran away and succeeded in getting clear, or if a slave killed his master, set fire to a barn, or did any thing very wrong in the mind of a slaveholder, it was spoken of as the fruit of *abolition*. Hearing the word in this connection very often, I set about learning what it meant. The dictionary afforded me little or no help. I found it was "the act of abolishing"; but then I did not know what was to be abolished. Here I was perplexed. I did not dare to ask any one about its meaning, for I was satisfied that it was something they wanted me to know very little about. After a patient waiting, I got one of our city papers, containing an account of the number of petitions from the north, praying for the abolition of slavery in the District of Columbia, and of the slave trade between the States. From this time I understood the words *abolition* and *abolitionist*, and always drew near when that word was spoken, expecting to hear something of importance to myself and fellow-slaves. The light broke in upon me by degrees. I went one day down on the wharf of Mr. Waters; and seeing two Irishmen unloading a scow of stone, I went, unasked, and helped them. When we had finished, one of them came to me and asked me if I were a slave. I told him I was. He asked, "Are ye a slave for life?" I told him that I was. The good Irishman seemed to be deeply affected by the statement. He said to the other that it was a pity so fine a little fellow as myself should be a slave for life. He said it was a shame to hold me. They both advised me to run away to the north; that I should find friends there, and that I should be free. I pretended not to be interested in what they said, and treated them as if I did not understand them; for I feared they might be treacherous. White men have been known to encourage slaves to escape, and then, to get the reward, catch them and return them to their masters. I was afraid that these seemingly good men might use me so; but I nevertheless remembered their advice, and from that time I resolved to run away. I looked forward to a time at which it would be safe for me to escape. I was too young to think of doing so immediately; besides, I wished to learn how to write, as I might have occasion to write my own pass. I consoled myself with the hope that I should one day find a good chance. Meanwhile, I would learn to write.

The idea as to how I might learn to write was suggested to me by being in Durgin and Bailey's ship-yard, and frequently seeing the ship carpenters, after hewing, and getting a piece of timber ready for use, write on the timber the name of that part of the ship for which it was intended. When a piece of timber was intended for the larboard side, it would be marked thus—"L." When a piece was for the starboard side, it would be marked thus—"S." A piece for the larboard side forward, would be marked thus—"L. F." When a piece was for starboard side forward, it would be marked thus—"S. F." For larboard aft, it would be marked thus—"L.A." For starboard aft, it would be marked thus—"S. A." I soon learned the names of these letters, and for what they were intended when placed upon a piece of timber in the ship-yard. I immediately commenced copying them, and in a short time was able to make the four letters named. After that, when I met with any boy who I knew could write, I would tell him I could write as well as he. The next word would be, "I don't believe you. Let me see you try it." I would then make the letters which I had been so fortunate as to learn, and ask him to beat that. In this way I got a good many lessons in writing, which it is quite possible I should never have gotten in any other way. During this time, my copy-book was the board fence, brick wall, and pavement; my pen and ink was a lump of chalk. With these, I learned mainly how to write. I then commenced and continued copying the Italics in Webster's Spelling Book, until I could make them all without looking on the book. By this time, my little Master Thomas had gone to school, and learned how to write, and had written over a number of copy-books. These had been brought home, and shown to some of our near neighbors, and then laid aside. My mistress used to go to class meeting at the Wilk Street meeting-house every Monday afternoon, and leave me to take care of the house. When left thus, I used to spend the time in writing in the spaces left in Master Thomas's copy-book, copying what he had written. I continued to do this until I could write a hand very similar to that of Master Thomas. Thus, after a long, tedious effort for years, I finally succeeded in learning how to write.

Responding to Reading

1. Douglass escaped from slavery in 1838 and became a leading figure in the antislavery movement. In what ways did reading and writing help him form his ideas about slavery?

2. Do you think education and slavery are compatible or incompatible? Why do you think slaveholders did not want slaves to learn to read and write?
3. What ideas about education does Douglass have that are different from yours? Which of his ideas have relevance for the society in which you live?

A HOMEMADE EDUCATION

Malcolm X

Writer, lecturer, and political activist Malcolm X (1925–1965) was born Malcolm Little in Omaha, Nebraska. His father, a Baptist minister, supported the back-to-Africa movement of the 1920s. Because of these activities the family was threatened by the Ku Klux Klan and forced to move several times. Eventually, his father was murdered, and his mother was committed to a mental institution. Malcolm X quit high school, preferring the street world of criminals and drug addicts. While he served time in prison from 1946 to 1952, he read books and studied the Black Muslim religion, finally becoming an articulate advocate of black separatism. Malcolm X later split with Elijah Muhammad, the Black Muslim leader, rejecting the notion that whites were evil and working for worldwide African-American unity and equality. For his defection, Malcolm X was assassinated. Some of his writings are *The Autobiography of Malcolm X* (1965), *Malcolm X Talks to Young People* (1969), and *Malcolm X on Afro-American Unity* (1970). "A Homemade Education" is from Malcolm X's autobiography, which was written with Alex Haley.

It was because of my letters that I happened to stumble upon starting to acquire some kind of a homemade education. 1

I became increasingly frustrated at not being able to express what I wanted to convey in letters that I wrote, especially those to Mr. Elijah Muhammad. In the street, I had been the most articulate hustler out there—I had commanded attention when I said something. But now, trying to write simple English, I not only wasn't articulate, I wasn't even functional. How would I sound writing in slang, the way I would *say* it, something such as, "Look, daddy, let me pull your coat about a cat, Elijah Muhammad—" 2

Many who today hear me somewhere in person, or on television, or those who read something I've said, will think I went to school far beyond the eighth grade. This impression is due entirely to my prison studies. 3

It had really begun back in the Charlestown Prison, when Bimbi[1] [4] first made me feel envy of his stock of knowledge. Bimbi had always taken charge of any conversations he was in, and I had tried to emulate him. But every book I picked up had few sentences which didn't contain anywhere from one to nearly all of the words that might as well have been in Chinese. When I just skipped those words, of course, I really ended up with little idea of what the book said. So I had come to the Norfolk Prison Colony still going through only book-reading motions. Pretty soon, I would have quit even these motions, unless I had received the motivation that I did.

I saw that the best thing I could do was get hold of a dictionary—to [5] study, to learn some words. I was lucky enough to reason also that I should try to improve my penmanship. It was sad. I couldn't even write in a straight line. It was both ideas together that moved me to request a dictionary along with some tablets and pencils from the Norfolk Prison Colony school.

I spent two days just riffling uncertainly through the dictionary's [6] pages. I'd never realized so many words existed! I didn't know *which* words I needed to learn. Finally, just to start some kind of action, I began copying.

In my slow, painstaking, ragged handwriting, I copied into my [7] tablet everything printed on that first page, down to the punctuation marks.

I believe it took me a day. Then, aloud, I read back, to myself, every- [8] thing I'd written on the tablet. Over and over, aloud, to myself, I read my own handwriting.

I woke up the next morning, thinking about those words—im- [9] mensely proud to realize that not only had I written so much at one time, but I'd written words that I never knew were in the world. Moreover, with a little effort, I also could remember what many of these words meant. I reviewed the words whose meanings I didn't remember. Funny thing, from the dictionary first page right now, that "aardvark" springs to my mind. The dictionary had a picture of it, a long-tailed, long-eared, burrowing African mammal, which lives off termites caught by sticking out its tongue as an anteater does for ants.

I was so fascinated that I went on—I copied the dictionary's next [10] page. And the same experience came when I studied that. With every succeeding page, I also learned of people and places and events from history. Actually the dictionary is like a miniature encyclopedia. Final- ly the dictionary's A section had filled a whole tablet—and I went on into the B's. That was the way I started copying what eventually became

---

[1] A fellow inmate. [Eds.]

the entire dictionary. It went a lot faster after so much practice helped me to pick up handwriting speed. Between what I wrote in my tablet, and writing letters, during the rest of my time in prison I would guess I wrote a million words.

I suppose it was inevitable that as my word-base broadened, I [11] could for the first time pick up a book and read and now begin to understand what the book was saying. Anyone who has read a great deal can imagine the new world that opened. Let me tell you something: from then until I left that prison, in every free moment I had, if I was not reading in the library, I was reading on my bunk. You couldn't have gotten me out of books with a wedge. Between Mr. Muhammad's teachings, my correspondence, my visitors—usually Ella and Reginald[2]—and my reading of books, months passed without my even thinking about being imprisoned. In fact, up to then, I never had been so truly free in my life.

The Norfolk Prison Colony's library was in the school building. A [12] variety of classes was taught there by instructors who came from such places as Harvard and Boston universities. The weekly debates between inmate teams were also held in the school building. You would be astonished to know how worked up convict debaters and audiences would get over subjects like "Should Babies Be Fed Milk?"

Available on the prison library's shelves were books on just about [13] every general subject. Much of the big private collection that Parkhurst[3] had willed to the prison was still in crates and boxes in the back of the library—thousands of old books. Some of them looked ancient: covers faded; old-time parchment-looking binding. Parkhurst, I've mentioned, seemed to have been principally interested in history and religion. He had the money and the special interest to have a lot of books that you wouldn't have in general circulation. Any college library would have been lucky to get that collection.

As you can imagine, especially in a prison where there was heavy [14] emphasis on rehabilitation, an inmate was smiled upon if he demonstrated an unusually intense interest in books. There was a sizable number of well-read inmates, especially the popular debaters. Some were said by many to be practically walking encyclopedias. They were almost celebrities. No university would ask any student to devour literature as I did when this new world opened to me, of being able to read and *understand*.

I read more in my room than in the library itself. An inmate who [15] was known to read a lot could check out more than the permitted maximum number of books. I preferred reading in the total isolation of my own room.

---

[2] Ella was Malcolm's half sister, and Reginald was his brother. [Eds.]

[3] A philanthropist. [Eds.]

When I had progressed to really serious reading, every night at [16] about ten P.M. I would be outraged with the "lights out." It always seemed to catch me right in the middle of something engrossing.

Fortunately, right outside my door was a corridor light that cast a [17] glow into my room. The glow was enough to read by, once my eyes adjusted to it. So when "lights out" came, I would sit on the floor where I could continue reading in that glow.

At one-hour intervals the night guards paced past every room. Each [18] time I heard the approaching footsteps, I jumped into bed and feigned sleep. And as soon as the guard passed, I got back out of bed onto the floor area of that light-glow, where I would read for another fifty-eight minutes—until the guard approached again. That went on until three or four every morning. Three or four hours of sleep a night was enough for me. Often in the years in the streets I had slept less than that.

The teachings of Mr. Muhammad stressed how history had been [19] "whitened"—when white men had written history books, the black man simply had been left out. Mr. Muhammad couldn't have said anything that would have struck me much harder. I had never forgotten how when my class, me and all of those whites, had studied seventh-grade United States history back in Mason,[4] the history of the Negro had been covered in one paragraph, and the teacher had gotten a big laugh with his joke, "Negroes' feet are so big that when they walk, they leave a hole in the ground."

This is one reason why Mr. Muhammad's teachings spread so swift- [20] ly all over the United States, among *all* Negroes, whether or not they became followers of Mr. Muhammad. The teachings ring true—to every Negro. You can hardly show me a black adult in America—or a white one, for that matter—who knows from the history books anything like the truth about the black man's role. In my own case, once I heard of the "glorious history of the black man," I took special pains to hunt in the library for books that would inform me on details about black history.

I can remember accurately the very first set of books that really im- [21] pressed me. I have since bought that set of books and I have it at home for my children to read as they grow up. It's called *Wonders of the World*. It's full of pictures of archeological finds, statues that depict, usually, non-European people.

I found books like Will Durant's *Story of Civilization*. I read H. G. [22] Wells' *Outline of History*. *Souls of Black Folk* by W. E. B. Du Bois gave me a glimpse into the black people's history before they came to this country. Carter G. Woodson's *Negro History* opened my eyes about black empires before the black slave was brought to the United States, and the early Negro struggles for freedom.

---

[4] The junior high school that Malcolm X attended. [Eds.]

J. A. Rogers' three volumes of *Sex and Race* told about race-mixing 23
before Christ's time; about Aesop being a black man who told fables;
about Egypt's Pharaohs; about the great Coptic Christian Empires;
about Ethiopia, the earth's oldest continuous black civilization, as China
is the oldest continuous civilization.

Mr. Muhammad's teaching about how the white man had been cre- 24
ated led me to *Findings in Genetics* by Gregor Mendel.[5] (The dictionary's
G section was where I had learned what "genetics" meant.) I really studied this book by the Austrian monk. Reading it over and over, especially certain sections, helped me to understand that if you started with a
black man, a white man could be produced; but starting with a white
man, you never could produce a black man—because the white chromosome is recessive. And since no one disputes that there was but one
Original Man, the conclusion is clear.

During the last year or so, in the *New York Times,* Arnold Toynbee[6] 25
used the word "bleached" in describing the white man. (His words
were: "White [i.e. bleached] human beings of North European origin. . . .") Toynbee also referred to the European geographic area as only
a peninsula of Asia. He said there is no such thing as Europe. And if you
look at the globe, you will see for yourself that America is only an extension of Asia. (But at the same time Toynbee is among those who have
helped to bleach history. He has written that Africa was the only continent that produced no history. He won't write that again. Every day
now, the truth is coming to light.)

I never will forget how shocked I was when I began reading about 26
slavery's total horror. It made such an impact upon me that it later became one of my favorite subjects when I became a minister of Mr.
Muhammad's. The world's most monstrous crime, the sin and the blood
on the white man's hands, are almost impossible to believe. Books like
the one by Frederick Olmstead[7] opened my eyes to the horrors suffered
when the slave was landed in the United States. The European woman,
Fannie Kimball, who had married a Southern white slaveowner, described how human beings were degraded. Of course I read *Uncle Tom's
Cabin.* In fact, I believe that's the only novel I have ever read since I started serious reading.

Parkhurst's collection also contained some bound pamphlets of the 27
Abolitionist Anti-Slavery Society of New England. I read descriptions of
atrocities, saw those illustrations of black slave women tied up and
flogged with whips; of black mothers watching their babies being
dragged off, never to be seen by their mothers again; of dogs after slaves,

---

[5] Austrian monk (1822–84) acknowledged as the father of modern genetics. [Eds.]

[6] English historian (1889–1975). [Eds.]

[7] American landscape architect and writer (1822–1903) who first achieved fame for his accounts of the South in the early 1850s. [Eds.]

and of the fugitive slave catchers, evil white men with whips and clubs and chains and guns. I read about the slave preacher Nat Turner, who put the fear of God into the white slavemaster. Nat Turner wasn't going around preaching pie-in-the-sky and "nonviolent" freedom for the black man. There in Virginia one night in 1831, Nat and seven other slaves started out at his master's home and through the night they went from one plantation "big house" to the next, killing, until by the next morning 57 white people were dead and Nat had about 70 slaves following him. White people, terrified for their lives, fled from their homes, locked themselves up in public buildings, hid in the woods, and some even left the state. A small army of soldiers took two months to catch and hang Nat Turner. Somewhere I have read where Nat Turner's example is said to have inspired John Brown to invade Virginia and attack Harper's Ferry nearly thirty years later, with thirteen white men and five Negroes.

I read Herodotus, "the father of History," or, rather, I read about [28] him. And I read the histories of various nations, which opened my eyes gradually, then wider and wider, to how the whole world's white men had indeed acted like devils, pillaging and raping and bleeding and draining the whole world's non-white people. I remember, for instance, books such as Will Durant's *The Story of Oriental Civilization*, and Mahatma Gandhi's accounts of the struggle to drive the British out of India.

Book after book showed me how the white man had brought upon [29] the world's black, brown, red, and yellow peoples every variety of the sufferings of exploitation. I saw how since the sixteenth century, the so-called "Christian trader" white man began to ply the seas in his lust for Asian and African empires, and plunder, and power. I read, I saw, how the white man never has gone among the non-white peoples bearing the Cross in the true manner and spirit of Christ's teachings—meek, humble, and Christlike.

I perceived, as I read, how the collective white man had been actu- [30] ally nothing but a piratical opportunist who used Faustian machinations to make his own Christianity his initial wedge in criminal conquests. First, always "religiously," he branded "heathen" and "pagan" labels upon ancient non-white cultures and civilizations. The stage thus set, he then turned upon his non-white victims his weapons of war.

I read how, entering India—half a *billion* deeply religious brown [31] people—the British white man, by 1759, through promises, trickery and manipulations, controlled much of India through Great Britain's East India Company. The parasitical British administration kept tentacling out to half of the subcontinent. In 1857, some of the desperate people of India finally mutinied—and, excepting the African slave trade, nowhere has history recorded any more unnecessary bestial and ruthless human carnage than the British suppression of the nonwhite Indian people.

Over 115 million African blacks—close to the 1930s population of [32] the United States—were murdered or enslaved during the slave trade. And I read how when the slave market was glutted, the cannibalistic white powers of Europe next carved up, as their colonies, the richest areas of the black continent. And Europe's chancelleries for the next century played a chess game of naked exploitation and power from Cape Horn to Cairo.

Ten guards and the warden couldn't have torn me out of those [33] books. Not even Elijah Muhammad could have been more eloquent than those books were in providing indisputable proof that the collective white man had acted like a devil in virtually every contact he had with the world's collective non-white man. I listen today to the radio, and watch television, and read the headlines about the collective white man's fear and tension concerning China. When the white man professes ignorance about why the Chinese hate him so, my mind can't help flashing back to what I read, there in prison, about how the blood forebears of this same white man raped China at a time when China was trusting and helpless. Those original white "Christian traders" sent into China millions of pounds of opium. By 1839, so many of the Chinese were addicts that China's desperate government destroyed twenty thousand chests of opium. The first Opium War was promptly declared by the white man. Imagine! Declaring *war* upon someone who objects to being narcotized! The Chinese were severely beaten, with Chinese-invented gunpowder.

The Treaty of Nanking made China pay the British white man for [34] the destroyed opium: forced open China's major ports to British trade; forced China to abandon Hong Kong; fixed China's import tariffs so low that cheap British articles soon flooded in, maiming China's industrial development.

After a second Opium War, the Tientsin Treaties legalized the rav- [35] aging opium trade, legalized a British-French-American control of China's customs. China tried delaying that Treaty's ratification; Peking was looted and burned.

"Kill the foreign white devils!" was the 1901 Chinese war cry in the [36] Boxer Rebellion. Losing again, this time the Chinese were driven from Peking's choicest areas. The vicious, arrogant white man put up the famous signs, "Chinese and dogs not allowed."

Red China after World War II closed its doors to the Western white [37] world. Massive Chinese agricultural, scientific, and industrial efforts are described in a book that *Life* magazine recently published. Some observers inside Red China have reported that the world never has known such a hate-white campaign as is now going on in this non-white country where, present birthrates continuing, in fifty more years Chinese will be half the earth's population. And it seems that some Chinese chickens will soon come home to roost, with China's recent successful nuclear tests.

Let us face reality. We can see in the United Nations a new world [38] order being shaped, along color lines—an alliance among the nonwhite nations. America's U.N. Ambassador Adlai Stevenson complained not long ago that in the United Nations "a skin game" was being played. He was right. He was facing reality. A "skin game" *is* being played. But Ambassador Stevenson sounded like Jesse James accusing the marshal of carrying a gun. Because who in the world's history ever has played a worse "skin game" than the white man?

Mr. Muhammad, to whom I was writing daily, had no idea of what [39] a new world had opened up to me through my efforts to document his teachings in books.

When I discovered philosophy, I tried to touch all the landmarks of [40] philosophical development. Gradually, I read most of the old philosophers, Occidental and Oriental. The Oriental philosophers were the ones I came to prefer; finally, my impression was that most Occidental philosophy had largely been borrowed from the Oriental thinkers. Socrates, for instance, traveled in Egypt. Some sources even say that Socrates was initiated into some of the Egyptian mysteries. Obviously Socrates got some of his wisdom among the East's wise men.

I have often reflected upon the new vistas that reading opened to [41] me. I knew right there in prison that reading had changed forever the course of my life. As I see it today, the ability to read awoke inside me some long dormant craving to be mentally alive. I certainly wasn't seeking any degree, the way a college confers a status symbol upon its students. My homemade education gave me, with every additional book that I read, a little bit more sensitivity to the deafness, dumbness, and blindness that was afflicting the black race in America. Not long ago, an English writer telephoned me from London, asking questions. One was, "What's your alma mater?" I told him, "Books." You will never catch me with a free fifteen minutes in which I'm not studying something I feel might be able to help the black man.

Yesterday I spoke in London, and both ways on the plane across the [42] Atlantic I was studying a document about how the United Nations proposes to insure the human rights of the oppressed minorities of the world. The American black man is the world's most shameful case of minority oppression. What makes the black man think of himself as only an internal United States issue is just a catch-phrase, two words, "civil rights." How is the black man going to get "civil rights" before first he wins his *human* rights? If the American black man will start thinking about his *human* rights, and then start thinking of himself as part of one of the world's great peoples, he will see he has a case for the United Nations.

I can't think of a better case! Four hundred years of black blood and ⁴³
sweat invested here in America, and the white man still has the black
man begging for what every immigrant fresh off the ship can take for
granted the minute he walks down the gangplank.

But I'm digressing. I told the Englishman that my alma mater was ⁴⁴
books, a good library. Every time I catch a plane, I have with me a book
that I want to read—and that's a lot of books these days. If I weren't out
here every day battling the white man, I could spend the rest of my life
reading, just satisfying my curiosity—because you can hardly mention
anything I'm not curious about. I don't think anybody ever got more out
of going to prison than I did. In fact, prison enabled me to study far more
intensively than I would have if my life had gone differently and I had
attended some college. I imagine that one of the biggest troubles with
colleges is there are too many distractions, too much panty-raiding, fra-
ternities, and boola-boola and all of that. Where else but in a prison
could I have attacked my ignorance by being able to study intensely
sometimes as much as fifteen hours a day?

Responding to Reading

1. Malcolm X began his education by copying words from the dictionary and
   learning their definitions. What are the advantages and the disadvantages of
   this strategy?
2. What comment do you think this essay makes about the status of African
   Americans in the 1950s? Do you think this essay still has relevance? Explain.
3. Have you, like Malcolm X, ever wanted to express an idea but not been able
   to because you could not find the exact words? In what way was your experience similar to and different from the one he describes?

LOST IN TRANSLATION

Eva Hoffman

Born in Cracow, Poland, Eva Hoffman (1946–) immigrated with her
family to Vancouver, British Columbia, in 1959. She attended Rice University and Harvard and taught literature before beginning a career as
a writer and journalist. She is an editor for the *New York Times Book Review* and has published two books: the autobiographical *Lost in Translation: A Life in a New Language* (1989) and *Exit into History: A Journey*

through the New Eastern Europe (1993), a report on the changing face of
eastern Europe after the fall of communism. Of writing, Hoffman has
said that it is a search through "layers of acquired voices, silly voices,
sententious voices, voices that are too cool and too overheated" to find
"silence . . . the white blank center, the level ground that was there before Babel was built, that is always there before the Babel of our multiple selves is constructed," from which can emerge "an even voice . . .
capable of saying things straight, without exaggeration or triviality." In
the following excerpt from *Lost in Translation,* Hoffman meditates on
her youthful experience as a new speaker and writer of English and on
the authority and satisfaction that come with linguistic mastery.

For my birthday, Penny gives me a diary, complete with a little lock   1
and key to keep what I write from the eyes of all intruders. It is that little lock—the visible symbol of the privacy in which the diary is meant
to exist—that creates my dilemma. If I am indeed to write something entirely for myself, in what language do I write? Several times, I open the
diary and close it again. I can't decide. Writing in Polish at this point
would be a little like resorting to Latin or ancient Greek—an eccentric
thing to do in a diary, in which you're supposed to set down your most
immediate experiences and unpremeditated thoughts in the most un-
mediated[1] language. Polish is becoming a dead language, the language
of the untranslatable past. But writing for nobody's eyes in English?
That's like doing a school exercise, or performing in front of yourself, a
slightly perverse act of self-voyeurism.

Because I have to choose something, I finally choose English. If I'm   2
to write about the present, I have to write in the language of the present,
even if it's not the language of the self. As a result, the diary becomes
surely one of the more impersonal exercises of that sort produced by an
adolescent girl. These are no sentimental effusions of rejected love, eruptions of familial anger, or consoling broodings about death. English is
not the language of such emotions. Instead, I set down my reflections on
the ugliness of wrestling; on the elegance of Mozart, and on how Dostoyevsky puts me in mind of El Greco[2] I write down Thoughts. I Write.

There is a certain pathos to this naïve snobbery, for the diary is an   3
earnest attempt to create a part of my persona that I imagine I would
have grown into in Polish. In the solitude of this most private act, I write,
in my public language, in order to update what might have been my
other self. The diary is about me and not about me at all. But on one
level, it allows me to make the first jump. I learn English through writing, and, in turn, writing gives me a written self. Refracted through the
double distance of English and writing, this self—my English self—be-

---

[1] Connected directly, rather than through some intervening agent. [Eds.]
[2] Dostoyevsky (1828–1881) was a Russian novelist, El Greco (1541–1614) a Spanish painter. [Eds.]

comes oddly objective; more than anything, it perceives. It exists more easily in the abstract sphere of thoughts and observations than in the world. For a while, this impersonal self, this cultural negative capability, becomes the truest thing about me. When I write, I have a real existence that is proper to the activity of writing—an existence that takes place midway between me and the sphere of artifice, art, pure language. This language is beginning to invent another me. However, I discover something odd. It seems that when I write (or, for that matter, think) in English, I am unable to use the word "I." I do not go as far as the schizophrenic "she"—but I am driven, as by a compulsion, to the double, the Siamese-twin "you."

My voice is doing funny things. It does not seem to emerge from the   4
same parts of my body as before. It comes out from somewhere in my throat, tight, thin, and mat—a voice without the modulations, dips, and rises that it had before, when it went from my stomach all the way through my head. There is, of course, the constraint and the self-consciousness of an accent that I hear but cannot control. Some of my high school peers accuse me of putting it on in order to appear more "interesting." In fact, I'd do anything to get rid of it, and when I'm alone, I practice sounds for which my speech organs have no intuitions, such as "th" (I do this by putting my tongue between my teeth) and "a," which is longer and more open in Polish (by shaping my mouth into a sort of arrested grin). It is simple words like "cat" or "tap" that give me the most trouble, because they have no context of other syllables, and so people often misunderstand them. Whenever I can, I do awkward little swerves to avoid them, or pause and try to say them very clearly. Still, when people—like salesladies—hear me speak without being prepared to listen carefully, they often don't understand me the first time around. "Girls' shoes," I say, and the "girls" comes out as a sort of scramble. "Girls' shoes," I repeat, willing the syllable to form itself properly, and the saleslady usually smiles nicely, and sends my mother and me to the right part of the store. I say "Thank you" with a sweet smile, feeling as if I'm both claiming an unfair special privilege and being unfairly patronized.

It's as important to me to speak well as to play a piece of music with-   5
out mistakes. Hearing English distorted grates on me like chalk screeching on a blackboard, like all things botched and badly done, like all forms of gracelessness. The odd thing is that I know what is correct, fluent, good, long before I can execute it. The English spoken by our Polish acquaintances strikes me as jagged and thick, and I know that I shouldn't imitate it. I'm turned off by the intonations I hear on the TV sitcoms—by the expectation of laughter, like a dog's tail wagging in supplication, built into the actors' pauses, and by the curtailed, cutoff rhythms. I like the way Penny speaks, with an easy flow and a pleasure in giving words a fleshly fullness; I like what I hear in some movies; and

once the Old Vic[3] comes to Vancouver to perform *Macbeth*, and though I can hardly understand the particular words, I am riveted by the tones of sureness and command that mold the actors' speech into such majestic periods.

Sociolinguists might say that I receive these language messages as   6
class signals, that I associate the sounds of correctness with the social status of the speaker. In part, this is undoubtedly true. The class-linked notion that I transfer wholesale from Poland is that belonging to a "better" class of people is absolutely dependent on speaking a "better" language. And in my situation especially, I know that language will be a crucial instrument, that I can overcome the stigma of my marginality, the weight of presumption against me, only if the reassuringly right sounds come out of my mouth.

Yes, speech is a class signifier. But I think that in hearing these va-   7
rieties of speech around me, I'm sensitized to something else as well—something that is a matter of aesthetics, and even of psychological health. Apparently, skilled chefs can tell whether a dish from some foreign cuisine is well cooked even if they have never tasted it and don't know the genre of cooking it belongs to. There seem to be some deep-structure qualities—consistency, proportions of ingredients, smoothness of blending—that indicate culinary achievement to these educated eaters' taste buds. So each language has its own distinctive music, and even if one doesn't know its separate components, one can pretty quickly recognize the propriety of the patterns in which the components are put together, their harmonies and discords. Perhaps the crucial element that strikes the ear in listening to living speech is the degree of the speaker's self-assurance and control.

As I listen to people speaking that foreign tongue, English, I can   8
hear when they stumble or repeat the same phrases too many times, when their sentences trail off aimlessly—or, on the contrary, when their phrases have vigor and roundness, when they have the space and the breath to give a flourish at the end of a sentence, or make just the right pause before coming to a dramatic point. I can tell, in other words, the degree of their ease or dis-ease, the extent of authority that shapes the rhythms of their speech. That authority—in whatever dialect, in whatever variant of the mainstream language—seems to me to be something we all desire. It's not that we all want to speak the King's English, but whether we speak Appalachian or Harlem English, or Cockney, or Jamaican Creole, we want to be at home in our tongue. We want to be able to give voice accurately and fully to ourselves and our sense of the world. John Fowles, in one of his stories in *The Ebony Tower*, has a young man cruelly violate an elderly writer and his manuscripts because the

---

[3] London-based theatrical company, specializing in Shakespeare. [Eds.]

legacy of language has not been passed on to the youthful vandal properly. This seems to me an entirely credible premise. Linguistic dispossession is a sufficient motive for violence, for it is close to the dispossession of one's self. Blind rage, helpless rage is rage that has no words—rage that overwhelms one with darkness. And if one is perpetually without words, if one exists in the entropy[4] of inarticulateness, that condition itself is bound to be an enraging frustration. In my New York apartment, I listen almost nightly to fights that erupt like brushfire on the street below—and in their escalating fury of repetitious phrases ("Don't do this to me, man, you fucking bastard, I'll fucking kill you"), I hear not the pleasures of macho toughness but an infuriated beating against wordlessness, against the incapacity to make oneself understood, seen. Anger can be borne—it can even be satisfying—if it can gather into words and explode in a storm, or a rapier-sharp attack. But without this means of ventilation, it only turns back inward, building and swirling like a head of steam—building to an impotent, murderous rage. If all therapy is speaking therapy—a talking cure—then perhaps all neurosis is a speech dis-ease.

Responding to Reading

1. Do you think Hoffman is overly concerned with correctness? Explain your answer.
2. Do you agree with Hoffman's contention that "speech is a class signifier" (7)? For example, do you believe people are judged by the way they pronounce words and the vocabulary they use? Should they be?
3. Hoffman says that the inability to communicate leads people to frustration and eventually to rage and violence. Do you think she is correct? What implications do her observations have for society?

MOTHER TONGUE

Amy Tan

Amy Tan (1952–) was born in Oakland, California, to parents who had emigrated from China only a few years earlier. (Her given name is actually An-mei, which means "blessing from America.") After receiving degrees from San Francisco State University (including a master's de-

---

[4] Disorder; uncertainty; chaos. [Eds.]

gree in linguistics), she became a business writer, composing speeches for corporate executives. A workaholic, Tan began writing stories as a means of personal therapy, and these eventually became the phenomenally successful *The Joy Luck Club* (1987), a novel about Chinese-born mothers and their American-born daughters that was later made into a widely praised film (an excerpt appears on p. 454). Tan's other books include a second novel, *The Kitchen God's Wife* (1991), which is set in China, and two illustrated children's books, *The Moon Lady* (1992) and *The Chinese Siamese Cat* (1994). In the following essay, which was originally delivered as a speech, Tan considers her relationship with her own mother, concentrating on the different "Englishes" they use to communicate with each other and with the world.

I am not a scholar of English or literature. I cannot give you much   1
more than personal opinions on the English language and its variations in this country or others.

I am a writer. And by that definition, I am someone who has always   2
loved language. I am fascinated by language in daily life. I spend a great deal of my time thinking about the power of language—the way it can evoke an emotion, a visual image, a complex idea, or a simple truth. Language is the tool of my trade. And I use them all—all the Englishes I grew up with.

Recently, I was made keenly aware of the different Englishes I do   3
use. I was giving a talk to a large group of people, the same talk I had already given to half a dozen other groups. The nature of the talk was about my writing, my life, and my book, *The Joy Luck Club*. The talk was going along well enough, until I remembered one major difference that made the whole talk sound wrong. My mother was in the room. And it was perhaps the first time she had heard me give a lengthy speech, using the kind of English I have never used with her. I was saying things like, "The intersection of memory upon imagination" and "There is an aspect of my fiction that relates to thus-and-thus"—a speech filled with carefully wrought grammatical phrases, burdened, it suddenly seemed to me, with nominalized forms, past perfect tenses, conditional phrases, all the forms of standard English that I had learned in school and through books, the forms of English I did not use at home with my mother.

Just last week, I was walking down the street with my mother, and   4
I again found myself conscious of the English I was using, and the English I do use with her. We were talking about the price of new and used furniture and I heard myself saying this: "Not waste money that way." My husband was with us as well, and he didn't notice any switch in my English. And then I realized why. It's because over the twenty years we've been together I've often used that same kind of English with him, and sometimes he even uses it with me. It has become our language of

intimacy, a different sort of English that relates to family talk, the language I grew up with.

So you'll have some idea of what this family talk I heard sounds 5
like, I'll quote what my mother said during a recent conversation transcribed. During this conversation, my mother was talking about a political gangster in Shanghai who had the same last name as her family's, Du, and how the gangster in his early years wanted to be adopted by her family, which was rich by comparison. Later, the gangster became more powerful, far richer than my mother's family, and one day showed up at my mother's wedding to pay his respects. Here's what she said in part:

"Du Yusong having business like fruit stand. Like off the street kind. 6
He is Du like Du Zong—but not Tsung-ming Island people. The local people call putong, the river east side, he belong to that side local people. The man want to ask Du Zong father take him in like become own family. Du Zong father wasn't look down on him, but didn't take seriously, until that man big like become a mafia. Now important person, very hard to inviting him. Chinese way, came only to show respect, don't stay for dinner. Respect for making big celebration, he shows up. Mean gives lots of respect. Chinese custom. Chinese social life that way. If too important won't have to stay too long. He come to my wedding. I didn't see, I heard it. I gone to boy's side, they have YMCA dinner. Chinese age I was nineteen."

You should know that my mother's expressive command of English 7
belies how much she actually understands. She reads the *Forbes* report, listens to *Wall Street Week*, converses daily with her stockbroker, reads all of Shirley MacLaine's[1] books with ease—all kinds of things I can't begin to understand. Yet some of my friends tell me they understand 50 percent of what my mother says. Some say they understand 80 to 90 percent. Some say they understand none of it, as if she were speaking pure Chinese. But to me, my mother's English is perfectly clear, perfectly natural. It's my mother tongue. Her language, as I hear it, is vivid, direct, full of observation and imagery. That was the language that helped shape the way I saw things, expressed things, made sense of the world.

Lately, I've been giving more thought to the kind of English my 8
mother speaks. Like others, I have described it to people as "broken" or "fractured" English. But I wince when I say that. It has always bothered me that I can think of no way to describe it other than "broken," as if it were damaged and needed to be fixed, as if it lacked a certain wholeness and soundness. I've heard other terms used, "limited English," for example. But they seem just as bad, as if everything

---

[1] Actress known for her autobiographical books in which she traces her many past lives. [Eds.]

is limited, including people's perceptions of the limited English speaker.

I know this for a fact, because when I was growing up, my mother's "limited" English limited *my* perception of her. I was ashamed of her English. I believed that her English reflected the quality of what she had to say. That is, because she expressed them imperfectly her thoughts were imperfect. And I had plenty of empirical evidence to support me: the fact that people in department stores, at banks, and at restaurants did not take her seriously, did not give her good service, pretended not to understand her, or even acted as if they did not hear her. [9]

My mother has long realized the limitations of her English as well. When I was fifteen, she used to have me call people on the phone to pretend I was she. In this guise, I was forced to ask for information or even to complain and yell at people who had been rude to her. One time it was a call to her stockbroker in New York. She had cashed out her small portfolio and it just so happened we were going to go to New York the next week, our very first trip outside California. I had to get on the phone and say in an adolescent voice that was not very convincing, "This is Mrs. Tan." [10]

And my mother was standing in the back whispering loudly, "Why he don't send me check, already two weeks late. So mad he lie to me, losing me money." [11]

And then I said in perfect English, "Yes, I'm getting rather concerned. You had agreed to send the check two weeks ago, but it hasn't arrived." [12]

Then she began to talk more loudly. "What he want, I come to New York tell him front of his boss, you cheating me?" And I was trying to calm her down, make her be quiet, while telling the stockbroker, "I can't tolerate any more excuses. If I don't receive the check immediately, I am going to have to speak to your manager when I'm in New York next week." And sure enough, the following week there we were in front of this astonished stockbroker, and I was sitting there red-faced and quiet, and my mother, the real Mrs. Tan, was shouting at his boss in her impeccable broken English. [13]

We used a similar routine just five days ago, for a situation that was far less humorous. My mother had gone to the hospital for an appointment, to find out about a benign brain tumor a CAT scan had revealed a month ago. She said she had spoken very good English, her best English, no mistakes. Still, she said, the hospital did not apologize when they said they had lost the CAT scan and she had come for nothing. She said they did not seem to have any sympathy when she told them she was anxious to know the exact diagnosis, since her husband and son had both died of brain tumors. She said they would not give her any more information until the next time and she would have to make another appointment for that. So she said she would not leave until the doctor [14] called her daughter. She wouldn't budge. And when the doctor finally called her daughter, me, who spoke in perfect English—lo and behold—we had assurances the CAT scan would be found, promises that a conference call on Monday would be held, and apologies for any suffering my mother had gone through for a most regrettable mistake.

I think my mother's English almost had an effect on limiting my 15 possibilities in life as well. Sociologists and linguists probably will tell you that a person's developing language skills are more influenced by peers. But I do think that the language spoken in the family, especially in immigrant families which are more insular, plays a large role in shaping the language of the child. And I believe that it affected my results on achievement tests, IQ tests, and the SAT. While my English skills were never judged as poor, compared to math, English could not be considered my strong suit. In grade school I did moderately well, getting perhaps B's, sometimes B-pluses, in English and scoring perhaps in the sixtieth or seventieth percentile on achievement tests. But those scores were not good enough to override the opinion that my true abilities lay in math and science, because in those areas I achieved A's and scored in the ninetieth percentile or higher.

This was understandable. Math is precise; there is only one correct 16 answer. Whereas, for me at least, the answers on English tests were always a judgment call, a matter of opinion and personal experience. Those tests were constructed around items like fill-in-the-blank sentence completion, such as, "Even though Tom was , Mary thought he was ." And the correct answer always seemed to be the most bland combinations of thoughts, for example, "Even though Tom was shy, Mary thought he was charming," with the grammatical structure "even though" limiting the correct answer to some sort of semantic opposites, so you wouldn't get answers like, "Even though Tom was foolish, Mary thought he was ridiculous." Well, according to my mother, there were very few limitations as to what Tom could have been and what Mary might have thought of him. So I never did well on tests like that.

The same was true with word analogies, pairs of words in which 17 you were supposed to find some sort of logical, semantic relationship—for example, "*Sunset* is to *nightfall* as is to ." And here you would be presented with a list of four possible pairs, one of which showed the same kind of relationship: *red* is to *stoplight, bus* is to *arrival, chills* is to *fever, yawn* is to *boring*. Well, I could never think that way. I knew what the tests were asking, but I could not block out of my mind the images already created by the first pair, "*sunset* is to *nightfall*"—and I would see a burst of colors against a darkening sky, the moon rising, the lowering of a curtain of stars. And all the other pairs of words—red, bus, stoplight, boring—just threw up a mass of confusing images, making it impossible for me to sort out something as logical as saying: "A sunset precedes nightfall" is the same as "a chill precedes a fever." The only way

I would have gotten that answer right would have been to imagine an associative situation, for example, my being disobedient and staying out past sunset, catching a chill at night, which turns into feverish pneumonia as punishment, which indeed did happen to me.

I have been thinking about all this lately, about my mother's English, about achievement tests. Because lately I've been asked, as a writer, why there are not more Asian Americans represented in American literature. Why are there few Asian Americans enrolled in creative writing programs? Why do so many Chinese students go into engineering? Well, these are broad sociological questions I can't begin to answer. But I have noticed in surveys—in fact, just last week—that Asian students, as a whole, always do significantly better on math achievement tests than in English. And this makes me think that there are other Asian-American students whose English spoken in the home might also be described as "broken" or "limited." And perhaps they also have teachers who are steering them away from writing and into math and science, which is what happened to me. [18]

Fortunately, I happen to be rebellious in nature and enjoy the challenge of disproving assumptions made about me. I became an English major my first year in college, after being enrolled as pre-med. I started writing nonfiction as a freelancer the week after I was told by my former boss that writing was my worst skill and I should hone my talents toward account management. [19]

But it wasn't until 1985 that I finally began to write fiction. And at first I wrote using what I thought to be wittily crafted sentences, sentences that would finally prove I had mastery over the English language. Here's an example from the first draft of a story that later made its way into *The Joy Luck Club*, but without this line: "That was my mental quandary in its nascent state." A terrible line, which I can barely pronounce. [20]

Fortunately, for reasons I won't get into today, I later decided I should envision a reader for the stories I would write. And the reader I decided upon was my mother, because these were stories about mothers. So with this reader in mind—and in fact she did read my early drafts—I began to write stories using all the Englishes I grew up with: the English I spoke to my mother, which for lack of a better term might be described as "simple"; the English she used with me, which for lack of a better term might be described as "broken"; my translation of her Chinese, which could certainly be described as "watered down"; and what I imagined to be her translation of her Chinese if she could speak in perfect English, her internal language, and for that I sought to preserve the essence, but neither an English nor a Chinese structure. I wanted to capture what language ability tests can never reveal: her intent, her passion, her imagery, the rhythms of her speech and the nature of her thoughts. [21]

Apart from what any critic had to say about my writing, I knew I [22] had succeeded where it counted when my mother finished reading my book and gave me her verdict: "So easy to read."

Responding to Reading

1. Do you, like Tan, use different Englishes? In what way do these various languages enable you to express your different selves?
2. Tan implies that some languages are more expressive than others. Do you agree? Are there some ideas you can express in one language that are difficult or impossible to express in another? Give examples if you can.
3. Do you believe that the kind of English spoken at home can have an effect on a student's performance on IQ tests and the SAT? Do you think the English you speak at home has had a positive or negative effect on your command of English?

THE HUMAN COST OF AN
~ ILLITERATE SOCIETY

Jonathon Kozol

For over thirty years, Jonathan Kozol (see p. 102) has written compassionately about many of the social problems confronting the United States, particularly those that affect the poor and the disadvantaged. In the following excerpt from his 1985 book *Illiterate America*, Kozol exposes the problems facing the sixty million Americans who are unable to read well enough to function in society and argues that their plight has important implications for the literate among us as well.

PRECAUTIONS. READ BEFORE USING.
Poison: Contains sodium hydroxide (caustic soda-lye).
Corrosive: Causes severe eye and skin damage, may cause blindness.
Harmful or fatal if swallowed.
If swallowed, give large quantities of milk or water.
Do not induce vomiting.
Important: Keep water out of can at all times to prevent contents from violently erupting . . .

—warning on a can of Drano

Questions of literacy, in Socrates' belief, must at length be judged as   1
matters of morality. Socrates could not have had in mind the moral compromise peculiar to a nation like our own. Some of our Founding Fathers did, however, have this question in their minds. One of the wisest
of those Founding Fathers (one who may not have been most compassionate but surely was more prescient than some of his peers) recognized the special dangers that illiteracy would pose to basic equity in the
political construction that he helped to shape.

"A people who mean to be their own governors," James Madison   2
wrote, "must arm themselves with the power knowledge gives. A popular government without popular information or the means of acquiring it, is but a prologue to a farce or a tragedy, or perhaps both."

Tragedy looms larger than farce in the United States today. Illiter-   3
ate citizens seldom vote. Those who do are forced to cast a vote of questionable worth. They cannot make informed decisions based on serious
print information. Sometimes they can be alerted to their interests by aggressive voter education. More frequently, they vote for a face, a smile,
or a style, not for a mind or character or body of beliefs.

The number of illiterate adults exceeds by 16 million the entire vote   4
cast for the winner in the 1980 presidential contest. If even one third of
all illiterates could vote, and read enough and do sufficient math to vote
in their self-interest, Ronald Reagan would not likely have been chosen
president. There is, of course, no way to know for sure. We do know
this: Democracy is a mendacious[1] term when used by those who are prepared to countenance the forced exclusion of one third of our electorate.
So long as 60 million people are denied significant participation, the government is neither of, nor for, nor by, the people. It is a government, at
best, of those two thirds whose wealth, skin color, or parental privilege
allows them opportunity to profit from the provocation and instruction
of the written word.

The undermining of democracy in the United States is one "ex-   5
pense" that sensitive Americans can easily deplore because it represents
a contradiction that endangers citizens of all political positions. The
human price is not so obvious at first.

Since I first immersed myself within this work I have often had the   6
following dream: I find that I am in a railroad station or a large department store within a city that is utterly unknown to me and where I cannot understand the printed words. None of the signs or symbols is familiar. Everything looks strange: like mirror writing of some kind.
Gradually I understand that I am in the Soviet Union. All the letters on
the walls around me are Cyrillic. I look for my pocket dictionary but I
find that it has been mislaid. Where have I left it? Then I recall that I for-

---

[1] Basely dishonest. [Eds.]

got to bring it with me when I packed my bags in Boston. I struggle to remember the name of my hotel. I try to ask somebody for directions. One person stops and looks at me in a peculiar way. I lose the nerve to ask. At last I reach into my wallet for an ID card. The card is missing. Have I lost it? Then I remember that my card was confiscated for some reason, many years before. Around this point, I wake up in a panic.

This panic is not so different from the misery that millions of adult illiterates experience each day within the course of their routine existence in the U.S.A.   7

Illiterates cannot read the menu in a restaurant.   8

They cannot read the cost of items on the menu in the *window* of the restaurant before they enter.   9

Illiterates cannot read the letters that their children bring home from their teachers. They cannot study school department circulars that tell them of the courses that their children must be taking if they hope to pass the SAT exams. They cannot help with homework. They cannot write a letter to the teacher. They are afraid to visit in the classroom. They do not want to humiliate their child or themselves.   10

Illiterates cannot read instructions on a bottle of prescription medicine. They cannot find out when a medicine is past the year of safe consumption; nor can they read of allergenic risks, warnings to diabetics, or the potential sedative effect of certain kinds of nonprescription pills. They cannot observe preventive health care admonitions. They cannot read about "the seven warning signs of cancer" or the indications of blood-sugar fluctuations or the risks of eating certain foods that aggravate the likelihood of cardiac arrest.   11

Illiterates live, in more than literal ways, an uninsured existence. They cannot understand the written details on a health insurance form. They cannot read the waivers that they sign preceding surgical procedures. Several women I have known in Boston have entered a slum hospital with the intention of obtaining a tubal ligation and have emerged a few days later after having been subjected to a hysterectomy.[2] Unaware of their rights, incognizant of jargon, intimidated by the unfamiliar air of fear and atmosphere of ether that so many of us find oppressive in the confines even of the most attractive and expensive medical facilities, they have signed their names to documents they could not read and which nobody, in the hectic situation that prevails so often in those overcrowded hospitals that serve the urban poor, had even bothered to explain.   12

Childbirth might seem to be the last inalienable right of any female citizen within a civilized society. Illiterate mothers, as we shall see, already have been cheated of the power to protect their progeny against   13

---

[2] A hysterectomy, the removal of the uterus, is a much more radical procedure than a tubal ligation, a method of sterilization, which is a common form of birth control. [Eds.]

the likelihood of demolition in deficient public schools and, as a result, against the verbal servitude within which they themselves exist. Surgical denial of the right to bear that child in the first place represents an ultimate denial, an unspeakable metaphor, a final darkness that denies even the twilight gleamings of our own humanity. What greater violation of our biological, our biblical, our spiritual humanity could possibly exist than that which takes place nightly, perhaps hourly these days, within such over-burdened and benighted institutions as the Boston City Hospital? Illiteracy has many costs; few are so irreversible as this.

Even the roof above one's head, the gas or other fuel for heating that [14] protects the residents of northern city slums against the threat of illness in the winter months become uncertain guarantees. Illiterates cannot read the lease that they must sign to live in an apartment which, too often, they cannot afford. They cannot manage check accounts and therefore seldom pay for anything by mail. Hours and entire days of difficult travel (and the cost of bus or other public transit) must be added to the real cost of whatever they consume. Loss of interest on the check accounts they do not have, and could not manage if they did, must be regarded as another of the excess costs paid by the citizen who is excluded from the common instruments of commerce in a numerate society.

"I couldn't understand the bills," a woman in Washington, D.C., re- [15] ports, "and then I couldn't write the checks to pay them. We signed things we didn't know what they were."

Illiterates cannot read the notices that they receive from welfare of- [16] fices or from the IRS. They must depend on word-of-mouth instruction from the welfare worker—or from other persons whom they have good reason to mistrust. They do not know what rights they have, what deadlines and requirements they face, what options they might choose to exercise. They are half-citizens. Their rights exist in print but not in fact.

Illiterates cannot look up numbers in a telephone directory. Even if [17] they can find the names of friends, few possess the sorting skills to make use of the yellow pages; categories are bewildering and trade names are beyond decoding capabilities for millions of nonreaders. Even the emergency numbers listed on the first page of the phone book—"Ambulance," "Police," and "Fire"—are too frequently beyond the recognition of nonreaders.

Many illiterates cannot read the admonition on a pack of cigarettes. [18] Neither the Surgeon General's warning nor its reproduction on the package can alert them to the risks. Although most people learn by word of mouth that smoking is related to a number of grave physical disorders, they do not get the chance to read the detailed stories which can document this danger with the vividness that turns concern into determination to resist. They can see the handsome cowboy or the slim Virginia lady lighting up a filter cigarette; they cannot heed the words that tell them that this product is (not "may be") dangerous to their health. Sixty million men and women are condemned to be the unalerted, high-risk candidates for cancer.

Illiterates do not buy "no-name" products in the supermarkets. [19] They must depend on photographs or the familiar logos that are print-ed on the packages of brand-name groceries. The poorest people, there-fore, are denied the benefits of the least costly products.

Illiterates depend almost entirely upon label recognition. Many la- [20] bels, however, are not easy to distinguish. Dozens of different kinds of Campbell's soup appear identical to the nonreader. The purchaser who cannot read and does not dare to ask for help, out of the fear of being stigmatized (a fear which is unfortunately realistic), frequently comes home with something which she never wanted and her family never tasted.

Illiterates cannot read instructions on a pack of frozen food. Pack- [21] ages sometimes provide an illustration to explain the cooking prepara-tions; but illustrations are of little help to someone who must "boil water, drop the food—*within* its plastic wrapper—in the boiling water, wait for it to simmer, instantly remove."

Even when labels are seemingly clear, they may be easily mistaken. [22] A woman in Detroit brought home a gallon of Crisco for her children's dinner. She thought that she had bought the chicken that was pictured on the label. She had enough Crisco now to last a year—but no more money to go back and buy the food for dinner.

Recipes provided on the packages of certain staples sometimes [23] tempt a semiliterate person to prepare a meal her children have not tast-ed. The longing to vary the uniform and often starchy content of low-budget meals provided to the family that relies on food stamps com-monly leads to ruinous results. Scarce funds have been wasted and the food must be thrown out. The same applies to distribution of food-sur-plus produce in emergency conditions. Government inducements to poor people to "explore the ways" by which to make a tasty meal from tasteless noodles, surplus cheese, and powdered milk are useless to non-readers. Intended as benevolent advice, such recommendations mock reality and foster deeper feelings of resentment and of inability to cope. (Those, on the other hand, who cautiously refrain from "innovative" recipes in preparation of their children's meals must suffer the oppro-brium of "laziness," "lack of imagination. . . .")

Illiterates cannot travel freely. When they attempt to do so, they en- [24] counter risks that few of us can dream of. They cannot read traffic signs and, while they often learn to recognize and to decipher symbols, they cannot manage street names which they haven't seen before. The same is true for bus and subway stops. While ingenuity can sometimes help a man or woman to discern directions from familiar landmarks, build-ings, cemeteries, churches, and the like, most illiterates are virtually immobilized. They seldom wander past the streets and neighborhoods they know. Geographical paralysis becomes a bitter metaphor for their entire existence. They are immobilized in almost every sense we can imagine. They can't move up. They can't move out. They cannot see beyond. Illiterates may take an oral test for drivers' permits in most sections of America. It is a questionable concession. Where will they go? How will they get there? How will they get home? Could it be that some of us might like it better if they stayed where they belong?

Travel is only one of many instances of circumscribed existence. [25] Choice, in almost all its facets, is diminished in the life of an illiterate adult. Even the printed TV schedule, which provides most people with the luxury of preselection, does not belong within the arsenal of options in illiterate existence. One consequence is that the viewer watches only what appears at moments when he happens to have time to turn the switch. Another consequence, a lot more common, is that the TV set remains in operation night and day. Whatever the program offered at the hour when he walks into the room will be the nutriment that he accepts and swallows. Thus, to passivity, is added frequency—indeed, almost uninterrupted continuity. Freedom to select is no more possible here than in the choice of home or surgery or food.

"You don't choose," said one illiterate woman. "You take your [26] wishes from somebody else." Whether in perusal of a menu, selection of highways, purchase of groceries, or determination of affordable enjoyment, illiterate Americans must trust somebody else: a friend, a relative, a stranger on the street, a grocery clerk, a TV copywriter.

"All of our mail we get, it's hard for her to read. Settin' down and [27] writing a letter, she can't do it. Like if we get a bill . . . we take it over to my sister-in-law . . . My sister-in-law reads it."

Billing agencies harass poor people for the payment of the bills for [28] purchases that might have taken place six months before. Utility companies offer an agreement for a staggered payment schedule on a bill past due. "You have to trust them," one man said. Precisely for this reason, you end up by trusting no one and suspecting everyone of possible deceit. A submerged sense of distrust becomes the corollary to a constant need to trust. "They are cheating me . . . I have been tricked . . . I do not know . . ."

Not knowing: This is a familiar theme. Not knowing the right word [29] for the right thing at the right time is one form of subjugation. Not knowing the world that lies concealed behind those words is a more terrifying feeling. The longitude and latitude of one's existence are beyond all easy apprehension. Even the hard, cold stars within the firmament above one's head begin to mock the possibilities for self-location. Where am I? Where did I come from? Where will I go?

"I've lost a lot of jobs," one man explains. "Today, even if you're a [30] janitor, there's still reading and writing . . . They leave a note saying, 'Go to room so-and-so . . .' You can't do it. You can't read it. You don't know."

"The hardest thing about it is that I've been places where I didn't [31] know where I was. You don't know where you are . . . You're lost."

"Like I said: I have two kids. What do I do if one of my kids starts [32] choking? I go running to the phone . . . I can't look up the hospital phone number. That's if we're at home. Out on the street, I can't read the sign. I get to a pay phone. 'Okay, tell us where you are. We'll send an ambulance.' I look at the street sign. Right there, I can't tell you what it says. I'd have to spell it out, letter for letter. By that time, one of my kids would be dead . . . These are the kinds of fears you go with, every single day . . ."

"Reading directions, I suffer with. I work with chemicals . . . That's [33] scary to begin with . . ."

"You sit down. They throw the menu in front of you. Where do you [34] go from there? Nine times out of ten you say, 'Go ahead. Pick out something for the both of us.' I've eaten some weird things, let me tell you!"

Menus. Chemicals. A child choking while his mother searches for a [35] word she does not know to find assistance that will come too late. Another mother speaks about the inability to help her kids to read: "I can't read to them. Of course that's leaving them out of something they should have. Oh, it matters. You *believe* it matters! I ordered all these books. The kids belong to a book club. Donny wanted me to read a book to him. I told Donny: 'I can't read,' He said: 'Mommy, you sit down. I'll read it to you.' I tried it one day, reading from the pictures. Donny looked at me. He said, 'Mommy, that's not right.' He's only five. He knew I couldn't read . . .'"

A landlord tells a woman that her lease allows him to evict her if [36] her baby cries and causes inconvenience to her neighbors. The consequence of challenging his words conveys a danger which appears, unlikely as it seems, even more alarming than the danger of eviction. Once she admits that she can't read, in the desire to maneuver for the time in which to call a friend, she will have defined herself in terms of an explicit impotence that she cannot endure. Capitulation in this case is preferable to self-humiliation. Resisting the definition of oneself in terms of what one cannot do, what others take for granted, represents a need so great that other imperatives (even one so urgent as the need to keep one's home in winter's cold) evaporate and fall away in face of fear. Even the loss of home and shelter, in this case, is not so terrifying as the loss of self.

"I come out of school. I was sixteen. They had their meetings. The [37] directors meet. They said that I was wasting their school paper. I was wasting pencils . . ."

Another illiterate, looking back, believes she was not worthy of her [38] teacher's time. She believes that it was wrong of her to take up space within her school. She believes that it was right to leave in order that somebody more deserving could receive her place.

Children choke. Their mother chokes another way: on more than chicken bones. [39]

People eat what others order, know what others tell them, struggle not to see themselves as they believe the world perceives them. A man in California speaks about his own loss of identity, of self-location, definition: [40]

"I stood at the bottom of the ramp. My car had broke down on the freeway. There was a phone. I asked for the police. They was nice. They said to tell them where I was. I looked up at the signs. There was one that I had seen before. I read it to them: ONE WAY STREET. They thought it was a joke. I told them I couldn't read. There was other signs above the ramp. They told me to try. I looked around for somebody to help. All the cars was going by real fast. I couldn't make them understand that I was lost. The cop was nice. He told me: "Try once more,' I did my best. I couldn't read. I only knew the sign above my head. The cop was trying to be nice. He knew that I was trapped. 'I can't send out a car to you if you can't tell me where you are.' I felt afraid. I nearly cried. I'm forty-eight years old. I only said: 'I'm on a one-way street . . .'" [41]

The legal problems and the courtroom complications that confront illiterate adults have been discussed above. The anguish that may underlie such matters was brought home to me this year while I was working on this book. I have spoken, in the introduction, of a sudden phone call from one of my former students, now in prison for a criminal offense. Stephen is not a boy today. He is twenty-eight years old. He called to ask me to assist him in his trial, which comes up next fall. He will be on trial for murder. He has just knifed and killed a man who first enticed him to his home, then cheated him, and then insulted him—as "an illiterate subhuman." [42]

Stephen now faces twenty years to life. Stephen's mother was illiterate. His grandparents were illiterate as well. What parental curse did not destroy was killed off finally by the schools. Silent violence is repaid with interest. It will cost us $25,000 yearly to maintain this broken soul in prison. But what is the price that has been paid by Stephen's victim? What is the price that will be paid by Stephen? [43]

Perhaps we might slow down a moment here and look at the realities described above. This is the nation that we live in. This is a society that most of us did not create but which our President and other leaders have been willing to sustain by virtue of malign neglect. Do we possess the character and courage to address a problem which so many nations, poorer than our own, have found it natural to correct? [44]

The answers to these questions represent a reasonable test of our be- ⁴⁵
lief in the democracy to which we have been asked in public school to
swear allegiance.

Responding to Reading

1. Do you agree with Kozol that illiteracy undermines democracy in the United States? Explain. What do think can be done to lessen the problem of illiteracy?
2. Do you think Kozol accurately describes the difficulties illiterates face in
   their daily lives, or does he seem to be exaggerating? If you think he is exaggerating, what motive might he have?
3. What specific activities would you be unable to carry out if you were illiterate? What tasks would you have little or no difficulty performing? How
   would your life be different?

THE NEW IMMIGRANTS

~

James Fallows

Praised for his fluid prose style and balanced perspective, James Fallows (1949–) received early attention for his books about corporate
degradation of the environment (*The Water Works,* 1971) and wasteful
Pentagon spending (*National Defense,* 1981). More recently he has focused on what the United States can—and cannot—learn from Japanese corporate and economic policies (*More Like Us: Making American
Great Again,* 1989, and *Looking at the Sun: The Rise of the New East Asian
Economic and Political System,* 1994). A former speech writer for President Jimmy Carter, Fallows since 1979 has been an editor at the *Atlantic
Monthly,* for which he writes on a variety of subjects. In the following
article, which originally appeared in that magazine in 1983, Fallows
looks at the controversial issue of bilingual education from the perspective of an admittedly "hostile observer" and concludes that the debate is in fact more inflammatory than it need be.

Assume for the moment that legal immigrants make an economy ¹
more efficient. Does that tell us all we need to know in order to understand their impact on our society? A national culture is held together by
official rules and informal signals. Through their language, dress, taste,
and habits of life, immigrants initially violate the rules and confuse the

signals. The United States has prided itself on building a nation out of diverse parts. *E Pluribus Unum* originally referred to the act of political union in which separate colonies became one sovereign state. It now seems more fitting as a token of the cultural adjustments through which immigrant strangers have become Americans. Can the assimilative forces still prevail?

The question arises because most of today's immigrants share one   2
trait: their native language is Spanish.

From 1970 to 1978, the three leading sources of legal immigrants to   3
the U.S. were Mexico, the Philippines, and Cuba. About 42 percent of legal immigration during the seventies was from Latin America. It is thought that about half of all illegal immigrants come from Mexico, and 10 to 15 percent more from elsewhere in Latin America. Including illegal immigrants makes all figures imprecise, but it seems reasonable to conclude that more than half the people who now come to the United States speak Spanish. This is a greater concentration of immigrants in one non-English language group than ever before.

Is it a threat? The conventional wisdom about immigrants and their   4
languages is that the Spanish-speakers are asking for treatment different from that which has been accorded to everybody else. In the old days, it is said, immigrants were eager to assimilate as quickly as possible. They were placed, sink or swim, in English-language classrooms, and they swam. But now the Latin Americans seem to be insisting on bilingual classrooms and ballots. "The Hispanics demand that the United States become a bilingual country, with all children entitled to be taught in the language of their heritage, at public expense," Theodore White has written. Down this road lie the linguistic cleavages that have brought grief to other nations.

This is the way many people think, and this is the way I myself   5
thought as I began this project.

6

The historical parallel closest to today's concentration of Spanish-speaking immigrants is the German immigration of the nineteenth century. From 1830 to 1890, 4.5 million Germans emigrated to the United States, making up one third of the immigrant total. The Germans recognized that command of English would finally ensure for them, and especially for their children, a place in the mainstream of American society. But like the Swedes, Dutch, and French before them, they tried hard to retain the language in which they had been raised.

The midwestern states, where Germans were concentrated, estab-   7
lished bilingual schools, in which children could receive instruction in German. In Ohio, German–English public schools were in operation by 1840; in 1837, the Pennsylvania legislature ordered that German-language public schools be established on an equal basis with English-language schools. Minnesota, Maryland, and Indiana also operated public

schools in which German was used, either by itself or in addition to English. In *Life with Two Languages*, his study of bilingualism, François Grosjean says, "What is particularly striking about German Americans in the nineteenth century is their constant efforts to maintain their language, culture, and heritage."

Yet despite everything the Germans could do, their language began [8] to die out. The progression was slow and fraught with pain. For the immigrant, language was the main source of certainty and connection to the past. As the children broke from the Old World culture and tried out their snappy English slang on their parents, the pride the parents felt at such achievements was no doubt mixed with the bittersweet awareness that they were losing control.

At first the children would act as interpreters for their parents; then [9] they would demand the independence appropriate to that role; then they would yearn to escape the coarse ways of immigrant life. And in the end, they would be Americans. It was hard on the families, but it built an assimilated English-language culture.

The pattern of assimilation is familiar from countless novels, as well [10] as from the experience of many people now living. Why, then, is the currently fashionable history of assimilation so different? Why is it assumed, in so many discussions of bilingual education, that in the old days immigrants switched quickly and enthusiastically to English?

One reason is that the experience of Jewish immigrants in the early [11] twentieth century was different from this pattern. German Jews, successful and thoroughly assimilated here in the nineteenth century, oversaw an effort to bring Eastern European Jews into the American mainstream as quickly as possible. In New York City, the Lower East Side's Hebrew Institute, later known as the Educational Alliance, defined its goal as teaching the newcomers "the privileges and duties of American citizenship." Although many Jewish immigrants preserved their Yiddish, Jews generally learned English faster than any other group.

Another reason that nineteenth-century linguistic history is so little [12] remembered lies in the political experience of the early twentieth century. As an endless stream of New Immigrants arrived from Eastern Europe, the United States was awash in theories about the threats the newcomers posed to American economic, sanitary, and racial standards, and the "100 percent Americanism" movement arose. By the late 1880s, school districts in the Midwest had already begun reversing their early encouragement of bilingual education. Competence in English was made a requirement for naturalized citizens in 1906. Pro-English-language leagues sprang up to help initiate the New Immigrants. California's Commission on Immigration and Housing, for example, endorsed a campaign of "Americanization propaganda," in light of "the necessity for all to learn English—the language of America." With the coming of World War I, all German-language activities were suddenly cast in a different light. Eventually, as a result, Americans came to believe that previous immigrants had speedily switched to English, and to view the Hispanics' attachment to Spanish as a troubling aberration.

The term "Hispanic" is in many ways deceiving. It refers to those [13] whose origins can be traced back to Spain (*Hispania*) or Spain's former colonies. It makes a bloc out of Spanish-speaking peoples who otherwise have little in common. The Cuban-Americans, concentrated in Florida, are flush with success. Some of them nurse dreams of political revenge against Castro. They demonstrate little solidarity with such other Hispanics as the Mexican-Americans of Texas, who are much less estranged from their homeland and who have been longtime participants in the culture of the Southwest. The Cuban-Americans tend to be Republicans; most Mexican-Americans and Puerto Ricans are Democrats. The Puerto Ricans, who are U.S. citizens from birth, and who have several generations of contact with American city life behind them, bear little resemblance to the Salvadorans and Guatemalans now pouring northward to get out of the way of war. Economically, the Puerto Ricans of New York City have more in common with American blacks than with most other Hispanic groups. Such contact as Anglo and black residents of Boston and New York have with Hispanic life comes mainly through Puerto Ricans; they may be misled about what to expect from the Mexicans and Central Americans arriving in ever increasing numbers. Along the southern border, Mexican-American children will razz youngsters just in from Mexico. A newcomer is called a "TJ," for Tijuana; it is the equivalent of "hillbilly" or "rube."

Still, "Hispanic" can be a useful word, because it focuses attention [14] on the major question about this group of immigrants: Will their assimilation into an English-speaking culture be any less successful than that of others in the past?

To answer, we must consider what is different now from the cir- [15] cumstances under which the Germans, Poles, and Italians learned English.

The most important difference is that the host country is right next [16] door. The only other non-English-speaking group for which this is true is the French-Canadians. Proximity has predictable consequences. For as long as the Southwest has been part of the United States, there has been a border culture in which, for social and commercial reasons, both languages have been used. There has also been a Mexican-American population accustomed to moving freely across the border, between the cultures, directing its loyalties both ways.

Because it has always been so easy to go home, many Mexicans and [17] Mexican-Americans have displayed the classic sojourner outlook. The more total the break with the mother country, the more pressure immigrants feel to adapt; but for many immigrants from Mexico, whose kin and friends still live across the border and whose dreams center on returning in wealthy splendor to their native villages, the pressure is weak.

Many people have suggested that there is another difference, perhaps more significant than the first. It is a change in the nation's self-confidence. The most familiar critique of bilingual education holds that the nation no longer feels a resolute will to require mastery of the national language. America's most powerful assimilative force, the English language, may therefore be in jeopardy.

It is true that starting in the early 1960s U.S. government policy began to move away from the quick-assimilation approach preferred since the turn of the century. After surveys of Puerto Rican students in New York City and Mexican-Americans in Texas revealed that they were dropping out of school early and generally having a hard time, educational theorists began pushing plans for Spanish-language instruction. The turning point came with *Lau* v. *Nichols*, a case initiated in 1971 by Chinese-speaking students in San Francisco. They sued for "equal protection," on grounds that their unfamiliarity with English denied them an adequate education. In 1974, the Supreme Court ruled in their favor, saying that "those who do not understand English are certain to find their classroom experience wholly incomprehensible and in no way meaningful." The ruling did not say that school systems had to start bilingual programs of the kind that the phrase is now generally understood to mean—that is, classrooms in which both languages are used. The court said that "teaching English to the students . . . who do not speak the language" would be one acceptable solution. But the federal regulations and state laws that implemented the decision obliged many districts to set up the system of "transitional" bilingual education that has since become the focus of furor.

The rules vary from state to state, but they typically require a school district to set up a bilingual program whenever a certain number of students (often twenty) at one grade level are from one language group and do not speak English well. In principle, bilingual programs will enable them to keep up with the content of, say, their math and history courses while preparing them to enter the English-language classroom.

The bilingual system is accused of supporting a cadre of educational consultants while actually retarding the students' progress into the English-speaking mainstream. In this view, bilingual education could even be laying the foundation for a separate Hispanic culture, by extending the students' Spanish-language world from their homes to their schools.

Before I traveled to some of the schools in which bilingual education was applied, I shared the skeptics' view. What good could come of a system that encouraged, to whatever degree, a language other than the national tongue? But after visiting elementary, junior high, and high schools in Miami, Houston, San Antonio, Austin, several parts of Los Angeles, and San Diego, I found little connection between the political debate over bilingual education and what was going on in these schools.

To begin with, one central fact about bilingual education goes large- [23] ly unreported. It is a *temporary* program. The time a typical student stays in the program varies from place to place—often two years in Miami, three years in Los Angeles—but when that time has passed, the student will normally leave. Why, then, do bilingual programs run through high school? Those classes are usually for students who are new to the district—usually because their parents are new to the country.

There is another fact about bilingual education, more difficult to [24] prove but impressive to me, a hostile observer. Most of the children I saw were unmistakably learning to speak English.

In the elementary schools, where the children have come straight [25] out of all-Spanish environments, the background babble seems to be entirely in Spanish. The kindergarten and first- to third-grade classrooms I saw were festooned with the usual squares and circles cut from colored construction paper, plus posters featuring Big Bird and charts about the weather and the seasons. Most of the schools seemed to keep a rough balance between English and Spanish in the lettering around the room; the most Spanish environment I saw was in one school in East Los Angeles, where about a third of the signs were in English.

The elementary school teachers were mostly Mexican-American [26] women. They prompted the children with a mixture of English and Spanish during the day. While books in both languages are available in the classrooms, most of the first-grade reading drills I saw were in Spanish. In theory, children will learn the phonetic principle of reading more quickly if they are not trying to learn a new language at the same time. Once comfortable as readers, they will theoretically be able to transfer their ability to English.

In a junior high school in Houston, I saw a number of Mexican and [27] Salvadoran students in their "bilingual" biology and math classes. They were drilled entirely in Spanish on the parts of an amoeba and on the difference between a parallelogram and a rhombus. When students enter bilingual programs at this level, the goal is to keep them current with the standard curriculum while introducing them to English. I found my fears of linguistic separatism rekindled by the sight of fourteen-year-olds lectured to in Spanish. I reminded myself that many of the students I was seeing had six months earlier lived in another country.

The usual next stop for students whose time in bilingual education [28] is up is a class in intensive English, lasting one to three hours a day. These students are divided into two or three proficiency levels, from those who speak no English to those nearly ready to forgo special help.

In Houston, a teacher drilled two-dozen high-school-age Cambodians, Indians, Cubans, and Mexicans on the crucial difference between the voiced *th* sound of "this" and the voiceless *th* of "thing." In Miami, a class of high school sophomores included youths from Cuba, El Salvador, and Honduras. They listened as their teacher read a Rockwellesque essay about a student with a crush on his teacher, and then set to work writing an essay of their own, working in words like "garrulous" and "sentimentalize."

One of the students in Miami, a sixteen-year-old from Honduras, [29] said that his twelve-year-old brother had already moved into mainstream classes. Linguists say this is the standard pattern for immigrant children. The oldest children hold on to their first language longest, while their younger sisters and brothers swim quickly into the new language culture.

The more I saw of the classes, the more convinced I became that [30] most of the students were learning English. Therefore, I started to wonder what it is about bilingual education that has made it the focus of such bitter disagreement.

For one thing, most immigrant groups other than Hispanics take a [31] comparatively dim view of bilingual education. Haitians, Vietnamese, and Cambodians are eligible for bilingual education, but in general they are unenthusiastic. In Miami, Haitian boys and girls may learn to read in Creole rather than English. Still, their parents push to keep them moving into English. "A large number of [Haitian] parents come to the PTA meetings, and they don't want interpreters," said the principal of Miami's Edison Park Elementary School last spring. "They want to learn English. They don't want notices coming home in three languages. When they come here, unless there is total noncommunication, they will try to get through to us in their broken English. The students learn the language *very* quickly."

Bilingual education is inflammatory in large part because of what it [32] symbolizes, not because of the nuts and bolts of its daily operation. In reality, bilingual programs move students into English with greater or lesser success; in reality, most Spanish-speaking parents understand that mastery of English will be their children's key to mobility. But in the political arena, bilingual education presents a different face. To the Hispanic ideologue,[1] it is a symbol of cultural pride and political power. And once it has been presented that way, with full rhetorical flourish, it naturally strikes other Americans as a threat to the operating rules that have bound the country together. . . .

⁓

---

[1] Strongly one-sided advocate. [Eds.]

But is this not a question for factual resolution rather than for bat- 33
tles about linguistic and ethnic pride? Perhaps one approach will succeed for certain students in certain situations and the other will be
best for others. The choice between bilingual programs and intensive-
English courses, then, should be a choice between methods, not ideologies. The wars over bilingual education have had a bitter, symbolic
quality. Each side has invested the issue with a meaning the other can
barely comprehend. To most Mexican-American parents and children,
bilingual education is merely a way of learning English; to Hispanic
activists, it is a symbol that they are at last taking their place in the
sun. But to many other Americans, it sounds like a threat not to assimilate. . . .

~

In only one respect does the Hispanic impulse seem to me to lead in 34
a dangerous direction. Hispanics are more acutely aware than most An-
glos that, as a practical reality, English is the national language of commerce, government, and mobility. But some have suggested that, in
principle, it should not be this way.

They invoke the long heritage of Mexican-Americans in the South- 35
west. As "Californios" or "Tejanos," the ancestors of some of these
families lived on and owned the territory before the Anglo settlers.
Others came across at the turn of the century, at a time of Mexican upheaval; still others came during the forties and fifties, as workers. They
have paid taxes, fought in wars, been an inseparable part of the region's culture. Yet they were also subject to a form of discrimination
more casual than the segregation of the Old South, but having one of
the same effects. Because of poverty or prejudice or gerry-mandered
school districts, many Mexican-Americans were, in effect, denied education. One result is that many now in their fifties and sixties do not
speak English well. Still, they are citizens, with the right of citizens to
vote. How are they to exercise their right if to do so requires learning
English? Do they not deserve a ballot printed in a language they can
understand?

In the early seventies, the issue came before the courts, and several 36
decisions held that if voters otherwise eligible could not understand
English, they must have voting materials prepared in a more convenient
language. In 1975, the Voting Rights Act amendments said that there
must be bilingual ballots if more than 5 percent of the voters in a district
were members of a "language minority group." The only "language minority groups" eligible under this ruling were American Indians,
Alaskan natives, Asian-Americans (most significantly, Chinese and Filipinos), and Spanish-speakers. A related case extracted from the Sixth
Circuit Court of Appeals the judgment that "the national language of the
United States is English."

So it is that ballots in parts of the country are printed in Spanish, or [37] Chinese, or Tagalog, along with English. This is true even though anyone applying for naturalization must still pass an English-proficiency test, which consists of questions such as "What are the three branches of government?" and "How long are the terms of a U.S. Senator and member of Congress?" The apparent inconsistency reflects the linguistic reality that many native-born citizens have not learned the national language.

By most accounts, the bilingual ballot is purely a symbol. The na- [38] tive-born citizens who can't read English often can't read Spanish, either. As a symbol, it points in the wrong direction, away from a single national language in which the public business will be done. Its only justification is the older generation, which was excluded from the schools. In principle, then, it should be phased out in several years.

But there are those who feel that even the present arrangement is too [39] onerous. Rose Matsui Ochi, an assistant to the mayor of Los Angeles, who served on the Select Commission, dissented from the commission's recommendation to keep the English-language requirement for citizenship. She wrote in her minority opinion, "Abolishing the requirement recognizes the inability of certain individuals to learn English." Cruz Reynoso, the first Mexican-American appointee to the California Supreme Court, was also on the Select Commission, and he too dissented. "America is a *political* union—not a cultural, linguistic, religious or racial union," he wrote. "Of course, we as individuals would urge all to learn English, for that is the language used by most Americans, as well as the language of the marketplace. But we should no more demand English-language skills for citizenship than we should demand uniformity of religion. That a person wants to become a citizen and will make a good citizen is more than enough."

Some Chicano activists make the same point in less temperate terms. [40] Twice I found myself in shouting matches with Mexican-Americans who asked me who I thought I was to tell them—after all the homeboys who had died in combat, after all the insults they'd endured on the playground for speaking Spanish—what language they "should" speak.

That these arguments were conducted in English suggests the theo- [41] retical nature of the debate. Still, in questions like this, symbolism can be crucial. "I have sympathy for the position that the integrating mechanism of a society is language," Henry Cisneros says. "The U.S. has been able to impose fewer such integrating mechanisms on its people than other countries, but it needs some tie to hold these diverse people, Irish, Jews, Czechs, together as a nation. Therefore, I favor people learning English and being able to conduct business in the official language of the country."

"The *unum* demands only certain things of the *pluribus*," Lawrence [42] Fuchs says. "It demands very little. It demands that we believe in the political ideals of the republic, which allows people to preserve their ethnic identity. Most immigrants come from repressive regimes; we say, we're asking you to believe that government should *not* oppress you. Then it only asks one other thing: that in the wider marketplace and in the civic culture, you use the official language. No other society asks so little.

"English is not just an instrument of mobility. It is a sign that you re- 43 ally are committed. If you've been here five years, which you must to be a citizen, and if you are reasonably young, you should be able to learn English in that time. The rest of us are entitled to that."

Most of the young people I met—the rank and file, not the intellec- 44 tuals who espouse a bilingual society—seemed fully willing to give what in Fuchs's view the nation asks. I remember in particular one husky Puerto Rican athlete at Miami Senior High School who planned to join the Navy after he got his diploma. I talked to him in a bilingual classroom, heard his story, and asked his name. He told me, and I wrote *"Ramon."* He came around behind me and looked at my pad. "No, no!" he told me. "You should have put R-A-Y-M-O-N-D."

Responding to Reading

1. What generally held assumption about Spanish-speaking immigrants does Fallows attempt to refute? Do you think Fallows effectively refutes this assumption, or do you believe he is overly optimistic?
2. Do you think English should be the official language of the United States, or do you agree that "we should no more demand English language skills for citizenship than we should demand uniformity of religion" (39)? Should ballots be printed (as they are now) in more than one language? Should highway signs be in different languages? How about the instructions on ATM machines and the like?
3. What are the social and political implications of encouraging a society in which there is more than one "official" language? What might the advantages and disadvantages of such an arrangement be?

SEXISM IN ENGLISH: A 1990S ∼ UPDATE

Alleen Pace Nilsen

Alleen Pace Nilsen (1936-) is an educator and essayist who has contributed to many journals and has taught English at Arizona State University and other schools. In 1967 Nilsen lived in Afghanistan, where for two years she observed the subordinate position of women in that society. When she returned to the United States, she began to study American English for its cultural biases toward men and women. She says of that project, "As I worked my way through the dictionary, I concentrated on the way that particular usages, metaphors, slang terms, and definitions reveal society's attitude towards males and females." Currently interested in what teenagers read, Nilsen has coauthored *Literature for Today's Young Adults* (1988). The following essay is an updated version of some of Nilsen's findings from her dictionary study.

Twenty years ago I embarked on a study of the sexism inherent in [1] American English. I had just returned to Ann Arbor, Michigan, after living for two years (1967–69) in Kabul, Afghanistan, where I had begun to look critically at the role society assigned to women. The Afghan version of the *chaderi*[1] prescribed for Moslem women was particularly confining. Afghan jokes and folklore were blatantly sexist, such as this proverb: "If you see an old man, sit down and take a lesson; if you see an old woman, throw a stone."

But it wasn't only the native culture that made me question [2] women's roles, it was also the American community.

Most of the American women were like myself—wives and moth- [3] ers whose husbands were either career diplomats, employees of USAID, or college professors who had been recruited to work on various contract teams. We were suddenly bereft of our traditional roles: some of us became alcoholics, others got very good at bridge, while still others searched desperately for ways to contribute either to our families or to the Afghans. The local economy provided few jobs for women and certainly none for foreigners; we were isolated from former friends and the social goals we had grown up with.

When I returned in the fall of 1969 to the University of Michigan in [4] Ann Arbor, I was surprised to find that many other women were also questioning the expectations they had grown up with. In the spring of 1970, a women's conference was announced. I hired a babysitter and attended, but I returned home more troubled than ever. The militancy of these women frightened me. Since I wasn't ready for a revolution, I decided I would have my own feminist movement. I would study the English language and see what it could tell me about sexism. I started reading a desk dictionary and making notecards on every entry that seemed to tell something about male and female. I soon had a dog-eared dictionary, along with a collection of notecards filling two shoe boxes.

Ironically, I started reading the dictionary because I wanted to avoid [5] getting involved in social issues, but what happened was that my note-

---

[1] A *chador* is a heavily draped cloth covering the entire head and body. [Eds.]

cards brought me right back to looking at society. Language and society are as intertwined as a chicken and an egg. The language a culture uses is telltale evidence of the values and beliefs of that culture. And because there is a lag in how fast a language changes—new words can easily be introduced, but it takes a long time for old words and usages to disappear—a careful look at English will reveal the attitudes that our ancestors held and that we as a culture are therefore predisposed to hold. My notecards revealed three main points. Friends have offered the opinion that I didn't need to read the dictionary to learn such obvious facts. Nevertheless, it was interesting to have linguistic evidence of sociological observations.

Women Are Sexy; Men Are Successful

First, in American culture a woman is valued for the attractiveness and sexiness of her body, while a man is valued for his physical strength and accomplishments. A woman is sexy. A man is successful.   6

A persuasive piece of evidence supporting this view are the eponyms—words that have come from someone's name—found in English. I had a two-and-a-half-inch stack of cards taken from men's names but less than a half-inch stack from women's names, and most of those came from Greek mythology. In the words that came into American English since we separated from Britain, there are many eponyms based on the names of famous American men: *Bartlett pear, boysenberry, diesel engine, Franklin stove, Ferris wheel, Gatling gun, mason jar, sideburns; sousaphone, Schick test,* and *Winchester rifle.* The only common eponyms taken from American women's names are *Alice blue* (after Alice Roosevelt Longworth), *bloomers* (after Amelia Jenks Bloomer), and *Mae West jacket* (after the buxom actress). Two out of the three feminine eponyms relate closely to a woman's physical anatomy, while the masculine eponyms (except for *sideburns* after General Burnsides) have nothing to do with the namesake's body but, instead, honor the man for an accomplishment of some kind.   7

Although in Greek mythology women played a bigger role than they did in the biblical stories of the Judeo-Christian cultures and so the names of goddesses are accepted parts of the language in such place names as *Pomona* from the goddess of fruit and *Athens* from Athena and in such common words as *cereal* from Ceres, *psychology* from Psyche, and *arachnoid* from Arachne, the same tendency to think of women in relation to sexuality is seen in the eponyms *aphrodisiac* from Aphrodite, the Greek name for the goddess of love and beauty, and *venereal disease* from Venus, the Roman name for Aphrodite.   8

Another interesting word from Greek mythology is *Amazon.* According to Greek folk etymology, the *a* means "without" as in *atypical* or *amoral,* while *mazon* comes from *mazos* meaning "breast" as still seen in   9 *mastectomy*. In the Greek legend, Amazon women cut off their right breasts so that they could better shoot their bows. Apparently, the storytellers had a feeling that for women to play the active, "masculine" role the Amazons adopted for themselves, they had to trade in part of their femininity.

This preoccupation with women's breasts is not limited to ancient 10 stories. As a volunteer for the University of Wisconsin's *Dictionary of American Regional English (DARE)*, I read a western trapper's diary from the 1930s. I was to make notes of any unusual usages or language patterns. My most interesting finding was that the trapper referred to a range of mountains as *The Teats*, a metaphor based on the similarity between the shapes of mountains and women's breasts. Because today we use the French wording, *The Grand Tetons*, the metaphor isn't as obvious, but I wrote to mapmakers and found the following listings: *Nippletop* and *Little Nipple Top* near Mount Marcy in the Adirondacks; *Nipple Mountain* in Archuleta County, Colorado; *Nipple Peak* in Coke County, Texas; *Nipple Butte* in Pennington, South Dakota; *Squaw Peak* in Placer County, California (and many other locations); *Maiden's Peak* and *Squaw Tit* (they're the same mountain) in the Cascade Range in Oregon; *Mary's Nipple* near Salt Lake City, Utah; and *Jane Russell Peaks* near Stark, New Hampshire.

Except for the movie star Jane Russell, the women being referred to 11 are anonymous—it's only a sexual part of their body that is mentioned. When topographical features are named after men, it's probably not going to be to draw attention to a sexual part of their bodies but instead to honor individuals for an accomplishment. For example, no one thinks of a part of the male body when hearing a reference to Pike's Peak, Colorado, or Jackson Hole, Wyoming.

Going back to what I learned from my dictionary cards, I was sur- 12 prised to realize how many pairs of words we have in which the feminine word has acquired sexual connotations while the masculine word retains a serious businesslike aura. For example, a *callboy* is the person who calls actors when it is time for them to go on stage, but a *callgirl* is a prostitute. Compare *sir* and *madam*. *Sir* is a term of respect, while *madam* has acquired the specialized meaning of a brothel manager. Something similar has happened to *master* and *mistress*. Would you rather have a painting by an *old master* or an *old mistress*?

It's because the word *woman* had sexual connotations, as in "She's 13 his woman," that people began avoiding its use, hence such terminology as *ladies' room, lady of the house*, and *girls' school* or *school for young ladies*. Feminists, who ask that people use the term *woman* rather than *girl* or *lady*, are rejecting the idea that *woman* is primarily a sexual term. They have been at least partially successful in that today *woman* is commonly used to communicate gender without intending implications about sexuality.

I found two hundred pairs of words with masculine and feminine [14] forms, e.g., *heir-heiress, hero-heroine, steward-stewardess, usher-usherette*. In nearly all such pairs, the masculine word is considered the base, with some kind of a feminine suffix being added. The masculine form is the one from which compounds are made, e.g., from *king-queen* comes *kingdom* but not *queendom*, from *sportsman-sportslady* comes *sportsmanship* but not *sportsladyship*. There is one—and only one—semantic area in which the masculine word is not the base or more powerful word. This is in the area dealing with sex and marriage. When someone refers to a *virgin*, a listener will probably think of a female, unless the speaker specifies *male* or uses a masculine pronoun. The same is true for *prostitute*.

In relation to marriage, there is much linguistic evidence showing [15] that weddings are more important to women than to men. A woman cherishes the wedding and is considered a bride for a whole year, but a man is referred to as a groom only on the day of the wedding. The word *bride* appears in *bridal attendant, bridal gown, bridesmaid, bridal shower*, and even *bridegroom*. *Groom* comes from the Middle English *groom*, meaning "man," and in the sense is seldom used outside of the wedding. With most pairs of male/female words, people habitually put the masculine word first, *Mr. and Mrs., his and hers, boys and girls, men and women, kings and queens, brothers and sisters, guys and dolls*, and *host and hostess*, but it is the *bride and groom* who are talked about, not the *groom and bride*.

The importance of marriage to a woman is also shown by the fact [16] that when a marriage ends in death, the woman gets the title of *widow*. A man gets the derived title of *widower*. This term is not used in other phrases or contexts, but *widow* is seen in *widowhood, widow's peak*, and *widow's walk*. A *widow* in a card game is an extra hand of cards, while in typesetting it is an extra line of type.

How changing cultural ideas bring changes to language is clearly [17] visible in this semantic area. The feminist movement has caused the differences between the sexes to be downplayed, and since I did my dictionary study two decades ago, the word *singles* has largely replaced such sex specific and value-laden terms as *bachelor, old maid, spinster, divorcee, widow*, and *widower*. And in 1970 I wrote that when a man is called *a professional* he is thought to be a doctor or a lawyer, but when people hear a woman referred to as *a professional* they are likely to think of a prostitute. That's not as true today because so many women have become doctors and lawyers that it's no longer incongruous to think of women in those professional roles.

Another change that has taken place is in wedding announcements. [18] They used to be sent out from the bride's parents and did not even give the name of the groom's parents. Today, most couples choose to list either all or none of the parents' names. Also it is now much more likely that both the bride and groom's picture will be in the newspaper, while a decade ago only the bride's picture was published on the "Women's" or the "Society" page. Even the traditional wording of the wedding ceremony is being changed. Many officials now pronounce the couple "husband and wife" instead of the old "man and wife," and they ask the bride if she promises "to love, honor, and cherish," instead of "to love, honor, and obey."

Women Are Passive; Men Are Active

The wording of the wedding ceremony also relates to the second [19] point that my cards showed, which is that women are expected to play a passive or weak role while men play an active or strong role. In the traditional ceremony, the official asks, "Who gives the bride away?" and the father answers, "I do." Some fathers answer, "Her mother and I do," but that doesn't solve the problem inherent in the question. The idea that a bride is something to be handed over from one man to another bothers people because it goes back to the days when a man's servants, his children, and his wife were all considered to be his property. They were known by his name because they belonged to him, and he was responsible for their actions and their debts.

The grammar used in talking or writing about weddings as well as [20] other sexual relationships shows the expectation of men playing the active role. Men *wed* women while women *become* brides of men. A man *possesses* a woman; he *deflowers* her; he *performs*; he *scores*; he *takes away* her virginity. Although a woman can *seduce* a man, she cannot offer him her virginity. When talking about virginity, the only way to make the woman the actor in the sentence is to say that "She lost her virginity," but people lose things by accident rather than by purposeful actions, and so she's only the grammatical, not the real-life, actor.

The reason that women tried to bring the term *Ms.* into the language [21] to replace *Miss* and *Mrs.* relates to this point. Married women resent being identified only under their husband's names. For example, when Susan Glascoe did something newsworthy, she would be identified in the newspaper only as Mrs. John Glascoe. The dictionary cards showed what appeared to be an attitude on the part of the editors that it was almost indecent to let a respectable woman's name march unaccompanied across the pages of a dictionary. Women were listed with male names whether or not the male contributed to the woman's reason for being in the dictionary or in his own right was as famous as the woman. For example, Charlotte Bronte was identified as Mrs. Arthur B. Nicholls, Amelia Earhart as Mrs. George Palmer Putnam, Helen Hayes as Mrs. Charles MacArthur, Jenny Lind as Mme. Otto Goldschmit, Cornelia Otis Skinner as the daughter of Otis, Harriet Beecher Stowe as the sister of Henry Ward Beecher, and Edith Sitwell as the sister of Osbert and Sacheverell.[2] A very small number of women got into the dictionary

---

[2] Charlotte Bronte' (1816–55), author of *Jane Eyre*; Amelia Earhart (1898–1937), first woman to fly over the Atlantic; Helen Hayes (1900–), actress; Jenny Lind (1820–87), Swedish soprano known as the "Swedish nightingale"; Cornelia Otis Skinner (1901–79), actress and writer; Harriet Beecher Stowe (1811–96), author of *Uncle Tom's Cabin*; and Edith Sitwell (1877–1964), English poet and critic. [Eds.]

without the benefit of a masculine escort. They were rebels and crusaders: temperance leaders Frances Elizabeth Caroline Willard and Carry Nation, women's rights leaders Carrie Chapman Catt and Elizabeth Cady Stanton, birth control educator Margaret Sanger, religious leader Mary Baker Eddy, and slaves Harriet Tubman and Phillis Wheatley.

Etiquette books used to teach that if a woman had *Mrs.* in front of [22] her name, then the husband's name should follow because *Mrs.* is an abbreviated form of *Mistress* and a woman couldn't be a mistress of herself. As with many arguments about "correct" language usage, this isn't very logical because *Miss* is also an abbreviation of *Mistress*. Feminists hoped to simplify matters by introducing *Ms.* as an alternative to both *Mrs.* and *Miss,* but what happened is that *Ms.* largely replaced *Miss,* to become a catch-all business title for women. Many married women still prefer the title *Mrs.,* and some resent being addressed with the term *Ms.* As one frustrated newspaper reporter complained, "Before I can write about a woman, I have to know not only her marital status but also her political philosophy." The result of such complications may contribute to the demise of titles, which are already being ignored by many computer programmers who find it more efficient to simply use names, for example in a business letter: "Dear Joan Garcia," instead of "Dear Mrs. Joan Garcia," "Dear Ms. Garcia," or "Dear Mrs. Louis Garcia."

The titles given to royalty provide an example of how males can be [23] disadvantaged by the assumption that they are always to play the more powerful role. In British royalty, when a male holds a title, his wife is automatically given the feminine equivalent. But the reverse is not true. For example, a *count* is a high political officer with a *countess* being his wife. The same is true for a *duke* and a *duchess* and a *king* and a *queen.* But when a female holds the royal title, the man she marries does not automatically acquire the matching title. For example, Queen Elizabeth's husband has the title of *prince* rather than *king,* but if Prince Charles should become king while he is still married to Lady or Princess Diana, she will be known as the queen. The reasoning appears to be that since masculine words are stronger, they are reserved for true heirs and withheld from males coming into the royal family by marriage. If Prince Phillip were called *King Phillip,* it would be much easier for British subjects to forget where the true power lies.

The names that people give their children show the hopes and [24] dreams they have for them, and when we look at the differences between male and female names in a culture, we can see the cumulative expectations of that culture. In our culture girls often have names taken from small, aesthetically pleasing items, e.g., *Ruby, Jewel,* and *Pearl. Esther* and *Stella* mean "star," *Ada* means "ornament," and *Vanessa* means "butterfly." Boys are more likely to be given names with meanings of power and strength, e.g., *Neil* means "champion," *Martin* is from Mars, the God of War, *Raymond* means "wise protection," *Harold* means "chief of the army," *Ira* means "vigilant," *Rex* means "king," and *Richard* means "strong king."

We see similar differences in food metaphors. Food is a passive sub- 25 stance just sitting there waiting to be eaten. Many people have recognized this and so no longer feel comfortable describing women as "delectable morsels." However, when I was a teenager, it was considered a compliment to refer to a girl (we didn't call anyone a *woman* until she was middle-aged) as a *cute tomato, a peach, a dish, a cookie, honey, sugar,* or *sweetie-pie.* When being affectionate, women will occasionally call a man *honey* or *sweetie,* but in general, food metaphors are used much less often with men than with women. If a man is called *a fruit,* his masculinity is being questioned. But it's perfectly acceptable to use a food metaphor if the food is heavier and more substantive than that used for women. For example pin-up pictures of women have long been known as *cheesecake,* but when Burt Reynolds posed for a nude centerfold the picture was immediately dubbed *beefcake,* c.f., *a hunk of meat.* That such sexual references to men have come into the language is another reflection of how society is beginning to lessen the differences between their attitudes toward men and women.

Something similar to the *fruit* metaphor happens with references to 26 plants. We insult a man by calling him a *pansy,* but it wasn't considered particularly insulting to talk about a girl being a *wallflower,* a *clinging vine,* or a *shrinking violet,* or to give girls such names as *Ivy, Rose, Lily, Iris, Daisy, Camellia, Heather,* and *Flora.* A plant metaphor can be used with a man if the plant is big and strong, for example, Andrew Jackson's nickname of *Old Hickory.* Also, the phrases *blooming idiots* and *budding geniuses* can be used with either sex, but notice how they are based on the most active thing a plant can do, which is to bloom or bud.

Animal metaphors also illustrate the different expectations for 27 males and females. Men are referred to as *studs, bucks,* and *wolves* while women are referred to with such metaphors as *kitten, bunny, beaver, bird, chick,* and *lamb.* In the 1950s we said that boys went *tomcatting,* but today it's just *catting around* and both boys and girls do it. When the term *foxy,* meaning that someone was sexy, first became popular it was used only for girls, but now someone of either sex can be described as *a fox.* Some animal metaphors that are used predominantly with men have negative connotations based on the size and/or strength of the animals, e.g., *beast, bullheaded, jackass, rat, loanshark,* and *vulture.* Negative metaphors used with women are based on smaller animals, *e.g., social butterfly, mousy, catty,* and *vixen.* The feminine terms connote action, but not the same kind of large scale action as with the masculine terms.

Women Are Connected with Negative Connotations; Men with Positive Connotations

The final point that my notecards illustrated was how many pos- [28]
itive connotations are associated with the concept of masculine, while
there are either trivial or negative connotations connected with the
corresponding feminine concept. An example from the animal
metaphors makes a good illustration. The word *shrew* taken from the
name of a small but especially vicious animal was defined in my dictionary as "an ill-tempered scolding woman," but the word *shrewd*
taken from the same root was defined as "marked by clever, discern-
ing awareness" and was illustrated with the phrase "a shrewd busi-
nessman."

Early in life, children are conditioned to the superiority of the mas- [29]
culine role. As child psychologists point out, little girls have much
more freedom to experiment with sex roles than do little boys. If a little girl acts like a *tomboy*, most parents have mixed feelings, being at
least partially proud. But if their little boy acts like a *sissy* (derived
from *sister*), they call a psychologist. It's perfectly acceptable for a little girl to sleep in the crib that was purchased for her brother, to wear
his hand-me-down jeans and shirts, and to ride the bicycle that he has
outgrown. But few parents would put a boy baby in a white and gold
crib decorated with frills and lace, and virtually no parents would have
their little boys wear his sister's hand-me-down dresses, nor would
they have their son ride a girl's pink bicycle with a flower-bedecked
basket. The proper names given to girls and boys show this same attitude. Girls can have "boy" names—*Cris, Craig, Jo, Kelly, Shawn, Teri,
Toni,* and *Sam*—but it doesn't work the other way around. A couple of
generations ago, *Beverley, Frances, Hazel, Marion,* and *Shirley* were common boys' names. As parents gave these names to more and more
girls, they fell into disuse for males, and some older men who have
these names prefer to go by their initials or by such abbreviated forms
as *Haze* or *Shirl*.

When a little girl is told to *be a lady,* she is being told to sit with her [30]
knees together and to be quiet and dainty. But when a little boy is told
to *be a man* he is being told to be noble, strong, and virtuous—to have all
the qualities that the speaker looks on as desirable. The concept of man-
liness has such positive connotations that it used to be a compliment to
call someone a *he-man,* to say that he was doubly a man. Today many
people are more ambivalent about this term and respond to it much as
they do to the word *macho*. But calling someone a *manly man* or a *virile
man* is nearly always meant as a compliment. *Virile* comes from the Indo-
European *vir* meaning "man," which is also the basis for *virtuous*. Contrast the positive connotations of both *virile* and *virtuous* with the nega-

tive connotations of *hysterical*. The Greeks took this latter word from their name for *uterus* (as still seen in *hysterectomy*). They thought that women were the only ones who experienced uncontrolled emotional outbursts, and so the condition must have something to do with a part of the body that only women have.

Differences in the connotations between positive male and negative [31] female connotations can be seen in several pairs of words that differ denotatively only in the matter of sex. *Bachelor* as compared to *spinster* or *old maid* has such positive connotations that women try to adopt them by using the term *bachelor-girl* or *bachelorette*. *Old maid* is so negative that it's the basis for metaphors: pretentious and fussy old men are called *old maids*, as are the leftover kernels of unpopped popcorn, and the last card in a popular children's game.

Patron and *matron* (Middle English for *father* and *mother* have such [32] different levels of prestige that women try to borrow the more positive masculine connotations with the word *patroness*, literally "female father." Such a peculiar term came about because of the high prestige attached to *patron* in such phrases as *a patron of the arts* or *a patron saint*. *Matron* is more apt to be used in talking about a woman in charge of a jail or a public restroom.

When men are doing jobs that women often do, we apparently try [33] to pay the men extra by giving them fancy titles, for example, a male cook is more likely to be called a *chef* while a male seamstress will get the title of *tailor*. The armed forces have a special problem in that they recruit under such slogans as "The Marine Corps builds men!" and "Join the Army! Become a Man," Once the recruits are enlisted, they find themselves doing much of the work that has been traditionally thought of as "women's work." The solution to getting the work done and not insulting anyone's masculinity was to change the titles as shown below:

waitress	orderly
nurse	medic or corpsman
secretary	clerk-typist
assistant	adjutant
dishwasher or kitchen helper	KP (kitchen police)

Compare *brave* and *squaw*. Early settlers in America truly admired [34] Indian men and hence named them with a word that carried connotations of youth, vigor, and courage. But they used the Algonquin's name for "woman" and over the years it developed almost opposite connotations to those of *brave*. *Wizard* and *witch* contrast almost as much. The masculine *wizard* implies skill and wisdom combined with magic, while the feminine *witch* implies evil intentions combined with magic. Part of the unattractiveness of both *witch* and *squaw* is that they have been used so often to refer to old women, something with which our culture is particularly uncomfortable, just as the Afghans were. Imagine my surprise when I ran across the phrases *grandfatherly advice* and *old wives' tales* and realized that the underlying implication is the same as the Afghan proverb about old men being worth listening to while old women talk only foolishness.

Other terms that show how negatively we view old women as com- [35] pared to young women are *old nag* as compared to *filly*, *old crow* or *old bat* as compared to *bird*, and of being *catty* as compared to being *kittenish*. There is no matching set of metaphors for men. The chicken metaphor tells the whole story of a woman's life. In her youth she is a *chick*. Then she marries and begins *feathering her nest*. Soon she begins feeling *cooped up*, so she goes to *hen parties* where she *cackles* with her friends. Then she has her *brood*, begins to *henpeck* her husband, and finally turns into an *old biddy*.

I embarked on my study of the dictionary not with the intention of [36] prescribing language change but simply to see what the language would tell me about sexism. Nevertheless I have been both surprised and pleased as I've watched the changes that have occurred over the past two decades. I'm one of those linguists who believes that new language customs will cause a new generation of speakers to grow up with different expectations. This is why I'm happy about people's efforts to use inclusive language, to say *he or she* or *they* when speaking about individuals whose names they do not know. I'm glad that leading publishers have developed guidelines to help writers use language that is fair to both sexes, and I'm glad that most newspapers and magazines list women by their own names instead of only by their husbands' names and that educated and thoughtful people no longer begin their business letters with "Dear Sir" or "Gentlemen," but instead use a memo form or begin with such salutations as "Dear Colleagues," "Dear Reader," or "Dear Committee Members." I'm also glad that such words as *poetess, authoress, conductress*, and *aviatrix* now sound quaint and old-fashioned and that *chairman* is giving way to *chair* or *head, mailman* to *mail carrier, clergyman* to *clergy*, and *stewardess* to *flight attendant*. I was also pleased when the National Oceanic and Atmospheric Administration bowed to feminist complaints and in the late 1970s began to alternate men's and women's names for hurricanes. However, I wasn't so pleased to discover that the change did not immediately erase sexist thoughts from everyone's mind, as shown by a headline about Hurricane David in a 1979 New York tabloid, "David Rapes Virgin Islands." More recently a similar metaphor appeared in a headline in the *Arizona Republic* about Hurricane Charlie, "Charlie Quits Carolinas, Flirts with Virginia."

What these incidents show is that sexism is not something existing [37] independently in American English or in the particular dictionary that I happened to read. Rather, it exists in people's minds. Language is like an X-ray in providing visible evidence of invisible thoughts. The best thing about people being interested in and discussing sexist language is that as they make conscious decisions about what pronouns they will use, what jokes they will tell or laugh at, how they will write their names, or how they will begin their letters, they are forced to think about the underlying issue of sexism. This is good because as a problem that begins in people's assumptions and expectations, it's a problem that will be solved only when a great many people have given it a great deal of thought.

Responding to Reading

1. What point is Nilsen making about the culture in which she lives? Does your experience support her conclusions?
2. Does Nilsen use enough examples to illustrate her claims? What others can you think of? In what way do her examples—and your own—illustrate the power of language to define and, in some cases, to cloud thought?
3. Many of the connotations of the words Nilsen discusses are hundreds of years old and found in languages other than English. Given the widespread and long-standing linguistic bias against women, do you think attempts by Nilsen and others to change this situation can succeed?

POLITICS AND THE ENGLISH
~ LANGUAGE

George Orwell

Eric Blair (1903–1950) was an Englishman, born in Bengal, India, who took the pen name George Orwell. He attended school in England and then joined the Indian Imperial Police in Burma, where he came to question the British methods of colonialism. (See his essay "Shooting an Elephant," page 716.) An enemy of totalitarianism in any form and a spokesman for the oppressed, Orwell criticized totalitarian regimes in his bitterly satirical novels *Animal Farm* (1945) and *1984* (1949). The following essay was written during the period between these two novels' publications, at the end of World War II when jingoistic praise for "our democratic institutions" and blindly passionate defenses of Marxist ideology were the two common extremes of public political discourse. Orwell's plea for clear thinking and writing at a time when "[p]olitical language . . . is designed to makes lies sound truthful and murder respectable, and to give an appearance of solidity to pure wind" is as relevant today as when it was written.

Most people who bother with the matter at all would admit that the [1] English language is in a bad way, but it is generally assumed that we cannot by conscious action do anything about it. Our civilization is decadent and our language—so the argument runs—must inevitably share in the general collapse. It follows that any struggle against the abuse of language is a sentimental archaism, like preferring candles to electric light or hansom cabs to airplanes. Underneath this lies the half-conscious belief that language is a natural growth and not an instrument which we shape for our own purposes.

Now, it is clear that the decline of a language must ultimately have [2] political and economic causes: it is not due simply to the bad influence of this or that individual writer. But an effect can become a cause, reinforcing the original cause and producing the same effect in an intensified form, and so on indefinitely. A man may take to drink because he feels himself to be a failure, and then fail all the more completely because he drinks. It is rather the same thing that is happening to the English language. It becomes ugly and inaccurate because our thoughts are foolish, but the slovenliness of our language makes it easier for us to have foolish thoughts. The point is that the process is reversible. Modern English, especially written English, is full of bad habits which spread by imitation and which can be avoided if one is willing to take the necessary trouble. If one gets rid of these habits one can think more clearly, and to think clearly is a necessary first step towards political regeneration: so that the fight against bad English is not frivolous and is not the exclusive concern of professional writers. I will come back to this presently, and I hope that by that time the meaning of what I have said here will have become clearer. Meanwhile, here are five specimens of the English language as it is now habitually written.

These five passages have not been picked out because they are especially bad—I could have quoted far worse if I had chosen—but because they illustrate various of the mental vices from which we now suffer. They are a little below the average, but are fairly representative samples. I number them so that I can refer back to them when necessary:

"(1) I am not, indeed, sure whether it is not true to say that the Milton who once seemed not unlike a seventeenth-century Shelley had not become, out of an experience ever more bitter in each year, more alien (*sic*) to the founder of that Jesuit sect which nothing could induce him to tolerate."

Professor Harold Laski (Essay in *Freedom of Expression*).

"(2) Above all, we cannot play ducks and drakes with a native battery of idioms which prescribes such egregious collocations of vocables as the Basic *put up with* for *tolerate* or *put at a loss* for *bewilder*."

Professor Lancelot Hogben (*Interglossa*).

"(3) On the one side we have the free personality: by definition it is not neurotic, for it has neither conflict nor dream. Its desires, such as they are, are transparent, for they are just what institutional approval keeps in the forefront of consciousness; another institutional pattern would alter their number and intensity; there is little in them that is natural, irreducible, or culturally dangerous. But *on the other side*, the social bond itself is nothing but the mutual reflection of these self-secure integrities. Recall the definition of love. Is not this the very picture of a small academic? Where is there a place in this hall of mirrors for either personality or fraternity?"

Essay on psychology in *Politics* (New York).

"(4) All the 'best people' from the gentlemen's clubs, and all the frantic fascist captains, united in common hatred of Socialism and bestial horror of the rising tide of the mass revolutionary movement, have turned to acts of provocation, to foul incendiarism, to medieval legends of poisoned wells, to legalize their own destruction of proletarian organizations, and rouse the agitated petty-bourgeoisie to chauvinistic fervor on behalf of the fight against the revolutionary way out of the crisis."

Communist pamphlet.

"(5) If a new spirit *is* to be infused into this old country, there is one thorny and contentious reform which must be tackled, and that is the humanization and galvanization of the B.B.C. Timidity here will bespeak cancer and atrophy of the soul. The heart of Britain may be sound and of strong beat, for instance, but the British lion's roar at present is like that of Bottom in Shakespeare's *Midsummer Night's Dream*— as gentle as any sucking dove. A virile new Britain cannot continue indefinitely to be traduced in the eyes or rather ears, of the world by the effete languors of Langham Place, brazenly masquerading as 'standard English'. When the Voice of Britain is heard at nine o'clock, better far and infinitely less ludicrous to hear aitches honestly dropped than the present priggish, inflated, inhibited, school-ma'amish arch braying of blameless bashful mewing maidens!"

Letter in *Tribune*.

Each of these passages has faults of its own, but, quite apart from   4
avoidable ugliness, two qualities are common to all of them. The first is
staleness of imagery: the other is lack of precision. The writer either has
a meaning and cannot express it, or he inadvertently says something
else, or he is almost indifferent as to whether his words mean anything
or not. This mixture of vagueness and sheer incompetence is the most
marked characteristic of modern English prose, and especially of any
kind of political writing. As soon as certain topics are raised, the concrete melts into the abstract and no one seems able to think of turns of
speech that are not hackneyed: prose consists less and less of *words* chosen for the sake of their meaning, and more and more of *phrases* tacked
together like the sections of a prefabricated hen-house. I list below, with
notes and examples, various of the tricks by means of which the work
of prose-construction is habitually dodged:

Dying Metaphors

A newly invented metaphor assists thought by evoking a visual   5
image, while on the other hand a metaphor which is technically "dead"
(e.g. *iron resolution*) has in effect reverted to being an ordinary word and
can generally be used without loss of vividness. But in between these
two classes there is a huge dump of worn-out metaphors which have
lost all evocative power and are merely used because they save people
the trouble of inventing phrases for themselves. Examples are: *Ring the
changes on, take up the cudgels for, toe the line, ride roughshod over, stand
shoulder to shoulder with, play into the hands of, no axe to grind, grist to the
mill, fishing in troubled waters, on the order of the day, Achilles' heel, swan
song, hotbed.* Many of these are used without knowledge of their meaning (what is a "rift," for instance),[1] and incompatible metaphors are frequently mixed, a sure sign that the writer is not interested in what he is
saying. Some metaphors now current have been twisted out of their
original meaning without those who use them even being aware of the
fact. For example, *toe the line* is sometimes written *tow the line.* Another
example is *the hammer and the anvil,* now always used with the implication that the anvil gets the worst of it. In real life it is always the anvil
that breaks the hammer, never the other way about: a writer who
stopped to think what he was saying would be aware of this, and would
avoid perverting the original phrase.

Operators or Verbal False Limbs

These save the trouble of picking out appropriate verbs and nouns,   6
and at the same time pad each sentence with extra syllables which give it

---

[1] Originally *rift* referred to a geological fault or fissure. Now it is commonly used to indicate a breach
or estrangement. [Eds.]

an appearance of symmetry. Characteristic phrases are: *render inoperative, militate against, make contact with, be subjected to, give rise to, give grounds for, have the effect of, play a leading part (role) in, make itself felt, take effect, exhibit a tendency to, serve the purpose of, etc., etc.* The keynote is the elimination of simple verbs. Instead of being a single word, such as *break, stop, spoil, mend, kill,* a verb becomes a *phrase,* made up of a noun or adjective tacked on to some general-purposes verb such as *prove, serve, form, play, render.* In addition, the passive voice is wherever possible used in preference to the active, and noun constructions are used instead of gerunds (*by examination of* instead of *by examining*). The range of verbs is further cut down by means of the *-ize* and *de-* formation, and the banal statements are given an appearance of profundity by means of the *not un-* formation. Simple conjunctions and prepositions are replaced by such phrases as *with respect to, having regard to, the fact that, by dint of, in view of, in the interests of, on the hypothesis that;* and the ends of sentences are saved from anticlimax by such resounding commonplaces as *greatly to be desired, cannot be left out of account, a development to be expected in the near future, deserving of serious consideration, brought to a satisfactory conclusion,* and so on and so forth.

Pretentious Diction

Words like *phenomenon, element, individual* (as noun), *objective, categorical, effective, virtual, basic, primary, promote, constitute, exhibit, exploit, utilize, eliminate, liquidate,* are used to dress up simple statements and give an air of scientific impartiality to biased judgments. Adjectives like *epoch-making, epic, historic, unforgettable, triumphant, age-old, inevitable, inexorable, veritable,* are used to dignify the sordid processes of international politics, while writing that aims at glorifying war usually takes on an archaic color, its characteristic words being: *realm, throne, chariot, mailed fist, trident, sword, shield, buckler, banner, jackboot, clarion.* Foreign words and expressions such as *cul de sac, ancien régime, deus ex machina, mutatis mutandis, status quo, gleichschaltung, weltanschauung,* are used to give an air of culture and elegance. Except for the useful abbreviations *i.e., e.g.,* and *etc.,* there is no real need for any of the hundreds of foreign phrases now current in English. Bad writers, and especially scientific, political and sociological writers, are nearly always haunted by the notion that Latin or Greek words are grander than Saxon ones, and unnecessary words like *expedite, ameliorate, predict, extraneous, deracinated, clandestine, subaqueous* and hundreds of others constantly gain ground from their Anglo-Saxon opposite numbers.[2] The jargon peculiar to

[7]

---

[2] An interesting illustration of this is the way in which the English flower names which were in use till very recently are being ousted by Greek ones, *snapdragon* becoming *antirrhinum, forget-me-not* becoming *myosotis,* etc. It is hard to see any practical reason for this change of fashion: it is probably due to an instinctive turning-away from the more homely word and a vague feeling that the Greek word is scientific.

Marxist writing (*hyena, hangman, cannibal, petty bourgeois, these gentry, lacquey, flunkey, mad dog, White Guard*, etc.) consists largely of words and phrases translated from Russian, German or French; but the normal way of coining a new word is to use a Latin or Greek root with the appropriate affix and, where necessary, the *-ize* formation. It is often easier to make up words of this kind (*deregionalize, impermissible, extra-marital, nonfragmentatory* and so forth) than to think up the English words that will cover one's meaning. The result, in general, is an increase in slovenliness and vagueness.

Meaningless Words

In certain kinds of writing, particularly in art criticism and literary [8] criticism, it is normal to come across long passages which are almost completely lacking in meaning.[3] Words like *romantic, plastic, values, human, dead, sentimental, natural, vitality*, as used in art criticism, are strictly meaningless in the sense that they not only do not point to any discoverable object, but are hardly ever expected to do so by the reader. When one critic writes, "The outstanding feature of Mr. X's work is its living quality", while another writes, "The immediately striking thing about Mr. X's work is its peculiar deadness", the reader accepts this as a simple difference of opinion. If words like *black* and *white* were involved, instead of the jargon words *dead* and *living*, he would see at once that language was being used in an improper way. Many political words are similarly abused. The word *Fascism* has now no meaning except in so far as it signifies "something not desirable." The words *democracy, socialism, freedom, patriotic, realistic, justice*, have each of them several different meanings which cannot be reconciled with one another. In the case of a word like *democracy*, not only is there no agreed definition, but the attempt to make one is resisted from all sides. It is almost universally felt that when we call a country democratic we are praising it: consequently the defenders of every kind of régime claim that it is a democracy, and fear that they might have to stop using the word if it were tied down to any one meaning. Words of this kind are often used in a consciously dishonest way. That is, the person who uses them has his own private definition, but allows his hearer to think he means something quite different. Statements like *Marshal Pétain was a true patriot, The Soviet Press is the freest in the world, The Catholic Church is opposed to persecution*, are almost always made with intent to deceive. Other words used

---

[3] Example: "Comfort's catholicity of perception and image, strangely Whitmanesque in range, almost the exact opposite in aesthetic compulsion, continues to evoke that trembling atmospheric accumulative hinting at a cruel, an inexorably serene timelessness. . . . Wrey Gardiner scores by aiming at simple bull's-eyes with precision. Only they are not so simple, and through this contended sadness— runs more than the surface bittersweet of resignation" (*Poetry Quarterly*).

in variable meanings, in most cases more or less dishonestly, are: *class, totalitarian, science, progressive, reactionary, bourgeois, equality.*

Now that I have made this catalogue of swindles and perversions, [9] let me give another example of the kind of writing that they lead to. This time it must of its nature be an imaginary one. I am going to translate a passage of good English into modern English of the worst sort. Here is a well-known verse from *Ecclesiastes:*

> "I returned and saw under the sun, that the race is not to the swift, nor the battle to the strong, neither yet bread to the wise, nor yet riches to men of understanding, nor yet favor to men of skill; but time and chance happeneth to them all."

Here it is in modern English: [10]

> "Objective consideration of contemporary phenomena compels the conclusion that success or failure in competitive activities exhibits no tendency to be commensurate with innate capacity, but that a considerable element of the unpredictable must invariably be taken into account."

This a parody, but not a very gross one. Exhibit (3), above, for in- [11] stance, contains several patches of the same kind of English. It will be seen that I have not made a full translation. The beginning and ending of the sentence follow the original meaning fairly closely, but in the middle the concrete illustrations—race, battle, bread—dissolve into the vague phrase "success or failure in competitive activities." This had to be so, because no modern writer of the kind I am discussing—no one capable of using phrases like "objective consideration of contemporary phenomena"—would ever tabulate his thoughts in that precise and detailed way. The whole tendency of modern prose is away from concreteness. Now analyze these two sentences a little more closely. The first contains forty-nine words but only sixty syllables, and all its words are those of everyday life. The second contains thirty-eight words of ninety syllables: eighteen of its words are from Latin roots, and one from Greek. The first sentence contains six vivid images, and only one phrase ("time and chance") that could be called vague. The second contains not a single fresh, arresting phrase, and in spite of its ninety syllables it gives only a shortened version of the meaning contained in the first. Yet without a doubt it is the second kind of sentence that is gaining ground in modern English. I do not want to exaggerate. This kind of writing is not yet universal, and outcrops of simplicity will occur here and there in the worst-written page. Still, if you or I were told to write a few lines on the uncertainty of human fortunes, we should probably come much nearer to my imaginary sentence than to the one from *Ecclesiastes.*

As I have tried to show, modern writing at its worst does not con- [12] sist in picking out words for the sake of their meaning and inventing images in order to make the meaning clearer. It consists in gumming to-gether long strips of words which have already been set in order by someone else, and making the results presentable by sheer humbug. The attraction of this way of writing is that it is easy. It is easier—even quick-er, once you have the habit—to say *In my opinion it is a not unjustifiable assumption that* than to say *I think.* If you use ready-made phrases, you not only don't have to hunt about for words; you also don't have to bother with the rhythms of your sentences, since these phrases are gen-erally so arranged as to be more or less euphonious. When you are com-posing in a hurry—when you are dictating to a stenographer, for in-stance, or making a public speech—it is natural to fall into a pretentious, Latinized style. Tags like a *consideration which we should do well to bear in mind* or a *conclusion to which all of us would readily assent* will save many a sentence from coming down with a bump. By using stale metaphors, similes and idioms, you save much mental effort, at the cost of leaving your meaning vague, not only for your reader but for yourself. This is the significance of mixed metaphors. The sole aim of a metaphor is to call up a visual image. When these images clash—as in *The Fascist octo-pus has sung its swan song, the jackboot is thrown into the melting pot*—it can't be taken as certain that the writer is not seeing a mental image of the objects he is naming; in other words he is not really thinking. Look again at the examples I gave at the beginning of this essay. Professor Laski (1) uses five negatives in fifty-three words. One of these is super-fluous, making nonsense of the whole passage, and in addition there is the slip *alien* for *akin,* making further nonsense, and several avoidable pieces of clumsiness which increase the general vagueness. Professor Hogben (2) plays ducks and drakes with a battery which is able to write prescriptions, and, while disapproving of the everyday phrase *put up with,* is unwilling to look *egregious* up in the dictionary and see what it means. (3), if one takes an uncharitable attitude towards it, is simply meaningless: probably one could work out its intended meaning by reading the whole of the article in which it occurs. In (4), the writer knows more or less what he wants to say, but an accumulation of stale phrases chokes him like tea leaves blocking a sink. In (5), words and meaning have almost parted company. People who write in this manner usually have a general emotional meaning—they dislike one thing and want to express solidarity with another—but they are not interested in the detail of what they are saying. A scrupulous writer, in every sen-tence that he writes, will ask himself at least four questions, thus: What am I trying to say? What words will express it? What image or idiom will make it clearer? Is this image fresh enough to have an effect? And he will probably ask himself two more: Could I put it more shortly? Have I said anything that is avoidably ugly? But you are not obliged to go to all this trouble. You can shirk it by simply throwing your mind open and letting the ready-made phrases come crowding in. They will construct your sentences for you—even think your thoughts for you, to a certain extent—and at need they will perform the important service of partially concealing your meaning even from yourself. It is at this point that the special connection between politics and the debasement of language becomes clear.

In our time it is broadly true that political writing is bad writing. [13] Where it is not true, it will generally be found that the writer is some kind of rebel, expressing his private opinions and not a "party line." Orthodoxy, of whatever color, seems to demand a lifeless, imitative style. The political dialects to be found in pamphlets, leading articles, manifestos, White Papers and the speeches of under-secretaries do, of course, vary from party to party, but they are all alike in that one almost never finds in them a fresh, vivid, home-made turn of speech. When one watches some tired hack on the platform mechanically repeating the familiar phrases—*bestial atrocities, iron heel, bloodstained tyranny, free peoples of the world, stand shoulder to shoulder*—one often has a curious feeling that one is not watching a live human being but some kind of dummy: a feeling which suddenly becomes stronger at moments when the light catches the speaker's spectacles and turns them into blank discs which seem to have no eyes behind them. And this is not altogether fanciful. A speaker who uses that kind of phraseology has gone some distance towards turning himself into a machine. The appropriate noises are coming out of his larynx, but his brain is not involved as it would be if he were choosing his words for himself. If the speech he is making is one that he is accustomed to make over and over again, he may be almost unconscious of what he is saying, as one is when one utters the responses in church. And this reduced state of consciousness, if not indispensable, is at any rate favorable to political conformity.

In our time, political speech and writing are largely the defence of [14] the indefensible. Things like the continuance of British rule in India, the Russian purges and deportations, the dropping of the atom bombs on Japan, can indeed be defended, but only by arguments which are too brutal for most people to face, and which do not square with the professed aims of political parties. Thus political language has to consist largely of euphemism, question-begging and sheer cloudy vagueness. Defenceless villages are bombarded from the air, the inhabitants driven out into the countryside, the cattle machine-gunned, the huts set on fire with incendiary bullets: this is called *pacification*. Millions of peasants are robbed of their farms and sent trudging along the roads with no more than they can carry: this is called *transfer of population* or *rectification of frontiers*. People are imprisoned for years without trial, or shot in the back of the neck or sent to die of scurvy in Arctic lumber camps: this is called *elimination of unreliable elements*. Such phraseology is needed if one wants to name things without calling up mental pictures of them. Consider for instance some comfortable English professor defending Russian totalitarianism. He cannot say outright, "I believe in killing off your opponents when you can get good results by doing so." Probably, therefore, he will say something like this:

"While freely conceding that the Soviet régime exhibits certain features which the humanitarian may be inclined to deplore, we must, I think, agree that a certain curtailment of the right to political opposition is an unavoidable concomitant of transitional periods, and that the rigors which the Russian people have been called upon to undergo have been amply justified in the sphere of concrete achievement." [15]

The inflated style is itself a kind of euphemism. A mass of Latin words falls upon the facts like soft snow, blurring the outlines and covering up all the details. The great enemy of clear language is insincerity. When there is a gap between one's real and one's declared aims, one turns as it were instinctively to long words and exhausted idioms, like a cuttlefish squirting out ink. In our age there is no such thing as "keeping out of politics." All issues are political issues, and politics itself is a mass of lies, evasions, folly, hatred and schizophrenia. When the general atmosphere is bad, language must suffer. I should expect to find—this is a guess which I have not sufficient knowledge to verify—that the German, Russian and Italian languages have all deteriorated in the last ten to fifteen years, as a result of dictatorship. [16]

But if thought corrupts language, language can also corrupt thought. A bad usage can spread by tradition and imitation, even among people who should and do know better. The debased language that I have been discussing is in some ways very convenient. Phrases like *a not unjustifiable assumption, leaves much to be desired, would serve no good purpose, a consideration which we should do well to bear in mind,* are a continuous temptation, a packet of aspirins always at one's elbow. Look back through this essay, and for certain you will find that I have again and again committed the very faults I am protesting against. By this morning's post I have received a pamphlet dealing with conditions in Germany. The author tells me that he "felt impelled" to write it. I open it at random, and here is almost the first sentence that I see: "(The Allies) have an opportunity not only of achieving a radical transformation of Germany's social and political structure in such a way as to avoid a nationalistic reaction in Germany itself, but at the same time of laying the foundations of a cooperative and unified Europe." You see, he "feels impelled" to write—feels, presumably, that he has something new to say—and yet his words, like cavalry horses answering the bugle, group themselves automatically into the familiar dreary pattern. This invasion of one's mind by ready-made phrases (*lay the foundations, achieve a radical transformation*) can only be prevented if one is constantly on guard against them, and every such phrase anaesthetizes a portion of one's brain. [17]

I said earlier that the decadence of our language is probably curable.   18
Those who deny this would argue, if they produced an argument at all,
that language merely reflects existing social conditions, and that we cannot influence its development by any direct tinkering with words and
constructions. So far as the general tone or spirit of a language goes, this
may be true, but it is not true in detail. Silly words and expressions have
often disappeared, not through any evolutionary process but owing to
the conscious action of a minority. Two recent examples were *explore*
every avenue and *leave no stone unturned,* which were killed by the jeers
of a few journalists. There is a long list of flyblown metaphors which
could similarly be got rid of if enough people would interest themselves
in the job; and it should also be possible to laugh the *not un-* formation
out of existence,[4] to reduce the amount of Latin and Greek in the average sentence, to drive out foreign phrases and strayed scientific words,
and, in general, to make pretentiousness unfashionable. But all these are
minor points. The defence of the English language implies more than
this, and perhaps it is best to start by saying what it does *not* imply.

To begin with it has nothing to do with archaism, with the salvaging   19
of obsolete words and turns of speech, or with the setting up of a "standard English" which must never be departed from. On the contrary, it
is especially concerned with the scrapping of every word or idiom
which has outworn its usefulness. It has nothing to do with correct
grammar and syntax, which are of no importance so long as one makes
one's meaning clear, or with the avoidance of Americanisms, or with
having what is called a "good prose style." On the other hand it is not
concerned with fake simplicity and the attempt to make written English
colloquial. Nor does it even imply in every case preferring the Saxon
word to the Latin one, though it does imply using the fewest and short-
est words that will cover one's meaning. What is above all needed is to
let the meaning choose the word, and not the other way about. In prose,
the worst thing one can do with words is to surrender to them. When
you think of a concrete object, you think wordlessly, and then, if you
want to describe the thing you have been visualizing you probably hunt
about till you find the exact words that seem to fit. When you think of
something abstract you are more inclined to use words from the start,
and unless you make a conscious effort to prevent it, the existing dialect
will come rushing in and do the job for you, at the expense of blurring
or even changing your meaning. Probably it is better to put off using
words as long as possible and get one's meaning as clear as one can
through pictures or sensations. Afterwards one can choose—not simply
accept—the phrases that will best cover the meaning, and then switch
round and decide what impression one's words are likely to make on

---

[4] One can cure oneself of the *not un-* formation by memorizing this sentence: *A not unblack dog was*
chasing a not unsmall rabbit across a not ungreen field.

another person. This last effort of the mind cuts out all stale or mixed images, all prefabricated phrases, needless repetitions, and humbug and vagueness generally. But one can often be in doubt about the effect of a word or a phrase, and one needs rules that one can rely on when instinct fails. I think the following rules will cover most cases:

   (i) Never use a metaphor, simile or other figure of speech which you are used to seeing in print.

  (ii) Never use a long word where a short one will do.

 (iii) If it is possible to cut a word out, always cut it out.

 (iv) Never use the passive where you can use the active.

  (v) Never use a foreign phrase, a scientific word or a jargon word if you can think of an everyday English equivalent.

 (vi) Break any of these rules sooner than say anything outright barbarous.

These rules sound elementary, and so they are, but they demand a [20] deep change of attitude in anyone who has grown used to writing in the style now fashionable. One could keep all of them and still write bad English, but one could not write the kind of stuff that I quoted in those five specimens at the beginning of this article.

I have not here been considering the literary use of language, but [21] merely language as an instrument for expressing and not for concealing or preventing thought. Stuart Chase[5] and others have come near to claiming that all abstract words are meaningless, and have used this as a pretext for advocating a kind of political quietism. Since you don't know what Fascism is, how can you struggle against Fascism? One need not swallow such absurdities as this, but one ought to recognize that the present political chaos is connected with the decay of language, and that one can probably bring about some improvement by starting at the verbal end. If you simplify your English, you are freed from the worst follies of orthodoxy. You cannot speak any of the necessary dialects, and when you make a stupid remark its stupidity will be obvious, even to yourself. Political language—and with variations this is true of all political parties, from Conservatives to Anarchists—is designed to make lies sound truthful and murder respectable, and to give an appearance of solidity to pure wind. One cannot change this all in a moment, but one can at least change one's own habits, and from time to time one can even, if one jeers loudly enough, send some worn-out and useless phrase—some *jackboot, Achilles' heel, hotbed, melting pot, acid test, veritable inferno* or other lump of verbal refuse—into the dustbin where it belongs.

---

[5] Author known for his advocacy of clear writing and clear thinking. [Eds.]

Responding to Reading

1. According to Orwell, what is the relationship between politics and the English language? Do you think he overstates his case?
2. What does Orwell mean in paragraph 14 when he says, "In our time, political speech and writing are largely a defence of the indefensible"? Do you believe his statement applies to current times as well? Find several present-day examples of political language that support your conclusion.
3. Look through a newspaper or magazine and pick out some examples of dying metaphors. Do you agree with Orwell that they undermine clear thought and expression? Why or why not?

THE LESSON

Toni Cade Bambara

Originally trained as a dancer and actor, Toni Cade Bambara (1939–) has taught African-American literature in universities all over the United States. In her essay "What It Is I Think I'm Doing Anyhow," she says, "Through writing, I attempt to celebrate the tradition of resistance, attempt to tap Black potential, and try to join the chorus of voices that argues that exploitation and misery are neither inevitable nor necessary." Bambara writes fiction and nonfiction, and her stories are often marked by colloquial dialogue and street talk. The following short story is from Bambara's collection *Gorilla, My Love*.

Back in the days when everyone was old and stupid or young and foolish and me and Sugar were the only ones just right, this lady moved on our block with nappy hair and proper speech and no makeup. And quite naturally we laughed at her, laughed the way we did at the junk man who went about his business like he was some big-time president and his sorry-ass horse his secretary. And we kinda hated her too, hated the way we did the winos who cluttered up our parks and pissed on our handball walls and stank up our hallways and stairs so you couldn't halfway play hide-and-seek without a goddamn gas mask. Miss Moore was her name. The only woman on the block with no first name. And she was black as hell, cept for her feet, which were fish-white and spooky. And she was always planning these boring-ass things for us to do, us being my cousin, mostly, who lived on the block cause we all moved North the same time and to the same apartment then spread out gradual to breathe. And our parents would yank our heads into some kinda shape and crisp up our clothes so we'd be presentable for travel with Miss Moore, who always looked like she was going to church, though she never did. Which is just one of things the grown-ups talked about when they talked behind her back like a dog. But when she came calling with some sachet she'd sewed up or some gingerbread she'd made or some book, why then they'd all be too embarrassed to turn her down and we'd get handed over all spruced up. She'd been to college and said it was only right that she should take responsibility for the young ones' education, and she not even related by marriage or blood. So they'd go for it. Specially Aunt Gretchen. She was the main gofer in the family. You got some ole dumb shit foolishness you want somebody to go for, you send for Aunt Gretchen. She been screwed into the go-along for so long, it's a blood-deep natural thing with her. Which is how she got saddled with me and Sugar and Junior in the first place while our mothers were in a la-de-da apartment up the block having a good ole time.

So this one day Miss Moore rounds us all up at the mailbox and it's puredee hot and she's knockin herself out about arithmetic. And school suppose to let up in summer I heard, but she don't never let up. And the starch in my pinafore scratching the shit outta me and I'm really hating this nappy-head bitch and her goddamn college degree. I'd much rather go to the pool or to the show where it's cool. So me and Sugar leaning on the mailbox being surly, which is a Miss Moore word. And Flyboy checking out what everybody brought for lunch. And Fat Butt already wasting his peanut-butter-and-jelly sandwich like the pig he is. And Junebug punchin on Q.T.'s arm for potato chips. And Rosie Giraffe shifting from one hip to the other waiting for somebody to step on her foot or ask her if she from Georgia so she can kick ass, preferably Mercedes'. And Miss Moore asking us do we know what money is, like we a bunch of retards. I mean real money, she say, like it's only poker chips or monopoly papers we lay on the grocer. So right away I'm tired of this and say no. And would much rather snatch Sugar and go to the Sunset and terrorize the West Indian kids and take their hair ribbons and their money too. And Miss Moore files that remark away for next week's lesson on brotherhood, I can tell. And finally I say we oughta get to the subway cause it's cooler and besides we might meet some cute boys. Sugar done swiped her mama's lipstick, so we ready.

So we heading down the street and she's boring us silly about what things cost and what our parents make and how much goes for rent and how money ain't divided up right in this country. And then she gets to the part about we all poor and live in the slums, which I don't feature. And I'm ready to speak on that, but she steps out in the street and hails two cabs just like that. Then she hustles half the crew in with her and hands me a five-dollar bill and tells me to calculate 10 percent tip for the driver. And we're off. Me and Sugar and Junebug and Flyboy hangin out the window and hollering to everybody, putting lipstick on each other cause Flyboy a faggot anyway, and making farts with our sweaty armpits. But I'm mostly trying to figure how to spend this money. But they all fascinated with the meter ticking and Junebug starts laying bets as to how much it'll read when Flyboy can't hold his breath no more. Then Sugar lays bets as to how much it'll be when we get there. So I'm stuck. Don't nobody want to go for my plan, which is to jump out at the next light and run off to the first bar-b-que we can find. Then the driver tells us to get the hell out cause we there already. And the meter reads eighty-five cents. And I'm stalling to figure out the tip and Sugar say give him a dime. And I decide he don't need it bad as I do, so later for him. But then he tries to take off with Junebug foot still in the door so we talk about his mama something ferocious. Then we check out that we on Fifth Avenue and everybody dressed up in stockings. One lady in a fur coat, hot as it is. White folks crazy.

"This is the place," Miss Moore say, presenting it to us in the voice [4] she uses at the museum. "Let's look in the windows before we go in."

"Can we steal?" Sugar asks very serious like she's getting the [5] ground rules squared away before she plays. "I beg your pardon," says Miss Moore, and we fall out. So she leads us around the windows of the toy store and me and Sugar screamin, "This is mine, that's mine, I gotta have that, that was made for me, I was born for that," till Big Butt drowns us out.

"Hey, I'm goin to buy that there." [6]

"That there? You don't even know what it is, stupid." [7]

"I do so," he say punchin on Rosie Giraffe. "It's a microscope." [8]

"Watcha gonna do with a microscope, fool?" [9]

"Look at things." [10]

"Like what, Ronald?" ask Miss Moore. And Big Butt ain't got the [11] first notion. So here go Miss Moore gabbing about the thousands of bacteria in a drop of water and the somethin or other in a speck of blood and the million and one living things in the air around us is invisible to the naked eye. And what she say that for? Junebug go to town on that "naked" and we rolling. Then Miss Moore ask what it cost. So we all jam into the window smudgin it up and the price tag say $300. So then she ask how long'd take for Big Butt and Junebug to save up their allowances. "Too long," I say. "Yeh," adds Sugar, "outgrown it by that time." And Miss Moore say no, you never outgrow learning instruments. "Why, even medical students and interns and," blah, blah, blah. And we ready to choke Big Butt for bringing it up in the first damn place.

"This here costs four hundred eighty dollars," say Rosie Giraffe. So [12] we pile up all over her to see what she pointin out. My eyes tell me it's a chunk of glass cracked with something heavy, and different-color inks dripped into the splits, then the whole thing put into a oven or something. But the $480 it don't make sense.

"That's a paperweight made of semi-precious stones fused together under tremendous pressure," she explains slowly, with her hands doing the mining and all the factory work. [13]

"So what's a paperweight?" asks Rosie Giraffe. [14]

"To weigh paper with, dumbbell," say Flyboy, the wise man from the East. [15]

"Not exactly," say Miss Moore, which is what she say when you warm or way off too. "It's to weigh paper down so it won't scatter and make your desk untidy." So right away me and Sugar curtsy to each other and then to Mercedes who is more the tidy type. [16]

"We don't keep paper on top of the desk in my class," say Junebug, figuring Miss Moore crazy or lyin one. [17]

"At home, then," she say. "Don't you have a calendar and a pencil case and a blotter and a letter-opener on your desk at home where you do your homework?" And she know damn well what our homes look like cause she nosys around in them every chance she gets. [18]

"I don't even have a desk," say Junebug. "Do we?" [19]

"No. And I don't get no homework neither," say Big Butt. [20]

"And I don't even have a home," say Flyboy like he do at school to keep the white folks off his back and sorry for him. Send this poor kid to camp posters, is his specialty. [21]

"I do," says Mercedes. "I have a box of stationery on my desk and a picture of my cat. My godmother bought the stationery and the desk. There's a big rose on each sheet and the envelopes smell like roses." [22]

"Who wants to know about your smelly-ass stationery," say Rosie Giraffe fore I can get my two cents in. [23]

"It's important to have a work area all your own so that . . ." [24]

"Will you look at this sailboat, please," say Flyboy, cuttin her off and pointin to the thing like it was his. So once again we tumble all over each other to gaze at this magnificent thing in the toy store which is just big enough to maybe sail two kittens across the pond if you strap them to the posts tight. We all start reciting the price tag like we in assembly. "Handcrafted sailboat of fiberglass at one thousand one hundred ninety-five dollars." [25]

"Unbelievable," I hear myself say and am really stunned. I read it again for myself just in case the group recitation put me in a trance. Same thing. For some reason this pisses me off. We look at Miss Moore and she lookin at us, waiting for I dunno what. [26]

Who'd pay all that when you can buy a sailboat set for a quarter at Pop's, a tube of glue for a dime, and a ball of string for eight cents? "It must have a motor and a whole lot else besides," I say. "My sailboat cost me about fifty cents." [27]

"But will it take water?" say Mercedes with her smart ass. [28]

"Took mine to Alley Pond Park once," say Flyboy. "String broke. [29] Lost it. Pity."

"Sailed mine in Central Park and it keeled over and sank. Had to ask [30] my father for another dollar."

"And you got the strap," laugh Big Butt. "The jerk didn't even have [31] a string on it. My old man wailed on his behind."

Little Q.T. was staring hard at the sailboat and you could see he [32] wanted it bad. But he too little and somebody'd just take it from him. So what the hell. "This boat for kids, Miss Moore?"

"Parents silly to buy something like that just to get all broke up," say [33] Rosie Giraffe.

"That much money it should last forever," I figure. [34]

"My father'd buy it for me if I wanted it." [35]

"Your father, my ass," say Rosie Giraffe getting a chance to finally [36] push Mercedes.

"Must be rich people shop here," say Q.T. [37]

"You are a very bright boy," say Flyboy. "What was your first clue?" [38] And he rap him on the head with the back of his knuckles, since Q.T. the only one he could get away with. Though Q.T. liable to come up behind you years later and get his licks in when you half expect it.

"What I want to know," I says to Miss Moore though I never talk to [39] her, I wouldn't give the bitch that satisfaction, "is how much a real boat costs? I figure a thousand'd get you a yacht any day."

"Why don't you check that out," she says, "and report back to the [40] group?" Which really pains my ass. If you gonna mess up a perfectly good swim day least you could do is have some answers. "Let's go in," she say like she got something up her sleeve. Only she don't lead the way. So me and Sugar turn the corner to where the entrance is, but when we get there I kinda hang back. Not that I'm scared, what's there to be afraid of, just a toy store. But I feel funny, shame. But what I got to be shamed about? Got as much right to go in as anybody. But somehow I can't seem to get hold of the door, so I step away for Sugar to lead. But she hangs back too. And I look at her and she looks at me and this is ridiculous. I mean, damn, I have never ever been shy about doing nothing or going nowhere. But then Mercedes steps up and then Rosie Giraffe and Big Butt crowd in behind and shove, and next thing we all stuffed into the doorway with only Mercedes squeezing past us, smoothing out her jumper and walking right down the aisle. Then the rest of us tumble in like a glued-together jigsaw done all wrong. And people lookin at us. And it's like the time me and Sugar crashed into the Catholic church on a dare. But once we got in there and everything so hushed and holy and the candles and the bowin and the handkerchiefs on all the drooping heads, I just couldn't go through with the plan. Which was for me to run up to the altar and do a tap dance while Sugar played the nose flute and messed around in the holy water. And Sugar kept givin me the elbow. Then later teased me so bad I tied her up in the shower and turned it on and locked her in. And she'd be there till this day if Aunt Gretchen hadn't finally figured I was lyin about the boarder takin a shower.

Same thing in the store. We all walkin on tiptoe and hardly touch-   41
in the games and puzzles and things. And I watched Miss Moore who is steady watchin us like she waitin for a sign. Like Mama Drewery watches the sky and sniffs the air and takes note of just how much slant is in the bird formation. Then me and Sugar bump smack into each other, so busy gazing at the toys, 'specially the sailboat. But we don't laugh and go into our fat-lady bump-stomach routine. We just stare at that price tag. Then Sugar run a finger over the whole boat. And I'm jealous and want to hit her. Maybe not her, but I sure want to punch somebody in the mouth.

"Watcha bring us here for, Miss Moore?"   42

"You sound angry, Sylvia. Are you mad about something?" Givin me   43
one of them grins like she tellin a grown-up joke that never turns out to be funny. And she's lookin very closely at me like maybe she plannin to do my portrait from memory. I'm mad, but I won't give her that satisfaction. So I slouch around the store bein very bored and say, "Let's go."

Me and Sugar at the back of the train watchin the tracks whizzin by   44
large then small then gettin gobbled up in the dark. I'm thinkin about this tricky toy I saw in the store. A clown that somersaults on a bar then does chin-ups just cause you yank lightly at his leg. Cost $35. I could see me askin my mother for a $35 birthday clown. "You wanna who that costs what?" she'd say, cocking her head to the side to get a better view of the hole in my head. Thirty-five dollars could buy new bunk beds for Junior and Gretchen's boy. Thirty-five dollars and the whole household could visit Grandaddy Nelson in the country. Thirty-five dollars would pay for the rent and the piano bill too. Who are these people that spend that much for performing clowns and $1,000 for toy sailboats? What kinda work they do and how they live and how come we ain't in on it? Where we are is who we are, Miss Moore always pointin out. But it don't necessarily have to be that way, she always adds then waits for somebody to say that poor people have to wake up and demand their share of the pie and don't none of us know what kind of pie she talkin about in the first damn place. But she ain't so smart cause I still got her four dollars from the taxi and she ain't gettin it. Messin up my day with this shit. Sugar nudges me in my pocket and winks.

Miss Moore lines us up in front of the mailbox where we started   45
from, seem like years ago, and I got a headache for thinkin so hard. And we lean all over each other so we can hold up under the draggy-ass lecture she always finishes us off with at the end before we thank her for borin us to tears. But she just looks at us like she readin tea leaves. Finally she say, "Well, what did you think of F.A.O. Schwarz?"

Rosie Giraffe mumbles, "White folks crazy."   46

"I'd like to go there again when I get my birthday money," says   47
Mercedes, and we shove her out the pack so she has to lean on the mailbox by herself.

"I'd like a shower. Tiring day," say Flyboy.   48

Then Sugar surprises me by sayin, "You know, Miss Moore, I   49
don't think all of us here put together eat in a year what that sailboat
costs." And Miss Moore lights up like somebody goosed her. "And?"
she say, urging Sugar on. Only I'm standin on her foot so she don't
continue.

"Imagine for a minute what kind of society it is in which some peo-   50
ple can spend on a toy what it would cost to feed a family of six or seven.
What do you think?"

"I think," say Sugar pushing me off her feet like she never done be-   51
fore, cause I whip her ass in a minute, "that this is not much of a democracy if you ask me. Equal chance to pursue happiness means an equal
crack at the dough, don't it?" Miss Moore is besides herself and I am disgusted with Sugar's treachery. So I stand on her foot one more time to
see if she'll shove me. She shuts up, and Miss Moore looks at me, sor-
rowfully I'm thinkin. And somethin weird is goin on, I can feel it in my
chest.

"Anybody else learn anything today?" lookin dead at me. I walk   52
away and Sugar has to run to catch up and don't even seem to notice
when I shrug her arm off my shoulder.

"Well, we got four dollars anyway," she says.   53

"Uh hunh."   54

"We could go to Hascombs and get half a chocolate layer and then   55
go to the Sunset and still have plenty money for potato chips and ice-
cream sodas."

"Uh hunh."   56

"Race you to Hascombs," she say.   57

We start down the block and she gets ahead which is O.K. by me   58
cause I'm going to the West End and then over to the Drive to think this
day through. She can run if she want to and even run faster. But ain't nobody gonna beat me at nuthin.

Responding to Reading

1. How does the narrator's level of diction differ from Miss Moore's? What
   does this difference suggest about their relative positions in society? About
   the terms of their relationship?
2. Who do you think has the upper hand in this story, the narrator or Miss
   Moore? Why?
3. How do you respond to the narrator? Do you like her? Do you admire her?
   Does her level of diction play any part in shaping your impression of her?

─────────────────── **WRITING** ───────────────────

The Politics of Language

1. Both Malcolm X and Frederick Douglass discuss how they undertook a program of self-education. Write an essay in which you discuss how their efforts are similar and how they are different. Make certain you discuss what they learned about themselves and about their respective societies by learning to read and write.

2. How do people's spoken and written language affect your response to them? Considering friends as well as public figures, write an essay in which you define and illustrate the criteria by which you evaluate the communication skills of others.

3. Write an editorial for your local newspaper in which you argue for or against a Constitutional amendment making English the official language of the United States. In your essay refer to James Fallows's "The New Immigrants" as well as any of the other essays in this chapter that might help you support your points.

4. Both Eva Hoffman in "Lost in Translation" and Amy Tan in "Mother Tongue" discuss how language connects an immigrant with his or her native culture. Write an essay in which you compare their attitudes toward their respective native languages with that of Richard Rodriguez in "The Fear of Losing a Culture" (p.402).

5. Both Richard Rodriguez in "Aria" and Barbara Mellix in "From Outside, In" talk about how education changed their use of language. Write an essay discussing the effect that education has had on your own spoken and written language. What do you think you have gained and lost as your language has changed?

6. Which of your daily activities would you be unable to carry out if, like the people Jonathan Kozol describes in "The Human Cost of an Illiterate Society," you could neither read nor write? Write an article for your local newspaper in which you report on a typical day. For example, begin by having breakfast and then driving or taking public transportation to school. Make sure you refer to specific tasks you cannot do because you are illiterate. In addition, explain some strategies you would use to hide the fact you couldn't read or write.

7. In "Aria" Richard Rodriguez distinguishes between his private and public languages. For him the private language is Spanish, and the public one is English. Write an essay in which you define and discuss the private and public languages in your family, community, or age cohort.

8. In "Lost in Translation" Eva Hoffman points out that when people speak, they send class signals—that is, the higher their social class, the more correctly they speak. Write an essay in which you compare the class signals sent by Miss Moore and the narrator in Toni Cade Bambara's "The Lesson."

9. In "Sexism in English: A 1990s Update" Alleen Pace Nilsen says that one way to eliminate sexism in American society is to eliminate sexism in the English language. Write an essay in which you discuss whether George Orwell would agree with this position. For example, in "Politics and the English Language" does Orwell imply that changing language also changes the way people think?

10. In "Separate Is Better" (p.132) Susan Estrich makes a case for women students attending special schools. In recent years, proposals have been advanced for providing separate educational experiences for other groups—for example, African-American men in inner-city neighborhoods, deaf students, students who do not speak English well, or gay and lesbian high school students. Write an essay in which you discuss which groups should and should not have separate educational facilities. In addition, consider whether separate facilities empower a group, as Estrich contends, or whether they actually accomplish the opposite result. Make sure you refer specifically to Estrich's essay.

4

THE MEDIA'S
MESSAGE

Student Voices

"I was born in 1975. I spent most of my formative years in front of the television watching cartoons and kids' shows. I learned just about everything I neeeded to know from TV, and if something important happened, there would be a break in the programming to tell me. My experience tells me that my generation is just waiting for that program break to let them know what to do next. And if the TV is going to tell us what's going on, there's no reason to go out and find out on our own."

—*Stephen Berger*

"The mass media create stereotypes and set impossible standards. Movies, television, and radio also have a tendency to romanticize immoral acts and bad habits. Because the media give a limited, inaccurate view of the world, they should not be treated as a reliable source of information.

"On TV we see Mexicans and Puerto Ricans often portrayed as loud and obnoxious, starting trouble everywhere they turn. They usually live in the slums and are unwilling to work at improving their lives. Such a representation of a group of people is racist.

"On all types of media we see or hear ads for skin cream, weight loss, hair color—perfection. The media present every woman as tall, with a tiny waist, a large chest, a flawless complexion, and bouncy hair and all men as lean, broad shouldered, and muscular. Very few people measure up to these ideals. Why is everyone searching for physical improvement, and why do the media promote it? The media promote what they think the people want, and the people want what the media show them is desireable.

"Often the media romanticize dangerous habits. Commercials commonly show attractive young people drinking together in the back of a Jeep on the beach. Do viewers stop to ask themselves who will be driving home and whether that person will be sober enough to do so responsibly?"

—*Megan A. Seely*

"When I was young, the movies definitely had an effect on me. I found role models in them. I was a kid who liked to be adventurous, who wanted to fly like Superman or be a pilot or a Jedi knight in *Star Wars*. My dreams of being a hero made life exciting to me."

—*Dave Zimecki*

"Movies are not a good source of role models or heroes. It appears that the majority of today's films focus on violence and crime. Since we live in a nation where crime is the cause of many social problems that exist, I do not think that portraying criminals and violent characters as heroes is good for children. By doing this, the film industry tells the audience that violent people are admirable and that their values should be embraced. I feel there should be more positive role models in movies and on television so that young people can actually have someone to look up to who represents positive values."

—*Celeste Armenti*

"Television and radio have changed the music scene. Alternative music seems to be becoming mainstream because people are having it shoved in their faces on MTV. It seems there is no underground. The punk generation in the past (not that I'm a huge fan) had a purpose. It was for outcasts who were rebelling against a commercial society. But now the media push punk as a cool thing, so punks are showing up all over. How can music rebel against society when everything is accepted?"

—*D. Scot Ackertman*

"My main source of news is the newspaper, which I try to buy every day. The only problem with this is that I only read the sports page. I start from the back and read all the sports and then flip through the other pages. I sometimes stop at the comics. The other stuff doesn't interest me."

—*Charles Guittar*

--------------------- **Preparing to Read and Write** ---------------------

The popular media—newspapers and magazines, radio, television, and movies—have been around for a long time, but in recent years they have come to have a particularly powerful and significant impact on our lives. Cable television has brought us literally hundreds of stations—along with sitcom reruns that endlessly recycle our childhoods (or our parents' childhoods). Satellites have brought immediacy: The Vietnam War was the first televised war, but we had to wait for the evening news to see it; during the Persian Gulf War, CNN brought us news as it happened. Talk radio has become so powerful that it may actually be shaping government policy. (In fact, some political commentators believe talk radio was responsible for the Republican victories in the House and Senate in the 1994 elections.) Other innovations have also appeared: film special effects that have the power to mystify or terrify, newspapers that seem to have more color and graphics than words, and, on television, tabloid journalism, home shopping, informercials, and music videos.

Many more innovations are coming to our world. In the near future, fiber-optic cables will redefine our relationship with the media, enabling us to bank, shop, participate in public opinion polls, and possibly even vote—all without ever leaving our homes. With this explosion of technology, however, come questions. Who will have access to this new technology? How will we cope with the flood of information this new technology will bring? What use will we make of it? And finally, who will control it? The government? Private industry? Individuals? How we answer these and other questions will determine whether the new technology will bring people of the world together or whether it will produce a world of isolated individuals mindlessly surfing through hundreds of channels and thousands of programs. The problem is, as the writers in this chapter remind us, that quantity and variety do not necessarily equal quality.

As you read and prepare to write about the selections in this chapter, you may consider the following questions.

- Does the selection focus on one particular medium or on the media in general?

- Does the writer see the media as a positive, negative, or neutral force? Why?

- If the writer sees negative effects, where does he or she place blame? Do you agree?

- Does the writer make any recommendations for change? Do these recommendations seem reasonable?

- Is the writer focusing on the media's effect on society or on the media's effect on his or her own life?

Two Perspectives on the Media's Message

The first two essays in this chapter look at television and its impact on viewers. Marie Winn's "Television: The Plug-In Drug," a chapter from her book *The Plug-In Drug: Television, Children, and the Family* (1977), is a highly critical examination of the effects of television on family life and parent-child relationships, which Winn sees as almost wholly negative. The author of children's books as well as several other critiques of television, Winn (1936–) is currently working on a book about urban wildlife. John Leonard's "Why Blame TV?" originally appeared in the liberal periodical *The Nation*. It is a response to legislation proposed by Congress in 1993 that would have severely limited the amount of violence broadcast by television networks, particularly during children's viewing hours. Leonard (1939–), a long-time staff writer at the *New York Times* and now a cultural critic for a number of publications, takes the position that television has little if any negative effect on its audience and that, in fact, television offers a surprising amount of beneficial programming.

TELEVISION: THE PLUG-IN DRUG

Marie Winn

A quarter of a century after the introduction of television into American society, a period that has seen the medium become so deeply ingrained in American life that in at least one state the television set has attained the rank of a legal necessity, safe from repossession in case of debt along with clothes, cooking utensils, and the like, television viewing has become an inevitable and ordinary part of daily life. Only in the early years of television did writers and commentators have sufficient perspective to separate the activity of watching television from the actual content it offers the viewer. In those early days writers frequently discussed the effects of television on family life. However, a curious myopia afflicted those early observers: almost without exception they regarded television as a favorable, beneficial, indeed, wondrous influence upon the family. 1

"Television is going to be a real asset in every home where there are children," predicts a writer in 1949. 2

"Television will take over your way of living and change your chil-   3
dren's habits, but this change can be a wonderful improvement," claims
another commentator.

"No survey's needed, of course, to establish that television has   4
brought the family together in one room," writes the *New York Times*
television critic in 1949.

Each of the early articles about television is invariably accompanied   5
by a photograph or illustration showing a family cozily sitting together
before the television set, Sis on Mom's lap, Buddy perched on the arm
of Dad's chair, Dad with his arm around Mom's shoulder. Who could
have guessed that twenty or so years later Mom would be watching a
drama in the kitchen, the kids would be looking at cartoons in their
room, while Dad would be taking in the ball game in the living room?

Of course television sets were enormously expensive in those early   6
days. The idea that by 1975 more than 60 percent of American families
would own two or more sets was preposterous. The splintering of the
multiple-set family was something the early writers could not foresee.
Nor did anyone imagine the numbers of hours children would eventually devote to television, the common use of television by parents as a
child pacifier, the changes television would effect upon child-rearing
methods, the increasing domination of family schedules by children's
viewing requirements—in short, the *power* of the new medium to dominate family life.

After the first years, as children's consumption of the new medium   7
increased, together with parental concern about the possible effects of so
much television viewing, a steady refrain helped to soothe and reassure
anxious parents. "Television always enters a pattern of influences that
already exist: the home, the peer group, the school, the church and culture generally," write the authors of an early and influential study of
television's effects on children. In other words, if the child's home life is
all right, parents need not worry about the effects of all that television
watching.

But television does not merely influence the child; it deeply influ-   8
ences that "pattern of influences" that is meant to ameliorate its effects.
Home and family life has changed in important ways since the advent
of television. The peer group has become television-oriented, and much
of the time children spend together is occupied by television viewing.
Culture generally has been transformed by television. Therefore it is improper to assign to television the subsidiary role its many apologists (too
often members of the television industry) insist it plays. Television is not
merely one of a number of important influences upon today's child.
Through the changes it has made in family life, television emerges as *the*
important influence in children's lives today.

Television's contribution to family life has been an equivocal one.   9
For while it has, indeed, kept the members of the family from dispersing, it has not served to bring them *together*. By its domination of the time families spend together, it destroys the special quality that distinguishes one family from another, a quality that depends to a great extent on what a family *does*, what special rituals, games, recurrent jokes, familiar songs, and shared activities it accumulates.

"Like the sorcerer of old," writes Urie Bronfenbrenner, "the televi-   10
sion set casts its magic spell, freezing speech and action, turning the living into silent statues so long as the enchantment lasts. The primary danger of the television screen lies not so much in the behavior it produces—although there is danger there—as in the behavior it prevents: the talks, the games, the family festivities and arguments through which much of the child's learning takes place and through which his character is formed. Turning on the television set can turn off the process that transforms children into people."

Yet parents have accepted a television-dominated family life so   11
completely that they cannot see how the medium is involved in whatever problems they might be having. A first-grade teacher reports:

"I have one child in the group who's an only child. I wanted to find   12
out more about her family life because this little girl was quite isolated from the group, didn't make friends, so I talked to her mother. Well, they don't have time to do anything in the evening, the mother said. The parents come home after picking up the child at the babysitter's. Then the mother fixes dinner while the child watches TV. Then they have dinner and the child goes to bed. I said to this mother. 'Well, couldn't she help you fix dinner? That would be a nice time for the two of you to talk,' and the mother said, 'Oh, but I'd hate to have her miss "Zoom."[1] It's such a good program!'"

Even when families make efforts to control television, too often its   13
very presence counterbalances the positive features of family life. A writer and mother of two boys aged 3 and 7 described her family's television schedule in an article in the *New York Times:*

> We were in the midst of a full-scale War. Every day was a new battle and every program was a major skirmish. We agreed it was a bad scene all around and were ready to enter diplomatic negotiations. . . . In principle we have agreed on 2 1/2 hours of TV a day, "Sesame Street," "Electric Company" (with dinner gobbled up in between) and two half-hour shows between 7 and 8:30 which enables the grown-ups to eat in peace and prevents the two boys from destroying one another. Their pre-bedtime choice is dreadful, because, as Josh recently admitted, "There's nothing much on I really like." So . . . it's "What's My

---

[1] An educational program broadcast on PBS. [Eds.]

Line" or "To Tell the Truth"[2] . . . Clearly there is a need for first-rate children's shows at this time. . . .

Consider the "family life" described here: Presumably the father [14] comes home from work during the "Sesame Street"—"Electric Company" stint. The children are either watching television, gobbling their dinner, or both. While the parents eat their dinner in peaceful privacy, the children watch another hour of television. Then there is only a half-hour left before bedtime, just enough time for baths, getting pajamas on, brushing teeth, and so on. The children's evening is regimented with an almost military precision. They watch their favorite programs, and when there is "nothing much on I really like," they watch whatever else is on—because *watching* is the important thing. Their mother does not see anything amiss with watching programs just for the sake of watching; she only wishes there were some first-rate children's shows on at those times.

Without conjuring up memories of the Victorian era with family [15] games and long, leisurely meals, and large families, the question arises: isn't there a better family life available than this dismal, mechanized arrangement of children watching television for however long is allowed them, evening after evening?

Of course, families today still do *special* things together at times: go [16] camping in the summer, go to the zoo on a nice Saturday, take various trips and expeditions. But their *ordinary* daily life together is diminished—that sitting around at the dinner table, that spontaneous taking up of an activity, those little games invented by children on the spur of the moment when there is nothing else to do, the scribbling, the chatting, and even the quarreling, all the things that form the fabric of a family, that define a childhood. Instead, the children have their regular schedule of television programs and bedtime, and the parents have their peaceful dinner together.

The author of the article in the *Times* notes that "keeping a family [17] sane means mediating between the needs of both children and adults." But surely the needs of adults are being better met than the needs of the children, who are effectively shunted away and rendered untroublesome, while their parents enjoy a life as undemanding as that of any childless couple. In reality, it is those very demands that young children make upon a family that lead to growth, and it is the way parents accede to those demands that builds the relationships upon which the future of the family depends. If the family does not accumulate its backlog of shared experiences, shared *everyday* experiences that occur and recur and change and develop, then it is not likely to survive as anything other than a caretaking institution.

---

[2] Long-running game shows. [Eds.]

Family Rituals

Ritual is defined by sociologists as "that part of family life that the [18] family likes about itself, is proud of and wants formally to continue." Another text notes that "the development of a ritual by a family is an index of the common interest of its members in the family as a group."

What has happened to family rituals, those regular, dependable, re- [19] current happenings that gave members of a family a feeling of *belonging* to a home rather than living in it merely for the sake of convenience, those experiences that act as the adhesive of family unity far more than any material advantages?

Mealtime rituals, going-to-bed rituals, illness rituals, holiday rituals, [20] how many of these have survived the inroads of the television set?

A young woman who grew up near Chicago reminisces about her [21] childhood and gives an idea of the effects of television upon family rituals:

"As a child I had millions of relatives around—my parents both [22] come from relatively large families. My father had nine brothers and sisters. And so every holiday there was this great swoop-down of aunts, uncles, and millions of cousins. I just remember how wonderful it used to be. These thousands of cousins would come and everyone would play and ultimately, after dinner, all the women would be in the front of the house, drinking coffee and talking, all the men would be in the back of the house, drinking and smoking, and all the kids would be all over the place, playing hide and seek. Christmas time was particularly nice because everyone always brought all their toys and games. Our house had a couple of rooms with go-through closets, so there was always kids running in a great circle route. I remember it was just wonderful.

"And then all of a sudden one year I remember becoming sud- [23] denly aware of how different everything had become. The kids were no longer playing Monopoly or Clue or the other games we used to play together. It was because we had a television set which had been turned on for a football game. All of that socializing that had gone on previously had ended. Now everyone was sitting in front of the television set, on a holiday, at a family party! I remember being stunned by how awful that was. Somehow the television had become more attractive."

As families have come to spend more and more of their time to- [24] gether engaged in the single activity of television watching, those rituals and pastimes that once gave family life its special quality have become more and more uncommon. Not since prehistoric times when cave families hunted, gathered, ate, and slept, with little time remaining to accumulate a culture of any significance, have families been reduced to such a sameness.

Real People

It is not only the activities that a family might engage in together [25] that are diminished by the powerful presence of television in the home. The relationships of the family members to each other are also affected, in both obvious and subtle ways. The hours that the young child spends in a one-way relationship with television people, an involvement that allows for no communication or interaction, surely affect his relationships with real-life people.

Studies show the importance of eye-to-eye contact, for instance, in [26] real-life relationships, and indicate that the nature of a person's eye-contact patterns, whether he looks another squarely in the eye or looks to the side or shifts his gaze from side to side, may play a significant role in his success or failure in human relationships. But no eye contact is possible in the child-television relationship, although in certain children's programs people purport to speak directly to the child and the camera fosters this illusion by focusing directly upon the person being filmed. (Mr. Rogers is an example, telling the child "I like you, you're special," etc.) How might such a distortion of real-life relationships affect a child's development of trust, of openness, of an ability to relate well to other *real* people?

Bruno Bettelheim writes: [27]

> Children who have been taught, or conditioned, to listen passively most of the day to the warm verbal communications coming from the TV screen, to the deep emotional appeal of the so-called TV personality, are often unable to respond to real persons because they arouse so much less feeling than the skilled actor. Worse, they lose the ability to learn from reality because life experiences are much more complicated than the ones they see on the screen. . . .

A teacher makes a similar observation about her personal viewing [28] experiences:

"I have trouble mobilizing myself and dealing with real people after [29] watching a few hours of television. It's just hard to make that transition from watching television to a real relationship. I suppose it's because there was no effort necessary while I was watching, and dealing with real people always requires a bit of effort. Imagine, then, how much harder it might be to do the same thing for a small child, particularly one who watches a lot of television every day."

But more obviously damaging to family relationships is the elimi- [30] nation of opportunities to talk, and perhaps more important, to argue, to air grievances, between parents and children and brothers and sisters. Families frequently use television to avoid confronting their problems, problems that will not go away if they are ignored but will only fester and become less easily resolvable as time goes on.

A mother reports: [31]

"I find myself, with three children, wanting to turn on the TV set [32] when they're fighting. I really have to struggle not to do it because I feel that's telling them this is the solution to the quarrel—but it's so tempting that I often do it."

A family therapist discusses the use of television as an avoidance [33] mechanism:

"In a family I know the father comes home from work and turns on [34] the television set. The children come and watch him and the wife serves them their meal in front of the set. He then goes and takes a shower, or works on the car or something. She then goes and has her own dinner in front of the television set. It's a symptom of a deeper-rooted problem, sure. But it would help them all to get rid of the set. It would be far easier to work on what the symptom really means without the television. The television simply encourages a double avoidance of each other. They'd find out more quickly what was going on if they weren't able to hide behind the TV. Things wouldn't necessarily be better, of course, but they wouldn't be anesthetized."

The decreased opportunities for simple conversation between par- [35] ents and children in the television-centered home may help explain an observation made by an emergency room nurse at a Boston hospital. She reports that parents just seem to sit there these days when they come in with a sick or seriously injured child, although talking to the child would distract and comfort him. "They don't seem to know *how* to talk to their own children at any length," the nurse observes. Similarly, a television critic writes in the *New York Times:* "I had just a day ago taken my son to the emergency ward of a hospital for stitches above his left eye, and the occasion seemed no more real to me than Maalot or 54th Street, south-central Los Angeles. There was distance and numbness and an inability to turn off the total institution. I didn't behave at all; I just watched. . . ."

A number of research studies substantiate the assumption that tele- [36] vision interferes with family activities and the formation of family relationships. One survey shows that 78 percent of the respondents indicated no conversation taking place during viewing except at specified times such as commercials. The study notes: "The television atmosphere in most households is one of quiet absorption on the part of family members who are present. The nature of the family social life during a program could be described as 'parallel' rather than interactive, and the set does seem to dominate family life when it is on." Thirty-six percent of the respondents in another study indicated that television viewing was the only family activity participated in during the week.

In a summary of research findings on television's effect on family in- [37] teractions James Gabardino states: "The early findings suggest that television had a disruptive effect upon interaction and thus presumably human development. . . . It is not unreasonable to ask: 'Is the fact that the average American family during the 1950s came to include two parents, two children and a television set somehow related to the psychosocial characteristics of the young adults of the 1970s?'"

Undermining the Family

In its effect on family relationships, in its facilitation of parental [38] withdrawal from an active role in the socialization of their children, and in its replacement of family rituals and special events, television has played an important role in the disintegration of the American family. But of course it has not been the only contributing factor, perhaps not even the most important one. The steadily rising divorce rate, the increase in the number of working mothers, the decline of the extended family, the breakdown of neighborhoods and communities, the growing isolation of the nuclear family—all have seriously affected the family.

As Urie Bronfenbrenner suggests, the sources of family breakdown [39] do not come from the family itself, but from the circumstances in which the family finds itself and the way of life imposed upon it by those circumstances. "When those circumstances and the way of life they generate undermine relationships of trust and emotional security between family members, when they make it difficult for parents to care for, educate and enjoy their children, when there is no support or recognition from the outside world for one's role as a parent and when time spent with one's family means frustration of career, personal fulfillment and peace of mind, then the development of the child is adversely affected," he writes.

But while the roots of alienation go deep into the fabric of American [40] social history, television's presence in the home fertilizes them, encourages their wild and unchecked growth. Perhaps it is true that America's commitment to the television experience masks a spiritual vacuum, an empty and barren way of life, a desert of materialism. But it is television's dominant role in the family that anesthetizes the family into accepting its unhappy state and prevents it from struggling to better its condition, to improve its relationships, and to regain some of the richness it once possessed.

Others have noted the role of mass media in perpetuating an un- [41] satisfactory *status quo*. Leisure-time activity, writes Irving Howe, "must provide relief from work monotony without making the return to work too unbearable; it must provide amusement without insight and pleasure without disturbance—as distinct from art which gives pleasure through disturbance. Mass culture is thus oriented towards a central aspect of industrial society: the depersonalization of the individual." Similarly, Jacques Ellul rejects the idea that television is a legitimate means of educating the citizen: "Education . . . takes place only incidentally. The clouding of his consciousness is paramount. . . ."

And so the American family muddles on, dimly aware that some- [42] thing is amiss but distracted from an understanding of its plight by an endless stream of television images. As family ties grow weaker and vaguer, as children's lives become more separate from their parents', as parents' educational role in their children's lives is taken over by television and schools, family life becomes increasingly more unsatisfying for both parents and children. All that seems to be left is Love, an abstraction that family members *know* is necessary but find great difficulty giving each other because the traditional opportunities for expressing love within the family have been reduced or destroyed.

For contemporary parents, love toward each other has increasingly [43] come to mean successful sexual relations, as witnessed by the proliferation of sex manuals and sex therapists. The opportunities for manifesting other forms of love through mutual support, understanding, nurturing, even, to use an unpopular word, *serving* each other, are less and less available as mothers and fathers seek their independent destinies outside the family.

As for love of children, this love is increasingly expressed through [44] supplying material comforts, amusements, and educational opportunities. Parents show their love for their children by sending them to good schools and camps, by providing them with good food and good doctors, by buying them toys, books, games, and a television set of their very own. Parents will even go further and express their love by attending PTA meetings to improve their children's schools, or by joining groups that are acting to improve the quality of their children's television programs.

But this is love at a remove, and is rarely understood by children. [45] The more direct forms of parental love require time and patience, steady, dependable, ungrudgingly given time actually spent *with* a child, reading to him, comforting him, playing, joking, and working with him. But even if a parent were eager and willing to demonstrate that sort of direct love to his children today, the opportunities are diminished. What with school and Little League and piano lessons and, of course, the inevitable television programs, a day seems to offer just enough time for a good-night kiss.

WHY BLAME TV?

John Leonard

Like a warrior-king of Sumer, daubed with sesame oil, gorged on [1] goat, hefting up his sword and drum, Senator Ernest Hollings looked down November 23 from a ziggurat to intone, all over the op-ed page of the *New York Times:* "If the TV and cable industries have no sense of shame, we must take it upon ourselves to stop licensing their violence-saturated programming."

Hollings, of course, is co-sponsor in the Senate, with Daniel Inouye, 2 of a ban on any act of violence on television before, say, midnight. Never mind whether this is constitutional, or what it would do to the local news. Never mind, either, that in Los Angeles last August, in the International Ballroom of the Beverly Hilton, in front of 600 industry executives, the talking heads—a professor here, a producer there, a child psychologist and a network veep for program standards—couldn't even agree on a definition of violence. (Is it only violent if it hurts or kills?) And they disagreed on which was worse, a "happy" violence that sugarcoats aggressive behavior or a "graphic" violence that at least suggests consequences. (How, anyway, does television manage somehow simultaneously to *desensitize* and to *incite?*) Nor were they really sure what goes on in the dreamy heads of our children as they crouch in the dark to commune with the tube while their parents, if they have any, aren't around. (*Road Runner?* Beep-beep.) Nor does the infamous scarlet V "parent advisory" warning even apply to cartoons, afternoon soaps, or Somalias.

Never mind, because everybody agrees that watching television 3 causes anti-social behavior, especially among the children of the poor; that there seems to be more violent programming on the air now than there ever was before; that *Beavis and Butt-head* inspired an Ohio 5-year-old to burn down the family trailer; that in the blue druidic light of television we will have spawned generations of toadstools and triffids.

In fact, there is less violence on network television than there used 4 to be; because of ratings, it's mostly sitcoms. The worst stuff is the Hollywood splatterflicks; they're found on premium cable, which means the poor are less likely to be watching. Everywhere else on cable, not counting the court channel or home shopping and not even to think about blood sports and Pat Buchanan, the fare is innocent to the point of stupefaction (Disney, Discovery, Family, Nickelodeon). That Ohio trailer wasn't even wired for cable, so the littlest firebird must have got his MTV elsewhere in the dangerous neighborhood. (And kids have been playing with matches since, at least, Prometheus. I recall burning down my very own bedroom when I was 5 years old. The fire department had to tell my mother that the evidence pointed to me.) Since the '60s, according to statistics cited by Douglas Davis in *The Five Myths of Television Power*, more Americans than ever before are going out to eat in restaurants, see films, plays, and baseball games, visit museums, travel abroad, jog, even *read*. Watching television, everybody does *something else* at the same time. While our children are playing with their Adobe Illustrators and Domark Virtual Reality Toolkits, the rest of us eat, knit, smoke, dream, read magazines, sign checks, feel sorry for ourselves, think about Hillary, and plot shrewd career moves or revenge.

Actually watching television, unless it's C-Span, is usually more in- 5
teresting than the proceedings of Congress. Or what we read in hysterical books like Jerry Mander's *Four Arguments for the Elimination of Television*, or George Gilder's *Life After Television*, or Marie Winn's *The
Plug-In Drug*, or Neal Postman's *Amusing Ourselves to Death*, or Bill
McKibben's *The Age of Missing Information*.[1] Or what we'll hear at panel
discussions on censorship, where right-wingers worry about sex and
left-wingers worry about violence. Or just lolling around an academic
deepthink-tank, trading mantras like "violence profiles" (George Gerb-
ner), "processed culture" (Richard Hoggart), "narcoleptic joys" (Michael
Sorkin), and "glass teat" (Harlan Ellison).

Of *course* something happens to us when we watch television; net- 6
works couldn't sell their millions of pairs of eyes to advertising agencies,
nor would ad agencies buy more than $21 billion worth of commercial
time each year, if speech (and sound, and motion) didn't somehow modify action. But what happens is far from clear and won't be much clari-
fied by lab studies, however longitudinal, of habits and behaviors isolated from the larger feedback loop of a culture full of gaudy
contradictions. The only country in the world that watches more television than we do is Japan, and you should see its snuff movies and
pornographic comic books; but the Japanese are pikers compared with
us when we compute per capita rates of rape and murder. Some critics
in India tried to blame the recent rise in communal violence there on a
state-run television series dramatizing the *Mahabharata*,[2] but not long
ago they were blaming Salman Rushdie,[3] as in Bangladesh they have decided to blame the writer Taslima Nasrin. No Turk I know of attributes
skinhead violence to German TV.[4] It's foolish to pretend that all behavior is mimetic, and that our only model is Spock or Brokaw. Or Mork
and Mindy. Why, after so many years of *M*A*S*H*, weekly in prime time
and nightly in reruns, aren't all of us out there hugging trees and mor-
phing dolphins? Why, with so many sitcoms, aren't all of us comedians?

But nobody normal watches television the way congressmen, aca- 7
demics, symposiasts, and Bill McKibbens do. We are less thrilling. For
instance:

On March 3, 1993, a Wednesday, midway through the nine-week 8
run of *Homicide* on NBC, in an episode written by Tom Fontana and directed by Martin Campbell, Baltimore detectives Bayliss (Kyle Secor)
and Pembleton (Andre Braugher) had 12 hours to wring a confession
out of "Arab" Tucker (Moses Gunn) for the strangulation and disem-

---

[1] Books critical of the effects of television. [Eds.]

[2] Epic poem describing the exploits of ancient kings and heroes. [Eds.]

[3] Indian-born novelist long in hiding because of a death sentence imposed by Islamic extremists, who deemed his novel *The Satanic Verses* sacrilegious. [Eds.]

[4] Turkish-born immigrants in Germany have been victims of violent attacks by neo-Nazi groups. [Eds.]

boweling of an 11-year-old girl. In the dirty light and appalling intimacy of a single claustrophobic room, with a whoosh of wind sound like some dread blowing in from empty Gobi spaces, among maps, library books, diaries, junk food, pornographic crime-scene photographs, and a single black overflowing ashtray, these three men seemed as nervous as the hand-held cameras—as if their black coffee were full of jumping beans, amphetamines, and spiders; as if God himself were jerking them around.

Well, you may think the culture doesn't really need another cop [9] show. And, personally, I'd prefer a weekly series in which social problems are solved through creative nonviolence, after a Quaker meeting, by a collective of vegetarian carpenters. But in a single hour, for which Tom Fontana eventually won an Emmy, I learned more about the behavior of fearful men in small rooms than from any number of better-known movies, plays, and novels on the topic by the likes of Don DeLillo, Mary McCarthy, Alberto Moravia, Heinrich Böll, and Doris Lessing.[5]

This, of course, was an accident, as it usually is when those of us [10] who watch television like normal people are startled in our expectations. We leave home expecting, for a lot of money, to be exalted, and almost never are. But staying put, slumped in an agnosticism about sentience itself, suspecting that our cable box is just another bad-faith credit card enabling us to multiply our opportunities for disappointment, we are ambushed in our lethargy. And not so much by "event" television, like Ingmar Bergman's *Scenes from a Marriage,* originally a six-hour miniseries for Swedish television; or Marcel Ophuls' *The Sorrow and the Pity,* originally conceived for French television; or Rainer Werner Fassbinder's *Berlin Alexanderplatz,* commissioned by German television; or *The Singing Detective;* or *The Jewel in the Crown.*[6] On the contrary, we've stayed home on certain nights to watch television, the way on other nights we'll go out to a neighborhood restaurant, as if on Mondays we ordered in for laughs, as on Fridays we'd rather eat Italian. We go to television—message center, mission control, Big Neighbor, electronic Elmer's glue-all—to look at Oscars, Super Bowls, moon shots, Watergates, Pearlygates, ayatollahs, dead Kings, dead Kennedys; and also, perhaps, to experience some "virtual" community as a nation. But we also go because we are hungry, angry, lonely, or tired, and television is always there for us, a 24-hour user-friendly magic box grinding out narrative, novelty, and distraction, news and laughs, snippets of high culture, remedial seriousness and vulgar celebrity, an incitement and a sedative, a place to celebrate and a place to mourn, a circus and a wishing well.

---

[5] Highly regarded modern writers. [Eds.]

[6] The first three of these are films by important European directors; the last two are popular and critically acclaimed British miniseries aired on PBS. [Eds.]

And suddenly Napoleon shows up, like a popsicle, on *Northern Ex-* 11
posure, while Chris on the radio is reading Proust. Or Roseanne is about
lesbianism instead of bowling. Or *Picket Fences* has moved on, from serial bathers and elephant abuse to euthanasia and gay-bashing.

Kurt Vonnegut on Showtime! David ("Masturbation") Mamet on 12
TNT! Norman Mailer wrote the TV screenplay for *The Executioner's Song,*
and Gore Vidal gave us *Lincoln* with Mary Tyler Moore as Mary Todd.
In just the past five years, if I hadn't been watching television, I'd have
missed *Tanner '88,* when Robert Altman and Garry Trudeau ran Michael
Murphy for president of the United States; *My Name Is Bill W.,* with
James Woods as the founding father of Alcoholics Anonymous; *The Final
Days,* with Theodore Bikel as Henry Kissinger; *No Place Like Home,* where
there wasn't one for Christine Lahti and Jeff Daniels, as there hadn't been
for Jane Fonda in *The Dollmaker* and Mare Winningham in *God Bless the
Child; Eyes on the Prize,* a home movie in two parts about America's second civil war; *The Last Best Year,* with Mary Tyler Moore and Bernadette
Peters learning to live with their gay sons and HIV; *Separate but Equal,*
with Sidney Poitier as Thurgood Marshall; and *High Crimes and Misdemeanors,* the Bill Moyers special on Irangate and the scandal of our intelligence agencies; Graham Greene, John Updike, Philip Roth, Gloria Nay-
lor, Arthur Miller, and George Eliot, plus Paul Simon and Stephen
Sondheim. Not to mention—guiltiest of all our secrets—those hoots without which any popular culture would be as tedious as a John Cage or an
Anaïs Nin, like Elizabeth Taylor in *Sweet Bird of Youth* and the Redgrave
sisters in a remake of *Whatever Happened to Baby Jane?*

What all this television has in common is narrative. Even network 13
news—which used to be better than most newspapers before the bean
counters started closing down overseas bureaus and the red camera
lights went out all over Europe and Asia and Africa—is in the storytelling business. And so far no one in Congress has suggested banning
narrative.

Because I watch all those despised network TV movies, I know more 14
about racism, ecology, homelessness, gun control, child abuse, gender
confusion, date rape, and AIDS than is dreamt of by, say, Katie Roiphe,
the Joyce Maynard of Generation X, or than Hollywood has ever bothered to tell me, especially about AIDS. Imagine, Jonathan Demme's
Philadelphia opened in theaters around the country well after at least a
dozen TV movies on AIDS that I can remember without troubling my
hard disk. And I've learned something else, too:

We were a violent culture before television, from Wounded Knee to 15
the lynching bee, and we'll be one after all our children have disappeared by video game into the pixels of cyberspace. Before television,
we blamed public schools for what went wrong with the Little People
back when classrooms weren't overcrowded in buildings that weren't
falling down in neighborhoods that didn't resemble Beirut, and whose

fault is that? *The A-Team?* We can't control guns, or drugs, and each year two million American women are assaulted by their male partners, who are usually in an alcoholic rage, and whose fault is that? *Miami Vice?* The gangs that menace our streets aren't home watching Cinemax, and neither are the sociopaths who make bonfires, in our parks, from our homeless, of whom there are at least a million, a supply-side migratory tide of the deindustrialized and dispossessed, of angry beggars, refugee children, and catatonic nomads, none of them traumatized by *Twin Peaks*. So cut Medicare, kick around the Brady Bill, and animadvert Amy Fisher movies. But children who are loved and protected long enough to grow up to have homes and respect and lucky enough to have jobs don't riot in the streets. Ours is a tantrum culture that measures everyone by his or her ability to produce wealth, and morally condemns anybody who fails to prosper, and now blames Burbank for its angry incoherence. Why not recessive genes, angry gods, lousy weather? The mafia, the zodiac, the *Protocols of the Elders of Zion?* Probability theory, demonic possession, Original Sin? George Steinbrenner? Sunspots?

Responding to Reading

1. Winn says, "Home and family life has changed in important ways since the advent of television" (8). How, according to Winn, has family life changed? How do you think your own family life would change if you were suddenly deprived of all access to television? Do you think the changes would be largely positive or negative?

2. What differences do you observe between the role television plays in your life and the role it plays in your parents' lives? Between the role it plays in your life and the role it plays in the lives of your younger siblings or your children? On whom do you think television has had the greatest impact? The most negative impact?

3. Do you agree with Winn that television is an evil, addictive drug that has destroyed cherished family rituals, undermined family relationships, and "[anesthetized] the family into accepting its unhappy state and [prevented] it from struggling to better its condition, to improve its relationships, and to regain some of the richness it once possessed" (40)? Or do you believe any decline in family values has been incidental to, rather than the result of, the rise of television? On what do you base your conclusions?

4. In paragraph 5 Leonard characterizes Marie Winn's book *The Plug-In Drug* (from which her essay on pages 257–265 was taken) as "hysterical." On what do you think he bases this statement? Do you agree with him? Do you find Leonard's own essay "hysterical"?

5. Leonard claims that "there is less violence on network television than there used to be" and that, other than on premium cable, "the fare is innocent to the point of stupefaction" (4). Do your observations support or challenge his conclusions?

6. Leonard says, "We were a violent culture before television, from Wounded Knee to the lynching bee . . ." (15). Could you argue that these acts of group

violence are different from the many individual acts of violence we see today? Do you believe television is in any way responsible for *individual* acts of violence? Explain.

WHAT'S BAD FOR POLITICS IS
~ GREAT FOR TELEVISION

Walter Goodman

Born in New York City, Walter Goodman (1927–) graduated from Syracuse University in 1947 with degrees in economics and journalism. A writer since 1954, Goodman has been on the staffs of *New Republic, Redbook, Playboy, Newsweek,* and the *New York Times,* and he has published several books, including *All Honorable Men: Corruption and Compromise in American Life* (1963) and *The Committee: The Extraordinary Career of the House Committee on Un-American Activities* (1968). In the 1980s Goodman also served as director of humanities programming for WNET, New York's public television station. The following opinion piece was originally published in the *New York Times,* where Goodman is currently a television reviewer. Writing in November 1994 in response to the "wretched campaign that the nation just endured," Goodman offers a highly critical look at television news's inability to deal effectively with the complex issues and problems that face our country and the world.

With Republican hopefuls already showing up in Iowa and New Hampshire, and with Democrats scrambling to position themselves for 1996, television gives signs of becoming the toxic-waste dump of politics. Most of the criticism of the wretched campaign that the nation just endured has been directed at the candidates and their hirelings who turned out those noisome 30-second spots. They deserve it, but negative advertising is only the tip of the sludge heap. [1]

Television, as it has developed in the United States, is not merely a passive instrument of the cheap-shot gang. The media manipulators are themselves controlled by the medium's conventions, and the audience is an accomplice to its own exploitation. [2]

Take the matter of crime, so much on voters' minds. Unlike issues like budgets and trade agreements, violent crime is made for the tube. Television without shoot-'em-ups is unimaginable. For years the natural concerns of viewers have been heightened by vivid nightly reports, [3] news-magazine body-baggers and plenty of tabloid-style agitation, not to mention the prime-time staples of murder and mayhem.

The small-screen world is composed largely of villains and victims. 4 Here is the rapist who is paroled so that he may go forth and rape again. There is the convicted murderer on death row who turns out to be innocent. Here are the grieving survivors, there the manacled felons. What excitement when, as in the case of Susan Smith, the victim is transformed into the villain (although she may become a talk-show victim again, this time a victim of depression)![1]

Melodramas invite simple solutions, and so the most popular crime 5 cures are capital punishment and gun control, although it is generally agreed among law enforcers that whatever the merits of those ideas, neither is likely to affect street crime very much. What television does not deal with particularly well is the demoralization of our inner cities, their disconnection from the larger society. Some of the elements are reported from time to time, but they are too resistant to ready remedies to deliver the good-guy-bad-guy kick. Instead, they deliver headaches to an audience that wants headache relievers.

So if you were in the business of concocting political advertisements 6 about crime, would you chance making your candidate sound like a wimp by mooning over the narrow choices for many young people in our cities or would you give him or her a manly three-strikes-and-you're-out line to spout? That's the sort of 30-second solution deemed safe for large audiences, and the peddlers know their customers. (Such quick and dirty answers to the dissatisfactions of daily life also serve as a sort of Prozac on radio talk shows, those encounter sessions for people on the edge.)

In this sour hour, the get-tough approach to nagging problems is a 7 hot seller. Take the much-discussed matter of welfare reform. Television producers, never averse to imitating one another, can't resist two sorts of welfare stories: the hustler who is robbing the system and the single mother striving to make her way through high school or college.

It's a tidy setup and invites a tidy fix. Workfare becomes the hard- 8 est-worked word of the moment; exactly how it will fare in practice, at what cost, remains vague. Maybe in some form or another it will get us where we want to go, and maybe not. That matters less to any candidate than the sales appeal of a promise to reward the enterprising and, even more satisfying, punish the indolent. Looking for a short, sweet immigration policy? Crack down on immigrants. Make it simple and, for the time being, make it tough.

Whether tough or soft, simplicity is the key. While the tough guys 9 are declaiming about cutting taxes and cutting programs (without going

---

[1] Smith admitted drowning her two sons, after first having claimed that they had been kidnapped by a black man. [Eds.]

into undue detail), television continues to come down on the soft side. The favored approach of news programs and documentaries to the urban malaise are heartwarmers like innovative schools, improved health care, safe playgrounds, anything having to do with children.

Hardly a week passes without a plug for a great new way to bright- 10 en life for the young or ease it for the needy, and it takes a mighty skeptical viewer to resist. So many of these experiments keep being trumpeted, usually by the caring-sharing cadre whose livelihoods depend on them, it is amazing that any problems still exist.

If the costs of all the proposed improvements were added up at the 11 end of the fiscal year, they would probably break what is left of a big-city budget. (But then, it remains to be seen what the tax cuts promised by the tough side will do to the Federal budget.) Fortunately for the news shows, they don't have to do the adding, and rarely feel obliged to follow up on how yesterday's educational or medical or social miracle actually turned out.

When it comes to brain busters like Federal subsidies, defense 12 spending or China, network news generally does a professional job, but even such dry and distant matters are often treated from a human-interest angle or like a sports event: Who's ahead? Programs like "The McLaughlin Group" and "Crossfire" are exercises in diversion and trivialization. No one has ever charged that the images that constitute television's power encourage sustained or probing analysis, and the concentration on personalities rather than policies only readies one for the quick fix before the credits.

Commercial television, so brilliant at giving people what they want, 13 has always been cautious, not to say craven, about giving people more than they know they want or stimulating them to want more. Despite the networks' accomplishments and pretensions, even their news departments tend to operate as much along show-business as educational lines. Mass education is not a profit center.

These are not novel observations; unfortunately, the condition is 14 chronic and, as became painfully evident in the late political season, it is not getting better. A medium that has shown it can bring information and even ideas effectively to millions is reduced every two years to a tool for stirring up emotions and shutting down minds. As they used to say, that is not healthy for living things. Like representative government.

Responding to Reading

1. Why, according to Goodman, do political candidates rely so heavily on negative campaign commercials? Whom does he blame for the state of television's political advertising? What do you think the long-term effects of such advertising will be?
2. In paragraph 7 Goodman cites two favorite themes of television news feature

stories that focus on the welfare system: "the hustler who is robbing the system and the single mother striving to make her way through high school or college." What do these two kinds of stories have in common? What do you see as the basic audience appeal of each? Why is Goodman critical of them?

3. Do you agree with Goodman that commercial television "has always been cautious . . . about giving people more than they want or stimulating them to want more" (13)? Do you agree that "what's bad for politics is great for television"? Give examples to support your conclusions.

THE TRIUMPH OF THE YELL

Deborah Tannen

A professor of linguistics at Georgetown University in Washington, D.C., Deborah Tannen (1945–) has written both scholarly and popular books examining the problems people encounter communicating across cultural and gender lines. Her three bestsellers—*That's Not What I Meant: How Conversational Style Makes or Breaks Your Relationships* (1987), *You Just Don't Understand: Women and Men in Conversation* (1990), and *Talking from 9 to 5* (1994)—have given her readers a new perspective on the way communication style can affect how a message is perceived. A frequent guest on television news and talk shows, Tannen—also the author of short stories and poems and a former college English teacher—successfully translates complex linguistic theory into language non-linguists can readily comprehend. Her "humanistic approach to linguistic analysis" was developed, she says, in order to help people everywhere understand and improve human communication. In the following essay focusing on public discourse, Tannen suggests that the media in the United States encourage public debate to degenerate into simple-minded, mean-spirited verbal fighting because "the spectacles that result when extremes clash are thought to get higher ratings or larger readership."

I put the question to a journalist who had written a vitriolic attack   1
on a leading feminist researcher: "Why do you need to make others wrong for you to be right?" Her response: "It's an argument!"

That's the problem. More and more these days, journalists, politi-   2
cians and academics treat public discourse as an argument—not in the sense of *making* an argument, but in the sense of *having* one, of having a fight.

When people have arguments in private life, they're not trying to   3
understand what the other person is saying. They're listening for weak-

nesses in logic to leap on, points they can distort to make the other look bad. We all do this when we're angry, but is it the best model for public intellectual interchange? This breakdown of the boundary between public and private is contributing to what I have come to think of as a culture of critique.

Fights have winners and losers. If you're fighting to win, the temptation is great to deny facts that support your opponent's views and present only those facts that support your own. 4

At worst, there's a temptation to lie. We accept this style of arguing because we believe we can tell when someone is lying. But we can't. Paul Ekman, a psychologist at the University of California at San Francisco, has found that even when people are very sure they can tell whether or not someone is dissembling, their judgments are as likely as not to be wrong. 5

If public discourse is a fight, every issue must have two sides—no more, no less. And it's crucial to show "the other side," even if one has to scour the margins of science or the fringes of lunacy to find it. 6

The culture of critique is based on the belief that opposition leads to truth: when both sides argue, the truth will emerge. And because people are presumed to enjoy watching a fight, the most extreme views are presented, since they make the best show. But it is a myth that opposition leads to truth when truth does not reside on one side or the other but is rather a crystal of many sides. Truth is more likely to be found in the complex middle than in the simplified extremes, but the spectacles that result when extremes clash are thought to get higher ratings or larger readership. 7

Because the culture of critique encourages people to attack and often misrepresent others, those others must waste their creativity and time correcting the misrepresentations and defending themselves. Serious scholars have had to spend years of their lives writing books proving that the Holocaust happened, because a few fanatics who claim it didn't have been given a public forum. Those who provide the platform know that what these people say is, simply put, not true, but rationalize the dissemination of lies as showing "the other side." The determination to find another side can spread disinformation rather than lead to truth. 8

The culture of critique has given rise to the journalistic practice of confronting prominent people with criticism couched as others' views. Meanwhile, the interviewer has planted an accusation in readers' or viewers' minds. The theory seems to be that when provoked, people are spurred to eloquence and self-revelation. Perhaps some are. But others are unable to say what they know because they are hurt, and begin to sputter when their sense of fairness is outraged. In those cases, opposition is not the path to truth. 9

When people in power know that what they say will be scrutinized for weaknesses and probably distorted, they become more guarded. As 10 an acquaintance recently explained about himself, public figures who once gave long, free-wheeling press conferences now limit themselves to reading brief statements. When less information gets communicated, opposition does not lead to truth.

Opposition also limits information when only those who are adept [11] at verbal sparring take part in public discourse, and those who cannot handle it, or do not like it, decline to participate. This winnowing process is evident in graduate schools, where many talented students drop out because what they expected to be a community of intellectual inquiry turned out to be a ritual game of attack and counterattack.

One such casualty graduated from a small liberal arts college, where [12] she "luxuriated in the endless discussions." At the urging of her professors, she decided to make academia her profession. But she changed her mind after a year in an art history program at a major university. She felt she had fallen into a "den of wolves." "I wasn't cut out for academia," she concluded. But does academia have to be so combative that it cuts people like her out?

In many university classrooms, "critical thinking" means reading [13] someone's life work, then ripping it to shreds. Though critique is surely one form of critical thinking, so are integrating ideas from disparate fields and examining the context out of which they grew. Opposition does not lead to truth when we ask only "What's wrong with this argument?" and never "What can we use from this in building a new theory, and a new understanding?"

Several years ago I was on a television talk show with a represen- [14] tative of the men's movement. I didn't foresee any problem, since there is nothing in my work that is anti-male. But in the room where guests gather before the show I found a man wearing a shirt and tie and a floor-length skirt, with waist-length red hair. He politely introduced himself and told me he liked my book. Then he added: "When I get out there, I'm going to attack you. But don't take it personally. That's why they invite me on, so that's what I'm going to do."

When the show began, I spoke only a sentence or two before this [15] man nearly jumped out of his chair, threw his arms before him in gestures of anger and began shrieking—first attacking me, but soon moving on to rail against women. The most disturbing thing about his hysterical ranting was what it sparked in the studio audience: they too became vicious, attacking not me (I hadn't had a chance to say anything) and not him (who wants to tangle with someone who will scream at you?) but the other guests: unsuspecting women who had agreed to come on the show to talk about their problems communicating with their spouses.

This is the most dangerous aspect of modeling intellectual inter- [16] change as a fight: it contributes to an atmosphere of animosity that spreads like a fever. In a society where people express their anger by shooting, the result of demonizing those with whom we disagree can be truly demonic.

I am not suggesting that journalists stop asking tough questions nec-   17
essary to get at the facts, even if those questions may appear challenging. And of course it is the responsibility of the media to represent serious opposition when it exists, and of intellectuals everywhere to explore potential weaknesses in others' arguments. But when opposition becomes the overwhelming avenue of inquiry, when the lust for opposition exalts extreme views and obscures complexity, when our eagerness to find weaknesses blinds us to strengths, when the atmosphere of animosity precludes respect and poisons our relations with one another, then the culture of critique is stifling us. If we could move beyond it, we would move closer to the truth.

Responding to Reading

1. Tannen has no quarrel with our tendency to argue in our private lives. Why, then, does she think this tendency, fostered by what she calls the "culture of critique," is a negative, even dangerous, force in "public intellectual debate" (3)? Do you agree with her?
2. Tannen says, "If public discourse is a fight, every issue must have two sides—no more, no less" (6). Why does she see this as a problem? Give some examples of issues that you believe have more than two sides. Can you think of any issues that have only one side?
3. In paragraphs 11–12 Tannen explains how the "culture of critique" has spread to graduate schools, where it has created "a ritual game of attack and counterattack" (11). Why do you think graduate schools foster this combative behavior? Do you see it in operation in your own undergraduate classes?

THE MOVIE THAT CHANGED
～ MY LIFE

Terry McMillan

Novelist Terry McMillan (1951–) was born in Port Huron, Michigan, and developed her interest in writing after taking a job shelving books at a local library. When she was seventeen, she set out on her own for the West Coast, later receiving a degree in journalism from the University of California at Berkeley. Soon afterward she moved to New

York City, where she worked as a word processor and joined the Harlem Writer's Guild, a workshop for mostly African-American writers. Her first novel, *Mama* (1987), written during this time, was a critical and popular success. It was followed by *Disappearing Acts* (1989) and the bestseller *Waiting to Exhale* (1992), a story of the romantic complications besetting four contemporary African-American women friends. She has also edited *Breaking the Ice: An Anthology of Contemporary African-American Fiction* (1990) and has taught at the universities of Wyoming and Arizona. In the following essay, from an anthology for which a number of writers were asked to remember a movie important to their lives, McMillan describes both her positive and negative reactions to MGM's classic *The Wizard of Oz* as a reflection of mainstream American values and culture.

I grew up in a small industrial town in the thumb of Michigan: Port Huron. We had barely gotten used to the idea of color TV. I can guess how old I was when I first saw *The Wizard of Oz* on TV because I remember the house we lived in when I was still in elementary school. It was a huge, drafty house that had a fireplace we never once lit. We lived on two acres of land, and at the edge of the backyard was the woods, which I always thought of as a forest. We had weeping willow trees, plum and pear trees, and blackberry bushes. We could not see into our neighbors' homes. Railroad tracks were part of our front yard, and the house shook when a train passed—twice, sometimes three times a day. You couldn't hear the TV at all when it zoomed by, and I was often afraid that if it ever flew off the tracks, it would land on the sun porch, where we all watched TV. I often left the room during this time, but my younger sisters and brother thought I was just scared. I think I was in the third grade around this time. [1]

It was a raggedy house which really should've been condemned, but we fixed it up and kept it clean. We had our German shepherd, Prince, who slept under the rickety steps to the side porch that were on the verge of collapsing but never did. I remember performing a ritual whenever *Oz* was coming on. I either baked cookies or cinnamon rolls or popped popcorn while all five of us waited for Dorothy to spin from black and white on that dreary farm in Kansas to the luminous land of color of Oz. [2]

My house was chaotic, especially with four sisters and brothers and a mother who worked at a factory, and if I'm remembering correctly, my father was there for the first few years of the *Oz* (until he got tuberculosis and had to live in a sanitarium for a year). I do recall the noise and the fighting of my parents (not to mention my other relatives and neighbors). Violence was plentiful, and I wanted to go wherever Dorothy was going where she would not find trouble. To put it bluntly, I wanted to escape because I needed an escape. [3]

I didn't know any happy people. Everyone I knew was either angry [4] or not satisfied. The only time they seemed to laugh was when they were drunk, and even that was short-lived. Most of the grown-ups I was in contact with lived their lives as if it had all been a mistake, an accident, and they were paying dearly for it. It seemed as if they were always at someone else's mercy—women at the mercy of men (this prevailed in my hometown) and children at the mercy of frustrated parents. All I knew was that most of the grown-ups felt trapped, as if they were stuck in this town and no road would lead out. So many of them felt a sense of accomplishment just getting up in the morning and making it through another day. I overheard many a grown-up conversation, and they were never life-affirming: "Chile, if the Lord'll just give me the strength to make it through another week . . ."; "I just don't know how I'ma handle this, I can't take no more. . . ." I rarely knew what they were talking about, but even a fool could hear that it was some kind of drudgery. When I was a child, it became apparent to me that these grown-ups had no power over their lives, or, if they did, they were always at a loss as to how to exercise it. I did not want to grow up and have to depend on someone else for my happiness or be miserable or have to settle for whatever I was dished out—if I could help it. That much I knew already.

I remember being confused a lot. I could never understand why no [5] one had any energy to do anything that would make them feel good, besides drinking. Being happy was a transient and very temporary thing which was almost always offset by some kind of bullshit. I would, of course, learn much later in my own adult life that these things are called obstacles, barriers—or again, bullshit. When I started writing, I began referring to them as "knots." But life wasn't one long knot. It seemed to me it just required stamina and common sense and the wherewithal to know when a knot was before you and you had to dig deeper than you had in order to figure out how to untie it. It could be hard, but it was simple.

The initial thing I remember striking me about *Oz* was how nasty [6] Dorothy's Auntie Em talked to her and everybody on the farm. I was used to that authoritative tone of voice because my mother talked to us the same way. She never asked you to do anything; she gave you a command and never said "please," and, once you finished it, rarely said "thank you." The tone of her voice was always hostile, and Auntie Em sounded just like my mother—bossy and domineering. They both ran the show, it seemed, and I think that because my mother was raising five children almost single-handedly, I must have had some inkling that being a woman didn't mean you had to be helpless. Auntie Em's husband was a wimp, and for once the tables were turned: he took orders from her! My mother and Auntie Em were proof to me that if you wanted to get things done you had to delegate authority and keep everyone apprised of the rules of the game as well as the consequences. In my house it was punishment—you were severely grounded. What little freedom we had was snatched away. As a child, I often felt helpless, powerless, because I had no control over my situation and couldn't tell my mother when I thought (or knew) she was wrong or being totally unfair, or when her behavior was inappropriate. I hated this feeling to no end, but what was worse was not being able to do anything about it except keep my mouth shut.

So I completely identified when no one had time to listen to   7 Dorothy. That dog's safety was important to her, but no one seemed to think that what Dorothy was saying could possibly be as urgent as the situation at hand. The bottom line was, it was urgent to her. When I was younger, I rarely had the opportunity to finish a sentence before my mother would cut me off or complete it for me, or, worse, give me something to do. She used to piss me off, and nowadays I catch myself—stop myself—from doing the same thing to my seven-year-old. Back then, it was as if what I had to say wasn't important or didn't warrant her undivided attention. So when Dorothy's Auntie Em dismisses her and tells her to find somewhere where she'll stay out of trouble, and little Dorothy starts thinking about if there in fact is such a place—one that is trouble free—I was right there with her, because I wanted to know, too.

I also didn't know or care that Judy Garland was supposed to have   8 been a child star, but when she sang "Somewhere Over the Rainbow," I *was* impressed. Impressed more by the song than by who was singing it. I mean, she wasn't exactly Aretha Franklin or the Marvelettes or the Supremes, which was the only vocal music I was used to. As kids, we often laughed at white people singing on TV because their songs were always so corny and they just didn't sound anything like the soulful music we had in our house. Sometimes we would mimic people like Doris Day and Fred Astaire and laugh like crazy because they were always so damn happy while they sang and danced. We would also watch square-dancing when we wanted a real laugh and try to look under the women's dresses. What I hated more than anything was when in the middle of a movie the white people always had to start singing and dancing to get their point across. Later, I would hate it when black people would do the same thing—even though it was obvious to us that at least they had more rhythm and, most of the time, more range vocally.

We did skip through the house singing "We're off to see the Wiz-   9 ard," but other than that, most of the songs in this movie are a blank, probably because I blanked them out. Where I lived, when you had something to say to someone, you didn't sing it, you told them, so the cumulative effect of the songs wore thin.

I was afraid for Dorothy when she decided to run away, but at the   10 same time I was glad. I couldn't much blame her—I mean, what kind of life did she have, from what I'd seen so far? She lived on an ugly farm out in the middle of nowhere with all these old people who did nothing but chores, chores, and more chores. Who did she have to play with besides that dog? And even though I lived in a house full of people, I knew how lonely Dorothy felt, or at least how isolated she must have felt. First of all, I was the oldest, and my sisters and brother were ignorant and silly creatures who often bored me because they couldn't hold a decent conversation. I couldn't ask them questions, like: Why are we living in this dump? When is Mama going to get some more money? Why can't we go on vacations like other people? Like white people? Why does our car always break down? Why are we poor? Why doesn't Mama ever laugh? Why do we have to live in Port Huron? Isn't there someplace better than this we can go live? I remember thinking this kind of stuff in kindergarten, to be honest, because times were hard, but I'd saved twenty-five cents in my piggy bank for hotdog-and-chocolate-milk day at school, and on the morning I went to get it, my piggy bank was empty. My mother gave me some lame excuse as to why she had to spend it, but all I was thinking was that I would have to sit there (again) and watch the other children slurp their chocolate milk, and I could see the ketchup and mustard oozing out of the hot-dog bun that I wouldn't get to taste. I walked to school, and with the exception of walking to my father's funeral when I was sixteen, this was the longest walk of my entire life. My plaid dress was starched and my socks were white, my hair was braided and not a strand out of place; but I wanted to know why I had to feel this kind of humiliation when in fact I had saved the money for this very purpose. Why? By the time I got to school, I'd wiped my nose and dried my eyes and vowed not to let anyone know that I was even moved by this. It was no one's business why I couldn't eat my hot dog and chocolate milk, but the irony of it was that my teacher, Mrs. Johnson, must have sensed what had happened, and she bought my hot dog and chocolate milk for me that day. I can still remember feeling how unfair things can be, but how they somehow always turn out good. I guess seeing so much negativity had already started to turn me into an optimist.

I was a very busy child, because I was the oldest and had to see to it that my sisters and brother had their baths and did their homework; I combed my sisters' hair, and by fourth grade I had cooked my first Thanksgiving dinner. It was my responsibility to keep the house spotless so that when my mother came home from work it would pass her inspection, so I spent many an afternoon and Saturday morning mopping and waxing floors, cleaning ovens and refrigerators, grocery shopping, and by the time I was thirteen, I was paying bills for my mother and felt like an adult. I was also tired of it, sick of all the responsibility. So yes, I rooted for Dorothy when she and Toto were vamoosing, only I wanted to know: Where in the hell was she going? Where would I go if I were to run away? I had no idea because there was nowhere to go. What I did know was that one day I would go somewhere—which is why I think I watched so much TV. I was always on the lookout for Par- 11 adise, and I think I found it a few years later on "Adventures in Paradise," with Gardner McKay, and on "77 Sunset Strip."[1] Palm trees and blue water and islands made quite an impression on a little girl from a flat, dull little depressing town in Michigan.

Professor Marvel really pissed me off, and I didn't believe for a minute that that crystal ball was real, even before he started asking Dorothy all those questions, but I knew this man was going to be important, I just couldn't figure out how. Dorothy was so gullible, I thought, and I knew this word because my mother used to always drill it in us that you should "never believe everything somebody tells you." So after Professor Marvel convinced Dorothy that her Auntie Em might be in trouble, and Dorothy scoops up Toto and runs back home, I was totally disappointed, because now I wasn't going to have an adventure. I was thinking I might actually learn how to escape drudgery by watching Dorothy do it successfully, but before she even gave herself the chance to discover for herself that she could make it, she was on her way back home. "Dummy!" we all yelled on the sun porch. "Dodo brain!" 12

The storm. The tornado. Of course, now the entire set of this film looks so phony it's ridiculous, but back then I knew the wind was a tornado because in Michigan we had the same kind of trapdoor underground shelter that Auntie Em had on the farm. I knew Dorothy was going to be locked out once Auntie Em and the workers locked the door, and I also knew she wasn't going to be heard when she knocked on it. This was drama at its best, even though I didn't know what drama was at the time. 13

In the house she goes, and I was frightened for her. I knew that house was going to blow away, so when little Dorothy gets banged in the head by a window that flew out of its casement, I remember all of us screaming. We watched everybody fly by the window, including the wicked neighbor who turns out to be the Wicked Witch of the West, and I'm sure I probably substituted my mother for Auntie Em and fantasized that all of my siblings would fly away, too. They all got on my nerves because I could never find a quiet place in my house—no such thing as peace—and I was always being disturbed. 14

It wasn't so much that I had so much I wanted to do by myself, but I already knew that silence was a rare commodity, and when I managed to snatch a few minutes of it, I could daydream, pretend to be someone else somewhere else—and this was fun. But I couldn't do it if someone was bugging me. On days when my mother was at work, I would often send the kids outside to play and lock them out, just so I could have the house to myself for at least fifteen minutes. I loved pretending that none of them existed for a while, although after I fin- 15

---

[1] 1950s television shows set in Hawaii and Southern California. [Eds.]

ished with my fantasy world, it was reassuring to see them all there. I think I was grounded.

When Dorothy's house began to spin and spin and spin, I was curi-   16
ous as to where it was going to land. And to be honest, I didn't know little Dorothy was actually dreaming until she woke up and opened the door and everything was in color! It looked like Paradise to me. The foliage was almost an iridescent green, the water bluer than I'd ever seen in any of the lakes in Michigan. Of course, once I realized she was in fact dreaming, it occurred to me that this very well might be the only way to escape. To dream up another world. Create your own.

I had no clue that Dorothy was going to find trouble, though, even   17
in her dreams. Hell, if I had dreamed up something like another world, it would've been a perfect one. I wouldn't have put myself in such a precarious situation. I'd have been able to go straight to the Wizard, no strings attached. First of all, that she walked was stupid to me; I would've asked one of those Munchkins for a ride. And I never bought into the idea of those slippers, but once I bought the whole idea, I accepted the fact that the girl was definitely lost and just wanted to get home. Personally, all I kept thinking was, if she could get rid of that Wicked Witch of the West, the Land of Oz wasn't such a bad place to be stuck in. It beat the farm in Kansas.

At the time, I truly wished I could spin away from my family and   18
home and land someplace as beautiful and surreal as Oz—if only for a little while. All I wanted was to get a chance to see another side of the world, to be able to make comparisons, and then decide if it was worth coming back home.

What was really strange to me, after the Good Witch of the North   19
tells Dorothy to just stay on the Yellow Brick Road to get to the Emerald City and find the Wizard so she can get home, was when Dorothy meets the Scarecrow, the Tin Man, and the Lion—all of whom were missing something I'd never even given any thought to. A brain? What did having one really mean? What would not having one mean? I had one, didn't I, because I did well in school. But because the Scarecrow couldn't make up his mind, thought of himself as a failure, it dawned on me that having a brain meant you had choices, you could make decisions and, as a result, make things happen. Yes, I thought, I had one, and I was going to use it. One day. And the Tin Man, who didn't have a heart. Not having one meant you were literally dead to me, and I never once thought of it as being the house of emotions (didn't know what emotions were), where feelings of jealousy, devotion, and sentiment lived. I'd never thought of what else a heart was good for except keeping you alive. But I did have feelings, because they were often hurt, and I was envious of the white girls at my school who wore mohair sweaters and box-pleat skirts, who went skiing and tobogganing and yachting and spent summers in Quebec. Why didn't white girls have to straight-

en their hair? Why didn't their parents beat each other up? Why were they always so goddamn happy?

And courage. Oh, that was a big one. What did having it and not [20] having it mean? I found out that it meant having guts and being afraid but doing whatever it was you set out to do anyway. Without courage, you couldn't do much of anything. I liked courage and assumed I would acquire it somehow. As a matter of fact, one day my mother *told* me to get her a cup of coffee, and even though my heart was pounding and I was afraid, I said to her pointblank, "Could you please say please?" She looked up at me out of the corner of her eye and said, "What?" So I repeated myself, feeling more powerful because she hadn't slapped me across the room already, and then something came over her and she looked at me and said, "Please." I smiled all the way to the kitchen, and from that point forward, I managed to get away with this kind of behavior until I left home when I was seventeen. My sisters and brother— to this day—don't know how I stand up to my mother, but I know. I decided not to be afraid or intimidated by her, and I wanted her to treat me like a friend, like a human being, instead of her slave.

I do believe that Oz also taught me much about friendship. I mean, [21] the Tin Man, the Lion, and the Scarecrow hung in there for Dorothy, stuck their "necks" out and made sure she was protected, even risked their own "lives" for her. They told each other the truth. They trusted each other. All four of them had each other's best interests in mind. I believe it may have been a while before I actually felt this kind of sincerity in a friend, but really good friends aren't easy to come by, and when you find one, you hold on to them.

Okay. So Dorothy goes through hell before she gets back to Kansas. [22] But the bottom line was, she made it. And what I remember feeling when she clicked those heels was that you have to have faith and be a believer, for real, or nothing will ever materialize. Simple as that. And not only in life but even in your dreams there's always going to be adversity, obstacles, knots, or some kind of bullshit you're going to have to deal with in order to get on with your life. Dorothy had a good heart and it was in the right place, which is why I supposed she won out over the evil witch. I've learned that one, too. That good *always* overcomes evil; maybe not immediately, but in the long run, it does. So I think I vowed when I was little to try to be a good person. An honest person. To care about others and not just myself. Not to be a selfish person, because my heart would be of no service if I used it only for myself. And I had to have the courage to see other people and myself as not being perfect (yes, I had a heart and a brain, but some other things would turn up missing, later), and I would have to learn to untie every knot that I encountered—some self-imposed, some not—in my life, and to believe that if I did the right things, I would never stray too far from my Yellow Brick Road.

I'm almost certain that I saw *Oz* annually for at least five or six years, [23] but I don't remember how old I was when I stopped watching it. I do know that by the time my parents were divorced (I was thirteen), I couldn't sit through it again. I was a mature teen-ager and had finally reached the point where Dorothy got on my nerves. Singing, dancing, and skipping damn near everywhere was so corny and utterly senti-mental that even the Yellow Brick Road became sickening. I already knew what she was in for, and sometimes I rewrote the story in my head. I kept asking myself, what if she had just run away and kept going, maybe she would've ended up in Los Angeles with a promising singing career. What if it had turned out that she hadn't been dreaming, and the Wizard had given her an offer she couldn't refuse—say, for instance, he had asked her to stay on in the Emerald City, that she could visit the farm whenever she wanted to, but, get a clue, Dorothy, the Emerald City is what's happening; she could make new city friends and get a hobby and a boyfriend and free rent and never have to do chores . . .

I had to watch *The Wizard of Oz* again in order to write this, and my [24] six-and-a-half-year-old son, Solomon, joined me. At first he kept asking me if something was wrong with the TV because it wasn't in color, but as he watched, he became mesmerized by the story. He usually squirms or slides to the floor and under a table or just leaves the room if some-thing on TV bores him, which it usually does, except if he's watching Nickelodeon, a high-quality cable kiddie channel. His favorite shows, which he watches with real consistency, and, I think, actually goes through withdrawal if he can't see them for whatever reason, are "In-spector Gadget," "Looney Tunes," and "Mr. Ed." "Make the Grade," which is sort of a junior-high version of "Jeopardy," gives him some kind of thrill, even though he rarely knows any of the answers. And "Garfield" is a must on Saturday morning. There is hardly anything on TV that he watches that has any real, or at least plausible, drama to it, but you can't miss what you've never had.

The Wicked Witch intimidated the boy no end, and he was afraid of [25] her. The Wizard was also a problem. So I explained—no, I just told him pointblank—"Don't worry, she'll get it in the end, Solomon, because she's bad. And the Wizard's a fake, and he's trying to sound like a tough guy, but he's a wus." That offered him some consolation, and even when the Witch melted he kind of looked at me with those *Home Alone* eyes and asked, "But where did she go, Mommy?" "She's history," I said. "Melted. Gone. Into the ground. Remember, this is pretend. It's not real. Real people don't melt. This is only TV," I said. And then he got that look in his eyes as if he'd remembered something.

Of course he had a nightmare that night and of course there was a [26] witch in it, because I had actually left the sofa a few times during this last viewing to smoke a few cigarettes (the memory bank is a powerful place—I still remembered many details), put the dishes in the dishwasher, make a few phone calls, water the plants. Solomon sang "We're off to see the Wizard" for the next few days because he said that was his favorite part, next to the Munchkins (who also showed up in his nightmare).

So, to tell the truth, I really didn't watch the whole movie again. I [27] just couldn't. Probably because about thirty or so years ago little Dorothy had made a lasting impression on me, and this viewing felt like overkill. You only have to tell me, show me, once in order for me to get it. But even still, the movie itself taught me a few things that I still find challenging. That it's okay to be an idealist, that you have to imagine something better and go for it. That you have to believe in *something*, and it's best to start with yourself and take it from there. At least give it a try. As corny as it may sound, sometimes I am afraid of what's around the corner, or what's not around the corner. But I look anyway. I believe that writing is one of my "corners"—an intersection, really; and when I'm confused or reluctant to look back, deeper, or ahead, I create my own Emerald Cities and force myself to take longer looks, because it is one sure way that I'm able to see.

Of course, I've fallen, tumbled, and been thrown over all kinds of [28] bumps on my road, but it still looks yellow, although every once in a while there's still a loose brick. For the most part, though, it seems paved. Perhaps because that's the way I want to see it.

Responding to Reading

1. How was McMillan's life in Port Huron like Dorothy's life in Kansas? How was it different? Why did Dorothy's escape to Oz have such great appeal for McMillan?
2. McMillan strongly identifies with Dorothy, yet she also feels impatient with her—even let down by her, and by the film's ending. Why? Do you think McMillan's reactions are justified?
3. How, according to McMillan, did *The Wizard of Oz* change her life? Can you identify any changes that McMillan does not see?

WHY WE CRAVE HORROR
∽ MOVIES

Stephen King

An immensely prolific master of horror fiction and one of the world's best-selling authors, Stephen King (1947–) began writing unusual sto-

ries about offbeat characters when he was a high school student—
early pieces were published in such magazines as *Startling Mystery
Stories*—and seemingly has never stopped. Born in Portland and a
graduate of the University of Maine, King taught high school English
and wrote two unpublished novels before the success of *Carrie* (1974),
which was turned into a popular film. Others among his dozens of
horror novels—many of which have been filmed—include *The Shining*
(1977), *Pet Sematery* (1983), *Misery* (1987), *Needful Things* (1991), and *Insomnia* (1994). King's short stories also provided the basis for two critically praised non-horror films: *Stand By Me* (1985) and *The Shawshank
Redemption* (1994). The following essay, which was originally published in *Playboy* in 1982, is an expert's attempt to explain the appeal
that horror holds for contemporary audiences.

I think that we're all mentally ill; those of us outside the asylums   1
only hide it a little better—and maybe not all that much better, after all.
We've all known people who talk to themselves, people who sometimes
squinch their faces into horrible grimaces when they believe no one is
watching, people who have some hysterical fear—of snakes, the dark,
the tight place, the long drop . . . and, of course, those final worms and
grubs that are waiting so patiently underground.

When we pay our four or five bucks and seat ourselves at tenth-row   2
center in a theater showing a horror movie, we are daring the nightmare.

Why? Some of the reasons are simple and obvious. To show that   3
we can, that we are not afraid, that we can ride this roller coaster.
Which is not to say that a really good horror movie may not surprise
a scream out of us at some point, the way we may scream when the
roller coaster twists through a complete 360 or plows through a lake at
the bottom of the drop. And horror movies, like roller coasters, have
always been the special province of the young; by the time one turns
40 or 50, one's appetite for double twists or 360-degree loops may be
considerably depleted.

We also go to re-establish our feelings of essential normality; the   4
horror movie is innately conservative, even reactionary. Freda Jackson
as the horrible melting woman in *Die, Monster, Die!* confirms for us that
no matter how far we may be removed from the beauty of a Robert Red-
ford or a Diana Ross, we are still light-years from true ugliness.

And we go to have fun.   5

Ah, but this is where the ground starts to slope away, isn't it? Be-   6
cause this is a very peculiar sort of fun indeed. The fun comes from seeing others menaced—sometimes killed. One critic has suggested that if
pro football has become the voyeur's version of combat, then the horror
film has become the modern version of the public lynching.

It is true that the mythic, "fairytale" horror film intends to take away   7
the shades of gray. . . . It urges us to put away our more civilized and
adult penchant for analysis and to become children again, seeing things

in pure blacks and whites. It may be that horror movies provide psychic relief on this level because this invitation to lapse into simplicity, irrationality and even outright madness is extended so rarely. We are told we may allow our emotions a free rein . . . or no rein at all.

If we are all insane, then sanity becomes a matter of degree. If your insanity leads you to carve up women like Jack the Ripper or the Cleveland Torso Murderer, we clap you away in the funny farm (but neither of those two amateur-night surgeons was ever caught, heh-heh-heh); if, on the other hand your insanity leads you only to talk to yourself when you're under stress or to pick your nose on your morning bus, then you are left alone to go about your business . . . though it is doubtful that you will ever be invited to the best parties.   8

The potential lyncher is in almost all of us (excluding saints, past and present; but then, most saints have been crazy in their own ways), and every now and then, he has to be let loose to scream and roll around in the grass. Our emotions and our fears form their own body, and we recognize that it demands its own exercise to maintain proper muscle tone. Certain of these emotional muscles are accepted—even exalted— in civilized society; they are, of course, the emotions that tend to maintain the status quo of civilization itself. Love, friendship, loyalty, kindness—these are all the emotions that we applaud, emotions that have been immortalized in the couplets of Hallmark cards and in the verses (I don't dare call it poetry) of Leonard Nimoy.   9

When we exhibit these emotions, society showers us with positive reinforcement; we learn this even before we get out of diapers. When, as children, we hug our rotten little puke of a sister and give her a kiss, all the aunts and uncles smile and twit and cry, "Isn't he the sweetest little thing?" Such coveted treats as chocolate-covered graham crackers often follow. But if we deliberately slam the rotten little puke of a sister's fingers in the door, sanctions follow—angry remonstrance from parents, aunts and uncles; instead of a chocolate-covered graham cracker, a spanking.   10

But anticivilization emotions don't go away, and they demand periodic exercise. We have such "sick" jokes as, "What's the difference between a truckload of bowling balls and a truckload of dead babies? (You can't unload a truckload of bowling balls with a pitchfork . . . a joke, by the way, that I heard originally from a ten-year-old.) Such a joke may surprise a laugh or a grin out of us even as we recoil, a possibility that confirms the thesis: If we share a brotherhood of man, then we also share an insanity of man. None of which is intended as a defense of either the sick joke or insanity but merely as an explanation of why the best horror films, like the best fairy tales, manage to be reactionary, anarchistic, and revolutionary all at the same time.   11

The mythic horror movie, like the sick joke, has a dirty job to do.   12
It deliberately appeals to all that is worst in us. It is morbidity un-

chained, our most base instincts let free, our nastiest fantasies realized
. . . and it all happens, fittingly enough, in the dark. For those reasons,
good liberals often shy away from horror films. For myself, I like to see
the most aggressive of them—*Dawn of the Dead,* for instance—as lifting
a trap door in the civilized forebrain and throwing a basket of raw
meat to the hungry alligators swimming around in that subterranean
river beneath.

Why bother? Because it keeps them from getting out, man. It keeps   13
them down there and me up here. It was Lennon and McCartney who
said that all you need is love, and I would agree with that.

As long as you keep the gators fed.   14

Responding to Reading

1. King characterizes his readers as "mentally ill" (1) and claims that "the potential lyncher is in almost all of us" (9). Is he being serious? Why do you
   think he uses such strong language? Does this language make you more or
   less receptive to his ideas?
2. In paragraph 4 King says, "the horror movie is innately conservative, even
   reactionary" (4). Later on, he says that "the best horror films, like the best
   fairy tales, manage to be reactionary, anarchistic, and revolutionary all at the
   same time" (11). What does he mean? Can you give your own examples of
   horror films—or fairy tales—to support his statements?
3. Why, according to King, do we crave horror movies? Do you think his explanation makes sense? Do you think he overstates his case? Does his essay
   explain why *you* like (or dislike) horror films? What other reasons can you
   think of?

WHERE THE BOYS ARE

~

Steven Stark

Steven Stark (1952–), a graduate of Harvard and the Yale Law School
and a former aide to President Jimmy Carter, writes frequently about
popular culture and contemporary political and social issues. He has
worked for the *Wall Street Journal, Boston Magazine,* the *Boston Phoenix,*
and the *Boston Globe,* and he is a featured contributor to the *Atlantic
Monthly* and many other publications, as well as a regular commentator on National Public Radio and CNN's "Showbiz Today." Stark is
currently working on a new book, *Fifty Television Shows Which Changed
America.* In the following essay, which originally appeared in the *Atlantic Monthly* in 1994, he looks at what he considers a disturbing ten-

dency of contemporary media to celebrate uncritically "the early-teen male sensibility."

Over the past several years American pop culture has spawned a [1] wide range of wildly popular offerings that appear remarkably similar in sensibility. Although at first glance little appears to link the infamous syndicated-radio talk-meisters Howard Stern and Don Imus with the movies *Jurassic Park* and *Field of Dreams,* the comedy of David Letterman and Jerry Seinfeld, the cartoon series *Beavis and Butt-head* and *The Simpsons,* and journalism's *The McLaughlin Group,* they in fact share a motif: though for the most part aimed at adults, these are all offerings that strongly echo the world of boys in early adolescence, ages eleven to fifteen. The unspoken premise of much of American pop culture today is that a large group of men would like nothing better than to go back to their junior high school locker rooms and stay there.

There is nothing new, of course, about men acting like boys, as any- [2] one who has read the *The Odyssey* or *Don Quixote*[1] knows. But something different is going on today: never before have so many seemed to produce so much that is so popular to evoke what is, after all, a brief and awkward stage of life. What's more, the trend spans the range of popular culture. Take talk radio: One of its most popular approaches today is to offer the listener a world of close-knit boyish pals. The style of Stern and Imus is that of the narcissistic class cutup in seventh grade: both sit in a playhouse-like radio studio with a bunch of guys and horse around for hours talking about sex or sports, along with political and show-biz gossip, all the while laughing at the gang's consciously loutish, subversive jokes. To the extent that women participate, they are often treated to a barrage of sexual and scatological humor. It's no wonder the audience for both shows is predominantly male.

Late Show With David Letterman and *Seinfeld* similarly echo the ethos [3] of young teenage boys. Late-night television has always been a chiefly male world, but until recently it wasn't a boy's world. One of Letterman's contributions to late-night entertainment has been to take its humor out of the nightclub-act tradition—replete with all of Johnny Carson's jokes about drinking or adult sex—and place it firmly in that prankish, subversive, back-of-the-classroom seventh-grade realm that has become so culturally prominent. Although Letterman rarely greets women guests with filthy jokes (you can't do that on network television), he often treats them with the exaggerated deference and shyness typical of fourteen-year-old boys.

Like a group of fourteen-year-olds, the men on *Seinfeld* seem not to [4] hold regular jobs, the better to devote time to "the gang." One woman, Elaine, is allowed to tag along with the boys, much like those younger

---

[1] Classic tales of adventurous quests. [Eds.]

sisters who are permitted to hang out with their brothers. It's not simply that everyone in Seinfeld's gang is unmarried and pushing fortysomething. It's that given their personas, it's difficult to imagine any of them having a real relationship with any woman but his mother. (Note how much more often parents of adult children appear here than on other shows.) Compare this situation comedy with the one that was roughly its cultural predecessor, *Cheers,* which appeared in the same time slot. On that show, too, the men didn't spend much time at work, but they did hang out in a traditional domain of adults (the tavern), and the hero, Sam Malone, spent many of his waking hours chasing women. Seinfeld is better known for sitting in a diner eating french fries with his pals. One of the show's most celebrated "risqué" episodes was about—what else?—masturbation.

And so it goes in various ways, as the early-teen male sensibility is 5 celebrated in everything from *Wayne's World* (the adventures of two adolescent goofballs) to *The Simpsons* (starring the proud underachiever Bart) to *Beavis and Butt-head* (MTV's notorious early-adolescent icons). The heavy-metal sound of bands with names like Danzig, Gwar, and Genitorturers is in vogue now, and with its constant evocation of sexism, violence, and hostility for hostility's sake, that rock genre has always reeked of the adolescent experience more than others have.

Like many recent cinema hits, ranging from the Indiana Jones series 6 to most Arnold Schwarzenegger offerings, last year's blockbuster film *Jurassic Park* was largely a traditional teenage "boys' movie"—heavy on adventure and violence, light on romance and relationships. Psychologists have observed that the culture-wide trend toward "pumped-up" male heroes—Schwarzenegger, Sylvester Stallone, and half the guys at your local health club—is a pre-teen male fantasy brought to life. Even popular "adult" movies, such as *City Slickers* and *Big,* often revolve around the premise that once a man has passed through puberty, it's pretty much all downhill.

The cult of baseball can be seen as an intensely nostalgic return to 7 early adolescence for many Americans. The rite of Rotisserie League baseball—an activity in which men spend hours every week poring over sheets of statistics, as they did when they were young—is part of this phenomenon, as are the wearing of baseball hats and the collecting of autographs and baseball cards by men of all ages. So, too, are baseball-movie parables like the quasi-religious *Field of Dreams,* in which male adolescence, the pastoral life, and baseball are linked in a way that would make both Jean Jacques Rousseau and Casey Stengel proud. In these visions of utopia, of course, women are again peripheral—except, perhaps, when baking cookies or waving in maternal fashion from the front porch as Dad and Son play catch. In the 1955 America that is usually the baseball lover's Paradise Lost, there are no Astroturf, no new stadiums, and no western teams to challenge the prominence of New

York and the eastern urban society it represents. That America is not only a man's world but also, by and large, a white man's world.

Today's early-adolescent attitude is certainly on display through-   8
out the news media. It's not simply that in a tabloid age many publications have adopted a kind of sneering, sophomoric attitude toward public affairs, or that shows such as *Crossfire* and *The McLaughlin Group*—with their mostly male screaming casts—resemble nothing so much as a junior high social-studies debate (in which the girls were always shouted down by the boys regardless of what they had to say). It's that today's journalism is obsessed with the kinds of things that tend to preoccupy thirteen-year-old boys: sports, sex, crime, and narcissism—that is, itself. Also in journalism as currently practiced, reporters often set themselves up as passive observers of events and then spend much of their time identifying with those who exercise real power—a point of view that is reminiscent of the way a young teenager views his parents. Moreover, if today's journalism has a driving principle, that principle centers on an obsession with hypocrisy. Journalism is about many things, but these days it is often about revealing that public figures are phonies. Covering Bill Clinton, or Prince Charles, or Michael Jackson, reporters frame their stories by saying implicitly, "These people aren't what they say they are. Look, they lied to you." Although there is a cultural role for balloon deflators, journalism has brought this characteristic attitude of the early adolescent to the adult world and elevated it to the status of cultural religion. That's why much of journalism today is really a form of institutionalized early adolescence.

Because the press tends to set the agenda for our culture, these sen-   9
timents have enormous ramifications. Whether in the form of the media's obsession with violence or its preoccupation with polls and popularity, the fantasy life of the adolescent male ends up defining much of our political reality. Political coverage tends to focus on gaffes, girlfriends, and youthful indiscretions while far more important, "adult" issues go underreported.

The press has also seen to it that the cardinal sin in American poli-   10
tics today is not to run up a deficit or lose an important court case but to change one's mind: like a fourteen-year-old, the press always takes a switch as evidence of hypocrisy. Thus George Bush was skewered by the media in 1990 for flip-flopping on the issue of taxes, and Bill Clinton was attacked unmercifully last year for going back on his promise of a tax cut for the middle class. Maybe both men had misled the voters during their campaigns, but a less iconoclastic press corps might have concluded that both men changed their minds for unselfish policy reasons. While an adolescent often looks at a change in direction and sees deceit, an adult realizes that life is usually more complex than that. Mature

leaders recognize their mistakes and often adjust accordingly—though not without peril in today's climate.

Admittedly, too much can be made of all this. Entertainment has always evoked certain stages of life in ways that appeal to the masses: think of *The Wizard of Oz* and *Rebel Without a Cause.* The fourteen-year-old sensibility is certainly not the only one celebrated in a culture that includes *The Golden Girls, Murphy Brown,* and Barney the dinosaur. And it's true that other eras in America have celebrated youth in various forms, from Shirley Temple to the Brady Bunch. But it's hard to make the case that the male early-adolescent mind-set was as pervasive or influential in those eras as it is in this one.   11

There are, of course, antecedents in our cultural life for this veneration of male early adolescence. The western often celebrated the young cowboy or outlaw like Billy the Kid, who, surrounded by his loyal gang in a world without commitment to women, broke the rules. In his recent book, *American Manhood,* E. Anthony Rotundo shows how American culture came to celebrate the misbehavior of boys as a way of idolizing the traits of childishness without idolizing children. In *Love and Death in the American Novel* (1960) Leslie Fiedler traces the evolution of the "bad boy" in American fiction from its roots in late-nineteenth-century best-sellers like *Peck's Bad Boy* and *The Story of a Bad Boy.* He also describes American fiction's traditional preoccupation with "The Good Bad Boy"—from Huckleberry Finn to Holden Caulfield to the characters in Jack Kerouac's *On the Road.* Fiedler wrote, "The Good Bad Boy is, of course, America's vision of itself, crude and unruly in his beginnings, but endowed by his creator with an instinctive sense of what is right."   12

Thirty-four years ago Fiedler wrote that from the Puritan-influenced Hawthorne and Melville on, Americans had been drawn to tales of boys and neutered women as a way of avoiding the subject of sex. In a tabloid era of penis-mutilation trials, prime-time network nudity, condom ads, and endless talk-show discussions of sexual fetishes, however, it's hard to continue to make his case. Still, if early-adolescent boys are notable for their inclinations to look at dirty pictures and talk about sex, they aren't quite ready to do something about it responsibly with a woman. That propensity to be in the world of sex but not really of it is certainly a sign of the times.   13

What's more, even if men aren't trying to avoid sex today, a retreat into teenhood may be a convenient way to avoid the opposite sex. As Susan Faludi and other writers have noted, the women's movement—perhaps the greatest social change of our time—has triggered something of a well-documented backlash. One result may be the creation of this boyish countermovement that looks with nostalgic longing on perhaps the last period in life when it's socially acceptable for males to exclude women, if not deride them.   14

The reasons for the cultural ubiquity of male early adolescence have [15] little to do with puritanism. Many psychologists consider that stage of life, when one is acutely aware of being powerless, to be the time when individuals are most subversive of the society at large. That idea also fits a wider cultural mood, always somewhat prevalent in America, that exalts the outsider. Such an anti-establishment mood, rooted in powerlessness, is particularly strong today, and the proof is not simply in the Ross Perot phenomenon. Whether the subject is how the tabloid press now eagerly tears down public figures or the pervasiveness of gossip masquerading as news (to demonstrate how the famous are no better than anyone else) or the rise of anti-establishment talk radio and comedy clubs where the humor grows more derisive by the day, America is full of the defiant, oppositional anger that often characterizes the early adolescent.

That anger is also an asset for TV programmers in the cable era. [16] Television, of course, tends to encourage a kind of passivity that isn't ultimately much different from the angry powerlessness early teens tend to feel: Beavis and Butt-head have become cultural symbols precisely because a nation of couch potatoes feels like a nation of fifteen-year-olds. Moreover, in an age of multiple offerings and channel surfing, what tends to draw these passive audiences is the irately outrageous and exhibitionistic—the Howard Sterns, not the Arthur Godfreys.[2] It also doesn't hurt that adolescents tend to be what advertisers call "good consumers"—narcissistic, with a fair amount of disposable income, and with no one but themselves to spend it on. A culture that is obsessed with this stage of life is arguably in a better frame of mind to buy—to run up the limit on Dad's (or Uncle Sam's) credit card—than one that worships, say, thrifty middle age.

In a country whose citizens have always had tendencies that remind [17] observers of those of a fourteen-year-old boy, it would be wrong to lay all the blame for society's vulgarity and violence, its exhibitionist inclinations, its fear of powerful women, its failure to grow up and take care of its real children, and its ambivalence about paternal authority at the feet of Howard Stern, John McLaughlin, and Jerry Seinfeld. But they have helped, and many of us have willingly obliged. After all, as Fiedler reminded us, boys will be boys.

Responding to Reading

1. In paragraph 1 Stark says that many popular films and television and radio programs, though aimed at adults, "strongly echo the world of boys in early adolescence, ages eleven to fifteen." Do you think he is correct?

---

[2] Host of a long-running television variety show in the 1950s and 1960s who projected a kindly, uncle-like image. [Eds.]

2. Can you think of movies and television shows that explore the female sensibility? Exactly how are they different from those Stark cites?
3. Stark sees not only television and films but journalism too as "obsessed with the kinds of things that tend to preoccupy thirteen-year-old boys: sports, sex, crime, and narcissism—that is, itself" (8). In fact, he sees much of today's journalism as "a form of institutionalized early adolescence" (8). Do you agree? What does he see as some of the negative results of this "retreat into teenhood" (14)? Can you think of others?

WE TALK, YOU LISTEN

Vine Deloria, Jr.

A Standing Rock Sioux born in South Dakota, Vine Deloria, Jr. (1933–) holds a B.S. from Iowa State University, a master's of theology from Rock Island Lutheran School, and a law degree from the University of Colorado. He was executive director of the National Congress of American Indians from 1964 to 1967, and his early books—including *Custer Died for Your Sins: An Indian Manifesto* (1969), *God Is Red: A Native View of Religion* (1973), and *Behind the Trail of Broken Treaties: An American Indian Declaration of Independence* (1974)—made him a leader in the "Red Power" movement of the 1970s. A professor at the University of Arizona since 1978 and a former chair of Native American Studies there, Deloria has argued for the establishment of new treaties between Native American tribes and the U.S. government "to ensure the survival of the tribes, their lands, and their ways of life." In the following essay from *We Talk, You Listen: New Tribes, New Turf* (1970), Deloria looks at media stereotypes of Native Americans and other minorities as well as at university ethnic studies programs.

One reason that Indian people have not been heard from until recently is that we have been completely covered up by movie Indians. Western movies have been such favorites that they have dominated the public's conception of what Indians are. It is not all bad when one thinks about the handsome Jay Silverheels bailing the Lone Ranger out of a jam, or Ed Ames rescuing Daniel Boone with some clever Indian trick. But the other mythologies that have wafted skyward because of the movies have blocked out any idea that there might be real Indians with real problems.

Other minority groups have fought tenaciously against stereotyping, and generally they have been successful. Italians quickly quashed the image of them as mobsters that television projected in *The Un-touchables*. Blacks have been successful in getting a more realistic picture of the black man in a contemporary setting because they have had standout performers like Bill Cosby and Sidney Poitier to represent them.

Since stereotyping was highlighted by motion pictures, it would 3 probably be well to review the images of minority groups projected in the movies in order to understand how the situation looks at present. Perhaps the first aspect of stereotyping was the tendency to exclude people on the basis of their inability to handle the English language. Not only were racial minorities excluded, but immigrants arriving on these shores were soon whipped into shape by ridicule of their English.

Traditional stereotypes pictured the black as a happy watermelon-eating darky whose sole contribution to American society was his indiscriminate substitution of the "d" sound for "th." Thus a black always said "dis" and "dat," as in "lift dat bale." The "d" sound carried over and was used by white gangsters to indicate disfavor with their situation, as in "dis is de end, ya rat." The important thing was to indicate that blacks were like lisping children not yet competent to undertake the rigors of economic opportunities and voting.

Mexicans were generally portrayed as shiftless and padded out for 5 siesta, without any redeeming qualities whatsoever. Where the black had been handicapped by his use of the "d," the Mexican suffered from the use of the double "e." This marked them off as a group worth watching. Mexicans, according to the stereotype, always said "theenk," "peenk," and later "feenk." Many advertisements today still continue this stereotype, thinking that it is cute and cuddly.

These groups were much better off than Indians were. Indians were 6 always devoid of any English whatsoever. They were only allowed to speak when an important message had to be transmitted on the screen. For example, "many pony soldiers die" was meant to indicate that Indians were going to attack the peaceful settlers who happened to have broken their three hundredth treaty moments before. Other than that Indian linguistic ability was limited to "ugh" and "kemo sabe" (which means honky in some obscure Indian language).

The next step was to acknowledge that there was a great American 7 dream to which any child could aspire. (It was almost like the train in the night that Richard Nixon heard as a child anticipating the dream fairy.) The great American dream was projected in the early World War II movies. The last reel was devoted to a stirring proclamation that we were going to win the war and it showed factories producing airplanes, people building ships, and men marching in uniform to the transports. There was a quick pan of a black face before the scene shifted to scenes of orchards, rivers, Mount Rushmore, and the Liberty Bell as we found out what we were fighting for.

The new images expressed a profound inability to understand why   8
minority groups couldn't "make it" when everybody knew what America was all about freedom and equality. By projecting an image of everyone working hard to win the war, the doctrine was spread that America was just one big happy family and that there really weren't any
differences so long as we had to win the war.

It was a rare war movie in the 1940s that actually showed a black or   9
a Mexican as a bona fide fighting man. When they did appear it was in
the role of cooks or orderlies serving whites. In most cases this was a
fairly accurate statement of their situation, particularly with respect to
the Navy.

World War II movies were entirely different for Indians. Each pla-   10
toon of red-blooded white American boys was equipped with its own
set of Indians. When the platoon got into trouble and was surrounded,
its communications cut off except for one slender line to regimental
headquarters, and that line tapped by myriads of Germans, Japanese, or
Italians, the stage was set for the dramatic episode of the Indians.

John Wayne, Randolph Scott, Sonny Tufts, or Tyrone Power would   11
smile broadly as he played his ace, which until this time had been hidden from view. From nowhere, a Navaho, Comanche, Cherokee, or
Sioux would appear, take the telephone, and in some short and inscrutable phraseology communicate such a plenitude of knowledge to
his fellow tribesman (fortunately situated at the general's right hand)
that fighting units thousands of miles away would instantly perceive the
situation and rescue the platoon. The Indian would disappear as mysteriously as he had come, only to reappear the next week in a different
battle to perform his esoteric rites. Anyone watching war movies during
the '40s would have been convinced that without Indian telephone op-
erators the war would have been lost irretrievably, in spite of John
Wayne.

Indians were America's secret weapon against the forces of evil. The   12
typing spoke of a primitive gimmick, and it was the strangeness of Indians that made them visible, not their humanity. With the Korean War
era and movies made during the middle '50s, other minority groups
began to appear and Indians were pushed into the background. This era
was the heyday of the "All-American Platoon." It was the ultimate conception of intergroup relations. The "All-American Platoon" was a "one
each": one black, one Mexican, one Indian, one farm boy from Iowa, one
Southerner who hated blacks, one boy from Brooklyn, one Polish boy
from the urban slums of the Midwest, one Jewish intellectual, and one
college boy. Every possible stereotype was included and it resulted in a
portrayal of Indians as another species of human being for the first time
in moving pictures.

The platoon was always commanded by a veteran of grizzled coun-   13
tenance who had been at every battle in which the United States had

ever engaged. The whole story consisted in killing off the members of the platoon until only the veteran and the college boy were left. The Southerner and the black would die in each other's arms singing "Dixie." The Jewish intellectual and the Indian formed some kind of attachment and were curiously the last ones killed. When the smoke cleared, the college boy, with a prestige wound in the shoulder, returned to his girl, and the veteran reconciled with his wife and checked out another platoon in anticipation of taking the same hill in the next movie.

While other groups have managed to make great strides since those [14] days. Indians have remained the primitive unknown quantity? Dialogue has reverted back to the monosyllabic grunt and even pictures that attempt to present the Indian side of the story depend upon unintelligible noises to present their message. The only exception to this rule is a line famed for its durability over the years. If you fall asleep during the Late Show and suddenly awaken to the words "go in peace, my son," it is either an Indian chief bidding his son good bye as the boy heads for college or a Roman Catholic priest forgiving Paul Newman or Steve McQueen for killing a hundred men in the preceding reel.

Anyone raising questions about the image of minority groups as [15] portrayed in television and the movies is automatically suspect as an un-American and subversive influence on the minds of the young. The historical, linguistic, and cultural differences are neatly blocked out by the fad of portraying members of minority groups in roles which formerly were reserved for whites. Thus Burt Reynolds played a Mohawk detective busy solving the crime problem in New York City. Diahann Carroll played a well-to-do black widow with small child in a television series that was obviously patterned after the unique single-headed white family.

In recent years the documentary has arisen to present the story of [16] Indian people and a number of series on Black America have been produced. Indian documentaries are singularly the same. A reporter and television crew hasten to either the Navaho or Pine Ridge reservation, quickly shoot reels on poverty conditions, and return East blithely thinking that they have captured the essence of Indian life. In spite of the best intentions, the eternal yearning to present an exciting story of a strange people overcomes, and the endless cycle of poverty-oriented films continues.

This type of approach continually categorizes the Indian as an in- [17] competent boob who can't seem to get along and who is hopelessly mired in a poverty of his own making. Hidden beneath these documentaries is the message that Indians really *want* to live this way. No one has yet filmed the incredible progress that is being made by the Makah tribe, the Quinaults. Red Lake Chippewas, Gila River Pima-Waricopas, and others. Documentaries project the feeling that reservations should be eliminated because the conditions are so bad. There is no effort to present the bright side of Indian life.

With the rise of ethnic studies programs and courses in minority- [18] group history, the situation has become worse. People who support these programs assume that by communicating the best aspects of a group they have somehow solved the major problems of that group in its relations with the rest of society. By emphasizing that black is beautiful or that Indians have contributed the names of rivers to the road map, many people feel that they have done justice to the group concerned.

One theory of interpretation of Indian history that has arisen in the [19] past several years is that all of the Indian war chiefs were patriots defending their lands. This is the "patriot chief" interpretation of history. Fundamentally it is a good theory in that it places a more equal balance to interpreting certain Indian wars as wars of resistance. It gets away from the tendency, seen earlier in this century, to classify all Indian warriors as renegades. But there is a tendency to overlook the obvious renegades. Indians who were treacherous and would have been renegades had there been no whites to fight. The patriot chiefs interpretation also conveniently overlooks the fact that every significant leader of the previous century was eventually done in by his own people in one way or another. Sitting Bull was killed by Indian police working for the government. Geronimo was captured by an army led by Apache scouts who sided with the United States.

If the weak points of each minority group's history are to be covered [20] over by a sweetness-and-light interpretation based on what we would like to think happened rather than what did happen, we doom ourselves to decades of further racial strife. Most of the study programs today emphasize the goodness that is inherent in the different minority communities, instead of trying to present a balanced story. There are basically two schools of interpretation running through all of these efforts as the demand for black, red, and brown pride dominates the programs.

One theory derives from the "All-American Platoon" concept of a [21] decade ago. Under this theory members of the respective racial minority groups had an important role in the great events of American history. Crispus Attucks, a black, almost single-handedly started the Revolutionary War, while Eli Parker, the Seneca Indian general, won the Civil War and would have concluded it sooner had not there been so many stupid whites abroad in those days. This is the "cameo" theory of history. It takes a basic "manifest destiny" white interpretation of history and lovingly plugs a few feathers, woolly heads, and sombreros into the famous events of American history. No one tries to explain what an Indian is who was helping the whites destroy his own people, since we are now all Americans and have these great events in common.

The absurdity of the cameo school of ethnic pride is self-apparent. [22]
Little Mexican children are taught that there were some good Mexicans
at the Alamo. They can therefore be happy that Mexicans have been involved in the significant events of Texas history. Little is said about the
Mexicans on the other side at the Alamo. The result is a denial of a substantial Mexican heritage by creating the feeling that "we all did it together." If this trend continues I would not be surprised to discover that
Columbus had a Cherokee on board when he set sail from Spain in
search of the Indies.

The cameo school smothers any differences that existed historical- [23]
ly by presenting a history in which all groups have participated through
representatives. Regardless of Crispus Attuck's valiant behavior during
the Revolution, it is doubtful that he envisioned another century of slavery for blacks as a cause worth defending.

The other basic school of interpretation is a projection backward of [24]
the material blessings of the white middle class. It seeks to identify where
all the material wealth originated and finds that each minority group *contributed* something. It can therefore be called the contribution school.
Under this conception we should all love Indians because they contributed corn, squash, potatoes, tobacco, coffee, rubber, and other agricultural products. In like manner, blacks and Mexicans are credited with
Carver's work on the peanut, blood transfusion, and tacos and tamales.

The ludicrous implication of the contribution school visualizes the [25]
minority groups clamoring to enter American society, lined up with an
abundance of foods and fancies, presenting them to whites in a never
ending stream of generosity. If the different minority groups were given
an overriding two-percent royalty on their contributions, the same way
whites have managed to give themselves royalties for their inventions,
this school would have a more realistic impact on minority groups.

The danger with both of these types of ethnic studies theories is that [26]
they present an unrealistic account of the role of minority groups in
American history. Certainly there is more to the story of the American
Indian than providing cocoa and popcorn for Columbus's landing party.
When the clashes of history are smoothed over in favor of a mushy to-
getherness feeling, then people begin to wonder what has happened in
the recent past that has created the conditions of today. It has been the
feeling of younger people that contemporary problems have arisen because community leadership has been consistently betraying them.
Older statesmen are called Uncle Toms, and the entire fabric of accumulated wisdom and experience of the older generation of minority
groups is destroyed. . . .

~

Under present conceptions of ethnic studies there can be no lasting [27]
benefit either to minority groups or to society at large. The pride that can
be built into children and youth by acknowledgment of the validity of

their group certainly cannot be built by simply transferring symbols and interpretations arising in white culture history into an Indian, black, or Mexican setting. The result will be to make the minority groups bear the white man's burden by using his symbols and stereotypes as if they were their own.

There must be a drive within each minority group to understand its own uniqueness. This can only be done by examining what experiences were relevant to the group, not what experiences of white America the group wishes itself to be represented in. As an example, the discovery of gold in California was a significant event in the experience of white America. The discovery itself was irrelevant to the western Indian tribes, but the migrations caused by the discovery of gold were vitally important. The two histories can dovetail around this topic but ultimately each interpretation must depend upon its orientation to the group involved. 28

What has been important and continues to be important is the Constitution of the United States and its continual adaptation to contemporary situations. With the Constitution as a framework and reference point, it would appear that a number of conflicting interpretations of the experience of America could be validly given. While they might conflict at every point as each group defines to its own satisfaction what its experience has meant, recognition that within the Constitutional framework we are engaged in a living process of intergroup relationships would mean that no one group could define the meaning of American society to the exclusion of any other. 29

Self-awareness of each group must define a series of histories about the American experience. Manifest destiny has dominated thinking in the past because it has had an abstract quality that appeared to interpret experiences accurately. Nearly every racial and ethnic group has had to bow down before this conception of history and conform to an understanding of the world that it did not ultimately believe. Martin Luther King, Jr., spoke to his people on the basis of self-awareness the night before he died. He told them that they as a people would reach the promised land. Without the same sense of destiny, minority groups will simply be adopting the outmoded forms of stereotyping by which whites have deluded themselves for centuries. 30

We can survive as a society if we reject the conquest-oriented interpretation of the Constitution. While some Indian nationalists want the whole country back, a guarantee of adequate protection of existing treaty rights would provide a meaningful compromise. The Constitution should provide a sense of balance between groups as it has between conflicting desires of individuals. 31

As each group defines the ideas and doctrines necessary to maintain its own sense of dignity and identity, similarities in goals can be drawn that will have relevance beyond immediate group aspirations. Stereotyping will change radically because the ideological basis for portraying 32 the members of any group will depend on that group's values. Plots in books and movies will have to show life as it is seen from within the group. Society will become broader and more cosmopolitan as innovative themes are presented to it. The universal sense of inhumanity will take on an aspect of concreteness. From the variety of cultural behavior patterns we can devise a new understanding of humanity.

The problem of stereotyping is not so much a racial problem as it is   33 problem of limited knowledge and perspective. Even though minority groups have suffered in the past by ridiculous characterizations of themselves by white society, they must not fall into the same trap by simply reversing the process that has stereotyped them. Minority groups must thrust through the rhetorical blockade by creating within themselves a sense of "peoplehood." This ultimately means the creation of a new history and not mere amendments to the historical interpretations of white America.

Responding to Reading

1. In paragraphs 1–17 Deloria focuses on media stereotypes; in paragraphs 18–33 his focus is on ethnic studies programs. What connection does he make between these two subjects?
2. Deloria's essay was first published in 1970. Based on what you see today, do you think the media's treatment of African Americans and Latinos has changed significantly since then? Has its treatment of Native Americans also changed? Or do you think Native Americans remain "the primitive unknown quantity" (14) Deloria believed they were in 1970?
3. Despite his thoughtful critique of the media's tendency to stereotype ethnic minorities, Deloria's essay does not mention Asians, even in his description of the "All-American Platoon"—which, he says, included "every possible stereotype" (12). How do you explain this omission? Are other important groups omitted?

CHALLENGING THE ASIAN
∼ ILLUSION

Gish Jen

Born in 1955, Gish Jen grew up in the New York City suburbs of Yonkers and Scarsdale, her parents having emigrated from China in the late 1940s. After receiving her B.A. from Harvard, Jen spent an unhappy year at the Stanford Business School before deciding to focus on writing. She then worked as a teacher in China, returning to the United States after a year to complete *Typical American* (1991), her well-received novel about a Chinese-American family much like her own. Jen has said of her writing, "I understand that the mainstream audience is Anglo, but there are things they have to understand. One is to recognize us (children of immigrants) as Americans—period—just as we are"; she wants the value of her work to lie "not in strangeness, but in what I am able to tell about life." In the following essay, she criticizes media stereotypes of Asians.

For a very long time, when people talked about race, they talked   1
about black America and white America. Where did that put Asian-Americans?

Spike Lee touches on the Asian-American dilemma in *Do the Right*   2
Thing when the Korean grocer, afraid of having his business attacked by rioting blacks, yells: "I not white! I black! Like you! Same!"

Unlike the grocer, though, my family and I identified mostly with   3
white America, which, looking back, was partly wishful thinking, partly racism and partly an acknowledgment that, whatever else we did face, at least we did not have to contend with the legacy of slavery.

Yet we were not white. We were somehow borderline; we did not   4
quite belong. Now, not only has the number of Asian-Americans in this country doubled in the last decade, we are growing faster than any other ethnic group. How meaningful it will ultimately prove to lump the Hmong[1] with the Filipinos with the Japanese remains to be seen. Still, to be perceived as a significant minority is a development for which I, at least, am grateful.

There is a sense that to be perceived at all, a minority group must be   5
plagued with problems—a problem in itself, to be sure. But what about our problems—were they significant enough to warrant attention? Who cared, for instance, that we did not see outselves reflected on movie screens? Until recently, it did not occur to most of us that the absence of Asian and Asian-American images was symptomatic of a more profound invisibility.

Today, though, it is shocking to behold how little represented we   6
have been, and in how blatantly distorted a manner. There has been some progress now that more Asian-Americans like David Henry Hwang and Philip Kan Gotanda have begun to write for stage and screen: also, some recent Caucasian-directed television shows, including *Shannon's Deal* and *Davis Rules,* are breaking new ground.

For the most part, however, film, television and theater, from *Miss*   7
Saigon to *Teen-Age Mutant Ninja Turtles,* have persisted in perpetuating

---

[1] Cambodian mountain people, many of whom have been displaced to the United States in the aftermath of civil war. [Eds.]

stereotypes. Mostly this has been through the portrayal of Asian characters; Asian-Americans have rarely been represented at all.

This invisibility is essentially linked to the process by which fanci- 8 ful ideas are superimposed onto real human beings. How are everyday Asians transformed into mysterious "Orientals," after all, if not by distance? Americans can be led to believe anything about people living in a far-off land, or even a distinctly unfamiliar place like Chinatown. It is less easy with a kid next door who plays hockey and air guitar.

Over the years, Asians have been the form onto which white writ- 9 ers have freely projected their fears and desires. That this is a form of colonialism goes almost without saying; it can happen only when the people whose images are appropriated are in no position to object.

For certainly anyone would object to being identified with a figure 10 as heartlessly evil and preternaturally cunning as Fu Manchu, a brilliant but diabolical force set on taking over the world. The character's prototype was invented in 1916, in a climate of hysteria over the "threat" that Asian workers posed to native labor. We behold its likeness in figures like Odd Job in *Goldfinger* (1964); his influence can be seen in depictions of Chinatown as a den of iniquity in movies like *The Year of the Dragon* (1985) and *True Believer* (1988). *Chinatown* (1974) used it as a symbol of all that is rotten in the city of Los Angeles, despite the fact that no Chinese person had much to do with the evil turnings of the plot.

What fuels these images is xenophobia. In periods of heightened po- 11 litical tension, they tend to recur; in more secure times, they are replaced by more benign images. Charlie Chan[2] for example, arose in 1926, shortly after the last of a series of laws restricting Chinese immigration had been passed and the "Yellow Peril" seemed to be over.

The benign images, however, are typically no more tied to reality 12 than their malign counterparts; vilification is merely replaced by glorification. The aphorism-spouting Charlie Chan (played by Warner Oland, a white actor in yellowface) is godlike in his intelligence, the original Asian whiz kid; you would not be surprised to hear he had won a Westinghouse prize in his youth. More message than human being, he recalls the ever-smiling black mammy that proliferated during Reconstruction: Don't worry, he seems to say, no one's going to go making any trouble.

One Good Guy, But He's a Rat

In today's social climate of multi-culturalism, movies like *Rambo,* 13 which made the Vietnamese out to be so much cannon fodder, seem to

---

[2] Fictional Chinese-American detective in a series of books and movies. [Eds.]

be behind us, at least temporarily. Instead, reflecting the American preoccupation with Japan, there is *Teen-Age Mutant Ninja Turtle*. Here the
Japanese enemy gang leader is once again purely demonic and bestial,
a hairless, barbaric figure who wears a metal claw for ornament. What
gives the movie a more contemporary stamp is the fact that Master
Splinter, the good-guy rodent leader of the Mutant Turtles, is also Japanese. It is as if Fu Manchu and Charlie Chan were cast into a single
movie—seemingly presenting a balanced view of the Japanese as good
and bad.

But the fact that the "good" Japanese is a rat means that slanty   14
eyes belong to the bad guy. And as individuals the Japanese are still
portrayed as sub- or superhuman, possessing fabulous abilities and
arcane knowledge that center on (another contemporary twist) mar-
tial arts.

Is it a sign of a fitness-crazed age that this single aspect of Asian cul-   15
ture is so enthralling? So perennially popular are movies like *The Karate
Kid* (1984) and this year's *Iron and Silk* that one begins to wonder
whether Asian males pop out of the womb doing mid-air gyrations. The
audience marvels: How fantastic, these people! Meanwhile, the non-
Asian roles are the more recognizably human ones.

Real humanity similarly eludes the Asian characters in the Broad-   16
way play *Miss Saigon*. As in *Teen-Age Mutant Ninja Turtles,* they are either simply evil or simply good, with the possible exception of the Engineer (Jonathan Pryce) who, loathsome as he is, seems more
self-interested than evil. Half-white, he seems to be, correspondingly,
halfway human. In contrast, Thuy, the major Vietnamese character, is
portrayed as so inhuman that he would kill a child in cold blood. Is this
what Communists do? Asians? When Kim (Lea Salonga), the heroine,
shoots her erstwhile loyal fiancé, the audience applauds, feeling no more
for him than for Rambo's victims. The subhuman brute has got what he
deserved.

At the same time, the audience does feel, horribly, for Kim, who has   17
been forced to pull the trigger and now must live with blood on her
hands. What a fate for a paragon of virtue! She is Madame Butterfly un-
pinned from her specimen board and let loose to flutter around the room
again: abandoned, virtuous, she waits faithfully for her white lover, only
to discover that he has married. He returns for his son (it's always a son);
she kills herself.

Isn't this a beautiful story? Annette Kolodny, a feminist critic, has   18
observed that when the Western mind feels free to remake a place and
people according to its liking, it conceives of that place and people as a
woman. This has been nowhere so true as in the case of the "Orient,"
and correspondingly, no woman, it seems, has been portrayed as more
exquisitely feminine than an Oriental.

Take any play in which both Oriental and Caucasian women ap- [19] pear—say, *South Pacific*—and it is immediately obvious which is more delicate, more willing to sacrifice for her man, more docile. Never mind that there are in the world real women who might object to having their image appropriated for such use.

But of course, women do object. I object, especially since the only [20] possible end for this invented Butterfly is suicide. For how would the white characters go on with their lives?

It is an irony of stage history that a musical as conventional in its use [21] of the Butterfly story should follow so closely on the heels of another play that turns the same narrative on its head. The 1988 Broadway play *M. Butterfly* offers not just the "beautiful story" itself, but also a white man who has been taken in by it. So enthralled is René Gallimard by the idea of his Butterfly, the projection of his own desire, that he forgets there is a real person—Song Liling, a man and a spy—upon which his notions are imposed.[3]

Ultimately, *M. Butterfly* makes clear that for the "game" of Orien- [22] talism, there is a price to pay, not only by those whose images are appropriated, but by the appropriators.

Do stereotypes lurk even here? It might seem so, but would a stereo- [23] type wonder, as does Song Liling, whether he and Gallimard might not continue on together, even after the truth has been revealed. When Song asks, "What do I do now?" he conveys how helpless he is too, how powerless. This is a human being. That he should be is maybe not so surprising, given that he was invented by David Henry Hwang, an Asian-American.

One Step Forward: Spoof the Stereotype

Are Asian-American writers the only hope for new forms of char- [24] acterization? Perhaps, when even directors as intelligent as Woody Allen portray Chinatown as having opium dens. In his most recent movie, *Alice*, Mr. Allen's recycling of an Aisan sage is likewise problematic. Could he not have created a spoof of a sage—a character who winked at the stereotype even as he played it—without any damage to the plot?

Spoofing the stereotype was the strategy taken last spring in an [25] episode of the now-cancelled television series *Shannon's Deal* that featured a pony-tailed Korean immigrant. Here were clear signs for hope: the immigrant at first appeared to be an all-knowing Charlie Chan, but turned out to be at once less and more. At moments way ahead of the in-

---

[3] In the play, based on a true story, Gallimard falls in love with Song Liling, a man who is impersonating a woman. [Eds.]

vestigator Shannon, he proved to be way behind at others; he knew all the aphorisms but had trouble passing the bar exam, and discussed his own tendency to drop pronouns.

Other signs of change include a jeans-wearing, face-making, poker- 26 playing Japanese character in *Davis Rules*. Unexotic Mrs. Yamagami (Tamayo Otsuki) even shows a sense of humor, characterizing a co-worker as "a rebel without a car." Similarly, in *Twin Peaks*, the figure of Jocelyn (Joan Chen), evil as she is, does not stand in contrast to the good, white characters the way a female Fu Manchu—a dragon lady—might. Neither, certainly, is she any Butterfly. She is, within the show's offbeat context, just one of the gang.

All these characters are heartening, since they are not simply un- 27 examined projections onto the Asian race. Still, as might be expected, directors like Wayne Wang and playwrights like Philip Kan Gotanda are not only more likely to present Asian-Americans in their work, but to present Asian-Americans who are not of the immigrant generation. In Mr. Wang's movie *Dim Sum* (1987) and Mr. Gotanda's film *The Wash* (1988), Asian-Americans are presented in far greater complexity than is typical of the mainstream media; the characters seem more captured than constructed, more like flesh-and-blood than cartoons. This is partly a matter of their status as protagonists rather than peripheral figures.

And more images are needed if the few that exist now are not to be- 28 come new stereotypes. Since the much publicized success of Connie Chung, for example, Asian-American anchorwomen have become a staple in films like *Year of the Dragon* and *Moscow on the Hudson*. With real-life repercussions: the San Francisco newscaster Emerald Yeh tells of an interview with CNN, during which she was more or less asked why she couldn't do her hair like Connie Chung's.

Ridiculous, right? And yet such is the power of image. We would 29 not have to insist that images reflect life, except that all too often we ask life to reflect images.

Responding to Reading

1. Jen believes that "the absence of Asian and Asian-American images [has been] symptomatic of a more profound invisibility" (5). How "visible" are Asians and Asian Americans on television? In films? In your community?
2. What stereotypes of Asians does Jen believe the media have perpetuated? Can you think of others? Which, if any, do you see as positive? Do you believe a stereotype can be damaging even if it is a positive one? Explain.
3. In her essay's last line Jen says, "We would not have to insist that images reflect life, except that all too often we ask life to reflect images" (29). What do you think she means? Do you agree with her?

PC AND THE PRESS

Huntly Collins

A native of Oregon, Huntly Collins (1947–) attended Portland State University and holds a master's degree in education from the University of Missouri at Kansas City. After two years as a high school teacher, she turned to journalism, first as a general assignment reporter with the Portland *Oregonian* and for the last twelve years as a reporter and editor with the *Philadelphia Inquirer*, covering business, education, and medicine. She wrote the following essay in 1991 for *Change*, the publication of the American Association for Higher Education. In it she critiques the press's coverage of the debate over "political correctness" in college curriculums, speech codes, and other areas. An excerpt from one book she mentions, Dinesh D'Souza's *Illiberal Education*, appears in Chapter 2 (p. 136).

As a higher education reporter at the *Philadelphia Inquirer*, I seem to have missed the biggest story on my beat last year: the rise of the "political correctness" movement on American college campuses. Somehow, I got caught up in less weighty matters like massive budget cuts at state-funded schools, the effort to improve undergraduate teaching at major research universities, and a month-long faculty strike at Temple University, the largest school in the Philadelphia area. [1]

It wasn't until I read *Newsweek's* cover story of December 24, 1990 (entitled "Thought Police: There's a 'Politically Correct' Way to Talk About Race, Sex and Ideas. Is This the New Enlightenment—or the New McCarthyism?") that I began to realize what was really happening in academe. [2]

The big news on campus had nothing to do with budget cuts, or the competing interests of undergraduate teaching and university research, or the faculty's role in academic decision-making. The big news was a left-wing conspiracy by college administrators and 1960s-era professors to stifle dissent and impose a "liberal orthodoxy" about race and gender. The goal: to capture the hearts and minds of the nation's 13 million college students. [3]

Such is the alarmist picture that has emerged from a significant segment of the popular press—especially magazines—over the past year. One need look only as far as the headlines and graphics to get the message. [4]

Following *Newsweek's* lead, *New York* magazine weighed in with John Taylor's January 21, 1991 story entitled "Are You Politically Correct?" It ran with a photograph of Red Guards jeering at Chinese aca- [5]

demics in dunce caps; another photo showed a public book burning by Hitler youth in Nazi Germany. The headline superimposed on the photos read: "Am I Misogynistic, Patriarchal, Gynophobic, Phallocentric, Logocentric? Am I Guilty of Racism, Sexism, Classism? Do I say 'Indian' Instead of 'Native American'? 'Pet' Instead of 'Animal Companion'?"

Then in March came the *Atlantic*'s excerpts from Dinesh D'Souza's   6 book, *Illiberal Education*. The cartoon-like cover illustration showed an aging white male professor about to be set afire as he lay sandwiched between the cracking covers of a Western classic. Hands representing different minority groups were shown tugging the professor in different directions by the arms and legs. In the foreground was an even more ominous image: a pile of books being doused with gasoline. The hand holding the gas canister was dark-skinned.

By April 1, *Time* magazine had jumped on the PC bandwagon.   7 "U.S. Campuses: The New Intolerance," said the teaser headline on the cover. Inside, readers were treated to "Upside Down in the Groves of Academe," an essay by William A. Henry III.[1] "Imagine a place where it is considered racist to speak of the rights of the individual when they conflict with the community's prevailing opinion," Henry began.

Magazine journalism, of course, isn't the only popular medium   8 where the nation's colleges and universities have been depicted as captive to a left-wing orthodoxy. Syndicated columnists like George Will have had a heyday with PC, as have editorial writers and cartoonists at newspapers across the country.

In an April 23rd editorial about the controversy over the diversity   9 standards of the Middle States Association of Colleges and Schools, the *Wall Street Journal* declared: "The truth is that we are far worse off now as regards the threat to intellectual freedom, the pressures to conform ideologically, than during the McCarthy era.

Today the most serious assault on that freedom comes from within   10 the universities themselves."

The tale being told by these and other publications reads the same   11 from one to another. It is a tale of how colleges and universities have adopted student conduct codes restricting free speech. A tale of how Third World and women's literature has supplanted the Western classics as requirements in the college curriculum. A tale of how conservative faculty members are being silenced and hounded out of their jobs by liberal colleagues and administrators. A tale of how unqualified black students are being admitted to elite private schools. A tale of how English professors have fallen captive to a strange brand of literary crit-

---

[1] Another essay by Henry appears in Chapter 2 (p. 121). [Eds.]

icism known as deconstructionism, which challenges the existence of "truth itself."

No matter that each of these topics is a complicated story, with its [12] own history, its own context at various schools, its own lineup of players on one side or another. Much of the popular press, taking a cue from D'Souza and others, has lumped the issues together to prove that "politically correct" thinking has gained a hammerlock on academic life. As *Newsweek* put it: "PC is, strictly speaking, a totalitarian philosophy. No aspect of university life is too obscure to come under its scrutiny."

There is one problem with the portrait that has dominated the main- [13] stream media: It grossly exaggerates the influence of PC, and badly distorts reality on the vast majority of American campuses. A recent survey by the American Council on Education (ACE), for instance, asked administrators on a representative sample of 444 campuses whether their schools had experienced controversy over the "political correctness" of courses, speeches, or faculty lectures. Ten percent or less of the 359 schools responding to the survey said "yes."

A reporter who visits almost any campus today would have to [14] deny his or her senses to conclude that women and minorities are in control of the curriculum. Even a cursory look at college catalogues shows that Western culture, including science and technology, is still the centerpiece.

While much ado has been made of deconstructionism, the debate [15] has generally failed to reach beyond English departments. The only segment of higher education where much heat has been generated by it is the highly selective private schools and the so-called public Ivys.

And while the raw number of black students on college campuses [16] has risen, that's primarily because of demographic changes, not skewed admissions policies. In fact, the percentage of black high school graduates attending college has declined, from 33.5 percent in 1976 to 30.8 percent in 1989—this, during a period when the proportion of blacks graduating from high school rose from 67.5 percent to 76.1 percent.

Even if there had been a left-wing conspiracy on campus, one would [17] have to conclude that it has been a monumental failure, at least judging by the predilections of students themselves. Business administration remains the most popular major among undergraduates. Surveys show that college graduates today are more concerned with landing a good job than changing the world. And, in recent years, the GOP has enjoyed new-found popularity among college-age students.

The number of campus Republican clubs went from several hun- [18] dred in the early 1980s to about 1,100 today. A recent poll by the Wirthin Group found that Republicans enjoyed their greatest strength among people aged 18 to 24. Forty-two percent—more than any other age group—said they thought of themselves as Republicans. Thirty-five percent identified themselves as Democrats, and 23 percent as independents.

Nonetheless, the press has made a case for a PC conspiracy by re- [19] lying almost exclusively on a litany of by-now-familiar anecdotes, recycled from one publication to another. Often, the yarns are oversimplified and incompletely reported. Sometimes they are simply false.

Many stories, for instance, cite the catchy chant of student pro- [20] testers at Stanford University: "Hey; hey, ho, ho, Western culture's got to go." The impression left is that the students were opposed to Western culture itself; in fact, they were referring to the school's Western culture requirement. As it turns out, Stanford's new "Culture, Ideas, and Values" (CIV) course, which replaced the Western culture course, retains the Western classics in seven of eight tracks. And even in the less traditional eighth track, "Europe and the Americas," students are required to read selections from the Bible and other works in the Western tradition.

"In fact, the West was not being 'phased out' at Stanford," wrote [21] Anthony Day, in a page-one piece for the *Los Angeles Times* on May 3, 1990. "In addition to 'Europe and the Americas,' which this year has about 100 students, the other seven CIV courses offered to freshmen remained much as they were."

Day's piece, which took an in-depth look at Stanford a year after the [22] curricular reform went into effect, is a fine example of on-site reporting, the kind of coverage that has been missing elsewhere. Unlike other reporters, Day actually spent time on campus, sat in classes, and interviewed a large number of faculty members and students.

Apart from anecdotes, statistical evidence of PC's reign on campus [23] is hard to find in most of the stories. And when numbers are cited, they are often cited inaccurately. For instance, many editorials—rightly concerned about First Amendment violations in student conduct codes—assert that 70 percent of the nation's colleges and universities have adopted such restrictive codes. The number, widely disseminated to the press by the American Civil Liberties Union, comes from a 1989 survey of student affairs officers that was published by the Carnegie Foundation for the Advancement of Teaching as part of its 1990 report, "Campus Life: In Search of Community."

In fact, the survey did not ask a single question about campus [24] speech codes. But it did ask whether schools had a "written policy on bigotry, racial harassment, or intimidation." The response: 60 percent had such a policy, 11 percent were developing one, and 29 percent had no policy. Of course, such policies could run the gamut from something as innocuous as a statement condemning racial bigotry to something as troubling as speech codes that infringe on First Amendment rights. The survey, however, did not ask about the content of the policies, so any conclusions about that are shaky at best. The point was totally missed by the mainstream press.

"I sent out a correction and clarification saying 'Buyer Beware,'" [25] said David Merkowitz, spokesman for the ACE, which co-sponsored the original survey. "But, as usual, the correction never catches up with the original story. We keep seeing this figure repeated everywhere."

To be sure, there are some campuses, such as The University of [26] Michigan, where speech codes have been found unconstitutional by the courts. There are also legitimate differences of opinion on every campus about affirmative action, curricular reform, and new forms of faculty scholarship. To write about each of these issues in separate stories is one thing; to mix them all together into catch-all pieces on political correctness is something else.

The best of the country's education reporters, including Kenneth J. [27] Cooper of *The Washington Post*, have picked off the issues one by one and attempted to take a careful and balanced look at how they have played out. In a May 27, 1991 page-one story, for instance, Cooper examined the new "American cultures" requirement for freshmen at The University of California-Berkeley. Although the controversial new requirement wasn't scheduled to take effect until this fall, Cooper sat in on three pilot courses taught last spring. There, he found "a range of lessons" being taught, not the politically correct line suggested by critics.

One of the lessons: "In a journalism course, 'News and the Under- [28] dog in American Society,' a dozen students discussed sympathetic photographs of migrant 'Okies' published during the Depression. One theme was that white folks can be victims too," Cooper wrote.

Although he interviewed scores of students, Cooper found few who [29] believed that the Berkeley faculty had caved in to left-wing ideology— quite the contrary. A number of students complained that the university was too conservative.

Other education reporters who have gone out to find the stifling [30] campus atmosphere described by *Newsweek* and others have come away dumbfounded. "When you are out there on the campuses and you don't see it, you wonder, am I crazy or are they?" said an education writer at a large West Coast newspaper.

The very debate over PC on college campuses would seem to signal [31] that a spirit of free inquiry is alive and well. And although some conservative faculty members and students may feel uncomfortable with multiculturalism, even Lynne V. Cheney, chairwoman of the National Endowment for the Humanities and one of the country's most strident critics of PC, admitted in a September 25th speech before the National Press Club that, to her knowledge, no professor had actually been fired over PC, though some, she asserted, had not been hired. While that may be true, it's a far cry from the Congressional investigations and loyalty

oaths of the McCarthy era that Cheney and many in the media continue to invoke.

What explains the abysmal performance of the press in covering the [32]
controversies that have arisen over issues of race and gender on campus? To some extent, schools themselves are to blame. There are at least
two things dear to every journalist's heart—the First Amendment and
the English language. When colleges and universities start pushing the
boundaries of either, they are, rightly or wrongly, inviting criticism.

What journalist could resist poking fun at mangled language like [33]
"lookism," "vertically challenged," and "differently abled"? The phrases are typical of the twisted rhetoric that has worked its way into official
policy on many campuses.

By contrast, the conservative critics of multiculturalism have spoken [34]
with a less tortured tongue, a language that is readily accessible to the
media as well as to the average reader. What's more, the conservatives
have organized—an occurrence that was duly noted by the reporters
who followed the formation of the National Association of Scholars, a
vocal critic of PC.

Beyond that, however, the distorted coverage of PC is part of a long [35]
tradition of anti-intellectualism in the popular press, which has tended
to put down what it doesn't understand. The annual meeting of the
Modern Language Association, for instance, produces a predictable
string of stories spanning the seemingly esoteric topics discussed in
scholarly papers.

When the press belatedly discovered deconstructionism, which has [36]
formed the philosophical underpinnings for at least some of the campus
debate over multiculturalism, it is not surprising that most reporters
didn't take the time to understand what the critique was all about.

"Journalists have sort of given up knowing what's going on (in [37]
scholarship)," says Mitchell Stephens, an associate professor of journalism at New York University. "The scholarship itself has gotten more
complicated. If we are talking about the latest Saul Bellow novel, journalists can read it, too. But if we are talking about deconstructing Hei-
degger, that's too much work."

Although a few papers, like the *New York Times* and *The Boston* [38]
Globe, have assigned specialists to cover "the egghead beat," as it's
known in the trade, those whose job it is to cover ideas are few and far
between. So are those assigned to cover higher education full time. Of
the 369 members of the Education Writers Association, just 13 identify
themselves as higher education writers. The dearth of beat reporters in
higher education has undoubtedly contributed to the lackluster coverage of multiculturalism and has allowed distortion of the PC issue to go
unchallenged.

One of the nation's few full-time higher education writers is An- [39] thony Flint of the *Boston Globe*. In a thoughtful piece on July 8, Flint cat- alogued the growing number of educators who were speaking out against the conservative critics of PC.

"Those who have been labeled politically correct—advocates of [40] greater sensitivity about race and gender awareness, for example—say they have been the victims of a right-wing smear campaign, exaggerat- ed by a pack-mentality media using a handful of damning anecdotes," Flint wrote. More than two months later, on September 25, the *New York Times'* Anthony DePalma wrote the same piece. The news peg was the formation of Teachers for a Democratic Culture, a group of 30 scholars waging a counteroffensive against their conservative critics.

These two stories were among the first in the mainstream press to [41] devote considerable space to telling the other side of the PC story. In the view of some media experts, the skewed reporting of PC and the belat- ed effort to right the balance stem from the rightward drift of the press in recent years. As the country has moved to the right, so has much of the media. Ever since the Reagan years, the press has been extremely sensitive to charges of a liberal bias; to compensate, many publications, including the *Philadelphia Inquirer*, have added strong conservative voic- es to their editorial pages.

More fundamentally, however, the press, like other institutions of [42] American society, is undergoing fundamental change as more women and minorities enter the journalism profession. Though minorities and women are still underrepresented, especially at the top (minorities now constitute 8.72 percent of the supervisors, editors, copy editors, re- porters, and photographers on the nation's newspapers, according to a 1991 survey by the American Society of Newspaper Editors), they have forced news organizations to confront their own racism and sexism.

For some of the white men whose world view is being challenged, [43] the change has proved discomfiting. "News executives are experiencing many of the same pressures within their own organizations as the uni- versities have felt," says Larry Gross, a professor of communications at The University of Pennsylvania's Annenberg School. "By jumping on the bash-academia bandwagon, they are putting down the forces of up- pity groups within their own circles."

At a time of declining readership, the alleged PC conspiracy has also [44] provided an irresistible opportunity to attract more readers with sensa- tionalized headlines, graphics, and stories that play on the deepest fears of white, middle-class Americans—the very segment of the population that newspapers and magazines must attract if they are to remain eco- nomically viable.

"We have begun to define success in the press the same way it [45] would be defined by Nike—profits before social obligation," laments Mercedes Lynn de Uriarte, an associate professor of journalism at The

University of Texas-Austin. "Why do you need the protection of the First Amendment when you are basically selling sneakers?"

Enough. I have to go write my first story about the PC conspiracy. [46] Make that my second.

Responding to Reading

1. Collins begins her essay by describing and illustrating popular press coverage of the impact of political correctness. What is her purpose in presenting this overview?

2. In paragraph 14 Collins observes that at most colleges "women and minorities are [not] in control of the curriculum. Even a cursory look at college catalogues shows that Western culture, including science and technology, is still the centerpiece." Is this situation true at your school? Explain.

3. In paragraph 32 Collins asks, "What explains the abysmal performance of the press in covering the controversies that have arisen over issues of race and gender on campus?" Where does she believe the explanation lies? Where do you believe it lies?

Magic and AIDS: Presumed
~ Innocent

Michael Bronski

A long-time activist and reporter on gay issues, Michael Bronski (1949–) has written reviews as well as articles about AIDS and other issues facing the gay community for a number of periodicals, including *The Advocate* and the *Village Voice*. His book *Culture Clash: The Making of a Gay Sensibility* (1984) is still in print. The following essay originally appeared in *Z Magazine*, a liberal periodical focusing on political and media issues, published by the Boston-based Institute for Social and Cultural Communication. In it Bronski looks at the way the media create "guilty" and "innocent" victims of this epidemic and suggests that such "pander[ing] to popular prejudice" can have seriously negative effects on public policy.

The buzz began sometime that morning. Television newsrooms and [1] sports desks began calling one another, checking out the almost unbelievable rumor that Magic Johnson was giving a press conference later that afternoon in which he was going to announce his retirement from the sports world because he had tested positively for the HIV virus. This was the sort of news story that held up the evening edition, caused radio DJs to scuttle their preordained playlist, and even interrupted the afternoon's installment of *The Guiding Light*. This was NEWS.

Sure enough on Thursday, November 7, basketball star Magic Johnson announced that after having tested positively for the HIV virus—or, as the *New York Times* insists, "the AIDS virus"—he would be leaving the Los Angeles Lakers and devoting his life to helping educate Americans, especially teenagers, about AIDS and safe sex.   2

After the initial announcement there was a moment of startled silence—not for the man himself, who was in apparent good health and made his public revelation in straightforward, unapologetic language—but in anticipation of the media response. The announcement of any public figure—not to mention one as famous and beloved as Magic Johnson—being HIV-positive does not, and cannot, happen in a judgment-free vacuum. Was the media going to embrace him as a poor unfortunate, an "innocent victim" who through no fault of his own had fallen prey to a dreadful calamity? Or was he going to be rejected as a diseased "guilty victim" who was being punished for his own evil actions?   3

That moment of silence ended relatively quickly when almost all of the print and electronic media declared Johnson, because of his honesty and courage, the new hero of the AIDS epidemic. But this declaration of support was not without its unspoken unrest. Initially Magic Johnson never stated, or even indicated, how he contracted the HIV virus. In the face of eventual illness and death such concerns might seem minor, or even insignificant, but in the United States both the quantity and quality of sympathy for people with AIDS has *always* been predicated upon an understanding of how they contracted the virus and their attendant status as "guilty" or "innocent" victims.   4

The breakdown between "guilty" and "innocent" has traditionally been simple: homosexuals (usually portrayed by the media as white) who get AIDS through "perverted" sex, prostitutes who sell their bodies, and people who shoot drugs (almost always portrayed by the media as black) were almost always "guilty"; children who are infected through their mothers, and hemophiliacs, or anyone who received the virus through a blood transfusion, were "innocent."   5

It is not surprising, therefore, that it took Magic Johnson little more than twenty-four hours to announce on the *Arsenio Hall Show* on Friday, November 8, that "he was the furthest thing from a homosexual" and that he got the HIV virus from "messing around with too many women." A statement which placed him in the discernible, if increasingly fragile, realm of the innocent. For after more than a decade of the AIDS pandemic, the once well-entrenched categories of "guilty" and "innocent" are now becoming less rigid. Not that they are disappear-   6 ing—they are as secure as any number of socially constructed categories which are used to punish, repress, or control certain socially proscribed behaviors—but as the visible profile of the "typical" person with AIDS is changing both the media and popular opinion are having a difficult time accommodating to the fact that the comforting simplicity (and lie) of "guilty" and "innocent" are now untenable categories. No matter that ACT UP has been saying for more than half a decade that "All People With AIDS Are Innocent," there is still a rush in the press, as well as the public imagination, to distinguish between those people with AIDS who are morally culpable for their illness and those who "truly" deserve sympathy and compassion.

The social structures that support this "guilty" and "innocent" di- 7 chotomy are so strong that there was probably no way for Magic Johnson—the private man or the public image—to transcend them. And although there has been increasing variance within the categories lately—the publicity generated by the cases of Marc Christian, Dr. Veronica Prego, and Kimberly Bergalis (and now Magic Johnson) has established the parameters of the debate—the basic structure still holds.

The association of moral guilt to physical disease is certainly not a 8 new one. When the great plagues ravaged Europe during the Middle Ages they were seen as divine punishment (as well as the onset of the millennium.) There were no "innocent victims" because strict Christian theology taught that all humankind, by nature of their incarnate state, was guilty. Later, during more "enlightened" times, other diseases too took on various moral meanings. TB, at least in upper-class Britain, was seen as a sign of sensitivity and artistic temperament. In the United States, however, it has always been viewed as a disease of the undeserving poor, and those who suffered from it were generally seen as being responsible for their illness as well as their state in life. More recently, diseases like cholera, which is airborne and spreads quickly (and across class lines), never became as stigmatizing as TB, probably because it killed so quickly there was little time for large-scale stigmatization to occur. Typhoid, in the late nineteenth and early twentieth century, on the other hand, was seen as a disease of "dirty" immigrants (morally as well as physically suspect) who were guilty of spreading it to the "general population." Mary Mallon, dubbed by the popular press as Typhoid Mary, was branded, hounded, and eventually arrested and quarantined—in 1907 and 1915—by New York health officials when she was suspected of "spreading" the disease to her wealthy employers. Later, polio became a nonstigmatizing disease (FDR, after all, suffered from it) and the polio scares of the mid-1950s—possibly because they involved children—never catered to popular prejudices of "guilt" and "innocence."

AIDS is probably the only disease to have spawned simultaneous 9 "guilty" and "innocent" associations in the popular imagination. At first—when it was called GRID (Gay-Related Immune Deficiency)—only sexually active gay men were being diagnosed, so *everyone* was guilty. The later addition of IV-drug users did not require any changes of popular perception: shooting drugs in the arm was as bad as taking it up the ass. The quick addition (and then removal) of Haitians from official listing of high-risk groups was accompanied with "factual" data of their immoral proclivities: from prostitution with U.S. gay men to massive uncleanliness to exotic, and dangerous, voodoo rites. When women were first diagnosed, they were generally seen as IV users or prostitutes.

It was probably the advent of "AIDS babies" in the early 1980s which [10] first stirred the idea of the truly "innocent victim" in the popular imagination. But when most of these children turned out to live in the inner city, the offspring of drug-using mothers, they lost not only their "innocence" but their media cachet. The search for the perfect "innocent victim" became, in time, a media obsession. White middle-class hemophiliacs were good choices, and for a long time Ryan White was the media choice. And although the press never turned on him, he did not in the end suit their purposes because he refused to fulfill one of the requirements of truly innocent victim status: to highlight and attack the "guilty victims."

The cult of the innocent AIDS victim exists to promote the idea that [11] AIDS is, in some profound sense, a moral fault and that the "general population" (as the mainstream press is fond of saying) is safe—not only from disease, but from moral wrongdoing. From a traditional Christian point of view, Ryan White was practicing the noblest form of "Christian charity"—forgiving the sins of others and helping to correct the wrongs of the world. But in our contemporary culture, which promotes a more judgmental, muscular Christianity, moral wrongdoing must be denounced and punished. That is why the moral outrage of Kimberly Bergalis was enormously appealing and persuasive to so many people.

Over the past six years it has become more and more apparent that [12] there is no one-size-suits-all perfect-great-white-innocent victim. Life, as it usually does, intruded on the theologizing and moralizing. Accommodations had to be made. The notions of "guilt" and "innocence" were modified, depending on circumstances and considerations; nuances surfaced and the notions of "guilt" and "innocence" became more byzantine.

The case of Rock Hudson and Marc Christian proved to be one of [13] the earliest chances for the popular press (as well as the attendant legal battles) to reconstruct and reinforce the idea of the "innocent victim." After Hudson's death in 1985 his surviving lover Marc Christian brought a lawsuit against the Hudson estate claiming that the movie star had never disclosed his AIDS diagnosis to him and that, even though he was not infected with the virus, this caused incredible emotional stress: $11 million worth, to be exact. The court awarded Christian a $5.5 million settlement two years later, a decision which was quickly appealed but upheld two months ago by a state appeals court.

It is impossible to understand the positive publicity that Christian [14] received with his initial lawsuit without first understanding the impact of Hudson's death on popular culture. When the news was first released that Rock Hudson—a living legend, an icon of Hollywood heterosexuality—was dying of AIDS the immediate response was disbelief. Although rumors of Hudson's homosexuality had long flourished both in and outside of the industry, most people believed he was straight. If Rock Hudson could be gay *and* could get AIDS, longstanding ideas of who was and who wasn't at risk from the disease were shattered.

Although most people accepted the fact that Hudson contracted the ⁱⁿᵈᵉⁿᵗ 15 disease through his own conscious homosexual sexual activity—thus making him a "guilty" victim—neither the press nor the public was willing to brand him a complete villain. That is why there was general relief and satisfaction when Marc Christian brought his lawsuit. The fact that he was HIV-negative—no physical harm had actually been done him by Hudson—was the perfect ironic twist of the situation. The social function of Marc Christian's lawsuit was to distinguish a truly *innocent* victim (Christian) from the guilty, but very well liked, victim (Hudson). The fact that Christian was an HIV-negative, open homosexual also addressed the attendant, widespread anxiety generated by the simultaneous understanding of Hudson's health status and his homosexuality.

The fact that Christian, four years later, could still be awarded a substantial sum of money for "emotional distress" speaks to the fact that the 16 images of "guilty" and "innocent" AIDS victims are still strongly embedded in our culture. And although these ideas are a baseline for much popular and media thinking, they are not without variants. In 1990 Dr. Veronica Prego, who had been diagnosed with PCP[1] in 1987, brought a $175 million suit against the New York City Health and Hospital Corporation as well as two doctors, claiming that the needle stick by which she had been infected was caused by one doctor's negligence and that her confidentiality had been violated by another physician. What should have been a trial about AIDS and safety in the workplace soon became a four-star television miniseries in which physicians were calling one another "liar" from the witness stand, and Dr. Prego's wardrobe became as important as her testimony.

By all accounts Dr. Prego should have been the ideal "innocent victim": a professional woman with no outstanding slurs against her good 17 name. And even though she wasn't, in media terms, "a white middle-class American" (she was born in Argentina), she was clearly much less culpable than your average junkie or queer. But reading through all of the accounts of the trial, it becomes apparent that the popular press was uncomfortable in presenting Prego as a completely "innocent victim." This had less to do with her ethnicity than with her gender, her professional standing, and what was perceived as her greed in asking for such a large settlement. Almost all the media accounts present Prego as an unfortunate victim of circumstances—"a terrible tragedy, an accident"—but there were always lingering doubts. What if Dr. Prego was lying?

---

[1] A type of pneumonia associated with AIDS. [Eds.]

What if she did it to herself and was only blaming the other doctor's negligence? The fact that both doctors were women added to the stereotyped image of a cat fight and unstable emotional responses. But beyond
that, $175 million seemed like a lot of money to the average New York-
er. In a city in the midst of a financial crisis, where the health care and
hospital system is always under great stress, and where the streets are
filled with disenfranchised people who need immediate mental and
physical care, the medical needs of Dr. Prego may have seemed, if not
inconsequential, at least not worth $175 million.

The Prego case was eventually settled out of court for an undis- [18]
closed sum but the social myths surrounding the case—the necessity to
differentiate "guilty" from "innocent"—remained in place. What was
important about the Prego case, however, was the cultural ambivalence
about the HIV risk that patients presented to their doctors. One of the
subtexts in the reporting on the Prego case was the fact that, although it
was a shame that she had AIDS, it was, or at least *may have been*, a risk
she ran as a health care provider. This was probably the last time this
specific problem was aired in public. And, in fact, since then the situation has been placed in quite the opposite context. The "innocent victim"
is no longer the doctor who has contracted AIDS from a patient, but
rather the "innocent" patient who is at risk from the "guilty" doctor. A
situation which the case of Kimberly Bergalis all too aptly illustrated
these past weeks and months.

Kimberly Bergalis first became a media sensation in late January [19]
1991, when she was publicly identified as one of five HIV-positive
clients of a Florida dentist who had recently died of AIDS. Although it
is unclear how the transmission occurred—the most recent, and widely accepted, theory is that the virus was passed along through nonster-
ile surgical equipment rather than from doctor to patient—Bergalis, who
was white, twenty-three years old, and middle class became the most
visible media example of the "innocent victim." The national media
played up the Florida story (without naming names) as the first example of AIDS transmitted by a health care worker and lost no time when
Bergalis came forward, in light of a $1 million malpractice settlement.
Clearly this was the perfect "innocent victim" for whom the media had
been waiting.

It wasn't just that she was white, middle class, not a prostitute, and [20]
moderately photogenic—Ryan White was all of those things as well as
being fourteen years old, really cute, and *really* photogenic. What Kimberly Bergalis had, which White was sorely missing, was an acute sense
of rage. White was willing to go on TV and say that his job for the rest
of his life was to eradicate AIDS prejudice and help inform all U.S. citizens about the risks of AIDS. But he refused to manifest the fear and
loathing that AIDS instills in the popular imagination. Not so Bergalis.
Upon being awarded the $1 million from her dentist's insurance com-
pany, she announced, "It's not going to buy me a cure." She soon,

helped immeasurably by a conservative political climate and the eager and willing media, began a one-woman campaign to mandate HIV testing for all health care providers.

Within two weeks, many newspapers began carrying tacitly homo- [21] phobic stories on how Bergalis further suffered because "people and organizations don't believe me; they want to believe you were using IV drugs; they want to believe you were sleeping around." Bergalis was clearly speaking of AIDS and gay rights groups who were worried that this single Florida incident would be the catalyst for mandatory HIV testing of health care providers. And they were right. By June 1991 Bergalis was calling for federal laws which would mandate such testing. Racked by physical and emotional pain, Bergalis began giving press conferences in which she used her own condition as the main reason to enact mandatory testing laws. "Who do I blame?" she wrote in a letter to the Florida state health investigators, "Do I blame myself? I sure don't. I never used IV drugs, never slept with anyone, never had a blood transfusion. I blame Dr. Acer [her dentist] and every one of you bastards. Anyone who knew Dr. Acer was infected and had full-blown AIDS and stood by not doing a damn thing about it. You are all just as guilty as he was."

What is most surprising about Bergalis is not that she does not iden- [22] tify with the "guilty victims" of AIDS; she doesn't even identify with the "innocent victims." The media has consistently played up Bergalis's sense of her own singularity—we never even hear about the other four clients of Dr. Acer who have been diagnosed—until they would have you believe that Bergalis's AIDS diagnosis epitomizes all of the social issues surrounding AIDS social policy. And while any AIDS diagnosis is tragic, none is more or less tragic than others. There are many social policy issues which might be raised by the Bergalis case—the treatment of women and AIDS, the lack of AIDS education in many nonurban locales, the need for safeguards in health care centers—but Bergalis and the media focused solely, despite overwhelming evidence to the contrary from the presidential AIDS commission as well as the AMA, on the need for mandatory testing of health care providers.

It is not surprising that the Bergalis case, as well as that of Prego and [23] Christian, would revolve around financial settlements. The idea of a monetary payment, a settlement, for physical or emotional harm, is common in our legal culture. But these cases—and the massive publicity which surrounds them—hint at a broader meaning. By singling out and rewarding these "innocent victims" the popular press is upholding the traditional, false dichotomy between "guilty" and "innocent" victims.

Although there was never any indication that monetary settlements [24] would be sought in the Magic Johnson case—there was no one to sue, for any reason—the matter of his beloved public persona and the attendant income from his commercial endorsements made it imperative for Johnson and his public relations people to situate the sports star firmly in the realm of the "innocent." Although he was recently married and his wife is pregnant, the rumors of Johnson's bisexuality (or homosexuality) were so strong that nearly every newspaper report felt obliged to mention them, even as they rushed to discount them. Johnson's possible drug and steroid use—rampant among some professional circles—also came under scrutiny as a possible cause of his HIV infection. But in the long run, Johnson's story of becoming infected because he "messed around with a lot of women" became not only the accepted version of how he contracted the virus, but also the main tenet in his status as an "innocent victim."

In the first flurry of praise for Johnson, almost all of the media noted [25] how he would be the ideal spokesperson for safe sex for younger people, since he is extremely popular among inner-city and African-American teenagers—a population which evidences the highest incidence of new AIDS diagnoses and which (because of government negligence) obtains very little, if any, safe sex and AIDS education. And certainly Johnson—being the only HIV-positive person of color the mainstream press has ever noticed—is in a unique cultural, historical, and political position. But as much as one would like to believe in the positive effect of Johnson's message on people's lives, there is reason to be cautious, if not weary, of his role as a spokesperson for safe sex and those living with the variety of conditions brought on by HIV infection.

The rush to confirm Johnson's status as an "innocent victim" by [26] reaffirming his heterosexuality (as opposed to, say, remaining silent on the possible source of infection) forces the topic of heterosexual transmission to the forefront of public discussion. And while the media have focused on this subject before—usually in the context of repressive, antisex sentiments—they have never really taken or presented it seriously or factually. Unfortunately, although hardly surprising, all of the coverage in the Magic Johnson case has focused on female-to-male transmission. Yet, statistically this is the least probable of all transmission scenarios. The probability of male-to-female transmission, for example, is roughly twenty times the probability of female-to-male transmission. The number of heterosexual males with AIDS who have contracted HIV from a female partner is less than 2 percent of the total AIDS population.

The constant media attention on Johnson contracting HIV from [27] "messing around with too many women" not only highlights heterosexual transmission but also works to demonize and brand women, especially sexually active women, as deadly disease carriers. This image has always been historically very popular: from Typhoid Mary through the anti-VD poster campaigns of the First and Second World Wars, to the 1950s film images of fallen women who get young men addicted to alcohol and drugs, the deadly, sexual temptress has been a stock figure in contemporary, misogynist morality plays. The innocent AIDS victim

as constructed by the mainstream media is contingent on the oppositional appearance of a "guilty victim." For Marc Christian it was Rock
Hudson, for Kimberly Bergalis it was Dr. Acer, for Magic Johnson it is
sexually active women.

This rush to confirm Magic Johnson's innocence by making his fe- 28
male partners dangerous disease carriers began only days after his original announcement. A November 10 *New York Sunday Times* sports page
ran a long piece entitled "Fast Lane Could Be AIDS Lane," which portrayed professional sports groupies as empty-headed sluts hankering for
a famous fuck: "In my day," they quote Walt Frazier, an ex-player and
broadcaster for the New York Knicks, "you at least had to go to parties
and have a rap to pick up women. Now you see them lining up against
the wall after a game. The stars just take their pick and the other guys
get the leftovers." So we shouldn't forget who is at risk, Frazier added,
"sex is a human need . . . but these guys need to use their heads." In the
November 18 *Sports Illustrated* an article entitled "Dangerous Games"
quoted numerous professional athletes on how easily available some
women make themselves to sports figures. "We come to town, and the
women come out in force. They call the hotel, they follow the bus. They
hover and wait to get you," claims Kevin Johnson, a guard with the
Phoenix Suns. The piece repeats the story, now an urban AIDS legend,
of the woman who had over one hundred pairs of autographed pro-bas-
ketball sneakers under her bed. A December 4 *Boston Globe* article reported that a Montreal physician has released information that a female
patient, who died of AIDS two years ago, told of having sexual relations
with fifty National Hockey League players. "If this revelation," claims
the doctor, "can save the life of any athlete in the future, my patient's
death will have some meaning." As if her death, and life, had no meaning in and of itself.

There is, of course, very little discussion about any of these men— 29
including Magic Johnson—infecting their female partners. There is no
question that AIDS consciousness in professional sports is on the rise
and that women are being blamed for spreading the disease.

While Magic Johnson might be doing the right thing in promoting 30
safe sex (and this remains to be seen), the lingering message that his own
personal life is communicating to teenagers who have no access to the
hard, realistic facts of HIV transmission, is that it is only bad girls—a socially constructed idea if there ever was one—who give you AIDS. If
such skewered notions of transmission and responsibility become attached, in any way, to Johnson's safe-sex information, they undermine
any good such education will do.

The day after the public announcement of his HIV status, Magic 31
Johnson volunteered to be on the presidential AIDS commission and
George Bush (after hesitating to sniff the political winds) quickly agreed.
It is ironic that Johnson will be taking the place of the recently deceased

Belinda Mason. Mason, a young mother who had contracted AIDS through a transfusion and served on the presidential AIDS commission, explicitly called for no mandatory testing, the lifting of all bans of HIV-positive immigrants, and consistently refused to make any distinction between "innocent" and "guilty" victims. Although Johnson has yet to make any statements on public policy, his visibility on the commission will put him under a great deal of pressure to conform to the most conservative tenets of the Bush social and public policy agenda. Already there is talk that Johnson is pulling away from his strong safe-sex line and easing into the more right-wing, Republican-authorized, "just say no" mode of AIDS advice. It is impossible to overestimate the pull of politics on the formation of AIDS education and policy. Last September, Kimberly Bergalis testified, on her deathbed, before the House, on a bill which called for mandatory testing of all health care workers. Not surprisingly, Bergalis's trip to Washington was paid for by the archconservative Representative William Dannemyer. As Tom Stoddard of Lambda Legal Defense wittily noted in the *New York Times*, "Kimberly Bergalis is the Willie Horton of AIDS."

The popular media have a clear economic interest in promoting [32] these images of "guilty" and "innocent" victims; they pander to popular prejudice and help sell papers and TV shows. On an even more dangerous level they not only reflect but help shape public policy—the massive attention Bergalis received for her recent press conferences and Senate appearance has set the stage for widespread mandatory testing and helped ease the way for Illinois Governor Jim Thompson to sign a draconian testing measure last September. The ability of the press to influence public policy adds immeasurably to its own sense of self-importance, and illustrates how susceptible it is to partisan politics and power-brokering.

But when all is said and done the problem with the press coverage [33] on all of these cases is that it relies on soap-opera scenarios and flash-and-trash sound-bite journalism. After almost a decade, the press still has no idea of how to write about AIDS clearly and honestly. People living with AIDS have to be labeled as either "guilty" or "innocent" victims; the failings of the health care system to deal with the range and variety of HIV infections is seen as idiosyncratic and not part of a larger social problem, and the reporting of personal tragedy is seen as more important than consistent and useful prevention guidelines and information.

The publicity surrounding the cases of Marc Christian, Veronica [34] Prego, Kimberly Bergalis, and now Magic Johnson are further indications that society and the media still have a deeply committed investment to making moral judgments about AIDS and to prove, again and again, that the world is divided into good and bad, us and them, even when those categories are not useful, applicable, or right.

Responding to Reading

1. Early in his essay Bronski introduces the concept of "guilty" and "innocent" AIDS victims. Define and illustrate each of these two categories. Why do the media promote this dichotomy? What dangers does Bronski see in the perpetuation of the idea of "guilty" and "innocent" victims?
2. Bronski acknowledges that although the "guilty" and "innocent" categories are not disappearing, they are becoming less rigid. Why do you suppose this is true? If you know someone with AIDS, does this person fit either stereotype?
3. In paragraph 22 Bronski says, "while any AIDS diagnosis is tragic, none is more or less tragic than others." Do you agree? Do you think most people would agree? Explain.

DEAR JOHN WAYNE

Louise Erdrich

Louise Erdrich (1954–), born in North Dakota, is the daughter of a German immigrant and a Chippewa Indian. She first gained her reputation as a writer through publication in magazines such as the *Atlantic Monthly* and *Redbook*. Erdrich has written three novels, *Love Medicine* (1984), *The Beet Queen* (1986), and *Tracks* (1988) and coauthored one, *The Crown of Columbus* (1991). Her most recent work is a nonfiction book, *The Blue Jay's Dance* (1995). In "Dear John Wayne," from *Jacklight* (1984), a collection of her poetry, Erdrich contrasts images of Native Americans on the movie screen with the images of Native American life around her.

August and the drive-in picture is packed.
We lounge on the hood of the Pontiac
surrounded by the slow-burning spirals they sell
at the window, to vanquish the hordes of mosquitoes.

Nothing works. They break through the smoke-screen for blood.   5
Always the look-out spots the Indians first,
spread north to south, barring progress.
The Sioux, or Cheyenne, or some bunch
in spectacular columns, arranged like SAC missiles,
their feathers bristling in the meaningful sunset.   10

The drum breaks. There will be no parlance.[1]
Only the arrows whining, a death-cloud of nerves

---
[1] Conversation. [Eds.]

swarming down on the settlers
who die beautifully, tumbling like dust weeds
into the history that brought us all here   15
together: this wide screen beneath the sign of the bear.

The sky fills, acres of blue squint and eye
that the crowd cheers. His face moves over us,
a thick cloud of vengeance, pitted
like the land that was once flesh. Each rut,   20
each scar makes a promise: *It is
not over, this fight, not as long as you resist.*

Everything we see belongs to us.
A few laughing Indians fall over the hood
slipping in the hot spilled butter.   25
The eye sees a lot, John, but the heart is so blind.
How will you know what you own?
He smiles, a horizon of teeth
the credits reel over, and then the white fields
again blowing in the true-to-life dark.   30
The dark films over everything.
We get into the car
scratching our mosquito bites, speechless and small
as people are when the movie is done.
We are back in ourselves.   35

How can we help but keep hearing his voice,
the flip side of the sound-track, still playing:
Come on, boys, we've got them
where we want them, drunk, running.
They will give us what we want, what we need: 40
The heart is a strange wood inside of everything
we see, burning, doubling, splitting out of its skin.

Responding to Reading

1. How are Native Americans characterized in the film the poem describes?
   How is this characterization different from the way Native Americans are
   portrayed in contemporary films?
2. Do you think the portrayals of Native Americans in old movies are so inaccurate and/or demeaning that the films should not be shown? Or can you
   accept them as relics of a less sensitive, less informed period in our history?
   Explain.
3. Do you think this poem is addressed to John Wayne simply because he was
   featured in films like the one described, or do you think he is meant to serve
   as a symbol for someone—or something—else? Explain.

WRITING

The Media's Message

1. Was there for you, as there was for McMillan, a movie that changed your life—opening a new world, introducing you to new ideas, or giving you new insight into your own life? Write a fan letter to the movie's director.

2. Deborah Tannen comments, "If public discourse is a fight, . . . it's crucial to show 'the other side' even if one has to scour the margins of science or the fringes of lunacy to find it" (6). She warns, however, that "[t]he determination to find another side can spread disinformation rather than lead to truth" (8). Apply these ideas and others in Tannen's essay to the situation Deborah Lipstadt describes in "Denying the Holocaust" in Chapter 10.

3. Discussing her six-year-old son's television habits, Terry McMillan says, "There is hardly anything on TV that he watches that has any real, or at least plausible, drama to it, but you can't miss what you've never had" (24). Evaluate this statement in light of McMillan's and Marie Winn's essays as well as your own experience as a viewer of television. Or, write an editorial for *TV Guide* in which you defend television against its critics.

4. Consider the sentiments voiced in "Dear John Wayne" in light of the two selections in this text by Chief Seattle—"We May Be Brothers" in Chapter 6 and "Letter to President Pierce, 1855" in Chapter 9. How do Chief Seattle's speeches help to explain the media images described in Erdrich's poem?

5. Reconsider the charges leveled at the media by several writers in this chapter, but apply them to the commercial messages that make most magazines and television programs possible. Are magazine ads and television commercials more or less guilty of the sins with which this chapter's writers charge the media?

6. Keep a daily log of the programs you listen to on the radio and watch on television, the movies you see, and the newspapers and magazines you read. After one week, review what you chose to read, listen to, and watch, and consider why you chose what you did and how these different kinds of media have informed, provoked, or entertained you. Chart your habits, including the time you spent and what you selected, and write a report evaluating the impact of various media on you.

7. Do the media present an accurate image of your gender, race, religion, or cultural group? In what ways, if any, is the image unrealistic? In what ways, if any, is it demeaning? You may refer to the selections in this chapter by Erdrich, Deloria, or Jen, but you should focus on specific examples from your own observations. If possible, include recommendations for improving the image of the group you discuss. What can be done to challenge—or change—simplistic or negative images?

8. Should the government continue to support public television and radio? What, if anything, do public radio and television provide that commercial programming does not offer?

9. Steven Stark says, "Whether in the form of the media's obsession with violence or its preoccupation with polls and popularity, the fantasy life of the adolescent male ends up defining much of our political reality" (9). Apply this statement to the observations made by Stephen King about moviegoers and by Deborah Tannen about politicians, journalists, and academics. Does Stark's theory help to explain the traits and behavior King and Tannen discuss?

10. Consider Bronski's ideas about guilty and innocent people with AIDS in light of Barbara Grizzuti Harrison's remarks about victims in "Getting Away with Murder" in Chapter 7. How do you think she might respond to Bronski?

5

WOMEN AND
MEN

Student Voices

"Being a woman in the work force can be difficult. Many women are discriminated against, sexually harassed, or just not taken seriously. Today, a woman needs to be self-confident and self-assured. She must know that she can go out and do her job well."

—*Kim Cerino*

"I don't see any real difficulty being a woman. I don't hate my body or feel weak because of my gender. Still, it does disturb me that the male-female ratio at my school isn't equal and that there are fewer female than male engineering students.

"Certainly there are difficulties being female. You have to have a thick skin. Some men have a hard time with certain assertions or demonstrations of will. Many of these attitudes seem to be going out with my father's generation, however."

—*Elizabeth Zaffarano*

"The entire gender issue confuses me. I know that I'll probably get many women upset by writing this, but it's my opinion. Women are constantly fighting for equal rights, but then they try to use their gender as an excuse not to do certain things or to change things in their favor."

—*John Buchinsky*

"There has definitely been a change in female-male roles since my parents' generation. Females of my generation have a difficult time because they look at their futures differently from the way they did forty years ago. A female is supposed to be not only the ultimate homemaker but also an independent, ambitious member of the working world. Even with all the talk of liberation, most males still only do one thing— earn a living. Sometimes I get really upset thinking about the situation."

—Jennifer Liebl

"During these times of political correctness, it's hard to be a white male. This is because the government has set quotas telling employers how many women and members of minority groups they must hire. White men are made out to be evil beings who are responsible for all the evils of the world. I am not saying that there are not bad men who have done horrible things. What I am saying is that there are a lot of men who are loving and kind, and I wish we would get some credit for this."

—Stephen Berger

"Men have traditionally been the breadwinners of the family. They gained a sense of pride when they were able to take care of their family. They displayed very little emotion even though they had a lot of emotion inside. Women played the more passive role and stayed home to care for their children. The difficulty of women's work was frequently overlooked.

"The feminist movement has helped women improve their status. There are now many more opportunities for women to succeed than there were before. Men continue to hold the majority of senior-level positions, however. There still hasn't been a female president, but there may be one soon."

—Jennifer Falk

---------------------------- **Preparing to Read and Write** ----------------------------

Attitudes about gender have changed dramatically over the past twenty-five years, and they continue to change. For some, the changes have produced confusion and anger as well as liberation. One reason for this confusion is that people no longer have fixed roles to tell them how to behave in public and how to function within their families. Still, many men and women—uncomfortable with the demands of confining gender roles and unhappy with the expectations those roles create—yearn for even less rigidity, for an escape from stereotypes into the flexibility and freedom of a society where roles are not defined solely by gender.

Unfortunately, many people still tend to see men and women in terms of outdated and unrealistic stereotypes: Men are strong, tough, and brave, and women are weak, passive, and in need of protection. Men understand mathematics and science and have a natural aptitude for mechanical tasks. They also have the drive, the aggressiveness, the competitive edge, and the power to succeed. They are never sentimental, and they never cry. Women are better at small, repetitive tasks than at bold, decisive actions. They enjoy, and are good at, domestic activities and have a natural aptitude for nurturing. They may like their jobs, but they will leave them without hesitation to devote themselves to husband and children.

As we read the preceding list of stereotypes, some of us may react neutrally (or even favorably) and others with annoyance; how we react tells us something about our society and something about ourselves. But as a number of writers in this section observe, stereotypes are not just inaccurate; they also limit the way people think, the opportunities to which they have access, the roles they chose to assume, and, ultimately, the positions they occupy in society.

As you read and prepare to write about the selections in this chapter, you may consider the following questions.

- Is the writer male or female? Are you able to tell without reading the author's name or the headnote? Does the writer's gender really matter?

- Is the writer's focus on males, on females, or on both sexes?

- When was the selection written? How do you think the date of publication affects its content?

- Does the selection seem fair-minded? Balanced?

- Does the writer discuss gender as a sexual, political, economic, or social issue?

- What does the writer suggest are the specific advantages or disadvantages of being male? Of being female?

- Does the writer support the status quo, or does he or she suggest that change is necessary? Possible? Inevitable?
- Does the writer recommend specific changes? What are they?
- Is your interpretation of the problem the same as the interpretation presented in the selection? Are your ideas about possible solutions similar to those presented?
- Does the work express the view that men and women are fundamentally different? If so, does it suggest that these differences can (or should) be overcome, or at least lessened?
- Does the writer see gender differences as the result of environment or of heredity?
- Does the work challenge any of your ideas about male-female roles?

TWO PERSPECTIVES ON WOMEN AND MEN

The following two essays both consider the subject of power and its relationship to gender roles and to identity. Barbara Lazear Ascher (1946–), a former attorney and now a columnist and critic, writes in "On Power," an essay from her book *The Habit of Loving* (1989), about her sense of powerlessness as a young associate at a prestigious, largely male law firm in the 1970s. Ascher's latest book is *Landscape without Gravity: A Memoir of Grief* (1993), written after her brother's death from AIDS-related illnesses. Scott Russell Sanders (1945–), author of novels, children's books, science fiction stories, and personal essays, looks at power from a different perspective—that of a poor rural boy who saw himself as having no more power than the women he met at college, who railed at the "joys and privileges of men." Sanders books include *The Paradise of Bombs* (1988), from which "The Men We Carry in Our Minds" is excerpted, *Secrets of the Universe: Scenes from the Journey Home* (1993), and *Staying Put: Making a Home in a Restless World* (1993).

ON POWER

Barbara Lazear Ascher

When I graduated from law school, I was hired by what is known [1] in the business as a Prestigious New York Law Firm. I felt privileged to be associated with talent and money and respectability, to be in a place that promised me four weeks vacation, my own secretary, an office with a window, and, above all, a shot at power. I would not have preferred working for a single practitioner who struggled to pay rent on his windowless, one-room office in the Bronx.

There's a lot to be said for the accouterments of power. Those who [2] asked where I worked immediately assumed, upon being told the name of the firm, that I must have been at the top of my class, an editor of the Law Review and a clerk for a federal judge. I was none of these, but being where the power is frees you from having to explain yourself.

The "outsider's" version of the "insider" is always distorted by the [3] mental glass through which they observe. The outsider tends to think that once inside the power structure the voyage is over, destination reached. No more struggle or strain. But in fact, once you have "arrived," you discover that there are power structures within the power. You may share office space and a central switchboard, but that doesn't mean you are at the controls.

In my firm, the partners (male) took the young associates (also male), resplendent in their red suspenders and newly sported cigars, to lunch, to Dallas, Los Angeles, and Atlanta to meet the clients. The "girl" associates were sent to the library to do research. Actually, they were sent to the library to stay out of trouble. 4

Soon the clients with whom the associates dined were calling them for advice. These associates were learning how to practice law. Those of us hidden away in the stacks were learning how to be invisible. 5

A friend at a similar Prestigious New York Law Firm told me that she had tried and failed to enlist the cooperation of the one woman partner. "I suggested that we, the women associates and she, have monthly luncheons to discuss some of the problems we faced. After all, she'd been one of us." But she was no longer "one of us" and feared that if her partners perceived her as an ally of women associates, they might forget that she was, first and foremost, one of "them." She knew that hanging out with weak sisters was no way to safeguard her tentative grasp of success. 6

Eight years later, when my friend became a partner, she learned that the woman she had approached for help was powerless within the partnership. She was, in the eyes of the men, their token "girl" partner, and power, like beauty, is in the eye of the beholder. She was a lady and that's how she was perceived. How could her mother have known as she trained her daughter for power in the drawing room that what she would want was power in the boardroom? 7

However, even if hers was a token acceptance, she had entered that heady realm, she was feted around town as "the first woman partner" and she proceeded to follow a pattern not unusual for women who achieve some semblance of power. She refused to reach behind to pull other women along. It was too risky. She might fall backwards. I blush to recall that when, in fourth grade I was the only girl on the boys' baseball team, I joined in their systematic "girl trashing." I enthusiastically participated in disparaging conversations about people who were "just girls." Who threw like girls. Who giggled like girls. Who couldn't whistle through their fingers, burp on command or slide into home plate. Then, all I knew was that my power depended on keeping other girls out. Now, I know about identification with the aggressor. 8

Not that it makes much difference. There are uncanny similarities between being the only girl on a fourth grade baseball team and the only woman in bigger boys' games. Take, for instance, the response of Harvard Business School's tenured, female professors when their former colleague, Barbara Bund Jackson, filed suit against the school for its refusal to grant her tenure. Nonsense, these women replied to Jackson's 9 charge of a sexist "institutional bias." Not so, they said of her contention that the school sets "impossible standards for female faculty members." Why shouldn't they? Why should Harvard deviate from the accepted wisdom that a man can occasionally goof off and still be perceived as powerful? It's kind of cute, we say. Oh, look, he's got nice human touches, an ability to have fun. How boyish. How charming. Not so for a woman. She who goofs off is a goof-off.

Tenured Harvard professor Regina E. Herzlinger's response to Jackson's claim of discrimination was, "I don't feel there is . . . friction caused by the fact that there are few women on the faculty . . . I don't think there is discrimination on the basis of sex." Of course there isn't friction for those "few women." And Regina'd better keep quiet if she thinks otherwise. Boys don't like girls who turn around and say, "But what about the other girls?" I certainly never invited my friend Linda to play baseball with us, even though she ran like the wind and threw overhand.   10

But power, who has it and who doesn't, is not limited to the realm of male/female strife. My husband, a physician in practice for many years, volunteers his time, one day a week at a hospital often described with the same breathless reverence as my law firm. This is the place to which ailing shahs and wealthy dowagers come to be healed. The full time attendings (those with the power) don't like the voluntary attendings (those without the power), and occasionally rise up to divest them of responsibility. How, you might ask, when wise and seasoned physicians are willing to give their time, free of charge, to teach students and treat patients, could there be a complaint? The volunteers are not part of the power structure. And power's particular drive is to grab more for itself, an act which invariably involves stripping others of any.   11

Recently, some of the voluntary attendings went to the head of their department and informed him, "You make us feel like second-class citizens." He listened, nodded, and assured: "You are second-class citizens."   12

Irrational, you say? Of course. But whoever thought that the power drive made sense?   13

In fifth grade, secret clubs were the order of the day. The purpose was, first of all, the secret. A secret name. Secret rules. Secret members. Secret meeting places. The purpose was to exclude, which is the first step in establishing a power base. The second is to create fear in those excluded. Those of us who assembled the group of meanest and most popular children had the run of the playground. We were a force to contend with.   14

Recently, when I went to choose a puppy from a litter, I was told, "Don't get the Alpha dog, whatever you do!" It seems that, like their ancestors the wolves, each litter has a leader. He or she is the power in the pack, and once the Alpha dog comes to live with your family, you become the pack.   15

What does the Alpha dog get for his trouble? A certain haughtiness. [16] A certain swagger. What did the Alpha attorneys in my firm get for their power? A certain haughtiness. A certain swagger. And an occasional invitation to the Piping Rock Country Club.

So who cares? We all did. We who sat in the library working on Blue [17] Sky[1] Memos, something my twelve-year-old daughter could have done, given the careful and patronizing instructions we received. We were enraged at being excluded from Making It Big. What we didn't know at the time is that the ones who Make It Big are always watching their backs, but then girls rarely have the opportunity to learn these finer points.

Power sanctions self-centeredness. (It could be argued that that's [18] why girls don't have it—"They're so giving.") It returns you, full circle, to the delicious years of being an infant and toddler when, it seemed, you were the center of the universe. But what is missing at thirty-five, forty, or fifty years of age is the innocence of the infant, the two- or three-year-old. It is a dangerous absence. Self-interest plus muscle power and experience combine to create a being more pervasively harmful than the sandbox bully.

Take, for instance, Manhattan real estate developers. They are cur- [19] rently a favorite target of the less powerful, and are, in some instances, a legitimate target. There are those who use their amassed fortunes to gain political sway by contributing to the campaign funds of elected officials. The elected officials then turn deaf ears to the complaints of less powerful constituents dispossessed from low rent buildings razed to make room for luxury high rises complete with Jacuzzis in every bath.

Donald Trump's song of himself is on the best-seller lists. *Vanity Fair* [20] featured a breathlessly infatuated profile of his wife. Why? Because if you can't be powerful, the next best thing is to fancy yourself on intimate terms with those who are. There is a hunger to know how they make their deals, shop for their children's Christmas presents, stay fresh and alert from five A.M. until Peter Duchin's orchestra plays its last charity ball waltz at midnight. All this, and not a wrinkle in the brow to show for it.

People read about power for the same reason that little girls read [21] *Cinderella*, they want to believe that someday a prince will come to deliver a subject into sovereignty.

One might ask whether adulation of those who are flagrantly self- [22] involved makes any sense when there are thousands of dispossessed sleeping in Grand Central and Pennsylvania Station. It certainly doesn't make mature sense.

---

[1] Hypothetical and thus valueless. [Eds.]

But then power is not necessarily in mature hands. It is most often [23] achieved, and clung to by those whose passion for it is fueled by child-like greed and self-interest. What they find, once they have it, is that being the proud possessor of power bears an uncanny similarity to being the two-year-old with the biggest plastic pail and shovel on the beach. It's a life of nervous guardianship.

I left the law because I wasn't motivated to engage in the struggle [24] required to move myself from library to the light of day and lunches with clients. The struggle would have required molding myself in the partners' images, a hard concept for them to visualize since I was female and they were male. It would have been necessary to remember when to speak and when to keep my mouth shut. I would have had to create an asexual aura. I would have had to work very, very hard.

I left the law because that wasn't the power that interested me. [25] Which is not to say that power itself doesn't interest me. I remember the full glory of being the only girl on the boy's baseball team. I remember the total sense of worthlessness that resulted when I grew breasts and the guys banished me from the pitcher's mound to the powerless world of hopscotch. Power is as tantalizing as a hypnotist's swinging pendulum. Power promises that you will never again be stuck with "the girls." Ask Regina Herzlinger. She knows.

The Men We Carry in Our Minds

Scott Russell Sanders

When I was a boy, the men I knew labored with their bodies. They [1] were marginal farmers, just scraping by, or welders, steelworkers, carpenters; they swept floors, dug ditches, mined coal, or drove trucks, their forearms ropy with muscle; they trained horses, stoked furnaces, built tires, stood on assembly lines wrestling parts onto cars and refrigerators. They got up before light, worked all day long whatever the weather, and when they came home at night they looked as though somebody had been whipping them. In the evenings and on weekends they worked on their own places, tilling gardens that were lumpy with clay, fixing broken-down cars, hammering on houses that were always too drafty, too leaky, too small.

The bodies of the men I knew were twisted and maimed in ways [2] visible and invisible. The nails of their hands were black and split, the hands tattooed with scars. Some had lost fingers. Heavy lifting had given many of them finicky backs and guts weak from hernias. Racing against conveyor belts had given them ulcers. Their ankles and knees ached from years of standing on concrete. Anyone who had worked for long around machines was hard of hearing. They squinted, and the skin of their faces was creased like the leather of old work gloves. There were times, studying them, when I dreaded growing up. Most of them coughed, from dust or cigarettes, and most of them drank cheap wine or whiskey, so their eyes looked bloodshot and bruised. The fathers of my friends always seemed older than the mothers. Men wore out sooner. Only women lived into old age.

As a boy I also knew another sort of men, who did not sweat and   3
break down like mules. They were soldiers, and so far as I could tell they scarcely worked at all. During my early school years we lived on a military base, an arsenal in Ohio, and every day I saw GIs in the guard-shacks, on the stoops of barracks, at the wheels of olive drab Chevrolets. The chief fact of their lives was boredom. Long after I left the Arsenal I came to recognize the sour smell the soldiers gave off as that of souls in limbo. They were all waiting—for wars, for transfers, for leaves, for promotions, for the end of their hitch—like so many braves waiting for the hunt to begin. Unlike the warriors of older tribes, however, they would have no say about when the battle would start or how it would be waged. Their waiting was broken only when they practiced for war. They fired guns at targets, drove tanks across the churned-up fields of the military reservation, set off bombs in the wrecks of old fighter planes. I knew this was all play. But I also felt certain that when the hour for killing arrived, they would kill. When the real shooting started, many of them would die. This was what soldiers were *for*, just as a hammer was for driving nails.

Warriors and toilers: those seemed, in my boyhood vision, to be the   4
chief destinies for men. They weren't the only destinies, as I learned from having a few male teachers, from reading books, and from watching television. But the men on television—the politicians, the astronauts, the generals, the savvy lawyers, the philosophical doctors, the bosses who gave orders to both soldiers and laborers—seemed as removed and unreal to me as the figures in tapestries. I could no more imagine growing up to become one of these cool, potent creatures than I could imagine becoming a prince.

A nearer and more hopeful example was that of my father, who had   5
escaped from a red-dirt farm to a tire factory, and from the assembly line to the front office. Eventually he dressed in a white shirt and tie. He carried himself as if he had been born to work with his mind. But his body, remembering the earlier years of slogging work, began to give out on him in his fifties, and it quit on him entirely before he turned sixty-five. Even such a partial escape from man's fate as he had accomplished did not seem possible for most of the boys I knew. They joined the Army, stood in line for jobs in the smoky plants, helped build highways. They

were bound to work as their fathers had worked, killing themselves or preparing to kill others.

A scholarship enabled me not only to attend college, a rare enough feat in my circle, but even to study in a university meant for the children of the rich. Here I met for the first time young men who had assumed from birth that they would lead lives of comfort and power. And for the first time I met women who told me that men were guilty of having kept all the joys and privileges of the earth for themselves. I was baffled. What privileges? What joys? I thought about the maimed, dismal lives of most of the men back home. What had they stolen from their wives and daughters? The right to go five days a week, twelve months a year, for thirty or forty years to a steel mill or a coal mine? The right to drop bombs and die in war? The right to feel every leak in the roof, every gap in the fence, every cough in the engine, as a wound they must mend? The right to feel, when the lay-off comes or the plant shuts down, not only afraid but ashamed?

I was slow to understand the deep grievances of women. This was because, as a boy, I had envied them. Before college, the only people I had ever known who were interested in art or music or literature, the only ones who read books, the only ones who ever seemed to enjoy a sense of ease and grace were the mothers and daughters. Like the men-folk, they fretted about money, they scrimped and made-do. But, when the pay stopped coming in, they were not the ones who had failed. Nor did they have to go to war, and that seemed to me a blessed fact. By comparison with the narrow, ironclad days of fathers, there was an ex-pansiveness, I thought, in the days of mothers. They went to see neighbors, to shop in town, to run errands at school, at the library, at church. No doubt, had I looked harder at their lives, I would have envied them less. It was not my fate to become a woman, so it was easier for me to see the graces. Few of them held jobs outside the home, and those who did filled thankless roles as clerks and waitresses. I didn't see, then, what a prison a house could be, since houses seemed to me brighter, handsomer places than any factory. I did not realize—because such things were never spoken of—how often women suffered from men's bullying. I did learn about the wretchedness of abandoned wives, single mothers, wid-ows; but I also learned about the wretchedness of lone men. Even then I could see how exhausting it was for a mother to cater all day to the needs of young children. But if I had been asked, as a boy, to choose be-tween tending a baby and tending a machine, I think I would have cho-sen the baby. (Having now tended both, I know I would choose the baby.)

So I was baffled when the women at college accused me and my sex of having cornered the world's pleasures. I think something like my baf-flement has been felt by other boys (and by girls as well) who grew up in dirt-poor farm country, in mining country, in black ghettos, in Hispanic barrios, in the shadows of factories, in Third World nations—any place where the fate of men is as grim and bleak as the fate of women. Toilers and warriors. I realize now how ancient these identities are, how deep the tug they exert on men, the undertow of a thousand generations. The miseries I saw, as a boy, in the lives of nearly all men I continue to see in the lives of many—the body-breaking toil, the tedium, the call to be tough, the humiliating powerlessness, the battle for a living and for territory.

When the women I met at college thought about the joys and priv- 9 ileges of men, they did not carry in their minds the sort of men I had known in my childhood. They thought of their fathers, who were bankers, physicians, architects, stockbrokers, the big wheels of the big cities. These fathers rode the train to work or drove cars that cost more than any of my childhood houses. They were attended from morning to night by female helpers, wives and nurses and secretaries. They were never laid off, never short of cash at month's end, never lined up for welfare. These fathers made decisions that mattered. They ran the world.

The daughters of such men wanted to share in this power, this 10 glory. So did I. They yearned for a say over their future, for jobs worthy of their abilities, for the right to live at peace, unmolested, whole. Yes, I thought, yes yes. The difference between me and these daughters was that they saw me, because of my sex, as destined from birth to become like their fathers, and therefore as an enemy to their desires. But I knew better. I wasn't an enemy, in fact or in feeling. I was an ally. If I had known, then, how to tell them so, would they have believed me? Would they now?

Responding to Reading

1. How does Ascher define power? Do you think she has a realistic definition of power? According to Ascher's definition, do you have power?
2. Do you think Ascher was right to leave the law? Could you argue that her decision to leave only helped to confirm her male bosses' opinion of women?
3. What do the men Sanders carries in his mind have in common? How have they helped shape his attitude toward gender? Do you know men like Sanders's father? Do you know men (or women) who have "made decisions that mattered" (9)?
4. Do you agree with Sanders that women believe all men have greater access to power than they themselves do? Do you agree that women who believe this are mistaken?
5. How do you think Ascher would react to Sanders's essay? Would she see him as an ally or as an enemy?
6. Whom do you see as the most—and least—powerful people in society? Why? Does their status have anything to do with gender?

MARY CASSATT

Mary Gordon

Novelist and critic Mary Gordon (1940–) was born in Far Rockaway, New York, and educated at Barnard and Syracuse universities. Her first novel, *Final Payments* (1978), was an immediate critical and popular success and was followed by the equally successful *The Company of Women* (1980), *Men and Angels* (1985), and *The Rest of Life* (1993). She lives and writes in upstate New York. In the following selection from her 1991 collection of essays *Good Boys and Dead Girls*, Gordon considers the life and career of American Impressionist painter Mary Cassatt (1845–1926), who "exemplified the paradoxes of the woman artist."

When Mary Cassatt's father was told of her decision to become a 1
painter, he said: "I would rather see you dead." When Edgar Degas saw a show of Cassatt's etchings, his response was: "I am not willing to admit that a woman can draw that well." When she returned to Philadelphia after twenty-eight years abroad, having achieved renown as an Impressionist painter and the esteem of Degas, Huysmans, Pissarro, and Berthe Morisot, the *Philadelphia Ledger* reported: "Mary Cassatt, sister of Mr. Cassatt, president of the Pennsylvania Railroad, returned from Europe yesterday. She has been studying painting in France and owns the smallest Pekingese dog in the world."

Mary Cassatt exemplified the paradoxes of the woman artist. Cut off 2
from the experiences that are considered the entitlement of her male counterpart, she has access to a private world a man can only guess at. She has, therefore, a kind of information he is necessarily deprived of. If she has almost impossible good fortune—means, self-confidence, heroic energy and dedication, the instinct to avoid the seductions of ordinary domestic life, which so easily become a substitute for creative work—she may pull off a miracle: she will combine the skill and surety that she has stolen from the world of men with the vision she brings from the world of women.

Mary Cassatt pulled off such a miracle. But if her story is particu- 3
larly female, it is also American. She typifies one kind of independent American spinster who keeps reappearing in our history in forms as various as Margaret Fuller and Katharine Hepburn. There is an astringency in such women, a fierce discipline, a fearlessness, a love of work. But they are not inhuman. At home in the world, they embrace it with a kind of aristocratic greed that knows nothing of excess. Balance, proportion, an instinct for the distant and the formal, an exuberance, a vividness, a

clarity of line: the genius of Mary Cassatt includes all these elements. The details of the combination are best put down to grace; the outlines may have been her birthright.

She was one of those wealthy Americans whose parents took the   4
children abroad for their education and medical care. The James family comes to mind and, given her father's attitude toward her career, it is remarkable that Cassatt didn't share the fate of Alice James.[1] But she had a remarkable mother, intelligent, encouraging of her children. When her daughter wanted to study in Paris, and her husband disapproved, Mrs. Cassatt arranged to accompany Mary as her chaperone.

From her beginnings as an art student, Cassatt was determined to follow the highest standards of craftsmanship. She went first to Paris, then to Italy, where she studied in Parma with Raimondi and spent many hours climbing up scaffolding (to the surprise of the natives) to study the work of Correggio and Parmigianino. Next, she was curious to visit Spain to look at the Spanish masters and to make use of the picturesque landscape and models. Finally, she returned to Paris, where she was to make her home, and worked with Degas, her sometime friend and difficult mentor. There has always been speculation as to whether or not they were lovers; her burning their correspondence gave the rumor credence. But I believe that they were not; she was, I think, too protective of her talent to make herself so vulnerable to Degas as a lover would have to be. But I suppose I don't believe it because I cherish, instead, the notion that a man and a woman can be colleagues and friends without causing an excuse for raised eyebrows. Most important, I want to believe they were not lovers because if they were, the trustworthiness of his extreme praise grows dilute.

She lived her life until late middle age among her family. Her   6
beloved sister, Lydia, one of her most cherished models, had always lived as a semi-invalid and died early, in Mary's flat, of Bright's disease. Mary was closely involved with her brothers and their children. Her bond with her mother was profound: when Mrs. Cassatt died, in 1895, Mary's work began to decline. At the severing of her last close familial tie, when her surviving brother died as a result of an illness he contracted when traveling with her to Egypt, she broke down entirely. "How we try for happiness, poor things, and how we don't find it. The best cure is hard work—if only one has the health for it," she said, and lived that way.

Not surprisingly, perhaps, Cassatt's reputation has suffered because   7
of the prejudice against her subject matter. Mothers and children: what could be of lower prestige, more vulnerable to the charge of sentimentality. Yet if one looks at the work of Mary Cassatt, one sees how tri-

---

[1] Alice James, a woman of Cassatt's generation and social rank, sublimated her own intellectual and artistic talents to those of her brothers, the novelist Henry and the philosopher William. [Eds.]

umphantly she avoids the pitfalls of sentimentality because of the astringent rigor of her eye and craft. The Cassatt iconography dashes in an instant the notion of the comfortable, easily natural fit of the maternal embrace. Again and again in her work, the child's posture embodies the ambivalence of his or her dependence. In *The Family*, the mother and child exist in positions of unease; the strong diagonals created by their postures of opposition give the pictures their tense strength, a strength that renders sentimental sweetness impossible. In *Ellen Mary Cassatt in a White Coat* and *Girl in the Blue Arm Chair*, the children seem imprisoned and dwarfed by the trappings of respectable life. The lines of Ellen's coat, which create such a powerful framing device, entrap the round and living child. The sulky little girl in the armchair seems about to be swallowed up by the massive cylinders of drawing room furniture and the strong curves of emptiness that are the floor. In *The Bath*, the little girl has all the unformed charming awkwardness of a young child: the straight limbs, the loose stomach. But these are not the stuff of Gerber babies—even of the children of Millais. In this picture, the center of interest is not the relationship between the mother and the child but the strong vertical and diagonal stripes of the mother's dress, whose opposition shape the picture with an insistence that is almost abstract.

Cassatt changed the iconography of the depiction of mothers and children. Hers do not look out into and meet the viewer's eye; neither supplicating nor seductive, they are absorbed in their own inner thoughts. Minds are at work here, a concentration unbroken by an awareness of themselves as objects to be gazed at by the world. [8]

The brilliance of Cassatt's colors, the clarity and solidity of her forms, are the result of her love and knowledge of the masters of European painting. She had a second career as adviser to great collectors: she believed passionately that America must, for the sake of its artists, possess masterpieces, and she paid no attention to the outrage of her European friends, who felt their treasures were being sacked by barbarians. A young man visiting her in her old age noted her closed mind regarding the movement of the moderns. She thought American painters should stay home and not become "café loafers in Paris. Why should they come to Europe?" she demanded. "When I was young it was different. . . . Our Museums had not great paintings for the students to study. Now that has been corrected and something must be done to save our young over here." [9]

One can hear the voice of the old, irascible, still splendid aunt in that comment and see the gesture of her stick toward the Left Bank.[2] Cassatt was blinded by cataracts; the last years of her life were spent in a fog. She became ardent on the subjects of suffragism, socialism, and spiritualism; the horror of the First World War made her passionate in her [10]

---

[2] Paris neighborhood populated by artists, students, and bohemians. [Eds.]

conviction that mankind itself must change. She died at her country estate near Grasse, honored by the French, recipient of the Légion d'honneur, but unappreciated in America, rescued only recently from misunderstanding, really, by feminist art critics. They allowed us to begin to see her for what she is: a master of line and color whose great achievement was to take the "feminine" themes of mothers, children, women with their thoughts alone, to endow them with grandeur without withholding from them the tenderness that fits so easily alongside the rigor of her art.

Responding to Reading

1. Gordon says Cassatt "exemplified the paradoxes of the woman artist" (2). What do you suppose she means? Do you think these paradoxes exist today? Explain.
2. As Gordon points out, Cassatt was wealthy. Do you believe she would have been able to accomplish what she did if she had been middle class or poor? Does the fact that she was wealthy make you less sympathetic to her?
3. In paragraph 3 Gordon says Cassatt's story is "particularly female, [but] it is also American." In what sense is her story "particularly female"? In what sense is it American?

FIGHTING BACK

Stanton L. Wormley, Jr.

Stanton L. Wormley, Jr. (1951–), who holds a B.A. in Spanish from Howard University and a master's in forensic science from George Washington University, has held various administrative positions at Howard and at the University of Southern Maine in Portland. Now a freelance writer based in Maine, Wormley has published technical writing pieces, video scripts for industrial training films, science articles, and three articles in *American Negro Biography* about a Washington, D.C., family. In addition, he has published a number of articles about shooting and firearms, subjects on which he says he plans to concentrate in the future. In the following essay Wormley talks about the lessons to be learned from fighting back—and from not fighting back— especially for members of minority groups who feel "disenfranchised and often victimized by discrimination and poverty."

In the spring of 1970, I was an 18-year-old army private at Fort Jackson, S.C. I had been in the Army for less than six months and was still   1 making the difficult transition from life as an only child in an upper-middle-class black family. One rite of passage was particularly intense: on a cool April night, a drunken white soldier whom I barely knew attacked me as I lay sleeping.

My recollection of the incident is, in some details, still hazy. Like the 2 seven other men in the squad bay, I was asleep in my bunk. I half-remember some vigorous off-key singing, the ceiling light going on and someone roughly shaking my foot. I sat up, drowsily irritated at being disturbed. Everything happened very quickly then: a voice began shouting, an arm tightened around my neck and a fist pounded the top of my head. I was still somewhat asleep and confused. Why was this happening to me? It didn't occur to me to fight. I simply covered my head as best I could. There was a hubbub, arms reaching in to separate us and then the sight of the man above me, struggling against the others holding him back, his face red with fury. By then I was fully awake, and I saw the strained tendons in the man's neck, the wormlike vein pulsing at his temple, the spittle that sprayed as he screamed obscenities at me. I wasn't hurt, at least not physically, and all I could do was stare, bewildered. I never did discover what had provoked him.

Afterward, I was angrily confronted by a young black streetwise 3 soldier named Morris. He eyed me with unconcealed contempt. "What the hell's wrong with you, man?" he demanded. "Why didn't you fight back? I would've killed that mother." I had no answer for him. How could I have made him understand the sheltered world of my childhood, in which violence was deplored and careful deliberation encouraged. I was brought up to *think,* not just react.

Nevertheless, that question—*Why didn't I fight back?*—haunted me 4 long after the incident had been forgotten by everyone else. Was I less of a man for not having beaten my attacker to a bloody pulp? Morris—and undoubtedly others—certainly thought so. And so, perhaps, would the majority of American men. The ability and the will to fight back are integral parts of our society's conception of manhood. It goes beyond mere self-defense, I think, for there is a subtle but significant difference between self-defense and fighting back. Self-defense is essentially passive; it involves no rancor, pride or ego. Running away from danger is what martial-arts instructors sometimes recommend as the appropriate response, the best self-defense strategy. Fighting back, on the other hand, is active and defiant. It involves the adoption of an attitude that one's retribution is morally justified—or even, at times, morally obligatory.

And we American men buy that attitude—especially those of us who 5 are members of minority groups. For us, largely disenfranchised and often victimized by discrimination and poverty, fighting back is a statement of individual potency and self-determination. It is the very antithesis of victimization: it is a sign of empowerment. The symbolic consequences of fighting back—or failing to do so—reflect upon the group as a whole. To Morris, I had disgraced the entire black American population.

I suppose that there are still situations in which immediate, violent retaliation is necessary. Sometimes it seems that fighting back is the only way to command respect in the world. Women are now learning that unfortunate lesson, as did blacks and other minorities in recent decades. I can't help feeling, however, that when one gains the ability to fight back one loses something as well. What that something is, I can't easily define: a degree of compassion, perhaps, or tolerance or empathy. It is a quality I hope is possessed by the men in Washington and Moscow who have the power to dispense the ultimate retribution.

Once in a great while, past events are repeated, granting people a chance either to redeem themselves or to relive their mistakes. Two years ago, in a small roadside diner in Virginia, a man—again white, again drunk—chanced to make a derogatory remark to me. I was sitting with my back to him and ignored it. Thinking I had not heard him, he drew close to repeat his taunt, grabbing my shoulder. I suppose I could have moved away, shaken his hand off or complained to the manager. But the accumulated frustrations of years of ignoring such remarks—plus the memory of the incident at Fort Jackson, dictated otherwise. Before I knew what was happening, I was up out of my chair. I hit the man hard in the stomach and he sank to one knee with a moan. Grasping his collar, I almost hit again, but it was obvious that he had had enough. He looked up at me, gasping, his face contorted with pain and fear. The man was perhaps 50, of average size, with a fleshy, florid face surmounted by close-cropped gray bristle. I noted that he had bad teeth, a fact that gave me a moment of spiteful satisfaction. Suddenly sober, he stammered something unintelligible—it might have been an apology—and I let him go.

As I walked away, I was filled with a feeling of exultation. I had not stopped to wonder why; I had not been checked by compassion or sympathy. I had retaliated and it had felt good. But later, my exhilaration passed, leaving a strange sensation of hollowness. I felt vaguely embarrassed, even ashamed. In my mind I was still confident I had acted rightly, but my heart was no longer sure. I remembered my fury, and the quiet way the people in the diner had watched me stalk angrily away. I remembered, too, the abject grimace on the man's face, partly from the pain of the blow and partly in anticipation of a second; and I realized that there was a trace of sadness in the knowledge that I, too, had learned to fight back.

Responding to Reading

1. Have you ever been in a situation in which you could have fought back and did not? Why did you choose not to fight? Did you regret your decision?
2. In many ways Wormley's initial situation is similar to that of a woman:

When first attacked, his instinctive response is to protect himself; it simply does not occur to him to fight back. Later he says, "When one gains the ability to fight back one loses something as well" (6). Do you think most women would agree with him? Do you agree?

3. Is the fact that Wormley is African American of any special significance in this essay? Is the fact that he is an only child? That he was 18 at the time of the incident he describes? That he comes from an upper-middle-class family? Does any of this information influence your expectations about how Wormley might respond to a physical challenge? If so, how?

WHY I WANT A WIFE

Judy Brady

Judy Brady (1937–) studied painting in college and wanted to pursue painting as a career. Instead, she has said, she was discouraged from an art career in higher education by her male teachers, and so she married and had a family. First a housewife, Brady began to write articles on social issues and became involved in the feminist movement. In recent years she has edited several books about women and cancer. Her popular essay "Why I Want a Wife" appeared in the preview issue of *Ms.* in 1972.

I belong to that classification of people known as wives. I am A 1
Wife. And, not altogether incidentally, I am a mother.

Not too long ago a male friend of mine appeared on the scene fresh 2
from a recent divorce. He had one child, who is, of course, with his ex-wife. He is looking for another wife. As I thought about him while I was ironing one evening, it suddenly occurred to me that I, too, would like to have a wife. Why do I want a wife?

I would like to go back to school so that I can become economically 3
independent, support myself, and, if need be, support those dependent upon me. I want a wife who will work and send me to school. And while I am going to school I want a wife to take care of my children. I want a wife to keep track of the children's doctor and dentist appointments. And to keep track of mine, too. I want a wife to make sure my children eat properly and are kept clean. I want a wife who will wash the children's clothes and keep them mended. I want a wife who is a good nurturant attendant to my children, who arranges for their schooling, makes sure that they have an adequate social life with their peers, takes them to the park, the zoo, etc. I want a wife who takes care of the children

when they are sick, a wife who arranges to be around when the children need special care, because, of course, I cannot miss classes at school. My wife must arrange to lose time at work and not lose the job. It may mean a small cut in my wife's income from time to time, but I guess I can tolerate that. Needless to say, my wife will arrange and pay for the care of the children while my wife is working.

I want a wife who will take care of *my* physical needs. I want a wife   4
who will keep my house clean. A wife who will pick up after me. I want a wife who will keep my clothes clean, ironed, mended, replaced when need be, and who will see to it that my personal things are kept in their proper place so that I can find what I need the minute I need it. I want a wife who cooks the meals, a wife who is a *good* cook. I want a wife who will plan the menus, do the necessary grocery shopping, prepare the meals, serve them pleasantly, and then do the cleaning up while I do my studying. I want a wife who will care for me when I am sick and sympathize with my pain and loss of time from school. I want a wife to go along when our family takes a vacation so that someone can continue to care for me and my children when I need a rest and change of scene.

I want a wife who will not bother me with rambling complaints   5
about a wife's duties. But I want a wife who will listen to me when I feel the need to explain a rather difficult point I have come across in my course of studies. And I want a wife who will type my papers for me when I have written them.

I want a wife who will take care of the details of my social life. When   6
my wife and I are invited out by friends, I want a wife who will take care of the babysitting arrangements. When I meet people at school that I like and want to entertain, I want a wife who will have the house clean, will prepare a special meal, serve it to me and my friends, and not interrupt when I talk about the things that interest me and my friends. I want a wife who will have arranged that the children are fed and ready for bed before my guests arrive so that the children do not bother us. I want a wife who takes care of the needs of my guests so that they feel comfortable, who makes sure that they have an ashtray, that they are passed the hors d'oeuvres, that they are offered a second helping of the food, that their wine glasses are replenished when necessary, that their coffee is served to them as they like it. And I want a wife who knows that sometimes I need a night out by myself.

I want a wife who is sensitive to my sexual needs, a wife who makes   7
love passionately and eagerly when I feel like it, a wife who makes sure that I am satisfied. And, of course, I want a wife who will not demand sexual attention when I am not in the mood for it. I want a wife who assumes the complete responsibility for birth control, because I do not want more children. I want a wife who will remain sexually faithful to me so that I do not have to clutter up my intellectual life with jealousies. And I want a wife who understands that *my* sexual needs may entail

more than strict adherence to monogamy. I must, after all, be able to relate to people as fully as possible.

If, by chance, I find another person more suitable as a wife than   8
the wife I already have, I want the liberty to replace my present wife with another one. Naturally, I will expect a fresh, new life; my wife will take the children and be solely responsible for them so that I am left free.

When I am through with school and have a job, I want my wife to   9
quit working and remain at home so that my wife can more fully and completely take care of a wife's duties.

My God, who *wouldn't* want a wife?   10

Responding to Reading

1. What is your definition of a wife? How closely does it conform to Brady's? Do you know any women who meet Brady's criteria?
2. This essay, written over twenty years ago, has been anthologized many times. To what do you attribute its continued popularity? Is the essay dated?
3. What is your emotional response to Brady's grievances? Are you sympathetic? Impatient? Explain your reactions.

THE GOOD NEWS IS: THESE
~ ARE NOT THE BEST YEARS
OF YOUR LIFE

Gloria Steinem

Feminist writer, editor, speaker, and political activist Gloria Steinem (1934–) was born in Toledo, Ohio. After graduation from college, she became active in the women's movement as an organizer and speaker, worked as a journalist, and founded *Ms.* magazine in 1971. Steinem came to national prominence with her essay "I Was a Playboy Bunny," a humorous and sarcastic exposé of the harassment she suffered on the job. Her most recent books are *Revolution from Within: A Book of Self-Esteem* (1992) and *Moving Beyond Words* (1993). Of social change, she has said, "When one member of a group changes, it shifts the balance for everyone, and when one group changes, it changes the balance of society." In the following essay, first published in *Ms.* in 1979, Steinem asserts that women, unlike men, grow "more radical with age."

If you had asked me a decade or more ago, I certainly would have [1] said the campus was the first place to look for the feminist or any other revolution. I also would have assumed that student-age women, like student-age men, were much more likely to be activist and open to change than their parents. After all, campus revolts have a long and well-publicized tradition, from the students of medieval France, whose "heresy" was suggesting that the university be separate from the church, through the anticolonial student riots of British India; from students who led the cultural revolution of the People's Republic of China, to campus demonstrations against the Shah of Iran. Even in this country, with far less tradition of student activism, the populist movement to end the war in Vietnam was symbolized by campus protests and mistrust of anyone over thirty.

It has taken me many years of traveling as a feminist speaker and or- [2] ganizer to understand that I was wrong about women; at least, about women acting on their own behalf. In activism, as in so many other things, I had been educated to assume that men's cultural pattern was the natural or the only one. If student years were the peak time of re- bellion and openness to change for men, then the same must be true for women. In fact, a decade of listening to every kind of women's group— from brown-bag lunchtime lectures organized by office workers to all- night rap sessions at campus women's centers; from housewives' self- help groups to campus rallies—has convinced me that the reverse is more often true. Women may be the one group that grows more radical with age. Though some students are big exceptions to this rule, women in general don't begin to challenge the politics of our own lives until later.

Looking back, I realize that this pattern has been true for my life, [3] too. My college years were full of uncertainties and the personal con- servatism that comes from trying to win approval and fit into the prop- er grown-up and womanly role whether that means finding a well-to- do man to be supported by or a male radical to support. Nonetheless, I went right on assuming that brave exploring youth and cowardly con- servative old age were the norms for everybody, and that I must be just an isolated and guilty accident. Though every generalization based on female culture has many exceptions, and should never be used as a crutch or excuse, I think we might be less hard on ourselves and each other as students, feel better about our potential for change as we grow older—and educate reporters who announce feminism's demise because its red-hot center is not on campus—if we figured out that for most of us as women, the traditional college period is an unrealistic and cautious time. Consider a few of the reasons.

As students, women are probably treated with more equality than [4] we ever will be again. For one thing, we're consumers. The school is only too glad to get the tuitions we pay, or that our families or government grants pay on our behalf. With population rates declining because of women's increased power over childbearing, that money is even more vital to a school's existence. Yet more than most consumers, we're too transient to have much power as a group. If our families are paying our tuition, we may have even less power.

As young women, whether students or not, we're still in the stage 5 most valued by male-dominant cultures: We have our full potential as workers, wives, sex partners, and childbearers.

That means we haven't yet experienced the life events that are most 6 radicalizing for women: entering the paid-labor force and discovering how women are treated there; marrying and finding out that it is not yet an equal partnership; having children and discovering who is responsible for them and who is not; and aging, still a greater penalty for women than for men.

Furthermore, new ambitions nourished by the rebirth of feminism 7 may make young women feel and behave a little like a classical immigrant group. We are determined to prove ourselves, to achieve academic excellence, and to prepare for interesting and successful careers. More noses are kept to more grindstones in an effort to demonstrate newfound abilities, and perhaps to allay suspicions that women still have to have more and better credentials than men. This doesn't leave much time for activism. Indeed, we may not yet know that it is necessary.

In addition, the very progress into previously all-male careers that 8 may be revolutionary for women is seen as conservative and conformist by outside critics. Assuming male radicalism to be the measure of change, they interpret any concern with careers as evidence of "campus conservatism." In fact, "dropping out" may be a departure for men, but "dropping in" is a new thing for women. Progress lies in the direction we have not been.

Like most groups of the newly arrived or awakened, our faith in ed- 9 ucation and paper degrees also has yet to be shaken. For instance, the percentage of women enrolled in colleges and universities has been increasing at the same time that the percentage of men has been decreasing. Among students entering college in 1978, women *outnumbered* men for the first time. This hope of excelling at the existing game is probably reinforced by the greater cultural pressure on females to be "good girls" and observe somebody else's rules.

Though we may know intellectually that we need to have new 10 games with new rules, we probably haven't quite absorbed such facts as the high unemployment rate among female Ph.D.s; the lower average salary among women college graduates of all races than among counterpart males who graduated from high school or less; the middle-management ceiling against which even those eagerly hired new business-school graduates seem to bump their heads after five or ten years; and the barrier-breaking women in nontraditional fields who become the first fired when recession hits. Sadly enough, we may have to personally experience some of these reality checks before we accept the idea that lawsuits, activism, and group pressure will have to accompany our individual excellence and crisp new degrees.

Then there is the female guilt trip, student edition. If we're not sail- [11] ing along as planned, it must be *our* fault. If our mothers didn't "do anything" with their educations, it must have been *their* fault. If we can't study as hard as we think we must (because women still have to be better prepared than men), and have a substantial personal and sexual life at the same time (because women are supposed to care more about relationships than men do), then we feel inadequate, as if each of us were individually at fault for a problem that is actually culture-wide.

I've yet to be on a campus where most women weren't worrying [12] about some aspect of combining marriage, children, and a career. I've yet to find one where many men were worrying about the same thing. Yet women will go right on suffering from the double-role problem and terminal guilt until men are encouraged, pressured, or otherwise forced, individually and collectively, to integrate themselves into the "women's work" of raising children and homemaking. Until then, and until there are changed job patterns to allow equal parenthood, children will go right on growing up with the belief that only women can be loving and nurturing, and only men can be intellectual or active outside the home. Each half of the world will go on limiting the full range of its human talent.

Finally, there is the intimate political training that hits women in the [13] teens and early twenties: the countless ways we are still brainwashed into assuming that women are dependent on men for our basic identities, both in our work and our personal lives, much more than vice versa. After all, if we're going to enter a marriage system that's still legally designed for a person and a half, submit to an economy in which women still average about fifty-nine cents on the dollar earned by men, and work mainly as support staff and assistants, or co-directors and vice-presidents at best, then we have to be convinced that we are not whole people on our own.

In order to make sure that we will see ourselves as half-people, and [14] thus be addicted to getting our identity from serving others, society tries hard to convert us as young women into "man junkies"; that is, into people who are addicted to regular shots of male-approval and presence, both professionally and personally. We need a man standing next to us, actually and figuratively, whether it's at work, on Saturday night, or throughout life. (If only men realized how little it matters *which* man is standing there, they would understand that this addiction depersonalizes them, too.) Given the danger to a male-dominant system if young women stop internalizing this political message of derived identity, it's no wonder that those who try to kick the addiction—and, worse yet, to help other women do the same—are likely to be regarded as odd or dangerous by everyone from parents to peers.

With all that pressure combined with little experience, it's no wonder that younger women are often less able to support each other. Even young women who espouse feminist goals as individuals may refrain from identifying themselves as "feminist": it's okay to want equal pay for yourself (just one small reform) but it's not okay to want equal pay for women as a group (an economic revolution). Some retreat into individualized career obsessions as a way of avoiding this dangerous discovery of shared experience with women as a group. Others retreat into the safe middle ground of "I'm not a feminist but. . . ." Still others become politically active, but only on issues that are taken seriously by their male counterparts. [15]

The same lesson about the personal conservatism of younger women is taught by the history of feminism. If I hadn't been conned into believing the masculine stereotype of youth as the "natural" time for freedom and rebellion, a time of "sowing wild oats" that actually is made possible by the assurance of power and security later on, I could have figured out the female pattern of activism by looking at women's movements of the past. [16]

In this country, for instance, the nineteenth-century wave of feminism was started by older women who had been through the radicalizing experience of getting married and becoming the legal chattel of their husbands (or the equally radicalizing experience of *not* getting married and being treated as spinsters). Most of them had also worked in the antislavery movement and learned from the political parallels between race and sex. In other countries, that wave was also led by women who were past the point of maximum pressure toward marriageability and conservatism. [17]

Looking at the first decade of this second wave, it's clear that the early feminist activist and consciousness-raising groups of the 1960s were organized by women who had experienced the civil rights movement, or homemakers who had discovered that raising kids and cooking didn't occupy all their talents. While most campuses of the late sixties were still circulating the names of illegal abortionists privately (after all, abortion could damage our marriage value), slightly older women were holding press conferences and speak-outs about the reality of abortions (including their own, even though that often meant confessing to an illegal act) and demanding reform or repeal of antichoice laws. Though rape had been a quiet epidemic on campus for generations, younger women victims were still understandably fearful of speaking up, and campuses encouraged silence in order to retain their reputation for safety with tuition-paying parents. It took many off-campus speakouts, demonstrations against laws of evidence and police procedures, and testimonies in state legislatures before most student groups began [18] to make demands on campus and local cops for greater rape protection. In fact, "date rape"—the common campus phenomenon of a young woman being raped by someone she knows, perhaps even by several students in a fraternity house—is just now being exposed. Marital rape, a more difficult legal issue, was taken up several years ago. As for battered women and the attendant exposé of husbands and lovers as more statistically dangerous than unknown muggers in the street, that issue still seems to be thought of as a largely noncampus concern, yet at many of the colleges and universities where I've spoken, there has been at least one case within current student memory of a young woman beaten or murdered by a jealous lover.

This cultural pattern of youthful conservatism makes the growing [19] number of older women going back to school very important. They are life examples and pragmatic activists who radicalize women young enough to be their daughters. Now that the median female undergraduate age in this country is twenty-seven because so many older women have returned, the campus is becoming a major place for cross-generational connections.

None of this should denigrate the courageous efforts of young [20] women, especially women on campus, and the many changes they've pioneered. On the contrary, they should be seen as even more remarkable for surviving the conservative pressures, recognizing societal problems they haven't yet fully experienced, and organizing successfully in the midst of a transient student population. Every women's history course, rape hot line, or campus newspaper that is finally covering *all* the news; every feminist professor whose job has been created or tenure saved by student pressure, or male administrator whose consciousness has been permanently changed; every counselor who's stopped guiding women one way and men another; every lawsuit that's been fueled by student energies against unequal athletic funds or graduate school requirements: all those accomplishments are even more impressive when seen against the backdrop of the female pattern of activism.

Finally, it would help to remember that a feminist revolution rarely [21] resembles a masculine-style one—just as a young woman's most radical act toward her mother (that is, connecting as women in order to help each other get some power) doesn't look much like a young man's most radical act toward his father (that is, breaking the father-son connection in order to separate identities or take over existing power).

It's those father-son conflicts at a generational, national level that [22] have often provided the conventional definition of revolution; yet they've gone on for centuries without basically changing the role of the female half of the world. They have also failed to reduce the level of violence in society, since both fathers and sons have included some degree of aggressiveness and superiority to women in their definition of masculinity, thus preserving the anthropological model of dominance.

Furthermore, what current leaders and theoreticians define as rev- 23
olution is usually little more than taking over the army and the radio stations. Women have much more in mind than that. We have to uproot the
sexual caste system that is the most pervasive power structure in society, and that means transforming the patriarchal values of those who
run the institutions, whether they are politically the "right" or the "left,"
the fathers or the sons. This cultural part of the change goes very deep,
and is often seen as too intimate, and perhaps too threatening, to be considered as either serious or possible. Only conflicts among men are "serious." Only a takeover of existing institutions is "possible."

That's why the definition of "political," on campus as elsewhere, 24
tends to be limited to who's running for president, who's demonstrating against corporate investments in South Africa, or which is the
"moral" side of some conventional revolution, preferably one that is
thousands of miles away.

As important as such activities are, they are also the most comfort- 25
able ones when we're young. They provide a sense of virtue without
much disruption in the power structure of our daily lives. Even when
the most consistent energies on campus are actually concentrated
around feminist issues, they may be treated as apolitical and invisible.
Asked "What's happening on campus?" a student may reply, "The an-
tinuke movement," even though that resulted in one demonstration of
two hours, while student antirape squads have been patrolling the campus every night for two years and women's studies have begun to transform the very textbooks we read.

No wonder reporters and sociologists looking for revolution on 26
campus often miss the depth of feminist change and activity that is really there. Women students themselves may dismiss it as not political
and not serious. Certainly, it rarely comes in the masculine sixties style
of bombing buildings or burning draft cards. In fact, it goes much deeper than protesting a temporary symptom—say, the draft—and challenges the right of one group to dominate another, which is the disease
itself.

Young women have a big task of resisting pressures and challeng- 27
ing definitions. Their increasing success is a miracle of foresight and
courage that should make us all proud. But they should know that they,
too, may grow more radical with age.

One day, an army of gray-haired women may quietly take over the 28
earth.

Responding to Reading

1. On the basis of your own experience, do you agree with Steinem that "women
   may be the one group that grows more radical with age" (2)? Explain.

2. Does the "female guilt trip, student edition" defined by Steinem in paragraph 11 accurately represent the feelings of the female college students you know? Is the characterization of young women as "man junkies" (14) accurate? If not, do you attribute the inaccuracies to the time that has passed since the essay was written, or to other factors?

3. Do you agree with Steinem's comment (25) that feminist thought has transformed America's college campuses? Do you see evidence of this transpormation on your campus?

WOMEN'S BRAINS

Stephen Jay Gould

Writer and lecturer Stephen Jay Gould (1941–) is a paleontologist and professor whose speciality is snails. As he explains in an interview for the *Contemporary Authors* series, "Snails suit my own interest because I'm concerned with the relationship between growth and evolution, and snails preserve in their shell the record of their growth from babyhood to adult." Gould is especially skilled at writing about science—particularly about evolution and biological determinism—for the layperson. He publishes a column in *Natural History* magazine and has collected his essays in *Ever Since Darwin* (1977), *The Panda's Thumb: More Reflections in Natural History* (1980), *An Urchin in the Storm* (1987), *Bully for Brontosaurus* (1991), and *Eight Little Piggies* (1993). "Women's Brains," which gives a historical account of how scientists have used data about brain size, is typical of Gould's informal and informative style.

In the prelude to *Middlemarch*, George Eliot lamented the unfulfilled   1
lives of talented women:

> Some have felt that these blundering lives are due to the inconvenient indefiniteness with which the Supreme Power has fashioned the natures of women: if there were one level of feminine incompetence as strict as the ability to count three and no more, the social lot of women might be treated with scientific certitude.

Eliot goes on to discount the idea of innate limitation, but while she   2
wrote in 1872, the leaders of European anthropometry were trying to measure "with scientific certitude" the inferiority of women. Anthropometry, or measurement of the human body, is not so fashionable a field these days, but it dominated the human sciences for much of the nineteenth century and remained popular until intelligence testing re-

placed skull measurement as a favored device for making invidious comparisons among races, classes, and sexes. Craniometry, or measurement of the skull, commanded the most attention and respect. Its unquestioned leader, Paul Broca (1824–80), professor of clinical surgery at the Faculty of Medicine in Paris, gathered a school of disciples and imitators around himself. Their work, so meticulous and apparently irrefutable, exerted great influence and won high esteem as a jewel of nineteenth-century science.

Broca's work seemed particularly invulnerable to refutation. Had he   3 not measured with the most scrupulous care and accuracy? (Indeed, he had. I have the greatest respect for Broca's meticulous procedure. His numbers are sound. But science is an inferential exercise, not a catalog of facts. Numbers, by themselves, specify nothing. All depends upon what you do with them.) Broca depicted himself as an apostle of objectivity, a man who bowed before facts and cast aside superstition and sentimentality. He declared that "there is no faith, however respectable, no interest, however legitimate, which must not accommodate itself to the progress of human knowledge and bend before truth." Women, like it or not, had smaller brains than men and, therefore, could not equal them in intelligence. This fact, Broca argued, may reinforce a common prejudice in male society, but it is also a scientific truth. L. Manouvrier, a black sheep in Broca's fold, rejected the inferiority of women and wrote with feeling about the burden imposed upon them by Broca's numbers:

> Women displayed their talents and their diplomas. They also invoked philosophical authorities. But they were opposed by *numbers* unknown to Condorcet[1] or to John Stuart Mill.[2] These numbers fell upon poor women like a sledge hammer, and they were accompanied by commentaries and sarcasms more ferocious than the most misogynist imprecations of certain church fathers. The theologians had asked if women had a soul. Several centuries later, some scientists were ready to refuse them a human intelligence.

Broca's argument rested upon two sets of data: the larger brains of   4 men in modern societies, and a supposed increase in male superiority through time. His most extensive data came from autopsies performed personally in four Parisian hospitals. For 292 male brains, he calculated an average weight of 1,325 grams; 140 female brains averaged 1,144 grams for a difference of 181 grams, or 14 percent of the male weight. Broca understood, of course, that part of this difference could be attributed to the greater height of males. Yet he made no attempt to measure

---

[1] Jean Antoine, Marquis de Condorcet (1743–94), one of a group of French writers, known as Les Philosophes, who examined religious, philosophical, and ethical issues. [Eds.]

[2] English economist, philosopher, and political theorist (1806–73). [Eds.]

the effect of size alone and actually stated that it cannot account for the entire difference because we know, a priori, that women are not as intelligent as men (a premise that the data were supposed to test, not rest upon):

> We might ask if the small size of the female brain depends exclusively upon the small size of her body. Tiedemann has proposed this explanation. But we must not forget that women are, on the average, a little less intelligent than men, a difference which we should not exaggerate but which is, nonetheless, real. We are therefore permitted to suppose that the relatively small size of the female brain depends in part upon her physical inferiority and in part upon her intellectual inferiority.

In 1873, the year after Eliot published *Middlemarch,* Broca measured 5 the cranial capacities of prehistoric skulls from L'Homme Mort cave. Here he found a difference of only 99.5 cubic centimeters between males and females, while modern populations range from 129.5 to 220.7. Topinard, Broca's chief disciple, explained the increasing discrepancy through time as a result of differing evolutionary pressures upon dominant men and passive women:

> The man who fights for two or more in the struggle for existence, who has all the responsibility and the cares of tomorrow, who is constantly active in combating the environment and human rivals, needs more brain than the woman whom he must protect and nourish, the sedentary woman, lacking any interior occupations, whose role is to raise children, love, and be passive.

In 1879, Gustave Le Bon, chief misogynist of Broca's school, used 6 these data to publish what must be the most vicious attack upon women in modern scientific literature (no one can top Aristotle).[3] I do not claim his views were representative of Broca's school, but they were published in France's most respected anthropological journal. Le Bon concluded:

> In the most intelligent races, as among the Parisians, there are a large number of women whose brains are closer in size to those of gorillas than to the most developed male brains. This inferiority is so obvious that no one can contest it for a moment; only its degree is worth discussion. All psychologists who have studied the intelligence of women, as well as poets and novelists, recognize today that they represent the most inferior forms of human evolution and that they are closer to children and savages than to an adult, civilized man. They excel in fickleness, inconstancy, absence of thought and logic, and incapacity to reason. Without doubt there exist some distinguished women, very superior to the average man, but they are as exceptional as the birth of

---

[3] In his philosophical writings, Aristotle (384–322 b.c.) notes that women are (among other things) "more dispirited, more despondent, more imprudent, and more given to falsehood" than men and also that they are "more envious, more querulous, more slanderous, and more contentious." [Eds.]

any monstrosity, as, for example, of a gorilla with two heads; consequently, we may neglect them entirely.

Nor did Le Bon shrink from the social implications of his views. He [7] was horrified by the proposal of some American reformers to grant women higher education on the same basis as men:

> A desire to give them the same education, and, as a consequence, to propose the same goals for them, is a dangerous chimera. . . . The day when, misunderstanding the inferior occupations which nature has given her, women leave the home and take part in our battles; on this day a social revolution will begin, and everything that maintains the sacred ties of the family will disappear.

Sound familiar?[4]

I have reexamined Broca's data, the basis for all this derivative pro- [8] nouncement, and I find his numbers sound but his interpretation ill-founded, to say the least. The data supporting his claim for increased difference through time can be easily dismissed. Broca based his contention on the samples from L'Homme Mort alone—only seven male and six female skulls in all. Never have so little data yielded such far ranging conclusions.

In 1888, Topinard published Broca's more extensive data on the [9] Parisian hospitals. Since Broca recorded height and age as well as brain size, we may use modern statistics to remove their effect. Brain weight decreases with age, and Broca's women were, on average, considerably older than his men. Brain weight increases with height, and his average man was almost half a foot taller than his average woman. I used multiple regression, a technique that allowed me to assess simultaneously the influence of height and age upon brain size. In an analysis of the data for women, I found that, at average male height and age, a woman's brain would weigh 1,212 grams. Correction for height and age reduces Broca's measured difference of 181 grams by more than a third, to 113 grams.

I don't know what to make of this remaining difference because I [10] cannot assess other factors known to influence brain size in a major way. Cause of death has an important effect: degenerative disease often entails a substantial diminution of brain size. (This effect is separate from the decrease attributed to age alone.) Eugene Schreider, also working with Broca's data, found that men killed in accidents had brains weighing, on average, 60 grams more than men dying of infectious diseases. The best modern data I can find (from American hospitals) records a full

---

[4] When I wrote this essay, I assumed that Le Bon was a marginal, if colorful, figure. I have since learned that he was a leading scientist, one of the founders of social psychology, and best known for a seminal study on crowd behavior, still cited today (*La psychologie des foules*, 1895), and for his work on unconscious motivation.

100-gram difference between death by degenerative arteriosclerosis and by violence or accident. Since so many of Broca's subjects were very elderly women, we may assume that lengthy degenerative disease was more common among them than among the men.

More importantly, modern students of brain size still have not [11] agreed on a proper measure for eliminating the powerful effect of body size. Height is partly adequate, but men and women of the same height do not share the same body build. Weight is even worse than height, because most of its variation reflects nutrition rather than intrinsic size—fat versus skinny exerts little influence upon the brain. Manouvrier took up this subject in the 1880s and argued that muscular mass and force should be used. He tried to measure this elusive property in various ways and found a marked difference in favor of men, even in men and women of the same height. When he corrected for what he called "sexual mass," women actually came out slightly ahead in brain size.

Thus, the corrected 113-gram difference is surely too large; the true [12] figure is probably close to zero and may as well favor women as men. And 113 grams, by the way, is exactly the average difference between a 5 foot 4 inch and a 6 foot 4 inch male in Broca's data. We would not (especially us short folks) want to ascribe greater intelligence to tall men. In short, who knows what to do with Broca's data? They certainly don't permit any confident claim that men have bigger brains than women.

To appreciate the social role of Broca and his school, we must rec- [13] ognize that his statements about the brains of women do not reflect an isolated prejudice toward a single disadvantaged group. They must be weighed in the context of a general theory that supported contemporary social distinctions as biologically ordained. Women, blacks, and poor people suffered the same disparagement, but women bore the brunt of Broca's argument because he had easier access to data on women's brains. Women were singularly denigrated but they also stood as surrogates for other disenfranchised groups. As one of Broca's disciples wrote in 1881: "Men of the black races have a brain scarcely heavier than that of white women." This juxtaposition extended into many other realms of anthropological argument, particularly to claims that, anatomically and emotionally, both women and blacks were like white children—and that white children, by the theory of recapitulation, represented an ancestral (primitive) adult stage of human evolution. I do not regard as empty rhetoric the claim that women's battles are for all of us.

Maria Montessori did not confine her activities to educational re- [14] form for young children. She lectured on anthropology for several years at the University of Rome, and wrote an influential book entitled *Pedagogical Anthropology* (English edition, 1913). Montessori was no egalitarian. She supported most of Broca's work and the theory of innate criminality proposed by her compatriot Cesare Lombroso. She measured the circumference of children's heads in her schools and inferred that the best prospects had bigger brains. But she had no use for Broca's conclusions about women. She discussed Manouvrier's work at length and made much of his tentative claim that women, after proper correction of the data, had slightly larger brains than men. Women, she concluded, were intellectually superior, but men had prevailed heretofore by dint of physical force. Since technology has abolished force as an instrument of power, the era of women may soon be upon us: "In such an epoch there will really be superior human beings, there will really be men strong in morality and in sentiment. Perhaps in this way the reign of women is approaching, when the enigma of her anthropological superiority will be deciphered. Woman was always the custodian of human sentiment, morality and honor."

This represents one possible antidote to "scientific" claims for the ¹⁵ constitutional inferiority of certain groups. One may affirm the validity of biological distinctions but argue that the data have been misinterpreted by prejudiced men with a stake in the outcome, and that disadvantaged groups are truly superior. In recent years, Elaine Morgan has followed this strategy in her *Descent of Woman,* a speculative reconstruction of human prehistory from the woman's point of view—and as farcical as more famous tall tales by and for men.

I prefer another strategy. Montessori and Morgan followed Broca's ¹⁶ philosophy to reach a more congenial conclusion. I would rather label the whole enterprise of setting a biological value upon groups for what it is: irrelevant and highly injurious. George Eliot well appreciated the special tragedy that biological labeling imposed upon members of disadvantaged groups. She expressed it for people like herself—women of extraordinary talent. I would apply it more widely—not only to those whose dreams are flouted but also to those who never realize that they may dream—but I cannot match her prose. In conclusion, then, the rest of Eliot's prelude to *Middlemarch:*

> The limits of variation are really much wider than anyone would imagine from the sameness of women's coiffure and the favorite love stories in prose and verse. Here and there a cygnet is reared uneasily among the ducklings in the brown pond, and never finds the living stream in fellowship with its own oary-footed kind. Here and there is born a Saint Theresa,⁵ foundress of nothing, whose loving heartbeats and sobs after an unattained goodness tremble off and are dispersed among hindrances instead of centering in some long-recognizable deed.

Responding to Reading

1. Although this essay is solidly grounded in scientific research and quotes researchers extensively, Gould uses the first person, contractions, and other

---

⁵ One of the principal saints of the Catholic Church (1515–82). [Eds.]

characteristics of informal style. Does this level of diction make you more or less receptive to his ideas?

2. In paragraph 6 Gould describes the remarks of Gustave Le Bon as "what must be the most vicious attack upon women in modern scientific literature." What shocks or angers you most about Le Bon's theory as Gould presents it?

3. In his analysis of the larger implications of Broca's theories, Gould says, "I do not regard as empty rhetoric the claim that women's battles are for all of us" (13). What does he mean? What application, if any, does this statement have to inequities that you see in modern society?

MARKED WOMEN

Deborah Tannen

Language researcher Deborah Tannen is widely known for her best-selling books on the problems people have communicating across gender and cultural lines (see p. 274). The following essay, written in 1993, is something of a departure from her usual work. Here she focuses not on different communication styles, but rather on the striking contrast she finds between the neutral way men in our culture are able to present themselves to the world and the more message-laden way women must generally do so.

Some years ago I was at a small working conference of four women and eight men. Instead of concentrating on the discussion I found myself looking at the three other women at the table, thinking how each had a different style and how each style was coherent.

One woman had dark brown hair in a classic style, a cross between Cleopatra and Plain Jane. The severity of her straight hair was softened by wavy bangs and ends that turned under. Because she was beautiful, the effect was more Cleopatra than plain.

The second woman was older, full of dignity and composure. Her hair was cut in a fashionable style that left her with only one eye, thanks to a side part that let a curtain of hair fall across half her face. As she looked down to read her prepared paper, the hair robbed her of bifocal vision and created a barrier between her and the listeners.

The third woman's hair was wild, a frosted blond avalanche falling over and beyond her shoulders. When she spoke she frequently tossed her head, calling attention to her hair and away from her lecture.

Then there was makeup. The first woman wore facial cover that ⁵
made her skin smooth and pale, a black line under each eye and mascara
that darkened already dark lashes. The second wore only a light gloss
on her lips and a hint of shadow on her eyes. The third had blue bands
under her eyes, dark blue shadow, mascara, bright red lipstick and
rouge; her fingernails flashed red.

I considered the clothes each woman had worn during the three ⁶
days of the conference: In the first case, man-tailored suits in primary
colors with solid-color blouses. In the second, casual but stylish black T-
shirts, a floppy collarless jacket and baggy slacks or a skirt in neutral colors. The third wore a sexy jump suit; tight sleeveless jersey and tight yellow slacks; a dress with gaping armholes and an indulged tendency to
fall off one shoulder.

Shoes? No. 1 wore string sandals with medium heels; No. 2, sensi- ⁷
ble, comfortable walking shoes; No. 3, pumps with spike heels. You can
fill in the jewelry, scarves, shawls, sweaters—or lack of them.

As I amused myself finding coherence in these styles, I suddenly ⁸
wondered why I was scrutinizing only the women. I scanned the eight
men at the table. And then I knew why I wasn't studying them. The
men's styles were unmarked.

The term "marked" is a staple of linguistic theory. It refers to the ⁹
way language alters the base meaning of a word by adding a linguistic
particle that has no meaning on its own. The unmarked form of a word
carries the meaning that goes without saying—what you think of when
you're not thinking anything special.

The unmarked tense of verbs in English is the present—for example, ¹⁰
visit. To indicate past, you mark the verb by adding *ed* to yield *visited*.
For future, you add a word: *will visit*. Nouns are presumed to be singular until marked for plural, typically by adding *s* or *es*, so *visit* becomes
visits and *dish* becomes *dishes*.

The unmarked forms of most English words also convey "male." ¹¹
Being male is the unmarked case. Endings like *ess* and *ette* mark words
as "female." Unfortunately, they also tend to mark them for frivolous-
ness. Would you feel safe entrusting your life to a doctorette? Alfre
Woodard, who was an Oscar nominee for best supporting actress, says
she identifies herself as an actor because "actresses worry about eyelashes and cellulite, and women who are actors worry about the characters we are playing." Gender markers pick up extra meanings that reflect common associations with the female gender: not quite serious,
often sexual.

Each of the women at the conference had to make decisions about ¹²
hair, clothing, makeup and accessories, and each decision carried meaning. Every style available to us was marked. The men in our group had

made decisions, too, but the range from which they chose was incomparably narrower. Men can choose styles that are marked, but they don't have to, and in this group none did. Unlike the women, they had the option of being unmarked.

Take the men's hair styles. There was no marine crew cut or oily [13] longish hair falling into eyes, no asymmetrical, two-tiered construction to swirl over a bald top. One man was unabashedly bald; the others had hair of standard length, parted on one side, in natural shades of brown or gray or graying. Their hair obstructed no views, left little to toss or push back or run fingers through and, consequently, needed and attracted no attention. A few men had beards. In a business setting, beards might be marked. In this academic gathering, they weren't.

There could have been a cowboy shirt with string tie or a three-piece [14] suit or a necklaced hippie in jeans. But there wasn't. All eight men wore brown or blue slacks and nondescript shirts of light colors. No man wore sandals or boots; their shoes were dark, closed, comfortable and flat. In short, unmarked.

Although no man wore makeup, you couldn't say the men didn't [15] wear makeup in the sense that you could say a woman didn't wear makeup. For men, no makeup is unmarked.

I asked myself what style we women could have adopted that [16] would have been unmarked, like the men's. The answer was none. There is no unmarked woman.

There is no woman's hair style that can be called standard, that says [17] nothing about her. The range of women's hair styles is staggering, but a woman whose hair has no particular style is perceived as not caring about how she looks, which can disqualify her for many positions, and will subtly diminish her as a person in the eyes of some.

Women must choose between attractive shoes and comfortable [18] shoes. When our group made an unexpected trek, the woman who wore flat, laced shoes arrived first. Last to arrive was the woman in spike heels, shoes in hand and a handful of men around her.

If a woman's clothing is tight or revealing (in other words, sexy), it [19] sends a message—an intended one of wanting to be attractive, but also a possibly unintended one of availability. If her clothes are not sexy, that too sends a message, lent meaning by the knowledge that they could have been. There are thousands of cosmetic products from which women can choose and myriad ways of applying them. Yet no makeup at all is anything but unmarked. Some men see it as a hostile refusal to please them.

Women can't even fill out a form without telling stories about them- [20] selves. Most forms give four titles to choose from. "Mr." carries no meaning other than that the respondent is male. But a woman who checks "Mrs." or "Miss" communicates not only whether she has been married but also whether she has conservative tastes in forms of address—and probably other conservative values as well. Checking "Ms."

declines to let on about marriage (checking "Mr." declines nothing since nothing was asked), but it also marks her as either liberated or rebellious, depending on the observer's attitudes and assumptions.

I sometimes try to duck these variously marked choices by giving [21] my title as "Dr."—and in so doing risk marking myself as either uppity (hence sarcastic responses like *"Excuse me!"*) or an overachiever (hence reactions or congratulatory surprise like "Good for you!").

All married women's surnames are marked. If a woman takes her [22] husband's name, she announces to the world that she is married and has traditional values. To some it will indicate that she is less herself, more identified by her husband's identity. If she does not take her husband's name, this too is marked, seen as worthy of comment: she has done something; she has "kept her own name." A man is never said to have "kept his own name" because it never occurs to anyone that he might have given it up. For him using his own name is unmarked.

A married woman who wants to have her cake and eat it too may [23] use her surname plus his, with or without a hyphen. But this too announces her marital status and often results in a tongue-tying string. In a list (Harvey O'Donovan, Jonathan Feldman, Stephanie Woodbury McGillicutty), the woman's multiple name stands out. It is marked.

I have never been inclined toward biological explanations of gender [24] differences in language, but I was intrigued to see Ralph Fasold bring biological phenomena to bear on the question of linguistic marking in his book "The Sociolinguistics of Language." Fasold stresses that language and culture are particularly unfair in treating women as the marked case because biologically it is the male that is marked. While two X chromosomes make a female, two Y chromosomes make nothing. Like the linguistic markers *s, es* or *ess*, the Y chromosome doesn't "mean" anything unless it is attached to a root form—an X chromosome.

Developing this idea elsewhere, Fasold points out that girls are born [25] with fully female bodies, while boys are born with modified female bodies. He invites men who doubt this to lift up their shirts and contemplate why they have nipples.

In his book, Fasold notes "a wide range of facts which demonstrates [26] that female is the unmarked sex." For example, he observes that there are a few species that produce only females, like the whiptail lizard. Thanks to parthenogenesis, they have no trouble having as many daughters as they like. There are no species, however, that produce only males. This is no surprise, since any such species would become extinct in its first generation.

Fasold is also intrigued by species that produce individuals not in- [27] volved in reproduction, like honeybees and leaf-cutter ants. Reproduction is handled by the queen and a relatively few males; the workers are sterile females. "Since they do not reproduce," Fasold says, "there is no reason for them to be one sex or the other, so they default, so to speak, to female."

Fasold ends his discussion of these matters by pointing out that if [28] language reflected biology, grammar books would direct us to use "she" to include males and females and "he" only for specifically male referents. But they don't. They tell us that "he" means "he or she," and that "she" is used only if the referent is specifically female. This use of "he" as the sex-indefinite pronoun is an innovation introduced into English by grammarians in the 18th and 19th centuries, according to Peter Mühlhäusler and Rom Harré in "Pronouns and People." From at least about 1500, the correct sex-indefinite pronoun was "they," as it still is in casual spoken English. In other words, the female was declared by grammarians to be the marked case.

Writing this article may mark me not as a writer, not as a linguist, [29] not as an analyst of human behavior, but as a feminist—which will have positive or negative, but in any case powerful, connotations for readers. Yet I doubt that anyone reading Ralph Fasold's book would put that label on him.

I discovered the markedness inherent in the very topic of gender after [30] writing a book on differences in conversational style based on geographical region, ethnicity, class, age and gender. When I was interviewed, the vast majority of journalists wanted to talk about the differences between women and men. While I thought I was simply describing what I observed—something I had learned to do as a researcher—merely mentioning women and men marked me as a feminist for some.

When I wrote a book devoted to gender differences in ways of [31] speaking, I sent the manuscript to five male colleagues, asking them to alert me to any interpretation, phrasing or wording that might seem unfairly negative toward men. Even so, when the book came out, I encountered responses like that of the television talk show host who, after interviewing me, turned to the audience and asked if they thought I was male-bashing.

Leaping upon a poor fellow who affably nodded in agreement, she [32] made him stand and asked, "Did what she said accurately describe you?" "Oh, yes," he answered. "That's me exactly." "And what she said about women—does that sound like your wife?" "Oh yes," he responded. "That's her exactly." "Then why do you think she's male-bashing?" He answered, with disarming honesty, "Because she's a woman and she's saying things about men."

To say anything about women and men without marking oneself as [33] either feminist or anti-feminist, male-basher or apologist for men seems as impossible for a woman as trying to get dressed in the morning without inviting interpretations of her character.

Sitting at the conference table musing on these matters, I felt sad to [34] think that we women didn't have the freedom to be unmarked that the men sitting next to us had. Some days you just want to get dressed and go about your business. But if you're a woman, you can't, because there is no unmarked woman.

Responding to Reading

1. Tannen notes that men "can choose styles that are marked, but they don't have to" (12); however, she believes that women do not have the "option of being unmarked." Do you agree? If possible, give some examples of women's styles that you believe are unmarked. (Note that in paragraph 16 Tannen says there are no such styles.)
2. In paragraph 33 Tannen says, "To say anything about women or men without marking oneself as either feminist or antifeminist, male-basher or apologist for men seems as impossible for a woman as trying to get dressed in the morning without inviting interpretation of her character." Do you think she is right? Do you think her statement also applies to men?
3. In paragraphs 24–28 Tannen discusses Ralph Fasold's book *The Sociolinguistics of Language.* Why does she include this material? Could she have made her point as effectively without it?

THE LOOKING-GLASS SHAME

Judith Ortiz Cofer

Born in Puerto Rico and raised in Paterson, New Jersey, Judith Ortiz Cofer (1952–) is an award-winning poet and novelist as well as an essayist. Her recent books include the novel *The Line of the Sun* (1989); *Silent Dancing* (1990), a collection of biographical essays; and *The Latin Deli: Prose and Poetry* (1993). A teacher of creative writing at the University of Georgia, she has said that she began writing because "as a native speaker of Spanish, I first perceived of language, especially the English language, as a barrier, a challenge to be met with the same kind of closed-eyed bravado that prompted me to jump into the deep end of the pool before taking my first swimming lesson." In the following essay from *Silent Dancing,* Cofer recalls her freshman year at a Catholic high school (where she was the only Puerto Rican student), her awakening hormones, and her first love, a handsome senior whom she worshipped from afar.

"At any rate, the looking-glass
shame has lasted all my life."

Virginia Woolf, Moments of Being

In her memoir, *Moments of Being,* Virginia Woolf tells of a frighten- ¹
ing dream she had as a young girl in which, as she looked at herself in
the mirror, she saw something moving in the background: ". . . a horrible face—the face of an animal . . ." over her shoulder. She never forgot
that "other face in the glass" perhaps because it was both alien and familiar. It is not unusual for an adolescent to feel disconnected from her
body—a stranger to herself and to her new developing needs—but I
think that to a person living simultaneously in two cultures this phenomenon is intensified.

Even as I dealt with the trauma of leaving childhood, I saw that ²
"cultural schizophrenia" was undoing many others around me at different stages of their lives. Society gives clues and provides rituals for
the adolescent but withholds support. As I entered my freshman year of
high school in a parochial school, I was given a new uniform to wear: a
skirt and blouse as opposed to the severe blue jumper with straps, to accommodate for developing breasts, I suppose, although I would have little to accommodate for an excruciatingly long time—being a "skinny
bones," as my classmates often called me, with no hips or breasts to
speak of. But the warnings began, nevertheless. At home my mother
constantly reminded me that I was now a "señorita" and needed to behave accordingly; but she never explained exactly what that entailed.
She had said the same thing when I had started menstruating a couple
of years before. At school the classrooms and the cafeteria were segregated into "boyside" and "girlside." The nuns kept a hawk-eye on the
length of the girls' skirts, which had to come to below the knee at a time
when the mini-skirt was becoming the microskirt out in the streets.

After school, I would see several of the "popular" girls walk down ³
to the corner out of sight from the school, and get into cars with public
school boys. Many of the others went down to the drugstore to have a
soda and talk loudly and irreverently about the school and the nuns.
Most of them were middle class Italian and Irish kids. I was the only
Puerto Rican student, having gotten in after taking a rigorous academic test and after the priest visited our apartment to ascertain that we
were a good Catholic family. I felt lost in the sea of bright white faces
and teased blond hair of the girls who were not unkind to me, but did
not, at least that crucial first year, include me in their groups that traveled together to skating rinks, basketball games, pizza parlors—those activities that they would talk about on Monday in their rapid-fire English
as we all awaited to be let into the building.

Not that I would have been allowed to go to these places. I lived in ⁴
the carefully constructed facsimile of a Puerto Rican home my mother
had created. Every day I crossed the border of two countries: I would
spend the day in the pine-scented parochial school building where exquisitely proper behavior was the rule strictly enforced by the soft spoken nuns, who could, upon observing an infraction of their many rules,

turn into despots—and never raise their voices—as they destroyed your peace of mind with threats of shameful exposure and/or expulsion. But there was order, quiet, respect for logic, and there, also, I received the information I was always hungry for. I liked reading books, and I took immense pleasure in the praise of the teachers for my attentiveness and my good grades. So what, I thought to myself, if I was not invited to the homes of my classmates who did not live in my neighborhood, anyway. I lived in the city core, in an apartment that may have housed an Italian or Irish family a generation before. Now they were prosperous and had moved to the suburbs and the Puerto Ricans had moved into the "immigrant" apartment buildings. That year I actually felt a sense of burning shame at the fact that I did not have to take a bus or be picked up in a car to go home. I lived only a few blocks away from the church and the school which had been built in the heart of the city by the original wave of Irish Catholics—for *their* convenience. The Puerto Ricans had built no churches.

I would walk home every day from school. I had fifteen minutes to   5
get home before my mother panicked and came after me. I did not want that to happen. She was so different from my classmates' mothers that I was embarrassed to be seen with her. While most of the other mothers were stoutly built women with dignified grey hair who exuded motherliness, my mother was an exotic young beauty, black hair down to her waist and a propensity for wearing bright colors and spike heels. I would have died of shame if one of my classmates had seen her sensuous walk and the looks she elicited from the men on our block. And she would have embraced me in public, too, for she never learned moderation in her emotions, or restraint for her gesturing hands and loud laughter. She kept herself a "native" in that apartment she rarely left, except on my father's arm, or to get one of us from school. I had had to have a shouting match with her to convince her that I no longer needed to be escorted back and forth from school in the ninth grade.

My mother carried the island of Puerto Rico over her head like the   6
mantilla she wore to church on Sunday. She was "doing time" in the U.S. She did not know how long her sentence would last, or why she was being punished with exile, but she was only doing it for her children. She kept herself "pure" for her eventual return to the island by denying herself a social life (which would have connected her too much with the place); by never learning but the most basic survival English; and by her ability to create an environment in our home that was a comfort to her, but a shock to my senses, and I suppose, to my younger brother's, both of us having to enter and exit this twilight zone of sights and smells that meant *casa* to her.

In our apartment we spoke Spanish, we ate rice and beans with   7
meats prepared in *adobo*, that mouth-watering mixture of spices, and we listened to romantic ballads sung by Daniel Santos which my mother

played on the record-player. She read letters from her family in Puerto Rico and from our father. Although she loved getting his letters, his descriptions of the Roman Coliseum or the Acropolis did not interest her as much as news from *casa*—her mother and her many brothers and sisters.

Most of my mother's sentences began with *En casa* . . . at her Mama's house things were done like this and like that. At any place in the world other than her beloved *Isla* my mother would have been homesick: perpetual nostalgia, constant talk of return, that was my mother's chosen method of survival. When she looked into her looking-glass, what did she see? Another face, an old woman nagging, nagging, at her—*Don't bury me in foreign soil* . . . 8

> *A sailor went to see, sea, sea,*
> *To see what he could see, see, see,*
> *And all that he could see, see, see,*
> *Was the bottom of the deep, blue*
> *Sea, sea, sea.*

The black girls sang this faster and faster in the concrete play yard of the public school, perhaps not thinking of the words, landlocked in the city, never having seen the deep, blue sea. I thought of my father when I heard it. 9

The deep blue sea for my father was loneliness. He had joined the U.S. Military service at eighteen, the very same year he had married, because for the young men of Puerto Rico who did not have money in 1951, it was the only promise of a future away from the cane fields of the island or the factories of New York City. He had been brought up to expect better things. My father had excelled in school and was president of his senior class. In my mother, whom he met when she was just fourteen, he must have seen the opposite of himself. He had forsaken his early dreams for her love, and later for the future of his children. 10

His absences from home seemed to be harder on him than on us. Whatever happened to him during those years, most of it, I will never know. Each time he came home he was a quieter man. It was as if he were drowning in silence and no one could save him. His main concern was our education, and I remember showing him my school papers, which he would pore over as if he were reading a fascinating book. 11

He would listen attentively while Mother recounted the ordinary routine of our days to him, taking it all in like nourishment. He asked endless questions. Nothing was too trivial for his ears. It was as if he were attempting to live vicariously each day he had missed with us. And he never talked about the past; unlike our mother, he had no yearning to return to the Island that held no promise for him. But he did not deprive her of her dream of home either. And her need to be with her family may have been what prompted him to devise the complex system of back-and-forth travel that I experienced most of my childhood. 12

Every time he went to Europe for six months, we went back with Mother to her mother's *casa;* upon his return to Brooklyn Yard, he would wire us, and we would come back. Cold/hot, English/Spanish; that was our life.

I remember my father as a man who rarely looked into mirrors. He 13 would even comb his hair looking down. What was he afraid of seeing? Perhaps the monster over his shoulder was his lost potential. He was a sensitive, intellectual man whose energies had to be entirely devoted to survival. And that is how many minds are wasted in the travails of immigrant life.

And so, life was difficult for my parents, and that means that it was 14 no more and no less painful than for others like them: for the struggle, *la lucha,* goes on all around for people who want to be a piece that fits in the American puzzle, to get a share in the big picture; but, of course, I see that in retrospect. At fourteen and for a few years after, my concerns were mainly focused on the alarms going off in my body warning me of pain or pleasure ahead.

I fell in love, or my hormones awakened from their long slumber in 15 my body, and suddenly the goal of my days was focused on one thing: to catch a glimpse of my secret love. And it had to remain secret, because I had, of course, in the great tradition of tragic romance, chosen to love a boy who was totally out of my reach. He was not Puerto Rican; he was Italian and rich. He was also an older man. He was a senior at the high school when I came in as a freshman. I first saw him in the hall, leaning casually on a wall that was the border line between girlside and boyside for underclassmen. He looked extraordinarily like a young Marlon Brando—down to the ironic little smile. The total of what I knew about the boy who starred in every one of my awkward fantasies was this: that he was the nephew of the man who owned the supermarket on my block; that he often had parties at his parents' beautiful home in the suburbs which I would hear about; that this family had money (which came to our school in many ways)—and this fact made my knees weak: and that he worked at the store near my apartment building on weekends and in the summer.

My mother could not understand why I became so eager to be the 16 one sent out on her endless errands. I pounced on every opportunity from Friday to late Saturday afternoon to go after eggs, cigarettes, milk (I tried to drink as much of it as possible, although I hated the stuff)—the staple items that she would order from the "American" store.

Week after week I wandered up and down the aisles, taking furtive 17 glances at the stock room in the back, breathlessly hoping to see my prince. Not that I had a plan. I felt like a pilgrim waiting for a glimpse of Mecca. I did not expect him to notice me. It was sweet agony.

One day I did see him. Dressed in a white outfit like a surgeon: 18 white pants and shirt, white cap, and (gross sight, but not to my love-glazed eyes) blood-smeared butcher's apron. He was helping to drag a side of beef into the freezer storage area of the store. I must have stood there like an idiot, because I remember that he did see me, he even spoke to me! I could have died. I think he said, "Excuse me," and smiled vaguely in my direction.

After that, I *willed* occasions to go to the supermarket. I watched my [19] mother's pack of cigarettes empty ever so slowly. I wanted her to smoke them fast. I drank milk and forced it on my brother (although a second glass for him had to be bought with my share of Fig Newton cookies which we both liked, but we were restricted to one row each). I gave my cookies up for love, and watched my mother smoke her L&M's with so little enthusiasm that I thought (God, no!) that she might be cutting down on her smoking or maybe even giving up the habit. At this crucial time!

I thought I had kept my lonely romance a secret. Often I cried hot [20] tears on my pillow for the things that kept us apart. In my mind there was no doubt that he would never notice me (and that is why I felt free to stare at him—I was invisible). He could not see me because I was a skinny Puerto Rican girl, a freshman who did not belong to any group he associated with.

At the end of the year I found out that I had not been invisible. I [21] learned one little lesson about human nature—adulation leaves a scent, one that we are all equipped to recognize, and no matter how insignificant the source, we seek it.

In June the nuns at our school would always arrange for some cul- [22] tural extravaganza. In my freshman year it was a Roman banquet. We had been studying Greek drama (as a prelude to church history—it was at a fast clip that we galloped through Sophocles and Euripedes toward the early Christian martyrs), and our young, energetic Sister Agnes was in the mood for spectacle. She ordered the entire student body (it was a small group of under 300 students) to have our mothers make us togas out of sheets. She handed out a pattern on mimeo pages fresh out of the machine. I remember the intense smell of the alcohol on the sheets of paper, and how almost everyone in the auditorium brought theirs to their noses and inhaled deeply—mimeographed handouts were the school-day buzz that the new Xerox generation of kids is missing out on. Then, as the last couple of weeks of school dragged on, the city of Paterson becoming a concrete oven, and us wilting in our uncomfortable uniforms, we labored like frantic Roman slaves to build a splendid banquet hall in our small auditorium. Sister Agnes wanted a raised dais where the host and hostess would be regally enthroned.

She had already chosen our Senator and Lady from among our [23] ranks. The Lady was to be a beautiful new student named Sophia, a recent Polish immigrant, whose English was still practically unintelligible, but whose features, classically perfect without a trace of makeup, enthralled us. Everyone talked about her gold hair cascading past her waist, and her voice which could carry a note right up to heaven in choir. The nuns wanted her for God. They kept saying that she had vocation. We just looked at her in awe, and the boys seemed afraid of her. She just smiled and did as she was told. I don't know what she thought of it all. The main privilege of beauty is that others will do almost everything for you, including thinking.

Her partner was to be our best basketball player, a tall, red-haired [24] senior whose family sent its many offsprings to our school. Together, Sophia and her senator looked like the best combination of immigrant genes our community could produce. It did not occur to me to ask then whether anything but their physical beauty qualified them for the starring roles in our production. I had the highest average in the church history class, but I was given the part of one of many "Roman Citizens." I was to sit in front of the plastic fruit and recite a greeting in Latin along with the rest of the school when our hosts came into the hall and took their places on their throne.

On the night of our banquet, my father escorted me in my toga to [25] the door of our school. I felt foolish in my awkwardly draped sheet (blouse and skirt required underneath). My mother had no great skill as a seamstress. The best she could do was hem a skirt or a pair of pants. That night I would have traded her for a peasant woman with a golden needle. I saw other Roman ladies emerging from their parents' cars looking authentic in sheets of material that folded over their bodies like the garments on a statue by Michaelangelo. How did they do it? How was it that I always got it just slightly wrong, and worse, I believed that other people were just too polite to mention it. "The poor little Puerto Rican girl," I could hear them thinking. But in reality, I must have been my worst critic, self-conscious as I was.

Soon, we were all sitting at our circle of tables joined together [26] around the dais. Sophia glittered like a golden statue. Her smile was beatific: a perfect, silent Roman lady. Her "senator" looked uncomfortable, glancing around at his buddies, perhaps waiting for the ridicule that he would surely get in the locker room later. The nuns in their black habits stood in the background watching us. What were they supposed to be, the Fates? Nubian slaves? The dancing girls did their modest little dance to tinny music from their finger cymbals, then the speeches were made. Then the grape juice "wine" was raised in a toast to the Roman Empire we all knew would fall within the week—before finals anyway.

All during the program I had been in a state of controlled hysteria. [27] My secret love sat across the room from me looking supremely bored. I watched his every move, taking him in gluttonously. I relished the shadow of his eyelashes on his ruddy cheeks, his pouty lips smirking sarcastically at the ridiculous sight of our little play. Once he slumped down on his chair, and our sergeant-at-arms nun came over and tapped him sharply on his shoulder. He drew himself up slowly, with disdain. I loved his rebellious spirit. I believed myself still invisible to him in my "nothing" status as I looked upon my beloved. But towards the end of the evening, as we stood chanting our farewells in Latin, he looked straight across the room and into my eyes! How did I survive the killing power of those dark pupils? I trembled in a new way. I was not cold— I was burning! Yet I shook from the inside out, feeling light-headed, dizzy.

The room began to empty and I headed for the girls' lavatory. I [28] wanted to relish the miracle in silence. I did not think for a minute that anything more would follow. I was satisfied with the enormous favor of a look from my beloved. I took my time, knowing that my father would be waiting outside for me, impatient, perhaps glowing in the dark in his phosphorescent white Navy uniform. The others would ride home. I would walk home with my father, both of us in costume. I wanted as few witnesses as possible. When I could no longer hear the crowds in the hallway, I emerged from the bathroom, still under the spell of those mesmerizing eyes.

The lights had been turned off in the hallway and all I could see was [29] the lighted stairwell, at the bottom of which a nun would be stationed. My father would be waiting just outside. I nearly screamed when I felt someone grab me by the waist. But my mouth was quickly covered by someone else's mouth. I was being kissed. My first kiss and I could not even tell who it was. I pulled away to see that face not two inches away from mine. It was he. He smiled down at me. Did I have a silly expression on my face? My glasses felt crooked on my nose. I was unable to move or to speak. More gently, he lifted my chin and touched his lips to mine. This time I did not forget to enjoy it. Then, like the phantom lover that he was, he walked away into the darkened corridor and disappeared.

I don't know how long I stood there. My body was changing right [30] there in the hallway of a Catholic school. My cells were tuning up like musicians in an orchestra, and my heart was a chorus. It was an opera I was composing, and I wanted to stand very still and just listen. But, of course, I heard my father's voice talking to the nun. I was in trouble if he had had to ask about me. I hurried down the stairs making up a story on the way about feeling sick. That would explain my flushed face and it would buy me a little privacy when I got home.

The next day Father announced at the breakfast table that he was [31] leaving on a six month tour of Europe with the Navy in a few weeks and, that at the end of the school year my mother, my brother, and I would be sent to Puerto Rico to stay for half a year at Mamá's (my mother's mother) house. I was devastated. This was the usual routine for us. We had always gone to Mamá's to stay when Father was away for long periods. But this year it was different for me. I was in love, and . . . my heart knocked against my bony chest at this thought . . . he loved me too? I broke into sobs and left the table.

In the next week I discovered the inexorable truth about parents. 32 They can actually carry on with their plans right through tears, threats, and the awful spectacle of a teenager's broken heart. My father left me to my mother who impassively packed while I explained over and over that I was at a crucial time in my studies and that if I left my entire life would be ruined. All she would say is, "You are an intelligent girl, you'll catch up." Her head was filled with visions of *casa* and family reunions, long gossip sessions with her mamá and sisters. What did she care that I was losing my one chance at true love?

In the meantime I tried desperately to see him. I thought he would 33 look for me too. But the few times I saw him in the hallway, he was always rushing away. It would be long weeks of confusion and pain before I realized that the kiss was nothing but a little trophy for his ego. He had no interest in me other than as his adorer. He was flattered by my silent worship of him, and he had *bestowed* a kiss on me to please himself, and to fan the flames. I learned a lesson about the battle of the sexes then that I have never forgotten: the object is not always to win, but most times simply to keep your opponent (synonymous at times with "the loved one") guessing.

But this is too cynical a view to sustain in the face of that over- 34 whelming rush of emotion that is first love. And in thinking back about my own experience with it, I can be objective only to the point where I recall how sweet the anguish was, how caught up in the moment I felt, and how every nerve in my body was involved in this salute to life. Later, much later, after what seemed like an eternity of dragging the weight of unrequited love around with me, I learned to make myself visible and to relish the little battles required to win the greatest prize of all. And much later, I read and understood Camus'[1] statement about the subject that concerns both adolescent and philosopher alike: if love were easy, life would be too simple.

Responding to Reading

1. Do you agree with Cofer when she says, "Society gives clues and provides rituals for the adolescent but withholds support" (2)? How are these "clues" and "rituals" different for males and females? Do you think the degree of support offered to adolescent boys and girls differs?
2. In paragraph 33 Cofer talks about "the battle of the sexes." Do you believe there is a battle between the sexes? Is its object, as Cofer says, "to keep your opponent . . . guessing"?

---

[1] Albert Camus (1913–1960), French writer whose works reflect a tough-minded humanism. [Eds.]

3. Was Cofer's adolescence different from yours? If so, do you think the fact that she is Puerto Rican has anything to do with the difference? The fact that she grew up in a different place or generation?

THE LANGUAGE OF MEN

Norman Mailer

Norman Mailer (1923–) won a fiction award from *Story* magazine while he was studying engineering in college. After serving in World War II, Mailer wrote *The Naked and the Dead* (1948), the story of an American invasion of a Japanese-held island, and this novel established his literary reputation. Mailer is a prolific and controversial writer who is influenced by an awareness of and concern for American culture. Among his novels are *The Deer Park* (1955), *The American Dream* (1965), and *Harlot's Ghost* (1992). His nonfiction—for which he has won two Pulitzer Prizes—includes *The Armies of the Night* (1968), about the 1967 march on the Pentagon to protest the Vietnam War; *Of a Fire on the Moon* (1970), about the space program; *Marilyn* (1973), a biography of Marilyn Monroe; *The Executioner's Song: A True Life Novel* (1979), about a convicted murderer; and *Oswald's Tale: An American Mystery*, about presidential assassin Lee Harvey Oswald. "The Language of Men," first published in 1953, is the story of an army cook who struggles to gain the respect of his fellow soldiers without resorting to physical force.

In the beginning, Sanford Carter was ashamed of becoming an [1] Army cook. This was not from snobbery, at least not from snobbery of the most direct sort. During the two and a half years Carter had been in the Army he had come to hate cooks more and more. They existed for him as a symbol of all that was corrupt, overbearing, stupid, and privileged in Army life. The image which came to mind was a fat cook with an enormous sandwich in one hand, and a bottle of beer in the other, sweat pouring down a porcine face, foot on a flour barrel, shouting at the K.P.'s, "Hurry up, you men, I ain't got all day." More than once in those two and a half years, driven to exasperation, Carter had been on the verge of throwing his food into a cook's face as he passed on the serving line. His anger often derived from nothing: the set of a pair of fat lips, the casual heavy thump of the serving spoon into his plate, or the resentful conviction that the cook was not serving him enough. Since life in the Army was in most aspects a marriage, this rage over apparently harmless details was not a sign of unbalance. Every soldier found some particular habit of the Army spouse impossible to support.

Yet Sanford Carter became a cook and, to elaborate the irony, did   2
better as a cook than he had done as anything else. In a few months he
rose from a Private to a first cook with the rank of Sergeant, Technician.
After the fact, it was easy to understand. He had suffered through all his
Army career from an excess of eagerness. He had cared too much, he
had wanted to do well, and so he had often been tense at moments when
he would better have been relaxed. He was very young, twenty-one, had
lived the comparatively gentle life of a middle-class boy, and needed
some success in the Army to prove to himself that he was not completely
worthless.

In succession, he had failed as a surveyor in Field Artillery, a clerk   3
in an Infantry headquarters, a telephone wireman, and finally a rifleman. When the war ended, and his regiment went to Japan, Carter was
still a rifleman; he had been a rifleman for eight months. What was more
to the point, he had been in the platoon as long as any of its members;
the skilled hard-bitten nucleus of veterans who had run his squad had
gone home one by one, and it seemed to him that through seniority he
was entitled to at least a corporal's rating. Through seniority he was so
entitled, but on no other ground. Whenever responsibility had been
handed to him, he had discharged it miserably, tensely, overconscien-
tiously. He had always asked too many questions, he had worried the
task too severely, he had conveyed his nervousness to the men he was
supposed to lead. Since he was also sensitive enough and proud enough
never to curry favor with the noncoms in the platoons, he was in no position to sit in on their occasional discussions about who was to succeed
them. In a vacuum of ignorance, he had allowed himself to dream that
he would be given a squad to lead, and his hurt was sharp when the
squad was given to a replacement who had joined the platoon months
after him.

The war was over, Carter had a bride in the States (he had lived with   4
her for only two months), he was lonely, he was obsessed with going
home. As one week dragged into the next, and the regiment, the company, and his own platoon continued the same sort of training which
they had been doing ever since he had entered the Army, he thought he
would snap. There were months to wait until he would be discharged
and meanwhile it was intolerable to him to be taught for the fifth time
the nomenclature of the machine gun, to stand a retreat parade three
evenings a week. He wanted some niche where he could lick his
wounds, some Army job with so many hours of work and so many
hours of complete freedom, where he could be alone by himself. He
hated the Army, the huge Army which had proved to him that he was
good at no work, and incapable of succeeding at anything. He wrote
long, aching letters to his wife, he talked less and less to the men around
him and he was close to violent attacks of anger during the most casual phases of training—during close-order drill or cleaning his rifle for in-

spection. He knew that if he did not find his niche it was possible that
he would crack.

So he took an opening in the kitchen. It promised him nothing ex-   5
cept a day of work, and a day of leisure which would be completely at
his disposal. He found that he liked it. He was given at first the job of
baking the bread for the company, and every other night he worked till
early in the morning, kneading and shaping his fifty-pound mix of
dough. At two or three he would be done, and for his work there would
be the tangible reward of fifty loaves of bread, all fresh from the oven,
all clean and smelling of fertile accomplished creativity. He had the rare
and therefore intensely satisfying emotion of seeing at the end of an
Army chore the product of his labor.

A month after he became a cook the regiment was disbanded, and   6
those men who did not have enough points to go home were sent to
other outfits. Carter ended at an ordnance company in another Japanese city. He had by now given up all thought of getting a non-com's
rating before he was discharged, and was merely content to work each
alternate day. He took his work for granted and so he succeeded at it.
He had begun as a baker in the new company kitchen; before long he
was the first cook. It all happened quickly. One cook went home on
points, another caught a skin disease, a third was transferred from the
kitchen after contracting a venereal infection. On the shift which
Carter worked there were left only himself and a man who was illiterate. Carter was put nominally in charge, and was soon actively in
charge. He looked up each menu in an Army recipe book, collected
the items, combined them in the order indicated, and after the proper time had elapsed, took them from the stove. His product tasted neither better nor worse than the product of all other Army cooks. But
the mess sergeant was impressed. Carter had filled a gap. The next
time ratings were given out Carter jumped at a bound from Private to
Sergeant T/4.

On the surface he was happy; beneath the surface he was overjoyed.   7
It took him several weeks to realize how grateful and delighted he felt.
The promotion coincided with his assignment to a detachment working
in a small seaport up the coast. Carter arrived there to discover that he
was in charge of cooking for thirty men, and would act as mess sergeant.
There was another cook, and there were four permanent Japanese K.P.'s,
all of them good workers. He still cooked every other day, but there was
always time between meals to take a break of at least an hour and often
two; he shared a room with the other cook and lived in comparative privacy for the first time in several years; the seaport was beautiful; there
was only one officer, and he left the men alone; supplies were plentiful
due to a clerical error which assigned rations for forty men rather than
thirty; and in general everything was fine. The niche had become a
sinecure.

This was the happiest period of Carter's life in the Army. He came   8
to like his Japanese K.P.'s. He studied their language, he visited their
homes, he gave them gifts of food from time to time. They worshiped
him because he was kind to them and generous, because he never shouted, because his good humor bubbled over into games, and made the
work of the kitchen seem pleasant. All the while he grew in confidence.
He was not a big man, but his body filled out from the heavy work; he
was likely to sing a great deal, he cracked jokes with the men on the
chow line. The kitchen became his property, it became his domain, and
since it was a warm room, filled with sunlight, he came to take pleasure
in the very sight of it. Before long his good humor expanded into a series of efforts to improve the food. He began to take little pains and
make little extra efforts which would have been impossible if he had
been obliged to cook for more than thirty men. In the morning he would
serve the men fresh eggs scrambled or fried to their desire in fresh butter. Instead of cooking sixty eggs in one large pot he cooked two eggs at
a time in a frying pan, turning them to the taste of each soldier. He baked
like a housewife satisfying her young husband; at lunch and dinner
there was pie or cake, and often both. He went to great lengths. He
taught the K.P.'s how to make the toast come out right. He traded excess
food for spices in Japanese stores. He rubbed paprika and garlic on the
chickens. He even made pastries to cover such staples as corn beef hash
and meat and vegetable stew.

It all seemed to be wasted. In the beginning the men might have no-   9
ticed these improvements, but after a period they took them for granted. It did not matter how he worked to satisfy them; they trudged
through the chow line with their heads down, nodding coolly at him,
and they ate without comment. He would hang around the tables after
the meal, noticing how much they consumed, and what they discarded;
he would wait for compliments, but the soldiers seemed indifferent.
They seemed to eat without tasting the food. In their faces he saw mirrored the distaste with which he had once stared at cooks.

The honeymoon was ended. The pleasure he took in the kitchen and   10
himself curdled. He became aware again of his painful desire to please
people, to discharge responsibility, to be a man. When he had been a
child, tears had come into his eyes at a cross word, and he had lived in
an atmosphere where his smallest accomplishment was warmly
praised. He was the sort of young man, he often thought bitterly, who
was accustomed to the attention and the protection of women. He
would have thrown away all he possessed—the love of his wife, the love
of his mother, the benefits of his education, the assured financial security of entering his father's business—if he had been able just once to dig
a ditch as well as the most ignorant farmer.

Instead, he was back in the painful unprotected days of his first en-   11
trance into the Army. Once again the most casual actions became the

most painful, the events which were most to be taken for granted grew into the most significant, and the feeding of the men at each meal turned progressively more unbearable.

So Sanford Carter came full circle. If he had once hated the cooks, he [12] now hated the troops. At mealtimes his face soured into the belligerent scowl with which he had once believed cooks to be born. And to himself he muttered the age-old laments of the housewife: how little they appreciated what he did.

Finally there was an explosion. He was approached one day by Cor- [13] poral Taylor, and he had come to hate Taylor, because Taylor was the natural leader of the detachment and kept the other men endlessly amused with his jokes. Taylor had the ability to present himself as inefficient, shiftless, and incapable, in such a manner as to convey that really the opposite was true. He had the lightest touch, he had the greatest facility, he could charm a geisha in two minutes and obtain anything he wanted from a supply sergeant in five. Carter envied him, envied his grace, his charmed indifference; then grew to hate him.

Taylor teased Carter about the cooking, and he had the knack of [14] knowing where to put the knife. "Hey, Carter," he would shout across the mess hall while breakfast was being served, "you turned my eggs twice, and I asked for them raw." The men would shout with laughter. Somehow Taylor had succeeded in conveying all of the situation, or so it seemed to Carter, insinuating everything, how Carter worked and how it meant nothing, how Carter labored to gain their affection and earned their contempt. Carter would scowl, Carter would answer in a rough voice, "Next time I'll crack them over your head." "You crack 'em, I'll eat 'em," Taylor would pipe back, "but just don't put your fingers in 'em." And there would be another laugh. He hated the sight of Taylor.

It was Taylor who came to him to get the salad oil. About twenty of [15] the soldiers were going to have a fish fry at the geisha house; they had bought the fish at the local market, but they could not buy oil, so Taylor was sent as the deputy to Carter. He was charming to Carter, he complimented him on the meal, he clapped him on the back, he dissolved Carter to warmth, to private delight in the attention, and the thought that he had misjudged Taylor. Then Taylor asked for the oil.

Carter was sick with anger. Twenty men out of the thirty in the de- [16] tachment were going on the fish fry. It meant only that Carter was considered one of the ten undesirables. It was something he had known, but the proof of knowledge is always more painful than the acquisition of it. If he had been alone his eyes would have clouded. And he was outraged at Taylor's deception. He could imagine Taylor saying ten minutes later, "You should have seen the grease job I gave to Carter. I'm dumb, but man, he's dumber."

Carter was close enough to giving him the oil. He had a sense of [17] what it would mean to refuse Taylor, he was on the very edge of mild acquiescence. But he also had a sense of how he would despise himself afterward.

"No," he said abruptly, his teeth gritted, "you can't have it." 18

"What do you mean we can't have it?" 19

"I won't give it to you." Carter could almost feel the rage which Tay- 20 lor generated at being refused.

"You won't give away a lousy five gallons of oil to a bunch of G.I.'s 21 having a party?"

"I'm sick and tired," Carter began. 22

"So am I." Taylor walked away. 23

Carter knew he would pay for it. He left the K.P.'s and went to 24 change his sweat-soaked work shirt, and as he passed the large dormitory in which most of the detachment slept he could hear Taylor's high-pitched voice. Carter did not bother to take off his shirt. He returned instead to the kitchen, and listened to the sound of men going back and forth through the hall and of a man shouting with rage. That was Hobbs, a Southerner, a big man with a big bellowing voice.

There was a formal knock on the kitchen door. Taylor came in. His 25 face was pale and his eyes showed a cold satisfaction. "Carter," he said, "the men want to see you in the big room."

Carter heard his voice answer huskily. "If they want to see me," 26 they can come into the kitchen."

He knew he would conduct himself with more courage in his own 27 kitchen than anywhere else. "I'll be here for a while."

Taylor closed the door, and Carter picked up a writing board to 28 which was clamped the menu for the following day. Then he made a pretense of examining the food supplies in the pantry closet. It was his habit to check the stocks before deciding what to serve the next day, but on this night his eyes ranged thoughtlessly over the canned goods. In a corner were seven five-gallon tins of salad oil, easily enough cooking oil to last a month. Carter came out of the pantry and shut the door behind him.

He kept his head down and pretended to be writing the menu when 29 the soldiers came in. Somehow there were even more of them than he had expected. Out of the twenty men who were going to the party, all but two or three had crowded through the door.

Carter took his time, looked up slowly. "You men want to see me?" 30 he asked flatly.

They were angry. For the first time in his life he faced the hostile ex- 31 pressions of many men. It was the most painful and anxious moment he had ever known.

"Taylor says you won't give us the oil," someone burst out. 32

"That's right, I won't," said Carter. He tapped his pencil against the 33 scratchboard, tapping it slowly and, he hoped, with an appearance of calm.

"What a stink deal," said Porfirio, a little Cuban whom Carter had ³⁴ always considered his friend.

Hobbs, the big Southerner, stared down at Carter. "Would you ³⁵ mind telling the men why you've decided not to give us the oil?" he asked quietly.

"'Cause I'm blowed if I'm going to cater to you men. I've catered ³⁶ enough," Carter said. His voice was close to cracking with the outrage he had suppressed for so long, and he knew that if he continued he might cry. "I'm the acting mess sergeant," he said as coldly as he could, "and I decide what goes out of this kitchen." He stared at each one in turn, trying to stare them down, feeling mired in the rut of his own failure. They would never have dared this approach to another mess sergeant.

"What crud," someone muttered. ³⁷

"You won't give a lousy five-gallon can of oil for a G.I. party," ³⁸ Hobbs said more loudly.

"I won't. That's definite. You men can get out of here." ³⁹

"Why, you lousy little snot," Hobbs burst out, "how many five-gal- ⁴⁰ lon cans of oil have you sold on the black market?"

"I've never sold any." Carter might have been slapped with the flat ⁴¹ of a sword. He told himself bitterly, numbly, that this was the reward he received for being perhaps the single honest cook in the whole United States Army. And he even had time to wonder at the obscure prejudice which had kept him from selling food for his own profit.

"Man, I've seen you take it out," Hobbs exclaimed. "I've seen you ⁴² take it to the market."

"I took food to trade for spices," Carter said hotly. ⁴³

There was an ugly snicker from the men. ⁴⁴

"I don't mind if a cook sells," Hobbs said, "every man has his own ⁴⁵ deal in this Army. But a cook ought to give a little food to a G.I. if he wants it."

"Tell him," someone said. ⁴⁶

"It's bull," Taylor screeched. "I've seen Carter take butter, eggs, ⁴⁷ every damn thing to the market."

Their faces were red, they circled him. ⁴⁸

"I never sold a thing," Carter said doggedly. ⁴⁹

"And I'm telling you," Hobbs said, "that you're a two-bit crook. You ⁵⁰ been raiding that kitchen, and that's why you don't give to us now."

Carter knew there was only one way he could possibly answer if he ⁵¹ hoped to live among these men again. "That's a goddam lie," Carter said to Hobbs. He laid down the scratchboard, he flipped his pencil slowly and deliberately to one corner of the room, and with his heart aching he lunged toward Hobbs. He had no hope of beating him. He merely intended to fight until he was pounded unconscious, advancing the pain and bruises he would collect as collateral for his self-respect.

To his indescribable relief Porfirio darted between them, held them 52
apart with the pleased ferocity of a small man breaking up a fight.
"Now, stop this! Now, stop this!" he cried out.

Carter allowed himself to be pushed back, and he knew that he had 53
gained a point. He even glimpsed a solution with some honor.

He shrugged violently to free himself from Porfirio. He was in a 54
rage, and yet it was a rage he could have ended at any instant. "All
right, you men," he swore, "I'll give you the oil, but now that we're at
it, I'm going to tell you a thing or two." His face red, his body perspiring, he was in the pantry and out again with a five-gallon tin.
"Here," he said, "you better have a good fish fry, 'cause it's the last
good meal you're going to have for quite a while. I'm sick of trying to
please you. You think I have to work—" he was about to say, my fingers to the bone— "well, I don't. From now on, you'll see what chow
in the Army is supposed to be like." He was almost hysterical. "Take
that oil. Have your fish fry." The fact that they wanted to cook for
themselves was the greatest insult of all. "Tomorrow I'll give you real
Army cooking."

His voice was so intense that they backed away from him. "Get out 55
of this kitchen," he said. "None of you has any business here."

They filed out quietly, and they looked a little sheepish. 56

Carter felt weary, he felt ashamed of himself, he knew he had not 57
meant what he said. But half an hour later, when he left the kitchen and
passed the large dormitory, he heard shouts of raucous laughter, and he
heard his name mentioned and then more laughter.

He slept badly that night, he was awake at four, he was in the 58
kitchen by five, and stood there white-faced and nervous, waiting for the
K.P.'s to arrive. Breakfast that morning landed on the men like a lead
bomb. Carter rummaged in the back of the pantry and found a tin of dehydrated eggs covered with dust, memento of a time when fresh eggs
were never on the ration list. The K.P.'s looked at him in amazement as
he stirred the lumpy powder into a pan of water. While it was still half-
dissolved he put it on the fire. While it was still wet, he took it off. The
coffee was cold, the toast was burned, the oatmeal stuck to the pot. The
men dipped forks into their food, took cautious sips of their coffee, and
spoke in whispers. Sullenness drifted like vapors through the kitchen.

At noontime Carter opened cans of meat and vegetable stew. He 59
dumped them into a pan and heated them slightly. He served the stew
with burned string beans and dehydrated potatoes which tasted like
straw. For dessert the men had a single lukewarm canned peach and
cold coffee.

So the meals continued. For three days Carter cooked slop, and suf- 60
fered even more than the men. When mealtime came he left the chow
line to the K.P.'s and sat in his room, perspiring with shame, determined
not to yield and sick with the determination.

Carter won. On the fourth day a delegation of men came to see him. [61]
They told him that indeed they had appreciated his cooking in the past,
they told him that they were sorry they had hurt his feelings, they listened to his remonstrances, they listened to his grievances, and with delight Carter forgave them. That night, for supper, the detachment celebrated. There was roast chicken with stuffing, lemon merinque pie and
chocolate cake. The coffee burned their lips. More than half the men
made it a point to compliment Carter on the meal.

In the weeks which followed the compliments diminished, but they [62]
never stopped completely. Carter became ashamed at last. He realized
the men were trying to humor him, and he wished to tell them it was no
longer necessary.

Harmony settled over the kitchen. Carter even became friends with [63]
Hobbs, the big Southerner. Hobbs approached him one day, and in the
manner of a farmer talked obliquely for an hour. He spoke about his father, he spoke about his girl friends, he alluded indirectly to the night
they had almost fought, and finally with the courtesy of a Southerner he
said to Carter, "You know, I'm sorry about shooting off my mouth. You
were right to want to fight me, and if you're still mad I'll fight you to
give you satisfaction, although I just as soon would not."

"No, I don't want to fight with you now," Carter said warmly. They [64]
smiled at each other. They were friends.

Carter knew he had gained Hobbs' respect. Hobbs respected him [65]
because he had been willing to fight. That made sense to a man like
Hobbs. Carter liked him so much at this moment that he wished the
friendship to be more intimate.

"You know," he said to Hobbs, "it's a funny thing. You know I re- [66]
ally never did sell anything on the black market. Not that I'm proud of
it, but I just didn't."

Hobbs frowned. He seemed to be saying that Carter did not have to [67]
lie. "I don't hold it against a man," Hobbs said, "if he makes a little
money in something that's his own proper work. Hell, I sell gas from the
motor pool. It's just I also give gas if one of the G.I.'s wants to take the
jeep out for a joy ride, kind of."

"No, but I never did sell anything." Carter had to explain. "If I ever [68]
had sold on the black market, I would have given the salad oil without
question."

Hobbs frowned again, and Carter realized he still did not believe [69]
him. Carter did not want to lose the friendship which was forming. He
thought he could save it only by some further admission. "You know,"
he said again, "remember when Porfirio broke up our fight? I was awful
glad when I didn't have to fight you." Carter laughed, expecting Hobbs
to laugh with him, but a shadow passed across Hobbs' face.

"Funny way of putting it," Hobbs said.   [70]

He was always friendly thereafter, but Carter knew that Hobbs 71
would never consider him a friend. Carter thought about it often, and
began to wonder about the things which made him different. He was no
longer so worried about becoming a man; he felt that to an extent he had
become one. But in his heart he wondered if he would ever learn the language of men.

Responding to Reading

1. The army "had proved to [Carter] that he was good at no work, and incapable of succeeding at anything" (4). How does his history of failure prepare
   you for the events that follow?
2. What does "becoming a man" mean to Carter? What does it mean to you?
   Do you agree that at the end of the story Carter has, at least "to an extent"
   (71), become a man? Explain.
3. The story's narrator tells us that Carter sees physical force as his only possible response: "Carter knew there was only one way he could possibly answer if he hoped to live among these men again" (51). Do you think Carter
   has any other alternative? Do you believe that resorting to physical force can
   be a solution, or do you see it simply as the stereotypical male way to resolve
   a problem?

BARBIE DOLL

Marge Piercy

The author of twelve novels and twelve collections of poetry, Marge
Piercy was born and educated in Michigan. Her recent works include
the novels *He, She, and It* (1991) and *The Longings of Women* (1994) and
the poetry collection *Mars and Her Children* (1992). Active in the
women's movement since 1969, Piercy says it "has been a great energy source (as well as energy sink!) and healer of the psyche for me."
Piercy wants her poems to be useful; she hopes, as she explains in *Circles on the Water* (1988), "that readers will find poems that speak to and
for them." "Barbie Doll," an ironic look at the influence of the controversial cultural icon, is from that collection.

This girlchild was born as usual
and presented dolls that did pee-pee
and miniature GE stoves and irons
and wee lipsticks the color of cherry candy.

Then in the magic of puberty, a classmate said: 5
You have a great big nose and fat legs.

She was healthy, tested intelligent,
possessed strong arms and back,
abundant sexual drive and manual dexterity.
'She went to and fro apologizing.   10
Everyone saw a fat nose on thick legs.

She was advised to play coy,
exhorted to come on hearty,
exercise, diet, smile and wheedle.
Her good nature wore out   15
like a fan belt.
So she cut off her nose and her legs
and offered them up.

In the casket displayed on satin she lay
with the undertaker's cosmetics painted on,   20
a turned-up putty nose,
dressed in a pink and white nightie.
Doesn't she look pretty? everyone said.
Consummation at last.
To every woman a happy ending.   25

Responding to Reading

1. Is Piercy exaggerating the effect of Barbie dolls and similar toys on girls? If so, why?
2. Can you think of toys that might define maleness for boys? What characteristics do these toys have that make them "male"? Do you think "male" toys can have a negative impact on a child's self-image and behavior as Piercy thinks female toys do?
3. What were your favorite toys? In what ways—if any—did they affect how you saw yourself? How did they define male and female roles for you?

WRITING

Women and Men

1. In her well-known *A Room of One's Own,* novelist and critic Virginia Woolf observes that "any woman born with a great gift in the sixteenth century would certainly have gone crazed, shot herself, or ended her days in some lonely cottage outside the village, half witch, half wizard, feared and mocked at." Write an essay in which you discuss how this statement applies to gifted women of your own generation and of your parents' generation. You may consider the essays by Ascher, Gordon, and Steinem and the poem "Barbie Doll" as you plan your paper.

2. List all the stereotypes of women—and of men—identified in the selections you read in this chapter. Then, write an essay in which you identify those that have had the most negative effects on your life and explain why. Do you consider these stereotypes to be just annoying, or actually dangerous?

3. Stephen Jay Gould says, "I do not regard as empty rhetoric the claim that women's battles are for all of us" (13). Do you agree with Gould? Use examples from your own experience to support your position.

4. Write an essay in which you identify the burdens society places on men—or on women—through its expectations, based solely on gender, that they will behave in a certain fashion. Referring to the selections in this chapter as well as to your own experience, explain who has it easier, men or women.

5. Write a letter to Judy Brady in which you develop further (or challenge) her characterization of a wife. Support your assertions with specific references to women you know as well as to Brady's essay.

6. In her memoir "The Looking-Glass Shame," Judith Ortiz Cofer says that at times she felt as if she were living in two worlds: one at home and one at school. Write an essay in which you discuss the various worlds in which you live. Be certain to point out how your experiences in these worlds are shaped by your gender. For example, one of your worlds, like Cofer's home, could encourage stereotypical gender roles; another, like the world of sports, could encourage less traditional behavior.

7. Several of the selections in this chapter draw distinctions, implicitly or explicitly, between "men's work" and "women's work." Write

an essay in which you consider the extent to which such distinctions exist today and how they have affected your professional goals.

8. Assuming there really is a language of men—and a language of women—define these languages. In your essay refer to Deborah Tannen's "Marked Women" and Norman Mailer's "The Language of Men" in this chapter and to Alleen Pace Nilsen's "Sexism in English: A 1990s Update" in Chapter 3. Consider whether these languages consist only of words, or of gestures, facial expressions, postures, and even behavior patterns as well. You may also consider whether such languages are necessary and what function, if any, they serve.

9. Stanton L. Wormley, Jr., and Norman Mailer express definite ideas about what it means to be male. Write an essay in which you define *maleness*. Refer to Wormley's "Fighting Back" and Mailer's "The Language of Men" in this chapter and to "Shooting an Elephant" in Chapter 10.

10. Do you think success means the same thing for men and for women? Do you believe it should? Use the readings in this chapter by Mary Gordon, Stanton L. Wormley, Jr., and Barbara Lazear Ascher, as well as your own observations to support your thesis.

6

THE AMERICAN DREAM

Student Voices

"The American dream to my Chinese-American family is more a vision than a dream. It is a vision of being financially prosperous, attaining a good future through a college education. Although my family has been lucky, the rest of my race was less fortunate. During the early years of Chinese immigration into this country, they were denied citizenship, and sometimes denied entrance into certain states; they were denied access to certain occupations, and even admission into the U.S. armed forces; they were also harassed by whites and even by the government itself; and they experienced segregation in schools and housing. Still, they had the vision."

—Jeff Hui

"My ethnic background helped to shape my identity. Although I was born in Canada and have grown up in the United States, there are many Filipino customs that are a part of my life. The Filipino food my family eats may seem very different to my American friends. There are also decorations in my house that have an Asian or Filipino flavor. This is an environment in which I have grown up, and it will always be a part of my life. I will always remember that my heritage is from the Philippines, and so will my children."

—Cynthia Denise Padilla

"I like to think of America not as a melting pot, but as a double boiler. On the bottom level you have the family, where tradition and heritage play a vital role. On this level cultures are separate. On the top level, the melting occurs. This is the social system, where heritage and tradition must sometimes be sacrificed. On this level individuality is sacrificed, but the overall product strengthens our nation."

—*Russell Jayne*

"Being a hyphenated American, such as an Italian-American, makes you feel like you are part of a group. Everyone strives to be part of a group. It's comforting and it gives you a sense of belonging as well as a sense of accomplishment. Being in a group gives you a feeling that you have something in common with others."

—*Pat DiStefano*

"I am a first-generation American who is a descendant of the Phoenicians. In defining who I am, I must first consider where I come from. This place, just northwest of Philadelphia, is the small town of Easton, which is also the home of Larry Holmes, the former heavyweight boxing champion of the world. Like my family, Easton is on the rebound after difficult economic hardships associated with the geographic area in general, including the strip mining of the western suburbs and, most of all, the demise of Bethlehem Steel.

"Easton is a melting pot, home to numerous immigrants from Europe and the Middle East. In the town, as in my family, it is no longer assumed that children will grow up to be laborers. As children, we were challenged to look up to the Hill where Lafayette College stands. The Hill remains a source of inspiration for me, reminding me to not accept what is given, but to challenge and excel in order to give."

—*Michael Karam*

"The American Dream once involved having a family with 2.5 children and a small house with a white picket fence. Now that dream has turned into a nightmare for many. People who once struggled to achieve lofty goals are now disillusioned. They have given up on their dreams. Many people don't dare to dream because they can see no way out of their situation. Many will never have a chance at the old dream. But I believe a new dream can take its place. The new dream may not be as lofty as the old one, but it's still a dream."

—*Jeff Morris*

"The American Dream is not only for Americans."

—*Ashley Shaner*

Preparing to Read and Write

The American Dream—of political and religious freedom, equal access to education, and, ultimately, success and wealth—is often elusive, but it still continues to attract many who have heard its call. In the process of working toward the dream, some individuals and groups struggle to overcome their status as newcomers, while others who have been "Americans" for many years try to overcome their status as outsiders—to fit in, to belong, to be accepted. As they work toward their goals, however, some must make a painful decision, for full realization of the dream all too often means assimilating, giving up language, custom, and culture to become more like others. Thus, although the American Dream may ultimately mean winning, it can also mean losing a vital part of oneself.

Most of the selections in this chapter are written from the point of view of outsiders looking in. All these writers want to be accepted; all believe that the American Dream's reward is worth the struggle. Still, while some eagerly anticipate (or even demand) full acceptance as "Americans," with all the rights and responsibilities that this entails, others are more cautious, afraid of the personal or cultural price they will have to pay for full acceptance into the American mainstream.

As you read and prepare to write about the selections in this chapter, you may consider the following questions.

- What does the American Dream mean to the writer?
- Has the writer's version of the dream changed over the years, or has it remained constant?
- Has the writer been able to achieve the American Dream? If so, how? If not, why not?
- What are the greatest obstacles that stand between the writer and the American Dream? Would you characterize these obstacles as primarily cultural, social, political, racial, economic, religious, linguistic, gender related, or behavioral?
- Which writers have the easiest access to the American Dream? For whom is access most difficult? Why? Does the writer blame anything or anyone for his or her inability to fit in?
- Is the writer looking at the United States from the point of view of an insider or an outsider?
- How does the writer react to his or her situation? For example, is he or she sad? Angry? Bitter? Confused? Resigned?
- Does the writer want to change his or her status? What steps, if any, does he or she take to win acceptance? What additional steps could he or she take?

- What is the writer's attitude toward the group of which he or she is not (or cannot be) a part? Toward his or her own group?
- Where does the writer seem to feel most comfortable? In what situations does the writer feel most alone? Most conspicuous? Most threatened?
- Does the writer present himself or herself as an individual or as a representative of a particular group?
- Which writers' views of the American Dream are most similar? Most different? Most like your own?

TWO PERSPECTIVES ON THE AMERICAN DREAM

Following are two of the most famous documents in American history. The first is The Declaration of Independence, which was drafted by founding father Thomas Jefferson and amended by the Continental Congress in 1776 as an announcement to the world that the American colonists were rejecting the tyrannical rule of the British crown, sparking the Revolutionary War. The opening of the second paragraph expresses the fundamental American ideal that "all men are created equal," which is deeply ironic in light of the fact that Jefferson himself and other signers were slave-holders at the time. (Jefferson's original draft included a strong statement against slavery, but the Congress deleted this passage.) The second is the famous "I Have a Dream" speech which Martin Luther King, Jr. (see also p. 741) delivered from the steps of the Lincoln Memorial during the 1963 civil rights march on Washington. One of the greatest orators of the century, King offers a stirring indictment of the lack of equality shared by black Americans almost two hundred years after the Declaration was written but also looks hopefully, almost joyfully, to a future when "all of God's children" will be free.

THE DECLARATION OF INDEPENDENCE

Thomas Jefferson

In Congress, July 4, 1776: The Unanimous Declaration of the Thirteen United States of America

When in the Course of human events it becomes necessary for one 1
people to dissolve the political bands which have connected them with another, and to assume among the powers of the earth, the separate and equal station to which the Laws of Nature and of Nature's God entitle them, a decent respect to the opinions of mankind requires that they should declare the causes which impel them to the separation.

We hold these truths to be self-evident, that all men are created 2
equal, that they are endowed by their Creator with certain unalienable Rights, that among these are Life, Liberty and the pursuit of Happiness. That to secure these rights, Governments are instituted among Men, de-

riving their just powers from the consent of the governed. That whenever any Form of Government becomes destructive of these ends, it is the Right of the People to alter or to abolish it, and to institute new Government, laying its foundation on such principles and organizing its powers in such form, as to them shall seem most likely to affect their Safety and Happiness. Prudence, indeed, will dictate that Governments long established should not be changed for light and transient causes; and accordingly all experience hath shewn that mankind are more disposed to suffer, while evils are sufferable, than to right themselves by abolishing the forms to which they are accustomed. But when a long train of abuses and usurpations, pursuing invariably the same Object evinces a design to reduce them under absolute Despotism, it is their right, it is their duty, to throw off such Government, and to provide new Guards for their future security. Such has been the patient sufferance of these Colonies; and such is now the necessity which constrains them to alter their former Systems of Government. The history of the present King of Great Britain is a history of repeated injuries and usurpations, all having in direct object the establishment of an absolute Tyranny over these States. To prove this, let Facts be submitted to a candid world.

He has refused his Assent to Laws, the most wholesome and nec- 3
essary for the public good.

He has forbidden his Government to pass laws of immediate and 4
pressing importance, unless suspended in their operation till his Assent should be obtained; and when so suspended, he has utterly neglected to attend to them.

He has refused to pass other Laws for the accommodation of large 5
districts of people, unless those people would relinquish the right of Representation in the Legislature, a right inestimable to them and formidable to tyrants only.

He has called together legislative bodies at places unusual, uncom- 6
fortable, and distant from the depository of their Public Records, for the sole purpose of fatiguing them into compliance with his measures.

He has dissolved Representative Houses repeatedly, for opposing 7
with manly firmness his invasions on the rights of the people.

He has refused for a long time, after such dissolutions, to cause oth- 8
ers to be elected; whereby the Legislative Powers, incapable of Annihilation, have returned to the People at large for their exercise; the State remaining in the mean time exposed to all the dangers of invasion from without, and convulsions within.

He has endeavored to prevent the population of these States; for 9
that purpose obstructing the Laws for Naturalization of Foreigners; refusing to pass others to encourage their migration hither, and raising the conditions of new Appropriations of Lands.

He has obstructed the Administration of Justice, by refusing his As- 10
sent to Laws for establishing Judiciary Powers.

He has made Judges dependent on his Will alone, for the tenure of [11] their offices, and the amount and payment of their salaries.

He has erected a multitude of New Offices, and sent hither swarms [12] of Officers to harass our people, and eat out their substance.

He has kept among us, in times of peace, Standing Armies without [13] the Consent of our legislatures.

He has affected to render the Military independent of and superior [14] to the Civil Power.

He has combined with others to subject us to a jurisdiction foreign [15] to our constitution, and unacknowledged by our laws; giving his Assent to their Acts of pretended Legislation: For quartering large bodies of armed troops among us: For protecting them, by a mock Trial, from punishment for any Murders which they should commit on the Inhabitants of these States: For cutting off our Trade with all parts of the world: For imposing Taxes on us without our Consent: For depriving us in many cases, of the benefits of Trial by Jury; For transporting us beyond Seas to be tried for pretended offenses: for abolishing the free System of English Laws in a neighboring Province, establishing therein an Arbitrary government, and enlarging its Boundaries so as to render it at once an example and fit instrument for introducing the same absolute rule into these Colonies: For taking away our Charters, abolishing our most valuable Laws and altering fundamentally and Forms of our Governments: For suspending our own Legislatures, and declaring themselves invested with power to legislate for us in all cases whatsoever.

He has abdicated Government here, by declaring us out of his Pro- [16] tection and waging War against us.

He has plundered our seas, ravaged our Coasts, burnt our towns, [17] and destroyed the lives of our people.

He is at this time transporting large Armies of foreign Mercenaries [18] to complete the works of death, desolation and tyranny, already begun with circumstances of Cruelty & Perfidy scarcely paralleled in the most barbarous ages, and totally unworthy the Head of a civilized nation.

He has constrained our fellow Citizens taken Captive on the high [19] Seas to bear Arms against their Country, to become the executioners of their friends and Brethren, or to fall themselves by their Hands.

He has excited domestic insurrections amongst us, and has en- [20] deavored to bring on the inhabitants of our frontiers, the merciless Indian Savages, whose known rule of warfare, is an undistinguished destruction of all ages, sexes, and conditions.

In every stage of these Oppressions We have Petitioned for Redress [21] in the most humble terms: Our repeated Petitions have been answered only by repeated injury. A Prince, whose character is thus marked by every act which may define a Tyrant, is unfit to be the ruler of a free people.

Nor have We been wanting in attention to our British brethren. We [22] have warned them from time to time of attempts by their legislature to extend an unwarrantable jurisdiction over us. We have reminded them of the circumstances of our emigration and settlement here. We have appealed to their native justice and magnanimity, and we have conjured them by the ties of our common kindred to disavow these usurpations, which would inevitably interrupt our connections and correspondence. They too have been deaf to the voice of justice and of consanguinity. We must, therefore, acquiesce in the necessity, which denounces our Separation, and hold them, as we hold the rest of mankind, Enemies in War, in Peace Friends.

We, THEREFORE the Representatives of the UNITED STATES OF AMERICA, [23] in General Congress, Assembled, appealing to the Supreme Judge of the world for the rectitude of our intentions, do, in the Name, and by Authority of the good People of these Colonies, solemnly publish and declare, That these United Colonies are, and of Right ought to be FREE AND INDEPENDENT STATES; that they are Absolved from all Allegiance to the British Crown, and that all political connection between them and the State of Great Britain, is and ought to be totally dissolved; and that as Free and Independent States, they have full Power to levy War, conclude Peace, contract Alliances, establish Commerce, and to do all other Acts and Things which Independent States may of right do. And for the support of this Declaration, with a firm reliance on the protection of Divine Providence, we mutually pledge to each other our Lives, our Fortunes, and our sacred Honor.

I HAVE A DREAM

Martin Luther King, Jr.

I am happy to join with you today in what will go down in histo- [1] ry as the greatest demonstration for freedom in the history of our nation.

Fivescore years ago, a great American, in whose symbolic shadow [2] we stand today, signed the Emancipation Proclamation. This momentous decree came as a great beacon light of hope to millions of Negro slaves who had been seared in the flames of withering injustice. It came as a joyous daybreak to end the long night of their captivity.

But one hundred years later, the Negro still is not free; one hundred [3] years later, the life of the Negro is still sadly crippled by the manacles of segregation and the chains of discrimination; one hundred years later, the Negro lives on a lonely island of poverty in the midst of a vast ocean of material prosperity; one hundred years later, the Negro is still languishing in the corners of American society and finds himself in exile in his own land.

So we've come here today to dramatize a shameful condition. In a sense we've come to our nation's capital to cash a check. When the architects of our republic wrote the magnificent words of the Constitution and the Declaration of Independence, they were signing a promissory note to which every American was to fall heir. This note was the promise that all men, yes, black men as well as white men, would be guaranteed the unalienable rights of life, liberty, and the pursuit of happiness. [4]

It is obvious today that America has defaulted on this promissory note in so far as her citizens of color are concerned. Instead of honoring this sacred obligation, America has given the Negro people a bad check; a check which has come back marked "insufficient funds." We refuse to believe that there are insufficient funds in the great vaults of opportunity of this nation. And so we've come to cash this check, a check that will give us upon demand the riches of freedom and the security of justice. [5]

We have also come to this hallowed spot to remind America of the fierce urgency of now. This is no time to engage in the luxury of cooling off or to take the tranquilizing drug of gradualism. Now is the time to make real the promises of democracy; now is the time to rise from the dark and desolate valley of segregation to the sunlit path of racial justice; now is the time to lift our nation from the quicksands of racial injustice to the solid rock of brotherhood; now is the time to make justice a reality for all God's children. It would be fatal for the nation to overlook the urgency of the moment. This sweltering summer of the Negro's legitimate discontent will not pass until there is an invigorating autumn of freedom and equality. [6]

Nineteen sixty-three is not an end, but a beginning. And those who hope that the Negro needed to blow off steam and will now be content, will have a rude awakening if the nation returns to business as usual. [7]

There will be neither rest nor tranquility in America until the Negro is granted his citizenship rights. The whirlwinds of revolt will continue to shake the foundations of our nation until the bright day of justice emerges. [8]

But there is something that I must say to my people who stand on the warm threshold which leads into the palace of justice. In the process of gaining our rightful place we must not be guilty of wrongful deeds. [9]

Let us not seek to satisfy our thirst for freedom by drinking from the cup of bitterness and hatred. We must forever conduct our struggle on the high plane of dignity and discipline. We must not allow our creative protest to degenerate into physical violence. Again and again we must rise to the majestic heights of meeting physical force with soul force. [10]

The marvelous new militancy which has engulfed the Negro community must not lead us to a distrust of all white people, for many of our [11] white brothers, as evidenced by their presence here today, have come to realize that their destiny is tied up with our destiny and they have come to realize that their freedom is inextricably bound to our freedom. This offense we share mounted to storm the battlements of injustice must be carried forth by a biracial army. We cannot walk alone.

And as we walk, we must make the pledge that we shall always [12] march ahead. We cannot turn back. There are those who are asking the devotees of civil rights, "When will you be satisfied?" We can never be satisfied as long as the Negro is the victim of the unspeakable horrors of police brutality.

We can never be satisfied as long as our bodies, heavy with fatigue [13] of travel, cannot gain lodging in the motels of the highways and the hotels of the cities. We cannot be satisfied as long as the Negro's basic mobility is from a smaller ghetto to a larger one.

We can never be satisfied as long as our children are stripped of [14] their selfhood and robbed of their dignity by signs stating "for whites only." We cannot be satisfied as long as a Negro in Mississippi cannot vote and a Negro in New York believes he has nothing for which to vote. No, we are not satisfied, and we will not be satisfied until justice rolls down like waters and righteousness like a mighty stream.

I am not unmindful that some of you have come here out of exces- [15] sive trials and tribulation. Some of you have come fresh from narrow jail cells. Some of you have come from areas where your quest for freedom left you battered by the storms of persecution and staggered by the winds of police brutality. You have been the veterans of creative suffering. Continue to work with the faith that unearned suffering is redemptive.

Go back to Mississippi; go back to Alabama; go back to South Car- [16] olina; go back to Georgia; go back to Louisiana; go back to the slums and ghettos of the northern cities, knowing that somehow this situation can, and will be changed. Let us not wallow in the valley of despair.

So I say to you, my friends, that even though we must face the dif- [17] ficulties of today and tomorrow, I still have a dream. It is a dream deeply rooted in the American dream that one day this nation will rise up and live out the true meaning of its creed—we hold these truths to be self-evident, that all men are created equal.

I have a dream that one day on the red hills of Georgia, sons of for- [18] mer slaves and sons of former slave-owners will be able to sit down together at the table of brotherhood.

I have a dream that one day, even the state of Mississippi, a state [19] sweltering with the heat of injustice, sweltering with the heat of oppression, will be transformed into an oasis of freedom and justice.

I have a dream my four little children will one day live in a nation [20] where they will not be judged by the color of their skin but by content of their character. I have a dream today!

I have a dream that one day, down in Alabama, with its vicious [21] racists, with its governor having his lips dripping with the words of interposition and nullification, that one day, right there in Alabama, little black boys and black girls will be able to join hands with little white boys and white girls as sisters and brothers. I have a dream today!

I have a dream that one day every valley shall be exalted, every hill [22] and mountain shall be made low, the rough places shall be made plain, and the crooked places shall be made straight and the glory of the Lord will be revealed and all flesh shall see it together.

This is our hope. This is the faith that I go back to the South with. [23]

With this faith we will be able to hew out of the mountain of despair [24] a stone of hope. With this faith we will be able to transform the jangling discords of our nation into a beautiful symphony of brotherhood.

With this faith we will be able to work together, to pray together, to [25] struggle together, to go to jail together, to stand up for freedom together, knowing that we will be free one day. This will be the day when all of God's children will be able to sing with new meaning—"my country 'tis of thee; sweet land of liberty; of thee I sing; land where my fathers died, land of the pilgrim's pride; from every mountain side, let freedom ring"—and if America is to be a great nation, this must become true.

So let freedom ring from the prodigious hilltops of New Hampshire. [26]

Let freedom ring from the mighty mountains of New York. [27]

Let freedom ring from the heightening Alleghenies of Pennsylvania. [28]

Let freedom ring from the snow-capped Rockies of Colorado. [29]

Let freedom ring from the curvaceous slopes of California. [30]

But not only that. [31]

Let freedom ring from Stone Mountain of Georgia. [32]

Let freedom ring from Lookout Mountain of Tennessee. [33]

Let freedom ring from every hill and molehill of Mississippi, from [34] every mountainside, let freedom ring.

And when we allow freedom to ring, when we let it ring from every [35] village and hamlet, from every state and city, we will be able to speed up that day when all of God's children—black men and white men, Jews and Gentiles, Catholics and Protestants—will be able to join hands and to sing in the words of the old Negro spiritual, "Free at last, free at last; thank God Almighty, we are free at last."

Responding to Reading

1. The Declaration of Independence was written in the eighteenth century, a time when logic and reason were thought to be the supreme achievements of human beings. Do you think it is as reasonably argued as it seems to be on the surface, or does it also include emotional appeals? Explain your position.

2. Do you think it is fair, as some have done, to accuse the framers of the Declaration of Independence of being racist? Sexist?

3. What exactly is King's dream? Do you believe it has come true in any sense?
4. Speaking as a representative of his fellow African-American citizens, King tells his audience that blacks find themselves "in exile in [their] own land" (3). Do you believe this is true for members of any minority groups today? Which groups? Why?
5. Jefferson wrote in the eighteenth century; King, in the twentieth. Jefferson wrote as an insider; King, as an outsider. What do their dreams have in common? How does each man intend to achieve his dream?
6. What does the American Dream mean to you?

WE MAY BE BROTHERS

Chief Seattle

Son of a Suquamish chief and a Duwamish chief's daughter, Sealth (1786?–1866) in 1810 became chief of the Suquamish, Duwamish, and other salt-water tribes occupying the area around Puget Sound in what is now the state of Washington. A skilled diplomat and orator, he helped maintain peace between his followers and the white settlers, who began arriving in the area around 1851. (Unable to pronounce his name in the original Salish tongue, the whites changed its pronunciation to "Seattle," eventually naming their new town after him.) In 1854, during treaty negotiations with the U.S. territorial governor, the Chief delivered a moving speech in which he described the inevitable displacement of his people by the better armed, more technologically advanced newcomers. This speech was not in fact transcribed until some thirty years later, and then by a white onlooker who wrote in the flowery English popular at the time; as a result, it is impossible to say how closely what we reprint here corresponds to Seattle's exact words. The message, however, is a timeless one about the relationship between human beings and the earth.

Yonder sky that has wept tears of compassion upon my people for [1] centuries untold, and which to us appears changeless and eternal, may change. Today is fair. Tomorrow it may be overcast with clouds. My words are like the stars that never change. Whatever Seattle says the great chief at Washington can rely upon with as much certainty as he can upon the return of the sun or the seasons. The White Chief says that Big Chief at Washington sends us greetings of friendship and goodwill. That is kind of him for we know he has little need of our friendship in return. His people are many. They are like the grass that covers vast prairies. My people are few. They resemble the scattering trees of a storm-swept plain. . . . I will not dwell on, nor mourn over, our untimely decay, nor reproach our paleface brothers with hastening it, as we too may have been somewhat to blame. . . .

Your God is not our God. Your God loves your people and hates mine. He folds his strong and protecting arms lovingly about the paleface and leads him by the hand as a father leads his infant son—but He has forsaken His red children—if they really are His. Our God, the Great Spirit, seems also to have forsaken us. Your God makes your people strong every day. Soon they will fill the land. Our people are ebbing away like a rapidly receding tide that will never return. The white man's God cannot love our people or He would protect them. They seem to be orphans who can look nowhere for help. How then can we be brothers? . . . We are two distinct races with separate origins and separate destinies. There is little in common between us.

To us the ashes of our ancestors are sacred and their resting place is hallowed ground. You wander far from the graves of your ancestors and seemingly without regret. Your religion was written upon tables of stone by the iron finger of your God so that you could not forget. The Red Man could never comprehend nor remember it. Our religion is the traditions of our ancestors—the dreams of our old men, given them in solemn hours of night by the Great Spirit; and the visions of our sachems; and it is written in the hearts of our people.

Your dead cease to love you and the land of their nativity as soon as they pass the portals of the tomb and wander way beyond the stars. They are soon forgotten and never return. Our dead never forget the beautiful world that gave them being.

Day and night cannot dwell together. The Red Man has ever fled the approach of the White Man, as the morning mist flees before the morning sun. However, your proposition seems fair and I think that my people will accept it and will retire to the reservation you offer them. Then we will dwell apart in peace. . . . It matters little where we pass the remnant of our days. They will not be many. A few more moons; a few more winters—and not one of the descendants of the mighty hosts that once moved over this broad land or lived in happy homes, protected by the Great Spirit, will remain to mourn over the graves of a people once more powerful and hopeful than yours. But why should I mourn at the untimely fate of my people? Tribe follows tribe, and nation follows nation, like the waves of the sea. It is the order of nature, and regret is useless. Your time of decay may be distant, but it will surely come, for even the White Man whose God walked and talked with him as friend with friend cannot be exempt from the common destiny. We may be brothers after all. We will see. . . .

Every part of this soil is sacred in the estimation of my people. Every hillside, every valley, every plain and grove, has been hallowed by some sad or happy event in days long vanished. The very dust upon which you now stand responds more lovingly to their footsteps than to yours, because it is rich with the blood of our ancestors and our bare feet are conscious of the sympathetic touch. Even the little children who lived here and rejoiced here for a brief season will love these somber solitudes and at eventide they greet shadowy returning spirits. And when the last Red Man shall have perished, and the memory of my tribe shall have become a myth among the White Men, these shores will swarm with the invisible dead of my tribe, and when your children's children think themselves alone in the field, the store, the shop, upon the highway, or in the silence of the pathless woods, they will not be alone. At night when the streets of your cities and villages are silent and you think them deserted, they will throng with the returning hosts that once filled and still love this beautiful land. The White Man will never be alone.

Let him be just and deal kindly with my people, for the dead are not   7
powerless. Dead, did I say? There is no death, only a change of worlds.

Responding to Reading

1. The point is made in paragraph 2 that Native Americans and whites are "two distinct races with separate origins and separate destinies." What differences are then identified? Can you identify any similarities?
2. Would you characterize the speech's tone as primarily hopeful, resigned, conciliatory, angry, or bitter? What dreams, if any, does it suggest for Seattle's people?
3. Paragraph 5 offers the observation, "We may be brothers after all. We will see." What do you suppose this means? Do you agree?

THE FEAR OF LOSING A CULTURE

Richard Rodriguez

Richard Rodriguez (see also p.169) has strong opinions about language and culture; he says in a *People* magazine interview: "I refuse to accept my generation's romanticism about discovering 'roots.' The trouble with that is it somehow holds children accountable for maintaining their culture, and freezes them into thinking of themselves as Mexicans or as Chinese or as blacks." In "The Fear of Losing a Culture," written in 1988, Rodriguez defines Hispanic-American culture, which stands "where the past meets the future," and argues that this culture has something essential to offer America.

What is culture?   1

The immigrant shrugs. Latin American immigrants come to the   2
United States with only the things they need in mind—not abstractions
like culture. Money. They need dollars. They need food. Maybe they
need to get out of the way of bullets.

Most of us who concern ourselves with Hispanic-American culture,   3
as painters, musicians, writers—or as sons and daughters—are the children of immigrants. We have grown up on this side of the border, in the
land of Elvis Presley and Thomas Edison; our lives are prescribed by the
mall, by the DMV and the Chinese restaurant. Our imagination yet vas-
cillates between and Edenic Latin America (the blue door)—which nevertheless betrayed our parents—and the repellent plate glass of a real
American city—which has been good to us.

Hispanic-American culture is where the past meets the future. His-   4
panic-American culture is not an Hispanic milestone only, not simply a
celebration at the crossroads. America transforms into pleasure what
America cannot avoid. Is it any coincidence that at a time when Americans are troubled by the encroachment of the Mexican desert, Americans discover a chic in cactus, in the decorator colors of the Southwest?
In sand?

Hispanic-American culture of the sort that is now showing (the teen   5
movie, the rock songs) may exist in an hourglass; may in fact be irrelevant to the epic. The U.S. Border Patrol works through the night to arrest the flow of illegal immigrants over the border, even as Americans
wait in line to get into "La Bamba." Even as Americans vote to declare,
once and for all, that English shall be the official language of the United States, Madonna starts recording in Spanish.

But then so is Bill Cosby's show irrelevant to the 10 o'clock news,   6
where families huddle together in fear on porches, pointing at the body
of the slain boy bagged in tarpoline. Which is not to say that Bill Cosby
or Michael Jackson are irrelevant to the future or without neo-Platonic[1]
influence. Like players within the play, they prefigure, they resolve.
They make black and white audiences aware of a bond that may not yet
exist.

Before a national TV audience, Rita Moreno tells Geraldo Rivera that   7
her dream as an actress is to play a character rather like herself: "I speak
English perfectly well . . . I'm not dying from poverty . . . I want to play
that kind of Hispanic woman, which is to say, an American citizen." This
is an actress talking, these are show-biz pieties. But Moreno expresses as
well the general Hispanic-American predicament. Hispanics want to belong to America without betraying the past.

---

[1] A philosophical and religious system developed in the third century A.D., based on doctrines of
Plato and other Greek philosophers, and incorporating elements of Oriental mysticism and some
Christian and Judaic ideas. [Eds.]

Hispanics fear losing ground in any negotiation with the American ⁸
city. We come from an expansive, an intimate culture that has been
judged second-rate by the United States of America. For reasons of
pride, therefore, as much as of affection, we are reluctant to give up our
past. Hispanics often express a fear of "losing" culture. Our fame in the
United States has been our resistance to assimilation.

The symbol of Hispanic culture has been the tongue of flame— ⁹
Spanish. But the remarkable legacy Hispanics carry from Latin America is not language—an inflatable skin—but breath itself, capacity of
soul, an inclination to live. The genius of Latin America is the habit of
synthesis.

We assimilate. Just over the border there is the example of Mexico, ¹⁰
the country from which the majority of U.S. Hispanics come. Mexico is
mestizo²—Indian and Spanish. Within a single family, Mexicans are
light-skinned and dark. It is impossible for the Mexican to say, in the
scheme of things, where the Indian begins and the Spaniard surrenders.

In culture as in blood, Latin America was formed by a rape that be- ¹¹
came a marriage. Due to the absorbing generosity of the Indian, European culture took on new soil. What Latin America knows is that people create one another as they marry. In the music of Latin America you
will hear the litany of bloodlines—the African drum, the German ac-
cordian, the cry from the minaret.

The United States stands as the opposing New World experiment. In ¹²
North America the Indian and the European stood apace. Whereas Latin
America was formed by a medieval Catholic dream of one world—of
meltdown conversion—the United States was built up from Protestant
individualism. The American melting pot washes away only embarrassment; it is the necessary initiation into public life. The American faith
is that our national strength derives from separateness, from "diversity."
The glamour of the United States is a carnival promise: You can lose
weight, get rich as Rockefeller, tough up your roots, get a divorce.

Immigrants still come for the promise. But the United States wavers ¹³
in its faith. As long as there was space enough, sky enough, as long as
economic success validated individualism, loneliness was not too high
a price to pay. (The cabin on the prairie or the Sony Walkman.)

As we near the end of the American century, two alternative cul- ¹⁴
tures beckon the American imagination—both highly communal cultures—the Asian and the Latin American. The United States is a literal
culture. Americans devour what we might otherwise fear to become.
Sushi will make us corporate warriors. Combination Plate #3, smoth-
ered in mestizo gravy, will burn a hole in our hearts.

Latin America offers passion. Latin America has a life—I mean *life*— ¹⁵
big clouds, unambiguous themes, death, birth, faith, that the United

---

² Any person of mixed blood, but particularly European and Native American. [Eds.]

States, for all its quality of life, seems without now. Latin America offers communal riches: an undistressed leisure, a kitchen table, even a full sorrow. Such is the solitude of America, such is the urgency of American need, Americans reach right past a fledgling, homegrown Hispanic-American culture for the real thing—the darker bottle of Mexican beer; the denser novel of a Latin American master.

For a long time, Hispanics in the United States withheld from the ¹⁶ United States our Latin American gift. We denied the value of assimilation. But as our presence is judged less foreign in America, we will produce a more generous art, less timid, less parochial. Carlos Santana, Luis Valdez, Linda Ronstadt[3]—Hispanic Americans do not have a "pure" Latin American art to offer. Expect bastard themes, expect ironies, comic conclusions. For we live on this side of the border, where Kraft manufactures bricks of "Mexican style" Velveeta, and where Jack in the Box serves "Fajita Pita."

The flame-red Chevy floats a song down the Pan American Highway: From ¹⁷ *a rolled-down window, the grizzled voice of Willie Nelson rises in disembodied harmony with the voice of Julio Iglesias. Gabby Hayes and Cisco[4] are thus resolved.*

Expect marriage. We will change America even as we will be ¹⁸ changed. We will disappear with you into a new miscegenation.[5]

Along the border, real conflicts remain. But the ancient tear sepa- ¹⁹ rating Europe from itself—the Catholic Mediterranean from the Protestant north—may yet heal itself in the New World. For generations, Latin America has been the place—the bed—of a confluence of so many races and cultures that Protestant North America shuddered to imagine it.

Imagine it.   20

Responding to Reading

1. What characteristics does Rodriguez consider central to his culture? Do you think non-Hispanics are likely to define Hispanic culture as Rodriguez does? Why or why not?
2. Rodriguez suggests in paragraphs 18 and 19 that he believes full assimilation of cultures is inevitable ("a new miscegenation"; "a confluence of . . . races and cultures"). Do you agree? Does he see such assimilation as a positive or negative development? What are your thoughts on this issue?
3. Do you believe it is possible for Hispanic Americans—or members of other ethnic minorities—to retain their culture *and* to assimilate into American society? Explain.

---

[3] Carlos Santana (1947–), guitarist and founder of the rock band Santana; Luis Valdez (1940–), playwright focusing on Chicano experience; Linda Ronstadt (1946–), popular singer [Eds.]
[4] George "Gabby" Hayes was an Anglo actor who appeared in movie and TV westerns beginning in the 1930s. The Cisco Kid was a popular Latino character in movie and TV westerns.
[5] Interbreeding between races. [Eds.]

THE LIBRARY CARD

Richard Wright

Born on a plantation near Natchez, Mississippi, Richard Wright (1908–1960) spent much of his childhood in an orphanage or with various relatives. He moved to Chicago in 1934 and worked at various unskilled jobs before joining the Federal Writer's Project. Wright's politics became radical at this time, and he wrote poetry for leftist publications. In 1938 he published his first book, *Uncle Tom's Children: Four Novellas.* His 1940 novel *Native Son* made him famous. After World War II, Wright lived as an expatriate in Paris, where he wrote his autobiography, *Black Boy* (1945), a book that celebrates black resilience and courage much as nineteenth-century slave narratives do. In this excerpt from *Black Boy,* Wright tells how he took advantage of an opportunity to feed his hunger for an intellectual life.

One morning I arrived early at work and went into the bank lobby [1]
where the Negro porter was mopping. I stood at a counter and picked up the Memphis *Commercial Appeal* and began my free reading of the press. I came finally to the editorial page and saw an article dealing with one H. L. Mencken.[1] I knew by hearsay that he was the editor of the *American Mercury,* but aside from that I knew nothing about him. The article was a furious denunciation of Mencken, concluding with one hot, short sentence: Mencken is a fool.

I wondered what on earth this Mencken had done to call down [2]
upon him the scorn of the South. The only people I had ever heard denounced in the South were Negroes, and this man was not a Negro. Then what ideas did Mencken hold that made a newspaper like the *Commercial Appeal* castigate him publicly? Undoubtedly he must be advocating ideas that the South did not like. Were there, then, people other than Negroes who criticized the South? I knew that during the Civil War the South had hated northern whites, but I had not encountered such hate during my life. Knowing no more of Mencken than I did at that moment, I felt a vague sympathy for him. Had not the South, which had assigned me the role of a non-man, cast at him its hardest words?

Now, how could I find out about this Mencken? There was a huge [3]
library near the riverfront, but I knew that Negroes were not allowed to patronize its shelves any more than they were the parks and playgrounds of the city. I had gone into the library several times to get books

---

[1] Henry Louis Mencken (1880–1956), journalist, critic, and essayist who was known for his pointed, outspoken, and satirical comments about the blunders and imperfections of democracy and the cultural awkwardness of Americans. [Eds.]

for the white men on the job. Which of them would now help me to get books? And how could I read them without causing concern to the white men with whom I worked? I had so far been successful in hiding my thoughts and feelings from them, but I knew that I would create hostility if I went about this business of reading in a clumsy way.

I weighed the personalities of the men on the job. There was Don, a   4
Jew; but I distrusted him. His position was not much better than mine and I knew that he was uneasy and insecure; he had always treated me in an offhand, bantering way that barely concealed his contempt. I was afraid to ask him to help me to get books; his frantic desire to demonstrate a racial solidarity with the whites against Negroes might make him betray me.

Then how about the boss? No, he was a Baptist and I had the sus-   5
picion that he would not be quite able to comprehend why a black boy would want to read Mencken. There were other white men on the job whose attitudes showed clearly that they were Kluxers or sympathizers, and they were out of the question.

There remained only one man whose attitude did not fit into an anti-   6
Negro category, for I had heard the white men refer to him as a "Pope lover." He was an Irish Catholic and was hated by the white Southern- ers. I knew that he read books, because I had got him volumes from the library several times. Since he, too, was an object of hatred, I felt that he might refuse me but would hardly betray me. I hesitated, weighing and balancing the imponderable realities.

One morning I paused before the Catholic fellow's desk.   7

"I want to ask you a favor," I whispered to him.   8

"What is it?"   9

"I want to read. I can't get books from the library. I wonder if you'd   10
let me use your card?"

He looked at me suspiciously.   11

"My card is full most of the time," he said.   12

"I see," I said and waited, posing my question silently.   13

"You're not trying to get me into trouble, are you, boy?" he asked,   14
staring at me.

"Oh, no, sir."   15

"What book do you want?"   16

"A book by H. L. Mencken."   17

"Which one?"   18

"I don't know. Has he written more than one?"   19

"He has written several."   20

"I didn't know that."   21

"What makes you want to read Mencken?"   22

"Oh, I just saw his name in the newspaper," I said.   23

"It's good of you to want to read," he said. "But you ought to read   24
the right things."

I said nothing. Would he want to supervise my reading? 25

"Let me think," he said. "I'll figure out something." 26

I turned from him and he called me back. He stared at me quizzi- 27
cally.

"Richard, don't mention this to the other white men," he said. 28

"I understand," I said. "I won't say a word." 29

A few days later he called me to him. 30

"I've got a card in my wife's name," he said. "Here's mine." 31

"Thank you, sir." 32

"Do you think you can manage it?" 33

"I'll manage fine," I said. 34

"If they suspect you, you'll get in trouble," he said. 35

"I'll write the same kind of notes to the library that you wrote when 36
you sent me for books," I told him. "I'll sign your name."

He laughed. 37

"Go ahead. Let me see what you get," he said. 38

That afternoon I addressed myself to forging a note. Now, what 39
were the names of books written by H. L. Mencken? I did not know any
of them. I finally wrote what I thought would be a foolproof note: *Dear
Madam: Will you please let this nigger boy*—I used the word "nigger" to
make the librarian feel that I could not possibly be the author of the
note—*have some books by H. L. Mencken?* I forged the white man's name.

I entered the library as I had always done when on errands for 40
whites, but I felt that I would somehow slip up and betray myself. I
doffed my hat, stood a respectful distance from the desk, looked as un-
bookish as possible, and waited for the white patrons to be taken care of.
When the desk was clear of people, I still waited. The white librarian
looked at me.

"What do you want, boy?" 41

As though I did not possess the power of speech, I stepped forward 42
and simply handed her the forged note, not parting my lips.

"What books by Mencken does he want?" she asked. 43

"I don't know, ma'am," I said, avoiding her eyes. 44

"Who gave you this card?" 45

"Mr. Falk," I said. 46

"Where is he?" 47

"He's at work, at the M—Optical Company," I said. "I've been in 48
here for him before."

"I remember," the woman said. "But he never wrote notes like this." 49

Oh, God, she's suspicious. Perhaps she would not let me have the 50
books? If she had turned her back at that moment, I would have ducked
out the door and never gone back. Then I thought of a bold idea.

"You can call him up, ma'am," I said, my heart pounding. 51

"You're not using these books, are you?" she asked pointedly. 52

"Oh, no, ma'am. I can't read." 53

"I don't know what he wants by Mencken," she said under her [54] breath.

I knew now that I had won; she was thinking of other things and the [55] race question had gone out of her mind. She went to the shelves. Once or twice she looked over her shoulder at me, as though she was still doubtful. Finally she came forward with two books in her hand.

"I'm sending him two books," she said. "But tell Mr. Falk to come [56] in next time, or send me the names of the books he wants. I don't know what he wants to read."

I said nothing. She stamped the card and handed me the books. Not [57] daring to glance at them, I went out of the library, fearing that the woman would call me back for further questioning. A block away from the library I opened one of the books and read a title: *A Book of Prefaces.* I was nearing my nineteenth birthday and I did not know how to pronounce the word "preface." I thumbed the pages and saw strange words and strange names. I shook my head, disappointed. I looked at the other book; it was called *Prejudices.* I knew what that word meant; I had heard it all my life. And right off I was on guard against Mencken's books. Why would a man want to call a book *Prejudices?* The word was so stained with all my memories of racial hate that I could not conceive of anybody using it for a title. Perhaps I had made a mistake about Mencken? A man who had prejudices must be wrong.

When I showed the books to Mr. Falk, he looked at me and frowned. [58]

"That librarian might telephone you," I warned him. [59]

"That's all right," he said. "But when you're through reading those [60] books, I want you to tell me what you get out of them."

That night in my rented room, while letting the hot water run over [61] my can of pork and beans in the sink, I opened *A Book of Prefaces* and began to read. I was jarred and shocked by the style, the clear, clean, sweeping sentences. Why did he write like that? And how did one write like that? I pictured the man as a raging demon, slashing with his pen, consumed with hate, denouncing everything American, extolling everything European or German, laughing at the weaknesses of people, mocking God, authority. What was this? I stood up, trying to realize what reality lay behind the meaning of the words . . . . Yes, this man was fighting, fighting with words. He was using words as a weapon, using them as one would use a club. Could words be weapons? Well, yes, for here they were. Then, maybe, perhaps, I could use them as a weapon? No. It frightened me. I read on and what amazed me was not what he said, but how on earth anybody had the courage to say it.

Occasionally I glanced up to reassure myself that I was alone in the [62] room. Who were these men about whom Mencken was talking so passionately? Who was Anatole France? Joseph Conrad? Sinclair Lewis, Sherwood Anderson, Dostoevski, George Moore, Gustave Flaubert, Maupassant, Tolstoy, Frank Harris, Mark Twain, Thomas Hardy,

Arnold Bennett, Stephen Crane, Zola, Norris, Gorky, Bergson, Ibsen, Balzac, Bernard Shaw, Dumas, Poe, Thomas Mann, O. Henry, Dreiser, H. G. Wells, Gogol, T. S. Eliot, Gide, Baudelaire, Edgar Lee Masters, Stendhal, Turgenev, Huneker, Nietzsche, and scores of others? Were these men real? Did they exist or had they existed? And how did one pronounce their names?

I ran across many words whose meanings I did not know, and I ei- 63
ther looked them up in a dictionary or, before I had a chance to do that, encountered the word in a context that made its meaning clear. But what strange world was this? I concluded the book with the conviction that I had somehow overlooked something terribly important in life. I had once tried to write, had once reveled in feeling, had let my crude imagination roam, but the impulse to dream had been slowly beaten out of me by experience. Now it surged up again and I hungered for books, new ways of looking and seeing. It was not a matter of believing or disbelieving what I read, but of feeling something new, of being affected by something that made the look of the world different.

As dawn broke I ate my pork and beans, feeling dopey, sleepy. I 64
went to work, but the mood of the book would not die; it lingered, coloring everything I saw, heard, did. I now felt that I knew what the white men were feeling. Merely because I had read a book that had spoken of how they lived and thought, I identified myself with that book. I felt vaguely guilty. Would I, filled with bookish notions, act in a manner that would make the whites dislike me?

I forged more notes and my trips to the library became frequent. 65
Reading grew into a passion. My first serious novel was Sinclair Lewis's *Main Street*.[2] It made me see my boss, Mr. Gerald, and identify him as an American type. I would smile when I saw him lugging his golf bags into the office. I had always felt a vast distance separating me from the boss, and now I felt closer to him, though still distant. I felt now that I knew him, that I could feel the very limits of his narrow life. And this had happened because I had read a novel about a mythical man called George F. Babbitt.[3]

The plots and stories in the novels did not interest me so much as 66
the point of view revealed. I gave myself over to each novel without reserve, without trying to criticize it; it was enough for me to see and feel something different. And for me, everything was something different. Reading was like a drug, a dope. The novels created moods in which I lived for days. But I could not conquer my sense of guilt, my feeling that

---

[2] *Main Street*, published in 1920, examines the smugness, intolerance, and lack of imagination that characterizes small-town American life. [Eds.]

[3] The central character in Sinclair Lewis's *Babbitt* (1922) who believed in the virtues of home, the Republican party, and middle-class conventions. To Wright, Babbitt symbolizes the mindless complacency of white middle-class America. [Eds.]

the white men around me knew that I was changing, that I had begun to regard them differently.

Whenever I brought a book to the job, I wrapped it in newspaper— 67 a habit that was to persist for years in other cities and under other circumstances. But some of the white men pried into my packages when I was absent and they questioned me.

"Boy, what are you reading those books for?"   68

"Oh, I don't know, sir."   69

"That's deep stuff you're reading, boy."   70

"I'm just killing time, sir."   71

"You'll addle your brains if you don't watch out."   72

I read Dreiser's *Jennie Gerhardt* and *Sister Carrie*[4] and they revived in 73 me a vivid sense of my mother's suffering; I was overwhelmed. I grew silent, wondering about the life around me. It would have been impossible for me to have told anyone what I derived from these novels, for it was nothing less than a sense of life itself. All my life had shaped me for the realism, the naturalism of the modern novel, and I could not read enough of them.

Steeped in new moods and ideas, I bought a ream of paper and tried 74 to write; but nothing would come, or what did come was flat beyond telling. I discovered that more than desire and feeling were necessary to write and I dropped the idea. Yet I still wondered how it was possible to know people sufficiently to write about them. Could I ever learn about life and people? To me, with my vast ignorance, my Jim Crow station in life, it seemed a task impossible of achievement. I now knew what being a Negro meant. I could endure the hunger. I had learned to live with hate. But to feel that there were feelings denied me, that the very breath of life itself was beyond my reach, that more than anything else hurt, wounded me. I had a new hunger.

In buoying me up, reading also cast me down, made me see what 75 was possible, what I had missed. My tension returned, new, terrible, bitter, surging, almost too great to be contained. I no longer *felt* that the world about me was hostile, killing; I *knew* it. A million times I asked myself what I could do to save myself, and there were no answers. I seemed forever condemned, ringed by walls.

I did not discuss my reading with Mr. Falk, who had lent me his 76 library card; it would have meant talking about myself and that would have been too painful. I smiled each day, fighting desperately to maintain my old behavior, to keep my disposition seemingly sunny. But some of the white men discerned that I had begun to brood.

"Wake up there, boy!" Mr. Olin said one day.   77

---

[4] Both *Jennie Gerhardt* (1911) and *Sister Carrie* (1900) tell the stories of working women who struggle against poverty and social injustice. [Eds.]

"Sir!" I answered for the lack of a better word. [78]

"You act like you've stolen something," he said. [79]

I laughed in the way I knew he expected me to laugh, but I resolved [80] to be more conscious of myself, to watch my every act, to guard and hide the new knowledge that was dawning within me.

If I went north, would it be possible for me to build a new life then? [81] But how could a man build a life upon vague, unformed yearnings? I wanted to write and I did not even know the English language. I bought English grammars and found them dull. I felt that I was getting a better sense of the language from novels than from grammars. I read hard, discarding a writer as soon as I felt that I had grasped his point of view. At night the printed page stood before my eyes in sleep.

Mrs. Moss, my landlady, asked me one Sunday morning: "Son, [82] what is this you keep on reading?"

"Oh, nothing. Just novels." [83]

"What you get out of 'em?" [84]

"I'm just killing time," I said. [85]

"I hope you know your own mind," she said in a tone which im- [86] plied that she doubted if I had a mind.

I knew of no Negroes who read the books I liked and I wondered if [87] any Negroes ever thought of them. I knew that there were Negro doctors, lawyers, newspapermen, but I never saw any of them. When I read a Negro newspaper I never caught the faintest echo of my preoccupation in its pages. I felt trapped and occasionally, for a few days, I would stop reading. But a vague hunger would come over me for books, books that opened up new avenues of feeling and seeing, and again I would forge another note to the white librarian. Again I would read and wonder as only the naïve and unlettered can read and wonder, feeling that I carried a secret, criminal burden about with me each day.

That winter my mother and brother came and we set up house- [88] keeping, buying furniture on the installment plan, being cheated and yet knowing no way to avoid it. I began to eat warm food and to my surprise found that regular meals enabled me to read faster. I may have lived through many illnesses and survived them, never suspecting that I was ill. My brother obtained a job and we began to save toward the trip north, plotting our time, setting tentative dates for departure. I told none of the white men on the job that I was planning to go north; I knew that the moment they felt I was thinking of the North they would change toward me. It would have made them feel that I did not like the life I was living, and because my life was completely conditioned by what they said or did, it would have been tantamount to challenging them.

I could calculate my chances for life in the South as a Negro fairly [89] clearly now.

I could fight the southern whites by organizing with other Negroes, [90] as my grandfather had done. But I knew that I could never win that way;

there were many whites and there were but few blacks. They were strong and we were weak. Outright black rebellion could never win. If I fought openly I would die and I did not want to die. News of lynchings were frequent.

I could submit and live the life of a genial slave, but that was impossible. All of my life had shaped me to live by my own feelings and thoughts. I could make up to Bess and marry her and inherit the house. But that, too, would be the life of a slave; if I did that, I would crush to death something within me, and I would hate myself as much as I knew the whites already hated those who had submitted. Neither could I ever willingly present myself to be kicked, as Shorty had done. I would rather have died than do that.   91

I could drain off my restlessness by fighting with Shorty and Harrison. I had seen many Negroes solve the problem of being black by transferring their hatred of themselves to others with a black skin and fighting them. I would have to be cold to do that, and I was not cold and I could never be.   92

I could, of course, forget what I had read, thrust the whites out of my mind, forget them; and find release from anxiety and longing in sex and alcohol. But the memory of how my father had conducted himself made that course repugnant. If I did not want others to violate my life, how could I voluntarily violate it myself?   93

I had no hope whatever of being a professional man. Not only had I been so conditioned that I did not desire it, but the fulfillment of such an ambition was beyond my capabilities. Well-to-do Negroes lived in a world that was almost as alien to me as the world inhabited by whites.   94

What, then, was there? I held my life in my mind, in my consciousness each day, feeling at times that I would stumble and drop it, spill it forever. My reading had created a vast sense of distance between me and the world in which I lived and tried to make a living, and that sense of distance was increasing each day. My days and nights were one long, quiet, continuously contained dream of terror, tension, and anxiety. I wondered how long I could bear it.   95

Responding to Reading

1. Do you think access to books brought Wright closer to achieving the American Dream? What new obstacles did books introduce?
2. In paragraph 74 Wright mentions his "Jim Crow station in life." The term *Jim Crow*, derived from a character in a minstrel show, refers to laws enacted in Southern states that legalized racial segregation. What is Wright's "station in life"? In what ways does he adapt his behavior to accommodate this Jim Crow image? In what ways does he defy this stereotype? How would you describe your "station in life"?

3. After World War II Wright left the United States to live in Paris. Given what you have read in this essay, does his decision surprise you? Would you have made the same decision?

MAY 29, 1942

Mary Tsukamoto

In the wake of the Japanese attack on Pearl Harbor (December 1941) that precipitated World War II, the U.S. government in March of the following year ordered all persons of Japanese ancestry living on the West Coast to be evacuated to one of ten relocation centers in Western states. Some 110,000 people, mostly loyal American citizens, were forcibly removed to these camps, where they were held as virtual prisoners for as long as four years. Among the internees were Mary Tsukamoto and her family, farmers from Florin, California. In the following chapter from her memoir *We the People: A Story of Internment in America*, written with Elizabeth Pinkerton, Tsukamoto recalls the painful day that she and her neighbors were forced to leave their homes. Tsukamoto would later become a teacher and a leader in the effort to make the U.S. government acknowledge the injustice of its actions toward Japanese Americans, a goal that was finally achieved in 1988 when President Reagan signed a bill granting surviving internees $20,000 each in reparations and a formal apology from the government.

May was always such a beautiful month in the Sacramento Valley. [1] The summer heat was yet to come; days were usually bright and clear. Fields were green from the winter's rain, and flowers bloomed everywhere. May was also harvest month for Florin's strawberries. The delicious, but fragile, red berries were ready to be placed in boxcars and shipped to Seattle, Portland and other major cities. In May of 1942, however, there were only a few Florin strawberries shipped to the breakfast tables of America. Florin's berries rotted in the fields that spring because there was no one to pick them, pack them, or ship them away. The work force that would have harvested them was boarding busses and trains for a journey that would take them far away. For many it was a final farewell to Florin's strawberry fields.

The day we left is like a crystal memory in time. In the darkness I [2] heard my husband call to us. It was time to get up even though the day was yet too early for the sun.

For a sweet fleeting moment, my body tingled with excitement. I ³
remembered other mornings when I had been awakened in just this
way, when Al had surprised us by transforming ordinary events into
memorable adventures for the Tsukamoto family. That day, though it
would be memorable, was not an ordinary day at all. It was the day of
our departure.

The cold wetness of my pillow shocked me into reality, and my ⁴
sleepy state was gone in an instant. Suddenly, I realized what was to
come as the horror of the day dawned and my heart began to pound like
thunder. My body was weak from fright, my throat, dry and sore from
yet another night of weeping. Though I had cried deep inside for
months, as a mother and responsible member of my family, I dared not
let my loved ones know how sick at heart I was. My angry tears came
forth only at night when there was no one there to see.

That last night, I heard my husband, usually so brave and strong, ⁵
sobbing under the blanket in the privacy of the quiet night. How hopeless it was, and how helpless we were! Our only course was to follow the
orders of the military.

With only a few hours left, we had much to do before it was time to ⁶
surrender the last bit of our freedom. Blessed sleep had for a brief moment erased the nightmare in which we were gripped, the nightmare
that controlled our destiny and clutched at our very souls. Every person
of Japanese ancestry on the west coast of the United States of America,
in California, Washington, Oregon, and Arizona in the winter and
spring of 1942 was caught up in that torment.

My muffled heart begged to cry out again and again—why? why? ⁷
why? What have I done? Why is this happening to me? What did I do?
What did *we* do?

I was an American citizen. So were my husband and my tiny daugh- ⁸
ter. We had broken no law, committed no criminal act. We were law-
abiding citizens, farmers, growers of strawberries and grapes. We loved
our country and only asked to prove our loyalty if we could but be given
the chance.

On this day we were to leave our homes—leave our farm and our ⁹
lives. No one knew where we were to go nor for how long we would be
gone. We were to take only what we could carry and be at the train station at nine or go to prison for crimes we knew nothing of. Our orders
were clear and supported by our president; it was our sad duty as residents of California in May of 1942. We were labeled as criminals because
our faces were Japanese.

Shocked into reality, I rolled off the mattress and touched the bare ¹⁰
floor. I quickly remembered why I had spent this night sleeping on a
mattress on the floor. Our furniture was already stored on the second
floor of our barn. This morning we had only enough time to put the mat-
tresses away, pack our bedding and eat the last breakfast in our house.

I packed a lunch for us to eat on the train, and we cleaned the house [11] thoroughly from end to end. This ritual of cleaning was important for we could not bear to leave our dear home dirty. This humble place had given us warmth and security, and as we brought back memories of past griefs and joys, our little house was made more dear to us. Here we felt safe; we belonged. We would no more know this feeling.

It was almost time to leave. I swept the kitchen floor for the last time [12] daring not to think about a return. Al mopped up each tiny bit of dust, and each family member did something to tidy up. We all wept silently, reluctant to leave. With this final act, we prayed to God that in His infinite mercy He would bless us to return to Florin and our farm home once again.

In Japanese, Ojiisan spoke the last words. "It is the darkest day of [13] our lives. We are about to lose our treasured liberty. Will we ever see this dear place again?"

Margaret and George Feil, our good friends, came to take us to the [14] train station in Elk Grove, eight miles away. Marielle hugged Uppie, her little dog, and fed him for the last time. Uppie was a perky, white dog with black spots, his tail especially curly as he pranced about the yard. I turned away with a lump in my throat knowing the grief that would tear our little daughter's heart. The orders were firm in regard to pets; Uppie was to be left behind.

"He'll miss us, Mommy," cried Marielle. "And I'll miss him too. [15] He'll feel forsaken here all alone."

"Not as forsaken as we feel," I replied, cheered somewhat by my [16] daughter's compassion and her brave attempt to use adult words. I could not think of any adult words that would explain to her the enormity of this day and what was taking place among us.

The last things were put away. Al loaded the numbered duffel bags [17] into the truck Bob Fletcher brought. There was one bag for each of us, each clearly marked with bright green stripes so we would be able to recognize them easily. On each bag was the military number given to the Tsukamoto family—#22076.

Grandpa stood quietly in the corner of the yard facing his acres of [18] beautiful green grape vines. They were the vines he had planted more than twenty years ago. Beyond him were row upon row of ripe strawberries, ready to be picked.

Grandma was in her garden crying. Lovely flowers bloomed in all [19] their glory in May. Nami and Marielle cried together, and Marielle could not let go of her Uppie. "It's time to go," called Al. "We must not be late. The papers said nine o'clock."

He was right. The stark words from the military posters tacked all [20] over Florin days earlier were vividly imprinted in my mind.

> *No Japanese person will be permitted to move into, or out of, the above area*
> *after 12 o'clock noon . . . both alien and non-alien will be evacuated . . . all per-*

sons of Japanese ancestry . . . no pets of any kind will be permitted . . . pack-
ages limited to that which can be carried by the individual or family group . . .

Our orders were from the WCCA and the Western Defense Com- 21
mand of the 4th Army. Did we ever consider not obeying? Never. We
never questioned it at all. It was our duty, and we had better be there on
time.

From the scant information on the posters, we had planned our ten- 22
tative future and decided what to take with us. Now we were on our
way.

We were all gravely silent as we drove away from the Tsukamoto 23
place. We knew it was not polite to weep in the presence of friends. How
interesting that age-old Japanese customs controlled our leaving just as
they had shaped our lives in bringing us to this tragic situation. Inwardly, we wept as we searched to make sense out of this abrupt departure from everything we loved.

I looked out across the Sacramento Valley, and as I did I caught a 24
view of the magnificent, snow-capped Sierra Nevada Mountains. How
often I had looked to the east with joy and faith. Though there was no
joy in my heart that day, I looked with faith.

Never had the words of the psalmist meant so much to me: 25

"I will lift up mine eyes unto the hills from whence cometh my help; My help
cometh from the Lord who made Heaven and Earth."

With this prayer in my heart, I left Florin enroute to Elk Grove to 26
board a train that would take us on the first part of our long journey into
the unknown.

Elk Grove-Florin Road, the seven mile stretch of road between the 27
sister towns of Elk Grove and Florin, was the scene of a strange procession that day. I felt as if I were in a movie theater watching an exodus
of a people. But these people were us—families of Japanese ancestry—
and we were crowded into the oddest collection of old vehicles I had
ever seen. There were huge pick-ups, ancient passenger cars, and trucks
loaded to capacity with personal belongings. We joined the strange parade and turned down Main Street. I wanted to laugh, but the sick
queasiness in my stomach stopped me. The incredible assortment of vehicles, piled high with colorful suitcases and hand luggage, was like
nothing I had ever seen before. Peeking out from among the piles of baggage were the familiar faces of friends and neighbors. They were coming to the station in whatever means of transportation they could manage to find at this late date. Often the new owner of what had been the
family car accompanied them helped them unload and then drove off
with his new purchase.

Entire families were on the road—stunned grandparents, some 28
barely able to walk; playful teenagers, more interested in seeing each

other than the solemn event taking place; tiny babies and frightened children; and among them all, Nisei[1] parents trying to find order in the confusion of the day.

Everyone was dressed in their Sunday best, men in suits and [29] women in dresses and hats. How strange to see so many wearing coats on such a warm May morning, but with so much to keep track of, it was wiser to wear a coat than to lose it in the crowd.

Children talked excitedly. Most had never been on a train before. [30] Growing up as they had in the age of the automobile, they were thrilled at the prospect of a train ride. Their excitement, however, turned to bewilderment as they saw the old people crying unashamedly as they sat on their suitcases and blankets in the middle of the hubbub. They had been brave before, but now their tears flowed freely, the only semblance of freedom at the station that day.

As each truck and car arrived, many hands helped with unloading. [31] An enormous pile of belongings was being packed into the baggage car. We had been instructed specifically to take only what each of us could carry. I was amazed at the mountain of luggage for the 500 people assigned to our train.

What if the soldiers would not let us take so much? What if they [32] refused to take it all? What would I do? I needed everything I had packed for my family's needs. I had followed the army's instructions to the letter.

It was not my problem, I suddenly realized. My eyes blurred as [33] I gazed at the bizarre drama of people being loaded on the train. It seemed like a dream, but they were all Japanese faces. At that very moment, my consciousness jarred into the harsh realization that we had become evacuees. My tongue turned dry, and I could not speak without choking. We were evacuees, leaving our homes—forever perhaps—and we were prisoners as well. This knowledge rushed through my soul with a jolt. A silent scream echoed through my heart.

Suddenly I noticed the guns! The soldiers were carrying rifles with [34] bayonets as if we were to be shot down if we tried to escape. They were young boys in brisk uniforms, perplexed by what was happening before them. I looked closely at the one nearest to me. He looked just as frightened as I, and there were tears in his eyes too.

Beyond him were the children, with large conspicuous numbers [35] pinned to the front of their clothes. We had all become numbered items for the government file.

In the midst of the crowd, Mrs. Okimoto began to have labor pains [36] and was ordered to the hospital. No one was allowed to go with her, a dismaying realization to her family, wrought with concerns for her well-

---

[1] First generation Japanese-American. [Eds.]

being and for the child about to be born. There was nothing that could be done, however, for the train was about to leave.

I moved about greeting friends I had known for a long time. I knew [37] not what to say, nor did they, but our collective grief was eased with the knowledge that we were going to the same camp. What a disappointment to hear, "They left for Manzanar two days ago . . ." "She has gone to Walerga . . ." "Tule Lake I think."[2] My heart sank a dozen times as I wondered if I would ever see those dear ones again.

There were all sorts of last minute problems in addition to the im- [38] pending birth. Some were minor, but others could not be ignored as families struggled to find solutions. Expectant mothers, some great with child and exhausted already from the ordeal, were worried and anxious. Elderly parents needed to be made comfortable. Some were ill and had to lie down; special places had to be arranged. Finally, we were ready to go; it was exactly nine o'clock.

Much to our surprise there was a small group of people who had [39] braved criticism to see us off—teachers, neighbors and friends. Some wept openly; others looked confused by what they saw. There was much hugging, but there were few words amidst the mass bewilderment. No one knew what to say in a situation like this.

Just as we were ready to board, Edith's children ran up to us shout- [40] ing, "Sonny's got the chicken pox."

"Mom says to tell you we can't ride with you." [41]

Sure enough, Sonny had the chicken pox. Patricia Thayer, the social [42] welfare worker, scurried around trying to arrange a special quarantine section for the Ouchida family. It was a hectic last minute emergency, but a solution was found. The entire family would be quartered in the ladies' restroom, the only isolated place that could be found. Women in that car had to use the next car for their toilet needs.

Al had made earlier arrangements for Grandma to have a Pullman [43] car and bed because she always got carsick when she traveled. This meant that she would ride apart from us, but we were pleased she could have the facilities she needed. Our sense of anxiety for each other increased when we were separated in these chaotic hours of our lives, but knowing Grandma was comfortable, we all relaxed a little.

I was grateful for the few, brave Caucasian friends who had come to [44] see us off. They brought us sandwiches and cookies for our trip. I was a marvelous testimony to the bond of friendship that had developed between the Japanese people and their Caucasian neighbors in our rural communities. They brought gifts and mementoes, packages of sandwiches, cakes and cookies, prepared for us with love. I forgot the hateful headlines as I looked out across the faces so different from ours, yet the same in that we were all children of God and we were all Americans.

---

[2] Sites of internment camps. [Eds.]

Soldiers reminded us that it was time to board the train. I held [45] hands tightly with dear friends who tearfully promised to wait for my safe return. I cried unashamedly as I said good-bye to classmates, teachers, neighbors and friends and stepped on board. I cried until I could hardly breathe. The train moved slowly southward; I strained to catch the last glimpse of the railroad station and the friends who stood transfixed at the spot where we had just parted.

I said goodbye to a part of my life the day we left Elk Grove. I could [46] not comprehend the forces that caused this strange departure from the community we loved. With breaking hearts, we were wrenched away from the only home we knew.

Our painful parting from friends and neighbors was more than we [47] could bear. Deep within all of us, however, invisible threads of friendship were slowly knitting into form. I hoped there would be letters and messages to strengthen our affection. I hoped that our song of faith, hope, and joy would eventually become a great affirmation.

Once again, I remembered Reverend Sasaki's words on that fateful [48] December day:

"All the darkness of the world cannot blot out the light from one [49] candle."

Thus we left Elk Grove and our Florin home. For all we knew it [50] would be forever. I sat in a stupor, exhausted and trembling all over from the emotional ordeal of parting. It was over now; we were on our way, the last people of Japanese ancestry to leave Florin, California on May 29, 1942.

The first-time travelers among us looked eagerly out the windows [51] of the train to watch the changing scenery of this great adventure as the train moved slowly down the San Joaquin Valley. Suddenly, though, there were military police in the cars. Quickly, they pulled down the blinds so we could not see. The lights were turned on so it would not be dark in the cars. Some among us protested and the truth was finally known—"We don't want anyone to see that this is a trainload of Japanese being moved."

Our departure was to be a secret! It was the first of many shocking [52] humiliations. I was sick with despair.

Suspected of crimes we never dreamed of committing, there was [53] clearly nothing we could do. We, the people of Florin, of Japanese ancestry, were on our way to become a chapter of American history. We had been singled out along with our brothers and sisters from the western coast of California, Washington and Oregon. There were 110,000 of us, a mass removal unprecedented in the annals of our country's story. How we ached to prove our loyalty to the only country we had ever known! Instead, even though we were American citizens, we were heading for prison because our country was at war with the land of our ancestors. We had been told that it was a military necessity and that we were a threat to national security, but it made no sense at all. Each and every one of us felt the loss of freedom and personal liberties.

I sat with Marielle and Al in the shrouded car and wondered with 54 traces of bitterness, "Where is the justice of it all?"

Responding to Reading

1. In paragraph 7 Tsukamoto asks, "Why is this happening to me? What did I do? What did *we* do?" Supply two sets of answers to her questions—one that might have been given in 1942 and one that might be given today.
2. What are the Tsukamotos giving up? Consider their emotional as well as their material sacrifices.
3. In paragraph 33 Tsukamoto describes those forced to leave Florin as "Japanese faces" and characterizes them as "evacuees" and "prisoners." In paragraph 44 she refers to "the bond of friendship that had developed between the Japanese people and their Caucasian neighbors" and comforts herself with the knowledge that they are all "children of God, . . . all Americans." Do you think she is contradicting herself, or do you believe it is possible for both these characterizations to be accurate? Explain.

LIMITED SEATING ON BROADWAY

~

John Hockenberry

John Hockenberry (1956–) is a news reporter who has covered stories ranging from the eruption of Mount St. Helens to the Persian Gulf war as a correspondent for National Public Radio. He is also a wheelchair-bound paraplegic, paralyzed since the age of nineteen as the result of an automobile accident when he was a student at the University of Chicago. Eventually a music major at the University of Oregon, Hockenberry began his journalistic career at an NPR affiliate in Eugene. In 1992 he joined ABC television's newsmagazine *Day One*, becoming the first—and only—network reporter to appear in a wheelchair. A fierce advocate of strict enforcement of laws that protect the disabled, Hockenberry has said, "For the struggles I've gone through to mean something, I have to be an activist." In the following opinion piece, written for the *New York Times* op-ed page in 1992, Hockenberry describes his outrage at being denied access to a Broadway theater. He later sued the theater, and under the terms of the settlement its owners installed a lift to allow wheelchair access.

The show at the Virginia Theater, "Jelly's Last Jam," is in previews, [1] and even though tickets are $60 for orchestra seats (the only option for patrons in wheelchairs), the price was a minor impediment to the prospect of an evening of Jelly Roll Morton's jazz.

The art community in New York City has a reputation for being pro- [2] gressive. It is the forum and agent for challenging America's hardened perceptions about race, politics, class, gender, religion and, more recently, AIDS and homophobia. In particular, the theater world likes to think of itself as a seeker of such challenges and is proudest when a play or musical becomes a vehicle for change.

I thought of this two Saturdays ago as I sat at the top of some stairs [3] in the Virginia Theater waiting to be helped into my seat. Because the Virginia, like virtually all Broadway theaters, refuses to take orders for wheelchair tickets over the phone, except for purchases well in advance, I had to make a special trip to the box office the day before to buy my ticket.

At the box office, I was told that a ticket was available but that I [4] would have to sit far from my friend. I was told the house manager would seat me when I arrived. Here again, minor hassles well worth bearing on the way to an evening of good theater.

But that didn't happen. Two minutes before curtain time the house [5] manager emerged from a white door with a copy of the theater's "Policy for Disabled Patrons." He abruptly told me to leave the theater. I was shocked and asked why. He asked if I could walk, something I thought was fairly clear when I had bought the ticket the day before. He mentioned stairs for the first time and noted that since I could not walk and had not brought my own crew with me that it was impossible to seat me. I said that there was no problem and that I would show him how to get me up the stairs with the help of the usher standing next to him.

He said in a loud voice audible to everyone around us: "Sir, we are [6] not allowed to touch you. Our staff is not allowed to do that." I reminded him that my friend had already taken her seat at the suggestion of the usher and would react with some alarm if she saw my seat empty after the show began. "I'm sorry, sir, you'll have to leave," was his only response.

Having had many close calls with the inaccessible infrastructure of [7] the world I still could not believe I would not be able to see the show. I recalled an incident some years before at the Hakawati Theater in East Jerusalem when four fellow patrons and the playwright, all strangers, helped me up 12 stairs to see a puppet show. They demanded that I be carried even when I was doubtful.

The theatergoers at the Virginia eyed me with the detached, craven [8] interest that New Yorkers reserve for the white chalk outline of a corpse at a crime scene. "You are a fire hazard, sir," the manager insisted. Only moments before I had been a component of his cash flow. I grabbed his collar and told him what he could do with his Policy for Disabled Patrons. I was easily overpowered and ushered, the only ushering I would experience that night, to the 52d Street sidewalk.

I sat powerless and humiliated; all dressed up, nowhere to go. Of   9 course, the Virginia Theater staff probably thought differently. They might recall a rude, angry man trying to get rules bent in his favor. But outside, it seemed as if I was the only one who thought that a few stairs shouldn't stand in the way of seeing a play. Certainly there was no one to complain to about the lack of ramps. There was no meaning to the incident at all.

The Virginia Theater was not my first such encounter with New   10 York City's art community. Some months ago on 10th Avenue I tried to empty a bottle of urine I had carried for 40 blocks. In the absence of any public restroom I rolled into a dirty parking lot to pour out the jar in a discreet corner. Two attendants with all the righteousness of crusaders grabbed me and threw me out of my chair and onto the sidewalk as people walked by.

Not long after the event I learned that a proposal for handicapped-   11 accessible public restrooms on city streets was opposed by the Public Art Commission, which had determined that the structures would be too ugly. (Uglier even than public defecation, and heaven knows the arts community knows best about that.)

Artists might shrink from taking blame for the insensitive acts of ar-   12 chitects, producers and theater owners. But as society's voice of protest, are artists to be excused for ignoring discrimination that hasn't yet made it to Broadway?

Maybe if I was an artist who daringly confronted whole flights of   13 stairs in front of a paying audience and who carried around bottles of urine just to make a point about society I might keep from wetting my pants and, better yet, get to see "Jelly's Last Jam." But then that wouldn't be honest. Art and theater are nothing if not honest.

Responding to Reading

1. Hockenberry is clearly angry in this piece. For whom does he reserve his greatest anger? Why? Do you share his anger?
2. What specific changes does Hockenberry feel must be made before he and other disabled people can participate fully in American society? Do you believe the changes he wants are reasonable? Possible? Do you believe he has a basic right to expect, or even demand, such accommodations?
3. Hockenberry is a well-educated white male with a prestigious job, and he is willing and able to pay $60 for a theater ticket. Could you argue that, despite his physical disability, he has achieved the American Dream? Or do you believe part of the dream has nonetheless eluded him?

THRIVING AS AN OUTSIDER, EVEN ~ AS AN OUTCAST, IN SMALLTOWN AMERICA

Louie Crew

A founder of Integrity, the national organization of gay and lesbian Episcopalians, Alabama native Louis Crew (1936–) has long been an active participant in the gay rights and civil rights movements, seeing in both the common goal of overcoming oppression and intolerance. Educated at Baylor University, Auburn University, and the University of Alabama, Crew is a teacher, lecturer, and writer, as well as a social and religious reformer. In the following essay he recalls the four years he and his African-American companion spent as residents of a small, conservative town in Georgia, living openly as a gay couple. Their methods of survival, he suggests, "should interest anyone who values the role of the dissident in our democracy."

From 1973 to 1979, my spouse and I lived in Fort Valley, a town of [1] 12,000 people, the seat of Peach County, sixty miles northeast of Plains, right in the geographic center of Georgia. I taught English at a local black college and my spouse was variously a nurse, hairdresser, choreographer for the college majorettes, caterer, and fashion designer.

The two of us have often been asked how we survived as a gay, [2] racially integrated couple living openly in that small town. We are still perhaps too close to the Georgia experience and very much caught up in our similar struggles in central Wisconsin to offer a definite explanation, but our tentative conjectures should interest anyone who values the role of the dissident in our democracy.

Survive we did. We even throve before our departure. Profession- [3] ally, my colleagues and the Regents of the University System of Georgia awarded me tenure, and the Chamber of Commerce awarded my spouse a career medal in cosmetology. Socially, we had friends from the full range of the economic classes in the community. We had attended six farewell parties in our honor before we called a halt to further fetes, especially several planned at too great a sacrifice by some of the poorest folks in the town. Furthermore, I had been away only four months when the college brought me back to address an assembly of Georgia judges, majors, police chiefs, and wardens. We are still called two to three times a week by scores of people seeking my spouse's advice on fashion, cooking, or the like.

It was not always so. In 1974 my spouse and I were denied housing   4
which we had "secured" earlier before the realtor saw my spouse's
color. HUD documented that the realtor thought that "the black man
looked like a criminal." Once the town was up in arms when a bishop
accused the two of us of causing a tornado which had hit the town early
in 1975, an accusation which appeared on the front page of the newspaper. "This is the voice of God. The town of Fort Valley is harboring
Sodomists. Would one expect God to keep silent when homosexuals are
tolerated? We remember what He did to Sodom and Gomorrah" (*The
Macon Herald*, March 20, 1975: 1). A year later my Episcopal vestry[1]
asked me to leave the parish, and my own bishop summoned me for discipline for releasing to the national press correspondence related to the
vestry's back-room maneuvers. Prompted in part by such officials, the
local citizens for years routinely heckled us in public, sometimes threw
rocks at our apartment, trained their children to spit on us from their bi-
cycles if we dared to jog, and badgered us with hate calls on an average
of six to eight times a week.

One such episode offers a partial clue to the cause of our survival.   5
It was late summer, 1975 or 1976. I was on my motorcycle to post mail
at the street-side box just before the one daily pickup at 6:00 P.M. About
fifty yards away, fully audible to about seventy pedestrians milling
about the court house and other public buildings, a group of police officers, all men, began shouting at me from the steps of their headquarters: "Louise! Faggot! Queer!"

Anyone who has ever tried to ease a motorcycle from a still position   6
without revving the engine knows that the feat is impossible: try as I did
to avoid the suggestion, I sounded as if I were riding off in a huff. About
half-way up the street, I thought to myself, "I'd rather rot in jail than feel
the way I do now." I turned around, drove back—the policemen still
shouting and laughing—and parked in the lot of the station. When I
walked to the steps, only the lone black policeman remained.

"Did you speak to me?" I asked him.   7

"No, sir," he replied emphatically.   8

Inside I badgered the desk sergeant to tell her chief to call me as   9
soon as she could locate him, and I indicated that I would press charges
if necessary to prevent a recurrence. I explained that the police miscon-
duct was an open invitation to more violent hoodlums to act out the officers' fantasies with impunity in the dark. Later, I persuaded a black city
commissioner and a white one, the latter our grocer and the former our
mortician, to threaten the culprits with suspension if ever such miscon-
duct occurred again.

Over a year later, late one Friday after his payday, a black friend of   10
my spouse knocked at our door to offer a share of his Scotch to celebrate

---

[1] Elected board that administers affairs in an Episcopal parish. [Eds.]

his raise—or so he said. Thus primed, he asked me, "You don't recognize me, do you?"

"No," I admitted.   11

"I'm the lone black policeman that day you were heckled. I came by   12
really because I thought you two might want to know what happened
inside when Louie stormed up to the sergeant."

"Yes," we said.   13

"Well, all the guys were crouching behind the partition to keep you   14
from seeing that they were listening. Their eyes bulged when you
threatened to bring in the F.B.I. and such. Then when you left, one
spoke for all when he said, 'But sissies aren't supposed to do things like
that!'"

Ironically, I believe that a major reason for our thriving on our own   15
terms of candor about our relationship has been our commitment to resist the intimidation heaped upon us. For too long lesbians and gay
males have unwillingly encouraged abuses against ourselves by serving
advance notice to any bullies, be they the barnyard-playground variety,
or the Bible-wielding pulpiteers, that we would whimper or run into
hiding when confronted with even the threat of exposure. It is easy to
confuse sensible nonviolence with cowardly nonresistance.

In my view, violent resistance would be counter-productive, espe-   16
cially for lesbians and gays who are outnumbered 10 to 1 by heterosexuals, according to Kinsey's statistics. Yet our personal experience suggests that special kinds of creative nonviolent resistance are a major
source of hope if lesbians and gay males are going to reverse the physical and mental intimidation which is our daily portion in this culture.

Resistance to oppression can be random and spontaneous, as in par   17
was my decision to return to confront the police hecklers, or organized
and sustained, as more typically has been the resistance by which my
spouse and I have survived. I believe that only organized and sustained
resistance offers much hope for long-range change in any community.
The random act is too soon forgotten or too easily romanticized.

Once we had committed ourselves to one another, my spouse and   18
I never gave much thought for ourselves to the traditional device most
gays have used for survival, the notorious "closet" in which one hides
one's identity from all but a select group of friends. In the first place, a
black man and a white man integrating a Georgia small town simply
cannot be inconspicuous. More importantly, the joint checking account
and other equitable economies fundamental to the quality of our marriage are public, not private acts. Our denial of the obvious would have
secured closet space only for our suffocation; we would have lied, "We
are ashamed and live in secret."

All of our resistance stems from our sense of our own worth, our   19
conviction that we and our kind do not deserve the suffering which heterosexuals continue to encourage or condone for sexual outcasts. Dr.

Martin Luther King used to say, "Those who go to the back of the bus, deserve the back of the bus."

Our survival on our own terms has depended very much on our [20] knowing and respecting many of the rules of the system which we resist. We are not simply dissenters, but conscientious ones.

For example, we are both very hard workers. As a controversial per- [21] son, I know that my professionalism comes under far more scrutiny than that of others. I learned early in my career that I could secure space for my differences by handling routine matters carefully. If one stays on good terms with secretaries, meets all deadlines, and willingly does one's fair share of the busy work of institutions, one is usually already well on the way towards earning collegial space, if not collegial support. In Georgia, I routinely volunteered to be secretary for most committees on which I served, thereby having enormous influence in the final form of the groups' deliberations without monopolizing the forum as most other molders of policy do. My spouse's many talents and sensibilities made him an invaluable advisor and confidante to scores of people in the community. Of course, living as we did in a hairdresser's salon, we knew a great deal more about the rest of the public than that public knew about us.

My spouse and I are fortunate in the fact that we like the enormous [22] amount of work which we do. We are not mere opportunists working hard only as a gimmick to exploit the public for lesbian and gay issues. Both of us worked intensely at our professional assignments long before we were acknowledged dissidents with new excessive pressures to excel. We feel that now we must, however unfairly, be twice as effective as our competitors just to remain employed at all.

Our survival has also depended very much on our thorough knowl- [23] edge of the system, often knowledge more thorough than that of those who would use the system against us. For example, when my bishop summoned me for discipline, I was able to show him that his own canons give him no authority to discipline a lay person except by excommunication. In fact, so hierarchical have the canons of his diocese become, that the only laity who exist worthy of their mention are the few lay persons on vestries.

Especially helpful has been our knowledge of communication pro- [24] cedures. For example, when an area minister attacked lesbians and gays on a TV talk show, I requested equal time; so well received was my response that for two more years I was a regular panelist on the talk show, thereby reaching most residents of the entire middle Georgia area as a known gay person, yet one speaking not just to sexual issues, but to a full range of religious and social topics.

When I was occasionally denied access to media, as in the parish or [25] diocese or as on campus when gossip flared, I knew the value of candid explanations thoughtfully prepared, xeroxed, and circulated to

enough folks to assure that the gossips would have access to the truthful version. For example, the vestry, which acted in secret, was caught
by surprise when I sent copies of their hateful letter to most other
parishioners, together with a copy of a psalm which I wrote protesting
their turning the House of Prayer into a Court House. I also was able to
explain that I continued to attend, not in defiance of their withdrawn invitation, but in obedience to the much higher invitation issued to us all
by the real head of the Church. In January, 1979, in the first open meeting of the parish since the vestry's letter of unwelcome three years earlier, the entire parish voted to censure the vestry for that action and to
extend to me the full welcome which the vestry had tried to deny. Only
three voted against censure, all three of them a minority of the vestry
being censured.

My spouse and I have been very conscious of the risks of our con-   26
victions. We have viewed our credentials—my doctorate and his professional licenses—not as badges of comfortable respectability, but as as-
sets to be invested in social change. Dr. King did not sit crying in the
Albany jail, "Why don't these folk respect me? How did this happen?
What am I doing here?" When my spouse and I have been denied jobs
for which we were the most qualified applicants, we have not naively
asked how such things could be, nor have we dwelt overly long on self-
pity, for we have known in advance the prices we might have to pay,
even if to lose our lives. Our realism about danger and risk has helped
us to preserve our sanity when everyone about us has seemed insane. I
remember the joy which my spouse shared with me over the fact that he
had just been fired for his efforts to organize other black nurses to
protest their being treated as orderlies by the white managers of a local
hospital.

Never, however, have we affirmed the injustices. Finally, we simply   27
cannot be surprised by any evil and are thus less likely to be intimidated by it. Hence, we find ourselves heirs to a special hybrid of courage,
a form of courage too often ignored by the heterosexual majority, but
widely manifest among sexual outcasts, not the courage of bravado on
battlegrounds or sportsfields, but the delicate courage of the lone person
who patiently waits out the stupidity of the herd, the cagey courage that
has operated many an underground railway station.

Our survival in smalltown America has been helped least, I suspect,   28
by our annoying insistence that potential friends receive us not only in
our own right, but also as members of the larger lesbian/gay and black
communities of which we are a part. Too many whites and heterosexuals are prepared to single us out as "good queers" or "good niggers," offering us thereby the "rewards" of their friendship only at too great a
cost to our integrity. My priest did not whip up the vestry against me the
first year we lived openly together. He was perfectly happy to have one
of his "clever queers" to dress his wife's hair and the other to help him

write his annual report. We became scandalous only when the two of us began to organize the national group of lesbian and gay-male Episcopalians, known as INTEGRITY; then we were no longer just quaint. We threatened his image of himself as the arbiter of community morality, especially as he faced scores of queries from brother priests elsewhere.

Many lesbians and gay males are tamed by dependencies upon [29] carefully selected heterosexual friends with whom they have shared their secret, often never realizing that in themselves alone, they could provide far more affirmation and discover far more strength than is being cultivated by the terms of these "friendships." Lesbians and gay males have always been taught to survive on the heterosexuals' terms, rarely on one's own terms, and almost never on the terms of a community shared with other lesbians and gay males.

Heterosexuals are often thus the losers. The heterosexual ac- [30] quaintances close to us early on when we were less visible who dropped us later as our notoriety spread were in most cases folks of demonstrably much less character strength than those heterosexuals who remained our friends even as we asserted our difference with thoughtful independence.

My spouse and I have never been exclusive nor aspired to move to [31] any ghetto. In December 1978, on the night the Macon rabbi and I had successfully organized the area's Jews and gays to protest a concert by Anita Bryant.[2] I returned home to watch the videotape of the march on the late news in the company of eight house guests invited by my spouse for a surprise party, not one of them gay (for some strange reason nine out of ten folks are not), not one of them obligated to be at the earlier march and not one of them uneasy, as most of our acquaintances would have been a few years earlier before we had undertaken this reeducation together.

Folks who work for social change need to be very careful to allow [32] room for it to happen, not to allow realistic appraisals of risks to prevent their cultivation of the very change which they germinate.

Our survival has been helped in no small way by our candor and [33] clarity in response to rumor and gossip, which are among our biggest enemies. On my campus in Georgia, I voluntarily spoke about sexual issues to an average of fifty classes per year outside my discipline. Initially, those encounters sharpened my wits for tougher national forums, but long after I no longer needed these occasions personally for rehearsal, I continued to accept the invitations, thereby reaching a vast majority of the citizens of the small town where we continued to live. I used to enjoy the humor of sharing with such groups facts which would make my day-to-day life more pleasant. For example, I routinely noted that

---

[2] Former beauty queen who during the late 1970s and early 1980s attempted to bolster a faltering singing career by becoming a visible opponent of gay rights. [Eds.]

when a male student is shocked at my simple public, "Hello," he would look both ways to see who might have seen him being friendly with the gay professor. By doing this he is telling me and all other knowledgeable folks far more new information about his own body chemistry than he is finding out about mine. More informed male students would reply, "Hello" when greeted. With this method I disarmed the hatefulness of one of their more debilitating weapons of ostracism.

All personal references in public discussions inevitably invade one's 34 privacy, but I have usually found the invasion a small price to pay for the opportunity to educate the public to the fact that the issues which most concern sexual outcasts are not genital, as the casters-out have so lewdly imagined, but issues of justice and simple fairness.

Resistance is ultimately an art which no one masters to perfection. 35 Early in my struggles, I said to a gay colleague living openly in rural Nebraska, "We must stamp on every snake." Wisely he counseled, "Only if you want to get foot poisoning." I often wish I had more of the wisdom mentioned in *Ecclesiastes,* the ability to judge accurately, "The time to speak and the time to refrain from speaking." Much of the time I think it wise to pass public hecklers without acknowledging their taunts, especially when they are cowardly hiding in a crowd. When I have faced bullies head-on, I have tried to do so patiently, disarming them by my own control of the situation. Of course, I am not guaranteed that their violence can thus be aborted every time.

Two major sources of our survival are essentially very private—one, 36 the intense care and love my spouse and I share, and the other, our strong faith in God as Unbounding Love. To these we prefer to make our secular witness, more by what we do than by what we say.

I am not a masochist. I would never choose the hard lot of the sex- 37 ual outcast in smalltown America. Had I the choice to change myself but not the world, I would return as a white male heterosexual city-slicker millionaire, not because whites, males, heterosexuals, city-slickers, and millionaires are better, but because they have it easier.

Yet everyone faces a different choice: Accept the world the way you 38 find it, or change it. For year after year I dissented, right in my own neighborhood.

America preserves an ideal of freedom, although it denies freedom 39 in scores of instances. My eighth-grade civics teacher in Alabama did not mention the price I would have to pay for the freedom of speech she taught me to value. I know now that the docile and ignorant dislike you fiercely when you speak truth they prefer not to hear. But I had a good civics class, one that showed me how to change our government. I rejoice.

Sometimes I think a society's critics must appreciate the society far 40 more than others, for the critics typically take very seriously the society's idle promises and forgotten dreams. When I occasionally see them, I certainly don't find many of my heterosexual eighth-grade classmates probing much farther than the issues of our common Form 1040 headaches and the issues as delivered by the evening news. Their lives seem often far duller than ours and the main adventures in pioneering they experience come vicariously, through television, the movies, and for a few, through books. In defining me as a criminal, my society may well have hidden a major blessing in its curse by forcing me out of lethargy into an on-going, rigorous questioning of the entire process. Not only do I teach *The Adventures of Huckleberry Finn*,[3] my spouse and I have in an important sense had the chance to be Huck and Jim fleeing a different form of slavery and injustice in a very real present.

Responding to Reading

1. In this essay's title Crew describes himself as "an outsider, even . . . an outcast." In what ways are he and his companion excluded from mainstream society? Do you think they were wise to move to a small town, or do you feel they should have taken up residence in a place that might have been more hospitable? Explain your views.
2. Which do you suppose the town objects to more, the idea of a gay couple or the idea of a racially integrated couple? Explain.
3. Again and again Crew uses the word *survival*. How do you think he would define this word? What specific tactics do Crew and his companion use to ensure that they survive in "smalltown America"? How is this "survival" different from the title's "thriving"?

SAFE AT HOME

Philip Roth

One of the dominant voices in modern American literature, Philip Roth (1933–) is a novelist and short story writer who grew up during World War II in a neighborhood of Jewish immigrants who inspired many of Roth's plots and characters. Roth once said that his fiction "is about people in trouble." He is known for sarcasm, wit, colloquial American speech, and stinging political satire. A film was made of the title piece in his collection *Goodbye, Columbus and Five Short Stories* (1959). Some

---

[3] Mark Twain tale (1884) of the exploits of a young white boy and a slave on the Mississippi River.

of his other works include *Portnoy's Complaint* (1969), *Our Gang,* (1971), *The Great American Novel* (1973), *The Ghost Writer* (1979), *The Counterlife* (1986), *Patrimony* (1990), and *Operation Shylock: A Confession* (1993). "Safe at Home," a reminiscence of Roth's childhood, is from *The Facts: A Novelist's Autobiography* (1988).

The greatest menace while I was growing up came from abroad, [1] from the Germans and the Japanese, our enemies because we were American. I still remember my terror as a nine-year-old when, running in from playing on the street after school, I saw the banner headline COR-REGIDOR[1] FALLS on the evening paper in our doorway and understood that the United States actually could lose the war it had entered only months before. At home the biggest threat came from the Americans who opposed or resisted us—or condescended to us or rigorously excluded us—because we were Jews. Though I knew that we were tolerated and accepted as well—in publicized individual cases, even specially esteemed—and though I never doubted that this country was mine (and New Jersey and Newark as well), I was not unaware of the power to intimidate that emanated from the highest and lowest reaches of gentile America.

At the top were the gentile executives who ran my father's compa- [2] ny, the Metropolitan Life, from the home office at Number One Madison Avenue (the first Manhattan street address I ever knew). When I was a small boy, my father, then in his early thirties, was still a new Metropolitan agent, working a six-day week, including most evenings, and grateful for the steady, if modest, living this job provided, even during the Depression; a family shoe store he'd opened after marrying my mother had gone bankrupt some years before, and in between he'd had to take a variety of low-paying, unpromising jobs. He proudly explained to his sons that the Metropolitan was "the largest financial institution in the world" and that as an agent he provided Metropolitan Life policyholders with "an umbrella for a rainy day." The company put out dozens of pamphlets to educate its policyholders about health and disease; I collected a new batch off the racks in the waiting room on Saturday mornings when he took me along with him to the narrow downtown street where the Essex district office of Newark occupied nearly a whole floor of a commercial office building. I read up on "Tuberculosis," "Pregnancy," and "Diabetes," while he labored over his ledger entries and his paperwork. Sometimes at his desk, impressing myself by sitting in his swivel chair, I practiced my penmanship on Metropolitan stationery; in one corner of the paper was my father's name and in the other a picture of the home-office tower, topped with the beacon that he

---

[1] Heavily fortified island known known as "the Rock" that guarded Manila Bay during World War II and was lost to the Japanese in May 1942 after a month-long fight. [Eds.]

described to me, in the Metropolitan's own phrase, as the light that never failed.

In our apartment a framed replica of the Declaration of Independence hung above the telephone table on the hallway wall—it had been awarded by the Metropolitan to the men of my father's district for a successful year in the field, and seeing it there daily during my first school years forged an association between the venerated champions of equality who signed that cherished document and our benefactors, the corporate fathers at Number One Madison Avenue, where the reigning president was, fortuitously, a Mr. Lincoln. If that wasn't enough, the home-office executive whom my father would trek from New Jersey to see when his star began to rise slightly in the company was the superintendent of agencies, a Mr. Wright, whose good opinion my father valued inordinately all his life and whose height and imposing good looks he admired nearly as much as he did the man's easygoing diplomacy. As my father's son I felt no less respectful toward these awesomely named gentiles than he did, but I, like him, knew that they had to be the very officials who openly and guiltlessly conspired to prevent more than a few token Jews from assuming positions of anything approaching importance within the largest financial institution in the world.

One reason my father so admired the Jewish manager of his own district, Sam Peterfreund—aside, of course, from the devotion that Peterfreund inspired by recognizing my father's drive early on and making him an assistant manager—was that Peterfreund had climbed to the leadership of such a large, productive office despite the company's deep-rooted reluctance to allow a Jew to rise too high. When Mr. Peterfreund was to make one of his rare visits for dinner, the green felt protective pads came out of the hall closet and were laid by my brother and me on the dining room table, it was spread with a fresh linen cloth and linen napkins, water goblets appeared, and we ate off "the good dishes" in the dining room, where there hung a large oil painting of a floral arrangement, copied skillfully from the Louvre by my mother's brother, Mickey; on the sideboard were framed photographic portraits of the two dead men for whom I'd been named, my mother's father, Philip, and my father's younger brother, Milton. We ate in the dining room only on religious holidays, on special family occasions, and when Mr. Peterfreund came—and we all called him Mr. Peterfreund, even when he wasn't there; my father also addressed him directly as "Boss." "Want a drink, Boss?" Before dinner we sat unnaturally, like guests in our own living room, while Mr. Peterfreund sipped his schnapps and I was encouraged to listen to his wisdom. The esteem he inspired was a tribute to a gentile-sanctioned Jew managing a big Metropolitan office as much as to an immediate supervisor whose goodwill determined my father's occupational well-being and our family fate. A large, bald-headed man with a gold chain across his vest and a slightly mysterious German ac-

3

4

cent, whose family lived (in high style, I imagined) in New York (*and* on Long Island) while (no less glamorously to me) he slept during the week in a Newark hotel, the Boss was our family's Bernard Baruch.[2]

Opposition more frightening than corporate discrimination came [5] from the lowest reaches of the gentile world, from the gangs of *lumpen*[3] kids who, one summer, swarmed out of Neptune, a ramshackle little town on the Jersey shore, and stampeded along the boardwalk into Bradley Beach, hollering "Kikes! Dirty Jews!" and beating up whoever hadn't run for cover. Bradley Beach, a couple of miles south of Asbury Park on the mid-Jersey coast, was the very modest little vacation resort where we and hundreds of other lower-middle class Jews from humid, mosquito-ridden north Jersey cities rented rooms or shared small bungalows for several weeks during the summer. It was paradise for me, even though we lived three in a room, and four when my father drove down the old Cheesequake highway to see us on weekends or to stay for his two-week vacation. In all of my intensely secure and protected childhood, I don't believe I ever felt more exuberantly snug than I did in those mildly anarchic rooming houses, where—inevitably with more strain than valor—some ten or twelve women tried to share the shelves of a single large icebox, and to cook side by side, in a crowded communal kitchen, for children, visiting husbands, and elderly parents. Meals were eaten in the unruly, kibbutzlike atmosphere—so unlike the ambiance in my own orderly home—of the underventilated dining room.

The hot, unhomelike, homey hubbub of the Bradley Beach rooming [6] house was somberly contrasted, in the early forties, by reminders all along the shore that the country was fighting in an enormous war: bleak, barbwired Coast Guard bunkers dotted the beaches, and scores of lonely, very young sailors played the amusement machines in the arcades at Asbury Park; the lights were blacked out along the boardwalk at night and the blackout shades on the rooming-house windows made it stifling indoors after dinner; there was even tarry refuse, alleged to be from torpedoed ships, that washed up and littered the beach—I sometimes had fears of wading gleefully with my friends into the surf and bumping against the body of someone killed at sea. Also—and most peculiarly, since we were all supposed to be pulling together to beat the Axis Powers—there were these "race riots," as we children called the hostile nighttime invasions by the boys from Neptune: violence directed against the Jews by youngsters who, as everyone said, could only have learned their hatred from what they heard at home.

Though the riots occurred just twice, for much of one July and Au- [7] gust it was deemed unwise for a Jewish child to venture out after supper alone, or even with friends, though nighttime freedom in shorts and

---

[2] American financier of German-Jewish descent (1870–1965). [Eds.]

[3] Ragamuffin. [Eds.]

sandals was one of Bradley's greatest pleasures for a ten-year-old on vacation from homework and the school year's bedtime hours. The morning after the first riot, a story spread among the kids collecting Popsicle sticks and playing ring-a-lievo on the LaReine Avenue beach; it was about somebody (whom nobody seemed to know personally) who had been caught before he could get away: the anti-Semites had held him down and pulled his face back and forth across the splintery surface of the boardwalk's weathered planks. This particular horrific detail, whether apocryphal or not—and it needn't necessarily have been—impressed upon me how barbaric was this irrational hatred of families who, as anyone could see, were simply finding in Bradley Beach a little inexpensive relief from the city heat, people just trying to have a quiet good time, bothering no one, except occasionally each other, as when one of the women purportedly expropriated from the icebox, for her family's corn on the cob, somebody else's quarter of a pound of salt butter. If that was as much harm as any of us could do, why make a bloody pulp of a Jewish child's face?

The home-office gentiles in executive positions at Number One [8] Madison Avenue were hardly comparable to the kids swarming into Bradley screaming "Kike!"; and yet when I thought about it, I saw that they were no more reasonable or fair: they too were against Jews for no good reason. Small wonder that at twelve, when I was advised to begin to think seriously about what I would do when I grew up, I decided to oppose the injustices wreaked by the violent and the privileged by becoming a lawyer for the underdog.

When I entered high school, the menace shifted to School Stadium, [9] then the only large football grounds in Newark, situated on alien Bloomfield Avenue, a forty-minute bus ride from Weequahic High. On Saturdays in the fall, four of the city's seven high schools would meet in a doubleheader, as many as two thousand kids pouring in for the first game, which began around noon, and then emptying en masse into the surrounding streets when the second game had ended in the falling shadows. It was inevitable after a hard-fought game that intense school rivalries would culminate in a brawl somewhere in the stands and that, in an industrial city of strongly divergent ethnic backgrounds and subtle, though pronounced, class gradations, fights would break out among volatile teenagers from four very different neighborhoods. Yet the violence provoked by the presence of a Weequahic crowd—particularly after a rare Weequahic victory—was unlike any other.

I remember being in the stands with my friends in my sophomore [10] year, rooting uninhibitedly for the "Indians," as our Weequahic teams were known in the Newark sports pages; after never having beaten Barringer High in the fourteen years of Weequahic's existence, our team was leading them 6–0 in the waning minutes of the Columbus Day game. The Barringer backfield was Berry, Peloso, Short, and Thompson;

in the Weequahic backfield were Weissman, Weiss, Gold, and fullback Fred Rosenberg, who'd led a sustained march down the field at the end of the first half and then, on a two-yard plunge, had scored what Fred, now a PR consultant in New Jersey, recently wrote to tell me was "one of the only touchdowns notched by the Indians that entire season, on a run that probably was one of the longer runs from scrimmage in 1947."

As the miraculous game was nearing its end—as Barringer, tied [11] with Central for first place in the City League, was about to be upset by the weakest high school team in Newark—I suddenly noticed that the rival fans on the other side of the stadium bowl had begun to stream down the aisles, making their way around the far ends of the stadium toward us. Instead of waiting for the referee's final whistle, I bolted for an exit and, along with nearly everyone else who understood what was happening, ran down the stadium ramp in the direction of the buses waiting to take us back to our neighborhood. Though there were a number of policemen around, it was easy to see that once the rampage was under way, unless you were clinging to a cop with both arms and both legs, his protection wouldn't be much help; should you be caught on your own by a gang from one of the other three schools waiting to get their hands on a Weequahic Jew—our school was almost entirely Jewish—it was unlikely that you'd emerge from the stadium without serious injury.

The nearest bus was already almost full when I made it on board; as [12] soon as the last few kids shoved their way in, the uniformed Public Service driver, fearful for his own safety as a transporter of Weequahic kids, drew the front door shut. By then there were easily ten of fifteen of the enemy, aged twelve to twenty, surrounding the bus and hammering their fists against its sides. Fred Rosenberg contends that "every able-bodied man from north Newark, his brother, and their offspring got into the act." When one of them, having worked his hands through a crevice under the window beside my seat, started forcing the window up with his fingers, I grabbed it from the top and brought it down as hard as I could. He howled and somebody took a swing at the window with a baseball bat, breaking the frame but miraculously not the glass. Before the others could join together to tear back the door, board the bus, and go straight for me—who would have been hard put to explain that the reprisal had been uncharacteristic and intended only in self-defense—the driver had pulled out from the curb and we were safely away from the postgame pogrom, which, for our adversaries, constituted perhaps the most enjoyable part of the day's entertainment.

That evening I fled again, not only because I was a fourteen-year-old [13] weighing only a little over a hundred pounds but because I was never to be one of the few who stayed behind for a fight but always among the many whose impulse is to run to avoid it. A boy in our neighborhood might be expected to protect himself in a schoolyard confrontation with another boy his age and size, but no stigma attached to taking flight from a violent melee—by and large it was considered both shameful and stupid for a bright Jewish child to get caught up in something so dangerous to his physical safety, and so repugnant to Jewish instincts. The collective memory of Polish and Russian pogroms[4] had fostered in most of our families the idea that our worth as human beings, even perhaps our distinction as a people, was embodied in the *incapacity* to perpetrate the sort of bloodletting, visited upon our ancestors.

For a while during my adolescence I studiously followed prize- [14] fighting, could recite the names and weights of all the champions and contenders, and even subscribed briefly to *Ring,* Nat Fleischer's colorful boxing magazine. As kids my brother and I have been taken by our father to the local boxing arena, where invariably we all had a good time. From my father and his friends I heard about the prowess of Benny Leonard, Barney Ross, Max Baer, and the clownishly nicknamed Slapsie Maxie Rosenbloom. And yet Jewish boxers and boxing aficionados remained, like boxing itself, "sport" in the bizarre sense, a strange deviation from the norm and interesting largely for that reason: in the world whose values first formed me, unrestrained physical aggression was considered contemptible everywhere else. I could no more smash a nose with a fist than fire a pistol into someone's heart. And what imposed this restraint, if not on Slapsie Maxie Rosenbloom, then on me, was my being Jewish. In my scheme of things, Slapsie Maxie was a more miraculous Jewish phenomenon by far than Dr. Albert Einstein.

The evening following our escape from School Stadium the ritual [15] victory bonfire was held on the dirt playing field on Chancellor Avenue, across from Syd's, a popular Weequahic hangout where my brother and I each did part-time stints selling hot dogs and french fries. I'd virtually evolved as a boy on that playing field; it was two blocks from my house and bordered on the grade school—"Chancellor Avenue"—that I'd attended for eight years, which itself stood next to Weequahic High. It was the field where I'd played pickup football and baseball, where my brother had competed in school track meets, where I'd shagged flies for hours with anybody who would fungo the ball out to me, where my friends and I hung around on Sunday mornings, watching with amusement as the local fathers—the plumbers, the electricians, the produce merchants—kibitzed their way through their weekly softball game. If ever I had been called on to express my love for my neighborhood in a single reverential act, I couldn't have done better than to get down on my hands and knees and kiss the ground behind home plate.

Yet upon this, the sacred heart of my inviolate homeland, our sta- [16] dium attackers launched a nighttime raid, the conclusion to the violence

---

[4] Organized massacres of Jews conducted by the Czar's army during the late nineteenth and early twentieth centuries in Russia. [Eds.]

begun that afternoon, their mopping-up exercise. A few hours after the big fire had been lit, as we happily sauntered around the dark field, joking among ourselves and looking for girls to impress, while in the distance the cartwheeling cheerleaders led the chant of the crowd encircling the fire—" And when you're up against Weequahic/you're upside down!"—the cars pulled up swiftly on Chancellor Avenue, and the same guys who'd been pounding on the sides of my bus (or so I quickly assumed) were racing onto the field, some of them waving baseball bats. The field was set into the slope of the Chancellor Avenue hill; I ran through the dark to the nearest wall, jumped some six feet down into Hobson Street, and then just kept going, through alleyways, between garages, and over backyard fences, until I'd made it safely home in less than five minutes. One of my Leslie Street friends, the football team water boy, who'd been standing in the full glare of the fire wearing his Weequahic varsity jacket, was not so quick or lucky; his assailants—identified in the neighborhood the next day as "Italians"—picked him up and threw him bodily toward the flames. He landed just at the fire's edge and, though he wasn't burned, spent days in the hospital recovering from internal injuries.

But this was a unique calamity. Our lower-middle-class neighbor-   17
hood of houses and shops—a few square miles of tree-lined streets at the corner of the city bordering on residential Hillside and semi-industrial Irvington—was as safe and peaceful a haven for me as his rural community would have been for an Indiana farm boy. Ordinarily nobody more disquieting ever appeared there than the bearded old Jew who sometimes tapped on our door around dinnertime; to me an unnerving specter from the harsh and distant European past, he stood silently in the dim hallway while I went to get a quarter to drop into his collection can for the Jewish National Fund[5] (a name that never sank all the way in: the only nation for Jews, as I saw it, was the democracy to which I was so loyally—and lyrically—bound, regardless of the unjust bias of the so-called best and the violent hatred of some of the worst). Shapiro, the immigrant tailor who also did dry cleaning, had two thumbs on one hand, and that made bringing our clothes to him a little eerie for me when I was still small. And there was LeRoy "the moron," a somewhat gruesome but innocuous neighborhood dimwit who gave me the creeps when he sat down on the front stoop to listen to a bunch of us talking after school. On our street he was rarely teased but just sat looking at us stupidly with his hollow eyes and rhythmically tapping one foot—and that was about as frightening as things ever got.

A typical memory is of five or six of us energetically traversing the   18
whole length of the neighborhood Friday nights on our way back from

---

[5] A private fund established to support the emerging nation of Israel. [Eds.]

a double feature at the Roosevelt Theater. We would stop off at the Watson Bagel Company on Clinton Place to buy, for a few pennies each, a load of the first warm bagels out of the oven—and this was four decades before the bagel became a breakfast staple at Burger King. Devouring three and four apiece, we'd circuitously walk one another home, howling with laughter at our jokes and imitating our favorite baritones. When the weather was good we'd sometimes wind up back of Chancellor Avenue School, on the wooden bleachers along the sidelines of the asphalt playground adjacent to the big dirt playing field. Stretched on our backs in the open night air, we were as carefree as any kids anywhere in postwar America, and certainly we felt ourselves no less American. Discussions about Jewishness and being Jewish, which I was to hear so often among intellectual Jews once I was an adult in Chicago and New York, were altogether unknown; we talked about being misunderstood by our families, about movies and radio programs and sex and sports, we even argued about politics, though this was rare since our fathers were all ardent New Dealers and there was no disagreement among us about the sanctity of F.D.R. and the Democratic Party. About being Jewish there was nothing more to say than there was about having two arms and two legs. It would have seemed to us strange *not* to be Jewish—stranger still, to hear someone announce that he wished he weren't a Jew or that he intended not to be in the future.

Yet, simultaneously, this intense adolescent camaraderie was the [19] primary means by which we were deepening our *Americanness*. Our parents were, with few exceptions, the first-generation offspring of poor turn-of-the-century immigrants from Galicia[6] and Polish Russia, raised in predominantly Yiddish[7]-speaking Newark households where religious Orthodoxy was only just beginning to be seriously eroded by American life. However unaccented and American-sounding their speech, however secularized their own beliefs, and adept and convincing their American style of lower-middle-class existence, they were influenced still by their childhood training and by strong parental ties to what often seemed to us antiquated, socially useless old-country mores and perceptions.

My larger boyhood society cohered around the most inherently [20] American phenomenon at hand—the game of baseball, whose mystique was encapsulated in three relatively inexpensive fetishes that you could have always at your side in your room, not only while you did your homework but in bed with you while you slept if you were a worshiper as primitive as I was at ten and eleven: they were a ball, a bat, and a glove. The solace that my Orthodox grandfather doubt-

---

[6] Region of southeastern Poland, including the cities of Kraków and Lvov. [Eds.]

[7] Language derived from German dialects and written in Hebrew characters. [Eds.]

less took in the familiar leathery odor of the flesh-worn straps of the old phylacteries[8] in which he wrapped himself each morning, I derived from the smell of my mitt, which I ritualistically donned every day to work a little on my pocket. I was an average playground player, and the mitt's enchantment had to do less with foolish dreams of becoming a major leaguer, or even a high school star, than with the bestowal of membership in a great secular nationalistic church from which nobody had ever seemed to suggest that Jews should be excluded. (The blacks were another story, until 1947.)[9] The softball and hardball teams we organized and reorganized obsessively throughout our grade-school years—teams we called by unarguably native names like the Seabees and the Mohawks and described as "social and athletic clubs"—aside from the opportunity they afforded to compete against one another in a game we loved, also operated as secret societies that separated us from the faint, residual foreignness still clinging to some of our parents' attitudes and that validated our own spotless credentials as American kids. Paradoxically, our remotely recent old-country Jewish origins may well have been a source of our especially intense devotion to a sport that, unlike boxing or even football, had nothing to do with the menace of brute force unleashed against flesh and bones.

The Weequahic neighborhood for over two decades now has been [21] part of the vast black Newark slum. Visiting my father in Elizabeth, I'll occasionally take a roundabout route off the parkway into my old Newark and, to give myself an emotional workout, drive through the streets still entirely familiar to me despite the boarded-up shops and badly decaying houses, and the knowledge that my white face is not at all welcome. Recently, snaking back and forth in my car along the one-way streets of the Weequahic section, I began to imagine house plaques commemorating the achievements of the boys who'd once lived there, markers of the kind you see in London and Paris on the residences of the historically renowned. What I inscribed on those plaques, along with my friends' names and their years of birth and of local residence, wasn't the professional status they had attained in later life but the position each had played on those neighborhood teams of ours in the 1940s. I thought that if you knew that in this four-family Hobson Street house there once lived the third baseman Seymour Feldman and that down a few doors had lived Ronnie Rubin, who in his boyhood had been our catcher, you'd understand how and where the Feldman and the Rubin families had been naturalized irrevocably by their young sons.

---

[8] Small leather boxes containing strips of parchment inscribed with quotations from the Hebrew scriptures, used in morning prayers. [Eds.]

[9] In 1947, professional baseball signed its first black player: Jackie Robinson of the Brooklyn Dodgers. [Eds.]

In 1982, while I was visiting my widowered father in Miami Beach [22] during his first season there on his own, I got him one night to walk over with me to Meyer Lansky's[10] old base of operations, the Hotel Singapore on Collins Avenue; earlier in the day he'd told me that wintering at the Singapore were some of the last of his generation from our neighborhood—the ones, he mordantly added, "still above-ground." Among the faces I recognized in the lobby, where the elderly residents met to socialize each evening after dinner, was the mother of one of the boys who also used to play ball incessantly "up the field" and who hung around on the playground bleachers after dark back when we were Seabees together. As we sat talking at the edge of a gin-rummy game, she suddenly took hold of my hand and, smiling at me with deeply emotional eyes—with that special heartfilled look that *all* our mothers had—she said, "Phil, the feeling there was among you boys—I've never seen anything like it again." I told her, altogether truthfully, that I haven't either.

Responding to Reading

1. In what respects does Roth—both as a child and as an adolescent—see himself as different from his non-Jewish counterparts? Do you think such feelings of differentness generally increase or decrease as members of minority groups become adults?

2. Roth sees himself "opposed," "resisted," "condescended to," and "rigorously excluded" by a powerful non-Jewish elite. Still, he finds the gentile children who call him names even more frightening than these powerful adults. Why? Which group do you see as more frightening?

3. When Roth speaks of being "safe at home," what does he mean by "safe"? By "home"? What does being "safe at home" mean to you?

CHOOSING A DREAM: ITALIANS ∾ IN HELL'S KITCHEN

Mario Puzo

Mario Puzo (1920–) had written two well-reviewed but commercially unsuccessful novels, *Time* magazine reported, when in 1965 a publisher "overheard him telling Mafia yarns and offered a $5,000 advance for

---

[10] Reputed underworld crime figure during the 1930s. [Eds.]

a book about the Italian underworld." The result was *The Godfather* (1969), the best-selling novel of the 1970s and the basis for several movies whose durable popularity is evidenced by television rebroadcasts and video rentals. (Puzo won Academy Awards for his first two *Godfather* screen adaptations.) If his later novels—including *The Sicilian* (1984) and *The Fourth K* (1991)—proved less spectacularly successful, they were bestsellers nonetheless. Born poor in the Manhattan neighborhood he describes in the following essay, Puzo wanted to be an artist from an early age, but the limitations of the world he grew up in demanded a long struggle before he was able to free himself to write. Even so, as he explains here, the dream he realized of escaping childhood poverty and achieving fame and material success sometimes seems less attractive to him now than the "happy" childhood he recalls through the filtering lens of memory.

As a child and in my adolescence, living in the heart of New York's 1 Neapolitan ghetto, I never heard an Italian singing. None of the grownups I knew were charming or loving or understanding. Rather they seemed coarse, vulgar, and insulting. And so later in my life when I was exposed to all the clichés of lovable Italians, singing Italians, happy-go-lucky Italians, I wondered where the hell the moviemakers and storywriters got all their ideas from.

At a very early age I decided to escape these uncongenial folk by be- 2 coming an artist, a writer. It seemed then an impossible dream. My father and mother were illiterate, as were their parents before them. But practicing my art I tried to view the adults with a more charitable eye and so came to the conclusion that their only fault lay in their being foreigners; I was an American. This didn't really help because I was only half right. I was the foreigner. They were already more "American" than I could ever become.

But it did seem then that the Italian immigrants, all the fathers and 3 mothers that I knew, were a grim lot; always shouting, always angry, quicker to quarrel than embrace. I did not understand that their lives were a long labor to earn their daily bread and that physical fatigue does not sweeten human natures.

And so even as a very small child I dreaded growing up to be like the 4 adults around me. I heard them saying too many cruel things about their dearest friends, saw too many of their false embraces with those they had just maligned, observed with horror their paranoiac anger at some small slight or a fancied injury to their pride. They were, always, too unforgiving. In short, they did not have the careless magnanimity of children.

In my youth I was contemptuous of my elders, including a few 5 under thirty. I thought my contempt special to their circumstances. Later when I wrote about these illiterate men and women, when I thought I understood them, I felt a condescending pity. After all, they had suffered, they had labored all the days of their lives. They had never tasted luxury, knew little more economic security than those ancient Roman slaves who might have been their ancestors. And alas, I thought, with new-found artistic insight, they were cut off from their children because of the strange American tongue, alien to them, native to their sons and daughters.

Already an artist but not yet a husband or father, I pondered omni- ⁶ sciently on their tragedy, again thinking it special circumstance rather than a constant in the human condition. I did not yet understand why these men and women were willing to settle for less than they deserved in life and think that "less" quite a bargain. I did not understand that they simply could not afford to dream; I myself had a hundred dreams from which to choose. For I was already sure that I would make my escape, that I was one of the chosen. I would be rich, famous, happy. I would master my destiny.

And so it was perhaps natural that as a child, with my father gone, ⁷ my mother the family chief, I, like all the children in all the ghettos of America, became locked in a bitter struggle with the adults responsible for me. It was inevitable that my mother and I became enemies.

As a child I had the usual dreams. I wanted to be handsome, specif- ⁸ ically as cowboy stars in movies were handsome. I wanted to be a killer hero in a world-wide war. Or if no wars came along (our teachers told us another was impossible), I wanted at the very least to be a footloose adventurer. Then I branched out and thought of being a great artist, and then, getting ever more sophisticated, a great criminal.

My mother, however, wanted me to be a railroad clerk. And that ⁹ was her *highest* ambition; she would have settled for less. At the age of sixteen when I let everybody know that I was going to be a great writer, my friends and family took the news quite calmly, my mother included. She did not become angry. She quite simply assumed that I had gone off my nut. She was illiterate and her peasant life in Italy made her believe that only a son of the nobility could possibly be a writer. Artistic beauty after all could spring only from the seedbed of fine clothes, fine food, luxurious living. So then how was it possible for a son of hers to be an artist? She was not too convinced she was wrong even after my first two books were published many years later. It was only after the commercial success of my third novel that she gave me the title of poet.

My family and I grew up together on Tenth Avenue, between Thir- ¹⁰ tieth and Thirty-first streets, part of the area called Hell's Kitchen. This particular neighborhood could have been a movie set for one of the Dead End Kid flicks or for the social drama of the East Side in which John Garfield played the hero. Our tenements were the western wall of the city. Beneath our windows were the vast black iron gardens of the New York Central Railroad, absolutely blooming with stinking boxcars freshly unloaded of cattle and pigs for the city slaughterhouse. Steers sometimes escaped and loped through the heart of the neighborhood followed by astonished young boys who had never seen a live cow.

The railroad yards stretched down to the Hudson River, beyond [11] whose garbagey waters rose the rocky Palisades of New Jersey. There were railroad tracks running downtown on Tenth Avenue itself to another freight station called St. Johns Park. Because of this, because these trains cut off one side of the street from the other, there was a wooden bridge over Tenth Avenue, a romantic-looking bridge despite the fact that no sparkling water, no silver flying fish darted beneath it; only heavy dray carts drawn by tired horses, some flat-boarded trucks, tin lizzie automobiles and, of course, long strings of freight cars drawn by black, ugly engines.

What was really great, truly magical, was sitting on the bridge, feet [12] dangling down, and letting the engine under you blow up clouds of steam that made you disappear, then reappear all damp and smelling of fresh ironing. When I was seven years old I fell in love for the first time with the tough little girl who held my hand and disappeared with me in that magical cloud of steam. This experience was probably more traumatic and damaging to my later relationships with women than one of those ugly childhood adventures Freudian novelists use to explain why their hero has gone bad.

My father supported his wife and seven children by working as a [13] trackman laborer for the New York Central Railroad. My oldest brother worked for the railroad as a brakeman, another brother was a railroad shipping clerk in the freight office. Eventually I spent some of the worst months of my life as the railroad's worst messenger boy.

My oldest sister was just as unhappy as a dressmaker in the garment [14] industry. She wanted to be a school teacher. At one time or another my other two brothers also worked for the railroad—it got all six males in the family. The two girls and my mother escaped, though my mother felt it her duty to send all our bosses a gallon of homemade wine on Christmas. But everybody hated their jobs except my oldest brother who had a night shift and spent most of his working hours sleeping in freight cars. My father finally got fired because the foreman told him to get a bucket of water for the crew and not to take all day. My father took the bucket and disappeared forever.

Nearly all the Italian men living on Tenth Avenue supported their [15] large families by working on the railroad. Their children also earned pocket money by stealing ice from the refrigerator cars in summer and coal from the open stoking cars in the winter. Sometimes an older lad would break the seal of a freight car and take a look inside. But this usually brought down the "Bulls," the special railroad police. And usually the freight was "heavy" stuff, too much work to cart away and sell, something like fresh produce or boxes of cheap candy that nobody would buy.

The older boys, the ones just approaching voting age, made their [16] easy money by hijacking silk trucks that loaded up at the garment factory on Thirty-first Street. They would then sell the expensive dresses door to door, at bargain prices no discount house could match. From this some graduated into organized crime, whose talent scouts alertly tapped young boys versed in strongarm. Yet despite all this, most of the kids grew up honest, content with fifty bucks a week as truck drivers, deliverymen, and white-collar clerks in the civil service.

I had every desire to go wrong but I never had a chance. The Italian [17] family structure was too formidable.

I never came home to an empty house; there was always the smell [18] of supper cooking. My mother was always there to greet me, sometimes with a policeman's club in her hand (nobody ever knew how she acquired it). But she was always there, or her authorized deputy, my older sister, who preferred throwing empty milk bottles at the heads of her little brothers when they got bad marks on their report cards. During the great Depression of the 1930s, though we were the poorest of the poor, I never remember not dining well. Many years later as a guest of a millionaire's club, I realized that our poor family on home relief ate better than some of the richest people in America.

My mother would never dream of using anything but the finest imported olive oil, the best Italian cheeses. My father had access to the fruits coming off ships, the produce from railroad cars, all before it went through the stale process of middlemen; and my mother, like most Italian women, was a fine cook in the peasant style.

My mother was as formidable a personage as she was a cook. She [20] was not to be treated cavalierly. My oldest brother at age sixteen had his own tin lizzie Ford and used it to further his career as the Don Juan of Tenth Avenue. One day my mother asked him to drive her to the market on Ninth Avenue and Fortieth Street, no more than a five-minute trip. My brother had other plans and claimed he was going to work on a new shift on the railroad. Work was an acceptable excuse even for funerals. But an hour later when my mother came out of the door of the tenement she saw the tin lizzie loaded with three pretty neighborhood girls, my Don Juan brother about to drive them off. Unfortunately there was a cobblestone lying loose in the gutter. My mother dropped her black leather shopping bag and picked up the stone with both hands. As we all watched in horror, she brought the boulder down on the nearest fender of the tin lizzie, demolishing it. Then she picked up her bag and marched off to Ninth Avenue to do her shopping. To this day, forty years later, my brother's voice still has a surprised horror and shock when he tells the story. He still doesn't understand how she could have done it.

My mother had her own legends and myths on how to amass a fortune. There was one of our uncles who worked as an assistant chef in a famous Italian-style restaurant. Every day, six days a week, this uncle brought home, under his shirt, six eggs, a stick of butter, and a small bag of flour. By doing this for thirty years he was able to save enough money to buy a fifteen-thousand-dollar house on Long Island and two smaller houses for his son and daughter. Another cousin, blessed with a college degree, worked as a chemist in a large manufacturing firm. By using the firm's raw materials and equipment he concocted a superior floor wax which he sold door to door in his spare time. It was a great floor wax and with his low overhead, the price was right. My mother and her friends did not think this stealing. They thought of it as being thrifty. [21]

The wax-selling cousin eventually destroyed his reputation for thrift by buying a sailboat; this was roughly equivalent to the son of a Boston brahmin[1] spending a hundred grand in a whorehouse. [22]

As rich men escape their wives by going to their club, I finally escaped my mother by going to the Hudson Guild Settlement House. Most people do not know that a settlement house is really a club combined with social services. The Hudson Guild, a five-story field of joy for slum kids, had ping pong rooms and billiard rooms, a shop in which to make lamps, a theater for putting on amateur plays, a gym to box and play basketball in. And then there were individual rooms where your particular club could meet in privacy. The Hudson Guild even suspended your membership for improper behavior or failure to pay the tiny dues. It was a heady experience for a slum kid to see his name posted on the billboard to the effect that he was suspended by the Board of Governors. [23]

The Hudson Guild was also responsible for absolutely the happiest times of my childhood. When I was about nine or ten they sent me away as a Fresh Air Fund kid. This was a program where slum children were boarded on private families in places like New Hampshire for two weeks. [24]

As a child I knew only the stone city. I had no conception of what the countryside could be. When I got to New Hampshire, when I smelled grass and flowers and trees, when I ran barefoot along the dirt country roads, when I drove the cows home from pasture, when I darted through fields of corn and waded through clear brooks, when I gathered warm brown speckled eggs in the henhouse, when I drove a hay wagon drawn by two great horses—when I did all these things—I nearly went crazy with the joy of it. It was quite simply a fairy tale come true. [25]

---

[1] A member of the cultural and social elite. [Eds.]

The family that took me in, a middle-aged man and woman, child- [26] less, were Baptists and observed Sunday so religiously that even check-er playing was not allowed on the Lord's day of rest. We went to church on Sunday for a good three hours, counting Bible class, then again at night. On Thursday evenings we went to prayer meetings. My guardians, out of religious scruple, had never seen a movie. They disapproved of dancing, they were no doubt political reactionaries; they were everything that I came later to fight against.

And yet they gave me those magical times children never forget. For [27] two weeks every summer from the time I was nine to fifteen I was happier than I have ever been before or since. The man was good with tools and built me a little playground with swings, sliding ponds, seesaws. The woman had a beautiful flower and vegetable garden and let me pick from it. A cucumber or strawberry in the earth was a miracle. And then when they saw how much I loved picnics, the sizzling frankfurters on a stick over the wood fire, the yellow roasted corn, they drove me out on Sunday afternoons to a lovely green grass mountainside. Only on Sundays it was never called a picnic, it was called "taking our lunch outside." I found it then—and now—a sweet hypocrisy.

From this Paradise I was flung into Hell. That is, I had to help sup- [28] port my family by working on the railroad. After school hours of course. This was the same railroad that had supplied free coal and free ice to the whole Tenth Avenue when I was young enough to steal with impunity. After school finished at 3 p.m. I went to work in the freight office as a messenger. I also worked Saturdays and Sundays when there was work available.

I hated it. One of my first short stories was about how I hated that [29] job. But of course what I really hated was entering the adult world. To me the adult world was a dark enchantment, unnatural. As unnatural to the human dream as death. And as inevitable.

The young are impatient about change because they cannot grasp [30] the power of time itself; not only as the enemy of flesh, the very germ of death, but time as a benign cancer. As the young cannot grasp really that love must be a victim of time, so too they cannot grasp that injustices, the economic and family traps of living, can also fall victim to time.

America may be a fascistic, warmongering, racially prejudiced [31] country today. It may deserve the hatred of its revolutionary young. But what a miracle it once was! What has happened here has never happened in any other country in any other time. The poor who had been poor for centuries—hell, since the beginning of Christ—whose children had inherited their poverty, their illiteracy, their hopelessness, achieved some economic dignity and freedom. You didn't get it for nothing, you had to pay a price in tears, in suffering, but why not? And some even became artists.

Not even my gift for retrospective falsification[2] can make my eigh- 32
teenth to twenty-first years seem like a happy time. I hated my life. I was
being dragged into the trap I feared and had foreseen even as a child. It
was all there, the steady job, the nice girl who would eventually get
knocked up, and then the marriage and fighting over counting pennies
to make ends meet. I noticed myself acting more unheroic all the time.
I had to tell lies in pure self-defense, I did not forgive so easily.

But I was delivered. When World War II broke out I was delighted. 33
There is no other word, terrible as it may sound. My country called. I
was delivered from my mother, my family, the girl I was loving passionately but did not love. And delivered WITHOUT GUILT. Heroically. My country called, ordered me to defend it. I must have been one of
millions, sons, husbands, fathers, lovers, making their innocent getaway
from baffled loved ones. And what an escape it was. The war made all
my dreams come true. I drove a jeep, toured Europe, had love affairs,
found a wife, and lived the material for my first novel. But of course that
was a just war as Vietnam is not, and so today it is perhaps for the best
that the revolutionary young make their escape by attacking their own
rulers.

Then why five years later did I walk back into the trap with a wife 34
and child and a civil service job I was glad to get? After five years of the
life I had dreamed about, plenty of women, plenty of booze, plenty of
money, hardly any work, interesting companions, travel, etc., why did
I walk back into that cage of family and duty and a steady job?

For the simple reason, of course, that I had never really escaped, not 35
my mother, not my family, not the moral pressures of our society. Time
again had done its work. I was back in my cage and I was, I think,
happy. In the next twenty years I wrote three novels. Two of them were
critical successes but I didn't make much money. The third novel, not as
good as the others, made me rich. And free at last. Or so I thought.

Then why do I dream of those immigrant Italian peasants as having 36
been happy? I remember how they spoke of their forebears, who spent
all their lives farming the arid mountain slopes of Southern Italy. "He
died in that house in which he was born," they say enviously. "He was
never more than an hour from his village, not in all his life," they sigh.
And what would they make of a phrase like "retrospective falsification"?

No, really, we are all happier now. It is a better life. And after all, as 37
my mother always said, "Never mind about being happy. Be glad
you're alive."

When I came to my "autobiographical novel," the one every 38
writer does about himself, I planned to make myself the sensitive,

---

[2] Remembering the good and not the bad. [Eds.]

misunderstood hero, much put upon by his mother and family. To my astonishment my mother took over the book and instead of my revenge I got another comeuppance. But it is, I think, my best book. And all those old-style grim conservative Italians whom I hated, then pitied so patronizingly, they also turned out to be heroes. Through no desire of mine. I was surprised. The thing that amazed me most was their courage. Where were their Congressional Medals of Honor? Their Distinguished Service Crosses? How did they ever have the balls to get married, have kids, go out to earn a living in a strange land, with no skills, not even knowing the language? They made it without tranquilizers, without sleeping pills, without psychiatrists, without even a dream. Heroes. Heroes all around me. I never saw them.

But how could I? They wore lumpy work clothes and handlebar   39
moustaches, they blew their noses on their fingers and they were so short that their high-school children towered over them. They spoke a laughable broken English and the furthest limit of their horizon was their daily bread. Brave men, brave women, they fought to live their lives without dreams. Bent on survival, they narrowed their minds to the thinnest line of existence.

It is no wonder that in my youth I found them contemptible. And   40
yet they had left Italy and sailed the ocean to come to a new land and leave their sweated bones in America. Illiterate Colombos, they dared to seek the promised land. And so they, too, dreamed a dream.

But maybe the young are on the right track this time. Maybe they   41
know that the dreams of our fathers were malignant. Perhaps it is true that the only real escape is in the blood magic of drugs. All the Italians I knew and grew up with have escaped, have made their success. We are all Americans now, we are all successes now. And yet the most successful Italian man I know admits that though the one human act he never could understand was suicide, he understood it when he became a success. Not that he ever would do such a thing; no man with Italian blood ever commits suicide or becomes a homosexual in his belief. But suicide has crossed his mind. And so to what avail the finding of the dream? He went back to Italy and tried to live like a peasant again. But he can never again be unaware of more subtle traps than poverty and hunger.

There is a difference between having a good time in life and being   42
happy. My mother's life was a terrible struggle and yet I think it was a happy life. One tentative proof is that at the age of eighty-two she is positively indignant at the thought that death dares approach her. But it's not for everybody that kind of life.

Thinking back I wonder why I became a writer. Was it the poverty   43
or the books I read? Who traumatized me, my mother or the Brothers

Karamazov? Being Italian? Or the girl sitting with me on the bridge as the engine steam deliciously made us vanish? Did it make any difference that I grew up Italian rather than Irish or black?

No matter. The good times are beginning, I am another Italian suc- [44] cess story. Not as great as DiMaggio or Sinatra but quite enough. It will serve. Yet I can escape again. I have my retrospective falsification (how I love that phrase). I can dream now about how happy I was in my childhood, in my tenement, playing in those dirty but magical streets—living in the poverty that made my mother weep. True, I was a deposed dictator at fifteen but they never hanged me. And now I remember, all those impossible dreams strung out before me, waiting for me to choose, not knowing that the life I was living then, as a child, would become my final dream.

Responding to Reading

1. What was Puzo's childhood dream? How did it change as he grew older? In what sense was his dream the typical American Dream?
2. In the last paragraph of his essay Puzo describes himself as "another Italian success story." What does *success* mean to him? What did it mean to his parents? Does your own concept of success differ from your parents'?
3. How is Puzo's childhood view of "all those old-style grim conservative Italians" (39), the hardworking, joyless men and women he knew when he was a child, different from his adult view of them? What do you think changed his opinion? Do you, like Puzo, see your parents differently now that you are an adult?

HOW IT FEELS TO BE COLORED
~ ME

Zora Neale Hurston

Folklorist and writer Zora Neale Hurston (1901–1969) grew up in Eatonville, Florida, the first incorporated African-American community in the United States, and Hurston herself was the first African-American woman admitted to Barnard College in New York City. There she developed an interest in anthropology, and she studied with Columbia University's famous anthropologist, Franz Boas. *Mules and Men* (1935) is her book of folklore about voodoo among southern blacks. During the Harlem Renaissance of the 1920s and 1930s, Hurston wrote stories celebrating the hope and joy of African-American life, music, and stories. Her most notable novel is *Their Eyes Were Watching God* (1937). The essay below, which features Hurston's strong personal voice, is from the collection *I Love Myself When I Am Laughing* (1979), edited by Alice Walker.

I am colored but I offer nothing in the way of extenuating circumstances except the fact that I am the only Negro in the United States whose grandfather on the mother's side was *not* an Indian chief.

I remember the very day that I became colored. Up to my thirteenth year I lived in the little Negro town of Eatonville, Florida. It is exclusively a colored town. The only white people I knew passed through the town going to or coming from Orlando. The native whites rode dusty horses, the Northern tourists chugged down the sandy village road in automobiles. The town knew the Southerners and never stopped cane chewing[1] when they passed. But the Northerners were something else again. They were peered at cautiously from behind curtains by the timid. The more venturesome would come out on the porch to watch them go past and got just as much pleasure out of the tourists as the tourists got out of the village.

The front porch might seem a daring place for the rest of the town, but it was a gallery seat for me. My favorite place was atop the gate-post. Proscenium[2] box for a born first-nighter. Not only did I enjoy the show, but I didn't mind the actors knowing that I liked it. I usually spoke to them in passing. I'd wave at them and when they returned my salute, I would say something like this: "Howdy-do-well-I-thank-you-where-you-goin'?" Usually automobile or the horse paused at this, and after a queer exchange of compliments, I would probably "go a piece of the way" with them, as we say in farthest Florida. If one of my family happened to come to the front in time to see me, of course negotiations would be rudely broken off. But even so, it is clear that I was the first "welcome-to-our-state" Floridian, and I hope the Miami Chamber of Commerce will please take notice.

During this period, white people differed from colored to me only in that they rode through town and never lived there. They liked to hear me "speak pieces" and sing and wanted to see me dance the parse-me-la, and gave me generously of their small silver for doing these things, which seemed strange to me for I wanted to do them so much that I needed bribing to stop. Only they didn't know it. The colored people gave no dimes. They deplored any joyful tendencies in me, but I was their Zora nevertheless. I belonged to them, to the nearby hotels, to the county—everybody's Zora.

---

[1] Chewing sugar cane. [Eds.]

[2] In the ancient Greek theater, the stage; in the modern theater, the area between the curtain and the orchestra. [Eds.]

But changes came in the family when I was thirteen, and I was sent   5
to school in Jacksonville. I left Eatonville, the town of the oleanders,[3] as
Zora. When I disembarked from the river-boat at Jacksonville, she was
no more. It seemed that I had suffered a sea change. I was not Zora of
Orange County any more, I was now a little colored girl. I found it out
in certain ways. In my heart as well as in the mirror, became a fast
brown—warranted not to rub nor run.

But I am not tragically colored. There is no great sorrow dammed up   6
in my soul, nor lurking behind my eyes. I do not mind at all. I do not belong to the sobbing school of Negrohood who hold that nature somehow has given them a lowdown dirty deal and whose feelings are all
hurt about it. Even in the helter-skelter skirmish that is my life, I have
seen that the world is to the strong regardless of a little pigmentation
more or less. No, I do not weep at the world—I am too busy sharpening
my oyster knife.[4]

Someone is always at my elbow reminding me that I am the grand-   7
daughter of slaves. It fails to register depression with me. Slavery is sixty
years in the past. The operation was successful and the patient is doing
well, thank you. The terrible struggle[5] that made me an American out of
a potential slave said "On the line!" The Reconstruction[6] said "Get set!";
and the generation before said "Go!" I am off to a flying start and I must
not halt in the stretch to look behind and weep. Slavery is the price I paid
for civilization, and the choice was not with me. It is a bully adventure
and worth all that I have paid through my ancestors for it. No one on
earth ever had a greater chance for glory. The world to be won and nothing to be lost. It is thrilling to think—to know that for any act of mine, I
shall get twice as much praise or twice as much blame. It is quite exciting to hold the center of the national stage, with the spectators not knowing whether to laugh or to weep.

The position of my white neighbor is much more difficult. No   8
brown specter pulls up a chair beside me when I sit down to eat. No
dark ghost thrusts its leg against mine in bed. The game of keeping what
one has is never so exciting as the game of getting.

I do not always feel colored. Even now I often achieve the uncon-   9
scious Zora of Eatonville before the Hegira.[7] I feel most colored when I
am thrown against a sharp white background.

For instance at Barnard. "Beside the waters of the Hudson" I feel my   10
race. Among the thousand white persons, I am a dark rock surged upon,

---

[3] Tropical flowers. [Eds.]

[4] Reference is to the expression "The world is my oyster." [Eds.]

[5] The Civil War. [Eds.]

[6] The period immediately following the Civil War. [Eds.]

[7] The flight of Mohammed from Mecca in A.D. 622; here, an escape from a dangerous situation. [Eds.]

and overswept, but through it all, I remain myself. When covered by the waters, I am; and the ebb but reveals me again.

Sometimes it is the other way around. A white person is set down 11
in our midst, but the contrast is just as sharp for me. For instance, when I sit in the drafty basement that is The New World Cabaret with a white person, my color comes. We enter chatting about any little nothing that we have in common and are seated by the jazz waiters. In the abrupt way that jazz orchestras have, this one plunges into a number. It loses no time in circumlocutions, but gets right down to business. It constricts the thorax and splits the heart with its tempo and narcotic harmonies. This orchestra grows rambunctious, rears on its hind legs and attacks the tonal veil with primitive fury, rending it, clawing it until it breaks through to the jungle beyond. I follow those heathen—follow them ex-ultingly. I dance wildly inside myself; I yell within, I whoop; I shake my assegai[8] above my head, I hurl it true to the mark *yeeeeooww!* I am in the jungle and living in the jungle way. My face is painted red and yellow and my body is painted blue. My pulse is throbbing like a war drum. I want to slaughter something—give paid, give death to what, I do not know. But the piece ends. The men of the orchestra wipe their lips and rest their fingers. I creep back slowly to the veneer we call civilization with the last tone and find the white friend sitting motionless in his seat, smoking calmly.

"Good music they have here," he remarks, drumming the table with 12
his fingertips.

Music. The great blobs of purple and red emotion have not 13
touched him. He has only heard what I felt. He is far away and I see him but dimly across the ocean and the continent that have fallen between us. He is so pale with his whiteness then and I am so colored.

At certain times I have no race, I am *me*. When I set my hat at a cer- 14
tain angle and saunter down Seventh Avenue, Harlem City, feeling as snooty as the lions in front of the Forty-Second Street Library, for in-stance. So far as my feelings are concerned, Peggy Hopkins Joyce[9] on the Boule Mich with her gorgeous raiment, stately carriage, knees knocking together in a most aristocratic manner, has nothing on me. The cosmic Zora emerges. I belong to no race nor time. I am the eternal feminine with its string of beads.

I have no separate feeling about being an American citizen and col- 15
ored. I am merely a fragment of the Great Soul that surges within the boundaries. My country, right or wrong.

---

[8] South American hunting spear. [Eds.]

[9] American known for setting trends in beauty and fashion in the nineteen-twenties. The Boule Mich (also Boul' Mich) is a street on Paris's Left Bank. [Eds.]

Sometimes, I feel discriminated against, but it does not make me 16 angry. It merely astonishes me. How *can* any deny themselves the pleasure of my company? It's beyond me.

But in the main, I feel like a brown bag of miscellany propped 17 against a wall. Against a wall in company with other bags, white, red and yellow. Pour out the contents, and there is discovered a jumble of small things priceless and worthless. A first-water diamond, an empty spool, bits of broken glass, lengths of string, a key to a door long since crumbled away, a rusty knife-blade, old shoes saved for a road that never was and never will be, a nail bent under the weight of things too heavy for any nail, a dried flower or two still a little fragrant. In your hand is the brown bag. On the ground before you is the jumble it held— so much like the jumble in the bags, could they be emptied, that all might be dumped in a single heap and the bags refilled without altering the contents of any greatly. A bit of colored glass more or less would not matter. Perhaps that is how the Great Stuffer of Bags filled them in the first place—who knows?

Responding to Reading

1. How, according to Hurston, does it feel to be "colored"? How do her feelings about her color change as she grows older? Why do they change?
2. In what sense does Hurston see herself as fundamentally different from the whites she encounters? Does she see this difference as a problem? Does her reaction surprise you?
3. When Hurston says, "At certain times I have no race, I am *me*" (14), does she mean she feels assimilated into the larger society, or does she mean something else? Do you think it is possible to be only yourself and not a member of any particular racial or ethnic group? Explain.

TWO KINDS

Amy Tan

Novelist Amy Tan (see p. 197) achieved immediate success with her first novel, *The Joy Luck Club* (1989), a collection of related stories in which four Chinese-born mothers and their four American-born daughters each narrates a significant story from her life. Tan has joked that her own mother wanted her to grow up to be a neurosurgeon while performing as an acclaimed concert pianist on the side; the following story from *The Joy Luck Club* explores a similar mother-daughter relationship.

My mother believed you could be anything you wanted to be in America. You could open a restaurant. You could work for the government and get good retirement. You could buy a house with almost no money down. You could become rich. You could become instantly famous.

"Of course you can be prodigy, too," my mother told me when I was nine. "You can be best anything. What does Auntie Lindo know? Her daughter, she is only best tricky."

America was where all my mother's hopes lay. She had come here in 1949 after losing everything in China: her mother and father, her family home, her first husband, and two daughters, twin baby girls. But she never looked back with regret. There were so many ways for things to get better.

We didn't immediately pick the right kind of prodigy. At first my mother thought I could be a Chinese Shirley Temple. We'd watch Shirley's old movies on TV as though they were training films. My mother would poke my arm and say, "Ni kan"—You watch. And I would see Shirley tapping her feet, or singing a sailor song, or pursing her lips into a very round O while saying, "Oh my goodness."

"Ni kan," said my mother as Shirley's eyes flooded with tears. "You already know how. Don't need talent for crying!"

Soon after my mother got this idea about Shirley Temple, she took me to a beauty training school in the Mission district[1] and put me in the hands of a student who could barely hold the scissors without shaking. Instead of getting big fat curls, I emerged with an uneven mass of crinkly black fuzz. My mother dragged me off to the bathroom and tried to wet down my hair.

"You look like Negro Chinese," she lamented, as if I had done this on purpose.

The instructor of the beauty training school had to lop off these soggy clumps to make my hair even again. "Peter Pan is very popular these days," the instructor assured my mother. I now had hair the length of a boy's, with straight-across bangs that hung at a slant two inches above my eyebrows. I liked the haircut and it made me actually look forward to my future fame.

In fact, in the beginning, I was just as excited as my mother, maybe even more so. I pictured this prodigy part of me as many different images, trying each one on for size. I was a dainty ballerina girl standing by the curtains, waiting to hear the right music that would send me floating on my tiptoes. I was like the Christ child lifted out of the straw manger, crying with holy indignity. I was Cinderella stepping from her pumpkin carriage with sparkly cartoon music filling the air.

---

[1] San Francisco neighborhood. [Eds.]

In all of my imagingings, I was filled with a sense that I would soon [10] become *perfect*. My mother and father would adore me. I would be beyond reproach. I would never feel the need to sulk for anything.

But sometimes the prodigy in me became impatient. "If you don't [11] hurry up and get me out of here, I'm disappearing for good," it warned. "And then you'll always be nothing."

Every night after dinner, my mother and I would sit at the Formica [12] kitchen table. She would present new tests, taking her examples from stories of amazing children she had read in *Ripley's Believe It or Not*, or *Good Housekeeping, Reader's Digest,* and a dozen other magazines she kept in a pile in our bathroom. My mother got these magazines from people whose houses she cleaned. And since she cleaned many houses each week, we had a great assortment. She would look through them all, searching for stories about remarkable children.

The first night she brought out a story about a three-year-old boy [13] who knew the capitals of all the states and even most of the European countries. A teacher was quoted as saying the little boy could also pronounce the names of the foreign cities correctly.

"What's the capital of Finland?" my mother asked me, looking at the [14] magazine story.

All I knew was the capital of California, because Sacramento was [15] the name of the street we lived on in Chinatown. "Nairobi!" I guessed, saying the most foreign word I could think of. She checked to see if that was possibly one way to pronounce "Helsinki" before showing me the answer.

The tests got harder—multiplying numbers in my head, finding the [16] queen of hearts in a deck of cards, trying to stand on my head without using my hands, predicting the daily temperatures in Los Angeles, New York, and London.

One night I had to look at a page from the Bible for three minutes [17] and then report everything I could remember. "Now Jehosphaphat had riches and honor in abundance and . . . that's all I remember, Ma," I said.

And after seeing my mother's disappointed face once again, some- [18] thing inside of me began to die. I hated the tests, the raised hopes and failed expectations. Before going to bed that night, I looked in the mirror above the bathroom sink and when I saw only my face staring back—and that it would always be this ordinary face—I began to cry. Such a sad, ugly girl! I made high-pitched noises like a crazed animal, trying to scratch out the face in the mirror.

And then I saw what seemed to be the prodigy side of me—because [19] I had never seen that face before. I looked at my reflection, blinking so I could see more clearly. The girl staring back at me was angry, powerful. This girl and I were the same. I had new thoughts, willful thoughts, or rather thoughts filled with lots of won'ts. I won't let her change me, I promised myself. I won't be what I'm not.

So now on nights when my mother presented her tests, I performed [20] listlessly, my head propped on one arm. I pretended to be bored. And I was. I got so bored I started counting the bellows of the foghorns out on the bay while my mother drilled me in other areas. The sound was comforting and reminded me of the cow jumping over the moon. And the next day, I played a game with myself, seeing if my mother would give up on be before eight bellows. After a while I usually counted only one, maybe two bellows at most. At last she was beginning to give up hope.

Two or three months had gone by without any mention of my being [21] a prodigy again. And then one day my mother was watching "The Ed Sullivan Show" on TV. The TV was old and the sound kept shorting out. Every time my mother got halfway up from the sofa to adjust the set, the sound would go back on and Ed would be talking. As soon as she sat down, Ed would go silent again. She got up, the TV broke into loud piano music. She sat down. Silence. Up and down, back and forth, quiet and loud. It was like a stiff embraceless dance between her and the TV set. Finally she stood by the set with her hand on the sound dial.

She seemed entranced by the music, a little frenzied piano piece [22] with this mesmerizing quality, sort of quick passages and then teasing lilting ones before it returned to the quick playful parts.

"*Ni kan,*" my mother said, calling me over with hurried hand ges- [23] tures. "Look here."

I could see why my mother was fascinated by the music. It was [24] being pounded out by a little Chinese girl, about nine years old, with a Peter Pan haircut. The girl had the sauciness of a Shirley Temple. She was proudly modest like a proper Chinese child. And she also did this fancy sweep of a curtsy, so that the fluffy skirt of her white dress cascaded slowly to the floor like the petals of a large carnation.

In spite of these warning signs, I wasn't worried. Our family had no [25] piano and we couldn't afford to buy one, let alone reams of sheet music and piano lessons. So I could be generous in my comments when my mother bad-mouthed the little girl on TV.

"Play note right, but doesn't sound good! No singing sound," com- [26] plained my mother.

"What are you picking on her for?" I said carelessly. "She's pretty [27] good. Maybe she's not the best, but she's trying hard." I knew almost immediately I would be sorry I said that.

"Just like you," she said. "Not the best. Because you not trying." She [28] gave a little huff as she let go of the sound dial and sat down on the sofa.

The little Chinese girl sat down also to play an encore of "Anitra's [29] Dance" by Grieg. I remember the song, because later on I had to learn how to play it.

Three days after watching "The Ed Sullivan Show," my mother [30] told me what my schedule would be for piano lessons and piano practice. She had talked to Mr. Chong, who lived on the first floor of our apartment building. Mr. Chong was a retired piano teacher and my mother had traded housecleaning services for weekly lessons and a piano for me to practice on every day, two hours a day, from four until six.

When my mother told me this, I felt as though I had been sent to [31] hell. I whined and then kicked my foot a little when I couldn't stand it anymore.

"Why don't you like me the way I am? I'm *not* a genius! I can't play [32] the piano. And even if I could, I wouldn't go on TV if you paid me a million dollars!" I cried.

My mother slapped me. "Who ask you be genius?" she shouted. [33] "Only ask you be your best. For you sake. You think I want you be genius? Hnnh! What for! Who ask you!"

"So ungrateful," I heard her mutter in Chinese. "If she had as much [34] talent as she has temper, she would be famous now."

Mr. Chong, whom I secretly nicknamed Old Chong, was very [35] strange, always tapping his fingers to the silent music of an invisible orchestra. He looked ancient in my eyes. He had lost most of the hair on top of his head and he wore thick glasses and had eyes that always looked tired and sleepy. But he must have been younger than I thought, since he lived with his mother and was not yet married.

I met Old Lady Chong once and that was enough. She had this peculiar smell like a baby that had done something in its pants. And her fingers felt like a dead person's, like an old peach I once found in the back of the refrigerator; the skin just slid off the meat when I picked it up.

I soon found out why Old Chong had retired from teaching piano. [37] He was deaf. "Like Beethoven!" he shouted to me. "We're both listening only in our head!" And he would start to conduct his frantic silent sonatas.

Our lessons went like this. He would open the book and point to different things, explaining their purpose: "Key! Treble! Bass! No sharps or flats! So this is C major! Listen now and play after me!"

And then he would play the C scale a few times, a simple chord, and [39] then, as if inspired by an old, unreachable itch, he gradually added more notes and running trills and a pounding bass until the music was really something quite grand.

I would play after him, the simple scale, the simple chord and then [40] I just played some nonsense that sounded like a cat running up and down on top of garbage cans. Old Chong smiled and applauded and then said, "Very good! But now you must learn to keep time!"

So that's how I discovered that Old Chong's eyes were too slow to 41
keep up with the wrong notes I was playing. He went through the motions in half-time. To help me keep rhythm, he stood behind me, pushing down on my right shoulder for every beat. He balanced pennies on
top of my wrists so I would keep them still as I slowly played scales and
arpeggios. He had me curve my hand around an apple and keep that
shape when playing chords. He marched stiffly to show me how to
make each finger dance up and down, staccato like an obedient little
solider.

He taught me all these things, and that was how I also learned I 42
could be lazy and get away with mistakes, lots of mistakes. If I hit the
wrong notes because I hadn't practiced enough, I never corrected myself. I just kept playing in rhythm. And Old Chong kept conducting his
own private reverie.

So maybe I never really gave myself a fair chance. I did pick up the 43
basics pretty quickly, and I might have become a good pianist at that
young age. But I was so determined not to try, not to be anybody different that I learned to play only the most ear-splitting preludes, the
most discordant hymns.

Over the next year, I practiced like this, dutifully in my own way. 44
And then one day I heard my mother and her friend Lindo Jong both
talking in a loud bragging tone of voice so others could hear. It was
after church, and I was leaning against the brick wall wearing a dress
with stiff white petticoats. Auntie Lindo's daughter, Waverly, who was
about my age, was standing farther down the wall about five feet away.
We had grown up together and shared all the closeness of two sisters
squabbling over crayons and dolls. In other words, for the most part,
we hated each other. I thought she was snotty. Waverly Jong had
gained a certain amount of fame as "Chinatown's Littlest Chinese
Chess Champion."

"She bring home too many trophy," lamented Auntie Lindo that 45
Sunday. "All day she play chess. All day I have no time do nothing but
dust off her winnings." She threw a scolding look at Waverly, who pretended not to see her.

"You lucky you don't have this problem," said Auntie Lindo with 46
a sigh to my mother.

And my mother squared her shoulders and bragged: "Our problem 47
worser than yours. If we ask Jing-mei wash dish, she hear nothing but
music. It's like you can't stop this natural talent."

And right then, I was determined to put a stop to her foolish 48
pride.

A few weeks later, Old Chong and my mother conspired to have me 49
play in a talent show which would be held in the church hall. By then,
my parents had saved up enough to buy me a secondhand piano, a

black Wurlitzer spinet with a scarred bench. It was the showpiece of our living room.

For the talent show, I was to play a piece called "Pleading Child" 50 from Schumann's *Scenes from Childhood*. It was a simple, moody piece that sounded more difficult than it was. I was supposed to memorize the whole thing, playing the repeat parts twice to make the piece sound longer. But I dawdled over it, playing a few bars and then cheating, looking up to see what notes followed, I never really listened to what I was playing. I daydreamed about being somewhere else, about being someone else.

The part I liked to practice best was the fancy curtsy: right foot out, 51 touch the rose on the carpet with a pointed foot, sweep to the side, left leg bends, look up and smile.

My parents invited all the couples from the Joy Luck Club[2] to wit- 52 ness my debut. Auntie Lindo and Uncle Tin were there. Waverly and her two older brothers had also come. The first two rows were filled with children both younger and older than I was. The littlest ones got to go first. They recited simple nursery rhymes, squawked out tunes on miniature violins, twirled Hula Hoops, pranced in pink ballet tutus, and when they bowed or curtsied, the audience would sigh in unison, "Awww," and then clap enthusiastically.

When my turn came, I was very confident. I remember my childish 53 excitement. It was as if I knew, without a doubt, that the prodigy side of me really did exist. I had no fear whatsoever, no nervousness. I re- member thinking to myself, This is it! I looked out over the audience, at my mother's blank face, my father's yawn, Auntie Lindo's stiff-lipped smile, Waverly's sulky expression. I had on a white dress layered with sheets of lace, and a pink bow in my Peter Pan haircut. As I sat down I envisioned people jumping to their feet and Ed Sullivan rushing up to introduce me to everyone on TV.

And I started to play. It was so beautiful. I was so caught up in how 54 lovely I looked that at first I didn't worry how I would sound: So it was a surprise to me when I hit the first wrong note and I realized something didn't sound quite right. And then I hit another and another followed that. A chill started at the top of my head and began to trickle down. Yet I couldn't stop playing, as though my hands were bewitched. I kept thinking my fingers would adjust themselves back, like a train switch- ing to the right track. I played this strange jumble through two repeats, the sour notes staying with me all the way to the end.

When I stood up, I discovered my legs were shaking. Maybe I had 55 just been nervous and the audience, like Old Chong, had seen me go through the right motions and had not heard anything wrong at all. I

---

[2] The club consists of four mothers who meet weekly to play Mah-Jongg, a popular Chinese game. [Eds.]

swept my right foot out, went down on my knee, looked up and smiled. The room was quiet, except for Old Chong, who was beaming and shouting, "Bravo! Bravo! Well done!" But then I saw my mother's face, her stricken face. The audience clapped weakly, and as I walked back to my chair, with my whole face quivering as I tried not to cry, I heard a little boy whisper loudly to his mother, "That was awful," and the mother whispered back, "Well, she certainly tried."

And now I realized how many people were in the audience, the 56 whole world it seemed. I was aware of eyes burning into my back. I felt the shame of my mother and father as they sat stiffly throughout the rest of the show.

We could have escaped during intermission. Pride and some 57 strange sense of honor must have anchored my parents to their chairs. And so we watched it all: the eighteen-year-old boy with a fake mustache who did a magic show and juggled flaming hoops while riding a unicycle. The breasted girl with white makeup who sang from *Madama Butterfly* and got honorable mention. And the eleven-year-old boy who won first prize playing a tricky violin song that sounded like a busy bee.

After the show, the Hsus, the Jongs, and the St. Clairs from the Joy 58 Luck Club came up to my mother and father.

"Lots of talented kids," Auntie Lindo said vaguely, smiling 59 broadly.

"That was somethin' else," said my father, and I wondered if he was 60 referring to me in a humorous way, or whether he even remembered what I had done.

Waverly looked at me and shrugged her shoulders. "You aren't a 61 genius like me," she said matter-of-factly. And if I hadn't felt so bad, I would have pulled her braids and punched her stomach.

But my mother's expression was what devastated me: a quiet, blank 62 look that said she had lost everything. I felt the same way, and it seemed as if everybody were now coming up, like gawkers at the scene of an accident, to see what parts were actually missing. When we got on the bus to go home, my father was humming the busy-bee tune and my mother was silent. I kept thinking she wanted to wait until we got home before shouting at me. But when my father unlocked the door to our apartment, my mother walked in and then went to the back, into the bedroom. No accusations. No blame. And in a way, I felt disappointed. I had been waiting for her to start shouting, so I could shout back and cry and blame her for all my misery.

I assumed by talent-show fiasco meant I never had to play the piano 63 again. But two days later, after school, my mother came out of the kitchen and saw me watching TV.

"Four clock," she reminded me as if it were any other day. I was 64 stunned, as though she were asking me to go through the talent-show torture again. I wedged myself more tightly in front of the TV.

"Turn off TV," she called from the kitchen five minutes later.   65

I didn't budge. And then I decided. I didn't have to do what my   66
mother said anymore. I wasn't her slave. This wasn't China. I had listened to her before and look what happened. She was the stupid one.

She came out from the kitchen and stood in the arched entryway of   67
the living room. "Four clock," she said once again, louder.

"I'm not going to play anymore," I said nonchalantly. "Why should   68
I? I'm not a genius."

She walked over and stood in front of the TV. I saw her chest was   69
heaving up and down in an angry way.

"No!" I said, and I now felt stronger, as if my true self had finally   70
emerged. So this was what had been inside me all along.

"No! I won't!" I screamed.   71

She yanked me by the arm, pulled me off the floor, snapped off the   72
TV. She was frighteningly strong, half pulling, half carrying me toward
the piano as I kicked the throw rugs under my feet. She lifted me up and
onto the hard bench. I was sobbing by now, looking at her bitterly. Her
chest was heaving even more and her mouth was open, smiling crazily
as if she were pleased I was crying.

"You want me to be someone that I'm not!" I sobbed. "I'll never be   73
the kind of daughter you want me to be!"

"Only two kinds of daughters," she shouted in Chinese. "Those who   74
are obedient and those who follow their own mind! Only one kind of
daughter can live in this house. Obedient daughter!"

"Then I wish I wasn't your daughter. I wish you weren't my moth-   75
er," I shouted. As I said these things I got scared. I felt like worms and
toads and slimy things were crawling out of my chest, but it also felt
good, as if this awful side of me had surfaced, at last.

"Too late change this," said my mother shrilly.   76

And I could sense her anger rising to its breaking point. I wanted to   77
see it spill over. And that's when I remembered the babies she had lost
in China, the ones we never talked about. "Then I wish I'd never been
born!" I shouted. "I wish I were dead! Like them."

It was as if I had said the magic words. Alakazam!—and her face   78
went blank, her mouth closed, her arms went slack, and she backed out
of the room, stunned, as if she were blowing away like a small brown
leaf, thin, brittle, lifeless.

It was not the only disappointment my mother felt in me. In the   79
years that followed, I failed her so many times, each time asserting my
own will, my right to fall short of expectations. I didn't get straight A's.
I didn't become class president. I didn't get into Stanford. I dropped out
of college.

For unlike my mother, I did not believe I could be anything I want-   80
ed to be. I could only be me.

And for all those years, we never talked about the disaster at the ⁸¹
recital or my terrible accusations afterward at the piano bench. All that
remained unchecked, like a betrayal that was now unspeakable. So I
never found a way to ask her why she had hoped for something so large
that failure was inevitable.

And even worse, I never asked her what frightened me the most: ⁸²
Why had she given up hope?

For after our struggle at the piano, she never mentioned my playing ⁸³
again. The lessons stopped. The lid to the piano was closed, shutting out
the dust, my misery, and her dreams.

So she surprised me. A few years ago, she offered to give me the ⁸⁴
piano, for my thirtieth birthday. I had not played in all those years. I saw
the offer as a sign of forgiveness, a tremendous burden removed.

"Are you sure?" I asked shyly. "I mean, won't you and Dad miss it?" ⁸⁵

"No, this your piano," she said firmly. "Always your piano. You ⁸⁶
only one can play."

"Well, I probably can't play anymore," I said. "It's been years." ⁸⁷

"You pick up fast," said my mother, as if she knew this was certain. ⁸⁸
"You have natural talent. You could been genius if you want to."

"No I couldn't." ⁸⁹

"You just not trying," said my mother. And she was neither angry ⁹⁰
nor sad. She said it as if to announce a fact that could never be dis-
proved. "Take it," she said.

But I didn't at first. It was enough that she had offered it to me. And ⁹¹
after that, every time I saw it in my parents' living room, standing in
front of the bay windows, it made me feel proud, as if it were a shiny trophy I had won back.

Last week I sent a tuner over to my parents' apartment and had the ⁹²
piano reconditioned, for purely sentimental reasons. My mother had died
a few months before and I had been getting things in order for my father,
a little bit at a time. I put the jewelry in special silk pouches. The sweaters
she had knitted in yellow, pink, bright orange—all the colors I hated—I
put those in moth-proof boxes. I found some old Chinese silk dresses, the
kind with little slits up the sides. I rubbed the old silk against my skin,
then wrapped them in tissue and decided to take them home with me.

After I had the piano tuned, I opened the lid and touched the keys. ⁹³
It sounded even richer than I remembered. Really, it was a very good
piano. Inside the bench were the same exercise notes with handwritten
scales, the same secondhand music books with their covers held together with yellow tape.

I opened up the Schumann book to the dark little piece I had played ⁹⁴
at the recital. It was on the left-hand side of the page. "Pleading Child."
It looked more difficult than I remembered. I played a few bars, surprised at how easily the notes came back to me.

And for the first time, or so it seemed, I noticed the piece on the right-hand side. It was called "Perfectly Contented." I tried to play this one as well. It had a lighter melody but the same flowing rhythm and turned out to be quite easy. "Pleading Child" was shorter but slower; "Perfectly Contented" was longer but faster. And after I played them both a few times, I realized they were two halves of the same song. ⁹⁵

Responding to Reading

1. What does the American Dream mean to the narrator's mother? Do you think the narrator herself believes in the American Dream? Why does she resist her mother's efforts to make her a success?
2. Is "Two Kinds" really about cultural conflict, or is it simply about a struggle of wills between parent and child? Explain your position.
3. Whom do you see as more "American," Jing-mei or her mother? Why?

WRITING

The American Dream

1. Write an essay in which you support the idea that the strength of the United States comes from its ability to assimilate many different groups. In your essay, discuss specific contributions various groups have made to American society.

2. When Philip Roth writes of "the power to intimidate that emanated from the highest and lowest reaches of gentile America" (1), he identifies a basic conflict that applies not only to Jews but also to many other groups excluded from the largely white, male, upper-class mainstream. Argue for or against the idea that the existence and dominance of this powerful class makes outsiders out of many—or even most—Americans.

3. To what extent can a person's estrangement from mainstream society be the very force that drives his or her life? Consider Zora Neale Hurston and any other writer or character—or person you know—whose separateness is a source of strength or power.

4. Roth, Hurston, and Rodriguez identify strongly with a culture that is not part of the mainstream. Compare and contrast their views about assimilation into the dominant culture. Then, consider whether your own ethnic group can—or should—assimilate. Will assimilating mean giving up its unique identity?

5. Some of the writers in this chapter—for example, Crew and Hockenberry—explicitly or implicitly connect their personal struggles to achieve the American Dream with the struggles of the American civil rights movement. Do you think this parallel between the struggles of African Americans for equality and the difficulties faced by other individuals or groups is a fair, or even a legitimate, one? Write a letter supporting your view to the writer of one of the essays in this chapter.

6. Rodriguez closes his essay by stating, "For generations, Latin America has been the place—the bed—of a confluence of so many races and cultures that Protestant North America shuddered to imagine it. Imagine it." Write an essay in which you explain what Rodriguez means and explore the possible effects on North America of the change he would have us imagine. Or, write about the way another cultural group has changed (or is likely to change) the United States.

7. The mother in "Two Kinds" sees television shows and popular magazines as inspirational literature. How do you think television programs (and their commercial messages) and the stories and advertisements in popular magazines "sell" the American Dream of wealth and success? You may refer to essays in this chapter and in Chapter 5, but most of your supporting examples should come from television programs and magazines with which you are familiar.

8. Some writers respond to their exclusion from mainstream society with anger and protest, others with resignation and acceptance. Considering several different writers and situations, write an essay in which you contrast these two kinds of responses. Does each response make sense? Why or why not?

9. What do you see as the greatest obstacle to full access to the American Dream? For example, is success most likely to depend on gender, race, language, social class, ethnicity, family, ability, education, income, or sexual orientation? Support your thesis with your own experiences or with references to selections in this chapter.

10. In paragraph 39 of "Thriving as an Outsider, Even as an Outcast, in Smalltown America" Louie Crew states, "America preserves an ideal of freedom, although it denies freedom in scores of instances." Use three or four of this chapter's essays to support this thesis—or to argue that it is not valid.

7

THE WAY WE LIVE NOW

Student Voices

"I see myself as part of the Why Bother? generation."

—Stephen Berger

"Whenever you look for me, I'm in chill mode. I enjoy almost everything I do. When I don't enjoy something, I just get it over with and never have to think of it again.

"My whole goal in life today is having fun. When I wake up in the morning, which is the worst part of the day, I imagine I'm going to have an excellent day. How I live may be immature, but I think it is beneficial and different. People admire my lifestyle. Friends try to mimic it. It's one I have planned out for a while. I hope to be in chill mode for the rest of my life."

—Todd Snellenburg

"We live in a world of violence. Violence surrounds us every day of our lives. We are told that violence doesn't solve problems and that violence is wrong. Even though this is instilled in us, we see that violence is used to entertain us from childhood to adulthood."

—Teren Brown

"As an African-American male, I see my people and generation as targets for violence. I believe I am stereotyped in ways that have a negative effect on my outlook on life.

"When I look back at the civil rights movement of the '60s, I see that our people fought for things like the right to an equal education. Now, in my generation, we do not even want to attend school. We have forgotten our past.

"We have problems now that our parents did not have—for example, drugs, teenage pregnancy, and gang violence. The old-fashioned family values of the past that kept families together seem to be diminishing. Where these values have gone, I am not certain. Maybe this society of fast money and quick fixes is to blame. Who knows?"

—*William Fulton*

"Basically, I think our generation doesn't want to be in the mainstream. I think people today are free thinkers. They do what they want to do. Kids want to be part of a group, but today there are so many different types of groups out there that almost nothing is mainstream."

—*Pat DiStefano*

"Our own city, once a city of clean streets and friendly people, now is a dirty cold place where fear is felt more often than happiness. Neighbors who once looked out for one another now look the other way. Streets lined with well-kept brick rowhomes are now overgrown, broken down, grafitti-covered eyesores."

—*Jeff Morris*

"My parents grew up in a time in which things were simpler. For example, people in my generation started doing things a lot earlier than my parents did. The things they were doing in college, I did in junior high."

—*Robin Michel*

"When I was growing up, my parents told me to try everything at least once. However, when I started trying things on my own, they would tell me not to."

—*Marko D'Avignon*

"My generation is a scary one. We are the target generation for AIDS and, according to some, are at an all-time moral low. Despite actions taken to inform and educate us, I know that even my best friends are still behaving carelessly and not being sexually responsible. Everyone's thinking, 'It won't happen to me.'"

—*Natalie Chepelevich*

Preparing to Read and Write

Because contemporary life in the United States is so diverse and so dynamic, it is extremely difficult to characterize. In fact, because we all have different experiences, it might be said that each of us lives in a different society—different even from that of our family members or close friends. Of course, we also have a good deal in common. We share concerns about issues like violence, racism, and homelessness; we are confused and curious (and, sometimes, exhilarated) about the way the world is changing; and we have hopes, dreams, and heroes to inspire us.

Each of the writers whose essays are collected in this chapter has a different way of looking at the world. Some look ahead; others look back. Some are optimistic; others are pessimistic. Perhaps your own view of present-day society is like one of theirs; more likely, you see the world from a different angle, one that is unlike the one any of them describes. And, because your perspective is unique, it will lead you to draw conclusions that are also unique.

As you read the selections in this chapter and prepare to write about them, you may consider the following questions.

- Does the writer present a primarily positive or negative picture of society?

- Is the writer looking forward or backward?

- On what issue or issues does the writer focus?

- Is there a connection between the writer's own social class, race, or gender—or his or her assumptions about class, race, or gender—and the issue he or she examines?

- Would you say the writer's primary objective is to understand an issue and its effect on him or her, to inform readers, or to change readers' minds?

- Does the writer have a personal stake in his or her subject? If so, does your awareness of this involvement weaken or strenthen the selection's impact on you?

- Is the writer's tone serious, humorous, ironic, or sarcastic?

- If the selection identifies a problem, does it focus on finding solutions, speculating about long-term effects, or warning about consequences?

- Does the writer focus on the need for change—for example, for changing basic attitudes, for changing habits, or for changing the law? Is the writer optimistic or pessimistic about the possibility of change?

- Does the selection focus on a narrow segment of the society—members of a particular age or ethnic group or residents of a particular geographical area, for example—or does it focus on the society at large?

- Do you recognize people and situations with which you are familiar, or are the issues under discussion unfamiliar to you? Are you emotionally connected to the issues, or are you relatively detached from them?

- What areas of common concern do writers explore? How are their views of life today alike? How are they different? In what ways are they like and unlike your own?

- How are the writers' hopes and dreams for the future alike? How are they different? In what ways are they like and unlike your own?

TWO PERSPECTIVES ON THE WAY WE LIVE NOW

The following two essays both focus on the influences that have shaped the current generation of young people in their late teens and twenties. In "Larger than Life," which originally appeared in the collection *Next: Young Americans Writers on the New Generation* (1994), Jenny Lyn Bader (1969–) argues that because her generation has lost faith in the idea of conventional heroes, it is now required "to steer a course between naivete and nihilism, to reshape vintage stories, to create stories of spirit without apologies." An editor and a contributor to the *New York Times*, Bader is also a theater director and author of the play *Shakespeare's Undiscovered One Act* (1992). The second essay originally appeared in 1993 in *Change,* the publication of the American Association for Higher Education. In it Arthur Levine (1948–) reports, based on interviews with focus groups conducted during the 1992–93 academic year, what undergraduates at twenty-eight U.S. colleges see as the five social and political events that have most influenced their generation. Currently on the faculty of the Harvard Graduate School of Education, Levine won the American Council of Education book of the year award for *Reform of Undergraduate Education* (1973) and is well-known for his many other books and articles focusing on higher education.

LARGER THAN LIFE

Jenny Lyn Bader

When my grandmother was young, she would sometimes spot the [1] emperor Franz Josef riding down the cobbled roads of the Austro-Hungarian Empire.

She came of age so long ago that the few surviving photographs are [2] colored cream and chestnut. Early on, she saw cars replace horses and carriages. When she got older, she marveled at the first televisions. Near the end of her life, she grew accustomed to remote control and could spot prime ministers on color TV. By the time she died, the world was freshly populated by gadgetry and myth. Her generation bore witness to the rise of new machinery created by visionaries. My generation has seen machinery break down and visionaries come under fire.

As children, we enjoyed collecting visionaries, the way we collect- 3
ed toys or baseball cards. When I was a kid, I first met Patrick Henry and
Eleanor Roosevelt, Abraham Lincoln and Albert Einstein. They could always be summoned by the imagination and so were never late for play
dates. I thought heroes figured in any decent childhood. I knew their
stats.

Nathan Hale. Nelson Mandela. Heroes have guts.   4

Michelangelo. Shakespeare. Heroes have imagination.   5

They fight. Alexander the Great. Joan of Arc.   6

They fight for what they believe in. Susan B. Anthony. Martin 7
Luther King.

Heroes overcome massive obstacles. Beethoven, while deaf, still 8
managed to carry an unforgettable tune. Homer, while blind, never
failed to give an excellent description. Helen Keller, both deaf and blind,
still spoke to the world. FDR, despite his polio, became president.
Moses, despite his speech impediment, held productive discussions
with God.

They inspire three-hour movies. They make us weepy. They do the 9
right thing while enduring attractive amounts of suffering. They tend to
be self-employed. They are often killed off. They sense the future. They
lead lives that make us question our own. They are our ideals, but not
our friends.

They don't have to be real. Some of them live in books and legends. 10
They don't have to be famous. There are lower-profile heroes who get
resurrected by ambitious biographers. There are collective heroes: fire-
fighters and astronauts, unsung homemakers, persecuted peoples. There
are those whose names we can't remember, only their deeds: "you
know, that woman who swam the English Channel," "the guy who died
running the first marathon," "the student who threw himself in front of
the tank at Tiananmen Square." There are those whose names we'll
never find out: the anonymous benefactor, the masked man, the under-
cover agent, the inventor of the wheel, the unknown soldier. The one
who did the thing so gutsy and terrific that no one will ever know what
it was.

Unlike icons (Marilyn, Elvis) heroes are not only sexy but noble, too. 11
Unlike idols (Gretzky, Streisand), who vary from fan to fan, they are almost universally beloved. Unlike icons and idols, heroes lack irony. And
unlike icons and idols, heroes are no longer in style.

As centuries end, so do visions of faith—maybe because the faithful 12
get nervous as the double zeroes approach and question what they've
been worshiping. Kings and queens got roughed up at the end of the
eighteenth century; God took a beating at the end of the nineteenth; and
as the twentieth century draws to a close, outstanding human beings are
the casualties of the moment. In the 1970s and 1980s, Americans started
feeling queasy about heroism. Those of us born in the sixties found our-

selves on the cusp of that change. A sweep of new beliefs, priorities, and headlines has conspired to take our pantheon away from us.

Members of my generation believed in heroes when they were [13] younger but now find themselves grasping for them. Even the word *hero* sounds awkward. I find myself embarrassed to ask people who their heroes are, because the word just doesn't trip off the tongue. My friend Katrin sounded irritated when I asked for hers. She said, "Oh, Jesus . . . Do people still have heroes?"

We don't. Certainly not in the traditional sense of adoring perfect [14] people. Frequently not at all. "I'm sort of intrigued by the fact that I don't have heroes right off the top of my head," said a colleague, Peter. "Can I get back to you?"

Some of us are more upset about this than others. It's easy to tell [15] which of us miss the heroic age. We are moved by schmaltzy political speeches, we warm up to stories of pets saving their owners, we even get misty-eyed watching the Olympics. We mope when model citizens fail us. My college roommate, Linda, remembers a seventh-grade class called "Heroes and She-roes." The first assignment was to write about a personal hero or she-ro. "I came home," Linda told me, "and cried and cried because I didn't have one. . . . Carter had screwed up in Iran and given the malaise speech. Gerald Ford was a nothing and Nixon was evil. My parents told me to write about Jane Fonda the political activist and I just kept crying."

Not everyone feels sentimental about it. A twentyish émigré raised [16] in the former Soviet Union told me: "It's kind of anticlimactic to look for heroes when you've been brought up in a culture that insists on so many heroes. . . . What do you want me to say? Lenin? Trotsky?" Even though I grew up in the relatively propaganda-free United States, I understood. The America of my childhood insisted on heroes, too.

Of all the myths I happily ate for breakfast, the most powerful one [17] was our story of revolution. I sang about it as early as kindergarten and read about it long after. The story goes, a few guys in wigs skipped town on some grumpy church leaders and spurned a loopy king to branch out on their own. The children who hear the story realize they don't have to believe in oldfangled clergy or a rusty crown—but they had better believe in those guys with the wigs.

I sure did. I loved a set of books known as the "Meet" series: *Meet* [18] *George Washington, Meet Andrew Jackson, Meet the Men Who Sailed the Seas,* and many more. I remember one picture of an inspired Thomas Jefferson, his auburn ponytail tied in a black ribbon, penning words with a feather as a battle of banners and cannon fire raged behind him.

A favorite "Meet" book starred Christopher Columbus. His resis- [19] tance to the flat-earth society of his day was engrossing, especially to a kid like me who had trouble trying new foods let alone seeking new land masses. I identified with his yearning for a new world and his difficulty with finding investors. Standing up to the king and queen of Spain was like convincing your parents to let you do stuff they thought was idiotic. Now, my allowance was only thirty-five cents a week, but that didn't mean I wasn't going to ask for three ships at some later date.

This is pretty embarrassing: I adored those guys. The ones in the [20] white powder and ponytails, the voluptuous hats, the little breeches and cuffs. They were funny-looking, but lovable. They did outrageous things without asking for permission. They invented the pursuit of happiness.

I had a special fondness for Ben Franklin, statesman and eccentric [21] inventor. Inventions, like heroes, made me feel as though I lived in a dull era. If I'd grown up at the end of the nineteenth century, I could have spoken on early telephones. A few decades later, I could have heard the new sounds of radio. In the sixties, I could have watched black-and-white TVs graduate to color.

Instead, I saw my colorful heroes demoted to black and white. Most- [22] ly white. By the time I finished high school, it was no longer hip to look up to the paternalistic dead white males who launched our country, kept slaves and mistresses, and massacred native peoples. Suddenly they weren't visionaries but oppressors, or worse—objects. Samuel Adams became a beer, John Hancock became a building, and the rest of the guys in wigs were knocked off one by one, in a whodunit that couldn't be explained away by the fact of growing up.

The flag-waving of my youth, epitomized by America's bicentenni- [23] al, was a more loving homage than I know today. The year 1976 rolled in while Washington was still reeling from Saigon, but the irony was lost on me and my second-grade classmates. The idea of losing seemed miles away. We celebrated July fourth with wide eyes and patriotic parties. Grown-ups had yet to tell themselves (so why should they tell us?) that the young nation on its birthday had suffered a tragic defeat.

Historians soon filled us in about that loss, and of others. Discover- [24] ing America was nothing compared to discovering the flaws of its discoverers, now cast as imperialist sleaze, racist and sexist and genocidal. All things heroic—human potential, spiritual fervor, moral resplendence—soon became suspect. With the possible exception of bodybuilding, epic qualities went out of fashion. Some will remember 1992 as the year Superman died. Literally, the writers and illustrators at *D.C. Comics* decided the guy was too old to keep leaping buildings and rescuing an aging damsel in distress. When rumors circulated that he would be resurrected, readers protested via calls to radio shows, letters to editors, and complaints to stores that they were in no mood for such an event.

A monster named Doomsday killed Superman, overcoming him not [25] with Kryptonite but with brute force. Who killed the others? I blame improved modes of character assassination, media hype artists, and scholars. The experts told me that Columbus had destroyed cultures and ravaged the environment. They also broke the news that the cowboys had brazenly taken land that wasn't theirs. In a way, I'm glad I didn't know that earlier; dressing up as a cowgirl for Halloween wouldn't have felt right. In a more urgent way, I wish I had known it then so I wouldn't have had to learn it later.

Just fifteen years after America's bicentennial came Columbus's [26] quincentennial, when several towns canceled their annual parades in protest of his sins. Soon other festivities started to feel funny. When my aunt served corn pudding last Thanksgiving, my cousin took a spoonful, then said drily that the dish was made in honor of the Indians who taught us to use corn before we eliminated them. Uncomfortable chuckles followed. Actually, neither "we" nor my personal ancestors had come to America in time to kill any Native Americans. Yet the holiday put us in the same boat with the pilgrims and anchored us in the white man's domain.

I am fascinated by how we become "we" and "they." It's as if sid- [27] ing with the establishment is the Alka-Seltzer that helps us stomach the past. To swallow history lessons, we turn into "we": one nation under God of proud but remorseful Indian killers. We also identify with people who look like us. For example, white northerners studying the Civil War identify both with white slaveholders and with northern abolitionists, aligning with both race and place. Transsexuals empathize with men and women. Immigrants identify with their homeland and their adopted country. Historians proposing a black Athena and a black Jesus have inspired more of such bonding.

I'll admit that these empathies can be empowering. I always un- [28] derstood the idea of feeling stranded by unlikely role models but never emotionally grasped it until I watched Penny Marshall's movie *A League of Their Own*. For the first time, I appreciated why so many women complain that sports bore them. I had enjoyed baseball before but never as intensely as I enjoyed the games in that film. The players were people like me. Lori Petty, petite, chirpy, wearing a skirt, commanded the pitcher's mound with such aplomb that I was moved. There's something to be said for identifying with people who remind us of ourselves, though Thomas Jefferson and Lori Petty look more like each other than either of them looks like me. I'll never know if I would've read the "Meet" books with more zeal if they'd described our founding mothers. I liked them as they were.

Despite the thrill of dames batting something on the big screen be- [29] sides their eyelashes, the fixation on look-alike idols is disturbing for those who get left out. In the movie *White Men Can't Jump*, Wesley Snipes tells Woody Harrelson not to listen to Jimi Hendrix, because "White people can't hear Jimi." Does this joke imply that black people can't hear Mozart? That I can admire Geena Davis's batting but never appreciate Carlton Fisk? Besides dividing us from one another, these emotional allegiances divide us from potential heroes too, causing us to empathize with, say, General Custer and his last stand instead of with Sitting Bull and the victorious Sioux.

Rejecting heroes for having the wrong ethnic credentials or sex or- 30 gans says less about our multicultural vision than our lack of imagination. By focusing on what we are instead of who we can become, by typecasting and miscasting our ideals—that's how we become "we" and "they." If heroes are those we'd like to emulate, it does make sense that they resemble us. But the focus on physical resemblance seems limited and racist.

Heroes should be judged on their deeds, and there are those with 31 plenty in common heroically but not much in terms of ethnicity, nationality, or gender. Just look at Harriet Tubman and Moses; George Washington and Simón Bolívar; Mahatma Gandhi and Martin Luther King; Murasaki and Milton; Cicero and Ann Richards. Real paragons transcend nationality. It didn't matter to me that Robin Hood was English—as long as he did good, he was as American as a barbecue. It didn't matter to Queen Isabella that Columbus was Italian as long as he sailed for Spain and sprinkled her flags about. The British epic warrior Beowulf was actually Swedish. Both the German hero Etzel and the Scandinavian hero Atli were really Attila, king of the Huns. With all this borrowing going on, we shouldn't have to check the passports of our luminaries; the idea that we can be like them not literally but spiritually is what's uplifting in the first place.

The idea that we can never be like them has led to what I call jeal- 32 ousy journalism. You know, we're not remotely heroic so let's tear down anyone who is. It's become hard to remember which papers are tabloids. Tell-all articles promise us the "real story"—implying that greatness can't be real. The safe thing about *Meet George Washington* was that you couldn't actually meet him. Today's stories and pictures bring us closer. And actually meeting your heroes isn't the best idea. Who wants to learn that a favorite saint is really just an egomaniac with a publicist?

Media maestros have not only knocked public figures off their 33 pedestals, they've also lowered heroism standards by idealizing just about everyone. Oprah, Geraldo, and the rest turn their guests into heroes of the afternoon because they overcame abusive roommates, childhood disfigurement, deranged spouses, multiple genitalia, cheerleading practice, or zany sexual predilections. In under an hour, a studio audience can hear their epic sagas told.

While TV and magazine producers helped lead heroes to their 34 graves, the academic community gave the final push. Just as my peers and I made our way through college, curriculum reformers were promoting "P.C." agendas at the expense of humanistic absolutes. Scholars invented their own tabloidism, investigating and maligning both dead professors and trusty historical figures. Even literary theory helped, when deconstructionists made it trendy to look for questions instead of answers, for circular logic instead of linear sense, for defects, contradictions, and the ironic instead of meaning, absolutes, and the heroic.

It was the generations that preceded ours who killed off our heroes. [35] And like everyone who crucified a superstar, these people thought they were doing a good thing. The professors and journalists consciously moved in a positive direction—toward greater tolerance, openness, and realism—eliminating our inspirations in the process. The death of an era of hero worship was not the result of the cynical, clinical materialism too often identified with my generation. It was the side effect of a complicated cultural surgery, of an operation that may have been necessary and that many prescribed.

So with the best of intentions, these storytellers destroyed bedtime [36] stories. Which is too bad for the kids, because stories make great teachers. Children glean by example. You can't tell a child "Be ingenious," or "Do productive things." You can tell them, "This Paul Revere person jumped on a horse at midnight, rode wildly through the dark, figured out where the mean British troops were coming to attack the warm, fuzzy, sweet, great-looking colonists, and sent messages by code, igniting our fight for freedom," and they'll get the idea. America's rugged values come gift wrapped in the frontier tales of Paul Bunyan, Daniel Boone, Davy Crockett—fables of independence and natural resources. Kids understand that Johnny Appleseed or Laura Ingalls Wilder would never need a Cuisinart. Pioneer and prairie stories convey the fun of roughing it, showing kids how to be self-reliant, or at least less spoiled.

Children catch on to the idea of imitating qualities, not literal feats. [37] After returning his storybook to the shelf, little Billy doesn't look around for a dragon to slay. Far-off stories capture the imagination in an abstract but compelling way, different from, say, the more immediate action-adventure flick. After watching a James Bond film festival, I might fantasize about killing the five people in front of me on line at the supermarket, while legends are remote enough that Columbus might inspire one to be original, but not necessarily to study Portuguese or enlist in the navy. In tales about conquerors and cavaliers, I first flirted with the idea of ideas.

Even Saturday-morning cartoons served me as parables, when I [38] woke up early enough to watch the classy Superfriends do good deeds. Sure, the gender ratio between Wonder Woman and the gaggle of men in capes seemed unfair, but I was rapt. I wonder whether I glued myself to my television and my high expectations with too much trust, and helped to set my own heroes up for a fall.

Some heroes have literally been sentenced to death by their own fol- [39] lowers. *Batman* subscribers, for example, were responsible for getting rid of Batman's sidekick, Robin. At the end of one issue, the Joker threatened to kill the Boy Wonder, and readers could decide whether Robin lived or died by calling one of two "900" numbers. The public voted overwhelmingly for his murder. I understand the impulse of those who dialed for death. At a certain point, eternal invincibility grows as dull and predictable as wearing a yellow cape and red tights every day of the year. It's not human. We get fed up.

My generation helped to kill off heroism as teenagers, with our language. We used heroic words that once described brave deeds—*excellent, amazing, awesome*—to describe a good slice of pizza or a sunny day. In our everyday speech, *bad* meant good. *Hot* meant cool. In the sarcastic slang of street gangs in Los Angeles, *hero* currently means traitor, specifically someone who snitches on a graffiti artist. [40]

Even those of us who lived by them helped shatter our own myths, which wasn't all negative. We discovered that even the superhero meets his match. Every Achilles needs a podiatrist. Every rhapsodically handsome leader has a mistress or a moment of moral ambiguity. We injected a dose of reality into our expectations. We even saw a viable presidential candidate under a heap of slung mud, a few imperfections, an alleged tryst or two. [41]

We're used to trysts in a way our elders aren't. Our parents and grandparents behave as if they miss the good old days when adulterers wore letter sweaters. They feign shock at the extramarital exploits of Thomas Jefferson, Frank Sinatra, JFK, Princess Di. Their hero worship is a romance that falters when beloved knights end up unfaithful to their own spouses. People my age aren't amazed by betrayal. We are suspicious of shining armor. Even so, tabloid sales escalate when a Lancelot gives in to temptation—maybe because the jerk who cheats on you somehow becomes more attractive. Other generations have gossiped many of our heroes into philanderers. The presumptuous hero who breaks your heart is the most compelling reason not to get involved in the first place. [42]

Seeing your legends discredited is like ending a romance with someone you loved but ultimately didn't like. However much you longed to trust that person, it just makes more sense not to. Why pine away for an aloof godlet who proves unstable, erratic, and a rotten lover besides? It's sad to give up fantasies but mature to trade them in for healthier relationships grounded in reality. [43]

We require a new pantheon: a set of heroes upon whom we can rely, who will not desert us when the winds change, and whom we will not desert. It's unsettling, if not down-right depressing, to go through life embarrassed about the identity of one's childhood idols. [44]

Maybe we should stick to role models instead. Heroes have become quaint, as old-fashioned as gas-guzzlers—and as unwieldy, requiring too much investment and energy. Role models are more like compact cars, less glam and roomy but easier to handle. They take up less parking space in the imagination. Role models have a certain degree of con- [45]

sciousness about their job. The cast members of "Beverly Hills 90210," for example, have acknowledged that they serve as role models for adolescents, and their characters behave accordingly: they refrain from committing major crimes; they overcome inclinations toward substance abuse; they see through adult hypocrisy; and any misdemeanors they do perpetrate are punished. For moral mediators we could do better, but at least the prime-time writing staff is aware of the burden of having teen groupies.

Heroes don't have the luxury of staff writers or the opportunity to endorse designer jeans. Hercules can't go on "Nightline" and pledge to stop taking steroids. Prometheus can't get a presidential pardon. Columbus won't have a chance to weep to Barbara Walters that he didn't mean to endanger leatherback turtles or monk seals or the tribes of the Lucayas. Elizabeth I never wrote a best-seller about how she did it her way. [46]

Role models can go on talk shows, or even host them. Role models may live next door. While a hero might be a courageous head of state, a saint, a leader of armies, a role model might be someone who put in a three-day presidential bid, your local minister, your boss. They don't need their planes to go down in flames to earn respect. Role models have a job, accomplishment, or hairstyle worth emulating. [47]

Rather than encompassing the vast kit and caboodle of ideals, role models can perform a little neat division of labor. One could wish to give orders like Norman Schwarzkopf but perform psychoanalysis like Lucy Van Pelt, to chair a round-table meeting as well as King Arthur but negotiate as well as Queen Esther, to eat like Orson Welles but look like Helen of Troy, and so forth. It was General Schwarzkopf, the most tangible military hero for anyone my age, who vied instead for role-model status by claiming on the cover of his book: *It Doesn't Take a Hero*. With this title he modestly implies that anyone with some smarts and élan could strategize and storm as well as he has. [48]

Role models are admirable individuals who haven't given up their lives or livelihoods and may even have a few hang-ups. They don't have to be prone to excessive self-sacrifice. They don't go on hunger strikes; they diet. They are therefore more likely than heroes to be free for lunch, and they are oftener still alive. [49]

Heroism is a living thing for many of my contemporaries. In my informal poll, I not only heard sob stories about the decline of heroes, I also discovered something surprising: the ascent of parents. While the founding fathers may be passé, actual mothers, fathers, grands, and great-grands are undeniably "in." An overwhelming number of those I polled named their household forebears as those they most admired. By choosing their own relatives as ideals, people in their twenties have replaced impersonal heroes with the most personal role models of all. Members of my purportedly lost generation have not only realized that it's time to stop believing in Santa Claus, they have chosen to believe in- [50]

stead in their families—the actual tooth fairy, the real Mr. and Mrs. Claus. They have stopped needing the folks from the North Pole, the guys with the wigs, the studs and studettes in tights and capes.

In a way it bodes well that Superman and the rest could be killed or [51] reported missing. They were needed to quash the most villainous folks of all: insane communists bearing nuclear weapons, heinous war criminals, monsters named Doomsday. The good news about Superman bleeding to death was that Doomsday died in the struggle.

If the good guys are gone, so is the world that divides down the [52] middle into good guys and bad guys. A world without heroes is a rigorous, demanding place, where things don't boil down to black and white but are rich with shades of gray; where faith in lofty, dead personages can be replaced by faith in ourselves and one another; where we must summon the strength to imagine a five-dimensional future in colors not yet invented. My generation grew up to see our world shift, so it's up to us to steer a course between naïveté and nihilism, to reshape vintage stories, to create stories of spirit without apologies.

I've heard a few. There was one about the woman who taught [53] Shakespeare to inner-city fourth graders in Chicago who were previously thought to be retarded or hopeless. There was the college groundskeeper and night watchman, a black man with a seventh-grade education, who became a contracts expert, wrote poetry and memoirs, and invested his salary so wisely that he bequeathed 450 acres of mountainous parkland to the university when he died. There was the motorcyclist who slid under an eighteen-wheeler at full speed, survived his physical therapy only to wind up in a plane crash, recovered, and as a disfigured quadriplegic started a business, got happily married, and ran for public office; his campaign button bore a caption that said "Send me to Congress and I won't be just another pretty face. . . ."

When asked for her heroes, a colleague of mine spoke of her great- [54] grandmother, a woman whose husband left her with three kids in Galicia, near Poland, and went to the United States. He meant to send for her, but the First World War broke out. When she made it to America, her husband soon died, and she supported her family; at one point she even ran a nightclub. According to the great-granddaughter, "When she was ninety she would tell me she was going to volunteer at the hospital. I would ask how and she'd say, 'Oh, I just go over there to read to the old folks.' The 'old folks' were probably seventy. She was a great lady."

My grandmother saved her family, too, in the next great war. She [55] did not live to see the age of the fax, but she did see something remarkable in her time, more remarkable even than the emperor riding down the street: she saw him walking down the street. I used to ask her, "Did you really see the emperor Franz Josef walking down the street?"

She would say, "Ya. Walking down the street." I would laugh, and [56] though she'd repeat it to amuse me, she did not see what was so funny.

To me, the emperor was someone you met in history books, not on the streets of Vienna. He was larger than life, a surprising pedestrian. He was probably just getting some air, but he was also laying the groundwork for my nostalgia of that time when it would be natural for him to take an evening stroll, when those who were larger than life roamed cobblestones.

Today, life is larger. 57

THE MAKING OF A GENERATION

Arthur Levine

Every college generation is defined by the social events of its age. 1 The momentous occurrences of an era—from wars and economics to politics and inventions—give meaning to lives of the individuals who live through them. They also serve to knit those individuals together by creating a collective memory and a common historic or generational identity.

In 1979, I went to 26 college and university campuses, selected to 2 represent the diversity of American higher education, and asked students what social or political events most influenced their generation. I told them that the children who came of age in the decade after World War I might have answered the Great Depression. The bombing of Pearl Harbor, World War II, or perhaps the death of Franklin Roosevelt might have stood out for those born a few years later. For my generation, born after World War II, the key event was the assassination of John F. Kennedy. We remember where we were when we heard the news. The whole world seemingly changed in its aftermath.

The Me Generation

I asked what stood out for that generation of undergraduates on the 3 eve of the 1980s. They said Vietnam and Watergate. These events had defined their world. Few could remember a time in their lives when there had been no war, and Watergate seemed a confirmation about the way the world worked in business, government, and all sectors of society. On Watergate, students' comments echoed one another:

"Government doesn't give a damn."

"All politicians are crooks."

"Nixon was like all of us, only he got caught."

"It happens all the time."

"I don't trust government as far as I can throw the Capitol building."

"Nixon was a victim, that's all."

"The whole thing was out of proportion."

For three out of four students, the effects of Watergate and Vietnam [4] had been distinctly negative, causing undergraduates to turn away from politics, politicians, and government. Most said they had no heroes.

Trust in all social institutions had declined among college students. [5] A plurality of undergraduates described the major social institutions of society—Congress, corporations, labor unions, and the rest—as dishonest and immoral. They expressed a belief that there was nothing left to hold onto: "Everything is bad."

In response, the students had turned inward, and the refuge they [6] had chosen was "me." They described the mood on campus this way:

"People only care about me, me, me."

"We're just interested in staying alive."

"We're part of the me generation."

"Concerns today are not about social issues, but about me."

"People are looking out for number one."

"The me generation is not concerned with the good of society, but with what's good for themselves."

Ninety-one percent of the undergraduates interviewed were opti- [7] mistic about their personal futures, but only 41 percent expressed hope about our collective future together. Student interests focused increasingly on being well-off financially. At the same time they had become more and more vocationally oriented, seeking careers in the platinum professions—law, medicine, and business. They had adopted what might be called a Titanic ethic: a sense that they were riding on a doomed ship called the United States or the world, and as long as it remained afloat, they would go first class.

The Current Generation

The findings of the 1979 study were so telling that I decided to re- [8] peat it this academic year. Once again I, along with several colleagues, visited a diverse selection of colleges and universities across the country. We followed the same approach as the original study, meeting with intentionally heterogeneous groups consisting of 8 to 10 students on each campus. The number of institutions was raised to 28 to reflect the changing character of higher education since 1979. (This was part of a larger study including a survey of 10,000 undergraduates, a survey of 300 chief student affairs officers, and interviews with undergraduate student body presidents, newspaper editors, vice presidents and deans of students, and others.) Again we asked the undergraduate groups what social and political events had most influenced their generation. They gave five common answers.

Challenger. The most frequent answer was the *Challenger* explosion. [9] Once a student mentioned it, members of the group commonly nodded in affirmation or said "yes." It was the equivalent of the Kennedy assassination for this generation. The students all knew where they had been when they heard the news. Many had watched it on television in school. Those who had not, saw it "on the news over and over and over again." Some had been scheduled to have teacher-astronaut Christa McAuliffe teach them from space. For a number it was the first time they had ever seen an adult, their own teacher, break down and cry. It was a first brush with death for quite a few.

That students answered the *Challenger* explosion surprised me. [10] When I thought about the responses students might give to my question, the Shuttle disaster was not on the list. My generation had witnessed other fatalities in the space program, and while the *Challenger* explosion was a very sad occurrence, it did not seem to me to be a defining moment for the nation.

I asked them why they had selected the *Challenger*. Beyond the fact [11] that it was the first shared generational tragedy, students talked of a shattering of both their idealism and their sense of safety:

> *"I always thought NASA was perfect."*
>
> *"There were smashed dreams because of it."*
>
> *"My hopes were in it. There was an Asian, a black, and a woman."*
>
> *"Thought America invincible."*
>
> *"Burst my bubble."*
>
> *"It was something good and then it blew up."*
>
> *"NASA fell off its pedestal."*

Students also said the *Challenger* explosion had marked a "wake-up call" or "reality check" for them and the nation. For some it was "a sign of a lot of things wrong" with the United States, such as in manufacturing, and for others it highlighted the decline of America due to its inability to compete economically and technologically. As one student put it, until then "I thought we were the best; we're really only second class."

End of the Cold War. The fall of communism was a second event [12] students cited. They spoke in terms of "pride," "hope," "drama," "energy," and "a closer world." The symbol that stood out for them was the razing of the Berlin Wall.

Today's undergraduates are the last Cold War generation. They had [13] studied Russia in school as an evil power to be feared. Although none of the 18-to-24-year-old undergraduates had seen Khrushchev bang his shoe at the U.N. or lived through the Cuban Missile Crisis, and only a small minority had engaged in duck-and-cover exercises in school, most had seen films like *The Day After*, which warned of the danger of a nuclear war. As a group, the students interviewed had been scared of the Soviet Union and afraid of the prospect of nuclear holocaust. In this sense the fall of communism was an extremely positive event.

However, the students were quite somber about the results. They [14] regularly talked of the instability of Central and Eastern Europe, but in recent months, their focus shifted to U.S. involvement in a potential Vietnam-like ground war in Bosnia. They noted almost as frequently the danger of a now uncontrolled Soviet nuclear arsenal. They often worried whether the world was, in retrospect, a better place because of the demise of communism. One student put it this way: "For my generation, every silver lining brings a cloud."

Persian Gulf War. The third event students mentioned was the 1991 [15] Gulf War, which they described as "our first war"—"Every generation has a war; this was ours." Like the *Challenger* explosion, they had watched it on television. TVs in student lounges, which were usually tuned to soap operas, had stayed fixed on the war. With the rise of CNN, students joked that friends would drop by and say, "You want to watch the war for a while?," and off they would go.

Despite fear of a draft and another potential Vietnam, students said [16] the Gulf War had pulled them together. Many knew people who had been called up to serve in the Gulf. On their campuses, demonstrations against the war had tended to be tiny or absent in comparison to those in favor. The initial student reaction was pride: "We're still number one"; and "We can get things done." This seemed to be generally true among both liberal and conservative undergraduates. Students talked of flags and yellow ribbons appearing in profusion on many campuses.

By the 1992–93 academic year, undergraduate reactions had [17] changed, with students becoming much more critical:

"It's still a mess."

"We didn't finish the job."

"We botched another one."

"No reason to be there."

"Only a political show."

"Bush just wanted to be a hero."

"People were risking their lives and then had to return and not get jobs."

"We were in there to keep our oil prices down."

"Did it for economic interest only."

Few students were willing to speak out in favor of the Gulf War in spring of 1993 or to offer non-economic rationales for it. In conversation after conversation, students disavowed the U.S. role as world peace officer. They rejected the notion that when "anything goes wrong, we have to straighten it out."

AIDS. A fourth event the students cited was the AIDS epidemic. [18] AIDS has been a fact of life for this generation as long as sexuality has been a possibility for them. Many reported lectures, pamphlets, films, and condom demonstrations in school. They commonly lamented, "I hear about it all the time"; "I'm tired of it."

But more than being tired, the students were often angry. They frequently compared their situation with that of the baby boomers, complaining, "When the boomers had sex, they got laid. When we have sex, we get AIDS." One student said it this way: "Free love is more expensive [now]." [19]

Nonetheless, even though undergraduates resented a sword dangling over their heads, they acted as if it were not there. Though most said they knew what constituted safe sex, only a minority said they practiced it consistently. Students interviewed felt AIDS could not happen to them. They felt immortal. Very few knew anyone who had been diagnosed as HIV positive. Women undergraduates regularly expressed a greater fear of rape and pregnancy than AIDS. [20]

Rodney King. The final event students mentioned was the verdict in the Rodney King beating trial and the riots that followed. Minorities— African-Americans, Hispanics, and Asian-Americans—cited it most frequently, but by no means exclusively. Students expressed polar opinions; some had been appalled by the verdict, and others repulsed by the subsequent violence. The only commonality was the strong negative reaction: [21]

"I lost faith in the judicial system."

"I lost faith in the police."

"I lost confidence in people."

"It was a lesson in how to buy off a jury."

"Everything is politics."

"I used to believe the civil rights movement made a difference."

"Racism lives."

"Laws were created, but minds were not changed."

"Another shock to the system."

"Rioting inexcusable."

"Lawless."

"Verdict really disturbed me."

"I was glad. It's the only way to get people to see."

"It reminded me that society treats me differently."

"Police jobs are stressful."

What Do These Events Mean?

What stands out about the five events the students cited is first how [22] recent they were. Most of today's freshmen were born in 1975—after John F. Kennedy's death, the end of the Great Society, the assassinations of Martin Luther King, Jr., and Robert Kennedy, the moon landing, the Watergate break-in and Richard Nixon's resignation, and the end of the war in Vietnam. They were a year old when Jimmy Carter was elected president, four when the hostages were taken in Iran, five when Ronald Reagan entered the White House, ten when Gorbachev came to power, and thirteen when George Bush became president. More than 40 percent have never heard of Hubert Humphrey, Ralph Nader, or Barry Goldwater.

As a consequence, the events that stand out to their parents and fac- [23] ulty have little meaning to current undergraduates. Those events do not stir the same anger, elation, frustration, or vivid emotions in students that they do in older adults. They are at best history to contemporary undergraduates.

Today's students really know only two presidents of the United [24] States, Ronald Reagan and George Bush. They have lived through three wars, Granada, Panama, and Iraq. The longest war in their lives lasted six weeks. They are living through a period of profound demographic, economic, global, and technological change.

In addition to being recent, the five events the students cited were [25] at least in part negative. They described three—the *Challenger* explosion, AIDS, and the Rodney King affair—in wholly negative terms, and their initial optimism about the fall of communism and the Gulf War has faded significantly. In general, students thought they were living in a deeply troubled nation in which intractable problems were multiplying and solutions were growing more distant:

"Our experience is of flaws, problems, decline. We're not number one in anything. Our generation grew up with that."

"The world seems to be falling apart."

"We don't have anything that stable to hold onto."

The students interviewed shared a sense that their "generation [26] would be called on to fix everything." As a group, they rejected the likelihood of broadscale solutions. For them the five events they cited showed that such solutions are unlikely to occur and unlikely to work. They also dismissed the possibility that answers would come from government. They saw Congress as bankrupt, but held out hope for the Clinton presidency in its earliest days.

An Increased, if Guarded, Optimism

Yet the students I interviewed expressed some optimism about the [27] future. Again, more than nine out of 10 were optimistic about their personal fates, but the level of optimism about our collective future shot up to 55 percent. This is in large measure because students have shifted their focus. While they were rather negative about the future of the country, they were remarkably optimistic about the future of their communities. Today's students emphasize the local in their thinking and their action.

Heroes are back too. More than three out of four students had heroes, but those heroes were local—Mom and Dad, my teacher, my neighbor, the person leading the community clean-up campaign. [28]

Participation in service activities increased dramatically as well. [29] Prior to coming to college about half of all current undergraduates had been engaged in some form of community service. Such programs are booming on college campuses today as well, particularly in the area of environmentalism, a common interest among today's undergraduates. Even on some campuses in which political action was low or absent, recycling bins have appeared at the behest of students.

Nonetheless, fear and anger were a part of the conversation with [30] every student group I interviewed. Current undergraduates were afraid of being unable to find jobs, of living in an economy in which they will do less well than their parents, of facing a mounting national debt, of having to contend with environmental disasters, and much, much more. They felt put upon, cheated, and robbed of the opportunity that had been given to previous generations. They especially resented the baby boomers for their advantages. They criticized the students of the 1980s for their "me-ism."

For most of the students interviewed the real struggle was choosing [31] between making money and performing good deeds. Six out of eight undergraduates said it was essential or very important to be very well-off financially, but five out of eight said it was essential or very important to have a career that would make a meaningful social contribution. The big issue facing students I interviewed was how to choose. Most didn't want to be Donald Trump, but the prospect of Mother Theresa was not all that appealing either. Above all, this is a generation torn between doing good and doing well.

Responding to Reading

1. What kinds of heroes does Bader say people of her generation—she was born in the late 1960s—have? What kinds of heroes does Levine say the students he studied—born in 1975—have? How are they alike? How are they different? How are they like and unlike your own heroes?
2. Are the five key political and social events Levine mentions the ones that had the greatest impact on your life? Are there others you consider more significant? How do you account for any differences between your choices and those of other students?
3. In paragraphs 29–31 Bader touches on a sensitive issue—the idea that one's heroes must be representatives of one's own gender, race, ethnic group, and nationality. Do you agree? Do you have heroes from backgrounds unlike your own?
4. Levine's conclusions reflect students' general optimism. Are you optimistic about your future? About the future of your community, your nation, and your world? What do you see that encourages (or discourages) you?
5. The last words in Bader's essay are, "Today, life is larger." What does she mean? Do you think she is correct? Would Levine agree with her?
6. In his conclusion Levine characterizes the generation he profiles as one "torn between doing good and doing well." Do you think this is an accurate characterization? Do you agree that "doing good" and "doing well" are mutually exclusive?

THE GLOBAL VILLAGE[1] FINALLY
~ ARRIVES

Pico Iyer

Born in England to parents who had emigrated from India, Pico Iyer (1957–) attended Oxford University and Harvard. During the 1980s he was a correspondent for *Time* magazine, focusing on international affairs, and he continues to contribute essays and reviews to that magazine as well as to the *Partisan Review*, the *Village Voice*, and the (London) *Times Literary Supplement*. His books include *Video Nights in*

---

[1] The term "global village" was coined in 1967 by Canadian cultural critic Marshall McLuhan to describe an increasingly interdependent world, linked by electronic technology.

Kathmandu and Other Reports from the Not-So-Far-East (1988), a humorous look at encounters between Eastern and Western cultures, and *The Lady and the Monk: A Season in Kyoto* (1991), a personal account of life in Japan. In the following essay, which was written for *Time* in 1993, Iyer suggests that the blending of international cultures he observes at home in southern California is becoming the paradigm for the entire world.

This is the typical day of a relatively typical soul in today's diversified world. I wake up to the sound of my Japanese clock radio, put on a T-shirt sent me by an uncle in Nigeria and walk out into the street, past German cars, to my office. Around me are English-language students from Korea, Switzerland and Argentina—all on this Spanish-named road in this Mediterranean-style town. On TV, I find, the news is in Mandarin; today's baseball game is being broadcast in Korean. For lunch I can walk to a sushi bar, a tandoori palace, a Thai café or the newest burrito joint (run by an old Japanese lady). Who am I, I sometimes wonder, the son of Indian parents and a British citizen who spends much of his time in Japan (and is therefore—what else?—an American permanent resident)? And where am I?

I am, as it happens, in Southern California, in a quiet, relatively uninternational town, but I could as easily be in Vancouver or Sydney or London or Hong Kong. All the world's a rainbow coalition, more and more; the whole planet, you might say, is going global. When I fly to Toronto, or Paris, or Singapore, I disembark in a world as hyphenated as the one I left. More and more of the globe looks like America, but an America that is itself looking more and more like the rest of the globe. Los Angeles famously teaches 82 different languages in its schools. In this respect, the city seems only to bear out the old adage that what is in California today is in America tomorrow, and next week around the globe.

In ways that were hardly conceivable even a generation ago, the new world order is a version of the New World writ large: a wide-open frontier of polyglot terms and postnational trends. A common multiculturalism links us all—call it Planet Hollywood, Planet Reebok or the United Colors of Benetton. *Taxi* and *hotel* and *disco* are universal terms now, but so too are *karaoke* and *yoga* and *pizza*. For the gourmet alone, there is *tiramisù* at the Burger King in Kyoto, echt[2] angel-hair pasta in Saigon and enchiladas on every menu in Nepal.

But deeper than mere goods, it is souls that are mingling. In Brussels, a center of the new "unified Europe," 1 new baby in every 4 is Arab. Whole parts of the Paraguayan capital of Asunción are largely Korean. And when the prostitutes of Melbourne distributed some pro-condom

1

2

3

4

---

[2] Real, authentic. [Eds.]

pamphlets, one of the languages they used was Macedonian.[3] Even Japan, which prides itself on its centuries-old socially engineered uni-culture, swarms with Iranian illegals, Western executives, Pakistani la-borers and Filipina hostesses.

The global village is defined, as we know, by an international youth   5 culture that takes its cues from American pop culture. Kids in Perth and Prague and New Delhi are all tuning in to *Santa Barbara* on TV, and wriggling into 501 jeans, while singing along to Madonna's latest in Eng-lish. CNN (which has grown 70-fold in 13 years) now reaches more than 140 countries; an American football championship pits London against Barcelona. As fast as the world comes to America, America goes round the world—but it is an America that is itself multi-tongued and many hued, an America of Amy Tan and Janet Jackson and movies with dia-logue in Lakota.[4]

For far more than goods and artifacts, the one great influence being   6 broadcast around the world in greater numbers and at greater speed than ever before is people. What were once clear divisions are now tangles of crossed lines: there are 40,000 "Canadians" resident in Hong Kong, many of whose first language is Cantonese. And with people come customs: while new immigrants from Taiwan and Vietnam and India—some of the so-called Asian Calvinists—import all-American values of hard work and family closeness and entrepreneurial energy to America, America is sending its values of upward mobility and individualism and melting-pot hopefulness to Taipei and Saigon and Bombay.

Values, in fact, travel at the speed of fax; by now, almost half the   7 world's Mormons live outside the U.S. A diversity of one culture quick-ly becomes a diversity of many: the "typical American" who goes to Japan today may be a third-generation Japanese American, or the son of a Japan-ese woman married to a California serviceman, or the offspring of a Sal-vadoran father and an Italian mother from San Francisco. When he goes out with a Japanese woman, more than two cultures are brought into play.

None of this, of course, is new: Chinese silks were all the rage in   8 Rome centuries ago, and Alexandria before the time of Christ was a par-adigm of the modern universal city. Not even American eclecticism is new: many a small town has long known Chinese restaurants, Indian doctors and Lebanese grocers. But now all these cultures are crossing at the speed of light. And the rising diversity of the planet is something more than mere cosmopolitanism: it is a fundamental recoloring of the very complexion of societies. Cities like Paris, or Hong Kong, have al-ways had a soigné, international air and served as magnets for exiles and émigrés, but now smaller places are multinational too. Marseilles speaks

---

[3] Melbourne is in Australia, Macedonia in Eastern Europe. [Eds.]
[4] Native American language used in *Dances with Wolves*. [Eds.]

French with a distinctly North African twang. Islamic fundamentalism has one of its strongholds in Bradford, England. It is the sleepy coastal towns of Queensland, Australia, that print their menus in Japanese.

The dangers this internationalism presents are evident: not for nothing did the Tower of Babel collapse. As national borders fall, tribal alliances, and new manmade divisions, rise up, and the world learns every day terrible new meanings of the word Balkanization.[5] And while some places are wired for international transmission, others (think of Iran or North Korea or Burma) remain as isolated as ever, widening the gap between the haves and the have-nots, or what Alvin Toffler has called the "fast" and the "slow" worlds. Tokyo has more telephones than the whole continent of Africa.

Nonetheless, whether we like it or not, the "transnational" future is upon us: as Kenichi Ohmae, the international economist, suggests with his talk of a "borderless economy," capitalism's allegiances are to products, not places. "Capital is now global," Robert Reich, the Secretary of Labor, has said, pointing out that when an Iowan buys a Pontiac from General Motors, 60% of his money goes to South Korea, Japan, West Germany, Taiwan, Singapore, Britain and Barbados. Culturally we are being re-formed daily by the cadences of world music and world fiction: where the great Canadian writers of an older generation had names like Frye and Davies and Laurence, now they are called Ondaatje and Mistry and Skvorecky.

As space shrinks, moreover, time accelerates. This hip-hop mishmash is spreading overnight. When my parents were in college, there were all of seven foreigners living in Tibet, a country the size of Western Europe, and in its entire history the country had seen fewer than 2,000 Westerners. Now a Danish student in Lhasa is scarcely more surprising than a Tibetan in Copenhagen. Already a city like Miami is beyond the wildest dreams of 1968; how much more so will its face in 2018 defy our predictions of today?

It would be easy, seeing all this, to say that the world is moving toward the *Raza Cósmica* (Cosmic Race), predicted by the Mexican thinker José Vasconcelos in the '20s—a glorious blend of mongrels and mestizos.[6] It may be more relevant to suppose that more and more of the world may come to resemble Hong Kong, a stateless special economic zone full of expats and exiles linked by the lingua franca[7] of English and the global marketplace. Some urbanists already see the world as a grid of 30 or so highly advanced city-regions, or technopoles, all plugged into the same international circuit.

9

10

11

12

---

[5] Breaking up of a region into smaller, often hostile groups. [Eds.]

[6] People of mixed race. [Eds.]

[7] A common language used for purposes of commerce among people who generally speak different languages. [Eds.]

The world will not become America. Anyone who has been to a 13
baseball game in Osaka, or a Pizza Hut in Moscow, knows instantly that
she is not in Kansas. But America may still, if only symbolically, be a
model for the world. *E Pluribus Unum*, after all, is on the dollar bill. As
Federico Mayor Zaragoza, the director-general of UNESCO, has said,
"America's main role in the new world order is not as a military superpower, but as a multicultural superpower."

The traditional metaphor for this is that of a mosaic. But Richard 14
Rodriguez, the Mexican-American essayist who is a psalmist for our
new hybrid forms, points out that the interaction is more fluid than
that, more human, subject to daily revision. "I am Chinese," he says,
"because I live in San Francisco, a Chinese city. I became Irish in
America. I became Portuguese in America." And even as he announces this new truth, Portuguese women are becoming American,
and Irishmen are becoming Portuguese, and Sydney (or is it Toronto?)
is thinking to compare itself with the "Chinese city" we know as San
Francisco.

Responding to Reading

1. Do you see any evidence in your community of the exchange of languages,
   goods, values, and people Iyer describes? Do you see it at your school?
   Give specific examples. What factors do you think have made this exchange possible?
2. Do you believe the global village Iyer describes has brought with it an increased understanding and knowledge of (or tolerance for) other cultures
   and nations? If so, how? If not, why not?
3. In paragraph 9 Iyer touches on some of the negative aspects of the global village. Can you think of others? For example, what *personal* price, if any, do we
   pay for the increasingly multicultural and multinational nature of our
   world?

GETTING AWAY WITH MURDER

Barbara Grizutti Harrison

A frequent contributor to periodicals such as *Harper's* and the *New Republic* and author of a monthly column for *Mademoiselle,* Barbara
Grizutti Harrison (1934–) has been noted for her "hard-edged journalism" which she "often combines with autobiography." For exam-

ple, her most famous book, *Visions of Glory: A History and Memory of Jehovah's Witnesses* (1978), is a critical but even-handed examination of the religious group, which Harrison joined at nine years old and was a member of for eleven years. A native of Brooklyn, New York, Harrison has written a novel, *Foreign Bodies* (1984), as well as a number of travel books and essay collections. A social critic with strong opinions, Harrison has said of contemporary society, "People may not be more selfish than they were before, but they're less ashamed of being selfish." In the following essay, which appeared in the magazine *Mirabella* in 1994, Harrison focuses her critical attention on another vexing issue: the increasing number of claims by those who commit crimes that they are themselves "victims" who don't deserve punishment.

There's a whole lot of blubbering going on these days; and there's a whole lot of support—even hysterical admiration—for the blubberers. [1]

The rich Menendez brothers, Lyle and Erik, bust into their family's den and fire off sixteen rounds from two 12-gauge shotguns at their parents, who are eating ice cream and strawberries and watching the tube. On the stand, the boys, who are in fact men, offer teary accounts of years of childhood sexual abuse—no corroboration, just awfully convenient allegations. Claiming self-defense, they are rewarded with deadlocked juries and with groupies. Erik's attorney calls the killers "adorable," never mind that the blood and guts of Mom and Pop Menendez had to be scraped off the walls. [2]

In Gainesville, Florida, one Danny Harold Rolling was convicted of having murdered four women and one man, all college students between seventeen and twenty-three years old. After killing one woman as she slept, he stabbed her roommate five times, saying, "Take the pain, bitch. Take the pain." He then stopped for a snack—a banana and an apple—before posing the bodies in "lewd positions." In the courtroom, Rolling was permitted to sing the little love ditties he had composed to a smitten female tabloid TV journalist. Rolling's defense attorney informed the jury that Danny Harold Rolling came from a dysfunctional family. [3]

So what.

Attorney William Kunstler is using what is being called the "black rage" defense on behalf of Colin Ferguson, who shot twenty-five unsuspecting people on a Long Island Rail Road commuter train, killing six and wounding nineteen. Ferguson was driven to a shooting rage because he'd been relegated to second-class citizenship, Kunstler says, and because he had a "pre-existing mental illness." (Maybe the attorney invokes Ferguson's "mental illness" in case any of us remembers that Martin Luther King, Jr., and Fannie Lou Hamer were also victims of racism—as a consequence of which they became prophets and [4] saints.) Tell me this: would *anybody* whose elevator went all the way to the top floor randomly shoot twenty-five dozing citizens?[1]

In *Race Matters,* Cornel West, a professor of religion and director of Afro-American studies at Princeton and the grandson of a Baptist minister, sensibly requires us to acknowledge "the lingering effect of black history—a history inseparable from though not reducible to victimization." But, he writes, to say that "More and more black people [are] vulnerable to daily lives endured with little sense of self and fragile existential moorings . . . is not the same as asserting that individual black people are not responsible for their actions—black murderers and rapists should go to jail."

Why is it not possible to say both that any murder is an insane act *and* that any murderer should pay for his crime?

I began obsessively to question our ability to hold these two thoughts in our heads simultaneously in the late 1970s, when a Yale graduate named Richard Herrin killed his girlfriend, twenty-year-old Bonnie Garland, with a claw hammer in her own bed, in her own house, in which her parents and brother and sister were sleeping: "Her head split open like a watermelon," Herrin said. For good measure he'd smashed her larynx and hammered her breast and throttled her. Herrin's lawyer, Jack Litman—the same sweetie pie who defended Robert Chambers, the "preppie murderer"—argued that his client was suffering from "overwhelming stress" and from "transient situational reaction," whatever that is. He managed to convince a malleable jury that Herrin was crazy enough to be excused from maximum responsibility but not so crazy as to be locked up forever: Herrin was found not guilty of murder in the second degree, guilty of manslaughter. His lawyer argued that Herrin's childhood had been traumatic: he'd been abandoned by his father and obliged to work for his stepfather in a flea market, he'd suffered from childhood eczema (otherwise known as a rash) and was a late bed wetter. So when Bonnie told him she wanted to date other guys, he snapped. Or, as Herrin himself put it, he killed Bonnie Garland because he was "out of touch with [his] feelings." And he got away with murder.

If every killer is "disturbed," is no killing a crime?

I want to go back for a moment to those Menendezes and to what *Newsweek*'s smart Meg Greenfield said about the alleged systematic abuse they endured: "Can anyone doubt that if such abuse did occur and that if the parents, while they lived, had been convincingly charged with it, they would have, in their turn, suggested that they had been abused as children themselves?"

She has it right.

---

[1] Ferguson, who eventually decided to defend himself, was convicted of multiple counts of murder in 1995.

Walter Goodman, the *New York Times*'s TV critic, offers us this daz- 11
zling TV vignette, which would be ever so funny if it were not ever so
true: a woman called Adrienne comes on a television talk show to speak
of having been forced to have oral sex with her father when she was
eight. A man called Michael talks of having had oral sex with his older
sister when he was seven. "But wait. Here comes Adrienne's father, with
roses, and he reveals that he was homosexually raped when he was five.
And here comes Michael's sister, with a doll and the announcement.
'I'm a victim, too.'"

How far back can we go? If you were victimized by your father who 12
was in turn victimized by his father who was . . . see what I mean? That
road leads to Adam and Eve. That road leads to a signpost: if everyone
is to blame, no one is to blame.

In a book called *What You Can Change and What You Can't,* Martin 13
E.P. Seligman, Ph.D., professor of clinical psychology at the University
of Pennsylvania, says that in studies claiming to demonstrate the effect
of major childhood traumas on adult personality "the influence is barely detectable. . . . Bad childhood events, contrary to the credo, do not
mandate adult troubles—far from it. There is no justification, according
to these studies, for blaming your adult depression, anxiety, bad marriage, drug use, sexual problems, unemployment, beating up your children, alcoholism, or anger on what happened to you as a child." In the
current love-the-victim/hug-the-inner-child climate, Seligman is not
likely to be given much talk-TV time.

But wait! Seligman says the studies were "methodologically inade- 14
quate anyway. They failed, in their enthusiasm for human plasticity, to
control for genes."

For *genes!* Genes are big now. 15

Writing in *Time,* columnist Dennis Overbye says: "Scientists say 16
they are on the verge of pinning down genetic and biochemical abnor-
malities that predispose their bearers to violence. An article in the journal *Science* last summer carried the headline EVIDENCE FOUND FOR A POSSI-
BLE 'AGGRESSION' GENE."

I say a predisposition (unproven) is not a life sentence or a doom. 17
I say we all know we can compensate for our weaknesses and even—
if they threaten other people—for our strengths. You are not permitted
to murder people. Period. No matter what the ideological flavor of the
day—environmental or genetic—you are not allowed, and that's that.

A ruthless Freudian determinism is yielding to a banal biological 18
determinism: if your mommy and daddy didn't do it, your genes did.
There is no room left for freedom or for grace; no room, for example, for
the arrival of the accidental person or event that changes, converts,

---

[2] An essay by Goodman appears in Chapter 4. [-Eds.]

transforms and lifts us. (Did you know that the man who wrote "Amazing Grace" was a slave trader—until he, who "was blind," saw, with life-changing light, the foul error of his ways?)

We have relentlessly and stupidly separated the individual and the [19] community; in effect, we have said that what is good for one is not necessarily good for all, and vice versa. I do not believe this. It is a gross and coarse polarization. We are all individuals within a community. We are accountable to that community, which requires, if it is to retain sanity, retribution. *Forgive yourself,* the talkshow gurus say—that's what one priest said to Bonnie Garland's killer. But accountability has to precede forgiveness for it not to be a rotten farce.

I can remember when we believed in Judgment Day—a day not [20] arranged by the Almighty to allow us to "get in touch with our feelings."

Cornel West argues, and I agree, for a return to spiritual values, [21] community values, for—conservatives don't have a lock on this—family values. These words make people nervous; they're afraid their liberty will be threatened. I say: how free are we now? How free are Jose and Kitty Menendez? How free are the man and the women killed in their youth by a self-romanticizing singing serial killer? Do you think Bonnie Garland's younger sister will ever feel free?

Suppose I'm wrong. Perhaps God is an invention; perhaps it's [22] naive to believe in free will. Albert Camus, who was quite sure there is no God and not at all sure that we are capable of exercising free will, had this formula: *act* as if you had free will. And, as my father used to say: don't let those suckers on the radio—or on the television—get to you.

The O.J. Simpson story broke as this issue was going to press. I do not [23] *know whether Mr. Simpson is guilty of double murder as charged, but—in keeping with the times—he was certainly positioning himself as victim when he, who made it a practice to beat his wife, wrote: "At times I have felt like a battered husband or boyfriend," standing truth on its head.*

Responding to Reading

1. Harrison is not an objective journalist in this essay. In paragraph 1, for example, she refers to those who claim victim status as "blubberers," and in paragraph 4 she suggests that Colin Ferguson is a man whose "elevator [doesn't go] all the way to the top floor." Find other examples of such casual, even irreverent, language in the essay. Do you think such language diminishes the strength of Harrison's arguments, or do you believe it gives her essay a refreshing honesty? Explain your position.
2. Do you believe the "dysfunctional family," "black rage," or "disadvantaged background" defense is ever a valid one? Under what circumstances, if any, should a murderer's background absolve him or her of guilt?

3. In paragraph 19 Harrison says, "accountability has to precede forgiveness for it not to be a rotten farce." What do you think she means? Do you agree with her?

JUST WALK ON BY

Brent Staples

Brent Staples (1951–) is an editor and writer who studied behavioral science and psychology, taught, and then turned to journalism writing for the *Chicago Sun-Times* and the *New York Times,* on whose editorial board he currently serves. He has also contributed essays to *Harper's* and *Ms.* His memoir, *Parallel Time* (1994), was sparked by his brother's murder in a dispute over a cocaine deal and describes Staple's own internal struggles in crossing back and forth between black and white worlds. In the following essay, which originally appeared in *Ms.* in 1986, Staples talks personally about white people's images of black men and how he deals with them.

My first victim was a woman—white, well dressed, probably in her early twenties. I came upon her late one evening on a deserted street in Hyde Park, a relatively affluent neighborhood in an otherwise mean, impoverished section of Chicago. As I swung onto the avenue behind her, there seemed to be a discreet, uninflammatory distance between us. Not so. She cast back a worried glance. To her, the youngish black man—a broad six feet two inches with a beard and billowing hair, both hands shoved into the pockets of a bulky military jacket—seemed menacingly close. After a few more quick glimpses, she picked up her pace and was soon running in earnest. Within seconds she disappeared into a cross street.

That was more than a decade ago. I was 22 years old, a graduate student newly arrived at the University of Chicago. It was in the echo of that terrified woman's footfalls that I first began to know the unwieldy inheritance I'd come into—the ability to alter public space in ugly ways. It was clear that she thought herself the quarry of a mugger, a rapist, or worse. Suffering a bout of insomnia, however, I was stalking sleep, not defenseless wayfarers. As a softy who is scarcely able to take a knife to a raw chicken—let alone hold it to a person's throat—I was surprised, embarrassed, and dismayed all at once. Her flight made me feel like an accomplice in tyranny. It also made it clear that I was indistinguishable from the muggers who occasionally seeped into the area from the surrounding ghetto. That first encounter, and those that followed, signified that a vast, unnerving gulf lay between nighttime pedestrians—particularly women—and me. And I soon gathered that being perceived as dangerous is a hazard in itself. I only needed to turn a corner into a dicey situation, or crowd some frightened, armed person in a foyer somewhere, or make an errant move after being pulled over by a policeman. Where fear and weapons meet—and they often do in urban America—there is always the possibility of death.

In that first year, my first away from my hometown, I was to become 3
thoroughly familiar with the language of fear. At dark, shadowy intersections in Chicago, I could cross in front of a car stopped at a traffic light and elicit the *thunk, thunk, thunk, thunk* of the driver—black, white, male, or female—hammering down the door locks. On less traveled streets after dark, I grew accustomed to but never comfortable with people who crossed to the other side of the street rather than pass me. Then there were the standard unpleasantries with police, doormen, bouncers, cab drivers, and others whose business it is to screen out troublesome individuals *before* there is any nastiness.

I moved to New York nearly two years ago and I have remained an 4
avid night walker. In central Manhattan, the near-constant crowd cover minimizes tense one-on-one street encounters. Elsewhere—visiting friends in SoHo, where sidewalks are narrow and tightly spaced buildings shut out the sky—things can get very taut indeed.

Black men have a firm place in New York mugging literature. Nor- 5
man Podhoretz in his famed (or infamous) 1963 essay, "My Negro Problem—And Ours," recalls growing up in terror of black males; they "were tougher than we were, more ruthless," he writes—and as an adult on the Upper West Side of Manhattan, he continues, he cannot constrain his nervousness when he meets black men on certain streets. Similarly, a decade later, the essayist and novelist Edward Hoagland extols a New York where once "Negro bitterness bore down mainly on other Negroes." Where some see mere panhandlers, Hoagland sees "a mugger who is clearly screwing up his nerve to do more than just *ask* for money." But Hoagland has "the New Yorker's quickhunch posture for broken-field maneuvering," and the bad guy swerves away.

I often witness that "hunch posture," from women after dark on the 6
warrenlike streets of Brooklyn where I live. They seem to set their faces on neutral and, with their purse straps strung across their chests bandolier style, they forge ahead as though bracing themselves against being tackled. I understand, of course, that the danger they perceive is not a hallucination. Women are particularly vulnerable to street violence, and young black males are drastically overrepresented among the perpetrators of that violence. Yet these truths are no solace against the kind of alienation that comes of being ever the suspect, against

being set apart, a fearsome entity with whom pedestrians avoid making eye contact.

It is not altogether clear to me how I reached the ripe old age of 22 7 without being conscious of the lethality nighttime pedestrians attributed to me. Perhaps it was because in Chester, Pennsylvania, the small, angry industrial town where I came of age in the 1960s, I was scarcely noticeable against a backdrop of gang warfare, street knifings, and murders. I grew up one of the good boys, had perhaps a half-dozen fist fights. In retrospect, my shyness of combat has clear sources.

Many things go into the making of a young thug. One of those 8 things is the consummation of the male romance with the power to intimidate. An infant discovers that random flailings send the baby bottle flying out of the crib and crashing to the floor. Delighted, the joyful babe repeats those motions again and again, seeking to duplicate the feat. Just so, I recall the points at which some of my boyhood friends were finally seduced by the perception of themselves as tough guys. When a mark cowered and surrendered his money without resistance, myth and reality merged—and paid off. It is, after all, only manly to embrace the power to frighten and intimidate. We, as men, are not supposed to give an inch of our lane on the highway; we are to seize the fighter's edge in work and in play and even in love; we are to be valiant in the face of hostile forces.

Unfortunately, poor and powerless young men seem to take all this 9 nonsense literally. As a boy, I saw countless tough guys locked away; I have since buried several, too. They were babies, really—a teenage cousin, a brother of 22, a childhood friend in his mid-twenties—all gone down in episodes of bravado played out in the streets. I came to doubt the virtues of intimidation early on. I chose, perhaps even unconsciously, to remain a shadow—timid, but a survivor.

The fearsomeness mistakenly attributed to me in public places often 10 has a perilous flavor. The most frightening of these confusions occurred in the late 1970s and early 1980s when I worked as a journalist in Chicago. One day, rushing into the office of a magazine I was writing for with a deadline story in hand, I was mistaken for a burglar. The office manager called security and, with an ad hoc posse, pursued me through the labyrinthine halls, nearly to my editor's door. I had no way of proving who I was. I could only move briskly toward the company of someone who knew me.

Another time I was on assignment for a local paper and killing time 11 before an interview. I entered a jewelry store on the city's affluent Near North Side. The proprietor excused herself and returned with an enormous red Doberman pinscher straining at the end of a leash. She stood, the dog extended toward me, silent to my questions, her eyes bulging nearly out of her head. I took a cursory look around, nodded, and bade her good night. Relatively speaking, however, I never fared as badly as another black male journalist. He went to nearby Waukegan, Illinois, a couple of summers ago to work on a story about a murderer who was born there. Mistaking the reporter for the killer, police hauled him from his car at gunpoint and but for his press credentials would probably have tried to book him. Such episodes are not uncommon. Black men trade tales like this all the time.

In "My Negro Problem—And Ours," Podhoretz writes that the ha-   12
tred he feels for blacks makes itself known to him through a variety of avenues—one being his discomfort with that "special brand of paranoid touchiness" to which he says blacks are prone. No doubt he is speaking here of black men. In time, I learned to smother the rage I felt at so often being taken for a criminal. Not to do so would surely have led to madness—via that special "paranoid touchiness" that so annoyed Podhoretz at the time he wrote the essay.

I began to take precautions to make myself less threatening. I   13
move about with care, particularly late in the evening. I give a wide berth to nervous people on subway platforms during the wee hours, particularly when I have exchanged business clothes for jeans. If I happen to be entering a building behind some people who appear skittish, I may walk by, letting them clear the lobby before I return, so as not to seem to be following them. I have been calm and extremely congenial on those rare occasions when I've been pulled over by the police.

And on late-evening constitutionals along streets less traveled by, I   14
employ what has proved to be an excellent tension-reducing measure: I whistle melodies from Beethoven and Vivaldi and the more popular classical composers. Even steely New Yorkers hunching toward night-time destinations seem to relax, and occasionally they even join in the tune. Virtually everybody seems to sense that a mugger wouldn't be warbling bright, sunny selections from Vivaldi's *Four Seasons*. It is my equivalent of the cowbell that hikers wear when they know they are in bear country.

Responding to Reading

1. Staples speaks quite matter-of-factly of the fear he inspires. Does your experience support his assumption that black men have the "ability to alter public space?" Why or why not? Do you believe white men also have this capacity?

2. In paragraph 13 Staples suggests some strategies that he believes make him "less threatening." What else, if anything, do you think he could do? Do you believe he *should* adopt such strategies? Explain your position.

3. Although Staples says he arouses fear in others, he also admits that he himself feels fearful. Why? Do you think he has reason to be fearful?

On Being Black and Middle
~ Class

Shelby Steele

Shelby Steele (1945–), professor of English at San Jose State University, writes thoughtfully about African Americans and his own experience growing up the son of a white mother and a black father. He produced the film documentary *Seven Days in Bensonhurst* (1990), about the murder of Yusef Hawkins, and has published a collection of essays called *The Content of Our Character: A New Vision of Race in America* (1990), which won the National Book Critics Circle Award. Of his work Steele has remarked, "Some people say I shine a harsh light on difficult social problems. But I never shine a light on anything I haven't experienced or write about fears I don't see in myself first." In this essay Steele argues that blacks must "move beyond the victim-focused black identity," recognizing that class as much as race explains people's place in American society.

Not long ago a friend of mine, black like myself, said to me that the term "black middle class" was actually a contradiction in terms. Race, he insisted, blurred class distinctions among blacks. If you were black, you were just black and that was that. When I argued, he let his eyes roll at my naiveté. Then he went on. For us, as black professionals, it was an exercise in self-flattery, a pathetic pretension, to give meaning to such a distinction. Worse, the very idea of class threatened the unity that was vital to the black community as a whole. After all, since when had white America taken note of anything but color when it came to blacks? He then reminded me of an old Malcolm X line that had been popular in the sixties. Question: What is a black man with a Ph.D.? Answer: A nigger.

For many years I had been on my friend's side of this argument. Much of my conscious thinking on the old conundrum[1] of race and class was shaped during my high school and college years in the race-charged sixties, when the fact of my race took on an almost religious significance. Progressively, from the mid-sixties on, more and more aspects of my life found their explanation, their justification, and their motivation in race. My youthful concerns about career, romance, money, values, and even styles of dress became a subject to consultation with various oracular

---

[1] A riddle in which a fanciful question is answered by a pun; a problem that has no satisfactory solution. [Eds.]

sources of racial wisdom. And these ranged from a figure as ennobling as Martin Luther King, Jr., to the underworld elegance of dress I found in jazz clubs on the South Side of Chicago. Everywhere there were signals, and in those days I considered myself so blessed with clarity and direction that I pitied my white classmates who found more embarrassment than guidance in the fact of *their* race. In 1968, inflated by my new power, I took a mischievous delight in calling them culturally disadvantaged.

But now, hearing my friend's comment was like hearing a priest   3
from a church I'd grown disenchanted with. I understood him, but my faith was weak. What had sustained me in the sixties sounded monotonous and off the mark in the eighties. For me, race had lost much of its juju, its singular capacity to conjure meaning. And today, when I honestly look at my life and the lives of many other middle-class blacks I know, I can see that race never fully explained our situation in American society. Black though I may be, it is impossible for me to sit in my single-family house with two cars in the driveway and a swing set in the back yard and *not* see the role class has played in my life. And how can my friend, similarly raised and similarly situated, not see it?

Yet despite my certainty I felt a sharp tug of guilt as I tried to explain   4
myself over my friend's skepticism. He is a man of many comedic facial expressions and, as I spoke, his brow lifted in extreme moral alarm as if I were uttering the unspeakable. His clear implication was that I was being elitist and possibly (dare he suggest?) anti-black—crimes for which there might well be no redemption. He pretended to fear for me. I chuckled along with him, but inwardly I did wonder at myself. Though I never doubted the validity of what I was saying, I felt guilty saying it. Why?

After he left (to retrieve his daughter from a dance lesson) I realized   5
that the trap I felt myself in had a tiresome familiarity and, in a sort of slow-motion epiphany, I began to see its outline. It was like the suddenly sharp vision one has at the end of a burdensome marriage when all the long-repressed incompatibilities come undeniably to light.

What became clear to me is that people like myself, my friend, and   6
middle-class blacks generally are caught in a very specific double bind that keeps two equally powerful elements of our identity at odds with each other. The middle-class values by which we were raised—the work ethic, the importance of education, the value of property ownership, of respectability, of "getting ahead," of stable family life, of initiative, of self-reliance, etc.—are, in themselves, raceless and even assimilationist. They urge us toward participation in the American mainstream, toward integration, toward a strong identification with the society—and toward the entire constellation of qualities that are implied in the word "individualism." These values are almost rules for how to prosper in a democratic, free-enterprise society that admires and rewards individual ef-

fort. They tell us to work hard for ourselves and our families and to seek our opportunities whenever they appear, inside or outside the confines of whatever ethnic group we may belong to.

But the particular pattern of racial identification that emerged in the   7
sixties and that still prevails today urges middle-class blacks (and all blacks) in the opposite direction. This pattern asks us to see ourselves as an embattled minority, and it urges an adversarial stance toward the mainstream, an emphasis on ethnic consciousness over individualism. It is organized around an implied separatism.

The opposing thrust of these two parts of our identity results in the   8
double bind of middle-class blacks. There is no forward movement on either plane that does not constitute backward movement on the other. This was the familiar trap I felt myself in while talking with my friend. As I spoke about class, his eyes reminded me that I was betraying race. Clearly, the two indispensable parts of my identity were a threat to each other.

Of course when you think about it, class and race are both similar   9
in some ways and also naturally opposed. They are two forms of collective identity with boundaries that intersect. But whether they clash or peacefully coexist has much to do with how they are defined. Being both black and middle class becomes a double bind when class and race are defined in sharply antagonistic terms, so that one must be repressed to appease the other.

But what is the "substance" of these two identities, and how does   10
each establish itself in an individual's overall identity? It seems to me that when we identify with any collective we are basically identifying with images that tell us what it means to be a member of that collective. Identity is not the same thing as the fact of membership in a collective; it is, rather, a form of self-definition, facilitated by images of what we wish our membership in the collective to mean. In this sense, the images we identify with may reflect the aspirations of the collective more than they reflect reality, and their content can vary with shifts in those aspirations.

But the process of identification is usually dialectical. It is just as nec-   11
essary to say what we are *not* as it is to say what we are—so that finally identification comes about by embracing a polarity of positive and negative images. To identify as middle class, for example, I must have both positive and negative images of what being middle class entails; then I will know what I should and should not be doing in order to be middle class. The same goes for racial identity.

In the racially turbulent sixties the polarity of images that came to   12
define racial identification was very antagonistic to the polarity that defined middle-class identification. One might say that the positive images of one lined up with the negative images of the other, so that to identify with both required either a contortionist's flexibility or a dangerous

splitting of the self. The double bind of the black middle class was in place.

The black middle class has always defined its class identity by [13] means of positive images gleaned from middle- and upper-class white society, and by means of negative images of lower-class blacks. This habit goes back to the institution of slavery itself, when "house" slaves both mimicked the whites they served and held themselves above the "field" slaves. But in the sixties the old bourgeois impulse to dissociate from the lower classes (the "we-they" distinction) backfired when racial identity suddenly called for the celebration of this same black lower class. One of the qualities of a double bind is that one feels it more than sees it, and I distinctly remember the tension and strange sense of dishonesty I felt in those days as I moved back and forth like a bigamist between the demands of class and race.

Though my father was born poor, he achieved middle-class stand- [14] ing through much hard work and sacrifice (one of his favorite words) and by identifying fully with solid middle-class values—mainly hard work, family life, property ownership, and education for his children (all four of whom have advanced degrees). In his mind these were not so much values as laws of nature. People who embodied them made up the positive images in his class polarity. The negative images came largely from the blacks he had left behind because they were "going nowhere."

No one in my family remembers how it happened, but as time went [15] on, the negative images congealed into an imaginary character named Sam, who, from the extensive service we put him to, quickly grew to mythic proportions. In our family lore he was sometimes a trickster, sometimes a boob, but always possessed of a catalogue of sly faults that gave up graphic images of everything we should not be. On sacrifice: "Sam never thinks about tomorrow. He wants it now or he doesn't care about it." On work: "Sam doesn't favor it too much." On children: "Sam likes to have them but not to raise them." On money: "Sam drinks it up and pisses it out." On fidelity: "Sam has to have two or three women." On clothes: "Sam features loud clothes. He likes to see and be seen." And so on. Sam's persona amounted to a negative instruction manual in class identity.

I don't think any of us believed Sam's faults were accurate repre- [16] sentations of lower-class black life. He was an instrument of self-definition, not of sociological accuracy. It never occurred to us that he looked very much like the white racist stereotype of blacks, or that he might have been a manifestation of our own racial self-hatred. He simply gave us a counterpoint against which to express our aspirations. If self-hatred was a factor, it was not, for us, a matter of hating lower-class blacks but of hating what we did not want to be.

Still, hate or love aside, it is fundamentally true that my middle-class [17] identity involved a dissociation from images of lower-class black life and a corresponding identification with values and patterns of responsibility that are common to the middle class everywhere. These values sent me a clear message: be both an individual and a responsible citizen; understand that the quality of your life will approximately reflect the quality of effort you put into it; know that individual responsibility is the basis of freedom and that the limitations imposed by fate (whether fair or unfair) are no excuse for passivity.

Whether I live up to these values or not, I know that my acceptance [18] of them is the result of lifelong conditioning. I know also that I share this conditioning with middle-class people of all races and that I can no more easily be free of it than I can be free of my race. Whether all this got started because the black middle class modeled itself on the white middle class is no longer relevant. For the middle-class black, conditioned by these values from birth, the sense of meaning they provide is as immutable as the color of his skin.

I started the sixties in high school feeling that my class-conditioning [19] was the surest way to overcome racial barriers. My racial identity was pretty much taken for granted. After all, it was obvious to the world that I was black. Yet I ended the sixties in graduate school a little embarrassed by my class background and with an almost desperate need to be "black." The tables had turned. I knew very clearly (though I struggled to repress it) that my aspirations and my sense of how to operate in the world came from my class background, yet "being black" required certain attitudes and stances that made me feel secretly a little duplicitous. The inner compatibility of class and race I had known in 1960 was gone.

For blacks, the decade between 1960 and 1969 saw racial identifica- [20] tion undergo the same sort of transformation that national identity undergoes in times of war. It became more self-conscious, more narrowly focused, more prescribed, less tolerant of opposition. It spawned an implicit party line, which tended to disallow competing forms of identity. Race-as-identity was lifted from the relative slumber it knew in the fifties and pressed into service in a social and political war against oppression. It was redefined along sharp adversarial lines and directed toward the goal of mobilizing the great mass of black Americans in this warlike effort. It was imbued with a strong moral authority, useful for denouncing those who opposed it and for celebrating those who honored it as a positive achievement rather than as a mere birthright.

The form of racial identification that quickly evolved to meet this [21] challenge presented blacks as a racial monolith, a singular people with a common experience of oppression. Differences within the race, no matter how ineradicable, had to be minimized. Class distinctions were one of the first such differences to be sacrificed, since they not only threatened racial unity but also seemed to stand in contradiction to the principle of equality which was the announced goal of the movement for racial progress. The discomfort I felt in 1969, the vague but relentless sense of duplicity, was the result of a historical necessity that put my race and class at odds, that was asking me to cast aside the distinction of my class and identify with a monolithic view of my race.

If the form of this racial identity was the monolith, its substance was [22] victimization. The civil rights movement and the more radical splinter groups of the late sixties were all dedicated to ending racial victimization, and the form of black identity that emerged to facilitate this goal made blackness and victimization virtually synonymous. Since it was our victimization more than any other variable that identified and unified us, moreover, it followed logically that the purest black was the poor black. It was images of him that clustered around the positive pole of the race polarity; all other blacks were, in effect, required to identify with him in order to confirm their own blackness.

Certainly there were more dimensions to the black experience than [23] victimization, but no other had the same capacity to fire the indignation needed for war. So, again out of historical necessity, victimization became the overriding focus of racial identity. But this only deepened the double bind for middle-class blacks like me. When it came to class we were accustomed to defining ourselves against lower-class blacks and identifying with at least the values of middle-class whites; when it came to race we were now being asked to identify with images of lower-class blacks and to see whites, middle class or otherwise, as victimizers. Negative lining up with positive, we were called upon to reject what we had previously embraced and to embrace what we had previously rejected. To put it still more personally, the Sam figure I had been raised to define myself against had now become the "real" black I was expected to identify with.

The fact that the poor black's new status was only passively earned [24] by the condition of his victimization, not by assertive, positive action, made little difference. Status was status apart from the means by which it was achieved, and along with it came a certain power—the power to define the terms of access to that status, to say who was black and who was not. If a lower-class black said you were not really "black"—a sellout, an Uncle Tom—the judgment was all the more devastating because it carried the authority of his status. And this judgment soon enough came to be accepted by many whites as well.

In graduate school I was once told by a white professor, "Well, but [25] . . . you're not really black. I mean, you're not disadvantaged." In his mind my lack of victim status disqualified me from the race itself. More recently I was complimented by a black student for speaking reasonably correct English, "proper" English as he put it. "But I don't know if I really want to talk like that," he went on. "Why not?" I asked.

"Because then I wouldn't be black no more," he replied without a pause.

To overcome his marginal status, the middle-class black had to iden- 26
tify with a degree of victimization that was beyond his actual experience. In college (and well beyond) we used to play a game called "nap
matching." It was a game of one-upmanship, in which we sat around
outdoing each other with stories of racial victimization, symbolically
measured by the naps of our hair. Most of us were middle class and so
had few personal stories to relate, but if we could not match naps with
our own biographies, we would move on to those legendary tales of victimization that came to us from the public domain.

The single story that sat atop the pinnacle of racial victimization for 27
us was that of Emmett Till, the Northern black teenager who, on a visit
to the South in 1955, was killed and grotesquely mutilated for supposedly looking at or whistling at (we were never sure which, though we
argued the point endlessly) a white woman. Oh, how we probed his
story, finding in his youth and Northern upbringing the quintessential
embodiment of black innocence, brought down by a white evil so por-
tentous and apocalyptic, so gnarled and hideous, that it left us with a
feeling not far from awe. By telling his story and others like it, we came
to *feel* the immutability of our victimization, its utter indigenousness, as
a thing on this earth like dirt or sand or water.

Of course, these sessions were a ritual of group identification, a 28
means by which we, as middle-class blacks, could be at one with our
race. But why were we, who had only a moderate experience of victimization (and that offset by opportunities our parents never had), so intent on assimilating or appropriating an identity that in so many ways
contradicted our own? Because, I think, the sense of innocence that is always entailed in feeling victimized filled us with a corresponding feeling of entitlement, or even license, that helped us endure our vulnerability on a largely white college campus.

In my junior year in college I rode to a debate tournament with three 29
white students and our faculty coach, an elderly English professor. The
experience of being the lone black in a group of whites was so familiar
to me that I thought nothing of it as our trip began. But then halfway
through the trip the professor casually turned to me and, in an isn't-the-
world-funny sort of tone, said that he had just refused to rent an apartment in a house he owned to a "very nice" black couple because their
color would "offend" the white couple who lived downstairs. His eyebrows lifted helplessly over his hawkish nose, suggesting that he too,
like me, was a victim of America's racial farce. His look assumed a kind
of comradeship: he and I were above this grimy business of race, though
for expediency we had occasionally to concede the world its madness.

My vulnerability in this situation came not so much from the pro- 30
fessor's blindness to his own racism as from his assumption that I would

participate in it, that I would conspire with him against my own race so that he might remain comfortably blind. Why did he think I would be amenable to this? I can only guess that he assumed my middle-class identity was so complete and all-encompassing that I would see his action as nothing more than a trifling concession to the folkways of our land, that I would in fact applaud his decision not to disturb propriety. Blind to both his own racism and to me—one blindness serving the other—he could not recognize that he was asking me to betray my race in the name of my class.

His blindness made me feel vulnerable because it threatened to expose my own repressed ambivalence. His comment pressured me to choose between my class identification, which had contributed to my being a college student and a member of the debating team, and my desperate desire to be "black." I could have one but not both; I was double-bound. [31]

Because double binds are repressed there is always an element of terror in them: the terror of bringing to the conscious mind the buried duplicity, self-deception, and pretense involved in serving two masters. This terror is the stuff of vulnerability, and since vulnerability is one of the least tolerable of all human feelings, we usually transform it into an emotion that seems to restore the control of which it has robbed us; most often, that emotion is anger. And so, before the professor had even finished his little story, I had become a furnace of rage. The year was 1967, and I had been primed by endless hours of nap-matching to feel, at least consciously, completely at one with the victim-focused black identity. This identity gave me the license, and the impunity, to unleash upon this professor one of those volcanic eruptions of racial indignation familiar to us from the novels of Richard Wright. Like Cross Damon in *Outsider*, who kills in perfectly righteous anger, I tried to annihilate the man. I punished him not according to the measure of his crime but according to the measure of my vulnerability, a measure set by the cumulative tension of years of repressed terror. Soon I saw that terror in *his* face, as he stared hollow-eyed at the road ahead. My white friends in the back seat, knowing no conflict between their own class and race, were astonished that someone they had taken to be so much like themselves could harbor a rage that for all the world looked murderous. [32]

Though my rage was triggered by the professor's comment, it was deepened and sustained by a complex of need, conflict, and repression in myself of which I had been wholly unaware. Out of my racial vulnerability I had developed the strong need of an identity with which to defend myself. The only such identity available was that of me as victim, him as victimizer. Once in the grip of this paradigm, I began to do far more damage to myself than he had done. [33]

Seeing myself as a victim meant that I clung all the harder to my racial identity, which, in turn, meant that I suppressed my class identi- [34]

ty. This cut me off from all the resources my class values might have offered me. In those values, for instance, I might have found the means to a more dispassionate response, the response less of a victim attacked by a victimizer than of an individual offended by a foolish old man. As an individual I might have reported this professor to the college dean. Or I might have calmly tried to reveal his blindness to him, and possibly won a convert. (The flagrancy of his remark suggested a hidden guilt and even self-recognition on which I might have capitalized. Doesn't confession usually signal a willingness to face oneself?) Or I might have simply chuckled and then let my silence serve as an answer to his provocation. Would not my composure, in any form it might take, deflect into his own heart the arrow he'd shot at me?

Instead, my anger, itself the hair-trigger expression of a long-re- 35 pressed double bind, not only cut me off from the best of my own resources, it also distorted the nature of my true racial problem. The righteousness of this anger and the easy catharsis[2] it brought buoyed the delusion of my victimization and left me as blind as the professor himself.

As a middle-class black I have often felt myself *contriving* to be 36 "black." And I have noticed this same contrivance in others—a certain stretching away from the natural flow of one's life to align oneself with a victim-focused black identity. Our particular needs are out of sync with the form of identity available to meet those needs. Middle-class blacks need to identify racially; it is better to think of ourselves as black and victimized than not black at all; so we contrive (more unconsciously than consciously) to fit ourselves into an identity that denies our class and fails to address the true source of our vulnerability.

For me this once meant spending inordinate amounts of time at 37 black faculty meetings, though these meetings had little to do with my real racial anxieties or my professional life. I was new to the university, one of two blacks in an English department of over seventy, and I felt a little isolated and vulnerable, though I did not admit it to myself. But at these meetings we discussed the problems of black faculty and students within a framework of victimization. The real vulnerability we felt was covered over by all the adversarial drama the victim/victimizer polarity inspired, and hence went unseen and unassuaged. And this, I think, explains our rather chronic ineffectiveness as a group. Since victimization was not our primary problem—the university had long ago opened its doors to us—we had to contrive to make it so, and there is not much energy in contrivance. What I got at these meetings was ultimately an object lesson in how fruitless struggle can be when it is not grounded in actual need.

---

[2] Intense emotional release. [Eds.]

At our black faculty meetings, the old equation of blackness with [38] victimization was ever present—to be black was to be a victim; therefore, not to be a victim was not to be black. As we contrived to meet the terms of this formula there was an inevitable distortion of both ourselves and the larger university. Through the prism of victimization the university seemed more impenetrable than it actually was, and we more limited in our powers. We fell prey to the victim's myopia, making the university an institution from which we could seek redress but which we could never fully join. And this mind-set often led us to look more for compensations for our supposed victimization than for opportunities we could pursue as individuals.

The discomfort and vulnerability felt by middle-class blacks in the [39] sixties, it could be argued, was a worthwhile price to pay considering the progress achieved during that time of racial confrontation. But what may have been tolerable then is intolerable now. Though changes in American society have made it an anachronism, the monolithic form of racial identification that came out of the sixties is still very much with us. It may be more loosely held, and its power to punish heretics has probably diminished, but it continues to catch middle-class blacks in a double bind, thus impeding not only their own advancement but even, I would contend, that of blacks as a group.

The victim-focused black identity encourages the individual to feel [40] that his advancement depends almost entirely on that of the group. Thus he loses sight not only of his own possibilities but of the inextricable connection between individual effort and individual advancement. This is a profound encumbrance today, when there is more opportunity for blacks than ever before, for it reimposes limitations that can have the same oppressive effect as those the society has only recently begun to remove.

It was the emphasis on mass action in the sixties that made the vic- [41] tim-focused black identity a necessity. But in the eighties and beyond, when racial advancement will come only through a multitude of individual advancements, this form of identity inadvertently adds itself to the forces that hold us back. Hard work, education, individual initiative, stable family life, property ownership—these have always been the means by which ethnic groups have moved ahead in America. Regardless of past or present victimization, these "laws" of advancement apply absolutely to black Americans also. There is no getting around this. What we need is a form of racial identity that energizes the individual by putting him in touch with both his possibilities and his responsibilities.

It has always annoyed me to hear from the mouths of certain ar- [42] biters of blackness that middle-class blacks should "reach back" and pull up those blacks less fortunate than they—as though middle-class status were an unearned and essentially passive condition in which one needed a large measure of noblesse oblige to occupy one's time. My own image is of reaching back from a moving train to lift on board those who have no tickets. A noble enough sentiment—but might it not be wiser to show them the entire structure of principles, effort, and sacrifice that puts one in a position to buy a ticket any time one likes? This, I think, is something members of the black middle class can realistically offer to other blacks. Their example is not only a testament to possibility but also a lesson in method. But they cannot lead by example until they are released from a black identity that regards that example as suspect, that sees them as "marginally" black, indeed that holds *them* back by catching them in a double bind.

To move beyond the victim-focused black identity we must learn to 43 make a difficult but crucial distinction: between actual victimization, which we must resist with every resource, and identification with the victim's status. Until we do this we will continue to wrestle more with ourselves than with the new opportunities which so many paid so dearly to win.

Responding to Reading

1. Steele believes he has achieved middle-class status in economic and educational terms. Do you think he is correct, or do you agree with his friend that the term *black middle class* is a contradiction in terms?
2. Have you ever experienced a similar conflict between class and racial or ethnic identity? If so, what did you do?
3. A May 30, 1990 *New York Times* article portrays Steele as a controversial figure: "To many whites and conservative blacks, Mr. Steele has given eloquent voice to painful truths that are almost always left unspoken in the nation's circumscribed public discourse on race. To many black politicians and civil rights figures, he is a turncoat, a privileged black man whose visibility and success stem from his ability to say precisely what white America most wants to hear." With whom do you agree? Why?

CHILDREN OF AFFLUENCE

Robert Coles

Robert Coles (1929–) has been involved in social reform since the 1960s and is best known for his five-volume study of children and poverty, *Children of Crisis* (1967–1978), which won a Pulitzer Prize in 1973. Coles, a professor of psychiatry at the Harvard Medical School, has written about child psychology, civil rights, and literature. His recent books include *The Spiritual Life of Children* (1990), a bestseller, and *The Call of Service: A Witness to Idealism* (1993). In "Children of Affluence," excerpted from *Children of Crisis,* Coles analyzes the effects of affluence on the young by presenting their words and experiences and then interpreting these in a social and psychological context.

It won't do to talk of *the* affluent in America. It won't do to say that in our upper-middle-class suburbs, or among our wealthy, one observes clear-cut, consistent psychological or cultural characteristics. Even in relatively homogeneous places there are substantial differences in home-life, in values taught, hobbies encouraged, beliefs advocated or sometimes virtually instilled. But it is the obligation of a psychological observer like me, who wants to know how children make sense of a certain kind of life, to document as faithfully as possible the way a common heritage of money and power affects the assumptions of particular boys and girls.   1

I started my work with affluent children by seeing troubled boys and girls; they were the ones I saw as a child psychiatrist *before* I began my years of "field work" in the South, then Appalachia, then the North, then the West. There are only a few hundred child psychiatrists in the United States, and often their time is claimed by those who have money. After a while, if one is not careful, the well-off and the rich come to be seen exclusively through a clinician's eye: homes full of bitterness, deceit, snobbishness, neuroses, psychoses; homes with young children in mental pain, and with older children, adolescents and young adults, who use drugs, drink, run away, rebel constantly and disruptively, become truants, delinquents, addicts, alcoholics, become compulsively promiscuous, go crazy, go wild, go to ruin.   2

We blame the alcoholism, insanity, meanness, apathy, drug usage, despondency, and, not least, cruelty to children we see or are told exists in the ghetto or among the rural poor upon various "socio-economic factors." All of those signs of psychological deterioration can be found among quite privileged families, too—and so we remind ourselves, perhaps, that wealth corrupts.   3

No—it is not that simple. Wealth does not corrupt nor does it ennoble. But wealth does govern the minds of privileged children, gives them a peculiar kind of identity which they never lose, whether they grow up to be stockbrokers or communards,[1] and whether they lead healthy or unstable lives. There is, I think, a message that virtually all quite well-off American families transmit to their children—an emotional expression of those familiar, classbound prerogatives, money and power. I use the word "entitlement" to describe that message.   4

---

[1] People who live in communes. [Eds.]

The word was given to me by the rather rich parents of a child I ⁵ began to talk with almost two decades ago, in 1959. I have watched those parents become grandparents, and have seen what they described as "the responsibilities of entitlement" handed down to a new generation. When the father, a lawyer and stockbroker from a prominent and quietly influential family, referred to the "entitlement" his children were growing up to know, he had in mind a social rather than a psychological phenomenon: the various juries or committees that select the Mardi Gras participants in New Orlean's annual parade and celebration. He knew that his daughter was "entitled" to be invited.

He wanted, however, to go beyond that social fact. He talked about ⁶ what he had received from his parents and what he would give to his children, "automatically, without any thought," and what they too would pass on. The father was careful to distinguish between the social entitlement and "something else," a "something else" he couldn't quite define but knew he had to try to evoke if he was to be psychologically candid: "I mean they should be responsible, and try to live up to their ideals, and not just sit around wondering which island in the Caribbean to visit this year, and where to go next summer to get away from the heat and humidity here in New Orleans."

He was worried about what a lot of money can do to a personality. ⁷ When his young daughter, during a Mardi Gras season, kept *assuming* she would one day become a Mardi Gras queen, he realized that his notion of "entitlement" was not quite hers. Noblesse oblige² requires a gesture toward others.

He was not the only parent to express such a concern to me in the ⁸ course of my work. In homes where mothers and fathers profess no explicit reformist persuasions, they nevertheless worry about what happens to children who grow up surrounded by just about everything they want, virtually on demand. "When they're like that, they've gone from spoiled to spoiled rotten—and beyond, to some state I don't know how to describe."

Obviously, it is possible for parents to have a lot of money yet avoid ⁹ bringing up their children in such a way that they feel like members of a royal family. But even parents determined not to spoil their children often recognize what might be called the existential (as opposed to strictly psychological) aspects of their situation. A father may begin rather early on lecturing his children about the meaning of money; a mother may do her share by saying no, even when yes is so easy to say. And a child, by the age of five or six, has very definite notions of what is possible, even if it is not always permitted. That child, in conversation, and without embarrassment or the kind of reticence and secretiveness that

---

² The obligation of the "nobility" to be generous to those less well-off. [Eds.]

come later, may reveal a substantial knowledge of economic affairs. A six-year-old girl I spoke to knew that she would, at twenty-one, inherit half a million dollars. She also knew that her father "only" gave her twenty-five cents a week, whereas some friends of hers received as much as a dollar. She was vexed; she asked her parents why they were so "strict." One friend had even used the word "stingy" for the parents. The father, in a matter-of-fact way, pointed out to the daughter that she did, after all, get "anything she really wants." Why, then, the need for an extravagant allowance? The girl was won over. But admonitions don't always modify the quite realistic appraisal children make of what they are heir to; and they don't diminish their sense of entitlement—a state of mind that pervades their view of the world.

In an Appalachian[3] home, for instance, a boy of seven made the [10] following comment in 1963, after a mine his father owned had suffered an explosion, killing two men and injuring seriously nine others: "I heard my mother saying she felt sorry for the families of the miners. I feel sorry for them, too. I hope the men who got hurt get better. I'm sure they will. My father has called in doctors from Lexington. He wants the best doctors in all Kentucky for those miners. Daddy says it was the miners' fault; they get careless, and the next thing you know, there's an explosion. It's too bad. I guess there are a lot of kids who are praying hard for their fathers. I wish God was nice to everyone. He's been very good to us. My daddy says it's been hard work, running the mine, and another one he has. It's just as hard to run a mine as it is to go down and dig the coal! I'm glad my father is the owner, though. I wouldn't want him to get killed or hurt bad down there, way underground. Daddy has given us a good life. We have a lot of fun coming up, he says, in the next few years. We're going on some trips. Daddy deserves his vacations. He says he's happy because he can keep us happy, and he does."

Abundance is this boy's destiny, he has every reason to believe, [11] abundance and limitless possibility. He may even land on the stars. Certainly he has traveled widely in this country. He associates the seasons with travel. In winter, there is a trip south, to one or another Caribbean island. He worries, on these trips, about his two dogs, and the other animals—the guinea pigs, hamsters, rabbits, chickens. There is always someone in the house, a maid, a handyman. Still it is sad to say goodbye. Now if the family owned a plane, the animals could come along on those trips!

The boy doesn't really believe that his father will ever own a Lear jet; [12] yet he can construct a fantasy: "I had this dream. In it I was walking through the woods with Daddy, and all of a sudden there was an open

---

[3] Appalachia is a mountainous region of the eastern United States known for its impoverished rural communities. [Eds.]

field, and I looked, and I saw a hawk, and it was circling and circling. I like going hunting with Daddy, and I thought we were hunting. But when I looked at him, he didn't have his gun. Then he pointed at the hawk, and it was coming down. It landed ahead of us, and it was real strange—because the hawk turned into an airplane! I couldn't believe it. We went toward the plane, and Daddy said we could get a ride anytime we wanted, because it was ours; he'd just bought it. That's when I woke up, I think."

Four years after the boy dreamed that his father owned a plane, the father got one. The boom of the 1970s in the coal fields made his father even richer. The boy was, of course, eager to go on flying trips; eager, also, to learn to fly. At thirteen, he dreamed (by day) of becoming an astronaut, or of going to the Air Force Academy and afterwards becoming a "supersonic pilot." [13]

He would never become a commercial pilot, however; and his reasons were interesting. "I've gone on a lot of commercial flights, and there are a lot of people on board, and the pilot has to be nice to everyone, and he makes all these announcements about the seat belts, and stuff like that. My dad's pilot was in the Air Force, and then he flew commercial. He was glad to get out, though. He says you have to be like a waiter; you have to answer complaints from the customers, and apologize to them, just because the ride gets bumpy. It's best to work for yourself, or work for another person, if you trust him and like him. If you go commercial, like our pilot says, you're a servant." [14]

Many of the children I have worked with are similarly disposed; they do not like large groups of people in public places—in fact, have been taught the value not only of privacy but of the quiet that goes with being relatively alone. Some of the children are afraid of those crowds, can't imagine how it would be possible to survive them. Of course, what is strange, unknown, or portrayed as unattractive, uncomfortable, or just to be avoided as a nuisance can for a given child become a source of curiosity, like an event to be experienced at all costs. An eight-year-old girl who lived on a farm well outside Boston wanted desperately to go to the city and see Santa Claus—not because she believed in him, but because she wanted to see "those crowds" she had seen on television. She got her wish, was excited at first, then became quite disappointed, and ultimately uncomfortable. She didn't like being jostled, shoved, and ignored when she protested. [15]

A week after the girl had gone through her Boston "adventure" (as she had called the trip *before* she embarked upon it), each student in her third-grade class was asked to draw a picture in some way connected to the Christmas season, and the girl obliged eagerly. She drew Santa Claus standing beside a pile of packages, presents for the many children who stood near him. They blended into one another—a mob scene. Watching them but removed from them was one child, bigger and on a high- [16]

er level—suspended in space, it seemed, and partially surrounded by a thin but visible line. The girl wrote on the bottom of the drawing, "I saw Santa Claus." She made it quite clear what she had intended to portray. "He was standing there, handing out these gifts. They were all the same, I think, and they were plastic squirt guns for the boys and little dolls for the girls. I felt sorry for the kids. I asked my mother why kids wanted to push each other, just to get that junk. My mother said a lot of people just don't know any better. I was going to force my way up to Santa Claus and tell him to stop being so dumb! My mother said he was probably a drunk, trying to make a few dollars so he could spend it in a bar that evening! I don't want to be in a store like that again. We went up to a balcony and watched, and then we got out of the place and came home. I told my mother that I didn't care if I ever went to Boston again. I have two friends, and they've never been to Boston, and they don't want to go there, except to ride through on the way to the airport."

She sounded at that moment more aloof, condescending, and snob- [17] bish than she ordinarily is. She spends her time with two or three girls who live on nearby estates. Those girls don't see each other regularly, and each of them is quite able to be alone—in fact, rather anxious for those times of solitude. Sometimes a day or two goes by with no formal arrangement to play. They meet in school, and that seems to be enough. Each girl has obligations—a horse to groom, a stall to work on. They are quite "self-sufficient," a word they have heard used repeatedly by their parents. Even with one's own social circle there is no point surrendering to excessive gregariousness!

Once up on her own horse, she is (by her own description) in her [18] "own world." She has heard her mother use that expression. The mother is not boasting, or dismissing others who live in other worlds. The mother is describing, as does the child, a state of progressive withdrawal from people, and the familiar routines or objects of the environment, in favor of a mixture of reverie and disciplined activity.

Nothing seems impossible, burdensome, difficult. There are no dis- [19] tractions, petty or boring details to attend to. And one is closer to one's "self." The mother talks about the "self," and the child does, too. "It is strange," the girl comments, "because you forget yourself riding or skiing, but you also remember yourself the way you don't when you're just sitting around watching television or reading or playing in your room."

None of the other American children I have worked with have [20] placed such a continuous and strong emphasis on the "self"—its display, its possibilities, its cultivation and development, even the repeated use of the word *self*. A ten-year-old boy who lived in Westchester County[4] made this very clear. I met him originally because his parents were lawyers, and active in the civil rights movement. His father, a pa-

---

[4] Region of wealthy suburban communities north of New York City. [Eds.]

trician Yankee, very much endorsed the students who went south in the early 1960s, and worked on behalf of integrated schools up north. The boy, however, attended private schools—a source of anguish to both father and son, who do not lend themselves to a description that suggests hypocrisy.

The boy knew that he, also, *would* be (as opposed to *wanted* to be)   21 a lawyer. He was quick to perceive and acknowledge his situation, and as he did so, he brought his "self" right into the discussion: "I don't want to tell other kids what to do. I told my father I should be going to the public schools myself. Then I could say anything. Then I could ask why we don't have black kids with us in school. But you have to try to do what's best for your own life, even if you can't speak up for the black people. When I'm grown up I'll be like my father; I'll help the black people all I can. It's this way: first you build *yourself* up. You learn all you can. Later, you can *give of yourself.* That's what Dad says: you can't help others until you've learned to help yourself. It's not that you're being selfish, if you're going to a private school and your parents have a lot of money. We had a maid here, and she wasn't right in the head. She lost her temper and told Daddy that he's a phony, and he's out for himself and no one else, and the same goes for my sister and me. Then she quit. Daddy tried to get her to talk with us, but she wouldn't. She said that's all we ever do—talk, talk. I told Daddy she was contradicting herself, because she told me a few weeks ago that I'm always doing something, and I should sit down and talk with her. But I don't know what to say to her! I think she got angry with me, because I was putting on my skis, for cross-country skiing, and she said I had too much, that was my problem. I asked her where the regular skis were, and she said she wouldn't tell me, even if she knew! It's too bad, what happened to her.

"I feel sorry for her, though. It's not fun to be a maid. The poor   22 woman doesn't look very good. She weighs too much. She's only forty, my mother thinks, but she looks as if she's sixty, and is sick. She should take better care of herself. Now she's thrown away this job, and she told my mother last year that it was the best one she'd ever had, so she's her own worst enemy. I wonder what she'll think when she looks at herself in the mirror."

This boy was no budding egotist. If anything, he was less self-cen-   23 tered at ten than many other children of his community and others like it. He was willing to think about those less fortunate than himself—the maid, and black people in general. True, he would often repeat uncritically his father's words, or a version of them. But he was trying to respond to his father's wishes and beliefs as well as his words. It was impossible for him, no matter how compassionate his nature, to conceive of life as others live it—the maid and, yes, millions of children his age, who don't look in the mirror very often, and may not even own one;

who don't worry about how one looks, and what is said, and how one sounds, and how one smells.

It is important that a child's sense of entitlement be distinguished [24] not only from the psychiatric dangers of narcissism but from the less pathological and not all that uncommon phenomenon known as being "spoiled." It is a matter of degree; "spoiled" children are self-centered all right, petulant and demanding—but not as grandiose or, alas, saddled with illusions (or delusions) as the children clinicians have in mind when using the phrase "narcissistic entitlement." The rich or quite well-to-do are all too commonly charged with producing spoiled children. Yet one sees spoiled children everywhere, among the very poor as well as the inordinately rich.

In one of the first wealthy families I came to know there was a girl [25] who was described by both parents as "spoiled." At the time, I fear, I was ready to pronounce every child in New Orleans's Garden District spoiled. Were they not all living comfortable, indeed luxurious, lives, as compared to the lives of the black or working-class white children I was getting to know in other sections of that city?

Nevertheless, I soon began to realize that it wouldn't do to charac- [26] terize without qualification one set of children as spoiled, by virtue of their social and economic background, as against another set of children who were obviously less fortunate in many respects. One meets, among the rich, restrained, disciplined, and by no means indulged children; sometimes, even, boys and girls who have learned to be remarkably self-critical, even ascetic—anything but "spoiled" in the conventional sense of the word. True, one can find a touch and more of arrogance, or at least sustained self-assurance, in those apparently spartan boys and girls who seem quite anxious to deny themselves all sorts of presumably accessible privileges if not luxuries. But one also finds in these children a consistent willingness to place serious and not always pleasant burdens on themselves—to the point where they often struck me, when I came to their homes fresh from visits with much poorer age-mates, as remarkably *less* spoiled: not so much whining or crying; fewer demands for candy or other sweets; even, sometimes, a relative indifference to toys, however near at hand and expensive they may have been; a disregard of television—so often demanded by the children that I was seeing.

A New Orleans black woman said to me in 1961: "I don't know how [27] to figure out these rich white kids. They're something! I used to think, before I took a job with this family, that the only difference between a rich kid and a poor kid is that the rich kid knows he has a lot of money and he grows up and becomes spoiled rotten. That's what my mother told me; she took care of a white girl, and the girl was an only child, and her father owned a department store in McComb, Mississippi, and that girl thought she was God's special creature. My mother used to come home and tell us about the 'little princess;' but she turned out to be no good. She was so pampered, she couldn't do a thing for herself. All she knew how to do was order people around.

"It's different with these two children. I've never seen such a boy [28] and such a girl. They think they're the best ones who ever lived—like that girl in McComb—but they don't behave like her. They're never asking me to do much of anything. They even ask if they can help me! They tell me that they want to know how to do everything. The girl says she wants to learn how to run the washing machine and the dishwasher. She says she wants to learn all my secret recipes. She says she'd like to give the best parties in the Garden District when she grows up, and she'd like to be able to give them without anyone's help. She says I could serve the food, but she would like to make it. The boy says he's going to be a lawyer and a banker, so he wants to know how much everything costs. He doesn't want to waste anything. He'll see me throw something away, and he wants to know why. I only wish that my own kids were like him!

"But these children here are special, and don't they know it! That's [29] what being rich is: you know you're different from most people. These two kids act as if they're going to be tops in everything, and they're pleased as can be with themselves, because there is nothing they can't do, and there's nothing they can't get, and there's nothing they can't win, and they're always showing off what they can do, and then before you can tell them how good they are, they're telling the same thing to themselves. It's confusing! They're not spoiled one bit, but oh, they have a high opinion of themselves!"

Actually, children like the ones she speaks of don't allow themselves [30] quite the unqualified confidence she describes, though she certainly has correctly conveyed the appearance they give. Boys and girls may seem without anxiety or self-doubt; they have been brought up, as the maid suggests, to feel important, superior, destined for a satisfying, rewarding life—and at, say, eight or nine they already appear to know all that. Yet there are moments of hesitation, if not apprehension. An eleven-year-old boy from a prominent and quite brilliant Massachusetts family told his teachers, in an autobiographical composition about the vicissitudes[5] of "entitlement": "I don't always do everything right. I'd like to be able to say I don't make any mistakes, but I do, and when I do, I feel bad. My father and mother say that if you train yourself, you can be right *almost* 100 percent of the time. Even they make mistakes, though. I like to be first in sports. I like to beat my brothers at skiing. But I don't always go down the slopes as fast as I could and I sometimes fall down. Last year I broke my leg. When I get a bad cold, I feel disappointed in myself. I don't think it's right to be easy on yourself. If you are, then you

---

[5] Difficulties or problems. [Eds.]

slip back, and you don't get a lot of the rewards in life. If you really work for the rewards, you'll get them."

A platitude—the kind of assurance his teachers, as a matter of fact, [31] have rather often given him. In the fourth grade, for instance, the teacher had this written on the blackboard (and kept it there for weeks): "Those who want something badly enough get it, provided they are willing to wait and work." The boy considers that assertion neither banal nor unrealistic. He has been brought up to believe that such is and will be (for him) the case. He knows that others are not so lucky, but he hasn't really met those "others," and they don't cross his mind at all. What does occur to him sometimes is the need for constant exertion, lest he fail to "measure up." One "measures up" when one tries hard and succeeds. If one slackens or stumbles, one ought to be firm with oneself—but not in any self-pitying or self-excusing or self-paralyzing way. The emphasis is on a quick and efficient moment of scrutiny followed by "a fast pick-up."

Such counsel is not as callous as it may sound—or, ironically, as it [32] may well have been intended to sound. The child who hears it gets, briefly, upset; but unless he or she stops heeding what has been said, quite often "a fast pick-up" does indeed take place—an effort to redeem what has been missed or lost, or only somewhat accomplished. Again, it is a matter of feeling entitled. A child who has been told repeatedly that all he or she needs to do is try hard does not feel inclined to allow himself or herself long stretches of time for skeptical self-examination. The point is to feel *entitled*—then act upon that feeling. The boy whose composition was just quoted from used the word "entitled" in another essay he wrote, this one meant to be a description of his younger (age five) brother. The writing was not, however, without an autobiographical strain to it: "I was watching my brother from my bedroom window. He was climbing up the fence we built for our corral. He got to the top, and then he just stood there and waved and shouted. No one was there. He was talking to himself. He was very happy. Then he would fall. He would be upset for a few seconds, but he would climb right back up again. Then he would be even happier! He was entitled to be happy. It is his fence, and he has learned to climb it, and stay up, and balance himself."

Responding to Reading

1. Does Coles believe that the message affluent families convey to their children—what he calls "entitlement"—is a privilege or a burden? Which do you believe it is? Why? Do you think you and your friends have this sense of entitlement? Explain.

2. The attitudes of affluent children toward their futures are very different

from the attitudes of their poorer counterparts. Have your attitudes about your future have been shaped by your economic status? If so, how?
3. Do you think the affluent children Coles describes are likely to make a valuable contribution to the world in which they live? Explain your conclusion.

ON DUMPSTER DIVING

Lars Eighner

When Lars Eighner (1948–) was eighteen years old, his mother threw him out of her house because she found out he was gay. Then a student at the University of Texas at Austin, Eighner began a series of part-time and dead-end jobs that ended in 1988 when he was fired from his position at an Austin mental hospital and soon after evicted from his apartment. At that point he headed for Los Angeles, spending three years homeless on the streets, shuttling between California and Texas with Lizbeth, his Labrador retriever. During his travels, he began to keep a journal, and these entries, along with letters he wrote to a friend, resulted in the remarkable document *Travels with Lizbeth: Three Years on the Road and on the Streets* (1993), portions of which were published previously in several different magazines and journals. In the following chapter from that book, originally published in *The Threepenny Review* in 1991, Eighner takes readers on a graphic yet lyrical voyage through the process of scavenging Dumpsters for food and other necessities.

This chapter was composed while the author was homeless. The present tense has been preserved.

Long before I began Dumpster diving I was impressed with [1] Dumpsters, enough so that I wrote the Merriam-Webster research service to discover what I could about the word *Dumpster*. I learned from them that it is a proprietary word belonging to the Dempsey Dumpster company. Since then I have dutifully capitalized the word, although it was lowercased in almost all the citations Merriam-Webster photocopied for me. Dempsey's word is too apt. I have never heard these things called anything but Dumpsters. I do not know anyone who knows the generic name for these objects. From time to time I have heard a wino or hobo give some corrupted credit to the original and call them Dipsy Dumpsters.

I began Dumpster diving about a year before I became homeless.   2

I prefer the word *scavenging* and use the word *scrounging* when I   3
mean to be obscure. I have heard people, evidently meaning to be polite,
use the word *foraging,* but I prefer to reserve that word for gathering
nuts and berries and such which I do also according to the season and
the opportunity. *Dumpster diving* seems to me to be a little too cute and,
in my case, inaccurate because I lack the athletic ability to lower myself
into the Dumpsters as the true divers do, much as their increased profit.

I like the frankness of the word *scavenging,* which I can hardly think   4
of without picturing a big black snail on an aquarium wall. I live from
the refuse of others. I am a scavenger. I think it a sound and honorable
niche, although if I could I would naturally prefer to live the comfortable
consumer life, perhaps—and only perhaps—as a slightly less wasteful
consumer, owing to what I have learned as a scavenger.

While Lizbeth and I were still living in the shack on Avenue B as my   5
savings ran out, I put almost all my sporadic income into rent. The necessities of daily life I began to extract from Dumpsters. Yes, we ate from
them. Except for jeans, all my clothes came from Dumpsters. Boom
boxes, candles, bedding, toilet paper, a virgin male love doll, medicine,
books, a typewriter, dishes, furnishings, and change, sometimes
amounting to many dollars—I acquired many things from the Dumpsters.

I have learned much as a scavenger. I mean to put some of what I   6
have learned down here, beginning with the practical art of Dumpster
diving and proceeding to the abstract.

What is safe to eat?   7

After all, the finding of objects is becoming something of an urban   8
art. Even respectable employed people will sometimes find something
tempting sticking out of a Dumpster or standing beside one. Quite a
number of people, not all of them of the bohemian type, are willing to
brag that they found this or that piece in the trash. But eating from
Dumpsters is what separates the dilettanti from the professionals. Eating safely from the Dumpsters involves three principles: using the senses and common sense to evaluate the conditions of the found materials,
knowing the Dumpsters of a given area and checking them regularly,
and seeking always to answer the question "Why was this discarded?"

Perhaps everyone who has a kitchen and a regular supply of gro-   9
ceries has, at one time or another, made a sandwich and eaten half of it
before discovering mold on the bread or got a mouthful of milk before
realizing the milk had turned. Nothing of the sort is likely to happen to
a Dumpster diver because he is constantly reminded that most food is
discarded for a reason. Yet a lot of perfectly good food can be found in
Dumpsters.

Canned goods, for example, turn up fairly often in the Dumpsters I 10
frequent. All except the most phobic people would be willing to eat from
a can, even if it came from a Dumpster. Canned goods are among the
safest of foods to be found in Dumpsters but are not utterly foolproof.

Although very rare with modern canning methods, botulism is a 11
possibility. Most other forms of food poisoning seldom do lasting harm
to a healthy person, but botulism is most certainly fatal and often the
first symptom is death. Except for carbonated beverages, all canned
goods should contain a slight vacuum and suck air when first punctured. Bulging, rusty, and dented cans and cans that spew when punctured should be avoided, especially when the contents are not very
acidic or syrupy.

Heat can break down the botulin, but this requires much more cook- 12
ing than most people do to canned goods. To the extent that botulism occurs at all, of course, it can occur in cans on pantry shelves as well as in
cans from Dumpsters. Need I say that home-canned goods are simply
too risky to be recommended.

From time to time one of my companions, aware of the source of my 13
provisions, will ask, "Do you think these crackers are really safe to eat?"
For some reason it is most often the crackers they ask about.

This question has always made me angry. Of course I would not 14
offer my companion anything I had doubts about. But more than that, I
wonder why he cannot evaluate the condition of the crackers for himself. I have no special knowledge and I have been wrong before. Since
he knows where the food comes from, it seems to me he ought to assume some of the responsibility for deciding what he will put in his
mouth. For myself I have few qualms about dry foods such as crackers,
cookies, cereal, chips, and pasta if they are free of visible contaminates
and still dry and crisp. Most often such things are found in the original
packaging, which is not so much a positive sign as it is the absence of a
negative one.

Raw fruits and vegetables with intact skins seem perfectly safe to 15
me, excluding of course the obviously rotten. Many are discarded for
minor imperfections that can be pared away. Leafy vegetables, grapes,
cauliflower, broccoli, and similar things may be contaminated by liquids
and may be impractical to wash.

Candy, especially hard candy, is usually safe if it has not drawn 16
ants. Chocolate is often discarded only because it has become discolored
as the cocoa butter de-emulsified. Candying, after all, is one method of
food preservation because pathogens do not like very sugary substances.

All of these foods might be found in any Dumpster and can be eval- 17
uated with some confidence largely on the basis of appearance. Beyond
these are foods that cannot be correctly evaluated without additional information.

I began scavenging by pulling pizzas out of the Dumpster behind a [18] pizza delivery shop. In general, prepared food requires caution, but in this case I knew when the shop closed and went to the Dumpster as soon as the last of the help left.

Such shops often get prank orders; both the orders and the products [19] made to fill them are called *bogus*. Because help seldom stays long at these places, pizzas are often made with the wrong topping, refused on delivery for being cold, or baked incorrectly. The products to be discarded are boxed up because inventory is kept by counting boxes: A boxed pizza can be written off; an unboxed pizza does not exist.

I never placed a bogus order to increase the supply of pizzas and I [20] believe no one else was scavenging in this Dumpster. But the people in the shop became suspicious and began to retain their garbage in the shop overnight. While it lasted I had a steady supply of fresh, sometimes warm pizza. Because I knew the Dumpster I knew the source of the pizza, and because I visited the Dumpster regularly I knew what was fresh and what was yesterday's.

The area I frequent is inhabited by many affluent college students. [21] I am not here by chance; the Dumpsters in this area are very rich. Students throw out many good things, including food. In particular they tend to throw everything out when they move at the end of a semester, before and after breaks, and around midterm, when many of them despair of college. So I find it advantageous to keep an eye on the academic calendar.

Students throw food away around breaks because they do not know [22] whether it has spoiled or will spoil before they return. A typical discard is a half jar of peanut butter. In fact, nonorganic peanut butter does not require refrigeration and is unlikely to spoil in any reasonable time. The student does not know that, and since it is Daddy's money, the student decides not to take a chance. Opened containers require caution and some attention to the question. "Why was this discarded?" But in the case of discards from student apartments, the answer may be that the item was thrown out through carelessness, ignorance, or wastefulness. This can sometimes be deduced when the item is found with many others, including some that are obviously perfectly good.

Some students, and others, approach defrosting a freezer by chuck- [23] ing out the whole lot. Not only do the circumstances of such a find tell the story, but also the mass of frozen goods stays cold for a long time and items may be found still frozen or freshly thawed.

Yogurt, cheese, and sour cream are items that are often thrown out [24] while they are still good. Occasionally I find a cheese with a spot of mold, which of course I just pare off, and because it is obvious why such a cheese was discarded, I treat it with less suspicion than an apparently perfect cheese found in similar circumstances. Yogurt is often discarded, still sealed, only because the expiration date on the carton had passed. This is one of my favorite finds because yogurt will keep for several days, even in warm weather.

Students throw out canned goods and staples at the end of semesters and when they give up college at midterm. Drugs, pornography, spirits, and the like are often discarded when parents are expected—Dad's day, for example. And spirits also turn up after big party weekends, presumably discarded by the newly reformed. Wine and spirits, of course, keep perfectly well even once opened, but the same cannot be said of beer.

My test for carbonated soft drinks is whether they still fizz vigorously. Many juices or other beverages are too acidic or too syrupy to cause much concern, provided they are not visibly contaminated. I have discovered nasty molds in vegetable juices, even when the product was found under its original seal; I recommend that such products be decanted slowly into a clear glass. Liquids always require some care. One hot day I found a large jug of Pat O'Brien's Hurricane mix. The jug had been opened, but it was still ice cold. I drank three large glasses before it became apparent to me that someone had added the rum to the mix, and not a little rum. I never tasted the rum, and by the time I began to feel the effects I had already ingested a very large quantity of the beverage. Some divers would have considered this a boon, but being suddenly intoxicated in a public place in the early afternoon is not my idea of a good time.

I have heard of people maliciously contaminating discarded food and even handouts, but mostly I have heard of this from people with vivid imaginations who have had no experience with the dumpsters themselves. Just before the pizza shop stopped discarding its garbage at night, jalapeños began showing up on most of the discarded pizzas. If indeed this was meant to discourage me it was a wasted effort because I am native Texan.

For myself, I avoid game, poultry, pork, and egg-based foods, whether I find them raw or cooked. I seldom have the means to cook what I find, but when I do I avail myself of plentiful supplies of beef, which is often in very good condition. I suppose fish becomes disagreeable before it becomes dangerous. Lizbeth is happy to have any such thing that is past its prime and, in fact, does not recognize fish as food until it is quite strong.

Home leftovers, as opposed to surpluses from restaurants, are very often bad. Evidently, especially among students, there is a common type of personality that carefully wraps up even the smallest leftover and shoves it into the back of the refrigerator for six months or so before discarding it. Characteristic of this type are the reused jars and margarine tubs to which the remains are committed. I avoid ethnic foods I am unfamiliar with. If I do not know what it is supposed to look like when it is good, I cannot be certain I will be able to tell if it is bad.

No matter how careful I am I still get dysentery at least once a [30] month, oftener in warm weather. I do not want to paint too romantic a picture. Dumpster diving has serious drawbacks as a way of life.

I learned to scavenge gradually, on my own. Since then I have ini- [31] tiated several companions into the trade. I have learned that there is a predictable series of stages a person goes through in learning to scavenge.

At first the new scavenger is filled with disgust and self-loathing. He [32] is ashamed of being seen and may lurk around, trying to duck behind things, or he may try to dive at night. (In fact, most people instinctively look away from a scavenger. By skulking around, the novice calls attention to himself and arouses suspicion. Diving at night is ineffective and needlessly messy.)

Every grain of rice seems to be a maggot. Everything seems to stink. [33] He can wipe the egg yolk off the found can, but he cannot erase from his mind the stigma of eating garbage.

That stage passes with experience. The scavenger finds a pair of run- [34] ning shoes that fit and look and smell brand-new. He finds a pocket calculator in perfect working order. He finds pristine ice cream, still frozen, more than he can eat or keep. He begins to understand: People throw away perfectly good stuff, a lot of perfectly good stuff.

At this stage, Dumpster shyness begins to dissipate. The diver, after [35] all, has the last laugh. He is finding all manner of good things that are his for the taking. Those who disparage his profession are the fools, not he.

He may begin to hang on to some perfectly good things for which [36] he has neither a use nor a market. Then he begins to take note of the things that are not perfectly good but are nearly so. He mates a Walkman with broken earphones and one that is missing a battery cover. He picks up things that he can repair.

At this stage he may become lost and never recover. Dumpsters are [37] full of things of some potential value to someone and also of things that never have much intrinsic value but are interesting. All the Dumpster divers I have known come to the point of trying to acquire everything they touch. Why not take it, they reason, since it is all free? This is, of course, hopeless. Most divers come to realize that they must restrict themselves to items of relatively immediate utility. But in some cases the diver simply cannot control himself. I have met several of these pack-rat types. Their ideas of the values of various pieces of junk verge on the psychotic. Every bit of glass may be a diamond, they think, and all that glisters, gold.

I tend to gain weight when I am scavenging. Partly this is because I [38] always find far more pizza and doughnuts than water-packed tuna, nonfat yogurt, and fresh vegetables. Also I have not developed much faith in the reliability of Dumpsters as a food source, although it has been proven to me many times. I tend to eat as if I have no idea where my next meal is coming from. But mostly I just hate to see food go to waste and so I eat much more than I should. Something like this drives the obsession to collect junk.

As for collecting objects, I usually restrict myself to collecting one [39] kind of small object at a time, such as pocket calculators, sunglasses, or campaign buttons. To live on the street I must anticipate my needs to a certain extent: I must pick up and save warm bedding I find in August because it will not be found in Dumpsters in November. As I have no access to health care, I often hoard essential drugs, such as antibiotics and antihistamines. (This course can be recommended only to those with some grounding in pharmacology. Antibiotics, for example, even when indicated are worse than useless if taken in insufficient amounts.) But even if I had a home with extensive storage space, I could not save everything that might be valuable in some contingency.

I have proprietary feelings about my Dumpsters. As I have men- [40] tioned, it is no accident that I scavenge from ones where good finds are common. But my limited experience with Dumpsters in other areas suggests to me that even in poorer areas, Dumpsters, if attended with sufficient diligence, can be made to yield a livelihood. The rich students discard perfectly good kiwifruit; poorer people discard perfectly good apples. Slacks and Polo shirts are found in the one place; jeans and T-shirts in the other. The population of competitors rather than the affluence of the dumpers most affects the feasibility of survival by scavenging. The large number of competitors is what puts me off the idea of trying to scavenge in places like Los Angeles.

Curiously, I do not mind my direct competition, other scavengers, [41] so much as I hate the can scroungers.

People scrounge cans because they have to have a little cash. I have [42] tried scrounging cans with an able-bodied companion. Afoot a can scrounger simply cannot make more than a few dollars a day. One can extract the necessities of life from the Dumpsters directly with far less effort than would be required to accumulate the equivalent value in cans. (These observations may not hold in places with container redemption laws.)

Can scroungers, then, are people who must have small amounts of [43] cash. These are drug addicts and winos, mostly the latter because the amounts of cash are so small. Spirits and drugs do, like all other commodities, turn up in Dumpsters and the scavenger will from time to time have a half bottle of a rather good wine with his dinner. But the wino cannot survive on these occasional finds; he must have his daily dose to stave off the DTs. All the cans he can carry will buy about three bottles of Wild Irish Rose.

I do not begrudge them the cans, but can scroungers tend to tear [44] up the Dumpsters, mixing the contents and littering the area. They become so specialized that they can see only cans. They earn my contempt by passing up change, canned goods, and readily hockable items.

There are precious few courtesies among scavengers. But it is common practice to set aside surplus items: pairs of shoes, clothing, canned goods, and such. A true scavenger hates to see good stuff go to waste, and what he cannot use he leaves in good condition in plain sight. [45]

Can scroungers lay waste to everything in their path and will stir one of a pair of good shoes to the bottom of a Dumpster, to be lost or ruined in the muck. Can scroungers will even go through individual garbage cans, something I have never seen a scavenger do. [46]

Individual garbage cans are set out on the public easement only on garbage days. On other days going through them requires trespassing close to a dwelling. Going through individual garbage cans without scattering litter is almost impossible. Litter is likely to reduce the public's tolerance of scavenging. Individual cans are simply not as productive as Dumpsters; people in houses and duplexes do not move so often and for some reason do not tend to discard as much useful material. Moreover, the time required to go through one garbage can that serves one household is not much less than the time required to go through a Dumpster that contains the refuse of twenty apartments. [47]

But my strongest reservation about going through individual garbage cans is that this seems to me a very personal kind of invasion to which I would object if I were a householder. Although many things in Dumpsters are obviously meant never to come to light, a Dumpster is somehow less personal. [48]

I avoid trying to draw conclusions about the people who dump in the Dumpsters I frequent. I think it would be unethical to do so, although I know many people will find the idea of scavenger ethics too funny for words. [49]

Dumpsters contain bank statements, correspondence, and other documents, just as anyone might expect. But there are also less obvious sources of information. Pill bottles, for example. The labels bear the name of the patient, the name of the doctor, and the name of the drug. AIDS drugs and antipsychotic medicines, to name but two groups, are specific and are seldom prescribed for any other disorders. The plastic compacts for birth-control pills usually have complete label information. [50]

Despite all of this sensitive information, I have had only one apartment resident object to my going through the Dumpster. In that case it turned out the resident was a university athlete who was taking bets and who was afraid I would turn up his wager slips. [51]

Occasionally a find tells a story. I once found a small paper bag containing some unused condoms, several partial tubes of flavored sexual lubricants, a partially used compact of birth-control pills, and the torn [52] pieces of a picture of a young man. Clearly she was through with him and planning to give up sex altogether.

Dumpster things are often sad—abandoned teddy bears, shredded [53] wedding books, despaired-of sales kits. I find many pets lying in state in Dumpsters. Although I hope to get off the streets so that Lizbeth can have a long and comfortable old age, I know this hope is not very realistic. So I suppose when her time comes she too will go into a Dumpster. I will have no better place for her. And after all, it is fitting, since for most of her life her livelihood has come from the Dumpster. When she finds something I think is safe that has been spilled from a Dumpster, I let her have it. She already knows the route around the best ones. I like to think that if she survives me she will have a chance of evading the dog catcher and of finding her sustenance on the route.

Silly vanities also come to rest in the Dumpsters. I am a rather ac- [54] complished needleworker. I get a lot of material from the Dumpsters. Evidently sorority girls, hoping to impress someone, perhaps themselves, with their mastery of a womanly art, buy a lot of embroider-by-number kits, work a few stitches horribly, and eventually discard the whole mess. I pull out their stitches, turn the canvas over, and work an original design. Do not think I refrain from chuckling as I make gifts from these kits.

I find diaries and journals. I have often thought of compiling a book [55] of literary found objects. And perhaps I will one day. But what I find is hopelessly commonplace and bad without being, even unconsciously, camp. College students also discard their papers. I am horrified to discover the kind of paper that now merits an A in an undergraduate course. I am grateful, however, for the number of good books and magazines the students throw out.

In the area I know best I have never discovered vermin in the [56] Dumpsters, but there are two kinds of kitty surprise. One is alley cats whom I meet as they leap, claws first, out of Dumpsters. This is especially thrilling when I have Lizbeth in tow. The other kind of kitty surprise is a plastic garbage bag filled with some ponderous, amorphous mass. This always proves to be used cat litter.

City bees harvest doughnut glaze and this makes the Dumpster at [57] the doughnut shop more interesting. My faith in the instinctive wisdom of animals is always shaken whenever I see Lizbeth attempt to catch a bee in her mouth, which she does whenever bees are present. Evidently some birds find Dumpsters profitable, for birdie surprise is almost as common as kitty surprise of the first kind. In hunting season all kinds of small game turn up in Dumpsters, some of it, sadly, not entirely dead. Curiously, summer and winter, maggots are uncommon.

The worst of the living and near-living hazards of the Dumpsters [58] are the fire ants. The food they claim is not much of a loss, but they are vicious and aggressive. It is very easy to brush against some surface of the Dumpster and pick up half a dozen or more fire ants, usually in some sensitive area such as the underarm. One advantage of bringing Lizbeth along as I make Dumpster rounds is that, for obvious reasons, she is very alert to ground-based fire ants. When Lizbeth recognizes a fire-ant infestation around our feet, she does the Dance of the Zillion Fire Ants. I have learned not to ignore this warning from Lizbeth, whether I perceive the tiny ants or not, but to remove ourselves at Lizbeth's first pas de bourrée.[1] All the more so because the ants are the worst in the summer months when I wear flip-flops if I have them. (Perhaps someone will misunderstand this. Lizbeth does the Dance of the Zillion Fire Ants when she recognizes more fire ants than she cares to eat, not when she is being bitten. Since I have learned to react promptly, she does not get bitten at all. It is the isolated patrol of fire ants that falls in Lizbeth's range that deserves pity. She finds them quite tasty.)

By far the best way to go through a Dumpster is to lower yourself ⁵⁹ into it. Most of the good stuff tends to settle at the bottom because it is usually weightier than the rubbish. My more athletic companions have often demonstrated to me that they can extract much good material from a Dumpster I have already been over.

To those psychologically or physically unprepared to enter a ⁶⁰ Dumpster, I recommend a stout stick, preferably with some barb or hook at one end. The hook can be used to grab plastic garbage bags. When I find canned goods or other objects loose at the bottom of a Dumpster, I lower a bag into it, roll the desired object into the bag, and then hoist the bag out—a procedure more easily described than executed. Much Dumpster diving is a matter of experience for which nothing will do except practice.

Dumpster diving is outdoor work, often surprisingly pleasant. It is ⁶¹ not entirely predictable; things of interest turn up every day and some days there are finds of great value. I am always very pleased when I can turn up exactly the thing I most wanted to find. Yet in spite of the element of chance, scavenging more than most other pursuits tends to yield returns in some proportion to the effort and intelligence brought to bear. It is very sweet to turn up a few dollars in change from a Dumpster that has just been gone over by a wino.

The land is now covered with cities. The cities are full of Dumpsters. ⁶² If a member of the canine race is ever able to know what it is doing, then Lizbeth knows that when we go around to the Dumpsters, we are hunting. I think of scavenging as a modern form of self-reliance. In any event, after having survived nearly ten years of government service, where everything is geared to the lowest common denominator, I find it refreshing to have work that rewards initiative and effort. Certainly I

---

[1] A short walking or running step in ballet. [Eds.]

would be happy to have a sinecure again, but I am no longer heartbroken that I left one.

I find from the experience of scavenging two rather deep lessons. 63 The first is to take what you can use and let the rest go by. I have come to think that there is no value in the abstract. A thing I cannot use or make useful, perhaps by trading, has no value however rare or fine it may be. I mean useful in a broad sense—some art I would find useful and some otherwise.

I was shocked to realize that some things are not worth acquiring, 64 but now I think it is so. Some material things are white elephants that eat up the possessor's substance. The second lesson is the transience of material being. This has not quite converted me to a dualist,[2] but it has made some headway in that direction. I do not suppose that ideas are immortal, but certainly mental things are longer lived than other material things.

Once I was the sort of person who invests objects with sentimental 65 value. Now I no longer have those objects, but I have the sentiments yet.

Many times in our travels I have lost everything but the clothes I 66 was wearing and Lizbeth. The things I find in Dumpsters, the love letters and rag dolls of so many lives, remind me of this lesson. Now I hardly pick up a thing without envisioning the time I will cast it aside. This I think is a healthy state of mind. Almost everything I have now has already been cast out at least once, proving that what I own is valueless to someone.

Anyway, I find my desire to grab for the gaudy bauble has been 67 largely sated. I think this is an attitude I share with the very wealthy— we both know there is plenty more where what we have came from. Between us are the rat-race millions who nightly scavenge the cable channels looking for they know not what.

I am sorry for them. 68

Responding to Reading

1. In paragraph 6 Eighner explains, "I have learned much as a scavenger. I mean to put some of what I have learned down here, beginning with the practical art of Dumpster diving and proceding to the abstract. . . ." Do you think Eighner's purpose goes beyond educating his readers? What other purpose do you think he might have?
2. What surprised you most about Eighner's essay? Did any information embarrass you? Repulse you? Make you feel guilty? Arouse your sympathy? Arouse your pity? Explain your response.
3. Does Eighner's essay succeed in putting a human face on an abstract prob-

---

[2] One who believes that material things also exist as spiritual ideals or abstractions. [Eds.]

lem, or does the fact that he was able to write and publish a book about his situation lead you to see him as an atypical example rather than as a respresentative of all homeless people? Does he change the way you feel about the homeless?

IT'S JUST TOO LATE

Calvin Trillin

Calvin Trillin (1935–) is probably best known for his humorous writing about food: *American Fried* (1974), *Alice, Let's Eat* (1978), and *Third Helpings* (1983). In fact, he is a versatile writer of fiction, reportage, and political commentary. Trillin was a reporter for *Time*, a staff writer for the *New Yorker*, and a columnist for the *Nation*. His collections include *Uncivil Liberties* (1982), *With All Due Disrespect* (1985), *If You Can't Say Something Nice* (1987), and *American Stories* (1991). His most recent book is *Remembering Denny* (1993) about a college friend who committed suicide. The following essay, in which Trillin looks at the tragic death of a teenage girl killed in a car chase, first appeared in his series "U.S. Journal," written for the *New Yorker*, and was collected in *Killings* (1984).

Knoxville, Tennessee

March 1979

Until she was sixteen, FaNee Cooper was what her parents some-   1
times called an ideal child. "You'd never have to correct her," FaNee's mother has said. In sixth grade, FaNee won a spelling contest. She played the piano and the flute. She seemed to believe what she heard every Sunday at the Beaver Dam Baptist Church about good and evil and the hereafter. FaNee was not an outgoing child. Even as a baby, she was uncomfortable when she was held and cuddled. She found it easy to tell her parents she loved them but difficult to confide in them. Particularly compared to her sister, Kristy, a cheerful, open little girl two and a half years younger, she was reserved and introspective. The thoughts she kept to herself, though, were apparently happy thoughts. Her eighth-grade essay on Christmas—written in a remarkably neat hand—talked of the joys of helping put together toys for her little brother, Leo, Jr., and the importance of her parents' reminder that Christmas is the birthday of Jesus. Her parents were the sort of people who might have been expected to have an ideal child. As a boy, Leo Cooper had been called "one of the greatest high-school basketball players ever de-

veloped in Knox County." He went on to play basketball at East Tennessee State, and he married the homecoming queen, JoAnn Henson. After college, Cooper became a high-school basketball coach and teacher and, eventually, an administrator. By the time FaNee turned thirteen, in 1973, he was in his third year as the principal of Gresham Junior High School, in Fountain City—a small Knox County town that had been swallowed up by Knoxville when the suburbs began to move north. A tall man, with curly black hair going on gray, Leo Cooper has an elaborate way of talking ("Unless I'm very badly mistaken, he has never related to me totally the content of his conversation") and a manner that may come from years of trying to leave errant junior-high-school students with the impression that a responsible adult is magnanimous, even humble, about invariably being in the right. His wife, a high-school art teacher, paints and does batik, and created the name FaNee because she liked the way it looked and sounded—it sounds like "Fawn*ee*" when the Coopers say it—but the impression she gives is not of artiness but of soft-spoken small-town gentility. When she found, in the course of cleaning up FaNee's room, that her ideal thirteen-year-old had been smoking cigarettes, she was, in her words, crushed. "FaNee was such a perfect child before that," JoAnn Cooper said some time later. "She was angry that we found out. She knew we knew that she had done something we didn't approve of, and then the rebellion started. I was hurt. I was very hurt. I guess it came through as disappointment."

Several months later, FaNee's grandmother died. FaNee had been devoted to her grandmother. She wrote a poem in her memory—an almost joyous poem, filled with Christian faith in the afterlife ("Please don't grieve over my happiness/Rejoice with me in the presence of the Angels of Heaven"). She also took some keepsakes from her grandmother's house, and was apparently mortified when her parents found them and explained that they would have to be returned. By then, the Coopers were aware that FaNee was going to have a difficult time as a teenager. They thought she might be self-conscious about the double affliction of glasses and braces. They thought she might be uncomfortable in the role of the principal's daughter at Gresham. In ninth grade, she entered Halls High School, where JoAnn Cooper was teaching art. FaNee was a loner at first. Then she fell in with what could only be considered a bad crowd.

Halls, a few miles to the north of Fountain City, used to be known as Halls Crossroads. It is what Knoxville people call "over the ridge"—on the side of Black Oak Ridge that has always been thought of as rural. When FaNee entered Halls High, the Coopers were already in the process of building a house on several acres of land they had bought in Halls, in a sparsely settled area along Brown Gap road. Like two or three other houses along the road, it was to be constructed basically of huge logs taken from old buildings—a house that Leo Cooper describes as being, like the name FaNee, "just a little bit different." Ten years ago, Halls Crossroads was literally a crossroads. Then some of the Knoxville expansion that had swollen Fountain City spilled over the ridge, planting subdivisions here and there on roads that still went for long stretches with nothing but an occasional house with a cow or two next to it. The increase in population did not create a town. Halls has no center. Its commercial area is a series of two or three shopping centers strung together on the Maynardville Highway, the four-lane that leads north into Union County—a place almost synonymous in east Tennessee with mountain poverty. Its restaurant is the Halls Freezo Drive-In. The gathering place for the group FaNee Cooper eventually found herself in was the Maynardville Highway Exxon station.

At Halls High School, the social poles were represented by the Jocks   4 and the Freaks. FaNee found her friends among the Freaks. "I am truly enlighted upon irregular trains of thought aimed at strange depots of mental wards," she wrote when she was fifteen. "Yes! Crazed farms for the mental off—Oh! I walked through the halls screams & loud laughter fill my ears—Orderlys try to reason with me—but I am unreasonable! The joys of being a FREAK in a circus of imagination." The little crowd of eight or ten young people that FaNee joined has been referred to by her mother as "the Union County group." A couple of the girls were from backgrounds similar to FaNee's, but all the boys had the characteristics, if not the precise addresses, that Knoxville people associate with the poor whites of Union County. They were the sort of boys who didn't bother to finish high school, or finished it in a special program for slow learners, or get ejected from it for taking a swing at the principal.

"I guess you can say they more or less dragged us down to their   5 level with the drugs," a girl who was in the group—a girl who can be called Marcia—said recently. "And somehow we settled for it. It seems like we had to get ourselves in the pit before we could look out." People in the group used marijuana and Valium and LSD. They sneered at the Jocks and the "prim and proper little ladies" who went with Jocks. "We set ourselves aside," Marcia now says. "We put ourselves above everyone. How we did that I don't know." In a Knox County high school, teenagers who want to get themselves in the pit need not mainline heroin. The Jocks they mean to be compared to do not merely show up regularly for classes and practice football and wear clean clothes; they watch their language and preach temperance and go to prayer meetings on Wednesday nights and talk about having a real good Christian witness. Around Knoxville, people who speak of well-behaved high-school kids often seem to use words like "perfect," or even "angels." For FaNee's group, the opposite was not difficult to figure out. "We were into wicked things, strange things," Marcia says. "It was like we were on some kind of devil trip." FaNee wrote about demons and vultures and rats. "Slithering serpents eat my sanity and bite my ass," she wrote in an essay called "The Lovely Road of Life," just after she turned sixteen, "while tornadoes derail and ever so swiftly destroy every car in my train of thought." She wrote a lot about death.

FaNee's girl friends spoke of her as "super-intelligent." Her English [6] teacher found some of her writing profound—and disturbing. She was thought to be not just super-intelligent but super-mysterious, and even, at times, super-weird—an introverted girl who stared straight ahead with deep-brown, nearly black eyes and seemed to have thoughts she couldn't share. Nobody really knew why she had chosen to run with the Freaks—whether it was loneliness or rebellion or simple boredom. Marcia thought it might have had something to do with a feeling that her parents had settled on Kristy as their perfect child. "I guess she figured she couldn't be the best," Marcia said recently. "So she decided she might as well be the worst."

Toward the spring of FaNee's junior year at Halls, her problems [7] seemed to deepen. Despite her intelligence, her grades were sliding. She was what her mother called "a mental dropout." Leo Cooper had to visit Halls twice because of minor suspensions. Once, FaNee had been caught smoking. Once, having ducked out of a required assembly, she was spotted by a favorite teacher, who turned her in. At home, she exchanged little more than short, strained formalities with Kristy, who shared their parents' opinion of FaNee's choice of friends. The Coopers had finished their house—a large house, its size accentuated by the huge old logs and a great stone fireplace and outsize "Paul Bunyan"-style furniture—but FaNee spent most of her time there in her own room, sleeping or listening to rock music through earphones. One night, there was a terrible scene when FaNee returned from a concert in a condition that Leo Cooper knew had to be the result of marijuana. JoAnn Cooper, who ordinarily strikes people as too gentle to raise her voice, found herself losing her temper regularly. Finally, Leo Cooper asked a counsellor he knew, Jim Griffin, to stop in at Halls High School and have a talk with FaNee—unofficially.

Griffin—a young man with a warm, informal manner—worked for [8] the Juvenile Court of Knox County. He had a reputation for being able to reach teenagers who wouldn't talk to their parents or to school administrators. One Friday in March of 1977, he spent an hour and a half talking to FaNee Cooper. As Griffin recalls the interview, FaNee didn't seem alarmed by his presence. She seemed to him calm and controlled—Griffin thought it was something like talking to another adult—and, unlike most of the teenagers he dealt with, she looked him in the eye the entire time. Griffin, like some of FaNee's friends, found her eyes unsettling—"the coldest, most distant, but, at the same time, the most knowing eyes I'd ever seen." She expressed affection for her parents, but she didn't seem interested in exploring ways of getting along better with them. The impression she gave Griffin was that they were who they were, and she was who she was, and there didn't happen to be any connection. Several times, she made the same response to Griffin's suggestions: "It's too late."

That weekend, neither FaNee nor her parents brought up the subject of Griffin's visit. Leo Cooper has spoken of the weekend as being particularly happy; a friend of FaNee's who stayed over remembers it as particularly strained. FaNee stayed home from school on Monday because of a bad headache—she often had bad headaches—but felt well enough on Monday evening to drive to the library. She was to be home at nine. When she wasn't, Mrs. Cooper began to phone her friends. Finally, around ten, Leo Cooper got into his other car and took a swing around Halls—past the teenage hangouts like the Exxon station and the Pizza Hut and the Smoky Mountain Market. Then he took a second swing. At eleven, FaNee was still not home. 9

She hadn't gone to the library. She had picked up two girl friends and driven to the home of a third, where everyone took five Valium tablets. Then the four girls drove over to the Exxon station, where they met four boys from their crowd. After a while, the group bought some beer and some marijuana and reassembled at Charlie Stevens's trailer. Charlie Stevens was five or six years older than everyone else in the group—a skinny, slow-thinking young man with long black hair and a sparse beard. He was married and had a child, but he and his wife had separated; she was back in Union County with the baby. Stevens had remained in their trailer—parked in the yard near his mother's house, in a back-road area of Knox County dominated by decrepit, unpainted sheds and run-down trailers and rusted-out automobiles. Stevens had picked up FaNee at home once or twice—apparently, more as a driver for the group than as a date—and the Coopers, having learned that his unsuitability extended to being married, had asked her not to see him. 10

In Charlie's trailer, which had no heat or electricity, the group drank beer and passed around joints, keeping warm with blankets. By eleven or so, FaNee was what one of her friends has called "super-messed-up." Her speech was slurred. She was having trouble keeping her balance. She had decided not to go home. She had apparently persuaded herself that her parents intended to send her away to some sort of home for incorrigibles. "It's too late," she said to one of her friends. "It's just too late." It was decided that one of the boys, David Munsey, who was more or less the leader of the group, would drive the Coopers' car to FaNee's house, where FaNee and Charlie Stevens would pick him up in Stevens's car—a worn Pinto with four bald tires, one light, and a dragging muffler. FaNee wrote a note to her parents, and then, perhaps because her handwriting was suffering the effects of beer and marijuana and Valium, asked Stevens to rewrite it on a large piece of paper, which 11 would be left on the seat of the Coopers' car. The Stevens version was just about the same as FaNee's, except that Stevens left out a couple of sentences about trying to work things out ("I'm willing to try") and, not having won any spelling championship himself, he misspelled a few words, like "tomorrow." The note said, "Dear Mom and Dad. Sorry I'm late. Very late. I left your car because I thought you might need it tomorrow. I love you all, but this is something I just had to do. The man talked to me privately for one and a half hours and I was really scared, so this is something I just had to do, but don't worry. I'm with a very good friend. Love you all. FaNee. P.S. Please try to understand I love you all very much, really I do. Love me if you have a chance."

At eleven-thirty or so, Leo Cooper was sitting in his living room, [12] looking out the window at his driveway—a long gravel road that runs almost four hundred feet from the house to Brown Gap Road. He saw the car that FaNee had been driving pull into the driveway. "She's home," he called to his wife, who had just left the room. Cooper walked out on the deck over the garage. The car had stopped at the end of the driveway, and the lights had gone out. He got into his other car and drove to the end of the driveway. David Munsey had already joined Charlie Stevens and FaNee, and the Pinto was just leaving, travelling at a normal rate of speed. Leo Cooper pulled out on the road behind them.

Stevens turned left on Crippen Road, a road that has a field on one [13] side and two or three small houses on the other, and there Cooper pulled his car in front of the Pinto and stopped, blocking the way. He got out and walked toward the Pinto. Suddenly, Stevens put the car in reverse, backed into a driveway a hundred yards behind him, and sped off. Cooper jumped in his car and gave chase. Stevens raced back to Brown Gap Road, ran a stop sign there, ran another stop sign at Maynardville Highway, turned north, veered off onto the old Andersonville Pike, a nearly abandoned road that runs parallel to the highway, and then crossed back over the highway to the narrow, dark country roads on the other side. Stevens sometimes drove with his lights out. He took some of the corners by suddenly applying his hand brake to make the car swerve around in a ninety-degree turn. He was in familiar territory—he actually passed his trailer—and Cooper had difficulty keeping up. Past the trailer, Stevens swept down a hill into a sharp left turn that took him onto Foust Hollow Road, a winding, hilly road not much wider than one car.

At a fork, Cooper thought he had lost the Pinto. He started to go [14] right and then saw what seemed to be a spark from Stevens's dragging muffler off to the left, in the darkness. Cooper took the left fork, down Salem Church Road. He went down a hill and then up a long, curving hill to a crest, where he saw the Stevens car ahead. "I saw the car airborne. Up in the air," he later testified. "It was up in the air. And then it completely rolled over one more time. It started to make another flip forward, and just as it started to flip to the other side it flipped back this way, and my daughter's body came out."

Cooper slammed on his brakes and skidded to a stop up against the [15] Pinto. "Book!" Stevens shouted—the group's equivalent of "Scram!" Stevens and Munsey disappeared into the darkness. "It was dark, no one around, and so I started yelling for FaNee," Cooper had testified. "I thought it was an eternity before I could find her body, wedged under the back end of that car. . . . I tried everything I could, and saw that I couldn't get her loose. So I ran to a trailer back up to the top of the hill back up there to try to get that lady to call to get me some help, and then apparently she didn't think that I was serious. . . . I took the jack out of my car and got under, and it was dark, still couldn't see too much what was going on . . . and started prying and got her loose, and I don't know how. And then I dragged her over to the side, and, of course, at the time I felt reasonably assured that she was gone, because her head was completely—on one side just as if you had taken a sledgehammer and just hit it and bashed it in. And I did have the pleasure of one thing. I had the pleasure of listening to her breathe about the last three times she ever breathed in her life."

David Munsey did not return to the wreck that night, but Charlie [16] Stevens did. Leo Cooper was kneeling next to his daughter's body. Cooper insisted that Stevens come close enough to see FaNee. "He was kneeling down next to her," Stevens later testified. "And he said, 'Do you know what you've done? Do you really know what you've done?' Like that. And I just looked at her, and I said, 'Yes,' and just stood there. Because I couldn't say nothing." There was, of course, a legal decision to be made about who was responsible for FaNee Cooper's death. In a deposition, Stevens said he had been fleeing for his life. He testified that when Leo Cooper blocked Crippen Road, FaNee had said that her father had a gun and intended to hurt them. Stevens was bound over and eventually indicted for involuntary manslaughter. Leo Cooper testified that when he approached the Pinto on Crippen Road, FaNee had a strange expression that he had never seen before. "It wasn't like FaNee, and I knew something was wrong," he said. "My concern was to get FaNee out of the car." The district attorney's office asked that Cooper be bound over for reckless driving, but the judge declined to do so. "Any father would have done what he did," the judge said. "I can see no criminal act on the part of Mr. Cooper."

Almost two years passed before Charlie Stevens was brought to [17] trial. Part of the problem was assuring the presence of David Munsey, who had joined the Navy but seemed inclined to assign his own leaves.

In the meantime, the Coopers went to court with a civil suit—they had "uninsured-motorist coverage," which requires their insurance company to cover any defendant who has no insurance of his own—and they won a judgment. There were ways of assigning responsibility, of course, which had nothing to do with the law, civil or criminal. A lot of people in Knoxville thought that Leo Cooper had, in the words of his lawyer, "done what any daddy worth his salt would have done." There were others who believed that FaNee Cooper had lost her life because Leo Cooper had lost his temper. Leo Cooper was not among those who expressed any doubts about his actions. Unlike his wife, whose eyes filled with tears at almost any mention of FaNee, Cooper seemed able, even eager to go over the details of the accident again and again. With the help of a school-board security man, he conducted his own investigation. He drove over the route dozens of times. "I've thought about it every day, and I guess I will the rest of my life," he said as he and his lawyer and the prosecuting attorney went over the route again the day before Charlie Stevens's trial finally began. "But I can't tell any alternative for a father. I simply wanted her out of that car. I'd have done the same thing again, even at the risk of losing her."

Tennessee law permits the family of a victim to hire a special prosecutor to assist the district attorney. The lawyer who acted for the Coopers in the civil case helped prosecute Charlie Stevens. Both he and the district attorney assured the jurors that the presence of a special prosecutor was not to be construed to mean that the Coopers were vindictive. Outside the courtroom, Leo Cooper said that the verdict was of no importance to him—that he felt sorry, in a way, for Charlie Stevens. But there were people in Knoxville who thought Cooper had a lot riding on the prosecution of Charlie Stevens. If Stevens was not guilty of FaNee Cooper's death—found so by twelve of his peers—who was? [18]

At the trial, Cooper testified emotionally and remarkably graphically about pulling FaNee out from under the car and watching her die in his arms. Charlie Stevens had shaved his beard and cut his hair, but the effort did not transform him into an impressive witness. His lawyer—trying to argue that it would have been impossible for Stevens to concoct the story about FaNee's having mentioned a gun, as the prosecution strongly implied—said, "His mind is such that if you ask him a question you can hear his mind go around, like an old mill creaking." Stevens did not deny the recklessness of his driving or the sorry condition of his car. It happened to be the only car he had available to flee in, he said, and he had fled in fear for his life. [19]

The prosecution said that Stevens could have let FaNee out of the car when her father stopped them, or could have gone to the commercial strip on the Maynardville Highway for protection. The prose- [20]

cution said that Leo Cooper had done what he might have been expected to do under the circumstances—alone, late at night, his daughter in danger. The defense said precisely the same about Stevens: he
had done what he might have been expected to do when being pursued by a man he had reason to be afraid of. "I don't fault Mr. Cooper for what he did, but I'm sorry he did it," the defense attorney said.
"I'm sorry the girl said what she said." The jury deliberated for eighteen minutes. Charlie Stevens was found guilty. The jury recommended a sentence of from two to five years in the state penitentiary.
At the announcement, Leo Cooper broke down and cried, JoAnn
Cooper's eyes filled with tears; she blinked them back and continued
to stare straight ahead.

In a way, the Coopers might still strike a casual visitor as an ideal   21
family—handsome parents, a bright and bubbly teenage daughter, a little boy learning the hook shot from his father, a warm house with some
land around it. FaNee's presence is there, of course. A picture of her,
with a small bouquet of flowers over it, hangs in the living room. One
of her poems is displayed in a frame on a table. Even if Leo Cooper continues to think about that night for the rest of his life, there are questions
he can never answer. Was there a way that Leo and JoAnn Cooper could
have prevented FaNee from choosing the path she chose? Would she
still be alive if Leo Cooper had not jumped into his car and driven to the
end of the driveway to investigate? Did she in fact tell Charlie Stevens
that her father would hurt them—or even that her father had a gun? Did
she want to get away from her family even at the risk of tearing around
dark country roads in Charlie Stevens's dismal Pinto? Or did she welcome the risk? The poem of FaNee's that the Coopers have displayed is
one she wrote a week before her death:

> I think I'm going to die
> And I really don't know why.
> But look in my eye
> When I tell you good-bye.
> I think I'm going to die.

Responding to Reading

1. In paragraph 1 Trillin introduces FaNee Cooper as "what her parents sometimes called an ideal child." Does this characterization of FaNee provide an
effective introduction to the case study the essay develops? Why or why not?
2. Whom do you hold responsible for FaNee's death? Do you believe anyone
had the power to "save" her? If so, who? How might her slide toward death
have been prevented?
3. Do you know anyone like FaNee? Did you feel this person's fate was inevitable? At what point in FaNee's life do you believe it really was "just too
late?"

WHERE ARE YOU GOING,
∼ WHERE HAVE YOU BEEN?

Joyce Carol Oates

One of the most prolific contemporary American writers, Joyce Carol Oates (1938–) was born in Lockport, New York, and received degrees from Syracuse University and from the University of Wisconsin. Her first collection of fiction, *By the North Gate,* was published in 1963. Since then she has published dozens of books, including novels, criticism, poetry, and plays. Oates's writing reflects her concern with violence in contemporary society and the hostility of modern culture toward the individual. She often mixes realism with the supernatural in her fiction. Her many novels include *Them* (1969), *Childwold* (1976), *Bellefleur* (1980), *American Appetites* (1989), and *Foxfire: Confessions of a Girl Gang* (1993). She first published the story that follows in her collection *The Wheel of Love and Other Stories* (1970). In this strange and frightening tale, Oates's protagonist stays home from a family outing, leaving herself vulnerable to a dangerous seduction.

For Bob Dylan[1]

Her name was Connie. She was fifteen and she had a quick nervous giggling habit of craning her neck to glance into mirrors, or checking other people's faces to make sure her own was all right. Her mother, who noticed everything and knew everything and who hadn't much reason any longer to look at her own face, always scolded Connie about it. "Stop gawking at yourself, who are you? You think you're so pretty?" she would say. Connie would raise her eyebrows at these familiar complaints and look right through her mother, into a shadowy vision of herself as she was right at that moment: she knew she was pretty and that was everything. Her mother had been pretty once too, if you could believe those old snapshots in the album, but now her looks were gone and that was why she was always after Connie.

"Why don't you keep your room clean like your sister? How've you   2
got your hair fixed—what the hell stinks? Hair spray? You don't see your sister using that junk."

Her sister June was twenty-four and still lived at home. She was a   3
secretary in the high school Connie attended, and if that wasn't bad enough—with her in the same building—she was so plain and chunky

---

[1] Oates has said that the story was inspired in part by Dylan's song "It's All Over Now, Baby Blue." [Eds.]

and steady that Connie had to hear her praised all the time by her mother and her mother's sisters. June did this, June did that, she saved money and helped clean the house and cooked and Connie couldn't do a thing, her mind was all filled with trashy daydreams. Their father was away at work most of the time and when he came home he wanted supper and he read the newspaper at supper and after supper he went to bed. He didn't bother talking much to them, but around his bent head Connie's mother kept picking at her until Connie wished her mother was dead and she herself was dead and it was all over. "She makes me want to throw up sometimes," she complained to her friends. She had a high, breathless, amused voice which made everything she said sound a little forced, whether it was sincere or not.

There was one good thing: June went places with girl friends of hers,   4
girls who were just as plain and steady as she, and so when Connie wanted to do that her mother had no objections. The father of Connie's best girl friend drove the girls the three miles to town and left them off at a shopping plaza, so that they could walk through the stores or go to a movie, and when he came to pick them up again at eleven he never bothered to ask what they had done.

They must have been familiar sights, walking around that shopping   5
plaza in their shorts and flat ballerina slippers that always scuffed the sidewalk, with charm bracelets jingling on their thin wrists; they would lean together to whisper and laugh secretly if someone passed by who amused or interested them. Connie had long dark blond hair that drew anyone's eye to it, and she wore part of it pulled up on her head and puffed out and the rest of it she let fall down her back. She wore a pullover jersey blouse that looked one way when she was at home and another way when she was away from home. Everything about her had two sides to it, one for home and one for anywhere that was not home: her walk that could be childlike and bobbing, or languid enough to make anyone think she was hearing music in her head, her mouth which was pale and smirking most of the time, but bright and pink on these evenings out, her laugh which was cynical and drawling at home—"Ha, ha, very funny"—but high-pitched and nervous anywhere else, like the jingling of the charms on her bracelet.

Sometimes they did go shopping or to a movie, but sometimes they   6
went across the highway, ducking fast across the busy road, to a drive-in restaurant where older kids hung out. The restaurant was shaped like a big bottle, though squatter than a real bottle, and on its cap was a revolving figure of a grinning boy who held a hamburger aloft. One night in mid-summer they ran across, breathless with daring, and right away someone leaned out a car window and invited them over, but it was just a boy from high school they didn't like. It made them feel good to be able to ignore him. They went up through the maze of parked and cruising cars to the bright-lit, fly-infested restaurant, their faces pleased and

expectant as if they were entering a sacred building that loomed out of the night to give them what haven and what blessing they yearned for. They sat at the counter and crossed their legs at the ankles, their thin shoulders rigid with excitement, and listened to the music that made everything so good: the music was always in the background like music at a church service, it was something to depend upon.

A boy named Eddie came in to talk with them. He sat backwards on 7 his stool, turning himself jerkily around in semi-circles and then stopping and turning again, and after a while he asked Connie if she would like something to eat. She said she did and so she tapped her friend's arm on her way out—her friend pulled her face up into a brave droll look—and Connie said she would meet her at eleven, across the way. "I just hate to leave her like that," Connie said earnestly, but the boy said that she wouldn't be alone for long. So they went out to his car and on the way Connie couldn't help but let her eyes wander over the windshields and faces all around her, her face gleaming with a joy that had nothing to do with Eddie or even this place; it might have been the music. She drew her shoulders up and sucked in her breath with the pure pleasure of being alive, and just at that moment she happened to glance at a face just a few feet from hers. It was a boy with shaggy black hair, in a convertible jalopy painted gold. He stared at her and then his lips widened into a grin. Connie slit her eyes at him and turned away, but she couldn't help glancing back and there he was still watching her. He wagged a finger and laughed and said, "Gonna get you, baby," and Connie turned away again without Eddie noticing anything.

She spent three hours with him, at the restaurant where they ate 8 hamburgers and drank Cokes in wax cups that were always sweating, and then down an alley a mile or so away, and when he left her off at five to eleven only the movie house was still open at the plaza. Her girl friend was there, talking with a boy. When Connie came up the two girls smiled at each other and Connie said, "How was the movie?" and the girl said, "*You* should know." They rode off with the girl's father, sleepy and pleased, and Connie couldn't help but look at the darkened shopping plaza with its big empty parking lot and its signs that were faded and ghostly now, and over at the drive-in restaurant where cars were still circling tirelessly. She couldn't hear the music at this distance.

Next morning June asked her how the movie was and Connie said, 9 "So-so."

She and that girl and occasionally another girl went out several 10 times a week that way, and the rest of the time Connie spent around the house—it was summer vacation—getting in her mother's way and thinking, dreaming, about the boys she met. But all the boys fell back and dissolved into a single face that was not even a face, but an idea, a feeling, mixed up with the urgent insistent pounding of the music and the humid night air of July. Connie's mother kept dragging her back to the daylight by finding things for her to do or saying, suddenly, "What's this about the Pettinger girl?"

And Connie would say nervously, "Oh, her. That dope." She al- [11] ways drew thick clear lines between herself and such girls, and her mother was simple and kindly enough to believe her. Her mother was so simple, Connie thought, that it was maybe cruel to fool her so much. Her mother went scuffling around the house in old bedroom slippers and complained over the telephone to one sister about the other, then the other called up and the two of them complained about the third one. If June's name was mentioned her mother's tone was approving, and if Connie's name was mentioned it was disapproving. This did not really mean she disliked Connie and actually Connie thought that her mother preferred her to June because she was pret- tier, but the two of them kept up a pretense of exasperation, a sense that they were tugging and struggling over something of little value to either of them. Sometimes, over coffee, they were almost friends, but something would come up—some vexation that was like a fly buzzing suddenly around their heads—and their faces went hard with contempt.

One Sunday Connie got up at eleven—none of them bothered with [12] church—and washed her hair so that it could dry all day long, in the sun. Her parents and sister were going to a barbecue at an aunt's house and Connie said no, she wasn't interested, rolling her eyes to let her mother know just what she thought of it. "Stay home alone then," her mother said sharply. Connie sat out back in a lawn chair and watched them drive away, her father quiet and bald, hunched around so that he could back the car out, her mother with a look that was still angry and not at all softened through the windshield, and in the back seat poor old June all dressed up as if she didn't know what a barbecue was, with all the running yelling kids and the flies. Connie sat with her eyes closed in the sun, dreaming and dazed with the warmth about her as if this were a kind of love, the caresses of love, and her mind slipped over onto thoughts of the boy she had been with the night before and how nice he had been, how sweet it always was, not the way someone like June would suppose but sweet, gentle, the way it was in movies and promised in songs; and when she opened her eyes she hardly knew where she was, the back yard ran off into weeds and a fence-line of trees and behind it the sky was perfectly blue and still. The asbestos "ranch house" that was now three years old startled her—it looked small. She shook her head as if to get awake.

It was too hot. She went inside the house and turned on the radio to [13] drown out the quiet. She sat on the edge of her bed, barefoot, and lis- tened for an hour and a half to a program called XYZ Sunday Jamboree, record after record of hard, fast, shrieking songs she sang along with, in- terspersed by exclamations from "Bobby King": "An' look here you girls at Napoleon's—Son and Charley want you to pay real close attention to this song coming up!"

And Connie paid close attention herself, bathed in a glow of slow-pulsed joy that seemed to rise mysteriously out of the music itself and lay languidly about the airless little room, breathed in and breathed out with each gentle rise and fall of her chest.   14

After a while she heard a car coming up the drive. She sat up at once, startled, because it couldn't be her father so soon. The gravel kept crunching all the way in from the road—the driveway was long—and Connie ran to the window. It was a car she didn't know. It was an open jalopy, painted a bright gold that caught the sunlight opaquely. Her heart began to pound and her fingers snatched at her hair, checking it, and she whispered "Christ. Christ," wondering how bad she looked. The car came to a stop at the side door and the horn sounded four short taps as if this were a signal Connie knew.   15

She went into the kitchen and approached the door slowly, then hung out the screen door, her bare toes curling down off the step. There were two boys in the car and now she recognized the driver: he had shaggy, shabby black hair that looked crazy as a wig and he was grinning at her.   16

"I ain't late, am I?" he said.   17

"Who the hell do you think you are?" Connie said.   18

"Toldja I'd be out, didn't I?"   19

"I don't even know who you are."   20

She spoke sullenly, careful to show no interest or pleasure, and he spoke in a fast bright monotone. Connie looked past him to the other boy, taking her time. He had fair brown hair, with a lock that fell onto his forehead. His sideburns gave him a fierce, embarrassed look, but so far he hadn't even bothered to glance at her. Both boys wore sunglasses. The driver's glasses were metallic and mirrored everything in miniature.   21

"You wanta come for a ride?" he said.   22

Connie smirked and let her hair fall loose over one shoulder.   23

"Don'tcha like my car? New paint job," he said. "Hey."   24

"What?"   25

"You're cute."   26

She pretended to fidget, chasing flies away from the door.   27

"Don'tcha believe me, or what?" he said.   28

"Look, I don't even know who you are," Connie said in disgust.   29

"Hey, Ellie's got a radio, see. Mine's broke down." He lifted his friend's arm and showed her the little transistor the boy was holding, and now Connie began to hear the music. It was the same program that was playing inside the house.   30

"Bobby King?" she said.   31

"I listen to him all the time. I think he's great."   32

"He's kind of great," Connie said reluctantly.   33

"Listen, that guy's *great*. He knows where the action is."   34

Connie blushed a little, because the glasses made it impossible for 35
her to see just what this boy was looking at. She couldn't decide if she
liked him or if he was just a jerk, and so she dawdled in the doorway
and wouldn't come down or go back inside. She said, "What's all that
stuff painted on your car?"

"Can'tcha read it?" He opened the door very carefully, as if he was 36
afraid it might fall off. He slid out just as carefully, planting his feet firmly on the ground, the tiny metallic world in his glasses slowing down
like gelatine hardening and in the midst of it Connie's bright green
blouse. "This here is my name, to begin with," he said. ARNOLD
FRIEND was written in tarlike black letters on the side, with a drawing
of a round grinning face that reminded Connie of a pumpkin, except it
wore sunglasses. "I wanta introduce myself, I'm Arnold Friend and
that's my real name and I'm gonna be your friend, honey, and inside the
car's Ellie Oscar, he's kinda shy." Ellie brought his transistor radio up to
his shoulder and balanced it there. "Now these numbers are a secret
code, honey," Arnold Friend explained. He read off the numbers 33, 19,
17 and raised his eyebrows at her to see what she thought of that, but she
didn't think much of it. The left rear fender had been smashed and
around it was written, on the gleaming gold background: DONE BY
CRAZY WOMAN DRIVER. Connie had to laugh at that. Arnold Friend
was pleased at her laughter and looked up at her. "Around the other
side's a lot more—you wanta come and see them?"

"No."   37

"Why not?"   38

"Why should I?"   39

"Don'tcha wanta see what's on the car? Don'tcha wanta go for a 40
ride?"

"I don't know."   41

"Why not?"   42

"I got things to do."   43

"Like what?"   44

"Things."   45

He laughed as if she had said something funny. He slapped his 46
thighs. He was standing in a strange way, leaning back against the car
as if he were balancing himself. He wasn't tall, only an inch or so taller
than she would be if she came down to him. Connie liked the way he
was dressed, which was the way all of them dressed: tight faded jeans
stuffed into black, scuffed boots, a belt that pulled his waist in and
showed how lean he was, and a white pull-over shirt that was a little
soiled and showed the hard small muscles of his arms and shoulders. He
looked as if he probably did hard work, lifting and carrying things. Even
his neck looked muscular. And his face was a familiar face, somehow:

the jaw and chin and cheeks slightly darkened, because he hadn't shaved for a day or two, and the nose long and hawk-like, sniffing as if she were a treat he was going to gobble up and it was all a joke.

"Connie, you ain't telling the truth. This is your day set aside for a ride with me and you know it," he said, still laughing. The way he straightened and recovered from his fit of laughing showed that it had been all fake. 47

"How do you know what my name is?" she said suspiciously. 48

"It's Connie." 49

"Maybe and maybe not." 50

"I know my Connie," he said, wagging his finger. Now she remembered him even better, back at the restaurant, and her cheeks warmed at the thought of how she sucked in her breath just at the moment she passed him—how she must have looked to him. And he had remembered her. "Ellie and I come out here especially for you," he said. "Ellie can sit in back. How about it?" 51

"Where?" 52

"Where what?" 53

"Where're we going?" 54

He looked at her. He took off the sunglasses and she saw how pale the skin around his eyes was, like holes that were not in shadow but instead in light. His eyes were chips of broken glass that catch the light in an amiable way. He smiled. It was as if the idea of going for a ride somewhere, to some place, was a new idea to him. 55

"Just for a ride, Connie sweetheart." 56

"I never said my name was Connie," she said. 57

"But I know what it is. I know your name and all about you, lots of things," Arnold Friend said. He had not moved yet but stood still leaning back against the side of his jalopy. "I took a special interest in you, such a pretty girl, and found out all about you like I know your parents and sister are gone somewheres and I know where and how long they're going to be gone, and I know who you were with last night, and your best girl friend's name is Betty. Right?" 58

He spoke in a simple lilting voice, exactly as if he were reciting the words to a song. His smile assured her that everything was fine. In the car Ellie turned up the volume on his radio and did not bother to look around at them. 59

"Ellie can sit in the back seat," Arnold Friend said. He indicated his friend with a casual jerk of his chin, as if Ellie did not count and she should not bother with him. 60

"How'd you find out all that stuff?" Connie said. 61

"Listen: Betty Schultz and Tony Fitch and Jimmy Pettinger and Nancy Pettinger," he said, in a chant. "Raymond Stanely and Bob Hutter—" 62

"Do you know all those kids?" 63

"I know everybody." [64]

"Look, you're kidding. You're not from around here." [65]

"Sure." [66]

"But—how come we never saw you before?" [67]

"Sure you saw me before," he said. He looked down at his boots, as [68] if he were a little offended. "You just don't remember."

"I guess I'd remember you," Connie said. [69]

"Yeah?" He looked up at this, beaming. He was pleased. He began [70] to mark time with the music from Ellie's radio, tapping his fists lightly together. Connie looked away from his smile to the car, which was painted so bright it almost hurt her eyes to look at it. She looked at that name, ARNOLD FRIEND. And up at the front fender was an expression that was familiar—MAN THE FLYING SAUCERS. It was an expression kids had used the year before, but didn't use this year. She looked at it for a while as if the words meant something to her that she did not yet know.

"What're you thinking about? Huh?" Arnold Friend demanded. [71] "Not worried about your hair blowing around in the car, are you?"

"No." [72]

"Think I maybe can't drive good?" [73]

"How do I know?" [74]

"You're a hard girl to handle. How come?" he said. "Don't you [75] know I'm your friend? Didn't you see me put my sign in the air when you walked by?"

"What sign?" [76]

"My sign." And he drew an X in the air, leaning out toward her. [77] They were maybe ten feet apart. After his hand fell back to his side the X was still in the air, almost visible. Connie let the screen door close and stood perfectly still inside it, listening to the music from her radio and the boy's blend together. She stared at Arnold Friend. He stood there so stiffly relaxed, pretending to be relaxed, with one hand idly on the door handle as if he were keeping himself up that way and had no intention of ever moving again. She recognized most things about him, the tight jeans that showed his thighs and buttocks and the greasy leather boots and the tight shirt, and even that slippery friendly smile of his, that sleepy dreamy smile that all the boys used to get across ideas they didn't want to put into words. She recognized all this and also the singsong way he talked, slightly mocking, kidding, but serious and a little melancholy, and she recognized the way he tapped one fist against the other in homage to the perpetual music behind him. But all these things did not come together.

She said suddenly, "Hey, how old are you?" [78]

His smile faded. She could see then that he wasn't a kid, he was [79] much older—thirty, maybe more. At this knowledge her heart began to pound faster.

"That's a crazy thing to ask. Can'tcha see I'm your own age?"   80

"Like hell you are."   81

"Or maybe a coupla years older, I'm eighteen."   82

"Eighteen?" she said doubtfully.   83

He grinned to reassure her and lines appeared at the corners of his   84
mouth. His teeth were big and white. He grinned so broadly his eyes became slits and she saw how thick the lashes were, thick and black as if
painted with a black tarlike material. Then he seemed to become embarrassed, abruptly, and looked over his shoulder at Ellie. "*Him*, he's
crazy," he said. "Ain't he a riot, he's a nut, a real character." Ellie was
still listening to the music. His sunglasses told nothing about what he
was thinking. He wore a bright orange shirt unbuttoned halfway to
show his chest, which was a pale, bluish chest and not muscular like
Arnold Friend's. His shirt collar was turned up all around and the very
tips of the collar pointed out past his chin as if they were protecting him.
He was pressing the transistor radio up against his ear and sat there in
a kind of daze, right in the sun.

"He's kinda strange," Connie said.   85

"Hey, she says you're kinda strange! Kinda strange!" Arnold Friend   86
cried. He pounded on the car to get Ellie's attention. Ellie turned for the
first time and Connie saw with shock that he wasn't a kid either—he had
a fair, hairless face, cheeks reddened slightly as if the veins grew too
close to the surface of his skin, the face of a forty-year-old baby. Connie
felt a wave of dizziness rise in her at this sight and she stared at him as
if waiting for something to change the shock of the moment, make it all
right again. Ellie's lips kept shaping words, mumbling along with the
words blasting in his ear.

"Maybe you two better go away," Connie said faintly.   87

"What? How come?" Arnold Friend cried. "We come out here to   88
take you for a ride. It's Sunday." He had the voice of the man on the
radio now. It was the same voice, Connie thought. "Don'tcha know it's
Sunday all day and honey, no matter who you were with last night
today you're with Arnold Friend and don't you forget it!—Maybe you
better step out here," he said, and this last was in a different voice. It was
a little flatter, as if the heat was finally getting to him.

"No. I got things to do."   89

"Hey."   90

"You two better leave."   91

"We ain't leaving until you come with us."   92

"Like hell I am—"   93

"Connie, don't fool around with me. I mean, I mean, don't fool   94
around," he said, shaking his head. He laughed incredulously. He placed
his sunglasses on top of his head, carefully, as if he were indeed wearing a wig, and brought the stems down behind his ears. Connie stared
at him, another wave of dizziness and fear rising in her so that for a mo-

ment he wasn't even in focus but was just a blur, standing there against his gold car, and she had the idea that he had driven up the driveway all right but had come from nowhere before that and belonged nowhere and that everything about him and even about the music that was so familiar to her was only half real.

"If my father comes and sees you—"   95

"He ain't coming. He's at a barbecue."   96

"How do you know that?"   97

"Aunt Tillie's. Right now they're—uh—they're drinking. Sitting 98
around," he said vaguely, squinting as if he were staring all the way to town and over to Aunt Tillie's backyard. Then the vision seemed to get clear and he nodded energetically. "Yeah. Sitting around. There's your sister in a blue dress, huh? And high heels, the poor sad bitch—nothing like you, sweetheart! And your mother's helping some fat woman with the corn, they're cleaning the corn—husking the corn—"

"What fat woman?" Connie cried.   99

"How do I know what fat woman. I don't know every goddam fat 100
woman in the world!" Arnold Friend laughed.

"Oh, that's Mrs. Hornby. . . . Who invited her?" Connie said. She felt 101
a little light-headed. Her breath was coming quickly.

"She's too fat. I don't like them fat. I like them the way you are, 102
honey," he said, smiling sleepily at her. They stared at each other for a while, through the screen door. He said softly, "Now what you're going to do is this: you're going to come out that door. You're going to sit up front with me and Ellie's going to sit in the back, the hell with Ellie, right? This isn't Ellie's date. You're my date. I'm your lover, honey."

"What? You're crazy—"   103

"Yes, I'm your lover. You don't know what that is but you will," he 104
said. "I know that too. I know all about you. But look: it's real nice and you couldn't ask for nobody better than me, or more polite. I always keep my word. I'll tell you how it is, I'm always nice at first, the first time. I'll hold you so tight you won't think you have to try to get away or pretend anything because you'll know you can't. And I'll come inside you where it's all secret and you'll give in to me and you'll love me—"

"Shut up! You're crazy!" Connie said. She backed away from the 105
door. She put her hands against her ears as if she'd heard something terrible, something not meant for her. "People don't talk like that, you're crazy," she muttered. Her heart was almost too big now for her chest and its pumping made sweat break out all over her. She looked out to see Arnold Friend pause and then take a step toward the porch lurching. He almost fell. But, like a clever drunken man, he managed to catch his balance. He wobbled in his high boots and grabbed hold of one of the porch posts.

"Honey?" he said. "You still listening?"   106

"Get the hell out of here!"   107

"Be nice, honey. Listen."   108

"I'm going to call the police—"   109

He wobbled again and out of the side of his mouth came a fast spat   110
curse, an aside not meant for her to hear. But even this "Christ!" sounded forced. Then he began to smile again. She watched this smile come,
awkward as if he were smiling from inside a mask. His whole face was
a mask, she thought wildly, tanned down onto his throat but then running out as if he had plastered make-up on his face but had forgotten
about his throat.

"Honey—? Listen, here's how it is. I always tell the truth and I   111
promise you this: I ain't coming in that house after you."

"You better not! I'm going to call the police if you—if you don't—"   112

"Honey," he said, talking right through her voice, "honey, I'm not   113
coming in there but you are coming out here. You know why?"

She was panting. The kitchen looked like a place she had never seen   114
before, some room she had run inside but which wasn't good enough,
wasn't going to help her. The kitchen window had never had a curtain,
after three years, and there were dishes in the sink for her to do—probably—and if you ran your hand across the table you'd probably feel
something sticky there.

"You listening, honey? Hey?"   115

"—going to call the police—"   116

"Soon as you touch the phone I don't need to keep my promise and   117
can come inside. You won't want that."

She rushed forward and tried to lock the door. Her fingers were   118
shaking. "But why lock it," Arnold Friend said gently, talking right into
her face. "It's just a screen door. It's just nothing." One of his boots was
at a strange angle, as if his foot wasn't in it. It pointed out to the left, bent
at the ankle. "I mean, anybody can break through a screen door and
glass and wood and iron or anything else if he needs to, anybody at all
and specially Arnold Friend. If the place got lit up with a fire honey
you'd come running out into my arms, right into my arms and safe at
home—like you knew I was your lover and'd stopped fooling around.
I don't mind a nice shy girl but I don't like no fooling around." Part of
those words were spoken with a slight rhythmic lilt, and Connie somehow recognized them—the echo of a song from last year, about a girl
rushing into her boy friend's arms and coming home again—

Connie stood barefoot on the linoleum floor, staring at him. "What   119
do you want?" she whispered.

"I want you," he said.   120

"What?"   121

"Seen you that night and thought, that's the one, yes sir. I never   122
needed to look any more."

"But my father's coming back. He's coming to get me. I had to wash [123] my hair first—" She spoke in a dry, rapid voice, hardly raising it for him to hear.

"No, your daddy is not coming and yes, you had to wash your hair [124] and you washed it for me. It's nice and shining and all for me, I thank you, sweetheart," he said, with a mock bow, but again he almost lost his balance. He had to bend and adjust his boots. Evidently his feet did not go all the way down; the boots must have been stuffed with something so that he would seem taller. Connie stared out at him and behind him Ellie in the car, who seemed to be looking off toward Connie's right, into nothing. This Ellie said, pulling the words out of the air one after another as if he were just discovering them, "You want me to pull out the phone?"

"Shut your mouth and keep it shut," Arnold Friend said, his face [125] red from bending over or maybe from embarrassment because Connie had seen his boots. "This ain't none of your business."

"What—what are you doing? What do you want?" Connie said. "If [126] I call the police they'll get you, they'll arrest you—"

"Promise was not to come in unless you touch that phone, and I'll [127] keep that promise," he said. He resumed his erect position and tried to force his shoulders back. He sounded like a hero in a movie, declaring something important. He spoke too loudly and it was as if he were speaking to someone behind Connie. "I ain't made plans for coming in that house where I don't belong but just for you to come out to me, the way you should. Don't you know who I am?"

"You're crazy," she whispered. She backed away from the door but [128] did not want to go into another part of the house, as if this would give him permission to come through the door. "What do you. . . . You're crazy, you . . ."

"Huh? What're you saying, honey?" [129]

Her eyes darted everywhere in the kitchen. She could not remem- [130] ber what it was, this room.

"This is how it is, honey: you come out and we'll drive away, have [131] a nice ride. But if you don't come out we're gonna wait till your people come home and then they're all going to get it."

"You want that telephone pulled out?" Ellie said. He held the radio [132] away from his ear and grimaced, as if without the radio the air was too much for him.

"I toldja shut up, Ellie," Arnold Friend said, "you're deaf, get a hear- [133] ing aid, right? Fix yourself up. This little girl's no trouble and's gonna be nice to me, so Ellie keep to yourself, this ain't your date—right? Don't hem in one me. Don't hog. Don't crush. Don't bird dog. Don't trail me," he said in a rapid meaningless voice, as if he were running through all the expressions he'd learned but was no longer sure which one of them was in style, then rushing on to new ones, making them up with his eyes closed, "Don't crawl under my fence, don't squeeze in my chipmunk hole, don't sniff my glue, suck my popsicle, keep your own greasy fingers on yourself!" He shaded his eyes and peered in at Connie, who was backed against the kitchen table. "Don't mind him honey he's just a creep. He's a dope. Right? I'm the boy for you and like I said you come out here nice like a lady and give me your hand, and nobody else gets hurt, I mean, your nice old bald-headed daddy and your mummy and your sister in her high heels. Because listen: why bring them in this?"

"Leave me alone," Connie whispered.   134

"Hey, you know that old woman down the road, the one with the   135
chickens and stuff—you know her?"

"She's dead!"   136

"Dead? What? You know her?" Arnold Friend said.   137

"She's dead—"   138

"Don't you like her?"   139

"She's dead—she's—she isn't here any more—"   140

"But don't you like her, I mean, you got something against her?   141
Some grudge or something?" Then his voice dipped as if he were conscious of a rudeness. He touched the sunglasses perched on top of his head as if to make sure they were still there. "Now you be a good girl."

"What are you going to do?"   142

"Just two things, or maybe three," Arnold Friend said. "But I   143
promise it won't last long and you'll like me that way you get to like people you're close to. You will. It's all over for you here, so come on out. You don't want your people in any trouble, do you?"

She turned and bumped against a chair or something, hurting her   144
leg, but she ran into the back room and picked up the telephone. Something roared in her ear, a tiny roaring, and she was so sick with fear that she could do nothing but listen to it—the telephone was clammy and very heavy and her fingers groped down to the dial but were too weak to touch it. She began to scream into the phone, into the roaring. She cried out, she cried for her mother, she felt her breath start jerking back and forth in her lungs as if it were something Arnold Friend were stabbing her with again and again with no tenderness. A noisy sorrowful wailing rose all about her and she was locked inside it the way she was locked inside the house.

After a while she could hear again. She was sitting on the floor with   145
her wet back against the wall.

Arnold Friend was saying from the door, "That's a good girl. Put the   146
phone back."

She kicked the phone away from her.   147

"No, honey. Pick it up. Put it back right."   148

She picked it up and put it back. The dial tone stopped.   149

"That's a good girl. Now you come outside."   150

She was hollow with what had been fear, but what was now just an   151
emptiness. All that screaming had blasted it out of her. She sat, one leg

cramped under her, and deep inside her brain was something like a pin-point of light that kept going and would not let her relax. She thought, I'm not going to see my mother again. She thought, I'm not going to sleep in my bed again. Her bright green blouse was all wet.

Arnold Friend said, in a gentle-loud voice that was like a stage [152] voice, "The place where you came from ain't there any more, and where you had in mind to go is cancelled out. This place you are now—inside your daddy's house—is nothing but a cardboard box I can knock down any time. You know that and always did know it. You hear me?"

She thought, I have got to think. I have to know what to do.   [153]

"We'll go out to a nice field, out in the country here where it smells [154] so nice and it's sunny," Arnold Friend said. "I'll have my arms around you so you won't need to try to get away and I'll show you what love is like, what it does. The hell with this house! It looks solid all right," he said. He ran a fingernail down the screen and the noise did not make Connie shiver, as it would have the day before. "Now put your hand on your heart, honey. Feel that? That feels solid too but we know better, be nice to me, be sweet like you can because what else is there for a girl like you but to be sweet and pretty and give in?—and get away before her people come back?"

She felt her pounding heart. Her hand seemed to enclose it. She [155] thought for the first time in her life that it was nothing that was hers, that belonged to her, but just a pounding, living thing inside this body that wasn't really hers either.

"You don't want them to get hurt," Arnold Friend went on. "Now [156] get up, honey. Get up all by yourself."

She stood.   [157]

"Now turn this way. That's right. Come over here to me—Ellie, put [158] that away, didn't I tell you? You dope. You miserable creepy dope," Arnold Friend said. His words were not angry but only part of an in-cantation. The incantation was kindly. "Now come out through the kitchen to me honey and let's see a smile, try it, you're a brave sweet lit-tle girl and now they're eating corn and hotdogs cooked to bursting over an outdoor fire, and they don't know one thing about you and never did and honey you're better than them because not a one of them would have done this for you."

Connie felt the linoleum under her feet; it was cool. She brushed her [159] hair back out of her eyes. Arnold Friend let go of the post tentatively and opened his arms for her, his elbows pointing in toward each other and his wrists limp, to show that this was an embarrassed embrace and a lit-tle mocking, he didn't want to make her self-conscious.

She put out her hand against the screen. She watched herself push [160] the door slowly open as if she were safe back somewhere in the other doorway, watching this body and this head of long hair moving out into the sunlight where Arnold Friend waited.

"My sweet little blue-eyed girl," he said, in a half-sung sigh that had [161] nothing to do with her brown eyes but was taken up just the same by the vast sunlit reaches of the land behind him and on all sides of him, so much land that Connie had never seen before and did not recognize except to know that she was going to it.

Responding to Reading

1. How is Connie like other fifteen-year-old girls? Is she atypical in any way?
2. Does Connie's relationship with her mother strike you as realistic? Why or why not? Is it in any way like the relationship you have (or had) with your own mother? If so, how?
3. Why is Connie so vulnerable to Arnold? What is the nature of his appeal for her?

WRITING

The Way We Live Now

1. Who are your heroes? Are they real or fictional? Are they famous? Are they living? Applying Bader's criteria as well as some criteria of your own to the figures you select, explain why they qualify as heroes.

2. What do people in your age group have to look forward to? Write an essay outlining your predictions. You may base your conclusions on personal experience or on information in this chapter's essays.

3. Identify several "signs of the times," familiar images and events that you believe typify the way we live now, and write an essay explaining what they tell you about your world.

4. How are FaNee, the real teenager profiled in Trillin's "It's Just Too Late," and Connie, the fictional teenage protagonist of Joyce Carol Oates's short story "Where Are You Going, Where Have You Been?" alike? How are they different? Pay particular attention to their relationships with their families and friends and to their stories' outcomes.

5. Several of the selections in this chapter suggest that some of modern-day society's problems are caused (or at least aggravated) by the media, which expose private lives and turn personal problems into economic commodities. Do you believe the media make social problems worse—or even create social problems? Support your conclusion with examples from essays in this chapter and in Chapter 4 as well as from your own experiences.

6. In "The Making of a Generation" Arthur Levine says, "Every . . . generation is defined by the social events of its age." Identify several pivotal social and political events—local or national—that had an impact on you and others your age, and explain how these events define your generation.

7. On the basis of your own observations, how easy do you think it is to move to a higher social class? For example, how do factors like race or geography limit or enhance social mobility? In developing your response, consider the selections by Steele, Staples, Coles, and Trillin.

8. In "Children of Affluence" Robert Coles equates entitlement with destiny: From birth, affluent children are aware that they are special and that their lives will therefore be different from others' lives. They are "destined for a satisfying and rewarding life" (paragraph

30), and they know it. How does this idea square with the traditional view of the American Dream, which sees the United States as a land of unlimited possibilities? How does this idea apply to your own plans for the future? You may support your thesis with material from essays in this chapter and from Chapter 6.

9. Do you believe the American family is deteriorating? Are the ties that connect family members weakening? If so, what forces do you hold responsible for this decline? Consider your own extended family as well as the situations presented in "It's Just Too Late" or "Where Are You Going, Where Have You Been?" If you like, you may also consider Marie Winn's comments about the American family in "The Plug-In Drug" in Chapter 4.

10. As selections like "Just Walk on By," "It's Just Too Late," and "Getting Away with Murder" reveal, we live in an increasingly violent society. Logically, then, we should be becoming more and more accustomed to violence. Do your own observations and experiences suggest that we *are* becoming accustomed to violence? Explain your views in a letter to a local or national government official.

MEDICAL
PRACTICE AND
RESPONSIBILITY

8

Student Voices

"I believe that medical research is extremely important to our society. In fact, medical research will become the main source of jobs over the next decade. In my opinion, there should be very few legal restrictions on what work a scientist should be able to do. However, I do feel that morality and common sense should play a major part in deciding what and how medical research is done.

"I believe people should suffer as little as possible if they have a terminal illness. If a person decides that pain and suffering is unbearable, that person should be able to end his or her life. It should be the person's decision, not someone else's."

—*Todd Lemon*

"Death is a word that frightens me. I prefer not to think of it."

—*Renee Higgins*

"My grandmother tells me that if she ever gets too feeble to take care of herself, I should take her behind the barn and shoot her. She doesn't think it is fair to keep someone alive when their time has come. I don't think most of my friends would agree with her. I suppose their attitudes are based on the fear of death we have in this culture. Since we view death as a permanent separation from those we love, we try our best to prevent it. We also look with awe upon those who we think can save us. I think this fear has made us think of doctors as some sort of gods."

—*Elizabeth Zaffarano*

"AIDS is unfortunately here with us, and we must deal with it. This disease affects everybody either directly or indirectly. For this reason, we must all take the responsibility to learn about this disease, to help slow it down, and someday to stop the virus completely."

—*Dave Zimecki*

"I think that AIDS is eventually going to make people really take notice. So far a lot of attention has been paid to AIDS by activists and scientists; however, I think everyday people have not been as concerned as they should be. But this situation will change when the death rate goes up. Perhaps then people will take the disease seriously and do what they can to stop its spread."

—*Yuval Ozer*

"I think AIDS is a problem that will always be with us. This means AIDS will get worse and become so widespread that millions will die from it. Sometimes I try to be positive about the disease, but I can't. Maybe it's because I'm a biology major, but I only see a nightmare that will never end."

—*Jennifer Liebl*

————————————— **Preparing to Read and Write** —————————————

Because medical science has made such great advances, it is easy to forget that until the 1930s, doctors did little more than diagnose most diseases. With the discovery of sulfa drugs and penicillin, the situation changed, and physicians were actually able to cure diseases that had decimated human populations for centuries. During the last two decades, medical science has gone even further, making tremendous advances toward understanding basic biological processes and prolonging human life. Recently, however, new diseases or new forms of old diseases have threatened to wipe out these gains. For example, AIDS, a disease almost unheard of fifteen years ago, afflicts over a million people worldwide, and tuberculosis in new drug-resistant forms (ironically, caused in part by the medications used to cure tuberculosis itself) is making a deadly comeback in American cities. Thus, twentieth-century science must face the uncomfortable fact that in the near future epidemics may be as common as they were a hundred years ago.

Like our gains against disease, our advances in medical technology have proved to be a mixed blessing. Although doctors are armed with an array of high-tech equipment, they must face problems this technology has created. For example, how far should doctors go to preserve human life? At what point, if any, does a life become not worth saving? Once this point has been reached, should the patient be allowed to end his or her life? The writers in this chapter struggle with these and other questions. In some cases they simply define the issues and acknowledge their difficulty. In other cases they offer answers that at best are tentative or incomplete. Still, writers—along with doctors, ethicists, and theologians—continue to search for answers, just as we do. If we do not, we run the risk of being overwhelmed by the very technology we developed to improve the human condition.

As you read and prepare to write about the selections in this chapter, you may consider the following questions.

- Is the writer a physician? A scientist? A layperson? Does the writer's background make you more or less receptive to his or her ideas?
- What is the writer's subject?
- Is the writer's attitude toward his or her subject positive or negative?
- What position does the writer take on the issues? Do you agree or disagree with this position?
- Is the writer's emphasis on the theory or practice of medicine?
- Does the writer consider ethical questions related to his or her subject?

- Does the writer deal primarily with his or her culture or with another culture? What differences, if any, does he or she see between cultures?

- What preconceptions do you have about the writer's subject? Does the selection reinforce or contradict your preconceptions?

- What background in science or medicine does the writer assume readers have?

- Does the selection present concepts in general terms, or does it use technical language? Could the writer have made his or her points as effectively with simpler language?

- Is the writer optimistic or pessimistic about the future of medicine? About the future in general?

- Is the writer's purpose to educate? To make readers think about a provocative idea? To persuade them? To warn them?

TWO PERSPECTIVES ON MEDICAL PRACTICE AND RESPONSIBILITY

In the following essays, two young doctors write about surprising encounters with unexpected pathologies. "My Own Country," the first
chapter of Abraham Verghese's book of the same name, recounts the
case of the first AIDS patient treated in Johnson City, Tennessee. Indian by birth, Verghese (1956–) studied medicine in Madras before coming to the U.S. in 1980. He had dealt with many AIDS cases while training in New York and Boston but didn't expect to find a similar
epidemic when he joined the staff of a hospital in rural Tennessee. He
has said of his experiences, "You are suddenly dealing with people
your own age whose plight makes you reflect on your ideas about sex,
about social issues, and, of course, about your own mortality." In the
second essay, American-trained pediatrician Perri Klass (1958–) recalls
her experiences working in a prestigious hospital in India, where patients suffer from ailments that are common there but that she found
unfamiliar, even mystifying. A graduate of Harvard Medical School,
Klass contributes articles to many popular magazines and has published novels and short stories as well as a book about her first year as
a medical student, *A Not Entirely Benign Procedure* (1987), from which
"India" is taken.

MY OWN COUNTRY

Abraham Verghese

Summer, 1985. A young man is driving down from New York to 1
visit his parents in Johnson City, Tennessee.

I can hear the radio playing. I can picture his parents waiting, his 2
mother cooking his favorite food, his father pacing. I see the young man
in my mind, despite the years that have passed; I can see him driving
home along a route that he knows well and that I have traveled many
times. He started before dawn. By the time it gets hot, he has reached
Pennsylvania. Three hundred or so miles from home, he begins to feel
his chest tighten.

He rolls up the windows. Soon, chills shake his body. He turns the 3
heater on full blast; it is hard for him to keep his foot on the accelerator
or his hands on the wheel.

By the time he reaches Virginia, the chills give way to a profuse   4
sweat. Now he is burning up and he turns on the air conditioner, but the
perspiration still soaks through his shirt and drips off his brow. His
lungs feel heavy as if laden with buckshot. His breath is labored, weight-
ed by fear and perhaps by the knowledge of the burden he is bringing
to his parents. Maybe he thinks about taking the next exit off Interstate
81 and seeking help. But he knows that no one can help him, and the
dread of finding himself sick and alone keeps him going. That and the
desire for home.

I know this stretch of highway that cuts through the Virginia moun-   5
tains; I know how the road rises, sheer rock on one side, how in places
the kudzu takes over and seems to hold up a hillside, and how, in the
early afternoon, the sun glares directly into the windshield. He would
have seen hay rolled into tidy bundles, lined up on the edges of fields.
And tobacco plants and sagging sheds with their rusted, corrugated-tin
roofs and shutterless side-openings. It would have all been familiar, this
country. His own country.

In the early evening of August 11, 1985, he was rolled into the emer-   6
gency room (ER) of the Johnson City Medical Center—the "Miracle Center," as we referred to it when we were interns. Puffing like an overheated steam engine, he was squeezing in forty-five breaths a minute. Or
so Claire Bellamy, the nurse, told me later. It had shocked her to see a
thirty-two-year-old man in such severe respiratory distress.

He sat bolt upright on the stretcher, his arms propped behind him   7
like struts that braced his heaving chest. His blond hair was wet and
stuck to his forehead; his skin, Claire recalled, was gun-metal gray, his
lips and nail beds blue.

She had slapped an oxygen mask on him and hollered for someone   8
to pull the duty physician away from the wound he was suturing. A
genuine emergency was at hand, something she realized, even as it over-
took her, she was not fully comprehending. She knew what it was not:
it was *not* severe asthma, status asthmaticus; it was *not* a heart attack.
She could not stop to take it all in. Everything was happening too
quickly.

With every breath he sucked in, his nostrils flared. The strap mus-   9
cles of his neck stood out like cables. He pursed his lips when he exhaled, as if he was loath to let the oxygen go, hanging on to it as long as
he could.

Electrodes placed on his chest and hooked to a monitor showed his   10
heart fluttering at a desperate 160 beats per minute.

On his chest X ray, the lungs that should have been dark as the night   11
were instead whited out by a veritable snowstorm.

My friend Ray, a pulmonary physician, was immediately sum-   12
moned. While Ray listened to his chest, the phlebotomist drew blood for
serum electrolytes and red and white blood cell counts. The respiratory

therapist punctured the radial artery at the wrist to measure blood oxygen levels. Claire started an intravenous line. And the young man slumped on the stretcher. He stopped breathing.

Claire punched the "Code Blue" button on the cubicle wall and an [13] operator's voice sounded through the six-story hospital building: "Code Blue, emergency room!"

The code team—an intern, a senior resident, two intensive care unit [14] nurses, a respiratory therapist, a pharmacist—thundered down the hallway.

Patients in their rooms watching TV sat up in their beds; visitors [15] froze in place in the corridors.

More doctors arrived; some came in street clothes, having heard the [16] call as they headed for the parking lot. Others came in scrub suits. Ray was "running" the code; he called for boluses of bicarbonate and epinephrine, for a second intravenous line to be secured, and for Claire to increase the vigor but slow down the rate of her chest compressions.

The code team took their positions. The beefy intern with Nautilus [17] shoulders took off his jacket and climbed onto a step stool. He moved in just as Claire stepped back, picking up the rhythm of chest compression without missing a beat, calling the cadence out loud. With locked elbows, one palm over the back of the other, he squished the heart between breastbone and spine, trying to squirt enough blood out of it to supply the brain.

The ER physician unbuttoned the young man's pants and cut away [18] the underwear, now soiled with urine. His fingers reached for the groin, feeling for the femoral artery to assess the adequacy of the chest compressions.

A "crash cart" stocked with ampules of every variety, its defibrilla- [19] tor paddles charged and ready, stood at the foot of the bed as the pharmacist recorded each medication given and the exact time it was administered.

The clock above the stretcher had been automatically zeroed when [20] the Code Blue was called. A code nurse called out the elapsed time at thirty-second intervals. The resident and another nurse from the code team probed with a needle for a vein to establish the second "line."

Ray "bagged" the patient with a tight-fitting mask and hand-held [21] squeeze bag as the respiratory therapist readied an endotracheal tube and laryngoscope.

At a signal from Ray, the players froze in midair while he bent the [22] young man's head back over the edge of the stretcher. Ray slid the laryngoscope in between tongue and palate and heaved up with his left hand, pulling the base of the tongue up and forward until the leaf-shaped epiglottis appeared.

Behind it, the light at the tip of the laryngoscope showed glimpses [23] of the voice box and the vocal cords. With his right hand, Ray fed the endotracheal tube alongside the laryngoscope, down the back of the throat, past the epiglottis, and past the vocal cords—this part done almost blindly and with a prayer—and into the trachea. Then he connected the squeeze bag to the end of the endotracheal tube and watched the chest rise as he pumped air into the lungs. He nodded, giving the signal for the action to resume.

Now Ray listened with his stethoscope over both sides of the chest [24] as the respiratory therapist bagged the limp young man. He listened for the muffled *whoosh* of air, listened to see if it was equally loud over both lungs.

He heard sounds only over the right lung. The tube had gone down [25] the right main bronchus, a straighter shot than the left.

He pulled the tube back an inch, listened again, and heard air en- [26] tering both sides. The tube was sitting above the carina, above the point where the trachea bifurcates. He called for another chest X ray; a radiopaque marker at the end of the tube would confirm its exact position.

With a syringe he inflated the balloon cuff at the end of the endo- [27] tracheal tube that would keep it snugly in the trachea. Claire wound tape around the tube and plastered it down across the young man's cheeks and behind his neck.

The blue in the young man's skin began to wash out and a faint pink [28] appeared in his cheeks. The ECG machine which had spewed paper into a curly mound on the floor, now showed the original rapid heart rhythm restored.

At this point the young man was alive again, but just barely. The [29] Code Blue had been a success.

In no time, the young man was moved to the intensive care unit [30] (ICU) and hooked up via the endotracheal tube to a machine that looked like a top-loading washer, gauges and dials covering its flat surface. Its bellows took over the work of his tired diaphragm.

He came awake an hour later to the suffocating and gagging sensa- [31] tion of the endotracheal tube lodged in his throat. Even as the respira-tor tried to pump oxygen into his lungs, he bucked and resisted it, tried to cough out the tube. One can only imagine his terror at this awaken-ing: naked, blazing light shining in his eyes, tubes in his mouth, tubes up his nose, tubes in his penis, transfixed by needles and probes stuck into his arms.

He must have wondered if this was hell. [32]

The Miracle Center ICU nurses who were experienced—at least in [33] theory—with this sort of fright and dislocation, reassured him in loud tones. Because of the tube passing between his vocal cords and because his hands were tied to prevent his snatching at the tube (an automatic gesture in this setting), he could not communicate at all. With every passing second, his terror escalated. His heart rate rose quickly.

He was immediately sedated with a bolus of morphine injected into [34]
one of his lines. He was paralyzed with a curarelike agent, a cousin of
the paste used on arrow-tips by indigenous tribes in the Amazon. As the
drug shot through his circulation and reached the billions of junctions
where nerve met and directed muscle, it blocked all signals and he lay
utterly still and flaccid.

The respirator sent breaths into him with rhythmic precision at the [35]
rate dialed in by Ray, even throwing in a mechanical sigh—a breath
larger than usual—to recruit and keep patent the air sacs in the base of
the lung.

The young man's parents now arrived at the hospital and were es- [36]
corted up to their son's bedside. They had been waiting for him at home.
Now they stood, I was told, in utter disbelief, trying to see their son
through the forest of intravenous poles and the thicket of tubing and
wires that covered him, asking again and again *what* had happened.
And *why?*

By the next day the pneumonia had progressed. His lungs were [37]
even stiffer, making the respirator work overtime to drive oxygen into
him. Ray performed a bronchoscopy, sliding a fiberoptic device into
the endotracheal tube. Through the bronchoscope he could see the
glossy red lining of the trachea and the bronchi. All looked normal. He
directed the bronchoscope as far out as it would go, then passed a
biopsy forceps through it and took a blind bite of the air sacs of the
lung.

Under the microscope, the honeycomblike air spaces of the lung [38]
were congealed with a syrupy outpouring of inflammatory fluid and
cells. Embedded in this matrix were thousands upon thousands of tiny,
darkly staining, flying-saucerlike discs that the pathologist identified as
Pneumocystis carinii.

The young man had no predisposing illness like leukemia or cancer [39]
that would explain this fulminant pneumonia caused by an innocuous
organism.

His immune system *had* to be abnormal. [40]

It was clear, though no one had yet seen a case, that he was Johnson [41]
City's first case of the acquired immune deficiency syndrome—AIDS.

Word spread like wildfire through the hospital. All those involved [42]
in his care in the ER and ICU agonized over their exposure.

The intern remembered his palms pressed against the clammy [43]
breast as he performed closed-chest massage.

Claire remembered starting the intravenous line and having blood [44]
trickle out and touch her ungloved skin.

The respiratory therapist recalled the fine spray that landed on his [45]
face as he suctioned the tracheal tube.

The emergency room physician recalled the sweat and the wet un- [46]
derwear his fingers encountered as he sought out the femoral artery.

Even those who had not touched the young man—the pharmacist, [47] the orderlies, the transport personnel—were alarmed.

Ray worried too; he had been exposed as much as anyone. In the [48] days to follow, he was stopped again and again in the corridor by people quizzing him about the danger, about their exposure. Ray even felt some anger directed at him. As if he, who had done everything right and diagnosed the case in short order, could have prevented this or warned them.

An ICU nurse told me that the young man's room took on a special [49] aura. In the way a grisly murder or the viewing of an apparition can transform an otherwise ordinary abode, so cubicle 7C was forever transformed. Doctors and others in the ICU peeked through the glass, watching the inert body of the young man. His father was seated beside him. The hometown boy was now regarded as an alien, the father an object of pity.

Ray told me how the parents took the news. The mother froze, star- [50] ing at Ray's lips as if he was speaking a foreign language. The father turned away, only the sound of his footsteps breaking the silence as he walked out into the corridor and on out into the parking lot, unable to stay in the building where that word had been uttered.

Much later, the father asked, "But *how* did he get it? How could he [51] have gotten this?"

Ray pointed out that he had had no time to get a history: perhaps [52] they could give him some information. Had their son been healthy in the past year and in the days preceding the trip? Lord, yes! (The father did all the answering.) Did he ever use intravenous drugs? Lord, no! And to their knowledge had he ever had a blood transfusion?

No.   [53]

Was he married?   [54]

No.   [55]

Did he live alone? No, he had a friend in New York.   [56]

A male friend? Yes . . . they had never met him.   [57]

"Oh Lord! Is that what you're saying? Is that how he got it? Is my [58] son a queer?"

Ray just stood there, unable to respond to the father's words.   [59]

The father turned to his wife and said, "Mother, do you hear this? [60] Do you hear this?"

She gazed at the floor, nodding slowly, confirming finally what she [61] had always known.

The mother never left the ICU or her son's side. And in a day or so, [62] the father also rallied around his son, spending long hours with him, holding his hand, talking to him. Behind the glass one could watch as the father bent over his son, his lips moving soundlessly.

He balked when his son's buddies flew down from New York. He [63] was angry, on the verge of a violent outburst. This was all too much.

This nightmare, these city boys, this new world that had suddenly engulfed his family.

Ray tried to mediate. But only when it seemed his boy's death was [64] inevitable did the father relent and allow the New Yorkers near him. He guarded the space around his son, marshaling his protection.

The two visitors were men with closely cut hair. One had a [65] pierced ear, purple suede boots, tight jeans and what the ICU ward clerk, Jennie, described to me as a "New York attitude—know what I mean?"

Jennie said the other friend, clearly the patient's lover, was dressed [66] more conservatively and was in his early forties. She thought he was "a computer person." She remembers the tears that trickled continuously down his cheeks and the handkerchief squeezed in his hand. Jennie thought the mother wanted to talk to her son's lover. He, in turn, needed badly to talk to anyone. But in the presence of the father there was no chance for them to speak.

Three weeks after his arrival, the young man died. [67]

The New Yorkers left before the funeral. [68]

The respirator was unhooked and rolled back to the respiratory [69] therapy department. A heated debate ensued as to what to do with it. There were, of course, published and simple recommendations for disinfecting it. But that was not the point. The machine that had sustained the young man had come to symbolize AIDS in Johnson City.

Some favored burying the respirator, deep-sixing it in the swampy [70] land at the back of the hospital. Others were for incinerating it. As a compromise, the machine was opened up, its innards gutted and most replaceable parts changed. It was then gas disinfected several times. Even so, it was a long time before it was put back into circulation.

About two months after the young man died, I returned to Johnson [71] City. I had previously worked there as an intern and resident in internal medicine and I was now coming back after completing my training in infectious diseases in Boston. People who knew me from my residency days stopped me and told me the sad story of this young man's homecoming.

But it was not always recounted as a sad story. "Did you hear what [72] happened to Ray?" a doctor asked me. He proceeded to tell me how a young man had dropped into the emergency room looking like he had pneumonia but turning out to be "a homo from New York with AIDS." The humor resided in what had happened to the unsuspecting Ray, the pie-in-your-face nature of the patient's diagnosis.

Some of the veteran ICU nurses, perhaps because this case broke [73] through their I've-seen-it-all-and-more-honey attitudes, astonished me with their indignation. In their opinion, this "homo-sex-shual" with AIDS clearly had no right to expect to be taken care of in our state-of-the-art, computerized ICU.

When I heard the story, the shock waves in the hospital had already [74]
subsided. Everyone thought it had been a freak accident, a one-time
thing in Johnson City. This was a small town in the country, a town of
clean-living, good country people. AIDS was clearly a big city problem.
It was something that happened in other kinds of lives.

INDIA

Perri Klass

The people look different. The examining room is crowded with chil- [1]
dren and their parents, gathered hopefully around the doctor's desk,
jockeying for position. Everyone seems to believe, if the doctor gets close
to *my* child everything will be okay. Several Indian medical students are
also present, leaning forward to hear their professor's explanations as
they watch one particular child walk across the far end of the room. I
stand on my toes, straining to see over the intervening heads so I, too,
can watch this patient walk. I can see her face, intent, bright dark eyes,
lips pinched in concentration. She's about ten years old. I can see her
sleek black head, the two long black braids pinned up in circles over her
ears in the style we used to call doughnuts. All she's wearing is a long
loose shirt, so her legs can be seen, as with great difficulty she wobbles
across the floor. At the professor's direction, she sits down on the floor
and then tries to get up again; she needs to use her arms to push her
body up.

I'm confused. This patient looks like a child with absolutely classic [2]
muscular dystrophy, but muscular dystrophy is a genetic disease carried
on the X chromosome, like hemophilia. It therefore almost never occurs
in girls. Can this be one of those one-in-a-trillion cases? Or is it a more
unusual form of muscle disease, one that isn't sex-linked in inheritance?

Finally the child succeeds in getting up on her feet, and her parents [3]
come forward to help her dress. They pull her over near to where I'm
standing, and as they're helping with the clothing, the long shirt slides
up over the child's hips. No, this isn't one of those one-in-a-trillion cases.
I've been watching a ten-year-old boy with muscular dystrophy; he
comes from a Sikh family, and Sikh males don't cut their hair. Adults
wear turbans, but young boys often have their hair braided and pinned
up in those two knots.

Recently I spent some time in India, working in the pediatric de- [4]
partment of an important New Delhi hospital. I wanted to learn about
medicine outside the United States, to work in a pediatric clinic in the
Third World, and I suppose I also wanted to test my own medical education, to find out whether my newly acquired skills are in fact trans-

ferable to any place where there are human beings, with human bodies, subject to their range of ills and evils.

But it wasn't just a question of my medical knowledge. In India, I 5 found that my cultural limitations often prevented me from thinking clearly about patients. Everyone looked different, and I was unable to pick up any clues from their appearance, their manner of speech, their clothing. This is a family of Afghan refugees. This family is from the south of India. This child is from a very poor family. This child has a Nepalese name. All the clues I use at home to help me evaluate patients, clues ranging from what neighborhood they live in to what ethnic origin their names suggest, were hidden from me in India.

The people don't just look different on the outside, of course. It 6 might be more accurate to say *the population is different.* The gene pool, for example: there are some genetic diseases that are much more common here than there, cystic fibrosis, say, which you have to keep in mind when evaluating patients in Boston, but which would be a show-offy and highly unlikely diagnosis-out-of-a-book for a medical student to suggest in New Delhi (I know—in my innocence I suggested it).

And all of this, in the end, really reflects human diversity, though 7 admittedly it's reflected in the strange warped mirror of the medical profession; it's hard to exult in the variety of human genetic defects, or even in the variety of human culture, when you're looking at it as a tool for examining a sick child. Still, I can accept the various implications of a world full of different people, different populations.

The diseases are different. The patient is a seven-year-old boy whose 8 father says that over the past week and a half he has become more tired, less active, and lately he doesn't seem to understand everything going on around him. Courteously, the senior doctor turns to me, asks what my assessment is. He asks this in a tone that suggests that the diagnosis is obvious, and as a guest I'm invited to pronounce it. The diagnosis, whatever it is, is certainly not obvious to me. I can think of a couple of infections that might look like this, but no single answer. The senior doctor sees my difficulty and offers a maxim, one that I've heard many times back in Boston. Gently, slightly reprovingly, he tells me, "Common things occur commonly. There are many possibilities, of course, but I think it is safe to say that this is almost certainly tuberculous meningitis."

Tuberculous meningitis? Common things occur commonly? Some- 9 where in my brain (and somewhere in my lecture notes) "the complications of tuberculosis" are filed away, and yes, I suppose it can affect the central nervous system, just as I can vaguely remember that it can affect the stomach and the skeletal system. . . . To tell the truth, I've never even seen a case of straightforward tuberculosis of the lung in a small child, let alone what I would have thought of as a rare complication.

And hell, it's worse than that. I've done a fair amount of pediatrics [10] back in Boston, but there are an awful lot of things I've never seen. When I was invited in New Delhi to give an opinion on a child's rash, I came up with quite a creative list of tropical diseases, because guess what? I had never seen a child with measles before. In the United States, children are vaccinated against measles, mumps, and rubella at the age of one year. There are occasional outbreaks of measles among college students, but the disease is now very rare in small children. ("Love this Harvard medical student. Can't recognize tuberculous meningitis. Can't recognize measles or mumps. What the hell do they teach them over there in pediatrics?")

And this, of course, is one of the main medical student reasons for [11] going to study abroad, the chance to see diseases you wouldn't see at home. The pathology, we call it, as in "I got to see some amazing pathology while I was in India." It's embarrassing to find yourself suddenly ignorant, but it's interesting to learn all about a new range of diagnoses, symptoms, treatments, all things you might have learned from a textbook and then immediately forgotten as totally outside your own experience.

The difficult thing is that these differences don't in any way, how- [12] ever tortured, reflect the glory of human variation. They reflect instead the sad partitioning of the species, because they're almost all preventable diseases, and their prevalence is a product of poverty, of lack of vaccinations, of malnutrition and poor sanitation. And therefore, though it's all very educational for the medical student (and I'm by now more or less used to parasitizing my education off of human suffering), this isn't a difference to be accepted without outrage.

The expectations are different. The child is a seven-month-old girl with [13] diarrhea. She has been losing weight for a couple of weeks, she won't eat or drink, she just lies there in her grandmother's arms. The grandmother explains: one of her other grandchildren has just died from very severe diarrhea, and this little girl's older brother died last year, not of diarrhea but of a chest infection. . . . I look at the grandmother's face, at the faces of the baby's mother and father, who are standing on either side of the chair where the grandmother is sitting with the baby. All these people believe in the possibility of death, the chance that the child will not live to grow up. They've all seen many children die. These parents lost a boy last year, and they know that they may lose their daughter.

The four have traveled for almost sixteen hours to come to this hospi- [14] tal, because after the son died last year, they no longer have faith in the village doctor. They're hopeful, they offer their sick baby to this famous hospital. They're prepared to stay in Delhi while she's hospitalized, the mother will sleep in the child's crib with her, the father and grandmother may well sleep on the hospital grounds. They've brought food, cooking pots, warm shawls because it's January and it gets cold at night. They're tough, and they're hopeful, but they believe in the possibility of death.

Back home, in Boston, I've heard bewildered, grieving parents say, [15] essentially, "Who would have believed that in the 1980s a child could just die like that?" Even parents with terminally ill children, children who spend months or years getting sicker and sicker, sometimes have great difficulty accepting that all the art and machinery of modern medicine are completely helpless. They expect every child to live to grow up.

In India, it isn't that parents are necessarily resigned, and certainly [16] not that they love their children less. They may not want to accept the dangers, but poor people, people living in poor villages or in urban slums, know the possibility is there. If anything, they may be even more terrified than American parents, just because perhaps they're picturing the death of some other loved child, imagining this living child going the way of that dead one.

I don't know. This is a gap I can't cross. I can laugh at my own in- [17] ability to interpret the signals of a different culture, and I can read and ask questions and slowly begin to learn a little about the people I'm trying to help care for. I can blush at my ignorance of diseases uncommon in my home territory, study up in textbooks, and deplore inequalities that allow preventable diseases to ravage some unfortunate populations while others are protected. But I can't draw my lesson from this grandmother, these parents, this sick little girl. I can't imagine their awareness, their accommodations of what they know. I can't understand how they live with it. I can't accept their acceptance. My medical training has taken place in a world where all children are supposed to grow up, and the exceptions to this rule are rare horrible diseases, disastrous accidents. That is the attitude, the expectation I demand from patients. I'm left most disturbed not by the fact of children dying, not by the different diseases from which they die, or the differences in the medical care they receive, but by the way their parents look at me, at my profession. Perhaps it is only in this that I allow myself to take it all personally.

Responding to Reading

1. Why do you think Verghese describes the examination and treatment of the patient in such detail? How does this description affect your feelings toward the patient?

2. How did Verghese's medical team react in 1985 when they heard the patient was gay and had AIDS? Do you think they would react the same way today? Why or why not?

3. Klass observes that in India "*The people look different* (1)," "*the diseases are different*" (7), and "*the expectations are different*" (13). Exactly how are they different? How do you account for the differences?

4. How are Klass's and Verghese's attitudes toward their patients alike? How are they different? Do their attitudes change? Do they ever get used to what they see?

5. Both Verghese and Klass have to deal with people's attitudes about death. How do these attitudes make it difficult for them to treat disease?
6. As you read these essays, do you identify with the doctors or with the patients? Explain.

IMELDA

Richard Selzer

A surgeon as well as an accomplished writer, Richard Selzer (1928–) was born in Troy, New York, where his father had a family medical practice until his death when Selzer was twelve. Following in his father's footsteps, he attended Albany Medical College and Yale Medical School, later serving on the faculty there as a professor of surgery. Influenced by his artistic mother, Selzer also took an early interest in literature but didn't himself begin writing for publication until he was in his forties. Since then he has published essays and stories in a variety of magazines and journals, and his collections include *Mortal Lessons* (1977), *Letters to a Young Doctor* (1982), and *Imagine a Woman* (1991). His latest book is a memoir, *Down from Troy: A Doctor Comes of Age* (1992). Of his two professions Selzer has written, "The surgeon sutures together the tissues of the body to make whole what is sick or injured; the writer sews words into sentences to fashion a new version of human experience." Selzer's work often focuses on the complex relationship between doctor and patient; in the following essay he recalls a surgeon he worked under in medical school whose compassionate gesture toward a young patient has remained with Selzer all his life.

I heard the other day that Hugh Franciscus had died. I knew him once. He was the Chief of Plastic Surgery when I was a medical student at Albany Medical College. Dr. Franciscus was the archetype of the professor of surgery—tall, vigorous, muscular, as precise in his technique as he was impeccable in his dress. Each day a clean lab coat monkishly starched, that sort of thing. I doubt that he ever read books. One book only, that of the human body, took the place of all others. He never raised his eyes from it. He read it like a printed page as though he knew that in the calligraphy there just beneath the skin were all the secrets of the world. Long before it became visible to anyone else, he could detect the first sign of granulation at the base of a wound, the first blue line of new epithelium at the periphery that would tell him that a wound would heal, or the barest hint of necrosis that presaged failure. This gave him the appearance of a prophet. "This skin graft will take," he would say, and you must believe beyond all cyanosis, exudation and inflammation that it would.

He had enemies, of course, who said he was arrogant, that he exalted activity for its own sake. Perhaps. But perhaps it was no more than the honesty of one who knows his own worth. Just look at a scalpel, after all. What a feeling of sovereignty, megalomania even, when you know that it is you and you alone who will make certain use of it. It was said, too, that he was a ladies' man. I don't know about that. It was all rumor. Besides, I think he had other things in mind than mere living. Hugh Franciscus was a zealous hunter. Every fall during the season he drove upstate to hunt deer. There was a glass-front case in his office where he showed his guns. How could he shoot a deer? we asked. But he knew better. To us medical students he was someone heroic, someone made up of several gods, beheld at a distance, and always from a lesser height. If he had grown accustomed to his miracles, we had not. He had no close friends on the staff. There was something a little sad in that. As though once long ago he had been flayed by friendship and now the slightest breeze would hurt. Confidences resulted in dishonor. Perhaps the person in whom one confided would scorn him, betray. Even though he spent his days among those less fortunate, weaker than he—the sick, after all—Franciscus seemed aware of an air of personal harshness in his environment to which he reacted by keeping his own counsel, by a certain remoteness. It was what gave him the appearance of being haughty. With the patients he was forthright. All the facts laid out, every question anticipated and answered with specific information. He delivered good news and bad with the same dispassion.

I was a third-year student, just turned onto the wards for the first time, and clerking on Surgery. Everything—the operating room, the morgue, the emergency room, the patients, professors, even the nurses—was terrifying. One picked one's way among the mines and booby traps of the hospital, hoping only to avoid the hemorrhage and perforation of disgrace. The opportunity for humiliation was everywhere.

It all began on Ward Rounds. Dr. Franciscus was demonstrating a cross-leg flap graft he had constructed to cover a large fleshy defect in the leg of a merchant seaman who had injured himself in a fall. The man was from Spain and spoke no English. There had been a comminuted fracture of the femur, much soft tissue damage, necrosis. After weeks of debridement and dressings, the wound had been made ready for grafting. Now the patient was in his fifth postoperative day. What we saw was a thick web of pale blue flesh arising from the man's left thigh, and which had been sutured to the open wound on the right thigh. When the surgeon pressed the pedicle with his finger, it blanched; when he let up, there was a slow return of the violaceous color.

"The circulation is good," Franciscus announced. "It will get better."   5
In several weeks, we were told, he would divide the tube of flesh at its
site of origin, and tailor it to fit the defect to which, by then, it would
have grown more solidly. All at once, the webbed man in the bed
reached out, and gripping Franciscus by the arm, began to speak rapidly, pointing to his groin and hip. Franciscus stepped back at once to dis-
engage his arm from the patient's grasp.

"Anyone here know Spanish? I didn't get a word of that."   6

"The cast is digging into him up above," I said. "The edges of the   7
plaster are rough. When he moves, they hurt."

Without acknowledging my assistance, Dr. Franciscus took a plas-   8
ter shears from the dressing cart and with several large snips cut away
the rough edges of the cast.

"*Gracias, gracias.*" The man in the bed smiled. But Franciscus had al-   9
ready moved on to the next bed. He seemed to me a man of immense
strength and ability, yet without affection for the patients. He did not
want to be touched by them. It was less kindness that he showed them
than a reassurance that he would never give up, that he would bend
every effort. If anyone could, he would solve the problems of their flesh.

Ward Rounds had disbanded and I was halfway down the corridor   10
when I heard Dr. Franciscus's voice behind me.

"You speak Spanish." It seemed a command.   11

"I lived in Spain for two years," I told him.   12

"I'm taking a surgical team to Honduras next week to operate on   13
the natives down there. I do it every year for three weeks, somewhere.
This year, Honduras. I can arrange the time away from your duties
here if you'd like to come along. You will act as interpreter. I'll show
you how to use the clinical camera. What you'd see would make it
worthwhile."

So it was that, a week later, the envy of my classmates, I joined the   14
mobile surgical unit—surgeons, anesthetists, nurses and equipment—
aboard a Military Air Transport plane to spend three weeks performing
plastic surgery on people who had been previously selected by an advance team. Honduras. I don't suppose I shall ever see it again. Nor do
I especially want to. From the plane it seemed a country made of clay—
burnt umber, raw sienna, dry. It had a deadweight quality, as though
the ground had no buoyancy, no air sacs through which a breeze might
wander. Our destination was Comayagua, a town in the Central High-
lands. The town itself was situated on the edge of one of the flatlands
that were linked in a network between the granite mountains. Above, all
was brown, with only an occasional Spanish cedar tree; below, patches
of luxuriant tropical growth. It was a day's bus ride from the airport. For
hours, the town kept appearing and disappearing with the convolutions
of the road. At last, there it lay before us, panting and exhausted at the
bottom of the mountain.

That was all I was to see of the countryside. From then on, there was ¹⁵
only the derelict hospital of Comayagua, with the smell of spoiling bananas and the accumulated odors of everyone who had been sick there
for the last hundred years. Of the two, I much preferred the frank smell
of the sick. The heat of the place was incendiary. So hot that, as we
stepped from the bus, our own words did not carry through the air, but
hung limply at our lips and chins. Just in front of the hospital was a
thirsty courtyard where mobs of waiting people squatted or lay in the
meager shade, and where, on dry days, a fine dust rose through which
untethered goats shouldered. Against the walls of this courtyard, gaunt,
dejected men stood, their faces, like their country, preternaturally
solemn, leaden. Here no one looked up at the sky. Every head was bent
beneath a wide-brimmed straw hat. In the days that followed, from the
doorway of the dispensary, I would watch the brown mountains sliding
about, drinking the hospital into their shadow as the afternoon grew
later and later, flattening us by their very altitude.

The people were mestizos, of mixed Spanish and Indian blood. They ¹⁶
had flat, broad, dumb museum feet. At first they seemed to me indistinguishable the one from the other, without animation. All the vitality,
the hidden sexuality, was in their black hair. Soon I was to know them
by the fissures with which each face was graven. But, even so, compared
to us, they were masked, shut away. My job was to follow Dr. Franciscus around, photograph the patients before and after surgery, interpret
and generally act as aide-de-camp. It was exhilarating. Within days I
had decided that I was not just useful, but essential. Despite that we
spent all day in each other's company, there were no overtures of friendship from Dr. Franciscus. He knew my place, and I knew it, too. In the
afternoon he examined the patients scheduled for the next day's
surgery. I would call out a name from the doorway to the examining
room. In the courtyard someone would rise. I would usher the patient
in, and nudge him to the examining table where Franciscus stood, always, I thought, on the verge of irritability. I would read aloud the case
history, then wait while he carried out his examination. While I took the
"before" photographs, Dr. Franciscus would dictate into a tape recorder:

"Ulcerating basal cell carcinoma of the right orbit—six by eight cen- ¹⁷
timeters—involving the right eye and extending into the floor of the
orbit. Operative plan: wide excision with enucleation of the eye. Later,
bone and skin grafting." The next morning we would be in the operating room where the procedure would be carried out.

We were more than two weeks into our tour of duty—a few days to ¹⁸
go—when it happened. Earlier in the day I had caught sight of her
through the window of the dispensary. A thin, dark Indian girl about
fourteen years old. A figurine, orange-brown, terra-cotta, and still attached to the unshaped clay from which she had been carved. An older,
sun-weathered woman stood behind and somewhat to the left of the

girl. The mother was short and dumpy. She wore a broad-brimmed hat with a high crown, and a shapeless dress like a cassock. The girl had long, loose black hair. There were tiny gold hoops in her ears. The dress she wore could have been her mother's. Far too big, it hung from her thin shoulders at some risk of slipping down her arms. Even with her in it, the dress was empty, something hanging on the back of a door. Her breasts made only the smallest imprint in the cloth, her hips none at all. All the while, she pressed to her mouth a filthy, pink, balled-up rag as though to stanch a flow or buttress against pain. I knew that what she had come to show us, what we were there to see, was hidden beneath that pink cloth. As I watched, the woman handed down to her a gourd from which the girl drank, lapping like a dog. She was the last patient of the day. They had been waiting in the courtyard for hours.

"Imelda Valdez," I called out. Slowly she rose to her feet, the cloth [19] never leaving her mouth, and followed her mother to the examining-room door. I shooed them in.

"You sit up there on the table," I told her. "Mother, you stand over [20] there, please." I read from the chart:

"This is a fourteen-year-old girl with a complete, unilateral, left- [21] sided cleft lip and cleft palate. No other diseases or congenital defects. Laboratory tests, chest X ray—negative."

"Tell her to take the rag away," said Dr. Franciscus. I did, and the [22] girl shrank back, pressing the cloth all the more firmly.

"Listen, this is silly," said Franciscus. "Tell her I've got to see it. Ei- [23] ther she behaves, or send her away."

"Please give me the cloth," I said to the girl as gently as possible. She [24] did not. She could not. Just then, Franciscus reached up and, taking the hand that held the rag, pulled it away with a hard jerk. For an instant the girl's head followed the cloth as it left her face, one arm still upflung against showing. Against all hope, she would hide herself. A moment later, she relaxed and sat still. She seemed to me then like an animal that looks outward at the infinite, at death, without fear, with recognition only.

Set as it was in the center of the girl's face, the defect was utterly [25] hideous—a nude rubbery insect that had fastened there. The upper lip was widely split all the way to the nose. One white tooth perched upon the protruding upper jaw projecting through the hole. Some of the bone seemed to have been gnawed away as well. Above the thing, clear almond eyes and long black hair reflected the light. Below, a slender neck where the pulse trilled visibly. Under our gaze the girl's eyes fell to her lap where her hands lay palms upward, half open. She was a beautiful bird with a crushed beak. And tense with the expectation of more shame.

"Open your mouth," said the surgeon. I translated. She did so, and [26] the surgeon tipped back her head to see inside.

"The palate, too. Complete," he said. There was a long silence. At [27] last he spoke.

"What is your name?" The margins of the wound melted until she [28] herself was being sucked into it.

"Imelda." The syllables leaked through the hole with a slosh and a [29] whistle.

"Tomorrow," said the surgeon, "I will fix your lip. *Mañana.*" [30]

It seemed to me that Hugh Franciscus, in spite of his years of ex- [31] perience, in spite of all the dreadful things he had seen, must have been awed by the sight of this girl. I could see it flit across his face for an instant. Perhaps it was her small act of concealment, that he had had to demand that she show him the lip, that he had had to force her to show it to him. Perhaps it was her resistance that intensified the disfigurement. Had she brought her mouth to him willingly, without shame, she would have been for him neither more nor less than any other patient.

He measured the defect with calipers, studied it from different an- [32] gles, turning her head with a finger at her chin.

"How can it ever be put back together?" I asked. [33]

"Take her picture," he said. And to her, "Look straight ahead." [34] Through the eye of the camera she seemed more pitiful than ever, her humiliation more complete.

"Wait!" The surgeon stopped me. I lowered the camera. A strand of [35] her hair had fallen across her face and found it way to her mouth, becoming stuck there by saliva. He removed the hair and secured it behind her ear.

"Go ahead," he ordered. There was the click of the camera. The girl [36] winced.

"Take three more, just in case." [37]

When the girl and her mother had left, he took paper and pen and [38] with a few lines drew a remarkable likeness of the girl's face.

"Look," he said. "If this dot is A, and this one B, this, C, and this, D, [39] the incisions are made A to B, then C to D. CD must equal AB. It is all equilateral triangles." All well and good, but then came X and Y and rotation flaps and the rest.

"Do you see?" he asked. [40]

"It is confusing," I told him. [41]

"It is simply a matter of dropping the upper lip into a normal posi- [42] tion, then crossing the gap with two triangular flaps. It is geometry," he said.

"Yes," I said. "Geometry." And relinquished all hope of becoming [43] a plastic surgeon.

In the operating room the next morning the anesthesia had already [44] been administered when we arrived from Ward Rounds. The tube emerging from the girl's mouth was pressed against her lower lip to be kept out of the field of surgery. Already, a nurse was scrubbing the face which swam in a reddish-brown lather. The tiny gold earrings were included in the scrub. Now and then, one of them gave a brave flash. The face was washed for the last time, and dried. Green towels were placed over the face to hide everything but the mouth and nose. The drapes were applied.

"Calipers!" The surgeon measured, locating the peak of the distort-   45
ed Cupid's bow.

"Marking pen!" He placed the first blue dot at the apex of the bow.   46
The nasal sills were dotted; next, the inferior philtral dimple, the ver-milion line. The *A* flap and the *B* flap were outlined. On he worked, pep-pering the lip and nose, making sense of chaos, realizing the lip that lay waiting in that deep essential pink, that only he could see. The last dot and line were placed. He was ready.

"Scalpel!" He held the knife above the girl's mouth.   47

"O.K. to go ahead?" he asked the anesthetist.   48

"Yes."   49

He lowered the knife.   50

"No! Wait!" The anesthetist's voice was tense, staccato. "Hold it!"   51

The surgeon's hand was motionless.   52

"What's the matter?"   53

"Something's wrong. I'm not sure. God, she's hot as a pistol. Blood   54
pressure is way up. Pulse one eighty. Get a rectal temperature." A nurse fumbled beneath the drapes. We waited. The nurse retrieved the ther-mometer.

"One hundred seven . . . no . . . eight." There was disbelief in her   55
voice.

"Malignant hyperthermia," said the anesthetist. "Ice! Ice! Get lots of   56
ice!" I raced out the door, accosted the first nurse I saw.

"Ice!" I shouted. *"Hielo!"*[1] Quickly! *Hielo!"* The woman's expression   57
was blank. I ran to another. *"Hielo! Hielo!* For the love of God, ice."

"Hielo?" She shrugged. *"Nada."*[2] I ran back to the operating room.   58

"There isn't any ice." I reported. Dr. Franciscus had ripped off his   59
rubber gloves and was feeling the skin of the girl's abdomen. Above the mask his eyes were the eyes of a horse in battle.

"The EKG is wild . . ."   60

"I can't get a pulse . . ."   61

"What the hell . . ."   62

The surgeon reached for the girl's groin. No femoral pulse.   63

"EKG flat. My God! She's dead!"   64

"She can't be."   65

"She is."   66

The surgeon's fingers pressed the groin where there was no pulse to   67
be felt, only his own pulse hammering at the girl's flesh to be let in.

---

[1] Ice. [Eds.]

[2] Nothing. [Eds.]

It was noon, four hours later, when we left the operating room. It [68] was a day so hot and humid I felt steamed open like an envelope. The woman was sitting on a bench in the courtyard in her dress like a cassock. In one hand she held the piece of cloth the girl had used to conceal her mouth. As we watched, she folded it once neatly, and then again, smoothing it, cleaning the cloth which might have been the head of the girl in her lap that she stroked and consoled.

"I'll do the talking here," he said. He would tell her himself, in what- [69] ever Spanish he could find. Only if she did not understand was I to speak for him. I watched him brace himself, set his shoulders. How could he tell her? I wondered. What? But I knew he would tell her everything, exactly as it had happened. As much for himself as for her, he needed to explain. But suppose she screamed, fell to the ground, attacked him, even? All that hope of love . . . gone. Even in his discomfort I knew that he was teaching me. The way to do it was professionally. Now he was standing above her. When the woman saw that he did not speak, she lifted her eyes and saw what he held crammed in his mouth to tell her. She knew, and rose to her feet.

"*Señora*," he began, "I am sorry." All at once he seemed to me short- [70] er than he was, scarcely taller than she. There was a place at the crown of his head where the hair had grown thin. His lips were stones. He could hardly move them. The voice dry, dusty.

"No one could have known. Some bad reaction to the medicine [71] for sleeping. It poisoned her. High fever. She did not wake up." The last, a whisper. The woman studied his lips as though she were deaf. He tried, but could not control a twitching at the corner of his mouth. He raised a thumb and forefinger to press something back into his eyes.

"*Muerte*,"[3] the woman announced to herself. Her eyes were human, [72] deadly.

"*Sí, muerte*." At that moment he was like someone cast, still alive, as [73] an effigy for his own tomb. He closed his eyes. Nor did he open them until he felt the touch of the woman's hand on his arm, a touch from which he did not withdraw. Then he looked and saw the grief corroding her face, breaking it down, melting the features so that eyes, nose, mouth ran together in a distortion, like the girl's. For a long time they stood in silence. It seemed to me that minutes passed. At last her face cleared, the features rearranged themselves. She spoke, the words coming slowly to make certain that he understood her. She would go home now. The next day her sons would come for the girl, to take her home for burial. The doctor must not be sad. God has decided. And she was happy now that the harelip had been fixed so that her daughter might

---

[3] Dead. [Eds.]

go to Heaven without it. Her bare feet retreating were the felted pads of a great bereft animal.

The next morning I did not go to the wards, but stood at the gate [74] leading from the courtyard to the road outside. Two young men in striped ponchos lifted the girl's body wrapped in a straw mat onto the back of a wooden cart. A donkey waited. I had been drawn to this place as one is drawn, inexplicably, to certain scenes of desolation—executions, battlefields. All at once, the woman looked up and saw me. She had taken off her hat. The heavy-hanging coil of her hair made her head seem larger, darker, noble. I pressed some money into her hand.

"For flowers," I said. "A priest." Her cheeks shook as though min- [75] utes ago a stone had been dropped into her navel and the ripples were just now reaching her head. I regretted having come to that place.

"Sí, sí," The woman said. Her own face was stitched with flies. "The [76] doctor is one of the angels. He has finished the work of God. My daughter is beautiful."

What could she mean! The lip had not been fixed. The girl had died [77] before he would have done it.

"Only a fine line that God will erase in time," she said. [78]

I reached into the cart and lifted a corner of the mat in which the girl [79] had been rolled. Where the cleft had been there was now a fresh line of tiny sutures. The Cupid's bow was delicately shaped, the vermilion border aligned. The flattened nostril had now the same rounded shape as the other one. I let the mat fall over the face of the dead girl, but not before I had seen the touching place where the finest black hairs sprang from the temple.

"Adiós, adiós. . . ." And the cart creaked away to the sound of hooves, [80] a tinkling bell.

There are events in a doctor's life that seem to mark the boundary [81] between youth and age, seeing and perceiving. Like certain dreams, they illuminate a whole lifetime of past behavior. After such an event, a doctor is not the same as he was before. It had seemed to me then to have been the act of someone demented, or at least insanely arrogant. An attempt to reorder events. Her death had come to him out of order. It should have come after the lip had been repaired, not before. He could have told the mother that, no, the lip had not been fixed. But he did not. He said nothing. It had been an act of omission, one of those strange lapses to which all of us are subject and which we live to regret. It must have been then, at that moment, that the knowledge of what he would do appeared to him. The words of the mother had not consoled him; they had hunted him down. He had not done it for her. The dire necessity was his. He would not accept that Imelda had died before he could repair her lip. People who do such things break free from society. They follow their own lonely path. They have a secret which they can never reveal. I must never let on that I knew.

How often I have imagined it. Ten o'clock at night. The hospital of [82]
Comayagua is all but dark. Here and there lanterns tilt and skitter up
and down the corridors. One of these lamps breaks free from the others
and descends the stone steps to the underground room that is the
morgue of the hospital. This room wears the expression as if it had waited all night for someone to come. No silence so deep as this place with
its cargo of newly dead. Only the slow drip of water over stone. The
door closes gassily and clicks shut. The lock is turned. There are four tables, each with a body encased in a paper shroud. There is no mistaking
her. She is the smallest. The surgeon takes a knife from his pocket and
slits open the paper shroud, that part in which the girl's head is enclosed. The wound seems to be living on long after she has died. Waves
of heat emanate from it, blurring his vision. All at once, he turns to peer
over his shoulder. He sees nothing, only a wooden crucifix on the wall.

He removes a package of instruments from a satchel and arranges [83]
them on a tray. Scalpel, scissors, forceps, needle holder. Sutures and
gauze sponges are produced. Stealthy, hunched, engaged, he begins.
The dots of blue dye are still there upon her mouth. He raises the scalpel,
pauses. A second glance into the darkness. From the wall a small lizard
watches and accepts. The first cut is made. A sluggish flow of dark blood
appears. He wipes it away with a sponge. No new blood comes to take
its place. Again and again he cuts, connecting each of the blue dots until
the whole of the zigzag slice is made, first on one side of the cleft, then
on the other. Now the edges of the cleft are lined with fresh tissue. He
sets down the scalpel and takes up scissors and forceps, undermining
the little flaps until each triangle is attached only at one side. He rotates
each flap into its new position. He must be certain that they can be
swung without tension. They can. He is ready to suture. He fits the tiny
curved needle into the jaws of the needle holder. Each suture is placed
precisely the same number of millimeters from the cut edge, and the
same distance apart. He ties each knot down until the edges are ap-
posed. Not too tightly. These are the most meticulous sutures of his life.
He cuts each thread close to the knot. It goes well. The vermilion border
with its white skin roll is exactly aligned. One more stitch and the
Cupid's bow appears as if by magic. The man's face shines with moisture. Now the nostril is incised around the margin, released, and sutured
into a round shape to match its mate. He wipes the blood from the face
of the girl with gauze the he has dipped in water. Crumbs of light are
scattered on the girl's face. The shroud is folded once more about her.
The instruments are handed into the satchel. In a moment the morgue
is dark and a lone lantern ascends the stairs and is extinguished.

Six weeks later I was in the darkened amphitheater of the Medical [84]
School. Tiers of seats rose in a semicircle above the small stage where
Hugh Franciscus stood presenting the case material he had encountered
in Honduras. It was the highlight of the year. The hall was filled. The

night before he had arranged the slides in the order in which they were to be shown. I was at the controls of the slide projector.

"Next slide!" he would order from time to time in that military voice [85] which had called forth blind obedience from generations of medical students, interns, residents and patients.

"This is a fifty-seven-year-old man with a severe burn contracture [86] of the neck. You will notice the rigid webbing that has fused the chin to the presternal tissues. No motion of the head on the torso is possible. . . . Next slide!"

"Click," went the projector. [87]

"Here he is after the excision of the scar tissue and with the head in full [88] extension for the first time. The defect was then covered. . . . Next slide!"

"Click." [89]

". . . with full-thickness drums of skin taken from the abdomen with [90] the Padgett dermatome. Next slide!"

"Click." [91]

And suddenly there she was, extracted from the shadows, sus- [92] pended above and beyond all of us like a resurrection. There was the oval face, the long black hair unbraided, the tiny gold hoops in her ears. And that luminous gnawed mouth. The whole of her life seemed to have been summed up in this photograph. A long silence followed that was the surgeon's alone to break. Almost at once, like the anesthetist in the operating room in Comayagua, I knew that something was wrong. It was not that the man would not speak as that he could not. The audience of doctors, nurses and students seemed to have been infected by the black, limitless silence. My own pulse doubled. It was hard to breathe. Why did he not call out for the next slide? Why did he not save himself? Why had he not removed this slide from the ones to be shown? All at once I knew that he had used his camera on her again. I could see the long black shadows of her hair flowing into the darker shadows of the morgue. The sudden blinding flash . . . The next slide would be the one taken in the morgue. He would be exposed.

In the dim light reflected from the slide, I saw him gazing up at her, [93] seeing not the colored photograph, I thought, but the negative of it where the ghost of the girl was. For me, the amphitheater had become Honduras. I saw again that courtyard littered with patients. I could see the dust in the beam of light from the projector. It was then that I knew that she was his measure of perfection and pain—the one lost, the other gained. He, too, had heard the click of the camera, had seen her wince and felt his mercy enlarge. At last he spoke.

"Imelda." It was the one word he had heard her say. At the sound [94] of his voice I removed the next slide from the projector. "Click" . . . and she was gone. "Click" again, and in her place the man with the orbital cancer. For a long moment Franciscus looked up in my direction, on his face an expression that I have given up trying to interpret. Gratitude?

Sorrow? It made me think of the gaze of the girl when at last she understood that she must hand over to him the evidence of her body.

"This is a sixty-two-year-old man with a basal cell carcinoma of the temple eroding into the bony orbit . . ." he began as though nothing had happened.   95

At the end of the hour, even before the lights went on, there was loud applause. I hurried to find him among the departing crowd. I could not. Some weeks went by before I caught sight of him. He seemed vaguely convalescent, as though a fever had taken its toll before burning out.   96

Hugh Franciscus continued to teach for fifteen years, although he operated a good deal less, then gave it up entirely. It was as though he had grown tired of blood, of always having to be involved with blood, of having to draw it, spill it, wipe it away, stanch it. He was a quieter, softer man, I heard, the ferocity diminished. There were no more expeditions to Honduras or anywhere else.   97

I, too, have not been entirely free of her. Now and then, in the years that have passed, I see that donkey-cart cortège, or his face bent over hers in the morgue. I would like to have told him what I now know, that his unrealistic act was one of goodness, one of those small, persevering acts done, perhaps, to ward off madness. Like lighting a lamp, boiling water for tea, washing a shirt. But, of course, it's too late now.   98

Responding to Reading

1. What do you think motivated Dr. Franciscus to repair Imelda's lip after she had died? Do you think he did the right thing?
2. What qualities do you associate with doctors? In what ways does Dr. Franciscus meet (or fail to meet) your criteria?
3. What does Selzer learn from the story of Imelda? What does he mean when he says, "I too, have not been entirely free of her" (98)? Do you thinks the true subject of the essay is Imelda, Dr. Franciscus, or Richard Seltzer? Explain.

HIV SUFFERERS HAVE A
~ RESPONSIBILITY

Amitai Etzioni

Born in Cologne, Germany, sociologist Amitai Etzioni (1929–) received degrees from Hebrew University in Jerusalem and the University of California at Berkeley. A long-time professor of sociology and director of the Center for Policy Research at Columbia University, Etzioni is currently on the faculty at George Washington University. He has written many scholarly works, as well as books for general audiences, on subjects ranging from modern organizations and political communities to the social implications of genetic research. Much of his recent writing has been on the subject of communitarianism, a movement he and others have founded to move people beyond the unproductive contentiousness Etzioni sees as characterizing much political debate today and to foster a greater sense of unity in the effort to effect positive social change. His book *The Spirit of Community: Rights, Responsibilities, and the Communitarian Agenda* (1993) focuses specifically on this movement as does the journal he edits, *Responsive Community*. In the following essay, which originally appeared in *Newsweek* in 1993, Etzioni argues that public policy in the battle against AIDS must include some specific preventive measures that currently find little support within the AIDS community.

A major drive to find a cure for AIDS was announced last week by [1] Donna Shalala, President Clinton's Secretary of Health and Human Services. Researchers from the private sector, gay activists and government officials were teamed up to accelerate the search for an effective treatment. Yet even highly optimistic observers do not expect a cure to be found before the end of this century. Still, as the Shalala announcement's exclusive focus on cure highlights, it is not acceptable to explore publicly the measures that could curb the spread of the disease by slowing the transmission of HIV, the virus that causes it. Indeed, before you can say What about prevention? the politically correct choir chimes in: You cannot call it a plague! You are feeding the fires of homophobia! Gay basher!

Case in point: a panel of seven experts fielded questions from 4,000 [2] personnel managers at a conference in Las Vegas. "Suppose you work for medical records. You find out that Joe Doe, who is driving the company's 18-wheeler, is back on the bottle. Will you violate confidentiality and inform his supervisor?" The panel stated unanimously, "I'll find a way." Next question: "Joe Smith is HIV positive; he is intimate with the top designer of the company but did not tell; will *you?*" "No way," the panel agreed in unison.

We need to break the silence. It is not antigay but fully compas- [3] sionate to argue that a massive prevention drive is a viable way to save numerous lives in the very next years. We must lay a moral claim on those who are likely to be afflicted with HIV (gays, drug addicts who exchange needles and anyone who received a blood transfusion before 1985) and urge them as a social obligation to come forward to be tested. If the test is positive, they should inform their previous sexual contacts and warn all potential new ones. The principle is elementary, albeit openly put: the more responsibly HIV sufferers act, the fewer dead they will leave in their trail.

HIV testing and contact tracing amount to "a cruel hoax," claims a 4 gay representative from the West Coast. "There are not enough beds to take care of known AIDS patients. Why identify more?" Actually, testing is cruel only in a world where captains of sinking ships do not warn passengers because the captains cannot get off. We must marshal the moral courage to tell those infected with HIV: It is truly tragic that currently we have no way to save your life, but surely you recognize your duty to try to help save the lives of others.

"Warning others is unnecessary because everybody should act safe- 5 ly all the time anyhow," argues Rob Teir, a gay activist in Washington. But human nature is such, strong data show, that most people cannot bring themselves to act safely all the time. A fair warning that they are about to enter a highly dangerous situation may spur people to take special precautions. The moral duty of those already afflicted, though, must be clearly articulated: being intimate without prior disclosure is like serving arsenic in a cake. And not informing previous contacts (or not helping public authorities trace them without disclosing your name) leaves the victims, unwittingly, to transmit the fatal disease to uncounted others.

Testing and contact tracing may lead to a person's being deprived 6 of a job, health insurance, housing and privacy, many civil libertarians fear. These are valid and grave concerns. But we can find ways to protect civil rights without sacrificing public health. A major AIDS-prevention campaign ought to be accompanied by intensive public education about the ways the illness is *not* transmitted, by additional safeguards on data banks and by greater penalties for those who abuse HIV victims. It may be harsh to say, but the fact that an individual may suffer as a result of doing what is right does not make doing so less of an imperative. Note also that while society suffers a tremendous loss of talent and youth and is stuck with a gargantuan bill, the first victims of nondisclosure are the loved ones of those already afflicted with HIV, even—in the case of infected women—their children.

"Not cost effective," intone the bean counters. Let's count. Take, for 8 example, a suggestion by the highly regarded Centers for Disease Control and Prevention that hospitals be required to ask patients whose blood is already being tested whether they would consent to having it tested for HIV as well. The test costs $60 or less and routinely identifies many who were unaware they had the virus. If those who are thus identified were to transmit the disease to only one less person on average, the suggested tests would pay for themselves much more readily than a coronary bypass, PSA tests and half the pills we pop. And society could continue to enjoy the lifelong earnings and social contributions of those whose lives would be saved.

There are other excuses and rationalizations. But it is time for some   8
plain talk: if AIDS were any other disease—say, hepatitis B or tuberculosis—we would have no trouble (and indeed we have had none) introducing the necessary preventive measures. Moreover, we should make
it clear that doing all you can to prevent the spread of AIDS or any other
fatal disease is part and parcel of an unambiguous commandment: Thou
shalt not kill.

Responding to Reading

1. Do you believe, as Etzioni does, that HIV sufferers have an obligation to
   come forward? Or do you believe they have a right to privacy? Explain your
   position.
2. Do you agree with Etzioni that ways can be found "to protect civil rights
   without sacrificing public health" (6)? Do you think preventive measures
   should be instituted even if no way can be found to protect the civil rights
   of HIV victims?
3. How would you respond to the moral dilemma presented in paragraph 2?
   Would you violate Joe Doe's or Joe Smith's confidentiality, or would you
   keep the condition of either man secret?

A PLEA FOR THE CHIMPS

Jane Goodall

English-born Jane Goodall (1934–) has spent most of her adult life
studying the behavior of wild chimpanzees in the jungles of Tanzania.
Shortly after graduating high school, she visited Kenya, where she met
naturalist and paleontologist Louis Leakey. Impressed by her love of
wildlife and despite her lack of formal training, Leakey arranged for
her to conduct a six-month field study of chimpanzees on a Tanzan-
ian reserve, a project which has stretched to almost four decades.
Goodall has described her fascinating observations in a number of
popular books, including *In the Shadow of Man* (1971; revised 1988), *The
Chimpanzees of Gombe: Patterns of Behavior* (1986), and *Through a Window: My Thirty Years with the Chimpanzees of Gombe* (1990). As she has
said, "Animals are like us. They feel pain like we do. We want people
to understand that every chimp is an individual, with the same kinds
of intellectual abilities." In the following 1987 article, Goodall makes
the case for more humane treatment of champanzees used for medical
research.

The chimpanzee is more like us, genetically, than any other animal. [1]
It is because of similarities in physiology, in biochemistry, in the immune system, that medical science makes use of the living bodies of chimpanzees in its search for cures and vaccines for a variety of human diseases.

There are also behavioral, psychological and emotional similarities between chimpanzees and humans, resemblances so striking that they raise a serious ethical question: are we justified in using an animal so close to us—an animal, moreover, that is highly endangered in its African forest home—as a human substitute in medical experimentation? [2]

In the long run, we can hope that scientists will find ways of exploring human physiology and disease, and of testing cures and vaccines, that do not depend on the use of living animals of any sort. A number of steps in this direction already have been taken, prompted in large part by a growing public awareness of the suffering that is being inflicted on millions of animals. More and more people are beginning to realize that nonhuman animals—even rats and guinea pigs—are not just unfeeling machines but are capable of enjoying their lives, and of feeling fear, pain and despair. [3]

But until alternatives have been found, medical science will continue to use animals in the battle against human disease and suffering. And some of those animals will continue to be chimpanzees. [4]

Because they share with us 99 percent of their genetic material, chimpanzees can be infected with some human diseases that do not infect other animals. They are currently being used in research on the nature of hepatitis non-A non-B, for example, and they continue to play a major role in the development of vaccines against hepatitis B. [5]

Many biomedical laboratories are looking to the chimpanzee to help them in the race to find a vaccine against acquired immune deficiency syndrome. Chimpanzees are not good models for AIDS research; although the AIDS virus stays alive and replicates within the chimpanzee's bloodstream, no chimp has yet come down with the disease itself. Nevertheless, many of the scientists involved argue that only by using chimpanzees can potential vaccines be safely tested. [6]

Given the scientists' professed need for animals in research, let us turn aside from the sensitive ethical issue of whether chimpanzees *should* be used in medical research, and consider a more immediate issue: how are we treating the chimpanzees that are actually being used? [7]

Just after Christmas I watched, with shock, anger and anguish, a videotape—made by an animal-rights group during a raid—revealing the conditions in a large biomedical research laboratory, under contract to the National Institutes of Health, in which various primates, including chimpanzees, are maintained. In late March, I was given permission to visit the facility. [8]

It was a visit I shall never forget. Room after room was lined with   9
small, bare cages, stacked one above the other, in which monkeys circled
round and round and chimpanzees sat huddled, far gone in depression
and despair.

Young chimpanzees, 3 or 4 years old, were crammed, two togeth-   10
er, into tiny cages measuring 22 inches by 22 inches and only 24 inches high. They could hardly turn around. Not yet part of any experiment, they had been confined in these cages for more than three
months.

The chimps had each other for comfort, but they would not remain   11
together for long. Once they are infected, probably with hepatitis, they
will be separated and placed in another cage. And there they will remain, living in conditions of severe sensory deprivation, for the next
several years. During that time, they will become insane.

A juvenile female rocked from side to side, sealed off from the out-   12
side world behind the glass doors of her metal isolation chamber. She
was in semidarkness. All she could hear was the incessant roar of air
rushing through vents into her prison.

In order to demonstrate the "good" relationship the lab's caretaker   13
had with this chimpanzee, one of the scientists told him to lift her from
the cage. The caretaker opened the door. She sat, unmoving. He reached
in. She did not greet him—nor did he greet her. As if drugged, she allowed him to take her out. She sat motionless in his arms. He did not
speak to her, she did not look at him. He touched her lips briefly. She did
not respond. He returned her to her cage. She sat again on the bars of the
floor. The door closed.

I shall be haunted forever by her eyes, and by the eyes of the other   14
infant chimpanzees I saw that day. Have you ever looked into the eyes
of a person who, stressed beyond endurance, has given up, succumbed
utterly to the crippling helplessness of despair? I once saw a little
African boy, whose whole family had been killed during the fighting in
Burundi. He too looked out at the world, unseeing, from dull, blank
eyes.

Though this particular laboratory may be one of the worst, from   15
what I have learned, most of the other biomedical animal-research facilities are not much better. Yet only when one has some understanding
of the true nature of the chimpanzee can the cruelty of these captive conditions be fully understood.

Chimpanzees are very social by nature. Bonds between individuals,   16
particularly between family members and close friends, can be affectionate, supportive, and can endure throughout their lives. The accidental separation of two friendly individuals may cause them intense
distress. Indeed, the death of a mother may be such a psychological
blow to her child that even if the child is 5 years old and no longer dependent on its mother's milk, it may pine away and die.

It is impossible to overemphasize the importance of friendly phys- [17] ical contact for the well-being of the chimpanzee. Again and again one can watch a frightened or tense individual relax if she is patted, kissed or embraced reassuringly by a companion. Social grooming, which provides hours of close contact, is undoubtedly the single most important social activity.

Chimpanzees in their natural habitat are active for much of the day. [18] They travel extensively within their territory, which can be as large as 50 square kilometers for a community of about 50 individuals. If they hear other chimpanzees calling as they move through the forest, or anticipate arriving at a good food source, they typically break into excited charging displays, racing along the ground, hurling sticks and rocks and shaking the vegetation. Youngsters, particularly, are full of energy, and spend long hours playing with one another or by themselves, leaping through the branches and gamboling along the ground. Adults sometimes join these games. Bunches of fruit, twigs and rocks may be used as toys.

Chimpanzees enjoy comfort. They construct sleeping platforms each [19] night, using a multitude of leafy twigs to make their beds soft. Often, too, they make little "pillows" on which to rest during a midday siesta.

Chimps are highly intelligent. They display cognitive abilities that [20] were, until recently, thought to be unique to humans. They are capable of cross-model transfer of information—that is, they can identify by touch an object they previously have only seen, and vice versa. They are capable of reasoned thought, generalization, abstraction and symbolic representation. They have some concept of self. They have excellent memories and can, to some extent, plan for the future. They show a capacity for intentional communication that depends, in part, on their ability to understand the motives of the individuals with whom they are communicating.

Chimpanzees are capable of empathy and altruistic behavior. They [21] show emotions that are undoubtedly similar, if not identical, to human emotions—joy, pleasure contentment, anxiety, fear and rage. They even have a sense of humor.

The chimpanzee child and the human child are alike in many ways; [22] in their capacity for endless romping and fun; their curiosity; their ability to learn by observation, imitation and practice; and, above all, in their need for reassurance and love. When young chimpanzees are brought up in a human home and treated like human children, they learn to eat at table, to help themselves to snacks from the refrigerator, to sort and put away cutlery, to brush their teeth, to play with dolls, to switch on the television and select a program that interests them and watch it.

Young chimpanzees can easily learn over 200 signs of the American [23] language of the deaf and use these signs to communicate meaningfully with humans and with one another. One youngster, in the laboratory of

Dr. Roger S. Fouts, a psychologist at Central Washington University, has picked up 68 signs from four older signing chimpanzee companions, with no human teaching. The chimp uses the signs in communication with other chimpanzees and with humans.

The chimpanzee facilities in most biomedical research laboratories [24] allow for the expression of almost none of these activities and behaviors. They provide little—if anything—more than the warmth, food and water, and veterinary care required to sustain life. The psychological and emotional needs of these creatures are rarely catered to, and often not even acknowledged.

In most labs the chimpanzees are housed individually, one chimp to [25] a cage, unless they are part of a breeding program. The standard size of each cage is about 25 feet square and about 6 feet high. In one facility, a cage described in the catalogue as "large," designed for a chimpanzee of up to 25 kilograms (55 pounds), measures 2 feet 6 inches by 3 feet 8 inches, with a height of 5 feet 4 inches. Federal requirements for cage size are dependent on body size; infant chimpanzees, who are the most active, are often imprisoned in the smallest cages.

In most labs, the chimpanzees cannot even lie with their arms and [26] legs outstretched. They are not let out to exercise. There is seldom anything for them to do other than eat, and then only when food is brought. The caretakers are usually too busy to pay much attention to individual chimpanzees. The cages are bleak and sterile, with bars above, bars below, bars on every side. There is no comfort in them, no bedding. The chimps, infected with human diseases, will often feel sick and miserable.

What of the human beings who administer these facilities—the care- [27] takers, veterinarians and scientists who work at them? If they are decent, compassionate people, how can they condone, or even tolerate, the kind of conditions I have described?

They are, I believe, victims of a system that was set up long before [28] the cognitive abilities and emotional needs of chimpanzees were understood. Newly employed staff members, equipped with a normal measure of compassion, may well be sickened by what they see. And, in fact, many of them do quit their jobs, unable to endure the suffering they see inflicted on the animals yet feeling powerless to help.

But others stay on and gradually come to accept the cruelty, believ- [29] ing (or forcing themselves to believe) that it is an inevitable part of the struggle to reduce human suffering. Some become hard and callous in the process, in Shakespeare's words, "all pity choked with custom of fell deeds."

A handful of compassionate and dedicated caretakers and veteri- [30] narians are fighting to improve the lots of the animals in their care. Vets are often in a particularly difficult position, for if they stand firm and try to uphold high standards of humane care, they will not always be welcome in the lab.

Many of the scientists believe that a bleak, sterile and restricting environment is necessary for their research. The cages must be small, the scientists maintain, because otherwise it is too difficult to treat the chimpanzees—to inject them, to draw their blood or to anesthetize them. Moreover, they are less likely to hurt themselves in small cages. [31]

The cages must also be barren, with no bedding or toys, say the scientists. This way, the chimpanzees are less likely to pick up diseases or parasites. Also, if things are lying about, the cages are harder to clean. [32]

And the chimpanzees must be kept in isolation, the scientists believe, to avoid the risk of cross-infection, particularly in hepatitis research. [33]

Finally, of course, bigger cages, social groups and elaborate furnishings require more space, more caretakers—and more money. Perhaps, then, if we are to believe these researchers, it is not possible to improve conditions for chimpanzees imprisoned in biomedical research laboratories. [34]

I believe not only that it is possible, but that improvements are absolutely necessary. If we do not do something to help these creatures, we make a mockery of the whole concept of justice. [35]

Perhaps the most important way we can improve the quality of life for the laboratory chimps is to increase the number of carefully trained caretakers. These people should be selected for their understanding of animal behavior and their compassion and respect for, and dedication to, their charges. Each caretaker, having established a relationship of trust with the chimpanzees in his care, should be allowed to spend time with the animals over and above that required for cleaning the cages and providing the animals with food and water. [36]

It has been shown that a chimpanzee who has a good relationship with his caretaker will cooperate calmly during experimental procedures, rather than react with fear or anger. At the Dutch Primate Research Center, at Rijswijk, for example, some chimpanzees have been trained to leave their group cage on command and move into small, single cages for treatment. At the Stanford Primate Center in California, a number of chimpanzees were taught to extend their arms for the drawing of blood. In return they were given a food reward. [37]

Much can be done to alleviate the pain and stress felt by younger chimpanzees during experimental procedures. A youngster, for example, can be treated when in the presence of a trusted human friend. Experiments have shown that young chimps react with high levels of distress if subjected to mild electric shocks when alone, but show almost no fear or pain when held by a sympathetic caretaker. [38]

What about cage size? Here we should emulate the animal protection regulations that already exist in Switzerland. These laws stipulate that a cage must be, at minimum, about 20 meters square and 3 meters high for pairs of chimpanzees. [39]

The chimpanzees should never be housed alone unless this is an es- [40]
sential part of the experimental procedure. For chimps in solitary confinement, particularly youngsters, three to four hours of friendly interaction with a caretaker should be mandatory. A chimp taking part in
hepatitis research, in which the risk of cross-infection is, I am told, great,
can be provided with a companion of a compatible species if it doesn't
infringe on existing regulations—a rhesus monkey, for example, which
cannot catch or pass on the disease.

For healthy chimpanzees there should be little risk of infection from [41]
bedding and toys. Stress and depression, however, can have deleterious
effects on their health. It is known that clinically depressed humans are
more prone to a variety of physiological disorders, and heightened
stress can interfere with immune function. Given the chimpanzee's similarities to humans, it is not surprising that the chimp in a typical laboratory, alone in his bleak cage, is an easy prey to infections and parasites.

Thus, the chimpanzees also should be provided with a rich and [42]
stimulating environment. Climbing apparatus should be obligatory.
There should be many objects for them to play with or otherwise manipulate. A variety of simple devices designed to alleviate boredom
could be produced quite cheaply. Unexpected food items will elicit great
pleasure. If a few simple buttons in each cage were connected to a computer terminal, it would be possible for the chimpanzees to feel they at
least have some control over their world—if one button produced a
grape when pressed, another a drink, or another a video picture. (The
Canadian Council of Animal Care recommends the provision of television for primates in solitary confinement, or other means of enriching
their environment.)

Without doubt, it will be considerably more costly to maintain chim- [43]
panzees in the manner I have outlined. Should we begrudge them the
extra dollars? We take from them their freedom, their health and often
their lives. Surely, the least we can do is try to provide them with some
of the things that could make their imprisonment more bearable.

There are hopeful signs. I was immensely grateful to officials of the [44]
National Institutes of Health for allowing me to visit the primate facility, enabling me to see the conditions there and judge them for myself.
And I was even more grateful for the fact that they gave me a great deal
of time for serious discussions of the problem. Doors were opened and
a dialogue begun. All who were present at the meetings agreed that, in
light of present knowledge, it is indeed necessary to give chimpanzees
a better deal in the labs.

Plans are now under way for a major conference to discuss ways [45]
and means of bringing about such change. Sponsored by the N.I.H. and
organized by Roger Fouts (who toured the lab with me) and myself, this
conference—which will be held in mid-December at the Jane Goodall Institute in Tucson, Ariz.—will bring together for the first time adminis-

trators, scientists and animal technicians from various primate facilities around the country and from overseas. The conference will, we hope, lead to the formulation of new, humane standards for the maintenance of chimpanzees in the laboratory.

I have had the privilege of working among wild, free chimpanzees 46 for more than 26 years. I have gained a deep understanding of chimpanzee nature. Chimpanzees have given me so much in my life. The least I can do is to speak out for the hundreds of chimpanzees who, right now, sit hunched, miserable and without hope, staring out with dead eyes from their metal prisons. They cannot speak for themselves.

Responding to Reading

1. Goodall says in paragraph 7 that she doesn't want to discuss the issue of whether chimpanzees should be used in medical research. Does she successfully sidestep this issue in her essay, or does she indirectly address it? Explain.

2. What arguments against Goodall's proposals could scientists who use chimpanzees in experiments make?

3. Some proponents of animal rights say that animals should not be used in experiments where human beings would not be used. Do you agree with this position? Do you think Goodall would agree?

MY WORLD NOW

≈

Anna Mae Halgrim Seaver

The following essay originally appeared as a "My Turn" column in *Newsweek* magazine in June of 1994. Anna Mae Halgrim Seaver (1919–1994) had recently died at the nursing home where she had been confined for some time, and her son discovered these notes in her room after her death.

This is my world now; it's all I have left. You see, I'm old. And, I'm 1 not as healthy as I used to be. I'm not necessarily happy with it but I accept it. Occasionally, a member of my family will stop in to see me. He or she will bring me some flowers or a little present, maybe a set of slippers—I've got 8 pair. We'll visit for awhile and then they will return to the outside world and I'll be alone again.

Oh, there are other people here in the nursing home. Residents, 2 we're called. The majority are about my age. I'm 84. Many are in wheelchairs. The lucky ones are passing through—a broken hip, a diseased heart, something has brought them here for rehabilitation. When they're well they'll be going home.

Most of us are aware of our plight—some are not. Varying stages of Alzheimer's have robbed several of their mental capacities. We listen to endlessly repeated stories and questions. We meet them anew daily, hourly or more often. We smile and nod gracefully each time we hear a retelling. They seldom listen to my stories, so I've stopped trying. [3]

The help here is basically pretty good, although there's a large turnover. Just when I get comfortable with someone he or she moves on to another job. I understand that. This is not the best job to have. [4]

I don't much like some of the physical things that happen to us. I don't care much for a diaper. I seem to have lost the control acquired so diligently as a child. The difference is that I'm aware and embarrassed but I can't do anything about it. I've had 3 children and I know it isn't pleasant to clean another's diaper. My husband used to wear a gas mask when he changed the kids. I wish I had one now. [5]

Why do you think the staff insists on talking baby talk when speaking to me? I understand English. I have a degree in music and am a certified teacher. Now I hear a lot of words that end in "y." Is this how my kids felt? My hearing aid works fine. There is little need for anyone to position their face directly in front of mine and raise their voice with those "y" words. Sometimes it takes longer for a meaning to sink in; sometimes my mind wanders when I am bored. But there's no need to shout. [6]

I tried once or twice to make my feelings known. I even shouted once. That gained me a reputation of being "crotchety." Imagine me, crotchety. My children never heard me raise my voice. I surprised myself. After I've asked for help more than a dozen times and received nothing more than a dozen condescending smiles and a "Yes, deary, I'm working on it," something begins to break. That time I wanted to be taken to a bathroom. [7]

I'd love to go out for a meal, to travel again. I'd love to go to my own church, sing with my own choir. I'd love to visit my friends. Most of them are gone now or else they are in different "homes" of their children's choosing. I'd love to play a good game of bridge but no one here seems to concentrate very well. [8]

My children put me here for my own good. They said they would be able to visit me frequently. But they have their own lives to lead. That sounds normal. I don't want to be a burden. They know that. But I would like to see them more. One of them is here in town. He visits as much as he can. [9]

Something else I've learned to accept is loss of privacy. Quite often I'll close my door when my roommate—imagine having a roommate at [10] my age—is in the TV room. I do appreciate some time to myself and be-lieve that I have earned at least that courtesy. As I sit thinking or writ-ing, one of the aides invariably opens the door unannounced and walks in as if I'm not there. Sometimes she even opens my drawers and begins rummaging around. Am I invisible? Have I lost my right to respect and dignity? What would happen if the roles were reversed? I am still a human being. I would like to be treated as one.

The meals are not what I would choose for myself. We get variety [11] but we don't get a choice. I am one of the fortunate ones who can still handle utensils. I remember eating off such cheap utensils in the Great Depression. I worked hard so I would not have to ever use them again. But here I am.

Did you ever sit in a wheelchair over an extended period of time? [12] It's not comfortable. The seat squeezes you into the middle and applies constant pressure on your hips. The armrests are too narrow and my arms slip off. I am luckier than some. Others are strapped into their chairs and abandoned in front of the TV. Captive prisoners of daytime television; soap operas, talk shows and commercials.

One of the residents died today. He was a loner who, at one time, [13] started a business and developed a multimillion-dollar company. His children moved him here when he could no longer control his bowels. He didn't talk to most of us. He often snapped at the aides as though they were his employees. But he just gave up; willed his own demise. The staff has made up his room and another man has moved in.

A typical day. Awakened by the woman in the next bed wheezing— [14] a former chain smoker with asthma. Call an aide to wash me and place me in my wheelchair to wait for breakfast. Only 67 minutes until break-fast. I'll wait. Breakfast in the dining area. Most of the residents are in wheelchairs. Others use canes or walkers. Some sit and wonder what they are waiting for. First meal of the day. Only 3 hours and 26 minutes until lunch. Maybe I'll sit around and wait for it. What is today? One day blends into the next until day and date mean nothing.

Let's watch a little TV. Oprah and Phil and Geraldo and who cares [15] if some transvestite is having trouble picking a color-coordinated wardrobe from his husband's girlfriend's mother's collection. Lunch. Can't wait. Dried something with puréed peas and coconut pudding. No wonder I'm losing weight.

Back to my semiprivate room for a little semiprivacy or a nap. I do [16] need my beauty rest, company may come today. What is today, again? The afternoon drags into early evening. This used to be my favorite time of the day. Things would wind down. I would kick off my shoes. Put my feet up on the coffee table. Pop open a bottle of Chablis and enjoy the fruits of my day's labor with my husband. He's gone. So is my health. *This* is my world.

Responding to Reading

1. Under what circumstances, if any, should a person be placed in a nursing home? Why do you think there are more people in nursing homes today than there were forty years ago?
2. Because Seaver's son compiled this essay from notes left in his mother's room after her death, it seems to jump from one subject to another. Are there any advantages to this somewhat choppy structure? Would a smoother, more unified structure have been more effective?
3. In paragraph 9 Seaver says "My children put me here for my own good.... But they have their own lives to lead.... I don't want to be a burden." How do you imagine Seaver's son reacted when he read these statements? What do you think he hoped to accomplish by publishing her notes?

ON THE FEAR OF DEATH

~

Elisabeth Kübler-Ross

Born in Zurich, Switzerland, psychologist and physician Elisabeth Kübler-Ross (1917–) has made a distinguished career of her interest in dying patients and their families. She established a pioneering interdisciplinary seminar in the care of the terminally ill when she taught at the University of Chicago, and for many years she headed a center for terminal patients in rural Virginia. Her first book on the subject was *On Death and Dying* (1969), and she has also written *Death: The Final State* (1974), *On Childhood and Death* (1985), and *AIDS: The Ultimate Challenge (1987)*. In recent years she has turned her attention to what happens after death, the subject of her most recent book, *On Life After Death* (1991). In the following 1969 essay, Kübler-Ross argues that we should confront death directly to reduce our fear of it.

Let me not pray to be sheltered from dangers but to be fearless in facing them.
    Let me not beg for the stilling of my pain but for the heart to conquer it.
    Let me not look for allies in life's battlefield but to my own strength.
    Let me not crave in anxious fear to be saved but hope for the patience to win my freedom.
    Grant me that I may not be a coward, feeling your mercy in my success alone; but let me find the grasp of your hand in my failure.

                                                    Rabindranath Tagore,

                                                            Fruit-Gathering

Epidemics have taken a great toll of lives in past generations. Death [1] in infancy and early childhood was frequent and there were few families who didn't lose a member of the family at an early age. Medicine has changed greatly in the last decades. Widespread vaccinations have practically eradicated many illnesses, at least in western Europe and the United States. The use of chemotherapy, especially the antibiotics, has contributed to an ever decreasing number of fatalities in infectious diseases. Better child care and education have effected a low morbidity and mortality among children. The many diseases that have taken an impressive toll among the young and middle-aged have been conquered. The number of old people is on the rise, and with this fact come the number of people with malignancies and chronic diseases associated more with old age.

Pediatricians have less work with acute and life-threatening situa- [2] tions as they have an ever increasing number of patients with psychosomatic disturbances and adjustment and behavior problems. Physicians have more people in their waiting rooms with emotional problems than they have ever had before, but they also have more elderly patients who not only try to live with their decreased physical abilities and limitations but who also face loneliness and isolation with all its pains and anguish. The majority of these people are not seen by a psychiatrist. Their needs have to be elicited and gratified by other professional people, for instance, chaplains and social workers. It is for them that I am trying to outline the changes that have taken place in the last few decades, changes that are ultimately responsible for the increased fear of death, the rising number of emotional problems, and the greater need for understanding of and coping with the problems of death and dying.

When we look back in time and study old cultures and people, we [3] are impressed that death has always been distasteful to man and will probably always be. From a psychiatrist's point of view this is very understandable and can perhaps best be explained by our basic knowledge that, in our unconscious, death is never possible in regard to ourselves. It is inconceivable for our unconscious to imagine an actual ending of our own life here on earth, and if this life of ours had to end, the ending is always attributed to a malicious intervention from the outside by someone else. In simple terms, in our unconscious mind we can only be killed; it is inconceivable to die of a natural cause or of old age. Therefore death in itself is associated with a bad act, a frightening happening, something that in itself calls for retribution and punishment.

One is wise to remember these fundamental facts as they are essen- [4] tial in understanding some of the most important, otherwise unintelligible communications of our patients.

The second fact that we have to comprehend is that in our uncon- [5] scious mind we cannot distinguish between a wish and a deed. We are all aware of some of our illogical dreams in which two completely opposite statements can exist side by side—very acceptable in our dreams but unthinkable and illogical in our wakening state. Just as our unconscious mind cannot differentiate between the wish to kill somebody in anger and the act of having done so, the young child is unable to make this distinction. The child who angrily wishes his mother to drop dead for not having gratified his needs will be traumatized greatly by the actual death of his mother—even if this event is not linked closely in time with his destructive wishes. He will always take part or the whole blame for the loss of his mother. He will always say to himself—rarely to others—"I did it, I am responsible, I was bad, therefore Mommy left me." It is well to remember that the child will react in the same manner if he loses a parent by divorce, separation, or desertion. Death is often seen by a child as an impermanent thing and has therefore little distinction from a divorce in which he may have an opportunity to see a parent again.

Many a parent will remember remarks of their children such as, "I will bury my doggy now and next spring when the flowers come up again, he will get up." Maybe it was the same wish that motivated the ancient Egyptians to supply their dead with food and goods to keep them happy and the old American Indians to bury their relatives with their belongings.   6

When we grow older and begin to realize that our omnipotence is really not so omnipotent, that our strongest wishes are not powerful enough to make the impossible possible, the fear that we have contributed to the death of a loved one diminishes—and with it the guilt. The fear remains diminished, however, only so long as it is not challenged too strongly. Its vestiges can be seen daily in hospital corridors and in people associated with the bereaved.   7

A husband and wife may have been fighting for years, but when the partner dies, the survivor will pull his hair, whine and cry louder and beat his chest in regret, fear and anguish, and will hence fear his own death more than before, still believing in the law of talion—an eye for an eye, a tooth for a tooth—"I am responsible for her death, I will have to die a pitiful death in retribution."   8

Maybe this knowledge will help us understand many of the old customs and rituals which have lasted over the centuries and whose purpose is to diminish the anger of the gods or the people as the case may be, thus decreasing the anticipated punishment. I am thinking of the ashes, the torn clothes, the veil, the *Klage Weiber*[1] of the old days—they are all means to ask you to take pity on them, the mourners, and are expressions of sorrow, grief, and shame. If someone grieves, beats his   9

---

[1] Wailing wives. [Eds.]

chest, tears his hair, or refuses to eat, it is an attempt at self-punishment to avoid or reduce the anticipated punishment for the blame that he takes on the death of a loved one.

This grief, shame, and guilt are not very far removed from feelings 10 of anger and rage. The process of grief always includes some qualities of anger. Since none of us likes to admit anger at a deceased person, these emotions are often disguised or repressed and prolong the period of grief or show up in other ways. It is well to remember that it is not up to us to judge such feelings as bad or shameful but to understand their true meaning and origin as something very human. In order to illustrate this I will again use the example of the child—and the child in us. The five-year-old who loses his mother is both blaming himself for her disappearance and being angry at her for having deserted him and for no longer gratifying his needs. The dead person then turns into something the child loves and wants very much but also hates with equal intensity for this severe deprivation.

The ancient Hebrews regarded the body of a dead person as some- 11 thing unclean and not to be touched. The early American Indians talked about the evil spirits and shot arrows in the air to drive the spirits away. Many other cultures have rituals to take care of the "bad" dead person, and they all originate in this feeling of anger which still exists in all of us, though we dislike admitting it. The tradition of the tombstone may originate in this wish to keep the bad spirits deep down in the ground, and the pebbles that many mourners put on the grave are left-over symbols of the same wish. Though we call the firing of guns at military funerals a last salute, it is the same symbolic ritual as the Indian used when he shot his spears and arrows into the skies.

I give these examples to emphasize that man has not basically 12 changed. Death is still a fearful, frightening happening, and the fear of death is a universal fear even if we think we have mastered it on many levels.

What has changed is our way of coping and dealing with death and 13 dying and our dying patients.

Having been raised in a country in Europe where science is not so 14 advanced, where modern techniques have just started to find their way into medicine, and where people still live as they did in this country half a century ago, I may have had an opportunity to study a part of the evolution of mankind in a shorter period.

I remember as a child the death of a farmer. He fell from a tree and 15 was not expected to live. He asked simply to die at home, a wish that was granted without questioning. He called his daughters into the bedroom and spoke with each one of them alone for a few moments. He arranged his affairs quietly, though he was in great pain, and distributed his belongings and his land, none of which was to be split until his wife should follow him in death. He also asked each of his children to share in the work, duties, and tasks that he had carried on until the time of the accident. He asked his friends to visit him once more, to bid good-bye to them. Although I was a small child at the time, he did not exclude me or my siblings. We were allowed to share in the preparations of the family just as we were permitted to grieve with them until he died. When he did die, he was left at home, in his own beloved home which he had built, and among his friends and neighbors who went to take a last look at him where he lay in the midst of flowers in the place he had lived in and loved so much. In that country today there is still no make-believe slumber room, no embalming, no false makeup to pretend sleep. Only the signs of very disfiguring illnesses are covered up with bandages and only infectious cases are removed from the home prior to the burial.

Why do I describe such "old-fashioned" customs? I think they are [16] an indication of our acceptance of a fatal outcome, and they help the dying patient as well as his family to accept the loss of a loved one. If a patient is allowed to terminate his life in the familiar and beloved environment, it requires less adjustment for him. His own family knows him well enough to replace a sedative with a glass of his favorite wine; or the smell of a home-cooked soup may give him the appetite to sip a few spoons of fluid which, I think is still more enjoyable than an infusion. I will not minimize the need for sedatives and infusions and realize full well from my own experience as a country doctor that they are sometimes life-saving and often unavoidable. But I also know that patience and familiar people and foods could replace many a bottle of intravenous fluids given for the simple reason that it fulfills the physiological need without involving too many people and/or individual nursing care.

The fact that children are allowed to stay at home where a fatality [17] has stricken and are included in the talk, discussions, and fears gives them the feeling that they are not alone in the grief and gives them the comfort of shared responsibility and shared mourning. It prepares them gradually and helps them view death as part of life, an experience which may help them grow and mature.

This is in great contrast to a society in which death is viewed as [18] taboo, discussion of it is regarded as morbid, and children are excluded with the presumption and pretext that it would be "too much" for them. They are then sent off to relatives, often accompanied with some unconvincing lies of "Mother has gone on a long trip" or other unbelievable stories. The child senses that something is wrong, and his distrust in adults will only multiply if other relatives add new variations of the story, avoid his questions or suspicions, shower him with gifts as a meager substitute for a loss he is not permitted to deal with. Sooner or later the child will become aware of the changed family situation and, depending on the age and personality of the child, will have an unresolved grief and regard this incident as a frightening, mysterious, in any case very traumatic experience with untrustworthy grownups, which he has no way to cope with.

It is equally unwise to tell a little child who lost her brother that God [19] loved little boys so much that he took little Johnny to heaven. When this little girl grew up to be a woman she never solved her anger at God, which resulted in a psychotic depression when she lost her own little son three decades later.

We would think that our great emancipation, our knowledge of sci- [20] ence and of man, has given us better ways and means to prepare ourselves and our families for this inevitable happening. Instead the days are gone when a man was allowed to die in peace and dignity in his own home.

The more we are making advancements in science, the more we [21] seem to fear and deny the reality of death. How is this possible?

We use euphemisms, we make the dead look as if they were asleep, [22] we ship the children off to protect them from the anxiety and turmoil around the house if the patient is fortunate enough to die at home, we don't allow children to visit their dying parents in the hospitals, we have long and controversial discussions about whether patients should be told the truth—a question that rarely arises when the dying person is tended by the family physician who has known him from delivery to death and who knows the weaknesses and strengths of each member of the family.

I think there are many reasons for this flight away from facing death [23] calmly. One of the most important facts is that dying nowadays is more gruesome in many ways, namely, more lonely, mechanical, and dehumanized; at times it is even difficult to determine technically when the time of death has occurred.

Dying becomes lonely and impersonal because the patient is often [24] taken out of his familiar environment and rushed to an emergency room. Whoever has been very sick and has required rest and comfort especially may recall his experience of being put on a stretcher and enduring the noise of the ambulance siren and hectic rush until the hospital gates open. Only those who have lived through this may appreciate the discomfort and cold necessity of such transportation which is only the beginning of a long order—hard to endure when you are well, difficult to express in words when noise, light, pumps, and voices are all too much to put up with. It may well be that we might consider more the patient under the sheets and blankets and perhaps stop our well-meant efficiency and rush in order to hold the patient's hand, to smile, or to listen to a question. I include the trip to the hospital as the first episode in dying, as it is for many. I am putting it exaggeratedly in contrast to the sick man who is left at home—not to say that lives should not be saved if they can be saved by a hospitalization but to keep the focus on the patient's experience, his needs and his reactions.

When a patient is severely ill, he is often treated like a person with [25] no right to an opinion. It is often someone else who makes the decision if and when and where a patient should be hospitalized. It would take so little to remember that the sick person too has feelings, has wishes and opinions, and has—most important of all—the right to be heard.

Well, our presumed patient has now reached the emergency room. [26] He will be surrounded by busy nurses, orderlies, interns, residents, a lab technician perhaps who will take some blood, an electrocardiogram technician who takes the cardiogram. He may be moved to X ray and he will overhear opinions of his condition and discussions and questions to members of the family. He slowly but surely is beginning to be treated like a thing. He is no longer a person. Decisions are made often without his opinion. If he tries to rebel he will be sedated and after hours of waiting and wondering whether he has the strength, he will be wheeled into the operating room or intensive treatment unit and become an object of great concern and great financial investment.

He may cry for rest, peace, and dignity, but he will get infusions, [27] transfusions, a heart machine, or tracheotomy[2] if necessary. He may want one single person to stop for one single minute so that he can ask one single question—but he will get a dozen people around the clock, all busily preoccupied with his heart rate, pulse, electrocardiogram or pulmonary functions, his secretions or excretions but not with him as a human being. He may wish to fight it all but it is going to be a useless fight since all this is done in the fight for his life, and if they can save his life they can consider the person afterwards. Those who consider the person first may lose precious time to save his life! At least this seems to be the rationale or justification behind all this—or is it? Is the reason for this increasingly mechanical, depersonalized approach our own defensiveness? Is this approach our own way to cope with and repress the anxieties that a terminally or critically ill patient evokes in us? Is our concentration on equipment, on blood pressure, our desperate attempt to deny the impending death which is so frightening and discomforting to us that we displace all our knowledge onto machines, since they are less close to us than the suffering face of another human being which would remind us once more of our lack of omnipotence, our own limits and failures, and last but not least perhaps our own mortality?

Maybe the question has to be raised: Are we becoming less human [28] or more human? . . . [I]t is clear that whatever the answer may be, the patient is suffering more—not physically, perhaps, but emotionally. And his needs have not changed over the centuries, only our ability to gratify them.

---

[2] An incision into the trachea in the neck to allow the insertion of a breathing tube. [Eds.]

Responding to Reading

1. Despite advances in medical science over the centuries, Kübler-Ross says, death remains "a fearful, frightening happening, and the fear of death is a universal fear even if we think we have mastered it on many levels" (12). Do you think she is correct? Are you afraid of death?
2. To what extent do you agree with Kübler-Ross that we should confront the reality of death directly—for example, by being honest with children, keeping terminally ill patients at home, and allowing dying patients to determine their own treatment? What arguments are there against each of her suggestions?
3. Instead of quoting medical authorities, Kübler-Ross supports her points with anecdotes. Do you find this support convincing? Would hard scientific data be more convincing? Explain.

THE ETHICS OF EUTHANASIA

Lawrence J. Schneiderman

Born in New York City, Lawrence J. Schneiderman (1932–) received his M.D. from Harvard Medical School in 1957 and has been on the staffs of Boston City Hospital, the National Institutes of Health, and Stanford University School of Medicine. Since 1970 he has been a professor at the University of California-San Diego School of Medicine, where he is director of the program in Medical Ethics. In addition to his contributions to medical journals, Schneiderman is the author of a novel, *Sea Nymphs by the Hour* (1972). In the following essay, which originally appeared in *The Humanist* in 1990, he considers the complex question, "What will become of a society that permits—indeed promotes—death as a social good?"

Should physicians be permitted to offer death among their therapeutic options? Should they be licensed to kill—not inadvertently or negligently but willfully, openly, and compassionately? This, on the most superficial level, is the euthanasia debate.

In California, a petition to put this matter before the voters failed to gain sufficient signatures. Perhaps this was because too many of those life-affirming hedonists cringed at the thought of signing their own death warrants, or—more likely in this land where almost everything has a price—because the sponsoring Hemlock Society did not hire enough solicitors.

In any case, euthanasia is being performed.

As a medical ethicist, when I give talks on this subject to physicians, 4
I always ask: "How many of you have ever hastened death to alleviate
the suffering of your patients?" Many hands are raised—uneasily; I can
offer them no legal immunity. Of all the humane acts physicians perform, euthanasia is the one we do most furtively.

But this is an old story. In 1537, while serving in the army of Fran- 5
cis I, the troubled surgeon Ambroise Paré confided in his diary:

> We thronged into the city and passed over the dead bodies and some
> that were not yet dead, hearing them cry under the feet of our horses,
> which made a great pity in my heart, and truly I repented that I had
> gone forth from Paris to see so pitiful a spectacle. Being in the city, I en-
> tered a stable, thinking to lodge my horse and that of my man, where
> I found four dead soldiers and three who were propped against the
> wall, their faces wholly disfigured, and they neither saw, nor heard,
> nor spoke, and their clothes yet flaming from the gun powder, which
> had burnt them. Beholding them with pity there came an old soldier
> who asked me if there was any means of curing them. I told him no. At
> once he approached them and cut their throats gently and without
> anger. Seeing this great cruelty I said to him that he was an evil man.
> He answered me that he prayed God that when he should be in such
> a case, he might find someone that would do the same for him, to the
> end that he might not languish miserably.

Today, the euthanasia debate takes place under the shadow of Nazi 6
doctors who appropriated the term to describe the "special treatment"
given first to the physically and mentally handicapped, then to the weak
and elderly, and, finally, to Jews, gypsies, and other "undesirables" as
part of the Final Solution—all in the name of social hygiene. In that monstrous orgy of evil, numbers replaced names, bodies replaced souls; all
were hauled by the trainload to work or to death, then converted to
ashes or merely dumped in such profusion that the very earth bubbled.
That was no *euthanasia*—no easy, pleasant death. That was ugly, debas-
ing death.

But we are different, are we not? Not like *them*. And yet, and yet . . . 7
didn't we American physicians commit atrocities of our own, such as allowing untreated blacks to succumb to the "natural course" of syphilis;
misleading Spanish-speaking women into thinking they were obtaining
contraceptives, when in fact they were receiving inactive dummy tablets
to distinguish drug side-effects, resulting in unwanted pregnancies; and
injecting cancer cells into unwitting elderly patients? All for the sake of
medical progress . . . we can only look back and shake our heads.

Worthy colleagues—with whom I respectfully disagree—are so 8
fearful of the "Naziness" in us all that they oppose withholding life-sustaining treatment from *anyone:* the malformed newborn with no hope of
survival, the permanently unconscious patient, the terminal cancer patient who begs to be allowed to die. Who would be next? they argue. The

physically and mentally handicapped? The weak and the elderly? And then? And then? This, of course, is the familiar "slippery slope" argument. Start with one exception and you inevitably skid down the moral slope of ever more exceptions. This also is the euthanasia debate, on a deeper level. What will become of a society that permits—indeed promotes—death as a social good?

An ethics consultation is where we ponder such questions at the bedside of a patient who perhaps is hopelessly ill. Not infrequently, back in the doctor's conference room, a harried resident will burst out: "*What good is it for us to keep him alive anyway?*" I don't regard this as a callous question for the simple reason that it is phrased intimately and in the singular: Why do *we* keep *him* alive? In contrast, you'd be surprised how often decent people who possess the most humane and compassionate sensibilities demand: "Why do *they* keep *them* alive?" That question, in my view, is morally indistinguishable from: "Why do *they* let *them* die?" 9

For, you see, the first question arises from *this* patient, this special case, *here.* The second question arises from a state of mind—*those* people. *There.* It is a state of mind that provides a dehumanizing abstraction appealing to both extremes of the political spectrum, and it has been applied to both ends of life. It can lead to the demand that *all* handicapped newborns be kept alive without regard to their specific agonies and that life-prolonging treatment be denied to *all* the elderly beyond a certain age. 10

What is so special about the special case? For those of us in medicine, it exerts a palpable moral power; the special case is our daily news, our gossip, a shaping force in our culture. Case studies and case reports are basic teaching tools. *Case* (from *casus*, "happening," "accident") in its original meaning refers to a unique person in unique circumstances. Physicians are molded by their particular autobiography of cases, by their own singular distressing experiences. My first physical diagnosis teacher said, "Make sure you examine the neck veins. Always. Once I missed a patient with congestive heart failure because I neglected to do so." Since then, I have heard many such honest confessions—covertly, for in the litigious world of contemporary medicine, it is almost treachery to reveal that this is how we learn best, by being wrong. To help my compulsively driven and terrified students get on with their duties, I tell them that, if it is true you learn from your mistakes, someday I will know everything. 11

And we do learn from our special cases, one by one—sometimes badly and incompletely, but each time the lesson is so painful that ultimately we do learn. For example, as a medical student, I was monitoring the blood pressure of a man dying of acute pulmonary edema and myocardial infarction.[1] The end of a gala evening for him. Next to me 12

---

[1] In lay person's terms, a severe heart attack. [Eds.]

was the man's wife—coiffed and elegantly gowned, cradling his head and crooning her love while the man blanched into death. It was a good death, since his physician, who was controlling the intravenous infusion on the other side of the bed, had made sure that the man was heavily sedated with morphine. It was a lesson I took with me to my internship, when I treated my first patient with terminal cancer of the bowel. She was tough, this woman, crusty, white-haired, and quite prepared to die. The searing looks she leveled at me made me very much aware of my youth, my health, my innocence.

Alas, she was right about my innocence. I had not yet learned every- 13
thing there was to know about morphine. Pumping in large doses to control her pain, I failed to deal with its paralytic effects on the intestine. As a result, her last day was a horror of acute intestinal obstruction. I shall never forget the curses she hurled at me between squalls of sewage. I doubt there was a soul in the world who knew or cared that she died, but, of course, she was for me immemorial, a special case. Am I forgiven now that countless others have received the blessing of her curses?— for you can be sure that I never fail to teach the importance of keeping the bowels open when caring for a cancer patient. Am I forgiven? I do not know.

Yet, you can see how easy it is to corrupt this experience, to slide 14
from the special case to a state of mind based upon dehumanizing abstractions. For it was a failure in mechanics that led to the poor woman's suffering, and it is merely with the hope of better attending to such mechanics that we have developed the powerful technology that now pervades medicine. Now we can better manage not only the bowels but also the hearts, livers, kidneys, lungs, and all combinations thereof. How do we know we manage them better? We do randomized, double-blind, prospective experimental trials in which patients are aggregated into treatment groups, outcomes are analyzed, and their differences compared by statistics—another state of mind (a related word, in fact), another set of abstractions. Bearing the weight of these massive studies like armies of pharaonic slaves, we plod step by step up federally funded pyramids of therapeutic progress. Read any good medical journal: It is filled with multiauthored, multi-institutional papers. Modern medicine; how dehumanizing, we are told.

And lo and behold, we are repelled into an opposite state of mind, 15
a sentimental longing to escape such cold-blooded modernity. We applaud the hit play *Whose Life Is It Anyway?*, which ends with the quadriplegic hero rejecting life-sustaining technology and going home to die. As the lights come up, we are left to assume that offstage he will effervesce nobly, wittily, free of hunger, thirst, and embarrassing bodily products—fulfilling Milan Kundera's[2] definition of *kitsch*.

---

[2] Czech novelist and essayist. *Kitsch* is anything that appeals to popular or middlebrow taste. [Eds.]

But the facts are not so vaporous, and the truth is not so clean-   16
shaven. For the truth is: Death is not an artist many of us admire. This
artist's work is often messy. Pretending otherwise is sentimentality—a
state of mind that we define as reaching sentiments too cheaply and easily. Of course, there is also the opposite state of mind, the reaction to sentimentality: cynicism, which can also be arrived at too cheaply and easily. Both of these states of mind are false. It is against both of these states
of mind that the special case protests.

This, I submit, is what the euthanasia debate is about: theoretical   17
and statistical abstractions versus the anguishing, messy particulars of
the special case. In illness, we are made exquisitely aware of what it
means to be ourselves, no other, alone—this is happening to *me*. Those
of us still healthy, if we are compassionate, acknowledge and even
honor the unbreachable solitude of those who are ill. It joins us in a
community of human feeling—notice that I do not use the word *state*.
Because it is truly human, such a community—unlike the totalitarian
state (of politics or of mind)—is as varied and unpredictable as the beings within it. And so, the argument goes, if we honor our fellow
human beings—their variety, each and every life—it follows that we
must honor how each person chooses to live that life, so long as it causes no harm to others. We must also honor—if fate so grants—whatever coda[3] each person sees fit to put on that life. In euthanasia, as in
abortion, this issue of choice gets lost in the rhetorical smoke. No one
is really *pro*-abortion. Similarly, no one claims to *like* euthanasia. Proponents merely want to have these options available in desperate circumstances.

But what will happen then? my worthy colleagues ask. Will things   18
fall apart? Is Nazi Germany our malign destiny? Or could it be, rather,
that peaceable kingdom, the Netherlands, where an estimated five to ten
thousand patients are administered euthanasia on request (and illegal-
ly) every year? Explicitly defined violations simply are not prosecuted.
The physician is permitted to administer painless death only when a
fully informed, rational patient voluntarily and repeatedly requests it in
a medical situation that is considered intolerable and hopeless and un-
responsive to any other means of medical relief. As a further safeguard,
two physicians must concur with a patient's request. At no time are social goals considered. Each patient is treated as a special case, and in
each case the act is voluntary.

But is it necessary to kill? my worthy colleagues argue, dubious that   19
a person in such extremity is capable of any voluntary act and drawing
a distinction between "active" and "passive" euthanasia. Can't we simply allow such a case to die? Such a distinction, in my view, makes no
sense, now that medicine has become so powerful that almost *any* life

---

[3] Concluding section of a musical or dramatic work. [Eds.]

can be prolonged, however briefly. And once a decision is made that death is preferable to existence, *any* choice—whether giving or withholding treatment, whether it be surgery or antibiotics or narcotics—is an act toward or against that end. So, the only relevant moral questions become *why* (the motive) and *how* (the method). One can have the cruelest motive and employ the kindest method; for example, slipping Gramps an overdose of sleeping medicine to get rid of him and get at his money. Or, one can have the kindest motive and employ the cruelest method: letting him "languish miserably" (in the words of Paré) out of a loving reluctance to hasten his death. Neither of these acts is as morally defensible, in my opinion, as the bloody dagger-thrust performed "gently and without anger" by that old unknown soldier.

And so, while the cautious Dutch carry on, several states—including California, once again—are preparing euthanasia initiatives. And the difficult questions will have to be faced. Can we be both merciful and just in matters of medically administered death? How? Do we keep the laws the way they are and grant no exceptions, thus publicly condemning (while at the same time insidiously perpetuating) unsupervised euthanasia? Or should we change the laws? And if we do so, can we craft them in such a way so as not to destroy hallowed and fragile values? Should we explicitly define and sanction certain acts of humane suicide assisted by physicians? Should we allow patients direct legal access to the necessary drugs? Or should we not attempt to change the laws but only openly acknowledge (as in the Netherlands) certain permissible violations—thus cautioning physicians to weigh each act as one they may have to defend in criminal court? The approach we take will reveal much about ourselves as a society. Are our moral cousins the Nazis or the Dutch? Can we keep our anguish fresh each time we contemplate the end of a fellow human being? Or will our anguish grow stale, allowing us to slide down the slope from "easy death" to "useful death," heaping *them* into nameless, faceless piles, saying there go *they*, not *I*, and discovering too late—as others have before—that if yesterday *they* were the retarded, the handicapped, the Jews, the blacks; and if today *they* are the elderly, the AIDS patient; then tomorrow *they* will be ourselves, wondering where all the others are—common waste requiring special treatment rather than special cases sharing a common fate.

Responding to Reading

1. Do you think physicians should be able to "offer death as one of their therapeutic options" (1)? Or do you think doctors should maintain life at all costs? What do you think of the "slippery slope" argument (8) offered by opponents of euthanasia?

2. What does Schneiderman mean when he says, "This, I submit, is what the euthanasia debate is about: theoretical and statistical abstractions versus the anguishing, messy particulars of the special case" (17)?
3. Schneiderman concludes with a series of questions. Why do you suppose he ends his essay in this way?

A CASE OF ASSISTED SUICIDE

Jack Kevorkian

Popularly known as "Dr. Death," Jack Kevorkian (1928–) has had a long interest in death and dying, which some critics trace to the fact that most of his Armenian family was annihilated by German soldiers during World War II. Trained in pathology at the University of Michigan, he was one of the earliest advocates of executing criminals by lethal injection, a practice which is followed in many states today. He has also argued in favor of using condemned criminals in medical experiments that would eventually kill them. Kevorkian's greatest notoriety, however, stems from his publicly acknowledged assistance in the suicides of a number of people with terminal or debilitatingly painful illnesses, actions for which he has been charged with murder in Michigan courts. In the following chapter from his book *Prescription: Medicide* (1991), Kevorkian describes in detail the first suicide in which he assisted using his "Mercitron," the device he invented for this purpose.

Amid the flurry of telephone calls in the fall of 1989 was one from a [1] man in Portland, Oregon, who learned of my campaign from an item in *Newsweek* (November 13, 1989). Ron Adkins's rich, baritone, matter-of-fact voice was tinged with a bit of expectant anxiety as he calmly explained the tragic situation of his beloved wife. Janet Adkins was a remarkable, accomplished, active woman—wife, mother, grandmother, revered friend, teacher, musician, mountain climber, and outdoorsperson—who, for some time, had noticed (as did her husband) subtle and gradually progressive impairment of her memory. The shock of hearing the diagnosis of Alzheimer's disease four months earlier was magnified by the abrupt and somewhat callous way her doctor announced it. The intelligent woman knew what the diagnosis portended, and at that instant decided she would not live to experience the horror of such a death.

Knowing that Janet was a courageous fighter, Ron and their three   2
sons pleaded with her to reconsider and at least give a promising new
therapy regimen a try. Ron explained to me that Janet was eligible to
take part in an experimental trial using the newly developed drug
Tacrine® or THA at the University of Washington in Seattle. I concurred
that Janet should enroll in the program because any candidate for the
Mercitron must have exhausted every potentially beneficial medical intervention, no matter how remotely promising.

I heard nothing more from the Adkinses until April 1990. Ron called   3
again, after Janet and he saw me and my device on a nationally televised
talk show. Janet had entered the experimental program in January, but
it had been stopped early because the new drug was ineffective. In fact,
her condition got worse; and she was more determined than ever to end
her life. Even though from a physical standpoint Janet was not immi-
nently terminal, there seemed little doubt that mentally she was—and,
after all, it is one's mental status that determines the essence of one's existence. I asked Ron to forward to me copies of Janet's clinical records,
and they corroborated what Ron had said.

I then telephoned Janet's doctor in Seattle. He opposed her planned   4
action and the concept of assisted suicide in general. It was his firm opinion that Janet would remain mentally competent for at least a year (but
from Ron's narrative I concluded that her doctor's opinion was wrong
and that time was of the essence). Because Janet's condition was deteriorating and there was nothing else that might help arrest it, I decided to
accept her as the first candidate—a qualified, justifiable candidate if not
"ideal"—and well aware of the vulnerability to criticism of picayune
and overly emotional critics.

A major obstacle was finding a place to do it. Because I consider   5
medicide to be necessary, ethical, and legal, there should be nothing
furtive about it. Another reason to pursue the practice above-board is to
avert the harrassment or vindictiveness of litigation. Consequently,
when searching for a suitable site I always explained that I planned to
assist a suffering patient to commit suicide. That posed no problem for
helping a Michigan resident in his or her own residence. But it was a different matter for an out-of-state guest who must rent temporary quarters.

And I soon found out how difficult a matter it could be. My own   6
apartment could not be used because of lease constraints, and the same
was true of my sister's apartment. I inquired at countless motels, funeral homes, churches of various denominations, rental office buildings,
clinics, doctors' offices for lease, and even considered the futile hope of
renting an emergency life-support ambulance. Many owners, propri-
etors, and landlords were quite sympathetic but fearful and envisioned
the negative public reaction that could seriously damage and even destroy their business enterprises. In short, they deemed it bad for public

relations. More dismaying yet was the refusal of people who are known supporters and active campaigners for euthanasia to allow Janet and me the use of their homes.

Finally, a friend agreed to avail us of his modest home in Detroit; I [7] immediately contacted Ron to finalize plans. My initial proposal was to carry out the procedure at the end of May 1990, but Ron and Janet preferred to avoid the surge of travel associated with the Memorial Day weekend. The date was postponed to Monday, June 4th.

In the meantime, my friend was warned by a doctor, in whom he [8] confided, not to make his home available for such a purpose. Soon thereafter the offer was quickly withdrawn. With the date set and airline tickets having been purchased by Janet, Ron, and a close friend of Janet's, I had to scamper to find another site. The device required an electrical outlet, which limited the possibilities.

I had made a Herculean effort to provide a desirable, clinical setting. [9] Literally and sadly, there was "no room at the inn." Now, having been refused everywhere I applied, the *only alternative* remaining was my 1968 camper and a suitable campground.

As expected, the owners of a commercial site refused permission, [10] even though they were sympathetic to the proposed scheme. They then suggested the solution by recommending that I rent space at a public camping site not too far away. The setting was pleasant and idyllic.

As with many other aspects of this extraordinary event, I was aware [11] of the harsh criticism that would be leveled at the use of a "rusty old van." In the first place, the twenty-two-year-old body may have been rusting on the outside, but its interior was very clean, orderly, and comfortable. I have slept in it often and not felt degraded. But carping critics missed the point: the essence and significance of the event are far more important than the splendor of the site where it takes place. If critics are thus deluded into denouncing the exit from existence under these circumstances, then why not the same delusional denunciation of entrance into existence when a baby is, of necessity, born in an old taxicab? On the contrary, the latter identical scenario seems to arouse only feelings of sentimental reverence and quaint joy.

But the dishonesty doesn't stop there. I have been repeatedly criti- [12] cized for having assisted a patient after a short personal acquaintance of two days. Overlooked or ignored is my open avowal to be the first practitioner in this country of a new and as yet officially unrecognized specialty. Because of shameful stonewalling by her own doctors, Janet was forced to refer herself to me. And acting as a unique specialist, of necessity self-proclaimed, solitary, and independent, I was obligated to scrutinize Janet's clinical records and to consult with her personal doctor. The latter's uncooperative attitude (tacitly excused by otherwise harsh critics) impaired but did not thwart fulfillment of my duties to a suffering patient and to my profession.

It is absurd even to imply, let alone to protest outright, that a med- 13
ical specialist's competence and ethical behavior are contingent upon
some sort of time interval, imposed arbitrarily or by fiat. When a doctor
refers a patient for surgery, in many cases the surgical specialist performs his *ultimate* duty after personal acquaintance with the patient
from a mere hour or two of prior consultation (in contrast to my having
spent at least twelve hours in personal contact with Janet). In a few instances the surgeon operates on a patient seen for the first time on the
operating table—and anesthetized to unconsciousness.

Moreover, in sharp contrast to the timorous, secretive, and even de- 14
ceitful intention and actions of other medical euthanasists on whom our
so-called bioethicists now shower praise, I acted openly, ethically, legally, with complete and uncompromising honesty, and—even more important—I remained in personal attendance during the second most
meaningful medical event in a patient's earthly existence. Were he alive
today, it's not hard to guess what Hippocrates[1] would say about all this.

My two sisters, Margo and Flora, and I met with Ron, Janet, and 15
Janet's close friend Carroll Rehmke in their motel room on Saturday afternoon, 2 June 1990. After getting acquainted through a few minutes of
conversation, the purpose of the trip was thoroughly discussed. I had already prepared authorization forms signifying Janet's intent, determination, and freedom of choice, which she readily agreed to sign. Here
again, while she was resolute in her decision, and absolutely mentally
competent, her impaired memory was apparent when she needed her
husband's assistance in forming the cursive letter "A." She could print
the letter but not write it, and the consent forms required that her sig-
nature be written. So her husband showed her on another piece of paper
how to form the cursive "A," and Janet complied. At this time, Ron and
Carroll also signed a statement attesting to Janet's mental competence.
Following this signing session, I had Flora videotape my interview with
Janet and Ron. The forty-five-minute taping reinforced my own conviction that Janet was mentally competent but that her memory had failed
badly. However, the degree of memory failure led me to surmise that
within four to six months she would be too incompetent to qualify as a
candidate. It should be pointed out that in medical terms loss of memory does not automatically signify mental incompetence. Any rational
critic would concede that a mentally sound individual can be afflicted
with even total amnesia.

Around 5:30 P.M. that same day all six of us had dinner at a well- 16
known local restaurant. Seated around the same table for many hours,
our conversation covered many subjects, including the telling of jokes.
Without appearing too obvious, I constantly observed Janet's behavior

---

[1] Ancient Greek physician, called the father of medicine. [Eds.]

and assessed her moods as well as the content and quality of her thoughts. There was absolutely no doubt that her mentality was intact and that she was not the least depressed over her impending death. On the contrary, the only detectable anxiety or disquieting demeanor was among the rest of us to a greater or lesser degree. Even in response to jokes, Janet's appropriately timed and modulated laughter indicated clear and coherent comprehension. The only uneasiness or distress she exhibited was due to her embarrassment at being unable to recall aspects of the topic under discussion at the time. And that is to be expected of intelligent, sensitive, and diligent individuals.

We left the restaurant at 12:30 A.M. Sunday. Janet and Ron enjoyed [17] their last full day by themselves.

At 8:30 A.M. the next day, Monday, 4 June 1990, I drove into a rent- [18] ed space at Groveland Park in north Oakland County, Michigan. At the same time, my sisters drove to the motel to fetch Janet, who had composed (and submitted to my sister) a brief and clear note reiterating her genuine desire to end her life and exonerating all others in this desire and the actual event. For the last time, Janet took tearful leave of her grieving husband and Carroll, both of whom were inconsolable. It was Janet's wish that they not accompany her to the park.

The day began cold, damp, and overcast. I took a lot of time in set- [19] ting up the Mercitron and giving it a few test runs. In turning to get a pair of pliers in the cramped space within the van, I accidentally knocked over the container of thiopental solution, losing a little over half of it. I was fairly sure that the remainder was enough to induce and maintain adequate unconsciousness, but I chose not to take the risk. I drove the forty-five miles home and got some more.

In the meantime, at about 9:30 A.M. my sisters and Janet had arrived [20] at the park. They were dismayed to learn of the accidental spill and opted to accompany me on the extra round trip, which required two and one-half hours. We reentered the park at approximately noontime. Janet remained in the car with Margo while Flora helped me with minor tasks in the van as I very carefully prepared and tested the Mercitron. Everything was ready by about 2:00 P.M., and Janet was summoned.

She entered the van alone through the open sliding side door and [21] lay fully clothed on the built-in bed covered with freshly laundered sheets. Her head rested comfortably on a clean pillow. The windows were covered with new draperies. With Janet's permission I cut small holes in her nylon stockings at the ankles, attached ECG electrodes to her ankles and wrists, and covered her body with a light blanket. Our conversation was minimal. In accordance with Janet's wish, Flora read to her a brief note from her friend Carroll, followed by a reading of the Lord's prayer. I then repeated my earlier instructions to Janet about how the device was to be activated, and asked her to go through the motions. In contrast to my sister and me, Janet was calm and outwardly relaxed.

I used a syringe with attached needle to pierce a vein near the [22] frontal elbow area of her left arm. Unfortunately, her veins were delicate and fragile; even slight movement of the restrained arm caused the needle to penetrate through the wall of the vein resulting in leakage. Two more attempts also failed, as did a fourth attempt on the right side. Finally an adequate puncture was obtained on the right arm. (It was reassuring to me to learn later that doctors in Seattle had had similar difficulty with her veins.)

The moment had come. With a nod from Janet I turned on the ECG [23] and said, "Now." Janet hit the Mercitron's switch with the outer edge of her palm. In about ten seconds her eyelids began to flicker and droop. She looked up at me and said, "Thank you, thank you." I replied at once as her eyelids closed, "Have a nice trip." She was unconscious and perfectly still except for two widely spaced and mild coughs several minutes later. Agonal complexes in the ECG tracing indicated death due to complete cessation of blood circulation in six minutes.

It was 2:30 P.M. Suddenly—for the first time that cold, dank day— [24] warm sunshine bathed the park.

Responding to Reading

1. What is Kevorkian's purpose in writing this essay? Do you think he accomplishes his goals?
2. Does Kevorkian convince you his actions were justified? If you were in his situation, would you have helped Janet Adkins commit suicide? Why or why not?
3. In paragraph 12 Kevorkian accuses his critics of intellectual dishonesty. Are there any points in this essay where you think Kevorkian is being less than honest with readers? With himself?

THE BLACK DEATH

Barbara Tuchman

Historical writer and journalist Barbara Tuchman (1912–1989) won Pulitzer Prizes for two of her books, *The Guns of August* (1962) and *Stillwell and the American Experience in China, 1911–1945* (1971). Known for both her literary approach and her factual accuracy, Tuchman once described herself as "a writer whose subject is history." Some of her many works are *The Proud Tower: A Portrait of the World Before the War, 1890–1914* (1966), *A Distant Mirror: The Calamitous Fourteenth Century*

(1978), and a collection of essays, *Practicing History* (1981). Tuchman was awarded the American Academy of Arts and Sciences gold medal for history in 1978. In the following excerpt from *A Distant Mirror*, she graphically describes the Black Death (or bubonic plague) without sentimentality or melodrama, using a variety of different sources to document this plague's horrifying effects.

In October 1347, two months after the fall of Calais, Genoese trading ships put into the harbor of Messina in Sicily with dead and dying men at the oars. The ships had come from the Black Sea port of Caffa (now Feodosiya) in the Crimea, where the Genoese maintained a trading post. The diseased sailors showed strange black swellings about the size of an egg or an apple in the armpits and groin. The swellings oozed blood and pus and were followed by spreading boils and black blotches on the skin from internal bleeding. The sick suffered severe pain and died quickly within five days of the first symptoms. As the disease spread, other symptoms of continuous fever and spitting of blood appeared instead of the swelling or buboes. These victims coughed and sweated heavily and died even more quickly, within three days or less, sometimes in 24 hours. In both types everything that issued from the body—breath, sweat, blood from the buboes and lungs, bloody urine, and blood-blackened excrement—smelled foul. Depression and despair accompanied the physical symptoms, and before the end "death is seen seated on the face." [1]

The disease was bubonic plague, present in two forms: one that infected the bloodstream, causing the buboes and internal bleeding, and was spread by contact; and a second, more virulent pneumonic type that infected the lungs and was spread by respiratory infection. The presence of both at once caused the high mortality and speed of contagion. So lethal was the disease that cases were known of persons going to bed well and dying before they woke, of doctors catching the illness at a bedside and dying before the patient. So rapidly did it spread from one to another that to a French physician, Simon de Covino, it seemed as if one sick person "could infect the whole world." The malignity of the pestilence appeared more terrible because its victims knew no prevention and no remedy. [2]

The physical suffering of the disease and its aspect of evil mystery were expressed in a strange Welsh lament which saw "death coming into our midst like black smoke, a plague which cuts off the young, a rootless phantom which has no mercy for fair countenance. Woe is me of the shilling in the armpit! It is seething, terrible . . . a head that gives pain and causes a loud cry . . . a painful angry knob . . . . Great is its seething like a burning cinder . . . a grievous thing of ashy color." Its eruption is ugly like the "seeds of black peas, broken fragments of brittle sea-coal . . . the early ornaments of black death, cinders of the peel- [3]

ings of the cockle weed, a mixed multitude, a black plague like half-pence, like berries. . . ."

Rumors of a terrible plague supposedly arising in China and spreading through Tartary (Central Asia) to India and Persia, Mesopotamia, Syria, Egypt, and all of Asia Minor had reached Europe in 1346. They told of a death so devastating that all of India was said to be depopulated, whole territories covered by dead bodies, other areas with no one left alive. As added up by Pope Clement VI at Avignon, the total of reported dead reached 23,840,000. In the absence of a concept of contagion, no serious alarm was felt in Europe until the trading ships brought their black burden of pestilence into Messina while other infected ships from the Levant carried it to Genoa and Venice.

By January 1348 it penetrated France via Marseille, and North Africa via Tunis. Shipborne along coasts and navigable rivers, it spread westward from Marseille through the ports of Languedoc to Spain and northward up the Rhône to Avignon, where it arrived in March. It reached Narbonne, Montpellier, Carcassonne, and Toulouse between February and May, and at the same time in Italy spread to Rome and Florence and their hinterlands. Between June and August it reached Bordeaux, Lyon, and Paris, spread to Burgundy and Normandy, and crossed the Channel from Normandy into southern England. From Italy during the same summer it crossed the Alps into Switzerland and reached eastward to Hungary.

In a given area the plague accomplished its kill within four to six months and then faded, except in the larger cities, where, rooting into the close-quartered population, it abated during the winter, only to reappear in spring and rage for another six months.

In 1349 it resumed in Paris, spread to Picardy, Flanders, and the Low Countries, and from England to Scotland and Ireland as well as to Norway, where a ghost ship with a cargo of wool and a dead crew drifted offshore until it ran aground near Bergen. From there the plague passed into Sweden, Denmark, Prussia, Iceland, and as far as Greenland. Leaving a strange pocket of immunity in Bohemia, and Russia unattacked until 1351, it had passed from most of Europe by mid-1350. Although the mortality rate was erratic, ranging from one fifth in some places to nine tenths or almost total elimination in others, the overall estimate of modern demographers has settled—for the area extending from India to Iceland—around the same figure expressed in Froissart's casual words: "a third of the world died." His estimate, the common one at the time, was not an inspired guess but a borrowing of St. John's figure for mortality from plague in Revelation, the favorite guide to human affairs of the Middle Ages.

A third of Europe would have meant about 20 million deaths. No one knows in truth how many died. Contemporary reports were an awed impression, not an accurate count. In crowded Avignon, it was said, 400 died daily; 7,000 houses emptied by death were shut up; a single graveyard received 11,000 corpses in six weeks; half the city's inhabitants reportedly died, including 9 cardinals or one third of the total, and 70 lesser prelates. Watching the endlessly passing death carts, chroniclers let normal exaggeration take wings and put the Avignon death toll at 62,000 and even at 120,000, although the city's total population was probably less than 50,000.

When graveyards filled up, bodies at Avignon were thrown into the Rhône until mass burial pits were dug for dumping the corpses. In London in such pits corpses piled up in layers until they overflowed. Everywhere reports speak of the sick dying too fast for the living to bury. Corpses were dragged out of homes and left in front of doorways. Morning light revealed new piles of bodies. In Florence the dead were gathered up by the Compagnia della Misericordia—founded in 1244 to care for the sick—whose members wore red robes and hoods masking the face except for the eyes. When their efforts failed, the dead lay putrid in the streets for days at a time. When no coffins were to be had, the bodies were laid on boards, two or three at once, to be carried to graveyards or common pits. Families dumped their own relatives into the pits, or buried them so hastily and thinly "that dogs dragged them forth and devoured their bodies."

Amid accumulating death and fear of contagion, people died without last rites and were buried without prayers, a prospect that terrified the last hours of the stricken. A bishop in England gave permission to laymen to make confession to each other as was done by the Apostles, "or if no man is present then even to a woman," and if no priest could be found to administer extreme unction, "then faith must suffice." Clement VI found it necessary to grant remissions of sin to all who died of the plague because so many were unattended by priests. "And no bells tolled," wrote a chronicler of Siena, "and nobody wept no matter what his loss because almost everyone expected death. . . . And people said and believed, 'this is the end of the world.'"

In Paris, where the plague lasted through 1349, the reported death rate was 800 a day, in Pisa 500, in Vienna 500 to 600. The total dead in Paris numbered 50,000 or half the population. Florence, weakened by the famine of 1347, lost three to four fifths of its citizens, Venice two thirds, Hamburg and Bremen, though smaller in size, about the same proportion. Cities, as centers of transportation, were more likely to be affected than villages, although once a village was infected, its death rate was equally high. At Givry, a prosperous village in Burgundy of 1,200 to 1,500 people, the parish register records 615 deaths in the space of fourteen weeks, compared to an average of thirty deaths a year in the previous decade. In three villages of Cambridgeshire, manorial records show a death rate of 47 percent, 57 percent, and in one case 70 percent. When the last survivors, too few to carry on, moved away, a deserted

village sank back into the wilderness and disappeared from the map altogether, leaving only a grass-covered ghostly outline to show where
mortals once had lived.

In enclosed places such as monasteries and prisons, the infection of [12]
one person usually meant that of all, as happened in the Franciscan con-
vents of Carcassonne and Marseille, where every inmate without exception died. Of the 140 Dominicans at Montpellier only seven survived.
Petrarch's brother Gherardo, member of a Carthusian monastery, buried
the prior and 34 fellow monks one by one, sometimes three a day, until
he was left alone with his dog and fled to look for a place that would
take him in. Watching every comrade die, men in such places could not
but wonder whether the strange peril that filled the air had not been sent
to exterminate the human race. In Kilkenny, Ireland, Brother John Clyn
of the Friars Minor, another monk left alone among dead men, kept a
record of what had happened lest "things which should be remembered
perish with time and vanish from the memory of those who come after
us." Sensing "the whole world, as it were, placed within the grasp of the
Evil One," and waiting for death to visit him too, he wrote, "I leave
parchment to continue this work, if perchance any man survive and any
of the race of Adam escape this pestilence and carry on the work which
I have begun." Brother John, as noted by another hand, died of the pestilence, but he foiled oblivion.

The largest cities of Europe, with populations of about 100,000, were [13]
Paris and Florence, Venice and Genoa. At the next level, with more than
50,000, were Ghent and Bruges in Flanders, Milan, Bologna, Rome,
Naples, and Palermo, and Cologne. London hovered below 50,000, the
only city in England except York with more than 10,000. At the level of
20,000 to 50,000 were Bordeaux, Toulouse, Montpellier, Marseille, and
Lyon in France, Barcelona, Seville, and Toledo in Spain, Siena, Pisa, and
other secondary cities in Italy, and the Hanseatic trading cities of the
Empire. The plague raged through them all, killing anywhere from one
third to two thirds of their inhabitants. Italy, with a total population of
10 to 11 million, probably suffered the heaviest toll. Following the Flo-
rentine bankruptcies, the crop failures and workers' riots of 1346–47, the
revolt of Cola di Rienzi that plunged Rome into anarchy, the plague
came as the peak of successive calamities. As if the world were indeed
in the grasp of the Evil One, its first appearance on the European main-
land in January 1348 coincided with a fearsome earthquake that carved
a path of wreckage from Naples up to Venice. Houses collapsed, church
towers toppled, villages were crushed, and the destruction reached as
far as Germany and Greece. Emotional response, dulled by horrors, underwent a kind of atrophy epitomized by the chronicler who wrote,
"And in these days was burying without sorrowe and wedding without
friendschippe."

In Siena, where more than half of the inhabitants died of the plague, [14]
work was abandoned on the great cathedral, planned to be the largest
in the world, and never resumed, owing to loss of workers and master
masons and "the melancholy and grief" of the survivors. The cathedral's
truncated transept still stands in permanent witness to the sweep of
death's scythe. Agnolo di Tura, a chronicler of Siena, recorded the fear
of contagion that froze every other instinct. "Father abandoned child,
wife husband, one brother another," he wrote, "for this plague seemed
to strike through the breath and sight. And so they died. And no one
could be found to bury the dead for money or friendship. . . . And I, Agnolo di Tura, called the Fat, buried my five children with my own hands,
and so did many others likewise."

There were many to echo his account of inhumanity and few to bal- [15]
ance it, for the plague was not the kind of calamity that inspired mutual help. Its loathsomeness and deadliness did not herd people together
in mutual distress, but only prompted their desire to escape each other.
"Magistrates and notaries refused to come and make the wills of the
dying," reported a Franciscan friar of Piazza in Sicily; what was worse,
"even the priests did not come to hear their confessions." A clerk of the
Archbishop of Canterbury reported the same of English priests who
"turned away from the care of their benefices from fear of death." Cases
of parents deserting children and children their parents were reported
across Europe from Scotland to Russia. The calamity chilled the hearts
of men, wrote Boccaccio in his famous account of the plague in Florence
that serves an introduction to the *Decameron.* "One man shunned another . . . kinsfolk held aloof, brother was forsaken by brother, often-
times husband by wife; nay, what is more, and scarcely to be believed,
fathers and mothers were found to abandon their own children to their
fate, untended, unvisited as if they had been strangers." Exaggeration
and literary pessimism were common in the 14th century, but the Pope's
physician, Guy de Chauliac, was a sober, careful observer who reported the same phenomenon: "A father did not visit his son, nor the son his
father. Charity was dead."

Yet not entirely. In Paris, according to the chronicler Jean de Venette, [16]
the nuns of the Hôtel Dieu or municipal hospital, "having no fear of
death, tended the sick with all sweetness and humility." New nuns repeatedly took the places of those who died, until the majority "many
times renewed by death now rest in peace with Christ as we may pi-
ously believe."

When the plague entered northern France in July 1348, it settled [17]
first in Normandy and, checked by winter, gave Picardy a deceptive in-
terim until the next summer. Either in mourning or warning, black flags
were flown from church towers of the worst-stricken villages of Normandy. "And in that time," wrote a monk of the abbey of Fourcarment,

"the mortality was so great among the people of Normandy that those of Picardy mocked them." The same unneighborly reaction was reported of the Scots, separated by a winter's immunity from the English. Delighted to hear of the disease that was scourging the "southrons," they gathered forces for an invasion, "laughing at their enemies." Before they could move, the savage mortality fell upon them too, scattering some in death and the rest in panic to spread the infection as they fled.

In Picardy in the summer of 1349 the pestilence penetrated the cas-   18
tle of Coucy to kill Enguerrand's[1] mother, Catherine, and her new husband. Whether her nine-year-old son escaped by chance or was perhaps living elsewhere with one of his guardians is unrecorded. In nearby Amiens, tannery workers, responding quickly to losses in the labor force, combined to bargain for higher wages. In another place villagers were seen dancing to drums and trumpets, and on being asked the reason, answered that, seeing their neighbors die day by day while their village remained immune, they believed that they could keep the plague from entering "by the jollity that is in us. That is why we dance." Further north in Tournai on the border of Flanders, Gilles li Muisis, Abbot of St. Martin's, kept one of the epidemic's most vivid accounts. The passing bells rang all day and all night, he recorded, because sextons were anxious to obtain their fees while they could. Filled with the sound of mourning, the city became oppressed by fear, so that the authorities forbade the tolling of bells and the wearing of black and restricted funeral services to two mourners. The silencing of funeral bells and of criers' announcements of deaths was ordained by most cities. Siena imposed a fine on the wearing of mourning clothes by all except widows.

Flight was the chief recourse of those who could afford it or arrange   19
it. The rich fled to their country places like Boccaccio's young patricians of Florence, who settled in a pastoral palace "removed on every side from the road" with "wells of cool water and vaults of rare wines." The urban poor died in their burrows, "and only the stench of their bodies informed neighbors of their death." That the poor were more heavily afflicted than the rich was clearly remarked at the time, in the north as in the south. A Scottish chronicler, John of Fordun, stated flatly that the pest "attacked especially the meaner sort and common people—seldom the magnates." Simon de Covino of Montpellier made the same observation. He ascribed it to the misery and want and hard lives that made the poor more susceptible, which was half the truth. Close contact and lack of sanitation was the unrecognized other half. It was noticed too that the young died in greater proportion than the old; Simon de Covi-

---

[1] Throughout *A Distant Mirror*, the book from which this excerpt is taken, Tuchman traces the impact of events on the life of a French nobleman named Enguerrand de Coucy. [Eds.]

no compared the disappearance of youth to the withering of flowers in the fields.

In the countryside peasants dropped dead on the roads, in the fields, [20] in their houses. Survivors in growing helplessness fell into apathy, leaving ripe wheat uncut and livestock untended. Oxen and asses, sheep and goats, pigs and chickens ran wild and they too, according to local reports, succumbed to the pest. English sheep, bearers of the precious wool, died throughout the country. The chronicler Henry Knighton, canon of Leicester Abbey, reported 5,000 dead in one field alone, "their bodies so corrupted by the plague that neither beast nor bird would touch them," and spreading an appalling stench. In the Austrian Alps wolves came down to prey upon sheep and then, "as if alarmed by some invisible warning, turned and fled back into the wilderness." In remote Dalmatia bolder wolves descended upon a plague-stricken city and attacked human survivors. For want of herdsmen, cattle strayed from place to place and died in hedgerows and ditches. Dogs and cats fell like the rest.

The dearth of labor held a fearful prospect because the 14th centu- [21] ry lived close to the annual harvest both for food and for next year's seed. "So few servants and laborers were left," wrote Knighton, "that no one knew where to turn for help." The sense of a vanishing future created a kind of dementia of despair. A Bavarian chronicler of Neuberg on the Danube recorded that "Men and women . . . wandered around as if mad" and let their cattle stray "because no one had any inclination to concern themselves about the future." Fields went uncultivated, spring seed unsown. Second growth with nature's awful energy crept back over cleared land, dikes crumbled, salt water reinvaded and soured the lowlands. With so few hands remaining to restore the work of centuries, people felt, in Walsingham's words, that "the world could never again regain its former prosperity."

Though the death rate was higher among the anonymous poor, the [22] known and the great died too. King Alfonso XI of Castile was the only reigning monarch killed by the pest, but his neighbor King Pedro of Aragon lost his wife, Queen Leonora, his daughter Marie, and a niece in the space of six months. John Cantacuzene, Emperor of Byzantium, lost his son. In France the lame Queen Jeanne and her daughter-in-law Bonne de Luxemburg, wife of the Dauphin, both died in 1349 in the same phase that took the life of Enguerrand's mother. Jeanne, Queen of Navarre, daughter of Louis X, was another victim. Edward III's second daughter, Joanna, who was on her way to marry Pedro, the heir of Castile, died in Bordeaux. Women appear to have been more vulnerable than men, perhaps because, being more housebound, they were more exposed to fleas. Boccaccio's mistress Fiammetta, illegitimate daughter of the King of Naples, died, as did Laura, the beloved— whether real or fictional—of Petrarch. Reaching out to us in the future,

Petrarch cried, "Oh happy posterity who will not experience such abysmal woe and will look upon our testimony as a fable."

In Florence Giovanni Villani, the great historian of his time, died at [23] 68 in the midst of an unfinished sentence: "... *e dure questo pistolenza fino a ...* (in the midst of this pestilence there came to an end ...)." Siena's master painters, the brothers Ambrogio and Pietro Lorenzetti, whose names never appear after 1348, presumably perished in the plague, as did Andrea Pisano, architect and sculptor of Florence. William of Ockham and the English mystic Richard Rolle of Hampole both disappear from mention after 1349. Francisco Datini, merchant of Prato, lost both his parents and two siblings. Curious sweeps of mortality afflicted certain bodies of merchants in London. All eight wardens of the Company of Cutters, all six wardens of the Hatters, and four wardens of the Goldsmiths died before July 1350. Sir John Pulteney, master draper and four times Mayor of London, was a victim, likewise Sir John Montgomery, Governor of Calais.

Among the clergy and doctors the mortality was naturally high be- [24] cause of the nature of their professions. Out of 24 physicians in Venice, 20 were said to have lost their lives in the plague, although, according to another account, some were believed to have fled or to have shut themselves up in their houses. At Montpellier, site of the leading medieval medical school, the physician Simon de Covino reported that, despite the great number of doctors, "hardly one of them escaped." In Avignon, Guy de Chauliac confessed that he performed his medical visits only because he dared not stay away for fear of infamy, but "I was in continual fear." He claimed to have contracted the disease but to have cured himself by his own treatment; if so, he was one of the few who recovered.

Clerical mortality varied with rank. Although the one-third toll of [25] cardinals reflects the same proportion as the whole, this was probably due to their concentration in Avignon. In England, in strange and almost sinister procession, the Archbishop of Canterbury, John Stratford, died in August 1348, his appointed successor died in May 1349, and the next appointee three months later, all three within a year. Despite such weird vagaries, prelates in general managed to sustain a higher survival rate than the lesser clergy. Among bishops the deaths have been estimated at about one in twenty. The loss of priests, even if many avoided their fearful duty of attending the dying, was about the same as among the population as a whole.

Government officials, whose loss contributed to the general chaos, [26] found, on the whole, no special shelter. In Siena four of the nine members of the governing oligarchy died, in France one third of the royal notaries, in Bristol 15 out of the 52 members of the Town Council or almost one third. Tax-collecting obviously suffered, with the result that Philip

VI was unable to collect more than a fraction of the subsidy granted him by the Estates in the winter of 1347–48.

Lawlessness and debauchery accompanied the plague as they had [27] during the great plague of Athens of 430 B.C., when according to Thucydides, men grew bold in the indulgence of pleasure: "For seeing how the rich died in a moment and those who had nothing immediately inherited their property, they reflected that life and riches were alike transitory and they resolved to enjoy themselves while they could." Human behavior is timeless. When St. John had his vision of plague in Revelation, he knew from some experience or race memory that those who survived "repented not of the work of their hands. . . . Neither repented they of their murders, nor of their sorceries, nor of their fornication, nor of their thefts."

Responding to Reading

1. Many passages of Tuchman's essay include graphic, unpleasant descriptions of the plague victims' symptoms. Is this kind of descriptive detail—for example, "the dead lay putrid in the streets" (9)—necessary? Why do you think Tuchman includes it? How do you react to this kind of detail?

2. Which kinds of supporting detail do you find most compelling in Tuchman's essay: statistics, quotations from contemporary sources, anecdotes, victims' names, or summaries of historical sources? What do you think Tuchman would gain by adding other kinds of support, such as artists' recreations of the scenes, quotations from modern-day historians, analysis by modern-day medical professionals, or a case study of one family?

3. This essay about the dead and dying is remarkably free of sentimentality. Where might another writer have become sentimental, even melodramatic? How do you think you would respond to a more emotional treatment?

THE YELLOW WALL-PAPER

Charlotte Perkins Gilman

Charlotte Perkins Gilman (1860–1935) was a social critic and feminist who wrote extensively about the need for equality in society, especially about women's need for economic independence. Born in Hartford, Connecticut, Gilman first worked as an art teacher and commercial artist. After a nervous breakdown following the birth of her daughter, and a failed marriage, she began to write on feminist issues. Her non-fiction includes *Women and Economics* (1898), *Concerning Children* (1900), and *The Man-Made World* (1911). Her novels include *Herland* (1915) and *With Her in Ourland* (1916). The short story "The Yellow Wall-Paper" (1899) describes the state of mind of a woman suffering from depression after childbirth.

It is very seldom that mere ordinary people like John and myself secure ancestral halls for the summer. 1

A colonial mansion, a hereditary estate, I would say a haunted house, and reach the height of romantic felicity—but that would be asking too much of fate! 2

Still I will proudly declare that there is something queer about it. 3

Else, why should it be let so cheaply? And why have stood so long untenanted? 4

John laughs at me, of course, but one expects that in marriage. 5

John is practical in the extreme. He has no patience with faith, an intense horror of superstition, and he scoffs openly at any talk of things not to be felt and seen and put down in figures. 6

John is a physician, and *perhaps*—(I would not say it to a living soul, of course, but this is dead paper and a great relief to my mind—) *perhaps* that is one reason I do not get well faster. 7

You see he does not believe I am sick! 8

And what can one do? 9

If a physician of high standing, and one's own husband, assures friends and relatives that there is really nothing the matter with one but temporary nervous depression—a slight hysterical tendency—what is one to do? 10

My brother is also a physician, and also of high standing, and he says the same thing. 11

So I take phosphates[1] or phosphites—whichever it is, and tonics, and journeys, and air, and exercise, and am absolutely forbidden to "work" until I am well again. 12

Personally, I disagree with their ideas. 13

Personally, I believe that congenial work, with excitement and change, would do me good. 14

But what is one to do? 15

I did write for a while in spite of them; but it *does* exhaust me a good deal—having to be so sly about it, or else meet with heavy opposition. 16

I sometimes fancy that in my condition if I had less opposition and more society and stimulus—but John says the very worst thing I can 17

---

[1] Phosphates are carbonated beverages of water, flavoring, and phosphoric acid that were believed to have medicinal properties. [Eds.]

do is to think about my condition, and I confess it always makes me feel bad.

So I will let it alone and talk about the house.   18

The most beautiful place! It is quite alone, standing well back from   19
the road, quite three miles from the village. It makes me think of English places that you read about, for there are hedges and walls and gates that lock, and lots of separate little houses for the gardeners and people.

There is a *delicious* garden! I never saw such a garden—large and   20
shady, full of box-bordered paths, and lined with long grape-covered arbors with seats under them.

There were greenhouses, too, but they are all broken now.   21

There was some legal trouble, I believe, something about the heirs   22
and co-heirs; anyhow, the place has been empty for years.

That spoils my ghostliness, I am afraid, but I don't care—there is   23
something strange about the house—I can feel it.

I even said so to John one moonlight evening, but he said what I felt   24
was a *draught,* and shut the window.

I get unreasonably angry with John sometimes. I'm sure I never   25
used to be so sensitive. I think it is due to this nervous condition.

But John says if I feel so, I shall neglect proper self-control; so I take   26
pains to control myself—before him, at least, and that makes me very tired.

I don't like our room a bit. I wanted one downstairs that opened on   27
the piazza and had roses all over the window, and such pretty old-fashioned chintz hangings! But John would not hear of it.

He said there was only one window and not room for two beds, and   28
no near room for him if he took another.

He is very careful and loving, and hardly lets me stir without special direction.   29

I have a schedule prescription for each hour in the day; he takes all   30
care from me, and so I feel basely ungrateful not to value it more.

He said we came here solely on my account, that I was to have perfect   31
rest and all the air I could get. "Your exercise depends on your strength, my dear," said he, "and your food somewhat on your appetite; but air you can absorb all the time." So we took the nursery at the top of the house.

It is a big, airy room, the whole floor nearly, with windows that look   32
all ways, and air and sunshine galore. It was nursery first and then play-room and gymnasium, I should judge; for the windows are barred for little children, and there are rings and things in the walls.

The paint and paper look as if a boys' school had used it. It is   33
stripped off—the paper—in great patches all around the head of my bed, about as far as I can reach, and in a great place on the other side of the room low down. I never saw a worse paper in my life.

One of those sprawling flamboyant patterns committing every artis- ³⁴ tic sin.

It is dull enough to confuse the eye in following, pronounced ³⁵ enough to constantly irritate and provoke study, and when you follow the lame uncertain curves for a little distance they suddenly commit suicide—plunge off at outrageous angles, destroy themselves in unheard of contradictions.

The color is repellent, almost revolting; a smouldering unclean yel- ³⁶ low, strangely faded by the slow-turning sunlight.

It is a dull yet lurid orange in some places, a sickly sulphur tint in ³⁷ others.

No wonder the children hated it! I should hate it myself if I had to ³⁸ live in this room long.

There comes John, and I must put this away,—he hates to have me ³⁹ write a word.

We have been here two weeks, and I haven't felt like writing before, ⁴⁰ since that first day.

I am sitting by the window now, up in this atrocious nursery, and ⁴¹ there is nothing to hinder my writing as much as I please, save lack of strength.

John is away all day, and even some nights when his cases are seri- ⁴² ous.

I am glad my case is not serious! ⁴³

But these nervous troubles are dreadfully depressing. ⁴⁴

John does not know how much I really suffer. He knows there is no ⁴⁵ *reason* to suffer, and that satisfies him.

Of course it is only nervousness. It does weigh on me so not to do ⁴⁶ my duty in any way!

I meant to be such a help to John, such a real rest and comfort, and ⁴⁷ here I am a comparative burden already!

Nobody would believe what an effort it is to do what little I am ⁴⁸ able,—to dress and entertain, and order things.

It is fortunate Mary is so good with the baby. Such a dear baby! ⁴⁹

And yet I *cannot* be with him, it makes me so nervous. ⁵⁰

I suppose John never was nervous in his life. He laughs at me so ⁵¹ about this wall-paper!

At first he meant to repaper the room, but afterwards he said that I ⁵² was letting it get the better of me, and that nothing was worse for a nervous patient than to give way to such fancies.

He said that after the wall-paper was changed it would be the heavy ⁵³ bedstead, and then the barred windows, and then that gate at the head of the stairs, and so on.

"You know the place is doing you good," he said, "and really, dear, ⁵⁴ I don't care to renovate the house just for a three months' rental."

"Then do let us go downstairs," I said, "there are such pretty rooms there." 55

Then he took me in his arms and called me a blessed little goose, and said he would go down cellar, if I wished, and have it white-washed into the bargain. 56

But he is right enough about the beds and windows and things. 57

It is an airy and comfortable room as any one need wish, and, of course, I would not be so silly as to make him uncomfortable just for a whim. 58

I'm really getting quite fond of the big room, all but that horrid paper. 59

Out of one window I can see the garden, those mysterious deep-shaded arbors, the riotous old-fashioned flowers, and bushes and gnarly trees. 60

Out of another I get a lovely view of the bay and a little private wharf belonging to the estate. There is a beautiful shaded lane that runs down there from the house. I always fancy I see people walking in these numerous paths and arbors, but John has cautioned me not to give way to fancy in the least. He says that with my imaginative power and habit of story-making, a nervous weakness like mine is sure to lead to all manner of excited fancies, and that I ought to use my will and good sense to check the tendency. So I try. 61

I think sometimes that if I were only well enough to write a little it would relieve the press of ideas and rest me. 62

But I find I get pretty tired when I try. 63

It is so discouraging not to have any advice and companionship about my work. When I get really well, John says we will ask Cousin Henry and Julia down for a long visit; but he says he would as soon put fireworks in my pillow-case as to let me have those stimulating people about now. 64

I wish I could get well faster. 65

But I must not think about that. This paper looks to me as if it *knew* what a vicious influence it had! 66

There is a recurrent spot where the pattern lolls like a broken neck and two bulbous eyes stare at you upside down. 67

I get positively angry with the impertinence of it and the everlast-ingness. Up and down and sideways they crawl, and those absurd, un-blinking eyes are everywhere. There is one place where two breadths didn't match, and the eyes go all up and down the line, one a little high-er than the other. 68

I never saw so much expression in an inanimate thing before, and we all know how much expression they have! I used to lie awake as a child and get more entertainment and terror out of blank walls and plain furniture than most children could find in a toy-store. 69

I remember what a kindly wink the knobs of our big, old bureau 70 used to have, and there was one chair that always seemed like a strong friend.

I used to feel that if any of the other things looked too fierce I could 71 always hop into that chair and be safe.

The furniture in this room is no worse than inharmonious, howev- 72 er, for we had to bring it all from downstairs. I suppose when this was used as a playroom they had to take the nursery things out, and no wonder! I never saw such ravages as the children have made here.

The wall-paper, as I said before, is torn off in spots, and it stick- 73 eth closer than a brother—they must have had perseverance as well as hatred.

Then the floor is scratched and gouged and splintered, the plaster it- 74 self is dug out here and there, and this great heavy bed which is all we found in the room, looks as if it had been through the wars.

But I don't mind it a bit—only the paper. 75

There comes John's sister. Such a dear girl as she is, and so careful 76 of me! I must not let her find me writing.

She is a perfect and enthusiastic housekeeper, and hopes for no bet- 77 ter profession. I verily believe she thinks it is the writing which made me sick!

But I can write when she is out, and see her a long way off from 78 these windows.

There is one that commands the road, a lovely shaded winding 79 road, and one that just looks off over the country. A lovely country, too, full of great elms and velvet meadows.

This wall-paper has a kind of sub-pattern in a different shade, a par- 80 ticularly irritating one, for you can only see it in certain lights, and not clearly then.

But in the places where it isn't faded and where the sun is just so— 81 I can see a strange, provoking, formless sort of figure, that seems to skulk about behind that silly and conspicuous front design.

There's sister on the stairs! 82

Well, the Fourth of July is over! The people are all gone and I am 83 tired out. John thought it might do me good to see a little company, so we just had mother and Nellie and the children down for a week.

Of course I didn't do a thing. Jennie sees to everything now. 84

But it tired me all the same. 85

John says if I don't pick up faster he shall send me to Weir Mitchell[2] 86 in the fall.

But I don't want to go there at all. I had a friend who was in his hands 87 once, and she says he is just like John and my brother, only more so!

---

[2] Silas Weir Mitchell (1829–1914), a Philadelphia neurologist-psychologist who introduced the "rest cure" for nervous diseases. [Eds.]

Besides, it is such an undertaking to go so far. [88]

I don't feel as if it was worth while to turn my hand over for any- [89]
thing, and I'm getting dreadfully fretful and querulous.

I cry at nothing, and cry most of the time. [90]

Of course I don't when John is here, or anybody else, but when I am [91]
alone.

And I am alone a good deal just now. John is kept in town very often [92]
by serious cases, and Jennie is good and lets me alone when I want her
to.

So I walk a little in the garden or down that lovely lane, sit on the [93]
porch under the roses, and lie down up here a good deal.

I'm getting really fond of the room in spite of the wall-paper. Per- [94]
haps *because* of the wall-paper.

It dwells in my mind so! [95]

I lie here on this great immovable bed—it is nailed down, I believe— [96]
and follow that pattern about by the hour. It is as good as gymnastics, I
assure you. I start, we'll say, at the bottom, down in the corner over there
where it has not been touched, and I determine for the thousandth time
that I *will* follow that pointless pattern to some sort of a conclusion.

I know a little of the principle of design, and I know this thing was [97]
not arranged on any laws of radiation, or alternation, or repetition, or
symmetry, or anything else that I ever heard of.

It is repeated, of course, by the breadths, but not otherwise. [98]

Looked at in one way each breadth stands alone, the bloated curves [99]
and flourishes—a kind of "debased Romanesque"[3]—with *delirium
tremens*[4] go waddling up and down in isolated columns of fatuity.

But, on the other hand, they connect diagonally, and the sprawling [100]
outlines run off in great slanting waves of optic horror, like a lot of wal-
lowing seaweeds in full chase.

The whole thing goes horizontally, too, at least it seems so, and I [101]
exhaust myself in trying to distinguish the order of its going in that
direction.

They have used a horizontal breadth for a frieze,[5] and that adds [102]
wonderfully to the confusion.

There is one end of the room where it is almost intact, and there, [103]
when the crosslights fade and the low sun shines directly upon it, I can
almost fancy radiation after all,—the interminable grotesques seem to
form around a common center and rush off in headlong plunges of
equal distraction.

It makes me tired to follow it. I will take a nap I guess. [104]

---

[3] Art characterized by solemnity, decorativeness, and symbolism. [Eds.]

[4] Mental confusion caused by alcohol poisoning and characterized by physical tremors and halluci-
nations. [Eds.]

[5] A richly ornamented band. [Eds.]

I don't know why I should write this.   105

I don't want to.   106

I don't feel able.   107

And I know John would think it absurd. But I *must* say what I feel 108
and think in some way—it is such a relief!

But the effort is getting to be greater than the relief.   109

Half the time now I am awfully lazy, and lie down ever so much.   110

John says I mustn't lose my strength, and has me take cod liver oil 111
and lots of tonics and things, to say nothing of ale and wine and rare
meat.

Dear John! He loves me very dearly, and hates to have me sick. I 112
tried to have a real earnest reasonable talk with him the other day, and
tell him how I wish he would let me go and make a visit to Cousin
Henry and Julia.

But he said I wasn't able to go, nor able to stand it after I got there; 113
and I did not make out a very good case for myself, for I was crying before I had finished.

It is getting to be a great effort for me to think straight. Just this ner- 114
vous weakness I suppose.

And dear John gathered me up in his arms, and just carried me up- 115
stairs and laid me on the bed, and sat by me and read to me till it tired
my head.

He said I was his darling and his comfort and all he had, and that I 116
must take care of myself for his sake, and keep well.

He says no one but myself can help me out of it, that I must use my 117
will and self-control and not let any silly fancies run away with me.

There's one comfort, the baby is well and happy, and does not have 118
to occupy this nursery with the horrid wall-paper.

If we had not used it, that blessed child would have! What a fortu- 119
nate escape! Why, I wouldn't have a child of mine, an impressionable little thing, live in such a room for worlds.

I never thought of it before, but it is lucky that John kept me here 120
after all, I can stand it so much easier than a baby, you see.

Of course I never mention it to them any more—I am too wise,—but 121
I keep watch of it all the same.

There are things in that paper that nobody knows but me, or ever 122
will.

Behind that outside pattern the dim shapes get clearer every day.   123

It is always the same shape, only very numerous.   124

And it is like a woman stooping down and creeping about behind 125
that pattern. I don't like it a bit. I wonder—I begin to think—I wish John
would take me away from here!

It is so hard to talk with John about my case, because he is so wise, 126
and because he loves me so.

But I tried it last night. [127]

It was moonlight. The moon shines in all around just as the sun [128] does.

I hate to see it sometimes, it creeps so slowly, and always comes in [129] by one window or another.

John was asleep and I hated to waken him, so I kept still and [130] watched the moonlight on that undulating wall-paper till I felt creepy.

The faint figure behind seemed to shake the pattern, just as if she [131] wanted to get out.

I got up softly and went to feel and see if the paper *did* move, and [132] when I came back John was awake.

"What is it, little girl?" he said. "Don't go walking about like that— [133] you'll get cold."

I thought it was a good time to talk, so I told him that I really was [134] not gaining here, and that I wished he would take me away.

"Why, darling!" said he, "our lease will be up in three weeks, and I [135] can't see how to leave before.

"The repairs are not done at home, and I cannot possibly leave town [136] just now. Of course if you were in any danger, I could and would, but you really are better, dear, whether you can see it or not. I am a doctor, dear, and I know. You are gaining flesh and color, your appetite is better, I feel really much easier about you."

"I don't weigh a bit more," said I, "nor as much; and my appetite [137] may be better in the evening when you are here, but it is worse in the morning when you are away!"

"Bless her little heart!" said he with a big hug, "she shall be as sick [138] as she pleases! But now let's improve the shining hours by going to sleep, and talk about it in the morning!"

"And you won't go away?" I asked gloomily. [139]

"Why, how can I, dear? It is only three weeks more and then we will [140] take a nice little trip of a few days while Jennie is getting the house ready. Really dear you are better!"

"Better in body perhaps—" I began, and stopped short, for he sat up [141] straight and looked at me with such a stern, reproachful look that I could not say another word.

"My darling," said he, "I beg of you, for my sake and for our child's [142] sake, as well as for your own, that you will never for one instant let that idea enter your mind! There is nothing so dangerous, so fascinating, to a temperament like yours. It is a false and foolish fancy. Can you not trust me as a physician when I tell you so?"

So of course I said no more on that score, and we went to sleep be- [143] fore long. He thought I was asleep first, but I wasn't, and lay there for hours trying to decide whether that front pattern and the back pattern really did move together or separately.

On a pattern like this, by daylight, there is a lack of sequence, a de- [144] fiance of law, that is a constant irritant to a normal mind.

The color is hideous enough, and unreliable enough, and infuriat- [145] ing enough, but the pattern is torturing.

You think you have mastered it, but just as you get well underway [146] in following, it turns back-somersault and there you are. It slaps you in the face, knocks you down, and tramples upon you. It is like a bad dream.

The outside pattern is a florid arabesque, reminding one of a fungus. [147] If you can imagine a toadstool in joints, an interminable string of toad-stools, budding and sprouting in endless convolutions—why, that is something like it.

That is, sometimes! [148]

There is one marked peculiarity about this paper, a thing nobody [149] seems to notice but myself, and that is that it changes as the light changes.

When the sun shoots in through the east window—I always watch [150] for that first long, straight ray—it changes so quickly that I never can quite believe it.

That is why I watch it always. [151]

By moonlight—the moon shines in all night when there is a moon— [152] I wouldn't know it was the same paper.

At night in any kind of light, in twilight, candlelight, lamplight, and [153] worst of all by moonlight, it becomes bars! The outside pattern I mean, and the woman behind it is as plain as can be.

I didn't realize for a long time what the thing was that showed be- [154] hind, that dim sub-pattern, but now I am quite sure it is a woman.

By daylight she is subdued, quiet. I fancy it is the pattern that keeps [155] her so still. It is so puzzling. It keeps me quiet by the hour.

I lie down ever so much now. John says it is good for me, and to [156] sleep all I can.

Indeed he started the habit by making me lie down for an hour after [157] each meal.

It is a very bad habit I am convinced, for you see I don't sleep. [158]

And that cultivates deceit, for I don't tell them I'm awake—O no! [159]

The fact is I am getting a little afraid of John. [160]

He seems very queer sometimes, and even Jennie has an inexplica- [161] ble look.

It strikes me occasionally, just as a scientific hypothesis,—that per- [162] haps it is the paper!

I have watched John when he did not know I was looking, and come [163] into the room suddenly on the most innocent excuses, and I've caught him several times *looking at the paper!* And Jennie too. I caught Jennie with her hand on it once.

She didn't know I was in the room, and when I asked her in a quiet, [164] a very quiet voice, with the most restrained manner possible, what she was doing with the paper—she turned around as if she had been caught stealing, and looked quite angry—asked me why I should frighten her so!

Then she said that the paper stained everything it touched, that she [165] had found yellow smooches on all my clothes and John's, and she wished we would be more careful!

Did not that sound innocent? But I know she was studying that pat- [166] tern, and I am determined that nobody shall find it out but myself!

Life is very much more exciting now than it used to be. You see I [167] have something more to expect, to look forward to, to watch. I really do eat better, and am more quiet than I was.

John is so pleased to see me improve! He laughed a little the other [168] day, and said I seemed to be flourishing in spite of my wall-paper.

I turned it off with a laugh. I had no intention of telling him it was [169] *because* of the wallpaper—he would make fun of me. He might even want to take me away.

I don't want to leave now until I have found it out. There is a week [170] more, and I think that will be enough.

I'm feeling ever so much better! I don't sleep much at night, for it is so [171] interesting to watch developments; but I sleep a good deal in the daytime.

In the daytime it is tiresome and perplexing. [172]

There are always new shoots on the fungus, and new shades of yel- [173] low all over it. I cannot keep count of them, though I have tried conscientiously.

It is the strangest yellow, that wall-paper! It makes me think of all [174] the yellow things I ever saw—not beautiful ones like buttercups, but old foul, bad yellow things.

But there is something else about that paper—the smell! I noticed it [175] the moment we came into the room, but with so much air and sun it was not bad. Now we have had a week of fog and rain, and whether the windows are open or not, the smell is here.

It creeps all over the house. [176]

If find it hovering in the dining-room, skulking in the parlor, hiding [177] in the hall, lying in wait for me on the stairs.

It gets into my hair. [178]

Even when I go to ride, if I turn my head suddenly and surprise it— [179] there is that smell!

Such a peculiar odor, too! I have spent hours in trying to analyze it, [180] to find what it smelled like.

It is not bad—at first, and very gentle, but quite the subtlest, most [181] enduring odor I ever met.

In this damp weather it is awful, I wake up in the night and find it [182] hanging over me.

It used to disturb me at first. I thought seriously of burning the [183] house—to reach the smell.

But now I am used to it. The only thing I can think of that it is like [184] is the *color* of the paper! A yellow smell.

There is a very funny mark on this wall, low down, near the mop- [185] board. A streak that runs round the room. It goes behind every piece of furniture, except the bed, a long, straight, even *smooch,* as if it had been rubbed over and over.

I wonder how it was done and who did it, and what they did it for. [186] Round and round and round—round and round and round!—it makes me dizzy!

I really have discovered something at last. [187]

Through watching so much at night, when it changes so, I have fi- [188] nally found out.

The front pattern *does* move—and no wonder! The woman behind [189] shakes it!

Sometimes I think there are a great many women behind, and some- [190] times only one, and she crawls around fast, and her crawling shakes it all over.

Then in the very bright spots she keeps still, and in the very shady [191] spots she just takes hold of the bars and shakes them hard.

And she is all the time trying to climb through. But nobody could [192] climb through that pattern—it strangles so; I think that is why it has so many heads.

They get through, and then the pattern strangles them off and turns [193] them upside down, and makes their eyes white!

If those heads were covered or taken off it would not be half so bad. [194]

I think that woman gets out in the daytime! [195]

And I'll tell you why—privately—I've seen her! [196]

I can see her out of every one of my windows! [197]

It is the same woman, I know, for she is always creeping, and most [198] women do not creep by daylight.

I see her in that long shaded lane, creeping up and down. I see her [199] in those dark grape arbors, creeping all around the garden.

I see her on that long road under the trees, creeping along, and when [200] a carriage comes she hides under the blackberry vines.

I don't blame her a bit. It must be very humiliating to be caught [201] creeping by daylight!

I always lock the door when I creep by daylight. I can't do it at night, [202] for I know John would suspect something at once.

And John is so queer now, that I don't want to irritate him. I wish [203] he would take another room! Besides, I don't want anybody to get that women out at night but myself.

I often wonder if I could see her out of all the windows at once. [204]

But, turn as fast as I can, I can only see out of one at one time. [205]

And though I always see her, she *may* be able to creep faster than I [206] can turn!

I have watched her sometimes away off in the open country, creep- [207] ing as fast as a cloud shadow in a high wind.

If only that top pattern could be gotten off from the under one! I [208] mean to try it, little by little

I have found out another funny thing, but I shan't tell it this time! It [209] does not do to trust people too much.

There are only two more days to get this paper off, and I believe [210] John is beginning to notice. I don't like the look in his eyes.

And I heard him ask Jennie a lot of professional questions about me. [211] She had a very good report to give.

She said I slept a good deal in the daytime. [212]

John knows I don't sleep very well at night, for all I'm so quiet! [213]

He asked me all sorts of questions, too, and pretended to be very [214] loving and kind.

As if I couldn't see through him! [215]

Still, I don't wonder he acts so, sleeping under this paper for three [216] months.

It only interests me, but I feel sure John and Jennie are secretly af- [217] fected by it.

Hurrah! This is the last day, but it is enough. John to stay in town [218] over night, and won't be out until this evening.

Jennie wanted to sleep with me—the sly thing! But I told her I [219] should undoubtedly rest better for a night all alone.

That was clever, for really I wasn't alone a bit! As soon as it was [220] moonlight and that poor thing began to crawl and shake the pattern, I got up and ran to help her.

I pulled and she shook, I shook and she pulled, and before morning [221] we had peeled off yards of that paper.

A strip about as high as my head and half around the room. [222]

And then when the sun came and that awful pattern began to laugh [223] at me, I declared I would finish it to-day!

We go away to-morrow, and they are moving all my furniture down [224] again to leave things as they were before.

Jennie looked at the wall in amazement, but I told her merrily that [225] I did it out of pure spite at the vicious thing.

She laughed and said she wouldn't mind doing it herself, but I must [226] not get tired.

How she betrayed herself that time! [227]

But I am here, and no person touches this paper but me,—not *alive!* [228]

She tried to get me out of the room—it was too patent! But I said it [229] was so quiet and empty and clean now that I believed I would lie down again and sleep all I could; and not to wake me even for dinner—I would call when I woke.

So now she is gone, and the servants are gone, and the things are [230] gone, and there is nothing left but that great bedstead nailed down, with the canvas mattress we found on it.

We shall sleep downstairs to-night, and take the boat home to- [231] morrow.

I quite enjoy the room, now it is bare again. [232]

How those children did tear about here! [233]

This bedstead is fairly gnawed! [234]

But I must get to work. [235]

I have locked the door and thrown the key down into the front path. [236]

I don't want to go out, and I don't want to have anybody come in, [237] till John comes.

I want to astonish him. [238]

I've got a rope up here that even Jennie did not find. If that woman [239] does get out, and tries to get away, I can tie her!

But I forgot I could not reach far without anything to stand on! [240]

This bed will *not* move! [241]

I tried to lift and push it until I was lame, and then I got so angry I [242] bit off a little piece at one corner—but it hurt my teeth.

Then I peeled off all the paper I could reach standing on the floor. [243] It sticks horribly and the pattern just enjoys it! All those strangled heads and bulbous eyes and waddling fungus growths just shriek with derision!

I am getting angry enough to do something desperate. To jump out [244] of the window would be admirable exercise, but the bars are too strong even to try.

Besides I wouldn't do it. Of course not. I know well enough that a [245] step like this is improper and might be misconstrued.

I don't like to *look* out of the windows even—there are so many of [246] those creeping women, and they creep so fast.

I wonder if they all come out of that wall-paper as I did? [247]

But I am securely fastened now by my well-hidden rope—you don't [248] get *me* out in the road there!

I suppose I shall have to get back behind the pattern when it comes [249] night, and that is hard!

It is so pleasant to be out in this great room and creep around as I [250] please!

I don't want to go outside. I won't, even if Jennie asks me to. [251]

For outside you have to creep on the ground, and everything is [252] green instead of yellow.

But here I can creep smoothly on the floor, and my shoulder just fits [253] in that long smooch around the wall, so I cannot lose my way.

Why there's John at the door! [254]

It is no use, young man, you can't open it! [255]

How he does call and pound! [256]

Now he's crying for an axe. 257

It would be a shame to break down that beautiful door! 258

"John dear!" said I in the gentlest voice, "the key is down by the 259 front steps, under a plaintain leaf!"

That silenced him for a few moments. 260

Then he said—very quietly indeed. "Open the door, my darling!" 261

"I can't," said I. "The key is down by the front door under a plain- 262 tain leaf!"

And then I said it again, several times, very gently and slowly, and 263 said it so often that he had to go and see, and he got it of course, and came in. He stopped short by the door.

"What is the matter?" he cried. "For God's sake, what are you 264 doing!"

I kept on creeping just the same, but I looked at him over my shoul- 265 der.

"I've got out at last," said I, "in spite of you and Jane. And I've 266 pulled off most of the paper, so you can't put me back!"

Now why should that man have fainted? But he did, and right 267 across my path by the wall, so that I had to creep over him every time!

Responding to Reading

1. The narrator is suffering from postpartum depression, a condition now un-derstood to be common in women who have just given birth. What other fac-tors contribute to her depression?
2. What is the attitude of the doctors toward the narrator? In what ways are the doctors in the story like and unlike doctors you have known?
3. Why do you think the doctors discourage the narrator from writing? What other parts of her treatment strike you as odd or inappropriate? In what ways do you think the doctors' ideas about women influence their medical judgment?

WRITING

Medical Practice and Responsibility

1. In a 1993 editorial in *Forbes* magazine, Malcolm S. Forbes, Jr., calls Dr. Jack Kevorkian a "serial killer" who should be "tried for murder—or at least manslaughter." Write an essay in which you agree with either Forbes or Kevorkian. Do you believe Kevorkian is a killer or a person who gives the terminally ill a chance to die with dignity?

2. Write an essay in which you describe your ideal doctor. Refer specifically to readings in this chapter to illustrate your points.

3. Assume you are either an animal rights activist or a person who believes animal experimentation is necessary. Write an editorial for your local newspaper in which you present your case. Be sure to cite information in Jane Goodall's essay in your editorial. If you like, you may also refer to Meir Shalev's "If Bosnians Were Whales" in Chapter 10.

4. Write an essay in which you compare your own ideas about disease with the ideas of Perri Klass's Indian patients. In what ways are your ideas similar to theirs? In what ways are they different?

5. Assume you are a teacher who has found out that one of your students is HIV positive. Write a confidential memo to the school principal in which you argue either for or against telling the other teachers (and other students and their parents) about the child's condition.

6. Abraham Verghese in "My Own Country," Perri Klass in "India," and Richard Selzer in "Imelda" all consider the limitations of medical science. Choose a medical problem and discuss how it presents challenges for both medical personnel and the general public. You may refer to the essays by Verghese, Klass, or Selzer if you like.

7. Identify a medical advance that has changed either your own life or the life of someone you know. Write an essay in which you discuss in what way this development has affected you or the person you know—and, possibly, society as a whole.

8. Assume you are the new director of Anna Mae Halgrim Seaver's nursing home. Write a memo in which you outline changes that would make life in the nursing home better for residents. In your memo respond specifically to the points Seaver mentions in her essay.

9. Perhaps because so many people are HIV positive or because so many people are afraid of the disease, the question of how to deal

with HIV sufferers is a compelling and controversial one. Write an essay in which you compare the way Abraham Verghese in "My Own Country," Amitai Etzioni in "HIV Sufferers Have a Responsibility," and Michael Bronski in "Magic and AIDS: Presumed Innocent" in Chapter 4 view AIDS. For example, how do they characterize people who are HIV positive—as innocent victims or as people who have contributed to their own problems? How do they think society should respond to the disease? What responsibility do they think HIV sufferers have to society?

10. In "The Yellow Wall-Paper," Charlotte Perkins Gilman describes the progression of a woman's mental illness, an illness that is made worse by her society's ideas about gender. Do you believe that attitudes about gender still influence doctors' judgment? What do you think male doctors need to know about their female patients? What attitudes do you believe they need to change?

EARTH IN THE
BALANCE

Student Voices

"I think there is a definite problem between human beings and nature. Human beings need the resources of nature in order to live, but we must use them in moderation. If we would just take the time to consider how important nature is to our survival, we would try harder to maintain the proper balance between us and nature."

—*Eric Forte*

"There are many opportunities to make the earth a cleaner and better place. Most damage to the earth's surface comes from industrial waste. For years industries have been dumping their wastes into the earth's waterways, thinking that it would wash out to sea and disappear. The truth, however, is that many of our lakes and waterways have become so polluted that they are unable to support life. Acid rain, caused by pollutants in the air, has also killed fish and plants in many lakes and streams.

"Landfills are another problem. Years ago, we thought the best way to get rid of the trash we create each year was to bury it in a landfill. Now toxic chemicals are leaking into the earth and polluting the groundwater many people use for drinking.

"Today we are starting to try to clean up the mess we have made. Laws have been passed to prohibit dumping in the oceans or in waterways. Landfills are being engineered to make them less likely to leak. And paper, aluminum, glass, and some plastics are being recycled."

—*Lauren Adair*

"One of the simplest ways a person can help save the environment is by recycling. Still, I don't think recycling will have much of an impact until industry uses recycled products on a much larger scale."

—*Robert Barr*

"Overpopulation destroys. When people overpopulate a piece of land, they destroy the resources they depend on— trees for shade and wood, land for grazing and farming, and animals for food. In addition, when their farm animals overgraze, they eat the grass down to its roots and kill the plants they need to survive."

—*Elisha Mark*

"The destruction of the earth is unavoidable. People will not make the changes or pay the price to save the planet. Some day they will look back and think how beautiful the earth was and how long it could have lasted if they only had cared more. But by then it will be too late."

—*Jeff Morris*

"People need to take the initiative and care for the earth. It's not ours to damage. We belong to the earth just as those before us did and just as those after us will. Each individual effort is one step toward preserving the earth. For example, I have stopped eating meat. I don't really think it will make a difference, but it's my way of showing I care. I don't think there is any need to cut down rain forests or kill animals for money. Individuals need to take a stand and do their part to save the planet."

—*Renee Higgins*

———————————— **Preparing to Read and Write** ————————————

Over a hundred years ago essayist Henry David Thoreau, already sensing the dangers of industrialism and expansionism, decided to live in the woods next to Walden Pond to reestablish his connections with nature. To one extent or another, *Walden,* Thoreau's account of his retreat, has influenced most of the writers in this section. Like Thoreau, they are concerned with examining the complex relationship between human beings and the environment. In addition, most argue that by ignoring this relationship, human beings cause the disappearance of scores of species each year, destroy thousands of acres of rain forest, and, ultimately, risk the extinction of all life on earth.

Apart from its majesty, nature serves as a counterforce to the technological culture in which we live. In such phenomena as grass pushing up through cracks in the pavement or dead animals littering the roads, nature reminds us that another, larger world exists outside our limited human sphere. It implies that the price we pay for living in society is our estrangement from the natural environment. Of course, we are not estranged in the literal sense of the word, for we are surrounded by the trees in our parks, the animals we keep as pets or in zoos, and the gardens we maintain in our yards. But these things are far removed from the untamed nature that Jack London presents in "To Build a Fire." The nature with which we have become familiar has become so domesticated that we have ceased to see it as alien or exotic.

Despite the gulf that seems to separate contemporary men and women from nature, one things remains clear: Nature continues to affect us in subtle and mysterious ways. For many of us nature can be refreshing and invigorating as well as fierce and mysterious. As Barry Lopez says in "Landscape and Narrative," "Each individual . . . undertakes to order his interior landscape according to the exterior landscape. To succeed in this means to achieve a balanced state of mental health." In this and other ways, we are dependent upon our natural environment, and we have a responsibility—perhaps even a duty—to preserve it.

As you read and prepare to write about the selections in this chapter, you may consider the following questions.

- What is the writer's attitude toward nature?
- Is nature seen as hostile or friendly?
- Does the writer present an objective or subjective description of nature?
- Do you think the writer is being realistic or idealistic? Reasonable or unreasonable?
- What relationship does the writer think people have with nature? What relationship does he or she think people *ought* to have with nature?

Two Perspectives on Earth in the Balance

Written more than a century apart, the following two statements make a surprisingly similar point about the effects of human "progress" on the environment. The first selection is an 1855 letter to U.S. President Franklin Pierce from Native American Chief Seattle (see p. 400), who served as a mediator between his tribes and the first white settlers in the area around Puget Sound; in it, Seattle warns the conquering white nation, "Continue to contaminate your bed, and you will one night suffocate in your own waste." Following this is an excerpt from *Earth in the Balance* (1992), Albert Gore's best-selling examination of a wide range of environmental problems. In his chapter entitled "The Wasteland," Gore looks specifically at the extent to which we are today suffocating in our own waste, as Seattle predicted. A graduate of Harvard and both the School of Religion and the School of Law at Vanderbilt, Gore was an investigative reporter at the Nashville *Tennessean* before following his father's footsteps and entering politics. He served Tennessee as a member of the U.S. House of Representatives (1977–85) and Senator (1985–1993), before assuming the Vice Presidency. Much of *Earth in the Balance* is based on research he conducted in the course of his work on congressional subcommittees.

Letter to President Pierce, 1855

Chief Seattle

We know that the white man does not understand our ways. One 1
portion of the land is the same to him as the next, for he is a stranger who comes in the night and takes from the land whatever he needs. The earth is not his brother, but his enemy, and when he has conquered it, he moves on. He leaves his fathers' graves, and his children's birthright is forgotten. The sight of your cities pains the eyes of the red man. But perhaps it is because the red man is a savage and does not understand.

There is no quiet place in the white man's cities. No place to hear the 2
leaves of spring or the rustle of insect's wings. But perhaps because I am a savage and do not understand, the clatter only seems to insult the ears. The Indian prefers the soft sound of the wind darting over the face of the pond, the smell of the wind itself cleansed by a mid-day rain, or scented

with the piñon pine. The air is precious to the red man. For all things share the same breath—the beasts, the trees, the man. Like a man dying for many days, he is numb to the stench.

What is man without the beasts? If all the beasts were gone, men ³ would die from great loneliness of spirit, for whatever happens to the beasts also happens to man. All things are connected. Whatever befalls the earth befalls the sons of the earth.

It matters little where we pass the rest of our days; they are not ⁴ many. A few more hours, a few more winters, and none of the children of the great tribes that once lived on this earth, or that roamed in small bands in the woods, will be left to mourn the graves of a people once as powerful and hopeful as yours.

The whites, too, shall pass—perhaps sooner than other tribes. Con- ⁵ tinue to contaminate your bed, and you will one night suffocate in your own waste. When the buffalo are all slaughtered, the wild horses all tamed, the secret corners of the forest heavy with the scent of many men, and the view of the ripe hills blotted by talking wires,[1] where is the thicket? Gone. Where is the eagle? Gone. And what is it to say goodby to the swift and the hunt, the end of living and the beginning of survival? We might understand if we knew what it was that the white man dreams, what he describes to his children on the long winter nights, what visions he burns into their minds, so they will wish for tomorrow. But we are savages. The white man's dreams are hidden from us.

THE WASTELAND

Al Gore

One of the clearest signs that our relationship to the global envi- ¹ ronment is in severe crisis is the floodtide of garbage spilling out of our cities and factories. What some have called the "throwaway society" has been based on the assumptions that endless resources will allow us to produce an endless supply of goods and that bottomless receptacles (i.e., landfills and ocean dumping sites) will allow us to dispose of an endless stream of waste. But now we are beginning to drown in that stream. Having relied for too long on the old strategy of "out of sight, out of mind," we are now running out of ways to dispose of our waste in a manner that keeps it out of either sight or mind.

In an earlier era, when the human population and the quantities of ² waste generated were much smaller and when highly toxic forms of waste were uncommon, it was possible to believe that the world's ab-

---

[1] Telegraph wires. [Eds.]

sorption of our waste meant that we need not think about it again. Now, however, all that has changed. Suddenly, we are disconcerted—even offended—when the huge quantities of waste we thought we had thrown away suddenly demand our attention as landfills overflow, incinerators foul the air, and neighboring communities and states attempt to dump their overflow problems on us.

The American people have, in recent years, become embroiled in debates about the relative merits of various waste disposal schemes, from dumping it in the ocean to burying it in a landfill to burning it or taking it elsewhere, anywhere, as long as it is somewhere else. Now, however, we must confront a strategic threat to our capacity to dispose of—or even recycle—the enormous quantities of waste now being produced. Simply put, the way we think about waste is leading to the production of so much of it that no method for handling it can escape being completely overwhelmed. There is only one way out: we have to change our production processes and dramatically reduce the amount of waste we create in the first place and ensure that we consider thoroughly, ahead of time, just how we intend to recycle or isolate that which unavoidably remains. But first we have to think clearly about the complexities of the predicament.

Waste is a multifaceted problem. We think of waste as whatever is useless, or unprofitable according to our transitory methods of calculating value, or sufficiently degraded so that the cost of reclamation seems higher than the cost of disposal. But anything produced in excess—nuclear weapons, for example, or junk mail—also represents waste. And in modern civilization, we have come to think of almost any natural resource as "going to waste" if we have failed to develop it, which usually means exploiting it for commercial use. Ironically, however, when we do transform natural resources into something useful, we create waste twice—once when we generate waste as part of the production process and a second time when we tire of the thing itself and throw it away.

Perhaps the most visible evidence of the waste crisis is the problem of how to dispose of our mountains of municipal solid waste, which is being generated at the rate of more than five pounds a day for every citizen of this country, or approximately one ton per person per year. But two other kinds of waste pose equally difficult challenges. The first is the physically dangerous and politically volatile material known as hazardous waste, which accompanied the chemical revolution of the 1930s and which the United States now produces in roughly the same quantities as municipal solid waste. (This is a conservative estimate, one that would double if we counted all the hazardous waste that is currently exempted from regulation for a variety of administrative and political reasons.) Second, one ton of industrial solid waste is created each week for every man, woman, and child—and this does not even count the gaseous waste steadily being vented into the atmosphere. (For example, each person in the United States also produces an average of twenty tons of CO_2[1] each year.) Incredibly, taking into account all three of these conservatively defined categories of waste, every person in the United States produces *more than twice his or her weight in waste every day.*

It's easy to discount the importance of such a statistic, but we can no   6
longer consider ourselves completely separate from the waste we help to produce at work or the waste that is generated in the process of supplying us with the things we buy and use.

Our cavalier attitude toward this problem is an indication of how   7
hard it will be to solve. Even the words we use to describe our behavior reveal the pattern of self-deception. Take, for example, the word *consumption,* which implies an almost mechanical efficiency, suggesting that all traces of whatever we consume magically vanish after we use it. In fact, when we consume something, it doesn't go away at all. Rather, it is transformed into two very different kinds of things: something "useful" and the stuff left over, which we call "waste." Moreover, anything we think of as useful becomes waste as soon as we are finished with it, so our perception of the things we consume must be considered when deciding what is and isn't waste. Until recently, none of these issues has seemed terribly important; indeed, a high rate of consumption has often been cited as a distinguishing characteristic of an advanced society. Now, however, this attitude can no longer be considered in any way healthy, desirable, or acceptable.

The waste crisis is integrally related to the crisis of industrial civi-   8
lization as a whole. Just as our internal combustion engines have automated the process by which our lungs transform oxygen into carbon dioxide (CO_2), our industrial apparatus has vastly magnified the process by which our digestive system transforms raw material (food) into human energy and growth—and waste. Viewed as an extension of our own consumption process, our civilization now ingests enormous quantities of trees, coal, oil, minerals, and thousands of substances taken from their places of discovery, then transforms them into "products" of every shape, kind, and description—and into vast mountain ranges of waste.

The chemical revolution has burst upon the world with awesome   9
speed. Our annual production of organic chemicals soared from 1 million tons in 1930 to 7 million tons in 1950, 63 million in 1970, and half a billion in 1990. At the current rate, world chemical production is now doubling in volume every seven to eight years. The amount of chemical waste dumped into landfills, lakes, rivers, and oceans is staggering. In the United States alone, there are an estimated 650,000 commercial and

---

[1] Carbon dioxide. [Eds.]

industrial sources of hazardous waste; the Environmental Protection Agency (EPA) believes that 99 percent of this waste comes from only 2 percent of the sources, and an estimated 64 percent of all hazardous waste is managed at only ten regulated facilities. Two thirds of all hazardous waste comes from chemical manufacturing and almost one quarter from the production of metals and machinery. The remaining 11 percent is divided between petroleum refining (3 percent) and a hundred other smaller categories. According to the United Nations Environment Programme, more than 7 million chemicals have now been discovered or created by humankind, and several thousand new ones are added each year. Of the 80,000 now in common use in significant quantities, most are produced in a manner that also creates chemical waste, much of it hazardous. While many kinds of hazardous chemical waste can be managed fairly easily, other kinds can be extremely dangerous to large numbers of people in even minute quantities. Unfortunately, there is such a wide range of waste labeled "hazardous" that the public is often misled about what is really dangerous and what is not. Most troubling of all, many of the new chemical waste compounds are never tested for their potential toxicity.

In addition, we now produce significant quantities of heavy metal [10] contaminants, like lead and mercury, and medical waste, including infectious waste. Nuclear waste, of course, is the most dangerous of all, since it is highly toxic and remains so for thousands of years. Indeed, the most serious waste problems appear to be those created by federal facilities involved in nuclear weapons production. These problems may have received less attention in the past because most federal facilities are somewhat isolated from their communities. In contrast, the public has become outraged by the dumping of hazardous waste into landfills, because numerous studies and disastrous events have shown that the practice is simply not safe. Basically, the technology for disposing of waste hasn't caught up with the technology of producing it.

Few communities want to serve as a dumping ground for toxic [11] waste; studies have noted the disproportionate number of landfills and hazardous waste facilities in poor and minority areas. For example, a major study, *Toxic Wastes and Race in the United States*, by the United Church of Christ, came to the following conclusion:

> Race proved to be the most significant among variables tested in association with the location of commercial hazardous waste facilities. This represented a consistent national pattern. Communities with the greatest number of commercial hazardous waste facilities had the highest composition of racial and ethnic residents. In communities with two or more facilities or one of the nation's five largest landfills, the average minority percentage of the population was more than three times that of communities without facilities (38% vs. 12%).

It's practically an American tradition: waste has long been dumped [12] on the cheapest, least desirable land in areas surrounded by less fortunate citizens. But the volume of hazardous waste being generated is now so enormous that it is being transported all over the country by haulers who are taking it wherever they can. A few years ago, some were actually dumping it on the roads themselves, opening a faucet underneath the truck and letting the waste slowly drain out as they crossed the countryside. In other cases, hazardous waste was being turned over to unethical haulers controlled by organized crime who dumped the waste on the side of the road in rural areas or into rivers in the middle of the night. There is some evidence that we have made progress in addressing these parts of the problem.

However, the danger we face as a result of improper waste hauling [13] is nothing compared to what happens in most older cities in America every time it rains heavily: huge quantities of raw, untreated sewage are dumped directly into the nearest river, creek, or lake. Since the so-called storm water sewers in these cities were built to connect to the sewer system (before the combined pipes reach the processing plant), the total volume of water during a hard rain is such that the processing plant would be overwhelmed if it didn't simply open the gates, forget about treating the raw sewage, and just dump it directly into the nearest large body of water. This practice is being allowed to continue indefinitely because local officials throughout the country have convinced Congress that the cost of separating the sewers that carry human waste from the sewers that carry rainwater would be greater than the cost of continuing to poison the rivers and oceans. But no effort has been made to calculate the cost of the growing contamination. Could it be because Congress, and indeed this generation of voters, seem to feel that this practice is acceptable because the cost of handling the waste properly will be borne by us, and much of the cost for fouling the environment can be shunted off on our children and their children?

Though federal law purports to prohibit the dumping of municipal [14] sewage and industrial waste into the oceans by 1991, it is obvious that the increasing volumes being generated and the enormous cost of the steps required to prevent ocean dumping will make that deadline laughably irrelevant. Currently, our coastal waters receive 2.3 trillion gallons of municipal effluent and 4.9 billion gallons of industrial wastewater each year, most of which fails to pass muster under the law. Nor are we the only nation guilty of this practice. Germany's river system carries huge quantities of waste toward the sea each day. Most rivers throughout Asia and Europe, Africa and Latin America, are treated as open sewers, especially for industrial waste and sewage. And, the first major tragedy involving chemical waste in the water was in Japan in the 1950s, at Minimata. International cooperative efforts have focused on regional ocean pollution problems, such as the Mediterranean, the North Sea, and the Caribbean.

The disposal of hazardous waste has received a good deal of atten- 15 tion in recent years, though there is still much to be done. For one thing, how do we know which waste is truly hazardous and which isn't? We produce more industrial waste than any other kind, but do we really know enough about it? Most industrial waste is disposed of on sites owned by the generator, often next to the facility that creates the waste. The landfills and dumps used by industry are therefore often far from public view and—especially because these companies create jobs—their waste is usually noticed only when it escapes from the site by means of underground water flow or dispersal by the winds.

~

Much more difficult to hide are the landfills used for municipal solid 16 waste. Many of us grew up assuming that although every town and city needed a dump, there would always be a hole wide enough and deep enough to take care of all our trash. But like so many other assumptions about the earth's infinite capacity to absorb the impact of human civilization, this one too was wrong. Which brings us to the second major change concerning our production of waste: the volume of garbage is now so high that we are running out of places to put it. Out of 20,000 landfills in the United States in 1979, more than 15,000 have since reached their permanent capacity and closed. Although the problem is most acute in older cities, especially in the Northeast, virtually every metropolitan area is either facing or will soon face the urgent need to find new landfills or dispose of their garbage by some other means.

Those landfills still in operation feature mountains of garbage that 17 are reaching heroic proportions: Fresh Kills Landfill on Staten Island, for instance, receives 44 million pounds of New York City garbage every single day. According to a study by a *Newsday* investigative team, it will soon become "the highest point on the Eastern Seaboard south of Maine." It will soon legally require a Federal Aviation Administration permit as a threat to aircraft.

Dr. W. L. Rathje, a professor of anthropology at the University of 18 Arizona and perhaps the leading "garbologist" in the world, testified to the epic scale of these modern landfills before one of my subcommittee hearings: "When I was a graduate student, I was told that the largest monument ever built by a New World civilization was the Temple of the Sun, constructed in Mexico around the time of Christ and occupying thirty million cubic feet of space. Durham Road Landfill near San Francisco is two mounds compiled since 1977 solely out of cover dirt and the municipal solid waste from three California cities. I can still remember my shock when my students calculated that each mound was seventy million cubic feet in volume, a total of nearly five Sun Temples. Landfills are clearly the largest garbage middens (i.e., refuse heaps) in the history of the world."

What is in these mountains? Various forms of paper, mostly news- [19] papers and packaging, take up approximately half the space. Another 20 percent or so is made up of yard waste, construction wood, and assorted organic waste, especially food. (Rathje found that 15 percent of all the solid food purchased by Americans ends up in landfills.) An unbelievable conglomeration of odds and ends accounts for the rest, with almost 10 percent made up of plastic, including the so-called biodegradable plastic. (Starch is added to the plastic compound as an appetizer for microorganisms, who will theoretically disassemble the plastic as they consume the starch.) Rathje dryly noted that he was skeptical of such claims: "In our landfill refuse from decades past we have uncovered corncobs with all their kernels still intact. If microorganisms won't eat corn-on-the-cob, I doubt whether they will dig cornstarch out of plastics."

But much organic waste does ultimately decompose, in the [20] process generating a great deal of methane,[2] which poses a threat of explosions and underground fires in older dumps that do not have proper venting or control. More significant, it contributes to the increased amount of methane entering the atmosphere. As we now know, rising levels of methane are one reason that the greenhouse effect has become so dangerous.

As existing landfills close, cities throughout the United States are [21] desperately searching for new ones. And they are not easy to find. In fact, in my home state of Tennessee, to take one example, the single hottest political issue in the majority of our ninety-five counties is where to locate a new landfill or incinerator. Since these problems have customarily been addressed at the local level, they have not been defined as national issues, even though they generate more political controversy nationwide than many other issues. Now, however, the accumulation of waste has gotten so out of hand that cities and states have begun shipping large quantities across state lines. The Congressional Research Service has estimated that more than 12 million tons of municipal solid waste were shipped across state lines in 1989. Although some of this volume is due to the fact that some major cities are next to a state line and some is due to formal interstate compacts for regional disposal facilities (which can be among the more responsible alternatives), there is an enormous growth in shipments by private haulers to landowners in poorer areas of the country who are ready to make a dollar by having garbage dumped on their property.

I remember the day that citizens from the small Tennessee town of [22] Mitchellville (pop. 500) called me to complain about four smelly boxcars dripping with garbage from New York City that had been sitting in the

---

[2] A flammable gas. [Eds.]

hot sun for a week on a railroad siding in their town. "What worries me," said one resident to a reporter from the *Nashville Banner*, "is that so many germs are carried through the air, viruses and this type of thing. When that wind is blowing that stuff all over town, them little germs are not saying, 'Now, we can't leave this boxcar, you know we've got to stay here,'" Mitchellville's vice mayor, Bill Rogers, said, "A lot of the time you can see water, or some kind of liquid, dripping out the bottom of the cars, and some of them contain pure New York garbage." As it turned out, the mayor had agreed to let the hauling company, Tuckasee Inc., bring trash from New York, New Jersey, and Pennsylvania to a landfill thirty-five miles from the railroad siding for a fee of $5 per boxcar, which looked like a good deal for a city whose annual budget is less than $50,000.

Small communities like Mitchellville throughout the Southeast and [23] Midwest are being deluged with shipments of garbage from the Northeast. Rural areas of the western United States are receiving garbage from large cities on the Pacific coast. No wonder that bands of vigilantes have formed to patrol the highways and backroads in areas besieged by trucks of garbage from larger population centers. One of my favorite spoofs on *Saturday Night Live* was a mock commercial for a product called the Yard-a-Pult, a scaled-down model of a medieval catapult, just large enough for the backyard patio, suitable for the launching of garbage bags into your neighbor's property. No need for recycling, incineration, or landfills. The Yard-a-Pult is the ultimate in "out of sight, out of mind" convenience. Unfortunately, the fiction is disturbingly like the reality of our policy for dealing with waste.

Sometimes truth is even stranger than fiction. One of the most [24] bizarre and disturbing consequences of this considerable shipment of waste is the appearance of a new environmental threat called backhauling. Truckers take loads of chemical waste and garbage in one direction and food and bulk liquids (like fruit juice) in the opposite direction—in the same containers. In a lengthy report, the *Seattle Post-Intelligencer* found hundreds of examples of food being carried in containers that had been filled with hazardous waste on the first leg of the journey. Although the trucks were typically washed between loads, the drivers (at some threat to their jobs) described lax inspections, totally inadequate washouts, and the use of liquid deodorizers, themselves dangerous, to mask left-over chemical smells. In 1990, Senators Jim Exon, Slade Gorton, and I joined with Congressman Bill Clinger to pass legislation prohibiting this practice.

But no legislation, by itself, can stop the underlying problem. When [25] one means of disposal is prohibited, the practice continues underground or a new method is found. And what used to be considered unthinkable becomes commonplace because of the incredible pressure from the mounting volumes of waste.

Responding to Reading

1. What relationship does Chief Seattle say Native Americans have to the land? In what way does this relationship differ from the white man's? Do you think his assessment of the white man's relationship to nature is accurate?
2. At the end of his letter Chief Seattle says, "But we are savages. The white man's dreams are hidden from us" (5). Why does he call himself a savage? Do you think he wants to be taken literally?
3. Do you think, as Gore does, that America is a "throwaway society" (1)? Has the situation improved since Gore published his book in 1992?
4. How is waste disposed of in the area in which you live? Does this method of disposal support or refute Gore's point?
5. How do you think Chief Seattle would react to Gore's essay? Would he be encouraged or discouraged? Explain.
6. Are you optimistic or pessimistic about people's ability to live in harmony with the environment? Which selection, Chief Seattle's or Gore's, more closely reflects your views?

THE OBLIGATION TO ENDURE

Rachel Carson

Naturalist and environmentalist Rachel Carson (1907–1964) was a specialist in marine biology. She won the National Book Award for *The Sea Around Us* (1951), which, like her other books, appeals to scientists and laypeople alike. While working as an aquatic biologist for the U.S. Fish and Wildlife Service, Carson became concerned with ecological hazards and wrote *Silent Spring* (1962), in which she warned readers about the indiscriminate use of pesticides. This book influenced President John F. Kennedy to begin investigations into this and other environmental problems. In the selection from *Silent Spring* that follows, Carson urges us to question the use of chemical pesticides.

The history of life on earth has been a history of interaction between [1] living things and their surroundings. To a large extent, the physical form and the habits of the earth's vegetation and its animal life have been molded by the environment. Considering the whole span of earthly time, the opposite effect, in which life actually modifies its surroundings, has been relatively slight. Only within the moment of time represented by the present century has one species—man—acquired significant power to alter the nature of his world.

During the past quarter century this power has not only increased   2
to one of disturbing magnitude but it has changed in character. The most
alarming of all man's assaults upon the environment is the contamination of air, earth, rivers, and sea with dangerous and even lethal materials. This pollution is for the most part irrecoverable; the chain of evil
it initiates not only in the world that must support life but in living tissues is for the most part irreversible. In this now universal contamination of the environment, chemicals are the sinister and little-recognized
partners of radiation in changing the very nature of the world—the very
nature of its life. Strontium 90, released through nuclear explosions into
the air, comes to earth in rain or drifts down in fallout, lodges in soil, enters into the grass or corn or wheat grown there, and in time takes up its
abode in the bones of a human being, there to remain until his death.
Similarly, chemicals sprayed on croplands or forests or gardens lie long
in soil, entering into living organisms, passing from one to another in a
chain of poisoning and death. Or they pass mysteriously by underground streams until they emerge and, through the alchemy of air and
sunlight, combine into new forms that kill vegetation, sicken cattle, and
work unknown harm on those who drink from once pure wells. As Albert Schweitzer[1] has said, "Man can hardly even recognize the devils of
his own creation."

It took hundreds of millions of years to produce the life that now   3
inhabits the earth—eons of time in which that developing and evolving and diversifying life reached a state of adjustment and balance
with its surroundings. The environment, rigorously shaping and directing the life it supported, contained elements that were hostile as
well as supporting. Certain rocks gave out dangerous radiation; even
within the light of the sun, from which all life draws its energy, there
were short-wave radiations with power to injure. Given time—time
not in years but in millennia—life adjusts, and a balance has been
reached. For time is the essential ingredient; but in the modern world
there is no time.

The rapidity of change and the speed with which new situations are   4
created follow the impetuous and heedless pace of man rather than the
deliberate pace of nature. Radiation is no longer merely the background
radiation of rocks, the bombardment of cosmic rays, the ultraviolet of
the sun that have existed before there was any life on earth; radiation is
now the unnatural creation of man's tampering with the atom. The
chemicals to which life is asked to make its adjustment are no longer
merely the calcium and silica and copper and all the rest of the minerals washed out of the rocks and carried in rivers to the sea; they are the

---

[1] French theologian (1875–1965) honored for his work as a scientist, humanitarian, musician, and religious thinker. In 1952 he was awarded the Nobel Peace Prize. [Eds.]

synthetic creations of man's inventive mind, brewed in his laboratories, and having no counterparts in nature.

To adjust to these chemicals would require time on the scale that is nature's; it would require not merely the years of a man's life but the life of generations. And even this, were it by some miracle possible, would be futile, for the new chemicals come from our laboratories in an endless stream; almost five hundred annually find their way into actual use in the United States alone. The figure is staggering and its implications are not easily grasped—500 new chemicals to which the bodies of men and animals are required somehow to adapt each year, chemically totally outside the limits of biologic experience.

Among them are many that are used in man's war against nature. Since the mid-1940s over 200 basic chemicals have been created for use in killing insects, weeds, rodents, and other organisms described in the modern vernacular as "pests"; and they are sold under several thousand different brand names.

These sprays, dusts, and aerosols are now applied almost universally to farms, gardens, forests, and homes—nonselective chemicals that have the power to kill every insect, the "good" and the "bad," to still the songs of birds and the leaping of fish in the streams, to coat the leaves with a deadly film, and to linger on in soil—all this though the intended target may be only a few weeds or insects. Can anyone believe it is possible to lay down such a barrage of poisons on the surface of the earth without making it unfit for all life? They should not be called "insecticides," but "biocides."

The whole process of spraying seems caught up in an endless spiral. Since DDT was released for civilian use, a process of escalation has been going on in which ever more toxic materials must be found. This has happened because insects, in a triumphant vindication of Darwin's principle of the survival of the fittest, have evolved super races immune to the particular insecticide used, hence a deadlier one has always to be developed—and than a deadlier one than that. It has happened also because, for reasons to be described later, destructive insects often undergo a "flare-back" or resurgence, after spraying in numbers greater than before. Thus the chemical war is never won, and all life is caught in its violent crossfire.

Along with the possibility of the extinction of mankind by nuclear war, the central problem of our age has therefore become the contamination of man's total environment with such substances of incredible potential for harm—substances that accumulate in the tissues of plants and animals and even penetrate the germ cells to shatter or alter the very material of heredity upon which the shape of the future depends.

Some would-be architects of our future look toward a time when it will be possible to alter the human germ plasm by design. But we may easily be doing so now by inadvertence, for many chemicals, like radiation, bring about gene mutations. It is ironic to think that man might determine his own future by something so seemingly trivial as the choice of an insect spray.

All this has been risked—for what? Future historians may well be [11] amazed by our distorted sense of proportion. How could intelligent beings seek to control a few unwanted species by a method that contaminated the entire environment and brought the threat of disease and death even to their own kind? Yet this is precisely what we have done. We have done it, moreover, for reasons that collapse the moment we examine them. We are told that the enormous and expanding use of pesticides is necessary to maintain farm production. Yet is our real problem not one of *overproduction?* Our farms, despite measures to remove acreages from production and to pay farmers *not* to produce, have yielded such a staggering excess of crops that the American taxpayer in 1962 in payout out more than one billion dollars a year as the total carrying cost of the surplus-food storage program. And is the situation helped when one branch of the Agriculture Department tries to reduce production while another states, as it did in 1958, "It is believed generally that reduction of crop acreages under provisions of the Soil Bank will stimulate interest in use of chemicals to obtain maximum production on the land retained in crops."

All this is not to say there is no insect problem and no need of con- [12] trol. I am saying, rather, that control must be geared to realities, not to mythical situations, and that the methods employed must be such that they do not destroy us along with the insects.

The problem whose attempted solution has brought such a train of [13] disaster in its wake is an accomplishment of our modern way of life. Long before the age of man, insects inhabited the earth—a group of extraordinarily varied and adaptable beings. Over the course of time since man's advent, a small percentage of the more than half a million species of insects have come into conflict with human welfare in two principal ways: as competitors for the food supply and as carriers of human disease.

Disease-carrying insects become important where human beings are [14] crowded together, especially under conditions where sanitation is poor, as in time of natural disaster or war or in situations of extreme poverty and deprivation. Then control of some sort becomes necessary. It is a sobering fact, however, as we shall presently see, that the method of massive chemical control has had only limited success, and also threatens to worsen the very conditions it is intended to curb.

Under primitive agricultural conditions the farmer had few insect [15] problems. These arose with the intensification of agriculture—the devotion of immense acreages to a single crop. Such a system set the stage for explosive increases in specific insect populations. Single-crop farming does not take advantage of the principles by which nature works; it is agriculture as an engineer might conceive it to be. Nature has introduced great variety into the landscape, but man has displayed a passion for simplifying it. Thus he undoes the built-in checks and balances by which nature holds the species within bounds. One important natural check is a limit on the amount of suitable habitat for each species. Obviously then, an insect that lives on wheat can build up its population to much higher levels on a farm devoted to wheat than on one in which wheat is intermingled with other crops to which the insect is not adapted.

The same thing happens in other situations. A generation or more [16] ago, the towns of large areas of the United States lined their streets with the noble elm tree. Now the beauty they hopefully created is threatened with complete destruction as disease sweeps through the elms, carried by a beetle that would have only limited chance to build up large populations and to spread from tree to tree if the elms were only occasional trees in a richly diversified planting.

Another factor in the modern insect problem is one that must be [17] viewed against a background of geologic and human history: the spreading of thousands of different kinds of organisms from their native homes to invade new territories. This worldwide migration has been studied and graphically described by the British ecologist Charles Elton in his recent book *The Ecology of Invasions*. During the Cretaceous Period, some hundred million years ago, flooding seas cut many land bridges between continents and living things found themselves confined in what Elton calls "colossal separate nature reserves." There, isolated from others of their kind, they developed many new species. When some of the land masses were joined again, about 15 million years ago, these species began to move out into new territories—a movement that is not only still in progress but is now receiving considerable assistance from man.

The importation of plants is the primary agent in the modern spread [18] of species, for animals have almost invariably gone along with the plants, quarantine being a comparatively recent and not completely effective innovation. The United States Office of Plant Introduction alone has introduced almost 200,000 species and varieties of plants from all over the world. Nearly half of the 180 or so major insect enemies of plants in the United States are accidental imports from abroad, and most of them have come as hitchhikers on plants.

In new territory, out of reach of the restraining hand of the natural [19] enemies that kept down its numbers in its native land, an invading plant or animal is able to become enormously abundant. Thus it is no accident that our most troublesome insects are introduced species.

These invasions, both the naturally occurring and those dependent [20] on human assistance, are likely to continue indefinitely. Quarantine and massive chemical campaigns are only extremely expensive ways of buying time. We are faced, according to Dr. Elton, "with a life-and-death need not just to find new technological means of suppressing this plant or that animal"; instead we need the basic knowledge of animal populations and their relations to their surroundings that will "promote an even balance and damp down the explosive power of outbreaks and new invasions."

Much of the necessary knowledge is now available but we do not [21] use it. We train ecologists in our universities and even employ them in our governmental agencies but we seldom take their advice. We allow the chemical death rain to fall as though there were no alternative, whereas in fact there are many, and our ingenuity could soon discover many more if given opportunity.

Have we fallen into a mesmerized state that makes us accept as in- [22] evitable that which is inferior or detrimental, as though having lost the will or the vision to demand that which is good? Such thinking, in the words of the ecologist Paul Shepard, "idealizes life with only its head out of water, inches above the limits of toleration of the corruption of its own environment . . . Why should we tolerate a diet of weak poisons, a home in insipid surroundings, a circle of acquaintances who are not quite our enemies, the noise of motors with just enough relief to prevent insanity? Who would want to live in a world which is just not quite fatal?"

Yet such a world is pressed upon us. The crusade to create a chem- [23] ically sterile, insect-free world seems to have engendered a fanatic zeal on the part of many specialists and most of the so-called control agencies. On every hand there is evidence that those engaged in spraying operations exercise a ruthless power. "The regulatory entomologists[2] . . . function as prosecutor, judge and jury, tax assessor and collector and sheriff to enforce their own orders," said Connecticut entomologist Neely Turner. The most flagrant abuses go unchecked in both state and federal agencies.

It is not my contention that chemical insecticides must never be [24] used. I do contend that we have put poisonous and biologically potent chemicals indiscriminately into the hands of persons largely or wholly ignorant of their potentials for harm. We have subjected enormous numbers of people to contact with these poisons, without their consent and often without their knowledge. If the Bill of Rights contains no guarantee that a citizen shall be secure against lethal poisons distributed either by private individuals or by public officials, it is surely only because our forefathers, despite their considerable wisdom and foresight, could conceive of no such problem.

I contend, furthermore, that we have allowed these chemicals to be [25] used with little or no advance investigation of their effect on soil, water, wildlife, and man himself. Future generations are unlikely to condone

---

[2] Scientists who study insects. [Eds.]

our lack of prudent concern for the integrity of the natural world that supports all life.

There is still very limited awareness of the nature of the threat. This [26] is an era of specialists, each of whom sees his own problem and is unaware of or intolerant of the larger frame into which it fits. It is also an era dominated by industry, in which the right to make a dollar at whatever cost is seldom challenged. When the public protests, confronted with some obvious evidence of damaging results of pesticide applications, it is fed little tranquilizing pills of half truth. We urgently need an end to these false assurances, to the sugar coating of unpalatable facts. It is the public that is being asked to assume the risks that the insect controllers calculate. The public must decide whether it wishes to continue on the present road, and it can do so only when in full possession of the facts. In the words of Jean Rostand, "The obligation to endure gives us the right to know."

Responding to Reading

1. Since this essay was written, DDT has been banned. Recently, however, some scientists have suggested that because some insects have developed resistance to safer insecticides, spraying of DDT should be reinstituted on a limited basis. Do you think health considerations and the need for food outweigh the environmental hazards of spraying DDT?

2. In recent years, the Mediterranean fruit fly has damaged fruit in California and Florida. In an effort to stop the damage, both states have aggressively sprayed malathion, an insecticide with relatively low toxicity to plants and animals. At the present time, however, these efforts have not stopped the spread of the fruit fly. How do you think Carson would suggest solving this problem?

3. Could Carson have made her point more forcefully by devoting more time to describing "the interaction between living things and their surroundings" (1)—that is, by showing what we have lost and what we have to lose? What in particular could she have described?

MY WOOD

~

E. M. Forster

British novelist, essayist, and short story writer E. M. Forster (1879–1969) first won wide recognition with his 1924 novel *Passage to India,* and his novels' popularity has continued, due in part to recent film versions of *Passage to India* and *Howard's End.* Forster also wrote biographies, literary criticism, and accounts of his travels as well as *Two Cheers for Democracy*, a 1951 collection of essays. In the following essay from his book *Abinger Harvest* (1936), Forster takes an ironic look at the effect of property ownership on individuals and on society.

A few years ago I wrote a book which dealt in part with the difficulties of the English in India. Feeling that they would have had no difficulties in India themselves, the Americans read the book freely. The more they read it the better it made them feel, and a check to the author was the result. I bought a wood with the check. It is not a large wood—it contains scarcely any trees, and it is intersected, blast it, by a public footpath. Still, it is the first property that I have owned, so it is right that other people should participate in my shame, and should ask themselves, in accents that will vary in horror, this very important question: What is the effect of property upon the character? Don't let's touch economics; the effect of private ownership upon the community as a whole is another question—a more important question, perhaps, but another one. Let's keep to psychology. If you own things, what's their effect on you? What's the effect on me of my wood? 1

In the first place, it makes me feel heavy. Property does have this effect. Property produces men of weight, and it was man of weight who failed to get into the Kingdom of Heaven. He was not wicked, that unfortunate millionaire in the parable, he was only stout; he stuck out in front, not to mention behind, and as he wedged himself this way and that in the crystalline entrance and bruised his well-fed flanks, he saw beneath him a comparatively slim camel passing through the eye of a needle and being woven into the robe of God.[1] The Gospels all through couple stoutness and slowness. They point out what is perfectly obvious, yet seldom realized: that if you have a lot of things you cannot move about a lot, that furniture requires dusting, dusters require servants, servants require insurance stamps, and the whole tangle of them makes you think twice before you accept an invitation to dinner or go for a bath in the Jordan. Sometimes the Gospels proceed further and say with Tolstoy[2] that property is sinful; they approach the difficult ground of asceticism here, where I cannot follow them. But as to the immediate effects of property on people, they just show straightforward logic. It produces men of weight. Men of weight cannot, by definition, move like the lightning from the East unto the West, and the ascent of a fourteen-stone[3] bishop into a pulpit is thus the exact antithesis of the coming of the Son of Man. My wood makes me feel heavy. 2

In the second place, it makes me feel it ought to be larger. 3

---

[1] "It is easier for a camel to go through the eye of a needle, than for a rich man to enter into the Kingdom of God." Matthew 19:246 [Eds.]

[2] Russian novelist. [Eds.]

[3] About two hundred pounds. [Eds.]

The other day I heard a twig snap in it. I was annoyed at first, for I   4
thought that someone was blackberrying, and depreciating the value of
the undergrowth. On coming nearer, I saw it was not a man who had
trodden on the twig and snapped it, but a bird, and I felt pleased. My
bird. The bird was not equally pleased. Ignoring the relation between us,
it took fright as soon as it saw the shape of my face, and flew straight
over the boundary hedge into a field, the property of Mrs. Henessy,
where it sat down with a loud squawk. It had become Mrs. Henessy's
bird. Something seemed grossly amiss here, something that would not
have occurred had the wood been larger. I could not afford to buy Mrs.
Henessy out, I dared not murder her, and limitations of this sort beset
me on every side. . . .

In the third place, property makes its owner feel that he ought to do   5
something to it. Yet he isn't sure what. A restlessness comes over him,
a vague sense that he has a personality to express—the same sense
which, without any vagueness, leads the artist to an act of creation.
Sometimes I think I will cut down such trees as remain in the wood, at
other times I want to fill up the gaps between them with new trees. Both
impulses are pretentious and empty. They are not honest movements toward money-making or beauty. They spring from a foolish desire to express myself and from an inability to enjoy what I have got. Creation,
property, enjoyment form a sinister trinity in the human mind. Creation
and enjoyment are both very, very good, yet they are often unattainable
without a material basis, and at such moments property pushes itself in
as a substitute, saying, "Accept me instead—I'm good enough for all
three." It is not enough. It is, as Shakespeare said of lust, "The expense
of spirit in a waste of shame": it is "Before, a joy proposed; behind, a
dream." Yet we don't know how to shun it. It is forced on us by our economic system as the alternative to starvation. It is also forced on us by
an internal defect in the soul, by the feeling that in property may lie the
germs of self-development and of exquisite or heroic deeds. Our life on
earth is, and ought to be, material and carnal. But we have not yet
learned to manage our materialism and carnality properly; they are still
entangled with the desire for ownership, where (in the words of Dante)
"Possession is one with loss."

And this brings us to our fourth and final point: the blackberries.   6

Blackberries are not plentiful in this meagre grove, but they are eas-   7
ily seen from the public footpath which traverses it, and all too easily
gathered. Foxgloves,[4] too—people will pull up the foxgloves, and ladies
of an educational tendency even grub for toadstools to show them on
the Monday in class. Other ladies, less educated, roll down the bracken
in the arms of their gentlemen friends. There is paper, there are tins.
Pray, does my wood belong to me or doesn't it? And, if it does, should

---

[4] A type of flower. [Eds.]

I not own it best by allowing no one else to walk there? There is a wood near Lyme Regis, also cursed by a public footpath, where the owner has not hesitated on this point. He had built high stone walls each side of the path, and has spanned it by bridges, so that the public circulate like termites while he gorges on the blackberries unseen. He really does own his wood, this able chap. And perhaps I shall come to this in time. I shall wall in and fence out until I really taste the sweets of property. Enormously stout, endlessly avaricious, pseudo-creative, intensely selfish, I shall weave upon my forehead the quadruple crown of possession until those nasty Bolshies[5] come and take it off again and thrust me aside into the outer darkness.

Responding to Reading

1. In this essay Forster shows how owning a piece of property has affected him. In what way has owning something affected you? What has it taught you about yourself?
2. Would you say that owning the wood has had positive or negative effects on Forster? Explain.
3. What general point is Forster implying about private property and ownership? Do you think he overstates his case? How valid are his conclusions?

THE TUGBOAT ON THE LAWN: A ～ TALE OF MAN AND NATURE

Hans Koning

A native of the Netherlands and a graduate of the University of Amsterdam and the University of Zurich, Hans Koningberger (1921–) immigrated to the United States when he was thirty. His first book, *Modern Dutch Painting: An Introduction* (1955), was followed by a series of novels, including *A Walk with Love and Death* (1961) and *Death of a Schoolboy* (1974), and travel books, including *Along the Roads of the New Russia* (1968) and *A New Yorker in Egypt* (1976). He has most recently written several books on the discovery of the Americas: *Columbus, His Enterprise: Exploding the Myth* (1982; revised 1991), *Rewriting Our History: Columbus and the New World Order* (1992), and *The Conquest of*

---

[5] Bolsheviks. Advocates of a proletarian dictatorship in Russia by the Soviets. Forster uses the word in a general sense to refer to Marxist revolutionaries. [Eds.]

America (1993). Most of his later works are published under the pseudonym Hans Koning. In the following essay, which appeared in the *International Herald Tribune* in 1994, Koning considers what we lose when we attempt to keep nature "sanitized and . . . at bay."

I was on my way to Montreal from New Haven, where I live. It was 1 dusk on a clear, early fall evening as I drove through Granby, a Quebec town an hour or so from Montreal. I decided to stay over and arrive fresh and shaven in Montreal the next morning. Granby has a nice-looking, recently built hotel.

I asked for a room on the top floor. It had a balcony and I stepped 2 out and looked at the last rays of the sun setting behind the hill of the La Yamaska nature park. Below me lay a lawn with white garden tables and chairs and the hotel swimming pool.

Suddenly, joltingly, a machine started up. I discovered that the three 3 vast, cement-encased cylinders against the hotel wall and facing the lawn were not abstract sculptures but funnels for the hotel air-conditioning system, now roaring like the engine of a tugboat pulling an ocean liner. I beat a hasty retreat and closed my balcony door and the curtains, which didn't much lessen the roar. It stopped and started again all night.

This is not an anti-noise complaint. But spending the night in that 4 room, I thought of the many small pleasures we are losing, how a new generation might never know of them or miss them. How many nights a year would a sleeper in Granby need air-conditioning?

And what had happened to people, to the guests on that lawn, that 5 they didn't mind swimming and sunning themselves or having a drink in the ambiance of a tugboat's engine room? Didn't they realize that they were losing out on the sound of bird song, the smells of nature, the caress of the breezes of the night?

I know these questions are largely rhetorical. No, these people don't 6 mind the roar of a machine because they live lives during which leisure is mostly filled with the roar of television or Walkmans. They don't miss the sounds and smells of nature because nature—subconsciously, maybe—has become an enemy except in very controlled circumstances.

Nature has to be sanitized and kept at bay, with guards, curfews 7 and a dizzying set of other rules and regulations, benches, white lines, parking lots, chemical outhouses. Even our own circumscribed little gardens are not kept for sitting in and, say, reading, but for dousing with insecticides and trimming and manicuring with mowers and the newest weapon, leaf blowers.

Once, nature was a legitimate enemy: Back when there were wolves 8 in the woods around Brussels, when travelers could lose their way and die of hunger and thirst on the plains of White Russia. But now, nature (aside from the weather) has long been tamed, and at such latitudes as New Haven and Granby it very rarely shows its old hidden strength.

To us here, nature becomes dangerous when we ourselves have first [9] polluted it. In fact, some might argue that we aren't protecting ourselves from nature but protecting nature from us. No doubt that is sometimes true, but it does nothing to change the perception that nature is "the other" of which we cannot be part.

That, we are told, is the price of progress. But progress does not have [10] to become a dirty word unless our lack of sense makes it so. The human body isn't happiest in a controlled, lukewarm environment of machine-made air. The wonder of nature may hit us at any time, but preferably not in a rest area with a dozen other cars under a sign, "Point Lookout. No Smoking. No Loitering. No Walking on the Grass." The night wind, perhaps too warm or too cold for "comfort," has its own mystery.

I don't know if it's true that the view of nature as an enemy or, at the [11] least an opponent, who has to be kept at arm's length, arranged and filtered, is a typically male trait. It is certainly a late 20th century human trait. It closes off a world of sensations for us and for our children.

Responding to Reading

1. Do you agree with Koning when he says that most people "don't mind the roar of a machine because they live lives during which leisure is mostly filled with the roar of televisions or Walkmans" (6)? Does his description apply to you?
2. In paragraph 8 Koning says, "nature (aside from the weather) has long been tamed." Do you agree? Is taming nature a desirable goal for human beings?
3. What is Koning's purpose in writing this essay? To entertain? To inform? To complain? To persuade? Something else? Do you think he accomplishes his purpose or purposes?

WHY SMALLER REFRIGERATORS ~ CAN PRESERVE THE HUMAN RACE

Appletree Rodden

Appletree Rodden has danced with the Staatstheatre Ballet Company and was at one time a biochemical researcher at Stanford University. His essay here, first published in *Harper's* in 1975, asks us to consider whether "bigger and more" necessarily means better when it comes to technology.

Once, long ago, people had special little boxes called refrigerators in which milk, meat, and eggs could be kept cool. The grandchildren of these simple devices are large enough to store whole cows, and they reach temperatures comparable to those at the South Pole. Their operating costs increase each year, and they are so complicated that few home handymen attempt to repair them on their own.   1

Why has this change in size and complexity occurred in America? It has not taken place in many areas of the technologically advanced world (the average West German refrigerator is about a yard high and less than a yard wide, yet refrigeration technology in Germany is quite advanced). Do we really need (or even want) all that space and cold?   2

The benefits of a large refrigerator are apparent: a saving of time (one grocery-shopping trip a week instead of several), a saving of money (the ability to buy expensive, perishable items in larger, cheaper quantities), a feeling of security (if the car breaks down or if famine strikes, the refrigerator is well stocked). The costs are there, too, but they are not so obvious.   3

Cost number one is psychological. Ever since the refrigerator began to grow, food has increasingly become something we buy to store rather than to eat. Few families go to market daily for their daily bread. The manna in the wilderness could be gathered for only one day at a time. The ancient distaste for making food a storage item is echoed by many modern psychiatrists who suggest that such psychosomatic disorders as obesity are often due to the patient's inability to come to terms with the basic transitoriness of life. Research into a relationship between excessive corpulence and the size of one's refrigerator has not been extensive, but we might suspect one to be there.   4

Another cost is aesthetic. In most of Europe, where grocery marketing is still a part of the daily rhythm, one can buy tomatoes, lettuce, and the like picked on the day of purchase. Many European families have modest refrigerators for storing small items (eggs, milk, butter) for a couple of days, but the concept of buying large quantities of food to store in the refrigerator is not widely accepted. Since fresh produce is easily available in Europe, most people buy it daily.   5

Which brings to mind another price the large refrigerator has cost us: the friendly neighborhood market. In America, time is money. A large refrigerator means fewer time-consuming trips to the grocery store. One member of a deep-freeze-owning family can do the grocery shopping once or twice a month rather than daily. Since shopping trips are infrequent, most people have been willing to forego the amenities of the little store around the corner in favor of the lower prices found in the supermarket.   6

If refrigerators weren't so large—that is, if grocery marketing were 7
a daily affair—the "entertainment surcharge" of buying farm-fresh food
in a smaller, more intimate setting might carry some weight. But as it is,
there is not really that much difference between eggs bought from
Farmer Brown's wife and eggs bought from the supermarket which in
turn bought them from Eggs Incorporated, a firm operated out of Los
Angeles that produces 200,000 eggs a day from chickens that are kept in
gigantic warehouses lighted artificially on an eighteen-hour light-and-
dark cycle and produce one-and-a-half times as many eggs—a special
breed of chickens who die young and insane. Not much difference if you
don't mind eating eggs from crazy chickens.

Chalk up Farmer and Mrs. Brown as cost number four of the big re- 8
frigerator. The small farmer can't make it in a society dominated by supermarkets and big refrigerators; make way for superfarmers, super
yields, and pesticides (cost number five).

Cost number six of the big refrigerator has been the diminution of 9
regional food differences. Of course the homogenization of American
fare cannot be blamed solely on the availability of frozen food. Nonetheless, were it not for the trend toward turning regional specialties into
frozen dinners, it might still be possible to experience novelty closer to
home.

So much for the disadvantages of the big refrigerator. What about 10
the advantages of the small one? First of all, it would help us to "think
small," which is what we must learn anyway if the scary predictions of
the Club of Rome[1] (*The Limits of Growth*) are true. The advent of smaller refrigerators would set the stage for reversing the "big-thinking"
trends brought on with the big refrigerator, and would eventually
change our lives.

Ivan Illich makes the point in *Tools for Conviviality* that any tool we 11
use (the automobile, standardized public education, public-health care,
the refrigerator) influences the individual, his society, and the relationship between the two. A person's automobile is a part of his identity.
The average Volkswagen owner has a variety of characteristics (income,
age, occupation) significantly different from those of the average Cadillac owner. American society, with more parking lots than parks, and
with gridded streets rather than winding lanes, would be vastly different without the private automobile. Similar conclusions can be drawn
about any of the tools we use. They change us. They change our society.
Therefore, it behooves us to think well before we decide which tool to
use to accomplish a given task. Do we want tools that usurp power unto
themselves, the ones called "non-convivial" by Illich?

---

[1] A non-political group of individuals from fifty-one countries who are concerned about problems
confronting society. The group periodically publishes reports, such as *The Limits of Growth,* which examine the effects of science and technology on society. [Eds.]

The telephone, a "convivial tool," has remained under control; it has [12] not impinged itself on society or on the individual. Each year it has become more efficient, and it has not prevented other forms of communication (letter writing, visits). The world might be poorer without the telephone, but it would not be grossly different. Telephones do not pollute, are not status symbols, and interact only slightly (if at all) with one's self-image.

So what about the refrigerator? Or back to the more basic problem [13] to which the refrigerator was a partial answer: what about our supply of food? When did we decide to convert the emotion-laden threat of starvation from a shared community problem (of societal structure: farm-market-home) to a personal one (of storage)? How did we decide to accept a thawed block taken from a supermarket's freezer as a substitute for the voluptuous shapes, smells, and textures of fresh fruits and vegetables obtained from complex individual sources?

The decision for larger refrigerators has been consistent with a [14] change in food-supply routes from highly diversified "trails" (from small farms to neighborhood markets) to uniform, standardized highways (from large farms to centrally located supermarkets). Desirable meals are quick and easy rather than rich and leisurely. Culinary artistry has given way to efficiency, the efficiency of the big refrigerator.

People have a natural propensity for running good things into the [15] ground. Mass production has been a boon to mankind, but its reliance on homogeneity precludes its being a paradigm for all areas of human life. Our forebears and contemporaries have made it possible to mass-produce almost anything. An equally challenging task now lies with us: to choose which things of this world should be mass-produced, and how the standards of mass production should influence other standards we hold dear.

Should houses be mass-produced? Should education? Should food? [16] Which brings us back to refrigerators. How does one decide how large a refrigerator to buy, considering one's life, one's society, and the world, and not simply the question of food storage?

As similar questions are asked about more and more of the things we [17] mass-produce, mass production will become less of a problem and more of a blessing. As cost begins to be measured not only in dollars spent and minutes saved, but in total richness acquired, perhaps smaller refrigerators will again make good sense. A small step backward along some of the roads of "technological progress" might be a large step forward for mankind, and one our age is uniquely qualified to make.

Responding to Reading

1. What issue is Rodden addressing in his essay? What position do you think he is taking on the environment? Do you agree with him?

2. Rodden concludes his essay by saying that a small step backward might result in a large step forward. Do you agree? Does this concept apply to other environmental issues? Explain.

3. Can you suggest another title that would convey the point of the essay more straightforwardly? Which title, the original one or the new one, is more effective?

OUR ANIMAL RITES

Anna Quindlen

Journalist and novelist Anna Quindlen (1953–) was born in Philadelphia, where she received what she calls "a liberal Catholic education." She attended college at Barnard and started her career as a reporter at *Time* magazine in 1977. She moved to the *New York Times* in the early 1980s, where she contributed to the newspaper's "Hers" column (1985-86) and eventually wrote the widely syndicated personal opinion columns "Life in the 30's" (1986–1988) and "Public and Private" (1990–1994); some of these columns have been collected in the books *Living Out Loud* (1988) and *Thinking Out Loud* (1993). In 1992 she won a Pulitzer Prize for journalism for her "Public and Private" columns. The success of Quindlen's two recent novels—*Object Lessons* (1991) and *One True Thing* (1994)—led her to retire from the *Times* and concentrate on fiction-writing. Of her nonfiction she has said, "Whenever my response to an important subject is rational and completely cerebral, I know there is something wrong with it. I have always been governed by my gut." In the following 1990 "Public and Private" column, Quindlen looks at the relationship between humans and the wild animals whose territory we are overtaking.

The bear had the adenoidal breathing of an elderly man with a passion for cigars and a tendency toward emphysema. My first thought, when I saw him contemplating me through tiny eyes from a rise just beyond the back porch, was that he looked remarkably bearlike, like a close-up shot from a public television nature program. 1

I screamed. With heavy tread—pad, pad, pad, harrumph, harrumph—the bear went off into the night, perhaps to search for garbage, cans inexpertly closed and apiaries[1] badly lighted. I sat on the porch, shaking. Everyone asks, "Was he big?" My answer is, "Compared to what?" 2

---

[1] Bee farms. [Eds.]

What I leave out when I tell the story is my conviction that the bear ³ is still watching. At night I imagine he is staring down from the hillside into the lighted porch, as though he had a mezzanine seat for a performance on which the curtain had already gone up. "A nice female, but not very furry," I imagine him thinking, "I see the cubs have gone to the den for the night."

Sometimes I suspect I think this because the peace and quiet of the ⁴ country have made me go mad, and if only I could hear a car alarm, an ambulance siren, the sound of a boom box playing "The Power" and its owner arguing with his girlfriend over whether or not he was flirting with Denise at the party, all that would drive the bear clear out of my head.

Sometimes I think it is because instead of feeling that the bear is tres- ⁵ passing on my property, in my heart I believe that I am trespassing on his.

That feeling is not apparent to city people, although there is some- ⁶ thing about the sight of a man cleaning up after a sheepdog with a sheet of newspaper that suggests a kind of horrible atonement. The city is a place built by the people, for the people. There we say people are acting like animals when they do things with guns and bats and knives that your ordinary bear would never dream of doing. There we condescend to our animals, with grooming parlors and cat carriers, using them to salve our loneliness and prepare us for parenthood.

All you who lost interest in the dog after the baby was born, you ⁷ know who you are.

But out where the darkness has depth, where there are no street ⁸ lights and the stars leap out of the sky, condescension, a feeling of supremacy, what the animal-rights types call speciesism, is impossible. Oh, hunters try it, and it is pathetic to consider the firepower they require to bring down one fair-sized deer. They get three bear days in the autumn, and afterward there is at least one picture in the paper of a couple of smiling guys in hats surrounding the carcass of an animal that looks, though dead, more dignified than they do.

Each spring, after the denning and the long, cold drowse, we wait ⁹ to see if the bear that lives on the hill above our house beat the bullets. We discover his triumph through signs: a pile of bear dung on the lawn, impossible to assign to any other animal unless mastodons still roam the earth. A garbage box overturned into the swamp, the cole slaw container licked clean. Symmetrical scratch marks five feet up on a tree.

They own this land. Once, long ago, someone put a house on it. That ¹⁰ was when we were tentative interlopers, when we put a farmhouse here and a barn there. And then we went nuts, built garden condos with pools and office complexes with parking garages and developments with names that always included the words Park, Acres, or Hills. You can't stop progress, especially if it's traveling 65 miles an hour. You notice that more this time of year, when the possums stiffen by the side of the road.

Sometimes the animals fight back. I was tickled by the people who 11 bought a house with a pond and paid a good bit of money for a little dock from which to swim. It did not take long for them to discover that the snapping turtles were opposed to the addition to their ecosystem of humans wearing sunscreen. An exterminator was sent for. The pond was dredged. A guest got bit. The turtles won.

I've read that deer use the same trails all their lives. Someone comes 12 along and puts a neo-Colonial house in the middle of their deer paths, and the deer will use the paths anyway, with a few detours. If you watch, you can see that it is the deer that belong and the house which does not. The bats, the groundhogs, the weasels, the toads—a hundred years from now, while our family will likely be scattered, their descendants might be in this same spot. Somewhere out there the bear is watching, picking his nits and his teeth, breathing his raggedy bear breath, and if he could talk, maybe he'd say, "I wonder when they're going back where they belong."

Responding to Reading

1. Do you think that human beings are guilty of "speciesism" (8)?
2. Do you think Quindlen is romanticizing nature? Does she give animals more insight and dignity than they actually possess or deserve?
3. If you were the owner of the house Quindlen describes in paragraph 11, would you try to exterminate the snapping turtles, or would you try to live with them? Explain the positive and negative consequences of your decision.

THE MYTH OF MAN AS HUNTER

Barbara Ehrenreich

An unabashed "feminist, populist, socialist, and secular humanist," Barbara Ehrenreich (1941–) was born in Butte, Montana, to a family of self-avowed "free-thinkers" and "fourth- or fifth-generation atheists." Now a resident of Long Island, she holds a Ph.D. from Rockefeller University and is one of the country's most controversial social critics, offering a decidedly liberal perspective on many political and economic issues. Her books of social criticism include *The Hearts of Men: American Dreams and the Flight from Commitment* (1983), *Fear of Falling: The Inner Life of the Middle Class* (1989), and *The Worst Years of Our Lives:*

Irreverent Notes on a Decade of Greed (1990), and she recently published her first novel, *Kipper's Game* (1993). She is also a featured essayist for *Time* magazine, where the following piece originally appeared in 1993. In it, Ehrenreich suggests that while early humans may have successfully made the transition from prey to predator, we are still prey to many enemies, including others of our own species.

It must seem odd to the duck and deer populations that Americans have paid more than $255 million this summer for the experience of being prey. In *Jurassic Park* we had the supreme thrill of being hunted for food by creatures far larger, faster, and—counting teeth and claws-better armed than we are. With the raptors closing in, we saw how vulnerable the human body is—no claws, no exoskeleton, no blinding poison sprays. Take away our guns and high-voltage fences and we are, from a typical predator perspective, tasty mounds of unwrapped meat.

If the experience resonates to the most ancient layers of our brains, it's probably because we spent our first million years or so not just hunting and gathering, but being hunted and gathered. *T. Rex* had been gone for 60 million years when our progenitors came along, but there were saber-toothed tigers, lions, cougars, leopards, bears, wolves and wild boars waiting at the edge of every human settlement and campground.

The myth of "man the hunter" has flatteringly obscured our true prehistory as prey. According to the myth, "man" climbed down from the trees one day, strode out into the savanna with a sharpened stick in his hand and started slaughtering the local ungulates.[1] After that, supposedly, the only violence prehumans had to worry about was from other stick-wielding bipeds like themselves. Thus some punctured australopithecine skulls found in Africa were at first chalked up to "intentional armed assault"—until someone pointed out that the punctures precisely fit the tooth gap of the leopard.

Humans didn't even invent effective action-at-a-distance weapons until a mere 40,000 or so years ago. Only with these new tools, like the bow and arrow and the spear thrower, could our ancestors begin to mimic the speed and sharpness of a big cat's claws. Even so, predator animals remained a major threat. As late as the 7th century B.C., a stela erected by the Assyrian King Assurbanipal recounts the ferocity of the lions and tigers after torrential rains had flushed them out of their lairs; the great King, of course, stamped out the beasts.

Our collective memory of the war against the predator beasts is preserved in myth and fairy tale. Typically, a mythical hero starts out by taking on the carnivorous monster that is ravaging the land: Perseus saves Andromeda from becoming a sea monster's snack. Theseus conquers the Minotaur who likes to munch on Athenian youth. Beowulf de-

---

[1] Hooved animals. [Eds.]

stroys the loathsome night-feeding Grendel. Heracles takes on a whole zoo of horrors: lions, hydras, boars. In European fairy tales it's the wolves you have to watch out for—if the cannibal witches don't get you first.

No doubt the greatest single leap in human prehistory was the one 6 we made from being helpless prey to becoming formidable predators of other living creatures, including, eventually, the ones with claws and fangs. This is the theme that is acted out over and over, obsessively, in the initiation rites of tribal cultures. In the drama of initiation, the young (usually men) are first humiliated and sometimes tortured, only to be "reborn" as hunters and warriors. Very often the initial torment includes the threat of being eaten by costumed humans or actual beasts. Orokai-va children in Papua New Guinea are told they will be devoured like pigs; among Indians of the Pacific Northwest, the initiates were kidnapped or menaced by wolves; young Norwegian men, at least in the sagas, had to tackle bears single-handedly.

As a species, we've been fabulously successful at predation. We en- 7 slaved the wild ungulates, turning them into our cattle and sheep, pushing them into ever narrower habitats. We tamed some of the wolves and big cats, trivializing them as household pets. We can dine on shark or alligator fillets if we want, and the only bears we're likely to know are the ones whose name is teddy. In fact, horror movies wouldn't be much fun if real monsters lurked outside our theaters. We can enjoy screaming at the alien or the raptor or the blob because we know, historically speaking, it was our side that won.

But the defeat of the animal predators was not a clear-cut victory for 8 us. With the big land carnivores out of the way, humans decided that the only worthwhile enemy was others like themselves—"enemy" individuals or tribes or nations or ethnic groups. The criminal stalking his victim, the soldiers roaring into battle, are enacting an archaic drama in which the other player was originally nonhuman, either something to eat or be eaten by. For millenniums now, the earth's scariest predator has been ourselves.

In our arrogance, we have tended to forget that our own most for- 9 midable enemies may still be of the nonhuman kind. Instead of hungry tigers or fresh-cloned dinosaurs, we face equally deadly microscopic life forms. It will take a whole new set of skills and attitudes to defeat HIV or the TB bacterium—not the raging charge on the field of battle, but the cunning ambush of the lab.

And then there are all the nonliving enemies—Pinatubo, Andrew, 10 the murderously bloated Mississippi—to remind us that the earth has not passively accepted our dominion over it. We will go down, locked in incestuous combat with our own kind, while the earth quakes, the meteors hit and the viruses mindlessly duplicate in our living organs. Or we will take another great leap like the one our protohuman ancestors took so long ago when the threat was still from predator beasts: We will marshal all our skills and resources, our tools and talents, and face the enemy without.

Responding to Reading

1. How do Ehrenreich's arguments relate to the sport of hunting—for example, for duck or deer—as we know it today? What position do you think she would take on recreational hunting?
2. Ehrenreich asserts that the idea of man as hunter is not accurate. How does she support her position? If, as she claims, the concept of man as hunter is inaccurate, why do you think it has endured?
3. In what sense are we predators today? In what sense are we prey?

DEATH IN THE RAIN FORESTS

~

Shawn Carlson

Shawn Carlson is a phycisist at Lawrence Berkeley Laboratories and a frequent contributor to *The Humanist* magazine's "Science and Society" column. In the following 1992 essay from *The Humanist,* Carlson argues that while tropical rain forests are unquestionably at serious risk, some ecologists and conservationists are exaggerating the potential loss of species and resorting to "scare tactics," which, he believes, may well backfire and "risk the credibility of the whole cause of rain-forest conservation."

Close your eyes and think of paradise. What do you see? Lush warm tropical forests, perhaps? Exotic birds and a plethora of strange creatures busily going about the business of survival? For me, nothing could come closer to paradise than a rain forest—a place of fantastic diversity, unfathomably rich in color and form.

Unfortunately, there is one particularly efficient primate going about its business in the rain forests as well. If the relentless industry of *Homo sapiens* proceeds unabated, it will ultimately devour these forests, forever eradicating at least half of all life on Earth. Fortunately, the situation is not as bleak as some people insist. All the vital signs suggest that the world's rain forests are in serious—but *not* critical—condition.

Surprisingly, these lavish forests grow in what biologists call *wet deserts*—extremely poor soil whose nutrients are quickly leached away by over 40 inches of rain each year. This perpetual soaking leaves behind those minerals which do not dissove in water and which, unhappily for the flora, cannot be absorbed by plant roots. Only about 0.1 percent of the nutrients released by the decaying matter on the forest floor ever feeds the next generation of vegetation. Furthermore, the struggle for sunlight favors the development of a network of high branches with broad expanses of large leaves to catch every morsel of the sun's nourishment. The branches of neighboring trees grow together into a thick canopy of leaves which absorbs rain water like green blotting paper and then slowly releases it to keep the air saturated with moisture. These canopies provide rich habitats for millions of organisms (mostly insects), which have evolved in such away that they spend their entire lives in the tree tops and are therefore almost never seen by humans.

It is not surprising then that most of the rain forests' inhabitants 4 have never been described by science. Just how many species do these forests harbor? Nobody knows—not even to within a factor of ten. Any estimate of biodiversity must be based upon surveys of areas which are small enough for biologists to personally scrutinize. To estimate the total number, the species count in these areas must somehow be extrapolated to the entire rain forest. Unfortunately, we have no model, no mathematical formula, which relates the number of species to rain-forest area. Still, assessing the damage now being wreaked on the forests requires some estimate to be made.

Although the species-area formula is not known for rain forests, it 5 is well known for so-called islands—relatively small and isolated habitats. In this context, an "island" can be a conventional island—an outcropping of land in an ocean—but it can also be a mountaintop above the timber line or an oasis surrounded by desert. On an island, the total number of species scales roughly as the fourth root of the island's area. Thus, if two islands had the same environment but one was 16 times larger than the other, the larger island would be roughly twice as species-rich as the smaller one. To estimate how many species make a particular island their home, a biologist could simply count all the species in some small but representative piece of the island and then extrapolate to the whole. Even if the species started out evenly distributed throughout the island, the destruction of habitat would put pressures on the surviving organisms. Put simply, any given area can only support so many species, and, if there are too many, competition for resources will drive some of them into extinction. But while the island model predicts that every acre cleared contributes to extinctions, keep in mind that a fourth-root dependence is very slow. The island model predicts that annihilating 50 percent of a habitat extinguishes only 16 percent of its inhabitants. If 99 percent of the island is destroyed, 32 percent of the species should still survive in the 1 percent remaining.

Since there are no good models for rain forests, most people use the 6 island model to estimate both rain-forest biodiversity and extinction rates. But since rain forests are not very much like islands, the island model can give only the crudest estimates for the rain forests' problems.

Just how badly does the island model do? Islands can be rather [7] sparse in species, but rain forests absolutely *brim* with biodiversity. It is not uncommon, for example, for a single leguminous tree in Peru to be home to more than 40 species of ants representing more than 25 genera. That's comparable to the total ant diversity found in the whole of Brittany! Most islands just don't compare.

Also, rain forests are usually *much* bigger than islands. They occu- [8] py gaping swaths of South America, Africa, and Indonesia and cover over 60 countries. Biologists do try to break up the rain forests into a number of smaller microclimates and use the island model to estimate the total number of species of each. Even so, the survey areas must be scaled to regions that are sometimes *millions* of times larger. In fact, the island model almost certainly fails for these huge extrapolations because, while new ecological niches (the engines which drive biodiversity) are easy to create on small islands, they are not so easily created in huge forests. A small island contains comparatively few niches. Adding area to an island adds lots of new niches and therefore enhances biodiversity, but adding area to a large forest tends only to duplicate the niches that are already available. And, according to University of Maryland rain-forest expert Patrick Kangas, this is what the rain-forest data actually show. In a recent issue of *Science,* he said, "There's a finite number of species within any community type. As you continue to move out, the number levels off." In other words, the number of species in a rain forest rises with area, but only to a point. And that's good news because it means that *any large rain forest should be able to withstand at least some clearing without any loss of species.*

And there's more good news. In the only available study on refor- [9] estation, J. P. Lanly showed in 1982 that over half of all virgin rain forest cleared turned not into wasteland but into second-generation forests. These new forests usually support less-diverse ecosystems than the virgin forests, but they do provide a buffer of support in which some endangered species can find safe haven. Furthermore, nearly 6 percent of the rain forests—about 1.8 million hectares—are in protected parks, and more land is being added all the time. Much of this land has been carefully chosen to protect both rare species and overall biodiversity. Also, several million rain-forest hectares are inaccessible to people or impractical for human use. These areas are not likely to be disturbed soon.

But all this good news isn't what some conservationists want you to [10] hear. Don't get me wrong: there are many good reasons to be opposed to cutting down the rain forests, and I am absolutely against any destruction of virgin woodlands. I have emphasized the positives simply because conservationists often downplay scientific uncertainties and manipulate the numbers to make things look far *worse* than they actually are.

The island-model estimates of the number of rain-forest organisms [11] vary greatly, running from 5 million to 100 million species. (By contrast, the total number of species which have been described by science, including microscopic organisms, is less than 1.4 million.) Clearly, the uncertainties in these calculations are huge.

Just how many species are becoming extinct each year is even more [12] uncertain. Even the experts disagree on how much of the forests we are devouring annually. The numbers I've found so far from "official" sources range from 0.5 percent to 1.8 percent forest cover lost each year. Some environmentalists—such as E. O. Wilson of Harvard University— estimate that we are "easily" losing 100,000 species every year. Others use the above deforestation rates to argue that the number is between 6,250 and 22,500. But even these guesses are likely to be too high, because they assume a species-area curve that we know *over-estimates* rain-forest biodiversity. What's more, to obtain these frightening rates, one must apply the island model in the most naive way—with no account of forest regeneration, the pattern of clearing, animal migration, or a host of other critical details. While it is true that continued clearing must at some point drive species to extinction, we simply don't know at what point that is. In some countries, the damage is so great that it is hard to imagine that some extinctions are not taking place; but in others, where large sections of forest remain intact, the extinction rates may be closer to zero.

Television ads targeted to elicit your financial support for one en- [13] vironmental group or another usually present the high extinction-rate numbers combined with footage of exotic animals and discussions of the cancer cures that might lie hidden in the plant species we are destroying. These ads create the impression that plants and higher animals are taking the brunt of the disaster, but that's all smoke and mirrors. Almost all of the rain forests' biodiversity lies within their bugs, and so even the island model predicts that the vast majority of species being extinguished are not plants that could cure cancer but *insects*. As unpopular as this may be to say, nature is so bug-abundant (more than 600,000 species of beetles have already been described and there are likely to be many more out there) that losing a few percent of these is not likely to cause an ecological collapse. However, resorting to scare tactics in our attempts to save the rain forests could wind up being ecologically disastrous.

In his masterful book *The Mismeasure of Man*, Stephen Jay Gould [14] documents just how badly biology has been misused by some scientists to prop up the prevailing prejudices of the day. Although Gould focuses on nineteenth-century biology, it would be folly to presume that no modern scientist perpetrates similar abuses.

Perhaps the field most abused these days is ecology, which some- 15
times seems to me more like a religious movement than a scientific discipline. Any "heretic" who dares stray from the most apocalyptic interpretations of the data risks the professional scorn of Mother Nature's
self-appointed, doctoral-wielding apostolates. Several biologists who
criticized the high species-extinction estimates have been snubbed at
professional conferences and vilified in print. A. E. Lugo, project leader
for the Institute of Tropical Forestry in Puerto Rico, reports that, after
giving a speech at the Smithsonian Institution in which he criticized the
high extinction rates usually quoted, a prominent conservationist verbally assaulted him in the cafeteria. Paul Ehrlich, the well-known Stanford biologist who is perhaps the new enviro-religion's foremost
spokesperson, has even declared that we must all undergo a "quasi-religious transformation" aimed at creating a "revolution in attitudes toward other people, population growth, the purpose of human life, and
the intrinsic value of organic diversity" if humanity is to survive.

This kind of rhetoric really frightens me. Why? Because the rain 16
forests *are* mortally imperiled. More than half the virgin forests have already been cleared and many areas have already been devastated. Stopping the destruction will require us to be very careful about our facts.
Alarmist statistics, dire predictions that don't come true, and petty self-
righteousness risk the credibility of the whole cause of rain-forest conservation. Without credibility, there is no persuasion, and, without persuasion, there is absolutely no hope for us to save the forests.

We cannot save the rain forests without addressing the problems of 17
their 100 million human inhabitants. It's pretty tough to sell hungry parents on the idea that the next acre of virgin forest they want to clear has
a greater right to exist than their own families, and professional conservationists know this. That's why most programs to save the rain forests
have the primary goal of improving agricultural productivity to reduce
the need for further forest-clearing. Modern land-management techniques—the use of fertilizers to replenish the nutrients leached from the
soil, tractors to break up the earth, careful crop rotation, and the judi-
cious use of pesticides to maintain soil viability and reduce destruction
from pests—could greatly reduce the need to clear virgin forests. Waste-
lands produced by logging can often be replanted with fast-growing native trees of high lumber value to provide loggers with a source of timber which can be more profitably harvested than virgin forests.
Although only about 13 percent of the cultivated land is currently being
managed to produce a sustainable yield, several comprehensive
plans—like the United Nations' Tropical Forestry Action Plan—are now
being implemented to slow the destruction. International strategies to
reverse the rampant destruction of the world's rain forests are in place.
We must now find the political will to implement them.

Thus, everything is not gloom and doom. The forces of social cor- 18
rosion—poverty, governmental corruption, and foreign debt—are still
hard at work conspiring to rid the world of our most biologically boun-
tiful treasures, but there is plenty of reason for hope. What may be most
dangerous and perhaps most difficult to overcome is our own tendency toward extremism. The winds of irrationality lash the public debate
and make impossible the clear-headed discussion of the reasoned and
practicable steps we must take to save the rain forests. We must choose
data over dogma if the rain forests are to stand a chance.

Responding to Reading

1. Carlson says that most researchers base their estimates of how much damage is being done to the rain forests on an "island model." Then, in paragraph 6, he suggests that because "rain forests are not very much like islands, the island model can give only the crudest estimates for the rain
   forests' problems." What is his point? How does this information serve his
   overall argument?
2. Is the tone of this essay optimistic or pessimistic? Do you think a conservationist would agree with Carlson's assessment of the severity of the problem? Do *you* agree?
3. What does Carlson mean when he says, "We must choose data over dogma
   if the rain forests are to stand a chance" (18)? Would activists succeed in raising money for their causes if they followed Carlson's advice?

IS A TREE WORTH A LIFE?

◇

Sally Thane Christensen

A native of Missoula, Montana, and a federal attorney who represents
the U. S. Forest Service, Sally Thane Christensen (1954–) contributed
the following essay to *Newsweek* magazine's "My Turn" column. "My
Turn" provides a forum in which readers offer their personal perspectives on a variety of social, cultural, political, and ethical issues.
(Another "My Turn" column appears in Chapter 8, p. 595.) In her column Christensen, who suffers from ovarian cancer, describes the potential cancer-fighting substance provided by the bark of the Pacific
yew tree and argues that it is wrong for environmentalists to block
harvesting of the tree out of a misplaced concern that it may be endangered.

For most of the last decade, federal timberlands in the West have   1
been held hostage in a bitter fight between environmental groups and
the timber industry. The environmentalists want to save the forests and
their wildlife occupants. The timber industry wants to cut trees and provide jobs in a depressed economy. Caught in the middle is the United
States Forest Service, which must balance the conflicting concepts of sustained yield and multiple use of national forest land.

The latest pawn in this environmental chess match is the Pacific   2
yew tree, a scrubby conifer found from southern Alaska to central California and in Washington, Oregon, Idaho and Montana. Historically
the yew has not been harvested for value but often has been treated as
logging slash and wasted. Not any longer. An extract of the bark of the
Pacific yew known as taxol has been found to have cancer-fighting
properties, particularly with ovarian cancer. As many as 30 percent of
those treated with taxol have shown significant response. Some researchers call taxol the most significant new cancer drug to emerge in
15 years.

For the first time, the environmental debate over the use of a natur-   3
al resource involves more than a question of the priority of the resource
versus economic considerations. At stake is the value of a species of tree
and the habitat it provides for wildlife as opposed to the value of the
greatest of all natural resources, human life.

When I was first diagnosed three years ago, no one had an inkling   4
that I would become caught in the center of what may become the most
significant environmental debate of my generation. Although as early as
1979 researchers had discovered that taxol killed cancer in a unique way,
imprisoning malignant cells in a cage of scaffoldlike rods called micro-
tubules, lab tests on animals were inconclusive. By 1985, however, a
woman with terminal ovarian cancer was treated with taxol and had a
dramatic response. Six years later, the once lowly yew tree is at the
threshold of a controversy that challenges the fundamental precepts of
even the most entrenched environmentalist.

It takes about three 100-year-old Pacific yew trees, or roughly 60   5
pounds of bark, to produce enough taxol to treat one patient. When the
bark is removed, the tree dies. Environmental groups like the Oregon
Natural Resources Council and the Audubon Society are concerned that
the Pacific yew as a species may be decimated by the demand for taxol.
But this year alone, 12,000 women will die from ovarian cancer. Breast
cancer will kill 45,000 women. Is preservation of the Pacific yew worth
the price?

It is sublimely ironic that my fate hinges so directly on the Pacific   6
yew. As a federal attorney representing the Forest Service, I have witnessed the environmental movement in the West from its embryonic
stages. I have seen such diverse groups as the National Wildlife Federation and the Sierra Club challenge the Forest Service's ability to sell and

harvest its trees. Win or lose, the forests are often locked up during the lengthy legal process.

The viability of the national forests does not rise or fall with the Pa-   7
cific yew. But, unfortunately for cancer victims, the tree is most abundant on national-forest lands which are subject to environmental review by the public. Already challenges to the federal harvest of the yew have begun. In Montana, the Save the Yaak Committee has protested the Kootenai National Forest's intention to harvest yew trees and make them available for experimental use. The committee contends that the yew may be endangered by overharvesting.

I have news for the Save the Yaak Committee. I am endangered, too.   8
I've had four major abdominal surgeries in two years. I've had the conventional chemotherapy for ovarian cancer, and it didn't work. Though I was in remission for almost a year, last August my cancer returned with a vengeance. Taxol may be my last hope.

Because of the scarcity of supply, taxol is not commercially avail-   9
able. It is available only in clinical trials at a number of institutions. Bristol-Myers, working with the National Cancer Institute in Bethesda, Md., is asking the Forest Service to provide 750,000 pounds of bark for clinical studies this year.

The ultimate irony of my story is that I am one of the lucky ones.   10
This May I was accepted by the National Cancer Institute for one of its clinical trials. On May 8 I was infused with my first treatment of taxol. Hospitalized in intensive care at NCI, I watched the precious, clear fluid drip into my veins and prayed for it to kill the cancer that has ravaged my body. I thought about the thousands of women who will die of cancer this year, who will not have my opportunity.

Every effort should be made to ensure that the yew tree is made   11
available for the continued research and development of taxol. Environmental groups, the timber industry and the Forest Service must recognize that the most important value of the Pacific yew is as a treatment for cancer. At the same time, its harvest can be managed in a way that allows for the production of taxol without endangering the continued survival of the yew tree.

The yew may be prime habitat for spotted owls. It may be estheti-   12
cally appealing. But certainly its most critical property is its ability to treat a fatal disease. Given a choice between trees or people, people must prevail. No resource can be more valuable or more important than a human life. Ask my husband. Ask my two sons. Ask me.

Responding to Reading

1. Christensen points out that before taxol the Pacific yew tree had not been of much value. In what way does this information support environmentalist arguments to preserve endangered habitats and species?

2. Christensen makes a compelling case in favor of harvesting the Pacific yew. What would be the short-term and long-term effects of her proposal? Do you think she overstates her case?

3. Do you agree or disagree with Christensen's contention that "Given a choice between trees or people, people must prevail" (12)? Do you think a plant or animal species is ever worth a human life?

LANDSCAPE AND NARRATIVE

Barry Lopez

In much of his writing, Barry Lopez (1945–) uses natural history as a metaphor for larger themes, such as the interaction between people and the landscape. Lopez says, "By landscape I mean the complete lay of the land—the animals that are there, the trees, the vegetation, . . . the sounds common to the region." His most popular book, *Of Wolves and Men* (1979), is considered a complete portrait of the wolf. He is also the author of *Arctic Dreams: Imagination and Desire in a Northern Landscape* (1986) and has retold many Native American stories. In "Landscape and Narrative," from *Crossing Open Ground* (1988), Lopez shows how oral stories can animate the landscape in which they are set and how storytelling generates an "inexplicable renewal of enthusiasm" in listeners.

One summer evening in a remote village in the Brooks Range of Alaska, I sat among a group of men listening to hunting stories about the trapping and pursuit of animals. I was particularly interested in several incidents involving wolverine,[1] in part because a friend of mine was studying wolverine in Canada, among the Cree, but, too, because I find this animal such an intense creature. To hear about its life is to learn more about fierceness.

Wolverines are not intentionally secretive, hiding their lives from view, but they are seldom observed. The range of their known behavior is less than that of, say, bears or wolves. Still, that evening no gratuitous details were set out. This was somewhat odd, for wolverine easily excite the imagination; they can loom suddenly in the landscape with authority, with an aura larger than their compact physical dimensions, drawing one's immediate and complete attention. Wolverine also have a de-

---

[1] The largest members of the weasel family, wolverines are extremely fierce and will attack nearly every animal except human beings. [Eds.]

served reputation for resoluteness in the worst winters, for ferocious strength. But neither did these attributes induce the men to embellish.

I listened carefully to these stories, taking pleasure in the sharply observed detail surrounding the dramatic thread of events. The story I remember most vividly was about a man hunting a wolverine from a snow machine in the spring. He followed the animal's tracks for several miles over rolling tundra in a certain valley. Soon he caught sight ahead of a dark spot on the crest of a hill—the wolverine pausing to look back. The hunter was catching up, but each time he came over a rise the wolverine was looking back from the next rise, just out of range. The hunter topped one more rise and met the wolverine bounding toward him. Before he could pull his rifle from its scabbard the wolverine flew across the engine cowl and the windshield, hitting him square in the chest. The hunter scrambled his arms wildly, trying to get the wolverine out of his lap, and fell over as he did so. The wolverine jumped clear as the snow machine rolled over, and fixed the man with a stare. He had not bitten, not even scratched the man. Then the wolverine walked away. The man thought of reaching for the gun, but no, he did not.

The other stories were like this, not so much making a point as evoking something about contact with wild animals that would never be completely understood.

When the stories were over, four or five of us walked out of the home of our host. The surrounding land, in the persistent light of a far northern summer, was still visible for miles—the striated, pitched massifs of the Brooks Range; the shy, willow-lined banks of the John River flowing south from Anaktuvuk Pass; and the flat tundra plain, opening with great affirmation to the north. The landscape seemed alive because of the stories. It was precisely these ocherous tones, this kind of willow, exactly this austerity that had informed the wolverine narratives. I felt exhilaration, and a deeper confirmation of the stories. The mundane tasks which awaited me I anticipated now with pleasure. The stories had renewed in me a sense of the purpose of my life.

This feeling, an inexplicable renewal of enthusiasm after storytelling, is familiar to many people. It does not seem to matter greatly what the subject is, as long as the context is intimate and the story is told for its own sake, not forced to serve merely as the vehicle for an idea. The tone of the story need not be solemn. The darker aspects of life need not be ignored. But I think intimacy is indispensable—a feeling that derives from the listener's trust and a storyteller's certain knowledge of his subject and regard for his audience. This intimacy deepens if the storyteller tempers his authority with humility, or when terms of idiomatic expression, or at least the physical setting for the story, are shared.

I think of two landscapes—one outside the self, the other within. The external landscape is the one we see—not only the line and color of the land and its shading at different times of the day, but also its plants and animals in season, its weather, its geology, the record of its climate and evolution. If you walk up, say, a dry arroyo[2] in the Sonoran Desert you will feel a mounding and rolling of sand and silt beneath your foot that is distinctive. You will anticipate the crumbling of the sedimentary earth in the arroyo bank as your hand reaches out, and in that tangible evidence you will sense a history of water in the region. Perhaps a black-throated sparrow lands in a paloverde bush—the resiliency of the twig under the bird, that precise shade of yellowish-green against the milk-blue sky, the fluttering whir of the arriving sparrow, are what I mean by "the landscape." Draw on the smell of creosote bush, or clack stones together in the dry air. Feel how light is the desiccated dropping of the kangaroo rat. Study an animal track obscured by the wind. These are all elements of the land, and what makes the landscape comprehensible are the relationships between them. One learns a landscape finally not by knowing the name or identity of everything in it, but by perceiving the relationships in it—like that between the sparrow and the twig. The difference between the relationships and the elements is the same as that between written history and a catalog of events.

The second landscape I think of is an interior one, a kind of projec- 8
tion within a person of a part of the exterior landscape. Relationships in the exterior landscape include those that are named and discernible, such as the nitrogen cycle, or a vertical sequence of Ordovician lime-stone, and others that are uncodified or ineffable, such as winter light falling on a particular kind of granite, or the effect of humidity on the frequency of a blackpoll warbler's burst of song. That these relationships have purpose and order, however inscrutable they may seem to us, is a tenet of evolution. Similarly, the speculations, intuitions, and formal ideas we refer to as "mind" are a set of relationships in the interior land-scape with purpose and order; some of these are obvious, many im-penetrably subtle. The shape and character of these relationships in a person's thinking, I believe, are deeply influenced by where on this earth one goes, what one touches, the patterns one observes in nature—the in-tricate history of one's life in the land, even a life in the city, where wind, the chirp of birds, the line of a falling leaf, are known. These thoughts are arranged, further, according to the thread of one's moral, intellectual, and spiritual development. The interior landscape responds to the char-acter and subtlety of an exterior landscape; the shape of the individual mind is affected by land as it is by genes.

In stories like those I heard at Anaktuvuk Pass about wolverine, the 9
relationship between separate elements in the land is set forth clearly. It is put in a simple framework of sequential incidents and apposite detail. If the exterior landscape is limned[3] well, the listener often feels that he

---

[2] Brook or stream. [Eds.]
[3] Depicted. [Eds.]

has heard something pleasing and authentic—trustworthy. We derive this sense of confidence I think not so much from verifiable truth as from an understanding that lying has played no role in the narrative. The storyteller is obligated to engage the reader with a precise vocabulary, to set forth a coherent and dramatic rendering of incidents—and to be ingenuous.

When one hears a story one takes pleasure in it for different reasons—for the euphony of its phrases, an aspect of the plot, or because one identifies with one of the characters. With certain stories certain individuals may experience a deeper, more profound sense of well-being. This latter phenomenon, in my understanding, rests at the heart of storytelling as an elevated experience among aboriginal peoples. It results from bringing two landscapes together. The exterior landscape is organized according to principles or laws or tendencies beyond human control. It is understood to contain an integrity that is beyond human analysis and unimpeachable. Insofar as the storyteller depicts various subtle and obvious relationships in the exterior landscape accurately in his story, and insofar as he orders them along traditional lines of meaning to create the narrative, the narrative will "ring true." The listener who "takes the story to heart" will feel a pervasive sense of congruence within himself and also with the world. [10]

Among the Navajo and, as far as I know, many other native peoples, the land is thought to exhibit a sacred order. That order is the basis of ritual. The rituals themselves reveal the power in that order. Art, architecture, vocabulary, and costume, as well as ritual, are derived from the perceived natural order of the universe—from observations and meditations on the exterior landscape. An indigenous philosophy—metaphysics, ethics, epistemology, aesthetics, and logic—may also be derived from a people's continuous attentiveness to both the obvious (scientific) and ineffable (artistic) orders of the local landscape. Each individual, further, undertakes to order his interior landscape according to the exterior landscape. To succeed in this means to achieve a balanced state of mental health. [11]

I think of the Navajo for a specific reason. Among the various sung ceremonies of this people—Enemyway, Coyoteway, Red Antway, Uglyway—is one called Beautyway. In the Navajo view, the elements of one's interior life—one's psychological makeup and moral bearing—are subject to a persistent principle of disarray. Beautyway is, in part, a spiritual invocation of the order of the exterior universe, that irreducible, holy complexity that manifests itself as all things changing through time (a Navajo definition of beauty, hózhǫ́ǫ́). The purpose of this invocation is to recreate in the individual who is the subject of the Beautyway ceremony that same order, to make the individual again a reflection of the myriad enduring relationships of the landscape. [12]

I believe a story functions in a similar way. A story draws on rela- [13] tionships in the exterior landscape and projects them onto the interior landscape. The purpose of storytelling is to achieve harmony between the two landscapes, to use all the elements of story—syntax, mood, figures of speech—in a harmonious way to reproduce the harmony of the land in the individual's interior. Inherent in story is the power to reorder a state of psychological confusion through contact with the pervasive truth of those relationships we call "the land."

These thoughts, of course, are susceptible to interpretation. I am [14] convinced, however, that these observations can be applied to the kind of prose we call nonfiction as well as to traditional narrative forms such as the novel and the short story, and to some poems. Distinctions between fiction and nonfiction are sometimes obscured by arguments over what constitutes "the truth." In the aboriginal literature I am familiar with, the first distinction made among narratives is to separate the authentic from the inauthentic. Myth, which we tend to regard as fictitious or "merely metaphorical," is as authentic, as real, as the story of a wolverine in a man's lap. (A distinction is made, of course, about the elevated nature of myth—and frequently the circumstances of myth-telling are more rigorously prescribed than those for the telling of legends or vernacular stories—but all of these narratives are rooted in the local landscape. To violate *that* connection is to call the narrative itself into question.)

The power of narrative to nurture and heal, to repair a spirit in dis- [15] array, rests on two things: the skillful invocation of unimpeachable sources and a listener's knowledge that no hypocrisy or subterfuge is involved. This last simple fact is to me one of the most imposing aspects of the Holocene[4] history of man.

We are more accustomed now to thinking of "the truth" as some- [16] thing that can be explicitly stated, rather than as something that can be evoked in a metaphorical way outside science and Occidental[5] culture. Neither can truth be reduced to aphorism or formulas. It is something alive and unpronounceable. Story creates an atmosphere in which it becomes discernible as a pattern. For a storyteller to insist on relationships that do not exist is to lie. Lying is the opposite of story. (I do not mean to confuse ignorance with deception, or to imply that a storyteller can perceive all that is inherent in the land. Every storyteller falls short of a perfect limning of the landscape— perception and language both fail. But to make up something that is not there, something which can never be corroborated in the land, to

---

[4] The period of the last 11,000 years. [Eds.]
[5] Western. [Eds.]

knowingly set forth a false relationship, is to be lying, no longer telling a story.)

Because of the intricate, complex nature of the land, it is not always [17] possible for a storyteller to grasp what is contained in a story. The intent of the storyteller, then, must be to evoke, honestly, some single aspect of all that the land contains. The storyteller knows that because different individuals grasp the story at different levels, the focus of his regard for truth must be at the primary one—with who was there, what happened, when, where, and why things occurred. The story will then possess similar truth at other levels—the integrity inherent at the primary level of meaning will be conveyed everywhere else. As long as the storyteller carefully describes the order before him, and uses his storytelling skill to heighten and emphasize certain relationships, it is even possible for the story to be more successful than the storyteller himself is able to imagine.

I would like to make a final point about the wolverine stories I heard [18] at Anaktuvuk Pass. I wrote down the details afterward, concentrating especially on aspects of the biology and ecology of the animals. I sent the information on to my friend living with the Cree. When, many months later, I saw him, I asked whether the Cree had enjoyed these insights of the Nunamiut into the nature of the wolverine. What had they said?

"You know," he told me, "how they are. They said, 'That could happen.'" [19]

In these uncomplicated words the Cree declared their own knowl- [20] edge of the wolverine. They acknowledged that although they themselves had never seen the things the Nunamiut spoke of, they accepted them as accurate observations, because they did not consider a story a context for misrepresentation. They also preserved their own dignity by not overstating their confidence in the Nunamiut, a distant and unknown people.

Whenever I think of this courtesy on the part of the Cree I think of [21] the dignity that is ours when we cease to demand the truth and realize that the best we can have of those substantial truths that guide our lives is metaphorical—a story. And the most of it we are likely to discern comes only when we accord one another the respect the Cree showed the Nunamiut. Beyond this—that the interior landscape is a metaphorical representation of the exterior landscape, that the truth reveals itself most fully not in dogma but in the paradox, irony, and contradictions that distinguish compelling narratives—beyond this there are only failures of imagination: reductionism in science; fundamentalism in religion; fascism in politics.

Our national literatures should be important to us insofar as they [22] sustain us with illumination and heal us. They can always do that so long as they are written with respect for both the source and the reader, and with an understanding of why the human heart and the land have been brought together so regularly in human history.

Responding to Reading

1. In the first five paragraphs of his essay, Lopez tells the story of a wolverine. What is the point of this story? What does it teach Lopez about the relationship between landscape and narrative?
2. How, according to Lopez, does the storyteller help connect our "inner landscapes" with the natural world around us? Do you believe stories and storytellers are as important as Lopez thinks they are?
3. Would the stories Lopez describes have the same effect on people who live in cities as on people who live in the country? How would you account for any differences?

TO BUILD A FIRE

Jack London

Jack London (1876–1916), born in San Francisco, left high school to become a sailor; he first bought his own boat and then signed aboard a sailing vessel for an expedition to the Pacific. At age twenty-one, after returning to California and graduating from high school, he journeyed to Alaska for the gold rush. London based the short stories in his first collection, *Son of Wolf* (1900), and the novel *Call of the Wild* (1903) on his experiences in Alaska. Many works followed these, including *Martin Eden* (1909), an autobiographical novel. The 1910 short story "To Build a Fire" tells of a battle between the frozen Yukon and a man's will to live.

Day had broken cold and gray, exceedingly cold and gray, when the   1
man turned aside from the main Yukon trail and climbed the high earthbank, where a dim and little-travelled trail led eastward through the fat spruce timberland. It was a steep bank, and he paused for breath at the top, excusing the act to himself by looking at his watch. It was nine o'clock. There was no sun nor hint of sun, though there was not a cloud in the sky. It was a clear day, and yet there seemed an intangible pall over the face of things, a subtle gloom that made the day dark, and that was due to the absence of sun. This fact did not worry the man. He was used to the lack of sun. It had been days since he had seen the sun, and he knew that a few more days must pass before that cheerful orb, due

south, would just peep above the sky line and dip immediately from view.

The man flung a look back along the way he had come. The Yukon lay a mile wide and hidden under three feet of ice. On top of this ice were as many feet of snow. It was all pure white, rolling in gentle undulations where the ice jams of the freeze-up had formed. North and south, as far as his eye could see, it was unbroken white, save for a dark hairline that curved and twisted from around the spruce-covered island to the south, and that curved and twisted away into the north, where it disappeared behind another spruce-covered island. This dark hairline was the trail—the main trail—that led south five hundred miles to the Chilcoot Pass, Dyea, and salt water; and that led north seventy miles to Dawson, and still on to the north a thousand miles to Nulato, and finally to St. Michael, on Bering Sea, a thousand miles and half a thousand more.

But all this—the mysterious, far-reaching hairline trail, the absence of sun from the sky, the tremendous cold, and the strangeness and weirdness of it all—made no impression on the man. It was not because he was long used to it. He was a newcomer in the land, a *chechaquo*, and this was his first winter. The trouble with him was that he was without imagination. He was quick and alert in the things of life, but only in the things, and not in the significances. Fifty degrees below zero meant eighty-odd degrees of frost. Such fact impressed him as being cold and uncomfortable, and that was all. It did not lead him to meditate upon his frailty as a creature of temperature, and upon man's frailty in general, able only to live within certain narrow limits of heat and cold; and from there on it did not lead him to the conjectural field of immortality and man's place in the universe. Fifty degrees below zero stood for a bite of frost that hurt and that must be guarded against by the use of mittens, ear flaps, warm moccasins, and thick socks. Fifty degrees below zero was to him just precisely fifty degrees below zero. That there should be anything more to it than that was a thought that never entered his head.

As he turned to go on, he spat speculatively. There was a sharp, explosive crackle that startled him. He spat again. And again, in the air, before it could fall to the snow, the spittle crackled. He knew that at fifty below spittle crackled on the snow, but this spittle had crackled in the air. Undoubtedly it was colder than fifty below—how much colder he did not know. But the temperature did not matter. He was bound for the old claim on the left fork of Henderson Creek, where the boys were already. They had come over across the divide from the Indian Creek country, while he had come the roundabout way to take a look at the possibilities of getting out logs in the spring from the islands in the Yukon. He would be in to camp by six o'clock; a bit after dark, it was true, but the boys would be there, a fire would be going, and a hot supper would be ready. As for lunch, he pressed his hand against the protruding bundle under his jacket. It was also under his shirt, wrapped up in a handkerchief and lying against the naked skin. It was the only way to keep the biscuits from freezing. He smiled agreeably to himself as he thought of those biscuits, each cut open and sopped in bacon grease, and each enclosing a generous slice of fried bacon.

He plunged in among the big spruce trees. The trail was faint. A foot   5
of snow had fallen since the last sled had passed over, and he was glad he was without a sled, travelling light. In fact, he carried nothing but the lunch wrapped in the handkerchief. He was surprised, however, at the cold. It certainly was cold, he concluded, as he rubbed his numb nose and cheekbones with his mittened hand. He was a warm-whiskered man, but the hair on his face did not protect the high cheek-bones and the eager nose that thrust itself aggressively into the frosty air.

At the man's heels trotted a dog, a big native husky, the proper   6
wolf dog, gray-coated and without any visible or temperamental difference from its brother, the wild wolf. The animal was depressed by the tremendous cold. It knew that it was no time for travelling. Its instinct told it a truer tale than was told to the man by the man's judgment. In reality, it was not merely colder than fifty below zero; it was colder than sixty below, than seventy below. It was seventy-five below zero. Since the freezing point is thirty-two above zero, it meant that one hundred and seven degrees of frost obtained. The dog did not know anything about thermometers. Possibly in its brain there was no sharp consciousness of a condition of very cold such as was in the man's brain. But the brute had its instinct. It experienced a vague but menacing apprehension that subdued it and made it slink along at the man's heels, and that made it question eagerly every unwonted movement of the man as if expecting him to go into camp or to seek shelter somewhere and build a fire. The dog had learned fire, and it wanted fire, or else to burrow under the snow and cuddle its warmth away from the air.

The frozen moisture of its breathing had settled on its fur in a fine   7
powder of frost, and especially were its jowls, muzzle, and eyelashes whitened by its crystalled breath. The man's red beard and mustache were likewise frosted, but more solidly, the deposit taking the form of ice and increasing with every warm, moist breath he exhaled. Also, the man was chewing tobacco, and the muzzle of ice held his lips so rigidly that he was unable to clear his chin when he expelled the juice. The result was that a crystal beard of the color and solidity of amber was increasing its length on his chin. If he fell down it would shatter itself, like glass, into brittle fragments. But he did not mind the appendage. It was the penalty all tobacco chewers paid in that country, and he had been out before in two cold snaps. They had not been so cold as this, he knew, but by the spirit thermometer at Sixty Mile he knew they had been registered at fifty below and at fifty-five.

He held on through the level stretch of woods for several miles,   8
crossed a wide flat of nigger heads,[1] and dropped down a bank to the
frozen bed of a small stream. This was Henderson Creek, and he knew
he was ten miles from the forks. He looked at his watch. It was ten o'-
clock. He was making four miles an hour, and he calculated that he
would arrive at the forks at half-past twelve. He decided to celebrate
that event by eating his lunch there.

The dog dropped in again at his heels, with a tail drooping dis-   9
couragement, as the man swung along the creek bed. The furrow of the
old sled trail was plainly visible, but a dozen inches of snow covered the
marks of the last runners. In a month no man had come up or down that
silent creek. The man held steadily on. He was not much given to thinking, and just then particularly he had nothing to think about save that
he would eat lunch at the forks and that at six o'clock he would be in
camp with the boys. There was nobody to talk to; and, had there been,
speech would have been impossible because of the ice muzzle on his
mouth. So he continued monotonously to chew tobacco and to increase
the length of his amber beard.

Once in a while the thought reiterated itself that it was very cold and   10
that he had never experienced such cold. As he walked along he rubbed
his cheekbones and nose with the back of his mittened hand. He did this
automatically, now and again changing hands. But, rub as he would, the
instant he stopped his cheekbones went numb, and the following instant
the end of his nose went numb. He was sure to frost his cheeks; he knew
that, and experienced a pang of regret that he had not devised a nose
strap of the sort Bud wore in cold snaps. Such a strap passed across the
cheeks, as well, and saved them. But it didn't matter much, after all.
What were frosted cheeks? A bit painful, that was all; they were never
serious.

Empty as the man's mind was of thoughts, he was keenly observant,   11
and he noticed the changes in the creek, the curves and bends and timber jams, and always he sharply noted where he placed his feet. Once,
coming around a bend, be shied abruptly, like a startled horse, curved
away from the place where he had been walking, and retreated several
paces back along the trail. The creek he knew was frozen clear to the bottom—no creek could contain water in that arctic winter—but he knew
also that there were springs that bubbled out from the hillsides and ran
along under the snow and on top of the ice of the creek. He knew that
the coldest snaps never froze these springs, and he knew likewise their
danger. They were traps. They hid pools of water under the snow that
might be three inches deep, or three feet. Sometimes a skin of ice half an
inch thick covered them, and in turn was covered by the snow. Sometimes there were alternate layers of water and ice skin, so that when one

---

[1] Knotted masses of roots projecting above the wet surface of a swamp. [Eds.]

broke through he kept on breaking through for a while, sometimes wetting himself to the waist.

That was why he had shied in such panic. He had felt the give under [12] his feet and heard the crackle of a snow-hidden ice skin. And to get his feet wet in such a temperature meant trouble and danger. At the very least it meant delay, for he would be forced to stop and build a fire, and under its protection to bare his feet while he dried his socks and moccasins. He stood and studied the creek bed and its banks, and decided that the flow of water came from the right. He reflected awhile, rubbing his nose and cheeks, then skirted to the left, stepping gingerly and testing the footing for each step. Once clear of the danger, he took a fresh chew of tobacco and swung along at his four-mile gait.

In the course of the next two hours he came upon several similar [13] traps. Usually the snow above the hidden pools had a sunken, candied appearance that advertised the danger. Once again, however, he had a close call; and once, suspecting danger, he compelled the dog to go on in front. The dog did not want to go. It hung back until the man shoved it forward, and then it went quickly across the white, unbroken surface. Suddenly it broke through, floundered to one side, and got away to firmer footing. It had wet its forefeet and legs, and almost immediately the water that clung to it turned to ice. It made quick efforts to lick the ice off its legs, then dropped down in the snow and began to bite out the ice that had formed between the toes. This was a matter of instinct. To permit the ice to remain would mean sore feet. It did not know this. It merely obeyed the mysterious prompting that arose from the deep crypts of its being. But the man knew, having achieved a judgment on the subject, and he removed the mitten from his right hand and helped tear out the ice particles. He did not expose his fingers more than a minute, and was astonished at the swift numbness that smote them. It certainly was cold. He pulled on the mitten hastily, and beat the hand savagely across the chest.

At twelve o'clock the day was at its brightest. Yet the sun was too [14] far south on its winter journey to clear the horizon. The bulge of the earth intervened between it and Henderson Creek, where the man walked under a clear sky at noon and cast no shadow. At half-past twelve, to the minute, he arrived at the forks of the creek. He was pleased at the speed he had made. If he kept it up, he would certainly be with the boys by six. He unbuttoned his jacket and shirt and drew forth his lunch. The action consumed no more than a quarter of a minute, yet in that brief moment the numbness laid hold of the exposed fingers. He did not put the mitten on, but, instead, struck the fingers a dozen sharp smashes against his leg. Then he sat down on a snow-covered log to eat. The sting that followed upon the striking of his fingers against his leg ceased so quickly that he was startled. He had had no chance to take a bite of biscuit. He struck the fingers repeatedly and returned them to the mitten, baring the other hand for the purpose of eating. He tried to take a mouthful, but the ice muzzle prevented. He had forgotten to build a fire and thaw out. He chuckled at his foolishness, and as he chuckled he noted the numbness creeping into the exposed fingers. Also, he noted that the stinging which had first come to his toes when he sat down was already passing away. He wondered whether the toes were warm or numb. He moved them inside the moccasins and decided that they were numb.

He pulled the mitten on hurriedly and stood up. He was a bit fright- 15 ened. He stamped up and down until the stinging returned into the feet. It certainly was cold, was his thought. That man from Sulphur Creek had spoken the truth when telling how cold it sometimes got in the country. And he had laughed at him at the time! That showed one must not be too sure of things. There was no mistake about it, it *was* cold. He strode up and down, stamping his feet and threshing his arms, until reassured by the returning warmth. Then he got out matches and proceeded to make a fire. From the undergrowth, where high water of the previous spring had lodged a supply of seasoned twigs, he got his firewood. Working carefully from a small beginning, he soon had a roaring fire, over which he thawed the ice from his face and in the protection of which he ate his biscuits. For the moment the cold of space was outwitted. The dog took satisfaction in the fire, stretching out close enough for warmth and far enough away to escape being singed.

When the man had finished, he filled his pipe and took his com- 16 fortable time over a smoke. Then he pulled on his mittens, settled the ear flaps of his cap firmly about his ears, and took the creek trail up the left fork. The dog was disappointed and yearned back toward the fire. This man did not know cold. Possibly all the generations of his ancestry had been ignorant of cold, of real cold, of cold one hundred and seven degrees below freezing point. But the dog knew; all its ancestry knew, and it had inherited the knowledge. And it knew that it was not good to walk abroad in such fearful cold. It was the time to lie snug in a hole in the snow and wait for a curtain of cloud to be drawn across the face of outer space whence this cold came. On the other hand, there was no keen intimacy between the dog and the man. The one was the toil slave of the other, and the only caresses it had ever received were the caresses of the whip lash and of harsh and menacing throat sounds that threatened the whip lash. So the dog made no effort to communicate its apprehension to the man. It was not concerned in the welfare of the man; it was for its own sake that it yearned back toward the fire. But the man whistled, and spoke to it with the sound of whip lashes, and the dog swung in at the man's heels and followed after.

The man took a chew of tobacco and proceeded to start a new amber 17 beard. Also, his moist breath quickly powdered with white his mustache, eyebrows, and lashes. There did not seem to be so many springs on the left fork of the Henderson, and for half an hour the man saw no signs of any. And then it happened. At a place where there were no signs, where the soft, unbroken snow seemed to advertise solidity beneath, the man broke through. It was not deep. He wet himself halfway to the knees before the floundered out to the firm crust.

He was angry, and cursed his luck aloud. He had hoped to get into [18] camp with the boys at six o'clock, and this would delay him an hour, for he would have to build a fire and dry out his footgear. This was imperative at that low temperature—he knew that much; and he turned aside to the bank, which he climbed. On top, tangled in the underbrush about the trunks of several small spruce trees, was a highwater deposit of dry firewood—sticks and twigs, principally, but also larger portions of seasoned branches and fine, dry, last year's grasses. He threw down several large pieces on top of the snow. This served for a foundation and prevented the young flame from drowning itself in the snow it otherwise would melt. The flame he got by touching a match to a small shred of birch bark that he took from his pocket. This burned even more readily than paper. Placing it on the foundation, he fed the young flame with wisps of dry grass and with the tiniest dry twigs.

He worked slowly and carefully, keenly aware of his danger. Grad- [19] ually, as the flame grew stronger, he increased the size of the twigs with which he fed it. He squatted in the snow, pulling the twigs out from their entanglement in the brush and feeding directly to the flame. He knew there must be no failure. When it is seventy-five below zero, a man must not fail in his first attempt to build a fire—that is, if his feet are wet. If his feet are dry, and he fails, he can run along the trail for half a mile and restore his circulation. But the circulation of wet and freezing feet cannot be restored by running when it is seventy-five below. No matter how fast he runs, the wet feet will freeze the harder.

All this the man knew. The old-timer on Sulphur Creek had told [20] him about it the previous fall, and now he was appreciating the advice. Already all sensation had gone out of his feet. To build the fire he had been forced to remove his mittens, and the fingers had quickly gone numb. His pace of four miles an hour had kept his heart pumping blood to the surface of his body and to all the extremities. But the instant he stopped, the action of the pump eased down. The cold of space smote the unprotected tip of the planet, and he, being on that unprotected tip, received the full force of the blow. The blood of his body recoiled before it. The blood was alive, like the dog, and like the dog it wanted to hide away and cover itself up from the fearful cold. So long as he walked four miles an hour, he pumped the blood, willy-nilly, to the surface; but now it ebbed away and sank down into the recesses of his body. The extremities were the first to feel its absence. His wet feet froze the faster, and his exposed fingers numbed the faster, though they had not yet begun to freeze. Nose and cheeks were already freezing, while the skin of all his body chilled as it lost its blood.

But he was safe. Toes and nose and cheeks would be only touched 21 by the frost, for the fire was beginning to burn with strength. He was feeding it with twigs the size of his finger. In another minute he would be able to feed it with branches the size of his wrist, and then he could remove his wet footgear, and, while it dried, he could keep his naked feet warm by the fire, rubbing them at first, of course, with snow. The fire was a success. He was safe. He remembered the advice of the old-timer on Sulphur Creek, and smiled. The old-timer had been very serious in laying down the law that no man must travel alone in the Klondike after fifty below. Well, here he was; he had had the accident; he was alone; and he had saved himself. Those old-timers were rather womanish, some of them, he thought. All a man had to do was to keep his head, and he was all right. Any man who was a man could travel alone. But it was surprising, the rapidity with which his cheeks and nose were freezing. And he had not thought his fingers could go lifeless in so short a time. Lifeless they were, for he could scarcely make them move together to grip a twig, and they seemed remote from his body and from him. When he touched a twig, he had to look and see whether or not he had hold of it. The wires were pretty well down between him and his finger ends.

All of which counted for little. There was the fire, snapping and 22 crackling and promising life with every dancing flame. He started to untie his moccasins. They were coated with ice; the thick German socks were like sheaths of iron halfway to the knees; and the moccasin strings were like rods of steel all twisted and knotted as by some conflagration. For a moment he tugged with his numb fingers, then, realizing the folly of it, he drew his sheath knife.

But before he could cut the strings, it happened. It was his own fault 23 or, rather, his mistake. He should not have built the fire under the spruce tree. He should have built it in the open. But it had been easier to pull the twigs from the brush and drop them directly on the fire. Now the tree under which he had done this carried a weight of snow on its boughs. No wind had blown for weeks, and each bough was fully freighted. Each time he had pulled a twig he had communicated a slight agitation to the tree—an imperceptible agitation, so far as he was concerned, but an agitation sufficient to bring about the disaster. High up in the tree one bough capsized its load of snow. This fell on the boughs beneath, capsizing them. This process continued, spreading out and involving the whole tree. It grew like an avalanche, and it descended without warning upon the man and the fire, and the fire was blotted out! Where it had burned was a mantle of fresh and disordered snow.

The man was shocked. It was as though he had just heard his own 24 sentence of death. For a moment he sat and stared at the spot where the fire had been. Then he grew very calm. Perhaps the old-timer on Sulphur Creek was right. If he had only had a trail mate he would have been in no danger now. The trail mate could have built the fire. Well, it was up to him to build the fire over again, and this second time there must be no failure. Even if he succeeded, he would most likely lose some toes. His feet must be badly frozen by now, and there would be some time before the second fire was ready.

Such were his thoughts, but he did not sit and think them. He was 25 busy all the time they were passing through his mind. He made a new foundation for a fire, this time in the open, where no treacherous tree could blot it out. Next he gathered dry grasses and tiny twigs from the highwater flotsam. He could not bring his fingers together to pull them out, but he was able to gather them by the handful. In this way he got many rotten twigs and bits of green moss that were undesirable, but it was the best he could do. He worked methodically, even collecting an armful of the larger branches to be used later when the fire gathered strength. And all the while the dog sat and watched him, a certain yearning wistfulness in its eyes, for it looked upon him as the fire provider, and the fire was slow in coming.

When all was ready, the man reached in his pocket for a second 26 piece of birch bark. He knew the bark was there, and, though he could not feel it with his fingers, he could hear its crisp rustling as he fumbled for it. Try as he would, he could not clutch hold of it. And all the time, in his consciousness, was the knowledge that each instant his feet were freezing. This thought tended to put him in a panic, but he fought against it and kept calm. He pulled on his mittens with his teeth, and threshed his arms back and forth, beating his hands with all his might against his sides. He did this sitting down, and he stood up to do it; and all the while the dog sat in the snow, its wolf brush of a tail curled around warmly over its forefeet, its sharp wolf ears pricked forward intently as it watched the man. And the man, as he beat and threshed with his arms and hands, felt a great surge of envy as he regarded the creature that was warm and secure in its natural covering.

After a time he was aware of the first faraway signals of sensations 27 in his beaten fingers. The faint tingling grew stronger till it evolved into a stinging ache that was excruciating, but which the man hailed with satisfaction. He stripped the mitten from his right hand and fetched forth the birch bark. The exposed fingers were quickly going numb again. Next he brought out his bunch of sulphur matches. But the tremendous cold had already driven the life out of his fingers. In his effort to separate one match from the others, the whole bunch fell in the snow. He tried to pick it out of the snow, but failed. The dead fingers could neither touch nor clutch. He was very careful. He drove the thought of his freezing feet, and nose, and cheeks, out of his mind, devoting his whole soul to the matches. He watched, using the sense of vision in place of that of touch, and when he saw his fingers on each side the bunch, he closed them—that is, he willed to close them, for the wires were down, and the fingers did not obey. He pulled the mitten on the right hand, and beat it fiercely against his knee. Then, with both mittened hands, he scooped the bunch of matches, along with much snow, into his lap. Yet he was no better off.

After some manipulation he managed to get the bunch between the 28 heels of his mittened hands. In this fashion he carried it to his mouth. The ice crackled and snapped when by a violent effort he opened his mouth. He drew the lower jaw in, curled the upper lip out of the way and scraped the bunch with his upper teeth in order to separate a match. He succeeded in getting one, which he dropped on his lap. He was no better off. He could not pick it up. Then he devised a way. He picked it up with his teeth and scratched it on his leg. Twenty times he scratched before he succeeded in lighting it. As it flamed he held it with his teeth to the birch bark. But the burning brimstone went up his nostrils and into his lungs, causing him to cough spasmodically. The match fell into the snow and went out.

The old-timer on Sulphur Creek was right, he thought in the mo- 29 ment of controlled despair that ensued: after fifty below, a man should travel with a partner. He beat his hands, but failed in exciting any sensation. Suddenly he bared both hands, removing the mittens with his teeth. He caught the whole bunch between the heels of his hands. His arm muscles not being frozen enabled him to press the hand heels tightly against the matches. Then he scratched the bunch along his leg. It flared into flame, seventy sulphur matches at once! There was no wind to blow them out. He kept his head to one side to escape the strangling fumes, and held the blazing bunch to the birch bark. As he so held it, he became aware of sensation in his hand. His flesh was burning. He could smell it. Deep down below the surface he could feel it. The sensation developed into pain that grew acute. And still he endured it, holding the flame of the matches clumsily to the bark that would not light readily because his own burning hands were in the way, absorbing most of the flame.

At last, when he could endure no more, he jerked his hands apart. 30 The blazing matches fell sizzling into the snow, but the birch bark was alight. He began laying dry grasses and the tiniest twigs on the flame. He could not pick and choose, for he had to lift the fuel between the heels of this hands. Small pieces of rotten wood and green moss clung to the twigs, and he bit them off as well as he could with his teeth. He cherished the flame carefully and awkwardly. It meant life, and it must not perish. The withdrawal of blood from the surface of his body now made him begin to shiver, and he grew more awkward. A large piece of green moss fell squarely on the little fire. He tried to poke it out with his fingers, but his shivering frame made him poke too far, and he disrupted the nucleus of the little fire, the burning grasses and the tiny twigs separating and scattering. He tried to poke them together again, but in spite of the tenseness of the effort, his shivering got away with him, and the twigs were hopelessly scattered. Each twig gushed a puff of smoke and went out. The fire provider had failed. As he looked apathetically about him, his eyes chanced on the dog, sitting across the ruins of the fire from him, in the snow, making restless, hunching movements, slightly lifting one forefoot and then the other, shifting its weight back and forth on them with wistful eagerness.

The sight of the dog put a wild idea into his head. He remembered [31] the tale of the man, caught in a blizzard, who killed a steer and crawled inside the carcass, and so was saved. He would kill the dog and bury his hands in the warm body until the numbness went out of them. Then he could build another fire. He spoke to the dog, calling it to him; but in his voice was a strange note of fear that frightened the animal, who had never known the man to speak in such way before. Something was the matter, and its suspicious nature sensed danger—it knew not what danger, but somewhere, somehow, in its brain arose an apprehension of the man. It flattened its ears down at the sound of the man's voice, and its restless, hunching movements and the liftings and shiftings of its forefeet became more pronounced; but it would not come to the man. He got on his hands and knees and crawled toward the dog. This unusual posture again excited suspicion, and the animal sidled mincingly away.

The man sat up in the snow for a moment and struggled for calm- [32] ness. Then he pulled on his mittens, by means of his teeth, and got upon his feet. He glanced down at first in order to assure himself that he was really standing up, for the absence of sensation in his feet left him unrelated to the earth. His erect position in itself started to drive the webs of suspicion from the dog's mind; and when he spoke peremptorily, with the sound of whip lashes in his voice, the dog rendered its customary allegiance and came to him. As it came within reaching distance, the man lost his control. His arms flashed out to the dog, and he experienced genuine surprise when he discovered that his hands could not clutch, that there was neither bend nor feeling in the fingers. He had forgotten for the moment that they were frozen and that they were freezing more and more. All this happened quickly, and before the animal could get away, he encircled its body with his arms. He sat down in the snow, and in this fashion held the dog, while it snarled and whined and struggled.

But it was all he could do, hold its body encircled in his arms and sit [33] there. He realized that he could not kill the dog. There was no way to do it. With his helpless hands he could neither draw nor hold his sheath knife nor throttle the animal. He released it, and it plunged wildly away, with tail between its legs, and still snarling. It halted forty feet away and surveyed him curiously, with ears sharply pricked forward.

The man looked down at his hands in order to locate them, and [34] found them hanging on the ends of his arms. It struck him as curious that one should have to use his eyes in order to find out where his hands were. He began threshing his arms back and forth, beating the mittened hands against his sides. He did this for five minutes, violently, and his heart pumped enough blood up to the surface to put a stop to his shivering. But no sensation was aroused in the hands. He had an impression that they hung like weights on the ends of his arms, but when he tried to run the impression down, he could not find it.

A certain fear of death, dull and oppressive, came to him. This fear [35] quickly became poignant as he realized that it was no longer a mere matter of freezing his fingers and toes, or of losing his hands and feet, but that it was a matter of life and death with the chances against him. This threw him into a panic, and he turned and ran up the creek bed along the old, dim trail. The dog joined in behind and kept up with him. He ran blindly, without intention, in fear such as he had never known in his life. Slowly, as he plowed and floundered through the snow, he began to see things again—the banks of the creek, the old timber jams, the leafless aspens, and the sky. The running made him feel better. He did not shiver. Maybe, if he ran on, his feet would thaw out; and, anyway, if he ran far enough, he would reach camp and the boys. Without doubt he would lose some fingers and toes and some of his face; but the boys would take care of him, and save the rest of him when he got there. And at the same time there was another thought in his mind that said he would never get to the camp and the boys; that he would soon be stiff and dead. This thought he kept in the background and refused to consider. Sometimes it pushed itself forward and demanded to be heard, but he thrust it back and strove to think of other things.

It struck him as curious that he could run at all on feet so frozen that [36] he could not feel them when they struck the earth and took the weight of his body. He seemed to himself to skim along above the surface, and to have no connection with the earth. Somewhere he had once seen a winged Mercury, and he wondered if Mercury felt as he felt when skimming over the earth.

His theory of running until he reached camp and the boys had one [37] flaw in it: he lacked the endurance. Several times he stumbled, and finally he tottered, crumpled up, and fell. When he tried to rise, he failed. He must sit and rest, he decided, and next time he would merely walk and keep on going. As he sat and regained his breath, he noted that he was feeling quite warm and comfortable. He was not shivering, and it even seemed that a warm glow had come to his chest and trunk. And yet, when he touched his nose and cheeks, there was no sensation. Running would not thaw them out. Nor would it thaw out his hands and feet. Then the thought came to him that the frozen portions of his body must be extending. He tried to keep this thought down, to forget it, to think of something else; he was aware of the panicky feeling that it caused, and he was afraid of the panic. But the thought asserted itself, and persisted, until it produced a vision of his body totally frozen. This was too much, and he made another wild run along the trail. Once he slowed down to a walk, but the thought of the freezing extending itself made him run again.

And all the time the dog ran with him, at his heels. When he fell [38] down a second time, it curled its tail over its forefeet and sat in front of him, facing him, curiously eager and intent. The warmth and security of the animal angered him, and he cursed it till it flattened down its ears appeasingly. This time the shivering came more quickly upon the man. He was losing in his battle with the frost. It was creeping into his body from all sides. The thought of it drove him on, but he ran no more than a hundred feet, when he staggered and pitched headlong. It was his last panic. When he had recovered his breath and control, he sat up and entertained in his mind the conception of meeting death with dignity. However, the conception did not come to him in such terms. His idea of it was that he had been making a fool of himself, running around like a chicken with its head cut off—such was the simile that occurred to him. Well, he was bound to freeze anyway, and he might as well take it decently. With this newfound peace of mind came the first glimmerings of drowsiness. A good idea, he thought, to sleep off to death. It was like taking an anesthetic. Freezing was not so bad as people thought. There were lots worse ways to die.

He pictured the boys finding his body next day. Suddenly he found [39] himself with them, coming along the trail and looking for himself. And, still with them, he came around a turn in the trail and found himself lying in the snow. He did not belong with himself any more, for even then he was out of himself, standing with the boys and looking at himself in the snow. It certainly was cold, was his thought. When he got back to the States he could tell the folks what real cold was. He drifted on from this to a vision of the old-timer on Sulphur Creek. He could see him quite clearly, warm and comfortable, and smoking a pipe.

"You were right, old hoss; you were right," the man mumbled to the [40] old-timer of Sulphur Creek.

Then the man drowsed off into what seemed to him the most com- [41] fortable and satisfying sleep he had ever known. The dog sat facing him and waiting. The brief day drew to a close in a long, slow twilight. There were no signs of a fire to be made, and, besides, never in the dog's experience had it known a man to sit like that in the snow and make no fire. As the twilight drew on, its eager yearning for the fire mastered it, and with a great lifting and shifting of forefeet, it whined softly, then flattened its ears down in anticipation of being chidden by the man. But the man remained silent. Later the dog whined loudly. And still later it crept close to the man and caught the scent of death. This made the animal bristle and back away. A little longer it delayed, howling under the stars that leaped and danced and shone brightly in the cold sky. Then it turned and trotted up the trail in the direction of the camp it knew, where were the other food providers and fire providers.

Responding to Reading

1. How would you describe the story's view of the natural world? Have you ever felt this way about nature? If so, under what circumstances?
2. What effect do the story's repetitive, almost monotonous style and the narrator's matter-of-fact tone have on you? How do these elements affect your reaction to the story?
3. Does the man ever have a chance, or is he doomed from the start? How does his attitude toward nature help determine his fate?

TRAVELING THROUGH THE DARK

William Stafford

William Stafford (1914–1993), a plain-talking poet of the western United States, was born in Hutchinson, Kansas, and earned an undergraduate degree from the University of Kansas and a doctorate from the University of Iowa. Although his poems hint at moral judgments, Stafford generally kept apart from trends and politics, following his own impulses. He once said that writing is like fishing in that the writer must be willing to fail. Some of his many collections of verse are *Allegiances* (1970), *The Design of the Oriole* (1977), and *An Oregon Message* (1987). From *Stories That Could Be True* (1960) comes his poem "Traveling through the Dark," about an encounter between nature and technology.

Traveling through the dark I found a deer
dead on the edge of the Wilson River road.
It is usually best to roll them into the canyon:
that road is narrow; to swerve might make more dead.

By glow of the tail-light I stumbled back of the car   5
and stood by the heap, a doe, a recent killing;
she had stiffened already, almost cold.
I dragged her off; she was large in the belly.

My fingers touching her side brought me the reason—
her side was warm; her fawn lay there waiting,   10
alive, still, never to be born.
Beside that mountain road I hesitated.

The car aimed ahead its lowered parking lights;
under the hood purred the steady engine.
I stood in the glare of the warm exhaust turning red;   15
around our group I could hear the wilderness listen.

I thought hard for us all—my only swerving—
then pushed her over the edge into the river.

Responding to Reading

1. In line 3 the speaker says, "It is usually best to roll them into the canyon." What information does this statement give you? Does it make it easier or more difficult to explain the speaker's initial hesitation? To understand his final action?
2. How does each of the following statements reveal the speaker's view of nature?
   - "Beside that mountain road I hesitated" (10)
   - "I could hear the wilderness listen" (16)
   - "I thought hard for us all" (17)
3. What meaning does the word *swerve* have in line 4? In line 17? Does "traveling through the dark" mean more to you than the fact that the encounter between man and deer took place at night? Explain.

WRITING

Earth in the Balance

1. Many writers, such as Hans Koning and Barry Lopez, believe that contact with nature has a beneficial effect on people, serving as a retreat from the pressures of civilization or helping to restore a lost innocence. Write an essay in which you describe the positive effects of nature on your life.

2. Appletree Rodden discusses one way in which the environment can be preserved. Write an essay in which you discuss how a specific change in governmental policy, social behavior, or industrial policy could improve the environment.

3. Reread one of the essays in this chapter. Then, write a letter to its author in which you argue against his or her position. Make sure you address the specific points the author makes in his or her essay, and support your position with references to your own observations and experiences.

4. The introduction to this chapter mentions a theme that is prevalent in much nature writing: the idea that human beings have somehow become separated from the natural world. Do you feel alienated from nature? How do you try to maintain a connection to the natural world? How successful are your attempts? If you like, you may also consider how some of the writers in this chapter attempt to maintain a connection with nature.

5. What responsibility do you believe each individual has for doing his or her part to save the planet? As you answer this question, you may consider what in particular is worth saving in the natural world and what forces you see as working to destroy it.

6. In "Our Animal Rites" Anna Quindlen makes an effort to confront nature on its own terms. Ultimately she fails, describing the bear in human terms and imagining what the bear would say if it could talk. Write an essay in which you objectively describe an animal, a place, or an environment. Make sure the picture you create does not include your subjective reactions or any descriptions that romanticize or humanize your subject.

7. E. M. Forster in "My Wood" seems to have a definite opinion about owning property. Summarize Forster's views and discuss in what ways they are or are not consistent with your own.

8. In "To Build a Fire" Jack London implies that nature, if not respected, can turn on human beings. What situations have you experi-

enced that called for you to meet a challenge in the natural world? How did you react?

9. Chief Seattle says that one day the white man will "suffocate in [his] own waste" (5). Write a letter from Al Gore to Chief Seattle in which you agree or disagree with this statement. Be specific, and refer to both essays.

10. In "Is a Tree Worth a Life?" Sally Thane Christensen says, "Given a choice between trees or people, people must prevail" (11). In "Our Animal Rites," Anna Quindlen says that human beings are interlopers on land owned by animals. And in "If Bosnians Were Whales" (Chapter 10), Meir Shalev says that if Bosnians were whales, the world would quickly come to their rescue. Write an essay in which you consider whether the welfare of plants or animals should ever take precedence over the welfare of human beings. Support your points with references to Christensen's, Quindlen's, and Shalev's essays as well as to any other essay in this chapter.

10
~

MAKING
CHOICES

Student Voices

"Making choices can be a very difficult thing to do, especially for a child or young adult. When adults make decisions, they have to think about what's best for them. When kids make decisions, they have to decide what's best for them and what will make their parents happy and proud—although it should be just what makes them happy. But when you're a kid or young adult, you want to make everyone else happy first. When you make the wrong choice, you are miserable. So making choices at this stage in life can be the most difficult thing you can do."

—*Kurt Banfi*

"Deciding whether to immigrate to the United States was the most complicated problem I have ever had. On one side of the scale was twenty years of life in a known and understood society with a pretty much predictable future; on the other, an unknown country with a different lifestyle, traditions, and language but offering a slim chance to make my life meaningful and to change my life through my abilities. I guess I just took a chance, which I have never regretted."

—*Gennadiy Levit*

"In my job, it seems as if no day is complete unless a difficult choice arises. As the budget officer for the student Programming Association, I am constantly faced with decisions about who to hire for a concert, lecture, or comedy event. Most recently, a vote was taken on whether or not to hire an alternative rock group to perform. Two factors went through my mind during the meeting: the cost and whether students would come and enjoy the event. Given the popularity of the group, I thought having students come out and enjoy the event outweighed the cost involved. I voted in favor of the concert. The show went off very well, but the number of students who attended was below what we expected. Still, I was glad to have been able to make that type of decision."

—*Michael Karam*

"Currently my daily habits are fairly regular and well established. The only choices that I make on a daily basis are what to wear and what to have for dinner. One of my more pressing choices is, 'Should I get a newer, more reliable car, or should I save my money?'"

—*Robert Barr*

"Until recently I lived a very sheltered life, thanks to my parents. All my choices and decisions were handled by them until I moved away to school. Now, most of the choices I make on a day-to-day basis deal with priorities in my life. For example, as a student athlete my first choice comes at 5AM: whether or not to get out of my warm bed and head down to the gym for swimming practice. If I take the easy way out and stay in bed, I will have many consequences to deal with. Other choices involve deciding whether to go to class or not, whether to drink at a party, and whether to say "No" to going out."

—*Natalie Chepelevich*

"Part of being responsible for our actions is knowing what our choices are and living with our decisions. Choosing to hit the snooze alarm can send shock waves through the rest of your life."

—*Matt Steigerwalt*

--------------------- **Preparing to Read and Write** ---------------------

As Robert Frost suggests in his poem, "The Road Not Taken" (p. 796), making choices is fundamental to our lives. The ability—and, in fact, the need—to make complex decisions is part of what characterizes us as human. On a practical level, we choose friends, mates, careers, and places to live. On a more theoretical level, we struggle to make the really important choices: the moral and ethical decisions that people have struggled with for thousands of years.

Many times complex questions have no easy answers; occasionally, they have no answers at all. For example, should we stand up to authority even if our stand puts us at risk? Should we help less fortunate individuals if such help weakens our own social or economic position? Should we act to save an endangered species if that action may put people out of work? Should we tell the truth even if the truth may hurt us— or hurt someone else? Which road should we take, the easy one or the hard one?

Most of the time, the choice we (and the writers whose works appear in this chapter) face is the same: to act or not to act. To make a decision, we must understand both the long- and short-term consequences of acting in a particular way or of choosing not to act. We must struggle with the possibility of compromise, and with the possibility of making a morally or ethically objectionable decision. And, perhaps most important, we must learn to take responsibility for our decisions.

As you read and prepare to write about the selections in this chapter, you may consider the following questions.

- On what specific choice or choices does the selection focus? Is the decision to be made moral? Ethical? Political?

- Does the writer introduce a **dilemma**, a choice between two equally problematic alternatives?

- Does the choice the writer presents apply only to one specific situation or case, or does it also have a wider application?

- Is the writer emotionally involved with the issue he or she is discussing? Does this involvement (or lack of involvement) make the selection more or less convincing?

- What social, political, or religious ideas influence the writer? How can you tell? Are these ideas similar to or different from your own views?

- Does the decision under discussion cause the writer to examine his or her own values? The values of others? The values of the society at large? Does the selection lead you to examine your own values?

- Does the writer offer a solution? Do you find it reasonable?

- What choice or choices do you believe should be made? Why?
- Which writers' views seem most alike? Which seem most at odds?

If Bosnians Were Whales

Meir Shalev

Jerusalem-based Israeli writer Meir Shalev is a journalist as well as the author of novels for both adults and children. Among his works that have been translated and published in the United States are the Israeli bestseller *The Blue Mountain* (1991); a story for young adults, *My Father Always Embarrasses Me* (1991); and his most recent novel, *Esau* (1994). The following essay was written for *Yedioth Aharonot,* an Israeli newspaper; it was later translated from the Hebrew by Marsha Weinstein and appeared on the op-ed page of the *New York Times* in 1992. In it Shalev turns a bemused eye on Americans' sympathetic obsession with the plight of whales and dolphins and suggests that if the Bosnian people in war-torn Yugoslavia were seen as a similarly endangered species of mammal, then perhaps greater U.S. efforts would be undertaken to save them.

Wherever I go, I always visit the zoo. That's where I get my pre- [1] conceived notions about the human race.

Not long ago, I visited a marine zoo, the aquarium of Baltimore. The [2] place was lavish and attractive, full of sharks, octopuses, eels and many other fish and varieties of marine life that I did not recognize at first, since they look so different on the grill. The aquarium's planners had obviously realized that a few of the exhibits would whet appetites, for despite the adage "no talking of charcoal in the sheep pen," here and there they'd placed mouth-watering gastronomic descriptions of seafoods.

Unlike sea bass and flounder, swordfish and lobster, there are some [3] sea creatures whose flesh Americans refuse to consider edible. In the U.S., quoting the recipe for whale steak from "Moby Dick" is like offering ham braised in butter to a Jew on Yom Kippur. A proud Baltimorean, (her mouth stuffed with clams) recently told me of a whale that had drifted too close to shore. It was immediately fished out, resuscitated and flown—at taxpayers' expense—to the Baltimore Aquarium, where it underwent extensive medical treatment, including psychological rehabilitation.

Anyone who remembers the whale stuck off Alaska a few years   4
back that had to be freed by an icebreaker and several million dollars
will find it difficult to shake the feeling that whales have simply learned
to know a sucker when they see one.

My visit to the aquarium ended with the dolphin pool. The trainers   5
talked to us about the social lives of marine mammals (most complex),
about their emotional virtues (they are full of love) and especially about
their astonishing intelligence. The brain of the dolphin, for those who
don't yet know it, is larger, more complex and, in particular, deeper than
the Silly Putty found in the human cranium.

Indeed, while we stupid land mammals sat in the bleachers munch-   6
ing popcorn, these gifted marine mammals were performing complex
somersaults in midair. Then we were told that dolphins have highly sophisticated "communications systems." As proof, one of them let out a
few shrill shrieks for a reward of two mackerel. (The mackerel, as we all
know, is not a marine mammal, but a fish and may therefore be eaten.)

We next heard a diatribe against the cruel Japanese tuna fisherman   7
who trap and kill innocent dolphins in their nets. We released a collective moan. It seems that the dolphins have better P.R. people than the
tuna: No one asked why it's O.K. to kill tuna.

At the end of my visit, I made a donation to save the dugong[1] and   8
the rain forests and then hurried back to my host's house to watch a
movie about the large primates of Africa on the Discovery Channel. It
was nice. Especially the end. As a gorilla vanished into the bush, the narrator said, "We have to make this world a better place for the mountain
gorilla."

Then he, too, vanished, never realizing that with these words he had   9
articulated the solution to the problem of U.S. intervention in Bosnia. It
would, after all, be a bit difficult to convince the public that the Bosnians are marine mammals. But if it were possible to convince them that
they are a land species in danger of extinction—a fact not far from the
truth—then it might be possible to make this world a better place for the
Bosnians, too.

News reports haven't helped the Bosnians. Or the Somalians. Amer-   10
icans have no energy for yet more images of murder, suffering and torture. If I were the leader of the Bosnians, I would kick all the news teams
out of Sarajevo and invite the guys from "Survival" to make a nature
film about my people. A documentary about the domestic habits of the
Bosnians, their mating dances, territorial marking practices, the way
they hollow out their lairs, would do the trick.

For a conclusion, the narrator could read: "Only a short time ago,   11
millions of Bosnians grazed the mountainsides of Yugoslavia. Now,

---

[1] An aquatic mammal, also known as the sea cow. [Eds.]

only a scant few remain. We have to make this world a better place for the Bosnians." Then, and only then, would the world awaken.

Responding to Reading

1. What do you think Shalev is suggesting when he says, "whales have simply learned to know a sucker when they see one" (4)? Whom does he imply are the suckers? Do you think he is overly cynical about humans' efforts to protect animals?
2. In paragraph 9 Shalev states the main point of his essay—that "if it were possible to convince [the public] that [Bosnians] are a land species in danger of extinction . . . then it might be possible to make this world a better place for the Bosnians, too." Do you think he is serious? Do you think he is right?
3. Although he does not say so in so many words, Shalev seems to be suggesting that some people—in particular many Americans—tend to feel more sympathy for animals than for fellow human beings. Do you agree with him?

THE DEER AT PROVIDENCIA

Annie Dillard

Known as a naturalist and essayist, Annie Dillard (1945–) won the Pulitzer Prize in 1974 for her first book, *Pilgrim at Tinker Creek,* a nonfiction work in which she records her explorations in the Roanoke Valley of Virginia. Dillard calls herself a "stalker" of nature and its mysteries and delights in both the wonders and terrors it inspires. She contributes to periodicals, such as *Harper's* and the *Atlantic Monthly,* and has also written *Teaching a Stone to Talk* (1982), *An American Childhood* (1987), *The Writing Life* (1989), and a novel, *The Living* (1992). In "The Deer at Providencia," first published in 1982, Dillard moves the setting away from familiar territory to Ecuador. Her critically observant eye is at work as she describes a captured deer, whose "skin looked virtually hairless, . . . almost translucent, like a membrane." Then Dillard deftly turns to a consideration of the paradoxical nature of suffering.

There were four of us North Americans in the jungle, in the Ecuadorian jungle on the banks of the Napo River in the Amazon watershed. The other three North Americans were metropolitan men. We stayed in tents in one riverside village, and visited others. At the village called Providencia we saw a sight which moved us, and which shocked the men.

The first thing we saw when we climbed the riverbank to the village   2
of Providencia was the deer. It was roped to a tree on the grass clearing
near the thatch shelter where we would eat lunch.

The deer was small, about the size of a whitetail fawn, but appar-   3
ently full-grown. It had a rope around its neck and three feet caught in
the rope. Someone said that the dogs had caught it that morning and the
villagers were going to cook and eat it that night.

This clearing lay at the edge of the little thatched-hut village. We   4
could see the villagers going about their business, scattering feed corn
for hens about their houses, and wandering down paths to the river to
bathe. The village headman was our host; he stood beside us as we
watched the deer struggle. Several village boys were interested in the
deer; they formed part of the circle we made around it in the clearing.
So also did four businessmen from Quito[1] who were attempting to
guide us around the jungle. Few of the very different people standing in
this circle had a common language. We watched the deer, and no one
said much.

The deer lay on its side at the rope's very end, so the rope lacked   5
slack to let it rest its head in the dust. It was "pretty," delicate of bone
like all deer, and thin-skinned for the tropics. Its skin looked virtually
hairless, in fact, and almost translucent, like a membrane. Its neck was
no thicker than my wrist; it was rubbed open on the rope, and gashed.
Trying to paw itself free of the rope, the deer had scratched its own neck
with its hooves. The raw underside of its neck showed red stripes and
some bruises bleeding inside the muscles. Now three of its feet were
hooked in the rope under its jaw. It could not stand, of course, on one
leg, so it could not move to slacken the rope and ease the pull on its
throat and enable it to rest its head.

Repeatedly the deer paused, motionless, its eyes veiled, with only its   6
rib cage in motion, and its breaths the only sound. Then, after I would
think, "It has given up; now it will die," it would heave. The rope
twanged; the tree leaves clattered; the deer's free foot beat the ground.
We stepped back and held our breaths. It thrashed, kicking, but only one
leg moved; the other three legs tightened inside the rope's loop. Its hip
jerked; its spine shook. Its eyes rolled; its tongue, thick with spittle,
pushed in and out. Then it would rest again. We watched this for fifteen
minutes.

Once three young native boys charged in, released its trapped legs,   7
and jumped back to the circle of people. But instantly the deer scratched
up its neck with its hooves and snared its forelegs in the rope again. It
was easy to imagine a third and then a fourth leg soon stuck, like Brer
Rabbit and the Tar Baby.

---

[1] Capital of Ecuador. [Eds.]

We watched the deer from the circle, and then we drifted on to   8
lunch. Our palm-roofed shelter stood on a grassy promontory from
which we could see the deer tied to the tree, pigs and hens walking
under village houses, and black-and-white cattle standing in the river.
There was even a breeze.

Lunch, which was the second and better lunch we had that day, was   9
hot and fried. There was a big fish called *doncella,* a kind of catfish,
dipped whole in corn flour and beaten egg, then deep fried. With our
fingers we pulled soft fragments of it from its sides to our plates, and ate;
it was delicate fish-flesh, fresh and mild. Someone found the roe, and I
ate of that too—it was fat and stronger, like egg yolk, naturally enough,
and warm.

There was also a stew of meat in shreds with rice and pale brown   10
gravy. I had asked what kind of deer it was tied to the tree; Pepe had answered in Spanish, *"Gama."* Now they told us this was *gama* too, stewed.
I suspect the word means merely game or venison. At any rate, I heard
that the village dogs had cornered another deer just yesterday, and it
was this deer which we were now eating in full sight of the whole article. It was good. I was surprised at its tenderness. But it is a fact that high
levels of lactic acid, which builds up in muscle tissues during exertion,
tenderizes.

After the fish and meat we ate bananas fried in chunks and served   11
on a tray; they were sweet and full of flavor. I felt terrific. My shirt was
wet and cool from swimming; I had had a night's sleep, two decent
walks, three meals, and a swim—everything tasted good. From time to
time each one of us, separately, would look beyond our shaded roof to
the sunny spot where the deer was still convulsing in the dust. Our meal
completed, we walked around the deer and back to the boats.

That night I learned that while we were watching the deer, the oth-   12
ers were watching me.

We four North Americans grew close in the jungle in a way that was   13
not the usual artificial intimacy of travelers. We liked each other. We
stayed up all that night talking, murmuring, as though we rocked on
hammocks slung above time. The others were from big cities: New York,
Washington, Boston. They all said that I had no expression on my face
when I was watching the deer—or at any rate, not the expression they
expected.

They had looked to see how I, the only woman, and the youngest,   14
was taking the sight of the deer's struggles. I looked detached, apparently, or hard, or calm, or focused, still. I don't know. I was thinking. I
remember feeling very old and energetic. I could say like Thoreau that
I have traveled widely in Roanoke, Virginia.[2] I have thought a great deal

---

[2] In *Walden* Henry David Thoreau (see p. 713) says, "I have traveled a good deal in Concord." [Eds.]

about carnivorousness; I eat meat. These things are not issues; they are mysteries.

Gentlemen of the city, what surprises you? That there is suffering [15] here, or that I know it?

We lay in the tent and talked, "If it had been my wife," one man said [16] with special vigor, amazed, "she wouldn't have cared *what* was going on; she would have dropped *everything* right at that moment and gone in the village from here to there to there, she would not have *stopped* until that animal was out of its suffering one way or another. She couldn't *bear* to see a creature in agony like that."

I nodded. [17]

Now I am home. When I wake I comb my hair before the mirror [18] above my dresser. Every morning for the past two years I have seen in that mirror, beside my sleep-softened face, the blackened face of a burnt man. It is a wire-service photograph clipped from a newspaper and taped to my mirror. The caption reads: "Alan McDonald in Miami hospital bed." All you can see in the photograph is a smudged triangle of face from his eyelids to his lower lip; the rest is bandages. You cannot see the expression in his eyes; the bandages shade them.

The story, headed MAN BURNED FOR SECOND TIME, begins: [19]

> "Why does God hate me?" Alan McDonald asked from his hospital bed.
>
> "When the gunpowder went off, I couldn't believe it," he said. "I just couldn't believe it. I said, 'No, God couldn't do this to me again.'"

He was in a burn ward in Miami, in serious condition. I do not even know if he lived. I wrote him a letter at the time, cringing.

He had been burned before, thirteen years previously, by flaming [20] gasoline. For years he had been having his body restored and his face remade in dozens of operations. He had been a boy, and then a burnt boy. He had already been stunned by what could happen, by how life could veer.

Once I read that people who survive bad burns tend to go crazy; [21] they have a very high suicide rate. Medicine cannot ease their pain; drugs just leak away, soaking the sheets, because there is no skin to hold them in. The people just lie there and weep. Later they kill themselves. They had not known, before they were burned, that the world included such suffering, that life could permit them personally such pain.

This time a bowl of gunpowder had exploded on McDonald. [22]

> "I didn't realize what had happened at first," he recounted. "And then I heard that sound from 13 years ago. I was burning. I rolled to put the fire out and I thought, 'Oh God, not again.'
>
> "If my friend hadn't been there, I would have jumped into a canal with a rock around my neck."

His wife concludes the piece, "Man, it just isn't fair."

I read the whole clipping again every morning. This is the Big Time 23 here, every minute of it. Will someone please explain to Alan McDonald in his dignity, to the deer at Providencia in his dignity, what is going on? And mail me the carbon.

When we walked by the deer at Providencia for the last time, I said 24 to Pepe, with a pitying glance at the deer, "*Pobrecito*"—"poor little thing." But I was trying out Spanish. I knew at the time it was a ridiculous thing to say.

Responding to Reading

1. Do you believe Dillard could have done anything to free the deer? Why do you think she chose to do nothing? Does she seem to regret her decision not to act? Do you think she *should* regret it?
2. In paragraph 14 Dillard says, "I have thought a great deal about carnivorousness; I eat meat. These things are not issues; they are mysteries." What does she mean? Do you find this statement to be a satisfactory explanation for her ability to eat and enjoy deer meat while she watches the trapped deer "convulsing in the dust" (11)? Why or why not?
3. What connection does Dillard see between Alan McDonald and the deer at Providencia? Do you see this as a valid, logical association, or do you believe Dillard has exploited (or even invented) a connection?

SHOOTING AN ELEPHANT

George Orwell

This detailed account of a cruel incident with an elephant in Burma is George Orwell's (see also p. 231) most powerful criticism of imperialism and the impossible position of British police officers—himself among them—in the colonies. Orwell says about the incident, "It was perfectly clear to me what I ought to do," but then he thinks of "the watchful yellow faces behind," and he realizes that his choice is not so simple.

In Moulmein, in lower Burma, I was hated by large numbers of people—the only time in my life that I have been important enough for this to happen to me. I was sub-divisional police officer of the town, and in an aimless, petty kind of way anti-European feeling was very bitter. No one had the guts to raise a riot, but if a European woman went through the bazaars alone somebody would probably spit betel juice over her dress. As a police officer I was an obvious target and was baited whenever it seemed safe to do so. When a nimble Burman tripped me up on the football field and the referee (another Burman) looked the other way, the crowd yelled with hideous laughter. This happened more than once. In the end the sneering yellow faces of young men that met me everywhere, the insults hooted after me when I was at a safe distance, got badly on my nerves. The young Buddhist priests were the worst of all. There were several thousands of them in the town and none of them seemed to have anything to do except stand on street corners and jeer at Europeans.

All this was perplexing and upsetting. For at that time I had already made up my mind that imperialism was an evil thing and the sooner I chucked up my job and got out of it the better. Theoretically—and secretly, of course—I was all for the Burmese and all against their oppressors, the British. As for the job I was doing, I hated it more bitterly than I can perhaps make clear. In a job like that you see the dirty work of Empire at close quarters. The wretched prisoners huddling in the stinking cages of the lock-ups, the grey, cowed faces of the long-term convicts, the scarred buttocks of the men who had been flogged with bamboos—all these oppressed me with an intolerable sense of guilt. But I could get nothing into perspective. I was young and ill-educated and I had had to think out my problems in the utter silence that is imposed on every Englishman in the East. I did not even know that the British Empire is dying, still less did I know that it is a great deal better than the younger empires that are going to supplant it.[1] All I knew was that I was stuck between my hatred of the empire I served and my rage against the evil-spirited little beasts who tried to make my job impossible. With one part of my mind I thought of the British Raj[2] as an unbreakable tyranny, as something clamped down, in *saecula saeculorum*,[3] upon the will of prostrate peoples; with another part I thought that the greatest joy in the world would be to drive a bayonet into a Buddhist priest's guts. Feelings like these are the normal by-products of imperialism; ask any Anglo-Indian official, if you can catch him off duty.

One day something happened which in a roundabout way was enlightening. It was a tiny incident in itself, but it gave me a better glimpse than I had had before of the real nature of imperialism—the real motives for which despotic governments act. Early one morning the sub-inspector at a police station the other end of the town rang me up on the phone and said that an elephant was ravaging the bazaar.

---

[1] This essay was written in 1936, three years before the start of World War II; Stalin and Hitler were in power. [Eds.]

[2] Sovereignty. [Eds.]

[3] From time immemorial. [Eds.]

Would I please come and do something about it? I did not know what I could do, but I wanted to see what was happening and I got on to a pony and started out. I took my rifle, an old .44 Winchester and much too small to kill an elephant, but I thought the noise might be useful in *terrorem*. Various Burmans stopped me on the way and told me about the elephant's doings. It was not, of course, a wild elephant, but a tame one which had gone "must." It had been chained up, as tame elephants always are when their attack of "must"[4] is due, but on the previous night it had broken its chain and escaped. Its mahout, the only person who could manage it when it was in that state, had set out in pursuit, but had taken the wrong direction and was now twelve hours' journey away, and in the morning the elephant had suddenly reappeared in the town. The Burmese population had no weapons and were quite help-less against it. It had already destroyed somebody's bamboo hut, killed a cow, and raided some fruit-stalls and devoured the stock; also it had met the municipal rubbish van and, when the driver jumped out and took to his heels, had turned the van over and inflicted violences upon it.

The Burmese sub-inspector and some Indian constables were wait-ing for me in the quarter where the elephant had been seen. It was a very poor quarter, a labyrinth of squalid bamboo huts, thatched with palm-leaf, winding all over a steep hillside. I remember that it was a cloudy, stuffy morning at the beginning of the rains. We began questioning the people as to where the elephant had gone and, as usual, failed to get any definite information. That is invariably the case in the East; a story al-ways sounds clear enough at a distance, but the nearer you get to the scene of events the vaguer it becomes. Some of the people said that the elephant had gone in one direction, some said that he had gone in an-other, some professed not even to have heard of any elephant. I had al-most made up my mind that the whole story was a pack of lies, when we heard yells a little distance away. There was a loud, scandalized cry of "Go away, child! Go away this instant!" and an old woman with a switch in her hand came round the corner of a hut, violently shooing away a crowd of naked children. Some more women followed, clicking their tongues and exclaiming; evidently there was something that the children ought not to have seen. I rounded the hut and saw a man's dead body sprawling in the mud. He was an Indian, a black Dravidian coolie,[5] almost naked, and he could not have been dead many minutes. The people said that the elephant had come suddenly upon him round the corner of the hut, caught him with its trunk, put its foot on his back, and ground him into the earth. This was the rainy season and the

---

[4] Frenzy. [Eds.]

[5] An unskilled laborer. [Eds.]

ground was soft, and his face had scored a trench a foot deep and a couple of yards long. He was lying on his belly with arms crucified and head sharply twisted to one side. His face was coated with mud, the eyes wide open, the teeth bared and grinning with an expression of unendurable agony. (Never tell me, by the way, that the dead look peaceful. Most of the corpses I have seen looked devilish.) The friction of the great beast's foot had stripped the skin from his back as neatly as one skins a rabbit. As soon as I saw the dead man I sent an orderly to a friend's house nearby to borrow an elephant rifle. I had already sent back the pony, not wanting it to go mad with fright and throw me if it smelt the elephant.

The orderly came back in a few minutes with a rifle and five cartridges, and meanwhile some Burmans had arrived and told us that the elephant was in the paddy fields below, only a few hundred yards away. As I started forward practically the whole population of the quarter flocked out of the houses and followed me. They had seen the rifle and were all shouting excitedly that I was going to shoot the elephant. They had not shown much interest in the elephant when he was merely ravaging their homes, but it was different now that he was going to be shot. It was a bit of fun to them, as it would be to an English crowd; besides they wanted the meat. It made me vaguely uneasy. I had no intention of shooting the elephant—I had merely sent for the rifle to defend myself if necessary—and it is always unnerving to have a crowd following you. I marched down the hill, looking and feeling a fool, with the rifle over my shoulder and an ever-growing army of people jostling at my heels. At the bottom, when you got away from the huts, there was a metalled road and beyond that a miry waste of paddy fields a thousand yards across, not yet ploughed but soggy from the first rains and dotted with coarse grass. The elephant was standing eight yards from the road, his left side towards us. He took not the slightest notice of the crowd's approach. He was tearing up bunches of grass, beating them against his knees to clean them and stuffing them into his mouth.

I had halted on the road. As soon as I saw the elephant I knew with perfect certainty that I ought not to shoot him. It is a serious matter to shoot a working elephant—it is comparable to destroying a huge and costly piece of machinery—and obviously one ought not to do it if it can possibly be avoided. And at that distance, peacefully eating, the elephant looked no more dangerous than a cow. I thought then and I think now that his attack of "must" was already passing off; in which case he would merely wander harmlessly about until the mahout came back and caught him. Moreover, I did not in the least want to shoot him. I decided that I would watch him for a little while to make sure that he did not turn savage again, and then go home.

But at that moment I glanced round at the crowd that had followed   7
me. It was an immense crowd, two thousand at the least and growing
every minute. It blocked the road for a long distance on either side. I
looked at the sea of yellow faces above the garish clothes—faces all
happy and excited over this bit of fun, all certain that the elephant was
going to be shot. They were watching me as they would watch a con-
jurer about to perform a trick. They did not like me, but with the magical rifle in my hands I was momentarily worth watching. And suddenly I realized that I should have to shoot the elephant after all. The
people expected it of me and I had got to do it; I could feel their two
thousand wills pressing me forward, irresistibly. And it was at this
moment, as I stood there with the rifle in my hands, that I first grasped
the hollowness, the futility of the white man's dominion in the East.
Here was I, the white man with his gun, standing in front of the unarmed native crowd—seemingly the leading actor of the piece; but in
reality I was only an absurd puppet pushed to and fro by the will of
those yellow faces behind. I perceived in this moment that when the
white man turns tyrant it is his own freedom that he destroys. He becomes a sort of hollow, posing dummy, the conventionalized figure of
a sahib. For it is the condition of his rule that he shall spend his life in
trying to impress the "natives," and so in every crisis he has got to do
what the "natives" expect of him. He wears a mask, and his face grows
to fit it. I had got to shoot the elephant. I had committed myself to
doing it when I sent for the rifle. A sahib has got to act like a sahib;[6] he
has got to appear resolute, to know his own mind and do definite
things. To come all that way, rifle in hand, with two thousand people
marching at my heels, and then to trail feebly away, having done nothing—no, that was impossible. The crowd would laugh at me. And my
whole life, every white man's life in the East, was one long struggle not
to be laughed at.

But I did not want to shoot the elephant. I watched him beating his   8
bunch of grass against his knees, with that preoccupied grand-mother-
ly air that elephants have. It seemed to me that it would be murder to
shoot him. At that age I was not squeamish about killing animals, but I
had never shot an elephant and never wanted to. (Somehow it always
seems worse to kill a *large* animal.) Besides, there was the beast's owner
to be considered. Alive, the elephant was worth at least a hundred
pounds; dead, he would only be worth the value of his tusks, five
pounds, possibly. But I had got to act quickly. I turned to some experienced looking Burmans who had been there when we arrived, and
asked them how the elephant had been behaving. They all said the same
thing: he took no notice of you if you left him alone, but he might charge
if you went to close to him.

---

[6] Term used by natives of colonial India when referring to a European of rank. [Eds.]

It was perfectly clear to me what I ought to do. I ought to walk up   9
to within, say, twenty-five yards of the elephant and test his behavior.
If he charged, I could shoot; if he took no notice of me, it would be safe
to leave him until the mahout came back. But also I knew that I was
going to do no such thing. I was a poor shot with a rifle and the ground
was soft mud into which one would sink at every step. If the elephant
charged and I missed him, I should have about as much chance as a toad
under a steam-roller. But even then I was not thinking particularly of my
own skin, only of the watchful yellow faces behind. For at that moment,
with the crowed watching me, I was not afraid in the ordinary sense, as
I would have been if I had been alone. A white man mustn't be frightened in front of "natives"; and so, in general, he isn't frightened. The
sole thought in my mind was that if anything went wrong those two
thousand Burmans would see me pursued, caught, trampled on, and reduced to a grinning corpse like that Indian up the hill. And if that happened it was quite probable that some of them would laugh. That would
never do. There was only one alternative. I shoved the cartridges into the
magazine and lay down on the road to get a better aim.

The crowd grew very still, and a deep, low, happy sigh, as of peo-   10
ple who see the theatre curtain go up at last, breathed from innumerable
throats. They were going to have their bit of fun after all. The rifle was
a beautiful German thing with cross-hair sights. I did not then know that
in shooting an elephant one would shoot to cut an imaginary bar running from ear-hole to ear-hole. I ought, therefore, as the elephant was
sideways on, to have aimed straight at his ear-hole; actually I aimed several inches in front of this, thinking the brain would be further forward.

When I pulled the trigger I did not hear the bang or feel the kick—   11
one never does when a shot goes home—but I heard the devilish roar of
glee that went up from the crowd. In that instant, in too short a time, one
would have thought, even for the bullet to get there, a mysterious, terrible change had come over the elephant. He neither stirred nor fell, but
every line of his body had altered. He looked suddenly stricken, shrunk-
en, immensely old, as though the frightful impact of the bullet had paral-
ysed him without knocking him down. At last, after what seemed a long
time—it might have been five seconds, I dare say—he sagged flabbily to
his knees. His mouth slobbered. An enormous senility seemed to have
settled upon him. One could have imagined him thousands of years old.
I fired again into the same spot. At the second shot he did not collapse
but climbed with desperate slowness to his feet and stood weakly upright, with legs sagging and head dropping. I fired a third time. That
was the shot that did for him. You could see the agony of it jolt his whole
body and knock the last remnant of strength from his legs. But in falling
he seemed for a moment to rise, for as his hind legs collapsed beneath
him he seemed to tower upward like a huge rock toppling, his trunk
reaching skywards like a tree. He trumpeted, for the first and only time.

And then down he came, his belly towards me, with a crash that seemed to shake the ground even where I lay.

I got up. The Burmans were already racing past me across the mud. 12 It was obvious that the elephant would never rise again, but he was not dead. He was breathing very rhythmically with long rattling gasps, his great mound of a side painfully rising and falling. His mouth was wide open—I could see far down into caverns of pale pink throat. I waited a long time for him to die, but his breathing did not weaken. Finally I fired my two remaining shots into the spot where I thought his heart must be. The thick blood welled out of him like red velvet, but still he did not die. His body did not even jerk when the shots hit him, the tortured breathing continued without a pause. He was dying, very slowly and in great agony, but in some world remote from me where not even a bullet could damage him further. I felt that I had got to put an end to that dreadful noise. It seemed dreadful to see the great beast lying there, powerless to move and yet powerless to die, and not even to be able to finish him. I sent back for my small rifle and poured shot after shot into his heart and down his throat. They seemed to make no impression. The tortured gasps continued as steadily as the ticking of a clock.

In the end I could not stand it any longer and went away. I heard 13 later that it took him half an hour to die. Burmans were bringing dahs[7] and baskets even before I left, and I was told they had stripped his body almost to the bones by the afternoon.

Afterwards, of course, there were endless discussions about the 14 shooting of the elephant. The owner was furious, but he was only an Indian and could do nothing. Besides, legally I had done the right thing, for a mad elephant has to be killed, like a mad dog, if its owner fails to control it. Among the Europeans opinion was divided. The older men said I was right, the younger men said it was a damn shame to shoot an elephant for killing a coolie, because an elephant was worth more than any damn Coringhee coolie. And afterwards I was very glad that the coolie had been killed; it put me legally in the right and it gave me a sufficient pretext for shooting the elephant. I often wondered whether any of the others grasped that I had done it solely to avoid looking a fool.

Responding to Reading

1. The central focus in this essay is Orwell's struggle to decide what action to take to control the elephant. Do you think he really has a choice? Explain.
2. What do you think you would have done in Orwell's place? Why?
3. Orwell says that his encounter with the elephant, although "a tiny incident in itself," gave him an understanding of "the real nature of imperialism—the real motives for which despotic governments act" (3). In light of this state-

---

[7] Large knives. [Eds.]

ment, do you think his purpose in this essay is to explore something about himself or something about the nature of British colonialism—or both?

CIVIL DISOBEDIENCE

Henry David Thoreau

American essayist, journalist, and intellectual Henry David Thoreau (1817–1862) was a social rebel who loved nature and solitude. A follower of transcendentalism, a philosophic and literary movement that flourished in New England, he contributed to *The Dial,* a publication that gave voice to the movement's romantic, idealistic, and individualistic beliefs. For three years, Thoreau lived in a cabin near Walden Pond in Concord, Massachusetts; his experiences there are recorded in his most famous book, *Walden* (1854). He left Walden, however, because he had "several more lives to live and could not spare any more for that one." A canoe excursion in 1839 resulted in the chronicle *A Week on the Concord and Merrimack Rivers,* and other experiences produced books about Maine and Cape Cod. The following impassioned and eloquent defense of civil disobedience, published in 1849, has influenced such leaders as Gandhi and Martin Luther King, Jr.

I heartily accept the motto,—"That government is best which governs least;" and I should like to see it acted up to more rapidly and systematically. Carried out, it finally amounts to this, which also I believe,— "That government is best which governs not at all;" and when men are prepared for it, that will be the kind of government which they will have. Government is at best but an expedient; but most governments are usually, and all governments are sometimes, inexpedient. The objections which have been brought against a standing army, and they are many and weighty, and deserve to prevail, may also at last be brought against a standing government. The standing army is only an arm of the standing government. The government itself, which is only the mode which the people have chosen to execute their will, is equally liable to be abused and perverted before the people can act through it. Witness the present Mexican war,[1] the work of comparatively a few individuals

1

---

[1] In December 1845, the United States annexed Texas, leading to a war between the U.S. and Mexico (1846–48). Thoreau opposed this war, thinking it served the interests of slaveholders, who believed that the land won from Mexico would be slave territory. In protest, he refused to pay the Massachusetts poll tax and was arrested for his act of civil disobedience. [Eds.]

using the standing government as their tool; for, in the outset, the people would not have consented to this measure.

This American Government,—what is it but a tradition, though a recent one, endeavoring to transmit itself unimpaired to posterity, but each instant losing some of its integrity? It has not the vitality and force of a single living man; for a single man can bend it to his will. It is a sort of wooden gun to the people themselves. But it is not the less necessary for this; for the people must have some complicated machinery or other, and hear its din, to satisfy that idea of government which they have. Governments show thus how successfully men can be imposed on, even impose on themselves, for their own advantage. It is excellent, we must all allow. Yet this government never of itself furthered any enterprise, but by the alacrity with which it got out of its way. *It* does not keep the country free. *It* does not settle the West. *It* does not educate. The character inherent in the American people has done all that has been accomplished; and it would have done somewhat more, if the government had not sometimes got in its way. For government is an expedient by which men would fain succeed in letting one another alone; and, as has been said, when it is most expedient, the governed are most let alone by it. Trade and commerce, if they were not made of India-rubber, would never manage to bounce over the obstacles which legislators are continually putting in their way; and, if one were to judge these men wholly by the effects of their actions and not partly by their intentions, they would deserve to be classed and punished with those mischievous persons who put obstructions on the railroads.

But, to speak practically and as a citizen, unlike those who call themselves no-government men, I ask for, not at once no government, but *at once* a better government. Let every man make known what kind of government would command his respect, and that will be one step toward obtaining it.

After all, the practical reason why, when the power is once in the hands of the people, a majority are permitted, and for a long period continue, to rule is not because they are most likely to be in the right, nor because this seems fairest to the minority, but because they are physically the strongest. But a government in which the majority rule in all cases cannot be based on justice, even as far as men understand it. Can there not be a government in which majorities do not virtually decide right and wrong, but conscience?—in which majorities decide only those questions to which the rule of expediency is applicable? Must the citizen ever for a moment, or in the least degree, resign his conscience to the legislator? Why has every man a conscience, then? I think that we should be men first, and subjects afterward. It is not desirable to cultivate a respect for the law, so much as for the right. The only obligation which I have a right to assume is to do at any time what I think right. It is truly enough said, that a corporation has no conscience; but a corporation of conscientious men is a corporation *with* a conscience. Law never made men a whit more just; and, by means of their respect for it, even the well-disposed are daily made the agents of injustice. A common and natural result of any undue respect for law is, that you may see a file of soldiers, colonel, captain, corporal, privates, powder-monkeys, and all, marching in admirable order over hill and dale to the wars, against their wills, ay, against their common sense and consciences, which makes it very steep marching indeed, and produces a palpitation of the heart. They have no doubt that it is a damnable business in which they are concerned; they are all peaceably inclined. Now, what are they? Men at all? or small movable forts and magazines, at the service of some unscrupulous man in power? Visit the Navy-Yard, and behold a marine, such a man as an American government can make, or such as it can make a man with its black arts,—a mere shadow and reminiscence of humanity, a man laid out alive and standing, and already, as one may say, buried under arms with funeral accompaniments, though it may be,—

> "Not a drum was heard, not a funeral note,
> As his corse to the rampart we hurried;
> Not a soldier discharged his farewell shot
> O'er the grave where our hero we buried."[2]

The mass of men serve the state thus, not as men mainly, but as machines, with their bodies. They are the standing army, and the militia, jailers, constables, posse comitatus, etc. In most cases there is no free exercise whatever of the judgment or of the moral sense; but they put themselves on a level with wood and earth and stones; and wooden men can perhaps be manufactured that will serve the purpose as well. Such command no more respect than men of straw or a lump of dirt. They have the same sort of worth only as horses and dogs. Yet such as these even are commonly esteemed good citizens. Others—as most legislators, politicians, lawyers, ministers, and office-holders—serve the state chiefly with their heads; and, as they rarely make any moral distinctions, they are as likely to serve the Devil, without *intending* it, as God. A very few, as heroes, patriots, martyrs, reformers in the great sense, and *men*, serve the state with their consciences also, and so necessarily resist it for the most part; and they are commonly treated as enemies by it. A wise man will only be useful as a man, and will not submit to be "clay," and "stop a hole to keep the wind away,"[3] but leave that office to his dust at least:—

> "I am too high-born to be propertied,
> To be a secondary at control,

5

---

[2] From "The Burial of Sir John Moore at Corunna," by Irish poet Charles Wolfe (1791–1823). [Eds.]
[3] From *Hamlet* (Act V, scene i) by William Shakespeare. [Eds.]

Or useful serving-man and instrument
To any sovereign state throughout the world."[4]

He who gives himself entirely to his fellow-men appears to them   6
useless and selfish; but he who gives himself partially to them is pronounced a benefactor and philanthropist.

How does it become a man to behave toward this American gov-   7
ernment to-day? I answer, that he cannot without disgrace be associated with it. I cannot for an instant recognize that political organization as
my government which is the *slave's* government also.

All men recognize the right of revolution; that is, the right to refuse   8
allegiance to, and to resist, the government, when its tyranny or its in-
efficiency are great and unendurable. But almost all say that such is not
the case now. But such was the case, they think, in the Revolution of '75.
If one were to tell me that this was a bad government because it taxed
certain foreign commodities brought to its ports, it is most probable that
I should not make an ado about it, for I can do without them. All machines have their friction; and possibly this does enough good to coun-
terbalance the evil. At any rate, it is a great evil to make a stir about it.
But when the friction comes to have its machine, and oppression and
robbery are organized, I say, let us not have such a machine any longer.
In other words, when a sixth of the population of a nation which has undertaken to be the refuge of liberty are slaves, and a whole country is unjustly overrun and conquered by a foreign army, and subjected to military law, I think that it is not too soon for honest men to rebel and
revolutionize. What makes this duty the more urgent is the fact that the
country so overrun is not our own, but ours is the invading army.

Paley,[5] a common authority with many on moral questions, in his   9
chapter on the "Duty of Submission to Civil Government," resolves all
civil obligation into expediency; and he proceeds to say, "that so long as
the interest of the whole society requires it, that is, so long as the established government cannot be resisted or changed without public incon-
veniency, it is the will of God that the established government be
obeyed, and no longer. . . . This principle being admitted, the justice of
every particular case of resistance is reduced to a computation of the
quantity of the danger and grievance on the one side, and of the probability and expense of redressing it on the other." Of this, he says, every
man shall judge for himself. But Paley appears never to have contemplated those cases to which the rule of expediency does not apply, in
which a people, as well as an individual, must do justice, cost what it
may. If I have unjustly wrested a plank from a drowning man, I must restore it to him though I drown myself. This, according to Paley, would

---

[4] From *King John* (Act V, scene ii) by William Shakespeare. [Eds.]
[5] William Paley (1743–1805), English clergyman and philosopher. [Eds.]

be inconvenient. But he that would save his life, in such a case, shall lose it. This people must cease to hold slaves, and to make war on Mexico, though it cost them their existence as a people.

In their practice, nations agree with Paley; but does any one think   10
that Massachusetts does exactly what is right at the present crisis?

> "A drab of state, a cloth-o'-silver slut,
> To have her train borne up, and her soul trail in the dirt."[6]

Practically speaking, the opponents to a reform in Massachusetts are not a hundred thousand politicians at the South, but a hundred thousand merchants and farmers here, who are more interested in commerce and agriculture than they are in humanity, and are not prepared to do justice to the slave and to Mexico, *cost what it may.* I quarrel not with far-off foes, but with those who, near at home, coöperate with, and do the bidding of, those far away, and without whom the latter would be harmless. We are accustomed to say, that the mass of men are unprepared; but improvement is slow, because the few are not materially wiser or better than the many. It is not so important that many should be as good as you, as that there be some absolute goodness somewhere; for that will leaven the whole lump. There are thousands who are *in opinion* opposed to slavery and to the war, who yet in effect do nothing to put an end to them; who, esteeming themselves children of Washington and Franklin, sit down with their hands in their pockets, and say that they know not what to do, and do nothing; who even postpone the question of freedom to the question of free-trade, and quietly read the prices-current along with the latest advices from Mexico, after dinner, and, it may be, fall asleep over them both. What is the price-current of an honest man and patriot to-day? They hesitate, and they regret, and sometimes they petition; but they do nothing in earnest and with effect. They will wait, well disposed, for others to remedy the evil, that they may no longer have it to regret. At most, they give only a cheap vote, and a feeble countenance and Godspeed, to the right, as it goes by them. There are nine hundred and ninety-nine patrons of virtue to one virtuous man. But it is easier to deal with the real possessor of a thing than with the temporary guardian of it.

All voting is a sort of gaming, like checkers or backgammon, with a   11
slight moral tinge to it, a playing with right and wrong, with moral questions; and betting naturally accompanies it. The character of the voters is not staked. I cast my vote, perchance, as I think right; but I am not vitally concerned that that right should prevail. I am willing to leave it to the majority. Its obligation, therefore, never exceeds that of expediency. Even voting *for the right* is *doing* nothing for it. It is only expressing to men feebly your desire that it should prevail. A wise man will not leave

---

[6] From Act IV, scene iv of Cyril Tourneur's *The Revenger's Tragedy* (1607). [Eds.]

the right to the mercy of chance, nor wish it to prevail through the power of the majority. There is but little virtue in the action of masses of men. When the majority shall at length vote for the abolition of slavery, it will be because they are indifferent to slavery, or because there is but little slavery left to be abolished by their vote. *They* will then be the only slaves. Only *his* vote can hasten the abolition of slavery who asserts his own freedom by his vote.

I hear of a convention to be held at Baltimore, or elsewhere, for the   12 selection of a candidate for the Presidency, made up chiefly of editors, and men who are politicians by profession; but I think, what is it to any independent, intelligent, and respectable man what decision they may come to? Shall we not have the advantage of his wisdom and honesty, nevertheless? Can we not count upon some independent votes? Are there not many individuals in the country who do not attend conventions? But no: I find that the respectable man, so called, has immediately drifted from his position, and despairs of his country, when his country has more reason to despair of him. He forthwith adopts one of the candidates thus selected as the only *available* one, thus proving that he is himself *available* for any purposes of the demagogue. His vote is of no more worth than that of any unprincipled foreigner or hireling native, who may have been bought. O for a man who is a *man,* and, as my neighbor says, has a bone in his back which you cannot pass your hand through! Our statistics are at fault: the population has been returned too large. How many *men* are there to a square thousand miles in this country? Hardly one. Does not America offer any inducement for men to settle here? The American has dwindled into an Odd Fellow,—one who may be known by the development of his organ of gregariousness, and a manifest lack of intellect and cheerful self-reliance; whose first and chief concern, on coming into the world, is to see that Almshouses[7] are in good repair; and, before yet he has lawfully donned the virile garb, to collect a fund for the support of the widows and orphans that may be; who, in short, ventures to live only by the aid of the Mutual Insurance company, which has promised to bury him decently.

It is not a man's duty, as a matter of course, to devote himself to the   13 eradication of any, even the most enormous wrong; he may still properly have other concerns to engage him; but it is his duty, at least, to wash his hands of it, and, if he gives it no thought longer, not to give it practically his support. If I devote myself to other pursuits and contemplations, I must first see, at least, that I do not pursue them sitting upon another man's shoulders. I must get off him first, that he may pursue his contemplations too. See what gross inconsistency is tolerated. I have heard some of my townsmen say, "I should like to have them order me out to help put down an insurrection of the slaves, or to march to

---

[7] Poorhouses; county homes that provided for the needy. [Eds.]

Mexico;—see if I would go;" and yet these very men have each, directly by their allegiance, and so indirectly, at least, by their money, furnished a substitute. The soldier is applauded who refuses to serve in an unjust war by those who do not refuse to sustain the unjust government which makes the war; is applauded by those whose own act and authority he disregards and sets at naught; as if the state were penitent to that degree that it hired one to scourge it while it sinned, but not to that degree that it left off sinning for a moment. Thus, under the name of Order and Civil Government, we are all made at last to pay homage to and support our own meanness. After the first blush of sin comes its indifference; and from immoral it becomes, as it were, *un*moral, and not quite unnecessary to that life which we have made.

The broadest and most prevalent error requires the most disinter- 14 ested virtue to sustain it. The slight reproach to which the virtue of patriotism is commonly liable, the noble are most likely to incur. Those who, while they disapprove of the character and measures of a government, yield to it their allegiance and support are undoubtedly its most conscientious supporters, and so frequently the most serious obstacles to reform. Some are petitioning the state to dissolve the Union, to disregard the requisitions of the President. Why do they not dissolve it themselves,—the union between themselves and the state,—and refuse to pay their quota into its treasury? Do not they stand in the same relation to the state that the state does to the Union? And have not the same reasons prevented the state from resisting the Union which have prevented them from resisting the state?

How can a man be satisfied to entertain an opinion merely, and 15 enjoy *it?* Is there any enjoyment in it, if his opinion is that he is aggrieved? If you are cheated out of a single dollar by your neighbor, you do not rest satisfied with knowing that you are cheated, or with saying that you are cheated, or even with petitioning him to pay you your due; but you take effectual steps at once to obtain the full amount, and see that you are never cheated again. Action from principle, the perception and the performance of right, changes things and relations; it is essentially revolutionary, and does not consist wholly with anything which was. It not only divides states and churches, it divides families; ay, it divides the *individual,* separating the diabolical in him from the divine.

Unjust laws exist: shall we be content to obey them, or shall we en- 16 deavor to amend them, and obey them until we have succeeded, or shall we transgress them at once? Men generally, under such a government as this, think that they ought to wait until they have persuaded the majority to alter them. They think that, if they should resist, the remedy would be worse than the evil. But it is the fault of the government itself that the remedy *is* worse than the evil. *It* makes it worse. Why is it not more apt to anticipate and provide for reform? Why does it not cherish its wise minority? Why does it cry and resist before it is hurt? Why does it not encourage its citizens to be on the alert to point out its faults, and *do* better than it would have them? Why does it always crucify Christ, and excommunicate Copernicus and Luther, and pronounce Washington and Franklin rebels?

One would think, that a deliberate and practical denial of its authority was the only offense never contemplated by government; else, why has it not assigned its definite, its suitable and proportionate penalty? If a man who has no property refuses but once to earn nine shillings for the state, he is put in prison for a period unlimited by any law that I know, and determined only by the discretion of those who placed him there; but if he should steal ninety times nine shillings from the state, he is soon permitted to go at large again. [17]

If the injustice is part of the necessary friction of the machine of government, let it go, let it go: perchance it will wear smooth,—certainly the machine will wear out. If the injustice has a spring, or a pulley, or a rope, or a crank, exclusively for itself, then perhaps you may consider whether the remedy will not be worse than the evil; but if it is of such a nature that it requires you to be the agent of injustice to another, then, I say, break the law. Let your life be a counter friction to stop the machine. What I have to do is to see, at any rate, that I do not lend myself to the wrong which I condemn. [18]

As for adopting the ways which the state has provided for remedying the evil, I know not of such ways. They take too much time, and a man's life will be gone. I have other affairs to attend to. I came into this world, not chiefly to make this a good place to live in, but to live in it, be it good or bad. A man has not everything to do, but something; and because he cannot do *everything*, it is not necessary that he should do *something* wrong. It is not my business to be petitioning the Governor or the Legislature any more than it is theirs to petition me; and if they should not hear my petition, what should I do then? But in this case the state has provided no way: its very Constitution is the evil. This may seem to be harsh and stubborn and unconciliatory; but it is to treat with the utmost kindness and consideration the only spirit that can appreciate or deserve it. So is all change for the better, like birth and death, which convulse the body. [19]

I do not hesitate to say, that those who call themselves Abolitionists should at once effectually withdraw their support, both in person and property, from the government of Massachusetts, and not wait till they constitute a majority of one, before they suffer the right to prevail through them. I think that it is enough if they have God on their side, without waiting for that other one. Moreover, any man more right than his neighbors constitutes a majority of one already. [20]

I meet this American government, or its representative, the state government, directly, and face to face, once a year—no more—in the person of its tax-gatherer; this is the only mode in which a man situat- [21]

ed as I am necessarily meets it; and it then says distinctly, Recognize me; and the simplest, the most effectual, and, in the present posture of affairs, the indispensablest mode of treating with it on this head, of expressing your little satisfaction with and love for it, is to deny it then. My civil neighbor, the tax-gatherer, is the very man I have to deal with,—for it is, after all, with men and not with parchment that I quarrel,—and he has voluntarily chosen to be an agent of the government. How shall he ever know well what he is and does as an officer of the government, or as a man, until he is obliged to consider whether he shall treat me, his neighbor, for whom he has respect, as a neighbor and well-disposed man, or as a maniac and disturber of the peace, and see if he can get over this obstruction to his neighborliness without a ruder and more impetuous thought or speech corresponding with his action. I know this well, that if one thousand; if one hundred, if ten men whom I could name;—if ten *honest* men only,—say if *one* HONEST man, in this State of Massachusetts, *ceasing to hold slaves,* were actually to withdraw from this copartnership, and be locked up in the county jail therefor, it would be the abolition of slavery in America. For it matters not how small the beginning may seem to be: what is once well done is done forever. But we love better to talk about it: that we say is our mission. Reform keeps many scores of newspapers in its service, but not one man. If my esteemed neighbor, the State's ambassador, who will devote his days to the settlement of the question of human rights in the Council Chamber, instead of being threatened with the prisons of Carolina, were to sit down the prisoner of Massachusetts, that State which is so anxious to foist the sin of slavery upon her sister,—though at present she can discover only an act of inhospitality to be the ground of a quarrel with her,—the Legislature would not wholly waive the subject the following winter.

Under a government which imprisons any unjustly, the true place ²² for a just man is also a prison. The proper place to-day, the only place which Massachusetts has provided for her freer and less desponding spirits, is in her prisons, to be put out and locked out of the State by her own act, as they have already put themselves out by their principles. It is there that the fugitive slave, and the Mexican prisoner on parole, and the Indian come to plead the wrongs of his race should find them; on that separate, but more free and honorable ground, where the State places those who are not *with* her, but *against* her,—the only house in a slave State in which a free man can abide with honor. If any think that their influence would be lost there, and their voices no longer afflict the ear of the State, that they would not be as an enemy within its walls, they do not know by how much truth is stronger than error, nor how much more eloquently and effectively he can combat injustice who has experienced a little in his own person. Cast your whole vote, not a strip of paper merely, but your whole influence. A minority is powerless while it conforms to the majority; it is not even a minority then; but it is irresistible when it clogs by its whole weight. If the alternative is to keep all just men in prison, or give up war and slavery, the State will not hesitate which to choose. If a thousand men were not to pay their tax-bills this year, that would not be a violent and bloody measure, as it would be to pay them, and enable the State to commit violence and shed innocent blood. This is, in fact, the definition of a peaceable revolution, if any such is possible. If the tax-gatherer, or any other public officer, asks me, as one has done, "But what shall I do?" my answer is, "If you really wish to do anything, resign your office." When the subject has refused allegiance, and the officer has resigned his office, then the revolution is accomplished. But even suppose blood should flow. Is there not a sort of blood shed when the conscience is wounded? Through this wound a man's real manhood and immortality flow out, and he bleeds to an everlasting death. I see this blood flowing now.

I have contemplated the imprisonment of the offender, rather than [23] the seizure of his goods,—though both will serve the same purpose,— because they who assert the purest right, and consequently are most dangerous to a corrupt State, commonly have not spent much time in accumulating property. To such the State renders comparatively small service, and a slight tax is wont to appear exorbitant, particularly if they are obliged to earn it by special labor with their hands. If there were one who lived wholly without the use of money, the State itself would hesitate to demand it of him. But the rich man—not to make any invidious comparison—is always sold to the institution which makes him rich. Absolutely speaking, the more money, the less virtue; for money comes between a man and his objects, and obtains them for him; and it was certainly no great virtue to obtain it. It puts to rest many questions which he would otherwise be taxed to answer; while the only new question which it puts is the hard but superfluous one, how to spend it. Thus his moral ground is taken from under his feet. The opportunities of living are diminished in proportion as what are called the "means" are increased. The best thing a man can do for his culture when he is rich is to endeavor to carry out those schemes which he entertained when he was poor. Christ answered the Herodians according to their condition. "Show me the tribute-money," said he;—and one took a penny out of his pocket;—if you use money which has the image of Caesar on it, which he has made current and valuable, that is, *if you are men of the State,* and gladly enjoy the advantages of Caesar's government, then pay him back some of his own when he demands it. "Render therefore to Caesar that which is Caesar's, and to God those things which are God's,"—leaving them no wiser than before as to which was which; for they did not wish to know.

When I converse with the freest of my neighbors, I perceive that, [24] whatever they may say about the magnitude and seriousness of the question, and their regard for the public tranquility, the long and the short of the matter is, that they cannot spare the protection of the existing government, and they dread the consequences to their property and families of disobedience to it. For my own part, I should not like to think that I ever rely on the protection of the State. But, if I deny the authority of the State when it presents its tax-bill, it will soon take and waste all my property, and so harass me and my children without end. This is hard. This makes it impossible for a man to live honestly, and at the same time comfortably, in outward respects. It will not be worth the while to accumulate property; that would be sure to go again. You must hire or squat somewhere, and raise but a small crop, and eat that soon. You must live within yourself, and depend upon yourself always tucked up and ready for a start, and not have many affairs. A man may grow rich in Turkey even, if he will be in all respects a good subject of the Turkish government. Confucius said: "If a state is governed by the principles of reason, poverty and misery are subjects of shame; if a state is not governed by the principles of reason, riches and honors are the subjects of shame." No: until I want the protection of Massachusetts to be extended to me in some distant Southern port, where my liberty is endangered, or until I am bent solely on building up an estate at home by peaceful enterprise, I can afford to refuse allegiance to Massachusetts, and her right to my property and life. It costs me less in every sense to incur the penalty of disobedience to the State than it would to obey. I should feel as if I were worth less in that case.

Some years ago, the State met me in behalf of the Church, and commanded me to pay a certain sum toward the support of a clergyman whose preaching my father attended, but never I myself. "Pay," it said, "or be locked up in the jail." I declined to pay. But, unfortunately, another man saw fit to pay it. I did not see why the schoolmaster should be taxed to support the priest, and not the priest the schoolmaster; for I was not the State's schoolmaster, but I supported myself by voluntary subscription. I did not see why the lyceum should not present its tax-bill, and have the State to back its demand, as well as the Church. However, at the request of the selectmen, I condescended to make some such statement as this in writing:—"Know all men by these presents, that I, Henry Thoreau, do not wish to be regarded as a member of any incorporated society which I have not joined." This I gave to the town clerk; and he has it. The State, having thus learned that I did not wish to be regarded as a member of that church, has never made a like demand on me since; though it said that it must adhere to its original presumption that time. If I had known how to name them, I should have then signed off in detail from all the societies which I never signed on to; but I did not know where to find a complete list.

I have paid no poll-tax for six years. I was put into a jail once on this account, for one night; and, as I stood considering the walls of solid stone, two or three feet thick, the door of wood and iron, a foot thick, and the iron grating which strained the light, I could not help being struck with the foolishness of that institution which treated me as if I were mere flesh and blood and bones, to be locked up. I wondered that it should have concluded at length that this was the best use it could put me to, and had never thought to avail itself of my services in some way. I say that, if there was a wall of stone between me and my townsmen, there was a still more difficult one to climb or break through before they could get to be as free as I was. I did not for a moment feel confined, and the walls seemed a great waste of stone and mortar. I felt as if I alone of all my townsmen had paid my tax. They plainly did not know how to treat me, but behaved like persons who are underbred. In every threat and in every compliment there was a blunder; for they thought that my chief desire was to stand the other side of that stone wall. I could not but smile to see how industriously they locked the door on my meditations, which followed them out again without let or hindrance, and *they* were really all that was dangerous. As they could not reach me, they had resolved to punish my body; just as boys, if they cannot come at some person against whom they have a spite, will abuse his dog. I saw that the State was half-witted, that it was timid as a lone woman with her silver spoons, and that it did not know its friends from its foes, and I lost all my remaining respect for it, and pitied it.

Thus the State never intentionally confronts a man's sense, intellec- [27] tual or moral, but only his body, his senses. It is not armed with superior wit or honesty, but with superior physical strength. I was not born to be forced. I will breathe after my own fashion. Let us see who is the strongest. What force has a multitude? They only can force me who obey a higher law than I. They force me to become like themselves. I do not hear of *men* being *forced* to live this way or that by masses of men. What sort of life were that to live? When I meet a government which says to me, "Your money or your life," why should I be in haste to give it my money? It may be in a great strait, and not know what to do: I cannot help that. It must help itself; do as I do. It is not worth the while to snivel about it. I am not responsible for the successful working of the machinery of society. I am not the son of the engineer. I perceive that, when an acorn and a chestnut fall side by side, the one does not remain inert to make way for the other, but both obey their own laws, and spring and grow and flourish as best they can, till one, perchance, overshadows and destroys the other. If a plant cannot live according to its nature, it dies; and so a man.

The night in prison was novel and interesting enough. The prison- [28] ers in their shirt-sleeves were enjoying a chat and the evening air in the doorway, when I entered. But the jailer said, "Come, boys, it is time to lock up;" and so they dispersed, and I heard the sound of their steps returning into the hollow apartments. My room-mate was introduced to me by the jailer as "a first-rate fellow and a clever man." When the door was locked, he showed me where to hang my hat, and how he managed matters there. The rooms were whitewashed once a month; and this one, at least, was the whitest, most simply furnished, and probably the neatest apartment in the town. He naturally wanted to know where I came from, and what brought me there; and, when I had told him, I asked him in my turn how he came there, presuming him to be an honest man, of course; and, as the world goes, I believe he was. "Why," said he, "they accuse me of burning a barn; but I never did it." As near as I could discover, he had probably gone to bed in a barn when drunk, and smoked his pipe there; and so a barn was burnt. He had the reputation of being a clever man, had been there some three months waiting for his trial to come on, and would have to wait as much longer; but he was quite domesticated and contented, since he got his board for nothing, and thought that he was well treated.

He occupied one window, and I the other; and I saw that if one ^{29} stayed there long, his principal business would be to look out the window. I had soon read all tracts that were left there, and examined where former prisoners had broken out, and where a grate had been sawed off, and heard the history of the various occupants of that room; for I found that even here there was a history and a gossip which never circulated beyond the walls of the jail. Probably this is the only house in the town where verses are composed, which are afterward printed in a circular form, but not published. I was shown quite a long list of verses which were composed by some young men who had been detected in an attempt to escape, who avenged themselves by signing them.

I pumped my fellow-prisoner as dry as I could, for fear I should ^{30} never see him again; but at length he showed me which was my bed, and left me to blow out the lamp.

It was like traveling into a far country, such as I had never expect- ^{31} ed to behold, to lie there for one night. It seemed to me that I never had heard the town-clock strike before, nor the evening sounds of the village; for we slept with the windows open, which were inside the grating. It was to see my native village in the light of the Middle Ages, and our Concord was turned into a Rhine stream, and visions of knights and castles passed before me. They were the voices of old burghers that I heard in the streets. I was an involuntary spectator and auditor of whatever was done and said in the kitchen of the adjacent village-inn,—a wholly new and rare experience to me. It was a closer view of my native town. I was fairly inside of it. I never had seen its institutions before. This is one of its peculiar institutions; for it is a shire town.[8] I began to comprehend what its inhabitants were about.

---

[8] County seat. [Eds.]

In the morning, our breakfasts were put through the hole in the [32] door, in small oblong-square tin pans, made to fit, and holding a pint of chocolate, with brown bread, and an iron spoon. When they called for the vessels again, I was green enough to return what bread I had left; but my comrade seized it, and said that I should lay that up for lunch or dinner. Soon after he was let out to work at haying in a neighboring field, whither he went every day, and would not be back till noon; so he bade me good-day, saying that he doubted if he should see me again.

When I came out of prison,—for some one interfered, and paid that [33] tax,—I did not perceive that great changes had taken place on the common, such as he observed who went in a youth and emerged a tottering and gray-headed man; and yet a change had to my eyes come over the scene,—the town, and State, and country,—greater than any that mere time could effect. I saw yet more distinctly the State in which I lived. I saw to what extent the people among whom I lived could be trusted as good neighbors and friends; that their friendship was for summer weather only; that they did not greatly propose to do right; that they were a distinct race from me by their prejudices and superstitions, as the Chinamen and Malays are; that in their sacrifices to humanity they ran no risks, not even to their property; that after all they were not so noble but they treated the thief as he had treated them, and hoped, by a certain outward observance and a few prayers, and by walking in a particular straight though useless path from time to time, to save their souls. This may be to judge my neighbors harshly; for I believe that many of them are not aware that they have such an institution as the jail in their village.

It was formerly the custom in our village; when a poor debtor came [34] out of jail, for his acquaintances to salute him, looking through their fingers, which were crossed to represent the grating of a jail window, "How do ye do?" My neighbors did not thus salute me, but first looked at me, and then at one another, as if I had returned from a long journey. I was put into jail as I was going to the shoemaker's to get a shoe which was mended. When I was let out the next morning, I proceeded to finish my errand, and, having put on my mended shoe, joined a huckleberry party, who were impatient to put themselves under my conduct; and in half an hour,—for the horse was soon tackled,—was in the midst of a huckleberry field, on one of our highest hills, two miles off, and then the State was nowhere to be seen.

This is the whole history of "My Prisons." [35]

I have never declined paying the highway tax, because I am as desirous of being a good neighbor as I am of being a bad subject; and as for supporting schools, I am doing my part to educate my fellow-countrymen now. It is for no particular item in the tax-bill that I refuse to pay it. I simply wish to refuse allegiance to the State, to withdraw and stand [36] aloof from it effectually. I do not care to trace the course of my dollar, if I could, till it buys a man or a musket to shoot one with,—the dollar is innocent,—but I am concerned to trace the effects of my allegiance. In fact, I quietly declare war with the State, after my fashion, though I will still make what use and get what advantage of her I can, as is usual in such cases.

If others pay the tax which is demanded of me, from a sympathy [37] with the State, they do but what they have already done in their own case, or rather they abet injustice to a greater extent than the State requires. If they pay the tax from a mistaken interest in the individual taxed, to save his property, or prevent his going to jail, it is because they have not considered wisely how far they let their private feelings interfere with the public good.

This, then, is my position at present. But one cannot be too much on [38] his guard in such a case, lest his action be biased by obstinacy or an undue regard for the opinions of men. Let him see that he does only what belongs to himself and to the hour.

I think sometimes, Why, this people mean well, they are only igno- [39] rant; they would do better if they knew how: why give your neighbors this pain to treat you as they are not inclined to? But I think again, This is no reason why I should do as they do, or permit others to suffer much greater pain of a different kind. Again, I sometimes say to myself, When many millions of men, without heat, without ill will, without personal feeling of any kind, demand of you a few shillings only, without the possibility, such is their constitution, of retracting or altering their present demand, and without the possibility, on your side, of appeal to any other millions, why expose yourself to this overwhelming brute force? You do not resist cold and hunger, the winds and the waves, thus obstinately; you quietly submit to a thousand similar necessities. You do not put your head into the fire. But just in proportion as I regard this as not wholly a brute force, but partly a human force, and consider that I have relations to those millions as to so many millions of men, and not of mere brute or inanimate things, I see that appeal is possible, first and instantaneously, from them to the Maker of them, and, secondly, from them to themselves. But if I put my head deliberately into the fire, there is no appeal to fire or to the Maker of fire, and I have only myself to blame. If I could convince myself that I have any right to be satisfied with men as they are, and to treat them accordingly, and not accordingly, in some respects, to my requisitions and expectations of what they and I ought to be, then, like a good Mussulman[9] and fatalist, I should endeavor to be satisfied with things as they are, and say it is the will of God. And, above all, there is this difference between resisting this and

---

[9] Moslem. [Eds.]

a purely brute or natural force that I can resist this with some effect; but I cannot expect, like Orpheus,[10] to change the nature of the rocks and trees and beasts.

I do not wish to quarrel with any man or nation. I do not wish to [40] split hairs, to make the fine distinctions, or set myself up as better than my neighbors. I seek rather, I may say, even an excuse for conforming to the laws of the land. I am but too ready to conform to them. Indeed, I have reason to suspect myself on this head; and each year, as the tax-gatherer comes round, I find myself disposed to review the acts and position of the general and State governments, and the spirit of the people, to discover a pretext for conformity.

> "We must affect our country as our parents,
> And if at any time we alienate
> Our love or industry from doing it honor,
> We must respect effects and teach the soul
> Matter of conscience and religion,
> And not desire of rule or benefit."[11]   [5]

I believe that the State will soon be able to take all my work of this sort out of my hands, and then I shall be no better a patriot than my fellow-countrymen. Seen from a lower point of view, the Constitution, with all its faults, is very good; the law and the courts are very respectable; even this State and this American government are, in many respects, very admirable, and rare things, to be thankful for, such as a great many have described them; but seen from a point of view a little higher, they are what I have described them; seen from a higher still, and the highest, who shall say what they are, or that they are worth looking at or thinking of at all?

However, the government does not concern me much, and I shall [41] bestow the fewest possible thoughts on it. It is not many moments that I live under a government, even in this world. If a man is thought-free, fancy-free, imagination-free, that which *is not* never for a long time appearing *to be* to him, unwise rulers or reformers cannot fatally interrupt him.

I know that most men think differently from myself; but those [42] whose lives are by profession devoted to the study of these or kindred subjects content me as little as any. Statesmen and legislators, standing so completely within the institution, never distinctly and nakedly behold it. They speak of moving society, but have no resting-place without it. They may be men of a certain experience and discrimination, and have no doubt invented ingenious and even useful systems, for which we sincerely thank them; but all their wit and usefulness lie

---

[10] Legendary Greek poet and musician who played the lyre so beautifully that wild beasts were transfixed by his music and rocks and trees moved. [Eds.]

[11] From *The Battle of Alcazar* (1594), a play by George Peele (1558?–97?). [Eds.]

within certain not very wide limits. They are wont to forget that the world is not governed by policy and expediency. Webster[12] never goes behind government, and so cannot speak with authority about it. His words are wisdom to those legislators who contemplate no essential reform in the existing government; but for thinkers, and those who legislate for all time, he never once glances at the subject. I know of those whose serene and wise speculations on this theme would soon reveal the limits of his mind's range and hospitality. Yet, compared with the cheap professions of most reformers, and the still cheaper wisdom and eloquence of politicians in general, his are almost the only sensible and valuable words, and we thank Heaven for him. Comparatively, he is always strong, original, and, above all, practical. Still, his quality is not wisdom, but prudence. The lawyer's truth is not Truth, but consistency or a consistent expediency. Truth is always in harmony with herself, and is not concerned chiefly to reveal the justice that may consist with wrong-doing. He well deserves to be called, as he has been called, the Defender of the Constitution. There are really no blows to be given to him but defensive ones. He is not a leader, but a follower. His leaders are the men of '87. "I have never made an effort," he says, "and never propose to make an effort; I have never countenanced an effort, and never mean to countenance an effort, to disturb the arrangement as originally made, by which the various States came into the Union." Still thinking of the sanction which the Constitution gives to slavery, he says, "Because it was a part of the original compact,—let it stand." Notwithstanding his special acuteness and ability, he is unable to take a fact out of its merely political relations, and behold it as it lies absolutely to be disposed of by the intellect,—what, for instance, it behooves a man to do here in America to-day with regard to slavery,—but ventures, or is driven, to make some such desperate answer as the following, while professing to speak absolutely, and as a private man,—from which what new and singular code of social duties might be inferred? "The manner," says he, "in which the governments of those States where slavery exists are to regulate it is for their own consideration, under their responsibility to their constituents, to the general laws of propriety, humanity, and justice, and to God. Associations formed elsewhere, springing from a feeling of humanity, or any other cause, have nothing whatever to do with it. They have never received any encouragement from me, and they never will."

They who know of no purer sources of truth, who have traced up its [43] stream no higher, stand, and wisely stand, by the Bible and the Constitution, and drink at it there with reverence and humility; but they who

---

[12] Daniel Webster (1782–1852), legendary American orator, lawyer, and statesman. [Eds.]

behold where it comes trickling into this lake or that pool, gird up their loins once more, and continue their pilgrimage toward its fountain-head.

No man with a genius for legislation has appeared in America. [44] They are rare in the history of the world. There are orators, politicians, and eloquent men, by the thousand; but the speaker has not yet opened his mouth to speak who is capable of settling the much-vexed questions of the day. We love eloquence for its own sake, and not for any truth which it may utter, or any heroism it may inspire. Our legislators have not yet learned the comparative value of free-trade and of freedom, of union, and of rectitude, to a nation. They have no genius or talent for comparatively humble questions of taxation and finance, commerce and manufacturers and agriculture. If we were left solely to the wordy wit of legislators in Congress for our guidance, uncorrected by the seasonable experience and the effectual complaints of the people, America would not long retain her rank among the nations. For eighteen hundred years, though perchance I have no right to say it, the New Testament has been written; yet where is the legislator who has wisdom and practical talent enough to avail himself of the light which it sheds on the science of legislation?

The authority of government, even such as I am willing to sub- [45] mit to,—for I will cheerfully obey those who know and can do better than I, and in many things even those who neither know nor can do so well,—is still an impure one: to be strictly just, it must have the sanction and consent of the governed. It can have no pure right over my person and property but what I concede to it. The progress from an absolute to a limited monarchy, from a limited monarchy to a democracy, is a progress toward a true respect for the individual. Even the Chinese philosopher was wise enough to regard the individual as the basis of the empire. Is a democracy, such as we know it, the last improvement possible in government? Is it not possible to take a further step towards recognizing and organizing the rights of man? There will never be a really free and enlightened State until the State comes to recognize the individual as a higher and independent power, from which all its own power and authority are derived, and treats him accordingly. I please myself with imagining a State at last which can afford to be just to all men, and to treat the individual with respect as a neighbor; which even would not think it inconsistent with its own repose if a few were to live aloof from it, not meddling with it, nor embraced by it, who fulfilled all the duties of neighbors and fellow-men. A State which bore this kind of fruit, and suffered it to drop off as fast as it ripened, would prepare the way for a still more perfect and glorious State, which also I have imagined, but not yet anywhere seen.

Responding to Reading

1. What moral or political choice does each of the following statements imply?

   "'That government is best which governs least' . . ." (1).

   "All men recognize the right of revolution . . ." (8).

   "All voting is a sort of gaming, like checkers or backgammon . . ." (11).

   "Under a government which imprisons any unjustly, the true place for a just man is also a prison" (22).

   "I did not see why the schoolmaster should be taxed to support the priest, and not the priest the schoolmaster . . ." (25).

2. Do you believe civil disobedience is ever necessary? If so, under what circumstances? Would you engage in it? Why or why not?

3. Do you see any advantages in conforming to a law, however unjust, rather than disobeying it? Explain.

LETTER FROM BIRMINGHAM JAIL

~

Martin Luther King, Jr.

One of the greatest civil rights leaders and orators of this century (see also p. 396), Martin Luther King, Jr. (1929–1968), was also a Baptist minister and winner of the 1964 Nobel Peace Prize. He was born in Atlanta, Georgia, and earned degrees from four institutions. Influenced by Thoreau and Gandhi, King altered the spirit of African-American protest in the United States by advocating nonviolent civil disobedience to achieve racial equality. King's books include *Letter from Birmingham Jail* (1963) and *Where Do We Go from Here: Chaos or Community?* (1967). King was assassinated on April 4, 1968. The following letter, written in 1963, is his eloquent and impassioned response to a public statement by eight fellow clergymen in Birmingham, Alabama, who appealed to the citizenry of the city to "observe the principles of law and order and common sense" rather than join in the principled protests that King was leading.

My Dear Fellow Clergymen:[1]

While confined here in the Birmingham city jail, I came across your   1
recent statement calling my present activities "unwise and untimely."
Seldom do I pause to answer criticism of my work and ideas. If I sought
to answer all the criticisms that cross my desk, my secretaries would
have little time for anything other than such correspondence in the
course of the day, and I would have no time for constructive work. But
since I feel that you are men of genuine good will and that your criticisms are sincerely set forth, I want to try to answer your statement in
what I hope will be patient and reasonable terms.

I think I should indicate that I am here in Birmingham, since you   2
have been influenced by the view which argues against "outsiders coming in." I have the honor of serving as president of the Southern Christian Leadership Conference, an organization operating in every southern state, with headquarters in Atlanta, Georgia. We have some
eighty-five affiliated organizations across the South, and one of them is
the Alabama Christian Movement for Human Rights. Frequently we
share staff, educational, and financial resources with our affiliates. Several months ago the affiliate here in Birmingham asked us to be on call
to engage in a nonviolent direct-action program if such were deemed
necessary. We readily consented, and when the hour came we lived up
to our promise. So I, along with several members of my staff, am here
because I was invited here. I am here because I have organizational ties
here.

But more basically, I am in Birmingham because injustice is here. Just   3
as the prophets of the eighth century B.C. left their villages and carried
their "thus saith the Lord" far beyond the boundaries of their home
towns, and just as the Apostle Paul left his village of Tarsus and carried
the gospel of Jesus Christ to the far corners of the Greco-Roman world, so
am I compelled to carry the gospel of freedom beyond my own home
town. Like Paul, I must constantly respond to the Macedonian call for aid.

Moreover, I am cognizant of the interrelatedness of all communities   4
and states. I cannot sit idly by in Atlanta and not be concerned about
what happens in Birmingham. Injustice anywhere is a threat to justice
everywhere. We are caught in an inescapable network of mutuality, tied
in a single garment of destiny. Whatever affects one directly, affects all
indirectly. Never again can we afford to live with the narrow, provincial

---

[1] This response to a published statement by eight fellow clergymen from Alabama (Bishop C. C. J.
Carpenter, Bishop Joseph A. Durick, Rabbi Milton L. Grafman, Bishop Paul Hardin, Bishop Holan
B. Harmon, the Reverend George M. Murray, the Reverend Edward V. Ramage and the Reverend
Earl Stallings) was composed under somewhat constricting circumstances. Begun on the margins of
the newspaper in which the statement appeared while I was in jail, the letter was continued on scraps
of writing paper supplied by a friendly Negro trusty, and concluded on a pad my attorneys were
eventually permitted to leave me. Although the text remains in substance unaltered, I have indulged
in the author's prerogative of polishing it for publication.

"outside agitator" idea. Anyone who lives inside the United States can never be considered an outsider anywhere within its bounds.

You deplore the demonstrations taking place in Birmingham. But your statement, I am sorry to say, fails to express a similar concern for the conditions that brought about the demonstrations. I am sure that none of you would want to rest content with the superficial kind of social analysis that deals merely with effects and does not grapple with underlying causes. It is unfortunate that demonstrations are taking place in Birmingham, but it is even more unfortunate that the city's white power structure left the Negro community with no alternative.

In any nonviolent campaign there are four basic steps: collection of the facts to determine whether injustices exist; negotiation; self-purification; and direct action. We have gone through all these steps in Birmingham. There can be no gainsaying the fact that racial injustice engulfs this community. Birmingham is probably the most thoroughly segregated city in the United States. Its ugly record of brutality is widely known. Negroes have experienced grossly unjust treatment in the courts. There have been more unsolved bombings of Negro homes and churches in Birmingham than in any other city in the nation. These are the hard, brutal facts of the case. On the basis of these conditions, Negro leaders sought to negotiate with the city fathers. But the latter consistently refused to engage in good-faith negotiation.

Then, last September, came the opportunity to talk with leaders of Birmingham's economic community. In the course of the negotiations, certain promises were made by the merchants—for example, to remove the stores' humiliating racial signs. On the basis of these promises, the Reverend Fred Shuttlesworth and the leaders of the Alabama Christian Movement for Human Rights agreed to a moratorium on all demonstrations. As the weeks and months went by, we realized that we were the victims of a broken promise. A few signs, briefly removed, returned; the others remained.

As in so many past experiences, our hopes had been blasted, and the shadow of deep disappointment settled upon us. We had no alternative except to prepare for direct action, whereby we would present our very bodies as a means of laying our case before the conscience of the local and the national community. Mindful of the difficulties involved, we decided to undertake a process of self-purification. We began a series of workshops on nonviolence, and we repeatedly asked ourselves: "Are you able to accept blows without retaliating?" "Are you able to endure the ordeal of jail?" We decided to schedule our direct-action program for the Easter season, realizing that except for Christmas, this is the main shopping period of the year. Knowing that a strong economic-withdrawal program would be the by-product of direct action, we felt that this would be the best time to bring pressure to bear on the merchants for the needed change.

Then it occurred to us that Birmingham's mayoral election was com-   9
ing up in March, and we speedily decided to postpone action until after
election day. When we discovered that the Commissioner of Public Safety, Eugene "Bull" Connor, had piled up enough votes to be in the run-
off, we decided again to postpone action until the day after the run-off
so that the demonstrations could not be used to cloud the issues. Like
many others, we wanted to see Mr. Connor defeated, and to this end we
endured postponement after postponement. Having aided in this community need, we felt that our direct-action program could be delayed no
longer.

You may well ask, "Why direct action? Why sit-ins, marches, and so   10
forth? Isn't negotiation a better path?" You are quite right in calling for
negotiation. Indeed, this is the very purpose of direct action. Nonviolent
direct action seeks to create such a crisis and foster such a tension that
a community which has constantly refused to negotiate is forced to confront the issue. It seeks so to dramatize the issue that it can no longer be
ignored. My citing the creation of tension as part of the work of the non-
violent-resister may sound rather shocking. But I must confess that I am
not afraid of the word "tension." I have earnestly opposed violent tension, but there is a type of constructive, nonviolent tension which is necessary for growth. Just as Socrates felt that it was necessary to create a
tension in the mind so that individuals could rise from the bondage of
myths and half-truths to the unfettered realm of creative analysis and
objective appraisal, so must we see the need for nonviolent gadflies to
create the kind of tension in society that will help men rise from the dark
depths of prejudice and racism to the majestic heights of understanding
and brotherhood.

The purpose of our direct-action program is to create a situation so   11
crisis-packed that it will inevitably open the door to negotiation. I therefore concur with you in your call for negotiation. Too long has our
beloved Southland been bogged down in a tragic effort to live in mono-
logue rather than dialogue.

One of the basic points in your statement is that the action that I and   12
my associates have taken in Birmingham is untimely. Some have asked:
"Why didn't you give the new city administration time to act?" The only
answer that I can give to this query is that the new Birmingham administration must be prodded about as much as the outgoing one, before it will act. We are sadly mistaken if we feel that the election of Albert Boutwell as mayor will bring the millennium to Birmingham. While
Mr. Boutwell is a much more gentle person than Mr. Connor, they are
both segregationists, dedicated to maintenance of the status quo. I have
hoped that Mr. Boutwell will be reasonable enough to see the futility of
massive resistance to desegregation. But he will not see this without
pressure from devotees of civil rights. My friends, I must say to you that
we have not made a single gain in civil rights without determined legal

and nonviolent pressure. Lamentably, it is an historical fact that privileged groups seldom give up their privileges voluntarily. Individuals may see the moral light and voluntarily give up their unjust posture; but, as Reinhold Niebuhr[2] has reminded us, groups tend to be more immoral than individuals.

We know through painful experience that freedom is never voluntarily given by the oppressor; it must be demanded by the oppressed. Frankly, I have yet to engage in a direct-action campaign that was "well timed" in the view of those who have not suffered unduly from the disease of segregation. For years now I have heard the word "Wait!" It rings in the ear of every Negro with piercing familiarity. This "Wait" has almost always meant "Never." We must come to see, with one of our distinguished jurists, that "justice too long delayed is justice denied."   13

We have waited for more than 340 years for our constitutional and God-given rights. The nations of Asia and Africa are moving with jetlike speed toward gaining political independence, but we still creep at horse-and-buggy pace toward gaining a cup of coffee at a lunch counter. Perhaps it is easy for those who have never felt the stinging darts of segregation to say, "Wait." But when you have seen vicious mobs lynch your mothers and fathers at will and drown your sisters and brothers at whim; when you have seen hate-filled policemen curse, kick, and even kill your black brothers and sisters; when you see the vast majority of your twenty million Negro brothers smothering in an airtight cage of poverty in the midst of an affluent society; when you suddenly find your tongue twisted and your speech stammering as you seek to explain to your six-year-old daughter why she can't go to the public amusement park that has just been advertised on television, and see tears welling up in her eyes when she is told that Funtown is closed to colored children, and see ominous clouds of inferiority beginning to form in her little mental sky, and see her beginning to distort her personality by developing an unconscious bitterness toward white people; when you have to concoct an answer for a five-year-old son who is asking, "Daddy, why do white people treat colored people so mean?"; when you take a cross-country drive and find it necessary to sleep night after night in the uncomfortable corners of your automobile because no motel will accept you; when you are humiliated day in and day out by nagging signs reading "white" and "colored"; when your first name becomes "nigger," your middle name becomes "boy" (however old you are) and your last name becomes "John," and your wife and mother are never given the respected title "Mrs."; when you are harried by day and haunted by night by the fact that you are a Negro, living constantly at tiptoe stance, never quite knowing what to expect next, and are plagued with inner fears and outer resentments; when you are forever fighting a degenerating sense   14

---

[2] American religious and social thinker (1892–1971). [Eds.]

of "nobodiness"—then you will understand why we find it difficult to wait. There comes a time when the cup of endurance runs over, and men are no longer willing to be plunged into the abyss of despair. I hope, sirs, you can understand our legitimate and unavoidable impatience.

You express a great deal of anxiety over our willingness to break [15] laws. This is certainly a legitimate concern. Since we so diligently urge people to obey the Supreme Court's decision of 1954 outlawing segregation in the public schools, at first glance it may seem rather paradoxical for us consciously to break laws. One may well ask: "How can you advocate breaking some laws and obeying others?" The answer lies in the fact that there are two types of laws: just and unjust. I would be the first to advocate obeying just laws. One has not only a legal but a moral responsibility to obey just laws. Conversely, one has a moral responsibility to disobey unjust laws. I would agree with St. Augustine that "an unjust law is no law at all."

Now, what is the difference between the two? How does one de- [16] termine whether a law is just or unjust? A just law is a man-made code that squares with the moral law or the law of God. An unjust law is a code this is out of harmony with the moral law. To put it in the terms of St. Thomas Aquinas:[3] An unjust law is a human law that is not rooted in eternal law and natural law. Any law that uplifts human personality is just. Any law that degrades human personality is unjust. All segregation statutes are unjust because segregation distorts the soul and damages the personality. It gives the segregator a false sense of superiority and the segregated a false sense of inferiority. Segregation, to use the terminology of the Jewish philosopher Martin Buber,[4] substitutes an "I-it" relationship for an "I-thou" relationship and ends up relegating persons to the status of things. Hence segregation is not only politically, economically, and sociologically unsound, it is morally wrong and sinful. Paul Tillich[5] has said that sin is separation. Is not segregation an existential expression of man's tragic separation, his awful estrangement, his terrible sinfulness? Thus it is that I can urge men to obey the 1954 decision of the Supreme Court, for it is morally right; and I can urge them to disobey segregation ordinances, for they are morally wrong.

Let us consider a more concrete example of just and unjust laws. An [17] unjust law is a code that a numerical or power majority group compels a minority group to obey but does not make binding on itself. This is *difference* made legal. By the same token, a just law is a code that a majority compels a minority to follow and that it is willing to follow itself. This is *sameness* made legal.

---

[3] Italian philosopher and theologian (1225–74). [Eds.]

[4] Austrian existentialist philosopher and Judaic scholar (1878–1965). [Eds.]

[5] American philosopher and theologian (1886–1965). [Eds.]

Let me give another explanation. A law is unjust if it is inflicted on 18 a minority that, as a result of being denied the right to vote, had no part in enacting or devising the law. Who can say that the legislature of Alabama which set up that state's segregation laws was democratically elected? Throughout Alabama all sorts of devious methods are used to prevent Negroes from becoming registered voters, and there are some counties in which, even though Negroes constitute a majority of the population, not a single Negro is registered. Can any law enacted under such circumstances be considered democratically structured?

Sometimes a law is just on its face and unjust in its application. For 19 instance, I have been arrested on a charge of parading without a permit. Now, there is nothing wrong in having an ordinance which requires a permit for a parade. But such an ordinance becomes unjust when it is used to maintain segregation and to deny citizens the First-Amendment privilege of peaceful assembly and protest.

I hope you are able to see the distinction I am trying to point out. In 20 no sense do I advocate evading or defying the law, as would the rabid segregationist. That would lead to anarchy. One who breaks an unjust law must do so openly, lovingly, and with a willingness to accept the penalty. I submit that an individual who breaks a law that conscience tells him is unjust, and who willingly accepts the penalty of imprisonment in order to arouse the conscience of the community over its injustice, is in reality expressing the highest respect for law.

Of course, there is nothing new about this kind of civil disobedience. 21 It was evidenced sublimely in the refusal of Shadrach, Meshach, and Abednego to obey the laws of Nebuchadnezzar, on the ground that a higher moral law was at stake.[6] It was practiced superbly by the early Christians, who were willing to face hungry lions and the excruciating pain of chopping blocks rather than submit to certain unjust laws of the Roman Empire. To a degree, academic freedom is a reality today because Socrates practiced civil disobedience.[7] In our own nation, the Boston Tea Party represented a massive act of civil disobedience.

We should never forget that everything Adolf Hitler did in Ger- 22 many was "legal" and everything the Hungarian freedom fighters[8] did in Hungary was "illegal." It was "illegal" to aid and comfort a Jew in Hitler's Germany. Even so, I am sure that, had I lived in Germany at the

---

[6] In the Book of Daniel, Nebuchadnezzar commanded the people to worship a golden statue or be thrown into a furnace of blazing fire. When Shadrach, Meshach, and Abednego refused to worship any god but their own, they were bound and thrown into a blazing furnace, but the fire had no effect on them. Their escape led Nebuchadnezzar to make a decree forbidding blasphemy against their god. [Eds.]

[7] The ancient Greek philosopher Socrates was tried by the Athenians for corrupting their youth through his use of questions to teach. When he refused to change his methods of teaching, he was condemned to death. [Eds.]

[8] The anti-Communist uprising of 1956 was quickly crushed by the Russian army. [Eds.]

time, I would have aided and comforted my Jewish brothers. If today I lived in a Communist country where certain principles dear to the Christian faith are suppressed, I would openly advocate disobeying that country's anti-religious laws.

I must make two honest confessions to you, my Christian and Jewish brothers. First, I must confess that over the past few years I have been gravely disappointed with the white moderate. I have almost reached the regrettable conclusion that the Negro's great stumbling block in his stride toward freedom is not the White Citizen's Counciler or the Ku Klux Klanner, but the white moderate, who is more devoted to "order" than to justice; who prefers a negative peace which is the absence of tension to a positive peace which is the presence of justice; who constantly says, "I agree with you in the goal you seek, but I cannot agree with your methods of direct action"; who paternalistically believes he can set the timetable for another man's freedom; who lives by a mythical concept of time and who constantly advises the Negro to wait for a "more convenient season." Shallow understanding from people of good will is more frustrating than absolute misunderstanding from people of ill will. Lukewarm acceptance is much more bewildering than outright rejection. [23]

I had hoped that the white moderate would understand that law and order exist for the purpose of establishing justice and that when they fail in this purpose they become the dangerously structured dams that block the flow of social progress. I had hoped that the white moderate would understand that the present tension in the South is a necessary phase of the transition from an obnoxious negative peace, in which the Negro passively accepted his unjust plight, to a substantive and positive peace, in which all men will respect the dignity and worth of human personality. Actually, we who engage in nonviolent direct action are not the creators of tension. We merely bring to the surface the hidden tension that is already alive. We bring it out in the open, where it can be seen and dealt with. Like a boil that can never be cured so long as it is covered up but must be opened with all its ugliness to the natural medicines of air and light, injustice must be exposed, with all the tension its exposure creates, to the light of human conscience and the air of national opinion, before it can be cured. [24]

In your statement you assert that our actions, even though peaceful, must be condemned because they precipitate violence. But is this a logical assertion? Isn't this like condemning a robbed man because his possession of money precipitated the evil act of robbery? Isn't this like condemning Socrates because his unswerving commitment to truth and his philosophical inquiries precipitated the act by the misguided populace in which they made him drink hemlock? Isn't this like condemning Jesus because his unique God-consciousness and never-ceasing devotion to God's will precipitated the evil act of crucifixion? We must come to see [25] that, as the federal courts have consistently affirmed, it is wrong to urge an individual to cease his efforts to gain his basic constitutional rights because the quest may precipitate violence. Society must protect the robbed and punish the robber.

I had also hoped that the white moderate would reject the myth   26 concerning time in relation to the struggle for freedom. I have just received a letter from a white brother in Texas. He writes: "All Christians know that the colored people will receive equal rights eventually, but it is possible that you are in too great a religious hurry. It has taken Christianity almost two thousand years to accomplish what it has. The teachings of Christ take time to come to earth." Such an attitude stems from a tragic misconception of time, from the strangely irrational notion that there is something in the very flow of time that will inevitably cure all ills. Actually, time itself is neutral; it can be used either destructively or constructively. More and more I feel that the people of ill will have used time much more effectively than have the people of good will. We will have to repent in this generation not merely for the hateful words and actions of the bad people, but for the appalling silence of the good people. Human progress never rolls in on wheels of inevitability; it comes through the tireless efforts of men willing to be co-workers with God, and without this hard work, time itself becomes an ally of the forces of social stagnation. We must use time creatively, in the knowledge that the time is always ripe to do right. Now is the time to make real the promise of democracy and transform our pending national elegy into a creative psalm of brotherhood. Now is the time to lift our national policy from the quicksand of racial injustice to the solid rock of human dignity.

You speak of our activity in Birmingham as extreme. At first I was   27 rather disappointed that fellow clergymen would see my nonviolent efforts as those of an extremist. I began thinking about the fact that I stand in the middle of two opposing forces in the Negro community. One is a force of complacency, made up in part of Negroes who, as a result of long years of oppression, are so drained of self-respect and a sense of "somebodiness" that they have adjusted to segregation; and in part of a few middle-class Negroes who, because of a degree of academic and economic security and because in some ways the profit by segregation, have become insensitive to the problems of the masses. The other force is one of bitterness and hatred, and it comes perilously close to advocating violence. It is expressed in the various black nationalist groups that are springing up across the nation, the largest and best-known being Elijah Muhammad's Muslim movement. Nourished by the Negro's frustration over the continued existence of racial discrimination, this movement is made up of people who have lost faith in America, who have absolutely repudiated Christianity, and who have concluded that the white man is an incorrigible "devil."

I have tried to stand between these two forces, saying that we need ²⁸
emulate neither the "do-nothingism" of the complacent nor the hatred
and despair of the black nationalist. For there is the more excellent way
of love and nonviolent protest. I am grateful to God that, through the influence of the Negro church, the way of nonviolence became an integral
part of our struggle.

If this philosophy had not emerged, by now many streets of the ²⁹
South would, I am convinced, be flowing with blood. And I am further
convinced that if our white brothers dismiss as "rabblerousers" and
"outside agitators" those of use who employ nonviolent direct action,
and if they refuse to support our nonviolent efforts, millions of Negroes
will, out of frustration and despair, seek solace and security in black-na-
tionalist ideologies—a development that would inevitably lead to a
frightening racial nightmare.

Oppressed people cannot remain oppressed forever. The yearning ³⁰
for freedom eventually manifests itself, and that is what has happened
to the American Negro. Something within has reminded him of his
birthright of freedom, and something without has reminded him that it
can be gained. Consciously or unconsciously, he has been caught up by
the *Zeitgeist*,⁹ and with his black brothers of Africa and his brown and
yellow brothers of Asia, South America, and the Caribbean, the United
States Negro is moving with a sense of great urgency toward the
promised land of racial justice. If one recognizes this vital urge that has
engulfed the Negro community, one should readily understand why
public demonstrations are taking place. The Negro has many pent-up
resentments and latent frustrations, and he must release them. So let him
march; let him make prayer pilgrimages to the city hall; let him go on
freedom rides—and try to understand why he must do so. If his repressed emotions are not released in nonviolent ways, they will seek expression through violence; this is not a threat but a fact of history. So I
have not said to my people, "Get rid of your discontent." Rather, I have
tried to say that this normal and healthy discontent can be channeled
into the creative outlet of nonviolent direct action. And now this approach is being termed extremist.

But though I was initially disappointed at being categorized as an ³¹
extremist, as I continued to think about the matter I gradually gained a
measure of satisfaction from the label. Was not Jesus an extremist for
love: "Love your enemies, bless them that curse you, do good to them
that hate you, and pray for them which despitefully use you, and per-
secute you." Was not Amos an extremist for justice: "Let justice roll
down like waters and righteousness like an ever-flowing stream." Was
not Paul an extremist for the Christian gospel: "I bear in my body the
marks of the Lord Jesus." Was not Martin Luther an extremist: "Here I

---

⁹ The spirit of the times. [Eds.]

stand; I cannot do otherwise, so help me God." And John Bunyan: "I will stay in jail to the end of my days before I make a butchery of my conscience." And Abraham Lincoln: "This nation cannot survive half slave and half free." And Thomas Jefferson: "We hold these truths to be self-evident, that all men are created equal. . . ." So the question is not whether we will be extremists, but what kind of extremists we will be. Will we be extremists for hate or for love? Will we be extremists for the preservation of injustice or for the extension of justice? In that dramatic scene on Calvary's hill three men were crucified. We must never forget that all three were crucified for the same thing—the crime of extremism. Two were extremists for immorality, and thus fell below their environment. The other, Jesus Christ, was an extremist for love, truth, and goodness, and thereby rose above his environment. Perhaps the South, the nation, and the world are in dire need of creative extremists.

I had hoped that the white moderate would see this need. Perhaps [32] I was too optimistic; perhaps I expected too much. I suppose I should have realized that few members of the oppressor race can understand the deep groans and passionate yearnings of the oppressed race, and still fewer have the vision to see that injustice must be rooted out by strong, persistent, and determined action. I am thankful, however, that some of our white brothers in the South have grasped the meaning of this social revolution and committed themselves to it. They are still all too few in quantity, but they are big in quality. Some—such as Ralph McGill, Lillian Smith, Harry Golden, James McBridge Dabbs, Ann Braden, and Sarah Patton Boyle—have written about our struggle in eloquent and prophetic terms. Others have marched with us down nameless streets of the South. They have languished in filthy, roach-infested jails, suffering the abuse and brutality of policemen who view them as "dirty nigger-lovers." Unlike so many of their moderate brothers and sisters, they have recognized the urgency of the moment and sensed the need for powerful "action" antidotes to combat the disease of segregation.

Let me take note of my other major disappointment. I have been so [33] greatly disappointed with the white church and its leadership. Of course, there are some notable exceptions. I am not unmindful of the fact that each of you has taken some significant stands on this issue. I commend you, Reverend Stallings, for your Christian stand on this past Sunday, in welcoming Negroes to your worship service on a nonsegregated basis. I commend the Catholic leaders of this state for integrating Spring Hill College several years ago.

But despite these notable exceptions, I must honestly reiterate that [34] I have been disappointed with the church. I do not say this as one of those negative critics who can always find something wrong with the church. I say this as a minister of the gospel, who loves the church; who was nurtured in its bosom; who has been sustained by its spiritual blessings and who will remain true to it as long as the cord of life shall lengthen.

When I was suddenly catapulted into the leadership of the bus [35] protest in Montgomery, Alabama, a few years ago, I felt we would be supported by the white church. I felt that the white ministers, priests, and rabbis of the South would be among our strongest allies. Instead, some have been outright opponents, refusing to understand the freedom movement and misrepresenting its leaders; all too many others have been more cautious than courageous and have remained silent behind the anesthetizing security of stainedglass windows.

In spite of my shattered dreams, I came to Birmingham with the [36] hope that the white religious leadership of this community would see the justice of our cause and, with deep moral concern, would serve as the channel through which our just grievances could reach the power structure. I had hoped that each of you would understand. But again I have been disappointed.

I have heard numerous southern religious leaders admonish their [37] worshipers to comply with a desegregation decision because it is the law, but I have longed to hear white ministers declare: "Follow this de-cree because integration is morally right and because the Negro is your brother." In the midst of blatant injustices inflicted upon the Negro, I have watched white churchmen stand on the sideline and mouth pious irrelevancies and sanctimonious trivialities. In the midst of a mighty struggle to rid our nation of racial and economic injustice, I have heard many ministers say: "Those are social issues, with which the gospel has no real concern." And I have watched many churches commit them-selves to a completely otherworldly religion which makes a strange, un-Biblical distinction between body and soul, between the sacred and the secular.

I have traveled the length and breadth of Alabama, Mississippi, and [38] all the other southern states. On sweltering summer days and crisp au-tumn mornings I have looked at the South's beautiful churches with their lofty spires pointing heavenward. I have beheld the impressive outlines of her massive religious-education buildings. Over and over I have found myself asking: "What kind of people worship here? Who is their God? Where were their voices when the lips of Governor Barnett dripped with words of interposition and nullification? Where were they when Governor Wallace gave a clarion call for defiance and hatred? Where were their voices of support when bruised and weary Negro men and women decided to rise from the dark dungeons of complacency to the bright hills of creative protest?"

Yes, these questions are still in my mind. In deep disappointment I [39] have wept over the laxity of the church. But be assured that my tears have been tears of love. There can be no deep disappointment where there is not deep love. Yes, I love the church. How could I do otherwise?

I am in the rather unique position of being the son, the grandson, and the great-grandson of preachers. Yes, I see the church as the body of Christ. But, oh! How we have blemished and scarred that body through social neglect and through fear of being nonconformists.

There was a time when the church was very powerful—in the time [40] when the early Christians rejoiced at being deemed worthy to suffer for what they believed. In those days the church was not merely a thermometer that recorded the ideas and principles of popular opinion; it was a thermostat that transformed the mores of society. Whenever the early Christians entered a town, the people in power became distrubed and immediately sought to convict the Christians for being "disturbers of the peace" and "outside agitators." But the Christians pressed on, in the conviction that they were "a colony of heaven," called to obey God rather than man. Small in number, they were big in commitment. They were too God-intoxicated to be "astronomically intimidated." By their effort and example they brought an end to such ancient evils as infanticide and gladiatorial contests.

Things are different now. So often the contemporary church is a [41] weak, ineffectual voice with an uncertain sound. So often it is an archdefender to the status quo. Far from being distrubed by the presence of the church, the power structure of the average community is consoled by the church's silent—and often even vocal—sanction of things as they are.

But the judgment of God is upon the church as never before. If [42] today's church does not recapture the sacrificial spirit of the early church, it will lose its authenticity, forfeit the loyalty of millions, and be dismissed as an irrelevant social club with no meaning for the twentieth century. Every day I meet young people whose disappointment with the church has turned into outright disgust.

Perhaps I have once again been too optimistic. Is organized religion [43] too inextricably bound to the status quo to save our nation and the world? Perhaps I must turn my faith to the inner spiritual church, the church within the church, as the true *ekklesia*[10] and the hope of the world. But again I am thankful to God that some noble souls from the ranks of organized religion have broken loose from the paralyzing chains of conformity and joined us as active partners in the struggle for freedom. They have left their secure congregations and walked the streets of Albany, Georgia, with us. They have gone down the highways of the South on tortuous rides for freedom. Yes, they have gone to jail with us. Some have been dismissed from their churches, have lost the support of their bishops and fellow ministers. But they have acted in the faith that right defeated is stronger than evil triumphant. Their witness has been the spiritual salt that has preserved the true meaning of the

---

[10] The Greek word for the early Christian church. [Eds.]

gospel in these troubled times. They have carved a tunnel of hope through the dark mountain of disappointment.

I hope the church as a whole will meet the challenge of this decisive [44] hour. But even if the church does not come to the aid of justice, I have no despair about the future. I have no fear about the outcome of our struggle in Birmingham, even if our motives are at present misunderstood. We will reach the goal of freedom in Birmingham and all over the nation, because the goal of America is freedom. Abused and scorned though we may be, our destiny is tied up with America's destiny. Before the pilgrims landed at Plymouth, we were here. Before the pen of Jefferson etched the majestic words of the Declaration of Independence across the pages of history, we were here. For more than two centuries our forebears labored in this country without wages; they made cotton king; they built the homes of their masters while suffering gross injustice and shameful humiliation—and yet out of a bottomless vitality they continued to thrive and develop. If the inexpressible cruelties of slavery could not stop us, the opposition we now face will surely fail. We will win our freedom because the sacred heritage of our nation and the eternal will of God are embodied in our echoing demands.

Before closing I feel impelled to mention one other point in your [45] statement that has troubled me profoundly. You warmly commended the Birmingham police force for keeping "order" and "preventing violence." I doubt that you would have so warmly commended the police force if you had seen its dogs sinking their teeth into unarmed, nonviolent Negroes. I doubt that you would so quickly commend the policemen if you were to observe their ugly and inhumane treatment of Negroes here in the city jail; if you were to watch them push and curse old Negro women and young Negro girls; if you were to see them slap and kick old Negro men and young boys; if you were to observe them, as they did on two occasions, refuse to give us food because we wanted to sing our grace together. I cannot join you in your praise of the Birmingham police department.

It is true that the police have exercised a degree of discipline in han- [46] dling the demonstrators. In this sense they have conducted themselves rather "nonviolently" in public. But for what purpose? To preserve the evil system of segregation. Over the past few years I have consistently preached that nonviolence demands that the means we use must be as pure as the ends we seek. I have tried to make clear that it is wrong to use immoral means to attain moral ends. But now I must affirm that it is just as wrong, or perhaps even more so, to use moral means to preserve immoral ends. Perhaps Mr. Connor and his policemen have been rather nonviolent in public, as was Chief Pritchett in Albany, Georgia, but they have used the moral means of nonviolence to maintain the immoral end of racial injustice. As T. S. Eliot has said, "The last temptation is the greatest treason: To do the right deed for the wrong reason."

I wish you had commended the Negro sit-inners and demonstra- 47
tors of Birmingham for their sublime courage, their willingness to suffer, and their amazing discipline in the midst of great provocation. One
day the South will recognize its real heroes. They will be the James
Merediths,[11] with the noble sense of purpose that enables them to face
jeering and hostile mobs, and with the agonizing loneliness that characterizes the life of the pioneer. They will be old, oppressed, battered
Negro women, symbolized in a seventy-two-year-old woman in Montgomery, Alabama, who rose up with a sense of dignity and with her
people decided not to ride segregated buses, and who responded with
ungrammatical profundity to one who inquired about her weariness:
"My feets is tired, but my soul is at rest." They will be the young high
school and college students, the young ministers of the gospel and a
host of their elders, courageously and nonviolently sitting in at lunch
counters and willingly going to jail for conscience' sake. One day the
South will know that when these disinherited children of God sat
down at lunch counters, they were in reality standing up for what is
best in the American dream and for the most sacred values in our Ju-
daeo-Christian heritage, thereby bringing our nation back to those
great wells of democracy which were dug deep by the founding fathers in their formulation of the Constitution and the Declaration of Independence.

Never before have I written so long a letter. I'm afraid it is much too 48
long to take your precious time. I can assure you that it would have been
much shorter if I had been writing from a comfortable desk, but what
else can one do when he is alone in a narrow jail cell, other than write
long letters, think long thoughts, and pray long prayers?

If I have said anything in this letter that overstates the truth and in- 49
dicates an unreasonable impatience, I beg you to forgive me. If I have
said anything that understates the truth and indicates my having a patience that allows me to settle for anything less than brotherhood, I beg
God to forgive me.

I hope this letter finds you strong in the faith. I also hope that cir- 50
cumstances will soon make it possible for me to meet each of you, not
as an integrationist or a civil-rights leader but as a fellow clergyman and
a Christian brother. Let us all hope that the dark clouds of racial prejudice will soon pass away and the deep fog of misunderstanding will be
lifted from our fear-drenched communities, and in some not too distant
tomorrow the radiant stars of love and brotherhood will shine over our
great nation with all their scintillating beauty.

Yours for the cause of Peace and Brotherhood,

MARTIN LUTHER KING, JR.

---

[11] First African American to enroll at the University of Mississippi. [Eds.]

Responding to Reading

1. What decision do the clergymen he addresses believe King should rethink? Do you believe King would be justified in arguing that he has no other alternative? Would you accept this argument?
2. In paragraph 30 King says, "Oppressed people cannot remain oppressed forever." Do you think world events of the last few years confirm or contradict this statement? Explain.
3. Throughout this letter King uses elaborate diction and a variety of rhetorical devices: He addresses his audience directly; makes frequent use of balance and parallelism, understatement, and metaphor; and makes many historical and religious allusions. What effect do you think King intended these rhetorical devices to have on the letter's original audience of clergymen? What is their effect on you—that is, do you find they enhance his argument, or do you think they just get in the way?

LIFEBOAT ETHICS: THE CASE
∽ AGAINST HELPING THE POOR

Garrett Hardin

Biologist Garrett Hardin (1915–) writes on moral and ethical issues in his field. His books include *Filters against Folly: How To Survive Despite Economists, Ecologists, and the Merely Eloquent* (1985) and *Living Within Limits: How Global Population Growth Threatens Widespread Social Disorder* (1992). He often takes unpopular positions on subjects such as ecology and the scarcity of resources, and he is a fierce advocate of population limits. He has said, "Population is not a global problem. It is produced in each bedroom, a very local activity. So population control needs to be local." In this essay, which originally appeared in 1974 in *Psychology Today*, Hardin uses the metaphor of the wealthy nations of the world as lifeboats to illustrate the rights of both the needy and the rich in the problem of distributing the world's food.

Environmentalists use the metaphor of the earth as a "spaceship" in [1] trying to persuade countries, industries and people to stop wasting and polluting our natural resources. Since we all share life on this planet, they argue, no single person or institution has the right to destroy, waste, or use more than a fair share of its resources.

But does everyone on earth have an equal right to an equal share of [2] its resources? The spaceship metaphor can be dangerous when used by misguided idealists to justify suicidal policies for sharing our resources through uncontrolled immigration and foreign aid. In their enthusiastic but unrealistic generosity, they confuse the ethics of a spaceship with those of a lifeboat.

A true spaceship would have to be under the control of a captain, since no ship could possibly survive if its course were determined by committee. Spaceship Earth certainly has no captain; the United Nations is merely a toothless tiger, with little power to enforce any policy upon its bickering members.   3

If we divide the world crudely into rich nations and poor nations, two thirds of them are desperately poor, and only one third comparatively rich, with the United States the wealthiest of all. Metaphorically each rich nation can be seen as a lifeboat full of comparatively rich people. In the ocean outside each lifeboat swim the poor of the world, who would like to get in, or at least to share some of the wealth. What should the lifeboat passengers do?   4

First, we must recognize the limited capacity of any lifeboat. For example, a nation's land has a limited capacity to support a population and as the current energy crisis has shown us, in some ways we have already exceeded the carrying capacity of our land.   5

So here we sit, say 50 people in our lifeboat. To be generous let us assume it has room for 10 more, making a total capacity of 60. Suppose the 50 of us in the lifeboat see 100 others swimming in the water outside, begging for admission to our boat or for handouts. We have several options: we may be tempted to try to live by the Christian ideal of being "our brother's keeper," or by the Marxist ideal of "to each according to his needs." Since the needs of all in the water are the same, and since they can all be seen as "our brothers," we could take them all into our boat, making a total of 150 in a boat designed for 60. The boat swamps, everyone drowns. Complete justice, complete catastrophe.   6

Since the boat has an unused excess capacity of 10 more passengers, we could admit just 10 more to it. But which 10 do we let in? How do we choose? Do we pick the best 10, the neediest 10, "first come, first served"? And what do we say to the 90 we exclude? If we do let an extra 10 into our lifeboat, we will have lost our "safety factor," an engineering principle of critical importance. For example, if we don't leave room for excess capacity as a safety factor in our country's agriculture, a new plant disease or a bad change in the weather could have disastrous consequences.   7

Suppose we decide to preserve our small safety factor and admit no more to the lifeboat. Our survival is then possible although we shall have to be constantly on guard against boarding parties.   8

While this last solution clearly offers the only means of our survival, it is morally abhorrent to many people. Some say they feel guilty about their good luck. My reply is simple: "Get out and yield your place to   9 others." This may solve the problem of the guilt-ridden person's conscience, but it does not change the ethics of the lifeboat. The needy person to whom the guilt-ridden person yields his place will not himself feel guilty about his good luck. If he did, he would not climb aboard. The net result of conscience-stricken people giving up their unjustly held seats is the elimination of that sort of conscience from the lifeboat.

This is the basic metaphor within which we must work out our solutions. Let us now enrich the image, step by step, with substantive additions from the real world, a world that must solve real and pressing problems of overpopulation and hunger. [10]

The harsh ethics of the lifeboat become even harsher when we consider the reproductive differences between the rich nations and the poor nations. The people inside the lifeboats are doubling in numbers every 87 years: those swimming around outside are doubling on the average, every 35 years, more than twice as fast as the rich. And since the world's resources are dwindling, the difference in prosperity between the rich and the poor can only increase. [11]

As of 1973, the U.S. had a population of 210 million people, who were increasing by 0.8 percent per year. Outside our lifeboat, let us imagine another 210 million people (say the combined populations of Colombia, Ecuador, Venezuela, Morocco, Pakistan, Thailand and the Philippines), who are increasing at a rate of 3.3 percent per year. Put differently, the doubling time for this aggregate population is 21 years, compared to 87 years for the U.S. [12]

Now suppose the U.S. agreed to pool its resources with those seven countries, with everyone receiving an equal share. Initially the ratio of Americans to non-Americans in this model would be one-to-one but consider what the ratio would be after 87 years, by which time the Americans would have doubled to a population of 420 million. By then, doubling every 21 years, the other group would have swollen to 354 billion. Each American would have to share the available resources with more than eight people. [13]

But, one could argue, this discussion assumes that current population trends will continue, and they may not. Quite so. Most likely the rate of population increase will decline much faster in the U.S. than it will in the other countries, and there does not seem to be much we can do about it. In sharing with "each according to his needs," we must recognize that needs are determined by population size, which is determined by the rate of reproduction, which at present is regarded as a sovereign right of every nation, poor or not. This being so, the philanthropic load created by the sharing ethic of the spaceship can only increase. [14]

The fundamental error of spaceship ethics, and the sharing it requires, is that it leads to what I call "the tragedy of the commons." Under a system of private property, the men who own property recognize their responsibility to care for it, for if they don't they will eventually suffer. [15]

A farmer, for instance, will allow no more cattle in a pasture than its carrying capacity justifies. If he overloads it, erosion sets in, weeds take over, and he loses the use of the pasture.

If a pasture becomes a commons open to all, the right of each to use [16] it may not be matched by a corresponding responsibility to protect it. Asking everyone to use it with discretion will hardly do, for the considerate herdsman who refrains from overloading the commons suffers more than a selfish one who says his needs are greater. If everyone would restrain himself all would be well; but it takes only one less than everyone to ruin a system of voluntary restraint. In a crowded world of less than perfect human beings, mutual ruin is inevitable if there are no controls. This is the tragedy of the commons.

One of the major tasks of education today should be the creation of [17] such an acute awareness of the dangers of the commons that people will recognize its many varieties. For example, the air and water have become polluted because they are treated as commons. Further growth in the population or per-capita conversion of natural resources into pollutants will only make the problem worse. The same holds true for the fish of the oceans. Fishing fleets have nearly disappeared in many parts of the world, technological improvements in the art of fishing are hastening the day of complete ruin. Only the replacement of the system of the commons with a responsible system of control will save the land, air, water and oceanic fisheries.

In recent years there has been a push to create a new commons [18] called a World Food Bank, an international depository of food reserves to which nations would contribute according to their abilities and from which they would draw according to their needs. This humanitarian proposal has received support from many liberal international groups, and from such prominent citizens as Margaret Mead, U.N. Secretary General Kurt Waldheim, and Senators Edward Kennedy and George McGovern.

A world food bank appeals powerfully to our humanitarian impulses. [19] But before we rush ahead with such a plan, let us recognize where the greatest political push comes from, lest we be disillusioned later. Our experience with the "Food for Peace program," or Public Law 480, gives us the answer. This program moved billions of dollars worth of U.S. surplus grain to food-short, population-long countries during the past two decades. But when P.L. 480 first became law, a headline in the business magazine *Forbes* revealed the real power behind it: "Feeding the World's Hungry Millions: How It Will Mean Billions for U.S. Business."

And indeed it did. In the years 1960 to 1970, U.S. taxpayers spent a [20] total of $7.9 billion on the Food for Peace program. Between 1948 and 1970, they also paid an additional $50 billion for other economic-aid programs, some of which went for food and food-producing machinery and technology. Though all U.S. taxpayers were forced to contribute to the cost of P.L. 480, certain special interest groups gained handsomely under the program. Farmers did not have to contribute the grain; the Government, or rather the taxpayers, bought it from them at full market prices. The increased demand raised prices of farm products generally. The manufacturers of farm machinery, fertilizers and pesticides benefited by the farmers' extra efforts to grow more food. Grain elevators profited from storing the surplus until it could be shipped. Railroads made money hauling it to ports, and shipping lines profited from carrying it overseas. The implementation of P.L. 480 required the creation of a vast Government bureaucracy, which then acquired its own vested interest in continuing the program regardless of its merits.

Those who proposed and defended the Food for Peace program in [21] public rarely mentioned its importance to any of these special interests. The public emphasis was always on its humanitarian effects. The combination of silent selfish interests and highly vocal humanitarian apologists made a powerful and successful lobby for extracting money from taxpayers. We can expect the same lobby to push now for the creation of a World Food Bank.

However great the potential benefit to selfish interests, it should not [22] be a decisive argument against a truly humanitarian program. We must ask if such a program would actually do more good than harm, not only momentarily but also in the long run. Those who propose the food bank usually refer to a current "emergency" or "crisis" in terms of world food supply. But what is an emergency? Although they may be infrequent and sudden, everyone knows that emergencies will occur from time to time. A well-run family, company, organization or country prepares for the likelihood of accidents and emergencies. It expects them, it budgets for them, it saves for them.

What happens if some organizations or countries budget for acci- [23] dents and others do not? If each country is solely responsible for its own well-being, poorly managed ones will suffer. But they can learn from experience. They may mend their ways, and learn to budget for infrequent but certain emergencies. For example, the weather varies from year to year, and periodic crop failures are certain. A wise and competent government saves out of the production of the good years in anticipation of bad years to come. Joseph taught this policy to Pharoah in Egypt more than 2,000 years ago. Yet the great majority of the governments in the world today do not follow such a policy. They lack either the wisdom or the competence, or both. Should those nations that do manage to put something aside be forced to come to the rescue each time an emergency occurs among the poor nations?

"But it isn't their fault!" Some kind-hearted liberals argue, "How [24] can we blame the poor people who are caught in an emergency? Why must they suffer for the sins of their governments?" The concept of blame is simply not relevant here. The real question is, what are the operational consequences of establishing a world food bank? If it is open to every country every time a need develops, slovenly rulers will not be motivated to take Joseph's advice. Someone will always come to their aid. Some countries will deposit food in the world food bank, and others will withdraw it. There will be almost no overlap. As a result of such solutions to food shortage emergencies, the poor countries will not learn to mend their ways, and will suffer progressively greater emergencies as their populations grow.

On the average, poor countries undergo a 2.5 percent increase in   25
population each year; rich countries, about 0.8 percent. Only rich countries have anything in the way of food reserves set aside, and even they do not have as much as they should. Poor countries have none. If poor countries received no food from the outside, the rate of their population growth would be periodically checked by crop failures and famines. But if they can always draw on a world food bank in time of need, their population can continue to grow unchecked, and so will their "need" for aid. In the short run, a world food bank may diminish that need, but in the long run it actually increases the need without limit.

Without some system of worldwide food sharing, the proportion of   26
people in the rich and poor nations might eventually stabilize. The overpopulated poor countries would decrease in numbers, while the rich countries that had room for more people would increase. But with a well-meaning system of sharing, such as a world food bank, the growth differential between the rich and the poor countries will not only persist, it will increase. Because of the higher rate of population growth in the poor countries of the world, 88 percent of today's children are born poor, and only 12 percent rich. Year by year the ratio becomes worse, as the fast-reproducing poor outnumber the slow-reproducing rich.

A world food bank is thus a commons in disguise. People will have   27
more motivation to draw from it than to add to any common store. The less provident and less able will multiply at the expense of the abler and more provident, bringing eventual ruin upon all who share in the commons. Besides, any system of "sharing" that amounts to foreign aid from the rich nations to the poor nations will carry the taint of charity, which will contribute little to the world peace so devoutly desired by those who support the idea of a world food bank.

As past U.S. foreign-aid programs have amply and depressingly   28
demonstrated, international charity frequently inspires mistrust and antagonism rather than gratitude on the part of the recipient nation [see "What Other Nations Hear When the Eagle Screams," by Kenneth J. and Mary M. Gergen, *Psychology Today,* June 1974].

The modern approach to foreign aid stresses the export of technol-   29
ogy and advice, rather than money and food. As an ancient Chinese proverb goes: "Give a man a fish and he will eat for a day; teach him

how to fish and he will eat for the rest of his days." Acting on this advice, the Rockefeller and Ford Foundations have financed a number of programs for improving agriculture in the hungry nations. Known as the "Green Revolution," these programs have led to the development of "miracle rice" and "miracle wheat," new strains that offer bigger harvests and greater resistance to crop damage. Norman Borlaug, the Nobel Prize winning agronomist who, supported by the Rockefeller Foundation, developed "miracle wheat," is one of the most prominent advocates of a world food bank.

Whether or not the Green Revolution can increase food production 30 as much as its champions claim is a debatable but possibly irrelevant point. Those who support this well-intended humanitarian effort should first consider some of the fundamentals of human ecology. Ironically, one man who did was the late Alan Gregg, a vice president of the Rockefeller Foundation. Two decades ago he expressed strong doubts about the wisdom of such attempts to increase food production. He likened the growth and spread of humanity over the surface of the earth to the spread of cancer in the human body, remarking that "cancerous growths demand food, but, as far as I know, they have never been cured by getting it."

Every human born constitutes a draft on all aspects of the environ- 31 ment: food, air, water, forests, beaches, wildlife, scenery and solitude. Food can, perhaps, be significantly increased to meet a growing demand. But what about clean beaches, unspoiled forests, and solitude? If we satisfy a growing population's need for food, we necessarily decrease its per capita supply of the other resources needed by men.

India, for example, now has a population of 600 million, which in- 32 creases by 15 million each year. This population already puts a huge load on a relatively impoverished environment. The country's forests are now only a small fraction of what they were three centuries ago, and floods and erosion continually destroy the insufficient farmland that remains. Every one of the 15 million new lives added to India's population puts an additional burden on the environment, and increases the economic and social costs of crowding. However humanitarian our intent, every Indian life saved through medical or nutritional assistance from abroad diminishes the quality of life for those who remain, and for subsequent generations. If rich countries make it possible, through foreign aid, for 600 million Indians to swell to 1.2 billion in a mere 28 years, as their current growth rate threatens, will future generations of Indians thank us for hastening the destruction of their environment? Will our good intentions be sufficient excuse for the consequences of our actions?

My final example of a commons in action is one for which the pub- 33 lic has the least desire for rational discussion—immigration. Anyone who publicly questions the wisdom of current U.S. immigration policy is promptly charged with bigotry, prejudice, ethnocentrism, chauvinism, isolationism or selfishness. Rather than encounter such accusations, one would rather talk about other matters, leaving immigration policy to wallow in the crosscurrents of special interests that take no account of the good of the whole, or the interests of posterity.

Perhaps we still feel guilty about things we said in the past. Two [34] generations ago the popular press frequently referred to Dagos, Wops, Polacks, Chinks and Krauts, in articles about how America was being "overrun" by foreigners of supposedly inferior genetic stock [see "The Politics of Genetic Engineering: Who Decides Who's Defective?" *Psychology Today*, June 1974]. But because the implied inferiority of foreigners was used then as justification for keeping them out, people now assume that restrictive policies could only be based on such misguided notions. There are other grounds.

Just consider the numbers involved. Our Government acknowl- [35] edges a net inflow of 400,000 immigrants a year. While we have no hard data on the extent of illegal entries, educated guesses put the figure at about 600,000 a year. Since the natural increase (excess of births over deaths) of the resident population now runs about 1.7 million per year, the yearly gain from immigration amounts to at least 19 percent of the total annual increase, and may be as much as 37 percent if we include the estimate for illegal immigrants. Considering the growing use of birth-control devices, the potential effect of educational campaigns by such organizations as Planned Parenthood Federation of America and Zero Population Growth, and the influence of inflation and the housing shortage, the fertility rate of American women may decline so much that immigration could account for all the yearly increase in population. Should we not at least ask if that is what we want?

For the sake of those who worry about whether the "quality" of the [36] average immigrant compares favorably with the quality of the average resident, let us assume that immigrants and nativeborn citizens are of exactly equal quality, however one defines that term. We will focus here only on quantity; and since our conclusions will depend on nothing else, all charges of bigotry and chauvinism become irrelevant.

World food banks *move food to the people*, hastening the exhaustion [37] of the environment of the poor countries. Unrestricted immigration, on the other hand, *moves people to the food*, thus speeding up the destruction of the environment of the rich countries. We can easily understand why poor people should want to make this latter transfer, but why should rich hosts encourage it?

As is the case of foreign-aid programs, immigration receives sup- [38] port from selfish interests and humanitarian impulses. The primary selfish interest in unimpeded immigration is the desire of employers for cheap labor, particularly in industries and trades that offer degrading work. In the past, one wave of foreigners after another was brought into the U.S. to work at wretched jobs for wretched wages. In recent years the

Cubans, Puerto Ricans and Mexicans have had this dubious honor. The interests of the employers of cheap labor mesh well with the guilty silence of the country's liberal intelligentsia. White Anglo-Saxon Protestants are particularly reluctant to call for a closing of the doors to immigration for fear of being called bigots.

But not all countries have such reluctant leadership. Most educated [39] Hawaiians, for example, are keenly aware of the limits of their environment, particularly in terms of population growth. There is only so much room on the islands, and the islanders know it. To Hawaiians, immigrants from the other 49 states present as great a threat as those from other nations. At a recent meeting of Hawaiian government officials in Honolulu, I had the ironic delight of hearing a speaker, who like most of his audience was of Japanese ancestry, ask how the country might practically and constitutionally close its door to further immigration. One member of the audience countered: "How can we shut the doors now? We have many friends and relatives in Japan that we'd like to bring here some day so that they can enjoy Hawaii too." The Japanese-American speaker smiled sympathetically and answered: "Yes, but we have children now, and someday we'll have grandchildren too. We can bring more people here from Japan only by giving away some of the land that we hope to pass on to our grandchildren some day. What right do we have to do that?"

At this point, I can hear U.S. liberals asking: "How can you justify [40] slamming the door once you're inside? You say that immigrants should be kept out. But aren't we all immigrants, or the descendants of immigrants? If we insist on staying, must we not admit all others?" Our craving for intellectual order leads us to seek and prefer symmetrical rules and morals: a single rule for me and everybody else; the same rule yesterday, today and tomorrow. Justice, we feel, should not change with time and place.

We Americans of non-Indian ancestry can look upon ourselves as [41] the descendants of thieves who are guilty morally, if not legally, of stealing this land from its Indian owners. Should we then give back the land to the now living American descendants of those Indians? However morally or logically sound this proposal may be, I, for one, am unwilling to live by it and I know no one else who is. Besides, the logical consequence would be absurd. Suppose that, intoxicated with a sense of pure justice, we should decide to turn our land over to the Indians. Since all our other wealth has also been derived from the land, wouldn't we be morally obliged to give that back to the Indians too?

Clearly, the concept of pure justice produces an infinite regression [42] to absurdity. Centuries ago, wise men invented statutes of limitations to justify the rejection of such pure justice, in the interest of preventing continual disorder. The law zealously defends property rights. Drawing a

line after an arbitrary time has elapsed may be unjust, but the alternatives are worse.

We are all the descendants of thieves, and the world's resources are ⁴³
inequitably distributed. But we must begin the journey to tomorrow
from the point where we are today. We cannot remake the past. We cannot safely divide the wealth equitably among all peoples so long as people reproduce at different rates. To do so would guarantee that our
grandchildren, and everyone else's grandchildren, would have only a
ruined world to inhabit.

To be generous with one's own possessions is quite different from ⁴⁴
being generous with those of posterity. We should call this point to the
attention of those who, from a commendable love of justice and equality, would institute a system of the commons, either in the form of a world
food bank, or of unrestricted immigration. We must convince them if we
wish to save at least some parts of the world from environmental ruin.

Responding to Reading

1. Hardin presents his problem as one with no comfortable solution: One alternative, welcoming all who wish to come into the lifeboat, is "complete justice, complete catastrophe" (6); the other, retaining the crucial "safety factor," is both "the only means of our survival" and "morally abhorrent to
   many people" (8–9). Does Hardin see these two alternatives as ethically and
   practically unacceptable? Do you? Is it really an either / or situation, or is
   there a middle ground? Are there some solutions he ignores?

2. Does Hardin's use of the lifeboat image make his arguments clearer and present the problem he describes more vividly? Or do you find it to be simplistic, distracting, or irrelevant?

3. In paragraph 2 Hardin asks, "But does everyone on earth have an equal right
   to an equal share of its resources?" That is, are some people more—or less—
   deserving than others? How would you answer him?

THE PERILS OF OBEDIENCE

Stanley Milgram

Social psychologist Stanley Milgram (1932–1984) is best known for experiments that study aggression and human conformity, especially
obedience. He has said that "it is only the person dwelling in isolation
who is not forced to respond, with defiance or submission, to the commands of others." Milgram uses Nazi Germany as a tragic example of

submission to obedience. The following selection is from his book, *Obedience to Authority* (1974). In this essay, Milgram's descriptions of some of his experiments on obedience raise perplexing moral questions.

Obedience is as basic an element in the structure of social life as one [1] can point to. Some system of authority is a requirement of all communal living, and it is only the person dwelling in isolation who is not forced to respond, with defiance or submission, to the commands of others. For many people, obedience is a deeply ingrained behavior tendency, indeed a potent impulse overriding training in ethics, sympathy, and moral conduct.

The dilemma inherent in submission to authority is ancient, as old [2] as the story of Abraham,[1] and the question of whether one should obey when commands conflict with conscience has been argued by Plato, dramatized in *Antigone*,[2] and treated to philosophic analysis in almost every historical epoch. Conservative philosophers argue that the very fabric of society is threatened by disobedience, while humanists stress the primacy of the individual conscience.

The legal and philosophic aspects of obedience are of enormous import, [3] but they say very little about how most people behave in concrete situations. I set up a simple experiment at Yale University to test how much pain an ordinary citizen would inflict on another person simply because he was ordered to by an experimental scientist. Stark authority was pitted against the subjects' strongest moral imperatives against hurting others, and, with the subjects' ears ringing with the screams of the victims, authority won more often than not. The extreme willingness of adults to go to almost any lengths on the command of an authority constitutes the chief finding of the study and the fact most urgently demanding explanation.

In the basic experimental design, two people come to a psychology [4] laboratory to take part in a study of memory and learning. One of them is designated as a "teacher" and the other a "learner." The experimenter explains that the study is concerned with the effects of punishment on learning. The learner is conducted into a room, seated in a kind of miniature electric chair; his arms are strapped to prevent excessive movement, and an electrode is attached to his wrist. He is told that he will be read lists of simple word pairs, and that he will then be tested on his ability to remember the second word of a pair when he hears the first one again. Whenever he makes an error, he will receive electric shocks of increasing intensity.

---

[1] Abraham, commanded by God to sacrifice his son Isaac, is ready to do so until an angel stops him. [Eds.]

[2] In Plato's *Apology* the philosopher Socrates provokes and accepts the sentence of death rather than act against his conscience; the heroine of Sophocles' *Antigone* risks a death sentence in order to give her brother a proper burial. [Eds.]

The real focus of the experiment is the teacher. After watching the ⁵
learner being strapped into place, he is seated before an impressive
shock generator. The instrument panel consists of thirty lever switches
set in a horizontal line. Each switch is clearly labeled with a voltage designation ranging from 15 to 450 volts. The following designations are
clearly indicated for groups of four switches, going from left to right:
Slight Shock, Moderate Shock, Strong Shock, Very Strong Shock, Intense
Shock, Extreme Intensity Shock, Danger: Severe Shock. (Two switches
after this last designation are simply marked XXX.)

When a switch is depressed, a pilot light corresponding to each ⁶
switch is illuminated in bright red; an electric buzzing is heard; a blue
light, labeled "voltage energizer," flashes; the dial on the voltage meter
swings to the right; and various relay clicks sound off.

The upper left-hand corner of the generator is labeled SHOCK GENER- ⁷
ATOR, TYPE ZLB, DYSON INSTRUMENT COMPANY, WALTHAM, MASS. OUTPUT 15
VOLTS–450 VOLTS.

Each subject is given a sample 45-volt shock from the generator be- ⁸
fore his run as teacher, and the jolt stregthens his belief in the authenticity of the machine.

The teacher is a genuinely naïve subject who has come to the labo- ⁹
ratory for the experiment. The learner, or victim, is actually an actor who
receives no shock at all. The point of the experiment is to see how far a
person will proceed in a concrete and measurable situation in which he
is ordered to inflict increasing pain on a protesting victim.

Conflict arises when the man receiving the shock begins to show ¹⁰
that he is experiencing discomfort. At 75 volts, he grunts; at 120 volts, he
complains loudly; at 150, he demands to be released from the experiment. As the voltage increases, his protests become more vehement and
emotional. At 285 volts, his response can be described only as an agonized scream. Soon thereafter, he makes no sound at all.

For the teacher, the situation quickly becomes one of gripping ten- ¹¹
sion. It is not a game for him; conflict is intense and obvious. The manifest suffering of the learner presses him to quit; but each time he heis-
tates to administer a shock, the experimenter orders him to continue. To
extricate himself from this plight, the subject must make a clear break
with authority.[3]

The subject, Gretchen Brandt,[4] is an attractive thirty-one-year-old ¹²
medical technician who works at the Yale Medical School. She had emigrated from Germany five years before.

On several occasions when the learner complains, she turns to the ¹³
experimenter coolly and inquires, "Shall I continue"? She promptly re-

---

[3] The ethical problems of carrying out an experiment of this sort are too complex to be dealt with
here, but they receive extended treatment in the book from which this article is adapted. [The book
is *Obedience to Authority* (New York: Harper and Row, 1974)—Eds.]

[4] Names of subjects described in this piece have been changed.

turns to her task when the experimenter asks her to do so. At the administration of 210 volts, she turns to the experimenter, remarking firmly, "Well, I'm sorry, I don't think we should continue."

> EXPERIMENTER: The experiment requires that you go on until he has learned all the word pairs correctly.
> BRANDT: He has a heart condition, I'm sorry. He told you that before.
> EXPERIMENTER: The shocks may be painful but they are not dangerous.
> BRANDT: Well, I'm sorry, I think when shocks continue like this, they are dangerous. You ask him if he wants to get out. It's his free will.
> EXPERIMENTER: It is absolutely essential that we continue . . .
> BRANDT: I'd like you to ask him. We came here of our free will. If he wants to continue I'll go ahead. He told you he had a heart condition. I'm sorry. I don't want to be responsible for anything happening to him. I wouldn't like it for me either.
> EXPERIMENTER: You have no other choice.
> BRANDT: I think we are here on our own free will. I don't want to be responsible if anything happens to him. Please understand that.

She refuses to go further and the experiment is terminated. [14]

The woman is firm and resolute throughout. She indicates in the interview that she was in no way tense or nervous, and this corresponds to her controlled appearance during the experiment. She feels that the last shock she administered to the learner was extremely painful and reiterates that she "did not want to be responsible for any harm to him." [15]

The woman's straightforward, courteous behavior in the experiment, lack of tension, and total control of her own action seem to make disobedience a simple and rational deed. Her behavior is the very embodiment of what I envisioned would be true for almost all subjects. [16]

Before the experiments, I sought predictions about the outcome from various kinds of people—psychiatrists, college sophomores, middle-class adults, graduate students and faculty in the behavioral sciences. With remarkable similarity, they predicted that virtually all subjects would refuse to obey the experimenter. The psychiatrists specifically predicted that most subjects would not go beyond 150 volts, when the victim makes his first explicit demand to be freed. They expected that only 4 percent would reach 300 volts, and that only a pathological fringe of about one in a thousand would administer the highest shock on the board. [17]

These predictions were unequivocally wrong. Of the forty subjects in the first experiment, twenty-five obeyed the orders of the experimenter to the end, punishing the victim until they reached the most potent shock available on the generator. After 450 volts were administered three times, the experimenter called a halt to the sessions. Many obedient subjects then heaved sighs of relief, mopped their brows, rubbed their fingers over their eyes, or nervously fumbled cigarettes. Others displayed only minimal signs of tension from beginning to end. [18]

When the very first experiments were carried out, Yale undergrad- [19]
uates were used as subjects, and about 60 percent of them were fully
obedient. A colleague of mine immediately dismissed these findings as
having no relevance to "ordinary" people, asserting that Yale undergraduates are a highly aggressive, competitive bunch who step on each
other's necks on the slightest provocation. He assured me that when "ordinary" people were tested, the results would be quite different. As we
moved from the pilot studies to the regular experimental series, people
drawn from every stratum of New Haven life came to be employed in
the experiment: professionals, white-collar workers, unemployed persons, and industrial workers. *The experimental outcome was the same as we
had observed among the students.*

Moreover, when the experiments were repeated in Princeton, Mu- [20]
nich, Rome, South Africa, and Australia, the level of obedience was invariably somewhat *higher* than found in the investigation reported in
this article. Thus one scientist in Munich found 85 percent of his subjects
obedient.

Fred Prozi's reactions, if more dramatic than most, illuminate the [21]
conflicts experienced by others in less visible form. About fifty years old
and unemployed at the time of the experiment, he has a good-natured,
if slightly dissolute, appearance, and he strikes people as a rather ordinary fellow. He begins the session calmly but becomes tense as it proceeds. After delivering the 180-volt shock, he pivots around in his chair
and, shaking his head, addresses the experimenter in agitated tones:

PROZI: I can't stand it. I'm not going to kill that man in there. You
    hear him hollering?

EXPERIMENTER: As I told you before, the shocks may be painful, but . . .

PROZI: But he's hollering. He can't stand it. What's going to happen
    to him?

EXPERIMENTER (his voice is patient, matter-of-fact): The experiment re-
    quires that you continue, Teacher.

PROZI: Aaah, but, unh, I'm not going to get that man sick in there—
    know what I mean?

EXPERIMENTER: Whether the learner likes it or not, we must go on,
    through all the word pairs.

PROZI: I refuse to take the responsibility. He's in there hollering!

EXPERIMENTER: It's absolutely essential that you continue, Prozi.

PROZI (indicating the unused questions): There's too many left here,
    I mean, Jeez, if he gets them wrong, there's too many of
    them left. I mean, who's going to take the responsibility if
    anything happens to that gentleman?

EXPERIMENTER: I'm responsible for anything that happens to him. Continue, please.

PROZI: All right. (Consults list of words.) The next one's "Slow—walk, truck, dance, music." Answer, please. (A buzzing sound indicates the learner has signaled his answer.) Wrong. A hundred and ninety-five volts. "Dance." (Zzumph!)

LEARNER (yelling): Let me out of here! My heart's bothering me! (Teacher looks at experimenter.)

EXPERIMENTER: Continue, please.

LEARNER: (screaming): Let me out of here! You have no right to keep me here! Let me out of here, my heart's bothering me, let me out!

PROZI (shakes head, pats the table nervously): You see, he's hollering. Hear that? Gee, I don't know.

EXPERIMENTER: The experiment requires . . .

PROZI (interrupting): I know it does, sir, but I mean—hunh! He don't know what he's getting in for. He's up to 195 volts! (Experiment continues, through 210 volts, 225 volts, 240 volts, 255 volts, 270 volts, at which point Prozi, with evident relief, runs out of word-pair questions.)

EXPERIMENTER: You'll have to go back to the beginning of that page and go through them again until he's learned them all correctly.

PROZI: Aw, no. I'm not going to kill that man. You mean I've got to keep going up with the scale? No sir. He's hollering in there. I'm not going to give him 450 volts.

EXPERIMENTER: The experiment requires that you go on.

LEARNER: Ohhh. I absolutely refuse to answer anymore. (Shouting urgently now.) Let me out of here! You can't hold me here! Get me out. Get-me-out-of-here!

EXPERIMENTER: Continue. The next word is "Green," please.

PROZI: "Green—grass, hat, ink, apple." (Nothing happens. No answering buzz. Just gloomy silence.)

PROZI: I don't think he is going to answer.

EXPERIMENTER: If the learner doesn't answer in a reasonable time, about four or five seconds, consider the answer wrong. And follow the same procedures you have been doing for wrong answers. Say, "Wrong," tell him the number of volts, give him the punishment, read him the correct answer. Continue, please.

PROZI: "Green—grass, hat, ink, apple." Answer, please. (More silence. Subject just sits there.)

EXPERIMENTER: Go on with the procedure, please.

PROZI: Three hundred and fifteen volts. The answer is "ink." (Zzumph!)

LEARNER: Ohh. Oooohh.

PROZI: (relieved to hear response): Next one . . .

LEARNER: I absolutely refuse to answer.

PROZI: You got to. You get a shock if you don't answer. (Experiment continues with learner refusing to answer, and, finally, failing even to grunt or groan. At 375 volts, the subject stands up.)

PROZI: I think something's happening to that fellow in there. I don't get no answer. He was hollering at less voltage. Can't you check in and see if he's all right, please?

EXPERIMENTER (with same detached calm): Not once we've started. Please continue, Teacher.

PROZI: (sits down, sighs deeply): "Cool—day, shade, water, paint." answer, please. Are you all right in there? Are you all right?

EXPERIMENTER: Please continue, Teacher. Continue, please. (Subject pushes lever. Zzumph!)

PROZI: (swiveling around in his chair): Something's happened to that man in there. (Swiveling back.) Next one. "Low—dollar, necklace, moon, paint." (Turning around again.) Something's happened to that man in there. You better check in on him, sir. He won't answer or nothing.

EXPERIMENTER: Continue. Go on, please.

PROZI: You accept all responsibility?

EXPERIMENTER: The responsibility is mine. Correct. Please go on. (Subject returns to his list, starts running through words as rapidly as he can read them, works through to 450 volts.)

PROZI: That's that.

EXPERIMENTER: Continue using the 450 switch for each wrong answer. Continue, please.

PROZI: But I don't get anything!

EXPERIMENTER: Please continue. The next word is "white."

PROZI: Don't you think you should look in on him, please?

EXPERIMENTER: Not once we've started the experiment.

PROZI: What if he's dead in there? (Gestures toward the room with the electric chair.) I mean, he told me he can't stand the shock, sir. I don't mean to be rude, but I think you should look in on him. All you have to do is look in on him. All you have to do is look in the door. I don't get no answer, no noise. Something might have happened to the gentleman in there, sir.

EXPERIMENTER: We must continue. Go on, please.

PROZI: You mean keep giving him what? Four-hundred-fifty volts, what he's got now?

EXPERIMENTER: That's correct. Continue. The next word is "white."

PROZI (now at a furious pace): "White—cloud, horse, rock, house." Answer, please. The answer is "horse." Four hundred and fifty volts. (Zzumph!) Next word, "Bag—paint, music, clown, girl." The answer is "paint." Four hundred and fifty volts. (Zzumph!) Next word is "Short—sentence, movie . . ."

EXPERIMENTER: Excuse me, Teacher. We'll have to discontinue the experiment.

Morris Braverman, another subject, is a thirty-nine-year-old social [22] worker. He looks older than his years because of his bald head and serious demeanor. His brow is furrowed, as if all the world's burdens were carried on his face. He appears intelligent and concerned.

When the learner refuses to answer and the experimenter instructs [23] Braverman to treat the absence of an answer as equivalent to a wrong answer, he takes his instruction to heart. Before administering 300 volts he asserts officiously to the victim, "Mr. Wallace, your silence has to be considered as a wrong answer." Then he administers the shock. He offers halfheartedly to change places with the learner, then asks the experimenter. "Do I have to follow these instructions literally?" He is satisfied with the experimenter's answer that he does. His very refined and authoritative manner of speaking is increasingly broken up by wheezing laughter.

The experimenter's notes on Mr. Braverman at the last few shocks [24] are:

Almost breaking up now each time gives shock. Rubbing face to hide [25] *laughter.*

Squinting, trying to hide face with hand, still laughing. [26]

Cannot control his laughter at this point no matter what he does. [27]

Clenching fist, pushing it onto table. [28]

In an interview after the session, Mr. Braverman summarizes the ex- [29] periment with impressive fluency and intelligence. He feels the experiment may have been designed also to "test the effects on the teacher of being in an essentially sadistic role, as well as the reactions of a student to a learning situation that was authoritative and punitive." When asked how painful the last few shocks administered to the learner were, he indicates that the most extreme category on the scale is not adequate (it read EXTREMELY PAINFUL) and places his mark at the edge of the scale with an arrow carrying it beyond the scale.

It is almost impossible to convey the greatly relaxed, sedate quality 30 of his conversation in the interview. In the most relaxed terms, he speaks about his severe inner tension.

> EXPERIMENTER: At what point were you most tense or nervous?

> MR. BRAVERMAN: Well, when he first began to cry out in pain, and I realized this was hurting him. This got worse when he just blocked and refused to answer. There was I. I'm a nice person, I think, hurting somebody, and caught up in what seemed a mad situation . . . and in the interest of science, one goes through with it.

When the interviewer pursues the general question of tension, Mr. 31 Braverman spontaneously mentions his laughter.

"My reactions were awfully peculiar. I don't know if you were 32 watching me, but my reactions were giggly, and trying to stifle laughter. This isn't the way I usually am. This was a sheer reaction to a totally impossible situation. And my reaction was to the situation of having to hurt somebody. And being totally helpless and caught up in a set of circumstances where I just couldn't deviate and I couldn't try to help. This is what got me."

Mr. Braverman, like all subjects, was told the actual nature and pur- 33 pose of the experiment, and a year later he affirmed in a questionnaire that he had learned something of personal importance: "What appalled me was that I could possess this capacity for obedience and compliance to a central idea, i.e., the value of a memory experiment, even after it became clear that continued adherence to this value was at the expense of violation of another value, i.e., don't hurt someone who is helpless and not hurting you. As my wife said, 'You can call yourself Eichmann.'[5] I hope I deal more effectively with any future conflicts of values I encounter."

One theoretical interpretation of this behavior holds that all people 34 harbor deeply aggressive instincts continually pressing for expression, and that the experiment provides institutional justification for the release of these impulses. According to this view, if a person is placed in a situation in which he has complete power over another individual,

---

[5] Nazi officer, executed in 1962, who engineered the mass extermination of Jews. Many concentration camp officials defended themselves afterwards as "just following orders." [Eds.]

whom he may punish as much as he likes, all that is sadistic and bestial in man comes to the fore. The impulse to shock the victim is seen to flow from the potent aggressive tendencies, which are part of the motivational life of the individual, and the experiment, because it provides social legitimacy, simply opens the door to their expression.

It becomes vital, therefore, to compare the subject's performance [35] when he is under orders and when he is allowed to choose the shock level.

The procedure was identical to our standard experiment, except that [36] the teacher was told that he was free to select any shock level on any of the trials. (The experimenter took pains to point out that the teacher could use the highest levels on the generator, the lowest, any in between, or any combination of levels.) Each subject proceeded for thirty critical trials. The learner's protests were coordinated to standard shock levels, his first grunt coming at 75 volts, his first vehement protest at 150 volts.

The average shock used during the thirty critical trials was less than [37] 60 volts—lower than the point at which the victim showed the first signs of discomfort. Three of the forty subjects did not go beyond the very lowest level on the board, twenty-eight went no higher than 75 volts, and thirty-eight did not go beyond the first loud protest at 150 volts. Two subjects provided the exception, administering up to 325 and 450 volts, but the overall result was that the great majority of people delivered very low, usually painless, shocks when the choice was explicitly up to them.

This condition of the experiment undermines another commonly [38] offered explanation of the subjects' behavior—that those who shocked the victim at the most severe levels came only from the sadistic fringe of society. If one considers that almost two-thirds of the participants fall into the category of "obedient" subjects, and that they represented ordinary people drawn from working, managerial, and professional classes, the argument becomes very shaky. Indeed, it is highly reminiscent of the issue that arose in connection with Hannah Arendt's 1963 book, *Eichmann in Jerusalem*. Arendt contended that the prosecution's effort to depict Eichmann as a sadistic monster was fundamentally wrong, that he came closer to being an uninspired bureaucrat who simply sat at his desk and did his job. For asserting her views, Arendt became the object of considerable scorn, even calumny. Somehow, it was felt that the monstrous deeds carried out by Eichmann required a brutal, twisted personality, evil incarnate. After witnessing hundreds of ordinary persons submit to the authority in our own experiments, I must conclude that Arendt's conception of the banality of evil comes closer to the truth than one might dare imagine. The ordinary person who shocked the victim did so out of a sense of obligation—an impression of his duties as a subject—and not from any peculiarly aggressive tendencies.

This is, perhaps, the most fundamental lesson of our study: ordinary [39] people, simply doing their jobs, and without any particular hostility on their part, can become agents in a terrible destructive process. Moreover, even when the destructive effects of their work become patently clear, and they are asked to carry out actions incompatible with fundamental standards of morality, relatively few people have the resources needed to resist authority.

Many of the people were in some sense against what they did to the [40] learner, and many protested even while they obeyed. Some were totally convinced of the wrongness of their actions but could not bring themselves to make an open break with authority. They often derived satisfaction from their thoughts and felt that—within themselves, at least—they had been on the side of the angels. They tried to reduce strain by obeying the experimenter but "only slightly," encouraging the learner, touching the generator switches gingerly. When interviewed, such a subject would stress that he had "asserted my humanity" by administering the briefest shock possible. Handling the conflict in this manner was easier than defiance.

The situation is constructed so that there is no way the subject can [41] stop shocking the learner without violating the experimenter's definitions of his own competence. The subject fears that he will appear arrogant, untoward, and rude if he breaks off. Although these inhibiting emotions appear small in scope alongside the violence being done to the learner, they suffuse the mind and feelings of the subject, who is miserable at the prospect of having to repudiate the authority to his face. (When the experiment was altered so that the experimenter gave his instructions by telephone instead of in person, only a third as many people were fully obedient through 450 volts.) It is a curious thing that a measure of compassion on the part of the subject—an unwillingness to "hurt" the experimenter's feelings—is part of those binding forces inhibiting his disobedience. The withdrawal of such deference may be as painful to the subject as to the authority he defies.

The subjects do not derive satisfaction from inflicting pain, but they [42] often like the feeling they get from pleasing the experimenter. They are proud of doing a good job, obeying the experimenter under difficult circumstances. While the subjects administered only mild shocks on their own initiative, one experimental variation showed that, under orders, 30 percent of them were willing to deliver 450 volts even when they had to forcibly push the learner's hand down on the electrode.

Bruno Batta is a thirty-seven-year-old welder who took part in the [43] variation requiring the use of force. He was born in New Haven, his parents in Italy. He has a rough-hewn face that conveys a conspicuous lack of alertness. He has some difficulty in mastering the experimental procedure and needs to be corrected by the experimenter several times. He shows appreciation for the help and willingness to do what is required.

After the 150-volt level, Betta has to force the learner's hand down on the shock plate, since the learner himself refuses to touch it.

When the learner first complains, Mr. Batta pays no attention to him. [44] His face remains impassive, as if to dissociate himself from the learner's disruptive behavior. When the experimenter instructs him to force the learner's hand down, he adopts a rigid, mechanical procedure. He tests the generator switch. When it fails to function he immediately forces the learner's hand onto the shock plate. All the while he maintains the same rigid mask. The learner, seated alongside him, begs him to stop, but with robotic impassivity he continues the procedure.

What is extraordinary is his apparent total indifference to the [45] learner; he hardly takes cognizance of him as a human being. Meanwhile, he relates to the experimenter in a submissive and courteous fashion.

At the 330-volt level, the learner refuses not only to touch the shock [46] plate but also to provide any answers. Annoyed, Batta turns to him, and chastises him: "You better answer and get it over with. We can't stay here all night." These are the only words he directs to the learner in the course of an hour. Never again does he speak to him. The scene is brutal and depressing, his hard, impassive face showing total indifference as he subdues the screaming learner and gives him shocks. He seems to derive no pleasure from the act itself, only quiet satisfaction at doing his job properly.

When he administers 450 volts, he turns to the experimenter and [47] asks, "Where do we go from here, Professor?" His tone is deferential and expresses his willingness to be a cooperative subject, in contrast to the learner's obstinacy.

At the end of the session he tells the experimenter how honored he [48] has been to help him, and in a moment of contrition, remarks, "Sir, sorry it couldn't have been a full experiment."

He has done his honest best. It is only the deficient behavior of the [49] learner that has denied the experimenter full satisfaction.

The essence of obedience is that a person comes to view himself as [50] the instrument for carrying out another person's wishes, and he therefore no longer regards himself as responsible for his actions. Once this critical shift of viewpoint has occurred, all of the essential features of obedience follow. The most far-reaching consequence is that the person feels responsible to the authority directing him but feels no responsibility *for* the content of the actions that the authority prescribes. Morality does not disappear—it acquires a radically different focus: the subordinate person feels shame or pride depending on how adequately he has performed the actions called for by authority.

Language provides numerous terms to pinpoint this type of moral- [51] ity: *loyalty, duty, discipline* all are terms heavily saturated with moral meaning and refer to the degree to which a person fulfills his obligations to authority. They refer not to the "goodness" of the person per se but to the adequacy with which a subordinate fulfills his socially defined role. The most frequent defense of the individual who has performed a heinous act under command of authority is that he has simply done his duty. In asserting this defense, the individual is not introducing an alibi concocted for the moment but is reporting honestly on the psychological attitude induced by submission to authority.

For a person to feel responsible for his actions, he must sense that   52
the behavior has flowed from "the self." In the situation we have studied, subjects have precisely the opposite view of their actions—namely, they see them as originating in the motives of some other person. Subjects in the experiment frequently said, "If it were up to me, I would not have administered shocks to the learner."

Once authority has been isolated as the cause of the subject's be-   53
havior, it is legitimate to inquire into the necessary elements of authority and how it must be perceived in order to gain his compliance. We conducted some investigations into the kinds of changes that would cause the experimenter to lose his power and to be disobeyed by the subject. Some of the variations revealed that:

The experimenter's physical presence has a marked impact on his authority. As cited earlier, obedience dropped off sharply when orders were given by telephone. The experimenter could often induce a disobedient subject to go on by returning to the laboratory.   54

Conflicting authority severely paralyzes action. When two experimenters of equal status, both seated at the command desk, gave incompatible orders, no shocks were delivered past the point of their disagreement.   55

The rebellious action of others severely undermines authority. In one variation, three teachers (two actors and a real subject) administered a test and shocks. When the two actors disobeyed the experimenter and refused to go beyond a certain shock level, thirty-six of forty subjects joined their disobedient peers and refused as well.   56

Although the experimenter's authority was fragile in some respects,   57
it is also true that he had almost none of the tools used in ordinary command structures. For example, the experimenter did not threaten the subjects with punishment—such as loss of income, community ostracism, or jail—for failure to obey. Neither could he offer incentives. Indeed, we should expect the experimenter's authority to be much less than that of someone like a general, since the experimenter has no power

to enforce his imperatives, and since participation in a psychological experiment scarcely evokes the sense of urgency and dedication found in warfare. Despite these limitations, he still managed to command a dismaying degree of obedience.

I will cite one final variation of the experiment that depicts a dilemma that is more common in everyday life. The subject was not ordered to pull the lever that shocked the victim, but merely to perform a subsidiary task (administering the word-pair test) while another person administered the shock. In this situation, thirty-seven of forty adults continued to the highest level of the shock generator. Predictably, they excused their behavior by saying that the responsibility belonged to the man who actually pulled the switch. This may illustrate a dangerously typical arrangement in a complex society: it is easy to ignore responsibility when one is only an intermediate link in a chain of action. 58

The problem of obedience is not wholly psychological. The form and shape of society and the way it is developing have much to do with it. There was a time, perhaps, when people were able to give a fully human response to any situation because they were fully absorbed in it as human beings. But as soon as there was a division of labor things changed. Beyond a certain point, the breaking up of society into people carrying out narrow and very special jobs takes away from the human quality of work and life. A person does not get to see the whole situation but only a small part of it, and is thus unable to act without some kind of overall direction. He yields to authority but in doing so is alienated from his own actions. 59

Even Eichmann was sickened when he toured the concentration camps, but he had only to sit at a desk and shuffle papers. At the same time the man in the camp who actually dropped Cyclon-b into the gas chambers was able to justify *his* behavior on the ground that he was only following orders from above. Thus there is a fragmentation of the total human act; no one is confronted with the consequences of his decision to carry out the evil act. The person who assumes responsibility has evaporated. Perhaps this is the most common characteristic of socially organized evil in modern society. 60

Responding to Reading

1. What is the "dilemma inherent in submission to authority" (2)? How do Milgram's experiments illustrate this dilemma? Why do you suppose virtually no one predicted that the subjects would continue to obey the orders of the experimenter?
2. Do you see the subjects as ordinary people—cooperative, obedient, and eager to please—or as weak individuals, too timid to defy authority? Explain.
3. In paragraph 51 Milgram says, "The most frequent defense of the individual who has performed a heinous act under command of authority is that he

has simply done his duty." In your opinion, can such a defense ever excuse a "heinous act"? If so, under what circumstances?

DIRTY NEEDLE

Nicholas Jenkins

A writer with a particular interest in the arts, Nicholas Jenkins was an associate editor with the monthly periodical *ARTnews* until 1993. Currently Jenkins is a freelancer based in New York City. In the following opinion essay, originally published in *The New Yorker* magazine in December 1994, Jenkins argues that proponents of the death penalty are hypocritical when they promote lethal injection as a "humane" form of execution; he believes they should "drop the cant about decency and concern" so the public can face the stark fact that "execution is still a killing, a legal homicide."

Conscience argues against its ethos, statistics confirm its racial bias, skepticism revolts from its finality, and economics warns of its costs, yet the death penalty, like some unkillable movie gorgon, keeps coming. To slow its progress, opponents call its social effectiveness a myth. Proponents, although they usually don't come out and say so, know that the mythical, phantasmal aspects of the death penalty are precisely what account for its persistence.   1

Part of the myth—the symmetrical-justice part—is obvious, even to the convicted. Robert Lowell,[1] imprisoned in 1943 as a conscientious objector, found himself in Manhattan's West Street Jail alongside Louis (Lepke) Buchalter, the boss of Murder, Inc., who was awaiting electrocution. The prospect of the chair, Lowell wrote in a poem, shimmered before the enfeebled gangster like a mysterious gateway back to the violent highs of his youth, "an oasis in his air / of lost connections." For sizable segments of the electorate, too, capital punishment is a mirage promising a return to a more "connected" world—a dream solution to a nightmare of social despair.   2

In order to survive, the death penalty must adapt to other fantasies as well, prominent among them the wish to kill without making a show of it and without assuming the guilt that comes with inflicting pain. The search for mechanisms that execute cleanly and, by prevailing stan-   3

---

[1] American poet (1917–1977). [Eds.]

dards, humanely, which has been going on ever since drawing-and-quartering[2] gave way to the guillotine, continually forces death-penalty enthusiasts to compromise their (demonstrably false) deterrence argument by finding venues that are ever more private and methods that seem ever less overtly cruel.

New York has a special niche in this history. Slightly more than a   4 century ago, the state's governor appointed a panel—popularly known as the Death Commission—to provide him with an acceptable alternative to hanging. (Among the options rejected at the time was lethal injection.) The commission recommended the application of electric current as the most rapid and painless method available. Electricity, the symbol of modern civilization, would dispatch that civilization's irredeemably corrupted elements like a light bulb banishing darkness. The world's first electrocution took place at Auburn State Prison on August 6, 1890. William Kemmler was the convict. In the days before the execution, newspapers hailed the new method as "euthanasia by electricity." (After seeing Kemmler convulsed in the chair, after smelling his burning flesh, and noticing the "purplish foam" that spilled from his mouth, witnesses were less certain.) The man who pulled the switch, Edwin F. Davis, New York's first state electrician, was accounted a gentle soul, dutiful but concerned for the creatures in his care. Davis's hobby was beekeeping—a pastime in which, as a hooded intruder pillaging the hive and suffering the stings of the enraged bee-citizens, he could act out a vivid rite of identification with his prisoners.

What could be just barely presented as humane a century ago—and   5 still survives as a method of execution in twelve states—is now widely felt to be repugnant, obsolete, barbarous. To do to animals what is routinely done to people can even be criminal: in California, Cynthia McFadden, of ABC News, reported not long ago, prosecutions are under way against chinchilla ranchers who electrocute their animals. The American Veterinary Medical Association's guidelines for animal euthanasia sternly specify that for a creature to be killed humanely it must be rendered unconscious before it is jolted.

As electrocution has lost favor, lethal injection has gained ground.   6 (It is now lawful in twenty-seven states—more than two-thirds of those that execute.) This method, drawing on the iconography of doctorly efficiency, kindness, and discretion, conforms to a national habit of medicalizing everything from laziness to incest. The lethal injection got its biggest public boost from the pioneer of high-tech, clean-war solutions to the nation's military needs. In 1973, when he was governor of California, Ronald Reagan likened executing a criminal with an injection to the best way of dealing with a doomed horse: "You call the veterinari-

---

[2] Medieval form of execution. The victim was first hanged and then split down the middle with a sword and chopped into four pieces. [Eds.]

an and the vet gives it a shot and the horse goes to sleep—that's it." Just as external enemies would be fought with lasers and "surgical" strikes, so, under the dispensation of the needle, the internal enemy could be made to glide away as smoothly as King Arthur in his barge, drifting into the mist.[3]

The fact is that lethal injections aren't uncomplicated or foolproof. In roughly one out of four cases, there are likely to be difficulties in locating a vein for the catheter through which a sedative, a paralytic agent, and a heart-stopping chemical must flow into the prisoner's body. When the probing fails, it can be necessary to perform a venous cutdown—a bloody procedure—to make a viable opening. (In 1985, in Texas, it took forty minutes of gurney time to pierce a vein in Stephen Peter Morin's body.) If the catheter misses a vein and instead penetrates subcutaneous tissue—always a possibility, since, despite the aura of medical ceremony surrounding lethal injections, doctors are forbidden to perform them—the sedative may wear off and the prisoner awaken while he or she is suffocating. In addition, just as the length of the drop was always a chancy calculation for the hangman, correct doses are difficult to assess for convicts with serious alcohol or drug histories.

The fantasy that electrocution and, now, injection are steps toward decency remains a powerful one. But what casts this humanitarianism in a different light and reveals the true object of its solicitude is some of the smaller procedures preceding an execution. In the states that electrocute, a prisoner may be invited (or forced) to put on a diaper before leaving the condemned cell for the last time. Muscle spasms mean that convicts usually defecate and urinate while they are in the all-powerful grip of the electric current. This sanitary etiquette has little to do with the needs of the prisoner and much to do with the sensibilities of those who carry out and witness the execution. Even more grotesque morally (because it involves an active denial of what is taking place) is the practice during execution by injection of swabbing the prisoner's forearm, as if to insure that the puncture wound won't become infected. It is hard to avoid the conclusion that an important part of the evolving technology of execution is driven by a need to find a process that seems bland enough to allow the death penalty itself to persist. The methods of execution have as much to do with a wish not to trouble our own tender consciences as with a desire not to cause pain to someone else.

Nobody yet knows whether it is to be back to the electric chair or in with the needle in New York. But, with Governor-elect Pataki[4] and the legislature preparing to reintroduce executions, it's a good time to drop

7

8

9

---

[3] In the medieval English legends, the noble Arthur, fatally wounded in battle, sails for the island of Avalon, never to return. [Eds.]

[4] In 1994 conservative George Pataki defeated Mario Cuomo, a staunch opponent of capital punishment, for the New York governorship. [Eds.]

the cant about decency and concern. However advanced the aesthetics of state death, an execution is still a killing, a legal homicide. That fact ought to be faced in all its starkness, not wrapped in a veil of morally neutral, medico-technical mystification. If history is a guide, the lethal injection will look as sickening a hundred years from now as the electric chair does today. Decency will not be served until everyone has come to understand that the only good death-penalty statute is a repealed one.

Responding to Reading

1. What does Jenkins mean when he calls the death penalty "a dream solution to a nightmare of social despair" (2)? What, according to Jenkins, is wrong with this "dream solution"?
2. Does your own position on the death penalty differ from Jenkins's? What do you see as the advantages and disadvantages of the death penalty?
3. Much of Jenkins's discussion describes the search for a humane method of execution. Why do you think people look so hard for a humane method? Do tyou think it is possible for an execution to be humane? Explain your reasoning.

DENYING THE HOLOCAUST

~

Deborah Lipstadt

Deborah Lipstadt (1947–) was born in New York City and attended Hebrew University of Jerusalem, City College in New York, and Brandeis University, where she received her Ph.D. She has been teaching the history of religion and Jewish studies since 1974 and currently holds an endowed chair in modern Jewish and Holocaust studies at Emory University in Atlanta. Her books include *Jewish Reflections on Death* (1975), *The Zionist Career of Louis Lipsky* (1982), *Beyond Belief: The American Press and the Coming of the Holocaust* (1986), and *Denying the Holocaust: The Growing Assault on Truth and Memory* (1993). In the latter she argues that Holocaust deniers are not presenting an "other side" of history; rather they are "extreme antisemites" whose aim is "to confuse the matter by making it appear as if they are engaged in genuine scholarly effort when, of course, they are not." The following chapter from *Denying the Holocaust* focuses specifically on Lipstadt's argument that by accepting advertisements in which Holocaust deniers outline their claims, college newspapers can inadvertently add legitimacy to those claims.

> This is not a public stagecoach that has to take everyone who buys a ticket.
>
> *Benjamin Franklin*

In the early 1990s American college campuses became loci of inten- [1]
sive activity by a small group of Holocaust deniers. Relying on creative
tactics and assisted by a fuzzy kind of reasoning often evident in academic circles, the deniers achieved millions of dollars of free publicity and
significantly furthered their cause. Their strategy was profoundly simple. Bradley Smith, a Californian who has been involved in a variety of
Holocaust denial activities since the early 1980s, attempted to place a
full-page ad claiming that the Holocaust was a hoax in college newspapers throughout the United States. The ad was published by papers at
some of the more prestigious institutions of higher learning in the United States.

Entitled "The Holocaust Story: How Much Is False? The Case for [2]
Open Debate," the ad provoked a fierce debate on many of the campuses approached by Smith. His strategy was quite straightforward:
He generally called a paper's advertising department to ascertain the
charge for publication of a full-page ad and then submitted camera-
ready copy and a certified check in the proper amount. On occasion
he inquired in advance whether a paper would be willing to run this
particular ad. Even when he was rejected, the attempt to place the ad
won him significant media attention. Campus newspapers began to
use his name in headlines without identifying him, assuming readers
would know who he was. Articles, letters, and op-ed pieces defended Holocaust denial's right to make its "views" known. But not all the
results were necessarily what Smith would have wanted. On some
campuses there was a backlash against him and Holocaust denial.
Courses on the Holocaust that had languished on the back burner for
an extended period materialized in the next semester's offerings.
Campus administrators admitted that the ad constituted the final
push necessary to move these courses from the planning stage to the
schedule books. Professors from a wide variety of disciplines included discussion of the Holocaust in their courses. Movies, speakers,
photographic exhibits and other presentations relating to the Holocaust were brought to campus. Students participated in rallies, teach-
ins, and protests.

This response prompted some observers to argue that the contro- [3]
versy had a positive impact. Students had become increasingly aware
not only of the Holocaust but of the contemporary attempt to subvert
history and spread antisemitism. While this may be a relatively accurate
analysis of the immediate outcome of Smith's endeavor, there is another more sobering and pessimistic aspect to the matter. Analysis of the

students', faculty's, and administration's responses reveals both a susceptibility to the worst form of historical revisionism and a failure to fully understand the implications of Holocaust denial, even among those who vigorously condemned it. . . .

∼

The ad Smith began to circulate in the spring of 1991 contained the   4
deniers' familiar litany of claims. It declared the gas chambers a fraud, photographs doctored, eyewitness reports "ludicrously unreliable," the Nuremberg trials a sham, and camp internees well fed until Allied bombings destroyed the German infrastructure in the most "barbarous form of warfare in Europe since the Mongol invasions," preventing food from being delivered and causing the inmates to starve. According to Smith the notion of a Nazi attempt to destroy the Jews was the product of Allied efforts to produce "anti-German hate propaganda." Today that same propaganda was used by powerful forces to "scape-goat old enemies," "seek vengeance rather than reconciliation," and pursue a "not-so-secret political agenda."

He repeated the familiar protest that his sole objective was to un-   5
cover the truth through an open debate on the Holocaust—debate that had been suppressed by a powerful but secret group on campus as part of their larger political agenda. "Let's ask these people—what makes such behavior a social good? Who benefits?"

The ad contended that denial was forcing "mainline Holocaust   6
historians" to admit the "more blatant examples" of Holocaust falsehoods. It was the deniers who had forced them to revise the "orthodox" Holocaust story. They had had to admit that the number of Jews killed at Auschwitz was far smaller than originally claimed, and had been made to confess that the Nazis did not use Jewish cadavers for the production of soap. It is correct that in recent years newly revealed documentation has allowed scholars to assess more precisely the number of Jews thought to have been murdered at Auschwitz.[1] It is also accurate that scholars have long written that despite wartime rumors to the contrary, the Nazis apparently did not use Jewish cadavers for soap. There has been a wide array of other "revelations" by Holocaust historians, all part of the attempt to uncover the full details of one of the most horrifying acts of human destruction. Smith suggested to his readers that scholars and others who work in this field, all of whom vigorously repudiate Holocaust denial, have been compelled to admit the truth of deniers' claims: "We are told that it is 'anti-Jewish' to question orthodox assertions about German criminality. Yet we find that it is Jews themselves like Mayer, Bauer, Hier, Hilberg, Lipstadt and others who beginning [sic] to challenge the es-

---

[1] The memorial stone at Auschwitz lists the number of victims of the camp as 4 million. Research now indicates that the number of people who died in the Auschwitz/Birkenau gas chambers was between 1.5 and 2 million, of whom 85 to 90 percent were Jews.

tablishment Holocaust story." This notion—that deniers have exposed the truth and mainline historians are scrambling to admit it—remains a linchpin of the deniers' strategy. It has two objectives: to make it appear that Jewish scholars are responding to the pressure of the deniers' findings and to create the impression that Holocaust deniers' "questions" are themselves part of a continuum of respectable scholarship. If establishment scholars, particularly those who are Jews, can question previously accepted truths, why is it wrong when Bradley Smith does the same?

Though much of the ad consisted of familiar rhetoric, Smith added 7 a new twist that had a particular resonance on American college campuses. Since the 1980s the concept of "political correctness" has been a source of academic conflict. Conservative political groups have accused the "liberal establishment" of labeling certain topics politically incorrect and therefore ineligible for inclusion in the curriculum. Smith framed his well-worn denial arguments within this rhetoric, arguing that Holocaust revisionism could not be addressed on campus because "America's thought police" had declared it out of bounds. "The politically correct line on the Holocaust story is, simply, it happened. You don't debate 'it.'" Unlike all other topics students were free to explore, the Holocaust story was off limits. The consequences, he charged, were antithetical to everything for which the university stood. "Ideology replaces free inquiry, intimidation represses open debate, and . . . the ideals of the university itself are exchanged for intellectual taboos." While most students who had to decide whether the ad should be published did not overtly succumb to CODOH's use of the political correctness argument, many proved prone to it, sometimes less than consciously—a susceptibility evident in their justifications for running the ad. Among the first universities to accept the ad were Northwestern, the University of Michigan, Duke, Cornell, Ohio State, and Washington University.[2]

At the University of Michigan the saga of the ad had a strange twist. 8 Smith mailed camera-ready copy directly to the *Michigan Daily*. According to the paper's business manager, the ad "slipped through without being read." When it appeared the business staff was appalled to learn what they had allowed to happen. On the following day they placed a six-column ad in the paper apologizing for running Smith's ad and acknowledging that its publication had been a mistake. They declared it a "sorrowful learning experience for the staff." The manager told the *Detroit Free Press*, "We make mistakes like any organization."

---

[2] The papers discussed in this chapter function as private newspapers. The courts have broadly defined their editorial discretion to accept or reject ads. In situations of "state action," where a state university administration controls the newspaper's content, the courts may prohibit content-based rejection of the ads. *Discretion of Student Editors to Accept or Reject Holocaust Revisionist Advertisements* (ADL Legal Affairs Dept., Feb. 1992).

The story might well have ended here—an example of faulty mon-   9
itoring by a segment of the staff of the *Michigan Daily*—but the issue became more complicated when, despite the fact that those responsible for
running the ad acknowledged doing so as a mistake, the editorial board
attempted to transform a blunder into a matter of principle. They recast
a snafu as an expression of freedom of speech. On the same day that the
advertising staff published its apology, the front page carried an editorial explaining that, though the editors found the ad "offensive and inaccurate," they could not condone the censorship of "unpopular views
from our pages merely because they are offensive or because we disagree with them." Editor in chief Andrew Gottesman acknowledged
that had the decision been in his hands, he would have printed the ad.
He argued that rejecting it constituted censorship, which the editorial
board found unacceptable.

The following day a campus rally attacked both Holocaust denial   10
and the paper's editorial policies. Stung by student and faculty condemnations and afraid that its editorial was being interpreted as an en-
dorsement of CODOH, the editorial board devoted the next issue's lead
editorial to the topic. Condemning Holocaust denial as "absurd" and
"founded on historical fiction and anti-Jewish bigotry," they dismissed
it as irrational, illogical, and ahistorical propaganda. The editors accurately assessed the ad as lacking intellectual merit. Nonetheless, they
continued to support its publication. Their powerful condemnation of
Holocaust denial in general and Smith's ad in particular appeared under
a banner quoting Supreme Court Justice Hugo Black's opinion on free
speech: "My view is, without deviation, without exception, without any
ifs, buts, or whereases, that freedom of speech means that you shall not
do something to people either for the views they have or the views they
express or the words they speak or write."

The strange set of circumstances at Michigan—snatching a consti-   11
tutional principle from the jaws of a mistake—was further complicated
by the entry of the university's president, James Duderstadt, into the debate. In a letter to the *Daily* he declared the ad the work of "a warped
crank" and proclaimed that denying the Holocaust was to "deny our
human potential for evil and to invite its resurgence." But he, too, defended the paper's decision, which was more of a nondecision, to run
the ad. The president asserted that the *Daily* had a long history of editorial freedom that had to be protected even when "we disagree either
with particular opinions, decisions, or actions." Most disturbing was
Duderstadt's elevation of Smith's prejudices to the level of opinions.

There was no doubt about the message the editors and the president   12
were trying to convey: As absurd, illogical, and bigoted as the ad may
be, First Amendment guarantees were paramount. The dictates of the
American Constitution compelled the *Daily* to publish. None of those involved seemed to have considered precisely what the First Amendment

said: "Congress shall make no law . . . abridging the freedom of speech or of the press." Those who argued that free speech guarantees acceptance of the ad ignored the fact that the First Amendment prevents *government* from interfering in any fashion with an individual's or group's right to publish the most outlandish argument. The *New York Times* made this point in an editorial when it adamantly repudiated the notion that this was a First Amendment question: "Government may not censor Mr. Smith and his fellow 'Holocaust revisionists,' no matter how intellectually barren their claims."

To call rejection of the ad censorship was to ignore the fact that, un- [13] like the government, whose actions are limited by the First Amendment, these papers do not have a monopoly of force. If the government denies someone the right to publish, they have no other option to publish in this country. But if a paper rejects someone's column, ad, or letter, there are always other publications. The First Amendment does not guarantee access to a private publication. It is designed to serve as a shield to protect individuals and institutions from government interference in their affairs. It is not a sword by which every person who makes an outlandish statement or notorious claim can invoke a Constitutional right to be published.[3] Nor did the *Michigan Daily* seem to notice how Justice Black, whom they quoted, framed it: "you shall not do something to people. . . ." No one was advocating "doing" anything to Smith.

One of the most ardent advocates of the free-speech argument was [14] the *Duke Chronicle*. In an editorial column the editor in chief, Ann Heimberger, justified the paper's decision by acknowledging that while the paper knew it could reject the ad, it "chose" to accept it as an expression of the paper's desire to "support the advertiser's rights." The editorial board believed that it was not the paper's responsibility to protect "readers from disturbing ideas," but to "disseminate them."

Echoing his Michigan colleague, Duke University president Keith [15] Brodie repeated the free-speech defense in a statement that, though it contained a strong refutation of the ad, was more vigorous in its support of the *Chronicle*'s publication of the ad. To have "suppressed" the ad, he argued, would have violated the university's commitment to free speech and contradicted its "long tradition of supporting First Amendment rights."

When the *Cornell Daily Sun* ran the ad, the editors justified the de- [16] cision in an editorial statement warning that "page twenty will shock most readers" but proclaimed that it was not the paper's role to "unjustly censor advertisers' viewpoints." Echoing their colleagues on many of the other campuses that printed the ad, the editors declared that they

---

[3] In 1931, in *Near v. Minnesota*, the Supreme Court struck down a state attempt to gag a paper's freedom to publish "malicious, scandalous or defamatory" material. Fred W. Friendly, *Minnesota Rag* (New York, 1981).

decided to print it because the "First Amendment right to free expression must be extended to those with unpopular or offensive ideas." Neeraj Khemlani, the editor in chief of the *Daily Sun,* said his role was not to "protect" readers. Cornell president Frank H. T. Rhodes joined his colleagues at Duke and Michigan in defending the paper's decision.

The University of Montana's paper, the *Montana Kaimin,* also used [17] the First Amendment to defend its publication of the ad. The editor contended that it was not the paper's place to "decide for the campus community what they should see." The University of Georgia's paper, the *Red and Black,* expressed the hope that publishing the ad would affirm America's unique commitment to "allowing every opinion to be heard, no matter how objectionable, how outright offensive, how clearly wrong that opinion may be." After the ad appeared the paper's editor defended the decision by describing it as "a business decision," arguing that "if the business department is set up to take ads, they darn well better take ads." Given the juxtaposition of these two explanations, there was, as Mark Silk, an editorial writer for the *Atlanta Constitution,* pointed out, something dubious about "this high-minded claim."

After an extensive debate Washington University's *Student Life* de- [18] cided to run the ad. When the ad appeared in the paper, Sam Moyn, the opinion editor, was responsible for conveying to the university community the reasoning behind the staff's "controversial action." The editors, he wrote, conceived of this as a free-speech issue: "The abridgement of Mr. Smith's rights endangers our own." The *St. Louis Post Dispatch* defended the students' actions. Declaring the ad "offensive, provocative and wrong," it praised the student newspaper's courage to print it and stated that its actions strengthened the cause of freedom of speech. The University of Arizona also depicted its actions as protecting the First Amendment. The editor in chief, Beth Silver, proclaimed that the mission of student newspapers is "to uphold the First Amendment and run things that are obviously going to be controversial and take the heat for it." This attitude—we have to do what is right irrespective of the costs—was voiced by a number of papers. Ironically, it echoed a theme frequently voiced by the deniers themselves: We will tell the truth, the consequences notwithstanding.

At Ohio State University the decision-making process was complex. [19] The *Lantern*'s advertising policy is in the hands of a publications committee comprising faculty, students, editorial board members, and the paper's business manager. University policy requires committee approval before acceptance of an ad designating a religious group. The committee voiced five to four to reject CODOH's submission. But the story did not end there. Enjoined by the committee's decision from running the ad, the *Lantern*'s editor, Samantha G. Haney, used her editorial powers to run it as an op-ed piece, explaining that the paper had an "obligation" to do so. This decision gave Smith added legitimacy and saved him the $1,134 it would have cost to place a full-page ad in the paper.

A lengthy editorial explaining the *Lantern*'s decision condemned [20] Bradley Smith and his cohorts as "racists, pure and simple" and the ad as "little more than a commercial for hatred." Nonetheless the newspaper had to publish it because it could not only "run things that were harmless to everyone." Haney and her staff rejected the suggestion that they turn to the Ohio State History Department to "pick apart" the ad fact by fact. That, they explained, might suggest that the ad had some "relevancy" and some "substance," which they were convinced it did not. Given that one of the rationales the *Lantern* offered for publishing the article was that "truth will always outshine any lie," its refusal to ask professional historians to elucidate how the ad convoluted historical fact seemed self-defeating. It seemed to reflect an understandable reluctance to accord denial legitimacy. There is no better example of the fragility of reason than the conclusion by these editorial boards that it was their obligation to run an ad or an op-ed column that, according to their *own* evaluation, was totally lacking in relevance or substance.

In contrast to the position adopted by James Duderstadt at the Uni- [21] versity of Michigan, Ohio State's president, Gordon Gee, attacked the decision to give Smith space in the newspaper, declaring the deniers' arguments "pernicious" and "cleverly disguised" propaganda that enhanced prejudice and distorted history.

When this issue was being debated at Ohio State, a CBS reporter [22] came to that campus to film a segment on Holocaust denial for a network show on hatred and extremism in the United States. Alerted in advance to the pending controversy, the cameras were conveniently present when the editor received a call from Smith congratulating her for running the ad and standing up for the principles of free speech and free press. When Haney hung up, the television reporter, who was standing nearby, asked how she felt. She turned and somewhat plaintively observed that she thought she had been had.

Not all the papers subscribed to the First Amendment argument; in- [23] deed, some explicitly rejected it. The University of Tennessee's *Daily Beacon* dismissed the idea that not running the ad harmed the deniers' interests: It was not "censorship or even damaging." Pennsylvania State University's *Daily Collegian*, which had been one of the first to receive an ad from Smith, denied that the issue was one of free speech. After seeing student leaders and numerous individuals on campus inundated with material by deniers, the paper reasoned that those behind the ad had sufficient funds to propagate their conspiracy theory of Jewish control without being granted space in the paper.

In an eloquent editorial the *Harvard Crimson* repudiated Smith's [24] claim to a free-speech right to publish his ad. To give CODOH a forum so that it could "promulgate malicious falsehoods" under the guise of open debate constituted an "abdication" of the paper's editorial responsibility. The University of Chicago *Maroon* agreed that while the deniers "may express their views," it had "no obligation at anytime to print their offensive hatred."

The argument that not publishing the ad constituted censorship was [25] not only a misinterpretation of the First Amendment but disingenuous. The editorial boards that reached this decision ignored the fact that they all had policies that prevented them from running racist, sexist, prejudicial, or religiously offensive ads. (Some of the papers in question even refuse cigarette ads.) How could they square their "principled" stand for absolute freedom of speech with policies that prevented them from publishing a range of ads and articles? Why was Bradley Smith entitled to constitutional protection while an ad for an X-rated movie, *Playboy*, the KKK, or Marlboros was not? Recognizing this inconsistency, some of the boards tried to reconcile these two seemingly contradictory positions by adopting a stance that drew them even further into the deniers' trap. They argued that Holocaust denial was not anti-semitic and therefore not offensive. The *Cornell Daily Sun* editorial board determined that the "ad does not directly contain racist statements about Jewish people." Valerie Nicolette, the *Sun*'s managing editor, told the *Chronicle of Higher Education* that the editors had evaluated the ad based on their standards of "obscenity and racism" and decided that it passed. When a group of Jewish students at Duke met with the editorial board of the *Duke Chronicle* to protest the running of the ad, they were told that the paper's policy was not to run any ad that was "racist or contained ethnic slurs" but that this ad did not fall into that category.

Andrew Gottesman, who vigorously argued that he could not con- [26] done "censorship" of Smith's advertisement and whose *Michigan Daily* published its ringing denunciation of Holocaust denial under Justice Hugo Black's interpretation of the First Amendment, admitted that there were ads he would not run in the paper. This ad, however, did not deserve to be "banned from the marketplace of ideas, like others might be." Among those he would ban were a Ku Klux Klan announcement of lynching or a beer ad with a woman holding a beer bottle between her breasts. For Gottesman keeping such sexist and racist ads out of the paper would not constitute censorship; keeping Smith's out would. When Washington University's *Student Life* published the ad, an editorial explained that it did so in the interest of preventing "freedom of ideas from disappearing from its newspapers." Yet the same paper includes the following policy statement on its advertising rate card: "*Student Life* reserves the right to edit or reject any advertisement which does not comply with the policies or judgment of the newspaper."

The claim that the rejection of the ad constituted censorship also re- [27] vealed the failure of editorial staffs and, in certain cases, university presidents to think carefully about what their papers did regularly: pick and choose between subjects they covered and those they did not, columns they ran and those they rejected, and ads that met their standards and those that did not. The *Daily Tar Heel*, the paper of the University of North Carolina, proclaimed that as soon as an editor "takes the first dangerous step and decides that an ad should not run because of its content, that editor begins the plunge down a slippery slope toward the abolition of free speech." What the *Tar Heel* failed to note was that newspapers continuously make such choices. As Tom Teepen, the editor of the *Atlanta Constitution*'s editorial page, observed, "Running a newspaper is mainly about making decisions, not about ducking them. In fact the *Duke Chronicle*, whose editor had wondered how newspapers founded on the principles of free speech and free press could "deny those rights to anyone," had earlier rejected an insert for *Playboy* and an ad attacking a fraternity.

While some papers justified their decision by arguing that the ad [28] was not antisemitic and others leaned on the censorship argument, an even more disconcerting rationale was offered by many papers. They argued that however ugly or repellent Smith's "ideas," they had a certain intellectual legitimacy. Consequently it was the papers' responsibility to present these views to readers for their consideration. Those editors who made this argument fell prey to denial's attempt to present itself as part of the normal range of historical interpretation. That they had been deceived was evident in the way they described the contents of the ad. The editor in chief of the *Cornell Daily Sun* described the ad as containing "offensive *ideas*." The *Sun* argued that it was not the paper's role to "unjustly censor advertisers' *viewpoints*" however "unpopular or offensive." In a similar vein the *University of Washington Daily* defended giving Smith op-ed space because the paper must constitute a "forum for diverse *opinions* and *ideas*." Ironically, six weeks earlier, when it rejected the ad, it had described Smith's assertions as "so obviously false as to be unworthy of serious debate." The paper insisted that the op-ed column it eventually published was different because it was Smith's "opinion" and did not contain the "blatant falsehoods" of the ad. In the column Smith asserted that for more than twelve years he has been unable to find "one bit of hard evidence" to prove that there was a plan to "exterminate" the Jews, and that the gas-chamber "stories" were "allegations" unsupported by "documentation or physical evidence."

The *Michigan Daily* engaged in the same reasoning. It would not cen- [29] sor "unpopular *views*" simply because readers might disagree with them. In a show of consistency, two weeks after Smith's ad appeared, the *Daily* supported the decision by Prodigy, the computer bulletin board, to allow subscribers to post Holocaust denial material. Prodigy, they contended, was similar to a newspaper, and like a newspaper it must be a *"forum for ideas."* In another suggestion that Smith's views were worthy of debate, the editor in chief of the *Montana Kaimin* argued that "this man's *opinions*, no matter how ridiculous they may be, need to be heard out there." According to the editor in chief of Washington University's *Student Life*, the board voted to run the ad because "we didn't feel comfortable censoring offensive *ideas*."

The *Ohio State Lantern*'s explanation of why it let Smith have his "public say" despite the fact that it condemned Smith and CODOH as "racist, pure and simple," was more disturbing than the decision itself. The *Lantern* argued that it was "repulsive to think that the quality, or total lack thereof, of any idea or opinion has any bearing on whether it should be heard." It is breathtaking that students at a major university could declare repulsive the making of a decision based on the "quality" of ideas. One assumes that their entire education is geared toward the exploration of ideas with a certain lasting quality. This kind of reasoning essentially contravenes all that an institution of higher learning is supposed to profess.   30

The editors of Washington University's *Student Life* demonstrated a similar disturbing inconsistency. They dismissed Smith's claim to be engaged in a quest for the truth, describing him as someone who "cloaks hate in the garb of intellectual detachment." They believed that Smith was posing as a "truth seeker crushed by a conspiratorial society." Given their evaluation of Smith, his tactics, and the way conspiracy theorists have captured the imagination of much of American society, what followed was particularly disconcerting. Notwithstanding all their misgivings, the editors decided that they must give "Mr. Smith the benefit of the doubt if we mean to preserve our own rights." In an assertion typical of the confused reasoning that student papers nationwide displayed on this issue, the *Student Life* editors acknowledged that they could have suppressed Smith's views "if we attributed motives to him that contradict his statements. But we cannot in good conscience tell Mr. Smith that we 'know' him and his true intentions." Was not the fact that he was denying a historical fact about whose existence there is no debate among any reputable scholars indicative of something significant? The editorial board had concluded that "if we refused Mr. Smith's advertisement, we could censor anyone based on ulterior motives that we perceive them to harbor." At what point would the board feel it was appropriate to make a decision based on the objective merits of the information contained in the ad?   31

In this instance what the paper considered to be ulterior motives is what scholars call coming to a conclusion based on a wide variety of facts, including historical data. In giving Smith the "benefit of the doubt," the editors fell prey to the notion that this was a rational debate. They ignored the fact that the ad contained claims that completely contravened a massive body of fact. They transformed what the *Harvard Crimson* described as "vicious propaganda" into iconoclasm.   32

The most controversial interpretation about precisely what this ad [33] represented was expressed by the *Duke Chronicle*. In a column justifying the paper's decision to run the ad, Ann Heimberger contended that "Revisionists are . . . reinterpreting history, a practice that occurs constantly, especially on a college campus." In a private meeting with Jewish student leaders on the Duke campus, the editors reiterated this argument. The students were told that the ad was neither racist nor antisemitic but was part of an ongoing "scholarly debate." The Duke editorial board viewed the advertisement more as "a political argument than as an ethnic attack." In editorials, articles, and interviews, those at helm of the *Duke Chronicle* repeatedly referred to Holocaust denial as "radical, unpopular *views*," and "disturbing *ideas*" and argued that the ad was not a "slur" but an "*opinion*." By doing so they not only clung to their First Amendment defense, they gave the ad historical and intellectual legitimacy. . . .

～

There were, of course, those college newspapers that had no prob- [34] lem evaluating the ad's intellectual value. The *Harvard Crimson* repudiated the idea that the ad was a "controversial argument based on questionable facts." In one of the most unequivocal evaluations of the ad, the *Crimson* declared it "vicious propaganda based on utter bullshit that has been discredited time and time again." More than "moronic and false," it was an attempt to "propagate hatred against Jews." The editorial board of the University of Pennsylvania's *Daily Pennsylvanian* argued that "running an ad with factual errors that fostered hate" was not in the best interests of the paper.

The *MIT Tech* simply decided that it would not accept an ad that it [35] knew "did not tell the truth." For the *Brown Daily Herald* the ad was "a pack of vicious, antisemitic lies" parading as "history and scholarship." The *Daily Nexus*, the publication of the University of California at Santa Barbara, refused the ad because of its "blatant distortions of truth and its offensive nature." The paper described receiving the ad itself and the more than one thousand dollars to print it as "chilling." The *Dartmouth Review*, no stranger to controversy, also rejected the ad. It acknowledged that by so doing it was denying "someone a forum through which to speak to the paper's readership" but explained that it had a "bond of trust" with the public, which expected it to abide by "standards of accuracy and decency." Accepting an ad "motivated by hatred and informed by total disregard to the truth" would be to violate that trust. The *Chicago Maroon* saw no reason why it should run an ad whose "only objective is to offend and incite hatred." The *Yale Daily News* "simply" let Smith know that it found the ad "offensive."

Some of the papers that ran the ad did so on the basis of what may [36] be called the light-of-day, defense, a corollary of the free-speech argument: In the light of day, truth always prevails over lies. Neeraj Khemlani of the *Cornell Sun* believed that by running the ad he had done the Jewish people a favor—reminding them that there were a "lot of people out to get [them]," which was something they needed to know. This attitude is reminiscent of the concept of "saving the Jews (or women, African Americans, or any other potentially vulnerable group) despite themselves. Michael Gaviser, business manager of the *Daily Pennsylvanian*, decided to run the ad because of his belief that Smith was a "dangerous neo-Nazi" of whom the public had to be aware. (His decision was reversed by the editorial board.)

∽

This assault on the ivory tower of academe illustrated how Holocaust denial can permeate that segment of the population that should be most immune to it. It was naive to believe that the "light of day" can dispel lies, especially when they play on familiar stereotypes. Victims of racism, sexism, antisemitism, and a host of other prejudices know of light's limited ability to discredit falsehood. Light is barely an antidote when people are unable, as was often the case in this investigation, to differentiate between reasoned arguments and blatant falsehoods. Most sobering was the failure of many of these student leaders and opinion makers to recognize Holocaust denial for what it was. This was particularly evident among those who argued that the ad contained ideas, however odious, worth of discussion. This failure suggests that correctly cast and properly camouflaged, Holocaust denial has a good chance of finding a foothold among coming generations. [37]

This chapter ends where it began. Given the fact that even the papers that printed the ad dismissed Smith's claims in the most derogatory of terms—absurd, irrational, racist, and a commercial for hatred—one might argue that the entire affair had a positive outcome. Rarely did the ad appear without an editorial or article castigating Holocaust denial. Students were alerted to a clear and present danger that can easily take root in their midst. Courses on the Holocaust increased in number. One could argue that all this is proof that CODOH's attempt to make Holocaust denial credible backfired. [38]

My assessment is far more pessimistic. It is probably the one issue about which I find myself in agreement with Bradley Smith. Many students read both the ad and the editorials condemning it. Some, including those who read neither but knew of the issue, may have walked away from the controversy convinced that there are two sides to this debate: the "revisionists" and the "establishment historians." They may know that there is tremendous controversy about the former. They may not be convinced that the two sides are of equal validity. They may even know that the deniers keep questionable company. But nonetheless they assume there *is* an "other side." That is the most frightening aspect of this entire matter. [39]

Responding to Reading

1. Do you believe the college newspapers Lipstadt discusses had a responsibility to publish the ad that branded the Holocaust a hoax, or do you believe they had the right (or even the responsibility) *not* to publish it? Explain your position. Do you see any possibility of compromise—for example, publishing the ad along with a detailed opposing viewpoint?
2. Holocaust scholar Raul Hilberg has criticized Lipstadt for writing her book, arguing that it gives the Holocaust deniers valuable publicity. Do you think this criticism of Lipstadt is valid?
3. Regardless of the legal definition of *free speech,* do you believe that every viewpoint should be allowed to reach an audience? Or do you think some ideas are so inaccurate, morally repugnant, or dangerous that they do not deserve to be heard? What kinds of views, if any, do you believe should *not* be aired?

TWO PERSPECTIVES ON MAKING CHOICES

The following poem and short story consider the issue of personal choice and responsibility and how their effects on individuals and on the larger world make "all the difference." "The Road Not Taken" is one the best-known works of Robert Frost (1874–1963), most widely read and beloved of twentieth-century American poets, whose language is familiar and accessible—though not simple—and whose poems are often rich in symbols and allusions. The speaker of this poem grapples in very concrete terms with the whole notion of personal choice and what it entails. "The Ones Who Walk Away from Omelas" by Ursula K. Le Guin (1929–) is a parable cast as a fantasy in which a mythical community strikes a grim bargain to achieve its "perfect" harmony. Best known for her works of science fiction and fantasy, LeGuin has written extensively about the sources of imaginative literature; her books include *The Left Hand of Darkness* (1969), *The Dispossessed* (1974), and the poetry collection *Hard Words* (1981).

THE ROAD NOT TAKEN

Robert Frost

Two roads diverged in a yellow wood,
And sorry I could not travel both
And be one traveller, long I stood
And looked down one as far as I could
To where it bent in the undergrowth;   5

Then took the other, as just as fair,
And having perhaps the better claim,
Because it was grassy and wanted wear;
Though as for that the passing there
Had worn them really about the same,   10

And both that morning equally lay
In leaves no step had trodden black.
Oh, I kept the first for another day!
Yet knowing how way leads on to way,
I doubted if I should ever come back.   15

I shall be telling this with a sigh
Somewhere ages and ages hence:
Two roads diverged in a wood, and I—
I took the one less travelled by,
And that has made all the difference.   20

THE ONES WHO WALK AWAY FROM OMELAS

Ursula K. Le Guin

With a clamor of bells that set the swallows soaring, the Festival of [1]
Summer came to the city Omelas, bright-towered by the sea. The rigging
of the boats in harbor sparkled with flags. In the streets between houses with red roofs and painted walls, between old moss-grown gardens
and under avenues of trees, past great parks and public buildings, processions moved. Some were decorous: old people in long stiff robes of
mauve and grey, grave master workmen, quiet, merry women carrying
their babies and chatting as they walked. In other streets the music beat
faster, a shimmering of gong and tambourine, and the people went
dancing, the procession was a dance. Children dodged in and out, their
high calls rising like the swallows' crossing flights over the music and
the singing. All the processions wound towards the north side of the
city, where on the great water-meadow called the Green Fields boys and
girls, naked in the bright air, with mud-stained feet and ankles and long,
lithe arms, exercised their restive horses before the race. The horses wore
no gear at all but a halter without bit. Their manes were braided with
streamers of silver, gold, and green. They flared their nostrils and
pranced and boasted to one another; they were vastly excited, the horse
being the only animal who had adopted our ceremonies as its own. Far
off to the north and west the mountains stood up half encircling Omelas on her bay. The air of morning was so clear that the snow still crown-
ing the Eighteen Peaks burned with white-gold fire across the miles of
sunlit air, under the dark blue of the sky. There was just enough wind
to make the banners that marked the racecourse snap and flutter now
and then. In the silence of the broad green meadows one could hear the
music winding through the city streets, farther and nearer and ever approaching, a cheerful faint sweetness of the air that from time to time
trembled and gathered together and broke out into the great joyous
clanging of the bells.

Joyous! How is one to tell about joy! How describe the citizens of [2]
Omelas?

They were not simple folk, you see, though they were happy. But [3]
we do not say the words of cheer much any more. All smiles have be-

come archaic. Given a description such as this one tends to make certain assumptions. Given a description such as this one tends to look next for the King, mounted on a splendid stallion and surrounded by his noble knights, or perhaps in a golden litter borne by great-muscled slaves. But there was no king. They did not use swords, or keep slaves. They were not barbarians. I do not know the rules and laws of their society, but I suspect that they were singularly few. As they did without monarchy and slavery, so they also got on without the stock exchange, the advertisement, the secret police, and the bomb. Yet I repeat that these were not simple folk, not dulcet shepherds, noble savages, bland utopians. They were not less complex than us. The trouble is that we have a bad habit, encouraged by pedants and sophisticates, of considering happiness as something rather stupid. Only pain is intellectual, only evil interesting. This is the treason of the artist: a refusal to admit the banality of evil and the terrible boredom of pain. If you can't lick 'em, join 'em. If it hurts, repeat it. But to praise despair is to condemn delight, to embrace violence is to lose hold of everything else. We have almost lost hold; we can no longer describe a happy man, nor make any celebration of joy. How can I tell you about the people of Omelas? They were not naïve and happy children—though their children were, in fact, happy. They were mature, intelligent, passionate adults whose lives were not wretched. O miracle! but I wish I could describe it better. I wish I could convince you. Omelas sounds in my words like a city in a fairy tale, long ago and far away, once upon a time. Perhaps it would be best if you imagined it as your own fancy bids, assuming it will rise to the occasion, for certainly I cannot suit you all. For instance, how about technology? I think that there would be no cars or helicopters in and above the streets; this follows from the fact that the people of Omelas are happy people. Happiness is based on a just discrimination of what is necessary, what is neither necessary nor destructive, and what is destructive. In the middle category, however—that of the unnecessary but undestructive, that of comfort, luxury, exuberance, etc.—they could perfectly well have central heating, subway trains, washing machines, and all kinds of marvelous devices not yet invented here, floating light-sources, fuelless power, a cure for the common cold. Or they could have none of that: It doesn't matter. As you like it. I incline to think that people from towns up and down the coast have been coming in to Omelas during the last days before the Festival on very fast little trains and double-decked trams, and that the train station of Omelas is actually the handsomest building in town, though plainer than the magnificent Farmers' Market. But even granted trains, I fear that Omelas so far strikes some of you as goody-goody. Smiles, bells, parades, horses, bleh. If so, please add an orgy. If an orgy would help, don't hesitate. Let us not, however, have temples from which issue beautiful nude priests and priestesses already half in ectasy and ready to copulate with any man or woman, lover or stranger, who desires union with the deep godhead of the blood, although that was my first idea. But really it would be better not to have any temples in Omelas— at least not manned temples. Religion yes, clergy no. Surely the beautiful nudes can just wander about, offering themselves like divine soufflés to the hunger of the needy and the rapture of the flesh. Let them join the processions. Let tambourines be struck above the copulations, and the glory of desire be proclaimed upon the gongs, and (a not unimportant point) let the offspring of these delightful rituals be beloved and looked after by all. One thing I know there is none of in Omelas is guilt. But what else should there be? I thought at first there were no drugs, but that is puritanical. For those who like it, the faint insistent sweetness of *drooz* may perfume the ways of the city, *drooz* which first brings a great lightness and brilliance to the mind and limbs, and then after some hours a dreamy languor, and wonderful visions at last of the very arcana and inmost secrets of the Universe, as well as exciting the pleasure of sex beyond all belief; and it is not habit-forming. For more modest tastes I think there ought to be beer. What else, what else belongs in the joyous city? The sense of victory, surely, the celebration of courage. But as we did without clergy, let us do without soldiers. The joy built upon successful slaughter is not the right kind of joy; it will not do; it is fearful and it is trivial. A boundless and generous contentment, a magnanimous triumph felt not against some outer enemy but in communion with the finest and fairest in the souls of all men everywhere and the splendor of the world's summer: This is what swells the hearts of the people of Omelas, and the victory they celebrate is that of life. I really don't think many of them need to take *drooz.*

Most of the processions have reached the Green Fields by now. A [4] marvelous smell of cooking goes forth from the red and blue tents of the provisioners. The faces of small children are amiably sticky; in the benign grey beard of a man a couple of crumbs of rich pastry are entangled. The youths and girls have mounted their horses and are beginning to group around the starting line of the course. An old woman, small, fat, and laughing, is passing out flowers from a basket, and tall young men wear her flowers in their shining hair. A child of nine or ten sits at the edge of the crowd, alone, playing on a wooden flute. People pause to listen, and they smile, but they do not speak to him, for he never ceases playing and never sees them, his dark eyes wholly rapt in the sweet, thin magic of the tune.

He finishes, and slowly lowers his hands holding the wooden flute. [5]

As if that little private silence were the signal, all at once a trumpet [6] sounds from the pavilion near the starting line: imperious, melancholy, piercing. The horses rear on their slender legs, and some of them neigh in answer. Sober-faced, the young riders stroke the horses' necks and soothe them, whispering, "Quiet, quiet, there my beauty, my hope. . . ." They begin to form in rank along the starting line. The crowds along the racecourse are like a field of grass and flowers in the wind. The Festival of Summer has begun.

Do you believe? Do you accept the festival, the city, the joy? No? [7] Then let me describe one more thing.

In a basement under one of the beautiful public buildings of Ome- [8] las, or perhaps in the cellar of one of its spacious private homes, there is a room. It has one locked door, and no window. A little light seeps in dustily between cracks in the boards, secondhand from a cobwebbed window somewhere across the cellar. In one corner of the little room a couple of mops, with stiff, clotted, foul-smelling heads, stand near a rusty bucket. The floor is dirt, a little damp to the touch, as cellar dirt usually is. The room is about three paces long and two wide: a mere broom closet or disused tool room. In the room a child is sitting. It could be a boy or a girl. It looks about six, but actually is nearly ten. It is feeble-minded. Perhaps it was born defective, or perhaps it has become imbecile through fear, malnutrition, and neglect. It picks its nose and occasionally fumbles vaguely with its toes or genitals, as it sits hunched in the corner farthest from the bucket and the two mops. It is afraid of the mops. It finds them horrible. It shuts its eyes, but it knows the mops are still standing there; and the door is locked; and nobody ever comes, except that sometimes—the child has no understanding of time or interval—sometimes the door rattles terribly and opens, and a person, or several people, are there. One of them may come in and kick the child to make it stand up. The others never come close, but peer in at it with frightened, disgusted eyes. The food bowl and the water jug are hastily filled, the door is locked, the eyes disappear. The people at the door never say anything, but the child, who has not always lived in the tool room, and can remember sunlight and its mother's voice, sometimes speaks. "I will be good," it says. "Please let me out. I will be good!" They never answer. The child used to scream for help at night, and cry a good deal, but now it only makes a kind of whining,"eh-haa-, ch-haa," and it speaks less and less often. It is so thin there are no calves to its legs; its belly protrudes; it lives on a half-bowl of corn meal and grease a day. It is naked. Its buttocks and thighs are a mass of festered sores, as it sits in its own excrement continually.

They all know it is there, all the people of Omelas. Some of them [9] have come to see it, others are content merely to know it is there. They all know that it has to be there. Some of them understand why, and some do not, but they all understand that their happiness, the beauty of their city, the tenderness of their friendships, the health of their children, the wisdom of their scholars, the skill of their makers, even the abundance of their harvest and the kindly weathers of their skies, depend wholly on this child's abominable misery.

This is usually explained to children when they are between eight [10] and twelve, whenever they seem capable of understanding; and most of those who come to see the child are young people, though often enough an adult comes, or comes back, to see the child. No matter how well the matter has been explained to them, these young spectators are always shocked and sickened at the sight. They feel disgust, which they had thought themselves superior to. They feel anger, outrage, impotence, despite all the explanations. They would like to do something for the child. But there is nothing they can do. If the child were brought up into and sunlight out of that vile place, if it were cleaned and fed and comforted, that would be a good thing, indeed; but if it were done, in that day and hour all the prosperity and beauty and delight of Omelas would wither and be destroyed. Those are the terms. To exchange all the goodness and grace of every life in Omelas for that single, small improvement: to throw away the happiness of thousands for the chance of the happiness of one: that would be to let guilt within the walls indeed.

The terms are strict and absolute; there may not even be a kind word [11] spoken to the child.

Often the young people go home in tears, or in a tearless rage, when [12] they have seen the child and faced this terrible paradox. They may brood over it for weeks or years. But as time goes on they begin to realize that even if the child could be released, it would not get much good of its freedom: a little vague pleasure of warmth and food, no doubt, but little more. It is too degraded and imbecile to know any real joy. It has been afraid too long ever to be free of fear. Its habits are too uncouth for it to respond to humane treatment. Indeed, after so long it would probably be wretched without walls about it to protect it, and darkness for its eyes, and its own excrement to sit in. Their tears at the bitter injustice dry when they begin to perceive the terrible justice of reality, and to accept it. Yet it is their tears and anger, the trying of their generosity and the acceptance of their helplessness, which are perhaps the true source of the splendor of their lives. Theirs is no vapid, irresponsible happiness. They know that they, like the child, are not free. They know compassion. It is the existence of the child, and their knowledge of its existence, that makes possible the nobility of their architecture, the poignancy of their music, the profundity of their science. It is because of the child that they are so gentle with children. They know that if the wretched one were not there snivelling in the dark, the other one, the flute-player, could make no joyful music as the young riders line up in their beauty for the race in the sunlight of the first morning of summer.

Now do you believe in them? Are they not more credible? But there [13] is one more thing to tell, and this is quite incredible.

At times one of the adolescent girls or boys who go to see the child [14] does not go home to weep or rage, does not, in fact, go home at all. Sometimes also a man or woman much older falls silent for a day or two, and then leaves home. These people go out into the street, and walk down the street alone. They keep walking, and walk straight out of the city of Omelas, through the beautiful gates. They keep walking across the farmlands of Omelas. Each one goes alone, youth or girl, man or woman. Night falls; the traveler must pass down village streets, between the houses with yellow-lit windows, and on out into the darkness of the fields. Each alone, they go west or north, towards the mountains. They go on. They leave Omelas, they walk ahead into the darkness, and they do not come back. The place they go towards is a place even less imaginable to most of us than the city of happiness. I cannot describe it at all. It is possible that it does not exist. But they seem to know where they are going, the ones who walk away from Omelas.

Responding to Reading

1. What is the difference between the two paths Frost's speaker considers? Why does he make the choice he does?
2. Is "The Road Not Taken" simply about two paths in the wood, or does it suggest something more? What makes you think so? To what larger choices might the speaker be alluding? What are the two paths that confront the citizens of Omelas?
3. What does the speaker mean by "That has made all the difference" (line 20)? Have you ever made a choice that made "all the difference"? Do those who walk away from Omelas make a difference?
4. Why do you think Le Guin's narrator keeps asking readers whether or not they "believe," whether they accept what she is saying as the truth? *Do* you "believe"? What do you find most unbelievable? What do you find most believable?
5. Are the ones who walk away from Omelas any less morally responsible for the child's welfare than those who keep the child imprisoned? Or do you believe there is a difference between actively doing something "wrong" and passively allowing it to happen?
6. Why does the logic of the story require that the child be present? Why must the child suffer? Might it be argued that our society has its own equivalent of the child locked in the closet and that we are all guilty of failing to act to save this child?

WRITING

Making Choices

1. What was the most important decision you ever made? Did you make the right choice? Would you make the same decision today?

2. The question of whether or not to act to end another's suffering—possibly at one's own expense—is explored, implicitly or explicitly, in "The Deer at Providencia," "Shooting an Elephant," "Lifeboat Ethics: The Case Against Helping the Poor" and "The Ones Who Walk Away from Omelas." What are your own feelings about this subject?

3. Thoreau says, "Unjust laws exist: shall we be content to obey them, or shall we endeavor to amend them, and obey them until we have succeeded, or shall we transgress them at once?" (16). Choose a law that you consider unjust, and write an essay in which you tell why you believe it should be disobeyed.

4. Is all life equally valuable? Explain your position on this issue, considering the ideas raised by Shalev and Dillard in this chapter and by Christensen in Chapter 9.

5. Milgram concludes that his study shows that "ordinary people, simply doing their jobs, and without any particular hostility on their part, can become agents in a terrible destructive process" (39). Cite examples from your own experience to illustrate his conclusion.

6. King, Milgram, and Thoreau all consider the difficulties of resisting majority rule, standing up to authority, and protesting against established rules and laws. Did you ever submit to authority even though you thought you should not have? What were the consequences of your act?

7. Describe a time when you stood up to authority. What motivated you? Was your resistance successful? Would you do the same thing again?

8. The writers represented in this chapter present some pessimistic scenarios. Shalev sees people more concerned about whales than about other suffering human beings; Hardin sees an overpopulated, underfed world; King sees a world corrupted by prejudice. What world problems are you most pessimistic about? Why?

9. Among the most important and difficult decisions facing human beings today are questions about how far we should go to preserve and protect life. Write an essay in which you give your personal re-

sponses to the ideas raised by Jenkins and Shalev in this chapter as well as to the positions expressed by Kevorkian and Schneiderman in Chapter 8.

10. How free should speech on your campus be? After reading Lipstadt's "Denying the Holocaust," write an editorial for your school newspaper in which you discuss the kinds of statements, if any, that should be censored and explain why.

APPENDIX:
STUDENT WRITING

Since the publication of the first edition of *The Blair Reader* in 1992, many students have responded in writing to its themes and readings. Five of these student responses appear on the pages that follow:

- "Morgan," by Summer Dawn Adams, University of Florida, explores the theme of gender in response to several of the selections in Chapter 5, "Women and Men." Notice that Summer does not refer to specific sources; instead, she examines the theme in general terms, directing her remarks to a three-year-old girl.

- Shari DeGroff, a student at the University of Memphis, also focuses on gender. In her essay "Fighting Back," she compares the way two writers, Gloria Steinem and Stanton L. Wormley, Jr., approach the issue of gender-based expectations. By setting these writers' words and ideas in opposition, Shari contrasts men's and women's expectations—and finds some common ground. (The essays by Steinem and Wormley appear in Chapter 5.)

- In "Lynching of the Mind," Adam Uriah Pickering, also of the University of Memphis, presents a thematic analysis of the subtle forms of racism discussed in Brent Staples's "Just Walk on By" (Chapter 7), Maya Angelou's "Graduation" (Chapter 2), and Richard Wright's "The Library Card" (Chapter 6). As Adam analyzes the way three different authors treat this single theme, he explores similarities and differences among their essays as well as his own responses to their ideas.

- In "After the Storm," Cherry Carnero, a student at the University of California at Irvine, explores the ways Martin Luther King, Jr.'s "I Have a Dream" and Zora Neale Hurston's "How It Feels to Be Colored Me" (both in Chapter 6) use similar images to develop different themes.

- finally, Hoang-Quyen N. Nguyen, in "To Live Again," does a close reading of a passage from "How It Feels to Be Colored Me." This paper analyzes Hurston's language choices and examines how these choices help her communicate her ideas to readers.

MORGAN

~

Summer Dawn Adams, University of Florida

"Sugar, and spice, and every thing nice, that's what little girls are made of. Snips, and snails, and puppy dog tails, that's what little boys are made of," recited Morgan. [1]

At the age of three Morgan already knows this harmless, traditional rhyme by heart. Harmless? At this impressionable time in Morgan's life, she is already separating "girls" and "boys" into different categories. As she progresses into adulthood, she will bring this mindset with her. No one can deny it; the imbalance between the sexes encompasses many areas of our lives. This aspect of our society is seen in schools, politics, and the workplace. Yet, no one, male or female, should be judged by which chromosome fell into place during conception. [2]

So what lies ahead for you, Morgan, when you become an active member of society? You are our future, but will the past discourage you as it limits our present? Granted, we have come a long way since medieval times when men considered women chattel, but look how long it took us to gain the basic right to vote. Politics—so many men, too few women. If statistics remain the same, sorry kid, you can probably forget about politics. Only a dozen women have held cabinet-level appointments in this country's two hundred years. So what happened to that right of suffrage we fought so hard for? Only about half of the women registered to vote actually make it to polls. Does this show our own apathy holding back progress? Well, Morgan, if we do not get our act together in the next few years, you can look forward to joining this centuries-old battle to gain political equality. [3]

We have all heard the saying, "Anything a man can do, a woman can do better." You may be able to, Morgan, but you sure can count on getting paid a lot less. The average female with five-plus years of college receives less money annually than a male with only a high school diplo- [4]

ma. This really hits home for me, because I am a photojournalist, a member of a profession traditionally dominated by men. This does not discourage me at all, though, just as I would not want you, Morgan, to be discouraged by anything. This only inspires me to strive even harder. I will shatter "glass ceilings" in pursuing my goals.

You do not need to concern yourself with the work place right now, [5] but in a few years you will begin your formal education. Not only will you have to cope with a new environment, but you will also have to face discrimination. Do boys get called on more in class than girls? Are girls less encouraged to go into careers in math and science? In this day these questions need to be asked. If our schools are not free from sexism, then what hope will we have of breaking out of our stereotypes? The school age is a time when people form their values and their ideas about others. There is no way we can promote equality when just the opposite is being instilled in children at such young ages. So, Morgan, if ever in recess you do not get picked for a game because you are a girl, or if a physical education coach is biased and makes you feel inferior, or an advisor gears you toward a " traditional" career even though you want to break away from the conventional, then stand up for yourself and demand that you be seen as an equal and a competitive player.

Morgan, I will leave you with a few words of advice: hold fast to [6] what you believe in, and never let anyone tell you your ideas do not have value. In your career plans pursue whatever you wish: law, nursing, construction, or teaching. If society accuses you of overstepping your bounds as a female, prove yourself by becoming the best and expanding those bounds for the rest of us.

FIGHTING BACK

~

Shari DeGroff,
University of Memphis

Society has certain ideas about how men and women should behave, [1] but ultimately one should allow his or her individual preferences and convictions to dictate personal behavior. This conclusion is reached by both Gloria Steinem in "The Good News Is: These Are Not the Best Years of Your Life" and Stanton L. Wormley, Jr., in "Fighting Back" as they examine society's narrow-minded expectations, the harmful repercussions of conforming, and the fulfillment that comes from being oneself.

Society expects men to be strong, tough, and courageous. In "Fight- 2
ing Back" Wormley tells how he was derided for not punching back
when he was rudely awakened from sleep by a drunken soldier looking
for a fight. He had been raised in a very peaceful home where violence
was discouraged, and he sought to understand why he was being
ridiculed. As he looks back at the incident, he questions his actions:
"Nevertheless, that question—*Why didn't I fight back?*—haunted me long
after the incident had been forgotten by everyone else. Was I less of a
man for not having beaten my attacker to a bloody pulp?" (345). Although his upbringing and his basic character told him to hold back, he
felt external pressure to do the "manly" thing.

Gloria Steinem in "The Good New Is: These Are Not the Best Years 3
of Your Life" observes that society defines women as "half-people, man
junkies; that is, people who are addicted to regular shots of male approval and presence, both professionally and personally" (352). She goes
on to state that a woman who tries to dispel this attitude, and help others to do the same, will be ridiculed by others and regarded as odd or
dangerous simply because the males will feel threatened by such a
courageous act. Like Wormley, she sees a basic conflict between doing
what she feels is right and doing what society expects of her.

Such pressure to conform is harmful because it causes many people 4
to act in ways contrary to their natures. Sometimes they regret their actions. Years later, for example, Wormley does fight back upon being provoked in a similar situation, and he feels sad because he has lost a certain innocence. For Steinem, "fighting back" does not mean using
physical power; it simply means resisting the stereotype rather than conforming to it. In this sense, she sees loss of innocence as a positive development. She believes it takes most women years to muster up the
courage to become who they truly are rather than simply live up to others' expectations. Still, she is hopeful: "One day, an army of gray-haired
women may quietly take over the Earth" (355).

Much of the process of sorting out what is "feminine" and "mascu- 5
line" is part of growing up and learning how one wants to conduct oneself, but we should be true to ourselves, not to our genders. Doing so allows others to realize that the stereotypes do not have to be played out.
Men and women as individuals have too much to contribute to limit
their action and discoveries.

Finally, the day has come where society is not as quick to define 6
roles on the basis of gender as it was in the past. Any modern office,
many with male secretaries and female supervisors, demonstrates that
change is taking place. But, even so, there is prejudice. Each man or
woman has a responsibility to himself or herself to be the best he or she
can be. By letting go of the stereotypes, refusing to conform for the sake
of fitting in, and focusing on being true to oneself, an individual can become part of the solution rather than part of the problem.

LYNCHING OF THE MIND

~

Adam Uriah Pickering, University of Memphis

Whenever racism is discussed, it invariably brings to mind images [1] of violence. Malcolm X., Louis Farrakhan, and, lately, Rodney King have all been viewed by some people as heroes. The actions of the KKK and white people (usually from the South) with violent tendencies have continuously been presented as examples of racism in action. The burning cross, the hanging man—these are the symbols of racism that come to mind. But racism is not always so obvious. Racism can be as subtle as the beating of raven's wings and just as dark. It is always there, lurking in the shadows, unnoticed, unacknowledged, but invariably present.

Brent Staples writes about a subtle, and probably unintended, form [2] of discrimination in his essay entitled "Just Walk on By." Staples is a rather large man who has the "audacity" to walk the city streets at night. He describes a time when he was walking alone and happened to encounter a woman. Despite the careful distance he maintained, "she picked up her pace and was soon running in earnest. It was clear that she thought herself the quarry of a mugger, a rapist, or worse" (497). Most likely this individual would not have been so panicked had the large man in the military field jacket been white. Being seen as a probable threat can be hazardous to one's health, especially in today's rather panicky atmosphere where mace, knives, and guns are commonplace. Staples took steps to alleviate the problem his appearance created. He no longer enters buildings behind people so they will not think he is following them; he often crosses the street rather than appearing to be approaching an individual with the intent of doing harm; and he whistles classical music, believing people will think it is unlikely for a mugger to know, much less be able, or inclined, to whistle such tunes (500). Why must an American citizen take such measures to prove he is not a threat primarily because of the color of his skin? Racism is not always violent.

Certainly, no one was violently beaten on the day of Maya An- [3] gelou's graduation. This occasion was intended to have been a joyous one, but due to a speech delivered by a white politician, the event was nearly ruined. The ceremony was to take place on the basketball field, because unlike the white Central School, Angelou's school had no lawn, hedges, tennis courts, or ivy (93). Edward Donleavy, a politician from Arkansas, arrived and began to speak. He praised the students and parents for the work they were doing—just like the work "going on . . . in the other schools" (98). He then proceeded to tell them of the "improvements" planned for their school (98). Where Central got new microscopes, the black school would get new sports equipment. Where Central got better classrooms, the black school would get a paved basketball court. He "praised" the school for the athletic achievements of its students while disregarding their educational achievements. Racism is not always violent.

No one burned a cross in Richard Wright's front yard when he   4
wanted to read. One day while reading through a copy of the *Commercial Appeal*, Wright saw the name of an author who was denounced as a fool. Wright wished to learn more about this "fool." Unfortunately, the Memphis Library would not allow blacks to use its materials, so Wright was forced to borrow a white man's card and convince the librarian that "this nigger boy" was sent there to retrieve books for the card's owner, who was busy (408–409). No one could understand why a black man would wish to read works by Mencken, Dreiser, and Sinclair Lewis. Surely such works would confuse him. Surely a mere black man wouldn't have the ability, or the wish, to read, and comprehend, and learn from such books. Racism is not always violent.

These are the attitudes that breed this subtle racism that must be   5
changed. They were present in the past, and they are still present today. They are the common attitudes of the ill-educated, the narrow-minded, the ignorant, the foolish. Violent action is the exception to the norm. It appears to be commonplace because the media present it so often. After all, bad news sells newspapers and magazines. It is far more important, however, that we put an end to the more pervasive, and more accepted, attitudes and misconceptions if we are to lay the spirit of divisiveness to rest once and for all. Racism may not always be violent, but it is always wrong.

AFTER THE STORM

~

Cherry Carnero, University of California at Irvine

Zora Neale Hurston's "How It Feels to Be Colored Me" and Martin   1
Luther King Jr.'s "I Have a Dream" both speak about racial identify, but they approach this issue quite differently. "How It Feels to Be Colored Me" speaks of an individual, Hurston, who defines herself as an African American. Hurston does not use race to totally define her identity. In-

stead, she wants to be judged on the basis of her character and deeds. On the other hand, "I Have a Dream" addresses African Americans as a group, and King urges them to rise from the ashes of injustice by coming together and working to change society. We might compare these two essays in order to learn how they use the same key images—*rock* and *storm*—to develop different themes.

The theme of Hurston's essay is the importance of being an individual. This theme is stated explicitly in paragraph 10: "Among the thousand white persons, I am a dark rock surged upon, and overswept, but through it all, I remain myself. When covered by the waters, I am; and the ebb but reveals me again (453)." Hurston speaks of the injustices and obstacles she faced as a result of the prejudicial treatment she received from the white students at Barnard. She has been able to clarify her identity as an African American and has become a stronger person— a rock—in the process. Her experiences at college helped mold her into a self-sufficient individual. Race became less important as her sense of her self grew stronger: "At certain times I have no race," she says. "I am *me* . . . I belong to no race nor time (453)." Although she knows she has roots she can trace back to slavery, this knowledge does not change the fact that she is her own person and can use her own intellect and determination to move forward.

In "How It Feels to Be Colored Me" two key images, *rock* and *water*, help develop the essay's theme. The rock refers to Hurston herself and the stability of her character. The water can be seen as the white students at her college who treated her so badly. Hurston is an individual who has overcome the tides of degrading treatment from her white college classmates; she has struggled through racial obstacles to define herself as an individual.

The theme of "I Have a Dream" is not the importance of individuality but the importance of unity; as King says in paragraph 6, "now is the time to lift our nation from the quicksands of racial injustice to the solid rock of brotherhood" (397). King also calls on African-American people to unite with people of other colors to change society's attitudes about civil rights, "for many of our white brothers . . . have come to realize that their destiny is tied up with our destiny and they have come to realize that their freedom is inextricably bound to our freedom" (398). These lines explain how unity is necessary to attain equal rights for minorities.

Rock and *storm* are two key images in "I Have a Dream." The rock represents the brotherhood of the African-American people. If they join as one, the rock can also reveal the strength of African-American brotherhood. In phrases like "storms of persecution" and "winds of police brutality" (398) the image of a storm is used as a metaphor for the persecution African Americans have experienced. In the phrase "whirlwinds of revolt" (397), however, the image of the storm suggests the coming upheaval. Through these key terms, "I Have a Dream" asserts that the "Negroes" of America should stand together and fight racism.

"How It Feels to Be Colored Me" and "I Have a Dream" use simi- 6
lar images, yet they communicate different themes. In "How It Feels to Be Colored Me" the rock refers to Hurston, an individual; in "I Have a Dream" King uses the word *rock* to mean the unified African-American population. The image of a storm (water) is also used differently. In "How It Feels to Be Colored Me" the water that surges around Hurston refers to the white population of her college, while the storm in "I Have a Dream" refers to more abstract ideas of racism and injustice.

"I Have a Dream" is written with a straightforward yet charismat- 7
ic tone. This essay is a speech designed to rally the people to take hold of their future by pressuring the government to change society. "Five score years ago," which is a phrase that starts off the essay, alludes to the Gettysburg Address, tying this speech to freedom from slavery. While "I Have a Dream" is a speech written to move the crowd strongly, "How It Feels to Be Colored Me" is a personal, autobiographical essay, and Hurston's references to her childhood and life experience give it a tone of intimacy. Unlike "I Have a Dream," "How It Feels to Be Colored Me" does not emphasize color and racial confrontations. Hurston is not saddened by her people's past. Rather, her roots have given her strength to do the best she can with her life. As she says in paragraph 6, "But I am not tragically colored. . . . No, I do not weep at the world—I am too busy sharpening my oyster knife (452)."

TO LIVE AGAIN

∾

Hoang-Quyen N. Nguyen, University of California at Irvine

In "How It Feels to Be Colored Me" Zora Neale Hurston attacks and 1
breaks down the preconceptions associated with being "colored" and opens up a world where the color of one's skin does not define one's value. By abandoning the prejudices associated with the word *colored*, the author gains a richer understanding of life as an African American. In paragraphs 11–13 of her essay, Hurston animates her life by personifying a jazz orchestra as a ferocious beast, comparing herself to an African native, and resurrecting "dead" words—language that is veiled with so many stereotypes that it has lost its true meaning. Using per-

sonification as her main literary device, the author brings to life her time-less message.

Hurston first assaults the biases associated with being "colored"   2
when she attributes human qualities to a rambunctious jazz perfor-mance. The jazz orchestra is personified as a wild beast that "rears on its hind legs and attacks the tonal veil with primitive fury, rending it, claw-ing it until it breaks through to the jungle beyond" (453). The barbaric animal symbolizes Hurston's wild nature, her restless passion and ef-fervescence. The author wants to tear down the veil that blocks the way to the jungle—the world where color is glorified, not rebuked; she wants to rip apart the subjectivities that "colored" denotes. The jazz perfor-mance attempts to break down the social and cultural stereotypes that view "colored" individuals as inferior and abominable. Stereotypical barriers are very difficult to destroy; therefore, the wild brute must struggle endlessly to break into the jungle. Because the image of the wild animal is so vivid, the reader is able to grasp Hurston's passion. When she personifies the orchestra, Hurston personifies herself. In other words, she brings herself—her color—to life and enlivens the emotion that is dormant within her and the reader.

During the dramatic jazz performance Hurston is filled with such   3
red, fiery emotion that she compares herself to a wild savage yearning to break through to the jungle beyond. The author writes: "I want to slaughter something—give paid, give death to what, I do not know" (453). There is something intangible that Hurston wants to destroy—that she must kill, but she is ignorant to what it is. Hurston, like the jazz or-chestra, is attempting to strike down the mysterious, invisible wall that keeps her "colored" people isolated from the rest of humanity. She once again wants to attack and break down the prejudices that are associat-ed with African Americans. Hurston is not ashamed of her race or of her ancestors. She passionately drives into the metaphor comparing herself to an uncivilized African native attacking societal standards. By doing so, Hurston takes images deadened with negative stereotypes and gives life and new meaning to them.

Hurston often takes words that have negative connotations and of-   4
fers new ways to interpret them. For example, African Americans gen-erally do not want to be associated with wild savages and the jungle, but Hurston purposely uses these same words to describe herself and how she feels. She writes: "I dance wildly inside myself; I yell within, I whoop; I shake my assegai above my head, I hurl it true to the mark *yeeeeooww!* I am in the jungle and living in the jungle way" (453). Al-though others are unable to fathom the emotion that lies within the primitive ceremony, Hurston sees the native lifestyle as something beau-tiful. Hurston's passion urges her to rip apart "dead" language. She brings to life words that have become deadened with stereotypical meanings. For instance, *primitive* is usually associated with being simple

or crude. Hurston, however, sees her *primitive* ancestors as the origin of the human race, the beginning of mankind. Hurston must strip words of their old, common meanings and give them new or different definitions. She does so literally by twisting the meanings of certain words and metaphorically by comparing herself to a wild native who tries to rip apart the "veil" that separates her from the jungle—the world where words are vivid and full of life. Thus, we see how Hurston masterfully takes words generally associated with different meanings and uses them to convey her message.

Not only does Hurston modify the connotations of certain words,   5 she also redefines words that are deadened with stereotypical meaning. For instance, while Hurston is dancing in the jungle and waving her hunting spear, her white friend sits motionless, only hearing what the author feels. Hurston ironically writes: "He is so pale with his whiteness then and I am so colored" (453). Hurston thus alters the meaning of the words *colored*. *Colored* usually denotes "belonging to a race other than the white, especially to the black race." However, Hurston rips apart the usual connotations of the word *colored* and twists its implications to relay her message. *Color* to Hurston simply means richness, having vivid or distinctive qualities. The author thus overcomes certain reader expectations by rewriting the evaluative associations of *colored*—taking it from simply meaning "not white" to making *colored* mean a variety of things. Hurston demonstrates the richness of her color when she writes: "My face is painted red and yellow and my body is painted blue" (453). She contrasts sharply with the colorless white friend at her side. *White* is often associated with purity and innocence, but Hurston describes *white* as lacking color, and thus lacking richness and vitality. Therefore, she attacks those who are colorless. Hurston feels that those who lack color are lifeless: "A white person is set down in our midst. . . ." The white person did not sit down; he was set down. The black person is active and alive; the white person is passive and quite "dead."

In personifying herself, the author loses all the prejudices she feels   6 against her fellow human beings. She forgets the old Zora, and a new, colored Zora emerges—a Zora who has learned to love herself and all of mankind. She breaks down many stereotypical barriers. For example, many "non-colored" individuals assume that they already know how a colored person feels—or how they should feel considering what they and their ancestors have been through—but Hurston challenges this "knowledge" when she writes of her white friend: "He has only heard what I felt" (453). And thus, in her essay, Hurston writes how it feels to be her, how it feels to be colored her. The author does not title her essay "How It *Is* to Be Colored Me," she titles it "How It *Feels* to Be Colored Me." Hurston does not simply tell the story of her life; she recounts humorous and original episodes and lets her readers feel how it is to be her. Through her words and images, we do experience a part of her life.

Hurston possesses a deep understanding of human life and charac- [7] ter and expresses this knowledge through her sensitive essay. The author makes a point that she feels rich being a colored person. Hurston rips apart the prejudices that are associated with being colored by personifying the jazz orchestra as a raging beast tearing its ways into the jungle; by metaphorically comparing herself to a wild native who, like the orchestra, must break down barriers to enter a world where color does not bear any significance to the value of a person; and last, by resuscitating words that are muffled with stereotypical meanings. Hurston acquires a profound love for her people and for all of humanity when she personifies her color. The reader is able to feel the emotions that the author vividly expresses; thus, Zora Hurston lives again.

ACKNOWLEDGMENTS

MAYA ANGELOU "Graduation" from *I Know Why the Caged Bird Sings* by Maya Angelou; copyright © 1969 by Maya Angelou. Reprinted by permission of Random House, Inc.

BARBARA LAZEAR ASCHER Excerpts from *The Habit of Loving* by Barbara Ascher; copyright © 1986, 1987, 1989 by Barbara Lazear Ascher. Reprinted by permission of Random House, Inc.

JENNY LYN BADER "Larger Than Life" from *Next: Young American Writers on the New Generation*, edited by Eric Liu; copyright © 1994 by Jenny Lyn Bader. Reprinted with permission of W. W. Norton, Inc.

TONI CADE BAMBARA "The Lesson" from *Gorilla, My Love* by Toni Cade Bambara; copyright © 1972 by Toni Cade Bambara. Reprinted by permission of Random House, Inc.

LYNDA BARRY "The Sanctuary of School"; copyright © 1992 by the New York Times Company. Used by permission.

CHARLES BAXTER "Gryphon" from *Through the Safety Net* by Charles Baxter; copyright © 1985 by Charles Baxter. Used by permission of Viking Penguin, a division of Penguin Books USA Inc.

JUDY BRADY "Why I Want a Wife" copyright © 1971. Reprinted by permission of the author.

MICHAEL BRONSKI "Magic and AIDS: Presumed Innocent" copyright © 1992 by Michael Bronski. Used by permission of the author.

SHAWN CARLSON "Death in the Rain Forests"; copyright © 1992 by American Humanist Association. From *The Humanist*, March/April 1992. Reprinted by permission of the American Humanist Association.

RACHEL CARSON "The Obligation to Endure" from *Silent Spring* by Rachel Carson; copyright © 1962 by Rachel Carson. copyright © renewed 1990 by Roger Christie. Reprinted by permission of Houghton Mifflin Co. All rights reserved.

STEPHEN A. CARTER "Racial Preferences? So What?" from *Reflections of an Affirmative Action Baby* by Stephen A. Carter; copyright © 1991 by Stephen A. Carter. Reprinted by permission of HarperCollins Publishers, Inc.

RAYMOND CARVER "My Father's Life"; copyright © 1984 by Raymond Carver. Reprinted by permission of Tess Gallagher.

SALLY THANE CHRISTIANSEN "Is a Tree Worth a Life?" copyright © 1991 by Sally Thane Christiansen. Reprinted by permission of the author.

JUDITH ORTIZ COFER "The Looking Glass Shame" from *Silent Dancing: A Partial Remembrance of a Puerto Rican Childhood*; copyright © 1990 by Judith Ortiz Cofer. Reprinted by permission of Arte Publico Press-University of Houston.

ROBERT COLES Adapted from "The Children of Affluence" from *Privileged Ones, Volume V of Children of Crises* by Robert Coles; copyright © 1977 by Robert Coles. Reprinted by permission of Little, Brown and Company.

HUNTLY COLLINS "PC and the Press" as printed in *Change Magazine* published by Heldref Publications; copyright © 1992. Reprinted with permission of the Helen Dwight Reid Educational Foundation.

LOUIE CREW "Thriving as an Outsider, Even as an Outcast, in Smalltown, America" copyright © 1981 by The University of Wisconsin, Stevens Point. Reprinted by permission of the author.

VINE DELORIA, JR. "We Talk, You Listen" from *We Talk, You Listen: New Tribes, New Trust* by Vine Deloria, Jr.; copyright © 1970 by Vine Deloria, Jr. Reprinted by permission of Simon & Schuster, Inc.

JOAN DIDION "On Going Home" and "On Keeping a Notebook" from *Slouching Toward Bethlehem* by Joan Didion; copyright © 1966, 1967 by Joan Didion. Reprinted by permission of Farrar, Straus and Giroux, Inc.

ANNIE DILLARD "The Deer at Providencia" from *Teaching a Stone to Talk* by Annie Dillard; copyright © 1982 by Annie Dillard. Reprinted by permission of HarperCollins Publishers, Inc.

DINESH D'SOUZA "The Visigoths in Tweeds"; copyright © 1991 by Dinesh D'Souza. Reprinted by permission of the author.

BARBARA EHRENREICH "The Myth of Man as Hunter"; copyright © 1993 by Time, Inc. Reprinted by permission of Time, Inc.

LARS EIGHNER "Dumpster Diving" from *Travels with Lizbeth*; copyright © 1993 by Lars Eighner. Reprinted by permission of St. Martin's Press.

LOUISE ERDRICH "Dear John Wayne" from *Jacklight* by Louise Edrich; copyright © 1984 by Louise Erdrich. Reprinted by permission of Henry Holt and Co., Inc.

SUSAN ESTRICH "Separate is Better"; copyright © 1994 by the New York Times Company. Reprinted by permission.

AMITAI ETZIONI "HIV Suffers Have a Responsibility"; copyright © 1993 by Time, Inc. Reprinted by permission of Time, Inc.

JAMES FALLOWS "The New Immigrants," as first published in *The Atlantic Monthly*; copyright © 1983 by James Fallows. Reprinted by permission of the author.

E. M. FORSTER "My Wood" from *Abinger Harvest* by E. M. Forster; copyright © 1936 by E. M. Forster; copyright renewed 1964 by E. M. Forster. Reprinted by permission of Harcourt Brace & Company, Inc.

JANE GOODALL "A Plea for the Chimps"; copyright © 1987 by the New York Times Company. Reprinted by permission.

WALTER GOODMAN "What's Bad for Politics is Great for Television"; copyright © 1994 by The New York Times Company. Reprinted by permission.

MARY GORDON "Mary Cassatt" from *Good Boys and Dead Girls* by Mary Gordon; copyright © 1993 by Mary Gordon. Reprinted by permission of Viking Penguin, a division of Penguin Books USA Inc.

AL GORE "The Wasteland" from *Earth in the Balance* by Al Gore; copyright © 1992 by Senator Al Gore. Reprinted by permission of Houghton Mifflin Co. All rights reserved.

STEPHEN JAY GOULD "Women's Brains" from *The Panda's Thumb: More Reflections in Natural History* by Stephen Jay Gould; copyright © 1990 by Stephen Jay Gould. Reprinted with the permission of W. W. Norton & Company, Inc.

GARRETT HARDIN "Lifeboat Ethics: The Case Against Helping the Poor"; copyright © 1974 by Sussex Publishers, Inc. Reprinted by permission from *Psychology Today Magazine*.

BARBARA GRIZUTTI HARRISON "Getting Away with Murder"; copyright © 1994 by Barbara Grizzutti Harrison. Reprinted with the permission of George Borchardt, Inc., for the author.

ROBERT HAYDEN "Those Winter Sundays" from *Angle of Ascent* by Robert Hayden; copyright © 1966 by Robert Hayden. Reprinted with the permission of Liveright Publishing Corporation.

SEAMUS HEANEY "Digging" from *Death of a Naturalist* by Seamus Heaney; copyright by Seamus Heaney. Reprinted by permission of Faber & Faber, Ltd. and Farrar, Straus and Giroux, Inc.

WILLIAM A. HENRY III "In Defense of Elitism"; copyright © 1994 by William A. Henry III. Used by permission of Doubleday, a division of Bantam Doubleday Dell Publishing Group, Inc.

JOHN HOCKENBERRY "Limited Seating on Broadway"; copyright © 1992 by The New York Times Company. Reprinted by permission.

EVA HOFFMAN Excerpt from *Lost in Translation* by Eva Hoffman; copyright © 1989 by Eva Hoffman. Used by permission of Dutton Signet, a division of Penguin Books USA Inc.

LINDA HOGAN "Heritage" from *Red Clay: Poems and Stories* by Linda Hogan; copyright © 1991 by Linda Hogan. Reprinted by permission of Greenfield Review Press.

JOYCE HOWE "Indelible Marks: Growing Up in a Chinese Laundry"; copyright © 1983. Reprinted by permission of the author.

PICO IYER "The Global Village Finally Arrives"; copyright © 1993 by Time, Inc. Reprinted by permission of Time, Inc.

GISH JEN "Challenging the Asian Illusion"; copyright © 1991 by Gish Jen. First published in the *New York Times*. Reprinted by permission of the author.

NICHOLAS JENKINS "Dirty Needle"; copyright © 1994 by Nicholas Jenkins. Reprinted by permission of the author.

DR. JACK KEVORKIAN "A Case of Assisted Suicide/The Birth of Medicide" from *Prescription: Medicide* by Dr. Jack Kevorkian; copyright © 1991 by Dr. Jack Kevorkian. Used by permission of Prometheus Books.

MARTIN LUTHER KING, JR. "I Have a Dream"; copyright © 1963 by Martin Luther King, Jr., copyright renewed 1991 by Coretta Scott King. Reprinted by arrangement with The Heirs to the Estate of Martin Luther King, Jr., c/o Joan Daves Agency as agent for the proprietor. "Letter from Birmingham Jail" from *Why We Can't Wait* by Martin Luther King, Jr.; copyright © 1964, 1964 by Martin Luther King, Jr. Reprinted by permission of HarperCollins Publishers, Inc.

STEPHEN KING "Why We Crave Horror Movies"; copyright © by Stephen King. Reprinted by permission of the author.

MAXINE HONG KINGSTON "No Name Woman" from *The Woman Warrior* by Maxine Hong Kingston; copyright © 1975, 1976 by Maxine Hong Kingston. Reprinted by permission of Alfred A. Knopf, Inc.

PERRI KLASS "India" from *A Not Entirely Benign Procedure* by Perri Klass; copyright © 1987 by Perri Klass. Reprinted by permission of the Putnam Publishing Group.

HANS KONING "The Tugboat on the Lawn: A Tale of Man and Nature"; copyright © 1994 by the *International Herald Tribune*. Reprinted by permission of the *International Herald Tribune*.

JONATHAN KOZOL "Savage Inequalities" from *Savage Inequalities* by Jonathan Kozol; copyright © 1991 by Jonathan Kozol. Reprinted by permission of Crown Publishers, Inc. "The Human Cost of an Illiterate Society" from *Illiterate America* by Jonathan Kozol; copyright © 1985 by Jonathan Kozol. Used by permission of Doubleday, a division of Bantam Doubleday Dell Publishing Group, Inc.

ELISABETH KÜBLER-ROSS "On the Fear of Death" from *On Death and Dying* by Elisabeth Kübler-Ross; copyright © 1969 by Elisabeth Kübler-Ross. Reprinted with the permission of Simon & Schuster, Inc.

JOHN LEONARD "Why Blame TV?" copyright © 1993 The Nation Company, L.P. Reprinted with permission from *The Nation Magazine*.

ARTHUR LEVINE "The Making of a Generation" as printed in *Change Magazine*, published by Heldref Publications; copyright 1993. Reprinted with permission of Helen Dwights Reid Educational Foundation.

DEBORAH LIPSTADT "The Battle for the Campus" from *Denying the Holocaust* by Deborah Lipstadt; copyright © 1983 by The Vidal Sassoon International Center for the Study of Antisemitism, The Hebrew University of Jerusalem. Reprinted with the permission of The Free Press, a Division of Simon & Schuster, Inc.

BARRY LOPEZ "Landscape and Narrative" from *Crossing Open Ground* by Barry Lopez; copyright © 1986 by Barry Holstun Lopez. Reprinted by permission of Sterling Lord Literistic, Inc.

NORMAN MAILER Excerpt from *The Language of Men* by Norman Mailer; copyright © 1960 by Norman Mailer. Used with the permission of Wylie, Aitken & Stone, Inc.

TERRI MCMILLAN "The Wizard of Oz" from *The Movie That Changed My Life* by David Rosenberg; copyright © 1991 by Terri McMillan. Used by permission of Viking Penguin, a division of Penguin Books USA, Inc.

BARBARA MELLIX "From Outside, In" as originally appeared in *The Georgia Review*, Volume XLI, No. 2 (Summer 1987); copyright © 1987 by *The Georgia Review* and Barbara Mellix. Reprinted by permission of Barbara Mellix and *The Georgia Review*.

STANLEY MILGRAM "The Perils of Obedience" abridged and adapted from *Obedience to Authority* by Stanley Milgram as published in *Harper's Magazine*; copyright © 1974 by Stanley Milgram. Reprinted by permission of HarperCollins Publishers, Inc.

N. SCOTT MOMADAY "The Way to Rainy Mountain" from *The Way to Rainy Mountain* by F. Scott Momaday; copyright © 1969 The University of New Mexico Press. Reprinted with the permission of the University of New Mexico Press.

ALLEEN PACE NILSEN "Sexism in English: A 1990s Update"; copyright © 1990 by Alleen Pace Nilsen. Reprinted by permission of the author.

JOYCE CAROL OATES "Where Are You Going, Where Have You Been?" from *The Wheel of Love and Other Stories* by Joyce Carol Oates; copyright © 1970 by Joyce Carol Oates. Reprinted by permission of John Hawkins & Associates, Inc.

GEORGE ORWELL "Politics and the English Language" by George Orwell from *Shooting an Elephant and Other Essays*; copyright © 1946 by Sonia Brownell Orwell; copyright renewed 1974 by Sonia Orwell; "Shooting an Elephant" from *Shooting an Elephant and Other Essays*; copyright © 1950 by Sonia Brownell Orwell; copyright renewed 1978 by Sonia Pitt-Rivers. Reprinted by permission of Harcourt Brace & Company and A. M. Heath & Company, Limited.

MARGE PIERCY "Barbie Doll" from *Circle on the Water* by Marge Piercy; copyright © 1982 by Marge Piercy. Reprinted by permission of Alfred A. Knopf, Inc.

MARIO PUZO "Choosing a Dream: Italians in Hell's Kitchen" from *The Immigrant Experience* by Thomas C. Wheeler; copyright © 1971 by Doubleday, a division of Bantam Doubleday Dell Publishing Group. Used by permission of Doubleday, a division of Bantam Doubleday Dell Publishing Group.

ANNA QUINDLEN "Our Animal Rites"; copyright © 1990 by The New York Times Company. Reprinted by permission.

APPLETREE RODDEN "Why Smaller Refrigerators Can Preserve the Human Race"; copyright © 1975 by *Harper's Magazine*. Reprinted by permission of *Harper's Magazine*.

RICHARD RODRIGUEZ "Aria" from *Hunger of Memory* by Richard Rodriguez; copyright © 1982 by Richard Rodriguez. Reprinted by permission of David R. Godine, Publisher. "The Fear of Losing a Culture"; copyright © 1988 by Richard Rodriguez. Reprinted by permission of Georges Borchardt, Inc.

KATIE ROIPHE "Date Rape's Other Victim" from *The Morning After* by Katie Roiphe; copyright © 1993 by Katherine Anne Roiphe. Reprinted by permission of Little, Brown and Company.

ABRAHAM VERGHESE Excerpt from *My Own Country* by Abraham Verghese; copyright © 1994 by Abraham Verghese. Reprinted by permission of Simon & Schuster, Inc.

ALICE WALKER "Beauty: When the Other Dancer is the Self" from *In Search of Our Mother's Gardens*; copyright © 1983 by Alice Walker. Reprinted by permission of Harcourt Brace & Company.

E. B. WHITE "Once More to the Lake" from *One Man's Meat* by E. B. White; copyright © 1941 by E. B. White. Reprinted by permission of HarperCollins Publishers, Inc.

MARION WINIK "Where Mommies Come From" from *Telling* by Marion Winik; copyright © 1994 by Marion Winik. Reprinted by permission of Villard Books, a division of Random House, Inc.

MARIE WINN "Family Life" from *The Plug-In Drug*, Revised Edition by Marie Winn; copyright © 1977, 1985 by Marie Winn Miller. Used by permission of Viking Penguin, a division of Penguin Books USA Inc.

STANTON L. WORMLEY, JR. "About Men: Fighting Back"; copyright © by The New York Times Company. Reprinted by permission.

RICHARD WRIGHT "The Library Card" from *Black Boy* by Richard Wright; copyright © 1937, 1942, 1944, 1945 by Richard Wright; copyright renewed 1973 by Ellen Wright. Reprinted by permission of HarperCollins Publishers, Inc.

MALCOLM X "A Homemade Education" from *The Autobiography of Malcolm X*, with Alex Haley; copyright © 1964 by Alex Haley and Malcolm X; copyright © 1965 by Alex Haley and Betty Shabazz. Reprinted by permission.Reprinted by permission of Random House, Inc.

WILLIAM ZINSSER "College Pressures," from *Blair & Kutchum's Country Journal*, April 1979; copyright © 1979 by William Zinsser. Reprinted by permission of the author.

TOPICAL CLUSTERS

Belief and Doubt

Conformity and Rebellion

Self-Image

Heritage

Fear and Courage

Property, Territoriality, and Space

"What's in a Name?"

Heroes and Role Models

Exiles

Teenage Wasteland

The Generation Gap

SUBSTANCE ABUSE

SUCCESS AND FAILURE

LAW AND JUSTICE

NATIONALISM AND PATRIOTISM

UNWISDOM IN GOVERNMENT

CIVIL DISOBEDIENCE

THE CIVIL RIGHTS MOVEMENT

Mother Tongues

Stereotypes

Developing Nations

The Global Village

The PC Debate

Free Speech and Censorship

Small-Town Life

The Cities

INDEX OF AUTHORS AND TITLES